CONTEMPORARIES OF ERASMUS
A BIOGRAPHICAL REGISTER OF THE
RENAISSANCE AND REFORMATION

VOLUME 2

F–M

Contemporaries of
ERASMUS

A BIOGRAPHICAL REGISTER OF THE

RENAISSANCE AND REFORMATION

VOLUME 2

F–M

Peter G. Bietenholz
University of Saskatchewan

Editor

Thomas B. Deutscher
University of Saskatchewan

Associate Editor

University of Toronto Press

Toronto / Buffalo / London

The research and publication costs of the
Collected Works of Erasmus are supported by the
Social Sciences and Humanities Research Council of Canada
(and previously by the Canada Council).
The publication costs are also assisted by
University of Toronto Press.

ISBN 0-8020-2571-4

Canadian Cataloguing in Publication Data
Main entry under title:
Contemporaries of Erasmus
Supplement to: Erasmus, Desiderius, d. 1536. Works.
Collected works of Erasmus.
Includes index.
Partial contents: v. 1. A–E – v. 2. F–M.
ISBN 0-8020-2507-2 (v. 1). – ISBN 0-8020-2571-4 (v. 2)
1. Erasmus, Desiderius, d. 1536 – Dictionaries,
indexes, etc. 2. Renaissance – Biography.
3. Reformation – Biography. I. Bietenholz, Peter G., 1933–
II. Deutscher, Thomas Brian, 1949–
III. Erasmus, Desiderius, d. 1536. Works.
Collected works of Erasmus.
PA8500 1975 suppl.   199.492   c85-098027-5

Collected Works of Erasmus

The aim of the Collected Works of Erasmus
is to make available an accurate, readable English text
of Erasmus' correspondence and his
other principal writings. The edition is planned
and directed by an Editorial Board, an Executive Committee,
and an Advisory Committee.

Contents

Editorial Notes

In assembling *Contemporaries of Erasmus*, the following principles have been applied, with an appropriate degree of flexibility in view of the diversity of available material and fields of scholarly specialization among contributors.

– No biography is offered unless the person in question could be plausibly identified. On the other hand, even persons known merely by their first names are included in the register, provided the references to them warranted investigation. It is hoped that our short notes will encourage further research and eventually lead to further identification of those so mentioned.
– Both first and second names are given in the appropriate vernacular, provided predominant forms could be established; Latin forms often seemed preferable for unidentified or obscure persons. Humanist names in Latin or Greek were preferred wherever they seemed less uncertain than their vernacular counterparts or were deemed to be more widely known.
– Persons known by place of birth rather than by family name are indexed under their first names, unless contemporaries already tended to use the place name as a surname.
– In accordance with English-language custom, popes, emperors, queens, and kings are indexed under their first names, given in English; other members of royal houses, both legitimate and illegitimate, are similarly indexed.
– All members of noble houses are listed together under the family name, with first names in the appropriate language. In some cases, however, the names of a house and a territory are identical or, as with many German princes, the territorial name, often in Anglicized form, is in general use, as with Albert of BRANDENBURG, archbishop of Mainz.
– Women are listed under their maiden names, when known, rather than under names adopted in marriage. Cross-references are provided to married names.
– Cross-references are provided to name forms and identifications proposed by Allen but now abandoned. Cross-references are also given for variant name forms, Latin or vernacular, wherever expedient.
– An asterisk has been used with the name of an individual to indicate that a biography on that individual is included in *Contemporaries of Erasmus*; the asterisk precedes the name under which the biography is indexed.

- For names of places, modern vernacular forms are used, with the exception of those for which there is a form commonly accepted in current English usage (for example The Hague, Brussels, Louvain, Cologne, Milan). Current political frontiers are respected in the choice of place names rather than historical geography; this practice was adopted as being the most acceptable to an international readership, despite the occasional anachronisms that result.
- References to the correspondence and works of Erasmus are incorporated in each article without an obligation to completeness. *Contemporaries of Erasmus* is not intended as a substitute for the indexes that complement the CWE.
- Contributors were given latitude in the preparation of the bibliographies that accompany their articles so that they could be arranged thematically, alphabetically, or chronologically, as was thought most appropriate for the particular biography.
- Abbreviated references are used for works frequently cited throughout *Contemporaries of Erasmus*. A list of these works, offering fuller data, will be found at the end of each volume. On occasion, however, the full reference to a work cited in abbreviated form in the text of an article will be found in the bibliography following that entry.

The biographies are signed with the names of their authors or co-authors. Initials identify the members of the team in the research office generously provided by the University of Saskatchewan:

| PGB | Peter G. Bietenholz | IG | Ilse Guenther |
| TBD | Thomas B. Deutscher | CFG | Catherine F. Gunderson |

The biographies contributed by members of this team frequently reflect their fields of competence, but just as often they had to be compiled with local research facilities because of limits on time and available funds.

BIOGRAPHIES

Volume 2

F–M

Jacobus FABER of Deventer,
19 August 1473–in or after 1517
Jacobus Faber, who should not be confused
with his friend and namesake Jacques *Lefèvre
d'Etaples (Ep 719), was a pupil of Alexander
*Hegius at his native Deventer and afterwards
remained at St Lebuin's school, serving it as a
teacher and as moderator of the *domus clericor-
um*. He is said to have recovered a Fulgentius
text on a visit to Louvain. Faber owned a fine
library (cf Jortin). *Alaard of Amsterdam tells
an amusing story of how in 1514 he was at first
refused admission to it after having travelled
all the way from Louvain in hopes of finding
what was supposed to be an excellent autograph manuscript of Rodolphus *Agricola's *De
inventione dialectica*. Unfortunately the manuscript turned out to be only a rough draft,
which needed laborious correction by Gerard
*Geldenhouwer and Maarten van *Dorp be-
fore it could be published (Louvain: D.
Martens 12 January 1515; NK 45).

Faber was the author of panegyrics on the
triumph of Christ (Deventer: R. Pafraet 15
September 1506; NK 918) and on the Virgin
Mary (Deventer: J. de Breda c 1509; NK 3013),
and he translated Basil's *Oratio in ebrietatem*
(Deventer: T. de Borne 19 January 1510; NK
253). He is said to have edited Cato's *Disticha* in
1511, but no copy of this edition seems to be
extant; he also contributed several letters and
poems to other books (cf NK 47, 107, 3831,
4122). More interesting, however, are his
editions of the *Carmina* (Deventer: R. Pafraet 29
July 1503; NK 1041) and the *Dialogi* (Deventer:
R. Pafraet 31 December 1503; NK 1042) of his
admired teacher, Hegius.

Faber dedicated the *Carmina* to Erasmus (Ep
174 of 9 July 1503). How the two became
acquainted is not clear; presumably they did
not see each other at Deventer, for Faber
remarked that they attended Hegius' school at
different times (Ep 174). Ep 719 shows that they
were still corresponding in 1517. Cornelis
*Gerard dedicated the first part of his 'Marias'
to Faber.

BIBLIOGRAPHY: Allen Ep 174, IV xxi / A.J. van
der Aa et al *Biographisch woordenboek der
Nederlanden* (Haarlem 1852–78,repr 1965) VI 1 /
P.C. Molhuysen in NNBW IV 595–6 / J. Jortin *The
Life of Erasmus* (London 1758–60) II 711–12 /
A.J. Kölker *Alardus Aemstelredamus en Cornelius
Crocus* (Nijmegen-Utrecht 1963) 23–6
                                    C.G. VAN LEIJENHORST

Jacobus FABER of Lorraine, documented
1518–c 1550
Faber (Lefèvre, Vérier) is known primarily as
an important and prolific metal engraver who
worked at Basel after designs by *Holbein and
Urs Graf. After training in Paris he was at work
in Basel in June 1518, or possibly earlier,
introducing engravings to the Basel presses,
which had hitherto used only woodcuts. He
signed his work with the monogram 'J.F.' He
worked primarily for Johann *Froben but also
collaborated with Thomas *Wolff, Johann
*Bebel, Johann *Schabler, and others. Through
Konrad *Resch his plates reached some Paris
printers. In the course of his years at Basel
Faber travelled a good deal. In July 1524 he encouraged *Oecolampadius to write to Antoine
*Morelet du Museau, having apparently met
the latter in Paris. Later in the year he went
to Lyon and circulated there a French treatise
by Guillaume *Farel which greatly irritated
Erasmus (Epp 1508, 1510).

Faber probably left Basel in 1525 or 1526 at
the time that Holbein moved to England.
Thereafter his work is documented in Paris
from about 1534 to 1550 and possibly also in
Lyon. On occasion he continued to supply the
Basel printers too, thus continuing to bring to
various printing centres the styles of artists not
normally found there. Faber is perhaps identical with Jacques le Fèvre, 'tailleur d'histoires,'
who was married to Marie Bienaisé and who in
Paris in January 1529 disposed of typographical material inherited from Marie's uncle, Jean
Bienaisé. Presumably the same person, now
called 'Jehan' or 'Jacques Lefèvre, dit le tailleur
d'histoires,' fled from Paris after the placards
affair of October 1534. If this was the engraver
from Lorraine, who had been connected with
supporters of the Reformation in his Basel
years, it is necessary to assume that he was able
to return to Paris shortly thereafter.

Either Jacobus or one Petrus Faber, who is
also mentioned in 1524 and is probably a
relative of Jacobus, may be the stammering
Lorrainer who carried a letter of Erasmus to
Constance (Epp 1416, 1423).

BIBLIOGRAPHY: H. Koegler in *Allgemeines Lexikon der bildenden Künstler* ed U. Thieme et al (Leipzig 1907–50) / H. Koegler 'Wechselbeziehungen zwischen dem Basler und Pariser Buchdruck in der ersten Hälfte des XVI. Jahrhunderts' *Festschrift zur Eröffnung des Kunstmuseums* ed Öffentliche Kunstsammlung Basel (Basel 1936) 159–230, esp 173–220 passim / Herminjard I 249, 309, 382n, III 237n / BRE Ep 58 (c 1520–1) / R. Wackernagel *Geschichte der Stadt Basel* (Basel 1907–54) III 279, 51*, and passim / G. Berthoud in BHR 25 (1963) 320   PGB

Jacobus FABER Stapulensis *See Jacques* LEFÈVRE d'Etaples

Johannes FABER, OP
d before 22 February 1531
The place and date of Faber's birth are not known with certainty. He may have been born at Augsburg around 1470 and may have matriculated at the University of Freiburg on 20 July 1489. It appears that he studied theology in Italy. In 1505 he supervised the students at the Dominican house of studies in Venice. In 1507 he obtained a doctorate in theology from the University of Padua. In the same year he went to Augsburg, where on 24 July he was appointed prior of the Dominican monastery. From 1511 on he was vicar-general of the conventual Dominicans in the province of Southern Germany. In the autumn of 1512 he was registered, and presumably taught, at the University of Freiburg.

In the winter of 1513–14 Faber went to Rome to solicit an indulgence for the rebuilding of his monastery's church. Pope *Leo X co-operated, and funds produced by the indulgence together with donations made by wealthy Augsburg families were sufficient to complete the new church in 1515.

On his way back from Rome Faber visited Bologna, where he publicly discussed questions regarding indulgences, usury, and predestination. In 1515 he was named councillor and court preacher by the Emperor *Maximilian. On the emperor's death he delivered the funeral oration for Maximilian (Augsburg: S. Grimm and M. Wirsung 1519). In 1520 he attended the court of *Charles V in the company of Cardinal Matthäus *Lang. When

the court visited Louvain in early October, Faber met Erasmus, who agreed to write several letters of recommendation on Faber's behalf so as to obtain for him from Charles V the same positions he had held under Maximilian (Epp 1149–52). It is uncertain whether these attempts were successful. A month later Faber and Erasmus met again when the court was at Cologne. In their meetings they discussed Faber's plan for a trilingual college in Augsburg and, above all, the *Luther question. Faber committed his views to writing, and they were shown to Cardinal Albert of *Brandenburg and Frederick the Wise, elector of *Saxony. In consultation with Erasmus, they were revised and published as the famous *Consilium* (n p, n d, *Opuscula* 338–61; cf Epp 1156, 1199, 1217, ASD IX-1 256–7). Although at that time Faber agreed with Erasmus in recommending an independent inquiry and arbitration as the only solution to the Luther controversy, he quickly came to change his mind. After the diet of Worms in 1521 he saw no further possibility of conciliation and fully endorsed a hard line against the Wittenberg reformers.

When the reform movement began to take root in Augsburg, Faber opposed it with the same determination. In 1524 he was forced to leave the city for a while after he had claimed that the evangelical preachers caused civic disorders. Shortly after his return the city council prohibited him from preaching (1 April 1525), and before long he was expelled from the city.

Just as from 1521 he had taken a stand against Luther and his cause, he later also turned against humanism. In August 1529 Erasmus complained (Ep 2205) that Faber had slandered him at Rome so as to curry favour with the curia.

Information on Faber's life after 1525 is scant. It appears that he again went to Rome (Ep 2205) and that he died 'in exile' (Ep 2430) – when and where is not clear.

BIBLIOGRAPHY: Allen and CWE Ep 1149 / NDB IV 721 / ADB VI 493 / *Matrikel Freiburg* I-1 96, 203 / T.A. Dillis 'Johannes Faber' in *Lebensbilder aus dem Bayerischen Schwaben* ed G. von Pölnitz et al (Munich 1952–) V 93–111 / P. Dirr 'Eine Gedächtnisschrift von Johannes Faber über die Erbauung der Augsburger Dominikaner-

Kirche' *Zeitschrift des historischen Vereins für Schwaben und Neuburg* 34 (1908) 164–78 / N. Paulus 'Der Dominikaner Johann Faber und sein Gutachten über Luther' *Historisches Jahrbuch* 17 (1896) 39–60 / F. Roth *Augsburger Reformationsgeschichte* I 2nd ed (Munich 1901) passim / *Deutsche Reichstagsakten* Jüngere Reihe (Gotha-Göttingen 1893–   ) II 484 and passim

RAINER VINKE & PGB

Johannes FABER Emmeus documented from 1526, d 1542

Johannes Faber of Emmerich, in the county of Jülich, became a citizen of Basel on 3 March 1526 and set up business as a printer, primarily serving the needs of the Roman party in Basel's Reformation controversy. Thus he printed works and pamphlets by *Glareanus, *Pelargus, and Augustinus *Marius. His publication in 1528 of a polemical tract by Johann *Eck enraged the Swiss diet as well as the owner of the premises he occupied, Heinrich *David, who expelled him. In 1529, when the reformers gained control of Basel, Faber was among the Catholic exiles who moved to Freiburg. There he continued his business, bringing to Freiburg an element of the humanistic tradition of Basel publishing. During his years in Basel Faber occasionally printed works by Erasmus, but at Freiburg Erasmus relied on him repeatedly, and a personal relationship developed between them which is documented in Epp 2321, 2412, 2827, 2865. Of the books Faber published for Erasmus the *Epistolae palaeonaeoi* of 1532 was the most important. Faber also corresponded with Tielmannus *Gravius, to whose son he had lent a sum of money (Ep 3040).

BIBLIOGRAPHY: Allen Ep 2321 / Grimm *Buchführer* 1411–12 / R. Wackernagel *Geschichte der Stadt Basel* (Basel 1907–54) III 443 and passim / z IX Ep 707 / AK III Ep 1441 / *Basler Chroniken* I 64–6 / *Aktensammlung zur Geschichte der Basler Reformation* ed E. Dürr et al (Basel 1921–50) II 677 / P. Heitz and C. Bernoulli *Basler Büchermarken* (Strasbourg 1895) xxix, 76 / Benzing *Buchdrucker* 33, 139   PGB

Jacobus FABRI of Reichshoffen, d 6 June 1519

Jacobus Fabri of Reichshoffen, in Lower Alsace, was provost of the chapter of St Thomas in Strasbourg and an old friend of *Wimpfeling. Fabri had been named provost by apostolic provision. His death opened the provostship at a moment of crisis in the church, and Erasmus was drawn into the controversy over the appointment of his successor. On the day of Fabri's death Johann Hepp, a member of the chapter, was elected to the provostship by his fellow canons. In 1521, however, Pope *Leo x moved to fill the provostship under papal provision, reserving the benefice for Wolfgang *Capito, although Capito had to overcome another threat to his claims in 1523 (Epp 1368, 1374) before he could be installed.

BIBLIOGRAPHY: Allen Ep 1374 / Paul Kalkoff *Wolfgang Capito im Dienste Erzbischof Albrechts von Mainz* (Berlin 1907) 7–9 / James M. Kittelson *Wolfgang Capito* (Leiden 1975) 54 and passim

MIRIAM U. CHRISMAN

Johannes FABRI of Leutkirch, 1478– 21 May 1541

Fabri was born in Leutkirch, Allgäu, in 1478, the son of a smith, Peter Heigerlin. Virtually nothing is known about the first twenty-seven years of his life, except that at the age of twelve he left home to pursue a course of studies first in Constance and then in Ulm. In the fall of 1505 Fabri, who was already a BA and possibly a MA, entered the University of Tübingen to study theology and law. Under the influence of his theology professor, Jakob Lemp, Fabri attached himself to the *via antiqua*; he was later referred to by his humanist friends as a Scotist. It was in Tübingen that Fabri was ordained a secular priest (not a Dominican, as is sometimes thought). On 26 July 1509 Fabri matriculated at the University of Freiburg, where he studied theology and law under Gregor *Reisch and Udalricus *Zasius. He graduated with a doctorate in civil and canon law, not in theology, some time in 1510 or 1511.

Fabri served in various minor ecclesiastical positions in Lindau, Leutkirch, and Basel. Making effective use of his legal and administrative training, Fabri rose to the position of vicar-general of Constance in 1517, and in 1521 he was appointed suffragan bishop of Constance.

In 1520 Fabri's first work, the *Declamationes divinae de humanae vitae miseria*, was published. This collection of sermons, first preached at Lindau in 1511, is the first indication we have

Johannes Fabri

---

of Fabri's intellectual propensities during this period. The sermons are made up almost entirely of quotations – most often from the Greek and Latin classics (eg 'the most holy philosopher Seneca'), but also occasionally from Scripture and the Fathers. In his preface addressed to Hugo von *Hohenlandenberg he praised Erasmus above all and also saw in *Capito and *Oecolampadius the overdue reformers of the art of preaching (BA *Oekolampads* I 89–90, 12 April 1519).

Initially Fabri had been sympathetic to what he saw as *Luther's efforts to renew the life of the church. This began to change, however, when Luther took his stand against the papacy and canon law at the Leipzig disputation of 1519. After a trip to Rome in the fall of 1521 Fabri was finally convinced that Luther's teachings demanded correction. Still his opposition to Luther at this stage was by no means adamant. The tone of his first work against the reformers, *Opus adversus dogmata Martini Lutheri* (1522) was friendly throughout. Using the form of a scholastic disputation and quoting primarily from Scripture and the Fathers, Fabri pointed out several errors to his

'most beloved Martin, select brother in Jesus. After reading the work, Luther, ridiculing Fabri's theological acumen and disdaining to reply personally, asked Justus *Jonas to reply. Jonas' reply was vicious and insulting. This abuse, of course, hardened Fabri's opposition, and in 1524 a new edition of the work appeared, this time under the title *Malleus in haeresim Lutheranam*.

Fabri's relationship with *Zwingli followed much the same pattern. Relations were cordial to begin with, and Fabri regarded Zwingli as a friend, supporting him in his opposition to the sale of indulgences. But it gradually became clear to Fabri that the reforms they sought had little in common. Before the Zürich disputation in 1523 Fabri had been convinced that these differences could be overcome. After this disputation, however, Fabri began to write refutations of Zwingli's errors, though it was not until after the Baden disputation of 1526 that he abandoned his hope that reunion could be achieved.

During this time Fabri's career was advanced by his appointment as an adviser to Archduke *Ferdinand in 1523. In this capacity Fabri took every opportunity to confirm Ferdinand's opposition to the Protestant heresy, and his influence can be discerned in some of the latter's edicts. Fabri also took part in the legal processing of heretics such as Kaspar Tauber and Balthasar *Hubmaier. He alerted the universities to the dangers of the new teaching, proposed candidates for bishoprics, and served as Ferdinand's censor of books. He also concerned himself with educational standards and financing, and diplomatic assignments took him to England and Spain.

His role as Ferdinand's adviser did not prevent Fabri from taking an equally active role in ecclesiastical politics. In 1530 he was consecrated bishop of Vienna. He used his office as bishop to establish the Collegium Trilingue of St Nicholas to which he donated his considerable library. Although accused by his contemporaries of ambition, vanity, and greed, he proved a zealous bishop, a tireless opponent of the Reformation, and a patron of scholarship until his death in Vienna.

It was probably soon after his graduation from the University of Freiburg in 1510 or 1511 that Fabri came into contact with the writings and personality of Erasmus. Certainly by 1513, when Fabri began serving as an ecclesiastical official in Basel, he had come to know Erasmus personally. Indications are that he immediately and enthusiastically welcomed Erasmus' work. In the following years, Fabri became increasingly interested in Scripture and the Fathers, joyfully greeting each new edition that Erasmus put out.

The first concrete evidence of friendly acquaintance between the two is a letter from Urbanus *Rhegius, a former fellow student at Freiburg, to Fabri dated February 1516. In this letter, Rhegius asked Fabri to try to persuade Erasmus to go to Ingolstadt to teach (Ep 386). On 24 February 1516 Erasmus reported to Rhegius that Fabri had delivered the invitation but that he had to decline (Ep 392). There is further evidence of friendship between the two in 1518, when Johann *Eck mentioned Fabri as a friend of Erasmus (Ep 769).

Their personal correspondence began with a letter from Fabri to Erasmus on 26 April 1519 (Ep 953). Fabri confessed that Erasmus had made a new person out of him: though he had been a follower of recent theological trends for some time, he now found much greater joy in working with Scripture and the Fathers. Erasmus sent a friendly reply in the following month (Ep 976).

The correspondence between the two, as we know it, then broke off for a number of years although the friendship did not, as is clear from Erasmus' amicable mention of 'my friend Fabri' in other letters (Epp 1103, 1294). Fabri again expressed his admiration for Erasmus in his *Declamationes* of 1520. In his opinion Erasmus was no less a blessing to Germany than Aristotle had been to Greece, and he expressed the wish that Germany had more such men.

From November 1521 Fabri was in Rome; Erasmus was told that unlike many others he had not come to chase after benefices (Ep 1260), and on 1 December 1522 Pope *Adrian VI himself informed Erasmus that Fabri was praising his humanist friend at every occasion and that Fabri would convey to him personally the pope's invitation to Rome (Ep 1324). It is more than likely that Fabri visited Erasmus early in 1523 when he was attending the Zürich disputation (BA *Oekolampads* I 203–4). Subsequently Fabri provided Erasmus with a copy of

the *Conclusiones* of Diego *López Zúñiga, as Erasmus recalled in the preface of his *Apologia contra Stunicam*, which he addressed to Fabri (Ep 1428). After Erasmus had received news of Fabri's appointment as adviser to Ferdinand I in 1523 (Epp 1382, 1388), the personal correspondence resumed, though not at a frequent rate. In a letter of 21 November 1523, Erasmus reported on his activities and advised Fabri to oppose at court the influence of militant and conservative theologians (Ep 1397; cf Ep 1398). In the spring of 1524 Fabri tried unsuccessfully to arrange an audience for Erasmus with Archduke Ferdinand, but relations must have remained cordial, for in April 1526 Erasmus asked Fabri to intervene in the case of Heinrich *Schürer of Waldshut, whose property had been confiscated in the wake of the peasant and Anabaptist troubles (Ep 1690).

The same letter sheds light on another side of their relationship. Fabri had often spoken of Erasmus as a true and loyal defender of the Catholic church and the papacy. But since Fabri had not heeded Erasmus' advice on moderation, Erasmus no doubt wished to dissociate his name, at least to some extent, from Fabri and other Catholic controversialists. Consequently in this letter Erasmus reminded Fabri that his position was more ambiguous than Fabri made it out to be and that the Catholic controversialists were not much better than the Lutherans. And he also asked Fabri not to irritate the latter by using his name in this connection (Ep 1437).

While attending the Baden disputation in May 1526, Fabri wrote about an Irenaeus manuscript which Erasmus evidently wished to borrow and promised to send it shortly. It was on Fabri's recommendation that Erasmus dedicated the Irenaeus to Bernhard von *Cles, bishop of Trent (Epp 1738, 1739, 1754, 1755, 1771). In 1528 Fabri attempted to persuade Erasmus to take up residence in Vienna (Ep 2000), but Erasmus declined for reasons of poor health (Ep 2006).

As for Erasmus, there is perhaps reason to suspect that his slight misgivings about his friend were reinforced by Fabri's harsh dealings with the Anabaptists (Ep 1926). At the diet of Speyer in 1529, although a protest was made on behalf of freedom of conscience, the position Fabri represented won the day, and the Anabaptists were placed under the penalty of death. Thus the diverging views of Erasmus and Fabri on this issue were thrown into sharp relief. Nothing, however, suggests that this topic was raised when they met that year at Freiburg (Epp 2158, 2196).

Fabri clearly remained enamoured with his friend, perhaps in part because he thought that Erasmus could be of great service to the Catholic cause. As bishop of Vienna, Fabri censured one of Erasmus' opponents, *Medardus, and admonished another, Eck (Ep 2503). As for Erasmus, he continued to refer to Fabri as a friend and to write to him occasionally, discussing current political developments (Ep 2750; cf Ep 3017). Although he may have differed with Fabri on the issue of tolerance and moderation, he could nevertheless commend Fabri in a letter of 1532/3 for his warm pastoral concern as bishop: with his many sermons to the common people Fabri has shown himself to be a true bishop, and, Erasmus adds, others would do well to follow his example (Ep 2750).

Fabri was the author of some eighty-one publications, most of which are either collections of sermons or polemical writings against the reformers. Among the sermons, the following may be seen as representative: *Declamationes divinae de humanae vitae miseria* (Augsburg: J. Miller August 1520) and *Etliche Sermonn von dem hochwirdigen Sacrament* (Vienna: J. Singriener July 1528). Among Fabri's writings against Luther, the following are the most significant: *Opus adversus dogmata Martini Lutheri* (Rome: M. Silber 1522), better known under the title of the second edition as *Malleus in haeresim Lutheranam* (Cologne: P. Quentel 1524) and re-edited in *Corpus Catholicorum* vols 23–6; *De antilogiis seu contradictionibus Martini Lutheri* (Cologne: G. Hittorp August 1523); and *Summarium ausz was Ursachen Fabri der Lutherischen Lere nit abhängig gewesen* (n p, n pr, August 1526). Fabri also wrote against Zwingli, Balthasar Hubmaier, and Kaspar Schwenkfeld: *Christliche Beweisung über sechs Artickel Ulrich Zwinglins* (Tübingen: U. Morhart 1526); *Ursach warum Balthasar Hubmayr verbrennet sey* (Dresden: W. Stöckel 1528); *Adversus Doctorem Balthasarum Pacimontanum* (Leipzig: M. Lotter 1528); *Christenliche Ablainung des erschröckenli-*

chen Yrsal so Caspar Schwenckfelder ... hat (Vienna: J. Singriener 1529).

BIBLIOGRAPHY: Allen Ep 386 / NDB IV 728–9 / LThK III 1333 / I. Staub *Dr. Johannes Fabri bis zum offenen Kampf gegen Luther* (Einsiedeln 1911) / L. Helbling *Dr Johann Fabri: Generalvikar von Konstanz und Bischof von Wien, 1478–1541* (Münster 1941) / *Helvetia sacra* ed A. Bruckner (Bern 1972–) I-1 254–5 / W. Köhler 'Zwingliana in Wildhaus und Einsiedeln' *Zwingliana* 6 (1934–8) 1–4 / BA *Oekolampads* I 89–90 and passim / BRE Ep 221 and passim / Pflug *Correspondance* I Ep 115 and passim

DENIS R. JANZ

FABRI *See also* FABER *and Johannes* RUFFUS *Fabri*

Petrus FABRICIUS (Epp 3099, 3100 of February 1536)
Erasmus refers to a dedicatory letter from Ulrich *Hugwald to one Petrus Fabricius who has not been identified.

Ulricus FABRICIUS of Koblenz, 1489–22 July 1526
Fabricius (Ulrich Windemacher) was born in Koblenz in the ecclesiastical principality of Trier, and matriculated in the summer term of 1506 at the University of Erfurt. He was soon in touch with the Erfurt humanist circles and gained a friend in the person of Ulrich von *Hutten. Subsequently he attended universities in Italy and France and obtained a doctorate of laws. Precise information on his years abroad is not available, however, nor is it known when he first entered the service of the archbishop of Trier, Richard von *Greiffenklau, whose tenure of the see began in 1511. Greiffenklau encouraged him to devote much time to searching for ancient manuscripts. He preferred to send his discoveries to Venice for publication by the press of Aldo *Manuzio and Francesco *Torresani, which failed to return some of Fabricius' treasures after his death (AK IV Ep 1623).

In the course of his activities Fabricius maintained an extensive correspondence, but unfortunately his letters appear to be lost. He also served as Greiffenklau's ambassador on several missions to Italy, France, and Spain. On his return from an embassy to *Charles V he fell ill and died in Genoa. In 1527 his widow married the lawyer Justin *Gobler, who continued to edit and publish Fabricius' manuscripts, among them the *Processus iudiciarius* (Basel [c 1542]). Gobler is probably the author of a life of Fabricius which was published in the preliminary material of this edition. In Ep 1946 Erasmus asked Gobler to lend him a text by Tertullian which he knew to exist among Fabricius' manuscripts.

BIBLIOGRAPHY: Allen Ep 1946 / ADB VI 524–5 / *Matrikel Erfurt* II 245 / AK III Ep 1117, IV Epp 1623, 1680, 1726   RAINER VINKE

Jan FAGE of Kortenberg, d 5 September 1526
Fage (Faets, Fagie, Hagius), a native of Kortenberg, near Louvain, became an Augustinian canon in 1491. He was for a time rector of the nunnery at Ekeren, near Antwerp, and spent the rest of his life in the monastery of St Maartensdal at Louvain.

In 1519 an anonymous attack upon Erasmus was sent to the Dominicans of Louvain. It was suspected that it had originated from St Maartensdal and that Fage, who was known to be critical of Erasmus, was the author. When Fage denied this accusation, Erasmus suggested that Edward *Lee was responsible (Ep 1049). He soon reaffirmed his suspicion of Fage (Ep 1052), although it was not shared by Maarten *Lips (Epp 1049, 1052 introductions).

BIBLIOGRAPHY: de Vocht MHL 561–2
CFG

Peter FALCK of Fribourg, d 6 October 1519
A son of Bernhard Falck (d 1482), city clerk of Fribourg, in Switzerland, Peter Falck (Faulcon, Falco) was born about 1468 and educated at first in his native city. From 1491 to 1492 he studied with the humanist Sebastian Murrho at the chapter school of St Martin's in Colmar. On his return to Fribourg, he established himself as a public notary and soon began to occupy public offices. About 1499 he married Anna von Garmiswil, the daughter of a well-to-do city councillor.

Thereafter, the city of Fribourg employed Falck on several diplomatic missions and also as administrator and judge. From 1500 to 1510 he served Fribourg as bailiff of the town of Murten (Morat). Subsequently he was often sent to the Swiss diets as one of Fribourg's representatives. As a city councillor he, like Cardinal Matthäus *Schiner, opposed Swiss co-operation with France and thus became a major protagonist in the so-called Arsent affair, which led in 1518 to the execution of Franz Arsent, former *Schultheiss* (burgomaster) of Fribourg. In accordance with his political orientation, Falck took part in the Italian campaign of 1511–12, fighting as a captain with the Swiss army that played a key role in expelling the French from Milan. From November 1512 to November 1514 he served as Swiss ambassador at the courts of Rome and Milan and was greatly favoured by both Pope *Julius II and Duke Massimiliano Sforza. In 1516 and 1517 he was instrumental in bringing about the peace treaty between the Swiss and *Francis I, king of France, who bestowed upon him the honour of knighthood. From 1515 to 1519, serving his city in the function of a *Schultheiss*, Falck was the undisputed head of Fribourg's city government.

A largely self-taught man of letters, excelling in his ready knowledge of Latin and other languages, Falck accumulated a considerable humanist library, while his frequent journeys and his correspondence kept him in touch with notable humanist friends such as *Glareanus, *Zwingli, *Vadianus, *Myconius, Andrea *Ammonio (Ep 450), Johannes *Dantiscus, and Johannes *Longicampianus.

In 1515 and 1519 Falck undertook pilgrimages to Jerusalem. On his first journey, he took passage on the same boat as a group of English pilgrims including John *Watson, who remembered him afterwards as a delightful and quite unusual companion (Ep 450). It is not known when he made the acquaintance of Erasmus, who by January 1517 had read a report of that same journey, identifying Watson as one of Falck's fellow pilgrims (Ep 512). On his return voyage from the second pilgrimage to the Holy Land Falck contracted the plague and died aboard ship. He was buried at Rhodes. Falck was portrayed in a Dance of Death painted by his contemporary, the Bernese painter, writer, and politician Niklaus Manuel. On 15 May 1516 Glareanus dedicated to Falck his *Isagoge in musicen* (Basel: J. Froben 1516).

BIBLIOGRAPHY: Allen Ep 450 / ADB VI 551 /

DHBS III 52 / Joseph Zimmermann *Peter Falck: Ein Freiburger Staatsmann und Heerführer* (Fribourg 1905, also in *Freiburger Geschichtsblätter* 12, 1905, 1–151) / Adalbert Wagner 'Peter Falcks Bibliothek und humanistische Bildung' *Freiburger Geschichtsblätter* 28 (1925) / Conrad André Beerli *Le Peintre-poète Nicolas Manuel et l'évolution sociale de son temps* (Geneva 1953) 58, 125–6   KASPAR VON GREYERZ

Johann von FALCKENBERG
d 12 September 1536

Johann, the brother of Otto von *Falckenberg, matriculated at the University of Erfurt in 1516 and on 26 June 1519 was appointed to a canonry of the chapter of Sts Germanus and Mauritius. At the beginning of August 1523 the papal nuncio Ennio *Filonardi provided him with a domiciliar's prebend at the Speyer cathedral chapter, and on 14 August 1527 he began his year of residence, thus meeting a prerequisite for his appointment to a full canonry, which followed on 5 November 1528. From 12 July 1529 he was active in the chapter's administration of finance, having charge of several offices including that of cellarer and the *cista cleri*, an archive of land titles. He occupied the canon's house 'am Fischertor' and at the time of his death the house 'zum Lobenstein.'

In 1532 Ludolf *Cock used Falckenberg's name as a forwarding address (Ep 2687).

BIBLIOGRAPHY: Allen Ep 2439 / *Matrikel Erfurt* II 295 / Michael Glaser 'Die Diözese Speyer in den päpstlichen Rechnungsbüchern 1317–1560' *Mitteilungen des historischen Vereins der Pfalz* 17 (1893) 81 / *Die Protokolle des Speyerer Domkapitels* ed Manfred Krebs (Stuttgart 1968–) II nos 6045, 6925, 7447, and passim / *Chorregel und jüngeres Seelbuch des alten Speyerer Domkapitels* ed K. von Busch and F.X. Glasschröder (Speyer 1923) I 478–9
                                    KONRAD WIEDEMANN

Otto von FALCKENBERG d 24 June 1532

Otto von Falckenberg matriculated at the University of Cologne on 23 May 1504. The register lists him as a cleric of the diocese of Paderborn, as does a later entry in the papal books of account (Glaser 76). Very likely he belonged to the Hessian family von Falckenberg auf Herstelle in the territory of Paderborn.

On 13 November 1514 he satisfied the cathedral chapter of Speyer as to his noble descent. On 15 May 1516 he began his year of residence at Speyer, thus meeting a prerequisite for his appointment as canon, which took place on 20 July 1517. On 29 January 1524 he is mentioned as provost of the chapter of St Mary's in Bruchsal, a position which he held until his death. From 7 September to 7 December 1527 he was pastor at Freisbach. On 21 March 1530 the Speyer chapter appointed him to the office of *custos* following a recommendation issued from the papal court.

Falckenberg was often engaged in legal business for the chapter, such as contesting candidates for prebends nominated by papal right of reservation. To settle time-consuming and costly legal disputes he undertook journeys to Rome in 1519 and from 1524 to 1525, while from November 1529 to March 1530 he went to Bologna with two fellow canons to obtain *Clement VII's confirmation of their new bishop, Philipp von Flersheim. As *custos* Falckenberg conducted the negotiations between the bishop and the cathedral chapter as well as concerning himself with building projects, rents, and payments for the war against the Turks.

Falckenberg's first residence was a house next to the 'Senfgarten' (1515). On 18 January 1522 he exchanged the house 'zum Wolf' for that 'zum Esel,' and from August 1525 to March 1527 he lived in a house 'am Fischertor.' In March 1531 Nikolaus *Winman was a guest in Falckenberg's house when he wrote to Erasmus (Ep 2439). On 9 July 1532 Ludolf *Cock proposed him as a forwarding address (Ep 2687), unaware of his death two weeks earlier.

BIBLIOGRAPHY: Allen Ep 2439 / *Matrikel Köln* II-2 561 / Michael Glaser 'Die Diözese Speyer in den päpstlichen Rechnungsbüchern 1317–1560' *Mitteilungen des historischen Vereins der Pfalz* 17 (1893) 76, 87 / *Die Protokolle des Speyerer Domkapitels* ed Manfred Krebs (Stuttgart 1968–) I no 4298 and passim / F. Pfaff 'Die Burg Herstelle und das hessische Rittergeschlecht von Falckenberg' *Hessenland* 35 (1921) Heft 4, 51 / *Acta reformationis catholicae* ed Georg Pfeilschifrer (Regensburg 1959–) I 249 / Franz Xaver Remling *Geschichte der Bischöfe zu Speyer* (Mainz 1852) II 271–2 / *Chorregel und*

jüngeres Seelbuch des alten Speyerer Domkapitels
ed K. von Busch and F.X. Glasschröder
(Speyer 1923) I   KONRAD WIEDEMANN

Johannes FALCO documented in Paris
1498–c 1499
Johannes Falco has not been identified. Erasmus met him in Paris by 1498 (Ep 80) and wrote
to him from Tournehem in February 1499 (Ep
87). By February 1500 he had left Paris (Ep 119).
It is possible that he had sisters living in
Antwerp (Ep 87), and he was clearly a good
friend of Jacob *Batt. Although he may thus
have been a Netherlander, it is unlikely that he
was identical with one Johannes de Falco (Jan
Valck?) Gandavus (or Gaudanus?), to whom
Josse *Bade dedicated his edition of Solinus, 12
July 1503.
    BIBLIOGRAPHY: Allen Ep 87
                           MARCEL A. NAUWELAERTS

Petrus FALCO *See Peter* FALCK

FALKENBERG *See* FALCKENBERG

Guillaume FAREL of Gap, 1489–
13 September 1565
Guillaume Farel (Pharellus) was born at Gap,
Dauphiné, in 1489 and was a son of Antoine
Farel, apostolic notary. From 1509 he studied at
Paris, where Gérard *Roussel (Ep 1407) and
*Lefèvre d'Etaples were among his teachers.
In 1517 he graduated MA and subsequently
received a professorship at the Collège du
Cardinal Lemoine. In 1521 he was called to the
court of Bishop Guillaume (II) *Briçonnet at
Meaux, where he joined the humanists and
reformers grouped around Lefèvre d'Etaples.
Inspired by the latter's biblical humanism and
by *Luther's first treatises, Farel became a
Protestant reformer by 1521. In 1522 he went
back to his native town to preach his new faith
but soon returned to Meaux and Paris by way
of Guyenne. When his evangelical radicalism
was no longer tolerated in France he emigrated
in the autumn of 1523 to Basel, where he joined
*Oecolampadius, *Pellicanus, and other re-
formers. From Basel, Farel probably visited the
Strasbourg reformers that autumn, and in May
1524 he made *Zwingli's acquaintance in

Guillaume Farel

Zürich. He returned to Basel by way of
Constance and there met Johann von *Botzheim (Ep 1454). On 3 March 1524 he held a
disputation at Basel, defending thirteen theses
which he had formulated for the occasion; the
event stirred up great public attention and
controversy. Shortly afterwards he was expelled from Basel because of his radical
preaching and the dispute with Erasmus that is
discussed below.
    Farel continued his preaching at Mont-
béliard and from April 1525 to October 1526 at
Strasbourg, where he was on friendly terms
with *Bucer and *Capito. From Strasbourg he
visited Metz to launch an evangelical campaign
there – an exercise he was to repeat in 1542 and
1543, and in 1565. In October 1526 he left
Strasbourg for Bern, where a former student of
his at Paris, Peter Cyro, had been appointed
town clerk in 1523. Farel was appointed
minister of Aigle, the centre of one of Bern's
western bailiwicks. His singleminded devotion
to his task, which often helped him to
overcome great resistance, soon made him the
foremost first-generation reformer of western

Switzerland. He participated at the Bern disputation (January 1528), became the reformer of Neuchâtel and Murten (Morat) in 1530, laid the groundwork for the reformation in Geneva between 1533 and 1538 (to which end he recruited Jean Calvin in 1538), and played the leading role during the Lausanne disputation of 1536. From 1538 to his death he was first minister at Neuchâtel. In 1558 he married Marie Torel, a young Huguenot refugee from Rouen.

Personal relations between Farel and Erasmus were precarious and short-lived. Farel reacted with enduring aversion to Erasmus' resistance to the increasing radicalism of the Reformation movement. Their antagonism first arose from Erasmus' opposition to the public disputation of Farel's thirteen theses of February 1524 and was aggravated by Erasmus' *Exomologesis*, which appeared in a French translation by Claudius *Cantiuncula (Basel: J. Froben April 1524). This work may have irritated Farel, and other factors (Ep 1496) prompted him to call Erasmus a venal 'Baalam' (Ep 1496; LB X 1618A). Erasmus learned of Farel's slanders and confronted him in the presence of others (May or June 1524), demanding an explanation. Farel reacted by composing pamphlets against his opponent – no fewer than three, according to Erasmus – but all are lost today (Epp 1496, 1510; Allen I 31). Thereafter Erasmus often called Farel 'Phallicus' or something similar. He also disapproved of Farel's anonymous attack on the Paris theologians, *Determinatio facultatis theologiae Parisiensis*, a pamphlet of rare violence (Ep 1496).

Farel's situation in Basel became precarious as a result of his sermons before a congregation of francophone exiles. His violent tone incensed the authorities, while his friends admonished him in vain to be more prudent (LB X 1616–18; Ep 1538). Erasmus, on the other hand, wrote to the Basel city council, denouncing what he considered Farel's seditious and slanderous activities. This undated letter (Ep 1508) helped to bring about Farel's immediate expulsion from Basel around 9 July 1524 (*Biographie nouvelle* 128) and must, therefore, be dated late June or early July rather than October 1524, as in Allen. Subsequently, Erasmus followed with great indignation

Farel's preaching at Montbéliard and Strasbourg and did not miss a chance to slur Farel as insane and a seditious liar (Epp 1510, 1522, 1531, 1534, 1548; the colloquy Ἰχθυοφαγία, published in February 1526, ASD I-3 521). Erasmus was quick to point out to *Melanchthon that any stings in *De libero arbitrio* were solely directed against Farel and those who were like him (Ep 1523). Erasmus also referred to a difference of opinion between Farel and Pellicanus (Ep 1644). After the placards affair of 1534 some of Erasmus' close friends believed that Farel had been the main instigator (AK IV Ep 1897), and as late as 1557 Farel caused a minor scandal when he passed through Basel in the company of Théodore de Bèze and fell to traducing Erasmus in a public inn.

A bibliography of Farel's writings is contained in *Biographie nouvelle* 36–47. Among them may be noted: *Gullielmus Farellus christianis lectoribus* (Basel: n pr February 1524; Farel's thirteen theses for the Basel disputation of 3 March 1524), *Determinatio facultatis theologiae Parisiensis super aliquibus propositionibus* (Nürnberg: J. Petreius 1524), and *Summaire et briefve declaration d'auculns lieux fort necesaires a ung chascun chrestien pour mettre sa confiance en dieu et ayder son prochain* (Turin: n pr 1524 and later editions; Farel's most important treatise). For extant portraits of Farel see *Biographie nouvelle* 60–76.

BIBLIOGRAPHY: Allen Ep 1407 / DHGE XVI 531–4 / DHBS III 57–9 / *Guillaume Farel 1489–1565, Biographie nouvelle* (Neuchâtel and Paris 1930, repr 1978) / Herminjard I Ep 91 and passim / BA *Oekolampads* I 268 and passim, II 100–1 and passim / E. Droz 'Pierre de Vingle, imprimeur de Farel' in *Aspects de la propagande religieuse* (Geneva 1957) 38–78 / Elfriede Jacobs *Die Sakramentslehre Wilhelm Farels* (Zürich 1979) / Rudolf Pfister *Kirchengeschichte der Schweiz* (Zürich 1964–74) II 139ff / Henri Tribout de Morembert *La Réforme à Metz I: Le Luthéranisme 1519–52* (Nancy 1969) / Nathaniel Weiss 'Guillaume Farel, ses premiers travaux 1521–24' *Bulletin de la Société de l'Histoire du Protestantisme français* 68 (1919) 179–214 / Nathaniel Weiss 'Guillaume Farel; la dispute de Bâle; le conflit avec Erasme' *Bulletin de la Société de l'Histoire du Protestantisme français* 69 (1920) 115–45 / P.G. Bietenholz *Basle and France in the*

Sixteenth Century (Geneva-Toronto 1971) 91–3
and passim   KASPAR VON GREYERZ

Ulrichus FARNBUL *See Ulrich* VARNBÜLER

Alessandro FARNESE of Valentano,
7 October 1520–4 March 1589
Alessandro, born at Valentano, near Viterbo,
was a son of Pier Luigi Farnese and Girolama
Orsini of Pitigliano, and a grandson of
Cardinal Alessandro Farnese, later Pope *Paul
III. He studied at Parma under Molossi da
Casalmaggiore and at Bologna. On 1 Novem-
ber 1534, only weeks after his elevation to the
papacy, Paul III named Alessandro bishop of
Parma. He created him cardinal of Sant' Angelo
on 18 December. Alessandro soon resigned
Parma to his cousin Cardinal Guido Ascanio
*Sforza, accepting Avignon in its stead on 13
August 1535. At the same time he was named
papal vice-chancellor and cardinal of San
Lorenzo in Damaso. His grandfather endowed
him with numerous other dioceses and benefices. In 1534 his education in ecclesiastical and
political matters was entrusted to Gian Pietro
Grassi, bishop of Viterbo. In 1538 he was ready
to assume control over official correspondence
and state affairs for Paul III, with Marcello
Cervini, later Pope Marcellus II, acting as his
first secretary. In addition to serving as legate
for Avignon from 1541 Farnese also undertook
a number of diplomatic missions to Germany
and France. From 1539 to 1540 and from 1543 to
1544 he was legate to *Charles V and *Francis I
in an effort to secure a lasting peace between
them. From June to November 1546 he was
legate to the imperial forces which defeated the
Schmalkaldic League at Mühlberg on 24 April
1547. After the death of Paul III in 1549 he was
unable to secure his own election to the papacy
but remained a powerful figure in Rome,
playing a decisive role in the conclave which
elected *Paul IV in 1555 and remaining a prime
candidate for the tiara in 1566. He was also a
patron of the Jesuit order and of the arts.
Although he fathered a daughter around 1556,
he increased in devotion in his later years, and
his death was much mourned by the Roman
populace.
    Erasmus was informed of Farnese's elevation
to the cardinalate by Conradus *Goclenius,

Alessandro Farnese, by Titian

who shared in the widespread disapproval
created by the nepotism of Paul III (Ep 2998).
    Portraits of Farnese by Titian are found in
the Museo di Capodimonte of Naples and in
the Galleria Corsini at Rome.
    BIBLIOGRAPHY: Allen Ep 2998 / DHGE XVI
608–15 / Eubel III 141, 288 / Pastor vols 11–21 *ad
indicem*   TBD

Heinrich FASTNACHT *See Henricus* URBANUS

Melchior FATTLIN of Trochtelfingen,
c 1490–25 October 1548
Melchior Fattlin (Fättlin, Vechtlin) of Trochtelfingen, in Sigmaringen matriculated in the
University of Freiburg on 23 February 1508.
Supporting himself as an assistant teacher at
the town school, he obtained the degrees of BA
in 1509 and MA in 1510. In 1516 he became a
member of the philosophical faculty and on 19
October 1518 he was awarded a theological
doctorate. Meanwhile he had become a priest
in 1514 and was soon preaching in the
cathedral. On 31 July 1518 he was appointed
suffragan bishop of Constance with the title of

bishop of Ascalon, consecutively serving in this office the bishops Hugo von *Hohenlandenberg, Balthasar *Merklin, Johann von Lupfen, and Johann von Weeze. From 1530 he was also canon of Constance and from 1532 dean of the chapter.

In Constance Johann von *Botzheim soon noted Fattlin's zeal in defence of the traditional faith (Ep 1401). In 1522 he debated in Zürich against *Zwingli, and in 1526 he participated in the disputation of Baden, producing at the same time a treatise in German against communion under both species, published by Ulrich Mohrhaupt in Tübingen in 1526. When the city of Constance went over to the Reformation, Fattlin and the chapter moved in April 1527 to Überlingen. There he preached many sermons that proved highly popular and included tirades against Erasmus (Epp 2516, 2640). When the chapter left Überlingen in 1542 over a disagreement with the city, Fattlin apparently stayed on, but he later held the office of town priest in Radolfszell. In 1543 he tried in vain to retire from his duties as a suffragan. In his will, signed at Radolfszell on 11 July 1546, he increased his earlier bequests for scholarships in the University of Freiburg. He was buried in the new cemetery of Überlingen.

BIBLIOGRAPHY: Allen Ep 1401 / J.A. Kraus in DHGE XVI 683–4 / J.A. Kraus 'Zu Weihbischof Melchior Fattlin' *Freiburger Diözesan-Archiv* 75 (1955) 307–14 / A. Semmler 'Weihbischof Melchior Fattlin in Überlingen' *Freiburger Diözesan-Archiv* 74 (1954) 181–94 / Rublack *Reformation in Konstanz* 217–18 and passim / *Matrikel Freiburg* I 181   PGB

John FAWNE documented 1494–1536
Fawne is documented as a student in Cambridge from 1494. In 1497 he was ordained deacon and elected a fellow of Queen's College. At Queen's he was dean of the chapel in 1498–9 and 1501–2 and vice-president of the college from 1511 to 1513. He obtained his degree of bachelor of theology in 1504 and his doctorate in 1510. Fawne was vice-chancellor of the university from 1512 until 1514, when he resigned his fellowship. He was appointed Lady *Margaret Beaufort preacher on 6 November 1515.

Fawne was admitted canon of Clynnog-fawr, Caernarvonshire, in 1520, vicar of St Cross, Southampton, in 1522, rector of Martyr Worthy, Hampshire, in 1523, prebendary of Middleton in Wherewell Abbey in 1527, and rector of Easton, Hampshire, in 1529. He held the last four benefices until his death, which had occurred by December 1536.

Fawne was acquainted with Erasmus, who sent him greetings through their common friends Robert *Aldridge and Henry *Bullock (Epp 456, 1656). He enjoyed the patronage of Bishop Richard *Foxe, in whose house he was resident from 1526 (Ep 1766).

BIBLIOGRAPHY: Allen and CWE Ep 456 / Emden BRUC 221, 675   CFG

Cassandra FEDELE of Venice, d 1558
Born in either 1456 or 1465 depending on her age at the time of death, which is variously quoted as 102 or 93, Cassandra was the daughter of a wealthy Venetian *cittadino* and a noted beauty who sat for Giovanni Bellini at the age of fifteen. In 1487 she won international fame by reciting a speech at Padua on the occasion of her cousin's doctorate and seems to have taught informally at the university thereafter. During the 1490s she became a legendary figure, corresponding with several European princes and numerous intellectuals. Drawing on the tributes of *Poliziano, Erasmus cited her as an example of learning in extreme youth (ASD I-2 76, 570), but since she was at least in her mid-twenties when Poliziano met her in 1491, the reference was barely appropriate. In 1500 she was implicated in a scandal involving counterfeit money (Sanudo *Diarii* III 1140) and immediately dropped out of social prominence. Probably soon afterwards she married a doctor named Mapellius, travelled extensively with him in the Eastern Mediterranean, suffered shipwreck, and was widowed in 1520. She made a final return to prominence in 1556, when she recited a speech of welcome to *Bona Sforza, queen of Poland, and she died in 1558 as superintendent of the hospital of San Domenico in Venice. She is said to have written a work entitled 'De scientiarum ordine,' but both this and Bellini's portrait have perished.

BIBLIOGRAPHY: *Cassandrae Fedelis epistolae et orationes* ed J. Tomasino (Padua 1636) / C. Cavazzana 'Cassandra Fedele, erudita vene-

ziana del rinascimento' *Ateneo veneto* anno
XXIX vol ii, fasc i (July–August 1906) 73–91,
249–74, 361–72   M.J.C. LOWRY

Johann FEIGE of Hessisch Lichtenau,
1482–20 March 1543
Johann Feige (Fyge, Fiegh, Veige, Ficinus), the
son of Heinz Feige and his wife, Margaret
Mergart, was born in the town of Lichtenau, in
Hesse. After a spell in the chancery of the
abbey of Fulda (1499), he studied at the
University of Erfurt (1501–3); there he was in
touch with Euricius *Cordus, who later dedicated verses to him, and *Eobanus Hessus,
whom he was later to appoint to the University
of Marburg (1536). After a few years in the
service of the landgrave of Hesse – in 1510 he
was secretary to the law court (*Hofgericht*) of
Marburg – he became secretary to the bishop of
Würzburg, Lorenz von Bibra (c 1512–14), but
returned to serve his own dynasty during the
difficult final years of the minority of Philip of
*Hesse (1508–18). He exercised considerable
influence over the young prince, who began
his rule before reaching the age of fourteen,
and was named chancellor in 1519. For a
quarter of a century he remained Philip's
leading adviser and, like the chancellors
Leonhard von *Eck in Bavaria, Gregor Brück in
electoral Saxony, and Simon *Pistorius in ducal
Saxony, was one of the ranking statesmen of
Germany. However, Landgrave Philip was
later at all times the master of his own
decisions, so that Feige was denied an independent role comparable to that of Chancellor
von Eck. From the time of the diet of Worms
(1521) Feige shared Philip's interest in Martin
*Luther and promoted the landgrave's grow-
ing commitment to the Lutheran Reformation.
In 1526 he organized the synod of Homberg,
which, after a theological dispute between
François *Lambert and Nikolaus *Ferber, opened the way for the creation of a Lutheran
church in Hesse. When the University of
Marburg was founded in 1527 Feige was asked
to take charge of its organization; he remained
the driving force behind the new institution
and after overcoming many obstacles finally
obtained the Emperor *Charles v's approval of
it in 1541. Feige, who was described as a cleric

in 1504, married Anna Sandmann in 1519 and,
after her death, Katharina Nusspicker in 1535.
    We have no knowledge of any direct
relations between Feige and Erasmus, but in
1532 Erasmus claimed that the chancellor of
Hesse was devoted to him (Ep 2728).
    BIBLIOGRAPHY: Allen Ep 2728 / NDB V 55–6 /
ADB VI 600–2 / B. Liebers *Johannes Feige*
(Hessisch Lichtenau 1960) / *Matrikel Erfurt* II
222   PGB

FELICE da Prato c 1458–5 November 1558
Felice (Felix Pratensis), born at Prato, was of
Jewish origin and was educated as a rabbi. He
converted to Christianity before 1506 and
entered the monastery of the Hermits of St
Augustine at Prato. He was transferred to
Rome and in 1515 obtained from *Leo X
permission to prepare a new Latin translation
of the Bible, but only the *Psalterium* was
published (Venice: D. Bomberg 1516). Gabriele
Veneto, the general of his order, appointed
him reader of theology and in 1522 sent him to
Spain to greet the new pope *Adrian VI. In 1523
Felice was named doctor of theology by papal
authority. From 1526 to 1528 he served as
procurator-general of his order, and for many
years he was a preacher, especially to the Jews,
of whom it is said he converted many. He knew
Egidio *Antonini of Viterbo personally and
taught Hebrew to the printer Daniel Bomberg.
He died in Rome.
    Erasmus mentioned Felice da Prato's *Psalte-
rium* in Ep 456 and in his preface to the 1535
edition of the New Testament (LB VI [22]).
    Felice da Prato also edited the *Biblia sacra
hebraea cum utraque Masora et Targum item cum
commentariis rabbinorum* (Venice: D. Bomberg
1518) and the polyglot *Psalterium sextuplex*
(Lyon: S. Gryphius 1530).
    BIBLIOGRAPHY: Allen Ep 456 / DHGE XVI 911 /
W. Hümpfner in LThK IV 70 / H. Hurter
Nomenclator literarius theologiae catholicae (Innsbruck 1906–11) II 1493 / J.F. Ossinger *Bibliotheca
Augustiniana* (Ingolstadt and Augsburg 1768)
716–7 / D.A. Perini *Bibliographia Augustiniana
cum notis biographicis* (Florence 1929–38) 100–2 /
J. Quetif and J. Echard *Scriptores ordinis
praedicatorum* (Paris 1719–21) II 340 / F. Secret
Les Kabbalistes chrétiens de la renaissance
(Paris 1964) 107   MARCO BERNUZZI

Francisco **FELIPE** or **FELIPEZ** *See Franciscus* PHILIPPI

Doctor **FELIX** *See Petrus* PHOENIX

Claude **FÉLIX** of Montigny-le-Roi, d 30 March 1543
Claude Félix was born in Montigny-le-Roi, near Langres. He studied arts at the Collège des Bons-Enfants in Paris, taking his MA about 1495, and was regent in arts and grammar at the same school. He was a *socius* of the Collège de Sorbonne, where he was the prior in 1506 and 1507. He obtained his licence in theology on 25 January, ranking third of eighteen, and his doctorate on 7 April 1508. He remained in Paris for two years, then returned to Langres, where he was a canon and later secretary and vicar-general to Bishop Michel *Boudet. He died in 1543 and was buried in the cathedral. He left two manuscript works: a history of the bishops of Langres and a poem on the life of Saint-Mammès, patron of Langres.
In Ep 1827 Erasmus returned the greetings Félix had sent him.
BIBLIOGRAPHY: Allen Ep 1827 / DBF XIII 961 / Farge no 179   JAMES K. FARGE

Pierre **FÉNIX** *See Petrus* PHOENIX

FELSENMEYER documented 1533–4
Felsenmeyer, a public messenger plying his trade between Freiburg and Basel, is probably the old man mentioned in Epp 2827 and 2259 (AK IV Ep 1783, October 1533); see AK IV Ep 1819. Felsenmeyer's first name is not known, nor do surviving records in Freiburg reveal whether he was identical with the Freiburg public messenger named Peter who in March 1533 carried letters from Erasmus to the Low Countries (Epp 2793, 2799).   PGB

Moritz **FERBER** of Gdansk, 1471–1 July 1537
Born of a patrician family in Gdansk (Danzig), Moritz was the son of the mayor of Gdansk, Johann Ferber, and of Barbara Tannenberg. Following a family tradition, he registered in 1508 at the German institution of Rome, Santa Maria dell'Anima. He studied in Rome and in Siena, where he obtained a doctorate in civil and canon law on 3 September 1515. Pope *Leo X granted him the titles of papal chamberlain

and notary of the Rota. He accumulated numerous church benefices, being a canon of Warmia (Ermland), Lübeck, Tallin (Reval), and Dorpat, and was a rector in the church of Our Lady in Gdansk. In 1516 he became *Domkustos* of Warmia. On 14 April 1523 he was elected bishop by the Warmian cathedral chapter in Frombork (Frauenburg) and strove successfully to keep his diocese free of Lutheran influences. From 1532 he was ailing and wished to appoint as his coadjutor Tiedemann *Giese, his relative and protégé (Ep 3112); however he could not secure the king's permission, and the appointment finally went to Johannes *Dantiscus. Ferber died in 1537 and was buried in the cathedral of Frombork.
BIBLIOGRAPHY: Allen Ep 3112 / NDB V 80 / PSB VI 417, 419–20 / *Altpreussische Biographie* ed Christian Krollmann (Kaliningrad 1941) I 181 / de Vocht *Dantiscus* 24, 422, and passim / *Liber confraternitatis S. Mariae de Anima* ed C. Jaenig (Rome 1875) 120   HALINA KOWALSKA

Nikolaus **FERBER** of Herborn, d 4 April 1535
Nothing is known about the early life of Nikolaus Ferber of Herborn, in Hesse. He joined the Franciscan Observants and from about 1512 may have studied theology at Cologne, but he is probably not identical with one Nicholas, a friar of the Observant monastery of Brühl near Cologne, who matriculated on 28 October 1512 and died in April 1533. From about 1520 Ferber was the warden of the Marburg Franciscans and engaged valiantly in the struggle to prevent Hesse from joining the reformed camp. In 1525 he published to this effect *Eyn Sendtbrieff ... an den ... Fürsten Philippen ... zu Hessen*. In 1526 at a synod at Homberg he faced François *Lambert, a former Franciscan who had become religious adviser to Philip of *Hesse and was also the target of Ferber's *Assertiones ... adversus Fr. Lamberti paradoxa impia* (Cologne: P. Quentel 1527), to which he replied the following year. Unable to change the course of Philip's religious policy, Ferber had to leave Hesse in the wake of the Homberg synod and from 1527 was warden of the monastery of Brühl. The city of Cologne appointed him preacher at the cathedral, and in his sermons he attacked the reformers, taking issue specifically with Archbishop Hermann von *Wied and Wilhelm von *Isen-

burg. In his Cologne years he was connected
with the influential Johann *Rinck and also
with Duke John III of *Cleves, both of whom
were admirers of Erasmus. In 1530 he was in
Denmark to oppose the reformers; his *Confutatio Lutheranismi Danici* was edited in 1902. From
1530 to 1532 he headed the Cologne province
of the Observants, and from 1532 he was
commissary-general for all provinces outside
Italy. In pursuit of his duties he travelled
extensively in Spain, France, and the Netherlands. The preface of his *Enarrationes* is dated
from Ypres on 10 October 1532, while Erasmus
later placed him at Bonn (Ep 2906). He was at
Toulouse when he died (Ep 3053).

Among Ferber's many writings the *Loci
communes adversus haereses* (Cologne: E. Cervicornus 1528) appeared repeatedly and were
re-edited in 1927, while the *Epitome convertendi
gentes Indiarum* (Cologne: M. von Neuss 1532)
was reprinted in Basel in 1555. Only one of
Ferber's works interested Erasmus: the *Enarrationes evangeliorum per sacrum quadragesimae
tempus occurrentium* (Antwerp: M. Hillen 1533
and Paris: A. Berthelin 1543). By 23 January
1534 Erasmus had received from the Netherlands a few pages pulled from this volume
which attacked him as a harbinger of the
Protestant Reformation. His letters show that
he was quite upset; he sent the offensive leaves
to Archbishop Jean de *Carondelet, demanding that the court of Brussels take action
against the unjustified attack, and endeavoured to secure a copy of the entire work as
well as more information about its author. In
both endeavours he eventually succeeded, but
he also learnt from Cornelius *Grapheus, who
sent the book in September 1535, that Ferber
had died in the mean time. Earlier Erasmus had
planned to answer Ferber's charges in the form
of a letter, and even the news of his death did
not entirely prevent the execution of this plan
(Epp 2896, 2898, 2899, 2912, 2915, 2961, 3053,
3100).

BIBLIOGRAPHY: Allen Ep 2896 / NDB V 80–1 /
ADB XII 42–5 / *Matrikel Köln* II 701 / A. Rebe
Nikolaus Herborn (Herborn 1869) / Patricius
Schlager *Geschichte der Kölner Franziskaner-
provinz während des Reformationszeitalters*
(Regensburg 1909) 33ff / Ludwig Schmitt *Die
Verteidigung der katholischen Kirche in Dänemark
gegen die Religionserneuerung im 16. Jahrhun-*

dert (Paderborn 1899) passim / Winand Virnich
'Nekrologium und Memorienbuch der Franzis-
kaner zu Brühl … ' *Annalen des historischen
Vereins für den Niederrhein* 34–5 (1879) 87–
166 especially 108
                                          EUGEN HOFFMANN & PGB

Emperor FERDINAND I
10 March 1503–25 July 1564
Ferdinand was born in Alcalá de Henares,
Castile. Unlike his older brother, the future
*Charles V, he was brought up in Castile at the
court of his grandfather, *Ferdinand II of
Aragon. After Charles was elected emperor,
Maximilian's territories were partitioned between the brothers in 1521 and 1522, and
Ferdinand began his rule over the Austrian
duchies. He also acted as Charles' deputy
when the latter was absent from the Empire. In
Austria he overcame initial resistance from the
estates and, continuing Maximilian's policy of
centralization, created important new organs
of government and administration: in 1522 a
privy council (*Zentraler Hofrat*) and in 1556 a
central military authority (*Hofkriegsrat*). After
the unexpected death of his brother-in-law,
King *Louis II, Ferdinand was elected king of
Hungary and Bohemia in 1526, but he was
unable to establish his authority in Hungary
because of the opposition of the Hungarian
rival king, *John Zápolyai, and the Turks. The
Hungarian question, linked in many ways with
the defence of central Europe against the
Turks, became Ferdinand's foremost political
and military concern.

In 1531 Ferdinand was elected Roman king.
This new dignity strengthened his hand in
imperial politics, especially after the Schmalkaldic war (1546–47), when Charles V began
gradually to withdraw from German affairs and
Ferdinand became more prominent, growing
into his role of successor to the imperial crown
without being disloyal to Charles. As Charles
refused to get involved, Ferdinand shouldered
the task of settling the religious issues in
Germany within the legal framework of the
peace of Augsburg (1555). The few years of his
rule as emperor (1558–64) were also dominated
by the religious question: he sought compromise with the Protestant princes and instructed
his envoys to the council of Trent to work for
the reform of ecclesiastical abuses and the

Emperor Ferdinand I, by Hans Maler

granting of concessions to the Protestants, including a married clergy and the chalice for the laity.

Ferdinand's education at the court of his grandfather and namesake, Ferdinand II of Aragon, lay in the hands of Dominican fathers and was fashioned by the methods of Spanish scholasticism and the ideals of the Spanish orders of chivalry. In addition one discerns a humanistic influence due to the physician Juan de la *Parra, who was one of the very few members of Ferdinand's Spanish entourage permitted to accompany the young prince to the Netherlands in the spring of 1518.

It was during this stay in the Netherlands (1518–21) that Ferdinand first met Erasmus in person. An excellent reputation preceded the fifteen-year old archduke (Ep 849), and Erasmus repeatedly expressed high hopes for the enlightened leadership expected of him (Epp 917, 952, 969). With the second edition of his *Institutio principis christiani* (July 1518) Erasmus had a first opportunity to offer Ferdinand the benefits of his thought and learning, although circumstances prevented the formal dedication of the book to him (CWE Ep 853 introduction).

Ferdinand read the *Institutio* with Juan de la Parra and was clearly impressed (Epp 943, 970, 1323), as he told Erasmus personally (LB IX 371E). It would be of great interest to know in what measure he accepted the ideas Erasmus had expressed in this book and whether they were subsequently reflected in his own political action. While this question remains to be studied, it can tentatively be suggested that Erasmus' ideas did indeed bear fruit in the circle of Ferdinand and his close advisers, especially after his elevation to Roman king in 1531 (Epp 2453, 2504), and that this influence proved enduring after the death of Erasmus.

Early in 1519 Erasmus was invited to become Ferdinand's teacher but declined, recommending instead Juan Luis *Vives (Ep 917). To his embarrassment efforts to make him reconsider continued for some time (CWE Ep 927 introduction), as did rumours that he was actually to join Ferdinand's entourage (Ep 932).

During the imperial election campaign of 1519 in which the Hapsburgs competed with the house of Valois, Erasmus was a keen observer of the discussions within the Hapsburg family over Ferdinand's place in the dynastic inheritance (CWE Ep 917 introduction) and of the wide range of speculations caused by those discussions (Ep 893).

In view of the outbreak of war between France and the Hapsburgs, Erasmus used the dedications of his paraphrases of the gospels to express concern for peace and stability in Europe. In line with the dedications of Matthew, Mark, and Luke to Charles V, *Francis I, and *Henry VIII respectively, John was dedicated to Ferdinand (Ep 1333). Addressing him in the preface, Erasmus praised Ferdinand's wisdom, moderation, clemency, and piety; he depicted him as a 'pastor populorum' and a model for the public conduct of a Christian prince. This dedication marked the beginning of the direct correspondence between Erasmus and Ferdinand, which continued intermittently until Erasmus' death. A number of letters are now missing (Epp 1386, 1505, 1553, 2161), perhaps because Erasmus was discreet enough not to publish them. On many other occasions trusted ministers and councillors of Ferdinand, such as Johannes *Fabri, Bernhard von *Cles, Jakob *Spiegel, Willibald *Pirckheimer, and Johann (II) *Paumgartner, were asked to relay messages. Erasmus was careful to obtain Ferdinand's consent before the paraphrase and its dedicatory letter went on sale (Epp 1323, 1343), and he was rewarded by a generous cash present (Ep 1376; LB IX 801D). Ferdinand also had a printer's privilege issued to protect the publications of Johann *Froben (Ep 1341, 1344). From then on Erasmus felt secure in Ferdinand's good favour (Epp 1415, 1488, 1596, 1608, 1697, 2211, 2299, 2514, 2577, 2792, 3087) – so secure, in fact, that he declined an invitation to meet the prince who was visiting Breisach and Freiburg in May 1524 (Ep 1452). The reason was that after the publication of his De libero arbitrio against *Luther he feared pressure to assume an even more polemical stance against the reformers, having persuaded himself of Ferdinand's special zeal in the religious question (Epp 1338, 1388). When Spiegel wrote to Erasmus on his master's instructions, Ferdinand was content with a very mild rebuke for Erasmus' failure to meet him and assured the beleaguered humanist of continued support against his Catholic critics (Ep 1505). At Erasmus' request Ferdinand even wrote to his aunt, *Margaret, requesting her to silence Nicolaas *Baechem Egmondanus (Epp 1515, 1553, 1581).

In June 1528 Ferdinand invited Erasmus to move to Vienna. He promised an annuity, scholarly freedom unencumbered by specific duties, and additional funds to make Vienna a centre for the study of the three ancient languages (Ep 2000). Erasmus declined the invitation (Epp 2005, 2006) but the fact that he appreciated it is shown by the frequency of his references to Ferdinand's offer in his subsequent correspondence. In January 1529, when Erasmus had made up his mind to leave Basel, he addressed a complimentary letter to Ferdinand, no doubt with the purpose of eliciting another invitation (Ep 2090). After some hesitation (Ep 2107) he accepted Ferdinand's offer of a haven at Freiburg (Epp 2130, 2145), which was accompanied by various efforts to facilitate his settlement there (Epp 2161, 2191–3), including rent-free accommodation (Allen Ep 2462 introduction), assistance in a legal matter (Ep 2317), and in 1533 a gift of cash (Epp 2801, 2808). Erasmus was delighted with his new surroundings (Ep 2193) and when he later prepared to leave Freiburg he knew that once again he could count on Ferdinand's assistance (Epp 2514, 2759, 2792).

Erasmus showed particular interest in Ferdinand's involvement in the troubles of Hungary and his wars against the Turks, returning to these subjects in many letters as well as in De bello turcico (LB V 352D–E, 363F). Due to his frequent exchanges of letters with the *Łaski brothers and other Polish informants, he saw the contention between Ferdinand and John Zápolyai in part at least from the latter's perspective, and in 1527 he aroused the anger of the court of Vienna when one of his letters was published in which he had referred to Zápolyai as king (Epp 1819, 2030, 2032). Erasmus endeavoured to remain neutral and save his ire for the Turks, but he also regretted the parsimony of the German princes (Ep 2211) and Ferdinand's lack of military experience (Ep 2295), while worrying in 1531 about the schemes of Francis I and *Clement VII (Epp 2480, 2481). In 1529 he noted Ferdinand's support for the Swiss Catholics (Ep 2173), and in 1534 he kept himself informed about the war that removed Württemberg from Ferdinand's control (Epp 2936, 2937, 2940, 2947, 2961).

Erasmus' greatest concern, however, was for Ferdinand's religious policy. He judged him to be a moderately scrupulous Catholic (Ep 2631) and, always retaining his role as Ferdinand's mentor, in September 1524 boldly advised him against the violent suppression of heresy (Ep 1515). In April 1526 he redoubled his pleas for moderation (Epp 1689, 1690), believing that they were having some effect (Ep 1608). By the end of 1527 he was alarmed by news indicating a hardening of Ferdinand's attitude, especially towards the Anabaptists (Epp 1924, 1926, 1977). He expressed his apprehension in a letter to Duke George of *Saxony, which was too frank to be published by Erasmus and is consequently lost, but which caused its recipient evident consternation (Ep 1983). The issue of freedom of conscience was raised at this very time at the diet of Speyer (February–April 1529), over which Ferdinand presided (Ep 2107). His intransigence prevailed, the protests of Philip of *Hesse and his supporters were overruled, and Erasmus' reaction changed from hope to despair (Epp 2123, 2130, 2133). At this diet some Protestants circulated statements by Erasmus on the question of capital

Ferdinand II of Aragon

punishment for heretics, which, Erasmus said, greatly irritated Ferdinand and were also brought to the attention of Charles v and Clement VII. In turn Erasmus reacted with visible anger in his *Epistola contra pseudevangelicos* (ASD IX-1 286–7, 290–1). Erasmus was again attacked at the diet of Augsburg the following year, his critic on this occasion being the preacher *Medardus, who was attached to Ferdinand's court. Erasmus appealed to his friends at court and also revenged himself on Medardus in a new edition of his *Colloquia*.

Despite the fact that Ferdinand did not, as Erasmus had hoped, put his ideas into practice, the Erasmian influence persisted at the court of Vienna even in later years. In his choice of councillors the monarch often relied on admirers of Erasmus such as Fabri, *Nausea, and Julius *Pflug. Especially in the early 1540s the Hapsburg rulers were committed to a serious search for religious concord, and in the years of his emperorship Ferdinand renewed that search with the religious colloquy of Worms (September 1557), in the aftermath of which such key documents of Erasmian irenism as Georg *Witzel's *Via regia*

and Georgius Cassander's *De officio pii ac publicae tranquillitatis vere amantis viri in hoc religionis dissidio* (Basel 1561) were composed.

BIBLIOGRAPHY: NDB V 81–3 / ADB VI 632–44 / Wilhelm Bauer *Die Anfänge Ferdinands* (Vienna 1907) / *Die Korrespondenz Ferdinands I.* ed W. Bauer et al (Vienna 1912–38) / Helmut Goetz 'Die geheimen Ratgeber Ferdinands I. ...' *Quellen und Forschungen aus italienischen Archiven und Bibliotheken* 42–3 (1963) 453–94 / Heinrich Lutz *Christianitas afflicta: Europa, das Reich und die päpstliche Politik im Niedergang der Hegemonie Karls v., 1552–1556* (Göttingen 1964) / Franz Bernhard von Bucholtz *Geschichte der Regierung Ferdinand des Ersten* new ed, with an introductory essay by Berthold Sutter (Graz 1971–) / Schottenloher III 66–75, VII 327 / Joseph Lecler *Histoire de la tolérance au siècle de la réforme* (Paris 1952) I 260–4, and passim (English trans, London 1960) / Heinz Eberdorfer 'Ferdinand I. und Erasmus von Rotterdam' (doctoral thesis, University of Graz 1977) / Paula S. Fichtner *Ferdinand I of Austria* (New York 1982) / Alfred Kohler *Antihabsburgische Politik in der Epoche Karls v.: die reichsständische Opposition gegen die Wahl Ferdinands I. ... (1524–1534)* (Göttingen 1982)

ALFRED KOHLER & PGB

FERDINAND II king of Aragon, 10 March 1452–23 January 1516
Ferdinand was born at Sos, in Aragon, the son of John II of Aragon and Juana Enríquez, the daughter of Fadrique, admiral of Castile. His teacher was the humanist Francisco Vidal de Noya. Intelligent, astute, and knowledgeable in law, Ferdinand was a true Renaissance prince. In 1469 he married *Isabella of Castile, the half-sister of Henry IV. On the death of Henry in 1474 Ferdinand had a claim to the crown of Castile on the grounds that he was the closest male relative. Although Isabella's claim to the throne prevailed, an agreement signed at Segovia on 28 April 1475 determined that both would govern Castile. They then conducted a successful war against a rival claimant, Juana la Beltraneja, and her allies, Alfonso v of Portugal and *Louis XI of France. In 1479, on the death of John II, Ferdinand inherited the crown of Aragon, thus uniting the two crowns for the first time in history. From 1482 he immersed himself in the conquest

of Granada, into whose capital he and Isabella
entered in triumph on 6 January 1492, thus
completing the reconquest of Spain from the
Moslems.

In domestic affairs in Castile, Ferdinand
collaborated with Isabella in using the Santa
Hermandad to crush rebellious nobles and
brigands. In Catalonia he solved the problem
of the *remensa* peasants, who were subject to
exorbitant feudal dues, the 'malos usos'; the
Sentence of Guadalupe (1486) abolished the
'malos usos' in return for monetary payments.
In the 1480s Ferdinand placed the inquisition
in Barcelona, thus causing many *converso*
merchants to emigrate to France.

In foreign affairs, Ferdinand's achievements
were many and enduring. In 1493, through the
treaty of Barcelona, he recovered Roussillon
from *Charles VIII of France in return for a
vague promise not to assist the king of Naples
if he was threatened by France. However, after
Charles invaded Italy and occupied Naples in
1494 and 1495 Ferdinand joined a Holy League
with the Emperor *Maximilian I, Venice, Milan,
and the papacy to drive out the French. His
intervention in this and subsequent Italian
wars laid the basis for Spanish hegemony in
the peninsula. Meanwhile, in 1512, Ferdinand
occupied the kingdom of Navarre and incorporated it into the kingdom of Castile in 1515. He
also campaigned in North Africa.

In 1504 Isabella died, naming Ferdinand
regent of Castile because of the mental
incapacity of their daughter, *Joanna. His
position was challenged by his son-in-law,
Philip the Handsome of *Burgundy, and
Ferdinand sought to strengthen his hand
through a French alliance involving his marriage to *Germaine de Foix. Although Ferdinand was forced to abandon Castile in 1506,
Philip's death in the same year allowed him to
return and continue to rule until his own
death.

Ferdinand is mentioned in the correspondence of Andrea *Ammonio with Erasmus: on
27 October 1511 Ammonio informed Erasmus of
the approaching war in Italy between Ferdinand and *Louis XII of France (Ep 236) and on
8 November 1511 of the formation of a league
including *Julius II, Ferdinand, and Venice
(Ep 239). In the *Panegyricus ad Philippum*
Erasmus mentioned the warm welcome given

by Ferdinand to his son-in-law, Philip the
Handsome, when the latter first visited Spain
in 1502 (ASD IV-1 42). In the *Julius exclusus* Pope
Julius is made to boast of how he had involved
Ferdinand and other rulers in war (*Opuscula*
112).

BIBLIOGRAPHY: Allen Ep 236 / J.N. Hillgarth
The Spanish Kingdoms, 1250–1516 (Oxford
1976–8) II / *Diccionario de historia de España*
2nd ed (Madrid 1968–9) II

MILAGROS RIVERA & TBD

FERDINANDUS *See Charles and Jean* FERNAND

Georgius FERIOTUS *See Georges* FERRIOT

Charles and Jean FERNAND of Bruges,
documented 1485–1517
Charles Fernand (Fernandus) was born at
Bruges in the middle of the fifteenth century.
His family moved to Paris, where he and his
younger brother, Jean, both very gifted Latin-
ists and musicians, were employed in the royal
chapel and became members of the circle of
humanists around Robert *Gaguin.

When Girolamo *Balbi arrived at Paris in
1485, Charles became one of his intimate
friends: they wrote laudatory poems for each
other and together they published an edition
of Seneca's tragedies. There can be little doubt
that Erasmus' distich *In caecum tragoediarum
castigatorem* (Reedijk poem 49) focuses on him
and not, as asserted by Reedijk, on the
Toulouse humanist Bernard *André. In the
Ciceronianus (ASD I-2 672) Erasmus mentioned
the two brothers briefly when examining the
style of Gaguin and Josse *Bade.

About 1492 Charles retired to the Benedictine monastery of Chezal-Benoît in Berry, and
Jean followed his example some three years
later. From 1508 or 1509 until his death in 1517
Charles stayed at the abbey of Saint-
Vincent-du-Mans. His main works are *Epistolae
familiares* (first published at Paris about 1488),
De animi tranquillitate (Paris: J. Bade and J. Petit
1512), *Epistola paraenetica observationis regulae
Benedictinae* (Paris: J. Bade and J. Petit 1512,
dedicated to Philippe de *Luxembourg), *Specu-
lum disciplinae monasticae* (Paris: J. Bade 1515),
and *Confabulationes monasticae* (Paris: J. Bade
1516). Moreover, a poem in honour of St
Catherine has been ascribed to him (Brussels,

Rui Fernandes de Almada, by Albrecht Dürer

Bibliothèque Royale, MS II 2112 ff 75–110). The same manuscript volume also contains several poems by Jean Fernand and one by Guy *Jouenneaux addressed to Charles (f 192 recto).

BIBLIOGRAPHY: E. Varenbergh in BNB VII 35–8 / U. Berlière 'La congrégation bénédictine de Chezal-Benoît' *Revue bénédictine* 17 (1900) 29–50, 113–27, 252–74, 337–61 (esp 261–74 and 337–47) / F. Simone 'Robert Gaguin ed il suo cenacolo umanistico' *Aevum* 13 (1939) 410–76 / L. Thuasne *Roberti Gaguini epistolae et orationes* (Paris 1903) / G. Tournoy 'Two poems written by Erasmus for Bernard André' *Humanistica Lovaniensia* 27 (1978) 45–51 / N. Loumyer 'Analyse d'un manuscrit du xve siècle – le Pseudo-Pindare – vers léonins inédits' *Bulletin du bibliophile belge* 2nd série 3 (1856) 305–20 / A. Scheler 'La passion de Sainte Cathérine' *Bulletin du bibliophile belge* 4 (1857) 286–306

GILBERT TOURNOY

Martín FERNANDES documented at Antwerp 1531–2

Martín Fernandes (Mertinus Ferrarius) is identified as the nephew of Rui *Fernandes in a letter from André de *Resende to Conradus *Goclenius dated 21 June 1531 and published in Resende's *Narratio rerum gestarum in India* (Louvain: S. Zassenus 1531).

From Erasmus' comments it is clear that Martín was not known to the humanist when he gave Erasmus *Schets in 1531 a letter for Erasmus together with a gift of candied fruits. Erasmus became rather exercised when the fruits failed to arrive. Not until December did they finally reach him in Freiburg, but by then he had mislaid Fernandes' letter, which had been delivered earlier; so Schets had to convey his thanks to Martín, who reacted by sending Erasmus another letter (Epp 2511, 2530, 2552, 2559, 2585, 2593). No more is known about Martín Fernandes.

BIBLIOGRAPHY: Allen Ep 2511   PGB

Rui FERNANDES de Almada documented 1512–37

Rui Fernandes (Rodericus Fernandius) served at the Portuguese Indiahouse in Antwerp beginning in 1512, a year after the house at the Kipdorf was opened. He represented Portuguese merchants as well as the Portuguese king (Ep 1681).

Since the beginning of the sixteenth century overseas goods had been transported from Lisbon to Antwerp, from where they were sold throughout Europe. The Portuguese factory was very much in the centre of Antwerp's economic activity. It attracted not only merchants but also foreign visitors who were curious to see the merchandise that came from far-away countries and to get news about the discoveries. One such visitor was Thomas *More. In 1515 he was appointed to a delegation that had to discuss a revision of the Anglo-Flemish commercial treaty in Bruges. He came to Antwerp and stopped at the Portuguese Indiahouse, where in conversation with the factors he showed much interest in the search for and contact with Christians overseas. It may well be that More suggested to his son, John (III) *More, that he translate Damião de *Gois' *Legatio* dealing with the message the Negus of Ethiopia had sent to King *Manuel in 1514. The translation was printed by William Rastell in 1533. It is noteworthy that the narrator in More's *Utopia* is a Portuguese, and it is possible that its setting was inspired by

More's conversations with the factors about the explorations.

Another famous visitor to the Indiahouse was *Dürer. Through the diary of his visit to Flanders (1520–1) we are well informed about his contacts with the two factors, João *Brandão and Rui Fernandes. Among the many presents he received from the Portuguese, Dürer mentioned sugar candy, silk, two parrots, nuts, corals, a pitcher, and cedar wood. Many of these items were new to Europeans and delighted Dürer. He showed his appreciation by presenting the factors with six paintings. One of them, the famous oil painting of St Jerome, is now among the treasures of Lisbon's ancient Museu das Janelas Verdas. Dürer also made drawings of the factors and of Brandão's negro servant or slave. In addition the Portuguese received many copper engravings and woodcuts. Joaquim de Vasconcellos counted 221 pieces in all.

In 1537 Rui Fernandes was ambassador in France. At that time he received a letter from André de Gouveia asking him to intervene in his favour with his uncle, Diogo de Gouveia. André was principal of the Collège de Guyenne at Bordeaux, where his religious views were suspect. Since he wanted to return to Portugal he was afraid that his uncle, who was a conservative and a great enemy of Erasmus, would warn the king not to offer him a position. Diogo actually did so, but the king nevertheless made André principal of the college of the arts. André thought of Fernandes as being a liberal, and his view is perhaps supported by the fact that Dürer, who was a religious suspect, was warmly received by him. There is no hard evidence regarding Fernandes' attitude towards Erasmus. Conceivably he was irritated by Erasmus' criticism of the spice monopoly (Ep 1800), but as he was the king's representative one can hardly blame him for that; nor can one draw conclusions from it as to his approval or disapproval of Erasmian humanism. He was, however, in close contact with Erasmus *Schets (Ep 1783), as was his nephew, Martín *Fernandes, who clearly admired Erasmus.

BIBLIOGRAPHY: Allen Ep 1681 / Maria do Rosário Themudo Barata *Rui Fernandes de Almada, diplomata português do seculo* XVI

(Lisbon 1971) / Marcel Bataillon 'Erasme et la Cour de Portugal' and 'Sur André de Gouvea' in *Etudes sur le Portugal au temps de l'humanisme* (Coimbra 1952) 49–99, 109–29 / J.A. Goris *Etude sur les colonies marchandes méridionales ... à Anvers de 1488 à 1567* (Louvain 1925) 219–21, 234–5, and passim / L. Guicciardini *Description de tous les Pays-Bas* (Antwerp 1568) / More Y v-2 344 / Artur Moreira de Sá *De re Erasmiana* (Braga 1977) 148–53 and passim

ELISABETH FEIST HIRSCH

Alonso FERNÁNDEZ de Madrid c 1475–18 August 1559
Alonso Fernández was a son of Pedro González de Madrid, himself a native of Palencia, *hijodalgo*, and treasurer of the Santa Cruzada and of the Santa Hermandad (1485–91). An elder brother of his was Francisco de Madrid, who translated Petrarch's *De remediis utriusque fortunae* into Spanish (Valladolid: Diego de Gumiel 1510). Alonso himself records that he was attached in his youth to the household of Fray Hernando de Talavera, first archbishop of Granada and a model Christian bishop in the eyes of Spanish Erasmians. Either in the boys' school that the archbishop established or in his 'college' for young men preparing for orders, Alonso received instruction in letters and religion, 'being a member of his household, his disciple and servant.' On Talavera's death in 1507, Alonso composed a eulogistic biography in his honour. This appears to have been the basis of an account of Talavera and his teaching prepared by Alonso years later at the urging of Luis *Núñez Cabeza de Vaca, then bishop of Salamanca (1530–6). The earliest surviving edition is that of Andrés de Burgos (Evora 1557). Renowned from an early age for his preaching and intellectual gifts, Alonso was a canon of Palencia cathedral by 1497 and followed his brother Francisco as archdeacon of Alcor there in August 1509. He spent the rest of his long life in these offices, serving both Luis Núñez Cabeza de Vaca and his predecessor, Bishop Francisco de *Mendoza y Cordoba, as vicar-general. The Palencia chapter minutes record the date of his death. It was from November 1506 that he added 'Fernández' to his name, possibly to lessen the *converso* overtones of plain 'Alonso de Madrid'.

Alonso's translation of Erasmus' *Enchiridion*

– by far the most important translation of any work by Erasmus to appear in Spain – was completed by the start of 1525 and after initial difficulties was soon to enjoy extraordinary success. The first edition, no copies of which are extant today, came out before September 1526, in which month, it seems, a second edition appeared (Alcalá: Miguel de Eguía), with a dedication to the inquisitor-general, Alonso *Manrique, whose arms it bore on its title-page. The dedicatory epistle repeats Erasmus' boldest remarks on the reading of the New Testament in the vernacular, set out by him in the *Paraclesis* and the preface to his *Paraphrasis in Matthaeum*. In 1529 Alonso wrote to Erasmus through Diego *Gracián de Alderete (Ep 1904). In his reply to Alonso (Ep 1969) and in a letter to Gracián (Ep 1970) Erasmus expressed gratification at Alonso's work and suggested other works of his own for translation, among them his commentaries on the Psalms. Bataillon judges it likely that the archdeacon or one of his friends was the author of the anonymous Spanish version of Erasmus' commentaries on Psalms 1 and 4 ([Toledo: J. de Ayala] 1531). In addition to the service-book *Passiones, Benedictiones, Lamentationes, et reliqua* (Palencia: Diego de Córdoba 1536) which he edited for his cathedral, the archdeacon wrote a historical miscellany, the *Silva Palentina*, whose contents include an enthusiastic reference to *Jiménez de Cisneros' encouragement of learning, a eulogy of Erasmus, and praise for the Spanish Inquisition and its 'purification' of Spain by means of its 'rigorous justice.' Existing in varying manuscript versions, this work was first published only in this century. If Alonso was in fact the translator, as accepted by Allen and Bataillon but questioned by Marín Martínez, his last publication in his own lifetime was his vernacular rendering of a work by Juan Bernal Díaz de Luco, bishop of Calahorra, *Doctrina y amonestación caritativa en la qual se demuestra no ser lícito a los cristianos ricos que dejen de socorrer con lo que les sobra a los pobres* (Estella: Guillermo de Millis 1547).

BIBLIOGRAPHY: The biographical information provided by Allen Ep 1904 now emerges as inaccurate at several points. See rather J. Galán *Diccionario de historia eclesiástica de España* (Madrid 1972–5) II 919; Erasmus *El Enquiridión*

o manual del caballero cristiano ed Dámaso Alonso, with prologue by Marcel Bataillon (Madrid 1932, repr 1971) 18–22; Bataillon *Erasmo y España* 191–2 and passim; P.E. Russell 'Francisco de Madrid y su traducción del *De remediis* de Petrarca' in *Estudios sobre literatura y arte dedicados al profesor Emilio Orozco Díaz* (Granada 1979) III 203–20; *Juan Bernal Díaz de Luco: soliloquio y carta desde Trento* ed T. Marín Martínez (Barcelona 1962) 114–16 / See also Alonso Fernández de Madrid *Silva palentina ...* ed Don Matías Vielva Ramos (Palencia 1932–42) esp I xi–xxviii, 447, 512, 529–30 and his *Vida de Fray Fernando de Talavera, primer arzobispo de Granada* ed Félix G. Olmedo, SJ (Madrid 1931) 22–8, 43, 79–84   R.W. TRUMAN

FERNANDO prince of Portugal, 1507–34 Dom Fernando was a son of King *Manuel I and his second wife, Maria of Castile. Sharing his father's interest in the arts and history, he commissioned a genealogy of the rulers of Spain and Portugal from prehistoric times to his own, which was embellished with drawings by António de Hollanda. Dom Fernando asked Damião de *Gois, who was in Antwerp, to find an artist who could make illuminations after Hollanda's drawings. The most famous illuminator at the time, in Gois' judgment, was Simon of Bruges. The latter was much in demand, but Gois preferred to wait until he was free rather than engage a lesser artist. Gois also purchased precious tapestries for the royal princes. Both Erasmus *Schets and Erasmus had good reasons to praise Fernando for his support of the sciences and the *belles-lettres* (Epp 1681, 1800). Dom Fernando was created duke of Guarda and Francoso in 1530 and in 1529 married a daughter of the count of Marialva.

Some folios of the genealogy are preserved in the British Museum as 'Portuguese Drawings.'

BIBLIOGRAPHY: Allen Ep 1681 / Francisco de Hollanda *Vier Gespräche über die Malerei geführt zu Rom, 1538* ed and trans Joaquim de Vasconcellos (Vienna 1899) deals with António's drawings (António was the father of Francisco)   ELISABETH FEIST HIRSCH

Jacques FERRAND documented 1516–30 Little is known as yet about Jacques Ferrand

(Ferrandus). A native of the diocese of Mende (archdiocese of Albi, Département de la Lozère), he matriculated in the University of Montpellier on 25 October 1516 and received a medical doctorate on 10 February 1527. He must have stayed on as a lecturer in the university, for in March 1527 and September 1530 newly arrived students selected him to be their mentor. When Petrus *Decimarius wrote to Erasmus, Ferrand sent greetings, and Erasmus returned them in September 1528 (Ep 2050).

BIBLIOGRAPHY: *Matricule de Montpellier* 29, 51, 60   PGB

Martinus FERRARIUS *See* Martín FERNANDES

Giovanni Stefano FERRERI of Biella, 31 December 1473–5 October 1510

Giovanni Stefano was born at Biella, in Piedmont, the son of Sebastiano Ferreri, who became the treasurer of *Louis XII in the duchy of Milan. Giovanni Stefano studied canon law and theology at the University of Paris. He became abbot of San Stefano, Ivrea, in 1489, bishop of Vercelli on 24 April 1493, and archbishop of Bologna on 24 January 1502, and on 18 September 1500 he was secretly appointed a cardinal; this was publicly announced on 28 June 1502. He voted for Giuliano della Rovere, who became Pope *Julius II in 1503, and subsequently enjoyed his favour accompanying Julius on his tour of the papal states in September and October 1505 and to Bologna in 1506. His palace in Rome had a garden and a fine collection of statuary.

Generally known as the cardinal of Bologna (for example, he was thus titled by Paris de Grassis when noting his death in Rome), he should not be confused with Cardinal Antonio de' Ferreri (d 23 July 1508), who was reviled for his extortions as legate at Bologna (19 February–15 July 1507), or with Cardinal Francesco *Alidosi. It seems probable that he was the cardinal of Bologna whom Erasmus recalled with gratitude in two letters of 1515 (Epp 296, 334), so that Allen's identification of Alidosi is questionable. Ferreri had been at Bologna when Erasmus was there in 1507 and in Rome when Erasmus stayed there in 1509. He promoted the edition of Aristotle's *Moralia* by Jacques *Lefèvre d'Etaples.

BIBLIOGRAPHY: DHGE XVI 1263–4 / J. Burchardus *Liber notarum* ed E. Celani (Città di Castello 1906–59) / Eubel II 265 (s v Vercelli) / Sanudo *Diarii* IV 306, 987, and passim / Also unpublished manuscripts of Paris de Grassis' *Diarium*   D.S. CHAMBERS

Georges FERRIOT of Porrentruy, documented 1493–1525

The Ferriots (Feriotus, Fereoti) were a good family of Porrentruy, in the Jura, where one Henri Ferriot was in this period one of the *maîtres-bourgeois*. Georges registered at the University of Basel in the winter term of 1493–4. He later lived at Porrentruy as a priest of the Confrèrie Saint-Michel, an institution comparable with a chapter of canons, which gave great encouragement to the cultural life of the region. In 1524 Ferriot accompanied Erasmus from Porrentruy to Besançon (Ep 1610), together with another priest of the same fraternity, Thiébaut *Biétry.

BIBLIOGRAPHY: *Matrikel Basel* I 227 / A. Chèvre 'Erasme, le prince des humanistes et ses amis de Porrentruy' *Actes de la Société jurassienne d'émulation* 77 (1974) 369–92, esp 371, 376, 392   PGB

Theobald FETTICH of Kaiserslautern, documented 1510–34

Theobald Fettich (Fettichius) of Kaiserslautern, in the Palatinate, seems to have studied at Cologne shortly after 1500. On 30 September 1510 he matriculated at the University of Heidelberg. In the second part of the *Epistolae obscurorum virorum* (1517) he is described as a doctor of medicine at Worms and a member of a humanistic circle composed mostly of assessors of the imperial court (*Reichskammergericht*). Among the friends of *Reuchlin he was seen as a supporter of their cause, and during the diet of Worms in 1521 he played host to Hermannus *Buschius. He was the physician of Wolfgang von *Affenstein, and in 1526 Erasmus directed to him a request for a manuscript from the Ladenburg library, which was under Affenstein's stewardship (Epp 1767, 1774). In the following year he was approached on behalf of Louis V, elector *Palatine, and asked for his advice concerning the appointment of a Protestant minister in Worms. Fettich was a friend of Otto *Brunfels, who praised his knowledge of Hebrew and history when dedicating to him in 1530 his *Catalogus illustrium medicorum* (Strasbourg: J. Schott). He also continued to be associated with the humanist printers as a supplier of manuscripts. In 1534 the Basel printer Henricus Petri dedicated to him an edition of Hrabanus Maurus' commentary on Jeremiah. Erasmus himself addressed to him a dedicatory preface (Ep 2760) for the first Greek edition of Ptolemy's *Geography* (Basel: H. Froben 1533), for which he had, without charge, supplied a copy of a manuscript.

BIBLIOGRAPHY: Allen Ep 1767 / *Matrikel Heidelberg* I 477 / Hutten *Operum supplementum* I 207 / David Friedrich Strauss *Ulrich von Hutten* new ed (Leipzig 1871) 425 / Adalbert Becker *Beiträge zur Geschichte der Frei- und Reichsstadt Worms* (Darmstadt 1880) 45–6

KONRAD WIEDEMANN

Eleanor van FEVIJN *See Robert* HELLIN

Jan van FEVIJN of Veurne, 10 May 1490–23 October 1555
Jan van Fevijn (Fevinus) was born at Veurne (Furnes), in Flanders. The Fevijn family was related to the Hedenbault family, and both were traditionally employed in the service of the dukes of Burgundy. When Jan lost his father at an early age, he and his sister were taken in charge by Filips van Hedenbault and, after Filips' death, by his brother, Karel van *Hedenbault. Thus from his childhood Jan had an intimate association with the Prinsenhof, the old ducal residence at Bruges, where Karel van Hedenbault lived and extended hospitality to Erasmus on several occasions. On 31 August 1506 Fevijn matriculated at the College of the Lily in Louvain, in due course taking his MA and turning to legal studies. By 1511 he was president of the law bachelors' association. Subsequently he completed his studies at Bologna and also visited Pavia and Rome before returning home with the degree of doctor of both laws.

While still a student at Louvain, Fevijn had been appointed to the twenty-fifth prebend of St Donatian's, Bruges, on 10 June 1510. He took holy orders and perhaps as early as 1523 was appointed scholaster (Ep 2278); he thus assumed responsibility for the famous chapter school, proposing staff appointments to his fellow-canons, conducting inspections, and administrating scholarship funds. In 1523 he also considered applying for the position of official but subsequently changed his mind because he did not wish to run against a friend.

As a canon Fevijn returned to live with Hedenbault in the Prinsenhof until his aged cousin and several other relatives died at short intervals in 1526 and 1527. Thereafter he moved to a house of his own on the Diver near the Gruthuis and the house of his friend Marcus *Laurinus, where he lived peacefully to his death, corresponding with his many friends and offering them his hospitality (Ep 2499), and on occasion even sketching their portraits, as he did with *Vives. He was particularly close to Frans van *Cranevelt, and from the time Cranevelt left Bruges for Mechelen in 1522 more than ninety letters to Cranevelt are preserved. He officiated at the wedding of Vives who praised him in his edition of Augustine's *De civitate Dei* (Basel: J. Froben 1522), while Adrianus Cornelii *Barlandus dedicated to him an edition of Terence's *Sex comoediae* (Louvain: R. Rescius 1530) and his *Compendiosae institutiones artis oratoriae* (Louvain: R. Rescius 1535). Hubertus *Barlandus inscribed to him his translation of Galen's *De paratu facilibus libellus* (Antwerp 1533).

Probably in 1519 Erasmus wrote to Fevijn after a highly enjoyable visit to the Prinsenhof (Ep 1012); likewise one of Fevijn's letters to Erasmus is preserved, written in 1530, apparently the first he had addressed to Erasmus in years (Ep 2278). In the mean time, however, they had exchanged greetings on many occasions (Epp 1145, 1303, 1317, 1665, 1792).

BIBLIOGRAPHY: Allen and CWE Ep 1012 / de Vocht *Literae ad Craneveldium* xci–xcix and passim / de Vocht *Dantiscus* 87–8 and passim / de Vocht CTL II 522 and passim PGB

Johann FICHARD of Frankfurt, 23 June 1512–7 June 1581
Johann Fichard (Fickard, Fichardus, Vicardus), the son of a school teacher in Frankfurt am Main, matriculated in Heidelberg on 17 May 1528. In the spring of 1530 he moved on to Freiburg in company with the son of Johann (1) *Lotzer, to study under *Zasius. Lotzer gave them a letter of introduction for delivery to

Erasmus (Ep 2306). In the autumn the plague drove them to Basel, where they stayed with the printer Andreas *Cratander. In December Fichard translated some short works by Galen for inclusion in Cratander's Latin edition of 1531; he also had friendly contacts with *Oecolampadius and Simon *Grynaeus. He returned to Freiburg in the spring of 1531, and on 28 November he obtained a legal doctorate together with Johann *Sichard, who had been his tutor for the past few months. In 1533 Fichard practised briefly as an advocate at the *Reichskammergericht* in Speyer but soon was appointed syndic in Frankfurt. In April 1536 he went to the imperial court with a letter of commendation from *Viglius Zuichemus. The preface of his *Virorum qui ... illustres fuerunt ... vitae* (Frankfurt: C. Egenolff 1536) was dated from Augsburg in 1536. He was in Padua from December 1536 to September 1537 and also visited Naples. After his return he was reappointed syndic in Frankfurt and became a well-known practising lawyer. He successfully represented Frankfurt on diplomatic missions and was instrumental in sparing the Protestant city from reprisals after the Schmalkaldic war. He married, was raised to the nobility in 1541, and remained in Frankfurt as a highly respected citizen until his death.

Fichard wrote on legal problems – *Tractatus cautelarum* (Frankfurt 1575), *Consilia* (Frankfurt 1590) – and added some recent lives to Bernardinus Rutilius' *Iuris consultorum vitae* (Basel: J. Oporinus [c 1539]). His biography of Sichard was included in Sichard's *Praelectiones in libros codicis* (Basel 1565).

BIBLIOGRAPHY: Allen Ep 2306 / NDB V 120–1 / ADB VI 757–9 / Paul Lehmann *Johannes Sichardus* (Munich 1912) passim / *Matrikel Heidelberg* I 543 / *Matrikel Freiburg* I-1 278 / BA *Oekolampads* II 800 / Winterberg 31–3   IG

Marsilio FICINO of Figline,
19 October 1433–1 October 1499
Marsilio Ficino (Marsilius Ficinus) was born in Figline, in the *contado* of Florence. His family, the Diotifeci of Castello di Feghine, belonged to the petty nobility and can be traced as far back as the twelfth century. His father was Diotifeci d'Agnolo di Giusto, born in 1401; his mother, Alexandra Giovanni di Lodovico Nannocio of Montevarchi, was born in 1413.

Marsilio Ficino, by Niccolò Fiorentino

His father, a student physician at Figline at the time of Marsilio's birth, developed a successful career in medicine in Florence and its environs, becoming the personal physician of Cosimo de' Medici and other Florentine notables. The surname assumed by Marsilio was derived from the diminutive of Diotifeci Fecino. In some of his early writings he was called Marsilius Feghinensis (that is, of Figline), but in the earliest extant document, of 28 October 1451, he is called 'Marsilio di maestro Fecino.'

Little is known of Ficino's early education, though biographers have not failed to speculate concerning it. The document of 1451, when he was just eighteen, shows him as a student of logic at the Studio of Florence and the tutor of a notable citizen, Piero de' Pazzi. Among his probable teachers were Niccolò Tignosi, an Aristotelian on the medical faculty, the theologians Lorenzo Pisano and Antonio Agli, and Francesco da Castiglione, presumed to be his teacher of Greek. Although he must be considered both a philosopher and a physician, and also a humanist for his translations of Plato and related ancient texts, there is no good evidence as to where he may have studied other than at Florence. The notion that he studied medicine at Bologna, though put forth by an early biographer, Giovanni Corsi, and repeated by both Della Torre and Marcel, his most notable modern biographers, is supported by no internal or external evidence.

A similar lack of precision characterizes modern understanding of the stages of development of Ficino's Platonism and of his connection with Cosimo de' Medici in this process. Some of his early writings have survived, and there is knowledge of others that have not. In 1454 or 1455 he wrote a series of short tracts on Aristotelian topics that were sent to Michele Mercati of San Miniato and were in the nature of school exercises, developed in connection with his university courses. In 1456 he wrote what seems to have been a more substantial work (now lost), the *Institutiones Platonicae*, based on Latin Platonic sources and the translations then available to him. This treatise, sent to Cosimo de' Medici and to Cristoforo *Landino, prompted them to urge Ficino to learn Greek and breathe in the authentic sources of Platonism. In 1457 and 1458 he wrote several treatises and letters of an eclectic nature indicating a broad interest in philosophical schools; included among them are *De voluptate* of Epicurean provenance, *De virtutibus moralibus, Di Dio et anima, De quatuor sectis philosophorum*, and *De furore divino*. It is possible that these works were revised by Ficino later. Some commentaries on Lucretius were later destroyed by Ficino, though traces of his Epicurean interests survive in his mature Platonist writings. These early writings exhibit a broad interest in a variety of currents befitting a developing philosophical mind. At the same time Ficino professed to have been drawn to Platonism from his early youth.

The connection with Cosimo is also unclear. Ficino claimed to have 'philosophized' with Cosimo for twelve years in 1464, which would have dated his relationship back to at least 1452. Yet we have seen him tutoring Piero de' Pazzi, of a rival house, in 1451. Certainly there were opportunities for contact with the Medici through his father's position. According to Ficino, Cosimo had resolved in 1439 at the urging of the Byzantine Platonist *Gemistos Plethon to found a new Platonic Academy. Yet it was only in the fall of 1462 that Cosimo

provided Ficino with a villa at Careggi, an income, and other properties. He also gave him a manuscript in Greek of the Hermetic work known as the Pimander. Within a year Ficino had translated it, and it was published at Treviso in 1471. By the spring of 1464 he had also translated ten dialogues he assumed were Plato's (only four are now considered genuine). Cosimo died shortly afterwards, on 1 August 1464. By 1469 Ficino had completed his translations of Plato. These were published later, after being polished and revised at Florence in 1484. Piero and then Lorenzo (1) de' *Medici took over Cosimo's role as patron; Lorenzo became actively involved in Ficino's so-called Platonic Academy.

In 1469 Ficino wrote the first of his mature philosophical works, his *Commentarium in Convivium Platonis, de amore*, first published with his edition of Plato of 1484. Other commentaries on the dialogues *Parmenides, Sophist, Timaeus, Phaedrus*, and *Philebus*, written and revised over the years, were published in his *Commentaria in Platonem* in Florence by Lorenzo de Alopa in 1496. Between 1469 and 1474 Ficino wrote his major philosophical and theological work, *Theologia Platonica, sive de immortalitate animorum*, first published in Florence by Antonio Miscomini in 1482. In December 1473 Ficino was ordained priest and the following year, in celebration of this event he wrote his *De christiana religione*, published in 1476 (Florence: N. Laurentii). His collection of letters in twelve books was published at Venice by Matteo Capcasa in 1495. Many of these were either short sermons or important moral and philosophical statements. His major medical work, which was also in part philosophical and theological, was written at various dates between 1480 and 1489 and published at Florence by Antonio Miscomini in the latter year (*De vita libri tres*). In March 1487 he became a canon of the cathedral of Santa Maria dei Fiori of Florence.

The so-called Platonic Academy founded by Ficino was not a formal educational or scholarly society but an informal association which met for discussions and celebrations of Plato's birthday and similar events. Nevertheless it was important in spreading a new kind of Christian-Platonic spirituality among laymen of the Florentine upper classes. It perhaps

contributed to some of the support offered to
*Savonarola's movement in the 1490s by
humanists and other intellectuals from this
group. Ficino himself offered limited support
to Savonarola, apparently on political rather
than intellectual grounds. Ficino's influence
upon other thinkers of his epoch spread
beyond Florence to other Italian and European
centres before the end of the fifteenth century,
the circles of *Lefèvre d'Etaples in France and
John *Colet in England being prominent
examples. Erasmus was well aware of Ficino's
importance (Ep 862), although the extent to
which his own spirituality was a form of
Christian Platonism has not been adequately
determined. His allusions to Plato in his
Enchiridion militis christiani have often been
observed but cannot be attributed directly to
Ficino.

Other works by Ficino included the *Consiglio
contro la pestilenza* (Florence: J. de Ripoli 1481),
De sole et lumine (Florence: A. Miscomini 1493),
In epistolas D. Pauli (late 1490s, *Opera omnia*
425–72), and *De comparatione solis ad Deum*
(Tübingen 1547). His *Opera omnia* were published at Basel in 1561 and 1576 (H. Petri) and
were reprinted at Turin in 1959. P.O. Kristeller
edited the *Opuscula inedita et dispersa* of Ficino
(Florence 1937), commonly called the *Supplementum Ficinianum*. A critical edition and
French translation of the *Theologia Platonica de
immortalitate animorum* was published by Raymond Marcel in three volumes (Paris 1964–70),
while members of the Language Department of
the School of Economic Science, London, have
translated two volumes of Ficino's letters into
English (London 1975–8). An edition and
English translation of *The Philebus Commentary*
was prepared by Michael J.B. Allen (Berkeley,
Los Angeles, London 1975). Ficino's commentary on the *Symposium* was edited and translated into English by Sears R. Jayne (Columbia,
Mo, 1944) and into French by Raymond Marcel
(Paris 1956).

Besides translating the Hermetic Pimander
and the complete works of Plato (including a
number of spurious or falsely attributed ones),
Ficino contributed to the renaissance of Platonism by his other translations of ancient Greek
neo-Platonists and of related texts. Of greatest
importance were the *Enneads* of Plotinus
(Florence: A. Miscomini 1492). Also translated

were Dionysius the Areopagite's *De mystica
theologia et de divinis nominibus* (Florence 1496),
Jamblichus' *De mysteriis et alia* (Venice 1497),
Athenagoras' *De resurrectione* (Paris: G.
Marchant 1498), Xenocrates' *De morte* (Paris
1498), Alcinous' *De doctrina Platonis* (Basel: M.
Isengrin 1532), and Synesius' *De somniis* (Lyon:
J. de Tournes 1549). Ficino also prepared an
Italian translation of Dante's *De monarchia*
(Florence 1839).

BIBLIOGRAPHY: Allen Ep 862 / Raymond
Marcel in DS V 295–362 / F. Vernet in DTC V
2277–91 / C. Carbonara in *Enciclopedia filosofica*
(Venice 1957–8) II 1327–31 / Giuseppe Saitta in
EI XV 221–3 / P.O. Kristeller in *Encyclopedia of
Philosophy* ed P. Edwards (New York 1967) III
196–201 / Arnaldo Della Torre *Storia dell'Acca-
demia Platonica di Firenze* (Florence 1902) / J.
Festugière *La Philosophie de l'amour de Marsile
Ficin et son influence sur la littérature française au
XVIe siècle* (Coimbra 1922; Paris 1941) / Walter
Dress *Die Mystik des Marsilio Ficino* (Leipzig-
Berlin 1929) / Giuseppe Saitta *Marsilio Ficino e
la filosofia dell'Umanesimo* rev 3d ed (Bologna
1954) / P.O. Kristeller *The Philosophy of Marsilio
Ficino* (New York 1943), *Il pensiero filosofico di
Marsilio Ficino* (Florence 1953), *Die Philosophie
des Marsilio Ficino* (Frankfurt 1972); Italian
version has texts in original Latin and Italian,
Italian and German versions have extended
indices / P.O. Kristeller *Studies in Renaissance
Thought and Letters* (Rome 1956); part ii,
'Marsilio Ficino and His Circle,' 35–253, has
important biographical papers used here / P.O.
Kristeller 'L'état présent des études sur Marsile
Ficin' in *Platon et Aristote à la Renaissance* (XVIe
Colloque International de Tours) (Paris 1976) /
Eugenio Garin *L'Umanesimo italiano, filosofia e
vita civile nel Rinascimento* (Bari 1952) chaps III
and IV / Eugenio Garin 'Immagine e simboli in
Marsilio Ficino' in *Medioevo e Rinascimento* (Bari
1961) 288–310 / André Chastel *Marsile Ficin et
l'art* (Geneva-Lille 1954) / Michele Schiavone
Problemi filosofici in Marsilio Ficino (Milan 1957) /
Raymond Marcel *Marsile Ficin* (Paris 1958)
contains important biographical documents;
should be used with caution / D.P. Walker
*Spiritual and Demonic Magic from Ficino to
Campanella* (London 1958) / Sears Jayne *John
Colet and Marsilio Ficino* (Oxford 1963) / Frances
A. Yates *Giordano Bruno and the Hermetic
Tradition* (London 1964) chaps I to IV / Charles

Trinkaus 'Humanist themes in Marsilio Ficino's philosophy of human immortality' in *In Our Image and Likeness: Humanity and Divinity in Italian Humanist Thought* (London-Chicago 1970) 461–504 / Samuel Jone Hough 'An early record of Marsilio Ficino' *Renaissance Quarterly* 30 (1977) 301–4   CHARLES TRINKAUS

Battista FIESCHI of Genoa, 1471–after 1535
Battista or Gian Battista Fieschi (Fliscus), the son of Luca di Daniele, belonged to one of the oldest, most powerful families of Genoa. He was a doctor of civil and canon law. His will, drawn up in November 1502, mentions a wife, Batina di Daniele, whose surname is unknown, and two sons, Luchetto and Giovanni Agostino. A later source states that he had two wives and three sons, among whom was perhaps Pietro, who was named bishop of Cervia in the will of Cardinal Niccolò Fieschi in 1524. On 20 November 1500 Battista participated in the foundation of the hospital for incurables that was connected with the Oratory of Divine Love, founded at Genoa by another member of Battista's family, St Caterina Fieschi Adorno. When the hospital for incurables was attacked by the patrons of the old hospital, Battista, acting as advocate, was deputized to plead its case before the Council of Ancients and obtained approval for the new institution on 27 November 1500. Fieschi also distinguished himself in the service of the commune: among other positions he was councillor in 1513, advocate for the incarcerated in 1515, and ambassador to Rome in 1517.

In a letter to Erasmus of 1535 Giovanni Angelo *Odoni stated that Fieschi was among Erasmus' most avid Italian supporters (Ep 3002).

Fieschi was a man of culture and a writer. Although most of his works are lost, a letter of his was published in an appendix to the polyglot *Psalterium hebraeum, graecum, arabicum et chaldaeum* of Agostino *Giustiniani (Genoa: P.P. Porro, 1516), the Latin sections of which Fieschi helped edit. In addition, Fieschi had ties with Guillaume *Budé, who sent him a letter on 15 December 1521, and with Cardinal Gregorio Cortese, the humanist and theologian.

Battista Fieschi may also have been the prominent Italian who entered into correspondence with Martin *Bucer under the pseudonym Eusebio Renato. In the early 1530s Renato led a small but active group of Italian sympathizers with the Reformation who sought to establish contacts with Strasbourg and Wittenberg. He also composed the 'Omelie sui vangeli di tutto l'anno,' which he sought to have published at Strasbourg and which would have spread the new religious ideas in Italy. The identification of Renato with Fieschi is supported by the contents of the above letter from Budé, which demonstrates that from 1521 the Genoese patrician was following the work of *Luther with profound interest. Eusebio Renato was last mentioned as alive in 1534, Fieschi in 1535.

BIBLIOGRAPHY: For Fieschi's will see Genoa, Archivio di Stato, Notaio Battista Strada, Filza 1, doc 29 / For his contacts with other scholars see Guillaume Budé *Epistolae* (Paris: J. Bade 1522) 64 recto–66 verso and Gregorio Cortese *Epistolarum familiarium liber* (Venice: F. dei Franceschi 1573) 93ff / For other biographical information see G. Banchero *Genova e le due Riviere* (Genoa 1846) I 87; N. Battilana *Genealogie delle famiglie nobili di Genova* [Genoa 1825–6] III 11 and passim; Cassiano Carpaneto da Langasco *Gli ospedali degli incurabili* (Genoa 1938) 68ff; F. Federici 'Alberi genealogici delle famiglie di Genova' Genoa, Biblioteca Franzoniana, Cod Urbani 127, 68 verso–69 recto; A. Oldoini *Athenaeum ligusticum seu syllabum scriptorum ligurum* (Perugia 1680) 84ff; S. Seidel Menchi 'Sulla fortuna di Erasmo in Italia' *Revue suisse d'histoire* 24 (1974) 543ff 630ff; S. Seidel Menchi 'Passione civile e aneliti erasmiani di riforma nel patriziato genovese nel primo cinquecento' *Rinascimento* 18 (1978) 113–16
                     SILVANA SEIDEL MENCHI

Lorenzo FIESCHI of Genoa, c 1466–13 February 1519
Lorenzo Fieschi (Fiesco, Fliscus) was an illegitimate son of Obieto Fieschi, a member of an old and powerful family of Genoa. He became bishop of Brugnato on 27 September 1502 and was translated to Ascoli on 24 May 1510 and to Mondovì on 15 October 1512. In August 1507 Pope *Julius II appointed him governor of Bologna after the disgrace of Cardinal Antonio de' Ferreri. Soon afterwards he became governor of Rome, but he returned

to Bologna in 1510 and – with the exception of a brief interlude in 1511 when Annibale (II) *Bentivoglio seized the city – remained there until his death.

In 1517 Ulrich von *Hutten informed Erasmus of an altercation between Germans and Lombards at the University of Bologna. Hutten was asked to present the Germans' case to an unsympathetic Fieschi (Ep 611).

BIBLIOGRAPHY: Allen Ep 611 / Eubel III 133, 156, 267 / Pastor VI 304 / Sanudo *Diarii* VII 154, X 81, 878–9, XI 81, XXV 491, XXVI 480, 509   TBD

Stefano FIESCHI documented c 1453
A native of Soncino, in Lombardy (36 kilometres north-east of Cremona), Stefano Fieschi (Fliscus, Philiscus) is said to have been rector of the Latin school of Dubrovnik (Ragusa) by 1453. He is known for his publications, including *De componendis epistolis* (Venice: D. de Mediolano 1494) and especially *Synonima seu variationes sententiarum*. The *Synonima* survive in many different editions, attesting to the popularity of this work in the late fifteenth century (Ep 260). Various editions were apparently adjusted to local demand by supplying synonyms in the appropriate vernacular language.

BIBLIOGRAPHY: Allen Ep 260 / Cosenza II 1434–5 / C.G. Jöcher *Allgemeines Gelehrtenlexicon* (Leipzig 1750, repr 1961) II 641 / J.-C. Brunet *Manuel du libraire* (Paris 1860–80, repr 1966–8) II 1291–2   PGB

Francesco FILELFO of Tolentino,
25 July 1398–31 July 1481
Francesco Filelfo (Philelphus) was born in Tolentino, near Ancona, apparently of very humble parents. At the age of eighteen he was studying in Padua under the guidance of Gasparino Barzizza and Paolo Veneto; shortly afterwards he started his teaching career as a private tutor of philosophy in Padua, Vicenza, and Venice. He was held in considerable esteem in Venetian aristocratic and political circles. In 1421 he was chosen as secretary to the Venetian ambassador in Constantinople, where he served the Emperor John Palaeologus in several missions and improved his knowledge of Greek; he frequented the school of Johannes Chrysoloras and married his daughter Theodora. On 24 August 1427 Filelfo

Francesco Filelfo

left Constantinople for Venice with a sound knowledge of Greek and a considerable number of Greek manuscripts, described in his letter of 13 June 1428 to Ambrogio Traversari. Venice was ravaged by the plague, but the enterprising humanist was able to obtain (13 February 1428) a chair of eloquence and moral philosophy at the University of Bologna. Soon after his arrival, however, the city was besieged by the army of Cardinal Capranica, and Filelfo left to seek his fortune in Florence as a teacher at the Studio.

Wide publicity was given to Filelfo's program of instruction even before his arrival. The humanist planned to devote the morning hours to reading Cicero (the rhetorical works and the *Tusculanae disputationes*), the first ten books of Livy's history, and the *Iliad*; the afternoon was to be devoted to studying the comedies of Terence and a treatise of moral philosophy, supplemented by selected readings from Cicero's orations and from the works of Thucydides and Xenophon. Initially his courses were attended by personalities such as Carlo Marsuppini and Niccolò Niccoli; however his contentious and arrogant nature soon provoked the resentment of numerous exponents of Florentine culture who were closely associated with Cosimo de' Medici. Mutual antagonism between Filelfo and Cosimo's supporters increased and assumed political overtones, and his tenure at the Studio was cancelled in October 1431. Later he was severely wounded by Filippo da Casale and attributed responsibility for the assault to Cosimo. In 1434 he was banished from Florence. He took refuge in Siena, where he taught Latin and Greek eloquence from 1434 to 1438 and continued his relentless campaign against Cosimo, trying to rally his political enemies against him. This provoked harsh rebuttals, famous among which are Poggio *Bracciolini's virulent *Invectivae in Franciscum Philelphum*. The unsafe proximity of Siena to Florence and the humanist's insatiable lust for money induced him to accept a highly lucrative offer (450 ducats for one semester) from the University of Bologna in 1439. Immediately afterwards Filelfo accepted Filippo Maria Visconti's invitation to teach at the University of Pavia and subsequently (11 February 1440) to join the ducal court in Milan.

During his seven years in the entourage of Filippo Maria Visconti, Filelfo wrote some of his best-known works: *Convivia Mediolaniensia* and works in Italian, among them the frequently reprinted commentary on Petrarch's *Canzoniere*. When Francesco Sforza took possession of the duchy of Milan (25 March 1450), Filelfo promptly offered him his services; the new and low-born duke offered him a chair of rhetoric – with a salary of six hundred florins per annum – and the humanist showed his gratitude by writing the epic poem *Sphortias*, in which his new master is cast in an atmosphere of classically conceived nobility. Greedy and restless, Filelfo did not remain quietly in Milan: on a tour to southern Italy he was well received by King Alfonso i in Naples and by Pope *Nicholas v in Rome, but he also managed to antagonize the college of cardinals with some of his ferocious epigrams. He was punished for this by Francesco Sforza and later recanted in order to obtain the favours of Cardinal Enea Silvio Piccolomini (later *Pius ii). After the death of Francesco Sforza, Filelfo considered a new offer from the University of Bologna but preferred the invitation extended by Pope *Sixtus iv to teach Greek and Latin eloquence

in Rome. Still vigorous in spite of his age, Filelfo returned to Milan after the assassination of Galeazzo Maria Sforza (1476). Meanwhile he had become reconciled with the Medici and was offered a chair of Greek eloquence at the Studio of Florence through the intervention of Lorenzo (i) de' *Medici ('il Magnifico'). Filelfo, who died in Florence, was married three times: his first wife, Theodora Chrysoloras, died on 3 May 1441, his second, Orsina Osnaga, on 6 January 1448, and his third, Lama Magiolini or Mazzorini, in 1476.

Erasmus was well acquainted with the activity of Filelfo, had extensive knowledge of his work (Ep 45), and was aware of the negative aspects of his personality (Ep 39). This fact, however, did not prevent him from appreciating Filelfo's contributions to the new learning (Epp 23, 182, 188; Allen i 4). Despite these tributes Erasmus' attitude towards Filelfo was not uncritical; it is evident that the Dutch scholar saw the Italian humanist in a precise historical perspective as a representative of the earlier phase of the humanistic movement (Ep 844). His consciousness of his own superiority is quite clear from Ep 3043, where he questioned the stylistic elegance of Filelfo's Latin prose and practically reiterated the position taken in the *Ciceronianus*, where he wondered about the appropriateness of defining Filelfo as a true Ciceronian (ASD I-2 661–2). In his later years Erasmus continued to pay tribute to Filelfo's translation of Plutarch's *Apophthegmata* (Epp 2422, 2431).

From 1485 to 1520 the letters of Filelfo appeared in at least twenty-nine editions, and some are still unpublished. Important modern editions of Filelfo's correspondence in Greek are: T. Klette *Die griechischen Briefe des Franciskus Philelphus* (Greifswald 1890) and E. Legrand *Cent-dix Lettres grecques de Filelfo* (Paris 1892). In addition to the works already quoted Filelfo's vast production includes the *De morali disciplina* (Venice 1552); the *Commentationes Florentinae de exilio*, the third book of which is now published in Eugenio Garin *Prosatori latini del quattrocento* (Milan-Naples 1952); the translations of Aristotle's *Rhetoric* (Cremona: B. de Misintis 1492), Xenophon's *De republica Lacedaemoniorum* (Bologna: B. Hector 1502) and *Cyropedia* (Rome: A. de Villa 1474); and *Exercitatiunculae latinae et italicae* (Milan: X.

Waldorfer 1483). Furthermore Filelfo wrote letters in Italian; orations in Latin and in Italian; satires; poems in Latin, Greek, and Italian; and additional translations from the Greek (notable among which are the translations from Plutarch's *Lives*). The manuscripts and the editions of these works are listed in Giovanni Benaducci *Contributo alla bibliografia di Francesco Filelfo* (Tolentino 1902), which also contains a vast bibliography on Filelfo, beginning in the sixteenth century and continuing to the beginning of the twentieth. Modern editions of Filelfo works include Eugenio Garin *Testi inediti e rari di Cristoforo Landino e Francesco Filelfo* (Florence 1949).

BIBLIOGRAPHY: Allen and CWE Ep 23 / The most important biographical study on Filelfo remains Carlo de'Rosmini *Vita di Francesco Filelfo* (Milan 1808) / A brief, but very accurate biographical profile is in Vittorio Rossi *Il quattrocento* (Milan 1956) 37–43, 69 / For the journey of Filelfo to Constantinople see G. Dalla Santa 'Di un patrizio veneziano del Quattrocento e di Francesco Filelfo suo debitore' *Archivio Veneto* n s 11 (1906) 63–4 / For the Tuscan period G. Zippel *Il Filelfo a Firenze [1429–1434]* (Rome 1899); L. De Feo Corso 'Il Filelfo in Siena' *Bullettino senese di storia patria* 47 (1940) 292–316 / For the Milanese period G. Biscaro 'Documenti milanesi inediti su Francesco Filelfo' *Archivio storico lombardo* 40 (1913) 215–20; A. Calderini 'I codici milanesi delle opere di Francesco Filelfo' *Archivio storico lombardo* 42 (1915) 355–411; A. Calderini 'Richerche intorno alla biblioteca e alla cultura greca di Francesco Filelfo' *Studi italiani di filologia classica* 20 (1913) 204–24; Eugenio Garin 'La cultura milanese nella prima metà del XV secolo' in *Storia di Milano* (Fondazione Treccani degli Alfieri) VI (Milan 1955) 600–608; Eugenio Garin 'Ambrogio Traversari e il Filelfo a Firenze' and 'Il Filelfo a Milano' in *Storia della letteratura italiana* III ed E. Cecchi and N. Sapegno (Milan 1966)

DANILO AGUZZI-BARBAGLI

Giovanni Mario FILELFO 24 July 1426–1480 Giovanni Mario Giacobbe was born in Constantinople, the son of Francesco *Filelfo, the famous humanist, and Theodora Chrysoloras. He probably received a doctoral degree in Milan in 1442 and soon began his restless wandering through Italy and France. After teaching for a brief period in Savona, he was a guest at the court of René, count of Provence, in Marseille (1450) and soon departed to spend some two years in various towns on the Ligurian coast. In 1452 Filelfo arrived at the court of Borso d'Este in Ferrara, where he met Battista Guarino and Aurispa; afterwards his travels took him to Turin (1454) and Paris (from 1456 till about 1458). In Venice in 1460 he unsuccessfully competed with George of *Trebizond and Pietro Pierleoni for the post of historiographer of the Venetian republic. After further visits to Bologna and Milan (1461–4), Filelfo accepted the hospitality extended by Pietro Alighieri, a descendant of Dante, in Verona. In this city he lectured on the *Divine Comedy* (1467) and composed a life of Dante (1468). From Verona Filelfo moved to Bergamo (1469) and Ancona (1470). During this period he worked at some of his numerous poems: a poem on Lorenzo (I) de *Medici, another on the fall of Constantinople, and three books of eclogues. In Urbino he composed his *Epistolarium seu de arte conficiendi epistolas opus* for his pupil Lodovico Mondello. In the *Epistolarium* are included summaries of rhetorical precepts applicable to the art of letter-writing, the study of twenty-four types of letters, instructions concerning the proper forms of address, and a series of sample letters. In 1479 Filelfo was invited to Mantua by the Marquis Federico Gonzaga, and there he died the following year.

Erasmus did not profess great admiration for the turbulent son of Francesco Filelfo, whose *Epistolarium* he called 'muddled and disorderly ... defective in both scholarship and suitability to the purpose in hand' (Ep 117; cf *De conscribendis epistolis* ASD I-2 265). It is uncertain whether a reference in Ep 2046 is to the father or the son.

Besides the *Epistolarium* (printed in Paris 1482, probably by Ulrich Gering, and again in Milan in 1484 by Leonard Pachel and Ulrich Scinzenzeler), the printed works of Giovanni Mario Filelfo include the following: *La traduzione in terza rima dell'Uffizio della Beata Vergine* (Venice 1488), *Epitoma ad illustrem Sigismundum Malatestam Arimini principem* (Wolfenbüttel 1662), a version of the Odyssey in Latin prose (Venice 1516), and *Vita Dantis Aligherii* (Florence 1828).

BIBLIOGRAPHY: Allen and CWE Ep 117 / The works of Giovanni Mario Filelfo still in manuscript are listed in Guillaume Favre 'Vie de Jean-Marius Philelphe' in *Mélanges d'histoire littéraire* I (Geneva 1856) 170–1 / Those in the possession of Italian libraries are recorded in P.O. Kristeller's *Iter Italicum* (London-Leiden 1965–   ) / Particularly notable among the latter is a novel in Italian prose, 'Glycephila', in the Biblioteca Estense MS 100 (alpha P 6 4) / Vittorio Rossi *Il quattrocento* (Milan 1956) 71 / A. Agostinelli - G. Benaducci *Biografia e bibliografia de Gio. Mario Filelfo* (Tolentino 1899) / F. Gabotto *Documenti intorno a Francesco e Giovanni Mario Filelfo* (Turin 1890) / Francesco Flamini *Versi inediti de G.M. Filelfo* (Livorno 1892) / G. Vinay *L'umanesimo subalpino nel secolo XV* (Turin 1935) / F. Patetta *Venturino de Prioribus umanista ligure del secolo XV* (Vatican City 1950)   DANILO AGUZZI-BARBAGLI

Antonio FILONARDI See Ennio FILONARDI

Ennio FILONARDI of Bauco, c 1466–19 December 1549

Born of humble parentage in the village of Bauco, in the Hernican mountains, in the diocese of Veroli, Filonardi studied at Rome, entering the curial service of *Sixtus IV at the age of eighteen. Better suited for diplomatic assignments than for spiritual or pastoral cares, he rose in the service of *Alexander VI and on 4 August 1503 was appointed bishop of Veroli. He served successive popes from *Julius II to *Paul III as a diplomat as well as in the administration of the papal states. In the course of his eight missions as a papal legate to the Swiss cantons, his tasks were to maintain peace in Switzerland, to preserve and strengthen the papal alliance with the cantons, and to raise troops. While he had considerable success in carrying out these functions, he failed to grasp the true significance of the reform movement and its effects upon Swiss politics. Erasmus exchanged confidential letters with him in 1522 (Epp 1282, 1342), and when visiting Constance in September he was warmly greeted by Filonardi (Epp 1316, 1342), who had recently transferred his residence from Zürich to Constance. Soon the nuncio invited him to join the papal curia and to write against *Luther (Ep 1387). Filonardi forwarded Erasmus' letters to Rome and recommended a physician for his stone ailment (Allen I 45). The exchange of friendly letters and notes continued until Erasmus reported in September 1525 that the nuncio felt threatened and had left Swiss territory (Ep 1606).

From 1526 Filonardi occupied important positions in the administration of the papal states before returning to the diplomatic service. From 1531 and 1534 he conducted his operations from Milan and Lucerne. His report about the victory of the Catholic cantons in the Kappel war (printed in *Zwingliana* 2) was read in the consistory of 11 December 1531, and his correspondence with Erasmus resumed when he resided in Lucerne from 1532 to 1533 (Epp 2712, 2738, 2779, 2780). Paul III, with whom he was on particularly good terms, made him prefect of the Castel Sant'Angelo in 1534 (Ep 3011), cardinal in 1536, bishop of Montefeltro in 1538, and bishop of Albano in 1546. In 1535 Filonardi supported Erasmus' nomination to the cardinalate (Ep 3011). Besides the evident diplomatic considerations inherent in this proposal, Filonardi may have been motivated by his admiration for the cause of humanism; in fact he was also instrumental in Pietro *Bembo's promotion to the cardinalate. But it does not seem that he had a better understanding of the postulates of the Catholic reform than he had of the Protestant one; in 1526 Gian Matteo *Giberti expressed contempt for him and in the conclave of 1549 Filonardi opposed the papal candidacy of Reginald *Pole.

In Ep 2738 Filonardi mentioned his nephew, who went back to Rome from Lucerne in the autumn of 1532 and took Erasmus' letters with him. By 13 November some replies had reached Lucerne. The nephew may have been either Antonio Filonardi (d before 19 June 1569), to whom the cardinal resigned the see of Veroli on 12 August 1538, or Ennio Filonardi (d before 6 July 1565), who succeeded the cardinal on 29 April 1549 as bishop of Montefeltro.

BIBLIOGRAPHY: Allen Ep 1282 / *Helvetia Sacra* ed A. Bruckner (Berne 1972) I-1 40 / J.C. Wirz *Ennio Filonardi* (Zürich 1894) / Pastor VII–XIII passim / *Amtliche Sammlung der älteren eidgenössischen Abschiede* ed F.K. Krütli et al (Lucerne 1839–82) III-2, IV-1a, IV-1b passim / *Korrespondenzen und Akten zur Geschichte des Kardinals Matth. Schiner* ed Albert Büchi (Basel 1920–5) /

Albert Büchi *Kardinal Matthaeus Schiner* (Zürich–Fribourg 1923–37) / Paul M. Krieg *Die Schweizergarde in Rom* (Lucerne 1960) / Adriano Prosperi *Tra evangelismo e controriforma: G.M. Giberti (1495–1543)* (Rome 1969) 66, 69 / Paolo Simoncelli *Il caso Reginald Pole* (Rome 1977) 65 / G. von Schulthess-Rechberg 'Die Schlacht von Kappel im Kardinalskollegium' *Zwingliana* 2 (1905–12) 434–9 / Eubel III 24, 195, 331
MANFRED E. WELTI

Wolfgang FILSER documented at Basel 1517–40
The merchant Wolfgang Filser (Vilsser, Füllser, Fylsner) acquired the citizenship of Basel in 1517 and membership in the 'Schlüssel' guild in 1518. With the militia detachment of this guild, the most distinguished in the city, he joined the Basel troops mobilized for the war in Württemberg in 1519, and in 1529 he belonged to the Basel contingent for the so-called first Kappel war. He was elected to the executive of his guild and was its secretary in 1533 and its treasurer from 1538; the account book he kept still exists.

In 1529 Bartholomäus *Welser advised Erasmus that Filser should be capable of cashing a bill of exchange for him (Ep 2153).

BIBLIOGRAPHY: Paul Koelner *Die Zunft zum Schlüssel in Basel* (Basel 1953) 91, 300, 318 / *Aktensammlung zur Geschichte der Basler Reformation* ed E. Dürr et al (Basel 1921–50) III 546
PGB

Eustachius a FINE *See Eustachius van der RIVIEREN*

Moritz FININGER of Pappenheim, documented 1499–1523
Fininger (Mauritius Finiger), an Austin friar, indicated Pappenheim, south of Weissenburg, Franconia, as his home town when he matriculated at the University of Basel in 1499. He obtained a theological doctorate in 1501 and a chair of theology in 1503, at a time when the Basel faculty of divinity consisted of no more than two or three teachers and enjoyed little distinction. From 1513 he was also prior of the Austin house. Both in his order and in the university he was known for his quarrelsome temper rather than for professional competence or interest in the new learning. After

his fierce defence of the traditional faith, especially against the popular preacher Johann *Lüthard, the city council suspended his salary on 11 April 1523. No more is known of him after this date.

Erasmus mentioned on 21 September 1514 (Ep 305) that on arriving at Basel he was invited to dinner by the dean of the theological faculty. No doubt he meant Fininger, who between 1502 and 1519 was appointed dean more often than any of his few colleagues and was, in fact, dean for the academic year October 1513 to September 1514. Erasmus was clearly more impressed by another theologian also present at the dinner, Ludwig *Baer, who was then the rector of the university.

BIBLIOGRAPHY: Allen and CWE Ep 305 / R. Wackernagel *Geschichte der Stadt Basel* (Basel 1907–54) II-2 585, III 128, 427, and passim / *Matrikel Basel* I 257, 369–70   PGB

Guihelmus FISCINIUS (Reedijk poem 10, of c 1487–9)
Guihelmus Fiscinius – perhaps a Latinization of Willem (de) Corver – is mentioned by Erasmus as the husband of one Margareta Honora. If Margareta Honora is identical with Margareta *Heyen, Fiscinius had married her just six weeks before her premature death. Otherwise nothing is known of him.

BIBLIOGRAPHY: Reedijk poem 10
C.G. VAN LEIJENHORST

Christopher FISHER d by October 1512
Fisher was rector of Avon Dossett, Warwickshire, from May 1500 until 1507, by which time he had received a doctorate in civil and canon law. He was king's clerk in 1500 and held the rectories of Towcester and Castleford from 1501 and 1505 respectively, both until his death. He was canon of York and prebendary of Hustwayte from 1507. By papal provision Fisher was made bishop of Elphin, Ireland, in 1506, but the provision may not have been effectual. He was in Rome as one of the king's solicitors at the curia from 1508 to 1510 (Ep 216); in 1510 he was also notary to Archbishop William *Warham. In the same year Pope *Julius II appointed him nuncio to convey the Golden Rose to *Henry VIII in an effort to prevent an English alliance with France; for this service Fisher received a gift of one

John Fisher, by Hans Holbein the Younger

hundred pounds from the king. During his years in Rome Fisher was warden of the English hospice of St Thomas the Martyr, and in 1510 he was clerk and secretary of the Sacred College.

Nothing is known about Fisher's stay in Paris in the winter of 1504–5 except that Erasmus was a guest in his household (Ep 181) and dedicated his edition of *Valla's *Adnotationes* on the New Testament to his patron, who had encouraged the work (Ep 182). Josse *Bade praised Fisher in the preface to his edition of Baptista *Mantuanus' *Georgius*, 15 October 1509.

BIBLIOGRAPHY: Allen Ep 182 and IV xxii / Emden BRUO II 686–7   CFG

John FISHER of Beverley, 1469–22 June 1535
A patron of learning, exemplary bishop, and martyr, John Fisher (Fycher, Fyschere, Fyshar, etc) was born in Beverley, Yorkshire, in 1469, the son of a prosperous mercer, Robert (d 1477). He was educated at Cambridge and rose to be chancellor of the university, where he guided Lady Margaret *Beaufort, the mother of *Henry VII, in her benefactions (Ep 3036). He

was a friend and correspondent of Erasmus, who admired his devotion to the preaching of the Gospel and his episcopal duties and respected his dedication to the revival of letters. An eminent spiritual figure in the circle around Thomas *More, he preceded More to the scaffold; on 22 June 1535, he was executed on Tower Hill for refusing to take the oath required of him in the administration of the Act of Succession. On 19 May 1935 he was canonized in Rome with More.

As a boy, Fisher attended the minster school at Beverley, then became a scholar of Michaelhouse, Cambridge, to which he was admitted about 1483; he was later a fellow, then master (1496–8) of that college. He took his BA in 1488 and his MA in 1491, in which year he was also priested on the title of his fellowship. He proceeded to the theological doctorate in 1510. In due course he was the first Lady Margaret reader in theology (1502), vice-chancellor (1501), and chancellor (from 1504 to 1514, when he was re-elected chancellor for life).

From about 1498, Fisher was chaplain and confessor to the Lady Margaret and to her household. It was Fisher who was chiefly responsible for the design and execution of her plans to endow learning at Cambridge, beginning with the refoundation of Godshouse as Christ's College in 1505. He was also president of Queen's College from 1505 to 1508. A second and even more ambitious scheme was the refoundation of St John's Hospital as St John's College, for which Fisher drew up the first set of statutes in 1516. On 14 October 1504 he was promoted bishop of Rochester and was consecrated by Archbishop *Warham on 25 November that year.

At the request of the Lady Margaret, Fisher preached the funeral sermon of Henry VII (9 May 1509), and later the same year he preached at the 'month mind' for the Lady Margaret herself (d 29 June). A strong opponent both of *Luther and of the royal divorce, he attracted the displeasure of the government by his published defences of Queen *Catherine of Aragon and by his involvement in the affair of Elizabeth Barton, the Holy Maid of Kent. On 6 April 1533 he was placed under house arrest and released only after the coronation of *Anne Boleyn on 1 June. As a consequence of his refusal to take the required oath, the see of

Rochester was declared vacant on 2 January 1535. While imprisoned in the Tower, he was created cardinal priest by Pope *Paul III on 31 May 1535. The chief events of his career can be gathered from any standard account of the English Reformation; here it is possible only to deal with his relations with Erasmus.

Fisher was almost certainly the chief sponsor of Erasmus' arrival in Cambridge in 1511 to succeed him as Lady Margaret reader. Erasmus had taught Robert *Fisher, the bishop's kinsman, in Paris, and it seems likely that even before his arrival in Cambridge he had been made known to Fisher by him and other common acquaintances – William *Blount, Lord Mountjoy, Bishop Richard *Foxe, or Richard *Whitford. The first letters, however, suggest that by 1511 their acquaintance was by no means intimate. Erasmus, who was then lecturing on the grammar of Manuel Chrysoloras (Ep 233), proposed to translate St Basil's commentary on Isaiah, acquired from *Grocyn's library, to present to Fisher in return for a gift of money. In the event, Erasmus grew suspicious of the authenticity of the work (Epp 227, 229, 237). A few weeks later, Fisher sent a small gift as requested, with the explanation that he had no funds to dispense from at will (Ep 242). This exchange suggests that Erasmus' position in the university was not yet secure, since Fisher assured him that he would not only help him as much as he could from his own resources but speak to others, like Mountjoy, on his behalf. In 1512 Fisher invited Erasmus to accompany him to the fifth Lateran council (Ep 252), and although Erasmus could not accept, he wrote glowing testimonials for Fisher to friends abroad (Epp 252–4). In the end Fisher himself was unable to attend.

By 1513 we have the first evidence of real familiarity in their common concern about Scripture and letters. A letter to John *Colet of 31 October suggests that Erasmus had lent his Latin translation of Matthew's Gospel to Fisher (Ep 278). In May 1515 Fisher wrote to Erasmus that he was reading Rodolphus *Agricola's De inventione dialectica, because it was praised both by Erasmus and by Ermolao *Barbaro, and he asked Erasmus to visit him on his way to Basel, perhaps to counsel him in the study of Greek (Ep 336). In a letter to Johann *Reuchlin in the previous March, Erasmus had quoted remarks

of Fisher in praise of Reuchlin (Ep 324; cf Ep 457), wishing that all of his works should be obtained. Fisher had been first among those to see the Augenspiegel when he learnt that Reuchlin was vindicated by the decision of the bishop of Speyer, George, count *Palatine (Ep 300, August 1514), and it seems (Ep 545) that Erasmus had paid to have the work translated into Latin so that Fisher could read it. By 1516 Fisher and Reuchlin were in touch directly (RE Ep 234; cf CWE Ep 457:27–8); indeed, Fisher apparently intended in 1516 to cross the Channel with Erasmus in order to meet Reuchlin (Epp 457, 471; ASD IX-1 144). His interest in Reuchlin's De arte cabalistica at this time emerges in a testimonial letter to Erasmus about his edition of the New Testament (Ep 592, c June 1517). In April 1518 Erasmus asked Fisher what he thought of the De arte cabalistica (Ep 824), and he continued to send Fisher and Reuchlin news of one another in later years (Epp 889, 1129, 1155, 1311).

The study of the New Testament is another recurrent theme in the correspondence. Erasmus apparently intended originally to dedicate his New Testament to Fisher, a natural consequence of his labours in Cambridge (cf CWE Ep 384 introduction). By June 1516 he had written to explain why he had changed his mind (Ep 413). Fisher's reply to that letter (Ep 432) showed no trace of resentment and indicated that he had already shown Erasmus' chief English patron, Archbishop Warham, the several passages where Erasmus paid tribute to him. Fisher was also one of those, with Warham, Colet, Christopher *Urswick, and More, to whom Erasmus sent copies of his edition of Jerome's letters when the volumes appeared in 1516 (Ep 474).

The publication of the New Testament posed fresh problems. Fisher wished that Erasmus had latinized more consistently (Ep 481), but his interest in studying Greek and Hebrew was clearly inspired by Erasmus' work. In a letter of June 1517 (Ep 592) Fisher commented on his pleasure in working through the new Greek text and signed himself Erasmus' grateful pupil, 'discipulus tuus.' He tried unsuccessfully to enlist Erasmus as a teacher of Greek; More and Erasmus in turn tried unsuccessfully to recruit William *Latimer for the task (Epp 481, 540). Fisher's Hebrew tutor was Robert *Wakefield. In August 1516, on his way back to the continent, Erasmus visited Rochester for ten days, when More also paid a visit (Epp 452, 455); he stayed again briefly in April 1517 (Ep 592). Erasmus' description of Fisher's library and the insalubrious location of his palace is preserved in Ep 1489 (4 September 1524).

In September 1517 Erasmus sent the manuscript of his edition of the second book of Theodorus *Gaza's grammar to Fisher to assist in his Greek studies; the parcel also included the *Apologia ad Fabrum* (Ep 653). In the following spring he sent the printed version of Gaza as well (Ep 784). A letter from Louvain at the same time suggests that Fisher had been thinking of publishing a harmony of the Gospels (Epp 667, 936). Erasmus sought Fisher's advice in his revision of the New Testament (Epp 784, 1030), apparently without strain, despite Fisher's contact with Edward *Lee. In this quarrel, Fisher tried to play the part of mediator. Lee submitted his notes to Fisher for arbitration in March 1519 but decided to proceed when the *Apologia contra Latomum* appeared at the end of that month (CWE Ep 1026; Rogers Ep 75). Erasmus' gratitude to Fisher is effusive in a letter of 2 April 1519 (Ep 936). On 16 October 1519 Erasmus told *Tunstall (Ep 1029) that he had no doubt of Fisher's attitude in the dispute. The next day (Ep 1030) he begged Fisher to send him a transcript of Lee's manuscript. On 1 February 1520 (Ep 1061) Lee told Erasmus that Fisher had been given a copy of Lee's annotations, and on 21 February 1520 (Ep 1068) Erasmus assured Fisher of his continuing friendship, even if he had not sent Lee's manuscript. On 2 August 1520 (Ep 1129), Erasmus told Fisher that there was a deluge of criticism of Lee appearing in Germany.

During the same period Erasmus was attempting to restrain Fisher in a controversy of his own with *Lefèvre d'Etaples. While Etienne *Poncher, the bishop of Paris, had been ambassador in England, he had drawn Fisher's attention to Lefèvre's *Disceptatio de Maria Magdalena et triduo Christi* (Paris: H. Estienne 1517), which opposed the traditional view that the three Marys of the New Testament were the same person. Fisher's treatise asserting their identity, the *De unica Magdalena* (Paris: J. Bade 1519), was sent to

Erasmus (Ep 936), who had had his own disagreements with Lefèvre. Erasmus thought that Fisher had the upper hand in the debate but that his attitude was too severe (Ep 1016), and he regretted that Fisher had not applied his talents to a more worthy subject, such as the commentary on the Gospels which Erasmus claimed to have seen.

Fisher published two rejoinders in the matter, developing views about the authority of tradition which he later used in his criticisms of Luther. His *Eversio munitionis quam Iodocus Clichtoveus erigere moliebatur adversus unicam Magdalenam* (Louvain: D. Martens [1519]) opposed Josse *Clichtove's defence of Lefèvre and was apparently sent to Erasmus for printing (Ep 1030). Against Lefèvre's own defence, *Disceptatio secunda* (Paris: H. Estienne 1518), Fisher brought out a *Confutatio*, published in Paris (J. Bade) in September 1519. On 17 October 1519 (Ep 1030) Erasmus told Fisher that he had been about to report on his first treatise when the next appeared, which he had not yet read. He begged Fisher to be satisfied with the victory which the learned had awarded him and pointed out that Lefèvre was much harassed by the Paris theologians, especially the Dominicans, for his suggested sympathy with Reuchlin – a point well calculated to win Fisher over. On 21 February 1520 (Ep 1068) Erasmus wrote that he hoped his attempts to restrain Fisher and Fisher's to reconcile him with Edward Lee had not created any coolness between them.

In June 1520 Fisher was at the Field of Cloth of Gold in attendance on Queen Catherine, and he also went to Gravelines for the meeting between *Henry VIII and *Charles V. Erasmus was there among the emperor's councillors, and the occasion provided a final reunion of the English humanist circle, with More, Warham, Tunstall, and Mountjoy also present. It was Fisher's last meeting with Erasmus.

In ensuing years their epistolary discourse continued on the same themes, with added concern about Luther and his followers. Both wrote against Luther, as both opposed *Oecolampadius' views of the Eucharist (cf Epp 1129, 1311, 1489, 1538, 1688, 1780, 1893 and LB X 1519F–20A). Fisher urged Erasmus to write the paraphrase on the Gospel of St John (Ep 1323) and to finish his treatise on preaching, the

Ecclesiastes or *De ratione concionandi*, which Erasmus promised to do (Ep 1332). In September 1524, in his last surviving letter to Fisher (Ep 1489), Erasmus told him that his efforts had been interrupted by illness and more urgent tasks, but that he would take them up again that winter. In the event the work did not appear until after Fisher's death, in 1535. Its prefatory epistle and another passage contain Erasmus' tribute to Fisher's career at Cambridge, to his preaching and zeal for training other preachers, and to his signal achievement as a bishop (Ep 3036; LB V 767–70, 812A).

In 1525 Fisher reappeared in Erasmus' letters to Noël *Béda as a scholar and theologian of stature who approved of Erasmus' New Testament scholarship (Epp 1571, 1581). In September 1525, Béda actually suggested that Erasmus send the disputed annotations to Fisher to ask for an objective evaluation, but it is not known whether Erasmus did this (Ep 1609).

There is a tradition that Erasmus translated the mass of St John Chrysostom into Latin for Fisher; certainly he presented Fisher with his edition of Chrysostom (Epp 2359, 2413). The mass was not published until 1537 (Surtz 152–3, 513 n14). Under interrogation Fisher acknowledged that he had received a letter from Erasmus in prison, brought by his brother Robert and shown by him first to *Cromwell, but this letter has been lost.

At Fisher's death Erasmus several times expressed his shock and sense of personal loss, but he refrained from criticism of the English government, a restraint that attracted criticism in turn, like that from Damião de *Gois (Ep 3085). Apart from the passages cited in the *Ecclesiastes*, Erasmus' esteem for Fisher is expressed in the *Hyperaspistes*, where he is cited as one of the few true bishops (LB X 1254C, 1297F, 1475C) and in the preface to the ten-volume Froben edition of St Augustine, to Alfonso *Fonseca (Allen Ep 2157: 608–16; cf Ep 2164). He was one of those whom Erasmus designated to receive a set of his *Opera omnia* in his will of 22 January 1527 (Allen VI 505). The portrait drawing by Hans *Holbein in the Royal Library, Windsor Castle, is the most important likeness of Fisher, from which all others are derived.

BIBLIOGRAPHY: Allen Ep 229 / DNB VII 58–63 / Emden BRUC 229–30 / T.E. Bridgett *Life of Blessed John Fisher* (London 1888) / E.E. Reynolds *Saint John Fisher* revised ed (Wheathampstead 1972) / E. Surtz *The Works and Days of John Fisher* (Cambridge, Mass, 1967) / J. Rouschausse *Erasmus and Fisher, their Correspondence 1511–1524* (Paris 1968) / D.F.S. Thompson and H.C. Porter *Erasmus and Cambridge* (Toronto 1963) / McConica 328 and passim / G.J. Gray 'Letters of Bishop Fisher, 1521–23' *Library* 3rd series 4 (1913) 133–45

JAMES K. MCCONICA

Robert FISHER d 14 February 1511(?)
A kinsman to John *Fisher, Robert (the name was a common one in the family) Fisher (Piscator, Fischerus) studied in Paris, where in 1497–8 he was a pupil of Erasmus (Epp 58, 62). He may actually have been responsible for introducing Erasmus to his first English patron, William *Blount, Lord Mountjoy (Ep 118). In the spring of 1498 he left Paris for Italy, where he took his doctorate of laws (Ep 71) and on 8 February 1503 was one of the witnesses listed on the doctoral diploma for Jérôme de *Busleyden issued by the University of Padua. On 10 May 1507 one of this name supplicated for incorporation at Oxford as a 'doctor transmarinus.'

Ep 71 is the preface to the original draft of *De conscribendis epistolis*, which was eventually printed without authorization by John *Siberch at Cambridge in 1521. In his preface to the revised and greatly enlarged version printed by Johann *Froben in 1522, Erasmus referred to Fisher, the original dedicatee, in a derogatory way (Epp 1284, 3100). But Ep 118 to Fisher (December 1499) is very friendly (cf CWE Ep 72:4n). Erasmus may also have written his paraphrase of Lorenzo *Valla's *Elegantiae* for Fisher (cf CWE Ep 23:108n). In Ep 2260 Erasmus disparaged the Englishman for whom it was written. Since the Valla too was pirated when first written, it may be that Erasmus blamed Fisher for both these unauthorized printings.

Allen's assertion that Fisher became the king's solicitor in Rome is certainly wrong. However, a cleric by this name became chaplain to *Henry VII and was present at the king's funeral in May 1509. He subsequently served *Henry VIII. In due course he obtained a canonry and prebend at Windsor, 18 May

1509. He was presented to the rectory of Gresford, Denbighshire, in the diocese of St Asaph, in November of the same year and to the living of Chedzoy, Somerset (Bath and Wells), in January 1511. Chedzoy became void by resignation on 16 January, and on 14 February Fisher died; three days later his canonry and prebend were granted to Thomas *Wolsey, then the king's almoner.

BIBLIOGRAPHY: Allen and CWE Ep 62 / Emden BRUO 1501-1540 677 / Register of the University of Oxford ed C.W. Boase (Oxford 1884) / LP I-1 20 (p 14), 54 (no 51), 82 (p 43), 257 (no 25), 682 (no 26), 709 (no 48) / de Vocht Busleyden 35, 38-9, 129 / G.B. Parks The English Traveler to Italy (Rome 1954–) I 627 and passim

JAMES K. MCCONICA

Johannes and Nicolaus FISTULA See Jan PIPE

Richard FITZJAMES of Redlynch, d 15 January 1522

Fitzjames was born at Redlynch, in the parish of Bruton, Somersetshire, where he later founded a school. He was a bachelor at Merton College, Oxford, from 1465, and was a fellow from about 1468 to about 1476. In 1473-4 he was a senior proctor at Oxford and in 1477 canon of Wells; in addition he held many other benefices. He was a MA and a doctor of theology by July 1481, vice-chancellor of Oxford in 1481, and warden of Merton College from 1483 to 1507. Fitzjames was chaplain to King Edward IV, from whom he received the rectory of Aller and the vicarage of Minehead, both in Somerset.

Fitzjames was granted a grace to incorporate his theological doctorate in 1495-6, at which time he was almoner to *Henry VII. From 1497 to 1503 he was bishop of Rochester and in 1499 was employed at Calais in negotiations for a commercial treaty with the Low Countries. He was one of the dignitaries who greeted *Catherine of Aragon when she arrived in England, and he attended the archbishop of Canterbury at her marriage to Prince *Arthur in 1501. He was chancellor of Oxford in 1502 and, on the king's nomination, was bishop of Chichester from 1503 to 1506. In 1506 he became bishop of London and held the office until his death. He left his library to Merton College.

Bishop Fitzjames restored and beautified St Paul's Cathedral and rebuilt the palace at Fulham. Fitzjames, who presided over the BA disputation of Erasmus' opponent Richard *Kidderminster on 17 February 1497, was unsympathetic to the new learning. He deprecated the reforms of John *Colet, whom he charged with holding heretical views and suspended from preaching from 1513 to 1514 (Epp 270, 278, 314, 1211).

BIBLIOGRAPHY: Allen Ep 1211 / DNB VII 180-1 / Emden BRUO II 691-2 and BRUC 233 / McConica 72 and passim

CFG

Johann FLAMING of Boppard, 1469– 24 July 1532

A native of Boppard, on the Rhine in the ecclesiastical principality of Trier, Johann Flaming (Flamming, Flamingus, Flaminius, Flamineus) was a priest and from about 1502 to the year of his death rector of the church of tertiary nuns of St Francis near the chapter of St Martin's at Boppard. He was buried in that church beneath a funeral inscription composed by himself. Flaming was a poet, and among the seventy-four short compositions by him preserved in a Trier manuscript there is (f 90 recto) a distich dedicated to Erasmus. On 31 December 1507 Johannes Adolphus Mullingus dedicated to him and another man his edition of some Libelli by Gregory Nazianzen (Strasbourg: J. Knobloch 13 January 1508). When Erasmus returned from Basel to Louvain in September 1518 Flaming accompanied him from Boppard to Koblenz and was rewarded with an honourable mention in Ep 867 and greetings in Ep 879. In the following month *Eobanus Hessus visited him on his way to Louvain and subsequently mentioned him as a fellow poet in his Hodoeporicon, while Adolf *Eichholz failed to meet him when passing through Boppard in 1528 (Ep 2071).

BIBLIOGRAPHY: Allen Ep 867 / Hansgeorg Molitor 'Johannes Flamingus' in Reformatio ecclesiae: Festgabe für Erwin Iserloh ed R. Bäumer (Paderborn 1980) 281-5 / Walter Röll 'Johannes Flamingus Boppardiensis und ein Glossator' in Verführung zur Geschichte: Festschrift zum 500. Jahrestag der Eröffnung einer Universität in Trier ed G. Droege et al (Trier 1973) 165-86 / L. Keil in Trierische Chronik 16 (1920) 146-51 / C. Browerus and J. Masenius Metropolis ecclesiae

Trevericae ... opus ed C. de Stramberg (Koblenz 1855–6) II 431–2 / Bonn, Universitätsbibliothek MS S 356 f 272: Johannes Butzbach 'Auctarium de scriptoribus ecclesiasticis' / Trier, Stadtbibliothek MS 1804/1814 ff 88–120: Flaming's poems   HANSGEORG MOLITOR

Louis of FLANDERS lord of Praet, 25 November 1488–7 October 1555
A descendant of the family of the counts of Flanders, Louis was born at Bruges, the son of another Louis and of Isabella of Burgundy. He was educated at the school of the Brethren of the Common Life in Ghent before matriculating on 8 February 1501 in the University of Louvain, where he met Erasmus (Ep 1191). In 1507 he fought in the war against Gelderland. From 1515 to 1522 he was *Charles v's grand bailiff in the city of Ghent and from 1523 to 1549 he held the same position with regard to Bruges and the surrounding free state (*vrije* or *franc*). In 1517 he joined Charles' privy council and in May 1522 was appointed resident ambassador to England (Epp 1281, 1286). When England prepared to repudiate her alliance with the Hapsburgs after the battle of Pavia and the capture of *Francis I, Louis of Flanders was exposed to harassment on the part of Cardinal *Wolsey. He was called back in May 1525, only to be sent on another embassy in August, this time to the regent of France, Louise of *Savoy. With the rank of a chamberlain, he thereafter attended the court of Charles v but was frequently sent on further diplomatic missions, acting as a troubleshooter both in the Netherlands and in Italy. He also received further military assignments, accompanying Charles v on the expedition to Tunis (1535) and also serving against France and Gelderland.

In 1531 Louis was received into the order of the Golden Fleece, and from about this time he normally lived in the Netherlands. One of the closest advisers to the regent, *Mary of Hungary, he was appointed to the council of state in 1536, and on 18 October 1540 he succeeded Antoine de *Lalaing as head of the council of finance. On 4 October 1544 he became governor of Holland, Zeeland, and Utrecht. His influence with both the emperor and the regent, and perhaps also a haughty temperament, exposed him to some antago-

nism on the part of other courtiers (Ep 1286). At a chapter of the Golden Fleece in 1545 he was described as 'hautain, ambitieux, brutal, indévot, avare et cognoissant d'autres femmes que la sienne.'

Louis' title to the lordship of Praet (Praat), near Sijsele, east of Bruges, derived from his marriage to Josine van Praat (Ep 1286), concluded at Bruges on 23 October 1517. Josine, who was the daughter of Karel van Praat, lord of Moerkerke, and of Passchina van Halewijn, died on 2 December 1546. She bore Louis a son, John of Flanders, who married Jacqueline, the daughter of Adolph of *Burgundy, lord of Veere and Beveren.

Louis of Flanders was a friend and patron of many scholars and writers; in particular he was clearly a genuine admirer of Erasmus (Ep 1281), even though Gerard *Bachuus' account (Ep 1286) appears hyperbolic. The printer Josse *Bade, who apparently knew Louis from their school-days at Ghent, dedicated to him part of his edition of Virgil (Paris 1507, reprinted in 1512) and addressed to him another dedicatory letter in Hendrik Goethals' *Summae quaestionum ordinarium* (Paris 1520). Bade's example was followed by a number of other authors and scholars. Both in Ghent and in Bruges Louis maintained contacts with such friends and supporters of Erasmus as Antonius *Clava, Willem de *Waele, Jan van *Fevijn, and above all Juan Luis *Vives, who dedicated to him *De consultatione* (1523) and stated in the preface of his important *De subventione pauperum* (1525) that it had been undertaken at Louis' request. He was a friend of Henricus Cornelius *Agrippa and Nicolaus *Olahus, while Alfonso de *Valdés in a letter to Johannes *Dantiscus called him jokingly 'Cato Pratensis': apparently he was not expected to judge an epigram by Dantiscus any more harshly than Valdés' *Lactancio*, which he examined at the request of Charles v and subsequently defended.

When Louis of Flanders was at Ghent, Erasmus resumed his relations with him by means of a letter written at the suggestion of Clava (Ep 1191). He sent him greetings in 1528 (Ep 1966) and a year later praised him in a dedicatory preface (Ep 2093); see also Epp 1847, 2810.

BIBLIOGRAPHY: Allen Ep 1191 / *Matricule de Louvain* III-1 211 / de Vocht *Literae ad Cranevel-*

dium Ep 150 and passim / de Vocht *Dantiscus* 38–9, 350, and passim / Michel Baelde *De Collaterale Raden onder Karel v en Filips ii* (Brussels1965) 327–8 and passim / F. Walser and R. Wohlfeil *Die spanischen Zentralbehörden und der Staatsrat Karls v.* (Göttingen 1959) 244 and passim / Karl Brandi *Kaiser Karl v.* new ed (Darmstadt 1959–67) I 217, 231, 234, and passim / Bataillon *Erasmo y España* 386 and passim / Eduard Boehmer 'Alfonsi Valdesii litteras xl ineditas …' in *Homenaje a Menéndez y Pelayo* (Madrid 1899) I 385–412 esp 397–8 / A. Henne *Histoire du règne de Charles-Quint en Belgique* (Brussels-Leipzig 1858–60) II 201 and passim   PGB

FLISCUS *See* FIESCHI

Etienne FLORIMOND, Stephanus FLORI-MUNDUS *See Etienne* DES GOUTTES

Agostino FOGIADENO or FOGLIETTA *See Augustinus* FOLIATUS

Augustinus FOLIATUS (Ep 2956, 31 July 1534)
Augustinus Foliatus, a resident of Ferrara greeted by Erasmus in Ep 2956, may have been the Augustinian monk Agostino Fogiadeno or Fogliato. Born at Cremona, Fogliato lived at the convent of Sant'Andrea and was known as an erudite scholar in the fields of the Scriptures, philosophy, and theology. On his death in 1533 or 1538 he left a number of works in manuscript.

Allen's identification of Foliatus with the Genoese patrician Agostino Foglietta (Foglieta) is erroneous. Foglietta, the uncle of Uberto and Paolo Foglietta, was attached to the papal court and died in the Sack of Rome of 1527.

BIBLIOGRAPHY: F. Arisi *Cremona literata* (Parma 1702–41) II 138 / T. Herrera *Alphabetum Augustinianum* (Madrid 1643–4) I 58 / G. Lanteri *Postrema saecula sex religionis Augustinianae* … (Tolentino-Rome 1858–60) II 170 / J.F. Ossinger *Bibliotheca Augustiniana* (Ingolstadt-Augsburg 1776) 354 / G. Pamfili *Chronica ordinis fratrum eremitarum S. Augustini* (Rome 1631) 111 / D.A. Perini *Bibliographia Augustiniana, cum notis biographicis* (Florence 1929–37) II 76 /

L. Torelli *Secoli Agostiniani* (Bologna 1659–86) VIII 219   PAOLO PISSAVINO

Girolamo FONDULO of Cremona, documented 1518–40
Girolamo Fondulo (Fundulus) was from a noble family of Cremona and studied Greek under Marcus *Musurus. In 1518 he was living at Venice with Jean de *Pins, whom he may have tutored in Greek. By 1520 he was in Paris, enjoying the patronage of Louise of *Savoy, the mother of *Francis I. In 1527 he received a pension from the crown; he later became a royal secretary. From 1536 to 1537 he was in the household of Cardinal François de *Tournon. In 1529 and from 1538 to 1540 the king sent him to Italy to collect Greek manuscripts and books for the library of the Collège Royal. He was probably in orders, for in 1538 he tried to obtain the priory of Suresnes, near Paris.

Fondulo was a teacher and friend of Germain de *Brie, who mentioned him in the preface to his Latin translation of Chrysostom's *De sacerdotio* (Paris: J. Bade 5 August 1526). Allen argued that he was the friend of Brie greeted by Erasmus in Ep 1736 of August 1526 and also the 'Balista,' a friend of Brie, who visited Erasmus at Basel in 1527 (Ep 1910). Cardinal Nikolaus von *Schönberg was another of Fondulo's acquaintances.

BIBLIOGRAPHY: Allen Ep 1733 / EI xv 622 for Fondulo's family / Cosenza II 1442–3 / M.-M. de la Garanderie 'Un érasmien français Germain de Brie' *Colloquia Erasmiana Turonensia* I 372 / Hans Striedel 'Der Humanist Johann Albrecht Widmanstetter … als klassischer Philologe' in *Festgabe der Bayerischen Staatsbibliothek* [for] *Emil Gratzl* (Wiesbaden 1953) 118   TBD

Alonso de FONSECA of Santiago de Compostela, c 1475–5 February 1534
Alonso de Fonseca, the son of the archbishop of the same name and of Maria de Ulloa, a lady from the Galician nobility, was born in Santiago de Compostela, his father's archdiocese. In 1490 he entered the University of Salamanca, and on finishing his studies he became a canon in his home city and then also archdeacon of Cornado. His father succeeded in naming him his successor as archbishop of Santiago in 1506; Fonseca took possession of

the see by proxy in 1508, entering in the archdiocese on the following year. Like his father, Fonseca was from his youth a leading and controversial figure in the Spanish court; he had a son by Juana Pimentel, Diego de Acevedo, for whom he founded a *mayorazgo* (hereditary estate), thus following a practice of nepotism for which the Fonseca family was well known. As archbishop of Santiago he founded two colleges, one in Salamanca and one in Santiago itself which bears his name, and soon was seen as a friend by Erasmus' admirers. In 1518 Juan de Oria dedicated to him his *Tractatus de immortalitate animae* (Salamanca), which was influenced by Erasmus. By 1523 Fonseca had become an obvious candidate for the archdiocese of Toledo, which was vacant after the death of the Cardinal Guillaume (II) de *Croy and had become a stronghold of Erasmus' supporters after the death of Cardinal *Jiménez. He was elected archbishop of Toledo and primate of Spain on 31 December 1523, and his first act was to choose as his secretary the Erasmian Juan de *Vergara, then an influential figure at the University of Alcalá. Fonseca took a personal interest in the affairs of that university and became a patron of the printer Miguel de Eguía, who dedicated to him several of his editions of Erasmus' works, mentioning Fonseca in one of them as an assiduous reader of Erasmus and a willing host should the latter decide to accept the invitation to visit Spain extended to him by the Emperor *Charles v (*Epistola nuncupatoria ad Carolum Caesarem ... Paraphrasis in Evangelium Matthaei*, Alcalá, 30 June 1525). In 1526 Fonseca joined the council of state as a supporter of the policies of Mercurino *Gattinara. He continued to play an important role in the government of Spain until his death.

Erasmus was aware of Fonseca's friendship, which he had already acknowledged in a letter to Guy *Morillon of 25 March 1524 (Ep 1431). On 3 September 1526 he wrote to thank Fonseca for his support against his detractors in Spain (Ep 1748). Erasmus' faith in Fonseca's allegiance was confirmed by Pedro Juan *Olivar, who in a letter of 13 March 1527 let him know that he could count on the archbishop's help against the attack launched by the Spanish monks on Erasmus' works (Ep 1791).

A month later Fonseca and his secretary, Vergara, confirmed Olivar's assurances, offering Erasmus four hundred ducats a year should he decide to come to Spain (Epp 1812, 1814). In his replies to both of them, and particularly in his letter to Vergara, Erasmus shows unreserved gratitude and admiration for Fonseca's efforts on his behalf (Epp 1874, 1875). Although Erasmus refused Fonseca's offer of patronage in Spain, in June 1528 the archbishop sent him two hundred ducats to facilitate his work in editing the writings of St Augustine and in combatting the Lutheran heresy (Epp 2003, 2004). Erasmus responded to this patronage by dedicating (Ep 2157) to Fonseca the Froben edition of Augustine (Basel 1529), perhaps following a suggestion of Alfonso de *Valdés (Ep 2109). Fonseca expressed his pleasure with the dedication in a letter of 31 October 1531 (Ep 2562). This is the last known letter exchanged by the two, but not the last proof of their friendship: between 1529 and 1534 Erasmus mentioned on several occasions new gifts received from Fonseca, and he never failed to show his concern for the archbishop's declining health (Epp 2198, 2208, 2253, 2297, 2348, 2879, 2904). Fonseca wrote a book, *Historia de linajes*, and is remembered partly for his contributions to the urban and civic development of Toledo and Alcalá, but above all because of his commitment to the Erasmian cause in Spain. His death was a serious blow to Spanish Erasmians, for it came at a time when the Inquisition had already arrested Bernardino *Tovar and Juan de Vergara on suspicion of heresy and would soon begin proceedings against Alonso Ruiz de *Virués and others. According to his own wishes, Fonseca was buried in Salamanca, his ancestral home.

BIBLIOGRAPHY: Allen Ep 1748 / *Enciclopedia universal ilustrada europeo-americana* (Barcelona, Madrid 1907?–) xxiv 314 / Bataillon *Erasmo y España* 157, 163–64, and passim / A. Bonilla y San Martín 'Erasmo en España' *Revue hispanique* 17 (1907) 526–27   ARSENIO PACHECO

Christophorus FONTANUS (Ep 2892 of 24 December 1533)
In a letter addressed to Pero and Cristóbal *Mexía Erasmus mentioned receiving a letter from Christophorus Fontanus. The letter was

so ardent in Erasmus' defence that Erasmus was happy it was not published because of the contention it would have aroused. Bataillon has tentatively suggested that Fontanus was really Constantino Ponce de la Fuente of Seville, who published a number of works influenced by Erasmian spirituality.

BIBLIOGRAPHY: Allen Ep 2892 / Bataillon *Erasmo y España* 492, 522–5, and passim   TBD

Conradus FONTANUS or FONTEIUS *See Konrad* BRUNNER

Benedetto de' FORNARI of Genoa, documented 1518–49
Benedetto de' Fornari (Benedictus de Furnariis), a member of a prominent Genoese banking family, seems to have been active in Antwerp in the spring of 1518 (Ep 823). In 1519 he and his partners loaned the Hapsburg government fifty-five thousand florins towards the financing of the election of *Charles v, while in 1549 Benedetto's firm incurred a penalty because in violation of imperial edicts it was continuing to do business at Lyon and was even dealing direct with the French crown.

BIBLIOGRAPHY: CWE Ep 823 / Richard Ehrenberg *Das Zeitalter der Fugger* (Jena 1896) I 327–8, II 95, 342, and passim / Götz von Pölnitz *Anton Fugger* (Tübingen 1958–   ) I 380, IV 49 / *Deutsche Reichstagsakten. Jüngere Reihe* (Gotha–Göttingen 1893–   ) I 220, 516, 530 PGB

FORSTER *See* FURSTER

Scipione FORTIGUERRA of Pistoia, 4 February 1466–16 October 1515
Scipione Fortiguerra, called Carteromachus, was born in Pistoia and was probably enabled to devote his life to research through the scholarships endowed by his uncle, Cardinal Niccolò. He studied for an uncertain period under *Poliziano in Florence but had definitely moved to Padua by 1493; cf A. Poliziano *Opera omnia* (Venice: A. Manuzio 1498) Epistolarum lib XII no 25. Whether or not Poliziano put him in touch with Aldo *Manuzio, it is clear that Scipione immediately became involved in the preparation of Greek first editions and devoted nearly ten years of his life to the project. From November 1495 he contributed introductory

epigrams or received honourable mentions in prefaces. Probably in 1502 he drafted the statute of the Aldine Academy, and the edition of Demosthenes which Aldus printed in 1504 closely followed a series of public lectures given by Scipione during the previous year. By October 1504 he had moved to Florence; he soon travelled to Rome, perhaps hoping to find in the service of powerful clerics a calm and security that free-lance teaching in Venice could not provide. But, as Erasmus later commented (Ep 1236), he failed to find it. Between 1504 and 1509 he served cardinals *Grimani, Farnese (later *Paul III), Franciotto della Rovere, and *Alidosi, following the latter to Bologna when he was appointed papal governor in 1509 and retreating hastily to Pistoia when the Bolognese rebelled and assassinated his patron in 1511 (Ep 217). Throughout this period Scipione kept in touch with his friends in Venice (Ep 251), collecting manuscripts and investigating the chances of establishing a more permanent Aldine Academy in Rome. This brought him increasingly under the influence of the Roman collector and dilettante Angelo *Colocci, whose patronage he enjoyed until his death in 1515. However, since he served for a while as Greek tutor to *Leo x's nephew Giulio de' Medici during 1513 and eventually died in Florence, it is evident that Scipione was too popular a teacher to be allowed the academic retirement he apparently craved.

In spite of Fortiguerra's close links with the Aldine circle, his friendship with Erasmus seems to have grown up independently. They first met in Bologna during 1506, before Erasmus went to Venice (Ep 1347), and it is unlikely that they met again before his visit to Rome early in 1509 (the 'Strategus' later mentioned in the colloquy *Opulentia sordida* as a member of the *Torresani household must be *Musurus' scribe Caesar *Strategus. But in Rome they quickly became intimate, meeting for discussions in the afternoon and sharing both board and bed (Ep 3032). Erasmus was impressed by Scipione's learning and by his lack of ostentation (ASD I-2 668), noting that he never tried to ape a narrowly Ciceronian style and remembering him with affection long after his friendship with other members of the Aldine circle had gone sour. His comments

appear to be justified: apart from a few
epigrams, Fortiguerra's only published work is
a short oration in praise of Greek literature,
delivered in Venice during January 1504 and
printed in May by Aldus. A short Latin treatise
on rabies survives in the Biblioteca Apostolica
Vaticana MS Graecus 1402, and a number of
other manuscripts, mostly extracts of Greek
grammatical or literary authors, were apparently copied by him and for his own use
(Biblioteca Apostolica Vaticana MSS Graeci
1386, 1405, etc). He was a respected scholar
who made little effort to capitalize upon his
reputation.

BIBLIOGRAPHY: Allen and CWE Ep 217 / A.
Chiti *Scipione Fortiguerra, il Carteromacho –
studio biografico con una raccolta di epigrammi,
sonetti e lettere di lui o a lui dirette* (Florence
1902) / M. Sicherl *Johannes Cuno* (Heidelberg
1978) 49–51 and passim   M.J.C. LOWRY

Johannes FORTIS documented 1510–23
Johannes Fortis (Fort, Fuertes, Furtas) of
Aragon was a student at the Collège de
Lisieux in Paris under Juan Dolz de Castellar in
1510. He was a room-mate of Juan Luis *Vives
during the latter's first stay in Paris, which
ended in 1512. Vives later made him a speaker
in the *Christi Jesu triumphus* (Paris: J. Lambert
1514) and on 31 March 1514, during a trip to
Paris, wrote him a letter later included in his
first edition of Hyginus' *Aureum opus* (Paris: J.
Lambert 1514). Vives' criticism of intellectual
life at the University of Paris, the *In pseudodialecticos* (Louvain: D. Martens 1519), was
written in the form of a letter to Fortis. When
Vives again visited Paris in 1520 he expected
to be chastised by his old friends; instead, as
he reported to Erasmus (Ep 1108), he was
relieved by the warm reception given him by
Fortis and the others. On 16 November 1523
Fortis matriculated in medicine at Montpellier.

BIBLIOGRAPHY: Allen Ep 1108 / J. IJsewijn
'J.L. Vives in 1512–1517: A reconsideration of
evidence' *Humanistica Lovaniensia* 26 (1977) 83,
93 / *Matricule de Montpellier* 44 / Ricardo Garcia
Villoslada *La universidad de Paris durante los
estudios de Francisco de Vitoria* (Rome 1938) 36,
404–5   TBD

FORTIS *See also Joachim van* RINGELBERG *and
Jan* STERKE

Matthaeus FORTUNATUS d 1528
Matthaeus Fortunatus (Pannonius), probably
of middle-class Slavonian or Dalmatian origin,
was born in Hungary some time after 1480.
Biographical information, especially about his
early career, is meagre. His statement that he
was moved to write a joyful greeting at the time
of the birth of the future King *Louis II in 1506
suggests that he was then no longer a child. In
1521 he met the humanist scholar István
*Brodarics at Buda and accompanied him when
he set out for Italy in early 1522 as royal
ambassador. After a brief stop at Venice
(April–May) they went to Padua, and, while
Brodarics continued on his diplomatic mission
to Rome, Fortunatus remained in Padua to
study Greek and Latin literature with the
encouragement and financial aid of the ambassador. He also found a new source of
support among the many students from Hungary who frequented the University of Padua
during the Renaissance period, namely Orbán
Batthyányi. This young man was a member of a
wealthy family of the Hungarian nobility and
was able to introduce Fortunatus to a number
of influential individuals at Padua, including
Prince Gianludovico Saluzzo, who was a
relative of King Louis II and had shown himself
to be a great friend of Hungarian students.

While continuing his studies at the university, Fortunatus prepared a critical edition of
Seneca's *Questiones naturales*. He used the
resources of Paduan and Venetian libraries
and, according to his own account, completed
the task in two months. He must have done
considerable work on this project prior to his
arrival at Padua, for it is improbable that he
could have completed such a large project in
two months while also attending lectures. The
book was published in February 1523 at the
famous press of Aldo *Manuzio. With the
encouragement of Batthyányi, Fortunatus dedicated the work to Saluzzo. The dedicatory
preface is the only important source on the life
of Fortunatus. He mentioned that he was also
preparing a critical edition of Pliny's *Historia
naturalis*, but there is no indication that he ever
published this work, possibly because Batthyányi returned to Hungary in April 1523.
Fortunatus soon found himself in dire financial
straits, which were not relieved until the end of
1524, when Batthyányi sent him a sum of

money. It is unclear exactly when Fortunatus left Padua and returned to Hungary or what he did in the troubled period before and after the battle of Mohács (29 August 1526). The last shred of information is a marginal entry in Erasmus' Seneca edition of 1529, now at the library of the University of Budapest, indicating that Matthaeus Fortunatus had died at Eger (Hungary) in 1528.

The Seneca edition of Fortunatus was based largely on the work published at Basel in 1515 by Erasmus. However, Fortunatus corrected a large number of mistakes which marred the Basel edition. Philologically his text was thus far superior to the 1515 edition, and Erasmus praised his achievement without reserve (Ep 1479). The ultimate recognition of Fortunatus' work is found in the 1529 Basel edition of Seneca, where Erasmus made Fortunatus co-editor of the volume: 'per Des. Erasmum Roterod. et Matthaeum Fortunatum ...' Erasmus also praised Fortunatus in the dedicatory letter to Piotr *Tomicki (Ep 2091). He did not seem to realize that Fortunatus had died the previous year.

BIBLIOGRAPHY: Allen Ep 1479 / *Magyar irodalmi lexikon* (Budapest 1963) I 359 / Rezsö Weiss 'Matthaeus Fortunatus' *Egyetemes Philologiai Közlöny* (1888) 346–62 / Rabán Gerézdi 'Aldus Manutius magyar barátai' *Magyar Könyvszemle* (1945) 84–98 / Imre Trencsényi-Waldapfel *Erasmus és magyar barátai* (Budapest 1941) / The preface dedicated to Gianludovico Saluzzo is reprinted in Andreas Veress *Matricula et acta Hungarorum in universitatibus Italiae studentium 1221–1864* (Budapest 1941) 467–76
L. DOMONKOS

Edward FOX of Dursley, c 1496–8 May 1538
Fox (Phoxus) was born at Dursley, in Gloucestershire, and was educated at Eton. On 27 March 1512 he was admitted to King's College, Cambridge. While serving as Thomas *Wolsey's secretary he was made prebendary of Osbaldwicke, York, in 1527 and in the spring of 1528 was sent with Stephen *Gardiner to Orvieto, where they attempted to overcome *Clement VII's objections to *Henry VIII's divorce. He was an almoner to Henry VIII and on the recommendation of the king and Wolsey he was elected provost of King's College in 1528. By this time he had received a doctorate

of theology, and in 1529, while at Waltham with the king, he discussed the divorce with Thomas *Cranmer and introduced him to Henry VIII.

Fox was sent on an embassy to Paris in October 1529, and early in 1530 he returned to Cambridge, where he intervened on William *Latimer's behalf in his controversy with the Romanists. Fox and Gardiner attempted to solicit support for the divorce at Cambridge and later at Oxford, in concert with Bishop John *Longland and John Bell, bishop of Worcester. Between 1532 and 1534 Fox was repeatedly dispatched to the French court and helped to keep relations with *Francis I friendly. He was appointed almoner to, and granted a benefice by, *Anne Boleyn. He treated for peace with Scotland in 1534 and was created archdeacon of Leicester (1531), dean of Salisbury and archdeacon of Dorset (1533), and finally bishop of Hereford (1535). In 1534 he published *De vera differentia regiae potestatis et ecclesiae* (London: T. Berthelet; STC 11218). Because of his extensive knowledge of the divorce issue, the transactions for its fulfilment were placed in his hands. In 1535 he supervised the collection of opinions from those universities which favoured the divorce. Fox was also sent to Germany to discuss the divorce with Protestant divines (Ep 3104) and met in Wittenberg with *Melanchthon and *Luther. Martin *Bucer appreciated his sympathetic attitude towards Lutheranism and addressed to him a dedicatory epistle published with his *In sacra quatuor evangelia enarrationes* (Basel: J. Herwagen 1536). As Erasmus seems to have mentioned Fox only once, it is unlikely that the two were personally acquainted.

BIBLIOGRAPHY: Allen Ep 3104 / DNB VII 553–5 / J.J. Scarisbrick *Henry VIII* (London 1968) passim / McConica 112, 127, and passim / C. Hopf *Martin Bucer and the English Reformation* (Oxford 1946) 6 and passim
CFG

Richard FOXE d 5 October 1528
Richard, the son of Thomas and Helena Foxe, was born at Pullock's Manor, Ropsley, near Grantham, Lincolnshire about 1448 and may have attended grammar school at nearby Boston. He may later have been a commoner at Magdalen College, Oxford, and is perhaps

identified with a Richard Foxe, 'gramatice magister ac eciam baccularius,' admitted to the Guild of Holy Cross, Stratford-on-Avon, Warwickshire, in 1477 or 1478. By 1477 Foxe was a bachelor of civil law, his degree probably having been taken on the continent, and by 1486 he was a doctor. On 5 July 1479 he had matriculated in the faculty of canon law at Louvain, and he later studied at Paris.

Foxe was in Paris and in the service of the future *Henry VII by January 1485, when Richard III delayed his institution as vicar of Stepney, Middlesex. In August 1485 he crossed to England with Henry and was present at Bosworth. Soon afterwards, like Christopher *Urswick, he began to receive the ecclesiastical and civil fruits of his support. He was king's councillor and secretary (1485–7) and keeper of the privy seal (1487–1516). He took part in negotiations with Scotland (1487), christened the future *Henry VIII (1491), was envoy to France (1490, 1492), headed or was a leading member of missions to Scotland (1494, 1496, 1497, 1498, 1499, 1503) and to Philip the Handsome, duke of *Burgundy (culminating in the *Intercursus magnus*, 1496), and helped to negotiate the marriage agreement of *Mary, the daughter of Henry VII, with the future *Charles V (1508). There is no evidence other than Francis Bacon's statement in his *History of Henry VII* that Foxe was responsible for the pageants at the entry of *Catherine of Aragon into London (1501). Foxe played an important role, by fortifying and arming Norham Castle and by other means, in frustrating the invasion of England by *James IV of Scotland (1497). Under Henry VIII he remained an important figure in affairs of state. He was an executor of the wills of both Henry VII and his mother, Lady Margaret *Beaufort (1509), was commissioner for the negotiation of peace with France (1510), crossed to that country with the English expeditionary force (1513), and took part in London in the treaties of marriage and of peace by which the war was concluded (1514). His advancement of Thomas *Wolsey and his resignation in Wolsey's favour of the keepership of the privy seal (1516) virtually mark the end of his career in civil offices, though he was appointed king's almoner in 1518. His relations with Wolsey, who was briefly to succeed him as bishop of Winchester, remained close. Foxe

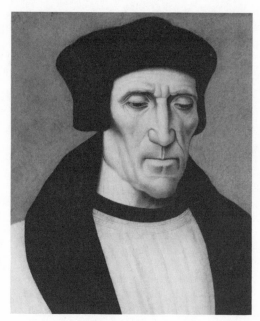

Richard Foxe, by 'Johannes Corvus'

and William *Warham jointly investigated the question of canonization for Henry VI; they were later in altercation over Canterbury's prerogatives (1510–13). Foxe was one of the bishops who opposed Henry VIII's demand for a subsidy at the convocation of 1523.

Foxe was ordained acolyte in 1477 and sub-deacon in 1486; he was canon of Sarum and prebendary of Bishopstone (to 1486) and of Grantham Borealis (1486–7), vicar of Stepney (1485), canon of Hereford and prebendary of Nonnington (1485–7), canon of St Paul's, London, and prebendary of Brownswood (1485–7). He was bishop of Exeter (1487–92) and of Bath and Wells (1492–4), though he did not reside in either diocese; he was also bishop of Durham (1494–1501) and of Winchester (1501–28). He was master of St Cross Hospital, Winchester (1500–17). For his registers as bishop see Emden BRUO.

Foxe was a notable builder, his civil architecture including the fortification of Norham Castle, the partial rebuilding of Durham Castle, the improvement of Calais harbour, and additions to Farnborough Castle, Surrey. At Winchester in 1524 and 1525 he rebuilt the cathedral presbytery in the Renaissance style, placing the chests with the bones of the Saxon and Danish kings on the cornice of the screens, and constructed a chantry chapel on the south side of the feretory. An important drawing for this is in the Royal Institute of British Architects. At Southwark Cathedral, London, he provided a stone reredos and painted glass; and at Cambridge he was the chief agent, in execution of the will of Henry VII, in commissioning the later stained glass for King's College Chapel. He built and endowed a school for Taunton, Somerset (1522), and a school and master's house at Grantham, Lincolnshire (1528). His most notable achievement was Corpus Christi College, Oxford, of which the chief building was completed in 1517.

Foxe had at first intended his 'beehive' to be an Oxford college for the student monks of Winchester, but he broadened its scope, perhaps under the influence of his friend Hugh Oldham, bishop of Exeter and founder of Manchester Grammar School, or of John *Fisher at St John's College, Cambridge. He provided for a president, twenty fellows, twenty scholars, two chaplains, and two clerks, as well as establishing public lectureships in Greek, Latin, and divinity. The royal licence for the establishment of the college is dated 26 November 1516, the charter 1 March 1517, and the statutes 20 June 1517, with supplementary statutes in 1528. It was not quite the equivalent of the trilingual colleges of Alcalá and Louvain, except in so far as Hebrew studies were comprehended in divinity, but Erasmus called it so when sending congratulations to John *Claymond, the first president (Ep 990; cf Ep 965), and it was certainly intended to foster good life through good letters, both Latin and Greek. Juan Luis *Vives, Nikolaus *Kratzer, Thomas *Lupset, John*Clement, and Reginald*Pole were among those closely connected with the college during Foxe's lifetime. To the college Foxe left his pastoral staff, gold chalice, and paten and plate (Trapp and Schulte Herbrüggen no 33) and the bulk of his library. He also gave at least one printed book to Magdalen College and in 1499 gave forty-one books to the Collegiate Church of Bishop Auckland, Durham (for details see Emden BRUO). Among his services to

learning was his patronage of John *Fawne (Ep 1766).

Foxe was blind for some years before his death, which probably occurred at Wolvesey Palace, Winchester; his will is dated 15 February 1528. He was buried, apparently on the day of his death, in his chantry chapel in Winchester Cathedral.

Erasmus and Foxe must have first met in 1500, and Foxe may have been Erasmus' host in London in 1505 (Epp 185, 186). He was certainly Erasmus' patron at about that time and received as a new year's gift for 1506 the dedication to Lucian's Toxaris, which Erasmus had translated from the Greek (Ep 187; ASD I-1 423–48). Eleven extant letters between Erasmus and Andrea *Ammonio of 1511–13 document Erasmus' attempts to get some material proof of Foxe's esteem (Epp 234, 236, 238–40, 243, 247–50, 282). According to Thomas *More, Foxe publicly declared Erasmus' translation of the New Testament worth ten commentaries (Ep 502). Foxe may have been responsible for the choice of Erasmus' translation for certain texts in the windows of King's College, Cambridge (CWE 3 220). It was this sympathy, perhaps as much as Edward *Lee's former membership in Foxe's household, that led Erasmus to appeal to Foxe as one of those who might be able to silence Lee's criticisms of his New Testament (Epp 973, 1099). An episode concerning Foxe is related in the Ecclesiastes (LB V 937 E–F).

There is only one authentic contemporary portrait of Foxe, by 'Johannes Corvus' (probably Jehan Raf/John Raven), in Corpus Christi College. There are replicas of this at Corpus Christi and elsewhere (Trapp and Schulte Herbrüggen no 32).

Foxe made a translation of the Benedictine rule at the request of four religious houses for women in the diocese of Winchester (STC 1859) and edited the Sarum processional (STC 16232.6, 16232.8, 16233, etc). The Contemplation of Sinners (STC 5643) was compiled and printed under his sponsorship, and there were dedicated to him Roger Collingwood's Arithmetica experimentalis, 1508 (Oxford, Corpus Christi College, MS 102); Baptista Fiera's Coena saluberrima, 1509; Philippus Albericus' (Filippo degli Alberici) De casu animae, 1509; and John Fisher's De veritate corporis et sanguinis

Christi ..., 1527. A presentation copy from *Linacre of his translation of Galen's *De sanitate tuenda*, 1517, is in the library of the Royal College of Physicians, London.

BIBLIOGRAPHY: Allen Ep 187 / Emden BRUC 239–41 / Emden BRUO II 715–19, III, xxiv / DNB VII 590–6 / T. Fowler *History of Corpus Christi College* Oxford Historical Society xxv (1893) 1–29 / P.S. and H.M. Allen *Letters of Richard Fox* (Oxford 1929) / Franklin B. Williams Jr *Index of Dedications and Commendatory Verses in English Books to 1641* (London 1962) 71 / McConica, especially 80–4 / S. Anglo *Spectacle, Pageantry and early Tudor Policy* (Oxford 1969) especially 43n, 58 / J.B. Trapp and H. Schulte Herbrüggen *'The King's Good Servant,' Sir Thomas More,* exhibition catalogue, National Portrait Gallery (London 1977) / H. Wayment *The Windows of King's College Chapel* (London 1972) 2–3, 123a / R.W. Chambers *Thomas More* (London 1935) 97–8   J.B. TRAPP

Girolamo FRACASTORO of Verona, 1479– 6 August 1553
Girolamo Fracastoro, the son of Paolo Filippo Fracastoro and Camilla Mascarelli, was born in Verona. While still a youth he entered the University of Padua, where he studied mathematics, astronomy, and philosophy with Pietro *Pomponazzi and Niccolò *Leonico Tomeo, medicine with Girolamo della Torre, Alessandro Achillini, Pietro Trapolini, and Alessandro Benedetti, and anatomy with Marco Antonio della Torre. By 1502 he was a lecturer in logic and *conciliarius anatomicus* at Padua and had married Elena Schiavi from Vicenza. From 18 September 1505 until his death he was a member of the college of physicians of Verona, serving as prior four times and as councillor eight times. For a time he followed the *condottiere* Bartolomeo *Alviano, serving as a physician in campaigns against the invading French armies. After the battle of Agnadello in 1509 he returned to Verona to practise medicine. His medical advice was sought throughout Italy, and in 1545 *Paul III appointed him 'Medicus conductus et stipendiatus' to the council of Trent with a salary of sixty golden scudi a month. In 1547 he and Balduino de' Balduini signed a statement in which they forecast an outbreak of a contagious disease ('morbus peticularis') at Trent, thus providing

an excuse for moving the council to Bologna. Fracastoro died at his villa of Incaffi, on the Lago di Garda near Verona. His friends included Paolo Giovio, Gaspare *Contarini, Andrea *Navagero, Marco Antonio della Torre, and Giovanni Battista Ramusio.

In addition to being a physician, Fracastoro was a poet of considerable fame in Italy, as Erasmus learnt from a letter from *Viglius Zuichemus of 2 August 1533 (Ep 2854). Fracastoro's most famous work was the *Syphilis sive de morbo gallico*, which dealt with the nature and cure of the disease in poetical form. First published by Niccolino and Stefano dei Sabbio at Verona in 1530, it was frequently reprinted and translated. Other works by Fracastoro included *Homocentrica sive de stellis* and *De dierum criticorum causis* (Venice: n pr 1538), *De contagione et contagionis morbis* (Venice: heirs of L.A. Giunta 1546), and *Naugerius sive de poetica dialogus*, which was published in his *Opera omnia* (Venice: heirs of L.A. Giunta 1555). Dionigi Atanagi included several of Fracastoro's letters to Giovanni Battista Ramusio in *Lettere di XIII huomini illustri* (Venice: F. Lorenzini 1560). Ramusio dedicated his *Delle navigationi et viaggi* (Venice: heirs of L.A. Giunta 1554–9) to him.

BIBLIOGRAPHY: Allen Ep 2854 / B. Zanobio in *Dictionary of Scientific Biography* ed C.C. Gillispie et al (New York 1970–9) V 104–7 / L. and F. Baumgartner *A Bibliography of the Poem 'Syphilis sive morbus gallicus' by Girolamo Fracastoro of Verona* (New Haven 1935) / G. Fracastoro *Scritti inediti* ed F. Pellegrini (Verona 1955) / Emilio di Leo *Scienza e umanesimo in Girolamo Fracastoro* (Salerno 1953) / F. Pellegrini *Fracastoro* (Trieste 1948) / G. Toffanin *Il Cinquecento* (Milan 1960) 513–5 and passim   VALERIA SESTIERI LEE

FRANCESCO of Crema *See Francesco da CREMA*

FRANCESCO of Padua (Ep 240 of 11 November [1511])
Francesco of Padua (Franciscus Patavinus), an Italian who was established in London and invited Erasmus to stay in his house in 1511, has not been identified. Allen suggested that he might be the Italian bookseller and agent for Aldo *Manuzio mentioned in Epp 219, 221.

Francis I, by Titian

FRANCIS I king of France, 12 September
1494–31 March 1547
Francis, the son of Charles d'Orléans, count of
Angoulême, and of Louise of *Savoy, was
betrothed in 1506 to *Claude, the daughter of
*Louis XII, at whose death in 1515 Francis
succeeded to the throne.

Francis has been called the 'restorer of arts
and letters.' Though *Charles VIII and Louis XII
had campaigned in Italy and had returned with
Italian artists and ideas, it was Francis who
brought Leonardo da Vinci and Benvenuto
Cellini to France and who established the
Fontainebleau school around Primaticcio and
Rosso. The châteaux on the Loire had already
acquired some classical motifs, but none was
on the scale of Chambord, which Francis built
from the ground up. He was a generous
patron, and he enjoyed conversing freely with
artists and men of letters.

Early in his reign Francis promised that he
would establish a trilingual college, like that
which had been created in accordance with
Erasmus' suggestion at Louvain, for the
dissemination of knowledge based on mastery
of Greek, Hebrew and classical Latin. Erasmus

was invited in 1517 to head the new institution
in Paris (Epp 522, 523), but he declined (Epp
529, 725). Lefranc, in his history of the Collège
de France, blames him for missing a great
opportunity and thus postponing the creation
of the new institution, but Erasmus correctly
anticipated that professors of the new methods
would be attacked by scholastic theologians of
the university (Epp 1434, 1435). The king's
intentions were good, but it was hard for a man
of letters to retain his attention long enough to
carry a project like this to fruition (*Budé to
*Lascaris, 12 June 1521, partially translated by
Lefranc, 77–9, from *Budaei epistolae graecae* ed
A. Pichon, Paris 1574, 93). In 1523 Erasmus
received a note in the king's own hand,
assuring him that he would indeed be welcome
if he came to France (Ep 1375), but the planned
visit of that year does not seem to have had
anything to do with the college, plans for
which were now in abeyance (see Ep 1342, and
Allen's introduction to Ep 1319). There was
never enough money, although it could always
be found for projects to which Francis attached
a higher priority. It was not until 1530 that he
finally fulfilled a part of his promise by
appointing five royal lecturers, two for Greek,
two for Hebrew and one for mathematics (Epp
2261, 2456), but there was no fine building or
any other evidence of a 'college.' Nevertheless,
the foundation had been laid for the teaching
of the new methods of scholarship and for
what was to become the Collège de France.
Francis deserves credit for taking the first step
towards breaking the monopoly of the citadel
of scholasticism.

What had priority, however, from the
beginning to the end of the reign was the
recovery of Milan and the great contest for
supremacy with *Charles V. In the first year of
the reign Francis succeeded in recovering
Milan by the victory at Marignano over the
Swiss (1515). The personal bravery and charis-
matic qualities which he displayed were an
important element in the victory. In recognition of his chivalric virtues he was knighted by
Bayard on the field of battle. Francis relied on
the same tactics throughout his life, but never
again with the same success. Milan was lost in
1520. After a great effort to regain it, the
catastrophic defeat at Pavia in 1525 exposed
Francis' incompetence as a strategist. He put

the blame on his subordinates and, after a year as the prisoner of Charles in Madrid, resumed the war until Andrea *Doria's defection led to another French disaster in 1528. By the treaty of Cambrai (1529) Francis had to concede Italy to Charles, who once more invested Francesco II *Sforza with the duchy of Milan. His death in 1535 encouraged Francis to resume the struggle, this time in alliance with the Turks, but the campaign was inconclusive. In Francis' last war with Charles (1542–4), French forces won a victory over the governor of Milan at Ceresole, but at the peace of Crépy (1544) Milan was still beyond French grasp. Since 1520 Francis had fought four wars without being able to regain the dominant position in Italy which had been his after Marignano, although he did hold on to Savoy and Piedmont.

Even had the wars been successful, Erasmus would have dissapproved. His first letter addressed to Francis after Marignano expressed the hope that he would henceforward foster peace (Ep 533). Alluding to the offers which Francis had made to the Swiss, Erasmus praised him as a king who was willing to pay for peace (*Querela pacis* LB IV 642B). In the dedication to Francis of his paraphrase of St Mark, Erasmus insisted that there was no calamity worse than war (Ep 1400, 1 December 1523).

After the victory of Marignano, Francis negotiated the concordat of Bologna with *Leo X (1516). At the expense of the liberties of the Gallican church he recognized the right of the pope once again to draw annates from France and in return was granted the right to nominate his candidates to most of the bishoprics and abbacies. The Parlement of Paris refused until 1518 to register the concordat, and then did so only under protest. When the king was the prisoner of Charles (1525–6), the Parlement seized the opportunity to challenge the concordat, and indeed the whole course of royal policy (articles of 10 April 1525). They even laid the blame for the spread of 'Lutheran' heresy at the door of the monarchy, for having allowed prisoners to escape the judgment of Parlement by evoking their cases to the king's council (*Berquin in 1523 was an example of this practice). The Parlement's articles furthermore suggested that persons infected by

heresy were being harboured at the royal court.

During the king's imprisonment vacancies occurred at the archbishopric of Sens and at the abbey of Saint-Benoît-sur-Loire. The queen regent conferred both upon the chancellor, Antoine *Duprat, claiming the authority to do so under the concordat. The canons at Sens and the monks at Saint-Benoît, however, declaring that they did not recognize the concordat, proceeded to elect their own candidates and asked the Parlement to sustain their cause. It did so, and this issue constituted one of the most serious sources of contention between crown and Parlement during the years 1525–7.

The Parlement had ideological as well as constitutional grounds for objecting to royally appointed bishops. Guillaume (II) *Briçonnet was one such royal appointee, and he, with the backing of the king's mother and sister, *Margaret of Angoulême, had undertaken the reform of his diocese at Meaux with the help of the humanist *Lefèvre d'Etaples. One of the Parlement's articles asked for the establishment of a new tribunal for the prosecution of heresy, so broadly defined as to lump evangelical humanists like Lefèvre and Lutherans together. The new tribunal acted under the direction of Parlement and at the expense of the usual jurisdiction of the bishops over matters of heresy. Lefèvre and others went into exile rather than submit to trial, and this was the end of the effort to achieve reform from within the church.

The works of Erasmus were under attack alongside those of Lefèvre and other reformers. Erasmus complained in letters to the king (Ep 1722, 16 June 1526) as well as to the Parlement (Ep 1721) and to the theological faculty of Paris (Ep 1723). On 4 August the king wrote the Parlement, criticizing the theological faculty for authorizing the printing of *Béda's *Adnotationes* of alleged heretical passages in the works of Lefèvre and Erasmus. At the king's request the *Adnotationes* were ordered confiscated, and the theological faculty was forbidden in future to publish books without the prior authorization of the Parlement (Archives Nationales, MS x^{1a} 1529, ff 367verso–369verso). Lefèvre was recalled from exile and made tutor to the king's children and royal librarian. There was, however, no further attempt to realize Lefèvre's ideal of peaceful reform of the church from within; henceforth the choice was to lie between militant Protestantism and the Counter-Reformation.

Francis responded to the parlementary challenge to his authority by forbidding the Parlement in a *lit de justice* (24 July 1527) to impose 'any limitations, modifications or restrictions upon his ordinances, edicts and charters.' It was not to meddle again in what he considered matters of state, but to confine itself to its strictly judicial functions. This did not prevent the Parlement, however, from continuing to play an important part in the prosecution of heresy.

Royal policy towards 'Lutheranism' veered back and forth in subsequent years. When a statue of the Virgin was mutilated in Paris in 1528, Francis felt it incumbent upon him to walk barefoot in the expiatory procession. In 1534 the placards affair produced a further wave of reaction; even court favourites like Clément Marot sought safety in exile. But in the following year Francis invited the exiles to return, provided they abjure heresy (edict of Coucy); he even invited prominent German Protestants like *Melanchthon and *Bucer to a conference in Paris (Ep 3043). Yet in the edict of Fountainbleau of 1540 Francis declared that his tolerance had been a mistake: the continued expansion of heresy required that the primary responsibility for its repression be given to the parlements and other royal judicial officers. In November of that year the Parlement of Provence condemned seventeen Waldensians of Mérindol to the fire and the town to destruction. Appeals from German Protestants helped to induce Francis to suspend the execution of this edict. By 1545, however, the pressure of the Provençal Parlement and bishops gained the upper hand, and Francis was persuaded to grant an order permitting the edict to be carried out (1 January). In April royal troops burned Mérindol, Cabrières, and twenty-two villages and killed more than eight hundred persons. Such was the atmosphere in the last years of a reign which Erasmus had hoped would usher in a new era of enlightenment.

Portraits of Francis by Titian and by the school of Clouet are in the Louvre. Illustrations of the reign drawn from paintings, drawings, miniatures, and coins may be found in the volume *François ier* in the series *Génies et réalités* published by Hachette (1967).

BIBLIOGRAPHY: Jules Isaac 'Francis I' *Encyclopaedia Britannica* 11th ed x (Cambridge 1910) 934–5 / DBF XIV 1005–12 / Auguste Bailly *François ier* (Paris 1954), without a scholarly apparatus, but the author shows mastery of the literature, and, unlike the other popular biographies, critical judgment / Henry Lemonnier *Histoire de France* ed Ernest Lavisse v-1 (Paris 1903), bibliographies of sources and published works / Henri Hauser and Augustin Renaudet *Les Débuts de l'âge moderne* (Paris 1929), bibliographies / Abel Lefranc *Histoire du Collège de France* (Paris 1893, repr 1970) / Roger Doucet *Etude sur le gouvernement de François ier dans ses rapports avec le Parlement de Paris* (Paris 1921, 1926) 2 vols, based on contemporary sources, especially the register of the Parlement of Paris in the Archives Nationales. Vol II is devoted to the crisis of 1525–7, marked by the struggle between monarchy and Parlement, regarded by the author as the turning point in the constitutional history of France, when it was determined that absolutism would triumph; but see Christopher W. Stocker 'The Politics of the Parlement of Paris in 1525' *French Historical Studies* 8 (1973) 191–212 / *Catalogue des actes de François ier* (Académie des sciences morales et politiques, Paris 1887–1907) / *Ordonnances des rois de France: Règne de François ier* ed Carléty, Marichal, and Bondois (Paris 1902–41) 7 vols: 1515–1535 / Jourdan, Decrusy, and Isambert *Recueil général des anciennes lois françaises* (Paris 1822–33) 30 vols, XII-1 and 2 for reign of Francis I / *Le Journal d'un bourgeois de Paris sous le règne de François ier* ed V.-L. Bourrilly (Paris 1910), the better edition of one of the more important of the many chronicles / *Poésies du roi François ier, de Louise de Savoie, etc* ed A. Champollion-Figeac (1847), whose attributions are, however, regarded as dubious

GORDON GRIFFITHS

FRANCIS dauphin of France, 28 February 1518–10 August 1536
Francis was the eldest son of *Francis I and his first queen, *Claude. Soon after his birth he was betrothed to *Mary, the daughter of *Henry VIII. The marriage project was con-

firmed in 1520 on the Field of Cloth of Gold but subsequently abandoned. Francis spent the years 1526–9 in Spain as a hostage for his father. On 14 August 1532 he was invested duke of Brittany. His sudden death, probably of tuberculosis, led to rumours that he had been poisoned, and his young Italian secretary, Count Montecucoli, was executed.

In 1529 Martin *Bucer published a commentary on the Psalms (*Psalmorum libri quinque*) at Strasbourg (G. Ulricher) with a preface addressed to the dauphin, signed with a fictitious name (Herminjard II Ep 260). Erasmus, who did not wish to be more specific, merely referred to this dedication in order to identify Bucer's work (ASD IX – 1 298, 332, 356).

BIBLIOGRAPHY: DBF XIV 1025–6 / Desmond Seward *Prince of the Renaissance* (New York 1973) 74, 148, 191–3, and passim (with portraits)   PGB

Francis, dauphin of France, by Corneille of Lyon

John FRANCIS documented 1518–26
John Francis (Franciscus) was one of Erasmus' long-time friends (Ep 1138). He was among the founders of the London College of Physicians in 1518 and appeared on its rolls as *consiliarius* in 1523. He attended Christopher *Urswick in 1520 and was physician to Thomas *Wolsey's household between 1524 and 1526. Erasmus corresponded with Francis, stating his own views on ways to improve public health in England (Ep 1532) and describing his stone ailment in the hope that Francis would be able to suggest a cure (Ep 1759).

BIBLIOGRAPHY: Allen Ep 1532 / CWE Ep 1138 / LP II 4450, III 1103, IV 1938, 2256, 2397, 2410 / H. Brabant 'Erasme, ses maladies et ses médicins' *Colloquia Erasmiana Turonensia* I 539–68 passim   CFG

FRANCISCUS (Epp 80, 123; 1498–1500)
Franciscus has not been identified. According to Erasmus he was a physician, conceivably in the service of the 'Grand Bâtard,' Anthony of *Burgundy. He may have resided at the castle of Tournehem amid the household of Anna van *Borssele.   ANDRÉ GODIN

FRANCISCUS (Ep 2886 of 8 December 1533)
Franz (Franciscus), who took Ep 2886 to Scotland, was one of the several nephews of Johannes *Cochlaeus, the son of one of his

sisters. He has not otherwise been identified.

BIBLIOGRAPHY: W. Friedensburg 'Beiträge zum Briefwechsel der katholischen Gelehrten Deutschlands im Reformationszeitalter' *Zeitschrift für Kirchengeschichte* 18 (1897) 233–97, esp 246, 254, 261; cf 235, 238 / Martin Spahn *Johannes Cochläus* (Berlin 1898) 186–7   PGB

FRANCISCUS See also Francesco da CREMA, FRANCESCO of Padua, John FRANCIS, Francisco QUIÑONES

Sebastian FRANCK of Donauwörth, 20 January 1499–1542-3
Sebastian Franck (Eleutherius) was born at Donauwörth, in Swabia, studied in Ingolstadt and Heidelberg, and took holy orders in the diocese of Augsburg. In 1527 he served as a Lutheran pastor near Nürnberg, but one year later he joined the Anabaptist community in the imperial city. This association did not last long either, and in 1529 Franck moved to Strasbourg, where he tried to settle down as a writer and private scholar. He maintained personal contacts with such radical religious thinkers as Kaspar Schwenckfeld, Hans

*Denck, Johannes Bünderlin, Johannes Campanus, and perhaps also with Michael *Servetus, who came to Strasbourg in 1531 to debate with *Capito and *Bucer. Denck and Bünderlin seem to have exerted a decisive influence upon Franck, who became more and more critical of all ecclesiastical institutions and adopted a fully spiritualist position. After having been expelled from Strasbourg in 1531 he spent some time at Esslingen, where he tried to make a living as a soap-boiler. In 1532 he moved to Ulm, where he set up a printing shop. His writings provoked the wrath of the Lutheran preachers, and on the initiative of Martin Frecht he was eventually banished again in 1539. After further wanderings he settled in Basel in 1541. He acquired citizenship and again started his printing business, but after little more than a year he died.

Franck's literary activity began in 1527–8 with a German translation of Andreas Althamer's *Diallage* against Hans Denck (Nürnberg 1528) and with the tract *Von dem grewlichen Laster der Trunckenheit* (Augsburg 1528). The *Paradoxa* (Ulm: J. Varnier 1534), the *Guldin Arch* (Augsburg: H. Steiner 1538), and the *Verbütschiert … Buch* (1539) are the main reflections of his spiritualism. His historical thought can be studied in the *Türkenchronik* (Nürnberg 1529) and in the *Germaniae Chronicon* (Frankfurt: C. Egenolff 1538) but above all in the *Chronica, Zeytbuch und Geschichtbybell* (Strasbourg: B. Beck 1531; Ulm J. Varnier 1536). Among his other writings are the cosmographic *Weltbuch* (1533), a Latin paraphrase of the *Theologia Deutsch*, and the *Kriegsbüchlein des Frides* (Augsburg: H. Steiner 1539), which became important as a landmark in the history of pacifist thought. A number of Franck's minor writings were published in Dutch editions only.

Sebastian Franck was one of the great religious individualists of his age; he was a lonely and isolated advocate of peace and an imperturbable critic of religious persecution, because he believed that God alone recognizes the true heretics. After many disappointing experiences with the Roman church, Lutheranism, and Anabaptism he dissociated himself from all religious parties; he had no followers and did not found his own religious movement. His life was a vagrant journey from one city to another because his attempts to settle down were thwarted almost everywhere.

Franck respected Erasmus very highly and often quoted from the humanist's writings. His scepticism of dogmatic formalism and his pacifist ideas clearly show marks of Erasmus' influence. In 1534 Franck wrote a German translation of the *Moria*. Erasmus, on the other hand, did not show much appreciation for Franck's work. Franck's expulsion from Strasbourg in 1531 was in fact due to a complaint which Erasmus had submitted to the city government because the author of the *Geschichtbybell* had listed him among the great and unjustly persecuted heretics of Christendom (Epp 2587, 2590, 2615, 2622). Cf also Erasmus' Ep 2441 to 'Eleutherius.'

BIBLIOGRAPHY: Allen Ep 2441 / NDB V 320–1 / RGG II 1012–13 / A. Hegler *Geist und Schrift bei Sebastian Franck* (Freiburg 1892) / Rufus M. Jones *Spiritual Reformers in the 16th and 17th Centuries* (New York 1914) / Will-Erich Peuckert *Sebastian Franck: ein deutscher Sucher* (Munich 1943) / R. Kommoss *Sebastian Franck und Erasmus von Rotterdam* (Berlin 1934) / W. Kaegi *Chronica mundi: Grundformen der Geschichtsschreibung seit dem Mittelalter* (Einsiedeln 1954) / A. Koyré 'Sebastian Franck, 1499–1542' *Mystiques, spirituels, alchimistes* (Paris 1955) / M. Barbers *Toleranz bei Sebastian Franck* (Bonn 1964) / S. Wollgast *Der deutsche Pantheismus im 16. Jahrhundert: Sebastian Franck und seine Wirkungen auf die Entwicklung der pantheistischen Philosophie in Deutschland* (Berlin 1972), contains a comprehensive bibliography of Sebastian Franck's writings and their editions and of modern research literature / But cf above all K. Kaczerowsky *Sebastian Franck: Bibliographie, Verzeichnisse von Francks Werken, der von ihm gedruckten Bücher sowie der Sekundärliteratur* (Wiesbaden 1976)   HANS R. GUGGISBERG

FRANÇOIS See FRANCISCUS

Peter FRAUENBERGER of Beinheim, Lower Alsace, documented 1520–8
Frauenberger (Frabenberger, Frobenberger, Gynoraeus) studied at Sélestat under Konrad *Witz. On the recommendation of *Beatus Rhenanus and Leo *Jud he was appointed parish priest at Einsiedeln in central Switzerland, early in 1520. In the spring of 1522 he

registered at the University of Basel, graduating MA the following year and henceforward enjoying a reputation for fine scholarship. Also in 1522 he took charge of the Basel parish of St Alban. Following the example of *Oecolampadius, he ceased to say mass and, finding no support among his parishioners, was expelled from Basel in November 1525. Until 1527 he lived in poverty at Augsburg and worked as a corrector for the printer Sigmund Grimm. When he returned to Basel, still without a position, Oecolampadius attempted to place him as a schoolmaster in Legnica (Liegnitz), Silesia, and *Zwingli recommended him to Bern. In the end he either returned to St Alban or was nominated to the parish of Rümlingen in the Basel territory. In the summer of 1528 he became the principal figure in a public scandal reported accurately by Erasmus in Ep 2054 and the *Epistola ad fratres Inferioris Germaniae* (ASD IX-1 396–7) and also in AK III Ep 1264, and with additional detail and perhaps bias by the Carthusian chronicler (*Basler Chroniken* I). Frauenberger was pilloried and led to the city gate by the hangman, leaving Oecolampadius and Zwingli disappointed and embarrassed. His moves thereafter are not known. If the Carthusian can be trusted, he seems to have favoured some form of concubinal arrangement for priests on a contractual basis, short of formal marriage. When accused before the authorities, he apparently blamed his offence on the unsettling influence of the reformers.

BIBLIOGRAPHY: F. Heusler 'Petrus Gynoraeus' *Zwingliana* 1 (1897–1904) 120–2 / K. Gauss 'Die Beziehungen Zwinglis zu den Pfarrherrn des Baselbiets' *Zwingliana* 3 (1913–20) 38 5–9, esp 387–8 / *Matrikel Basel* I 350 / BRE Epp 151, 444, and passim / Z VII Ep 114, IX Ep 610, and passim / BA *Oekolampads* II 199–200, 332, and passim / *Basler Chroniken* I 445–6
                                                                                      PGB

Emperor FREDERICK III 21 September 1415–19 August 1493
Frederick, a son of Duke Ernest of Austria (d 1424) and Cimburgis of Masovia (d 1429) and a cousin of Albert II, the Roman king (d 1439), was brought up by his guardian, Duke Frederick of Tirol. When he had come of age in 1435 he made a pilgrimage to the Holy Land,

where he became a knight of the Holy Sepulchre on 8 September 1436. In 1439 he was the head of the Hapsburg family and the guardian of Duke Sigmund of Tirol (the son of his own former guardian); in 1440 he also became the guardian of Ladislaus Posthumus, the son of his cousin Albert, whose claims to the throne of Hungary and Bohemia were recognized in May 1445. Frederick was elected Roman king on 2 February 1440 and crowned in Aachen on 17 June 1442. In Rome he married Eleanor of Portugal and was crowned emperor by Pope *Nicholas V on 16–18 March 1452. At that time, however, imperial power was at a low point. Frederick III was powerless to prevent the untimely release of Ladislaus Posthumus from his guardianship in 1452, the installation of *Matthias Corvinus as king of Hungary after Ladislaus' death in 1457, or the division of Austria over disputes between himself and his brother Albert of Styria; at the same time insecurity and lawlessness in Austria was leading to general unrest. Only after the death of Albert in 1463 was he gradually able to gain control of the whole of Austria, and the marriage of his son, the future *Maximilian I, to Mary, the daughter of Charles the Rash of *Burgundy, on 19 August 1477 increased the power and prestige of the house of Hapsburg. Battles against Matthias Corvinus continued until 1491 (the peace of Bratislava), when the conditional rights of the Austrian ruler to the succession of Hungary were recognized. Two years later Frederick III died in Linz.

The Emperor Frederick III is mentioned in Epp 205, 2879 and LB V 726c; his moderation and wisdom in administration are praised in Erasmus' *Panegyricus ad Philippum* (ASD IV-1 54, 82).

BIBLIOGRAPHY: NDB V 484–7 / ADB VII 448–52 / Hermann Wiesflecker *Kaiser Maximilian I* (Munich 1971) I 48, 50–87, and passim / F.M. Mayer, R. Kaindl, H. Pirchegger, et al *Geschichte und Kulturleben Österreichs* 5th ed (Vienna 1958–65) 110–15 and passim   IG

Jeroen FREDERIKS of Groningen, d 26 August 1558
Jeroen, the son of Willem *Frederiks, matriculated at the University of Freiburg on 5 February 1522, presumably to study law under

Udalricus *Zasius. He did in fact obtain a doctorate of laws, but it is not known from which university. In 1521 Erasmus, who was then at Louvain, had an opportunity to be of service to Jeroen (Ep 1200). The grateful father sent Erasmus a gilt cup through *Gozewijn of Halen, the master of the Groningen school. Conceivably Jeroen might also have been the youth mentioned in Ep 838, who was sent to Louvain by the same Gozewijn in 1518 and became a student of Maarten van *Dorp. This hypothesis, however, is not supported by the *Matricule de Louvain*.

His studies completed, Jeroen returned to Groningen, where he married and had children. His illegitimate birth notwithstanding, he was appointed municipal *rentmeester* or steward. The date of his death is recorded in a note added to his father's history of Friesland.

BIBLIOGRAPHY: Allen Ep 1200 and IV 617 / *Matrikel Freiburg* I-1 617 / J. Reitsma in *Bijdragen tot de geschiedenis en oudheidkunde, inzonderheid van de provincie Groningen* 4 (1867) 303–5

C.G. VAN LEIJENHORST

Willem FREDERIKS d 3 August 1527

Willem Frederiks (Frederici, Fredericus) may have been born around 1455, probably at Groningen. On 19 or 20 May 1471 he matriculated at the University of Cologne and subsequently went to Ferrara, where he graduated MA on 15 February 1474 and doctor of medicine on 20 October 1475. At Ferrara he also attended the lectures of Rodolphus *Agricola. On 23 June 1485 he was a curate of St Martin's at Groningen, and from 1489 to 1525 he was one of the two parsons (*personae*) of that church. During his early years at Groningen he was a regular visitor to Wessel *Gansfort's 'Academy' at nearby Aduard; at the same time he was deeply involved in municipal affairs and often acted as a negotiator on behalf of the town council. The last two years of his life he spent in retirement, living with his natural son, Jeroen *Fredericks.

In 1521 Erasmus, who was at Louvain, had an opportunity to be of service to Jeroen. The grateful father sent him a gilt cup, which arrived together with a letter by *Gozewijn of Halen introducing the donor. In his reply Erasmus expressed his gratitude and praised Willem's integrity, piety, and zeal for good

learning (Ep 1200). In matters of faith the parson of Groningen seems to have adopted a middle course, not unlike Erasmus' own. While his own orthodoxy was never suspect, he arranged a theological debate on 12 March 1523 between Groningen Dominicans and their Lutheran opponents. In 1498 he had begun to write a history of Friesland, of which a fragment has been preserved and was published by Zuidema (139–52). In 1513 he drafted a set of rules for the appointment of his successor: 'Forma eligendi pastoris' (Zuidema 152–6). His library, of which Erasmus had written with admiration (Ep 1200), was left to St Martin's and is now in the library of the University of Groningen.

BIBLIOGRAPHY: Allen Ep 1200 / *Matrikel Köln* I 822 / W. Zuidema *Wilhelmus Frederici, persona van Sint-Maarten te Groningen* (Groningen 1888) / P.F. Wolfs *Das Groninger 'Religionsgespräch' (1523) und seine Hintergründe* (Nijmegen 1959) passim / E.H. Waterbolk *Twee eeuwen Friese geschiedschrijving* (Groningen 1952) passim

C.G. VAN LEIJENHORST

Christoph FREISLEBEN of Linz, documented 1517–after 1551

Christoph Freisleben (Eleutherobios) of Linz, Upper Austria, was enrolled at the University of Vienna in 1517 and afterwards became a schoolmaster in Wels. In 1521 he began to be interested in the reform movement; at first he was a Lutheran, and he or his brother Leonhard may be the author of an evangelical church ordinance for Loket (Elbogen), in Bohemia, printed in 1522. Both brothers belonged in 1527 to an Anabaptist circle whose leader was Johann Bünderlin, and on 15 November 1527 they fled to Passau when Archduke *Ferdinand sent soldiers to Wels to punish people known for their adherence to the reformers. Christoph Freisleben was in Esslingen in late 1527, and his pamphlet *Vom warhafftigen Tauff Joannis, Christi und der Aposteln* (n p, n pr) was printed in Strasbourg in 1528. Soon after that, however, he forsook Anabaptism, returned to the Catholic faith, and was appointed teacher at the chapter school of St Maurice in Augsburg in 1530. When the reformers gained the upper hand, he left Augsburg early in 1537 and may have become a schoolmaster in Ingolstadt, where he translated Plautus' *Stichus* for a scholastic production (published Augsburg: P. Ulhart 1539).

In 1544–5 Freisleben studied law at Bourges and received the licence and probably also the legal doctorate to which he laid claim later on. In the same year Sebastianus *Gryphius published three small books by him at Lyon *Precationes aliquot, Ad iuris utriusque titulos,* and *E divi Justiniani Institutionibus erotemata.* Later in 1545 he was appointed syndic at the University of Vienna and procurator-in-ordinary to the government of Vienna. In addition Fridericus *Nausea appointed him official and syndic to the bishop of Vienna. He assumed this office on 20 August 1547 and was confirmed in it by Nausea's successor on 9 March 1551. On 1 December 1549 he also obtained a benefice at Mistelbach. In this period he probably became a priest. He composed a collection of 172 sermons (*Harmonia quatuor evangelistarum*) which was published at Basel by Johannes Oporinus (n d, new edition 1557), who also printed works by Nausea. Freisleben further wrote a German translation of sermons by Gregory of Nanzianzus and Gregory of Nyssa (n p, n d).

In 1531 Freisleben introduced himself to Erasmus in Ep 2475 from Augsburg, referring to his return to the Catholic faith, his scholarly efforts, and friends of Erasmus whom he had met at Augsburg; no reply is known.

BIBLIOGRAPHY: Allen Ep 2475 / Luther w Briefwechsel IV Ep 1226 / Matrikel Wien II-1 439 / Ulrich Gäbler 'Eine unbeachtete Übersetzung des Leonhard Freisleben genannt Eleutherobius' ARG 61 (1970) 70–6 / Gustav Bossert 'Christoph Eleutherobius ...' *Jahrbuch der Gesellschaft für die Geschichte des Protestantismus in Österreich* 29 (1908) 1–12   IG

Konrad FRICK abbot of Schuttern, d 3 April 1535
Frick was elected abbot of the Benedictine abbey of Schuttern, near Lahr, on 12 July 1518. He joined with Lorenz *Effinger, abbot of Ettenheimmünster, in efforts to stop the attacks of Count Gangolf von *Geroldseck (Epp 1120, 1148) and in 1521 won a short-lived reprieve when Gangolf was threatened with prosecution and Schuttern came under the protection of the Hapsburg government at

Ensisheim. In February 1522 he was at Nürnberg, perhaps after a summons had gone out for a diet which did not in the end materialize, and was expected to return home shortly. In 1525 he joined other abbots of the region in taking flight before the rebelling peasants. Until the danger had passed he remained in Freiburg, where the abbey owned a house in which Johann von *Botzheim had stayed in 1519. When the peasants besieged Freiburg Frick took up arms and participated in a sally.

Frick promoted the continuation of a chronicle of Schuttern begun by Paul *Volz, and in 1526 he went to Ensisheim to negotiate with Volz and other parties about the future of the abbey of Hügshofen. Ottmar *Nachtgall spoke of him as an old friend and gave an example of his sense of humour in *Ioci et sales* (Augsburg 1524).

BIBLIOGRAPHY: Allen Ep 1120 / G. Mezler and J.G. Mayer 'Monumenta historico-chronologica monastica' *Freiburger Diözesan-Archiv* 14 (1881) 141–67, esp 162–3 / *Germania Benedictina* v: *Baden-Württemberg* ed F. Quarthal et al (Augsburg 1975) 562–72 / BRE Ep 255 / *Udalrici Zasii epistolae* (Ulm 1774) ed J.A. Riegger Epp 243, 266, I p 492   PGB

Franz FRIEDLIEB *See Franciscus* IRENICUS

Anna FRIES *See Conradus* PELLICANUS

Enno II, count of Eastern FRIESLAND *See Enno II* CIRKSENA

Erasmius FROBEN of Basel, c 1515–49
Johannes Erasmius, generally called Erasmius, the youngest son of Johann *Froben and Gertrud *Lachner, was born before 16 October 1515 (AK II Ep 538), either in the winter of 1514–15 or more likely in the summer of 1515. His godfathers were *Beatus Rhenanus and Erasmus, who was in Basel at the time and who, with affection and great expectations, followed the progress of the child named after him (Epp 635, 1226). When Erasmius was six Erasmus dedicated to him a new edition of the *Colloquia,* and the proud father printed a copy on vellum for the boy (Ep 1262; cf Ep 1476, Allen I 9). Erasmius also appears as a speaker in some dialogues and is mentioned otherwise. At his confirmation, before March 1522, *Ca-

pito was his sponsor. In the spring of 1522 Erasmius was sent to Freiburg, where Konrad *Heresbach became his tutor (Ep 1316; AK II Epp 874, 879). In March 1527 he was being tutored together with Valentin *Furster by Ludovicus *Carinus, apparently at Koblenz (Epp 1798, 1799). In his preface to the great edition of St Augustine of 1529 (Ep 2157), Erasmus suggested that after the recent death of his father some responsibility for the firm had fallen on Erasmius' shoulders, but there is no evidence that he was ever to play a prominent role in the 'officina Frobeniana.' Erasmus loved his godson tenderly and in 1529 after Basel's reformation had Erasmius with him in Freiburg until the beginning of November, when Hieronymus *Froben came to fetch him back, to Erasmus' bitter disappointment. Various plans were discussed for his further education, and he was finally sent to the Collegium Trilingue at Louvain, no doubt in an effort to appease Erasmus, who feared above all that he might be put to work in the Basel press or apprenticed to a business friend in Lyon (Epp 2229, 2231, 2235, 2236). At Louvain he at first lodged with Karl *Harst and by the summer of 1530 in the Trilingue, but Conradus *Goclenius was shocked by his deficient Latin and pessimistic about his academic prospects (Epp 2352, 2369, 2412). By November 1531 Erasmius had moved to Lille to study French (Ep 2573). Afterwards he no doubt returned to Basel and presumably lived and worked in the great publishing house. Plans for him to earn a degree had perhaps not quite been abandoned, though, for in 1534 he went to Freiburg with recommendations to Erasmus and *Zasius (Ep 2978; AK IV Epp 1885, 1886, 1892). Soon, however, more practical arrangements were made for the young man. In January 1536 he renewed his father's membership in the 'Schlüssel' and 'Safran' guilds and on 23 August he married Katharina Weckhart (BRE Ep 296; AK IV Ep 2055) and entered the printing business of his stepfather, Johann *Herwagen, who later said that his arm had been twisted to accept him (AK V Ep 2264). In 1538 and 1539 he is found riding to nearby towns on various errands (AK V Epp 2236, 2237, 2276). Eventually adultery between his wife and Herwagen led to Erasmius' divorce, on 6 December 1541. In 1548 he is mentioned on the roll of Basel's

militia, but otherwise the sources are silent. One may perhaps presume that he continued to live and work on the fringes of the great publishing firm.

BIBLIOGRAPHY: Allen Ep 635 / AK II Ep 538 and passim / Paul Koelner Die Zunft zum Schlüssel in Basel (Basel 1953) 314 / de Vocht CTL III 227–32 and passim   PGB

Gertrud FROBEN *See Gertrud* LACHNER

Hieronymus FROBEN of Basel, 1501–13 March 1563
Hieronymus, the eldest son of Johann *Froben, was born in the summer of 1501 (6 August?), apparently the first child born in Basel after the city had joined the Swiss Confederation. In 1515 he matriculated in the University of Basel, but his MA was bestowed upon him in 1520 by the papal legate, Antonio *Pucci (BRE Epp 149, 152), rather than earned. Although the printing firm claimed his undivided attention from an early age (AK II Ep 631; BRE Ep 149), there cannot be any doubt about his grasp of the scholarly side of the business. As an example his efforts concerning Chrysostom might be mentioned. In the summer of 1526 he went to Milan, Venice, and Padua and brought back manuscripts that were used and partly translated by Erasmus for the great Chrysostom edition of 1530 (Epp 1705–7, 1720), and as late as 3 March 1545 Froben was writing in a scholarly fashion to Wolfgangus Musculus about the collation of Chrysostom manuscripts (MS Basel). Later in 1526 he subjected the famous *Dalberg library at Ladenburg to a thorough scrutiny (Epp 1767, 1774; BRE Ep 264).

Towards the end of 1518 young Froben was at Louvain but did not allow himself to be retained in Erasmus' house as a famulus (BRE Ep 416). Business took him to Louvain and Antwerp on three more occasions between the autumn of 1519 and August 1521 (CWE Ep 1226 introduction; BRE Ep 132; AK II Ep 764). On 2 June 1521 he became a member of the 'Safran' guild and on 18 November 1544 of the prestigious 'Schlüssel' guild. On 7 January 1524 he married Anna, a daughter of Wolfgang *Lachner and a sister of his stepmother, Gertrud *Lachner. Anna had been living in the Froben house since her father's death, and it seems that the marriage did not spring solely from business strategy (AK II Ep 942, 945). After Anna's death Hieronymus married Barbara Brand, the daughter of a Basel burgomaster, in the spring of 1544; she survived him. Under Hieronymus' direction the family firm, which was later carried on by his sons Ambrosius and Aurelius, underwent a number of changes (Ep 2108), while retaining its outlook on fundamentals. The firm's precious *Rechnungsbuch* shows that towards the end of his life sales at the Frankfurt fair accounted for two-thirds and more of general revenue. Froben himself normally attended the fairs (Epp 1769, 1972, 2063, 2126; AK VII Ep 3337), selling as well as collecting orders for books he planned to print (Ep 1994 A). While the number of copies in each edition was large, the number of titles published each year no longer reached the levels of Johann's last decade. In the thirty-five years between the death of Johann and Hieronymus' own death, about four hundred titles were published. The firm gradually lost most of the exceptional reputation it had enjoyed in the days of Johann and Erasmus, but it seems to have become more profitable. It was reorganized on the basis of partnerships, from 1528 to 1529 with Johann *Herwagen, Hieronymus' stepfather, and thereafter either with his brother-in-law, Nicolaus *Episcopius, or on occasions with both men. Later Froben's sons were also active in the firm, but Hieronymus was normally responsible for all major initiatives. In 1531 he moved with his family to the newly acquired house 'zum Luft' in the Bäumleingasse, leaving the Nadelberg premises to Herwagen and Episcopius. Printing continued in both locations.

Froben and Episcopius were for the most part content to use the typographical material developed in the days of Johann Froben. They continued faithfully to reprint individual works by Erasmus together with the great editions of the classics and the Fathers launched in the earlier days; however, they added a number of significant new titles to the firm's list, some in co-operation with the scholar Simon *Grynaeus. As in the earlier days the most prestigious undertakings were still folio-sized and scholarly editions of the complete works of an author, such as the Latin Plato of 1532. Between 1535 and 1539 Froben

Hieronymus Froben

and Episcopius pursued an action against Eucharius *Cervicornus and Gottfried Hittorp before the imperial law court at Speyer for having pirated their edition of Flavius Josephus (AK V Ep 2239). The press also continued to avoid the works of Protestant theologians but, in keeping with general intellectual trends in Basel and elsewhere, was paying more attention to science, publishing, among others, important editions of Galen (1542), Hippocrates (1538), and Georgius *Agricola, the pioneer of mining literature. Finally the fundamental edition of the collected works of Erasmus (1538–40) could not have succeeded without Hieronymus' personal initiative and attention to many details (AK V Epp 2123, 2156, 2206).

As a scholar and printer combined, Hieronymus probably worked more closely with Erasmus than his father ever had. After Johann's death Erasmus wrote that he and Hieronymus had jointly to shoulder the responsibility for the press (Ep 1921) and even from Freiburg he continued to take his moral obligations to the Froben press very seriously (Epp 2305, 2328, 2569, 2628, 2757). He also praised Hieronymus publicly for his zeal and courage (Epp 2022, 2773) and persuaded him to invest in a larger Greek type (Ep 2062) and undertake with it specific ventures such as the Greek Basil of 1532 (Epp 2526, 2611). However, when he feared that Hieronymus might have to do battle in the first Kappel campaign in 1529, he withdrew the modest part of his savings he had left with the firm (Epp 2183, 2194). Hardly anything negative about Hieronymus can be found in Erasmus' letters (Ep 2040) until his plans for the education of Erasmius *Froben momentarily enraged the ageing scholar (Ep 2231); however, complete trust was soon restored and was never thereafter in question (Epp 2481, 2488, 2501, 2628, 2748, 2818). It seems that it was chiefly Hieronymus who on his frequent visits to Freiburg persuaded Erasmus that he should return to Basel (Epp 2755, 2756) and it was in his house 'zum Luft' (Ep 3028) that Erasmus spent the last thirteen months of his life. In company with Episcopius he visited Erasmus in his final days, and it seems certain that he was present when he died (BRE Ep 299; AK IV Ep 2036). He also helped with the arrangements for Erasmus' tombstone (AK IV Ep 2075, V Epp 2118, 2119). Erasmus' affection is also shown by his will (Allen XI 364), in which he left Froben and his wife personal and treasured objects. Froben and Episcopius were the executors and in this capacity were often consulted by Bonifacius *Amerbach about subsidies he proposed to pay from the bequest of Erasmus, such as a loan to Johann Ulrich *Zasius to save his father's library in 1545 and a grant to Sebastianus Castellio in 1546 (AK VI Epp 2685, 2851, 2891, 2949).

Like his father, Hieronymus had allowed his friendship with *Zwingli to end at an early date (Z VII Ep 118), but Zwingli's successor, Heinrich Bullinger, was among his many correspondents and there is no indication that the victory of Basel's reform party represented a dilemma for him. However, on 20 September 1557 he joined Amerbach and Episcopius in publishing a dignified reply to *Farel and Beza, who had spoken irreverently of Erasmus in a Basel inn. Froben died of a stomach ailment and was buried in the cathedral, close to his home. A small portrait in the collection of the Kunstmuseum Basel shows him in advanced years.

BIBLIOGRAPHY: Allen Ep 903 / AK II Ep 631 and passim / A. Pfister in NDB V 637–8 / Grimm *Buchführer* 1376–8 / *Rechnungsbuch der Froben und Episcopius ... 1557–1564* ed R. Wackernagel (Basel 1881) / R. Wackernagel *Geschichte der Stadt Basel* (Basel 1907–54) III 439–40, 90–91 / I. Stockmeyer and B. Reber *Beiträge zur Basler Buchdruckergeschichte* (Basel 1840) 115–22 / P. Heitz and C.C. Bernoulli *Basler Büchermarken bis zum Anfang des 17. Jahrhunderts* (Strasbourg 1895) xxi, 36–41 / J. Tonjola *Basilea sepulta* (Basel 1661) 19 / A few MS letters addressed to him by Johann Ammann, Gualtherus Scottus and Conradus *Goclenius are in the Öffentliche Bibliothek of the University of Basel   PGB

Johann FROBEN of Hammelburg, c 1460–26 October 1527

A native of Hammelburg, north of Würzburg, Johann Froben was probably the most celebrated printer of his generation north of the Alps, but in some aspects he remains a surprising, and in others an elusive, figure. As he knew very little Latin (Epp 629, 802, 885), it must be assumed that his formal education was limited. Erasmus once called him 'stupid' (Ep 886) and judged him to be excessively naïve (Epp 733, 885, 902A, 1560, 1900). Moreover, not until the last decade of his life does Froben appear to have succeeded in fully freeing himself from the dominating influence of others. But if slow perseverance was his outstanding quality, he knew how to apply it to the technical mastery of his trade and how to combine it with warmth and a guileless trust in his associates. He was seldom disappointed and was well beloved by all who came to know him, including Erasmus. The emblem he used in his books is an apt reflection on the man. The staff of Mercury is guarded by the wary snake and the innocent dove of Matthew 10:16 (*Adagia* II i 1; V 34). A similar assessment of himself is revealed by a device which he used occasionally: 'prudens simplicitas amorque recti.'

Nothing is known of the first twenty-five years of Froben's life. In 1486 he was by his own testimony employed by Anton Koberger, a printer and publisher in Nürnberg. His move to Basel was no doubt facilitated by Koberger's business contacts with an older native of Froben's own region, Johann *Amerbach, who was already established in the Rhenish city as a successful printer of great prestige. In 1491 a record in Basel's Carthusian monastery calls Froben a former famulus of Amerbach. On 13 November 1490 he acquired the citizenship of Basel, on 13 May 1492 the membership of the 'Safran' guild, and on 6 December 1522 that of the more distinguished 'Schlüssel' guild. The earliest known book he produced, a Latin Bible, is dated 27 June 1491, and until 1496 approximately one more book each year appeared over his own imprint. From 1494, however, he tackled some voluminous folio editions in partnership with Johannes *Petri, and from 1500 they collaborated often with Amerbach, who remained the senior partner in their joint enterprises. With the deaths of Petri in 1511 and Amerbach in 1513, and above all with Froben's marriage to the daughter of Wolfgang *Lachner in 1510, his business was subject to further changes.

Until his death in 1518 the commercial direction of the publishing house was in Lachner's hands; since it was his responsibility to sell Froben's production he had the final say in what should be published. In the past he had liked to handle some of the Bibles and other bulky folios of Amerbach and his partners and he knew that north of the Alps, at any rate, expensive and voluminous works were not likely to succeed unless they appealed to the clerical market; thus he showed a preference for theological summae and similar works. Although Amerbach's appreciation of humanism was basically alien to Lachner, he brought his own aggressive pragmatism to Froben's business, and if he did not himself discover Erasmus, he certainly spared no efforts to accomodate him (Ep 305) as soon as he recognized his potential for sales. The sound businessman in him did not balk excessively at the additional expense of securing and collating manuscripts and employing humanistically trained editors and proof-readers (Ep 1341).

Erasmus may not have been a party to the famous deal in which Franz *Birckmann put into the hands of Lachner and Froben the material for a new edition of the *Adagia* (Epp 219, 263, 283), but he certainly liked the result, Froben's volume of 1513, handsomely set in Roman type. It is not likely that he came to

Johann Froben, by Hans Holbein the Younger

Basel in the fall of 1514 (Ep 305) without an invitation of some kind since the Froben firm was then anxious to secure a new academic director for the great edition of Jerome (Epp 326, 396; Allen I 63–4). Prior to the *Adagia* Froben had hardly published a title outside the field of theology and possibly none at all to satisfy the requisites of the new learning. Although not published until 1516, the Jerome edition had been planned by Amerbach in his final years as a work of scholarship as well as theological appeal (AK II Epp 501, 538). The new scholarly criteria introduced by Erasmus in the Jerome edition were also reflected in his own works that were printed while he was at Basel, and those of other humanists approached to work on the Jerome. All were indicative of the new direction of the press, and henceforward Froben's annual crop of publications was unthinkable without titles of interest to humanist scholars. However, scholastic works were well in evidence until the death of Lachner in spite of the 'sodalitas' of humanistic talent that the press now began to assemble, including the Amerbach sons, *Beatus Rhenanus, *Glareanus, *Pellicanus,

Wilhelm *Nesen, *Angst, *Listrius, *Bentinus, *Nepos, and *Gelenius, and also consultants among the university professors such as *Capito and Ludwig *Baer. Lachner's policies were at times bitterly opposed by Beatus Rhenanus, who, after Erasmus, was Froben's leading scholarly adviser. Only after Lachner's death, in the last decade of Johann Froben's life, when the influence of his son, Hieronymus *Froben, was growing (Ep 1707), did the press perhaps fully live up to its reputation for scholarly publishing *par excellence* and justify its image of being a nordic counterpart to that of Aldo *Manuzio, a reputation and an image carefully nurtured by Erasmus and his friends (Epp 635, 852, 925, 1304, 1465, 1544, 1659; *Adagia* II i 1, v 34).

Froben all but ignored the lucrative trade in popular and polemical pamphlets. He did launch a most important first collection of *Luther's Latin writings in 1518, but partly under pressure from Erasmus (Epp 904, 1033, 1143, 1634) and partly perhaps by personal preference, he soon refrained from publishing the authors of the Protestant Reformation. He used to give many books to Huldrych *Zwingli (z VII Ep 60), but their relations ended in 1523 when Zwingli's stance became uncompromising. Froben himself did not live to be confronted with the choices resulting from the victory of the reform party in Basel. As Erasmus had shown his hand in shaping Froben's editorial policy, he also made a most loyal effort to help Froben succeed with his publications; he wrote prefaces and letters in his name (Epp 602, 1304, 1702, 1736), applied for protective privileges (Epp 1341, 1392), and tried to prevent rival editions (Epp 815, 1623, 1628).

Lachner's death not only affected Froben's editorial policy but also caused his commercial tactics to be streamlined, a process which in turn facilitated the changes of editorial policy. Apart from his significant stake in Froben's press Lachner had continued independently his importation and distribution of Italian books, many of them Aldine products (AK II Ep 538) and Greek and Roman authors. Without Lachner Froben found a new freedom to compete with the Italians in their own chosen field. The firm's production of classical authors and other books of Italian humanist inspiration gained momentum and reached a climax after

Johann's death and the reform in Basel, although the major emphasis on religious subjects was never abandoned. Indeed, it too was reinforced during Johann's last decade through printing in Hebrew and through Erasmus' great editions of the Christian Fathers. Without Lachner it seems that Froben for the most part was content with offering his books at the Frankfurt fairs (Epp 801, 1654, 1681, 1682, 1750, 1900) to both bulk and retail buyers, although he did continue to supply such international traders as the *Schabler and Birckmann consortia (Epp 1560, 1704) and Francesco Giulio *Calvo. Froben's retail sales of books published by other presses do not appear to have been significant. While Lachner's independent book trade had been taken over by Schabler, whose capital and influence in the press, while still viewed with concern by Beatus Rhenanus (CWE Epp 885, 1014), was much smaller than Lachner's had been. Another economic matter, the remuneration of Erasmus, was settled satisfactorily soon after Lachner's death. Erasmus well understood the seriousness of the problems facing Froben at the time (Epp 795, 796), and two years later he had nothing but praise for Froben's generous intentions and his own altruism (Allen I 45; cf LB X 1612E, 1617E). Looking back from Freiburg, he was aware of the economic advantages he had enjoyed at Basel through his arrangements with the Froben press (Ep 2215).

While Johann Froben apparently preferred a simplified commercial structure for his firm and for his editiorial policy depended on the advice of others, his correspondence with Bonifacius *Amerbach shows him personally in charge of matters related to the operation of the press. He attended to the securing of copy once the scholars had advised him on what was needed, and he chose his staff carefully. There is some evidence that he should also be given credit for policy changes in the typographical sector. The outward appearance of his books was a matter of great importance; the firm's prestige and the renown of his own name depended heavily on it (Epp 1733, 1900; Rogers Ep 67; BRE Ep 26).

Froben's first independent production, the 1491 Bible, was printed in a newly designed 'rotunda' type of Italian inspiration. In spite of its very small size Froben achieved a printed page of great neatness. He also added a title page and a glossary of Hebrew terms, rare distinctions at the time. The *Adagia* of 1513 opened a new phase in the typographical history of the firm. The book was set in a newly created Roman type of Aldine inspiration, which was used by Froben in six different sizes and aroused great admiration north of the Alps. So did his elegant and highly readable Greek italic, which was created for Erasmus' *Novum instrumentum* in 1516. In a noticeable departure from both the Italian humanist tradition and all typographical precedents at Basel, Froben commissioned the best available artists, Urs Graf, Hans *Holbein the Younger, and the latter's brother Ambrosius, to design further embellishments for his books such as fine figurative borders for the title page, a vast array of decorated initials, and dozens of variations of his emblematic imprint, the woodcuts of 1516–17 being supplemented between 1520 and 1522 with metal engravings. Meanwhile a third typographical style began to appear in 1519, when Froben introduced an italic type, often thought to surpass its Aldine model, for use in the less expensive octavo size. Both italics and octavo were employed predominantly after 1523, normally without any supplementary decorations, to produce handy books of classical harmony and clarity. In all, Johann Froben's editions exceeded five hundred, and in the peak years of his production around 1520 as many as fifty new titles were published annually.

Turning to Froben's private life, nothing is known of his first wife, the mother of Hieronymus, not even her name. Perhaps it was not a happy marriage; rumours circulated about the identity of Hieronymus' father (Ep 2231), while Froben himself had a natural daughter, Margarete. His second marriage in November 1510 to Gertrud *Lachner was of great benefit to the firm. In personal matters too the resolution and confidence of his wife may have complemented to good advantage his own slow and kindly disposition. There were bound to be tensions, however; Gertrud's personal wealth and acumen for business were at odds with the inclinations of her husband who despite his fame never grew wealthy (Allen I 45) and probably did not care. The pride of the elderly father is unmistakable, however, when his last child was born only

four years before his death, although he was disappointed that it was a girl; she was named Ursula (AK III Epp 912, 916). In 1507 Froben acquired the property 'zum Sessel' consisting of several houses and a yard reaching from the Nadelberg to the Totengässlein. This complex was further extended in October 1522 when the house 'zur alten Treu,' on the Nadelberg to the other side of the yard, was purchased for use by Erasmus (Epp 1316, 1371). On 12 June 1526 Froben purchased a garden against the city wall only a short walk away from his house. This was greatly appreciated by Erasmus (Epp 1756, 2147). In 1521 Froben fell from a ladder, and late in 1526 suffered great pain in his right ankle (Epp 1769, 1900). Guaiac brought no relief (AK III Ep 1157), but after treatment by *Paracelsus he recovered sufficiently to travel twice more to the Frankfurt fair (Epp 1875, 1900). His ambition was to complete the great edition of St Augustine which had caused him much anxiety, but this was denied him (Epp 1921, 2033, 2157). He died of a stroke and was buried close to his home in the church of St Peter under a funeral inscription in Hebrew, Greek, and Latin verses. The latter two were composed by Erasmus, who also commemorated him in Ep 1900. Portraits by Hans *Holbein are in the Kunstmuseum Basel and in Hampton Court.

BIBLIOGRAPHY: Allen Ep 419 / A. Pfister in NDB V 638–40 / Benzing *Buchdrucker* 30 / Grimm *Buchführer* 1372–4 / P.S. Allen *Erasmus: Lectures and Wayfaring Sketches* (Oxford 1934) 123–37 passim / H. Koegler in Gewerbemuseum Basel *Johann Froben 1460?-1527: Gedächtnis-Ausstellung* (Basel [1927]) / A. Hernandez in Gewerbemuseum Basel *Johann Froben und der Basler Buchdruck des 16. Jahrhunderts: Ausstellung* (Basel 1960) / I. Stockmeyer and B. Reber *Beiträge zur Basler Buchdruckergeschichte* (Basel 1840) 86–115 / P. Heitz and C.C. Bernoulli *Basler Büchermarken bis zum Anfang des 17. Jahrhunderts* (Strasbourg 1895) xx, 22–43 / R. Wackernagel *Geschichte der Stadt Basel* (Basel 1907–54) III 166–9 and passim / AK I Ep 167 and passim / BRE Ep 26 and passim / Z Ep 80 and passim / Luther w *Briefwechsel* I Ep 146 / E. Hilgert 'Johann Froben and the Basel university scholars, 1513–1523' *The Library Quarterly* 41 (1971) 141–69   PGB

Justina FROBEN of Basel, 1512–
27 September 1564
Little is known about the eldest daughter of
Johann *Froben and Gertrud *Lachner. She
grew up in the bustle of the great publishing
house under the eyes of Erasmus, who
expressed delight with the fine qualities of the
child and later the girl. In the summer of 1527
she suffered from an infectious nerve disease
but recovered (Ep 2176) to marry Nicolaus
*Episcopius in the summer of 1529. Nicolaus
was joining the press as a partner of her
half-brother, Hieronymus *Froben, and the
couple was to occupy lodgings in the premises
on the Nadelberg vacated by Erasmus. Erasmus meant to give them a present but in the
confusion of moving to Freiburg had to be
content with leaving an epigram for them
together with some chickens that remained in
the yard (Reedijk poem 125), as he explained in
an affectionate letter subsequently sent from
Freiburg (Ep 2202). In his last will he left
Justina two rings, one with a diamond and the
other with a turquoise (Allen xi 364). She bore
her husband twelve children and survived him
by a few months, dying of the plague together
with four of her children. She was buried by
his side.

BIBLIOGRAPHY: Allen Ep 2033 / W.R. Staehelin *Wappenbuch der Stadt Basel* (Basel [1917-30])
s v Bischof   PGB

Francis FROWICK documented 1517
Frowick (Frowycus) was the provincial of the
Franciscan Observants in England and attend-
ed the general chapter of the order held in
Rome in May 1517. On his return he visited
Erasmus in Louvain and showed him newly
edited works from Italy (Epp 642, 643). At one
time Frowick was Lenten preacher before
*Henry viii. No more seems to be known about
him.

BIBLIOGRAPHY: Allen Ep 642 / LP ii 3370, 3374 /
J.H. Lupton *A Life of John Colet* 2nd ed (London
1909) 91n, 224n   CFG

Leonhard FUCHS of Neuenburg,
d summer of 1546
Fuchs was burgomaster of Neuenburg, a small
town situated on the Rhine halfway between
Basel and Freiburg. He was a staunch Catholic,
and from the time of Erasmus' move to Freiburg
(1529) frequent contacts with Fuchs are documented in his correspondence, although no
direct exchange of letters is known today.
Fuchs corresponded with Ludwig *Baer (Ep
2543) and regaled Erasmus' famulus, Felix
*Rex, with wine (Ep 2130). He acted as a carrier
of letters and books between Bonifacius
*Amerbach, his son-in-law, at Basel and
Erasmus at Freiburg (Ep 2280), and in 1531
Erasmus envisaged the possibility of staying
for a while in his house at Neuenburg (Epp
2490, 2519, 2531, 2532, 2538, 2539), but the visit
was cancelled when the plague struck in
Fuchs' house (Epp 2541–3, 2546, 2547, 2556).
After the death of his first wife, Margarete
Zscheckenbürlin, Fuchs had a son by Küngolt
Fischer; Erasmus was among those consulted
before he married Küngolt in 1534 (Epp 2940,
2943, 2946). When Erasmus died, he had nine
hundred gold crowns deposited with Fuchs.

BIBLIOGRAPHY: Allen Ep 2179 / AK ii Ep 966, iv
Epp 1682, 1947, vi Ep 2825, and passim / Emil
Major *Erasmus von Rotterdam* (Basel [1925]) 54
MANFRED E. WELTI

Martha FUCHS of Neuenburg, 1 May 1505–
14 December 1541
At the instigation of Uldalricus *Zasius, marriage negotiations between the daughter of the
wealthy burgomaster of Neuenburg, on the
Rhine, Leonhard *Fuchs, and Bonifacius
*Amerbach began in the summer of 1524 and
culminated in the wedding on 25 February
1527. Martha Fuchs' mother was Margarete, a
sister of Hieronymus *Zscheckenbürlin, the
prior of the Basel Carthusian monastery, with
which the Amerbachs entertained close contact. When her husband was considering
leaving Basel after the victory of the reform
party, Martha and her family exercised a
restraining influence (Epp 2267, 2649) which
may have facilitated his final accomodation
with the new regime at Basel. She frequently
exchanged greetings with Erasmus as he
corresponded with her husband, and on one
occasion he sent her sweetmeats (Ep 2740).
Martha died in December 1541, having born
her husband five children. Despite many
opportunities Amerbach did not marry again.

BIBLIOGRAPHY: Allen Ep 2179 / AK ii Ep 966,
iii Ep 1179, and passim   MANFRED E. WELTI

Juan FUERTES *See Johannes* FORTIS

Anton FUGGER of Augsburg, 10 June 1493–
14 September 1560
Anton Fugger was a descendant of the famous
banking family of Augsburg. In 1367 Hans
Fugger (d 1408), a farmer and weaver, had
migrated to Augsburg from Graben am Lech-
feld and obtained his citizenship by marriage.
He soon acquired a fortune and considerable
property. His sons, Andreas and Jakob,
founded the two branches of the Fugger family
'vom Reh' and 'von der Lilie.' In the following
generation, Jakob Fugger the Rich (d 1525)
amassed a fortune extraordinary even by
Augsburg standards. He also held important
offices in the civic administration which in turn
benefited his extensive network of business
connections throughout Europe. By 1489
Lukas Fugger (vom Reh) had become involved
in dealings with *Maximilian I, but the transactions brought disgrace on the family because
the imperial ban was invoked against him, and
this signalled the ruin of this branch of the
Fuggers.

Anton Fugger, by Albrecht Dürer

The interests of the other branch, 'von der
Lilie,' focused on trade in copper, silver,
mercury, cinnabar, and at times also in gold. By
comparison commodities such as spices and
textiles were of secondary importance. The
Fuggers were able to establish monopolies in
many areas and to open branches in such
economic centres as the Tirol, Hungary, Italy,
England, the Netherlands, and Spain. The fact
that their branch offices were spread all over
Europe permitted them to function as an
important news agency, circulating the so-
called *Fugger-Zeitungen*.

The unequalled success of the Fuggers was
due mainly to the business acumen of Jakob
Fugger the Rich and his nephew Anton. After
the death of Anton family interests shifted
increasingly to the patronage of artists and
scholars. Active involvement in business gave
way to the management of their vast estates
and the pursuit of high-ranking military and
ecclesiastical careers. In fact as early as 1560
Anton had proposed to disband the family
business. Despite the world-wide recession
towards the end of the sixteenth century and
the great losses suffered in Spain and elsewhere, the Fuggers (unlike the Welsers)

escaped complete financial ruin through skilful
political manoeuvering and the acquisition of
landed property.

Anton Fugger received a thorough humanistic education leading up to a sojourn of several
years in Rome, where Pope *Leo x conferred a
knighthood upon him in 1519. In 1525 he
assumed the general direction of the firm after
he had devoted himself to the development of
the branch offices in Nürnberg, Wrocław, and
Budapest, as well as those in Italy and the
Tirol. In 1526, shortly before the death of King
*Louis II, he gave proof of his diplomatic skills
by re-establishing good relations between his
family and the Hungarian crown. In the same
year *Charles v raised him to the rank of a
count of the Empire since he needed the
financial backing of the Fuggers in his war
against the Turks. Anton loyally supported
King *Ferdinand's claims to Hungary and
Bohemia and thus incurred the enmity of *John
Zápolyai. In spite of this Ferdinand preferred
to deal with Anton's competitors, such as the
Höchstetters, also of Augsburg. On the other
hand, the Fuggers maintained good relations
with Charles v, whose election they had

Anna Rehlinger, wife of Anton Fugger,
by Albrecht Dürer

financed in 1519 (CWE Epp 927, 1009). With his
help they were able to expand their business
empire in a new direction as far as the West
Indies, Mexico and Buenos Aires. Their loyal
co-operation with Charles v led to the liquida-
tion of their branch office at Rome following
the Sack of 1527.

In 1527 Anton married Anna (d 1548), a
daughter of Johann *Rehlinger von Horgau,
who was to bear him five sons and six
daughters. By that time the Fuggers owned a
fortune of 1.6 million gold florins on which
they could draw to defend German economic
interests in Italy and to finance the Hapsburg's
wars against the Turks. By extending credit to
King Ferdinand in 1529 Anton helped to save
Vienna from the Ottoman siege. Two years
later the Fuggers and Welsers jointly provided
1.5 million ducats to secure Ferdinand's election as Roman king.

By 1533 Anton began to reduce his involvement in American ventures, a wise move
bound to pay off in decades ahead as the
economic climate began to change for the
worse. He willingly invested his money to
defend the Hapsburgs and Catholicism but

was unable to stand his ground against
*Zwingli's supporters in Augsburg. Because of
the religious conflict (Ep 2961) he retired in July
1533 to his estate in the small town of
Weissenhorn, in Swabia (Epp 2936, 2937,
2947).

In 1532 Anton's hand within the firm was
further strengthened with the renewal of the
partnership agreement. He continued to support and bankroll Hapsburg policies in Württemberg and elsewhere, financing the purchase of Donauwörth in 1536 and in the
following years some of the activities of
Cardinal Reginald *Pole. On the other hand,
while lending Charles v money for his expedition against Tunis in 1535, he gave offence to
Ferdinand by terminating the firm's engage-
ment in Hungary, judging the Balkans to be
permanently unstable. He secured his interests
with the English Tudors, the divorce question
notwithstanding, and did business in the
Netherlands, Sweden, and Sicily.

As the prospect of religious war in Germany
grew, Anton promoted reconciliation between
the emperor and the Protestants at the diet of
Regensburg in 1546, albeit on the basis of a
return to the Catholic church. When this failed
he retreated first to Bavaria, then to Schwaz in
the Tirol. In the ensuing war against the
Schmalkaldic League he deliberately delayed
supplies for the Hapsburg forces, hoping to
bring about a stalemate. At the height of the
crisis he returned to Augsburg (15 January
1547) and subsequently persuaded Charles v
to grant the city his pardon on moderate terms.
In the following years Fugger's relations with
the Hapsburgs continued to cool while new
economic and personal interests developed,
such as the trade connections with England
and the Levant, the acquisition of the mar-
graviate of Burgau in Swabia and other estates,
the segregation of the Tirolian and Carinthian
interests from the Fugger company, and the
personal withdrawal of Anton from business
ventures in Spain.

In 1550 Anton signed his second will, which
further reflected his intentions to lessen his
dependence on the Hapsburgs and concen-
trate on trade with England and Portugal. Yet
his long-standing connections with the imperial house were not easily severed; in 1552 he
once again gave his financial support to

Charles v for the war against Maurice of
Saxony and his French allies. Between 1553
and 1555 Hans Dernschwam, a senior company
agent, was in Turkey on a journey designed to
benefit scholarship and also explore the
feasibility of trade connections with the Far
East, but because of his continued liaison with
Austria Anton was unable to follow up this
overture.

As deteriorating health forced Anton to
retire progressively from business, his interests shifted from cultural to religious matters.
In 1559 his close contact with Ignatius of
Loyola prompted him to approach Petrus
Canisius, who had come to Augsburg as
cathedral preacher and begun to reorganize
the Catholic party. His profound loyalty to the
church of Rome was never in question.

Although Anton and his firm are mentioned
frequently in the correspondence of Erasmus,
it does not appear that the two ever met. From
1529 Fugger tried for several years, writing
direct and also through Johann *Koler, to
induce Erasmus to move his permanent residence to Augsburg (Epp 2145, 2159, 2192,
2193, 2195, 2196, 2525, 2561, 2594), but
Erasmus declined despite the generosity of
Fugger's financial offers; however, he reacted
to Anton's gift of a gold cup (Ep 2192) by
dedicating to him his Latin rendering of
Xenophon's *Hieron* (Ep 2273). Fugger's pleasure at this mark of honour was genuine (Ep
2307, 2308), and he was happy to assist
Erasmus in his recurrent search for wine that
would agree with his health (Epp 2330, 2415,
2437). Many letters point to the paramount
importance of the Fugger network in remitting
money and forwarding mail, and Erasmus
repeatedly praised Anton for his honesty and
reliability on both counts (Epp 2403, 2701).
Finally, Erasmus lauded Fugger again in the
prefatory letter of his last great work, the
Ecclesiastes (Ep 3036).

BIBLIOGRAPHY: Allen Ep 2145 / ADB VIII
179–84, especially 181–2 / NDB V 707–19 /
Schottenloher I nos 6769–6809, VII nos 54668–
719 / Götz von Pölnitz *Anton Fugger* (Tübingen
1958–   ) I-IV passim / J.G. Schellhorn Jr 'Anton
Fuggers Freundschaft gegen den Erasmus' in
his *Beyträge zur Erleuterung der Geschichte*
(Memmingen 1772–7) I-2 99–102
                                   ROSEMARIE AULINGER

Jakob Fugger, by Albrecht Dürer

Georg FUNCK of Augsburg, documented
1510–40
Georg Funck of Augsburg matriculated at the
University of Freiburg on 7 October 1510. His
marriage to Catharina, the elder daughter of
Udalricus *Zasius, is recorded in a minute of
the university senate of 6 December 1513, and
on 4 January 1517 he is mentioned there again
as Zasius' son-in-law. A year earlier Funck and
his brother-in-law Johannes *Sutor apparently
called on Erasmus in Basel, handing him Ep 390
from Zasius, who described Funck as 'a
member of the best business circles in Augsburg, an educated man, especially in the law,
and one whose character deserves respect' (Ep
390). In 1518 Zasius urged again that Funck,
evidently on another visit to Basel, be given a
friendly reception by the scholars of the Froben
press, since he was unfamiliar with Basel (AK II
Ep 641). In 1520 he was a doctor of law when
Zasius recommended him warmly to *Beatus
Rhenanus at Sélestat (BRE Ep 445). In a letter of
20 October 1540 he signed himself as councillor
and town secretary, perhaps of Augsburg,
when requesting the legal advice of Bonifacius
*Amerbach in matters concerning the estate of

his brother-in-law Joachim *Zasius (AK V Ep 2412).

BIBLIOGRAPHY: Allen Ep 390 / *Matrikel Freiburg* I-1 194 / AK II Ep 641 / Freiburg, Universitätsarchiv, MSS Senatsprotokolle II 417
STEVEN ROWAN & PGB

Hieronymus FUNDULUS *See Girolamo* FONDULO

Benedictus de FURNARIIS *See Benedetto de'* FORNARI

Ludwig and Valentin FURSTER of Kassel, d 1528/9 and 1555
In March 1527 Erasmus wrote a short letter of encouragement to Valentin Furster, a youth tutored at Koblenz by Ludovicus *Carinus, apparently together with Erasmius *Froben (Epp 1798, 1799).

The youth was most likely the son of Ludwig Furster (Forster, Förster), chancellor of Richard von *Greiffenklau, archbishop of Trier. Ludwig was the son of Heinrich Furster (d 1515), burgomaster of Kassel, and Margaret, the natural daughter of Landgrave Louis II of Hesse. Ludwig matriculated at the University of Cologne on 29 October 1504 as a law student and in 1506 proceeded to Bologna in the company of his brother, Johann, who later succeeded him as chancellor of Brunswick-Lüneburg. Ludwig was appointed to that office in 1515 by Duke Henry II, having by then acquired a doctorate in civil and canon law. He was the first layman to hold the chancellorship. He subsequently resigned, possibly in connection with the disgrace of Duke Henry II, who in 1522 was forced to abdicate formally in favour of his sons, Otto, Ernest, and Francis of *Brunswick-Lüneburg. In 1524 Philip of *Hesse named Ludwig *Burgmann* of Kassel, a position in which he was later succeeded by his son, Valentin. It seems that by then he had already been appointed chancellor of the electorate of Trier. As chancellor of Trier he had some contacts with Erasmus in 1527 and 1528 when Carinus tutored Valentin (Ep 1799) and enlisted Ludwig's help in securing for Erasmus and Hieronymus *Froben a manuscript of Tertullian's treatise *De spectaculis* (Ep 1946; Allen tentatively identified the chancellor with one Henricus Duntginus). The

news of Ludwig's death reached Carinus at Besançon on 10 January 1529 (Ep 2085).

Valentin Furster later entered the service of Philip of Hesse. Apart from succeeding his father as *Burgmann* of Kassel, he accompanied the landgrave on his campaign in Württemberg in 1534, holding the office of clerk of the chancery. From 1539 to 1554 he was receiver, or *Rentmeister*, at Nidda. By the time of his death the following year he had probably returned to Kassel.

BIBLIOGRAPHY: Allen Ep 2085, abandoning the erroneous identification suggested in Ep 1798 / NDB V 735–6 / *Matrikel Köln* I 568 / Knod 130 / Franz Gundlach *Die hessischen Zentralbehörden von 1247 bis 1604* (Marburg 1930–2) III 72 / Willy Brändly in *Innerschweizer Jahrbuch für Heimatkunde* 19/20 (1959–60) 60–1
MICHAEL ERBE & PGB

Johann FUST of Mainz, d 30 October 1466
Johann Fust, born in Mainz around 1400, was an advocate and money lender between 1426 and 1462. In 1449 he was able to lend money to Johann Gutenberg, enabling him to set up a printing press. He demanded no interest until 1455, when he requested repayment of the loan. Gutenberg had to assign part of his business equipment to Fust, who set up the *Schöffer printing press in Mainz with the help of Gutenberg's assistant, Peter (I) Schöffer (1457–1502). Schöffer married Fust's daughter, Christine, in 1467, the year after Fust had died of the plague while visiting Paris.

Erasmus mentions him as the founder of the Schöffer press, calling him 'Faustus' (Ep 919).

BIBLIOGRAPHY: Allen and CWE Ep 919 / NDB V 743–4 / ADB VIII 267–71 / Benzing *Buchdrucker* 296
IG

Wolfgang FYLSNER *See Wolfgang* FILSER

Jean GACHI documented 1524–57
Probably a native of Cluses, Haute-Savoie, Jean Gachi (Gacy, Gacchus, perhaps Gatty, Gathy) was a highly respected member of the Franciscan monastery at Cluses. Twice he was elected provincial of his order, by a provincial chapter in Montferrand in 1540 and by another in Cluses in 1557. In 1524 he published in French verse the *Trialogue nouveau contenant l'expression des erreurs de Martin Luther* (Geneva:

Wygand Köln). By the summer of 1527 his popular sermons were directed against Erasmus (Ep 1852), and soon he possessed an additional source of information on Erasmus' presumed errors. The Musée de l'histoire de la Réforme in Geneva owns a copy (F. Ere. 1) of the first edition of Ep 1858 (*Epistola in tyrologum,* August 1527) which belonged to Gachi and has marginal notes, probably in his hand. From about that time he lived in Geneva as the last confessor of the nuns of St Clare and as their spiritual director. At a time of popular turbulence, great difficulties for the clergy, and the arrival of Bernese troops, he was inevitably a controversial figure. Meanwhile, in March-April 1529 he visited and comforted the nuns of Orbe whose own confessor was in prison while the Reformation gained ground in that town south-west of Lake Neuchâtel. In 1535 he opposed *Farel and Pierre Viret at the disputation of Rive, and a year later he published *La Déploration de la cité de Genefve* (new edition, Geneva 1882).

Warned by the *Alardet brothers of Gachi's outbursts against him (Ep 1852), Erasmus complained to Duke Charles III of *Savoy (Ep 1886) and wrote a long letter to Gachi himself (Ep 1891). Apparently he received a conciliatory answer and though he did not trust Gachi's assurances he evidently considered the matter settled (Epp 2033, 2045, 2126, 2205).

BIBLIOGRAPHY: Allen Ep 1891 / Jean-Marie Lavorel *Cluses et le Faucigny, étude historique* (Annecy 1888–9; also in *Mémoires et documents publiés par l'Académie salésienne*) 176, 318 / Henri Naef *Les Origines de la réforme à Genève* 2nd ed (Geneva 1968) I 435–40, II 257–8, and passim / Jean Barnaud *Pierre Viret et son oeuvre* (St Amans 1911) 97 / Herminjard VI 466–7.

Some manuscript notes for this article were prepared by the late Henry Meylan.   PGB

Bernardino GADOLO of Pontevio,
22 February 1463–22 April 1499
Bernardino Gadolo (Gadolus) of Pontevio, near Brescia, studied at the University of Padua, where he acquired a doctorate in canon law and also a taste for classical literature. At the age of eighteen he entered the Camaldolese abbey of San Michele on the island of Murano (Venice), and on 28 June 1482 he made his profession there. The abbot of San Michele,

Pietro Delfino, directed his energies to the study of Scripture and the Fathers; at the same time he was given administrative responsibilities and sent to Rome on the abbey's business. In 1498 he was appointed prior of Santa Maria degli Angeli at Florence but died prematurely in the following year.

For his edition of the entire Bible in four volumes (Venice: P. de Paganinis 1495) Gadolo compared preceding printed editions with some manuscripts; he also included the *Glossa ordinaria* and the commentary of Nicholas of Lyra. Two years later he edited St Jerome's commentaries on Genesis and the prophets (Venice: G. de Gregoriis 1497), winning Erasmus' praise for his learning and his diligence (*Liber quo respondet annotationibus Lei* LB IX 140C). Other writings in manuscript remained in San Michele and appear to be lost today.

BIBLIOGRAPHY: G.M. Cacciamani in DS VI 28–9 / Johannes Trithemius *Opera historica* (Frankfurt 1601, repr 1966) I 401   PGB

Robert GAGUIN of Colline-Beaumont,
c 1423–22 May 1501
Robert Gaguin was born at Colline-Beaumont, Pas-de-Calais. He was educated in a school belonging to the Trinitarians or Mathurins and eventually joined that order at the monastery of Préavins, near Arras. By 1457 he had moved to Paris for further study, but because he gave much of his time to the business of his order he did not receive a doctorate in canon law until 1480. In 1483 and often thereafter he was elected dean of the faculty of canon law for a term. Meanwhile, from 1465 on he undertook many journeys on behalf of his order, whose principal business was to ransom captives of the Turks and other prisoners of war. Until 1472 he repeatedly visited Spain and Italy and also undertook a trip to Germany. In 1473 he was elected general of his order. Subsequently he was also sent on diplomatic missions for the French crown, visiting Germany on very delicate missions in 1477 and 1492, Italy in 1484 and 1486, and England in 1491. He assisted his friend Guillaume Fichet in establishing the first printing press in Paris and may have been instrumental in attracting Josse *Bade to the capital. A leading exponent of the first humanist movement in Paris, Gaguin wrote a considerable number of works, including

Robert Gaguin, by Nicolas Ier de Larmessin

French translations of Caesar (1485; Paris:
A. Vérard n d) and the third decade of Livy
(1493; Paris: A. Vérard n d). His most
celebrated work was a chronicle which exhibited a measure of historical criticism, *Compendium de origine et gestis Francorum*, first
published in 1497 (Paris: D. Gerlier) and
revised until the end of his life. By 1586 it had
run through nineteen editions, while seven
translations had been published by 1514. It
was particularly noted in England, in part
because of its strong patriotic emphasis (Ep 46;
for Thomas *More's reaction see Rogers Ep 15).
John *Colet wrote about it to the author (Ep
106), and John *Skelton wrote against it his
poem *Recule against Gaguyne*.

Gaguin was an important patron of Erasmus
from the time of his arrival in Paris (Epp 43, 44).
Erasmus soon found occasion to write a
complimentary letter for publication on a blank
leaf at the end of Gaguin's *Compendium* (Ep 45)
as well as verses in praise of his historical talent
(Reedijk poem 39; cf poem 38). Gaguin shared
with Erasmus his knowledge as well as his
books (Epp 67, 68, 121); he read and approved
an early version of the *Antibarbari* (Ep 46) and

encouraged Erasmus to continue work on the
Adagia (Ep 531). Contacts continued (Epp 106,
136), and Gaguin was finally recalled in
Erasmus' *Ciceronianus* (ASD I-2 672).

BIBLIOGRAPHY: Allen and CWE Ep 43 / DBF XV
55–6 / R. Gaguin *Epistolae et orationes* ed L.
Thuasne (Paris 1903) / Renaudet *Préréforme*
114–15 and passim / Franco Simone *Il Rinascimento francese* (Turin 1961) 50 and passim / S.
Moreau-Rendu *Les Captifs libérés: Les Trinitaires
et Saint-Mathurin de Paris* (Paris 1974) 105–35 /
James Westfall Thompson *A History of Historical
Writing* (New York 1942) I 514–17 / R.J. Schoeck
in *New Catholic Encyclopedia* (New York
1967–79) VI 240   MICHEL REULOS & PGB

Jean de GAIGNY d 15 November 1549
Jean de Gaigny is almost certainly the correspondent of Erasmus (Ep 2807) whom Allen,
reluctantly following Herminjard, conjectured
to be Etienne Loret (d c1541). The only basis for
this conjecture was that Loret was known to be
grand master of the Collège de Navarre in
Paris at the time. However, Gaigny was
lecturing on the epistles of St Paul at Navarre in
1532–3 and is thus quite likely to be the
unnamed theologian lecturing on St Paul at
Navarre to whom Erasmus referred in a letter to
Bonifacius *Amerbach in May 1533 (Ep 2805)
and to whom Erasmus consequently wrote in
his own defence (Ep 2807).

Gaigny was born in the diocese of Paris. He
studied arts at Navarre under the famous
Pierre *Danès from about 1516 to 1520, taking
his MA about 1520, and then was regent in arts
for several years. He was the rector of the
University of Paris in the last quarter of 1531, at
which time he was said to be proficient in the
three languages. He was a *bursarius theologus*
at the Collège de Navarre, ranking second of
twenty-eight in the theology licentiate class of
30 January 1532, and received his doctorate on
20 March 1532. In addition to the lectures on St
Paul in 1532–3, Gaigny was also very involved
in the affairs of the faculty of theology at this
unusually crucial period. When King *Francis I
asked the faculty to send three of its most
competent doctors to explain the faculty's
objections to the preaching of Gérard *Roussel,
Gaigny was one of the three delegates. In July
1533, Gaigny acted as syndic of the faculty

during the imprisonment of Noël *Béda and continued the faculty's attack on *Cajetanus' commentaries on the Psalms and the New Testament. He probably drafted the faculty's letter to Cajetanus and the twenty-four censures of his work. This letter, known only through the 1534 Wittenberg printing by Nikolaus Schirlentz, reproaches Cajetanus for daring to comment on Scripture without a knowledge of Hebrew or an adequate knowledge of Greek and for abandoning the traditional Vulgate in favour of versions by Erasmus, *Lefèvre d'Etaples, and even *Luther.

Gaigny came under the patronage of Francis I around 1536 and at that time composed an elegy on the death of the dauphin *Francis. He was librarian, almoner, and chaplain to the king, who rewarded him with benefices *in commendam*. Gaigny was abbot of Saint-Jorre near Rouen, of Notre-Dame de 'Silva-Millonis' or Coëtmalouen (diocese of Quimper), and of the Cistercian abbey of Longvilliers. He was also called prior of Vincennes. Finally, he was a canon of the diocese of Paris and of the Sainte-Chapelle in Paris. From 1546 he was chancellor of the church of Paris, and therefore chancellor of the University of Paris. In 1548 Robert Estienne accused Gaigny, along with two other doctors, of responsibility for the allegations of heresy which led to Estienne's flight to Geneva, but Gaigny had apparently supported Estienne up to 1547.

As librarian to the king, Gaigny enthusiastically collected books and manuscripts which he found lying in priories and monasteries, and he published or sponsored the publication of several of these. He commissioned nine woodcut illustrations, four of which contain his own portrait, for his 1528 *Livre des sept parolles* and made innovations in the use of rubric and italic type. He eventually set up a printing press in his own house, hired his nephew Nicolas Le Riche to direct it, and brought Charles Chiffin, a type-founder from Tours, to copy the matrixes of Aldo *Manuzio. He was a patron of Claude Garamond and encouraged him to produce his italic types. Gaigny died on 15 November 1549, and was buried in the Collège de Navarre. His last will and testament is extant.

His works include: *Le Livre des sept parolles que Jesus Christ dist en l'arbre de la croix* (Paris:

Simon Du Bois for Chrétien Wechel 1528 and six further printings before 1546); *Le Livre de vraye et parfaite oraison* (Paris: Simon Du Bois for Chrétien Wechel 1529, Jean Kaerbriand for Chrétien Wechel 1530); *Le Livre contenant devote exposition sur le cinquantiesme pseaulme* (Paris: Denis Janot 1532, Nicolas Barbou 1541); *Epitome paraphrastica enarrationum in epistolam divi Pauli apostoli ad Romanos* (Paris: Michel Vascosan 1533, Jean Quesnel 1633); *Mars et Mors* (a mythological elegy on the death of the Dauphin François; Lyon: François Juste 1536). He edited Avitus and Claudius Marius *Poemata* (Lyon: Vincent Portonario for Melchior and Gaspar Trechsel 1536; Paris: Pierre Drouart 1545); Primasius *In omnes divi Pauli epistolas commentarii* (Lyon: Sébastien Gryphius 1537; Cologne: Johann Gymnicus 1538; Paris: Charlotte Guillard 1543; Lyon 1543; French trans Paris: Etienne Roffet 1540); *Divi Pauli apostoli epistolae brevissimis scholiis illustratae* (Paris: Simon de Colines and Galliot Du Pré 1538, 1539, 1543); Guerricus, abbot of Igny *Sermones antiqui* (Paris: Gervais Chevallon 1539, Nicolas Le Riche 1547, Gabriel Buon 1561; Antwerp 1576; French trans Paris: Simon de Colines for Etienne Roffet c 1540); Pietro Apollonio Collazio *Excidii Jeresolymitani libri IV* (Paris: Jean Loys and Nicolas Le Riche 1540). He further wrote *Brevissima et facillima in omnes divi Pauli epistolas scholia [et] in septem canonicas epistolas et D. Joannis Apocalypsin* (Paris: Simon de Colines 1543; nine later editions in Paris and Antwerp by 1633); *Sermon des six paroles de Jésus-Christ en croix* (Lyon: Jean de Tournes 1543); *Pia et admodum religiosa peccatoris meditatio in sacrosanctum Jesu Christi servatoris nostri crucem et vulnera* (Paris: Jacques Bogard 1546). He also edited *Epigrammata* of Marcantonio Flaminio, Francesco Maria Molza, et al (Paris: Nicolas Le Riche c 1547) and Eusebius of Emesa *Homeliae ad populum et monachos* (Paris: Nicolas Le Riche; Louvain: P. Sangrius 1560; Paris 1589). He composed *Psalmi Davidici septuaginta quinque in lyricos versus* (Paris: Nicolas Le Riche 1547) and edited Gaspare Contarini *De elementis et eorum mixtionibus libri quinque* and Scipione Capece *De principiis rerum poema* (Paris: Nicolas Le Riche 1548, André Wechel 1564). His *In quatuor sacra Jesu Christi evangelia, necnon in actus apostolicos scholia* were edited by Jean Benoist (Paris: G. Perier, Charlotte Guillard, and

Guillaume Des Boys 1552; Antwerp: J. Lotti 1559; Paris 1630, 1631).

BIBLIOGRAPHY: Farge no 199 / Jean de Launoy *Regii Navarrae gymnasii Parisiensis historia* (Paris 1677) II 681–5 / M.-H. Laurent 'Quelques documents des archives vaticanes concernants Cajétan' *Revue Thomiste* n s 17, 86–7 (Nov 1934) 111–17 / Philippe Renouard 'Le *Livre des sept parolles* (1528)' *Byblis* 8 (1928) 60–5 / For Loret see Farge no 315; Allen Ep 2807; Herminjard III Ep 418   JAMES K. FARGE

Petrus GALATINUS of Galatina, c 1460–1539/40

Petrus Galatinus (Monggius, Mongio, Columna, Colonna) is best known under the name derived from his native town of Galatina, south-west of Lecce. He became a Franciscan Observant in the province of Bari and was living in the monastery of Otranto, near his home town, when the Turks sacked Otranto in 1480.

Little detail is known about Galatinus' life. In the first half of 1515 he was in Rome and wrote to Johann *Reuchlin from the Vatican (RE Ep 211). At the request of cardinals Lorenzo *Pucci and Adriano *Castellesi he was working on his great defence of Reuchlin, the *Opus ... de arcanis catholicae veritatis* (Ortona: G. Soncino 15 February 1518). The good tidings quickly spread among the friends and supporters of Reuchlin (RE Epp 212, 216); on 31 August Nikolaus *Gerbel passed the news on to Erasmus but did not mention Galatinus by name (Ep 349). In 1517 Hermann von *Neuenahr cited his name among the defenders of Reuchlin, when prefacing Giorgio *Benigno's *Defensio* of Reuchlin (Cologne: E. Cervicornus 1517). No doubt Benigno and Galatinus, fellow Franciscans and supporters of Reuchlin, were intimates at Rome. Benigno interested Galatinus in a cabbalistic work, the 'Apocalypsis nova' attributed to the Blessed Amadeus, which greatly influenced the author of *De arcanis*. So likewise did Raimundus Martini's *Pugio fidei*, which Galatinus plagiarized. *De arcanis* also involved him in other controversies, but it was reprinted a number of times and became perhaps the most influential work of Christian cabbalism in the Renaissance.

When *De arcanis* was published Galatinus was the head of the Franciscan province of

Bari. He also seems to have advocated the creation of a bishopric in his native town in the hope of becoming the first bishop of Galatina. Lorenzo Pucci, cardinal penitentiary from 1520, continued to be his patron, and he was named an apostolic penitentiary. He also exercised some influence on Cardinal Egidio *Antonini of Viterbo. He seems to have spent the rest of his life in Rome, where he lived in the principal Franciscan monastery of Santa Maria in Araceli. On 11 May 1539 he obtained a papal brief protecting the manuscripts which he intended to leave to Araceli, and died there shortly afterwards. Several manuscript works of his are preserved in the Biblioteca Apostolica Vaticana; they include 'De sacra scriptura recte interpretanda' dedicated to King *Henry VIII of England in view of the latter's admiration for *De arcanis*, and a commentary on Revelation. In these works he often referred to Erasmus with frank disapproval, taking issue, for instance, with his rendering of the beginning of the Gospel of St John (Morisi 216).

BIBLIOGRAPHY: Allen and CWE Ep 349 / DTC VI-1 1052–4 / RE Epp 279, 280 / *Encyclopedia Judaica* (Jerusalem 1971–2) VII 262–3 / Arduinus Kleinhans in *Antonianum* 1 (1926) 145–79 / Anna Morisi 'Galatino et la Kabbale chrétienne' in *Kabbalistes chrétiens* Cahiers de l'hermétisme (Paris 1979) 207–31 / François Secret *Les Kabbalistes chrétiens de la Renaissance* (Paris 1964) 102–4 and passim / John W. O'Malley *Giles of Viterbo on Church and Reform* (Leiden 1968) 76 and passim / Ludwig Geiger *Johann Reuchlin* (Leipzig 1871, repr 1964) 399–400 and passim   PGB

GALBA (Epp 123 and 135 of 1500)

Galba, who has not been identified, may have been an agent in London. Erasmus complained about him in connection with the confiscation of his money at Dover and also suspected him of being behind the sudden parsimoniousness of Charles *Blount, Lord Mountjoy.

BIBLIOGRAPHY: Allen Ep 123
                                         MORDECHAI FEINGOLD

Eucharius GALLINARIUS of Bretten, documented 1475–1531

Eucharius Gallinarius (Henner, Hemmer, Heimerius), of Bretten in the Palatinate, perhaps a relative of Johannes *Gallinarius, matriculated at the University of Heidelberg on 13 November 1475 and graduated MA in 1479. From February 1501 Eucharius is frequently mentioned in the records of the Speyer cathedral chapter, which have been published down to 1531. In 1509, being a chaplain, or *Martinensis*, he was twice granted a short leave to preach in Weil der Stadt and Strasbourg. In April 1515 he is first mentioned in the position of a parish priest ('plebanus S. Crucis'), an office he did not always administer to the full satisfaction of his superiors; in 1528 he seems to have been besieged by his creditors. In September 1531, he finally received the more lucrative benefice of a vicar at the cathedral.

As a pupil of Jakob *Wimpfeling, who lived at Speyer during the years 1484–98, Gallinarius contributed a commendatory letter to Wimpfeling's *Stilpho* (Speyer: K. Hist 1495), dating it from Speyer, 1 September 1494. Eight years later he joined other students of Wimpfeling in defending their master against Thomas *Murner in a *Defensio Germaniae Jacobi Wympfelingii* (Freiburg [ie, Strasbourg: J. Grüninger 1502]). According to Allen, Gallinarius himself spent some time at Strasbourg between 1500 and 1502 as a chaplain at the hospital. In 1505 and 1506 he corresponded with Johannes *Trithemius, and in 1509 the Strasbourg printer Matthias *Schürer published at Gallinarius' expense an *Annotatiuncula pro confessoribus* by Georg von Gemmingen, provost of the Speyer cathedral chapter.

In October 1518, shortly after a visit to Speyer, Erasmus conveyed greetings to 'that charming Eucharius' in a letter sent to that city (Ep 882). The hypothesis that Gallinarius was intended is corroborated by the fact that on 27 August 1520 the latter dated from Speyer a letter in support of Erasmus, which was published in the *Epistolae aliquot eruditorum virorum* against Edward *Lee (Basel: J. Froben 1520; Ep 1083 introduction). The same volume has a reply to Gallinarius by Hermannus *Buschius, in which he described his friend not only as pastor of the Holy Cross but also as professor of canon law.

BIBLIOGRAPHY: Allen Ep 882 / ADB VIII 337–8 / *Matrikel Heidelberg* I 347, II 412 / *Die Protokolle des Speyerer Domkapitels* ed Manfred Krebs (Stuttgart 1968–) I 254, 277, 409–10, II 235, 396–8, and passim / Schmidt *Histoire littéraire* I

42, II 332 / Joseph Knepper *Jakob Wimpfeling* (Freiburg 1902) 35, 152   PGB

Johannes GALLINARIUS of Heidelberg, documented 1495–1525
Johannes Gallinarius (Henlin) was a member of the Alsatian humanist circle, a kinsman and intimate of Jakob *Wimpfeling. Born in Heidelberg, he matriculated at the university on 1 April 1495, received his MA, and subsequently taught there. His appointment as schoolmaster of Jung St Peter's chapter school in Strasbourg in 1503 reflected the concerted efforts of Wimpfeling and his friends to introduce humanist methods of instruction. The attempt was not fully successful. Gallinarius left and went to Cologne, where he matriculated in 1509 and in the same year translated Lucian's *Palinurus*. In 1512 he began to teach grammar and rhetoric at the Sélestat grammar school and established a reputation as a scholar. In 1516 he was appointed priest to the parish at Breisach, on the Rhine near Freiburg, where he may have remained until his death, despite an effort to find another parish in 1521.

Gallinarius knew Erasmus through Wimpfeling. Erasmus reported that he failed to see him on the famous journey from Basel to Louvain in 1518 (Ep 867). In August 1522 Gallinarius wrote to express his approval of *Henry VIII's *Assertio* against *Luther (Ep 1307). The following February Erasmus stayed with Gallinarius during an attack of the stone (Ep 1342). Gallinarius' literary production was limited to a few letters, translations, and an edition of Wimpfeling's *Adolescentia* which appeared in 1505 (Strasbourg: J. Knobloch).

BIBLIOGRAPHY: Allen and CWE Ep 305 / ADB VIII 336–7 / *Matrikel Heidelberg* I 414 / *Matrikel Köln* II 642 / J. Wimpfeling *Adolescentia* (*Opera selecta* I) ed O. Herding (Munich 1968) 13–26, 105–10, and passim   MIRIAM U. CHRISMAN

GALTERUS See *GUALTERUS*

Wilhelm GAMSHORN (Ep 2857 of 11 August 1533)
Wilhelm Gamshorn, a doctor of law, who visited Freiburg in 1533 and afterwards wrote to Udalricus *Zasius, has not been identified. A Wilhelm Ganshorn of Würzburg matricu-

lated at the University of Leipzig in the summer term of 1524.

BIBLIOGRAPHY: *Matrikel Leipzig* I 589 PGB

Joachim GANDAVUS *See Joachim* MARTENS

Antonius GANG (Ep 23 of 1489?)
Among the outstanding men of letters of his time Erasmus mentioned a certain Antonius Gang, a name otherwise unknown. As this letter is known only from a version printed in 1603 which corrupts the name of *Mormann, following that of Gang, Allen tentatively proposed to read 'Lang' or 'Langen' and suggested that Erasmus might have confused Rudolf von *Langen and Antonius Liber (Vrije), who died in 1506 or 1507 and, like Langen, was a friend of Alexander *Hegius and Rodolphus *Agricola.

BIBLIOGRAPHY: For Liber see ADB XVIII 532 / H.E. van Gelder *Geschiedenis der Latijnsche School te Alkmaar* (Alkmaar 1905) I 83–6
C.G. VAN LEIJENHORST

Wessel GANSFORT of Groningen, 1419–4 October 1489
Wessel was born at Groningen, a son of Herman Gansfort. Around 1432 he went to Zwolle to live in the *domus parva* of the Brethren of the Common Life, first as a pupil, then as a teacher. He remained at Zwolle at least until 1440, but perhaps even up to the end of 1449, when he matriculated at Cologne. He received his BA on 1 December 1450 and his MA around March 1452. He then continued his travels, staying for longer or shorter periods at Louvain, Paris (c 1454–5), Cologne (where he taught after 15 August 1455), Heidelberg (where he matriculated 1 June 1456), Zwolle, Rome, Venice, and Florence. He was at Paris almost continuously from 1458 to 1470, and there he gradually evolved from a realist in theology to formalist to Occamist. Well trained in Latin, Greek, and Hebrew, he returned to the Netherlands around 1475. The last years of his life he spent alternately at Mount St Agnes near Zwolle (the former dwelling place of his old friend Thomas à Kempis), at the Cistercian monastery of Aduard, near Groningen, and at the Groningen Poor Clares' convent, where he died. During his travels he became acquainted with many of the leading scholars of his time,

not the least of whom he and Abbott Hendrik van Rees sheltered in the so-called Academy of Aduard: Rodolphus *Agricola, Alexander *Hegius, Antonius Liber (Vrije), Willem *Fredericks, Rudolf von *Langen, Friedrich *Mormann, Jan *Canter, and others. Erasmus, who owned some work of Gansfort (cf F. Husner in *Gedenkschrift zum 400. Todestage* Basel 1936, 238 no 56), mentions him in the *Epistola ad fratres Inferioris Germaniae* (ASD IX-1 405–6), asserting that though Gansfort had much in common with *Luther (a fact acknowledged by Luther himself), he was infinitely more modest than Luther. Gansfort's works, including the *Tractatus de oratione, Scala meditationis, De causis incarnationis et de magnitudine Dominicae passionis*, and *De sacramento eucharistiae*, were published at Basel (A. Petri) and Wittenberg (M. Lotter) in 1522 under the title *Farrago rerum theologicarum uberrima*. His *Opera quae inveniri potuerunt omnia* were edited by Petrus Pappus (Groningen: J. Sassius 1614, repr 1963).

BIBLIOGRAPHY: A.J. van der Aa et al *Biographisch woordenboek der Nederlanden* (Haarlem 1852–78, repr 1965) VII 35–8 / M. van Rhijn in NNBW V 195–7 / M. van Rhijn *Wessel Gansfort* (The Hague 1917) / M. van Rhijn *Studiën over Wessel Gansfort en zijn tijd* (Utrecht 1933) / *Biographisch-Bibliographisches Kirchenlexikon* II (Hamm, Westphalia 1976) 176–7 / M.H. Ogilvie 'Wessel Gansfort's Theology of Church Government' *Nederlands Archief voor Kerkgeschiedenis* new series 55 (1975) 125–50
C.G. VAN LEIJENHORST

Stephen GARDINER of Bury St Edmunds, c 1497–12 November 1555
Stephen Gardiner was born at Bury St Edmunds, the son of John Gardiner, a clothmaker. After the death of his father in 1507, the boy was entrusted to one *Edenus, with whom he was residing in Paris in 1511. Later that same year Gardiner returned to England, where he matriculated at Trinity Hall, Cambridge, for the study of civil and canon law. Taking the degrees of bachelor and doctor of civil law and doctor of canon law in 1518, 1521, and 1522 respectively, Gardiner lectured in the faculties of civil and canon law from 1521 to 1524, served as university examiner in these faculties in 1523–4, and represented

Cambridge in a mission to *Wolsey in the summer of 1523. Having attracted the attention of Wolsey, Gardiner was engaged as his secretary in 1524. In 1525 he was elected master of Trinity Hall, a post he retained until his death except for a short interval during Edward VI's reign. By 1526 he was also archdeacon of Taunton.

As secretary to Wolsey, Gardiner was active in the divorce proceedings of *Henry VIII, joining Wolsey on his mission to *Francis I in 1527 and twice journeying to the papal court in 1528 and 1529. Gardiner's services to the king were handsomely rewarded; in addition to being made the principal secretary to the king, he was made archdeacon of Worcester in 1528, of Norfolk in 1529, and of Leicester in 1531. He was consecrated bishop of Winchester on 3 December 1531 as well. Shortly afterwards, on 29 December, Gardiner was dispatched as an ambassador to Francis I, remaining at the French court until March 1532. Between September and November 1533 he was again dispatched to France, this time to meet with *Clement VII at Marseille. Following his return to England, Gardiner fell from favour owing to his opposition to the ecclesiastical policy during the first session of the 1534 Parliament and retired to his diocese. On 10 February 1535, however, Gardiner renounced the jurisdiction of the Roman See, shortly thereafter publishing his *De vera obedientia oratio* (London: T. Berthelet; STC 11585) – a well-formulated defence of the king's case – which helped to restore him to favour. Consequently, in October 1535 he was again dispatched as an ambassador to the French court. In 1538 King Henry recalled him to England, suspecting him of favouring the imperial interests. Gardiner's diplomatic skills, however, caused the king to dispatch him to Germany in 1539. Gardiner is also credited as the moving force behind the Act of the Six Articles, which was promulgated shortly after his return to England. The year 1540 witnessed the fall of Gardiner's rival, Thomas *Cromwell, and Gardiner succeeded him both as the most influential man at court and as chancellor of Cambridge, in which capacity he attempted to check the advance of the Reformation. Gardiner served as King Henry's chief counsellor in the divorce of Anne of Cleves, and from

Stephen Gardiner

November 1540 to September 1541 he was engaged as the ambassador to *Charles V. The following year he was involved in an abortive attempt to produce a translation of the New Testament as well as in a heated debate with Thomas Smith and John Cheke on Greek pronunciation. In 1544 he joined the invasion into France, while in late 1544 and in the winter of 1545–6 he was dispatched on two embassies to Charles V, who mediated the peace negotiations.

Following Henry VIII's death on 28 January 1547 and the accession to the throne of Edward VI, Gardiner returned to his diocese. On 25 September he was committed to the Fleet prison for having refused to accept the new Homilies and Injunctions and remained there until 7 January 1548. On 30 June he was imprisoned in the Tower, where he remained until August 1553, when *Mary I entered London. During Edward's reign Gardiner was deprived of the chancellorship of Cambridge (1547), the mastership of Trinity Hall (1549), and the bishopric of Winchester (1551), all of which offices were restored to him in 1553. On 23 August 1553 he was made lord high chancellor. He crowned Mary on 1 October, and, although he initially objected to her intended marriage with Philip II, he bowed to her will and performed the ceremony on 25 July 1554. In November of that year he was instrumental in bringing about the renewal of the allegiance with Rome as well as being responsible for reinstating various heresy laws and ecclesiastical courts.

Gardiner met Erasmus in 1511 in Paris, when both were residing in the house of the Englishman Edenus. On 28 February 1526 Gardiner wrote to Erasmus (Ep 1669), reminding the latter of the delight he had taken in the salads Gardiner had prepared for him. In his reply of 3 September (Ep 1745) Erasmus confirmed that he indeed remembered Gardiner and the salads. From Gardiner's letter it also emerges that some time after his enrollment as a student at Cambridge, Erasmus had offered to engage him, via the Cambridge bookseller Garret *Godfrey, in his service, an offer which Gardiner declined. In this context Allen (Ep 277 note) suggests that Gardiner is the unnamed person to whom Erasmus referred in his letter of October 1513 to Roger *Wentford as one whom he hoped to acquire as his servant.

Gardiner's published works also included polemics with Martin *Bucer (Louvain: R. Rescius 1544; Cologne: Melchior von Neuss 1545), William Turner (1543–4), George Joye (London: J. Herford 1546; STC 11588), and Cranmer (1551), as well as a book of sermons (Rome: A. Bladus 1555).

BIBLIOGRAPHY: Allen Ep 1669 / DNB VII 859–65 / J.A. Muller *Stephen Gardiner and the Tudor Reaction* (New York 1926, repr 1970) with a catalogue of his writings / *The Letters of Stephen Gardiner* ed J.A. Muller (Cambridge 1933, repr 1970) / *Obedience in Church and State: Three Political Tracts by Stephen Gardiner* ed P. Janelle (Cambridge 1930) / *A Machiavellian Treatise by Stephen Gardiner* ed P.S. Donaldson (Cambridge 1975)

MORDECHAI FEINGOLD

William GARRARD documented 1519–21
William Garrard (Gerardus) served John *Colet in London as his steward (Ep 1229) and was one of the executors of his will. Erasmus

had probably met Garrard personally during his visits to England and at the time of Colet's death felt that he owed him a letter (Epp 1027). Erasmus connected him with two protégés of Colet who were teaching at Oxford, William *Dancaster and Thomas *Lupset (Epp 1027, 1229), and he may perhaps be identical with a student by the name of William Garrad documented at Oxford twenty years earlier. Garrad, who was at Canterbury College in 1501 and a Cardinal Morton scholar, received his MA at Oxford, though it is not known at what date. The name William Garrard is also documented in the diocese of Canterbury, where its bearer, in possession of an Oxford MA, was ordained subdeacon on 19 April 1495 and deacon at St Helen's, Abingdon, Berkshire, on 26 February 1496.

BIBLIOGRAPHY: Allen and CWE Ep 1027 / S. Knight *The Life of Dr John Colet* (Oxford 1823) 401, 409 / Emden BRUO II 744

CFG & PGB

Mercurino Arborio di GATTINARA
10 June 1465–5 June 1530
Mercurino Arborio di Gattinara (Gattinaria) was born near Vercelli, Piedmont, the son of Paolino Arborio di Gattinara and Felicita Ranzo, the daughter of Count Mercurino Ranzo, president of the council of Savoy. Despite the uninformed remarks in some of the older sources the family was among the more prominent of Piedmont. A second misconception surrounding the background of Gattinara involves the myth that the family derived from Arbois, in the Jura, and came to Arboro, near Vercelli, in the twelfth century. The myth was formally established by the same diploma of the Emperor *Maximilian I of 22 September 1513 that created him count and would be rehearsed in Gattinara's autobiography. There is no basis in fact for this Burgundian origin to the family. Indeed their role as local lords in Arboro and the vicinity goes back to the eleventh century. Without primogeniture, however, the lines had proliferated and fallen into low estate, with the result that Mercurino's parents lived in straitened circumstances in the castle. The poverty of his immediate family was made more acute by the early death of his father in 1478;

cf Antonio Manno *Il patriziato subalpino: Dizionario genealogico* (Florence 1906) II 67–8; Bornate *Vita* 239–40.

Gattinara's taste for letters derived from his mother, who introduced him to humanistic literature, the elegancies of Latin, and some natural philosophy; cf Alphonsus Ciaconius *Vitae et res gestae pontificum romanorum et S.R.E. cardinalium ...* (Rome 1677) III 504–5. But as the eldest male child in a large family, Mercurino's sense of responsibility for the family drove him to the rash action of betrothing himself at the age of thirteen to a wealthy orphan, Andreeta Avogadro, who was seven years older than himself. His relatives intervened to prevent this 'scandal,' and the chastened boy was sent off to live with his uncle Bartholomeo Ranzo. In the ensuing years of disgrace young Mercurino came to be introduced to the practicalities of political and administrative life and was encouraged to study law. From his mother's piety and his uncle's instruction the boy derived those principles that were to shape his life: a passionate devotion to work, a solid piety, an austere sense of honour, and a proud independence; cf Bornate *Vita* 240; M. Huart *Le Cardinal Arborio de Gattinara* (Besançon 1886) 8–9. In later marrying Andreeta, by whom he had one daughter, Elisa, Gattinara managed at once to apply his growing knowledge of law to securing and enhancing his wife's inheritance and to use part of her wealth for his own formal education. He studied under such jurists as Claude de Seyssel and received his doctorate from the University of Turin in 1493. During the subsequent decade Gattinara built up a reputation for himself as a leading lawyer of Piedmont (Bornate *Vita* 240–4).

With the marriage of *Margaret of Austria to Philibert II, duke of *Savoy, on 26 September 1501, Gattinara was commended to the Hapsburg princess as legal counsel, and from this moment he entered increasingly into the service of the dynasty. After Philibert's untimely death on 10 September 1504, Gattinara litigated successfully in defence of the dowry rights of his mistress. Following the death of her brother, Philip the Handsome of *Burgundy, Margaret had entrusted to her the tutelage of his children and the governorship of the Netherlands. Gattinara continued to protect her interests in each instance, and for his loyal, effective service he received on 12 February 1508 as a reward from the Emperor-elect Maximilian and his daughter, Margaret, the presidency of the Parlement at Dole in the Franche-Comté (Bornate *Vita* and 'Note' 245–9).

In the Franche-Comté the new president of Burgundy encountered a fractious nobility, and in the course of the next decade his austere sense of justice and his reforming efforts led to the outbreak of disorder and disobedience. Concurrently Gattinara served as president of Margaret's private council and played a critical role in the negotiations that culminated at Blois in the final understanding between Maximilian and *Ferdinand II of Aragon which determined the inheritance of the young Archduke *Charles to the Iberian kingdoms. Gattinara was also instrumental in forming the League of Cambrai (Bornate *Vita* 249), and from July 1510 to April 1511 he attended Ferdinand in Spain to oversee the implementation of the Blois agreement. He returned to a tense situation in the Franche-Comté which was soon complicated and embittered by litigation involving his purchase of the estate of Chevigny; the case ultimately reached the highest court, the grand council at Mechelen. An adverse judgment coincided with his deposition at the request of the fractious segment of the county's nobility while he was fulfilling a vow in the charterhouse of Scheut, outside Brussels. But the death of Jean *Le Sauvage in June led to the appointment and installation of Gattinara as Charles of Spain's grand chancellor at Saragossa on 15 October 1518 (Bornate *Vita* 257–70 and 'Note' 272).

In Spain Gattinara decisively supported the efforts of Las Casas to effect the reform of the administration of the Indies; cf M. Giménez Fernández *Bartolomé de las Casas* (Seville 1960) II passim. He promoted the election of his master as Holy Roman Emperor and on 30 November 1519 at Molina del Rey presented the official justification for Charles' election; cf P.F. Hane *Memoria viri politici ...* (Kiel 1728) 57. Despite formal co-operation with Guillaume de *Croy, seigneur de Chièvres, he was not compromised by the revolt of the *comuneros*. At Maastricht in mid-October 1520, while accompanying Charles back to the Netherlands, Gattinara had his first attack of gout (Bornate *Vita* 283). Yet, despite this recurring ailment that sapped his energies, in the succeeding decade the councils of the emperor responded more to the initiative of Gattinara than to any other dynastic servant. At the Calais negotiations of August to December 1521 he talked chancellors *Wolsey and *Duprat to a standstill (Weiss I 126–241). Back in Spain he was the driving force behind the reorganization of the central administration that would last down to the Bourbons; cf F. Walser *Die spanischen Zentralbehörden* ... (Göttingen 1959) passim. To his friend and frequent correspondent Pietro Martire d'Anghiera in the first years of his chancellorship Gattinara was the 'arcanorum Caesaris archivum' (*Opus epistolarum*, Amsterdam 1670, Ep 669). In shaping imperial diplomacy Gattinara worked for the constriction or even dismantling of France and for the European hegemony of the new Charlemagne based upon Italy as Dante's 'giardin dell'imperio.' Thus in January 1526 Gattinara refused to apply the seals of his office to the treaty of Madrid principally because he understood it to be an alliance of the emperor with the French king to the detriment of the Italian powers. Although his warning that *Francis I would not keep his promises proved correct, Gattinara's relations with the emperor had deteriorated so far that he could not capitalize on the correctness of his judgment. Except for permission to accept from the duke of Milan the county of Valenza and Sartirana on 12 December 1522 and the marquisate of Romagnano on 24 April 1525 (Bornate 'Note' 287–8) Charles granted his chancellor no relief from mounting debts. He had often asked to resign or at least to have a leave of absence to attend to his estates in Italy. The crisis with the papacy in September 1526, when Gattinara ended by appealing to the college of cardinals for a council, postponed his trip to Italy until 30 March 1527 (Bornate 'Documenti' 526). Chased by French galleys and besieged in Genoa, Gattinara never reached his estates and rejoined the imperial court on 4 October (Bornate *Vita* 354). His absence, however, had served its purpose in making the emperor more tractable. The remaining months of his chancellorship saw the solid accomplishments of the treaty of

Barcelona with the pope, the pacification of Italy, and the coronation at Bologna. Upon arriving in Italy he received the long-desired elevation to the cardinalate on 13 August 1529. En route to the diet of Augsburg Gattinara died at Innsbruck (Le Glay 216).

It is reasonable to conjecture that Gattinara encountered Erasmus at the meeting between Henry VIII and Charles at Calais between 10 and 14 July 1520 (Epp 1106, 1118) or at Bruges between 25 and 29 July (Ep 1129). The first surviving letter between them, dated 4 October 1520, in which the humanist commends to the care of the chancellor both himself and his enterprise of advancing the glory of Christ and good letters, mentions a brief conversation that they had recently had (Ep 1150). Gattinara responded six months later to a possible second letter by assuring him of his total support, while recognizing Erasmus as the unique expositor of the orthodox faith (Ep 1197). Awareness of such prominent defenders at the imperial court considerably reassured Erasmus (Epp 1299, 1331, 1342). That the chancellor should have received a letter at first misaddressed to 'Gulielmum' indicates little, given Erasmus' difficulty in remembering Christian names. More important is the extreme delight, even reverence, with which, according to *Vives in the same letter, Gattinara received the communication from Erasmus (Ep 1281). Perhaps in order not to sour his relationship with Gattinara by referring to monetary matters, Erasmus applied to Gattinara's subordinate *Lalemand rather than to the chancellor for his pension, which was already much in arrears, and coupled his request with the opening hint that the imperial court should take action against the relentless theologians of Louvain (Ep 1554). It was Gattinara, however, who replied towards the end of 1525, congratulating the humanist on having come out against the pestilential Lutheran faction and reassuring him of his support and the payment of the pension (Ep 1643). Throughout 1526 Erasmus complained of the factions that fragmented Germany and oppressed him; he asked that the emperor give public evidence of supporting humanistic studies and silence the Louvain theologians (Epp 1700, 1747). On receipt of the last of these requests Gattinara immediately responded with the most important letter of their entire correspondence: after declaring himself a regular reader of Erasmus' works, he presented his vision of the Christian republic fragmented into three parties – the Romanists, the Erasmians, and the Lutherans – and ended by identifying himself with the second as the only solution to current ills and calling for the complete extirpation of the Lutheran faction (Ep 1757). Erasmus was apparently impressed, for he circulated copies of this letter (Epp 1805, 1806). Meanwhile Gattinara turned on the Louvain theologians, calling them to order. His letter (Ep 1784A) incorporated a large section of Erasmus' – a fact that did not go unnoticed (Ep 1837). Nevertheless it had the desired effect (Ep 1784A introduction). Finally, before departing for Italy Gattinara sought to commit his friend to the imperial cause and that of universal monarchy by asking him to edit and publish Dante's *Monarchia* (Ep 1790A). Erasmus demurred. He held a different view of monarchy and of Christian polity, and he apparently made this view clear to the chancellor as well as to his subordinate Alfonso de *Valdés (Ep 2126; cf also Ep 586). Erasmus' letter of 1 September 1527 may well have served to moderate the chancellor's attitude towards the Lutherans and prepare his position just before the diet of Augsburg immediately prior to his death: Erasmus here called for prudence amidst the intransigence of sects and warned that if the Lutheran sect were removed, a worse tumult might develop (Ep 1872).

The friendship between Erasmus and Gattinara began as a matter of political convenience but eventually became more substantive. Gattinara was obviously pleased to have such a friend (Ep 1281) and soon came to see him as the paladin of orthodoxy and to treat him with almost reverential respect and devotion (Epp 1791, 1839). He allowed Erasmus to inform the later development of his moderate policy of accomodating the Lutherans and in his last moments was apparently reading several of Erasmus' works for instruction in this regard (Ep 2336). As for Erasmus, he began by sniffing at Gattinara's Latin (Ep 1197 introduction), but took obvious pride as well as comfort in being well connected (Epp 1796, 1805, 1806). Furthermore, he deeply appreciated Gattinara's intervention with the Louvain

theologians, wherein he sensed the stout support and candour of the man (Ep 1815). He included Gattinara among his five Spanish patrons to receive copies of his edition of Augustine (Epp 2126, 2253A). He took genuine pleasure in learning that his friend had been elevated to the cardinalate and showed real anxiety and distress when a letter from him was lost (Ep 2241). Three months after Gattinara's death, oppressed with fractious opponents, Erasmus lamented that he had lost an outstanding friend (Ep 2375).

At the suggestion of Wolsey Gattinara composed in Latin an account of the discussions held at Calais in 1521; a copy of the hitherto lost Latin original was discovered in 1980 in the Scheurl family archive in Nürnberg. However, a contemporary French translation by the Burgundian Claude de Chassey circulated widely, and several manuscript copies still exist, for example at the Bibliothèque Royale Albert 1er of Brussels, the Bibliothèque Nationale of Paris, the Archives du Nord of Lille, the Provinciale Archief at Ghent, the Bibliothèque Municipale de Besançon, and the Haus-, Hof-, und Staatsarchiv of Vienna. The translation was published in *Papiers d'état du Cardinal de Granvelle*, edited by Charles Weiss (Paris 1841) and condensed in LP III-2 1816, cf 2786. In the polemical replies to *Clement VII and to Francis I in late 1526 appearing in *Pro divo Carolo ...* (Mainz: J. Schöffer, 9 September 1527) Gattinara was as much the author of the imperial responses as Alfonso de Valdés. The autobiography, together with valuable notes, additions, and documents here referred to, was published by Carlo Bornate in *Miscellanea di storia italiana* 17 (1915) 231–585. Bornate also published *Mémoire de Chancelier de Gattinara sur les droits de Charles-Quint au duché de Bourgogne* (Brussels 1907). Parts of his political correspondence have been published in LP; *Calendar of State Papers, Spain and Venice*; L.M.G. Kooperberg *Margaretha van Oostenrijk* (1908) 373–463; and A. Le Glay 'Études biographiques' *Société Royale des Sciences ... Lille: Mémoires* 31 (1847) 183–260.

In the family castle at Albano-Vercelli there was until recently a portrait of Gattinara as cardinal that was often misattributed to Titian. He was buried in the parish church of San

Pietro at Gattinara before the altar; his interesting epitaph is published in Le Glay 215–16. Shortly after his death a medal was struck bearing his effigy and apotheosizing *fides* (Le Glay 217; *Die wöchentliche historische Münz-Belustigung*, 12 January 1735, 9).

BIBLIOGRAPHY: Besides the excellent biographical sketch in Allen's preface to Ep 1150 there are short articles in DHGE III 1473–4 and EI XVI 451. None of the eighteenth- and nineteenth-century biographies are adequate. In connection with the international conference in 1980 to celebrate the 450th anniversary of the chancellor's death a very useful modern biography was published by Franco Ferretti entitled *Un Maestro di politica* (Milan 1980). For other studies and the most complete bibliographical statement see John M. Headley 'The Hapsburg world empire and the revival of Ghibellinism' in *Medieval and Renaissance Studies* ed Siegfried Wenzel VII (Chapel Hill 1978) 93–127; John M. Headley 'The conflict between nobles and magistrates in Franche-Comté, 1508–18' *The Journal of Medieval and Renaissance Studies* 9 (1979) 49–80; John M. Headley 'Gattinara, Erasmus and the imperial configuration of Humanism' ARG 71 (1980) 64–98

JOHN M. HEADLEY

Luca GAURICO of Gauro, 12 March 1475–6 March 1558
Luca Gaurico, the son of Bernardino Linguisto and his wife, Cerelia, derived his surname from his native village, Gauro in the district of Giffoni. The humanist Pomponio Gaurico was his brother. Around 1500, after studying with their father, a teacher of grammar, Luca and Pomponio went to Padua, where Pietro *Pomponazzi was among their teachers. Luca received a doctorate in arts around 1502. His main interest lay in astrology, and in 1501 he published at Venice the first of many prognostications, this one for the year 1502. He taught astrology at Padua in 1503 and at the University of Bologna in 1506. At Bologna, however, he was publicly whipped and imprisoned for twenty-five days for predicting the fall of Giovanni (II) *Bentivoglio. He was freed through the efforts of Cristoforo Madrucci, later bishop of Trent and Brescia, and in 1507 and 1508 taught mathematics and astrology at Ferrara. After stops in Rome and Mantua, he

settled in Venice by 1524. In 1525 he was given a benefice by Don Ferdinando Sanseverino of Salerno, who referred to him as an apostolic protonotary. In 1529 and 1532 Gaurico predicted the election of Alessandro Farnese to the papacy, and he moved to Rome in 1534 after the cardinal became *Paul III. Paul made him his table companion and knighted him. In 1539 or shortly thereafter Gaurico became bishop of Giffoni and on 14 December 1545 bishop of Civitate, in the Capitanata. After the death of Paul in 1549 he returned to Venice, resigning his diocese in 1550. In 1552 he left Venice rather than retract certain libellous statements made against the city, going to Bologna and by 1556 to Rome. His will was dated 5 March 1558 and he was buried in the church of Santa Maria de Aracoeli in Rome.

According to *Viglius Zuichemus' letter to Erasmus of August 1533 (Ep 2854), Gaurico travelled to Germany in the early 1530s and on his return to Italy spoke in praise of *Luther and *Melanchthon. Gaurico's work was certainly known to Melanchthon, who addressed the Italian astrologer in a letter of dedication written for Joachim *Camerarius' *Norica sive de ostentis libri duo* (Wittenberg 1532).

Gaurico, perhaps the most renowned astrologer of the first half of the sixteenth century, composed many works, the most famous of which was the *Tractatus astrologicus* (Venice: B. Casano 1552), which gave prognostications for cities, popes, cardinals, rulers, artists, and men of letters. His other original works on astrology and astronomy included a prognostication for the years 1513–35 dedicated to Francesco Gonzaga of Mantua (Mantua 1512), the *Stellarum fixarum longitudinum ac latitudinum tabulae* (Venice 1524), *De eclipsi solis miraculosa in passione Domini observata* (Rome: A. Bladus 1539), the *Praedictiones super omnibus futuris luminarium deliquiis* (Rome: A. Bladus 1539), the *Trattato di astrologia giudiziaria sopra la natività degli uomini e donne* (Rome: V. Dorici 1539; Latin edition Nürnberg: J. Petreius 1540), the *Opera nuova astronomica intitolata Arbore del bene e del male* (Genoa 1548), and *De sorte hominum* (Venice 1549). He also edited *De rebus coelestibus* of Lorenzo Buonincontro (Venice: G.A. Nicolini da Sabbio 1526), the *Almagest* of Ptolemy (Venice: L.A. Giunta 1528), the *Spherae tractatus* of John of Holywood (Venice:

L.A. Giunta 1531), and the *Tabulae primi mobili*
of Giovanni Bianchini (Bologna 1554). Gaurico
also composed works on grammar and poetry:
the *Grammatices libellus isagogicus* (Rome 1540),
the *Ars metrica* (Rome: B. Cartolari 1541), and
the *Aureus liber de illustrium poetarum auctori-*
tatibus (Rome 1557), bound with the dialogue
De ocio liberali. His *Opera omnia* were published
at Basel in 1575 by Sebastian Henricpetri.

BIBLIOGRAPHY: Allen Ep 2854 / EI XVI 459 /
Eubel III I 83 / *Melanchthons Briefwechsel* II Ep
1223 / E. Percopo 'Luca Gàurico ultimo degli
astrologi: Notizie biografiche e bibliografiche'
in *Pomponio Gàurico umanista napoletano*
(Naples 1891) / Lynn Thorndike *A History of*
Magic and Experimental Science (New York and
London 1923–58) v 51 and passim, VI 21 and
passim   TBD

Jodocus GAVERIUS or GAVERUS *See* Joost
VROYE

Theodorus GAZA of Salonike, 1400–c 1476
After early studies in Constantinople, Gaza
(Theodoros Gazes) came to Italy for the council
of Ferrara-Florence in 1438. He decided to
remain there permanently, studying under
Vittorina da Feltre. He then taught Greek at the
University of Ferrara (1447–9) before being
called to Rome to enter the service of *Nicholas
v, under whose patronage he made important
translations from Greek into Latin. Upon the
death of Nicholas he entered the service of
Alfonso I at Naples, and later he returned
to Rome under the patronage of Cardinal
*Bessarion. After Bessarion's death (1472)
Gaza divided his time between Rome and
Calabria. His most important Latin translations
were of Aristotle's *De animalibus* and *Proble-*
mata and Theophrastus' *De causis plantarum*
and *De historia plantarum*, all of which remained
standard throughout the sixteenth century. He
also translated works of Caesar and Cicero into
Greek and composed a number of philosophical works, orations, and letters.

Erasmus considered Gaza to be the best of
the Greek grammarians (ASD I-2 114, 148) and
translated the first two books of Gaza's Greek
grammar (Venice 1495) into Latin (Louvain: D.
Martens 1516 and Basel: J. Froben 1518; LB I
117–63). On the whole Erasmus praises Gaza
(eg *Opuscula* 181–2), considering him to be

superior to George of *Trebizond in his
learning and agreeing with most other contemporaries that no one had translated Aristotle
better than Gaza (ASD I-2 665; Ep 2432). Gaza is
frequently mentioned as a translator in the
Adagia (I i 2, i 43–4, ix 67, etc) and elsewhere
(*Colloquia* ASD I-3 624, 626; Ep 2466), often in
terms of praise, though at one point Erasmus
sided with George of Trebizond in castigating
him (Ep 1479). On the whole Erasmus had a
very high opinion of Gaza and used his
grammar for his teaching at Cambridge (Ep
233).

BIBLIOGRAPHY: Allen Ep 233 / *Catalogus
translationum et commentariorum* (Washington
1960–   ) I 130 (bibliography) / C. Pizzi 'La
grammatica greca di T. Gaza e Erasmo' *Studi
bizantini e neoellenici* 7 (1953) 183–8 / G.
Salanitro 'Teodoro Gaza e Cicerone' *Siculorum
Gymnasium* 21 (1968) 76–92 / L. Labowsky
'An Unknown Treatise by Theodorus Gaza'
Mediaeval and Renaissance Studies 6 (1968)
173–98   CHARLES B. SCHMITT

Hieronymus GEBWILER of Kaysersberg,
c 1473–21 June 1545
Hieronymus Gebwiler (Gebuilerius), born in
the Alsatian town of Kaysersberg, matriculated
at Basel in 1492 and at Paris received a BA in
February 1493 and a MA in 1495. From 1501 he
directed the famous Latin school at Sélestat,
attracting to it *Beatus Rhenanus, *Sapidus,
and many pupils from Basel, among them
Bonifacius *Amerbach, who remained a faithful friend. In 1509 Gebwiler was called to
Strasbourg by the cathedral chapter, which, in
deference to the wishes of Geiler von Kaysersberg and *Wimpfeling, was determined to
reform the school. Gebwiler was not only a
humanist but a married layman. He attempted
to make the school a model Gymnasium,
preparing the students for university: they
were given exercises in etymology, syntax, and
prosody; they composed discourses, verses,
and letters following classical models; and they
were instructed in dialectics and given practice
in disputation. To improve the Latin style of his
pupils Gebwiler replaced the *Doctrinale* of
Alexander de Villa Dei with Johannes *Cochlaeus' new Latin grammar. In 1514 he edited
the Epistles of Horace and five comedies of
Plautus to introduce the students to the

sources. His scientific interests were reflected in the preparation of an annotated edition of *Lefèvre d'Etaples' commentaries on Aristotle's *Physics* (Strasbourg: R. Beck 1514) and an edition of Polidoro *Virgilio's *De inventoribus rerum* (Strasbourg: M. Schürer 1508). Like other Alsatian humanists, he was passionately interested in history, espousing the cause of German nationalism with vigour. He met Erasmus in 1514 through the Strasbourg literary circle (Epp 302, 305), was greeted by him in Epp 633, 883, and generously received him when he passed through Strasbourg in 1518 (Ep 867). In 1521 Gebwiler is mentioned in a polemical pamphlet as an adversary of the Reformation. He took up the role of champion of the Roman church and in 1525 left Strasbourg to become director of the school of St Georg in Haguenau. He remained in this post until his death in 1545.

BIBLIOGRAPHY: Allen and CWE Ep 302 / Schmidt *Histoire littéraire* II 159–73; complete bibliography of Gebwiler's work II 407–11 / ADB VIII 486–7 / AK I Ep 375 and passim / Rice *Prefatory Epistles* Ep 80 and passim / BRE Ep 4 and passim   MIRIAM U. CHRISMAN

Johann GEBWILER of Colmar, documented 1465–1530
Johann Gebwiler of Colmar, Upper Alsace, was the son of the blacksmith attached to the monastery of St Catherine at Colmar and most likely a relative of Hieronymus *Gebwiler (AK I Ep 375). In the autumn of 1465 he matriculated in the University of Freiburg and four years later in Basel. As he was poor, his academic progress was slowed down by his having to teach at the municipal Latin school. In 1470 he received his BA, in 1476 his MA, and in 1507 his doctorate in divinity. In the same year he was appointed canon of St Peter, professor of theology, and also rector of the university, a dignity which he held again in 1515 and 1522; he was also dean of the theological faculty at frequent intervals from 1508. Until the appointment of Ludwig *Baer his only colleague was Moritz *Fininger, whose reputation was as modest as Gebwiler's own. The beginning of disturbances caused by the reform party at Basel inspired him to violent denunciations from the pulpit of St Alban, where he was parish priest, and on 11 April 1523 his academic

salary was suspended by the city council. In 1526 he participated in the disputation of Baden, and subsequently he left Basel, probably at the time of the exodus of Catholics in February 1529. He is last documented as priest of Eichstetten, near Freiburg. He also held a benefice at Turckheim, Upper Alsace. He compiled *Magistralis totius Parvuli artis logices compilatio* (Basel: A. Petri 1511).

Conradus *Pellicanus mentioned Gebwiler among the scholastic doctors (Ep 1639), and Erasmus insisted in the *Spongia* that, contrary to *Hutten's suggestion, his acquaintance with Gebwiler was slight (ASD IX-1 158–9).

BIBLIOGRAPHY: Allen Ep 1639 / *Matrikel Freiburg* I-1 34 / *Matrikel Basel* I 78–9, 284, 328, 350, 369–70 / Wilhelm Vischer *Geschichte der Universität Basel* (Basel 1860) 223–5 / Rudolf Wackernagel *Geschichte der Stadt Basel* (Basel 1907–54) III 129 and passim   PGB

Thomas GEIERFALK *See Thomas* GYRFALK

Gerard GELDENHOUWER of Nijmegen, 1482–10 January 1542
Gerard Geldenhouwer (Geldenhauer, Noviomagus, Neocomus) was born at Nijmegen. His father, Gerrit, a valet in the service of successive dukes of Gelderland, was on good terms with Herman van Cranevelt, the duke's secretary, and so arranged for his son to be taught privately with Herman's son, Frans van *Cranevelt (born 1485). Soon the young Gerard was sent to Deventer, where a school was flourishing under the enthusiastic leadership of Alexander *Hegius. A number of important humanists passed through the Deventer school, among them Hermannus *Buschius, Conradus *Goclenius, Johannes *Murmellius, *Alaard of Amsterdam, and Gerardus *Listrius. Later Geldenhouwer went to Louvain, having in the meantime entered the order of the Crozier canons. At Louvain he again met his friend Frans van Cranevelt, who had arrived in 1501 and took his doctoral degree in 1510. In 1514 Geldenhouwer entered the service of the future *Charles V and was attached to the admiral of Flanders, Philip of *Burgundy, who afterwards became bishop of Utrecht.

In this period Geldenhouwer was very active as a humanistic author, publishing *De situ Zeelandiae* in 1514, followed by *Satyrae octo* *ad verae religionis cultores* (1515), *Pompa ex-equiarum Catholici Hispaniarum regis Ferdinandi* (Strasbourg: M. Schürer 1516), *De ingressu Philippi de Burgundia in ditionem suam* (1517), and *De Batavorum insula* (1520). Like Pieter *Gillis he was employed at Louvain by the printer Dirk *Martens; he corrected Martens' editions of Erasmus' *De constructione* (1514), *Parabolae* (1515), *Opuscula aliquot* (1515), and *Institutio principis christiani* (1516). These last two contain the same laudatory epigram by Geldenhouwer. He also assisted in the production of a number of other important works, such as the 1516 edition of Thomas *More's *Utopia*, with three distichs by Geldenhouwer among the introductory pieces. Together with *Dorp and Alaard of Amsterdam he edited Rodolphus *Agricola's *De inventione dialectica*. At this time Geldenhouwer maintained close relations with many outstanding humanists, among them Cranevelt, Dorp, Adrianus Cornelii *Barlandus, Cornelius *Grapheus, Pieter Gillis, Jean *Desmarez, and, naturally, Erasmus. In 1517 he was crowned poet laureate by the Emperor *Maximilian I at Tienen.

Geldenhouwer soon began sympathizing with the ideas of the Reformation, though for several years he managed to conceal this from his friends. It was only after the death of his 'Maecenas,' Bishop Philip of Utrecht (7 April 1524), that he decided gradually to lift the mask. On 17 September 1525 he left Antwerp and went to Germany, attending the lectures of *Luther, *Melanchthon and other reformers at Wittenberg, and was deeply impressed with what he heard. In March 1526 Cranevelt provided him with fresh travelling money, enabling him to move along the Rhine, eventually reaching the Strasbourg of *Bucer and *Capito. From Worms, where he married on 13 November 1526 (Ep 1778), he wrote to Adolph of *Burgundy, lord of Veere, and about the same time to Cranevelt, attempting to justify his conduct.

The following years proved very difficult for Geldenhouwer, who was kept on the move, living for short periods in Antwerp, Strasbourg, and Augsburg. Nevertheless, he managed to write and publish more historical works, such as *Vita Philippi a Burgundia* (Strasbourg: C. Egenolff 1529), *Historia Batavica* (1530, published by Petrus Scriverius in *Batavia*

illustrata, Leiden 1690), and *Germaniae inferioris historia* (1531, published together with *Pirkheimer's *Descriptio Germaniae utriusque*, Antwerp: C. Plantin 1585). Finally, in 1532, he was appointed professor of history, and in 1534 professor of theology, at the University of Marburg, where he lived quietly until his death in 1542. The only new work he published in this period was a pedagogical treatise, *Institutio scholae christianae* (Frankfurt: C. Egenolff 1534). His *Germanicarum historiarum illustratio*, a mere compilation of some earlier historical tracts on the Netherlands, was posthumously published at Marburg by Christian Egenolff in 1542.

Geldenhouwer's relationship with Erasmus was at first very friendly. We may safely assume that their acquaintance began early in the sixteenth century, most probably through the intercession of mutual friends, such as Dorp and Gillis. There is no trace of correspondence between them, however, before November 1516, when Geldenhouwer announced to Erasmus that Martens was very pleased to publish Thomas More's *Utopia* (Ep 487). When Geldenhouwer was publishing his description of Bishop Philip's entry into Utrecht (*De ingressu Philippi de Burgundia*), Erasmus wrote a commendatory letter dated 31 August 1517 (Ep 645). Some months later he let Geldenhouwer know that he was totally absorbed by his work on the New Testament and must decline the invitation from Philip of Burgundy (Ep 682). The following letters (Epp 714, 727, 759, 811, 812, 837) also reflect Geldenhouwer's connection with Philip, to whom Erasmus was dedicating his *Querela pacis*.

Geldenhouwer and Erasmus probably met at Mechelen in August 1519 (Ep 1001) and at Bruges in September 1520, when Erasmus shared with him his thoughts about the origin and progress of the Reformation (Ep 1141). In the spring of 1524 Geldenhouwer requested confidentially a summary of Erasmus' life, pointing out that others were about to write a biography; Erasmus allowed Goclenius to give Geldenhouwer orally all the information requested (Allen Ep 1437: 212–15). Allen's hypothesis that Ep 1436 is precisely the composition requested by Geldenhouwer thus seems rather unlikely, although Geldenhouwer did apparently have access to the very private Ep 296.

It seems that an estrangement between Geldenhouwer and Erasmus had already begun when Geldenhouwer published *D. Erasmi annotationes in leges pontificias et Caesareas de haereticis*, together with his *Epistolae aliquot de re evangelica et haereticorum poenis* (Strasbourg: C. Egenolff 1529), trying to connect Erasmus' name with the Reformation. Naturally Erasmus was upset; he reported the matter to several friends (Epp 2293, 2294, 2321, 2324, 2329, 2355, 2358, 2371, 2441, 2587) and replied vigorously in his *Epistola contra pseudevangelicos* (ASD IX-1 263–309). In his letters he called Geldenhouwer 'Vulturius,' explaining this by connecting the first part of the Christian name *Ger-ardus* with the Dutch *Gier* 'vulture' (Ep 2441; cf Ep 2238).

In this context Geldenhouwer's *Collectanea* must be considered. This manuscript (Brussels, Bibliothèque Royale, MS II.53; edited by Prinsen) is a collection of notes concerning a variety of matters, mainly covering the years 1520–32. Originally it also contained several autograph pieces by Erasmus, and it still contains a shorter version of an outrageous poem against Pope *Julius II, now reliably ascribed to Erasmus.

BIBLIOGRAPHY: Allen Ep 487 / J. Prinsen *Gerardus Geldenhauer Noviomagus: Bijdrage tot de kennis van zijn leven en werken* (The Hague 1898) / *Collectanea van Gerardus Geldenhauer Noviomagus, gevolgd door den herdruk van eenige zijner werken* ed J. Prinsen (Amsterdam 1901) / de Vocht *Literae ad Craneveldium* Ep 240 and passim / Olaf Hendriks 'Gerardus Geldenhouwer Noviomagus (1482–1542)' *Studia Catholica* 31 (1956) 129–49 and 176–96 / C. Reedijk 'Een schimpdicht van Erasmus op Julius II' in *Opstellen ... aan Dr. F.K.H. Kossmann* (The Hague 1958) 186–207 / Catalogue: *Tentoonstelling Dirk Martens 1473–1973* (Aalst 1973) / C. Augustijn 'Gerard Geldenhouwer und die religiöse Toleranz' ARG 69 (1978) 132–56　　　　GILBERT TOURNOY

Charles, duke of GELDERLAND or GUELDERS *See Karel van* EGMOND

Sigismundus GELENIUS of Prague, c 1498–early 1554

Zikmund Hrubý z Jelení, better known as Gelenius, was born into a family of Bohemian nobles. His father, Řehoř Hrubý (1460–1514), was a friend of Jan *Šlechta and translated into Czech Erasmus' *Moria* and likewise works by Petrarch (published 1501) and Cicero (*British Library General Catalogue of Printed Books to 1975* 154:164).

A canon of Prague, Václav Písecký (Wenceslas of Pisek), became Sigismund's tutor in 1505 and accompanied him to Bologna in 1509. According to his first biographer, Gelenius at one time studied Greek under Marcus *Musurus and visited Sicily, Sardinia, Corsica, and France before returning to Prague, where he lectured privately on Greek authors and entered into correspondence with *Melanchthon (*Melanchthons Briefwechsel* Ep 281, before 31 July 1523). Probably in 1524 he moved to Basel, where he lived at first in Erasmus' household (Allen Ep 1544 introduction). He spent the remainder of his life working for the *Froben press as a scholar, editor, corrector, and translator from the Greek, even declining a position as professor of Greek at Nürnberg for which he was recommended by Melanchthon in 1525 and 1526 (cf Ep 1717). His sedentary life-style led to corpulence, and Erasmus described him on occasion as lazy (Epp 2033, 3043, 3076). But in his day there cannot have been many major productions of the Froben press which did not benefit from his selfless scholarly devotion. He translated into Latin the *Periplus* of Arrian et al (1533) and Philo Judaeus (1554) and at his death left a nearly complete translation of Appian for Celio Secondo Curione to edit (1554, with a meagre biographical sketch of Gelenius). He took part in the Greek editions of Josephus (1544) and the *Epigrams* (1549). His edition of Aristophanes, likewise in Greek, is dedicated to Melanchthon (1549). He edited the thorny Velleius Paterculus (1546) and also prepared the first complete edition of the *Notitia dignitatum* (1552). He also produced a *Lexicum symphonum* (1537, 1544) in which he attempted to describe linguistic affinities between Greek, Latin, German, and Slavonic. There is also evidence that he collaborated on a number of editions by Erasmus such as Pliny's *Historia naturalis* (1525; Ep 1544), Ambrose (1527; Ep 2033), the second edition of Seneca (1529; Ep 2091), the fourth edition of the New Testament (1527; Ep 1571; LB IX 986F), the *Ecclesiastes* (1535; Ep 3044), and the *Opera omnia* (1538–40; AK V Ep 2123).

Erasmus held Gelenius in high regard as is attested to by himself and others (Epp 1702, 1767, 2901; AK VII 37–8); among his friends were Gilbert *Cousin, Damião de *Gois, and especially Anselmus *Ephorinus. Although he registered at the University of Basel in 1534 he did not teach there. In 1535 he visited Cracow (Ep 3000), presumably travelling by way of Prague. The name of his wife is not known; of his five children three survived him.

BIBLIOGRAPHY: Allen Ep 1702 / NDB VI 173 / O. Clemen 'Briefe aus Basel an Melanchthon' *Basler Zeitschrift für Geschichte und Altertumskunde* 43 (1944) 17–33 / Bierlaire *Familia* 67–8 / *Matrikel Basel* II 6, 20, 79 / AK IV Epp 1532, 1804, and passim / *Melanchthons Briefwechsel* I Ep 281 and passim / I.N. Goleniščev-Kutuzov *Il Rinascimento italiano e le letterature slave dei secoli xv e xvi* (Milan 1973) / J.K. Zeman *The Hussite Movement and the Reformation in Bohemia, Moravia and Slovakia, A Bibliographical Study Guide* (Ann Arbor 1977) 168   PGB

Georgius GEMISTOS PLETHON
of Constantinople, c 1360–26 May 1452
Georgius Gemistos was born into a great priestly family of Constantinople; his father was probably a protonotary of the cathedral of St Sophia. Through a Jewish teacher named Elijah he was exposed to the ideas of Arab and Latin commentators on Aristotle and to neo-Platonism. He assumed the name 'Plethon' in honour of Plato. For a time he studied at a foreign court, perhaps that of the Ottoman Turks, and on his return to Constantinople became an influential teacher. Around 1405 the Emperor Manuel II Palaeologus exiled him from Constantinople at the insistence of the clergy, who were outraged by his unorthodox doctrines. He settled in the Peloponnesian city of Mistra, an almost autonomous part of the Byzantine empire. Here Gemistos Plethon became the central figure in a renaissance of Hellenism and neo-Platonism. Among his students was Cardinal *Bessarion. Although he developed his neo-Platonic ideas to the degree that he defended polytheism, as the leading spokesman of one of the greatest

intellectual centres of the empire he was asked to attend the ecumenical council of Ferrara and Florence in 1438 and 1439 with the Emperor John VIII Palaeologus and members of the orthodox hierarchy. At the council he was among the minority who opposed union with the Latin church, for this conflicted with his hope for a Greek political and military resurgence. However, while in Italy he engaged in discussions with Leonardo Bruni, Francesco *Filelfo, and other Italian humanists, defending the merits of Plato against those of Aristotle and thus helping prepare for the neo-Platonic revival in Florence in the second half of the fifteenth century. After the council Gemistos Plethon returned to Mistra to complete his scholarly work and to continue to write against the union of the Greek and Latin churches. The school of Mistra endured for several years after his death but was doomed by the fall of the city to the Turks in 1460.

Erasmus mentions Gemistos Plethon only in passing in the *Vita Hieronymi* (*Opuscula* 181) and in *Adagia* II vi 24.

The most important writings of Gemistos Plethon were the *Laws*, which were burned by the patriarch of Constantinople in the 1460s and survived only in fragments. These were published in a French translation by C. Alexandre (Paris 1858). Beginning in 1413 Gemistos Plethon also wrote a series of memorials to Manuel II Palaeologus and the rulers of Mistra on the affairs of the Peloponnese and steps to be taken for a rejuvenation of Greece. His work on the differences between Plato and Aristotle, addressed to the Italian humanistic community and commonly called *De differentis*, was published in a Latin paraphrase at Venice (G. Scoto) in 1540 and in the original Greek at Basel (P. Perna) in 1574. Other works included treatises on the virtues and fortune (Basel: J. Oporinus 1552) and polemics against Bessarion and Georgius Scholarius.

BIBLIOGRAPHY: Deno John Geanakoplos *Interaction of the 'Sibling' Byzantine and Western Cultures in the Middle Ages and Italian Renaissance (330–1600)* (New Haven and London 1976) 49, 52, and passim / B. Kotter in LThK VIII 561–2 / François Masai *Pléthon et le platonisme de Mistra* (Paris 1956) / E. Stéphanou in DTC XII 2393–404   TBD

Hieronymus GEMUSEUS of Mulhouse,
1505–19 January 1544
From 1517 Gemuseus (Gschmus, Gmües), the
son of a leading official of the town of
Mulhouse, attended the school of Sélestat
under *Sapidus and in 1522 entered the
University of Basel, attaching himself to
*Glareanus. After graduating MA in 1525, he
directed his attention towards mathematics,
science, and medicine. While continuing his
studies he was the tutor and travelling
companion of Pierre de *Mornieu between
1526 and 1529. Erasmus evidently knew him a
little and reacted with warm praise when
Mornieu wrote to him about his tutor (Ep
2162). He continued his travels and studies,
acceding to the medical doctorate at Turin in
1533 and writing to Bonifacius *Amerbach
between 1534 and 1536 from Turin, Milan, and
Lyon. After lengthy negotiations Amerbach
succeeded in securing him an appointment as
professor of physics at Basel. In this capacity
he lectured on Aristotle from the spring of
1537. Gemuseus did not object to the Reformation and evidently showed some diplomatic
skill. He established ties with Guillaume Du
Bellay, sieur de Langey, and Germain de *Brie.
In 1543 he went again to Italy, in part at least as
an envoy of the Basel city council to the
government of Savoy. While he was absent, his
wife, Sibylle, the daughter of Andreas *Cratander, gave birth to a fourth child, Hieronymus,
baptized on 17 November 1543. When Gemuseus returned home he was ill, and before
long he died.

Gemuseus' significance lies chiefly in his
scholarly publications. He produced a Latin
epitome of Strabo (Basel: F. Walder 1539) and
edited Ptolemy's moral works (Basel: H. Petri
1541) and Paul of Aegina (Basel: A. Cratander
1538, revised 1543). He also contributed
prominently to editions of Galen in Greek
(1537–8) and Aristotle in Latin (1542, 1548),
undertaken by several Basel printers together.

BIBLIOGRAPHY: Allen Ep 2162 / Auguste
Stoeber *Jérôme Gemuseus* 2nd ed (Mulhouse
1881) / Albrecht Burckhardt *Geschichte der
medizinischen Fakultät zu Basel* (Basel 1917)
42–3 / AK III Ep 1178, IV Epp 1875, 1934, V Epp
2223, 2532, 2597, VI Ep 2611 and passim /
Matrikel Basel I 351   PGB

Andreas van GENNEP *See Andreas* BALENUS

Hieronymus de GENUTIIS *See Girolamo*
GHINUCCI

GEORGE of Austria 1504–5 May 1557
George, an illegitimate son of the Emperor
*Maximilian I, grew up at the court of
*Margaret of Austria in the Low Countries,
where he was educated at first with the future
*Charles V and subsequently with Maximilian's
other grandson, *Ferdinand. He studied at
Alcalá with some success. On 21 October 1525
he was elected bishop of Bressanone; he was a
good administrator but was often absent from
his diocese visiting the courts of his relatives.
In 1530 he was with the Emperor Charles V in
Augsburg and Bologna, and in 1531 he was
attached to the household of Queen *Mary of
Hungary in the Low Countries. In 1539 he
became archbishop of Valencia and resigned
the see of Bressanone. Two years later he set
out for Liège on a promise of succession to that
see when it fell vacant but was captured by the
French and held prisoner until he was released
for ransom in 1543. In 1544 he was appointed
prince-bishop of Liège, and resided in his
principality until his death.

George of Austria probably never met
Erasmus personally but took an interest in his
writings. In 1528, not long after he had become
bishop of Bressanone, he invited Erasmus to
stay at his residence there. Erasmus politely
declined the invitation (Ep 1938) in spite of the
proximity between Bressanone and Trent,
where Bernhard von *Cles, another supporter
of his, was bishop. It seems that George
continued to read and admire Erasmus'
writings after he had joined the court of Mary
of Hungary (Epp 2566, 3047). In 1535 he
worked with Ambrosius von *Gumppenberg
in securing for Erasmus the provostship of
Deventer (Ep 3047).

BIBLIOGRAPHY: Allen Ep 1938 / NDB VI 210 /
ADB VIII 637–8 / de Vocht CTL II 132 / Karl Brandi
Kaiser Karl v. new ed (Darmstadt 1959–67) II
316 / Léon-H. Halkin *Histoire religieuse des
règnes de Corneille de Berghes et de Georges
d'Autriche, princes-évêques de Liège* (Liège-Paris
1936) / Valentin von Tetleben *Protokoll des
Augsburger Reichstages 1530* ed H. Grundmann
(Göttingen 1958) 68 and passim   IG

GEORGE of Masevaux abbot of Murbach,
d 10 January 1542
George of Masevaux (Masmünster), north of
Belfort, was elected Benedictine abbot of Lure
(Haute-Saône), between Belfort and Vesoul, in
1511. In the following year he was also elected
prince-abbot of Murbach, in the Upper Alsace.
On 7 January 1514 *Leo x confirmed the joint
appointments. The two offices were united
from then on. Around 1520 George rebuilt the
towers of Lure. In 1525 he and his troops
defeated rebellious peasants who had taken
the town of Guebwiller, near Murbach, but
subsequently he was himself involved in a
conflict with Guebwiller. Murbach's famous
library provided many important manuscripts
for the Basel humanists and printers, and also
for the great edition of Jerome (AK I Ep 391)
which brought Erasmus to Basel in 1514. In
1527 or 1528, however, Johann *Sichard was
refused a volume because he had addressed his
request to the dean rather than to Abbot
George himself (AK III Ep 1224).

In 1529 Claudius *Cantiuncula asked Erasmus to write to George in connection with the
plans of a young relative of his (Ep 2240).

BIBLIOGRAPHY: Allen Ep 2240 / *Gallia christi-
ana* xv 170, 535, 556 / AK II Ep 742, v Ep 2444
and passim / A. Gatrio *Die Abtei Murbach*
(Strasbourg 1895) II 113–73 / Julius Kindler von
Knobloch and O. von Stotzingen *Oberbadisches
Geschlechterbuch* (Heidelberg 1894–1919) III 41
                                                    PGB

Doctor GEORGIUS
(Ep 1946 of 5 February 1528)
In a letter from Koblenz, Justin *Gobler
mentions Doctor Georgius as having received a
letter from Erasmus shortly before his recent
death; he has not been identified.

GEORGIUS
Georgius was a messenger sent by Erasmus to
the Low Countries with letters and verbal
messages. He left Basel by 8 June 1522 and
returned the following month (Epp 1292, 1296,
1303, 1306). He is probably not the Georgius
who was on his way from Poland to Basel in
October 1527. The latter had been sent by
Erasmus' Polish friends and carried their
letters. In Basel he worked for a while in the
Froben press. On his return to Poland he

claimed, according to Erasmus, to have been
his famulus. He made another trip to Basel in
1529 (Epp 1895, 1915, 1916, 2033, 2173).
                                                    PGB

GEORGIUS Trapezuntinus or Trapezuntius
See George of TREBIZOND

GERARD father of Erasmus *See* ERASMUS'
family

GERARD of Friesland
Besides what is learnt from two letters he wrote
to Erasmus (Epp 2232, 2815), nothing is known
about one Gerard of Friesland the younger
('Gerardus Phrysius minor'). A former pupil of
Gerardus *Listrius, he was by November 1529
in the service of Thomas *Boleyn and had
evidently met Erasmus before. In June 1533 he
was still in England and in Boleyn's service.
This virtually precludes an identification with
another Gerard, a young man of Friesland
('Gerardus quidam Phrysius, optimae spei
adulescens'), who had passed several months
in Paris in the household of Alberto *Pio when
the printer Gerard *Morrhy met him in the
spring of 1530 (Ep 2311). He also has not been
identified.

BIBLIOGRAPHY: Allen Ep 2232
                                    C.G. VAN LEIJENHORST

GERARD of Kloster, documented 1499–1520
Gerard, a native of Kloster, near Wittmund
(Ostfriesland), was an Augustinian canon of St
Agnietenberg (Mount St Agnes), the famous
convent near Zwolle which once accomodated
Thomas à Kempis. He is said to have learnt
Greek and Hebrew from Wessel *Gansfort,
who spent some time at St Agnietenberg
during his retirement. Around 1499 Gerard
succeeded Derick (Theodorus) Wanynck as
prior. A fervent admirer of Erasmus, he was
probably the prior who willingly yielded a
Greek text of the Gospels to his friend
Gerardus *Listrius to be forwarded to Erasmus
(Epp 504, 515). Afterwards Erasmus sent him
greetings several times in letters to Listrius (Ep
697; CWE Ep 1013A). On 23 November 1519
Listrius dedicated his *De figuris et tropis*
(Zwolle: S. Corver, 1 December 1519; NK 3408)
to Gerard. Gerard was at Louvain in the
summer of 1520, but Erasmus was too ill to meet

him and had to excuse himself (Ep 1116); not long afterwards they did see each other, and during their meeting the prior seems to have gently reproached Erasmus for not praising St Augustine enough (Ep 1140). After 1520 little is known of the 'Prior Montanus,' but since Albert Hardenberg, born in 1510, consulted him on the life of Wessel *Gansfort, he probably lived on for quite a few years.

BIBLIOGRAPHY: Allen Ep 504 / J.H.E. van der Zandt in *Verzameling van stukken* with regard to *Overijsselsch regt en geschiedenis* 2nd division 5 (1870) 76–83 / M. van Rijn *Wessel Gansfort* (The Hague 1917) 256, LV

C.G. VAN LEIJENHORST

Cornelis GERARD of Gouda, c 1460–before December 1531

Cornelis Gerard (Cornelius Aurelius, Aurotinus, Lopsenus, Duncenus) was born around 1460; when writing the prologue to his paraphrase of the Psalms (soon after 1517) he stated that he was over sixty. The name of Gouda, his native city, induced him to adopt the Latin surname 'Aurelius' or 'Aurotinus,' the Dutch and Latin words for *gold* being *goud* and *aurum*. Gerard had a brother, Jacob; Willem *Hermans was their cousin. There is some evidence to connect him with St Lebuin's school at Deventer in that he dedicated the first part of his 'Marias' to Jacobus *Faber (IJsewijn 384–9), but it is by no means certain that he was actually educated there: he should not be confused with *Cornelis of Woerden. He joined the Augustinian canons at the monastery of St Martin's at Den Donk or Hemsdonk (hence Duncenus), near Schoonhoven, a house belonging to the chapter of Sion. When he and Erasmus exchanged a series of letters (Epp 17–30, tentatively dated 1489 by Allen), he had moved and resided at Hieronymusdal or Lopsen (hence Lopsenus), just outside Leiden. How and when they had first met is not clear; in his letter prefacing Gerard's *Batavia* *Alaard of Amsterdam called Gerard Erasmus' 'praeceptor,' which implies that Erasmus was younger and could learn a good deal from his more experienced friend. Perhaps they had seen each other during the years Erasmus spent at Gerard's native town (c 1473–7), but it is also possible that their intermediary, brother *Martinus, played a

decisive part in the development of their friendship (Ep 21).

Apart from outpourings of their mutual love, Epp 17–30 are chiefly concerned with literature and their own efforts in that field. Gerard recast Erasmus' *Apologia* (Reedijk poems 14, 15) into the form of a dialogue (Epp 19, 20, 22, 23); he sent his own *De improvisa morte* (Molhuysen 72) for Erasmus to revise (Epp 19, 20) and wrote a history of the Utrecht war and a life of St Nicholas, both lost (Epp 20, 21). Erasmus addressed an ode to Gerard (Ep 21) and was inspired by him to write the first version of the *Antibarbari* (Ep 30). Perhaps in the same period Erasmus dedicated his *Oratio de pace* (LB VII 545–52) to Gerard. He also drew his friend's attention to Lorenzo *Valla, the author of the *Elegantiae*. Gerard did not, however, find Valla quite as important as Erasmus did and preferred the contemporary poet Girolamo *Balbi (Epp 23–7). Their disagreements over such matters seem to have spoiled a visit Gerard paid Erasmus (Ep 29) and may have contributed to a gradual cooling of their friendship. Only three letters (Epp 37, 40, 78) have been preserved from the time after 1489, and these suggest the waning of their former intimacy. Nevertheless, the influence Gerard had exercised upon Erasmus would seem to be profound: it may well be that Erasmus' reorientation towards theology was largely due to him.

In 1493 Gerard was still in Lopsen but subsequently seems to have returned to St Martin's, where he became steward and prior (1494; Epp 36, 37). There he possibly began his 'Marias.' By 1497 he seems to have been living again in the Lopsen monastery, which belonged to the chapter of Windesheim. As a result of the endeavours of Jan *Standonck, in particular, the Parlement of Paris invited the chapter of Windesheim by letter of 18 April 1497 to assist in the reform of St Victor's, Paris, and Gerard was among the six Windesheim canons sent to Paris in response. On 30 October 1497 they were introduced at St Victor's. It was hoped that their example might restore order and decorum to the convent, but they met with quiet opposition on the part of Abbot Nicaise *Delorme and his monks. Gerard's personal success (Ep 74) – Bishop Jean *Simon de Champigny regretted seeing him leave – did not help, and on 16 August

1498 the six were asked to return home. For Gerard personally the months spent in Paris were not wholly fruitless; they permitted intensive study and allowed him to make some distinguished friends, as is shown by his subsequent correspondence with Robert *Gaguin, Johannes *Trithemius, and Arnoldus *Bostius. A letter and a poem by Gerard were printed in a new edition of Gaguin's *Compendium* of Frankish history (Paris: A. Bocard 31 March 1498), a volume which also contained Erasmus' Ep 45. Undoubtedly Gerard and Erasmus met again, but perhaps they had drifted too far apart to make the renewal of their contact really satisfactory. It seems that Ep 78, which Erasmus addressed to Gerard, was never answered (Ep 81).

Having returned to Lopsen Cornelis Gerard finished his 'Marias' (Ep 40), an 'Alphabetum redemptorum,' and the first part of his 'Ter quinae in psalterium Davidicum decades' (finished after 1517). Perhaps in 1508, while staying with Gerard's patron Jan van *Heemstede at the castle of Liesveld, the Emperor *Maximilian sent him the poet's laurel. Immediately afterwards Gerard is found living in St Michael's, near Schoenhoven, the motherhouse of St Martin's, but he was at Lopsen again when he wrote his 'Vita Hieronymi' (1516; Ep 433), his important *Cronychke van Hollandt, Zeelandt en Vrieslant* (the so-called Divisiekroniek; Leiden: J. Seversen 18 August 1517; NK 613), and the two parts of his *Batavia*. The latter took issue with the theories of Gerard *Geldenhouwer; it was dedicated to Reyner *Snoy but was not printed until later (Antwerp: C. Plantinus 1586). Having returned to Hemsdonk he composed the *Diadema imperatorium* (on *Charles v's coronation in 1519), the *Apocalypsis* (1522), a dialogue addressed to Cornelis *Hoen expressing the hope he set on his former acquaintance, the new pope, *Adrian vi (inaccurately edited by C. Burmannus in *Hadrianus vi*, Utrecht 1727, 259–317), and 'De patientia' (1523), again addressed to Hoen, who was in prison at the time on charges of heresy.

In his old age Cornelis Gerard was severely criticized by his superiors and tried to move his manuscripts to safety, especially by entrusting them to Jan van der *Haer. The catalogue of Haer's library lists nineteen works by Gerard,

and thanks to him a substantial part of Gerard's writings has survived and is now in the library of the University of Leiden. His poems on the death of Jan van Wassenaar (d 6 December 1523) were long considered to be the terminus post quem for his own death, but his professed involvement in the editing of Erasmus' *Paraphrasis* and *Croock's *Farrago* (Cologne: J. Gymnich 1529) suggests that he was still alive in 1529 and believed his old friendship with Erasmus to be intact. Erasmus, on the other hand, voiced disapproval of Gerard's action (Epp 2260, 2354). It is certain, however, that Gerard died before December 1531, when a poem addressed to him after his death by Alaard of Amsterdam was published (Allen 1 xxiii).

BIBLIOGRAPHY: Allen and CWE Epp 17, 78 / P.C. Molhuysen in *Nederlands Archief voor Kerkgeschiedenis* n s 2 (1903) 1–35 and 4 (1907) 54–73 (summarized in NNBW 1 196) / H.E. van Gelder in *Bijdragen voor Vaderlandsche Geschiedenis en Oudheidkunde* 4th ser 7 (1909) 385–8 / P. Debognie in *Nederlands Archief voor Kerkgeschiedenis* n s 17 (1924) 161–78 / J. Romein *Geschiedenis van de Noord-Nederlandsche geschiedschrijving* (Haarlem 1932) no 86 / A. Renaudet 'Jean Standonck' *Bulletin de la Société de l'histoire du Protestantisme français* 57 (1908) 5–81, esp 47–51 / A. Renaudet *Préréforme* 221–8 and passim / M.E. Kronenberg 'Werken van Cornelius Aurelius (Donckanus) in de Bibliothek van Kanunnik Mr. Jan Dircsz. van der Haar (A° 1531)' *Het Boek* 3rd ser 36 (1963–4) 69–79 / J. IJsewijn 'Erasmus ex poeta theologus' in *Scrinium Erasmianum* 1 375–89 / Charles Béné *Erasme et Saint Augustin* (Geneva 1969) 37–57

C.G. VAN LEIJENHORST

Pieter GERARD *See* ERASMUS' *family*

GERARDUS (Epp 673, 792 of 1517–18)
In September 1517, and probably again in October 1518, Erasmus sent greetings to Saint-Omer for 'humanissimum dominum Gerardum,' perhaps an old friend whose acquaintance he had made fifteen years earlier when he spent some time in that region. However that may be, it is most unlikely that the 'dominus Gerardus' can be identified with Gérard d'Haméricourt, as Allen proposed.

Gérard d'Haméricourt, 1504–17 March 1577,

Nikolaus Gerbel

---

there. In May 1508 he was at Tübingen, studying Aquinas in the Dominican convent, but despite this he supported *Reuchlin against the Dominicans (RE Ep 98). He continued to travel, going in 1514 to Italy, where he visited Aldo *Manuzio at Venice and received his doctorate in canon law from Bologna. In January 1515 he was appointed a lawyer in the ecclesiastical administration at Strasbourg, where he settled for life. By 1521 he had become secretary to the cathedral chapter but also served as an editor and corrector for the printer Matthias *Schürer. He was an active member of the Strasbourg literary society and probably first met Erasmus when that group welcomed him as he was passing through Strasbourg in the summer of 1514 and the spring of 1515. Apparently they met again soon thereafter at Frankfurt when Gerbel attended the spring book fair in the company of Schürer. Erasmus commented, 'No man's society has given me the same pleasure' (CWE Ep 366B). Gerbel immediately entered into correspondence with Erasmus (Ep 342) and by September was offering him advice on the format of the New Testament, urging him to separate the Greek and Latin texts rather than present them side by side (Ep 352). Later in that month Gerbel went to Basel to work as a corrector on the great enterprise (Epp 351, 358). When the edition was nearly completed Erasmus complained that although Gerbel and *Oecolampadius had been hired at great expense, they had done a poor job and the text was filled with errors (Epp 417, 421). In addition to the work in Basel, Gerbel personally supervised the Schürer editions of the *Lucubrationes* and the *Parabolae* (Epp 343, 349, 369).

In 1517 Gerbel considered devoting himself to the reform of the church by becoming a priest, but the following year, reflecting the influence of *Luther on his life and thought, he married. Nevertheless Erasmus was still writing to him warmly in 1518 (Ep 883). From December 1522 to December 1529 Gerbel kept a diary, mostly in Latin, recording the religious changes which occurred in these years. He was a convinced Lutheran and thus rejected the theological formulations of *Capito and *Bucer. He remained in close friendship with Caspar *Hedio, who had been a childhood companion

---

was a great-nephew of Antoon van *Bergen, abbot of St Bertin. He made his profession in the abbey on 27 May 1519 and may conceivably have lived there at the time Erasmus sent his greetings, but the form of these greetings rather seems to preclude a lad of about thirteen years of age. Gérard d'Haméricourt rose to be abbot of St Bertin in 1544 and in 1562 first bishop of the new diocese of Saint-Omer; in both these offices he acted vigorously in the spirit of the Tridentine reform.

BIBLIOGRAPHY: The data for Gérard d'Haméricourt were kindly supplied by André Godin / Allen Ep 673 / H. de Laplane *Les Abbés de Saint Bertin* (Saint-Omer 1855) II 103–52 / O. Bled *Les Evêques de Saint-Omer* (Saint-Omer 1898) 67–207   PGB

GERARDUS *See also* GERARD

Nikolaus GERBEL of Pforzheim, c 1485–20 January 1560
Born in Pforzheim (Baden), Gerbel (Gerbellius, Musophilus) studied under Conradus Celtis at Vienna from 1501 to 1505. He matriculated at Cologne on 16 June 1506 and received his MA

in Pforzheim. When Hedio publicly preached Bucerian doctrine in 1527, Gerbel felt isolated and abandoned. He was never close to the Strasbourg reformers, but the founding of the Strasbourg Gymnasium in 1538 gave him a new focus for his scholarly work. He continued his grammatical studies and in 1541 became the first occupant of the chair of history. In 1545 he published his *Descriptio Graeciae* (Basel: J. Oporinus), an important compilation from ancient authors of sources on the geography of classical Greece.

Among Gerbel's many publications the following may be noted: preface to Virgil's *Aeneid* (Strasbourg: M. Schürer 1515, J. Knobloch 1525); preface to Sallust's *Bellum Catilinae* (Strasbourg: M. Schürer 1517); life of Cuspinianus in Johannes Cuspinianus *De caesaribus atque imperatoribus romanis* (Strasbourg: Christian Mylius 1540). He has also been proposed as the author of the anonymous lampoon *Hochstratus ovans* (1520; Ep 1165).

BIBLIOGRAPHY: Allen and CWE Ep 342 / NDB VI 249–50 / ADB VIII 716–18 / Matrikel Tübingen I 164 / Matrikel Wien II-1 298 / Marie-Joseph Bopp *Die evangelischen Geistlichen und Theologen in Elsass und Lothringen von der Reformation bis zur Gegenwart* (Neustadt a.d. Aisch 1959) 179 / AK II Epp 535, 628 / BRE Ep 54 and passim / *Melanchthons Briefwechsel* I Ep 183 and passim / de Vocht CTL I 437 / Jean Rott 'L'humaniste strasbourgeois Nicolas Gerbel et son diaire (1522–1529)' *Bulletin philologique et historique* (1946–7) 69–78 / Strasbourg, Archives municipales MS Strasbourg 39 cart. 21.1
MIRIAM U. CHRISMAN

Christoph GERING of Augsburg, documented 1534–41
Christoph Gering, secretary to Johann (II) *Paumgartner (Epp 2949, 2989) belonged to the privileged class of citizens in Augsburg who were called *Mehrer*, below the rank of the proper patriciate. In 1537 he married Sabina Arzt. He was a trusted member of the Paumgartner household, authorized to sign letters on behalf of his master. On 10 March 1541, when Johann Paumgartner's sons signed an agreement of inheritance, Gering signed as witness.

In 1534 and 1535 Gering wrote several letters to Erasmus on behalf of his master (Epp 2900,

2949, 2989) and arranged for some wine to be sent to him as a present (Ep 2989). In Ep 2906 Erasmus instructed Johann *Kohler to hand over his letters to Gering, should his master be out of town. In a similar fashion Gering also corresponded in 1536 and 1537 with Bonifacius *Amerbach. Gering may conceivably be identical with a Christoph Geringer of Auerbach, north-east of Nürnberg, who matriculated at Vienna in the spring of 1503.

BIBLIOGRAPHY: Allen Ep 2900 / AK IV Ep 2066, V Epp 2105, 2152, 2175 / Wilhelm Krag *Die Paumgartner von Nürnberg und Augsburg* (Munich and Leipzig 1919) 72, 82 / *Matrikel Wien* II-1 310   IG

GERMAINE de Foix Queen of Aragon and Naples, c 1488–18 October 1538
Germaine was the daughter of Jean de Foix, viscount of Narbonne and count of Étampes, and of Marie d'Orléans, the sister of *Louis XII of France. Gaston de Foix, the victor of the battle of Ravenna of 1512, was her brother. In the treaty of Blois of 12 October 1505 Germaine was betrothed to her recently widowed granduncle, *Ferdinand II, king of Aragon, who desired a French alliance to strengthen his position in Castile against the pretensions of his son-in-law, Philip the Handsome of *Burgundy. As part of the treaty Louis XII renounced his claim to Naples to Germaine, and Ferdinand agreed to recognize publicly her right to the kingdom – a promise he never kept. With a papal dispensation, the wedding took place in March 1506 at Denia in Valencia. Germaine's only child by Ferdinand, a boy named Juan, died almost immediately after birth in 1509, thus preventing a possible separation of the crowns of Aragon and Castile. After the death of Ferdinand in 1516 Germaine served as vice-regent of Valencia, a post she again held in 1524. In 1519 she married John, margrave of Brandenburg and governor of Valencia, and on his death Ferdinand of Aragon, duke of Calabria. She died at Valencia.

In Ep 1169 Erasmus mentioned a trip Germaine made to Aachen.

BIBLIOGRAPHY: Allen Ep 1169 / DBF XIV 208, 210 / *Nouvelle Biographie générale* (Paris 1853–66) XVIII 48–50 / J.M. Doussinague *Fernando el Católico y Germana de Foix* (Madrid 1944) / J.N.

Hilgarth *The Spanish Kingdoms 1250–1516*
(Oxford 1976–8) II 559–60 and passim / John
Lynch *Spain under the Hapsburgs* (Oxford
1964–9) I 41 / J.M. Batista I Roca in *New
Cambridge Modern History* (Cambridge 1957–70)
I 327   TBD

Gangolf von GEROLDSECK d 1523
The counts of Hohengeroldseck had been
prominent in the Ortenau (the right bank of the
upper Rhine) since the thirteenth century.
Lands and titles lost to the family in the
Bavarian succession war (1504–8) were partially restored by *Maximilian I in 1512. The
'bands of soldiery' Erasmus encountered
while travelling along the Rhine in May 1516
(Ep 412) were probably part of the struggle
between Duke Antoine of *Lorraine and
Hapsburg forces commanded by Gangolf von
Geroldseck. In 1520 the abbots of two monasteries in the vicinity of Lahr besought Erasmus, as councillor to *Charles V, to inter-
cede with the emperor to prevent the count of
Geroldseck from enforcing upon them the
rights of advowson he had regained in 1512
(Ep 1120).
    BIBLIOGRAPHY: Allen and CWE Ep 1120 / ADB
IX 43–4 / NDB VI 316–17 / H. Ullmann *Franz von
Sickingen* (Leipzig 1872)   JAMES D. TRACY

Gentil GERSON (Ep 55, of [spring] 1497)
Gentil Gerson was apparently the nickname of
a herald in the service of *Charles VIII of
France.

Franz GERSTER of Basel, d September 1535
Franz Gerster was a son of Johann, the
influential secretary to the city of Basel who
had rendered valuable services and provided
confidential information to papal diplomats
and the Hapsburg government and thus was in
a position to request favours for his sons as
well as himself. Franz matriculated at Basel in
the spring of 1505 but did not receive his BA
until 1512. *Cantiuncula recommended him to
*Zasius in Freiburg since he wished to obtain a
legal doctorate, but in December 1518 Zasius
refused his candidature because of insufficient
qualifications. Franz became a chaplain at the
Basel cathedral (documented 1525, 1527) and a
canon of Jung St Peter's in Strasbourg. His
brother Paul was in the service of the

Strasbourg merchant Friedrich *Prechter in
1515. After Franz had died Erasmus was
induced to recommend Franz (II) *Baer as a
successor for his canonry at Jung St Peter's (Ep
3065).
    BIBLIOGRAPHY: Allen Ep 3065 / *Matrikel Basel* I
278 / Rudolf Wackernagel *Geschichte der Stadt
Basel* (Basel 1907–54) III 124, 17*–18*
                         MIRIAM U. CHRISMAN & PGB

Franz GESTERS *See Franz* GERSTER

Martin GEUDER of Nürnberg, d 1532
On 19 March 1520 Erasmus wrote to Willibald
*Pirckheimer that he had recently met at
Antwerp the husband of Pirckheimer's sister
(Ep 1085). Juliana Pirckheimer was the wife of
Martin Geuder von Heroldsberg, burgomaster
of Nürnberg; however, he was probably not
the person Erasmus had in mind; cf CWE Ep
1085.

Willem GHEERSHOVEN d 5 April 1547
Willem Gheershoven, also called Willem of
Louvain (Guilelmus Lovaniensis), was a canon
regular of St Augustine at the monastery of
Groenendal at Hoeilaart, near Brussels, which
belonged to the Windesheim congregation. For
twenty years he was in charge of the library,
and his fellow monks remembered him as a
keen emendator of ancient manuscripts. Today
he is known from the seven preserved letters
of his correspondence with another Austin
canon, Maarten *Lips, which date from 1525–6
and deal with two manuscripts of St Augustine
in the Groenendal library. One of them recalls
that as a young man Erasmus had visited
Groenendal and its library and had astonished
his hosts by studying the two Augustine
manuscripts day and night (Allen I 590).
    In July 1524 Erasmus meant to write to
Gheershoven, whose learning and sincerity he
had not forgotten, by way of Maarten Lips,
and in June 1527 a letter was actually sent to
him in this way (Epp 1473, 1837). Gheershoven
may be identical with Wilhelmus Gherkoven of
Hasselt, fifty kilometers east of Louvain, who
matriculated at Louvain on 27 February 1495,
being too poor to be charged his fees and too
young to swear the customary oath.
    BIBLIOGRAPHY: Allen Ep 1473 / W. Lourdaux
Moderne devotie en christelijk humanisme: de

geschiedenis van Sint Maarten te Leuven van 1433 tot het einde der XVIe eeuw (Louvain 1967) 215–17, 226–8, 293, 300–1 / *Matricule de Louvain* III-1 116   PGB

Theoderich von GHEL documented 1532
Theoderich von Ghel (Gehl, Geel, Gele) is mentioned in Ep 2687 of July 1532 as a canon of Osnabrück sympathetic to humanistic learning. Other than his name nothing about him has been found in the sparse diocesan archives that have escaped destruction.

ROBERT STUPPERICH

Pieter GHERINX documented at Louvain
c 1521–34
Pieter Gherinx (Busconius) was perhaps a native of 's Hertogenbosch. In the early 1520s he attended lectures at the Collegium Trilingue at Louvain and seems to have been in contact with Erasmus before the latter left Louvain in 1521. Gherinx was a prolific writer of verse, earning from Erasmus the nickname of 'Metrarius.' After graduating MA and licentiate of law, Gherinx opened a legal practice in Louvain but also continued to write curious, though inadequate, verse, which later earned him a contemptuous mention on the part of the accomplished Latin scholar Petrus Nannius. He published a selection of verses in *Metrariolus vel Busconianus* (Louvain: R. Rescius 25 August 1534; NK 2586). Gherinx also took an interest in theological questions and discovered errors not only in the work of Cornelius *Agrippa of Nettesheim but also in that of Jan *Driedo.
In 1533 *Goclenius had occasion to remind Erasmus of his old acquaintance with Gherinx (Ep 2851).

BIBLIOGRAPHY: Allen Ep 2851 / de Vocht CTL II 208–9, III 116, 142–3, and passim   PGB

Girolamo GHINUCCI of Siena, d 3 July 1541
Girolamo Ghinucci (de Genutiis) was from a Sienese banking family. He became canon of the cathedral of Siena, secretary to *Julius II at the fifth Lateran council, and on 16 October 1512 bishop of Ascoli. After serving as prefect of the papal chancery, Ghinucci was appointed auditor of the apostolic camera by *Leo x on 15 May 1514. During the summer of 1518 Leo entrusted him with the preliminary investiga-

tion of Martin *Luther, whom he cited unsuccessfully to appear in Rome within sixty days (August 1518). In a consistory held on 9 January 1520 Ghinucci attacked Frederick of *Saxony as an enemy of the clergy and of the whole Christian religion.
On 30 April 1520 Leo x and Giulio de' Medici (*Clement VII) sent Ghinucci to England to investigate the foreign policy of Cardinal Thomas *Wolsey and the spread of Lutheran ideas in England. As nuncio he was present at Wolsey's burning of Lutheran books in May 1521. On 26 September 1522 he received the bishopric of Worcester, one of the English appointments usually given to Italian agents, but he had to share the revenues with Wolsey. Dispatched by *Henry VIII to Spain as his representative, Ghinucci attracted the attention of the newly elected *Adrian VI and became one of his closest advisers. He became the bishop of Malta on 10 September 1523. While returning to England in May 1525 he was taken prisoner by German peasants, to whom he had to pay a ransom of twelve hundred crowns. In September 1526 Clement VII used Ghinucci to solicit the support of Henry against *Charles v. Wolsey employed him until 1529 to search for books and to obtain copies of Greek manuscripts from Italian libraries. Ghinucci undertook delicate diplomatic missions as English ambassador to both Charles v in Spain and Clement VII in Rome, where he played an important part in the divorce negotiations. Despite Henry VIII's requests, Clement VII refused to make Ghinucci a cardinal because of imperial opposition. During 1530 he was in charge of obtaining favourable opinions on the divorce from Italian universities. As a result of Henry's break with Rome in 1534, he was deprived of the see of Worcester.
Returning to papal service, Ghinucci was raised to the cardinalate by *Paul III on 21 May 1535. For the next six years he served on various reform commissions and on committees to call a council. Besides earning a reputation as a conservative curialist, he objected to the foundation of the Jesuits because he was suspicious of their novel forms of asceticism. On 7 July 1537 he acquired the bishopric of Cavaillon in France and on 14 June 1538 that of Tropea in Italy. Despite imperial animosity

based on his strong advocacy of Henry VIII against *Catherine of Aragon, Paul III employed him to negotiate between *Francis I and Charles V in 1538 and 1539. His register as bishop of Worcester survives. He died at Rome and was buried in San Clemente. Piotr *Tomicki informed Erasmus of Ghinucci's elevation to the cardinalate (Ep 3066).

BIBLIOGRAPHY: Allen Ep 3066 / G. Opitz in LThK IV 882 / A. Ferrari in *Enciclopedia cattolica* (Vatican City 1949–54) VI 301–2 / Cosenza II 1593 / A. Ciaconius *Vitae et res gestae pontificium romanorum et S.R.E. cardinalium* (Rome 1677) III 569–70 / L. Cardella *Memorie storiche de' cardinali* (Rome 1793) IV 147–8 / J.-P. Migne *Dictionnaire des cardinaux* (Paris 1857) 984 / Eubel III 23, 119, 161, 244, 320, 334 / P. Kalkoff *Forschungen zu Luthers römischen Prozess* (Rome 1905) 50 / Pastor VI–XII / H. Jedin *A History of the Council of Trent* trans E. Graf (London 1957–   ) I 170 and passim / W.E. Wilkie *The Cardinal Protectors of England: Rome and the Tudors before the Reformation* (Cambridge 1974) 85–6 and passim / G. de C. Parmiter *The King's Great Matter: A Study of Anglo-Papal Relations, 1527–1534* (London 1967) passim / *Nuntiaturberichte aus Deutschland, 1533–59* ed W. Friedensburg and L. Cardaunus (Gotha-Berlin 1892–1910) I–VI / *Calendar of State Papers, Spanish* I–V / *Calendar of State Papers, Milan* I / *Calendar of State Papers, Venetian* I–IV   EDWARD ENGLISH

GHISBERT documented at Saint-Omer, 1499–1521
Ghisbert (Ghysbertus) may probably be identified with Ghisbert or Ghysbrecht Hessels, who was appointed physician to Philip the Handsome, duke of *Burgundy, (1503) and surgeon to the future *Charles V (1513). Ghisbert lived in Saint-Omer from 1499 (Ep 95) or earlier as physician to the town and the abbey of St Bertin (Ep 273). Still active and alert in 1521 (Ep 1211), he was a close friend to *Antonius of Luxembourg, steward of St Bertin and canon of Saint-Omer, and also to the Franciscan Jean *Vitrier and to Erasmus himself, who felt free to make a joke at the expense of his wife (Ep 673). It is surprising and unfortunate that Ghisbert has left no trace in the local sources, for his profession and his piety place him right in the centre of the town's material and spiritual life.

According to Juliusz Domanski (ASD I-4 147–9) Ghisbert may not only have asked Erasmus to write the *Encomium medicinae* for him (Allen I 18) but may also have delivered this oration, in the autumn of 1499, to an academic audience in Paris. The date of Ghisbert's visit to Paris (Ep 95) does, in fact, coincide with the composition of the *Encomium*; unfortunately we know nothing about the purpose of his journey. If some passages of the *Encomium* seem to suggest a speaker invited from outside Paris, these might also be explained as rhetorical fiction. However that may be, the friendship with Ghisbert was bound to stimulate Erasmus' interest in medical questions, an interest he was to display so often after the composition of the *Encomium*. In the same way his interest in Origen may be traced back to his friendship with Vitrier, who held Ghisbert too under the spell of his vigorous spirituality (Ep 1211). No evidence has been produced so far to show that Ghisbert was a kinsman of Jacob *Hessele.

BIBLIOGRAPHY: Allen and CWE Ep 95 / L.P. Gachard *Collection des voyages des souverains des Pays-Bas* (Brussels 1874–82) I 364 / *Correspondance de Maximilien I et Marguerite d'Autriche* ed A.J.G. Le Glay (Paris 1839) II 132
ANDRÉ GODIN

Gian Matteo GIBERTI of Palermo, 20 September 1495–30 December 1543
Gian Matteo, the son of Franco Giberti, a Genoese grain merchant and later a curial official and cardinal, was born out of wedlock at Palermo. Little is known of his education other than that he studied law and loved literature, especially poetry. He became the secretary of Cardinal Giulio de' Medici, the future *Clement VII, and was legitimized by *Leo X on 20 December 1514. He received a number of posts in the curia, including those of notary of the apostolic chancery and abbreviator, as well as enjoying the revenues of numerous abbeys and benefices. In 1519 he became secretary to Leo X and one of his most trusted advisers. On the death of Leo and the election of *Adrian VI in 1521 both Giulio de' Medici and Giberti were out of favour at Rome. The cardinal sent Giberti on visits to Alfonso I d'*Este, *Charles V, and Cardinal Thomas *Wolsey to win friends and support. Immedi-

ately after the election of Giulio to the papacy in November 1523 Giberti was named datary, in charge of distributing benefices, and in 1524 he became bishop of Verona. He was also one of Clement VII's principal political advisers, promoting an anti-imperial, pro-French policy as the means of securing the independence of Italy and of the church. His bitter opponent was the imperialist Cardinal Nikolaus von *Schönberg. After the French were crushed at Pavia in February 1525 Giberti was instrumental in fashioning the anti-imperial League of Cognac in 1526. His manoeuvres ended in the disastrous Sack of Rome of May 1527, and he himself was turned over to German mercenaries as a hostage. After being threatened with execution he managed to flee his captors and joined Clement VII at Orvieto in December 1527. However he was widely held responsible for the disasters of the preceding year, and in 1528 he left the curia for Verona.

Even before 1527 Giberti had been a member of the religious confraternity known as the Oratory of Divine Love and had taken a keen interest in the affairs of his diocese; now he dedicated himself to pastoral reform, leaving Verona only for brief intervals. In 1534 he served as nuncio to Venice, in 1536 he was a member of a commission of nine cardinals and prelates which drafted the important *Consilium de emendanda ecclesia* (Rome, Milan 1538), and in 1537 he made a short trip to France as legate with Cardinal Reginald *Pole. At Verona he sought to recall the clergy to the dignity of the ancient church by encouraging the study of the Gospels and Pauline Epistles. In 1528 he established a Latin and Greek press in his episcopal palace from which issued patristic works beginning with Chrysostom's commentaries on the Epistles of Paul in three volumes (1529). Giberti also attempted to enforce a strict code of conduct on the clergy. Although the Venetian government and the canons of his own cathedral challenged his authority as bishop, he surmounted these obstacles and left behind an important collection of reforming decrees and a model of episcopal action which would later be an inspiration to Carlo Borromeo, Gabriele Paleotti, and other bishops of the Italian Catholic Reformation.

In his days at Rome Giberti was a patron of the arts and letters and frequented the Roman

Gian Matteo Giberti, by Bernardino India

Academy which met at the villa of Johannes *Corycius. Pietro *Bembo, Girolamo *Vida, Lazzaro *Bonamico, and others addressed poems to him, and a number of books were dedicated to him, including several printed by Francesco Giulio *Calvo. His learned friends included Girolamo *Aleandro, Romolo Quirino *Amaseo, Jacopo *Sadoleto, and Reginald Pole. Given Giberti's cultural background – and his desire to enlist Erasmus in the battle against Martin *Luther – it is hardly surprising that on 24 April 1524, shortly after he became datary, Giberti wrote to the humanist praising him and offering his assistance (Ep 1443A). On 2 September 1524 Erasmus sent Giberti a copy of his *De libero arbitrio* against Luther and asked him to help obtain confirmation of the rights of the University of Louvain to nominate scholars to certain vacant benefices (Ep 1481). Giberti soon replied that Clement VII had already guaranteed the university's privileges (Ep 1509). Erasmus also asked the datary to protect him against Nicolaas *Baechem and other enemies (Ep 1481, 1506), but in this Giberti was ultimately less successful in satisfying Erasmus' wishes. In 1525 Giberti, acting for

Tiedemann Giese

Clement VII, sent Theodoricus *Hezius to silence Erasmus' detractors in the theological faculty at Louvain (Ep 1589A). Hezius, however, was soon won over by Baechem and Jacobus *Latomus and sent secret reports to Rome recommending that the opponents of Erasmus not be chastised publicly. Although Giberti remained friendly towards Erasmus, whom he described as the best antidote against the Lutheran poison (Ep 1650A), he accepted Hezius' advice for the sake of tranquility. By May 1526 Erasmus had heard of Hezius' mission and how its purpose had been undermined with the approval of Giberti (Ep 1717, 1735, 1747). In his last known letter to Giberti, dated 21 May 1526, Erasmus complained of the continuing attacks of his enemies, who disregarded papal censures, and once again begged the prelate for support (Ep 1716). In July 1527 Erasmus was informed of a rumour that Giberti had died at Rome (Ep 1848), but by 1530 he had heard reports of the bishop's exemplary life at Verona and of his Greek edition of Chrysostom (Epp 2340, 2379, 2648). Having recently completed his own

edition of the Father, Erasmus tried to obtain a copy (Ep 2526).

BIBLIOGRAPHY: Allen Ep 1443A / L. Bopp in LThK IV 885 / Pastor VIII–XII *ad indicem* / Adriano Prosperi *Tra evangelismo e contro-riforma: G.M. Giberti (1495–1543)* (Rome 1969) / de Vocht CTL II 267–82 and passim   TBD

Tiedemann GIESE of Gdansk, 1 June 1480–28 October 1550

Tiedemann Bartholomäus Giese (Gisius) was the son of Albert, burgomaster of Gdansk (Danzig), and the nephew of Moritz *Ferber, bishop of Warmia (Ermland). From 1492 he studied at Leipzig, obtaining his BA in 1495 and his MA in 1498. In 1504 he became a canon of Warmia in Frombork (Frauenburg), where he resided for the greater part of his adult life. From 1512 he was rector of the parish of Steblewo (Stüblau), near Gdansk, and from 1515 to 1527 also of the parish of Sts Peter and Paul in Gdansk. The Warmia chapter appointed him chancellor and *custos*, or administrator of its properties. As such he advocated close co-operation between Warmia and the Polish crown. Bishop Ferber would have liked to name Giese his coadjutor, but in the end he had to appoint Johannes *Dantiscus. When Dantiscus succeeded Ferber as bishop in 1538, Giese received the see of Chełmno (Kulm) as Dantiscus' successor and resided in Lubawa (Löbau). On 20 May 1549 he succeeded Dantiscus as bishop of Warmia and moved for his remaining days to the episcopal residence of Lidzbark (Heilsberg).

Giese professed a liberal theology but never quite came to side with the Protestants. He wrote against the Lutheran theologian Johann Briesmann a *Flosculorum Lutheranorum ...* ἀνθηλογικόν (Cracow: H. Wietor 1525). However, in 1536 he sought the friendship of *Melanchthon. In his unpublished 'Hyper-aspisticon' (now lost) he defended the helio-centric theory of his close friend and fellow canon in Frombork, Nicolaus Copernicus, apparently pointing out that Erasmus had expressed a highly favourable view of Copernicus. Copernicus, in turn, mentioned Giese's persistent support in the dedicatory preface of his *De revolutionibus orbium coelestium* (Nürnberg: J. Petreius 1543). Giese's last work, 'De

regno Christi' in three volumes, remained
unfinished. Through his nephew Eberhard
*Rogge he sent Erasmus a manuscript of it,
hoping to obtain a favourable opinion. The accompanying letter (Ep 3112) expressed Giese's
warm admiration for Erasmus, but the latter
was by then too ill to give the book his full
attention (Ep 3120) and died soon afterwards.
The work, which again exposed Giese's liberal
views, was classified as heretical by Stanislaus
*Hosius, his successor in the see of Warmia.
The manuscript later disappeared in Sweden.
Jan Brozek (Broscius, 1585–1652), who mentioned Erasmus' favourable judgment of
Copernicus recorded in Giese's 'Hyperaspis-
ticon,' also published two of Giese's letters in
his *Epistolae ad naturam ordinatarum figurarum
plenius intelligendum pertinentes* (Cracow 1615)
and was in possession of others now lost.

BIBLIOGRAPHY: Allen Ep 3112 / NDB VI 379 /
Melanchthons Briefwechsel II Ep 1713 / Andrzej
Kempfi 'Erasme et la vie intellectuelle en
Warmie au temps de Nicolas Copernic' *Collo-
quia Erasmiana Turonensia* I 397–406 / de Vocht
Dantiscus 173 and passim.

Some further notes were kindly supplied to
us by Professor Edward Rosen of the City
University of New York.   IG & PGB

Margaret GIGGS d 6 July 1570
Margaret Giggs (Gigs, Gygia), the foster-
daughter of Sir Thomas *More, was born by
1508 and was brought up as part of the More
family. She was related to More in some way,
though the degree and nature of relationship is
still unknown. She was educated along with
the More children and was a notable member of
the 'school' of More; she is mentioned by
*Vives in the *Institutio feminae christianae* (I iv),
as well as by John Coxe in *The Debate* (1550),
which extolled the superiority of learned
women in England over those in France. She
married John *Clement in 1530 and had three
children: Winifred (who married William Rastell), Thomas, and Margaret. She is included in
the *Holbein drawing of the More household
and is mentioned in *The Twelve Jests of the
Widow Edith*, published by John Rastell in 1525.
Having followed her husband into exile a
second time in 1563, Margaret died at
Mechelen.

Margaret Giggs, by Hans Holbein the Younger

Erasmus mentioned Margaret Giggs together with the More daughters in Epp 1233,
1402.

BIBLIOGRAPHY: Allen Ep 999 / DNB IV 489 /
R.J. Schoeck 'Two notes on Margaret Gigs
Clement, foster-daughter of Sir Thomas More'
Notes and Queries 194 (10 December 1949)
532–3 / R.J. Schoeck 'Thomas Gygges, Tudor
Lawyer' *Notes and Queries* 195 (24 June 1950)
269–71 / R.J. Schoeck in *New Catholic Encyclo-
pedia* (New York 1967–78) IX 1142 / E.E.
Reynolds *Margaret Roper* (London 1960) 10,
14, 47, 51–2, and passim   R.J. SCHOECK

Silvestro GIGLI of Lucca, 1463–18 April 1521
Silvestro Gigli was born at Lucca. He was a
nephew of Giovanni Gigli, the ambassador of
*Henry VII of England at Rome and in 1497
bishop of Worcester. Silvestro assisted his
uncle in his diplomatic duties and when he
died in 1498 succeeded him as ambassador and
on 24 December 1498 as bishop of Worcester,
by provision of *Alexander VI. He was en-
throned by proxy in April 1499. He soon
entered into a bitter personal rivalry with

Adriano *Castellesi, papal collector for England. Their clashes, which weakened English interests in Rome, were settled for a time by Castellesi's flight from Rome in 1507.

Meanwhile in 1505 Pope *Julius II sent Gigli to England as papal nuncio with tokens of his favour for Henry VII, and Gigli remained at the English court. In 1509 *Henry VIII sent Christopher Bainbridge, archbishop of York and later cardinal, as ambassador to Rome. Gigli followed in 1512 as ambassador to the fifth Lateran council and assistant to Bainbridge. Although relations between Bainbridge and Gigli were initially good, they soon became enemies, as Gigli came increasingly to serve the interests of Thomas *Wolsey, who was then rising rapidly in influence in England and who viewed Bainbridge as his rival. When Bainbridge died suddenly on 14 July 1514 poison was suspected, and one of his servants confessed under torture to the alleged crime, naming Gigli as its instigator. An inquiry failed to uncover new evidence against Gigli, who was absolved of all blame. Gigli continued to serve as the ambassador of England in Rome, and as the agent of Wolsey. He was instrumental in securing the cardinalate (1515) and legatine powers (1518) for his master. In 1517 and 1518 he collaborated in the final disgrace of Castellesi and became papal collector for England. However, in the last years of his life he lost influence at the papal court because of his subservience to Wolsey. He failed to obtain promotion to the rank of cardinal at least in part because Wolsey and Henry VIII did not press his case.

As English ambassador to Rome Gigli was extremely helpful to Erasmus on a number of occasions. In 1516 and 1517 he helped procure dispensations from *Leo x allowing Erasmus to set aside the habit of the canons regular and to hold more than one ecclesiastical benefice (Epp 521, 649). In 1520 he helped Erasmus obtain a papal diploma, probably permitting him to eat meat during Lent (Epp 1079, 1080). In January 1521 Erasmus dedicated his paraphrase of the Epistle to the Hebrews to Gigli (Ep 1181).

BIBLIOGRAPHY: Allen Ep 521 / DNB VII 1190–1 / D.S. Chambers *Cardinal Bainbridge in the Court of Rome* (Oxford 1965) 7–9 and passim / William E. Wilkie *The Cardinal Protectors of England:* *Rome and the Tudors before the Reformation* (Cambridge 1974) 24, 51, and passim   TBD

Pierre GILLES of Albi, 1490–1555
Little is known about the youth of Pierre Gilles (Gyllius) of Albi. He is said to have taken an early interest in ichthyology and to have studied fish along the coasts of France and Italy. He also edited Elio Antonio de *Nebrija's *Dictionarium oppidorum* (Paris n d) and Lorenzo *Valla's *Historiae Ferdinandi regis Aragoniae* (Paris: S. de Colines 1521). Around that time he became mentor to the young Georges d'*Armagnac, (Ep 2665), to whom his *Lexicon graecolatinum* (Basel: V. Curio 1532) was dedicated. In the following year he published a translation of Theodoret's commentary on the twelve minor prophets (Lyon 1533) and of texts by Aelian and others: *Ex Aeliani historia ... libri* xvi *de vi et natura animalium*, with his own additions and with his *Liber unus de Galicis et Latinis nominibus piscium* (Lyon: S. Gryphius 1533), the latter work dedicated to *Francis I at the suggestion of Georges d'Armagnac. As a result Gilles was put in a position to visit the Ottoman empire, since cultural missions of this kind could only help to improve the European image of France's political ally. After many adventures he eventually returned to France in 1553 with the ambassador, Gabriel d'Aramon. He died at Rome, again in the service of Cardinal d'Armagnac, who had also secured his appointment as prior of Durenque (Département Aveyron). Two fruits of his sojourn in Constantinople, *De Bosporo Thracio* and *De topographia Constantinopoleos et illius antiquitatibus*, the most successful of all his works, were published posthumously (Lyon G. de Rovillius 1561).

BIBLIOGRAPHY: Allen 2665 / Louis Delaruelle *Répertoire ... de la correspondance de Guillaume Budé* (Toulouse-Paris 1907, repr 1962) Epp 135, 167 / *Nouvelle Biographie universelle* ed A. and H. Firmin-Didot (Paris 1852–66) xx 542–3
MICHEL REULOS & PGB

Pierre or Peter GILLES *See also Pieter* GILLIS

Frans GILLIS of Antwerp, documented in 1526
Frans, a son of Nicolaas (I) *Gillis and a brother

of Erasmus' friend Pieter *Gillis, is known only
from the correspondence of Erasmus. In the
spring of 1526 he visited the Frankfurt book fair
and handed to Johann *Froben, or his representative, a sum of money for payment to
Erasmus, which had been kept in trust by
Pieter Gillis (Epp 1654, 1681, 1682, 1696). As
Erasmus knew as early as December 1525 that
Frans would take his bags to the fair, one may
perhaps assume that he was a merchant who
attended the fair with some regularity. It
would seem that in the autumn he travelled
again to Frankfurt, or even to Basel; Erasmus
expected him to bring linen, books or manuscripts, and the remainder of his money, while
on his return he took a bundle of letters to
Louvain (Epp 1740, 1765).
    BIBLIOGRAPHY: de Vocht CTL II 67
          MARCEL A. NAUWELAERTS & PGB

Gillis GILLIS of Antwerp, documented
1510–d circa 1534
Erasmus' friend Pieter *Gillis had a brother
who was canon and precentor of Our Lady's in
Antwerp. Erasmus sent him greetings in 1526
(Ep 1740) and wrote to him in January 1534,
after the death of Pieter (Ep 2896). In February
1535 Jan van *Campen informed Johannes
*Dantiscus that their common friends Pieter
Gillis and his brother, the precentor of
Antwerp, had both died in the preceding year.
Henry de Vocht identified the latter with one
Aegidius Nicolai (thus called after his father's
Christian name) who was a canon and became
the precentor in 1510.
  · BIBLIOGRAPHY: de Vocht CTL II 67 / de Vocht
Dantiscus 234   PGB

Michiel GILLIS of Antwerp, documented
1520–4
Michiel was probably a kinsman of Erasmus'
friend Pieter *Gillis. He is mentioned in 1520 by
Cornelius *Grapheus as a young citizen of
Antwerp who had for some time been among
the secretaries of *Maximilian I. He served
*Charles v in the same capacity. In March 1524
Erasmus had either recently met him or
received a letter from him (Ep 1432). In the same
year he was present at the diet of Nürnberg,
and Erasmus expected him to take some letters
back with him to Spain. He was in Madrid on

19 December 1524 when he wrote to *Spalatinus to introduce himself.
    BIBLIOGRAPHY: Allen Ep 1432 / *Correspondenz
des Kaisers Karl v.* ed Karl Lanz (Leipzig
1844–6) I Ep 55   MARCEL A. NAUWELAERTS

Nicolaas (I) GILLIS of Antwerp, c 1438–
c November 1517
Nicolaas (Claes, Nicolaus Egidius) was the
father of Erasmus' good friend Pieter *Gillis.
He was a candlemaker and master of the
mercers' guild of Antwerp and for some time
held the office of second treasurer of Antwerp.
By 1505, if not earlier, Erasmus had met him
personally (Ep 184); he showed great respect
for him (Ep 476) and after his death wrote a
sincere letter in his praise and memory (Epp
712, 715; cf Epp 726, 794). Greetings were
exchanged between them in Epp 491, 515, 526.
    BIBLIOGRAPHY: Allen Ep 715
          MARCEL A. NAUWELAERTS

Nicolaas (II) GILLIS of Antwerp, born c 1515
Late in 1517 Erasmus mentioned Nicolaas, a
son – apparently then the only one – of his
friend Pieter *Gillis (Ep 715). Nicolaas must
have been born some time after his father's
marriage to Cornelia *Sandrien and before the
arrival of a daughter by about January 1517 (Ep
515). In April 1518 Erasmus sent greetings to
Pieter's children (Ep 818). Unlike his younger
brothers Nicolaas is not mentioned later on.
          MARCEL A. NAUWELAERTS

Pieter GILLIS of Antwerp, c 1486–6 (or 11)
November 1533
Pieter Gillis (Gilles, Aegidius), a son of
Nicolaas (I) *Gillis, learnt his Latin in the
chapter school of Our Lady's at Antwerp and
by 1503 was a corrector in the press of Dirk
*Martens in his native city. In June 1504 he
matriculated at the University of Louvain;
subsequently he received a bachelor of law
degree at Orléans on 11 April 1512. Meanwhile, he had entered the service of the city of
Antwerp on 28 November 1509 and in 1512 was
appointed clerk to the city. In July 1514 he
married Cornelia *Sandrien, who bore him
nine children. After her death in 1526 he took a
second wife, Maria *Denys, who died late in
1529 or early in 1530. A last child was born from

Pieter Gillis, by Quentin Metsys

his third marriage with Katheline Draeckx. Finally, in 1532 he retired from his post as clerk. At Antwerp Gillis lived in his paternal house 'De Spiegel' on the Grand'Place and Oude Beurs, where he played host to Erasmus, Thomas *More, and many others.

Erasmus must have met Gillis in Martens' press, and early in 1505 they were corresponding (Ep 184). Soon Gillis counted among the closest friends of Erasmus, who stayed often in his house at Antwerp. Later on, however, financial issues cast a cloud over their warm relations, and from 1525 Erasmus *Schets replaced Gillis as the man who looked after the sums of money Erasmus was receiving or investing at Antwerp (Ep 1654). The correspondence between Erasmus and Gillis continued, however, until 1531 (Ep 2512), or possibly longer, although no letters survive after Ep 2260 of February 1530. Of thirty-one preserved letters in their correspondence only six were written by Gillis. In 1512 Erasmus involved his friend in the negotiations with Franz *Birckmann and Josse *Bade about a new edition of the *Adagia* (Ep 264); two years later when leaving England he had his baggage

directed to Gillis (Ep 294), and from Basel he dedicated to him the first edition of the *Parabolae* (Ep 312). In May 1515 he sent Gillis a short account of his journey to London (Ep 332), and in September he announced from Basel a new edition of the *Enchiridion* and reported on progress made in preparing the *Novum instrumentum* (Ep 356). Erasmus was again at Antwerp in the summer of 1515, when he composed his reply to Maarten *Dorp (Ep 337) and when, amid contacts with both Gillis and Erasmus, Thomas More composed a large part of his *Utopia*, in which Gillis appears as a speaker in the dialogue. He also wrote a preface to it. He and his wife played host to Erasmus again in the autumn of 1516 (Epp 476, 477). In November Erasmus invited Gillis to Brussels so that he might meet *Tunstall and announced that More's *Utopia* was in the printer's hands (Ep 491). Gillis in turn, in his first two preserved letters of early 1517 (Epp 515, 526), invited Erasmus to his house again – an invitation that was quickly accepted. Throughout this year, Gillis' poor health and its possible causes and remedies take up much space in the correspondence between him, Erasmus, and More (Ep 584, CWE 5 index); a more gratifying topic, however, is the diptych with the portraits of Gillis and Erasmus which the two friends commissioned from Quinten *Metsys as a gift for Thomas More (Epp 654, 681, 684). Towards the end of the year, Erasmus' letters deal largely with the final illness and death of Gillis' father (Epp 702, 708, 712, 715).

In 1516 and 1517 Gillis had rendered his friend an important service by editing two collections of Erasmus' letters (CWE 4 348–52). A casual critical remark (Ep 730) notwithstanding, it is clear that Erasmus was pleased with the response and continued to have friends edit his correspondence. When More's *Utopia* was being reprinted in Basel Erasmus caused Gillis' preface to be omitted (Ep 732); on the other hand, their references to financial matters, especially with regard to Erasmus' English benefice (Epp 712), and also Erasmus' frank language concerning the Antwerp physician Henricus *Afinius and his promised gift show that Gillis still enjoyed his full confidence. Gillis' prominent position among Erasmus' friends is also indicated by the frequency with which he is referred to, greeted, or praised or assistance for him is sought in the letters exchanged between Erasmus and his other friends. From the time of Erasmus' final departure from the Netherlands in 1521 financial transactions form the principal subject of his contacts with Gillis, and even after 1525, when Schets had taken Gillis' place as Erasmus' agent, Erasmus did not question the sincerity of Gillis' friendship for him (Epp 1654, 2260). It should also be borne in mind that our knowledge of their correspondence is by no means complete. In Ep 849 Gillis mentioned four of his letters which Erasmus had not yet answered; three of these four are now lost. In fact, between June 1518 (Ep 849) and April 1526 (Ep 1696) not a single letter they exchanged has been preserved. It may be that Erasmus destroyed some letters because of his dissatisfaction with the way Gillis took care of his money or because they referred to the Lutheran agitation at Antwerp in terms Erasmus later thought to be compromising. As early as June 1522 Erasmus had heard to his dismay that Gillis had been arrested as a Lutheran (Epp 1293, 1296). However, the information he had received no doubt concerned not Gillis but his colleague in the city hall of Antwerp, Cornelius *Grapheus, and on 26 June 1522 *Goclenius stated that the story Erasmus had heard was no more than a malicious rumour (Ep 1296).

In his last preserved letter (Ep 2089) Gillis invited his old friend once again to come and stay in his house; evidently he knew about Erasmus' decision to leave Basel because of the Reformation there. However, they were not to meet again. There is no record of how Erasmus reacted to Gillis' death, although in 1535 he mentioned him when listing the friends who had passed away (Ep 3013). His attitude then would seem in noticeable contrast with his affection in earlier days when he had written his *Epithalamium* in Gillis' honour (*Colloquia* ASD I-3 411–16); as recently as 1530 he had composed epitaphs for Gillis' wives (Reedijk poems 126–8).

The list of works edited for Martens by Pieter Gillis includes the letters of *Poliziano (Antwerp 1510), the *Opuscula* of Rodolphus *Agricola (Antwerp 1511), Aesop's fables in Latin translation (Antwerp 1513), two collec-

tions of Erasmus' letters (Louvain 1516 and 1517), and More's *Utopia* (Louvain 1516). He also edited a juridical work, *Summae sive argumenta legum* (Louvain 1517), of which a manuscript is preserved in the library of the University of Leiden (MS BPL 191 ba). It was re-edited by Gerard Meersman as *Institutionum summarium* (The Hague 1743 and 1751; cf R. Dekkers *Bibliotheca Belgica juridica*, Brussels 1951, 62). Two circumstantial publications by Gillis are his *Threnodia ... in funus imperatoris ... Maximiliani* (Antwerp 1519) and *Hypotheses sive argumenta spectaculorum* (Antwerp 1520) in honour of *Charles v. No copies are known today of a work by Gillis and Cornelius Grapheus published posthumously, *Enchiridion principis ac magistrati christiani* (Cologne 1541). Apart from his correspondence with Erasmus, we have three letters addressed to Gillis by More (Rogers Epp 25, 41a, 47) and Gillis' prefatory letter for the first edition of More's *Utopia*, addressed to Jérôme de *Busleyden (de Vocht *Busleyden* Ep 80). There is also a letter to Gillis by *Beatus Rhenanus (BRE Ep 426).

Gillis' portrait by Metsys, now in Longford Castle, is reproduced in CWE 4 371; an ancient copy is in Antwerp. Three other portraits of Gillis in Rotterdam, London, and Oldenburg are mentioned in W. Müller-Wulckow *Vier Bildnisse des Petrus Aegidius von Gossart, Massys, Dürer, Holbein* (Oldenburg n d).

BIBLIOGRAPHY: Allen Ep 184 / BNB VII 780–3 / NBW IV 4–8 / *Matricule de Louvain* III-1 276 / *Matricule d'Orléans* II-1 217–19 / J. Britz 'Aegidius Pierre' *Messager des sciences historiques* (Ghent 1864) 181–208 / F. Prims in *Antwerpiensia* 10 (1937) 176–99 and 12 (1939) 159–64 / M.A. Nauwelaerts in *Moreana* 15–16 (1967) 83–6 / M.A. Nauwelaerts in *Antwerpen: Tijdschrift der stad Antwerpen* 15 (1969) 38–46 / Y. Charlier *Erasme et l'amitié d'après sa correspondance* (Liège 1977) 209–12 and passim
MARCEL A. NAUWELAERTS

GILLIS of Delft See Gillis van DELFT

Aymon de GINGINS c 1465–June 1537
According to Ep 1413 Erasmus had sent a letter to Geneva for Philibert de *Lucinge to forward to an unnamed abbot. Allen suggested this might refer to Aymon de Gingins, seigneur of

Divonne, abbot of Bonmont, west of Nyon on
Lake Geneva. Gingins was acquainted with
the Lucinge family.

BIBLIOGRAPHY: Allen Ep 1413 / Henri Naef
Les Origines de la réforme à Genève 2nd ed
(Geneva 1968) I 63, 316–18, and passim / Henri
Vuilleumier *Histoire de l'église réformée du pays
de Vaud* (Lausanne 1927–37) I 198   PGB

Benedetto GIOVIO of Como, c 1471–c 1545
Benedetto Giovio (Jovius), the elder brother of
the historian Paolo (1483–1552), bishop of
Nocera, was born at Como. He studied Greek
by himself but went to Milan to learn how it
was pronounced from Demetrius *Chalcondyles. He spent almost all of his life at Como,
where he practised law – not medicine, as
Erasmus believed (Ep 1535). He was married
and had at least five children. He wrote a
history of Como to 1532 (Venice 1629), as well
as poems and antiquarian studies found in the
Biblioteca Ambrosiana of Milan, the Biblioteca
Comunale of Como, and other collections. His
letters, addressed to *Charles v, Pope *Paul III,
Andrea *Alciati, Pietro *Bembo, and numerous
other important figures, were published by
Santo Monti in 1891.

In 1525, prompted by his relative Paolo
*Benzi, Giovio wrote to Erasmus concerning
the grammatical correctness of his interpretation of John 8:25 and other matters (Ep 1634A).
Erasmus replied with Ep 1635.

BIBLIOGRAPHY: Allen Ep 1635 / *La Correspondance d'Erasme* ed A. Gerlo et al (Brussels
1967–) VI 584–7 / Ida Calabi Limentani 'La
lettera di Benedetto Giovio ad Erasmo' *Acme* 25
(1972) 5–37 / P.O. Kristeller *Iter Italicum*
(London-Leiden 1965–) I 46–8 and passim, II
70 and passim / Santo Monti 'Lettere di
Benedetto Giovio' *Periodico della societa storica
comense* 8 (1891) 91–259 / Paolo Giovio *Opera:
Epistolae* I and II ed G.G. Ferrero (Rome
1956–) I Ep 43 and passim, II Ep 346   TBD

Agostino GIUSTINIANI of Genoa,
c 1470–1536
Pantaleone Giustiniani (Justinianus) was born
into a patrician family of Genoa. His grandfather was Andreolo Giustiniani, a humanist
and a friend of Ambrogio Traversari. Pantaleone entered a Dominican house in 1484, but
was withdrawn by his family and sent abroad;

in 1488 he returned definitively to the order,
taking the name Agostino. His vocation for
studies was recognized and encouraged, and
he developed a proficiency in biblical and
cognate languages. For a time he taught in
Bologna. The patronage of his kinsman,
Cardinal Bandinello *Sauli, secured for Giustiniani in 1514 the bishopric of Nebbio, in
Corsica, whence his occasional surname
Nebiensis. His most significant contribution to
biblical studies came in 1516 with the publication of his so-called *Psalterium octuplex*, properly *Psalterium hebraeum, graecum, arabicum et
chaldaeum cum tribus latinis interpretationibus et
glossis* (Genoa: P.P. Porro), bearing a dedication to Pope *Leo x. The volume set in parallel
columns the Massoretic Hebrew, Septuagint,
Arabic, and Aramaic Targum (not the Syriac as
has been alleged), with Latin renderings of all
but the Arabic, and in the eighth column, a
collection of scholia garnered from rabbinic
sources, including the Midrash on the Psalms
and cabbalistic texts. Giustiniani's ambition to
continue the project towards a polyglot Bible
was frustrated by this volume's lack of commercial success and the loss of his patron when
Cardinal Sauli fell into disgrace. Accepting the
invitation of *Francis I (Ep 810), he lectured on
Hebrew in Paris for at least five years
(1517/18–22). A journey to England and the
Netherlands permitted a visit with Erasmus in
Louvain in early autumn 1518. The Paris years
saw a number of publications: additional
Hebraica and translations from the Greek
classics. His death came by shipwreck on a
voyage to visit his diocese. He willed his
library to his native city, but it was ultimately
dispersed.

In the *Apologia ad Fabrum* of 1517 Erasmus
made disparaging reference to Giustiniani's
psalter (LB IX 25C–26A) in the context of
Erasmus' argument with *Lefèvre d'Etaples
over the sense of Psalm 8:6. On the heels of
Giustiniani's visit with him the next year,
Erasmus commented favourably upon the man
(Epp 877, 878, 886), and in a letter to Guillaume
*Budé he expressed regret over his earlier
criticism (Ep 906). However, a few months
later Erasmus was annoyed by a rumour that
Giustiniani was criticizing him (Ep 931).
He complained to the inquisitor Jacob of
*Hoogstraaten that the Inquisition persecuted

Johann *Reuchlin and his friends while over-
looking the faults of Dominicans like Giustiniani (Ep 1006).

Beyond the *Psalterium octuplex*, Giustiniani's
publications include in particular at least two
editions of the Hebrew grammar of Moses
Kimhi (after Giustiniani failed to interest
Johann *Froben of Basel in the text these
appeared in Haguenau in 1519 and Paris in
1520), a Latin translation of Moses Maimon-
ides' *Guide of the Perplexed* (Paris: J. Bade 1520),
and an edition of the *Adversus impios Hebraeos*
(Paris: G. Des Plains 1520) of Porchetus de
Salvaticis, a fourteenth-century Genoan monk.
In later years he completed a description of
Corsica dedicated to Andrea *Doria, and an
edition of the *Annali* of Genoa which appeared
posthumously (Genoa: A. Bellono 1537). His
pride of homeland stands revealed, too, in a
striking gloss to Psalm 19:4 ('in fines orbis
terrae verba eorum') in his 1516 *Psalterium*: the
exploits of Columbus, his fellow-countryman,
are recited as evidence of the fulfilment of the
biblical text.

BIBLIOGRAPHY: Allen and CWE Ep 810 / AK II
Epp 643, 644 / L. Delaruelle 'Le séjour d'A.
Giustiniani à Paris (1518–1522)' *Revue du 16e
siècle* 12 (1925) 322–37 / F. Secret 'Les gram-
maires hébraïques d'Augustinus Justinianus'
Archivum Fratrum Praedicatorum 33 (1963) 269–
79 / F. Secret *Les Kabbalistes chrétiens de la
Renaissance* (Paris 1964) 99–102 / Giustiniani's
autobiography in his *Annali* bk 5, sub anno
1470   R. GERALD HOBBS

Sebastiano GIUSTINIANI of Venice, 1460–
13 March 1543
Giustiniani (Zustinian, Justinianus) was a
member of a Venetian family which claimed
descent from Justinian II. His parents were
Marino Giustiniani and a daughter of Piero
Gradenigo. In 1498 he was appointed Venetian
ambassador to the Emperor *Maximilian I; from
1500 to 1503 he was ambassador to Hungary
and in 1505 to Poland. He was governor of
Brescia in 1509 and of Illyria from 1511 to 1512.
On 27 December 1514 he was appointed
ambassador to England, where he remained
until 1519. Upon his return to Venice he made
his formal report for the senate on 10 October
1519. In 1526 he was appointed ambassador to
*Francis I. He returned to France in 1529 and in

November 1530 was at Blois, where he
remonstrated with the English ambassador, Sir
Francis Bryan, against the treatment to which
*Catherine of Aragon was being subjected. He
returned to Venice in 1532 and in 1540 was
rewarded for his services with the prestigious
office of procurator of St Mark. He died at the
advanced age of eighty-three. Giustiniani was
twice married; one of his three sons, Marino,
also became a noted diplomat. Of his writings
only an oration delivered before *Vladislav II of
Hungary was published.

Giustiniani probably met Erasmus in England in 1515 or 1516; in the latter year
Erasmus sent him a copy of his New Testament
(Ep 461). In 1517 Giustiniani wrote Erasmus
from London two long and learned letters,
expressing admiration for the *Adagia* and
sending greetings to Gianpietro Carafa, later
Pope *Paul IV (Epp 559, 591).

Giustiniani was a friend of Richard *Pace
and Thomas *More, who called him a 'learned
and holy man' and forwarded Giustiniani's
letters and greetings to Erasmus (Epp 461, 601).
His dispatches, preserved in manuscript at
Venice, provide detailed, shrewd, and objective descriptions of the affairs of the countries
which he visited. A selection of his dispatches
from England has been published in English
translation.

BIBLIOGRAPHY: Allen Ep 559 / *Four Years at the
Court of Henry VIII: Selection of Despatches written
by ... Sebastian Giustinian* ed Rawdon Brown
(London 1854, repr 1970) / Sanudo *Diarii* IV
858–67 and passim   CFG

Stanislaus GLANDINUS *See Stanisław
AICHLER*

Johann GLANDORP *See Cornelius
KEISEPREISTER*

Jean GLAPION d 14 September 1522
Jean Glapion was born at the end of the
fifteenth century in Northern France (probably
in Maine). He entered the Franciscan order as
an Observant at Le Mans and studied at the
University of Paris. Other information about
his early life is either unreliable or manifestly
false. On 22 July 1511 Glapion became warden
of an Observant house just outside Bruges and
soon was involved in a struggle with the

Conventual Franciscans who held the Bramberg monastery inside the city. From March to July 1515 he was in Rome and won his case: a subsequent papal bull enabled the Observants to take over and reform the Bramberg house. Glapion then served a term as provincial of the Observants of Burgundy and in the summer of 1517, while attending the general chapter at Rome, was appointed commissary-general for the Observants outside Italy. In that capacity he remained in Rome until elected provincial of the French province of all Franciscans on 17 July 1519. In 1520 he was the Lenten preacher at the court of Lorraine and later in that year was appointed confessor to the Emperor *Charles v, probably on the recommendation of Francisco de *Quiñones, who had met Glapion in the Netherlands. In June 1521 he was allowed to resign his offices in the order on account of his court appointment.

He remained in attendance at Charles v's court, and his influence upon the young monarch was considerable. He attended the diet of Worms, and as exponent of the policies of *Gattinara and Guillaume de *Croy, lord of Chièvres, he did not always see eye to eye with the papal legate, Girolamo *Aleandro (Ep 2639; cf Ep 1482). In private talks with the Saxon chancellor, Gregor Brück, in February 1521 he showed himself sympathetic to *Luther, hoping to secure his recantation. Eventually, however, he took a firm line and helped to bring about Luther's condemnation, earning himself a letter of thanks from Pope *Leo x. Even so, a man as open-minded as *Capito could afterwards express approval of Glapion's position (Ep 1241). In connection with the negotiations at Worms he had been sent on a mission to Franz von *Sickingen and Ulrich von *Hutten at the Ebernburg, where he also met Martin *Bucer (Hutten Opera II 210–11; ASD IX-1 154).

On 25 April 1521, only days after Luther's appearance before the diet, Leo x appointed Glapion on a mission to convert the American Indians. It is not clear whether this project reflected a personal calling or whether it had to do with the rivalry of opposing court factions. It is conceivable, of course, that the confessor and his opponents were actually united in their desire to see him depart for the Indies. For the time being, however, he continued to

accompany the emperor; no preparations were made for his American journey while Chièvres was alive. The powerful Chièvres appears to have been Glapion's patron, and after his death the Franciscan acted as an executor of his will. Charles v himself appointed Glapion as an executor when making a will in preparation for his second journey to Spain. Prior to their departure, Glapion debated in Brussels with the imprisoned Jacob *Proost and was present at Proost's public recantation in February 1522. After the court had reached Valladolid preparations for Glapion's departure to the Indies were taken in hand but were cut short by his death. In addition to a number of writings solely extant in manuscript (listed by Lippens), Glapion composed a 'Passe-temps du pélerin de vie humaine' which was printed in a Flemish version around 1540 (NK 3101) and prohibited at Louvain in 1550.

Glapion and Erasmus met only once, apparently in Brussels during the summer of 1521 (ASD IX-1 154). Thereafter they exchanged letters, but only one, written by Erasmus, is known today (Ep 1275). Glapion undertook to advocate Erasmus' cause before the emperor and his court; he also urged Erasmus to attack Luther in writing, while Erasmus, through the confessor, attempted to reach the emperor's ear with his counsels of moderation (Epp 1269, 1515; Allen I 35). Much later he presented Glapion's insistence that he take a public stand against Luther as a reason for moving his residence from the Netherlands to Basel (Ep 2792). In April 1522, when writing direct to Glapion about the related questions of his residence and his attitude to Luther, he had recourse to ambiguity (Ep 1275). It seems that first reports about Glapion's death reaching the Netherlands were not confirmed, but on 24 November 1522 Jan *Stercke let Erasmus know that the matter was certain (Ep 1322).

BIBLIOGRAPHY: Allen Ep 1275 / Hugolin Lippens 'Jean Glapion, défenseur de la réforme de l'Observance – conseiller de l'empereur Charles-Quint' in Archivum Franciscanum historicum 44 (1951) 3–70 and 45 (1952) 3–71 / Karl Brandi Kaiser Karl v. new ed (Darmstadt 1959–67) I 106–7, 146, and passim / Otto Lehnhoff Die Beichtväter Karls v. (Alfeld 1932) 20–33 / André Godin 'Jean Glapion: "Le passe-temps du pélerin de vie humaine"'

Bulletin trimestriel de la Société académique des antiquaires de la Morinie 20 (Saint-Omer 1965–6) 367–80, 427–30   PGB

Henricus GLAREANUS of Glarus, June 1488–27/8 March 1563

Heinrich Loriti, born at Mollis, near Glarus (Switzerland), is better known under the Latin name Henricus Glareanus, which is found from 1511 and was soon universally adopted. Not a great deal is known about the other members of his family (Ep 766). His father, whose Christian name is not recorded, was born by 1428 and seems to have known St Nicholas of Flüe, who fought on the side of Glareanus' grandfather in the so-called Old Zürich war (1436–50). For forty years Glareanus' father was a member of Glarus' ruling council. He was about ninety when he died early in January 1518 (Ep 766). Glareanus had two brothers, whose Christian names are also not known; one died before 6 August 1518; the other married a girl of the Aebli family, whose sister was the mother of Peter *Tschudi and his more famous brother, Aegidius. He seems to have died before 5 June 1537. In general, the Loriti seem to have been clients of the powerful Tschudi family.

Glareanus may have received his first schooling in Glarus and later was a student of Michael Rubellus (Röteli), perhaps at first in Bern, but certainly during the years 1501–6 in Rottweil in Württemberg, where he was given instruction in Latin and music in company with *Myconius, Berchtold Haller, and Melchior Volmar. In 1507 he matriculated at the University of Cologne as a resident of the Bursa Montis, obtaining his BA in 1508 and his MA in 1510. He was originally intended for the priesthood, as can be seen from three of his poems published in 1949 by Müller: a description of his journey from Cologne to Glarus, a panegyric on the Bursa Montis, and an autobiographical poem. These works show him as a disciple of such old-fashioned Cologne theologians as Remigius a Porta and Valentin Egelhart, but also of humanists and theological innovators such as Johannes *Caesarius and Matthias Cremer of Aachen, who played an important role in Glareanus' shift from scholastic theology to humanism and may in part have determined his subsequent atti-

tude towards the Protestant Reformation. Other determining factors in Glareanus' turn towards humanism were the controversy surrounding *Reuchlin, his friendship with *Zwingli, who was active in Glarus from 1506 to 1516, and his patriotism. In 1512 the Emperor *Maximilian I named him poet laureate in Cologne. This was the crowning moment of his humanistic transformation, and an honour which he cherished throughout his life.

When Glareanus moved to Basel in 1514 Erasmus welcomed him at once as the foremost of the Swiss humanists. In the following years he remained a prominent figure, as director of private residential schools (*bursae*) in Basel (1514–17), Paris (1517–22), again in Basel (1522–9), and finally in Freiburg (1529–63), where his reputation as an excellent and versatile teacher also earned him an academic appointment as professor of poetry. The *bursae* were lively centres of learning where the director cared in every way for the students entrusted to him. This enabled Glareanus to realize his humanistic goals and, more specifically, to educate an important group of young Swiss in the spirit of humanism.

Erasmus, with whom Glareanus maintained a lifelong association despite occasional disagreements (Ep 604) and differences in character, considered him the most important Swiss humanist. He mentioned Glareanus in highly complimentary terms in letters to Urbanus *Rhegius (Ep 394), Zwingli (Ep 404), and Etienne *Poncher, bishop of Paris (Ep 529), and later to Nikolaus von *Wattenwyl (Ep 1264), Charles *Blount, Lord Mountjoy (Ep 2435), and Bernhard von *Cles (Ep 2651). To Rhegius he emphasized Glareanus' even mastery of every 'department of sound learning'; to Zwingli he praised him as the 'leader and standard-bearer' of humanistic education in Switzerland. In his letter to Poncher he repeated these points and added that in view of the 'frigid quibbling' of scholastic theologians, Glareanus 'retreated, deciding to draw Christ from the fountain-head ... Against those prickly sophisters ... Glareanus does battle with no less spirit than Hercules.' In a letter to Glareanus himself (Ep 440) he likewise expressed his sincere devotion to his young friend and his appreciation for Glareanus' elegy *Ad Erasmum Roterodamum immortale*

Belgarum decus. He invited Glareanus' criticism of one of his own writings (Ep 604) and was eager to consult some notes Glareanus had made on the New Testament (Ep 707); he also offered his condolences on the death of Glareanus' father (Ep 766). In 1535, shortly before his death, Erasmus seems to have confirmed once more their long-standing and intimate friendship (Ep 3054).

Glareanus' importance as a humanist is evident from the testimony of his pupils and friends (cf Büchi, Sieber); from the chosen circle of men who received the dedications of his writings (among others Heinrich Utinger, Peter *Falck, Zwingli, Jan (II) *Łaski, Balthasar *Merklin, King *Ferdinand, Johannes *Fabri, Nikolaus von *Diesbach, Anton *Fugger, Otto Truchsess von Waldburg, and Jodok von Meggen); and, of course, from his writings themselves, some of which were printed in several editions. His writings developed from his lectures and represent innovative work in several areas. This is particularly true of his editions of classical authors and to a lesser degree of his poems such as the *Descriptio Helvetiae*, the *Panegyricum*, and two books of elegies dedicated to Zwingli. While Erasmus concentrated his philological efforts primarily on critical editions of theological source material (the New Testament, the Church Fathers), Glareanus concerned himself with the much wider field of secular classical literature, especially history, mathematics, and music. He edited Tacitus, Livy (pioneering an improved chronology), Dionysius of Halicarnassus, Horace, Ovid, Caesar (*Bellum Gallicum* and *Bellum civile*, with many geographical explanations), Sallust, Terence, Cicero (*De senectute*), Boethius (*Capita de arithmetica et musica*), Lucian (*Pharsalia*), Valerius Maximus, Eutropius, Quintus Curtius Rufus, and Suetonius (see Fritzsche 88ff). Among his philological works one might also include *De ratione syllabarum brevis isagoge* (Basel: A. Petri 1516), scholia to the *Methodus* of Donatus with numerous corrections derived from the preparation of his daily lectures (1535), notes to the vocabulary of Homer (1547), and a commentary on Johannes Caesarius.

Glareanus' geographical studies deserve special mention. In 1510 he published a map of the world based on an earlier map, now lost, by the humanist cosmographer Martin Waldseemüller. Glareanus' map not only presented the eastern coast-line of America with reasonable accuracy and correct nomenclature but also exhibited remarkably exact latitudes and longitudes. In 1527 he followed this up with his *De geographia* (Basel: J. Faber Emmeus), a mathematical-physical description of Asia, Africa, and Europe, complete with an appendix *De regionibus extra Ptolemaeum*. He dealt with mathematical problems in *De sex arithmeticae practicae speciebus epitome* (Freiburg: J. Faber Emmeus 1539) and in his *Liber de asse* (Basel: M. Isengrin 1550), which had its origin in discussions with Guillaume *Budé in Paris.

It is Glareanus' musical theories that won him a lasting reputation. In 1516 he published his *Isagoge in musicen* (Basel: J. Froben), in 1547 the *Dodecachordon* (Basel: H. Petri), written between 1519 and 1533. According to recent studies, especially those of Meier and Lichtenhahn, these works present an important facet of Renaissance humanism. Both the *Isagoge* and to an even greater extent the *Dodecachordon* reflect Glareanus' understanding of the classical culture and of recent shortcomings. According to Meier, the *Dodecachordon* is based on the idea of an erstwhile harmony between Christian religion and classical education, followed by the decay of the *bonae literae*, and stresses the necessity of renewing the original synthesis. The *Dodecachordon*, as the title indicates, increases the traditional eight to twelve modes, that is, six authentic and six plagal. This extension concerned the Aeolian and Ionian modes and in later practice led to the replacement of the medieval modes by the dualism of the keys of A minor and C major. More specifically Glareanus dealt with the double (that is, harmonic and arithmetical) division of the octave, using it as a point of departure rather than an end. Glareanus' observations on the history and the aesthetics of music are at least as important as his theory of the modes. The numerous musical examples given in the *Dodecachordon* illustrate his humanistic preference for models he thought to be classical or early Christian (that is, Ambrosian). He favoured plainsong no less than polyphonic compositions, as can be seen from his ambivalent, but in the end positive, assessment of Josquin des Prés. Thus Glareanus stopped short of a radical reform (see Meier) and rather aimed to lead students of music to true *eruditio* and *pietas* (see Lichtenhahn). In fact, it was Josquin's example that led Glareanus to go beyond questions of music training and to emphasize creative individuality in terms of genius and talent (see Kirsch). Glareanus' theory of the modes, as adopted by Ponthus de Tyard, Zarlino, and Gallus Dressler, was put to the test by Herpol, Utendal, and others, and thus found a wider dissemination.

Like Erasmus, Glareanus was cosmopolitan in his thought and led an itinerant life until he settled down in Freiburg. Nevertheless he felt a special vocation to become the *praeceptor Helvetiae* and was indeed the most important champion of Swiss national consciousness. In addition to its political freedom and military fame, he wanted the Swiss confederation to acquire cultural prominence and an independent place in the humanistic world. Glareanus' outstanding contribution to this goal was the *Descriptio Helvetiae*, to which was joined the *Panegyricum*, a eulogy of the thirteen Swiss cantons composed in 1514 (Basel: A. Petri 1515). He officially presented these poems to the representatives of the cantons assembled at a diet in Zürich – a symbolic encounter between the scholar-poet and the state (Näf). As the name indicates, the *Descriptio* is a geographical description of the Confederation in which Glareanus presents one region after the other. But more than that, the work presents a vision of Helvetia as the summit and centre of Europe, her snow-covered mountains sending forth rivers to all four directions, like Olympus, like a paradise from which flow the streams of the world (Näf). In the end he uses the four rivers, Thur, Limmat, Reuss, and Aare, as a basic grid for the presentation of four regions, each with its separate characteristics. In the *Panegyricum* Glareanus uses the example of individual cantons to describe the grandeur and free spirit, the awe-inspiring scenery, and the cultural achievements of his fatherland. Other poems exhibiting Glareanus' patriotism include the description of his return from Cologne (1511) and especially a heroic account of the battle of Näfels, neither published during his lifetime, the latter for political reasons.

In all his work Glareanus considered himself

Erasmus' friend and comrade in arms but also his admirer. It is significant that his enthusiasm for Erasmus was mainly generated by the latter's theological writings and views of Christianity. Glareanus wrote that he loved no one more dearly than Erasmus because through him he came to know Christ, 'to imitate Him, to worship Him, to love Him' (Ep 463; cf Epp 490, 618, 3054, 3055). It is certainly owing to his unwavering respect for Erasmus and for a life spent in the service of the *philosophia Christi* that Glareanus overcame his initial sympathy for friends like Myconius, *Vadianus, and Zwingli and finally chose to remain with the church of Rome. From the beginning he shared Erasmus' concern lest theology and church politics should jeopardize the revival of learning. Following Erasmus' lead, he severed his relations with Zwingli and later *Oecolampadius but remained on friendly terms with *Beatus Rhenanus, *Pirckheimer, and *Zasius. In his Freiburg years he supported the Catholic reform movement as a layman, for example, through his friendship with Aegidius Tschudi and his support of efforts to strengthen the Catholic party in Switzerland. Although he opposed the establishment of a Catholic university in the Confederation, he was active in the recruitment of capable teachers for Fribourg and Solothurn and encouraged the Catholic cantons to endow scholarships for young Swiss to study in Paris and Cologne.

A fine funeral inscription for Glareanus is found in the cathedral of Freiburg, opposite the university chapel.

Glareanus' works include, apart from those previously mentioned, his *Duo elegiarum libri* (Basel: J. Froben 1516), and commentaries on Sallust (Basel: A. Cratander 1538) and Livy (Basel: M. Isengrin 1540). To the lists of Glareanus' works in Fritzsche and Müller the following should be added: *Helvetiae descriptio*, *Panegyricum* ed and trans Werner Näf (St Gallen 1948); *Das Epos vom Heldenkampf bei Näfels und andere bisher ungedruckte Gedichte* ed E.F.J. Müller et al (Glarus 1949); *Dodecachordon* German trans by Peter Bohn (Leipzig 1888–90); *Dodecachordon* ed and trans Clement A. Miller (Rome, American Institute of Musicology 1965).

BIBLIOGRAPHY: Allen Ep 440 / Heinrich

Schreiber *Heinrich Loriti Glareanus, seine Freunde und seine Zeit* (Freiburg 1837) / Otto Fridolin Fritzsche *Glarean, sein Leben und seine Schriften* (Frauenfeld 1890) / Josef Bütler *Männer im Sturm: Vier Lebensbilder mit ergänzenden Texten* (Lucerne 1948) 15–88 / E.F.J. Müller 'Glarean und Aegidius Tschudi: Ihre menschlichen und gelehrten Beziehungen' *Zeitschrift für schweizerische Kirchengeschichte* 27 (1933) 107–31, 215– 29, 217–94, publishing 38 letters / Marc Sieber 'Glarean in Basel' *Jahrbuch des historischen Vereins des Kantons Glarus* 60 (1963) 53–75 / Albert Büchi 'Glareans Schüler in Paris' in *Aus Geschichte und Kunst … Robert Durrer … dargeboten* (Stans 1928) 372–431, publishing 15 letters / Werner Näf 'Schweizerischer Humanismus: Zu Glareans "Helvetiae Descriptio"' *Schweizer Beiträge zur allgemeinen Geschichte* 5 (1947) 186–98 / Ernst Kirsch 'Studie zum Problem des Heinrich Loriti (Glarean)' in *Festschrift A. Schering* (Berlin 1937) 125–36 / Frances B. Turrell 'The "Isagoge in Musicen" of Henry Glarean' *Journal of Music Theory* 3 (1959) 97–139 / Bernhard Meier 'Heinrich Loriti Glareanus als Musiktheoretiker' *Beiträge zur Freiburger Wissenschafts- und Universitätsgeschichte* 22 (1960) 65–112 / Ernst Lichtenhahn '"Ars Perfecta," zu Glareans Auffassung der Musikgeschichte' in *Festschrift A. Geering* ed Victor Ravizza (Bern 1972) 129–38 / Gustav Reese *Music in the Renaissance* rev ed (New York 1959) 185–6 and passim / Hans Albrecht in *Die Musik in Geschichte und Gegenwart* ed F. Blume (Basel-Kassel 1949–79) v 215–21 / Rudolf Aschmann et al *Der Humanist Heinrich Loriti genannt Glarean, 1488–1563* (Mollis 1983) / For Glareanus' father and brothers see Robert Durrer *Bruder Klaus* (Sarnen 1917–21) I 13, II 612   FRITZ BÜSSER

Anna van GLIMES

Anna van Glimes (Glymes) was the daughter of Filips van Glimes (Grimbergen), lord of Rode on Grimbergen (1422–69), a younger brother of Jan (II) van *Bergen ('metten lippen'). She married Filips van Spangen the elder on 4 February 1476 and had at least two children, Filips and Engelbert van *Spangen. She is mentioned in Ep 291 of 1514 but had apparently died by the time that letter was written.

BIBLIOGRAPHY: Allen and CWE Ep 291 / On Anna's father: C.J.F. Slootmans *Jan metten*

lippen (Rotterdam-Antwerp [1945]) 9 and passim   PGB

Johannes GLOGOVIENSIS *See* JAN *of Głogow*

Johannes GNOSTOPOLITANUS *See Johannes* CELLARIUS

Justin GOBLER of St Goar, d 21 April 1567
Justin Gobler (Göbler, Gobel, Gobelus) was born and educated in St Goar on the Rhine, near Boppard. He obtained a law degree and married the widow of Ulricus *Fabricius. For a few years he was in Koblenz for additional studies in law, supported by the archbishops of Trier, Richard von *Greiffenklau and Johann von *Metzenhausen; in 1535 he was town secretary of Koblenz. In January 1536 he moved to Trier, where he composed for Johann *Fichard's *Vitae* (Frankfurt: C. Egenolff 1536) a short life of Petrus *Mosellanus, whom he had known personally. His *Prosopographiae*, descriptions of famous men from classical sources, were printed in Mainz in 1537 by Peter II *Schöffer. Two years later he went to Minden as councillor to Duke Eric I of Brunswick-Calenberg, who died in 1540. Gobler at first stayed on in the service of his son Eric II, but then became chancellor to Franz von *Waldeck, bishop of Münster, Osnabrück, and Minden. During the religious wars he was in the service of the county of Nassau, but he retired after he had suffered an injury to his knee on 24 April 1559. He settled in Frankfurt, engaged in writing and scholarship until his death.

Gobler, who was interested in the history of his own time, composed *Brevis narratio de bello Hildesheimense inter Ericum ducem Brunswicensem et episcopum Hildesheimensem* (1519), printed in Simon Schard's *Historicum opus* (Basel: press of Henricpetri 1574), and a *Chronicon novum* for the years 1556–7 (published with Sleidanus' *De statu religionis*, Frankfurt: P. Fabricius 1568). However, his main work lay in the field of legal writings; he translated the so-called *Carolina* into Latin – *Augustissimi Imperatoris Caroli Quinti de capitalibus iudiciis constitutio* (Basel: J. Oporinus 1543) – and composed *Der Rechten Spiegel*

(Frankfurt: C. Egenolff 1550), many times reprinted.

In 1528 Gobler wrote to Erasmus (Ep 1946), who desired to borrow a manuscript of Tertullian's *De spectaculis* from Fabricius' library (cf BRE Ep 266).

BIBLIOGRAPHY: Allen Ep 1946 / ADB IX 301 / AK III Ep 1117, IV Ep 1623, and passim / P. Lehmann *Johannes Sichardus* (Munich 1912) 185, 193, 196   IG

Conradus GOCLENIUS
of Mengeringhausen, d 25 January 1539
Conrad Wackers, a native of Mengeringhausen, in the county of Waldeck (Westphalia), had an alternative surname, Gockelen, which he latinized to Goclenius. Only fragmentary information is available about his youth. As a young boy, for example, he enjoyed Alexander *Hegius' lectures at Deventer. In November 1510, he started university studies at Cologne and afterwards went to Louvain, where he enrolled as a poor student of the College of the Castle on 28 February 1512. After proceeding to MA on 10 November 1515, he provided for himself by private teaching.

Availing himself of the privilege granted the university by *Leo x, on 3 October 1518 Goclenius accepted nomination by the faculty of arts to a benefice vacated by the abbot of Floreffe; to become eligible for this nomination he was ordained. When in October 1519 Adrianus Cornelii *Barlandus left the chair of Latin at the Collegium Trilingue, Goclenius was appointed by the executors professor of Latin (de Vocht CTL I 484–7). Although in the beginning Erasmus did not back Goclenius' candidature, he soon came to support him and even defended him against the criticism of Barlandus and the rage and frustration of one of the other candidates for the chair (Epp 1050, 1051). Erasmus appreciated the quality of Goclenius' teaching and two months earlier had recommended him to Floris van *Egmond as a private teacher for his son, Maximilian van *Egmond (Ep 1018).

Perhaps at Goclenius' own request, Erasmus later recommended him most warmly to Thomas *More, who intended to visit the Netherlands (Ep 1220). In this letter Erasmus presented his friend as a skilful writer of both

prose and poetry and a gifted teacher who could make literature popular even with those who had previously been repelled by it. A similar eulogy to Goclenius is found in Erasmus' letter to Bernard Bucho van *Aytta, written on 24 September 1521 (Ep 1237). In August 1521, More did come to the Netherlands, attending Cardinal *Wolsey, who was going to meet *Charles v on a diplomatic mission. In the discharge of his duties as an imperial councillor Erasmus joined the emperor's court at Bruges and wrote to Goclenius about his meetings with More (Ep 1223). Acting upon Erasmus' suggestion, Goclenius dedicated to More his Latin translation of Lucian's *Hermotimus* (Louvain: D. Martens 1522). In return, More sent him a cup filled with gold coins and a letter of thanks (Rogers Ep 113). Goclenius' thorough knowledge of both Latin and Greek was also praised by Erasmus in an addition to adage II vii 59 in the 1520 edition of the *Adagia*.

Erasmus' public appreciation of Goclenius' excellent qualities was largely recompensed by the professor's enduring devotion and painstaking service in practical as well as scholarly matters. After Erasmus had settled at Basel in the autumn of 1521, Goclenius became, along with the banker *Schets, his representative and manager in the Netherlands, entrusted with a large amount of money (Allen x 406). At first Erasmus had intended to return quickly, and he continued to hope that he might spend the last years of his life in Louvain. With that aim he charged Goclenius in consultation with *Dorp, to look for a suitable house with a garden (Ep 1209).

Goclenius is also the man to whom Erasmus, in a mood of depression in 1524, committed his autobiography, the *Compendium vitae* (Allen I 46–52), to safeguard his name against future detraction (Ep 1437). In the same letter he asked Goclenius to help publish a collected edition of his works; he also announced a bequest of four hundred gold florins to Goclenius and gave him instructions about other bequests. Besides the deposit he had left in Goclenius' custody at his departure, Erasmus had also left a considerable sum with Jan de *Neve, the president of the Lily. In the summer of 1522 Erasmus charged his amanuensis, Hilarius *Bertholf, with the recovery of the money from de Neve. Goclenius took care that a detailed statement of the ensuing transaction was drawn up and sent a copy to Erasmus, who eight years later mistook it for a receipt for money actually paid de Neve rather than the opposite (de Vocht CTL III 385–6). On 14 July 1530 Goclenius reminded Erasmus of the way in which things really happened (Ep 2352), and Erasmus obviously believed him. He remembered his friend in his first will of 1527 by leaving him all the money he had left on deposit with him and six silver vessels (Allen VI 504). The bequest was later converted into a deed of donation (Ep 2836). In return Goclenius, by a deed of 17 September 1533, handed everything back to Erasmus in case he should die earlier than Erasmus. In addition Goclenius bequeathed to him twenty ducats (Allen X 409–10). In a memorandum of 8 April 1534, to which Erasmus attributed the value of a will (Allen X 410), he added more specific instructions for the disposal of the money turned over to Goclenius. In his last will, written at Basel on 12 February 1536, Erasmus stipulated that the money left with Goclenius should be spent only in Brabant. Further, he bequeathed to him a silver cup with the image of Fortuna. Goclenius, for unaccountable reasons, left the money untouched after Erasmus' death; thus, at Goclenius' own death in 1539, the funds became the subject of protracted litigation between Goclenius' family, the university, and the treasury of Brabant. The matter was finally settled in favour of the university (Allen X 406–24; de Vocht CTL IV 17–31).

Erasmus' concern about the welfare of his closest friend in Louvain is inseparable from his continuing solicitude for the prosperity of the Collegium Trilingue (CTL II 91–4). He never ceased encouraging the professors in the face of opposition and abuse; he rejoiced in their successes and congratulated them on the modesty and uprightness of their lives and the purity of their teaching (Ep 1856). Meanwhile, the fame of the Collegium Trilingue and Goclenius' excellent teaching attracted a large number of students and also visitors. Not only did the latter claim a great deal of the professors' research and teaching time, but the costs arising from their entertainment also absorbed a large part of their scanty wages. Erasmus was well aware of the danger that

might result for the college from the precarious financial position of its professors and intervened with Gilles de *Busleyden to improve their conditions. However, his pleas met with no palpable results (Allen Ep 2353:330–1). Goclenius himself, though he was able to complement his income handsomely by tutoring the sons of wealthy families, could hardly bear the cost of his social obligations (Ep 1994A; de Vocht CTL II 610–11, III 94). As did so many of his colleagues, Goclenius tried to provide for the increased expenses by securing himself a prebend, according to the *ius nominationis* granted by Pope Leo X to the Louvain faculty of arts. In April 1525, Goclenius was appointed to a canonry of Our Lady's at Antwerp. However, as that nomination was contested by a candidate backed by the curia, Goclenius was involved in a lawsuit lasting over eight years (Epp 1994A, 2352, 2573, 2587, 2644; de Vocht CTL III 95–103). His hopes of a favourable outcome were time and again thwarted by the stubbornness of his opponents. Much more fruitful was a nomination to the first vacancy at the collation of the provost of Hoegaarden, which he was able to secure about 1534 as a result of the intercession of Johannes *Dantiscus with Alfonso de *Valdés, the imperial secretary (de Vocht CTL III 97–8, 563–4).

Erasmus' gratitude to Goclenius applied not only to his friend's diligence in managing his belongings at Louvain but also to his active interest in Erasmus' work; it was Goclenius, for example, who helped Erasmus get back a manuscript of Augustinus' *De Trinitate* he had left with *Dorp (Epp 1547, 1890, 1899). Meanwhile Goclenius kept Erasmus informed of his own work. In 1527 he was preparing an edition of Donatus' commentaries on Terence. When he heard that Johann *Sichard was doing likewise he was willing to give up his plan, but in case Sichard did not succeed in his project, Goclenius was still disposed to send his manuscript whenever *Froben asked for it (Ep 1899). Eventually, however, heavy teaching duties prevented him from completing his edition. In fact his contemporaries considered him rather indolent because he published so little (ASD I-2 683–4).

In May 1519 Goclenius published a metrical version of the catalogue of Erasmus' works (Allen I 1–46) entitled *Lucubrationum Erasmi-*

carum elenchus. It was published with the reprint of Helius *Eobanus Hessus' Hodoeporicon* (Louvain: D. Martens; NK764). The same volume contains a letter by Pieter *Gillis in praise of Goclenius. Some months later Goclenius published a commendatory poem in Erasmus' *Familiarium colloquiorum formulae* (Louvain: D. Martens, November 1519; NK 2869). In 1522 he published his Latin rendering of Lucian's *Hermotimus*. In 1520 Froben offered him a copy of Erasmus' edition of Cicero's *De officiis*, which he probably used for his lessons. He added marginal notes to it (it is still preserved in the library of the University of Göttingen), which probably served for *M.T. Ciceronis officia – De amicitia ... per D. Erasmum et Conradum Goclenium deprehensis ac restitutis aliquot locis non cuilibet obviis* (Basel: J. Herwagen and H. Froben 1528). Three years later Goclenius published a corrected text of Lucan's *Pharsalia* (Antwerp: M. Hillen 1531). In 1534, he took temporary charge of the college after the death of the president, Joost van der *Hoeven. As a result he abandoned the complete edition of Quintilian on which he had already worked for several years.

Goclenius exercised considerable influence on posterity by educating a whole generation of fine Latin scholars (de Vocht CTL III 540–1, 552–60). His pedagogical qualities were eloquently praised by his old pupil *Viglius Zuichemus in his autobiography. The Portuguese André de *Resende, one of Goclenius' favourite students, dedicated to him his *Encomium urbis et academiae Lovaniensis* (Antwerp: J. Grapheus 1530) and his *Epitome rerum gestarum in India a Lusitanis anno* MDXXX (Louvain: S. Zassenus 1531) and wrote several poems in Goclenius' honour (de Vocht CTL III 559–60). His fame as a teacher occasioned the offering of appointments at Corpus Christi College, Oxford, (in succession to *Vives) and at the Danish court, where a tutor for the son of *Christian II was required (Ep 1765). Goclenius stayed at Louvain till his death, active, open-minded, and serving the interests of others, most of all those of his dear friend Erasmus, to whom he wrote his last letter on 21 March 1536. Although he was more than twenty years younger than Erasmus, he died barely three years after his friend. At the beginning of January 1539, he suddenly fell ill.

As he felt that the malignant illness was rapidly exhausting his forces, he invited his seven brothers, who lived in the county of Waldeck, to witness the making of a will. Long before they could arrive, however, he died of bronchial congestion (de Vocht CTL III 565–9). He was laid to rest in St Peter's church, Louvain. His successor, Petrus Nannius, delivered a funeral oration which is pedestrian and uninformative: *Funebris oratio habita pro mortuo Conrado Goclenio* (Louvain: S. Zassenus 1542). But in the funeral inscription for the monument erected in St Peter's church, Goclenius was called 'alter Erasmus,' a compliment he richly deserved.

BIBLIOGRAPHY: Allen Ep 1209, x 406–24 / NK passim / *Matrikel Köln* II 669 / de Vocht CTL passim / P. Reekmans and F.A. Lefever 'De grafmonumenten en epitafen van de Leuvense Sint-Pieterskerk' *Mededelingen van de Geschieden Oudheidkundige kring voor Leuven em omgeving* 14 (1974) 57–9 / R. Crahay 'Recherches sur le *Compendium Vitae*, attribué à Erasme' *Humanisme et Renaissance* 6 (1939) 7–19 and 135–53 / F. Meuser 'Conrad Goclenius aus Mengeringhausen (1489–1539)' *Geschichtsblätter für Waldeck* 60 (1968) 10–23

GODELIEVE TOURNOY-THOEN

Garret GODFREY documented at Cambridge 1503–d 1539

Garret (Gerardus) Godfrey (as he was known in English) was born in Graten, in Limburg (Holland). By 1503 he was resident at Cambridge, where he remained until his death. As a stationer and bookseller he was closely associated with the university; in 1503 he was among those accounted 'a common minister and servant' of the university and therefore came under the protection of its privileges. His duties as a stationer included binding, repairing, and chaining books. He was a churchwarden of Great St Mary's parish in 1516 and 1521 and gave some gifts to the church.

Godfrey carried letters and messages for Erasmus (Epp 248, 249, 1669), who may at one time have lodged with him at Cambridge and who often sent greetings to his 'old host Garret' (Epp 456, 777, 1656, 1766). To Roger Asham he described in 1530 how Erasmus used to ride 'about the Markette hill' when he was 'sore at his boke.'

BIBLIOGRAPHY: Allen and CWE Epp 248, 456 / *Erasmus and Cambridge* ed D.F.S. Thomson and H.C. Porter (Toronto 1963) 221 and passim
CFG

Aert van der GOES 1475–1 November 1545
Aert van der Goes, the son of Maarten van der Goes and Maria Hak van Oudheusden, was pensionary of Delft until, in 1525, he was appointed advocate, or *raadpensionaris*, of Holland and West Friesland. He was sent on many missions abroad and was a delegate when the peace of Cambrai, the 'Ladies Peace,' was patched up in 1529; in March of that year he addressed a speech of welcome to *Charles V on behalf of the states of Holland. Naturally he played a role when the states of Holland sent a gift to Erasmus in 1533; out of distrust of their agent, Pieter van *Montfoort, Erasmus exchanged some letters, now lost, with Goes (cf Epp 2819 and 2896), but their acquaintance hardly went so far as to enable Erasmus to give his name correctly. Goes retired in 1544 and was succeeded by his son Adriaan, who, like his father, kept a register of the delegates' assemblies (*Daghvaerten*), the whole of which was printed around 1750 at The Hague. Less than two months after Goes' death his wife, Margaretha van Binchem, followed him to the grave. Aert and Margaretha were portrayed on two fine paintings now to be seen in the Prinsenhof of Delft. Their daughter Genoveva was married to Everardus *Nicolai.
BIBLIOGRAPHY: Allen Ep 2819 / A.J. van der Aa et al *Biographisch woordenboek der Nederlanden* (Haarlem 1852–78, repr 1965) VII 254–5 / ADB IX 322 / N. van der Blom *Erasmus en Rotterdam* (Rotterdam-The Hague 1969) 15–18
C.G. VAN LEIJENHORST

Damianus de GOES *See Damião de GOIS*

Jan GOETGEBUER d before 24 September 1519
Jan Goetgebuer (Goetghebeur, Bonvicini) was a canon of St Donatian's, Bruges. He and Joris van *Themseke were candidates for the deanship of the chapter, but an election on 29 May 1499 ended in a tie, so that the curia annulled the election and appointed Cardinal Antonio Trivulzio on an interim basis; he resigned on 5 May 1502 in favour of Goetgebuer. Goetgebuer

remained dean to his death in 1519 and was succeeded on 24 September by Erasmus' friend Marcus *Laurinus, who had been his coadjutor since 1515. Erasmus repeatedly sent greetings to Goetgebuer in his letters to Laurinus (Epp 651, 666, 789).
Razo Goetgebuer or Bonvicini (d 1509), presumably a relative of Jan, had been Premonstratensian abbot of Drongen, near Ghent.
BIBLIOGRAPHY: Allen Ep 651 / *Gallia christiana* v 238, 258 / de Vocht CTL I 517, II 179 / de Vocht *Literae ad Craneveldium* 13
PGB

Johann GOGREVE d 17 February 1554
Johann Gogreve (Ghogreve, Gogreff, Hochgreif, Ghogravius) was born into an influential family (Ep 2298) of the duchy of Berg around 1499. In April 1514 he matriculated at the University of Cologne, graduating BA the following year. It seems probable that his acquaintance with his later friends and collaborators Johann von *Vlatten und Konrad *Heresbach dates back to when they were students at Cologne. In 1515 Gogreve continued his legal studies at Orléans, and in 1520 he registered in the University of Bologna. Apparently without a higher degree he returned home and, probably in 1524, perhaps simultaneously with Vlatten, entered the service of Duke John III of *Cleves as a councillor. As Heresbach too had been called to the duke's court in 1523 as tutor to the sons of John III, the government of Jülich-Cleves was visibly committed to a policy of religious and educational reform according to the ideas of Erasmus (Epp 2298, 3031, 3031A). These connections and the influential position of Gogreve were further emphasized when Heresbach dedicated to him his editions of *De genere vitaque Homeri* and of Lorenzo *Valla's translation of Herodotus (both Cologne 1526).
Meanwhile in 1524 Gogreve had carried out important missions for the duke to the imperial vicar and Reichsregiment at Esslingen and to the diet of Nürnberg. His ecclesiastical career also progressed with his appointment in 1526 as provost of the chapter of St George at Cologne, a position which he resigned in 1530 prior to his marriage. In 1528 Gogreve was named chancellor of Jülich and Berg, an office he retained until his death, while Vlatten, with the title of vice-chancellor, exercised analo-

gous functions for the duchy of Jülich from about 1530. In his imaginative and diplomatic move towards Erasmian reform Vlatten was loyally supported by the reliable and efficient Gogreve. Both share with Heresbach the principal credit for the fact that for half a century, and indirectly for much longer, the duchies of Jülich-Cleves remained a model for political government based on Erasmianism. Gogreve's share in this achievement resulted primarily from his many diplomatic missions, both domestic and foreign, such as his embassy of May 1546 to Regensburg in preparation for the marriage of Duke William v of *Cleves to a daughter of *Ferdinand I. His untiring diplomacy also served the goal of gaining recognition for the Erasmian church policy of the duchies. *Melanchthon and *Bucer saw – quite correctly – in Gogreve and his fellow councillors the principal obstacle to Protestant expansion in the region of the Nether Rhine. Gogreve's resignation as provost of St George's, Cologne, is clearly a result of his commitment to an Erasmian church policy which was opposed by Hermann von *Wied, the archbishop of Cologne, who endeavoured to assert and retain his authority over the church of Jülich-Cleves. Gogreve's activity extended both to negotiations with the archbishop and the preparation of the famous Jülich-Cleves church ordinance of 1532. Over his protests he was also appointed to conduct the subsequent visitation in the duchy of Berg, a task which he accomplished conscientiously and judiciously. Erasmus' advice in the matter of the church ordinance was rewarded with an annuity of thirty guilders, and the official patent issued to this effect – now in the Öffentliche Bibliothek of the University of Basel – bears Gogreve's signature.

From 1540 to 1542 Gogreve played a leading part in the negotiations for an alliance with France. The eventual defeat of the duchies by the Hapsburgs and the loss of Gelderland did not discourage the Erasmian councillors. In 1545 Gogreve participated in the drafting of a 'Christian Reformation' in accordance with the instructions issued at the diet of Speyer in 1544. This document re-emphasizes, perhaps with even greater precision, the principles of Erasmian reform.

Gogreve's letters to Erasmus (Ep 2804) are

now lost; in general the countless traces of his activity are found exclusively in official documents and letters, in drafts and his visitation reports. Gogreve died in office and was succeeded as chancellor by Vlatten. Heresbach commented on Gogreve's lively intelligence and, perhaps slightly amused by the chancellor's amateurish taste for scholarship, reported how he liked to recite Homer to the accompaniment of musicians.

BIBLIOGRAPHY: Allen Ep 2298 / Knod 162 / *Matrikel Köln* II 724 / *Matricule d'Orléans* II-1 336–8 / Pflug *Correspondance* I Ep 11 and passim / *Landtagsakten von Jülich-Berg, 1400–1610* ed Georg von Below (Düsseldorf 1895) I 803 and passim / August Franzen 'Das Schicksal des Erasmianismus am Niederrhein '*Historisches Jahrbuch* 83 (1964) 84–112 / Anton Gail 'Johann von Vlatten ...' *Düsseldorfer Jahrbuch* 45 (1951) 1–109 passim / *Briefe von Andreas Masius und seinen Freunden* ed Max Lossen (Leipzig 1886) Ep 55 / Albrecht Wolters *Konrad von Heresbach* (Elberfeld 1867) passim / *Das Stift zu St. Georg in Köln* ed A.D. von den Brincken (Cologne 1966) 111–12, 207 / Günter Bers *Die Allianz Frankreich-Kleve während des Geldrischen Krieges (1539–1543)* (Cologne 1969) 23–5 and passim / Otto R. Redlich *Staat und Kirche am Niederrhein zur Reformationszeit* (Leipzig 1938) 26, 58, 71, 79, and passim / Otto R. Redlich *Jülich-Bergische Kirchenpolitik am Ausgang des Mittelalters und in der Reformationszeit* (Bonn 1907–15) passim   ANTON J. GAIL

Damião de GOIS of Alenquer, 1502–30 January 1574

Gois (Goes) was born in Alenquer, the son of Rui Dias de Gois, who belonged to the lower nobility, and his fourth wife, Isabel Gomes de Limi. His father died in 1513, two years after Damião had entered the court of King *Manuel I as a page. Young Gois was endowed with a keen sense of observation. None of the thrilling overseas events that marked Manuel's reign escaped him. He was fascinated by Matthew, who was the emissary of *Lebna Dengal, emperor of Ethiopia, and his mother. In 1514 and 1515 the envoy had several conversations with Gois, who listened with sympathy to the complaint that Ethiopia's Christian faith was not recognized by the pope. The many foreigners and overseas

Damião de Gois

---

envoys he met at court taught Gois to respect other peoples' customs and beliefs. Inspired by the king's dedication to the arts, Gois became a noted art collector in his later life. Manuel attracted many outstanding musicians to his palace, who played for him even when he was at work. Gois discovered his own talent for music at an early age: he played several instruments and composed motets and madrigals in the Flemish tradition. Only a few have come down to us, but *Glareanus, who published one motet in his *Dodecachordon* (Basel: H. Petri 1547), had flattering words for Gois as a composer.

In 1521 King Manuel selected Gois for a highly responsible position abroad, but that same year the king died. *John III, his successor, appointed Gois secretary of the Indiahouse in Antwerp in 1523. The Portuguese factory was an important centre of the city's economic activity, and the factors were busy taking care of the king's commercial interests. In addition, Gois undertook diplomatic missions for John III. On one such assignment he went to England (1528), where he may have met Thomas *More whose

execution in 1535 filled him with great sorrow. He joined Erasmus' devotees in Italy, where he was then residing, in urging the great scholar to write an eulogy for his friend (Ep 3085).

Antwerp offered Gois a stimulating intellectual atmosphere. He was exposed to lively discussions of humanism and church reform and developed a strong interest in these movements. He was fortunate to meet Cornelius *Grapheus, the former secretary of Antwerp, a noted poet and geographer, who was able to satisfy his newly aroused intellectual curiosity. Grapheus had just come back to Antwerp after a period (April – November 1523) of imprisonment and confinement in Brussels because of 'heresy.' He had known Albrecht *Dürer (whose orthodoxy was also suspect) and gave him *Luther's *Babylonian Captivity* on his return to Germany after an extended visit to Flanders (1521). His choice of Grapheus as his teacher of Latin speaks for Gois' religious open-mindedness. It is not surprising that in 1531 he stopped over in Wittenberg on one of his diplomatic missions which took him from Denmark to Prussia, Poland, and Russia. Although he did not know German, he listened to a sermon by Luther in his church and was invited to his house for dinner. Whereas Luther's personality did not appeal to him, he liked *Melanchthon; they parted as friends and corresponded over a period of seven years, although only one letter has come down to us: *Philippi Melanchthonis epistolae* ... ed H.E. Bindseil (Halle 1874) Ep 517.

Gois was in doubt as to whether he should resign his diplomatic position and devote himself to humanist studies, and Johannes *Magnus, the exiled archbishop of Upsala, whom Gois met twice (1529, 1531) in Gdansk, helped him to overcome his uncertainty. Magnus had become a noted historian and supported Gois' humanist inclinations. He also encouraged him to publish the letters which the Ethiopian envoy, Matthew, had brought to Portugal. Finally, Magnus aroused Gois' compassion for the Lapps, who, exploited by their overlords, refused to become Christians.

When he returned to Antwerp Gois carried out Magnus' suggestions. Grapheus assisted him in his first Latin publication: the *Legatio ... Presbyteri Joannis ad Emanuelem* (Antwerp: J.

Grapheus 1532), which contained the Ethiopian message to Manuel of 1514, to which Gois appended *De Pilapiis*, a strong appeal for better treatment of the Lapps. Soon after the completion of these works he enrolled as a student at the University of Louvain in 1531. Rutgerus *Rescius and Conradus *Goclenius of the Collegium Trilingue became his friends; like Grapheus, they were both devoted to Erasmus. Gois was eager to meet the man of whom he had heard so much, so, with a letter of introduction from Rescius and a copy of the *Legatio*, he arrived in Freiburg in the spring of 1533. Erasmus invited him for a meal, but he failed to read Rescius' letter and did not look at the *Legatio*. Gois bore him no ill will, and in June of the same year sent him a gilded cup to remember him by (Ep 2826). Erasmus replied that he had been unaware of who his guest was and apologized for the cool reception he had accorded the Portuguese (Ep 2846).

During his visit with Erasmus, the question of *Henry VIII's divorce had come up. Gois thought that Erasmus condemned it, but on his return to Louvain he heard rumours to the contrary. Gois wrote and asked Erasmus to clear up the matter for him, promising that on his forthcoming visit to Portugal he would act as his friend. He wanted Erasmus' assurance that he was against the divorce since the subject would surely come up (Ep 2826). Erasmus gave a cautious reply asserting that nobody heard him approve or reject it; he further remarked that Henry had manoeuvred himself into a 'labyrinth.' In the same letter (Ep 2846) Erasmus asked Gois to help correct the bad impression he had made in his preface to his edition of St John Chrysostom, dedicated to John III, in which he had criticized the king's spice monopoly (Ep 1800). Gois was evidently pleased with Erasmus' letter, and must have spoken convincingly for Erasmus since John III offered him a post at the University of Coimbra, which he hoped to open shortly.

The Portuguese king had called Gois home in order to appoint him treasurer of the Indiahouse in Lisbon (Ep 2826), but after serious soul-searching Gois decided to pursue his humanist studies rather than continue in the king's service. The king gave his consent, and Gois returned to Louvain convinced that he had made the right decision. Erasmus wrote

to Grapheus that he hoped Gois had used wise judgment (Ep 2916). He had grown fond of Gois and invited him to be his house-guest in Freiburg. On 23 April 1534 he reported Gois' arrival to Erasmus *Schets (Ep 2924).

The friendship between Gois and Erasmus had its source in agreement on issues vital to both of them – among others a concern for the problems faced by small nations. In his first long letter to Erasmus, Gois wrote about the Ethiopians' bitter complaint that they were not recognized as Christians and about the ill-treatment of the Lapps (Ep 2826), and they explored those subjects further in conversations in Freiburg. Although he did not write a pamphlet dealing with these matters as Gois had hoped, Erasmus inserted in the *Ecclesiastes* (LB V 813–15) a paragraph calling attention to the Lapps and expressed his regret at the pope's utter disregard of the Ethiopians. He was instrumental in having the *Legatio* and the *De Pilapiis* translated into German, although he was unable to find a publisher (Epp 2846, 2914). Gois was a patriotic Portuguese, but unlike most of his contemporaries he was not blind to the military valour of Portugal's enemies and to the cruelties committed on both sides. Thus in a letter to him Erasmus felt free to condemn the way the Portuguese robbed the coastal towns of Africa (Ep 2846).

In temperament the two friends differed widely. Whereas Erasmus had learned to be cautious in his utterances, Gois was impulsive and given to frank expression of his thoughts. Even in strictly Catholic Freiburg he openly endorsed certain Protestant tenets. To his great chagrin his conduct ended his stay with Erasmus because he had antagonized the authorities and was advised to leave the city. It is likely that Erasmus had warned his guest to be prudent in his public statements, albeit apparently without success. In private the two men found they were in agreement on some basic religious views, for example that faith in Christ was more important than ceremonies and rituals. Gois expressed this thought in his *Fides, religio moresque Aethiopium* (Louvain: R. Rescius 1540), which contained a plea for religious tolerance.

Gois still needed to improve his knowledge of ancient languages. In an act of friendship Erasmus gave him some of his notes on rhetoric in Greek and Latin. Gois later thought of having them published, but Erasmus begged him not to do so since they were written quickly and only for him (Epp 2987, 3019). However years later Rescius printed the Latin notes under the title *Compendium rhetorices ad Damianum a Goes* (Louvain 1544), with a preface by Willem Bernaerts of Thielt justifying the publication (reprinted in Allen x 396–405).

In August 1534 Gois left Freiburg for Italy, where on Erasmus' recommendation he continued his studies at Padua. His teacher was Lazzaro *Bonamico, with whom he established a happy association. Erasmus advised him to attend his public lectures and not to engage him as a private teacher (Ep 2987). In a letter of introduction to *Bembo, Erasmus lauded Gois' modesty despite his noble background (Ep 2958). In Italy Gois came under the influence of the Ciceronians and in a letter that is no longer extant suggested that Erasmus perfect his style. In his answer Erasmus defended himself at length, for instance making the point that Cicero's 'perfume' did not suit religious topics (Ep 3043).

During his residence in Italy Gois received news of Erasmus' failing health. He wrote to Erasmus suggesting that after his death all his writings should be reprinted in a comprehensive edition and offering to pay for such an undertaking; he also urged Erasmus to leave a catalogue of his secular and religious writings which he wished to be printed (Ep 3085). The two men were not to meet again, because the next time Gois was on his way to visit Erasmus he heard in Nürnberg of disturbances in Switzerland which made it impossible for him to proceed to Basel. After Erasmus' death Bonifacius *Amerbach informed Gois that no catalogue such as he suggested was found among Erasmus' papers, so he reluctantly withdrew from the project of publishing his writings (AK IV Epp 2087, 2093). Contact between Amerbach and Gois ended in December 1536. Although Hartmann has suggested that Amerbach terminated the correspondence because he considered Gois' action 'disgraceful' (AK IV Ep 2093 note 7), it is equally possible that Gois was the one who ended the correspondence, offended by Amerbach's publication in 1537 of Erasmus' *Catalogi duo*

operum … ab ipso conscripti (Basel: H. Froben and N. Episcopius). In remembrance of his great mentor and because Erasmus had expressed to him his approval of the vernacular, Gois translated Cicero's *De senectute* (of which Erasmus was especially fond) into Portuguese and published it at Venice in 1538. In 1544 he published a collection of his essays, *Aliquot opuscula*, with Rescius at Louvain.

In 1538 Gois was again at the University of Louvain. He married Johanna van Hargen, who came from a prominent Dutch Catholic family and bore him three sons. When Louvain was attacked by the French in July 1542, Gois took part in the defence and was captured. After an imprisonment of fourteen months, he paid a large ransom and was recalled to Portugal by John III. Gois and his family finally landed in Lisbon in 1545, and John III appointed him royal archivist with the special task of bringing order to the national archives. He was commissioned to write the chronicles of the reigns of John II and Manuel I and established himself as a noted historian (*Chronica do Principe Dom Joam*, Lisbon 1567, and *Chronica do Felicissimo Rei Dom Emanuel*, Lisbon 1566–7). Nevertheless, his life in his native country was less happy than the years he had spent abroad. Simon Rodrigues, the Jesuit leader in Portugal, was present in Padua when Gois had spoken of his good relations with Wittenberg. He denounced him several times before the high tribunal of the Inquisition, but as long as John III ruled Gois was safe. After his death, however, the Jesuits exerted great influence on King Sebastian, who ascended the throne in 1568. In 1572 Gois was called before the Inquisition and found guilty of heresy because of his former contacts with Wittenberg and Erasmus. He was imprisoned and died two years later.

The memory of his friendship with Erasmus must have sustained Gois in his darkest hour. Twenty years after Erasmus' death he wrote to the humanist Jeronimo Cardoso: 'At the very moment when the youth whom you had asked to bring me your letter entered my chamber, I had in my hand the portrait of the great Erasmus of Rotterdam by Albrecht Dürer, the distinguished German sculptor [sic] of his time. When I began looking at it, the happiest memory of such a man, of such a host, evoked deepest emotions...' (J. Cardoso *Epistolarum familiarum libellus*, Lisbon 1556, Ep 65).

Dedications to Gois are found in: Cornelius Grapheus *Carmina aliquot* (Antwerp 1532) and *Flores, seu Latinissimae formulae loquendi ... Ex P. Terentii comoediis excerptae* ... (Antwerp 1529); Justus Velsius *Hippocratis Coi de insomniis liber* (Antwerp 1541); Bertram von *Damm *Pauli epistola ad Titum carmine heroico* ... (Louvain 1533); and Sigismundus *Gelenius *Annotationes Plinii* ... (Basel 1535).

The Albertina in Vienna possesses a drawing by Dürer which was thought to represent Gois (see bibliography below).

BIBLIOGRAPHY: Allen Ep 2826 / Marcel Bataillon 'Le cosmopolitisme de Damião de Gois' in *Etudes sur le Portugal au temps de l'humanisme* (Coimbra 1952) 149–96 / Elisabeth Feist Hirsch *Damião de Gois: The Life and Thought of a Portuguese Humanist, 1502–1574* (The Hague 1967) / de Vocht 'Damião de Gois and his Oratio Postliminio ...' MHL 611–98, gives details about Gois' part in the defence of Louvain and his captivity / Erwin Panofsky *Albrecht Dürer* (Princeton 1948) II no 1081; Panofsky believes that the Albertina drawing does not represent Gois but that it is a work by Dürer / Joaquim de Vasconcellos 'Albrecht Dürer e a sua influencia na peninsula' in *Renascenca Portuguesa* (Coimbra 1929) 164–70; the author believes the drawing in the Albertina does represent Gois and that it is a work of Dürer; cf Hirsch 25–6 and Mario de Sampayo Ribeiro in *Publicacões do Instituto Alemão da Universidade de Coimbra* (Coimbra 1943) II 99–143

ELISABETH FEIST HIRSCH

Álvar GÓMEZ of Ciudad Real, 1488– 14 July 1538

Álvar was probably born at Guadalajara, the only child of Pero Gómez, Señor de Pioz, and Catarina Arias, and grandson of Álvar Gómez de Ciudad Real, secretary to *Jiménez de Cisneros and Henry IV of Castile. Little is known of Álvar's studies and early years in the army. He was an accomplished Latinist. He distinguished himself in the wars of Naples (1504) and Florence (1512) and fought in the battle of Pavia (1525). In 1514 he married Brianda de Mendoza, an illegitimate daughter of the third duke del Infantado; in 1516 he was a page of the future *Charles v in the Burgundian court, where he must have seen Erasmus repeatedly; in 1530 he was in Bologna with the Spanish entourage for the coronation of Charles v as king of Lombardy and emperor. Álvar was apparently granted a pension by *Ferdinand II of Aragon, which Charles v later recognized and continued, but neither his learning, nor his family's contacts, nor his war services helped him advance in the court, where he never occupied an office of consequence. Disenchanted with the court he retired to his estates, devoting himself entirely to his writings until his death at Toledo. In 1516 Álvar sent a brief letter to Erasmus under the pseudonym Alvarus Nemo (Ep 506), clearly noting that Erasmus did not know him, and enclosing a poem (LB III[b] 1857–8) congratulating Luigi *Marliano on his appointment to the bishopric of Tuy in Galicia. Álvar must also have shown Erasmus his *De militia velleris aurei*, written in Flanders after Prince Charles was declared king of Spain in April 1516 and before he set out for Spain in September 1517. Erasmus praised *De militia* with a short poem (Reedijk poem 105) which was published with Álvar's work at Toledo by Juan de Ayala in 1540. In his introduction to Álvar's *Thalichristia* (Alcalá 1522) dedicated to *Adrian vi, *Nebrija called Álvar the Christian Virgil. Álvar's other principal works are *Musa Paulina* (Alcalá: M. de Eguía 1529) dedicated to *Clement vii, *Proverbia Salomonis* (Alcalá 1536), *Septem elegiae in septem poenitentiae psalmos* (Toledo 1538), *Theologica descriptión de los misterios sagrados* (Toledo: J. de Ayala 1541), and a translation of Petrarch's *Trionfi*, published with Montemayor's *Diana* (Cuenca 1561).

BIBLIOGRAPHY: Allen Ep 506 / Bataillon *Erasmo y España* 607 / *Biographie universelle* rev ed XVII 133–4 / J. Catalina García *Biblioteca de escritores de Guadalajara* (Madrid 1899) 157–66 / B.J. Gallardo *Ensayo de una biblioteca española de libros raros y curiosos* (Madrid 1863–89) III 61–6 / F.K.H. Kossmann 'Een vergeten lofdicht van Erasmus op de Orde van het Gulden Vlies door Alvar Gomez 1517' *Het Boek* 26 (1942) 357–64 / Nicolás Antonio *Biblioteca Hispana nova* (Madrid 1783– 8) I 59–60 / A. Palau y Dulcet

Manual del librero Hispano-Americano 10 (1957)
96   R.M. FLORES

William GONNELL of Landbeach,
d 28 August 1560
Gonnell (Gonell) was born at Landbeach,
Cambridgeshire. His parents were on hand
and perhaps living with their son at the time of
his association with Erasmus in Cambridge
(Epp 279, 287, 289 of 1513–14), where he did
copying for Erasmus and cared for his horse
when the master was away (Epp 274, 276, 287,
289). Gonnell may also have been in charge of a
school (Ep 275). He was a friend of Robert
*Smith (Epp 276, 277, 279) whose son, John
*Smith, became a member of Erasmus' house-
hold and subsequently of Thomas *More's.
Erasmus loved young Gonnell tenderly and
followed his progress with great solicitude.
Perhaps on Erasmus' recommendation he was
employed as a tutor in More's household in
1517 and 1518 (Ep 601; Rogers Ep 63);
thereafter he appears to have been in the
service of Cardinal *Wolsey (Ep 820; also Epp
1138, 1229, where Erasmus associates him with
*Burbank and *Lupset). Meanwhile, on 6
September 1517 he received a benefice at
Conington, near Landbeach, which he held
until his death. John *Palsgrave treated him as
an authority in the teaching of Latin and Greek
when consulting him in 1529 about the
curriculum of *Henry VIII's bastard son, Henry
Fitzroy, duke of Richmond (Rogers Ep 168).

BIBLIOGRAPHY: Allen and CWE Ep 274 / DNB
VIII 106 / For a Thomas Gunnell documented at
Oxford 1489–91, d 1504, see Emden BRUC
275   CFG & PGB

Jean GONTHIER *See Johannes* GUINTERIUS

Federico GONZAGA duke of Mantua,
17 May 1500–28 June 1540
Federico was the son of Francesco Gonzaga,
marquis of Mantua, and of Isabella d'Este. His
younger brother was the imperial commander
Ferrante Gonzaga. Nothing is known of his
education, although his personal library suggests a degree of literary sensibility. His father
died on 29 March 1519, and he was officially
recognized as marquis on 3 April, receiving the
imperial investiture from *Charles V in 1521.
Gonzaga was a skilful soldier. On 1 July 1521,

through the diplomacy of Baldesar *Castiglione, *Leo X appointed him captain-general of
the church with an annual stipend of twelve
thousand ducats. He founded the pro-imperial
policy which guaranteed the survival of his
dynasty through the vicissitudes of the first
half of the sixteenth century. During the
struggles of Charles and *Francis I of France
for the duchy of Milan he distinguished
himself in a number of military engagements,
including the siege of Parma in 1521 and that of
Piacenza in 1522. Also in 1522 he forced the
French troops of Lautrec to retreat from the
vicinity of Pavia towards Monza. In recognition of his services Charles V named him
captain of one hundred lances in May 1522,
with an annual stipend of ten thousand francs.
During the battle of Pavia of 1525 he was
among the allies of the emperor. In 1526 he
joined the League of Cognac promoted by
*Clement VII against Charles, but through
clever diplomacy he was able to avoid any real
commitment to the league. In 1529 Charles
named him general commandant of the imperial
troops in Italy and on 8 April 1530 gave him the
title of duke.

The next six years of Gonzaga's life were
occupied with the questions of his marriage
and succession to the state of Monferrato. In
1517 he had married Maria Paleologo, then
only eight, in the hope that her father,
Bonifacio, marquis of Monferrato, would soon
die. In 1527 Gonzaga, no longer desiring this
marriage – which was never consummated –
obtained an annulment. In April 1530 he was
betrothed to Giulia of Aragon, Charles V's
aunt. On 6 June 1530, however, the marquis of
Monferrato finally died, to be succeeded by his
sickly brother Giangiorgio. Once again Gonzaga reversed his marriage policy, seeking to
break his promise to Giulia and marry Margherita Paleologo, the sister of the now
deceased Maria. After securing the consent of
Charles V by the payment of a large subsidy,
Gonzaga married Margherita on 3 October
1531. On Giangiorgio's death in 1533 he laid
claim to Monferrato, contesting it with Charles
II of *Savoy. In 1536 the emperor decided in
Gonzaga's favour. In his final years Gonzaga
distinguished himself as a patron of artists,
including Titian and Giulio Romano, who
designed the celebrated palace of Tè for him.

Gonzaga died at Mormirolo and was succeeded by his son Francesco.

In November 1535 *Viglius Zuichemus informed Erasmus that Gonzaga would be meeting Charles v at Naples (Ep 3071).

BIBLIOGRAPHY: C. Coniglio *I Gonzaga* (Milan 1967) 253–84 / P. Litta *Famiglie celebri italiane* (Milan 1835) IV table v   MARCO BERNUZZI

Johannes GORCUMENSIS *See Jan Dirksz van der HAER*

Johann GORITZ *See Johannes CORYCIUS*

GORRA (ASD I-2 220)
Although Erasmus frequently referred to Robert Holcot and Thomas Bricot as representatives of decadent scholasticism, his reference to 'Holcot, Bricot, and Gorra' in the *De conscribendis epistolis* is the sole mention of 'Gorra,' who was probably (like Holcot and Bricot) a theologian. Erasmus perhaps refers here to a certain Johannes Gorre, an Augustinian friar, who ranked seventeenth of twenty-one in the Paris theology licentiate class of 15 February 1472 and received his doctorate on 16 November 1472. This Johannes Gorre could plausibly still have been teaching when Erasmus arrived in Paris and wrote the original version of *De conscribendis epistolis* in 1498.

BIBLIOGRAPHY: ASD I-2 220 / Paris, Bibliothèque Nationale MS Latin 5657-A f 24 verso
                                         JAMES K. FARGE

Johannes GORRE *See GORRA*

Laurent de GORREVOD d 1529
Hieronymus *Artolf, a visitor to Besançon, formed the impression that the Maréchal de Bourgogne (*marisgallus*) was responsible for a régime of increased vigilance throughout the Franche-Comté, the Hapsburg county of Burgundy (Ep 2012, 22 July 1528). Allen suggested that this might be a reference to Philippe Chabot, lieutenant-general in French Burgundy, but the title of Maréchal de Bourgogne was held from 1521 by Laurent de Gorrevod, who preceded Nicolas *Perrenot de Granvelle as the principal architect of Hapsburg policy in the Comté.

From his ancestors Gorrevod inherited the lordship of Marnay (Doubs) as well as estates in Bresse, which belonged to Savoy. In 1497 he was *écuyer* of duke Philibert II of *Savoy and in 1504 governor of Bresse. He went to the Netherlands with Philibert's widow, *Margaret of Austria, and rose rapidly in her service as a financial expert and a member of her councils. In 1513 he was at the side of *Maximilian I during the siege of Thérouanne, and in 1518 he was present at the coronation of the future *Charles v in Valladolid. In the spring of 1521 he reported to Margaret from the diet of Worms, where he wielded great influence. He advocated *Gattinara's appointment as chancellor and as *grand-maître de l'hôtel* occupied a leading position at the court of Charles v (1522). In 1526 he signed the Treaty of Madrid that ended the captivity of *Francis I of France.

In 1516 Gorrevod was made a knight of the Golden Fleece, in 1520 viscount of Salins, and in 1521 count of Pont-de-Vaux. During his frequent visits to the Comté he acted (1521–8) as one of Charles v's arbitrators in the conflict between the archbishop and the city of Besançon. In 1527 he signed a will at his castle of Marnay. He died at Barcelona after participating in the negotiations leading to the peace of Cambrai.

BIBLIOGRAPHY: Fritz Walser and Rainer Wohlfeil *Die spanischen Zentralbehörden und der Staatsrat Karls v.* (Göttingen 1959) 132–3 / *Correspondance politique et administrative de Laurent de Gorrevod* ed André Chagny (Mâcon 1913) / J. Gauthier in *Mémoires de la société d'émulation du Doubs* IV-5 (1869) 344–6 / A. Castan 'Granvelle et le petit empereur de Besançon' *Revue historique* 1 (1876) 78-139, esp 81, 85, 93 / Henri Jougla de Morenne *Grand Amorial de France* (Paris 1934–52) 54 / Max Bruchet *Marguerite d'Autriche* (Lille 1927) 48 and passim / A.J.G. Le Glay *Négociations entre la France et l'Autriche* (Paris 1845) I xxiv, 534–8, II 420 / A.J.G. Le Glay *Correspondance de Maximilien I et de Marguerite d'Autriche* (Paris 1839) II 196–7, 230, 314 / *Deutsche Reichstagsakten Jüngere Reihe* (Gotha-Göttingen 1893–   ) II 26, 903–4, 939–40, 948, and passim / Karl Brandi *Kaiser Karl v.* 2nd ed (Darmstadt 1959–67) passim   PGB

GOSWIN *See GOZEWIJN of Halen*

Artus Gouffier, by Jean Clouet

GOUDANUS *See Cornelis* GERARD, *Willem* HERMANS, *and Herman* LETHMAET

Artus GOUFFIER d 13 May 1519
Born around 1475, Artus Gouffier (Boisy) was the eldest son of Guillaume by his second marriage, with Philippe de Montmorency. Guillaume was a rich crown official and from him Artus inherited the lordship of Boisy and most of his other properties, adding to them in due course the estates belonging to his wife, Hélène de Hangest, and the considerable rewards of his own service to three consecutive kings. He took part in the Italian campaigns of *Charles VIII and *Louis XII. He was mentor of the young *Francis I, who on 7 January 1515 appointed him *grand maître de France*, or chief superintendant of the royal household, an officer particularly visible at key ceremonies such as royal funerals. He was bailiff of Vermandois from 1503 but resigned in 1512 to become bailiff of Valois. He went to Italy again in 1515 and fought with Francis I at Marignano. He was employed on a number of diplomatic missions. Together with Etienne *Poncher he was one of the chief French negotiators of the

treaty of Noyon in 1516, and the reconciliation with Hapsburg-Burgundy, but he died suddenly of a urinary disorder during the abortive follow-up negotiations at Montpellier in May 1519 (Ep 924). Immensely wealthy, Gouffier was a patron of both pious institutions and of artists and poets such as Clément Marot, who wrote an epitaph for him. Gouffier's wife did crayon sketches and assembled an important collection of portraits.

BIBLIOGRAPHY: Allen Ep 924 / *Nouvelle Biographie générale* ed A. and H. Firmin-Didot (Paris 1855–66) VI 473–5 / Y.-M. Bercé 'Artus Gouffier' in Roland Mousnier et al *Le Conseil du Roi de Louis XII à la Révolution* (Paris 1970) 207–30   PGB

Gilles de GOURMONT of Saint-Germain-de-Varreville, documented 1499–1533
Gilles de Gourmont (Gromontius, Gurmontius), of Saint-Germain-de-Varreville, in Normandy, is documented as living in Paris until 1533; he was a bookseller licensed by the University of Paris (*libraire-juré*) and a printer. He often did business in partnership with his two brothers, Robert and Jean, who were also booksellers. At first his shop was in rue Saint-Jean-de-Latran in front of the Collège de Cambrai, but in 1518 he moved to the rue Saint-Jacques, where he operated under the sign of the Three Crowns near the church of St Benoît. He stocked books printed at Antwerp and himself maintained a branch store in Louvain.

Gourmont's activities were of special benefit to the study of the ancient languages since he published alphabets, grammars, lexica, and, of course, texts by classical authors. In 1507 he began to print in Greek type and in 1508 in Hebrew type, in each case being the first Paris printer to do so. In 1512 he published Girolamo *Aleandro's *Lexicon graeco-latinum*, the first Greek dictionary to be printed in Paris. An enlarged edition, which Gourmont launched in 1523, prompted Erasmus to compare it with the Greek dictionary edited by Jacobus *Ceratinus for the press of Johann *Froben (Ep 1460).

In 1511 Gourmont printed and published in partnership with the bookseller Jean *Petit the first edition of Erasmus' *Moria* (Ep 263). The manuscript may have been edited by Erasmus' young friend Richard *Croke, but Erasmus later expressed dissatisfaction with Croke's work and with the type used by Gourmont (Allen I 19). Gourmont subsequently published several more works by Erasmus, but he also saw fit to print in 1531 Julius Caesar *Scaliger's *Oratio pro M. Tullio Cicerone*, which was directed against Erasmus; this greatly irritated Erasmus, who requested that the book be suppressed by the Paris authorities (Ep 2577).

BIBLIOGRAPHY: Allen Ep 263 / Renouard *Répertoire* 177–8 / Henry Omont 'Essai sur les débuts de la typographie grecque à Paris (1507–1516)' *Mémoires de la Société de l'histoire de Paris et de l'Ile-de-France* 18 (1891) 1–72

       GENEVIÈVE GUILLEMINOT

Marcial de GOUVEIA b 1496
In two letters, one addressed to Erasmus *Schets, the other to Damião de *Gois, Erasmus mentioned a Portuguese who had given him information about the king and princes of Portugal (Epp 2370, 2846). There are strong indications that the informant was Marcial de Gouveia. In a letter to *Melanchthon written in the same month as the one to Schets, August 1530, Erasmus referred to a Portuguese who had come to see him after a visit with the German reformer (Ep 2358). At his trial before the Inquisition in Portugal Marcial admitted that he had known both Melanchthon and Erasmus, although he confused the dates of their respective meetings.

Marcial belongs to the Gouveia family, which produced many noted scholars, among them André, principal of the College of Guyenne at Bordeaux and later of the College of the Arts in Coimbra. Marcial studied at the Collège de Sainte-Barbe in Paris when his uncle Diogo was principal there. On his return to Portugal in 1539 he taught first at the school in Braga, succeeding the humanist historian Johannes Vasaeus, who in turn had replaced Nicolaus *Clenardus. He was finally appointed professor at the College of the Arts in Coimbra. Together with the other professors formerly from Guyenne he was called before the Inquisition and testified against his colleagues, with whom – for personal reasons, it seems – he did not get along.

BIBLIOGRAPHY: Antonio Baião 'O Processo desconhecido da Inquisicão contra o lente do

Colégio das Artes, Mestre Marcial de Gouveia' in *Anais da Academia Portuguesa da História* 9 (1944), 30–1 / Marcel Bataillon 'Erasme et la cour de Portugal' in *Etudes sur le Portugal au temps de l'humanisme* (Coimbra 1952) 82–3 / Mário Brandão 'Marcial de Gouveia und seine Beziehungen zu Erasmus und Melanchthon' *Revista do Instituto de Cultura Alemão em Lisboa* 1 (1944) 13 / Mário Brandão *O Processo na Inquisicão de Mestre Diogo de Teive* (Coimbra 1943) 48–9, 136–9, and passim / Mário Brandão *O Processo na Inquisicão de Mestre João da Costa* (Coimbra 1944) passim

     ELISABETH FEIST HIRSCH

GOZEWIJN of Halen, d 1530
Gozewijn (Gosuinus, Goswinus) was born about 1468 in the rural village of Halen and at first went to school in the neighbouring village of Roermond, although, according to his own statement, he did not learn much there. By 1481 he was taken to Groningen – perhaps by Rodolphus *Agricola – to become Wessel *Gansfort's famulus. He was present at the conversations of the learned men who met in the 'Academy' at Aduard and often accompanied Agricola to his home and helped the drunken father of northern humanism to pull off his boots. Gansfort sent him to Deventer to continue his education, and there he heard Alexander *Hegius read out the news of Agricola's death (27 October 1485). Shortly before Gansfort's death (4 October 1489) Gozewijn gave away his wordly goods and entered the house of the Brethren of the Common Life at Groningen (25 June 1489). In 1497 he was chosen rector of this house. In April 1518 he took a youth to Louvain and left him in the charge of Maarten van *Dorp. He also met Erasmus, who thought highly of him (Epp 838, 839). On a subsequent visit to Louvain early in 1521 he handed Erasmus a gift from Willem *Frederiks (Ep 1200).

Gozewijn was a friend of Gerardus *Listrius, who dedicated to him his *Commentarioli* (Zwolle: S. Corver 1520), and also of Augustijn *Agge and *Melanchthon, at whose request he wrote a life of Agricola. He also was the author of a life of Wessel Gansfort and of some letters published as preliminary pieces in Gansfort's *Opera* (Groningen 1614).

BIBLIOGRAPHY: Allen Ep 839 / M. van Rhijn in

his *Studiën over Wessel Gansfort en zijn tijd*
(Utrecht 1933) 137–59 and in NNBW VII 516–17 /
The two lives were edited by J.B. Kan in
Erasmiani Gymnasii programma litterarium
(Rotterdam 1894)   C.G. VAN LEIJENHORST

Diego GRACIÁN de Alderete documented
c1517–63
Diego Gracián (Jacobus Gratianus), of Alder-
ete, near Tordesillas, was the son of Diego
García, at one time the chief armourer to
*Ferdinand II of Aragon and *Isabella of
Castile. He studied for eight years at Paris and
Louvain, where he was a pupil of Juan Luis
*Vives. Probably late in 1525 he entered the
service of Maximilianus *Transsilvanus and
attended the court of *Margaret of Austria.
Around 1527 he returned to Spain in search of
promotion and, on the recommendation of
Alfonso de *Valdés, the imperial secretary,
obtained employment at the imperial court. He
served Don *Juan Manuel, lord of Belmonte,
and Francisco de *Mendoza y Córdoba, bishop
of Zamora, and was employed by *Charles v
and Philip II as secretary and translator. On 10
April 1539 he was rewarded with a knighthood. On 30 June 1537 he married Juana, the
natural daughter of Johannes *Dantiscus, who
lived with her mother in Valladolid; they had
twelve children. In 1562 and 1563 Gracián was
a secretary to Bernardo de Fresneda, bishop of
Cuenca and royal confessor. He lived to be
ninety.
   In his youth Gracián was an enthusiastic
Erasmian. In the late 1520s and early 1530s he
corresponded with Erasmus (Epp 1913, 1970,
2297), recommending Don Juan Manuel and
his other employers and friends to the Dutch
humanist and pledging support against the
enemies of Erasmus in Spain. He also exchanged stories about monks with Juan de
*Valdés and Francisco de *Vergara. Other
correspondents included Dantiscus, Alfonso
de Valdés, and Alonso *Fernández, whose
letter to Erasmus of 13 November 1527 (Ep
1904) Gracián abridged.
   Gracián translated many Greek and Latin
works into Spanish, including Plutarch's
Apophthegmata (Alcalá: Miguel de Eguia 1533)
and *Moralia* (Alcalá 1548), works of Xenophon
(Salamanca: J. de Junta 1552), *The Peloponnesian
War* of Thucydides (Salamanca 1564), and

Isocrates' speech *Ad Nicoclem* (Salamanca: M.
Gast 1570). He also translated Johannes Sleidanus' abridgment of the chronicles of Froissart
(Munich, Bayerische Staatsbibliothek, MS hisp.
10). Around 1552 he wrote the *Speravi, sive de
falsa et vera spe* (ed A. Bonilla y San Martín in
Revue hispanique 8, 1901, 189–90, 268–78), in
which he listed all the dignitaries he had
served and the disappointments they had
caused him.

BIBLIOGRAPHY: Allen Ep 1913 / Bataillon
Erasmo y España 268–9 and passim / Milagros
Ezquerro *Diego Gracián de Alderete* (Toulouse
1968) / John E. Longhurst *Erasmus and the
Spanish Inquisition: The Case of Juan de Valdés*
(Albuquerque, New Mexico, 1950) passim / A.
Paz y Mélia 'Otro erasmista español: Diego
Gracián de Alderete' *Revista de archivos, biblio-
tecas y museos* ser 3 vol 5 (1901) 27–36, 125–39,
608–25 / de Vocht CTL II 408–12 and passim / de
Vocht *Danticus* 286–8 and passim
                                    LUIS A. PÉREZ & TBD

Gabriel de GRAMONT d 26 May or
7 June 1534
A son of Roger de Gramont and Aliénor de
Béarn, Gabriel became a protégé of Constable
Anne de Montmorency and one of *Francis I's
most able diplomats. By 1520 his brother
Charles had resigned to him the see of
Couserans in the Pyrenees, which he exchanged in 1524 for Tarbes, another diocese in
the Pyrenees. From 1525 he undertook one
diplomatic mission after another, negotiating
in England and at the imperial court. On 14 July
1529 he was elected archbishop of Bordeaux
but resigned the following year in favour of
Charles. On 8 June 1530 he was named cardinal
together with François de *Tournon, and
thereafter Rome was the principal scene of his
diplomatic activity (Ep 2753), which culminated in 1533 with the espousal of *Catherine de'
Medici to the future *Henry II. This match was
particularly welcome as a counterpoise to the
formidable influence *Charles v had gained
with *Clement VII since 1530. Gramont was,
however, less successful in pleading at Rome
the cause of his king's ally, *Henry VIII of
England. In 1532 he had been named bishop of
Poitiers and finally, in 1533, he gained the
archbishopric of Toulouse, of which his representative took possession on 27 October.

BIBLIOGRAPHY: Allen Ep 2753 / *Gallia christiana* I 1140, 1239–40, II 847, 1203–4, XIII 54–5 / Eubel III 21 and passim / Pastor x 101, 210–12, and passim   PGB

GRANVELLA, GRANVELLE *See Nicholas* PERRENOT

Cornelius GRAPHEUS of Aalst, d 19 December 1558

Cornelius Grapheus (Scribonius) was the name commonly used by Cornelis, a son of Joost de Schrijver, born about 1482 in Aalst, between Brussels and Ghent. Since he is later given the title of *magister* it may be assumed that he studied at a university, as yet undetermined. It may be that he obtained a MA during his visit to Italy. By 1515 he had returned from there and settled in Antwerp, marrying Adriana Philips. By 1520 he was one of the secretaries of the city of Antwerp and susceptible to the ideas of Martin *Luther. He edited two works by Jan Pupper van Goch, *Epistola apologetica* (1520) and *De libertate christiana* (March 1521), the latter with a preface in support of church reform that was soon to gain the attention of the Inquisition. In June 1521 Albrecht *Dürer met him while on a visit to Antwerp and received from him a copy of Luther's *De captivitate Babylonica*. On 5 February 1522 he was arrested at the request of the inquisitors Frans van der *Hulst and Nicolaas *Baechem Egmondanus. Although he retracted his views in writing and submitted to public recantations in Brussels and Antwerp (April–May 1522), he was jailed for some time in Brussels, where he wrote an unpublished 'Querimonia in carceris angustia' addressed to his friend Gerard *Geldenhouwer and an appeal to Jean de *Carondelet. In the autumn of 1523 he was allowed to return to Antwerp, where he was a schoolteacher and assisted his brother Johannes *Grapheus in the latter's print shop (Ep 2114) before he was finally reinstated as a town secretary in 1540.

A Latin poet of wide reputation, Grapheus maintained friendly contacts with Pieter *Gillis, who was his colleague in the chancery, Adrianus Cornelii *Barlandus, Thomas *More (Ep 1087), and many other humanists. Erasmus clearly knew him well; from Basel he followed Grapheus' tribulations in 1522 and 1523 (Epp 1299, 1302, 1306, 1318, 1351). After learning that his friend had regained his freedom (Epp 1358, 1394), Erasmus informed *Goclenius of a bequest he had set out for the needy poet (Ep 1437). In 1529 he thanked Grapheus for a poem which the latter had evidently sent him but declined to publish it, in part for the poet's own safety (Ep 2114). In 1534 Erasmus asked Grapheus to send him a new famulus (Ep 2916); the Antwerp secretary recommended Johannes *Clauthus and later calmly justified his choice in response to Erasmus' unreasonable suspicions against the poor famulus (Epp 3028, 3053).

Among Grapheus' publications the following may be noted: *Carmen pastorale* (Louvain 1515), *De magnificentissimis urbis Antverpiae spectaculis Carolo Imperatore designato aeditis* (Antwerp 1519), *Caroli Imperatore ex Hispania in Germaniam reditus* (Antwerp 1520) dedicated to Mercurino *Gattinara, *De nomine florentissimae civitatis Antverpiensis* (Antwerp 1528), *Conflagratio templi D. Mariae Antverpiensis* (Antwerp 1534), *Monstrum anabaptisticum* (Antwerp 1535), *Aeglogae tres* (Antwerp 1536), *Pacis inter Carolum V et Franciscum I descriptio* (Antwerp 1540), and, in collaboration with Pieter Gillis, *Enchiridion principis et magistratus christiani* (Cologne 1541).

BIBLIOGRAPHY: Allen Ep 1087 / J. Roulez in BNB V 721–6 / de Vocht *Literae ad Craneveldium* 484–6 and passim / de Vocht CTL I 438 and passim / Floris Prims *Geschiedenis van Antwerpen* (Brussels-Antwerp 1927–49) XVIII 188–9, 289
                                MARCEL A. NAUWELAERTS

Johannes GRAPHEUS of Aalst, d before 29 November 1571

Johannes Grapheus (Jan de Schrijver) was a younger brother of Erasmus' friend Cornelius *Grapheus. Born around 1502, Johannes married Elisabeth Amersfoort, who bore him a son, Baptista, and two daughters. Two sisters of his wife were married to Franz *Birckmann and John *Siberch respectively. Johannes owned a press at Antwerp and between 1527 and 1569 printed some three hundred works, partly on his own account and partly for other publishers in Flanders and abroad. In addition to books in Latin, Greek, and Hebrew, he printed works in French, Spanish, English, and Flemish, including some that were put on the Index.

Writing to Cornelius in March 1529, Erasmus regretted that circumstances seemed to rule out any collaboration between himself and Johannes (Ep 2114).

BIBLIOGRAPHY: Allen Ep 2114 / A. Rouzet *Dictionnaire des imprimeurs, libraires et éditeurs des xve et xvie siècles dans les limites de la Belgique actuelle* (Nieuwkoop 1975) 79–80 (with bibliography)   MARCEL A. NAUWELAERTS

Acchille de' GRASSI *See Annibale (II)* *BENTIVOGLIO*

Johannes GRATIANUS *See Diego GRACIÁN*

Ortwinus GRATIUS of Holtwick,
d 22 May 1542
Ortwinus Gratius (van Graes, van Grass, Gracius Daventriensis), the son of Friedrich and Gertrud, was born by 1480 in Holtwick, near Coesfeld, Westphalia. He was descended from a Dutch noble family that had settled in the region of Münster. The family was no longer well off; of Ortwinus' five younger half-sisters three became nuns. Ortwinus himself, who had lost his mother soon after birth, was taken to Deventer by his uncle, Jan van Graes, who was a priest there and was prepared to pay for the boy's support and education. In Deventer Ortwinus attended the Latin school under the direction of Alexander *Hegius; he may have been a teacher himself until 1501, when he matriculated at the University of Cologne, unable to pay the registration fee. He was admitted to the Kuck college, whose regent, Gerard of Zutphen, was later ridiculed in the *Epistolae obscurorum virorum* as 'Magister Scotphi.' On the eve of Corpus Domini 1502 he was promoted BA, and on 1 April 1506 MA. On 3 July 1507 he became a member of the faculty of arts, where he continued to teach until his death, having taken holy orders between 1512 and 1514. Little is known about his private life. His position appears to have been a modest one: in 1533 and 1534 he tried without success to better himself (*Epistolae ad Nauseam* 145ff).

Gratius took a lively interest in the promotion of printing. It seems that he persuaded the bookseller Heinrich of Neuss to acquire a press of his own, among whose earliest productions one notes Gratius' *Orationes quodlibeticae* (1508)

and *In laudem divi Swiberti epigrammata*. A quarrel with Hermannus *Buschius over the use of a commentary on Donatus eventually caused Gratius to end his collaboration with Heinrich's press. It is true that the latter published Gratius' Latin rendering of Johann *Pfefferkorn's *Beschirmung* in 1516 (Ep 487), but this appears to be an isolated occurrence. Gratius' own books were henceforward published by the Quentel brothers, and from August 1509 he also worked for this press as a corrector. In general, his considerable merits as a teacher, author, and editor in the fields of humanism and theology tend to be overlooked as a result of his involvement in the *Reuchlin controversy. In 1515 he edited for Quentel Cicero's *De officiis*, etc, with the commentaries of Erasmus, which he praised. In his *Fasciculus rerum expetendarum ac fugiendarum* (Cologne 1535) he argued in favour of moderate church reform, pointing specifically to the legacy of Erasmus.

Gratius' role amid the opponents of Reuchlin was perhaps more marginal than is commonly assumed in view of the violent attacks unleashed against him in the *Epistolae obscurorum virorum ad Magistrum Ortvinum Gratium* (1515, Epp 363, 487). It is true that he translated Pfefferkorn's *Judenfeind* and *Osterbuch* (1509) into Latin and edited with a commendatory poem the *Opus aureum* of Viktor of Carben, a converted rabbi. He also voiced his opposition to Reuchlin in an epigram printed with the *Articuli* by Albert of *Tongeren (1512) and in his *Praenotamenta* (1514). On the other hand, there seems to be no substance to the charges that he collaborated with Pfefferkorn over the production of the *Handspiegel*, and he did not otherwise initiate attacks upon the Reuchlinists, although he defended himself at length against their strictures in his *Lamentationes obscurorum virorum* (1518) and *Epistola apologetica* (1518).

Erasmus appears to have known Gratius personally. While he was disgusted with the *Lamentationes*, especially in view of the unauthorized inclusion of one of his own letters (Epp 622, 830; cf Ep 852), and suspected Gratius of collusion with Jacob of *Hoogstraten as well as Pfefferkorn (Ep 1006), he also expressed surprise and regret at seeing a talented scholar join the anti-Reuchlinist camp

(Ep 856); in 1519 he appealed to him to exercise moderation, while at the same time using Gratius' wide contacts in Cologne for a personal reason (Ep 1022). Others were unsparing in their comments on Gratius. Buschius called him the shadow of Pfefferkorn (RE Ep 182), while Reuchlin himself described him as a monkey, a barbarian, and the scum of mankind in his *Defensio contra calumniatores Colonienses* (1513). *Luther likened him to a dog, a wolf in sheep's clothing, and a crocodile (Luther W I 21, XII 69).

The *Gemma prenosticationum* published under Gratius' name (Ep 526) is no longer thought to be his work.

BIBLIOGRAPHY: Allen and CWE Ep 526 / L. Geiger in ADB IX 600–2 / D. Reichling *Ortwin Gratius: Sein Leben und sein Wirken* (Heiligenstadt 1884; repr 1963) reviewed by Geiger in *Vierteljahresschrift für Kultur und Literatur der Renaissance* 1 (1886) 402 / L. Geiger *Johann Reuchlin* (Leipzig 1871, repr 1964) 274 and passim / J. Hashagen 'Hauptrichtungen des rheinischen Humanismus' *Annalen des Historischen Vereins für den Niederrhein* 106 (1922) 1–56 especially 43–4 / H. Harthausen 'Der Kölner Buchdrucker Heinrich von Neuss' *Annalen des Historischen Vereins für den Niederrhein* 171 (1969) 81–174 / *Epistolae ad Nauseam* 108–11 and passim   DIETER RIESENBERGER

Bernardus GRAVIUS of Cologne, documented 1533–44(?)
Very little is known about Bernardus, one of the eight children of Tielmannus *Gravius. In the spring or summer of 1533 he joined Erasmus' household in Freiburg for a while; according to his father, he also studied in Basel and became acquainted with Bonifacius *Amerbach (AK IV Ep 2056). As the attractions of Freiburg taverns proved irresistible to the youth, he soon had to borrow money from the printer Johannes *Faber Emmeus. Eventually he was called home after Erasmus had written to complain about his conduct. By Christmas 1533 he had been back in Cologne for a while when his heartbroken father made him write a letter of apology to Erasmus (Epp 2893, 2894). Bernardus wrote again in the spring to ask for Erasmus' support in persuading Tielmannus to give him another chance and let him study at Louvain (Ep 2910), but there is no record of

Bernardus in the Louvain matriculation register. In the summer of 1535 Tielmannus was still worried about how he was to satisfy the incensed Faber Emmeus (Ep 3040). Bernardus may be identical with a Bernardus Gravius a Fossa who matriculated on 19 May 1544 in Cologne to study law.

BIBLIOGRAPHY: Allen Ep 2893 / AK IV Ep 2056 / *Matrikel Köln* II 985

FRANK GOLCZEWSKI & PGB

Tielmannus GRAVIUS documented 1496–1544
Tielmannus Gravius (a Fossa, Grave, von Graben) matriculated as a poor student in arts at the University of Cologne on 27 September 1496, where he graduated BA on 11 December 1497 and MA in 1499. From about 1503 he was employed in the chancery of the archbishops of Cologne; his notarial mark is found on a document dated 23 September 1504. From 1530 he was notary to the chapter of the cathedral of Cologne, and from 1535 to 1544 he was the chapter's secretary. Notes in his hand are found in a number of other documents; in a copy-book of the cathedral chapter, 1542–3, he annotated the correspondence between chapter and Archbishop Hermann von *Wied, also listing the names of the canons of that time. From letters to Erasmus in the years 1532–6 it may be gathered that he occupied a position of some significance at the court of Hermann von Wied (Epp 2626, 2894, 3128). Of his eight children (Ep 1865) two daughters were married to lawyers, while his son Leonardus married a daughter of the physician Heinrich Andreas Sittard. In 1535 he must have been a widower since he was about to take holy orders and had already received a modest benefice (Ep 3041). He owned a fine library and was a friend of Adolf *Eichholz (Ep 2071) and Henricus Cornelius *Agrippa (Epp 2626, 2737) and a patron of Jacobus *Omphalius, whose appointment to Cologne he promoted. He was also a patron of the printer Eucharius *Cervicornus. Johann Oldendorp dedicated to him *De iure et aequitate forensis disputatio* (Cologne: J. Gymnich 1541).

Contacts between Erasmus and Gravius may have been brought about by a common friend, Johannes *Caesarius (Ep 610). The fact that Helias *Marcaeus was also a common acquaintance raises the possibility of contacts when Erasmus was passing through Cologne in 1518 (Epp 842, 1865). The correspondence between them seems to have begun in 1527, when Erasmus wrote to thank Gravius for a gift (Ep 1829) and the latter responded eagerly with letters and more gifts (Epp 1865, 2068). They continued to write to each other until Erasmus' death; Gravius was frequently asked to forward Erasmus' letters to other destinations, and more than once he looked after Erasmus' servant and letter carrier Felix *Rex (Epp 2068, 2728). In February 1529 Erasmus dedicated to Gravius his edition of Lactantius' *De opificio Dei* (Ep 2103), and in 1535 he received one of his sons, Bernardus *Gravius, into his household for some months (Epp 2893, 2894), while the father informed him repeatedly about the Anabaptists of Münster (Epp 2990, 3041; AK IV Ep 1900). In his modest way Gravius was a fervent and faithful admirer of Erasmus, and Hieronymus *Froben found it appropriate to inform him personally of Erasmus' death (Ep 3136).

BIBLIOGRAPHY: Allen Ep 610 / AK IV Epp 2055–6, 2063, 2076 / Leonard Ennen *Geschichte der Stadt Köln* (Cologne-Neuss 1863–80) IV 111, 370 / *Briefe und Documente aus der Zeit der Reformation im 16. Jahrhundert* ed K. and W. Krafft (Elberfeld 1875) 166 / Conrad Varrentrapp *Hermann von Wied und sein Reformationsversuch in Köln* (Leipzig 1878) I 90, II 53 / *Matrikel Köln* II 408 / J. Hashagen 'Hauptrichtungen des rheinischen Humanismus' *Annalen des Historischen Vereins für den Niederrhein* 106 (1922) 1–56, esp 52–3

FRANK GOLCZEWSKI & PGB

Thomas GREEN d 1529
Thomas Green (Grene, Greanus) is documented as being at Cambridge in 1492–3. In 1499–1500 he was a fellow of Jesus College, and from 1507 to his death he was master of Catherine Hall. He graduated bachelor of theology on 31 May 1504. From 1504 he studied towards a higher degree in theology and incepted in 1511–12. In 1514 he was apparently commissary of the University of Cambridge, that is, a judge acting in cases involving students (Ep 289). To crown his career he was vice-chancellor in 1523–4. When he died in 1529 he left Catherine Hall ten pounds sterling.

Erasmus, who had evidently met Green at Cambridge, sent him greetings through William *Gonnell (Epp 287, 289) and also corresponded with him in 1514, doing him the honour of quoting his words to Gonnell (Ep 292).

BIBLIOGRAPHY: Allen and CWE Ep 287 / Emden BRUC 270 / D.F.S. Thomson and H.C. Porter *Erasmus and Cambridge* (Toronto 1963) 222 and passim   PGB

Gregorio de' GREGORI of Forlì, documented 1496–1527
When rebutting the charges of Edward *Lee (*Liber quo respondet annotationibus Lei* LB IX 140C), Erasmus mentioned Gregorio de' Gregori (de Gregoriis), although not by name, as the publisher of Bernardino *Gadolo's edition of St Jerome's commentaries on Genesis and the prophets (1497).

Gregorio is documented as a publisher in Venice from 1496 to 1527, printing in part with his brother, Giovanni, who is documented from 1482 to 1503. Gregorio, himself a skilled wood engraver, is noted above all for his outstanding achievements in the field of book illustration. He printed mainly classical authors and humanists, but also liturgial and scientific books. In September 1514 he seems to have operated a press at Fano, near Pesaro.

Gregori published a number of Erasmus' works in Venice in the 1520s: *Institutio principis christiani* (1522), *Institutum hominis christiani* (1522), *Parabolae* (1522), Dionysius Cato *Disticha moralia, cum scholiis Erasmi* (1522), *Enchiridion* (1523), *Auctarium selectarum epistolarum* (1524), and *Encomium matrimonii* printed with *Encomium medicinae* (1526).

BIBLIOGRAPHY: G. Fumagalli *Dictionnaire géographique d'Italie pour servir à l'histoire de l'imprimerie* (Florence 1905) 120, 464, 477, 480–2 / *Editori e stampatori italiani del Quattrocento* introduction by R. Bertieri (Milan 1929) 56–8 and passim / *Short-Title Catalogue of Books Printed in Italy ... from 1465 to 1600 now in the British Museum* (London 1958) 854–5 and passim / Marcella and Paul Grendler 'The Survival of Erasmus in Italy' *Erasmus in English* 8 (1976) 2–22, esp 17–20   PGB

GREGORIO da Tifernate *See Gregorius* TIPHERNAS

Gerard GREGORISZ, Guerard GREGOIRE
See ERASMUS' *family*

Richard von GREIFFENKLAU 1467–
15 March 1531
Richard was the son of the steward Johann von
Greiffenklau, from an ancient noble family of
the Rhineland, and Klara von Rathsamhausen.
His family directed him towards an ecclesiastical career, and in 1487 he received a canonry of
the cathedral of Trier, where he had been
domiciliar from 1482. On 14 April 1488 the
chapter granted him leave to attend the University of Paris for two or three years, but his
name has not been found in the Paris matriculation register. After his return he was appointed precentor, and on 15 May 1511 the chapter
elected him archbishop of Trier. In preparation
for the imperial election of 1519 Greiffenklau
led the princes opposed to the aspirations of
the Hapsburgs. In 1522 and 1523 he had to
ward off Franz von *Sickingen and his rebel
knights, who were attacking the principality of
Trier. In the two years preceding the diet of
Worms in 1521 Greiffenklau had repeatedly
been proposed as a mediator in the conflict
between Martin *Luther and the church.
Although Luther was willing to accept him in
this role, no such mediation process was set in
operation. When the diet actually met, Greiffenklau advocated moderation and compromise and privately arranged for a debate of the
religious issues in which Luther could participate on equal terms with his opponents.
  His moderation notwithstanding, Greiffenklau never departed from his firm adherence to
the church of Rome, and during his tenure of
the archdiocese the Reformation failed to make
any inroads in the ecclesiastical principality of
Trier. This success was partly due to the
absence of printers in the territory of Trier.
After 1526, however, Greiffenklau lost ecclesiastical jurisdiction over some of the secular
principalities which formed part of the archdiocese, among them Hesse, Nassau-Weilburg,
and Hohensolms. The archbishop died at
Ottenstein, near Wittlich.
  It appears that Greiffenklau had invited
Erasmus to meet him when both were at
Cologne in November of 1520 and that he
extended another invitation to the humanist in
the autumn of 1521, when Erasmus passed

through Koblenz on his way to Basel (Ep 1342).
No personal contacts resulted, however, conceivably because of Greiffenklau's previous
opposition to the Hapsburgs. Later the arch-
bishop was occasionally mentioned by one of
Erasmus' correspondents (Epp 1454, 2714).
Greiffenklau was also a patron of Bartholo-
maeus *Latomus, who published in his honour a
Declamatio funebris (Cologne 1531).
  BIBLIOGRAPHY: Allen Ep 1342 / ADB XXVIII
413–18 / Aloys Schmidt 'Richard von Greiffen-
klau, Erzbischof und Kurfürst zu Trier' in
Nassauische Lebensbilder VI (Wiesbaden 1961)
1–25 / Aloys Schmidt 'Der Trierer Kurfürst
Erzbischof Richard von Greiffenklau und die
Auswirkungen des Wormser Edikts in Kur-
trier' in *Der Reichstag zu Worms von 1521* ed Fritz
Reuter (Worms 1971) 271–96 / Paul Rettberg
*Studien zum Verständnis der Politik des Kurfürsten
Richard von Trier in den Jahren 1519–1526*
(Greifswald 1901) / Benedikt Caspar *Das
Erzbistum Trier im Zeitalter der Glaubensspaltung*
(Münster 1966)   ROLF DECOT

Karel GRENIER *See* CAROLUS *(Ep 1092)*

Johannes GREPPERUS *See Johann* GROPPER

Heinrich GRESBECK of Münster,
documented 1530–5
A citizen of Münster, in Westphalia, Gresbeck
returned to his native city in 1534 after an
absence of four years. He married and joined
the Anabaptist community which controlled
the city. On 27 February 1534 he was baptized.
During the defence of the city Gresbeck was on
watch at the Kreuz gate during the night of 23
May 1535 when he deserted with Hans *Eck
von der Langenstrate and three others (Ep
3031). Captured by the besieging army of
Bishop Franz von *Waldeck, Gresbeck revealed the weakest spots in the city's defences
and thus contributed to the success of the final
assault. His *Bericht von der Wiedertaufe in
Münster*, written in Low German, was edited
by C.A. Cornelius in *Die Geschichtsquellen des
Bistums Münster* (Münster 1851–   ) II 1–214.
  BIBLIOGRAPHY: Allen Ep 3031 / *The Mennonite
Encyclopedia* (Scottdale 1955–9) II 578 / Ugo
Gastaldi *Storia dell'anabattismo dalle origini a
Münster, 1525–1535* (Turin 1972) 531, 556
                                                    PGB

Adolf Greverade

Matthias GRETZ *See Matthias* KRETZ

Adolf GREVERADE of Lübeck,
d January 1501
On 18 December 1497 or 1498 (?) Erasmus
addressed a letter to one 'Greveradus advocatus,' which was to be delivered by Augustinus Vincentius *Caminadus (Ep 141). In this
letter Erasmus suggested that Greveradus
collaborate with him in the great enterprise of
editing Jerome, perhaps both as a scholar and
as a well-to-do patron. Greveradus was not
personally known to Erasmus but was clearly
an old acquaintance of Erasmus' friend Heinrich *Northoff of Lübeck.
   This letter was very likely addressed to
Adolf Greverade (Odolfus, Greverode), a
descendant of a leading merchant family of
Lübeck whose origins in the fourteenth century can perhaps be traced back to an immi-
grant from Greverath, north-east of Trier.
Adolf Greverade was the son of Heinrich (d
1468/9) and the brother of another Heinrich (d c
1509). On 19 September 1477 the two orphaned
brothers were declared of age by Lübeck
council; by Lübeck law this meant that they

must have attained the age of twenty-five. In
1484 Adolf acted as one of the executors of the
will of another Adolf Greverade, a city
councillor, who had died in 1481. He continued for some time in the commercial tradition of his family and with his brother managed
the Lübeck currency exchange. As late as 1494
Adolf was mentioned as a merchant, but soon
thereafter he must have resolved to enter the
church. On 4 September 1495 he matriculated
at the University of Louvain. By 1497 he was in
orders when Pope *Alexander VI nominated
him to a canonry in Lübeck. He was in
Louvain, however, at the time of his death.
   Soon after Adolf's matriculation in Louvain
two younger Greverades arrived there, presumably to continue their studies under
Adolf's supervision. On 30 April 1497 Ludolf
and (the younger) Adolf Greverade registered
as students of the College of the Lily. This
Adolf and his brother Heinrich are documented as the sons of the elder Heinrich (d c
1509). The younger Heinrich and Ludolf had
matriculated together at Rostock in July 1493
(*Matrikel Rostock* I 267). In 1504 the younger
Heinrich is also mentioned as executor of the
will of his uncle, the canon Adolf. It is possible
that Ludolf may be addressed in Erasmus' Ep
94.
   A tradition of pious devotion and munificence ran in the Greverade family. The canon's
father and his brother Heinrich both endowed
the choir chapel of St Mary's church, and in
1497 the latter helped found a lay fraternity
associated with this chapel. Above all the
brothers Adolf and Heinrich Greverade provided their city with the finest of its many altar
triptychs, a crucifixion painted by Hans Memling as his last major work and dated 1491.
Memling executed this work in Bruges, where
Heinrich Greverade seems to have been active
in business for some time. The composition
indicates that Memling worked to the specific
instructions of the Greverade brothers, one of
whom must be the man portrayed in the typical
donor's pose. It is assumed that a period of
unsettled conditions involving the bishop and
chapter of Lübeck at first discouraged the
Greverades from placing the triptych in the
cathedral for which it seems to have been
intended from the outset. Not until 1504 did
the family endow vicaries from Adolf's estate to

ensure regular mass services in the chapel that came to be known as the Greverade chapel, a step that normally precedes the presentation of an altar piece.

While their plans for the cathedral remained temporarily in suspense, Adolf and Heinrich Greverade continued the family patronage of St Mary's, providing on 23 February 1494 for a vicary and an altar in a chapel of that church, likewise to be known as the Greverade chapel. They had the Lübeck painter Hermann Rode execute a diptych for St Mary's which was clearly inspired by the same devotional and artistic ideas as were already expressed in Memling's great altar piece. The most striking similarity between the two works is the prominence given to St Jerome. In Ep 141 Erasmus speaks of the 'constant and special affection' the addressee had shown for St Jerome, so Erasmus must have had a clear understanding of the Greverades' special concern. In 1504 the family commissioned a further painting for St Mary's from the Lübeck painter Bernt Notke, which again exhibited features untypical of the artistic tradition of Lübeck. It showed St Gregory I celebrating mass and included the portraits of the late Adolf, dressed as a canon, and his nephew and executor, Heinrich. While Rode's and Notke's works in St Mary's church were destroyed in 1942, the Memling altar survived the war and is at present in the St. Annen-Museum, Lübeck.

In their patronage of St Mary's the Greverades were closely associated with the *Schinkel and Northoff families, some of whose members were likewise connected with Erasmus. Within this milieu of commerce and religious culture Adolf Greverade must indeed have been a striking figure. That Ep 141 was addressed to Adolf in Louvain rather than another Greverade seems probable in view of his scholarly interests and the fact that Erasmus refers to him as 'so near a neighbour.' Caminadus, who was expected to deliver Ep 141, travelled repeatedly to the Netherlands. The 'advocatus' in the title of Ep 141, if not simply an erroneous reading of 'Adolphus,' could point either to the patronage Erasmus hoped to obtain or to another ecclesiastical office held by Greverade.

BIBLIOGRAPHY: *Matricule de Louvain* III-1 129, 158 / Max Hasse *Hans Memlings Lübecker*

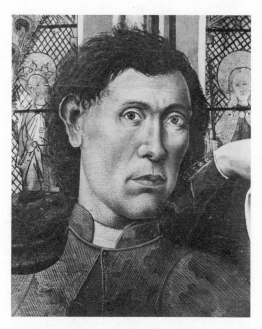

Heinrich Greverade, brother of Adolf

Passionsaltar 2nd ed (Lübeck 1979) / *Die Bau- und Kunstdenkmäler der Freien und Hansestadt Lübeck* (Lübeck 1906–   ) II 171, 211, 216, 320–2, III 63, 132, 144–6, and plates / K.B. McFarlane *Hans Memling* (Oxford 1971) 35, 40, plates 111–30 / Lübeck, Archiv der Hansestadt Lübeck, MS Personenkartei 112 passim

PGB

Thomas GREY documented 1497–1527/8
Thomas Grey (Greyus, Leucophaeus) is known exclusively from the correspondence of Erasmus, which reveals little about his external circumstances. He evidently came from a good family, and in 1497 in Paris he and Robert *Fisher were pupils of Erasmus, who lived in the same house with them. Their guardian entertained suspicions concerning Erasmus' feelings towards Grey and requested him to leave. Erasmus voiced his grief and anger in Ep 58, while Grey and his friends desired Erasmus' return (Ep 61), and despite all the two retained a close friendship (Epp 63, 64). About 1497 Erasmus apparently dedicated his *De ratione studii* to Grey (Epp 66, 69; ASD I-2

146–51), although subsequently in 1512 he re-dedicated it to Grey's close friend Pierre *Vitré. Meanwhile Grey appears to have been in London in 1511, sending greetings to Erasmus through Andrea *Ammonio (Ep 221).

From 1516 to 1518 Grey, having married and having fathered two children, was again at Paris, where he was connected with Vitré (Epp 445, 503, 528, 768). From Paris he also corresponded with *Beatus Rhenanus (Epp 445, 460, 581), who may have met him there between 1503 and 1507. In the spring of 1518 Grey left Paris and visited Erasmus at Louvain on his way to England (Epp 768, 777, 817, 827), taking Ep 829 to Thomas *More. He hoped that More would help him recover ancestral lands then in the possession of John *Colt (Ep 829). An Edmundus Grecius of London who matriculated at Louvain on 31 August 1518 as an inmate of Erasmus' own College of the Lily may have been a son of Thomas. In the autumn of 1525 Grey set out for the continent once more. In the company of his youngest son he visited Erasmus at Basel and apparently kept him informed of some conversations he had had with Guillaume *Farel (Epp 1624, 1640). He intended to take his son to the University of Louvain (Ep 1641), but their presence there is not documented. Grey's visit led to contacts between Erasmus and the Franciscan nuns of Denny near Cambridge, and by 1527 or 1528 he appears to have been living in England again (Ep 1925; LB V 609–14).

BIBLIOGRAPHY: Allen and CWE Ep 58 / de Vocht CTL II 365–7 / Matricule de Louvain III-1 594   CFG & PGB

Florens van GRIBOVAL of Bruges, 1512–8 November 1562

Florens van Griboval (Grebovallius, Guboval), the son of Pieter van *Griboval, matriculated at the University of Louvain on 24 February 1527 and studied at the Collegium Trilingue under Pieter de *Vriendt and Conradus *Goclenius (Ep 2716). Subsequently he went to Orléans, where he matriculated on 17 December 1529 and boarded with Nicolas *Bérault. Thereafter he joined *Viglius Zuichemus as both continued their legal studies in Bourges under Andrea *Alciati. By September 1532 Florens had followed Viglius to Padua (Ep 2716). In the summer of 1533 he visited Rome, intending to

return home afterwards (Ep 2854), but before long he was again in Orléans, where he obtained a licence in civil law in the second quarter of 1535. His studies completed, he settled in Bruges and was mayor of the free state (vrije, franc) of Bruges from 1539 to 1540. On 11 October 1540 he was appointed to the council of Flanders, and on 9 October 1543 he was appointed councillor and master of requests of the grand council of Mechelen, a position he held until his death. He was buried at St Rombout's, Mechelen.

Florens was lord of Berquin, Plessy, and Jumelles, and a 'Golden Knight.' His first wife was Cornelia le Fèvre, lady of Hemstede, a niece of Jérôme de *Busleyden. After her death in 1542 he married Adrienne van Halewijn, lady of Zwevegem (1522–70), who bore him several children. He is portrayed on a painting representing the grand council in session in 1559 (illustration in de Vocht Literae ad Craneveldium lxvi: the original is now in the municipal museum 'Hof van Busleyden' in Mechelen).

Writing from Padua in 1532, Viglius introduced Florens to Erasmus as a younger friend of outstanding qualities, who was extremely well-connected and eager to assist Erasmus in his efforts to secure payment of his annuity from the imperial court (Epp 2716, 2767). Following Florens' démarches, Erasmus wrote in the spring of 1533 to his father, the treasurer, and also corresponded with Florens himself (Epp 2791, 2810, 2829), but none of these letters have been preserved.

BIBLIOGRAPHY: Allen Ep 2716 / Matricule de Louvain III-1 771 / Matricule d'Orléans II-2 no 806 / de Vocht CTL II 155–8 / de Vocht Busleyden 16, 29 / Arthur Merghelynck Recueil de généalogies inédites de Flandre (Bruges 1877) I 20–2 / Jean Jacques Gaillard Bruges et le Franc (Bruges 1857–64) I 243, 391, 457, III 87, V 337 / O. Delepierre and F.-P. Priem Précis analytique des documents que renferme le dépôt des archives de la Flandre occidentale à Bruges (Bruges 1843–58) II-7 245 / J.F. Foppens Histoire du Conseil de Flandre (Brussels 1869) 152 / L. Stroobant 'Les Magistrats du Grand Conseil de Malines' Annales de l'Academie royale d'archéologie de Belgique 54 (1903) 460   HILDE DE RIDDER-SYMOENS

Pieter van GRIBOVAL d 26 June 1554
Pieter, the son of Louis van Griboval, lord of

Baquerode (Bakelroot), and Adrienne de Berquin, came to inherit Berquin and other family
estates in the part of Flanders which is now in
France (Département du Nord). From 1510 to
1513 he was tax collector for the region of
Namen, in Flanders, and from 1515 to 1524
clerk of the treasurer of the free state (vrije /
franc) of Bruges. Following in the footsteps
of an illustrious predecessor, Hieronymus
*Laurinus, who had also progressed from the
treasury of the vrije to the treasury of Flanders,
Griboval was head of the latter from 1524 to
1543, with the title quaestor Flandriae (Ep 2799).
From 1530 to his death he was also an
alderman, and in 1535, 1543, and 1552 one of
the four burgomasters in the vrije of Bruges
(representing the north section). He also held
the titles of councillor and chamberlain to
*Charles v. His succession to the lordship of
Berquin was finally upheld in court after a law
suit against Jean de Berquin which continued
through the greater part of the 1530s. Pieter
married twice. The name of his first wife, the
mother of his son Florens van *Griboval, is
uncertain; his second wife was Françoise
Joigny de Pamel.
   Florens van Griboval introduced himself to
Erasmus from Padua in 1532. Encouraged by
the acquaintance with his son, Erasmus wrote
to the influential father in the hope of securing
payment of his annuity from the imperial court
(Epp 2793, 2799), but he soon decided that
Pieter was in no position to help (Ep 2810),
although in the meantime Pieter appears to
have written to Florens in this matter (Ep 2829).
   BIBLIOGRAPHY: de Vocht CTL II 155–6 / Jean
Jacques Gaillard Bruges et le Franc (Bruges
1857–64) I 302–3 / C. Douxchamps-Lefèvre
Inventaire des archives du Fonds de Corroy-le-
Château (Brussels 1962) 142, 303, 305 / O.
Delepierre and F.-P. Priem Précis analytique des
documents que renferme le dépôt des archives de la
Flandre occidentale à Bruges (Bruges 1843–58)
II-7, 230–70   PAUL VAN PETEGHEM

Pietro GRIFFI of Pisa, January 1469–
7 November 1516
Pietro Griffi (Grifus, Grifius, Gryphus), the
son of Giovanni Griffi, count of Sasso, and of
Bandeca Sampanti, was born into the patriciate
of Pisa and studied law at the Studio of his
native city, receiving a doctorate in civil and

canon law by 1494. In the period of restored
independence from Florence he served Pisa in
political offices and on diplomatic missions. In
November 1494 he escorted *Charles VIII of
France from Florence to Pisa, and in 1495 and
1496 he undertook two more embassies to the
French king, meeting him in northern Italy and
in France. After remaining in Milan until early
1500, Griffi was elected gonfalonier of Pisa and
a member of the council of Anziani for the term
September-October 1500. In May 1502 he was
sent to Rome as the Pisan envoy and quickly
gained the confidence of Pope *Alexander VI,
who took him into his service. He became a
priest and an apostolic protonotary and continued to serve under *Julius II, but in 1508 he also
gave what assistance he could to Pisa in her
desperate efforts to preserve her independence from Florence.
   Earlier, in 1504 and 1505, the papal curia had
sent him on missions to Venice and Germany;
in 1506 he was dispatched to England with
credentials dated 15 May, referring specifically
to the papal alum monopoly, which Griffi was
expected to defend against Turkish competition. The English failed to co-operate and Griffi
was called back. In June 1507 he was sent to
Bologna with the new papal governor, Lorenzo *Fieschi; his specific task was to liquidate
the *Bentivoglio fortune and with the proceeds
to compensate the victims of the corruption
practised by the preceding papal administration. In February 1509 he arrived in England for the second time, temporarily replacing Adriano *Castellesi and Polidoro *Virgilio
as the agent in charge of collecting papal revenue, but he was also expected to win English support for the pope's political moves.
Having been called back to Rome in the
summer of 1512, he was made bishop of Forlì
on 10 November and participated in some
sessions of the fifth Lateran council before
undertaking some more diplomatic missions. In March 1514 he was appointed papal
referendarius, and the following year he was
again for some time in Bologna, now as the
papal vice-legate. He died at Forlì, and his
funeral monument and inscription are preserved in the church of Sant'Agostino, Rome.
   In the course of his second mission to
England Griffi encountered not only the
jealousy of Virgilio but also some misgivings on

the part of *Henry VIII; on the other hand, he was compensated with the friendship of Andrea *Ammonio, who suggested at one point that Erasmus should become Griffi's client and move to the envoy's house (Epp 243, 249). Erasmus preferred his independence, but he seems to have appreciated Griffi (Ep 250), who was also in friendly contact with John *Colet. On 1 January 1512 *Remaclus Arduenna dedicated to Griffi his comedy *Palamedes*. It was in England that Griffi wrote the most important of his own works, *De officio*, a manual for papal tax collectors in England, composed for practical ends but also exhibiting Griffi's thorough knowledge of canon law.

BIBLIOGRAPHY: Allen Ep 243 / *Il De officio collectoris in regno Angliae di Pietro Griffi (1469-1516)* ed Michele Monaco (Rome 1973) with exhaustive biography, bibliography, and excellent illustrations / LP I passim   PGB

Francesco GRIFFOLINI of Arezzo, b 1420–d after 1465
Francesco Griffolini (Aretino) was born at Arezzo to Mariotto Biasgio Griffolini, a merchant once engaged in trade with Hungary, and Bartolommea Piccino. On 19 May 1431 Mariotto and four other citizens of Arezzo were executed by the Florentine government for conspiring to betray Arezzo to the invading army of Milan, and all possessions of their families were confiscated. Bartolommea appears to have taken her children to Ferrara, where Francesco studied Latin and Greek under Guarino *Guarini of Verona and Theodorus *Gaza. Around 1447/8 Francesco went to Rome, where he studied under Lorenzo *Valla, taught grammar, and began in earnest the task of translating Greek works into Latin. He probably spent some time at Naples but returned to Rome and remained through the pontificates of Calixtus III (1455–8) and *Pius II (1458–64). In 1461 Pius tried to confer a benefice in Florentine territory on Griffolini, but the Florentine Signoria rejected him because of his father's treason. Griffolini received a post in the curia in 1463 as a member of the college of abbreviators, but this too turned sour when the next pope, Paul II, abolished the college in December 1464. In 1465 Griffolini · went to Naples as tutor to Alfonso of Calabria, the son of King Ferdinand. He died at an

unknown date, it is said as the result of a fall from his horse. His friends included Antonio Beccadelli, called Panormita. Usually called Francesco Aretino, Griffolini has often been confused with the jurist Francesco Accolti of Arezzo.

Although Erasmus was at times critical of Griffolini's translations (Epp 2263, 2291, 2611, 3043), he used his version of Chrysostom's homilies on 1 Corinthians in preparing the Froben edition of Chrysostom of 1530. The manuscript was loaned to Erasmus by John *Fisher, bishop of Rochester (Ep 2359).

Griffolini also translated the letters of Phalaris, dedicated to Malatesta Novello dei Malatesti and later to Alfonso I of Naples (Rome 1470?; Treviso: G. de Lisa 1471); the letters of Diogenes the Cynic, dedicated to Pius II (Florence c 1475, 1487); Chrysostom's homilies on the gospel of John, dedicated to Jean Geoffroi, bishop of Arras, and later printed with a dedication to Cosimo de' Medici (Rome: G. Lauer 1470); and Lucian's *De calumnia*, dedicated to John Tiptoft of Worcester and found in manuscript at the Biblioteca Laurenziana of Florence and St John's College, Cambridge. At the request of Pius II Griffolini also completed Lorenzo Valla's translation of the *Iliad* into Latin prose and translated the *Odyssey*. Manuscripts are found in the Barberini collection of the Biblioteca Apostolica Vaticana, the Biblioteca Casanatense of Rome, and the Bibliothèque Nationale, Paris. Latin editions of the *Iliad* were printed at Brescia in 1474 and 1497, attributed only to Valla although they contain Griffolini's work.

BIBLIOGRAPHY: Allen Ep 2226 / Cosenza II 1479–82 / Girolamo Mancini *Francesco Griffolini cognominato Francesco Aretino* (Florence (1890)
                                                TBD

Jean GRILLOT *See* GRYLLARDUS

Domenico GRIMANI of Venice,
22 February 1461–27 August 1523
Domenico Grimani (Grymanus) was a son of the Venetian patrician Antonio Grimani, who was doge from 1521 to 1523. He studied at the University of Padua, receiving his doctorate apparently in canon law, by 1487. He gained a reputation as a logician, and his contemporary Antonio Pizzamano, the editor of the works of

St Thomas Aquinas, praised his Aristotelian scholarship. His interests extended more widely, however: *Sabellico, for instance, referred to his understanding of the elder Pliny, and in 1489 *Poliziano introduced him to Giovanni *Pico della Mirandola, whose library of over a thousand books he bought in February 1498. Domenico's library contained fifteen thousand books by his death.

Domenico became a papal secretary in October 1491 and on 20 September 1493 a cardinal. (There were allegations that his father paid up to thirty thousand ducats for this.) On 13 September 1497 he became patriarch of Aquileia; he was ordained a priest on 21 March 1498 and bishop on 25 April 1498. He enjoyed *Julius II's favour and from 1505 inhabited the palazzo San Marco in Rome, though he also had a villa on the Quirinal. He accompanied the pope to Perugia and Bologna in 1506 and was promoted to the cardinal bishoprics of Albano (22 September 1508), Tusculum (3 June 1509), and Porto (20 January 1511). After a visit to Venice, by Easter 1508 Domenico had returned to Rome, where Erasmus met him in 1509.

Domenico Grimani

Although ill with tertian fever, Grimani helped to reconcile Julius II with Venice in the winter of 1509–10; one result was the political rehabilitation of his father, who had hitherto been exiled from Venice. Grimani accompanied Julius II to Bologna in October 1510, but according to Paolo Giovio he was sceptical of the pope's claim to be the liberator of Italy and warned him of the danger of Spanish power. Domenico did not vote for *Leo x in March 1513 and fell increasingly out of sympathy with him. At first he took an active part in events, regularly attending sessions of the fifth Lateran council and accompanying the papal court to Florence in November 1515 and to Bologna for Leo's meeting with *Francis I. However, he refused to renounce the bishopric of Urbino (which he had held since May 1514) in favour of Cardinal Giulio de' Medici (the future *Clement VII) in order to smooth the Medici take-over of the duchy in August 1516, and he bitterly opposed the closing of the Lateran council. He was in Padua from October 1517 until June 1518, then visited Ceneda near Treviso (assuming the bishopric from his nephew Marino *Grimani from 1517 to 1520),

and spent much of the remainder of Leo's pontificate at Murano. Though ill, in December 1521 he returned to Rome for the conclave and nearly died. In April 1522 he went back to Venice and Murano in the Venetian Lagoon, and in spite of *Adrian VI's summons he never reached Rome again. He died on 27 August 1523, his last will being dated 16 August; Marino received his ancient coins and gems. Domenico bequeathed his collection of ancient sculpture to the Signoria, but not his books, in view, it appears, of the neglectful treatment Cardinal *Bessarion's bequest of his library had been given. The bulk of Grimani's library went to the Venetian monastery of Sant'Antonio di Castello.

In spite of being a voracious bibliophile and collector and having wide personal contacts with humanist scholars within and beyond the Aldine circle, Domenico remained intellectually committed to his original training in Aristotelian logic, as the titles of his few known treatises suggest. There are several portraits of Domenico on medals (Hill nos. 443, 455, 863).

Writing to Grimani in 1515, Erasmus recalled his courtesy, eloquence, and learning and his friendly invitation to remain in Rome, which he had had to refuse; he also asked him for manuscripts of St Jerome's works and requested him to intercede for *Reuchlin (Ep 334). As late as 1531 Erasmus recalled in great detail their meeting in 1509: he had spent an afternoon at Domenico's palace; during their conversation the cardinal had invited him to join his household and become the tutor of his nephew Marino; then he showed him the library (Ep 2465).

Having failed to keep his promise to Domenico that he would return to Rome in the winter of 1515–16 (Ep 334), Erasmus tried, without much success, to carry on a correspondence with him about work in progress. Grimani's lost answer to Ep 334 caused Erasmus some anxiety (Epp 619, 701, 835). In November 1517 he dedicated the *Paraphrasis in Romanos* (Ep 710) to Domenico and hoped for his help in obtaining the pope's sanction for the 1519 edition of the New Testament (Epp 835, 860). Erasmus apparently did not know that Domenico was no longer in Rome until *Bombace wrote to tell him in October 1518 (Ep 865). Erasmus wrote again in October 1519 asking Domenico for a copy of Origen's commentary on the Psalms if he possessed it (Ep 1017). Although Domenico eventually thanked Erasmus for the dedication of the *Paraphrasis* (LB IX 801D, 1132B), Erasmus complained to *Botzheim that Domenico never sent him any money (Allen I 43).

BIBLIOGRAPHY: Allen and CWE Ep 334 / P. Paschini *Domenico Grimani, Cardinale di San Marco* (Rome 1943) / J. Buchardus *Liber notarum* ed E. Celani (Città di Castello 1906–59) passim / Eubel II 22 and passim / P. Grassi *Le due spedizioni militari di Giulio II* ed L. Frati (Bologna 1886) passim / Pastor V–VIII passim / Sanudo *Diarii* I–XXXIV passim / M.J.C. Lowry 'Two great Venetian libraries in the age of Aldus Manutius' *Bulletin of the John Rylands Library* 42 (1974–5) 128–66 / M. Perry 'Cardinal Domenico Grimani's legacy of ancient art to Venice' *Journal of the Warburg and Courtauld Institutes* 41 (1978) 215–44   D.S. CHAMBERS

Marino GRIMANI of Venice,
d 11 September 1546
Born about 1488, Marino was the son of Girolamo Grimani and the nephew of Cardinal

Domenico *Grimani, in whose household he was educated by Gregorio Amaseo, Girolamo *Aleandro and probably Marcus *Musurus; Erasmus was invited to be Marino's tutor in 1509 (Ep 2465). In August 1508 his uncle obtained for him the administration of the bishopric of Ceneda, north of Treviso, which he retained until 19 January 1517, when it was assumed by Domenico; Marino became patriarch of Aquileia in his place. From 1531 to 1546 Marino again administered Ceneda, where the reputed harshness of his regime caused the Venetian government to intervene. He was created a cardinal in secret on 3 May 1527 and publicly on 7 February 1528, being promoted to the cardinal bishoprics of Tusculum (13 March 1541) and Porto (24 September 1543).

Marino followed his uncle between Venice and Rome (though he was presumably by himself in Rome in December 1519, when he was recorded as singing mass, an indication that he was already ordained). He inherited some of Domenico's books, including for his lifetime the famous illustrated breviary, as well as his collection of coins and gems. He was favoured by *Clement VII, who permitted him to visit Aquileia and Friuli in 1524 and 1525; he was also there during the pope's captivity, until January 1528. Marino accompanied the pope to Bologna in October 1529 and was also present at his meetings with *Charles v from December 1532 to February 1533. He was appointed by *Paul III to serve on a commission of inquiry into officials of the papal states on 20 November 1534, and on 15 September 1535 was appointed legate of Perugia and Umbria. In December 1537 he discussed with the Venetian doge the possibility of locating a church council at Vicenza. He had returned to Rome before the end of December 1538. A bull of 21 September 1539 empowered him to proceed against heretics in the dioceses of Ceneda and Concordia, and in the patriarchate of Aquileia. In October 1539 he received Cardinal Aleandro at San Daniele in Friuli, and they probably travelled to Rome together; on 27 August 1540 they were both placed on a commission for the reform of the papal chancery. Alternating between Friuli and the papal court, Marino accompanied Paul III in his meeting with Charles v at Busseto, near Parma, on 24 June 1543 and exhorted the emperor to peace. On 5

March 1544 he was nominated legate in
Lombardy, including Parma and Piacenza, and
on 14 August 1544 legate to *Francis I, with
whom he negotiated the treaty of Crespy. He
returned to Venice and Friuli at the end of 1544;
he died at Orvieto.

Grimani left a son and two daughters. Of his
large collection of books, those in Greek and
Hebrew went to the monastery of San Giorgio
Maggiore, Venice, and others went to his
nephew, the protonotary Giulio Grimani.
Marino had been the patron of a number of
painters, such as Pordenone, Sebastiano del
Piombo, Giovanni da Udine, and the miniaturist Giulio Clovio. He wrote a commentary on
Romans and Galatians (printed at the Aldine
press in Venice in 1542 with a dedication to
Paul III) and received many dedications including the *Recognitio veteris testamenti ad hebraicam
veritatem* (Venice: press of A. Manuzio and A.
Torresani 1529) of *Steuco, the custodian of his
late uncle's library.

BIBLIOGRAPHY: Allen Ep 2465 / Eubel III 19
and passim / Pastor IX 7–8 and passim / Sanudo
Diarii XIX 158, XX 250, and passim / P. Paschini
'Il mecenatismo artistico del Cardinale Marino
Grimani' in *Miscellanea in onore di Roberto Cessi*
(Rome 1958) 79–88 / P. Paschini *Il Cardinale
Marino Grimani* (Rome 1960)

D.S. CHAMBERS

Petrus GRIPHIUS *See Pietro* GRIFFI

Alvise GRITTI 1501–autumn of 1534
Born at Constantinople in 1501, the son of the
future Venetian doge Andrea Gritti by a Greek
mistress, Alvise was barred by the taint of his
birth from promotion in Venetian society and
sought an alternative outlet for his ambitions in
Ottoman service. Versatile, determined, and
fluent in several languages, he became a
confidant of Ibrahim Pasha and *Suleiman the
Magnificent, secured valuable government
contracts, and amassed a fortune by trading in
gems. His palace in Constantinople soon
became the resort of all western agents in
search of confidential information, and his
access to the highest diplomatic sources in
Venice was equally useful to the sultan:
references to secret contact between Gritti and
the Council of Ten became frequent during the

later 1520s. After a successful defence of Buda
against the imperial counter-attack of 1529, he
became the pivotal figure in Suleiman's plans
for the pacification of Hungary under the
pro-Turkish regime of *John Zápolyai, receiving the titles of bishop of Agria and lieutenant-
general of the kingdom of Hungary. In 1531 he
was rumoured to have abandoned Christianity
for Islam, perhaps to forward his own claims
to the crown of a Hungarian state that would
be effectively an Ottaman province. In February
1532 Anselmus *Ephorinus reported that Suleiman had sent Gritti to the Polish court in a bid
to restore peace between *Sigismund I and the
princes of Wallachia, who were Ottoman vassals (Ep 2606). Gritti met his death when his
attempt to pacify Transylvania led to the
murder of the *voivode*, Cibacho of Waradin, by
one of his partisans and the resulting upheaval
took the form of a blood-feud against his own
person. An ambiguous and exotic character,
Gritti easily attracted the attention even of
those who, like Erasmus, had never met him
(Ep 2971). But since Erasmus wrongly suspected
that his friend Hieronim *Łaski had died with
Gritti, he perhaps had more cause for interest
than others who followed this meteoric and
tragic career (Ep 3049).

BIBLIOGRAPHY: Allen Ep 2971 / T. Kardos
'Dramma satirico cavalleresco su Alvise Gritti,
governatore dell'Ungheria' in *Venezia e
l'Ungheria nel Rinascimento* ed V. Branca (Florence 1973) / P. Preto *Venezia e i Turchi* (Florence
1975) / Tranquillus *Andronicus *De rebus in
Hungaria gestis ab Ludovico Gritti* was edited by
B. Banfi in *Archivio storico per la Dalmazia* 18
(1934–5) 419–68 / R.W. Seton-Watson *A History
of the Roumanians* (Cambridge 1934) 55–6

M.J.C. LOWRY

William GROCYN d 1519
William Grocyn was probably born at Colerne,
Wiltshire. In 1463 he was a scholar of
Winchester College, Oxford, being described
in the register as 'son of a tenant of the college,
residing at Colerne.' In 1465 he entered New
College, Oxford, and was a full fellow of that
college in 1467; at one time he was tutor to
William *Warham, who later, as archbishop of
Canterbury, granted Grocyn much prefer-
ment, including a prebend at Lincoln, which
he had held from 1485 to 1514. He received his

MA by 1474 and was admitted to the degree of bachelor of theology in 1491.

In 1483 Grocyn was appointed divinity reader at Magdalen College, where he held a theological disputation before Richard III on 25 July. In 1488 he resigned and left for Italy, where he spent two years, studying for a while in Florence under Angelo *Poliziano and Demetrius *Chalcondyles (Ep 520). He kept company with Thomas *Linacre and William *Latimer, who had arrived in Italy in 1485 and 1489 respectively. He also met the great Venetian printer Aldo *Manuzio.

Grocyn had begun to study Greek at Oxford before he went to Italy. On his return to Oxford in 1491 he rented rooms at Exeter College and introduced a regular lecture in Greek, the first to be offered at the university. When Erasmus first visited Oxford in 1499 he found that Grocyn and John *Colet were closely associated in spreading the new learning. In 1496 Grocyn was appointed rector of St Lawrence Jewry in London and thereafter spent increasing portions of his time in London. Thomas *More and Richard *Croke were among his pupils there (Epp 227, 1117). Erasmus and Grocyn were already close friends when the latter introduced Erasmus to his patron, William Warham, at Lambeth in 1506 (Ep 188; Allen I 5). During his visit in 1511 Erasmus apparently lodged with Grocyn in London (Ep 241) and, when he went on to Cambridge, borrowed his copy of St Basil's commentary on Isaiah (Ep 229). Grocyn was gathering an outstanding library; inventories made after his death listed some 105 printed books and 17 manuscripts (a list is in Emden).

In the autumn of 1501 Grocyn delivered in St Paul's, London, a series of lectures in the course of which he came to reject the established tradition, defended by Colet, that the biblical Dionysius Areopagita was identical with Dionysius, the author of the *Hierarchia ecclesiastica* (LB VI 503E–F; cf IX 446D, 676A, 917B–C). In general, however, his religious views were rather more conservative than those of his fellow-humanists, and his preference for Aristotle over Plato caused frequent comment. Grocyn did not choose to write for publication (Ep 540), a fact which Erasmus tried to excuse by referring to his failing eye-sight (*Ciceronianus* ASD I-2 676). The only

work to appear in print in his lifetime was a letter to Aldus, who affixed it to the preface of Linacre's edition of Proclus in 1499 (Ep 534). Grocyn's epigram on a lady who had thrown a snowball at him is recorded in Thomas Fuller's *History of the Worthies of England* (1662).

Erasmus admired Grocyn and recognized his leading position among the older English humanists (Ep 118; ASD IX-1 196–8). He was pleased to note that Grocyn had approved of his translations of two of Euripides' tragedies (Epp 207, 1479). Grocyn also promised to organize the sale of a hundred copies of the *Adagia* Erasmus had sent to England in 1500 (Ep 181). Erasmus was distressed when Grocyn suffered a disabling stroke of paralysis in 1518 (Epp 781, 784, 786, 821). His death must have occurred between June and October 1519. He bequeathed most of his property to Linacre, and John *Claymond purchased some of his manuscripts for Corpus Christi College, Oxford.

BIBLIOGRAPHY: Allen and CWE Ep 118 / DNB VIII 709–12 / Emden BRUO II 827–30 / Roberto Weiss *Humanism in England during the Fifteenth Century* 2nd ed (Oxford 1957) 173–4 and passim / McConica 49–53 and passim / Rogers Ep 2 and passim   CFG & PGB

Heinrich GROENKEN *See Heinrich* GRUNTGEN

Jakub GROFFIK of Felsztyn, d after 1538

Groffik (Grophicius) came from Felsztyn, in Little Poland. He was first a parish priest of Czchow in Little Poland, then prebendary at the Cracow cathedral and *custos* of the collegiate church of St Giles in Cracow. From his enthusiastic letter to Erasmus (Ep 2811) written on 15 May 1533, we learn that he accompanied the abbot of Mogiła, Erazm *Ciołek, on a trip to Rome and was present when his master visited Erasmus in Freiburg on the way home late in 1532.

BIBLIOGRAPHY: Allen Ep 2811 / *Zródła do dziejów Wawelu* v: *Wypisy źródłowé do dziejów Wawelu z archiwaliów kapitulnych i kurialnych krakowskich, 1516–1525* ed B. Przybyszewski (Cracow 1970) 197   HALINA KOWALSKA

Jean GROLIER of Lyon, 1479– 22 October 1565

Jean Grolier, subsequently viscount of Aigisy,

was born of a family originally from Verona. Little is known about his life in Paris until 1510, when he had already succeeded his father, Etienne, as treasurer of Milan under French occupation. He continued to serve in this position until 1512, when the French lost Milan temporarily, and again from 1515 to 1521, when they lost it for good. Grolier continued his career as treasurer of the army (1522), ambassador to Rome (1534), treasurer of the Ile-de-France (1537), treasurer of France (1545), and treasurer-general from 1547 to his death.

Grolier is mostly known today as a great bibliophile who had his books bound in impeccable taste. He was a great patron of scholars as well, and his protégés north of the Alps included *Beatus Rhenanus, who in 1519 dedicated to him an edition of Maximus Tyrius in Latin (BRE Ep 86). In the previous year the bookseller Francesco Giulio *Calvo had urged Erasmus to approach him. Reluctantly, Erasmus produced and published a flattering letter; Grolier replied, but his answer had not reached Erasmus by August 1519 and is still missing today (Epp 831, 1002).

BIBLIOGRAPHY: Allen Ep 831 / G.D. Hobson in EI XVII 983–5 / A.-J.-V. Le Roux de Lincy *Recherches sur Jean Grolier, sur sa vie et sa bibliothèque* (Paris 1866) / *Bookbindings from the Library of Jean Grolier: A Loan Exhibition* (British Museum, London 1965) / BRE Ep 86 and passim / *Catalogue des actes de François I* (Paris 1887–1908) I, II, IV passim   MICHEL REULOS

Aegidius GROMONTIUS *See Gilles de* GOURMONT

Pierre GROMORS documented c 1514–45
A native of Champagne, Gromors studied civil and canon law. He began working at the presses of his cousin Berthold Rembolt and by 1516 had set up shop of his own as a bookseller. From 1521 he lived in the rue du Mont-Saint-Hilaire, near the church of Saint Hilaire, of which he was a warden. In 1525 he moved to a house he had built 'au coing de la rue d'Escoce.'

From 1517 to 1545 Gromors published about one hundred books, some of them in association with other Paris publishers. He also printed several of Erasmus' works: the *Adagia*

(1523), *Dulce bellum inexpertis* (1523), the *Parabolae* (for Jean *Petit 1523), *De conscribendis epistolis* (for Pierre de la Motte c 1524), the *Formula* (1524–5), and *Breviores aliquot epistolae* (with Jean Petit 1525). In 1525 Erasmus complained to Noël *Béda, a leading member of the faculty of theology of the University of Paris (Ep 1581), and to Jean de *Selve, first president of the Parlement of Paris (Epp 1591, 1598), about Gromors' publication of his *Colloquia* with a preface by the Dominican Lambertus *Campester, who had made many changes in his text.

BIBLIOGRAPHY: Allen Ep 1581 / Renouard *Répertoire* 184–5 / M.M. de la Garanderie 'Recueils parisiens de lettres d'Erasme' BHR 31 (1969) 449–65, especially 452 / ASD I-3 11
                                                  GENEVIÈVE GUILLEMINOT

Martin GRÖNING of Bremen, d 1521
Martin Gröning (Groningus, Gruningk) of Bremen matriculated at Bologna in 1511 and received a legal doctorate in Siena. In his native city he received prebends as a lector, and subsequently the precentor, of the cathedral chapter, but he may have remained in Italy after the completion of his studies. He was in Rome in January 1515 and on behalf of *Reuchlin translated the German sections of his *Augenspiegel* into Latin. This translation was accepted as authoritative by the court hearing Reuchlin's case. It may also have been published in Rome; at any rate Gröning's preface for it was printed in *Illustrium virorum epistolae ... ad Joannem Reuchlinum* (Haguenau: T. Anshelm 1519). He remained in Rome until the summer of 1517, speaking on behalf of Reuchlin. After his return to Germany (Ep 615), he presented Giorgio *Benigno's *Defensio Reuchlini* to the Emperor *Maximilian I at Cologne (Gröning's preface is dated 1 August 1517). Gröning is mentioned several times in the *Epistolae obscurorum virorum* as an opponent of Jacob of *Hoogstraten.

Gröning wrote a chronicle of Bremen (unprinted), and in 1521 he offered to sell to Pope *Leo X a manuscript of Livy, alleged to contain some lost books, that he had received from a monastery in Norway. The death of Leo X on 1 December 1521 delayed the reply. By the time Filippo (II) *Beroaldo wrote to Gröning to say that he would like to buy the manuscript,

Gröning had died and the manuscript could no longer be found.

BIBLIOGRAPHY: Allen and CWE Ep 615 / ADB IX 719–20 / RE Epp 201, 206 / Ludwig Geiger *Johann Reuchlin* (Leipzig 1871 repr 1964) 314–15, 402–3, and passim / Knod 173 / Hutten *Operum supplementum* II 385–6   IG

GRONSELLUS (Ep 1347 of 1 March [1523])
In Ep 1347 Erasmus recalls a 'senator Mechliniensis' by the name of Gronsellus whom he associates with the physician *Bogardus. Both are said to have lived to an advanced age, with Gronsellus surviving the other by a few years. Erasmus had been a guest in his house at Mechelen and later had been told by his sons how their father had faced his approaching death with a calm and composure worthy of Christ.

Gronsellus was perhaps Gerard van Gronsselt (Gronsfelt, Gronsele), who may have been a son of Jan van Gronsselt (d 1463), a professor of civil law at Louvain. Gerard died at Mechelen on 7 January 1514. There is also his son Jan, who became a councillor on the grand council of Mechelen on 4 March 1505 and died on 8 February 1519.

BIBLIOGRAPHY: Allen Ep 1347 / L. Stroobant 'Les magistrats du Grand Conseil de Malines' *Annales de l'Académie Royale d'Archéologie de Belgique* 54 (1902) 448 / *Matricule d'Orléans* II-1 193   MARCEL A. NAUWELAERTS

Gerard and Jan van GRONSFELT or GRONSSELT *See* GRONSELLUS

Johann GROPPER of Soest, 24 February 1503–13 March 1559
Johann Gropper (Gropperus, Grepperus) was the son of another Johann (d after 1533) who was elected burgomaster of Soest, in Westphalia, for a term in 1522 and another in 1531. Gropper's mother, Anna Hugen, was the daughter of a Soest patrician; his youngest brother, Kaspar Gropper (1519–94), was to serve as papal nuncio in Germany on repeated occasions in the 1560s and 1570s. On 17 June 1516 Johann matriculated at the University of Cologne to begin his studies in the faculty of arts. On 17 March 1519 he graduated MA. He was also promoted licentiate and doctor of civil

law on 3 September 1523 and 7 November 1525 respectively.

Meanwhile, in September 1525, Gropper was appointed the official to Hermann von *Neuenahr, provost of the Cologne cathedral chapter. In 1526 the archbishop of Cologne, Hermann von *Wied, appointed him keeper of the seals. Around that time he also took holy orders without any formal course of study in theology. He went on to accumulate a good deal of preferment, being scholaster of St Gereon's, Cologne (1527), canon of St Andrew's, Cologne (1528), and of St Patroclus', Soest (1528), priest of St Peter's, Soest (1531), canon of Xanten (1532), and canon priest of the Cologne cathedral chapter (1534).

Gropper accompanied the archbishop of Cologne to the diets of 1529 and 1530. The intensive debate on religious issues that took place at the diet of Augsburg in 1530 prompted him to probe more deeply than hitherto into questions of theology. The results of these efforts were his collection of statutes prepared for a reforming synod of the archdiocese of Cologne in 1536, *Canones concilii provincialis Coloniensis*, and especially the *Institutio compendiaria doctrinae christianae*, his principal contribution to the field of theology (both Cologne: P. Quentel 1538). At the colloquy of Regensburg in 1541, Gropper and Julius *Pflug were the leading Catholic advocates of conciliation.

From 1542 Gropper played a central role in organizing the opposition to Hermann von Wied, who on the advice of Martin *Bucer was attempting to lead Cologne into the Protestant camp. After von Wied had been obliged to resign, Gropper assisted the new archbishop, Adolf von *Schaumburg, in his efforts to reform the archdiocese. He resigned all his benefices except the deanery of Soest, although in 1548 he accepted in addition the office of archdeacon of Bonn. From 1551 to 1552 Gropper accompanied Adolf von Schaumburg to the second session of the council of Trent. In 1555 he declined an offer of appointment to the college of cardinals. In 1558 he went to Rome in an effort to persuade Pope *Paul IV not to confirm the election of Johann Gebhard von Mansfeld as archbishop of Cologne since Mansfeld opposed the concerns of Catholic reform. Gropper's elevation to the cardinalate was imminent when he died in Rome. To honour him, Paul IV personally proclaimed his funeral oration. According to Walter Lipgens, Gropper may well have been the outstanding Catholic theologian of Germany in the sixteenth century, on account of both the theological depth and the historical impact of his work.

There is no evidence of direct connections between Gropper and Erasmus, but in June 1531 Erasmus was pleased to hear about Gropper from Tielmannus *Gravius and promised to write to the theologian in due course (Ep 2508).

BIBLIOGRAPHY: Allen Ep 2508 / Walter Lipgens in NDB VII 133–6 / ADB IX 734–40 / Walter Lipgens *Kardinal J. Gropper, 1503–1559, und die Anfänge der katholischen Reform in Deutschland* (Münster 1951), listing (pp 224–9) Gropper's published writings, thirty-seven in number; it may be noted that the *Dogmatic articles* listed as number 26, are probably not by Gropper; see *Acta reformationis catholicae* VI (Regensburg 1974) 88–9 / Pflug *Correspondance* II Ep 281 and passim / Leonard Ennen *Geschichte der Stadt Köln* (Cologne and Neuss 1863–80) IV / Wilhelm van Gulik *Johannes Gropper (1503 bis 1559)* (Freiburg 1906) / Reinhard Braunisch *Die Theologie der Rechtfertigung im 'Enchiridion' (1538) des Johannes Gropper* (Münster 1974) / Reinhard Braunisch 'Cardinalis designatus: Zur Ablehnung des Roten Hutes durch Johannes Gropper' *Annalen des Historischen Vereins für den Niederrhein* 176 (1974) 58–82 / Johannes Meier *Der priesterliche Dienst nach Johannes Gropper (1503–1559)* (Münster 1977) / Johann Gropper *Briefwechsel* ed Reinhard Braunisch (Münster 1977–) I   ROLF DECOT

Johann GROSS of Nürnberg, documented 1501–d December 1536
Johann Gross is documented as organist of the cathedral of Basel from 1501. In June 1515 he was called for service in the militia, together with other lay staff of the chapter and the bishop; thus he probably fought in the battle of Marignano. Armed with a halberd and accompanied by his servant, he still did military service in 1529. He did not at first go to the communion table after the fashion established by Basel's reformers, but when admonished in 1530 he promised to conform. Gross lived from 1528 on the St Albanvorstadt and received

paying guests into his house. Among them were Daniel *Stiebar (AK III Ep 1303) and in 1531 Anselmus *Ephorinus and his party (AK IV Epp 1547, 1761). Ephorinus described him to Erasmus as a kindly old man, a lover of the old faith and of learning, whose greatest wish was to receive a line from Erasmus, acknowledging a service he had rendered the scholar in the course of a journey to Nürnberg (Epp 2539, 2606). Other references (Epp 2755, 2788) further confirm the existence of friendly relations between Gross, Bonifacius *Amerbach, and Erasmus; in particular they concern the formula for a medicinal powder which proved equally beneficial to Erasmus and to Gross (Epp 2740, 2749; AK IV Ep 1897).

BIBLIOGRAPHY: AK I Ep 350, III Ep 1041, IV Ep 1547, and passim / *Basler Chroniken* VII 222 / *Aktensammlung zur Geschichte der Basler Reformation* ed E. Dürr et al (Basel 1921–50) III 563, IV 485 / R. Wackernagel *Geschichte der Stadt Basel* (Basel 1907–54) II-2 175*   PGB

Nicolaus GRUDIUS of Louvain, 1503/4–1570/1
A son of Nicolaas *Everaerts, Nicolaus (Nicolaus Nicolai or Everardi) derived his usual surname from the Grudii, the ancient occupants of his native Louvain. At The Hague he was trained by Rombout Steynemolen (Stenemola) and Jacob *Volkaerd (Volcardus); from 1522 Volkaerd tutored and lodged *Viglius Zuichemus, Grudius, and his younger brothers Johannes Secundus and Hadrianus Marius at Louvain; the 'tres fratres Belgae' owed much to the Collegium Trilingue, in particular to Conradus *Goclenius. Before May 1532, when his *Carmen sepulchrale* for *Margaret of Austria was published (Louvain: S. Zassenus; NK 1029), Grudius was named secretary to *Charles V; in Ep 2785 *Olahus styled him the successor of Alfonso de *Valdés, although the latter did not die until October 1532. Grudius went to Spain, where in 1534 he lost his first wife, Anna Coebels. In 1535 he returned to Holland and was appointed councillor in the council of Holland at The Hague. Before September 1536 he married Johanna Moys of Antwerp, who bore him two daughters, Maria and Helena. On 11 September 1538 he succeeded Willem Pensart as secretary to the council of state and at the same time was ap-

pointed secretary to the privy council; he held these posts until 1548 and 23 July 1545 respectively. He was also griffier of the order of the Golden Fleece, and he refused to resign this office when, in his post as receiver-general of Brabant, he was suspected of embezzlement and arrested by order of *Mary of Austria on 1 December 1553. Some time after his release in October 1555 he went abroad. He died at Venice and is thought to be buried at Alsemberg, south of Brussels.

Though less famous than Johannes Secundus, Grudius was a neo-Latin poet of merit. He wrote *Epigrammata* on Charles v's entry in Valencia (Louvain: S. Zassenus 1540; NK 3129), an *Apotheosis* of Maximilian van *Egmond (Louvain: E. of Diest 1549), *Poemata pia* (Antwerp: G. Silvius 1566) and other works. In 1609 Bonaventura Vulcanius produced an important edition of Grudius and Hadrianus Marius (Leiden: J. Patius), which was reprinted in 1612 with the poems of Secundus (Leiden: L. Elzevier).

BIBLIOGRAPHY: Allen Ep 2785 / BNB VI 756–9 / NNBW X 306–7 / C.M.G. ten Raa in NBW VII 662–72 / de Vocht CTL II 430–53 / M. Baelde *De Collaterale Raden* (Brussels 1965) 261–2 / G. Ellinger *Geschichte der neulateinischen Lyrik in den Niederlanden* (Berlin-Leipzig 1933) 79–83 / J. Hutton *The Greek Anthology in France ...* (Ithaca 1946) 229–30   C.G. VAN LEIJENHORST

Leonardus a GRUERIIS *See Léonard de* GRUYÈRES

Henricus GRUINGIUS *See Heinrich* GRUNTGEN

Johann GRÜNINGER of Markgröningen, c 1455–c 1533
Johann Grüninger (Reinhard, Greiniger), born in Markgröningen, in Württemberg, received part of his training as a printer in Basel, probably in the shop of Johann *Amerbach. In 1481 he established his own shop in Strasbourg, where he acquired citizenship in 1482 and became one of the most important printers, publishing at least 389 books during the forty-nine years of his active career. His work covered a broad repertory: collections of sermons; editions of the classics; dictionaries; medical and surgical manuals; and popular

legends and tales. He was one of the few in the early decades of printing who published for both the vernacular market and the scholarly market. He was interested in profit and pushed editions through his presses with great rapidity. Although reputable humanists like Matthias Ringmann, Johann Adelphus Müling, and Gervasius Sopher worked for him as proof-readers, the completed volumes were often slipshod, with mistakes in pagination, inexact dates, and an unusual number of orthographic errors. Thus Johannes *Gallinarius' comment that Grüninger's edition of *Henry VIII's *Assertio septem sacramentorum* (9 August 1522) was unworthy (Ep 1307) voiced a typical criticism of Grüninger's work. *Pirckheimer struggled with Grüninger over his edition of Ptolemy's *Cosmographia* because Grüninger added to the maps borders which Pirckheimer felt were in bad taste.

Whatever Grüninger's failings, he was the only Strasbourg printer who remained firmly loyal to the Roman church at the time of the Reformation. All the polemic for the Catholic side printed in Strasbourg came from his press. He printed Thomas *Murner's *Von dem grossen Lutherischen Narren* in 1522, but the magistrates forbade him to sell it. Grüninger pointed out that Murner was only replying to *Luther, but the city council confiscated his entire press run. Grüninger was shattered, because he was the dean of the printing community and had been respected and well regarded in the city. As a result he withdrew from active work at the press, and until his death the shop was carried on by his son Bartholomäus.

BIBLIOGRAPHY: Allen Ep 1307 / François Ritter in NDB VII 201 / François Ritter *Histoire de l'imprimerie alsacienne* (Strasbourg 1955) 81–111 / Benzing *Buchdrucker* 410–11
                                            MIRIAM U. CHRISMAN

GRUNNIUS (Ep 2440 of 5 March 1531)
This pseudonym, perhaps already found in the lost pamphlet to which Erasmus' letter is a reply, has not been identified.

Lambertus GRUNNIUS (Ep 447 of [August 1516])
Ep 447 is addressed to one Lambertus Grunnius, said in the salutation to be a papal scribe. The name is probably fictitious.

Heinrich GRUNTGEN of Kalkar,
d 20 November 1547

Heinrich Gruntgen (Groenken, Groentkens, Gruingius) came from a good family of Kalkar, near Emmerich on the Lower Rhine, where an Elbert and a Gerit Gruntgen were burgomasters in 1489 and 1532 respectively. Little is known about him otherwise. On 28 October 1480 he matriculated in the University of Cologne, obtaining a licence in arts on 3 March 1483. After the death of the previous holder of that office on 6 October 1515 he was appointed dean of Emmerich and retained this position until his death. His literary interests are indicated by the fact that he owned a copy of Johannes Turrecremata's *Summa de ecclesia* (Rome: E. Silber 1489), which Allen located in the Bodleian Library, Oxford, and by his emendation of a text published by Erasmus (Ep 1076).

BIBLIOGRAPHY: Allen and CWE Ep 1076 / *Matrikel Köln* II 88 / H.F. van Heussen *Historia episcopatuum foederati Belgii* (Leiden 1719) I 286 / *Annalen des historischen Vereins für den Niederrhein* 51 (1891) 142, 64 (1897) 135–6, 141   PGB

Léonard de GRUYÈRES d 2/3 April 1540

Léonard de Gruyères (Gruere, a Grueriis) belonged to a noble family from the region of Fribourg, Switzerland, of which a branch was established at Le Landeron, Neuchâtel. Léonard's father, Jean, was mayor of Neuchâtel. Léonard matriculated at Freiburg on 3 December 1508 and studied under Udalricus *Zasius. Lukas *Klett later praised his knowledge of the law and consulted him and Bonifacius *Amerbach about a legal problem (AK III Ep 1471). On 3 March 1507 he became a canon of Besançon, and on 24 September 1516 he was present at Besançon and demanded his share of revenues. He rose in the chapter to the rank of archdeacon of Salins. In about 1520 Antoine de *Vergy, archbishop of Besançon, appointed him his official; thus he came to live with Vergy at the castle of Gy, where in August 1531 he fell ill and almost died. Although he lived in Burgundy he maintained contacts with his family in Neuchâtel and Fribourg and in 1537 sold the fief of Gruyères to a cousin. He was also given the title of an apostolic protonotary and completed several diplomatic missions in the service of *Charles V, going to the court of

France in 1530 (Epp 2348, 2401A) and working among the Swiss cantons from 1533 to 1536, from February 1536 as official ambassador. In Switzerland he proved himself a competent and intelligent diplomat, working to counterbalance the French influence in the turbulent period of an Italian war and Bern's conquest of the Vaud. In October 1536 he and Jakob *Stürtzel were at Basel with Joachim *Zasius, who negotiated on behalf of Savoy. A month later he appeared before the Swiss diet at Baden and sent Bonifacius Amerbach a silver cup in return for an edition of Origen that Amerbach had given him (AK IV Ep 2085). He died at Ghent on a mission to the imperial court undertaken with Pierre *Richardot on behalf of the chapter.

Erasmus met Gruyères during his visit to Besançon in the spring of 1524 (Ep 1610); from then on they corresponded (Epp 1534, 2870, 3084) and perhaps exchanged verses (Ep 2241). Gruyères supplied Erasmus with Burgundian wine; Erasmus consulted him about a possible move to Besançon in 1529 (Ep 2112) and again in 1535, when he warmly offered hospitality (Epp 3063, 3075). His patronage was also acknowledged by Erasmus' former famulus Gilbert *Cousin (Ep 3123).

BIBLIOGRAPHY: Allen Ep 1534 / DHBS III 656 / AK III Ep 1471 and passim / *Matrikel Freiburg* I 186 / C. Gilliard 'La politica di Carlo V al principio del 1536' *Archivio storico italiano* 97 (1939) 229–35 / *Amtliche Sammlung der älteren eidgenössischen Abschiede* ed K. Krütli et al (Lucerne 1839–86) IV-1C 109 and passim / F.A.M. Jeanneret *Biographie neuchâteloise* (Le Locle 1863) I 431–2 / Gauthier 124–6, 132 / Besançon Archives du Doubs MS G 250

PGB

GRYLLARDUS (Ep 64 of [August 1497])

Erasmus' use of the name Gryllard (Gryllardus) is probably a playful corruption (cf French *griller* and *grillon*) of the name of one of his professors in Paris. The description of him as lecturing to Scotists suggests a Franciscan, since – apart from Pierre *Tartaret – the Franciscans were the main promoters of Scotism in Paris at that time. Erasmus perhaps intends here Jean Grillot, a Franciscan, whose licence in theology was granted on 20 December 1485 (he ranked ninth of twenty-one) and

Simon Grynaeus

who took his doctorate in theology on 21 November 1486. Grillot had obtained some notoriety in December 1495 and February 1496 (about a year before Erasmus' mention of him) in preaching at Saint-Germain-l'Auxerrois in Paris certain propositions about the Immaculate Conception of Mary. Grillot is documented in Paris until November 1497. With Antoine Capel he edited John Duns Scotus' *Aurea quarti Sententiarum expositio cum questionibus* (Paris 1497, Jean Barbier for Claude Chevallon 1512).

BIBLIOGRAPHY: Allen and CWE Ep 64 / C. Du Plessis d'Argentré *Collectio judiciorum de novis erroribus* (Paris 1725–36) I-2 332 / Paris, Bibliothèque Nationale, MS Latin 5657-A f 27 verso / Renaudet *Préréforme* 248, 251

JAMES K. FARGE

Simon GRYNAEUS of Veringendorf, c 1494– 1 August 1541
Simon Grynaeus (Griener, Griner) was descended from a peasant family of Veringendorf, north of Sigmaringen in Swabia. Together with Philippus *Melanchthon, a lifelong friend, he was educated in the Latin school of Pforzheim under Nikolaus *Gerbel and Georg

*Simler before attending an undetermined university. On 13 October 1511 he matriculated at Vienna, where he obtained his MA. For several years thereafter he directed a grammar school at Buda, the residence of the kings of Hungary, which was inhabited largely by German settlers. When his opposition to the conservative clergy forced him to leave Buda, he went to Wittenberg, where in April 1523 his name appears in the university register.

In 1524 Grynaeus was called to a chair of Greek in the University of Heidelberg, which by then had lost much of its earlier academic prominence. His religious views were not popular with the majority of his colleagues, but his talents were badly needed. To supplement his annual salary of sixty florins by another twenty, he had to teach mathematics as well as Greek in 1526, and when Hermannus *Buschius left the chair of Latin he was again asked to fill in, with a corresponding strain on his health. At Heidelberg his religious views evolved towards those of *Zwingli; in particular he abandoned *Luther's eucharistic doctrine after a meeting with *Karlstadt in 1524, and after Christmas 1525 he defended his newly formed convictions in a debate with Johann *Brenz. At the time of the diet in 1529 he visited Speyer, the native town of his first wife, and renewed his old friendship with Melanchthon, who had likewise gone to Speyer; he also clashed with the Catholic apologist Johannes *Fabri. In June 1529 he moved to Basel, where he was to live for most of his remaining years. There his activities gained a new importance, and biographical information, which had been scant hitherto, is abundant from that point on.

As soon as the reform party was in command at Basel its religious leader, *Oecolampadius, and his political counterpart, Jakob *Meyer, who had met Grynaeus a year earlier, persuaded the city council to offer him a chair of Greek (8 May 1529). In the preceding negotiations Oecolampadius also held out hopes for his eventual advancement to a medical professorship. Grynaeus accepted all the more eagerly because the Basel government agreed to pay the modest debts he had incurred at Heidelberg. If Grynaeus recommended himself to the Basel authorities by his religious views, the humanist and printing circles around Erasmus and Hieronymus *Froben also had every reason to welcome his appointment. He brought with him a well-founded reputation for scholarship and admirable skill in locating rare manuscripts and books. As early as 1525 and 1526 he had supplied some of his newly found material to Sebastian Münster, who used it especially to improve successive Froben editions of Elias *Levita's Hebrew grammar. Above all it was his famous discovery of five of the missing books of Livy (41–5) in the Benedictine abbey of Lorsch that excited the scholars associated with the Froben press, and in September 1526 the precious new text was in the hands of the Basel printer (AK III Ep 1141), who published it in his Livy edition of 1531. At the time of Erasmus' departure for Freiburg in the wake of the Reformation, with turmoil in the university and uncertainty in the printing industry, Grynaeus' arrival must indeed have had a reassuring effect. Perhaps Simon's move had been anticipated by a relative, for one Johannes Grynaeus died in 1525 as the priest of Münchenstein, close to the walls of Basel. The Grynaeus family's ties with Basel were further strengthened by Simon's nephew, Thomas Grynaeus, who matriculated at Basel at the same time as his uncle after studying in Heidelberg under his guidance. From both Simon and Thomas was to descend a remarkable dynasty of Basel professors and divines.

At Basel Grynaeus at once began his lectures on Aristotle's *Rhetoric* (z x Ep 870), and it seems that he also expounded the Greek New Testament (Ep 2539). But it was soon evident that the university could not be expected to resume regular academic courses for a while, and Grynaeus resolved that for the moment his time would be better spent in the pursuit of scholarship. The printers welcomed, and possibly financed, his plans, while Erasmus supported their execution. It is true that he did not favour Grynaeus' religious views and in November 1529 was very angry at the thought of him tutoring Erasmius *Froben at the orders of Oecolampadius (Ep 2231), but he recognized and appreciated Grynaeus' learning. There is ample evidence of friendly co-operation between the two scholars by letter and no doubt also in person, for Grynaeus visited Freiburg, where he earned the respect of *Zasius except in the matter of religion (AK III Ep 1470, IV Ep 1512). At short

notice he translated for Erasmus some of Chrysostom's homilies on 1 Corinthians and also helped the Froben press with the editorial work so that the long-awaited Latin edition of Chrysostom in five volumes could finally be published in the autumn of 1530; Grynaeus' assistance was publicly acknowledged by Erasmus on several occasions (Epp 2359, 2379, 2422, 2433, 2434). In turn, Erasmus contributed a commendatory preface to the equally ambitious Greek Aristotle edited by Grynaeus and published by Johann *Bebel in May 1531 (Epp 2432–4). In Ep 2433 Grynaeus told Erasmus how eagerly he welcomed both his requests and his suggestions. In fact his patience was tested when a preface was required for his newly discovered books of Livy. He had drafted a dedication to his friend and fellow-reformer Melanchthon but had to agree to have this replaced in the printed edition by a letter from Erasmus to Charles *Blount (Ep 2435) which was less likely to arouse the suspicions of Catholic readers. Another link between the two scholars was provided by Grynaeus' protégé *Claudius, who was treated generously by Erasmus although he could not be given a place in his house at Freiburg.

In the spring of 1531 Grynaeus undertook a journey to England in the company of Bebel, the printer. Erasmus prepared for his good reception with prefaces to Blount in Froben's Livy and to John *More in Bebel's Aristotle, thus honouring the sons of two old and close friends. He also provided personal letters of introduction for the travellers (Epp 2459, 2460), and they visited his friends along their way as they proceeded through Cologne, Antwerp, Ghent, and Bruges to Calais and London (Epp 2488, 2494, 2499, 2502, 2508). Joining Bebel on his business trip gave Grynaeus an opportunity to hunt for manuscripts; moreover he was presented to *Henry VIII on 6 June 1531 and also met Reginald *Pole (Ep 2526), Thomas *Cranmer, and other dignitaries. Thomas *More, then the lord chancellor, received him with his usual generosity, and thanks to his introductions Grynaeus' visits to the libraries of the Oxford colleges were exceptionally fruitful. He was shown much friendship by John *Claymond, the head of Corpus Christi, and permitted to take back with him to Basel a number of medieval manuscripts, especially of

Proclus. The importance of these borrowings, and of the English journey in general, is indicated by the subsequent dedications to his English patrons of some significant works of scholarship. Bebel's Greek Proclus (1531) he dedicated to John *Clement, Johann *Herwagen's Greek Euclid (1533) to Cuthbert *Tunstall (Ep 2878), and to Cranmer Bebel's edition of a work by Plutarch in Grynaeus' Latin translation (1534). He also seems to have considered dedicating to Thomas More a Froben edition of Plato in Latin (1532) for which he had made a careful revision of *Ficino's translation (Ep 2878; cf AK IV Ep 1648). In March 1534, he actually did dedicate Walder's Greek Plato to John *More, although the father had by then resigned his chancellorship.

These editions and also some others that were prepared or inspired by Grynaeus, such as several works by Aristotle and an important collection of sources on the discovery of America, Herwagen's Novus orbis regionum et insularum (1532), indicate a new, as it were post-Erasmian, orientation in scholarly printing at Basel and also show Grynaeus to be a protagonist of this development. A similar shift of emphasis towards scientific method, and indeed science, was propagated by Melanchthon in Wittenberg and in one form or another would soon be recognizable in many European centres of learning. Grynaeus' contribution to it is further indicated by a letter on scientific method which he addressed to Johann *Fichard (AK V Ep 1680a, IV Ep 1706), and also by his interest in medicine (AK V Ep 2100) and music (AK IV Epp 1862, 1870, 1997).

On his return from England Grynaeus reached Basel shortly before 25 July 1531, this time without having visited Antwerp (Epp 2526, 2558), and quickly resumed his teaching in the university, which was once more ready to offer normal courses. No doubt in accordance with his own interests, he used his Greek lectures to acquaint students with the logical and scientific works of Aristotle, and at the time of his death he was still lecturing on the Organon. In 1536–7 he was dean of the philosophical faculty; his rectorate from 1 May 1541 was cut short by his death. From about 1536 Grynaeus lectured in the theological faculty on the Greek New Testament (AK IV Ep

2015). Like other professors he lodged students as paying guests, among them several Frenchmen and Italians, and at times was suspected of paying too much attention to this form of supplemental duty and income (AK V Epp 2162, 2288, 2296, 2298). In the autumn of 1534 he was allowed to interrupt his academic teaching in Basel. Duke Ulrich of *Württemberg had recently been restored to his duchy; with the help of Ambrosius *Blarer, who was Grynaeus' friend, and the Strasbourg theologians, he persuaded the Basel council to grant Grynaeus leave for three months in order to visit Tübingen and help direct the reorganization of Württemberg's university. Grynaeus arrived in Tübingen on 28 October and set to work, gathering around him a new team of professors. His success is indicated by the fact that his leave was extended three times and he did not return to Basel until the city council finally sent *Phrygio to Tübingen as his replacement, riding the horse that was to carry Grynaeus back to Basel; he arrived on 13 July 1535 and was welcomed with a banquet. A subsequent request for a second visit was refused at the insistence of Grynaeus' academic colleagues, who were not prepared to spare him again (AK IV Ep 1927 and pp 481–3).

The invitation to Tübingen also reflected the duke's desire to balance Lutheran and Zwinglian influences in the reformation of Württemberg. Grynaeus, who would take the side of the Zwinglian Blarer, soon found himself involved in another controversy on the Eucharist. This caused him distress, for, inspired by the example of *Bucer, he was striving to reduce the disagreements between Wittenberg and the reformed cities of Switzerland and Alsace. For this purpose he organized a colloquy at Tübingen on 28 May 1535 which confirmed a compromise reached earlier at Stuttgart on the basis of Luther's Marburg proposals (which Zwingli had rejected). The Lutheran party was the stronger and in the long run would come to control the Württemberg church completely.

Grynaeus likewise worked to promote concord among the Swiss protestant churches. He was a member of the commission which prepared the Basel confession of 1534, and he assisted in the drafting of the first Helvetic Confession of 1536. Especially after his return from Tübingen it became apparent to what degree the intellectual direction of the Basel church had fallen to him because *Myconius, the *antistes*, depended heavily on his advice. At the synod of Bern in 1537, Grynaeus defended Strasbourg's concessions to the Lutherans and yet managed to retain the personal friendship of Calvin, whose final return to Geneva in 1541 he helped to prepare. Together with his friends in Strasbourg he also reacted positively to the efforts gaining momentum in the later 1530s to bring about an understanding between Lutherans and Catholics. He supported these efforts when representing Basel at the inconclusive colloquy of Worms from November 1540 to January 1541. In Basel he advocated the freedom of the ministry from secular control and supported Myconius in a conflict with the university and the city council, which insisted that the ministers should seek academic degrees. In this matter Grynaeus and Bonifacius *Amerbach, who had been very close for some time (AK IV Epp 1729, 1793), stood on opposite sides. The conflict was resolved in the new university statutes of 26 July 1539. The ministers had to give way, but their opposition did not end at once and it is possible that Grynaeus' elevation to the rectorate in 1541 was above all a gesture of reconciliation (AK V Epp 2162, 2389, 2436).

Grynaeus' relations with Erasmus took a sudden turn for the worse after his journey to England. When he set out Erasmus had fully trusted him, and in consultation with Erasmus *Schets he was given letters and oral instructions to request the redemption of Erasmus' English annuity by way of a lump-sum payment, a step which seemed desirable in view of *Warham's health and age (Epp 2488, 2494). When Grynaeus returned and reported on his efforts Erasmus was upset and angry (Ep 2574), but his suspicions were not based on firm evidence, and when Grynaeus, assisted by Amerbach remonstrated with him he hastened to send reassuring replies (Ep 2575, 2576). Cordial relations resumed (Epp 2580, 2597, 2605), but Erasmus remained suspicious, and reports he received from England were apt to reinforce his misgivings. It seems that in England Grynaeus had displayed a lack of sensitivity. In small things but also in such delicate matters as the religious controversies

and Erasmus' annuity, which was in some ways connected with the religious conflict, he had chosen to be forthright and as a result had seemed tactless, even arrogant, to some of his English contacts (Epp 2496, 2526, 2659, 2662). When Erasmus heard about this, his reaction was predictable, if probably disproportionate (Ep 2878). On quite different grounds Grynaeus' lack of regard for the complexity of certain issues was also noted by his friend Bucer.

When Grynaeus was received at court Henry VIII and Cranmer invited him to poll the intellectual lights of Protestant Germany about the king's intended divorce (Z XI Epp 1259, 1262, 1269). In no doubt as to what Henry VIII wanted to hear, Grynaeus approached a number of scholars, including Melanchthon, who consulted Luther, and Bonifacius Amerbach, who had already been consulted by Erasmus (Ep 2267; AK IV Epp 1550, 1551). By the end of August 1531 Grynaeus dispatched a first dossier to London which contained letters exchanged between himself and Zwingli, Oecolampadius, Phrygio, Bucer, and *Capito. On the whole it favoured the king's wishes, although some letters did so considerably more than others. In October he followed up by sending a summary of the opinions of Luther and Melanchthon which, alas, were not likely to please his majesty. Personally Grynaeus thought that the divorce presented an admissible solution, whereas Erasmus and Amerbach gradually came to believe that it did not. However, Grynaeus primarily played the role of an honest broker, and there is no evidence that his action disturbed Erasmus, although it is difficult to think that it did not adversely affect the opinion of Thomas More, who in turn criticized Grynaeus when writing to Erasmus (Epp 2659, 2831). A minor misunderstanding may have irritated Erasmus somewhat (Epp 2779, 2788), but all things considered, no adequate reasons are known today for his frank animosity towards Grynaeus late in 1533 which he privately expressed in Ep 2878. At the same time he went out of his way to publish More's Epp 2659 and 2831, whose criticism of Grynaeus was hardly intended for any but himself and was also quite transparent although he suppressed the name. That he published these letters together with his *De* *praeparatione ad mortem*, written to please Thomas *Boleyn, is another indication that he was then not greatly troubled by the divorce question. In spite of this animosity, it is not impossible that Grynaeus was present six months later when Erasmus died in Froben's house. His presence is indicated by letters of Bucer and Capito to Luther (Luther w *Briefwechsel* VII Epp 3048, 3050), but the Strasbourg reformers may have drawn on hearsay and were probably anxious to establish that a Protestant divine was present at Erasmus' deathbed.

Nothing is known of Grynaeus' first wife, Magdalena, except that she was a native of Speyer and that he married her in Heidelberg. After her death he married a rich widow, Katherine Lompart (AK VI Ep 2648), the sister of Jakob *Lompart, at Basel in September 1538. His only son, Samuel (1539–99), followed his example and became an esteemed professor at Basel. In 1539 two members of Grynaeus' household died of the plague, although his wife recovered (AK V Epp 2296, 2313). Grynaeus himself died of the plague two years later and was subsequently honoured by a funeral inscription in the cathedral cloister which commemorates him together with Oecolampadius and Meyer.

BIBLIOGRAPHY: Allen Ep 1657 / NDB VII 241–2 / J.V. Pollet *Martin Bucer* (Paris 1958–62) II 370–400, 439–59 (reproducing a portrait medal) / M. Welti 'Der Gräzist Simon Gryneus und England' *Archiv für Kulturgeschichte* 45 (1963) 232–52 / G.T. Streuber in *Basler Taschenbuch* (Basel 1853) 1–43 / *Simonis Grynaei ... epistolae* ed G.T. Streuber (Basel 1847) / A partly different collection of letters is in the appendix of S. Grynaeus *In librum octavum Topicorum Aristotelis ... commentaria* (Basel: J. Oporinus 1556) / AK III Ep 1434 and passim / *Melanchthons Briefwechsel* I Epp 277, 323, 587, 773 / z VIII Ep 469, x Ep 1043, and passim / *Blarer Briefwechsel* I Ep 218 and passim / *Matrikel Wien* II-1 383 / *Matrikel Wittenberg* I 116 / *Matrikel Basel* II 2, 26 / BA *Oekolampads* I 449–50 and passim / C. Reedijk 'Das Lebensende des Erasmus' *Basler Zeitschrift für Geschichte und Altertumskunde* 57 (1958) 23–66, esp 63–4 / W.R. Staehelin *Wappenbuch der Stadt Basel* (Basel [1917–30]) / J. Tonjola *Basilea sepulta* (Basel 1661) 14 / Max Geiger *Die Basler Kirche und Theologie im*

Zeitalter der Hochorthodoxie (Zollikon-Zürich 1952) 11–12 and passim   PGB

Sebastianus GRYPHIUS of Reutlingen, c 1493–7 September 1556
Gryphius (Sébastien Gryphe) was the son of Michael Greyff (Greif), a printer established at Reutlingen, in Swabia. After learning the book trade in Germany and Venice Gryphius moved by 1520 to Lyon, where he first worked as an agent for Venetian printers before setting up his own press in 1524. Taking his cues from Aldo *Manuzio, he was soon the leading humanistic publisher of Lyon. Both Etienne *Dolet and François *Rabelais worked for him as correctors, and he published some of their writings. His reprints of works by Erasmus included a complete edition of Jerome in 1530 and editions of the *Adagia* in 1528 and 1529 (Ep 2135) and 1548. A certain rivalry between Gryphius and the *Froben press is also indicated by the fact that Jacopo *Sadoleto hesitated to offer a manuscript to Froben because of his good relations with Gryphius (Ep 2816).

BIBLIOGRAPHY: Allen Ep 2135 / NDB VII 55–6 / L. Febvre and H.-J. Martin *L'Apparition du livre* (Paris 1958) 227–9 and passim / J. and H. Baudrier *Bibliographie lyonnaise* (Lyon 1895–1921) VIII / AK III Ep 1374, IV Ep 1446, and passim   MICHEL REULOS

Petrus GRYPHUS *See Pietro* GRIFFI

GUALTERUS (Ep 13, of c 1488)
In Ep 13 addressed to Servatius *Rogerus in Gouda, Erasmus mentioned a certain Gualterus as a common friend. Rogerus, he said, should follow the example of this persevering student. Mention of Gualterus does not recur in Erasmus' correspondence, but the reference in Ep 13 has been connected with other data. At some time before 1497 Willem *Hermans wrote two epitaphs (*Sylva odarum* nos 7 and 8; also in LB VIII 584B–E; cf Reedijk 395) for a fellow-townsman of his named Galterus, who had been devoted to learning and had died prematurely. And soon after his arrival at Ferrara in 1476, Rodolphus *Agricola addressed a letter to one Gualterus de Wouda – for which one might read Gouda – who was then staying at Fano. It is probable that

Herman's epitaphs concern the Gualterus of Ep 13; Allen has argued that Agricola's letter concerned the Gualterus of Herman's epitaphs. If these conjectures are well founded we may conclude that Gualterus was a citizen of Gouda acquainted with Erasmus, Hermans, and Rogerus and that he had presumably met Agricola when they were both staying in Italy (about 1476). Afterwards he must have returned to Holland, where he died at an early age between about 1488 (Ep 13) and 1497 (*Sylva odarum*).

BIBLIOGRAPHY: Allen Ep 13 / P.S. Allen 'The letters of Rudolf Agricola' *English Historical Review* 21 (1906) 302–17, esp 311 on the letter from Agricola, printed by K. Hartfelder in *Festschrift der Badischen Gymnasien* (Karlsruhe 1886) as no 8   C.G. VAN LEIJENHORST

GUALTERUS (Ep 2587 of 14 December 1531) In November or December 1531 Erasmus met in Freiburg one Gualterus, a former canon of Maastricht and Liège, and gave him letters for Conradus *Goclenius, Maarten *Lips, and Theodoricus *Hezius (Ep 2587). Gualterus has not been identified.

Pier Paolo GUALTIERI of Arezzo, 1501–72 Pier Paolo Gualtieri (Gualterius) was born at Arezzo. By 1532 he was in Rome, where from 1532 to 1544 he kept a diary, now in the Biblioteca Apostolica Vaticana (MS Barberini no 1105). On 1 June 1535, encouraged by Ludwig *Baer and Ambrosius von *Gumppenberg, he sent a note of friendship to Erasmus (Ep 3024). In a letter to Erasmus of 21 August 1535, Gumppenberg stated that Gualtieri was serving as a substitute for Blosius *Palladius as apostolic secretary of briefs (Ep 3047), and on 28 October 1535 Pope *Paul III referred to him as 'familiaris noster.' Gualtieri was one of several literary figures surrounding Cardinal Marcello Cervini; with Mariano Vittori, later bishop of Rieti, he learnt the Ethiopic language from Peter the Ethiopian or Peter the Abbot, whose name in Ethiopic was Tasfa Sion Malbazo and who was under the patronage of Cervini (see Vittori's dedication to Cervini for the *Institutiones linguae chaldeae, sive aethiopicae*, Rome: V. Dorici 1551). Gualtieri and Vittori helped Peter the Ethiopian translate into Ethiopic the *Testamentum Novum cum epistola Pauli ad Hebreos tantum, cum concordantiis evangelistarum Eusebii* (Rome: V. and L. Dorici 1548). Gualtieri also translated the Ethiopian rite of the mass, published in a single volume with translations of the rites of baptism and confirmation, under the title *Modus baptizandi* ... (Rome: A. Bladus, 1549; Brussels and Louvain 1550). In addition he is credited with translating into Italian in classical metres Horace *Ode* 1.8. Gualtieri served as secretary of Latin letters and adviser to Cervini when the latter became Pope Marcellus II in 1555. He became archdeacon of Arezzo in 1564 and was buried at Rome in Santa Maria in Via Lata, where a monument was dedicated to him. Peter the Ethiopian called him his 'maggábîna' or custodian (*Testamentum Novum*, f 176 verso), and in the dedication to the *Institutiones linguae chaldeae, sive aethiopicae* Vittori praised him for his knowledge of Ethiopic.

BIBLIOGRAPHY: Allen Ep 3024 / Pietro Polidori *De vita, gestis et moribus Marcelli II pontificis maximi commentarius* (Rome 1774) 120 / I. Guidi 'La prima stampa del Nuovo Testamento in etiopico fatta a Roma nel 1548–1549' *Archivio della Società Romana di storia patria* 9 (1886) 273–8 / G. Curcio *Q. Orazio Flacco studiato in Italia dal secolo XIII al XVII* (Catania 1913) 158–9
PAOLO PISSAVINO

Guarino GUARINI of Verona, 1374– 4 December 1460 Guarino Guarini (Guarinus Veronensis) was born in Verona. After initial studies at Verona he moved to Padua, where he studied the notarial arts and from 1392 the humanities under Giovanni di Conversino da Ravenna and Pier Paolo Vergerio the Elder. By 1403 he was in Venice, where he taught grammar. He met the Greek teacher Manuel Chrysoloras, whom he followed to Constantinople in 1403. He studied in Constantinople and Greece until 1408, returning to Venice and Verona in 1409. In 1410 he went to Bologna, where he met Poggio *Bracciolini and Leonardo Bruni, then attached to the papal curia. On the recommendation of Bruni, Guarino was invited to Florence as a teacher of Greek and Latin. In 1412 the Florentine Studio reopened with Guarino occupying the chair formerly held by Chrysoloras. In 1414 Guarino returned to Venice and opened a school for young

Guarino Guarini, by Matteo de' Pasti

patricians. Vittorino da Feltre came to him to learn Greek; other pupils included George of *Trebizond, who studied Latin under him, and Francesco Barbaro. During this period Guarino wrote a popular Latin grammar, the *Regulae grammatices*. In 1419 he moved to Verona, where he married Taddea Cendrata di Niccolò by whom he had thirteen children. At Verona he was public professor of rhetoric and taught Ermolao Barbaro, Giovanni Lamola, Bartolomeo Facio, and others. In 1429 Marquis Niccolò III d'Este invited Guarino to Ferrara to serve as his son's tutor. Guarino also opened a public school and from 1436 lectured at the Studio, retaining his post until his death at the age of eighty-six. His students at Ferrara included Iacopo Ammannati, Ludovico Carbone, and his own son Battista.

Guarino's great contribution was a system of literary education, adapted from Quintilian, which emphasized three graduated stages of instruction: the elementary, the grammatical, and the rhetorical. Respected both as a scholar and as a teacher, he made a thorough knowledge of the classics the basis of humanistic education. He translated into Latin works of

Isocrates, Plutarch, and Strabo, and edited works of Pliny the Elder, Pliny the Younger, and Julius Caesar. His letters were edited in three volumes by Remigo Sabbadini (Venice 1915–19, repr 1959) and his *Alda ... carmen elegiacum* by Willem H.D. Suringer (Leiden 1865).

In Ep 23 (June 1489) Erasmus included Guarino among Italian humanists whom he considered to be models of eloquence, but in Ep 3043 (18 August 1535) he qualified his praise by saying that Guarino and a number of other Italian humanists fell short of Ciceronian polish, although he still felt they could be read with profit (cf *Ciceronianus* ASD I-2 662). In the *Ecclesiastes* Erasmus emphasized Guarino's preference for a uniform style of declamation (LB V 957F). According to *Beatus Rhenanus, Erasmus' teacher Alexander *Hegius had attended Guarino's lectures. The *Compendium vitae* (Allen I 48; CWE IV 404) states that Erasmus' father, Gerard, heard Guarino lecture. This reference appears to be garbled; or it would have to concern one of Guarino's sons, perhaps Lionello or Battista.

BIBLIOGRAPHY: Allen and CWE Ep 23 / EI XVIII 27–8 / R. Sabbadini *La scuola e gli studi di Guarino Guarini Veronese* (Catania 1896) and *Vita di Guarino Veronese* (Genoa 1891) repr together in 1964 as *Guariniana / Il pensiero pedagogico dello umanesimo* ed E. Garin (Florence 1958) 306–503 (selections of Guarino's letters and documents about his school) / William H. Woodward *Studies in Education during the Age of the Renaissance 1400–1600* (Cambridge 1924) 26–47 / Vespasiano da Bisticci *Le vite* ed A. Greco (Florence 1970) I 555–87

DE ETTA V. THOMSEN

Guillaume GUÉRARD of Besançon, d 21 January 1529
Guillaume Guérard (Guerardus) was a canon of Besançon from 22 March 1514 and the official of the archdeacon, Ferry *Carondelet. When Erasmus visited Besançon in the spring of 1524 he was received and offered hospitality by Guérard until Carondelet himself had returned from his abbey (Ep 1610). Erasmus consulted Guérard in the spring of 1529, when he had made up his mind to leave Basel and was considering a move to Besançon (Ep 2112). Five years after his death Guérard was accused by

Etienne *Desprez of having spread a malicious rumour about Erasmus in the wake of his visit in 1524 (Ep 2895).

BIBLIOGRAPHY: Allen Ep 1534 / Gauthier 128 / Besançon, Archives du Doubs, MS G 250   PGB

Robert GUIBÉ 1459–9 November 1513
Robert Guibé was the nephew of Pierre Landais, treasurer of Brittany and the favourite of Duke Francis II. He became abbot of St Denis, near Paris, in 1477, bishop of Tréguier on 16 May 1483, and bishop of Rennes on 24 March 1502. He represented Duchess Anne of Brittany in a mission to congratulate Innocent VIII on his accession, arriving in Rome on 20 April 1485, and gave an oration of which copies survive. Guibé was again in Rome as Breton ambassador in October 1491 and in 1499, when *Louis XII recommended him to the pope's special favour; he remained in the curia as resident ambassador of the king of France. A guardian in both the papal conclaves of 1503, he was created a cardinal on 1 December 1505, becoming known as the cardinal of Nantes after his promotion to that see on 29 January 1507.

In 1506 Guibé accompanied *Julius II to Perugia and Bologna, where Erasmus may first have met him; in 1509 he assisted Erasmus during his journey to Rome and his stay there, as Erasmus gratefully recalled in a letter of 8 February 1512 offering to recommend him to Archbishop *Warham (Ep 253). In 1510 Guibé dissociated himself from the French cardinals who defied Julius II. He remained with the pope who exempted Brittany from his interdict against France, but the revenues of two of Robert's abbeys were confiscated by the French crown. *Leo X appointed him legate to Avignon and the Comtat Venaissin on 13 July 1513, but he died in Rome a few months later.

Information is lacking about his personality and intellectual interests, but Erasmus repeatedly recalled his kindness and hospitality at Rome (Epp 296, 334).

BIBLIOGRAPHY: Allen and CWE Ep 253 / Eubel II 222, 254, III 10, 252 / Pastor VI 221 and passim / Sanudo Diarii V 77, 80–1 and passim / J. Burchardus Liber notarum ed E. Celani (Città di Castello 1906–59) passim / L. Frati Le due spedizioni militari di Giulio II (Bologna 1886) / A.

Renaudet Le Concile gallican de Pise-Milan (Paris 1922) 665 / B.-A. Pocquet du Haut-Jussé Les Papes et les ducs de Bretagne (Paris 1928) 767 and passim   D.S. CHAMBERS

Johannes GUIDA of Sélestat, documented 1514–15
Very little is known about Johannes Guida, who appears in *Wimpfeling's list of the members of the Strasbourg literary society (Ep 302). A native of Sélestat, Guida was a pupil of Wimpfeling and assisted the latter in preparing his edition of the Germania of Aeneas Sylvius, subsequently *Pius II (Strasbourg: R. Beck 1515). In his letter of thanks to the Strasbourg circle after his celebrated visit, Erasmus included Guida with two others, referring to them as 'those elegant characters' (Ep 305).

BIBLIOGRAPHY: Allen and CWE Ep 302 / Schmidt Histoire littéraire I xvii / BRE Ep 54   MIRIAM U. CHRISMAN

Agazio GUIDACERIO of Rocca, 1477–1542
Born at Rocca, in Calabria, Agazio Guidacerio became a secular priest. He learnt Hebrew from the Portuguese rabbi Jacob Gabbai in Rome and in 1514 became a professor at the Roman university, the Sapienza. His studies were favoured by *Leo X, to whom he dedicated his first published work, the Grammatica hebraicae linguae (Rome: S. Guileretus 1520), and by *Clement VII, to whom, on the advice of the datary, Gian Matteo *Giberti, he dedicated a commentary on the Song of Solomon (Rome: A. Bladus 1524). After the Sack of Rome in 1527 he fled to Avignon, then to Paris, where he enjoyed the patronage of *Francis I and in 1530 was appointed to the chair of Hebrew which the king established in the Royal College. He died in Paris.

According to Erasmus' letter of 5 July 1521 to Daniël *Tayspil, Guidacerio received an offer to teach Hebrew at the Collegium Trilingue of Louvain (Ep 1221). However, he did not accept.

Convinced that the study of Hebrew and other near-eastern languages was of the utmost importance in winning over the adversaries of Christianity (see his dedications to the Grammatica hebraicae linguae and other works), Guidacerio published numerous other works of grammar and of scriptural commentary. His

Henry Guildford, by Hans Holbein the Younger

publications at Paris included *De laudibus et materia psalmorum. Et in primum psalmum secundum veritatem hebraicam expositio* (C. Garamond 1528), *In hoc libello continetur: de literis hebraicis, de punctis, de accentibus, de quantitate syllabarum, deque vera linguae hebraicae pronunciandi ratione* (C. Wechel 1537), *Grammaticae in sanctam Christi linguam institutiones* (1539), a Latin translation of the *Liber Michol grammatices linguae sanctae* of David Kimhi (1540), and other commentaries on various Psalms (in 1536, 1538, 1540) and on the Sermon on the Mount (1531).

BIBLIOGRAPHY: Allen Ep 1221 / P.A. Spera *De nobilitate professorum grammaticae ... libri quinque* (Naples 1641) v 548 / N. Toppi *Biblioteca napoletana* (Naples 1678) 2 / C. Minieri Riccio *Memorie storiche degli scrittori nati nel regno di Napoli* (Naples 1844) 163 / A. Lefranc *Histoire du Collège de France* (Paris 1893) 144 and passim / A. Lefranc 'Les origines du Collège de France' *Revue internationale de l'enseignement* 10 (1890) 457–81 / A. Tilley 'Humanism under Francis I' *English Historical Review* 15 (1900) 464 / H. Galliner 'Agazio Guidacerio, an early Hebrew grammarian in Rome and Paris' *Historia Judaica* 2 (1940) 85–101 / F. Secret *Les Kabbalistes* *chrétiens de la Renaissance* (Paris 1964) 166 and passim   PAOLO PISSAVINO

Henry GUILDFORD 1489–May 1532
Sir Henry was the son of Sir Richard Guildford and Lady Joan *Vaux. Owing to his parents' position he became closely connected with the royal court and was a close friend of *Henry VIII, partly because of his successes in tournaments and at war. As a young man he went crusading and was knighted by *Ferdinand II of Aragon on 15 September 1511 (and again by Henry VIII in 1512) for his exploits against the Moors. In the latter year he married Margaret, the daughter of Sir Thomas Bryan. He received manors in Warwickshire and Lincolnshire in 1512, the first of many grants from the king, but most of his family's estates were in Kent. He was the king's standard-bearer during the invasion of France in 1513 and was created master of the horse on 6 November 1515.

In October 1518 Guildford signed the protocol of the treaty of London along with the rest of the king's council, and also the treaty of marriage between Princess *Mary, the future queen of England, and the French dauphin, *Francis. Erasmus probably did not know him personally in 1519 when he addressed to him two letters in praise of the English court; one of them also recommended Antoon (III) van *Bergen (Epp 966, 1032). Guildford attended Henry VIII at the Field of Cloth of Gold in 1520 and the following year received a manor in Kent and the lordship of Langley. In May 1521 he was one of the justices receiving indictments against Edward *Stafford, duke of Buckingham, and in 1522 he received the duke's manor of Hadlow, Kent. In August 1521 he accompanied Thomas *Wolsey to Calais on his round of continental diplomacy but returned to England prematurely to attend the king in the privy chamber. Together with Wolsey, he greeted the Emperor *Charles V when he arrived at Dover in May 1522. In 1524 permits were granted to Guildford to export large quantities of woollen cloth and wheat. By 1525 he was appointed controller of the king's household. Two years later he accompanied Wolsey to France again and was saluted as 'ambassador' by *Francis I. He met Cardinal Lorenzo *Campeggi when he arrived in England in 1528 and a year later was called as a

witness to the consummation of *Catherine of
Aragon's marriage to Prince *Arthur; since
Guildford had been only twelve years old at
the time, the value of his testimony is
questionable.

Guildford represented Kent in Parliament in
1529. He signed the articles against Wolsey late
that year and early in 1530 signed the English
nobles' letter to *Clement VII urging agreement
to the divorce. Yet he opposed the divorce
contracted without papal sentence, and also
the French alliance. He discussed his views
with Eustache *Chapuys; when *Anne Boleyn
discovered this she warned Guildford that on
becoming queen she would deprive him of his
office of controller. Despite the king's remon-
strances he chose to retire from court for a
while; he remained a member of the king's
council until his death in 1532. He was
survived by his second wife, Mary, the
daughter of Sir Robert Wotton. His portrait by
Hans *Holbein is at Windsor Castle.

BIBLIOGRAPHY: Allen Ep 966 / DNB VIII
767–70   CFG

*Lady Mary Guildford, by Hans Holbein the
Younger*

Lady Joan GUILDFORD *See Joan* VAUX

GUILHELMUS (Ep 89 of 4 February 1499)
In a letter to Richard *Whitford, who was then
in Paris, Erasmus sent greetings to one Canon
Guilhelmus (William), a fellow countryman of
Whitford, who had sometimes dined with
Erasmus. In the same sentence Erasmus added
greetings to the prior of the Augustinian abbey
of St Geneviève. The wording does not
exclude the possibility that the prior and
Canon William were one and the same person,
although more likely they were not. On the
other hand, William may well have been, like
Erasmus, a canon regular of St Augustine. It
has not proved possible to identify the prior of
St Geneviève.   PGB

GUILHELMUS (Ep 1184 of 16 February 1521)
Guilhelmus has not been identified. A friend of
Erasmus, he set out from Louvain for Paris and
was given this letter for Guillaume *Budé.

GUILHELMUS Conradus *See Willem*
COLGHENENS

GUILHELMUS Goudanus *See Willem*
HERMANS

GUILHELMUS Harlemus *See* WILLEM *of*
Haarlem

GUILHELMUS Lovaniensis *See Willem*
GHEERSHOVEN

Louis GUILLARD of Paris, 1491–
19 November 1565
Louis Guillard (Guillart) was the son of
Charles, seigneur d'Epichellière, president of
the Parlement of Paris, and his wife, Jeanne de
Vignancourt. When Charles de Haultbois
vacated the episcopal see of Tournai, Guillard
succeeded him, having obtained the royal
nomination on 8 June 1513 and the confirmation of *Leo X and the archbishop of Reims on
19 June and 11 September. He was twenty-two
at the time and had only received minor orders.
Loyalty to King *Louis XII prevented him,
however, from taking possession of his see,
since on 23 September the English had
occupied Tournai. At their request the pope
appointed Thomas *Wolsey administrator of
Tournai (5 June 1514). Guillard appealed and
after the accession of *Francis I to the French
throne obtained a bull (15 January 1515) which

referred the matter to a French tribunal. Guillard claimed at once that the pope had confirmed him as administrator of Tournai but he preferred to remain in Paris for another two years, installing himself at the Collège de Navarre while Josse *Clichtove directed his theological studies. While the pope continued to vacillate, recognizing Guillard's rights in early 1517 and Wolsey's on 18 April 1518, Guillard resided from 1517 in the house of his vicar-general, Jacob van *Thielt, at Courtrai and the following year, defying the English occupation, visited his diocese in the company of Clichtove. His troubles were ended by the treaty of London (4 October 1518) which returned Tournai to France, and on 12 February 1519 he was finally able to take possession of his see. Erasmus must have watched this struggle with some interest, for he had at one time been promised a Tournai canonry by Wolsey (Epp 360, 388) and was soon to hold a benefice at Courtrai (Ep 1094).

Guillard began his episcopate with an important synod (17–18 April 1520), attempting with Clichtove's assistance to restore discipline and to forestall the spread of *Luther's ideas. In the wake of this synod Guillard's suffragan, Nicolas *Bureau, attacked Erasmus in public. Through Pieter de *Vriendt, Erasmus appealed to Guillard for redress, but a letter from the bishop gave him little satisfaction, and to Guillard's suggestion that he write against Luther Erasmus pointedly replied that this task would be better left to Clichtove (Ep 1212).

At the outbreak of war between Francis I and *Charles V, Guillard and Clichtove returned to Paris, and on 3 December 1521 imperial troops occupied Tournai. On 15 December Francis I nominated Guillard to the see of Chartres in succession to the deposed Erard de la *Marck. Again he had to endure four years of litigation before he could take possession of the see on 2 July 1525. Soon he was joined there by Clichtove and, as previously in Tournai, they endeavoured to govern the diocese in an exemplary fashion, with the bishop regularly in residence. On 16 October 1553 Guillard was transferred to the see of Chalons-sur-Saône (until 14 April 1561), and on 4 September 1560 he was nominated to that of Senlis. Blindness

prompted his resignation (19 September 1561) against an annuity of twelve hundred crowns. He also reserved to himself the right to collate benefices.

Guillard's qualities were publicly acknowledged by Clichtove, who dedicated to him ten of his works. Jean Chéradame, a Greek professor of Paris, inscribed to him his *Grammatica isagogica* (Paris 1521), and Louise of *Savoy and the Carthusian Petrus Blommevena held him in high esteem.

BIBLIOGRAPHY: Allen Ep 360 / Eubel III 143, 300, 316, 336 / J.-P. Massaut *Josse Clichtove, l'humanisme et la réforme du clergé* (Paris 1968) I 40–3 and passim / A. Hocquet *Tournai et le Tournaisis au XVIe siècle* (Brussels 1906) 23, 29–34, 48, 51, 52 / A. Hocquet 'Tournai et l'occupation anglaise' *Annales de la Société historique et archéologique de Tournai* (Tournai 1900) 327ff / C.G. Cruickshank *The English Occupation of Tournai 1513–1519* (Oxford 1971) 62, 143–87, 215, 264 / P. Declerck 'Deux ordonnances destinées aux doyens de chrétienté du diocèse de Tournai (1515–1534)' in *Horae Tornacenses 1171–1971* (Tournai 1971) 142–53 / *Le Journal d'un bourgeois de Tournai: le second livre des chroniques de Pasquier de le Barre* ed G. Moreau (Brussels 1975) 16, 36, 65 / G. Moreau *Histoire du Protestantisme à Tournai ...* (Paris 1962) 54, 57–9, 63 / *Journal d'un bourgeois de Paris* ed V.L. Bourrilly (Paris 1910) 52, 82, 83, 177 / Léon-E. Halkin *Les Conflits de juridiction entre Erard de la Marck et le chapitre cathédral de Chartres* (Liège 1933) 61–74 / H. Dubief 'Les opérations commerciales de Louis Guillart ... ' *Revue du Nord* 43 (1961) 151 / J.B. Souchet *Histoire du diocèse et de la ville de Chartres* (Chartres 1869) 528 / M.E. de Lépinois 'Mémoires de Guillaume Laisné' in *Mémoires de la Société archéologique d'Eure et Loir* (Chartres 1860) 2, 112, 116–17, 121–2 / A. Artonne, L. Guizardet, and O. Pontal *Répertoire des statuts synodaux des diocèses de l'ancienne France ...* (Paris 1963) 191, 201–3, 449 / Paris, Bibliothèque Mazarine, MS 1068 f 280 recto

GÉRARD MOREAU

Johannes GUINTERIUS of Andernach, d 4 October 1574

Johannes Guinterius Andernacus (Günther, Gonthier, Winter, Handernaique) was born at

Andernach, on the Rhine below Koblenz, probably around 1497. He is said to have studied and taught in various places before his arrival at Louvain, in or before the spring of 1523. Very likely he was the young man from Cologne called Johannes Andernacus who had been hired by Conradus *Goclenius, a professor at the Collegium Trilingue, to take a part of Juan Luis *Vives' manuscript for his edition of Augustine's *De civitate Dei* to Basel, leaving Louvain on 15 July 1522 (Ep 1303, 1306).

In Louvain Guinterius was teaching Greek as well as pursuing his own studies; among his students there was Johannes Sturm of Strasbourg, who later followed him to Paris. Guinterius went to Paris by 1526 and there graduated bachelor (1528), licentiate (1530), and finally doctor of medicine (29 October 1532). On 7 November 1534 he was appointed to one of the two medical chairs at the University of Paris, and the following year he was one of the royal physicians. Earlier, in 1532 and 1533, Guinterius had received scholarships from the king, probably at the instigation of Cardinal Jean *Du Bellay and his powerful brother, Guillaume Du Bellay. In 1530 and 1532 Guinterius dedicated to each brother one of his early medical publications; it may be expected, however, that his services to them were of a political as well as a medical nature.

Guinterius' academic duties included a course on anatomy, which he taught in the traditional manner so that Andreas Vesalius, a student of his, had reason to be severly critical of his teacher. Guinterius at least recognized Vesalius' talent and praised him in his *Institutiones anatomicae* (Paris: S. de Colines 1536). Two years later Vesalius himself edited an enlarged and corrected second edition of his teacher's work (Venice 1538). Guinterius' strength lay in his knowledge of Greek – by 1527 he had published in Paris (G. de Gourmont) an excellent *Syntaxis graeca* (dedicated to Antoine de la *Marck) – and in the untiring application with which he used his Greek to translate medical authors. Among the more important of his many translations were parts of Galen's *De anatomicis administrationibus* (Paris 1531), Paul of Aegina's *Opus de re medica* (Paris: S. de Colines 1532), and Galen's *De*

Hippocratis et Platonis placitis (Paris: S. de Colines 1534). In November 1533 Erasmus mentioned Guinterius' presence in Paris in a letter to Goclenius (Ep 2876).

Perhaps on account of his evangelical faith Guinterius left Paris around 1538. At first he seems to have divided his time between Strasbourg and Metz, where he lost his first wife, a native of Paris. He married again in 1543; his second wife was a wealthy widow, Felicitas Frosch, née Scher. She and Martin *Bucer were no doubt instrumental in securing him in the autumn of 1544 a teaching position at the Strasbourg Gymnasium where he taught the classics and – later exclusively – medicine. He also practised as a physician and continued to publish. His later publications, in particular those dealing with the plague, actually reflect a shift from academic to practical medicine. Thanks to the wealth of his wife and his own success as a physician Guinterius lived in comfort; some problems resulted for him, however, from the growing sympathy of his wife for the sectarian followers of Kaspar Schwenckfeld. Guinterius himself, who had been an elder in Strasbourg's French church, may have come to share her religious propensities to a degree; at any rate both were good friends of the remarkable Katharina Zell, a great defender of liberal religious attitudes in Strasbourg.

BIBLIOGRAPHY: Allen Ep 2876 / *Dictionary of Scientific Biography* ed C.C. Gillispie (New York 1970–80) v 585–6 / de Vocht CTL II 529–30 and passim / J. Bernays 'Zur Biographie Johann Winthers von Andernach' *Zeitschrift für die Geschichte des Oberrheins* 55 (1901) 28–58 / V.-L. Bourrilly *Guillaume Du Bellay* (Paris 1905) 119–20, 219 / G. Schaff in *Médecine et assistance en Alsace (xvie – xxe siècles)* (Strasbourg 1976) 21–40 / AK v Ep 2532 and passim / R. Hoven 'Antoine de la Marck, dédicataire d'Erasme, d'Amerot et de Gonthier d'Andernach' *Leodium* 57 (1970) 14–17
                                                KASPAR VON GREYERZ & PGB

Claude de Lorraine, first duke of GUISE *See Antoine duke of* LORRAINE

Anton GULDENMÜNSTER *See Antonius* PYRATA

Ambrosius von GUMPPENBERG
d 4 September 1574

Ambrosius von Gumppenberg (Gumpenbergius), the son of Walter and Magdalena von Kammer, was descended from a noble family with hereditary claims to the title of marshal of Upper Bavaria. He studied from 1514 in Tübingen and Ingolstadt and received ample ecclesiastical preferment. Eventually he came to hold nine canonries in Regensburg (1519), Würzburg, Augsburg, Eichstätt, and other chapters including that of Basel, where he was provost of the exiled chapter from 1541 to 1574. From 1525 he lived for twenty years in Rome as papal notary, acting as an agent for many princes and bishops. He was, moreover, attached to the household of Cardinal *Cajetanus. As an able diplomat he enjoyed the favour of popes *Clement VII and *Paul III. In 1527 he was sent by Clement on a mission to the dukes of Bavaria; when he returned, the imperial army was besieging Rome. During the Sack he shared the pope's refuge in the Castel Sant'Angelo. Gumppenberg's knowledge of German enabled him to mediate between the pope and the *Landsknechte*. Later he described these events in fragments of an autobiography (ed F. Gregorovius in *Sitzungsberichte der Königlichen baierischen Akademie der Wissenschaften* 1877 I Philosophisch-philologische Klasse 329–97). In 1530 Gumppenberg accompanied Cardinal Cajetanus to the diet of Augsburg. In 1545 he returned to Germany, living mainly in Augsburg and Eichstätt.

Wealthy and influential, Gumppenberg was a patron of the arts and a collector of ancient coins, but he became increasingly quarrelsome. A lawsuit with Johann Albrecht *Widmanstetter, begun in 1540, led to Gumppenberg's brief imprisonment and continued until 1552. The papal nomination to the Basel provostship involved him in a lengthy conflict with the Basel city council, which supported the Protestant incumbent. As legal consultant to the Basel council Bonifacius *Amerbach produced no fewer than four reports in this matter (September 1549–October 1555) and at one time was approached by Johann Ulrich *Zasius on behalf of Gumppenberg (AK VI 2920). Gumppenberg also quarrelled with Daniel *Stiebar in 1552 at Augsburg. His hopes of obtaining one of Germany's episcopal sees

were not realized, nor did his bid for the abbacy of Heilbronn (1548) succeed.

Although Erasmus never met Gumppenberg, his assessment of the Roman courtier as diligent and unsophisticated (Ep 2728) appears to be justified, at least in his dealings with Erasmus. Their connection sprang from Erasmus' contacts with Cajetanus (Epp 2619, 2690). As their correspondence developed and continued until Erasmus' death (Ep 3091), Gumppenberg was regularly involved in any contacts Erasmus had with Rome in the final years of his life. He forwarded letters and books sent to Erasmus by *Sepúlveda (Epp 2905, 3016) and others. He encouraged Erasmus' contacts with Pier Paolo *Gualtieri as well as with Dom *Martinho of Portugal (Epp 3024, 3047) and with Widmanstetter in the years prior to their bitter feud (Ep 3047). Despite Johann *Koler's pointed remarks about Gumppenberg's cunning and selfishness (Ep 2993), the latter's admiration for the renowned Dutch scholar was no doubt sincere. At the same time it was naïve, as when he urged Erasmus to put ambiguity aside and attack the reformers bluntly (Ep 2929). When working hard to secure for his Dutch friend the provostship of Deventer (Epp 3023, 3047), he may have misjudged Erasmus' priorities in the light of his own (cf Koler's remark in Ep 3050), but he appraised him quite correctly when doing his best to prevent the printing of Pietro *Corsi's attack (Epp 3007, 3015, 3016). He also seems to have been of real service to Erasmus' old friend Ludwig *Baer (Epp 3011, 3023), and in October 1547, after *Charles V's triumph over the Schmalkaldic League, he approached Baer on the emperor's behalf with a request for any works by Erasmus that might serve the cause of religious concord (AK VI Epp 3001, 3002).

BIBLIOGRAPHY: Allen Ep 2619 / ADB X 122–3 / NDB VII 310–11 / AK III Ep 1918, V Ep 2202, VI Ep 2920, and passim / *Matrikel Tübingen* I 202 / *Liber confraternitatis B. Mariae de Anima* ed C. Jaenig (Rome 1875) 134 / A.J. Schmidlin *Geschichte der deutschen Nationalkirche in Rom, S. Maria dell'Anima* (Freiburg - Vienna 1906) 274 / Aloys Schulte *Die Fugger in Rom 1495–1523* (Leipzig 1904) 210–11 / Pflug *Correspondance* I Ep 35 and passim / *Helvetia Sacra* ed A. Bruckner (Bern 1972–) I-1 284   IG

Petrus GYLLIUS *See Pierre* GILLES

Petrus GYNORAEUS *See Peter* FRAUENBERGER

Thomas GYRFALK of Munster, d 1560
A native of the region of Munster (Val
Saint-Grégoire), Upper Alsace, Gyrfalk (Geierfalk, Girfalck) was the preacher of the Augustinian friars at Fribourg, Switzerland, in 1523.
He was noted for the moderately Lutheran
stance of his sermons. In 1524 he was forced to
leave Fribourg and went to Basel with a
recommendation from Henricus Cornelius
*Agrippa, again assuming the function of
preacher at the Augustinian house. Soon he
emerged as a prominent spokesman of the
reform party. In 1526 he was among the few
remaining Austin friars to surrender their
monastery to the civic authorities against
personal rents. After the reformation of 1529 he
was appointed second minister – the first being
*Oecolampadius – at the cathedral, first with
the title of deacon, later with that of archdeacon and minister of St Elisabethen. In 1539 he
matriculated at the university with Johann
*Lüthard. Erasmus noted on 1 October 1528
(Ep 2054) that he had followed Oecolampadius'
example in getting married.

BIBLIOGRAPHY: Allen Ep 2054 / *Matrikel Basel*
II 22 / *Aktensammlung zur Geschichte der Basler
Reformation* ed E. Dürr et al (Basel 1921–50) II
398 and passim / R. Wackernagel *Geschichte der
Stadt Basel* (Basel 1907–54) III 340 and passim / z
VIII Epp 302, 367, and passim / BA *Oekolampads*
I / H.C. Agrippa *Opera* (Lyon [c 1601]; repr
1970) II 756–7: Agrippa's letter (Fribourg 5
January 1524) to an unnamed friend, perhaps
*Cantiuncula (cf Herminjard I 99n)   PGB

Christoph HACK documented at Erfurt
from 1509
Christoph Hack (Hacke, Hacus) was probably
born in Grossenehrich, one of the oldest towns
of Thuringia, 40 kilometres north of Erfurt. The
register of the University of Erfurt lists him as
'Hack de Erich,' but in humanist fashion he
preferred to style himself 'of Jericho.' He
matriculated at Erfurt in the spring term of 1509
and received his BA in the autumn of 1512, but
he did not obtain a MA, nor are any publications by him known. However, his poetry was
praised in 1515 by *Eobanus Hessus and

Euricius *Cordus. Later Joachim *Camerarius
paid him the compliment that his lyrical poems
were unsurpassed among his contemporaries
(J. Camerarius *Narratio de H. Eobano Hesso* ed
J.T. Kreyssig, Meissen 1843, 23). In May 1518
he joined Johannes *Cellarius for a visit to
*Reuchlin, whom they found at Bad Zell in the
Black Forest. Cellarius showed Reuchlin his
Isagogicon in hebraeas literas, which was subsequently printed with poems by *Melanchthon
and Hack (Haguenau: Thomas Anshelm 1518).
Reuchlin gave Hack a letter for *Mutianus
Rufus (RE Ep 261), and *Hutten, whom Hack
met at Mainz that same summer, added his
voice to those praising his poems (Hutten
Opera I Ep 104). When a rumour of Erasmus'
death reached Erfurt, Mutianus dedicated to
Hack an elegy on his passing, and subsequently a *Palinodia* when the rumour turned
out to be unfounded. In August 1519 Erasmus
wrote to Hack after he had received the first of
these poems (Ep 1008). Subsequent references
to Hack are scant; according to Eobanus he was
in orders by 1523 when he got married and
joined the evangelical camp, and by the end of
March 1523 *Melanchthon congratulated him
on his marriage (*Melanchthons Briefwechsel* I Ep
274).

BIBLIOGRAPHY: Allen and CWE Ep 1008 / Carl
Krause *Helius Eobanus Hessus* (Gotha 1879) I
146, 236–7, 299, 336 / Luther w *Briefwechsel* I
Ep 179   ERICH KLEINEIDAM

Lukas HACKFURT *See Lucas* BATHODIUS

Nicolas de HACQUEVILLE d December 1500
Nicolas de Hacqueville belonged to a large and
well-established family and owned estates in
Normandy. He was canon of Notre Dame of
Paris from 1482 and was also one of the
ecclesiastical members of the Parlement of Paris
and from December 1490 to his death president
of the Chambre des enquêtes. In the collegiate
church of St Martin, Tours, he held the
position of provost. He took a lively interest in
the University of Paris and was regularly
appointed as one of the official visitors to the
Paris colleges under the jurisdiction of the
cathedral chapter. A champion of ecclesiastical
and especially monastic reform, he pressed for
firm action in the spring of 1497 in the case of
the abbey of St Victor and its free-wheeling

abbot, Nicaise *Delorme. Admiring the work of Jan *Mombaer in Château-Landon, Hacqueville and his friends, including Jan *Standonck, succeeded in having a group of Dutch Augustinians settled at St Victor. From 1496 he also attempted to reform the Augustinian abbey of Livry-en-Launnois and to make this attempt effective he contrived by 1499 to bring about his own appointment as commendatory abbot. A volume of *Sermones dominicales* (n p, n d, Paris, Bibliothèque Nationale Rés. 67946) attributed to him was edited by the elder Jean Quintin.

Erasmus was in touch with Hacqueville in 1498 and delivered to him a letter from Mombaer (Ep 73).

BIBLIOGRAPHY: Allen and CWE Ep 73 / Renaudet *Préréforme* 182–3 and passim
MICHEL REULOS

Jan Dirksz van der HAER of Gorkum, d 1538–40
Jan Dirksz van der Haer (Johannes Theodorici, or Theodoricus, Harius) was a canon of his native town of Gorinchem (Gorkum), east of Dordrecht. He is best known for his amazing library of no fewer than 3849 volumes, which he offered to give *Charles v in 1530 in exchange for a prebend in The Hague. The offer was accepted, and in September 1531 the books were transferred to the court of Holland at The Hague. Van der Haer himself also moved to The Hague, and under the terms of the agreement the books remained at his disposal for the rest of his life. He made an inventory, which he presented on 14 March 1534; a copy of it is extant, and so is the original of a supplement dated 4 November 1536. Sadly this magnificent collection was partly dispersed and partly destroyed during the wars for Dutch independence.

Described as an old man in 1530, Van der Haer may well be identical with the 'dominus Johannes' mentioned in Epp 20, 21, 23 of 1489(?). That Johannes was a common friend of Erasmus and Cornelis *Gerard and seems to have owned a library since he was in a position to lend Gerard a volume of Lorenzo *Valla (Ep 23). Van der Haer is more likely to have moved about, taking letters with him, than the prior of the Steyn monastery, Jan Christiaan, with whom Allen tentatively identified Johannes (Ep 1). Many years later Cornelis Gerard

dedicated his paraphrase of the Psalms to Van der Haer and also entrusted a number of his writings to his safe-keeping. In September 1520 Erasmus wrote to Van der Haer, politely declining an invitation to visit him and his library (Ep 1141A). Had he chosen to go, he would have encountered many of his own books. Kronenberg has shown that of Erasmus' writings published prior to 1530 only four were missing from Van der Haer's library according to the inventory.

Van der Haer could also be identical with a Johannes Gorcumensis whom Erasmus apparently met at Paris in 1505 (Ep 184).

BIBLIOGRAPHY: Allen Ep 184, IV xxii, v xxiii / A.J. van der Aa et al *Biographisch woordenboek der Nederlanden* (Haarlem 1852–78, repr 1965) VIII-1 214 / J.L. van der Gouw 'De librye van den Hove van Holland' *Het Boek* 29 (1947–8) 117–30 / M.E. Kronenberg 'Nederlandse drukken in de Catalogus der Librye van het Hof van Holland' *Het Boek* 31 (1952–4) 22–40 and 121 / M.E. Kronenberg 'Erasmus-uitgaven A° 1531 in het bezit van kanunnik Mr Jan Dircsz van der Haer te Gorkum' in *Opstellen ... aangeboden aan Dr F.K.H. Kossmann* (The Hague 1958) 99–117
C.J. VAN LEIJENHORST

Bernhard von HAGEN of Geseke, d 3 October 1556
Bernhard, the son of Konrad von Hagen (Hagius) and his wife, Elisabeth, was born in Geseke, in Westphalia, before 1490. On 3 October 1503 he matriculated at the University of Cologne and began his study in the faculty of arts, graduating BA in 1504 and MA in 1506. From 1505 until before 1530 he was priest of St Peter's at Geseke, but he left the care of his parish to a vicar while he pursued his academic career. He took up jurisprudence and in 1518 was promoted licentiate and doctor of civil law. In 1518 he was dean of law in the University of Cologne, where he continued to teach until 1526.

On 3 October 1518 Hagen received one of the canonries reserved for priests in the cathedral chapter of Cologne, and in the same year Archbishop Hermann von *Wied appointed him keeper of the seals, promoting him to the office of chancellor in 1526, while his friend Johann *Gropper succeeded him as keeper of the seals. Hagen retained the chancellorship under the following archbishop, Adolf von

*Schaumburg. Among his other benefices, he held a canonry of St Severinus', Cologne, and was provost of the chapter of Holy Apostles, also in Cologne, a position to which he was appointed by Hermann von Wied despite the papal provision secured by another candidate, Adolf Norden of Krefeld.

In 1530 Hagen accompanied Hermann von Wied to the diet of Augsburg, where he was a member of both the first and second committees attempting to produce a formula for religious concord. In 1540 he participated in the religious colloquies of Haguenau and Worms. He strongly opposed the efforts of Hermann von Wied, who was attempting to lead Cologne into the Protestant camp. Martin *Bucer, who advised the archbishop, referred to him appreciatively as a 'bell-wether' amid the majority of canons who had remained Catholic. In 1549 Hagen participated in the synod of the archdiocese of Cologne, but although he retained the office of chancellor his role became less conspicuous during the last years of his life.

In June 1531 Erasmus was pleased to have heard about Hagen from Tielmannus *Gravius and promised to write the chancellor in due course (Ep 2508).

BIBLIOGRAPHY: Allen Ep 2508 / ADB XLIX 698–700 / Matrikel Köln II 530 / 'Bernhard von Hagen, kurfürstlicher Kanzler und Propst zum hl. Andreas in Köln' Sauerländisches Familienarchiv ed Franz Honselmann 5 (1906) 119–130 / F.X. Barth 'Literaturbericht für 1908 und 1909' Annalen des Historischen Vereins für den Niederrhein 90 (1911) 139–229 / Leonard Ennen Geschichte der Stadt Köln (Cologne-Neuss 1863–80) IV / Wilhelm van Gulik Johannes Gropper (1503–1559) (Freiburg 1906) / Johannes Gropper Briefwechsel ed Reinhard Braunisch (Münster 1977–   ) I / Hermann Keussen Regesten und Auszüge zur Geschichte der Universität Köln 1388–1559 (Cologne 1918) / Conrad Varrentrapp Hermann von Wied und sein Reformationsversuch in Köln (Leipzig 1878)

ROLF DECOT

Quirinus HAGIUS See QUIRINUS Hagius

HAIO HERMAN of Emden, 1498/1500–1539/40
Haio Herman (Hermannus Phrysius) was born at Emden, in Ostfriesland, and was a son of

Haio Ubbena and Eiske Hompen (after whom he called himself Humpius) and a brother of Wilhelm Ubbena, chancellor of Ostfriesland. He is not to be confused with Haio *Cammingha of Friesland, with whom he was acquainted (Ep 2261). On 19 December 1515 Haio matriculated at Cologne, where Konrad *Heresbach was one of his fellow students. He then went to Paris (Ep 903) and in June and July 1519 to Louvain, in the company of Wilhelm *Nesen. He was probably the courier who carried Ep 989 from Nicolas *Bérault to Erasmus, for in August he returned with Erasmus' reply to Bérault (Ep 1002), which included a glowing recommendation of Haio. At Paris Haio made the acquaintance of Guillaume *Budé (Epp 1011, 1015), but fear of the plague forced him back to Louvain, where he stayed for eight months at the College of the Lily, where Erasmus also lived. In March 1520 Haio was again in Paris, where he edited three dialogues of Lucian (Giles de Gourmont, March 1520) and was asked by Erasmus to help resolve the differences between Thomas *More and Germain de *Brie (Ep 1131). After February 1521 (Ep 1185) he travelled to Italy. He was at Perugia and Rome in 1522 (Epp 1294, 1342) with Caspar *Ursinus Velius, and in 1524 was at Padua, whence he corresponded with Erasmus (Ep 1479).

Having obtained a doctorate in civil and canon law, Haio returned north by the end of 1525. Apparently Erasmus and he had fallen out of contact for some time, for only on 20 March 1528 did Erasmus write to congratulate him on his return and on his recent (March 1528) marriage to Anna, the daughter of Pompeius *Occo (Ep 1978). On 10 July 1528 Haio was appointed to the council of Friesland; Erasmus wrote to him again on 1 October (Ep 2056), sending letters of introduction to Erard de la *Marck (Ep 2054) and Jean (II) de *Carondelet (Ep 2055) at the imperial court at Mechelen. At about this time Haio had gained access to important books and manuscripts by Rodolphus *Agricola, a relative of his, which had passed to Pompeius Occo through his uncle Adolph. Thinking highly of Haio, and certain that he would succeed to the fame of Agricola (Epp 2073, 2091, 2586), Erasmus considered it Haio's duty to edit his kinsman's writings (Ep 1978). Although Haio wanted to undertake the work, his political and administrative duties were too heavy and he could only edit Agricola's translation of Lucian's *De non facile credendis delationibus* (Louvain: R. Rescius and J. Sturm 4 July 1530; NK 558). In 1528, however, he loaned Erasmus Agricola's copy of the Treviso Seneca (1478) to assist in Erasmus' second edition of Seneca's works (Epp 2056, 2091, 2108). The task of editing the *Opera omnia* of Agricola was left to *Alaard of Amsterdam.

Erasmus again wrote to Haio on 31 January 1530 (Ep 2261), but thereafter direct correspondence between the two men ceased. One reason for this was the friction that arose over Erasmus' failure to mention Haio in the first edition of the *Ciceronianus* (Basel: H. Froben 1528). When Ursinus confronted Erasmus with this omission, his first reaction was to reply that Haio did not belong in the *Ciceronianus* because he had published nothing (Ep 2008). However, by the spring of 1529 Erasmus decided to add several lines in praise of Haio to the second Froben edition of the work (ASD I-2 683; Ep 2108). Although he continued to praise Haio's Latin style in later letters, Erasmus grew increasingly suspicious that Haio was not happy with him (Epp 2682, 2791, 2810), and on one occasion he stated that Haio had conceived a mortal hatred for him because of his omission from the *Ciceronianus* (Ep 2587). However, it is possible that Haio's hatred for Erasmus was imagined rather than real. Haio's willingness to provide materials from the Agricola library in 1528 and 1529 – the same years as the *Ciceronianus* affair – was not what one would expect from a man recently alienated. It is possible that Haio's failure to contact Erasmus arose from his involvement in administrative affairs and his increasing distance from literary pursuits.

On 29 February 1532 Haio became a member of the council of Utrecht. In 1534 he saw his old friend Heresbach at the court of Cleves. By then he was suffering from angina, which seems to have caused his death. Alaard of Amsterdam wrote an epitaph for him in 1541. Two fine portraits of Haio Herman and Anna, by Dirck Jacobszoon, are in Occo's hofje, Amsterdam.

BIBLIOGRAPHY: Allen Ep 903 / *Matrikel Köln* II 757 / *Naamrol der Edele Mogende Heeren Raden 's Hoffs van Friesland* (Leeuwarden 1742) 9 / J.F.M.

Sterck *Onder Amsterdamsche humanisten* (Hilversum-Amsterdam 1934) / de Vocht CTL I 393, II 13–15   C.G. VAN LEIJENHORST

Petrus HALCIONIUS *See Pietro* ALCIONIO

Joris van HALEWIJN c 1470–1536/7
Joris van Halewijn (Halewyn, Haloinus) was the son of Jan (d 1473) and of Jeanne de la Clyte (d 1512). In his annotations on Virgil he calls himself 'Georgius Haloini Cominiique dominus,' having inherited the lordship of Halewijn (now Halluin, near Lille) from his father and that of Comines or Komen (now on the Franco-Belgian border, near Lille) from his mother. As a member of the high nobility, he was educated at the Burgundian court; not until 1493 did he enrol in the College of the Lily at Louvain, and in general his humanistic learning was acquired independently through private study. He remained attached to the court, was sent on several diplomatic missions, and travelled a good deal, knowing Dutch, French, Spanish, Latin, and probably German. He had no Greek, however, and his vernacular translations of Greek authors are based on Latin versions. Although he belonged to the social élite, his fame rests on his cultural efforts. With his humanistic education he was a rare bird among his fellow-courtiers (Ep 1220), whom he attempted to win over to the new ideas. He gathered a famous library which later passed to Charles de Croy (d 1612) and was sold by auction in 1614. He also wrote works of his own and translations, but above all he was a patron of writers and scholars. Among his protégés the most significant were Johannes Despauterius, *Vives, and Erasmus. He was buried in the church of Comines and his epitaph was recorded by A. Le Pippre (*Intentions morales, civiles et militaires*, Antwerp 1625, 251–2).

Of Halewijn's Latin and French writings only the *Restauratio linguae latinae* (Antwerp: S. Coquus 1533) is to be found in print. Others, however, survive in manuscript: Brussels, Bibliothèque Royale MS 15.585: 'Annotationes super Virgilii codicem' (probably to be dated 1533–36/7); Paris, Bibliothèque Nationale MS Fr 20.312: a French translation, with additions, of Suetonius' *Vita Iulii* (to be dated c 1514); Paris, Bibliothèque Nationale MS Fr 24.725, containing 'Des Triumphes des Rommains' (1514; intended as an introduction to his translations of Suetonius' *Vitae*, but only that of the *Vita Iulii* is preserved) and a French translation of Aelian's *Tactica* (1517), both with dedications to the future *Charles v. Halewijn also translated Erasmus' *Moria* into French, but the work is not known to exist today; in the view of this writer it cannot be identified with the anonymous French translation published in Paris in 1520 by Pierre Vidoue for Galliot du Pré.

A small number of letters to and from Halewijn have survived; his correspondents are Despauterius, *Dorp, Josse *Bade, *Remaclus Arduenna, Prince Charles, Adrianus Cornelii *Barlandus, Vives, and Erasmus. On the other hand, his correspondence with Jacobus Papa, Hugues de Maubus, Luigi *Marliano, and Pieter *Gillis is lost; see C. Matheeussen in *Handelingen van de Kon. Zuidnederlandse Maatschappij vor Taal- en Letterkunde en Geschiedenis* 30 (Brussels 1976) 109–27. We also know some titles of other lost works by Halewijn, both in Latin and in French, including a *Trilinguis vocabularius*, presumably a Latin-French-Dutch dictionary.

Halewijn's relations with Erasmus are documented in the latter's correspondence. Two letters from Erasmus to him have survived (Epp 641 and 1115) and one of his to Erasmus (Ep 1269); further references can be found in a number of letters between 1517 (Ep 597) and 1525 (Ep 1585). The most interesting of these deal with Halewijn's translation of the *Moria*, which did not satisfy Erasmus completely (Epp 597, 641, 660, 739, 1115; cf also Ep 3101). Another noteworthy discussion concerns the use of grammar in the teaching of Latin. Ep 1115 can be related to Halewijn's preparation of the *Restauratio linguae latinae*, although this work was not to be published for another thirteen years. Halewijn held that grammar should be abandoned once and for all, and this radical view was not accepted by Erasmus. In Ep 1269 Halewijn expressed *Glapion's desire that Erasmus should publish a work against *Luther; in this regard one should notice that Halewijn himself was the author of a work (now lost) against Luther, which was criticized by *Clichtove in 1533. In general, Erasmus' correspondence characterizes Halewijn as his reliable friend and patron at court (Epp 794, 1256, 1331, 1342, 1585).

BIBLIOGRAPHY: Allen Ep 641 / CWE Ep 1115 / Georgius Haloinus *De restauratione linguae latinae libri III* ed C. Matheeussen (Leipzig 1978) / C. Matheeussen in NBW VII 310–16 / C. Matheeussen 'La traduction française de l'*Eloge de la Folie* ... ' *Humanistica Lovaniensia* 28 (1979) / de Vocht *Literae ad Craneveldium* Ep 56
C. MATHEEUSSEN

Thomas von HALLE (Ep 2687 of 9 July 1532) According to Erasmus' correspondent, Ludolf *Cock, Thomas von Halle was then the dean of the cathedral chapter of Minden. A member of a noble Westphalian family, he is not otherwise known.

BIBLIOGRAPHY: Allen Ep 2687
ROBERT STUPPERICH

Hartmann von HALLWYL
14 December 1503–February 1573
Hartmann, the son of Dietrich von Hallwyl, was educated at Basel under the care of his older cousin, Johann Rudolf von *Hallwyl. He matriculated at the university in the spring of 1518, but by 1516 he had already been studying the Greek language and reading Greek Fathers with *Capito (Ep 561) and *Oecolampadius. The former dedicated to him his *Hebraicae institutiones* (Basel: J. Froben 1518) and the latter his *Dragmata graecae literaturae* (Basel: A. Cratander 1518). In the summer of 1521 he registered at the University of Leipzig, where he is also documented in May 1523, when Petrus *Mosellanus attested to his serious approach to his studies. The winter of 1520–1 he spent in Mainz with Capito, like him taking an intermediate position in the Lutheran controversy (Ep 1165; Basel MSS). From about 1538 to 1544 he addressed some letters in elegant Latin to Matthias Erb, then minister at Riquewihr (Basel MSS). From 1545 he seems to have resided at Brugg (Aargau); in connection with two estates he owned in that region he obtained a mining concession in 1547.

The nobles of Hallwyl had been burghers of Bern for generations. Hartmann was active in the diplomatic service of Bern and attended several German diets as an observer for his government. In 1546, being Bern's ablest diplomat at the time, he was sent to negotiate with the Protestant princes of Germany on the eve of the Schmalkaldic war. In 1563 he was Bern's administrator for the territory of Aargau.

BIBLIOGRAPHY: Allen Ep 561 and IV xxvi / DHBS III 756–7 / *Matrikel Basel* I 337 / R. Wackernagel *Geschichte der Stadt Basel* (Basel 1907–54) III 160, 25* / *Aktensammlung zur Geschichte der Basler Reformation* ed E. Dürr et al (Basel 1921–50) IV 315–16 / BA *Oekolampads* I 30, 67–9 / W. Brändly in *Innerschweizerisches Jahrbuch für Heimatkunde* 19–20 (1959–60) 54–6 / Öffentliche Bibliothek of the University of Basel, MSS Ki.Ar. 25^a ff 34, 82; 25^c ff 2–7
                                                            PGB

Johann Rudolf von HALLWYL
d 12 February 1527
Johann Rudolf von Hallwyl (Hallwil) belonged to a noble family whose stately castle in the canton of Aargau is today an important historical monument. Following in the footsteps of an uncle, he received a pledge for a Basel canonry in 1476 and actually joined the chapter in 1484. In 1500 the same uncle resigned to him the provostship of St Ursanne in the Jura, and from 1504 he was provost of the Basel chapter, a charge which he exchanged in 1510 for that of *custos*. While Nikolaus von *Diesbach was bargaining over his resignation as coadjutor to the bishop of Basel, Hallwyl was nominated to succeed him in January 1527, but he died before Diesbach's resignation became effective and was buried in the cathedral.

He had registered at the University of Basel in 1485; thirty years later, in the heyday of the Basel humanist movement, he was studying Greek despite his advanced years (Ep 556) and to Erasmus' surprise giving enthusiastic support to his ideas (Ep 561). His devotion to classical studies was reflected in the careful education he offered to his young cousin Hartmann von *Hallwyl (Ep 561).

In 1517 *Capito dedicated to Johann Rudolf an *Epistola de formando a pueris theologo*, and in 1521 Hallwyl was to arrange with Johann *Froben the printing of Leo *Jud's German translation of Erasmus' *Querela pacis*, but in the end the book was published in Zürich.

BIBLIOGRAPHY: Allen Ep 556 / DHBS III 756 / *Helvetia sacra* ed A. Bruckner (Bern 1972–   ) I-1 201–2, 283 / *Matrikel Basel* I 190 / BRE Ep 188 / Z

VII Ep 173 / R. Wackernagel *Geschichte der Stadt Basel* (Basel 1907–54) III 159–60, 25*, and passim / *Aktensammlung zur Geschichte der Basler Reformation* ed E. Dürr et al (Basel 1921–50) I 468–9 and passim   PGB

Jaspar van HALMALE of Antwerp, c 1475–c 1530
Jaspar van Halmale (Halmalus) was the son of Costen and Katharina van Werve. His first wife, Maria, a daughter of Willem Andriessen, bore him a son and a daughter; his second wife, Cornelia de Heyter, bore him four more sons. From 1501 he studied law at Orléans together with his friend Pieter *Gillis, who later dedicated to Halmale the *Epistolae aliquot ... ad Erasmum* (Louvain: D. Martens October 1516; the dedication, of 26 September 1516, is reprinted in Allen II 601 and translated in CWE 3 350–1). Halmale completed his studies in Padua, where in 1507 he obtained a doctorate in civil and canon law. A member of the Antwerp city council from 1510 until 1527, he was also elected one of the city's burgomasters in 1524, 1526, and 1528. In 1514 he and Jacob de *Voecht negotiated a trade agreement between Antwerp, Lübeck, and Hamburg on behalf of *Margaret of Austria. He contributed some important notes to the Halmale family chronicle, which covers the years 1301–1530.

In view of Halmale's association with Pieter Gillis he may have been the 'Gaspar' mentioned by Erasmus in Ep 474; 'a priest called Simon, of the family of ... Caspar van Halmale' (Ep 570) has not been identified.

BIBLIOGRAPHY: Allen Ep 570 / H. de Ridder-Symoens in NBW IV 390–1 / H. de Ridder-Symoens in *Matricule d'Orléans* II-1 215–16 / H. de Ridder-Symoens in *Varia historica Brabantica* 7–8 ('s Hertogenbosch 1978) 72, 84
                                    MARCEL A. NAUWELAERTS

Gregorius HALOANDER of Zwickau, d 7 September 1531
Haloander, the son of a clothier, Philip Meltzer, and Margarethe Schneider, received a good education in his native Zwickau, Saxony, and matriculated in 1521 at the University of Leipzig, where he obtained a BA in 1522. A scholarship from the town of Zwickau and financial assistance from Julius *Pflug enabled him to go to Italy for advanced legal studies from 1525 to 1527, during which he en-

deavoured to apply the humanistic methods of textual criticism to the *Corpus iuris civilis*. The success of his efforts was ensured when he gained access to the papers of Ludovico Bolognini in Bologna. In 1527 at Venice he met Giambattista *Egnazio, who recommended him warmly to *Pirckheimer. Haloander next went to Nürnberg, where Pirckheimer at once took a keen interest in his projects, persuading the town council to finance Haloander's critical edition of the entire *Corpus iuris civilis*. The four parts of the 'Haloandrina,' *Digest, Institutiones, Codex*, and *Novellae*, were published by Johann Petreius at Nürnberg between 1529 and 1531. It was a pioneering effort and at the time a work of great significance, highly praised by *Melanchthon and appreciated by Bonifacius *Amerbach (AK III Ep 1369, IV Ep 1680). In 1531 Haloander again went to Italy, hoping to obtain his doctorate there, but he ran into difficulties when all his money was stolen soon after his arrival in Venice. He went to Ferrara (27 May 1531) and stayed for a few days with Jakob *Ziegler; after a few weeks in Bologna he returned to Ziegler on 5 August and stayed with him for another eleven days, copying a manuscript. After his departure he fell ill but continued his journey to Venice, where he died, deeply mourned by the German scholars. The circumstances leading to his sudden death are related in Ep 2568.

BIBLIOGRAPHY: Allen Ep 2568 / NDB VII 571–2 / ADB X 449–51 / Knod 182 / *Matrikel Leipzig* I 580, II 575 / *Melanchthons Werke in Auswahl* ed R. Stupperich et al (Gütersloh 1961–75) VII-2 Ep 128 and passim / Carl Krause *Helius Eobanus Hessus* (Gotha 1879) II 53 / AK III Ep 1369 and passim / Karl Schottenloher *Jakob Ziegler* (Münster 1910) 112–15 / Pflug *Correspondance* I Epp 37, 40, and passim   IG

Georgius HALOINUS *See Joris van* HALEWIJN

Thomas HALSEY d by February 1522
Halsey (Alsay, Halseius, Hulsay, etc) came from Lincolnshire and was admitted a fellow of All Souls College, Oxford, in 1495. He was a bachelor of civil law by 1498 and in the spring of 1499 received all orders from acolyte to priest. He went to Bologna in 1504 and took his doctorate in civil law there on 20 December 1510. By 1513 he had also received a doctorate of canon law. He visited Rome in 1504 and 1505

and from 1509 was one of the resident English representatives at the curia. He was closely associated with Cardinal Christoper Bainbridge, probably as a member of his household, and was one of his agents in controlling the English hospice, of which he became chamberlain and then (1513–14) warden. Among his other offices at the curia he was penitentiary of the English nation (not itself a rich post) in 1512, protonotary for Ireland, and a papal *familiaris*. At this period he was often active in cases before the Rota. *Julius II provided him with two Italian churches and in 1512 the deanery of Raphoe in Ireland. In the next year he became, on Bainbridge's referral in consistory, bishop of Leighlin in Ireland. He never visited his see. After Bainbridge's demise Halsey served Cardinal Adriano *Castellesi, in whose house he resided in 1515 and 1516 during the Lateran council. In July 1518 he accompanied Cardinal Lorenzo *Campeggi to London and sought Cardinal *Wolsey's patronage. But when in August 1520 the earl of Surrey, then lord-lieutenant of Ireland, recommended Halsey's promotion to the see of Cork, Wolsey selected another candidate. Halsey died at Westminister by February 1522 and was buried in the Savoy Palace.

Halsey incurred the enmity of Bishop Silvestro *Gigli but was a friend of humanists such as Richard *Pace, to whom Erasmus sent greetings in a letter to Halsey of February 1512 in which he praised John *Fisher and William *Warham (Ep 254). Halsey may also have been the 'Thomas' with whom Jacobus *Piso had claimed intimacy three years before (Ep 216). Writing to Warham in August 1521, Erasmus assured him that Halsey (whom he mistakenly called bishop of Elphin) could fill in the details of his diplomatic news (Ep 1228).

BIBLIOGRAPHY: Allen Ep 254 / Emden BRUO II 857–8 / D.S. Chambers *Cardinal Bainbridge in the Court of Rome, 1509 to 1514* (Oxford 1965) 8n, 74n, 76n, 77n, 79–80, 117, 119 / W.E. Wilkie *The Cardinal Protectors of England* (Cambridge 1974) 41, 79, 109, 160n, 165, 171 / LP II 2446, 2888, 3876   C.S. KNIGHTON

Gérard d'HAMÉRICOURT *See* GERARDUS (*Epp 673, 792*)

Johann HANER of Nürnberg, c 1480–c 1545
Born of a poor Nürnberg family, Haner

probably began his studies at the University of Ingolstadt. He was already a MA when he matriculated at the University of Freiburg on 6 October 1507. After his return to Nürnberg the city council appointed him warden of the hospital of the Holy Ghost on 16 November 1513; it was in the hospital that he celebrated his first mass, on 1 October 1514. In addition to his wardenship he received the parish of Grossgründlach, north of Nürnberg, in 1517, and after personal presentation in Rome the parish of Fürth, west of Nürnberg, to which he continued to lay claim until 1542 although he had never taken charge of it. On 31 July 1521, after he had resigned the hospital wardenship, the council approved his appointment as 'vicar of the altar of St Anne in the chapel of the graveyard next to the parish church of St Laurence.'

At first Haner had welcomed *Luther's call for reform, but he soon assigned himself the task of mediating between the religious parties. He claimed that on his visit to Rome in 1519 he had personally presented his proposals for reconciliation to Pope *Leo x, and on 5 January 1524 he wrote to *Clement VII, again offering his mediation and suggesting a series of minor reforms and concessions to the Lutherans. In the same vein he addressed himself to Erasmus on 17 February, urging him to speak up for the church in its hour of need (Ep 1421). At the same time he launched some sharp attacks upon Andreas *Osiander, a Lutheran preacher at Nürnberg, whom he denounced publicly as a heretic. On 14 February 1525 he was appointed preacher at the cathedral of Würzburg, but after returning to his initial position of support for the reformers he was compelled to leave Würzburg in November. He lost his benefices in Nürnberg and Grossgründlach in the same year. He returned to Nürnberg in the autumn of 1526 after an approach to Philip of *Hesse during the diet of Speyer had failed to bring results. While his fellow-citizens paid little attention to his admonitions and did not offer him another office, he entered into a correspondence with *Zwingli and *Oecolampadius in an attempt to resolve the controversy between the Swiss and the Lutherans concerning the Eucharist.

Nürnberg was by now fully on the side of the Protestants, but some questionable practices within its church and also his rejection of Luther's doctrine of justification led Haner once again to revise his personal stand. In 1532 he went to Regensburg to meet the papal legate Girolamo *Aleandro and subsequently returned to the church of Rome. In a bid for patronage, on 16 June 1533 he dedicated his *Prophetia vetus ac nova*, a critique of the evangelical doctrine of justification, to Duke George of *Saxony. Against the author's wishes it was edited in 1534 at Leipzig (M. Blum) by Johannes *Cochlaeus, while in the same year the Nürnberg minister Thomas *Venatorius published a firm response to Haner under the title *De sola fide iustificante nos in oculis Dei* (Nürnberg: J. Petreius). Haner's position in Nürnberg finally became untenable when Georg *Witzel published an exchange of letters in which Haner spoke out against the reformers in unmistakable terms and even proceeded to insult Luther: *Epistolae duae … Haneri et … Wicelii de causa Lutherana* (n p 1534). Compelled to leave Nürnberg at the beginning of 1535, he moved to Bamberg, where he was appointed vicar at the cathedral on 9 November 1535 and received another benefice. Between 29 December 1541 and 4 July 1544 he also held the position of cathedral preacher. He continued to argue his views in the religious controversy in writings and letters which went largely unnoticed. He died at Bamberg.

BIBLIOGRAPHY: Allen Ep 1421 / ADB X 511–12 / RGG III 66 / *Matrikel Freiburg* I-1 179 / Walter Friedensburg 'Zur Korrespondenz Johannes Haners' *Beiträge zur bayerischen Kirchenge-schichte* 5 (1899) 164–191 / Theodor Kolde 'Thomas Venatorius, sein Leben und seine literarische Tätigkeit' *Beiträge zur bayerischen Kirchengeschichte* 13 (1907) 97–121, 157–95, esp 171ff / Andreas Osiander *Gesamtausgabe* I *Schriften und Briefe 1522 bis März 1525* ed Gerhard Müller (Gütersloh 1975) 123–5 / Gerhard Pfeiffer *Quellen zur Nürnberger Refor-mationsgeschichte* (Nürnberg 1968) passim / Matthias Simon *Nürnbergisches Pfarrerbuch* (Nürnberg 1965) no 477a / Karl Schornbaum 'Beiträge zur Geschichte des Reformationszeit-alters in Nürnberg' *Mitteilungen des Vereins für Geschichte der Stadt Nürnberg* 44 (1953) 294–304 / *Realenzyklopädie für protestantische Theologie und Kirche* ed J.J. Herzog et al, 3rd ed (Leipzig 1896–1908) VII 400–4 (Theodor Kolde) /

Johannes Kist *Die Matrikel der Geistlichkeit im Bistum Bamberg 1400–1556* (Würzburg 1956) no 2374 / *Epistolae ad Nauseam* 122–3

STEPHAN FÜSSEL

Philippe HANETON d 18 April 1522 (or 1528)
Nothing appears to be known about the origins of Philippe Haneton, seigneur of Lindt. In 1494 he was appointed secretary to the grand council at Mechelen; from 1500 to 1522 he was first secretary as well as *audiencier*. In 1520 he was also appointed treasurer of the Golden Fleece. In 1500 and 1501 Haneton participated in the unsuccessful attempts to negotiate a marriage between the future *Charles v and *Claude, the future queen of France. In 1504 he attended the meetings at Blois. On 21 October 1504 he witnessed Erasmus' signature on a receipt for a grant in aid of his studies given to him by Philip the Handsome, duke of *Burgundy, in the wake of the presentation of his *Panegyricus* (Allen Ep 181 introduction). From 1506 until 1514(?) Haneton was also treasurer and keeper of the archives of Flanders. In the negotiations with England that took place at Calais in 1507 he revealed his sympathy for France. He assisted in negotiating the treaties of Noyon (1516) and Cambrai (1517) and was greatly esteemed by *Margaret of Austria. On account of his advanced years he did not go to Spain with Prince Charles (Marburg MS) but again participated in the negotiations with France at Paris and Montpellier in 1519 and with England in 1521. He died on 18 April, but his tomb in St Gudula's, Brussels, no longer exists, and the question as to the year of his death has not been completely resolved (cf Reedijk). Probably by 1528 Erasmus obliged his friend Maarten *Davidts by composing an epitaph for Haneton (Reedijk poem 120; Allen Ep 1280).

Haneton was married to Marguerite, the daughter of Gerard Numan; among their children were Charles, secretary to Charles v, and Anne, who married Jean *Lalemand as her second husband. Haneton composed a 'Recueil en forme d'histoire ... contenant les titres, actes et traitez faicts entre le roy Louis XII et ledicte roy de Castille' (1498–1507), which is preserved in Paris, Bibliothèque Nationale, and partly published in L.P. Gachard and C.

Piot *Collection des voyages des souverains des Pays-Bas* (Brussels 1874–82) I 341–4.

BIBLIOGRAPHY: Allen Ep 1280 / Reedijk poem 120 / BNB VIII 682–4 / Fritz Walser and R. Wohlfeil *Die spanischen Zentralbehörden und der Staatsrat Karls v.* (Göttingen 1959) 20 / Michel Baelde *De collaterale raden onder Karel v en Filips II* (Brussels 1965) 266 / *Négociations diplomatiques entre la France et l'Autriche durant les trente premières années du XVIe siècle* ed A.J.G. Le Glay (Paris 1845) I xv–xvi and passim / On Haneton's 'Recueil' see C.R. von Höfler 'Das diplomatische Journal des Andrea del Burgo ... und des ... Philippe Haneton Gedenkschrift über die Verhandlungen K. Philipps und K. Ludwigs XII. 1498–1506' in *Sitzungsberichte der kaiserlichen Akademie der Wissenschaften: Philosophisch-historische Klasse* 108 (Vienna 1884) 411–502 / Marburg on the Lahn, Staatsarchiv, MSS Bestand 3, Fasz. 3 / 390–2 ff 79–85

PETER KRENDL

Jérôme de HANGEST of Compiègne, d 8 September 1538
Jérôme de Hangest was born in Compiègne, in the diocese of Noyon. His position in the illustrious Hangest family in that region has not been clearly established. Hangest took his MA about 1502 in Paris at the Collège de Reims, where he was a student of the leading Scotist, Pierre *Tartaret, and he then taught arts at the same college. Admitted to the Collège de Sorbonne as *hospes* in 1507, he was a *socius* in 1510 and prior in 1513. Hangest was rector of the university from 11 October 1513 to mid-December. He ranked first of twenty-five in his licentiate class of 26 January 1514, and his doctorate in theology was completed on 22 March 1514. The faculty of theology added Hangest to its committee investigating *Reuchlin in 1514 (Renaudet's misreading of the manuscript has created a non-existent Marcel de Hangest). After 1514, however, Hangest took no part in the faculty's affairs. He is especially important for his prolific writings on logic (four titles in twelve editions) and ethics (two titles in fourteen editions) and for his anti-Lutheran polemic (eight titles in eleven editions). Imbart de La Tour says Hangest's *De libero arbitrio* drew heavily from Erasmus without acknowledging the source, but the notion of free will was

already one of the foundations of Hangest's *Moralia* in 1519. Erasmus felt that Hangest's polemic was not helpful, even though more restrained and factual than *Béda's (Ep 2134; LB IX 448D).

Hangest declined an invitation to serve Bishop János Gosztonyi in Hungary in 1519, instead attaching himself to Cardinal Louis de Bourbon, for whom he became vicar-general *in spiritualibus et temporalibus* in the diocese of Le Mans from 1521 until his death in 1538. In this position Hangest had a hand in the foundation and the drafting of statutes of the Collège du Mans in Paris. He preached frequently against heretics. His two polemical works in 1534 were intended to answer the famous placards attributed to Antoine Marcourt. Hangest was buried in the cathedral of Le Mans in the Chapelle du Sépulchre. His epitaph is extant.

Hangest's works include: *Problemata logicalia* (Paris: Gaspard Philippe for Jean Petit 1504); *Problemata exponibilium* (Paris: Jean Barbier for Jean Petit 1507); *Liber proportionum* (Paris: Jean Barbier for Jean Petit 1508); *Introductorium morale* (Paris: Jean Petit 1515); *Liber de causis* (Paris: Berthold Rembolt for Jean Petit); *Moralia* (Paris: Jean Petit 1519, eleven editions in Paris, Lyon, and Caen); *Adversus nonnullos articulos antilogia* (Paris: Pierre Vidoue for Jean Petit 1523); *De libero arbitrio in Lutherum* (Paris: Josse Bade for Jean Petit 1527); *De possibili praeceptorum divinorum impletione in Lutherum* (Paris: Josse Bade for Jean Petit 1528); *Praeconiorum sacrosanctae Christi matris ... adversus antimarianos propugnaculum* (Paris: Josse Bade for Jean Petit 1529); *De academiis in Lutherum* (Paris: Josse Bade for Jean Petit 1532); *Contre les tenebrions lumiere evangelicque* (Paris: Jean Petit 1534); and *De Christifera Eucharistia adversus nugiferos symbolistas* (Paris: Jean Petit 1534).

BIBLIOGRAPHY: Allen Ep 2134 / G. Berthoud *Antoine Marcourt* (Geneva 1973) 162–4 / DTC VI-2 2042 / Farge no 234 / P.-Y. Féret *La Faculté de théologie de Paris et ses docteurs les plus célèbres, époque moderne* (Paris 1900–10) II 25–30 / P. Imbart de La Tour *Les Origines de la réforme* (Paris 1914) III 210–12 / M.-M. de la Garanderie *Christianisme et lettres profanes* (Paris-Lille 1976) I 216–26 / Renaudet *Préréforme* 648

JAMES K. FARGE

Catherine HANNOT *See Lieven* ALGOET

Martinus HARDENUS *See Maerten van* NAERDEN

Eleuthère HARDY of Tournai,
d 11 November 1525
Eleuthère Hardy (Audax) is first documented as a student in Paris on 14 October 1487, being then a bachelor of theology and a student of the Collège de Navarre. On 28 June 1495 he passed his *Sorbonnique*, or third test for the licence in theology, ranking seventh among the thirty candidates. He obtained his licence on 28 January 1496, and on 7 November a doctorate in theology. He also seems to have received a doctorate in canon law. As a professor in the Collège de Navarre he formed a friendship with Josse *Clichtove, who may initially have been his student and was then working with *Lefèvre d'Etaples.

In 1498 Hardy returned to Tournai and was appointed canon of the chapter of Our Lady, at first occupying the position of hosteler (1498–1503) and subsequently that of scholaster (1503–25). In the years of the English occupation (1513–18) he also served as a lecturer in the college of classical languages founded by Pierre *Cotrel. It was probably in Tournai that he became acquainted with Willem *Bollart, who was appointed abbot of Saint-Amand following Hardy's recommendation. It was likewise in Tournai that Erasmus seems to have met him (Ep 755) when visiting his friends Johannes de *Molendino – like Hardy a canon – and Richard *Sampson. In 1519 and 1520 Hardy also met in Tournai his old friend Clichtove, with whom he had retained contacts after his departure from Paris. For example, in May 1515 he and his fellow-canon Georgius Civis (Bourgeois?) had sent Clichtove a book printed in French, asking him for a critique of heterodox statements it contained.

BIBLIOGRAPHY: CWE Ep 755 / de Vocht CTL I 521 / C. de Borman *Chronique de l'abbaye de Saint-Trond* (Liège 1877) II 359 / J. Vos *Les Dignités et les fonctions de l'ancien chapitre de Notre Dame de Tournai* (Bruges 1899) II 118, 157 / A. Clerval *De Jodoci Clichtovei Neoportuensis vita et operibus* (Paris 1894) 6 / J.-P. Massaut *Josse Clichtove, l'humanisme et la réforme du clergé* (Paris 1968) I 187, II 117

GÉRARD MOREAU

de HARENA, HARENACEUS *See Andrea*
AMMONIO, *Levinus and Johannes* AMMONIUS

Johannes HARIUS *See Jan Dirksz van der* HAER

Guilhelmus HARLEMUS *See* WILLEM *of
Haarlem*

William HARRIS of London, documented
1507–9
William Harris (Harrisius, Herisius, Harisius
Mela Anglus) matriculated at the University of
Cologne on 29 December 1507 and took his
licence in civil law on 27 January 1509. He
became a friend of Petrus Ravennas and
Ortwinus *Gratius, penning commendatory
letters to the former's *Alphabetum aureum* and
the latter's *Orationes quodlibeticae*, both of
which were published in 1508 at Cologne. He
also met *Remaclus Arduenna there and
became a good friend of Johannes *Cochlaeus,
who recalled him in 1529 (Ep 2120). No more is
known about Harris.
    BIBLIOGRAPHY: Allen Ep 2120 / *Matrikel Köln*
II 621 / D. Reichling *Ortwin Gratius* (Heiligenstadt 1884, repr 1963) 7, 22, 89 / Martin Spahn
Johannes Cochlaeus (Berlin 1898, repr 1964) 11 /
de Vocht *Busleyden* 219
                                    MORDECHAI FEINGOLD

Karl HARST of Wissembourg, 1492–1563
The son of an episcopal official at Wissembourg
(Weissenburg) in the bishopric of Speyer (now
in Lower Alsace), Karl Harst matriculated at
the University of Cologne on 28 October 1510
and a few years later was at Orléans (Allen Ep
866:5n), where he met Adolf *Eichholz and the
future chancellor of Jülich, Johann *Gogreve.
Later he moved to Louvain, where he studied
under Conradus *Goclenius and met Ludovicus *Carinus, Wilhelm *Nesen, Juan Luis
*Vives (Ep 1303, 1306), and, of course, Erasmus
himself, who wrote him a letter of encouragement on 22 June 1521 (Ep 1215) and may have
used him as a messenger (CWE Ep 1241A Allen
Ep 2680). By the end of October 1521, while still
studying at Louvain, he accompanied Erasmus
on his journey from Louvain to Basel as far as
Koblenz and then returned to the Low
Countries, carrying Erasmus' letters (Ep 1342).
Apparently he could not act at once upon his
intention to follow Erasmus to Basel (Epp 1296,

1303, 1306), but by April 1524 he had joined
Erasmus as a famulus (Ep 1437) and, being well
liked by his master, stayed with him for over a
year (Ep 1538; AK II Epp 961, 964, 965) before
being sent on important missions abroad.
Towards the middle of May 1525 he left for
Venice, Padua, and Rome by way of Innsbruck. He took to Venice Erasmus' revisions
for a new Aldine edition of the *Adagia*, but
Gianfrancesco *Torresani declined to undertake the work. However, Harst did bring back
from Rome a papal dispensation permitting
Erasmus to make a will (Epp 1575, 1576, 1588,
1589A, 1594, 1602, 2740; AK IV Ep 2068). He also
visited Erasmus' friends at Padua and Ferrara
(Epp 1587, 1594, 1595) and by 21 September
had returned to Basel (Herminjard I Ep 161).
Two weeks later he was sent once more to
Venice and Padua to recover the printer's copy
of the *Adagia* left with Torresani and to fetch a
Chrysostom he had been expected to bring on
his former trip (Epp 1623–8). By the end of
November he had left Venice on his way back
to Erasmus (Epp 1645, 1649, 1650; AK III Ep
1076). After Christmas he was again on the
move, this time to the Low Countries and
England (Epp 1654, 1656). Travelling in the
company of Frans van der *Dilft, he visited
Louvain and Antwerp before spending the
end of February and the beginning of March in
England (Epp 1666, 1671). On his way back he
revisited Antwerp and Mechelen, where he
attempted to effect a payment of Erasmus' court
annuity (Epp 1676, 1681, 1682). By way of
Cologne, where he met his old friend Eichholz,
he finally reached Basel on 19 April 1526 (Epp
1695, 1697, 1704; AK III Ep 1136).
    Harst had for some time planned to get
married (Ep 1437), and Erasmus let him go,
probably in June 1526, when he recommended
him to Frans van *Cranevelt (Ep 1724). By the
end of the year he was in Louvain, and on 8
January 1527 he married Katharina van der
*Klusen (Epp 1768, 1778, 1788). For more than
three years he remained in Louvain and lodged
and tutored pupils in his house (Ep 2231). He
also remained in touch with his friends in Basel
(AK III Epp 1204, 1281), and his charges
included Erasmus' godson, Erasmius *Froben
(Epp 2231, 2352).
    In the spring of 1530 Harst entered the
service of Duke John III of *Cleves as a

councillor (Ep 2352). At about this time he wished to enhance his standing by obtaining a legal doctorate. He made inquiries at the University of Basel (AK IV Ep 1607) and later on is normally styled doctor, but where he actually received the degree is not yet known. In the administration of Jülich and Cleves he joined his old fellow-students from Orléans, Gogreve and Heinrich Olisleger, and also Johann von *Vlatten and Konrad *Heresbach to form an influential circle of convinced Erasmians. In the summer of 1533 he was sent on a mission to visit Erasmus at Freiburg. He brought the first annual instalment of a pension his duke had accorded Erasmus together with an 'Erklärung' of the new church ordinance of the duchies, which had been drawn up along Erasmian lines (Epp 2804, 2845). Harst continued to be used on missions of great importance to Jülich-Cleves. In 1535 he attended the diet of Worms (Ep 3071) and in September and December 1536 and in August 1537 he wrote to Bonifacius *Amerbach from Speyer, the seat of the imperial law court (Reichskammergericht); he voiced disappointment at not being remembered in Erasmus' will and mentioned another visit to Basel in the summer of 1537 (AK IV Epp 2068, 2092, V Ep 2146). In 1540 he accompanied Anne of Cleves, the new queen of *Henry VIII, to England and remained at the English court until 1544. He undertook several missions to the courts of King *Ferdinand and the Emperor *Charles V and in 1548 went to Brussels in an unsuccessful attempt to obtain an exemption for the duchies from the stern religious decrees of the diet of Augsburg of 1547. He also undertook new missions to England in 1547 and in 1556. In the latter year he joined Vlatten and Heresbach in signing an exposé on the consequences for the duchies of the Augsburg articles of 1555. From 1552 he lived in Düsseldorf but was at Xanten at the time of his death.

BIBLIOGRAPHY: Allen Ep 1215 / NDB VII 705–6 / ADB X 647–9 / Matrikel Köln II 666 / Bierlaire Familia 62–4 / de Vocht CTL II 142–5 and passim / de Vocht Literae ad Craneveldium Ep 172 and passim / Otto R. Redlich Staat und Kirche am Niederrhein zur Reformationszeit (Leipzig 1938) 78 and passim / August Franzen Die Kelchbewegung am Niederrhein im 16. Jahrhundert (Münster 1955) 57, 63 / AK II Ep 961, VIII Ep 3479, and passim   FRANZ BIERLAIRE & PGB

Al-HASAN ben Muhammad Hafsid sultan of Tunisia, ruled 1526–42

Al-Hasan was a son of Muhammad ben al-Hasan. By the beginning of his reign as *mawlay* or sultan the Hafsid monarchy was in irreversible decline: Annaba (Bone) and Constantine had been lost to *Khair ad-Din (Barbarossa) of Algiers, and al-Hasan's authority was being challenged in the southern part of the country by the al-Shabi family. His uncertain authority did not extend much beyond Tunis, and he remained a spectator in the conflict between the Ottomans and the Spaniards for mastery in North Africa. In 1534 an Ottoman fleet of eighty-four ships under Khair ad-Din captured La Goulette and on 18 August 1534 entered Tunis, which al-Hasan had abandoned. Al-Hasan was later defeated by Khair ad-Din at al-Kayrawan, thus losing his entire kingdom. He then went to Spain to seek help. In June 1535 *Charles V expelled Khair ad-Din from Tunis and installed al-Hasan as a Spanish protégé (Epp 3047, 3061). He was, however, hated by his subjects, especially following the massacres that accompanied his reinstatement, and he could maintain his authority in the north only through the presence of a Spanish garrison at La Goulette. His unpopularity enabled his son Ahmad to depose and blind him in 1542.

BIBLIOGRAPHY: There is no adequate biography, short or full-scale. Useful information might be obtained from Charles-André Julien Histoire de l'Afrique du Nord (Paris 1956); Jamil M. Abun-Nasr A History of the Maghrib 2nd ed (Cambridge 1975); A.S. Ilter Simali Afrikada Türkler (Istanbul 1937) I   FEHMI ISMAIL

Jacques and Julien HASARD of Enghien, documented 1502–25

Very little is known about the brothers Jacques and Julien Hasard (Hassart, Hasert) of Enghien, in Hainaut. Julien matriculated at the University of Louvain on 31 July 1502, and Jacques may perhaps have done likewise in 1497. By 1520 Jacques had become a Dominican and Julien a Carmelite, and both were lectors in their respective monasteries. In December 1520 Erasmus reported that they had sent him a pamphlet critical of him, which he had 'arranged to have published to bring them glory' (Ep 1165). It is the Apologia F. Iacobi Hasardi Angiani (Louvain D. Martens 1520; NK 3142),

which according to the colophon was written
by the hand of Julien Hasard. While the author
presents in a rather abstruse fashion his own
interpretation of the beginning of the gospel of
St John in opposition to Erasmus', he never
attacks Erasmus and even defends the value of
biblical scholarship as long as the place of the
Vulgate in the liturgy is respected. Julien, who
died at Enghien in 1525, is credited with
several writings by the *Bibliotheca Carmelitana*,
but all that has been traced is a dedicatory
preface, dated from Enghien, to *Determinatio
optima quorundam doctorum super articulis pri-
vilegiorum fratrum mendicantium* (Antwerp: W.
Vorsterman c 1518; NK 2773).

BIBLIOGRAPHY: Allen Ep 1165 / *Matricule de
Louvain* III-1 153 (no 145), 239 / Irenaeus Rosier
*Biographisch en bibliographisch overzicht van de
vroomheid in de Nederlandse Carmel* (Tielt 1950)
69 / C. de Villiers et al *Bibliotheca Carmelitana*
(Orléans 1752) II 207–8   PGB

Aegidius HASEBART documented
1483–1539
Aegidius Hasebart (Hasenbaert) from the
diocese of Thérouanne, near Saint-Omer,
matriculated at the University of Louvain on 19
February 1483.

He was appointed *vicarius regius* at St Mary's
in Aachen on 3 December 1515. On 22
September 1524 Quirinus Hellinx succeeded
him in this function, but Hasebart seems to
have kept a canonry at St Mary's. He also held
the rectorate in the village church of Hergarten
within the collation of the chapter of Bonn but
resigned this post before 1 June 1539, when a
successor was nominated by the church's
patron, Duke William V of *Cleves. Hasebart
figures among the first members of Aachen's
prestigious Brotherhood of the Sacrament
founded in 1522. It is not known when he died
or when a successor was appointed to his
canonry at St Mary's.

Erasmus probably made Hasebart's acquaintance during his brief visit to Aachen in
September 1518 (Ep 867), for in May 1519 the
canon Leonardus *Priccardus extended greetings from Hasebart to Erasmus and to Hasebart's fellow-countryman, Jan de *Neve, at
Louvain (Ep 972).

BIBLIOGRAPHY: Allen Ep 972 / *Matricule de
Louvain* II-1 468 / Joseph Gaspers *Die Sakra-
mentsbruderschaft von St. Foillan in Aachen, 1521*

bis 1921 (Aachen 1921) 53 / *Nomina admodum
reverendorum perillustrium atque generosorum
dominorum canonicorum regalis ecclesiae B.M.V.
Aquisgranensis* ed Antonius Heusch (Berlin
1892) 12, 15 / *Jülich-Bergische Kirchenpolitik am
Ausgange des Mittelalters und in der Reformationszeit* ed Otto R. Redlich II-1 (Bonn 1911) 612
                                    KASPAR VON GREYERZ

Johann HASENBERG or HASENBURG *See*
Jan HORÁK

Franciscus HASSELTENSIS *See*
Frans TITELMANS

Maternus HATTEN of Speyer, d 4 March 1546
Maternus Hatten (Hatt, Hatto) was a vicar at
the cathedral of Speyer when in 1514 or 1515 he
extended hospitality to Erasmus, who was
travelling either to or from Basel (Epp 355, 361).
Fragmentary information about him is available
from the records of the Speyer cathedral
chapter. On 1 September 1517 he was appointed curate of Loffenau, resigning this benefice
at the end of 1518. In March 1519 he sold a
house to his friend and colleague Johann
*Kierher, and in March 1525 the chapter had to
take measures in view of his accumulating
debts. There is an early indication of Hatten's
sympathy with the religious reformers; in
January 1520 Martin *Bucer found refuge in his
house at Speyer while seeking permission to
leave the Dominican order (BRE Ep 146). In June
1527 Hatten was denounced for Lutheranism
and failure to say mass; the dean of the chapter
accepted the validity of these charges and in
July Hatten was suspended from office. He
appealed the suspension but according to the
chapter's records was still not willing to
resume saying mass. Instead he withdrew to
Strasbourg, where he received a canonry in the
reformed chapter of St Thomas and where he
lived until his death. From 31 August 1527 he
was a citizen of Strasbourg; at an unknown
date he married Barbara Heger.

Erasmus visited Hatten again at Speyer in
September 1518 and afterwards thanked him
and his friends for their hospitality (Epp 867,
882). In 1522 Hatten reassured Erasmus of his
affection in view of the attacks of Diego *López
Zúñiga, whose book was then circulating in
Speyer (Ep 1289). There is no evidence of
subsequent contacts between Erasmus and

Hatten; however, Hatten supplied a manuscript for Erasmus' perusal when he was editing Hilary (Basel: J. Froben 1523; cf Ep 1289) and had rendered similar services to the Froben press on an earlier occasion, as is shown by the dedication to him of Johann *Froben's edition of Luigi Bigi (Pictorius) *Sacra et satyrica epigrammata* in May 1518. In Strasbourg Hatten was a close friend of Jacobus Gallus and as the executor of his will he sent Gallus' nephew, Conradus *Pellicanus, some manuscript notes left by his uncle.

BIBLIOGRAPHY: Allen Ep 355 / Martin Krebs *Die Protokolle des Speyerer Domkapitels* (Stuttgart 1968–) I 396–7, II 25, 183–4, and passim / J.-V. Pollet *Martin Bucer* (Paris 1958–62) II 4 / Luther w *Briefwechsel* I Ep 250 and passim / *Das Chronikon des Konrad Pellikan* ed B. Riggenbach (Basel 1877) 2–3, 70–1 / Marie-Joseph Bopp *Die evangelischen Geistlichen und Theologen in Elsass und Lothringen von der Reformation bis zur Gegenwart* (Neustadt an der Aisch 1959) 216

IG & PGB

Marquard von HATTSTEIN c 1488–
13 June 1522
The ancestral castle of the nobles of Hattstein is situated south of Schmitten in the Taunus highlands, north of Frankfurt am Main. Marquard was the son of another Marquard, an official at Usingen, and of Maria Weissin von Feuerbach. In 1502 he matriculated at the University of Erfurt, and on 26 February 1509 he was promised an appointment to a prebend at the chapter of Mainz. From 1511 to 1514 Hattstein studied in Paris, where he was honoured by Jacques *Lefèvre d'Etaples with a letter that was addressed to Marquard and two other German students and published in Lefèvre's *Liber trium virorum* (1513; Rice Ep 99). Hattstein next went to Mainz to absolve a year of residence required by the chapter (14 March 1514–15 March 1515) and then went to Italy, moving from Rome in the summer of 1516 to Bologna, where he studied for a year. On 3 November 1519 he was appointed canon of the cathedral chapter and also canon of St Alban's at Mainz, and on 26 February 1522 he obtained an imperial recommendation (*preces primariae*) to a canonry at the chapter of St Stephan at Mainz. He occupied one of the canons' residences, the house 'zum Körblin,' and there

offered hospitality to Hermannus *Buschius in the summer of 1520 (Ep 1109). Hattstein was a kinsman of Ulrich von *Hutten, with whom he corresponded in 1515 (Hutten *Opera* I Ep 25). By June 1521 his health began to fail; in spite of this he served the chapter as the official of Hochheim, but a year later he died at the age of thirty-four.

Hattstein endeavoured to be of service to Erasmus on two occasions. He defended him against Edward *Lee in a letter dated 26 April 1520 addressed to John *Colet and published in a collection of similar protests, the *Epistolae aliquot eruditorum virorum* (Basel: J. Froben 1520; cf Ep 1083); Hattstein's letter, which was perhaps inspired by Hermannus Buschius, is his only publication. And when Erasmus was passing through Mainz on his way to Basel in November 1521, Hattstein offered to send armed men with him (Ep 1342).

BIBLIOGRAPHY: Allen and CWE Ep 1109 / NDB VIII 61 / *Matrikel Erfurt* II 225 / Johannes Maximilian Humbracht *Die höchste Zierde Teutsch-Landes und Vortrefflichkeit des Teutschen Adels* (Frankfurt 1767) no 35 / *Die Protokolle des Mainzer Domkapitels* ed Fritz Hermann (Paderborn 1932) III 8, 28, 84, 182, 229–30, and passim / Adam B. Gottron 'Johann von Hattstein, ein Mainzer Domherr im Zeitalter des Humanismus' *Archiv für hessische Geschichte und Altertumskunde* n s 24 (1951) 53 / Georgius Christianus Joannis *Rerum Moguntiacarum volumen secundum* (Frankfurt am Main 1727) 367 / *Die Reichsregisterbücher Karls v.* ed Lother Gross (Vienna 1913–30) I no 2183 / Georg Hellwich *Nobilitas ecclesiae: hoc est, omnium canonicorum metropolitanae ecclesiae Moguntinae nomina ab anno 1500 usque ad presentem annum 1614* (Munich 1614) f y^2 verso / Knod 187 / Rice *Prefatory Epistles* Ep 99 Appendix

KONRAD WIEDEMANN

ab HAUBITZ (Epp 1522, 1561)
A young man named ab Haubitz (Haubitzius) visited Erasmus at Basel late in 1524 in the company of Jindřich *Berka; both had been recommended by Heinrich *Stromer, a professor at Leipzig (Ep 1522). Haubitz returned to Saxony early in 1525, carrying a letter to Duke George of *Saxony (Ep 1561). He was perhaps Valentin Albert von Haubitz, a nobleman who had matriculated in the universities of Frank-

furt an der Oder in 1517 and Leipzig in 1520; he
also studied from 1525 to 1528 at Bologna,
where he associated with Andreas von *Könneritz. Haubitz is a village south-east of
Leipzig, near Grimma; since three more students bearing this name were matriculated at
Leipzig in 1521–2, the identity of Erasmus'
visitor remains uncertain.

BIBLIOGRAPHY: Allen Ep 1522 / *Matrikel
Leipzig* III 298 and passim / *Matrikel Frankfurt* I
47 / Knod 187   MICHAEL ERBE & PGB

Ulric des HAZARDS d 17 June 1527

Ulric was a brother of Hugues des Hazards,
bishop of Toul from 1506 to 1517. Ulric was a
canon of Toul and a doctor of civil and canon
law, but he was also appointed canon of Metz
in Lorraine on 17 January 1509 and, upon the
resignation of Hugues, who had held this
position, dean of the Metz chapter on 4
November 1514. When Ulric died Hugues had
his heart buried and erected a monument to
him in the cathedral of Toul. Erasmus referred
to the dean in the address of a letter to the
chapter of Metz (Ep 997, 11 July 1519).

BIBLIOGRAPHY: Allen Ep 997 / *Gallia christiana*
XIII 813, 1045 / Martin Meurisse *Histoire des
évesques de l'église de Metz* (Metz 1634) 601
                                                    PGB

Karel van HEDENBAULT c 1444–
28 August 1527

Karel, the son of Jan van Hedenbault and
Jossyne van Fevijn, had been in the service of
the Burgundian court from his childhood.
From 1473 to 1487, when Karel van *Egmond,
duke of Gelderland, lived as a hostage at the
Burgundian court, Hedenbault was in attendance to the boy, and thereafter he continued
to feel fatherly affection for Egmond in spite of
his alliance with the French. For years he
planned to visit him in Gelderland and actually
went there in 1525. In times of war between
Gelderland and the Hapsburg Netherlands he
defended the duke to the point of antagonizing
some Bruges citizens (1527).

Perhaps from the turn of the century
Hedenbault was living at Bruges, holding the
titular office of *concierge* of the Prinsenhof, an
old ducal residence that was still occasionally
visited by members of the dynasty. It was also
used for diplomatic conferences and thus

received such visitors as Thomas *Wolsey and
Thomas *More. Hedenbault shared his quarters in the Prinsenhof with two younger
relatives, Jan van *Fevijn and his sister,
Eleanor. Erasmus was a guest in this household during a vacation week in the summer of
1519 (or 1520) and no doubt a visitor on many
other occasions; he even made serious inquiries about the availability of permanent lodgings there (Ep 1012). Many years later he was
informed by Fevijn of Hedenbault's death (Ep
2278). 'Old Hedenbault' is fondly mentioned in
many of Fevijn's letters to Frans van
*Cranevelt.

BIBLIOGRAPHY: Allen and CWE Ep 1012 / de
Vocht *Literae ad Craneveldium* xciii, xcvi, Epp
22, 29, 223, and passim   PGB

Caspar HEDIO of Ettlingen, 1494–
17 October 1552

Caspar Hedio (Heyd, Bock, Böckel) was born
in Ettlingen, Baden, the son of a ropemaker.
He attended the Latin school at Pforzheim,
where *Melanchthon, *Irenicus, and Nikolaus
*Gerbel were his fellow-students. Matriculat-
ing at the University of Freiburg in 1513, he
received his BA in 1514 and his MA in 1516.
From 1518 on he was at the University of Basel,
while at the same time he held an appointment
as vicar. Under the guidance of *Capito he
completed his licence in theology in 1519. In
Basel he was quickly drawn into the humanist
circle – he knew Erasmus, the *Amerbach
brothers, *Oecolampadius, *Pellicanus, and
*Beatus Rhenanus. When Capito left Basel to
become the preacher at the cathedral of Mainz,
Hedio left to serve as his assistant (Ep 1308).
After Capito had been appointed provost of St
Thomas' chapter at Strasbourg, Hedio accepted the post of preacher at the Strasbourg
cathedral with the promise that he would
preach 'inoffensively.' Capito, who wanted
the appointment, felt betrayed by his former
student. However, by 1524 the incident was
forgotten and Capito and Hedio had joined
*Bucer and Matthias Zell in their efforts to
reform the Strasbourg church.

Erasmus respected Hedio until he identified
himself with the Reformation. In March 1524,
when he was still embroiled with *Brunfels in
the controversy over *Hutten, Erasmus referred the Strasbourg magistrate to Hedio to

Caspar Hedio, by Hans Baldung Grien

present his side of the case (Ep 1429), but Hedio failed to treat the matter with the discretion Erasmus had expected; as a result Erasmus' attitude to him changed. In June he noted Hedio's recent marriage with evident disapproval (Epp 1452, 1459). Instead of supporting Erasmus' request for the punishment of Johann *Schott, 'that terrible printer,' Hedio had defended him on the excuse that he had a wife and children (Epp 1459, 1496). In another letter, written that same day, Hedio was lumped together with Capito, Oecolampadius, and *Zwingli as promoters of anonymous libel (Ep 1497). Hedio's disloyalty still agitated Erasmus in 1528 (Ep 1934).

Hedio combined his scholarly interests with his pastoral responsibilities. He vigorously supported the project for a new school in Strasbourg as early as 1530 and served on the visitors' committee which supervised all the schools from 1526 to 1552. This became a particularly important post after the founding of the new Gymnasium in 1538. Through his efforts the income of the Wilhelmite convent was used to create a foundation to support theological students. The foundation has persisted to this day.

Hedio's own scholarly work was devoted to history. He translated into German much of Eusebius' ecclesiastical history and Platina's lives of the popes. He continued the *Enneades* of *Sabellico and the Ursberg chronicle, bringing the latter up to date from 1230. He collected a wide variety of documents, letters, speeches, and edicts to use as sources. His accounts of the councils of Constance and Basel were exceptionally well documented, including the speeches of the theologians and all the edicts issued by the councils. His humanist training was applied to the exploration of these historical sources, and, while his work was not original, he brought a new rigour to historical research.

Hedio's works include: *Chronica der alten Christlichen Kirchen ausz Eusebio, Ruffino, Sozomeno, Theodoreto, Tertulliano, Justino, Cypriano, und Plinio* (Strasbourg: G. Ulricher 1530, W. Köpfel 1545, 1558); Juan Luis *Vives *Von Almuosen geben zwey Büchlin* trans Caspar Hedio ([Strasbourg? 1533?]); Juan Luis Vives *Wannenher Ordnung*, a collection of works, trans Caspar Hedio ([Strasbourg] 1534); *Ein auszerleszne Chronik von anfang der Welt bis auff das jar nach Christi unsers eynigen Heylands geburt MDXXXIX* (Strasbourg: C. Mylius 1539, The Ursberg Chronicle); Johannes Cuspinianus *Chronika von C. Julio Cesare dem ersten, bisz auff Carolum quintum diser zeit Rhömischen Keyser, auch von allen orientischen oder Griechischen und Türckischen Keysern* trans Caspar Hedio (Strasbourg: C. Mylius 1541); Baptista Platina *Historia von der Bäbst und Keiser Leben* trans Caspar Hedio (Strasbourg: W. Rihel 1546, J. Rihel 1565).

BIBLIOGRAPHY: Allen Ep 1459 / R. Stupperich in NDB VIII 188–9 / Gustav Adolf Benrath 'Gaspard Hedion, historien de l'église' in *Strasbourg au coeur religieux de XVIe siècle* (Strasbourg 1977) 109–10 / Johann Ficker and Otto Winckelmann *Handschriftproben des sechzehnten Jahrhunderts* (Strasbourg 1905) passim / Emil Himmelheber *Caspar Hedio: Ein Lebensbild aus der Reformationsgeschichte* (Karlsruhe 1881) / James Kittelson *Wolfgang Capito: From Humanist to Reformer* (Leiden 1975) 95–6

MIRIAM U. CHRISMAN

Jan HEEMS of Armentières, d 1 July 1560

Jan Heems (Johannes Armentheriensis, de Armenteria) of Armentières, near Lille

(Départment du Nord), was the son of Christiaan and Johanna Mareschal. He studied in
Louvain, perhaps from 1512, and became a
priest. He had obtained a MA prior to 1521 and
began to study medicine. He shared the
direction of the college of the Lily in Louvain
with Jan de *Neve in 1521–2 and from
November 1522 with Pieter de *Corte, but he
resigned on 1 November 1525. He was appointed canon of St Peter's and professor of
medicine on 23 November 1525 and obtained a
doctorate of medicine on 25 April 1526. Heems
was elected rector in August 1529 and in
February of 1532, 1535, and 1550. On 30
September 1541 he was elected dean of arts.
From 1545 he was rector of the parish of
Meerbeek, near Louvain. In April or May 1531
Pieter de Corte resigned the regency of the Lily
to Heems, who between 1550 and 1560
defended his rights and financial benefits
connected with that position in a prolonged
litigation against the faculty of arts. He
founded several scholarships in the college
and gave to the chapel of clerics (now St
Antony's) a stained-glass window with his
coat of arms and the device 'Nil invita
Minerva.'

Since Heems had been co-regent of the Lily
with Jan de Neve, Erasmus sent greetings to
him through Joost *Vroye in a letter of
condolence after Neve's death (Ep 1347).

BIBLIOGRAPHY: Allen Ep 1347 / de Vocht CTL I
94, II 83, III 261, and passim / de Vocht Epistolae
ad Craneveldium Ep 26 and passim / de Vocht
MHL 604   IG

Jan of HEEMSTEDE documented in
Louvain 1520–33
Jan Symons was better known under the name
of his native village of Heemstede (Hemstedi-
us), near Haarlem. He may have matriculated
in Cologne as a law student in November 1514.
By 1520 he had obtained a MA from the
University of Louvain and, following the
example of his better-known brother, Dirk,
entered the charterhouse of Louvain. He made
his profession on 10 June 1521 and celebrated
his first mass on 24 June 1522. Like his brother
he gained a reputation as a painter and
illuminator, but at the same time he established
contacts among the circle of humanist scholars.
In 1528 he was appointed to the office of
procurator, or steward, of his convent.

Nothing is known about contacts between
him and Erasmus until after the death of
Maarten van *Dorp, when he wrote to Erasmus, whose answer (Ep 1646, of 8 November
1527) is preserved and was accompanied by an
epitaph for Dorp's tomb in the charterhouse
(Reedijk poem 113). Two years later Erasmus
honoured him by addressing to him a formal
letter in memory of Johann *Froben, which was
likewise followed by two epitaphs (Ep 1900;
Reedijk poems 116, 117). Meanwhile there are
also traces of personal letters that Erasmus had
sent to Heemstede (Epp 1837, 1994). In July
1530 he reported to Erasmus the gathering of
such common friends as *Vives, Marcus *Laurinus and *Goclenius to celebrate the solemn
promotion of Pieter de *Corte (Ep 2353); in turn
Erasmus dedicated to him an edition of the
commentaries on the Psalms attributed to
Haimo of Halberstadt (Freiburg: J. Faber
Emmeus 1533; Ep 2771).

BIBLIOGRAPHY: Allen Ep 1646 / de Vocht CTL
III 75–7 and passim / de Vocht MHL 284–5 and
passim   PGB

Steven van HEETVELDE of Brussels,
documented 1521–8
Steven van Heetvelde (Heetvelt), a canon
regular of St Augustine, succeeded Jan Ram-
paert in 1521 as prior of the Roode Clooster
(Rubea Vallis) in the Soignes forest near
Brussels and remained in office until 1528. He
was a supporter of the conservative theologians of Louvain and showed his opposition to
Erasmus by having an attack on him, the
Apologia published under the name Godefridus
Ruysius Taxander, read to the monks in the
refectory of his monastery (Ep 1804). On 6
November 1525 Erasmus' friend Maarten *Lips
reminded Heetvelde of the papal injunction
imposing silence on Erasmus' critics at
Louvain.

BIBLIOGRAPHY: Allen Ep 1804 / de Vocht CTL
II 281–2   IG

Christoph HEGENDORFF of Leipzig, 1500–
8 August 1540
Christoph Hegendorff (Hegendorfer, Hegen-
dorfinus) was educated in his native city of
Leipzig, at first in the school attached to the
Augustinian monastery of St Thomas and
subsequently at the university, where he
matriculated in 1513. As early as 1518 he broke

into print, publishing an edition of *Hutten's *Stichologia* and, in the following year, his own *Carmen de disputatione Lipsiensi* in praise of Martin *Luther. He took up the study of divinity under the guidance of the prior of St Thomas while at the same time teaching in a local school, probably St Nicholas'. For the benefit of his pupils he published in 1519 and 1520 *Dragmata in dialecticam Petri Hispani*, a *Ratio conscribendarum epistolarum compendiaria*, and a collection of *Dialogi pueriles*. In two consecutive reprints new parts were added to this collection, and two dialogues reappeared, soon after their publication, appended to an edition of Erasmus' *Familiarium colloquiorum formulae* (Strasbourg: J. Knobloch April 1520). This volume may have provided Hegendorff with an excuse for addressing a letter to Erasmus. It is unfortunately lost, but from Erasmus' answer we learn that Hegendorff had compared himself to Thersites daring to challenge Ulysses; not one word, however, did Erasmus say about Hegendorff's addition to a work of his own (Ep 1168). At any rate Knobloch, undeterred, went on to publish Hegendorff's *Dialogi pueriles* together with the *Paedologia* of Petrus *Mosellanus, and this combination was retained in all subsequent reprints.

In 1521 Hegendorff had taken his MA and began to teach at the University of Leipzig, where he was elected rector in 1523. He also lectured on the Scriptures, although he soon moved from theology to legal studies. His legal works, which were evidently much appreciated by his contemporaries, began to appear in 1529. By the end of 1530 Hegendorff was invited by the bishop of Poznan to go and teach classical literature as a salaried professor (*professor mercennarius*). After several years in this position he was obliged to leave Poznan during the second half of 1535 in the wake of a long and violent controversy with the archdeacon, who had accused him of Lutheranism. He next obtained a doctorate in canon and civil law and joined the University of Frankfurt an der Oder as professor of civil law. In 1537 he was in Lüneburg as legal consultant to the city, and in 1539 he assisted in the reorganization of the University of Rostock. He did return to Lüneburg, though, this time as church superintendent, and there he died while still engaged in his theological studies.

The list of publications of this travelling salesman of humanism and reform is endless, but the following may be noted: *Explicatio locorum implicatissimorum in Colloquiis Erasmi* (Haguenau: J. Setzer 1526), an edition of Erasmus' *De copia* (Haguenau: J. Setzer 1528) which was reprinted several times, and *Methodus conscribendi epistolas* (Haguenau: J. Setzer 1526), inspired by Erasmus' *De conscribendis epistolis*. In fact Hegendorff expressed the highest regard for Erasmus, calling him 'optimarum literarum princeps' and 'theologorum nostri temporis columen.' Placing Erasmus' educational writings on the same level as Quintilian, he often borrowed from them and also edited them with commentaries for the benefit of students; however, at the same time he appreciated the theologian, reading the *Enchiridion* with his pupils so that they might learn 'true religion jointly with good Latin style.'

BIBLIOGRAPHY: Allen and CWE Ep 1168 / NDB VIII 227–8 / Otto Günther *Plautuserneuerungen in der Deutschen Litteratur des XV.–XVII. Jahrhunderts* (Leipzig 1886) 70–91 / A. Henschel 'Christophorus Hegendorf' *Zeitschrift der historischen Gesellschaft für die Provinz Posen* 7 (1892) 337–43 / R. Stintzing *Geschichte der Deutschen Rechtswissenschaft* (Munich-Leipzig 1880) I 249–53 / *Matrikel Leipzig* I 529, II 503, 556, 560, 561, 564, 568, 569, 574, 577, 579, 581, 583 / *Matrikel Rostock* II 100 / *Die Evangelischen Katechismusversuche vor Luthers Enchiridion* ed F. Cohrs (Berlin 1901) III 347–414 / A. Bömer *Die lateinischen Schülergespräche der Humanisten* (Berlin 1897) I 108–112 / G. Bauch *Die Anfänge der Universität Frankfurt a. O. und die Entwicklung des wissenschaftlichen Lebens an der Hochschule (1506–1540)* (Berlin 1900) 72–8 / S. Kossowski 'Christophorus Hegendorphinus in der bischöflichen Akademie zu Posen (1530–1535)' *Jahresbericht des K.K. zweiten Obergymnasiums in Lemberg* (1903) 3–43 / Karol Mazurkiewicz *Poczatki Akademij Lubranskiego w Poznaniu (1519–1535)* (Poznan 1921) / O. Krabbe *Die Universität Rostock im fünfzehnten und sechzehnten Jahrhundert* (Rostock 1854) 421 ff / Franz Bierlaire 'Un livre du maître au XVIᵉ siècle: Erasme expliqué par Hegendorf' *Quaerendo* 2 (1972) 200–20 / Franz Bierlaire 'Les *Dialogi pueriles* de Christophe Hegendorff' in *Acta conventus neo-latini Turonensis* I (Tours 1980) 389–401   FRANZ BIERLAIRE

Alexander HEGIUS of Heek,
d 27 December 1498
Alexander Hegius was born at Heek – whence
his name – in Westphalia shortly after 1433.
Nothing is known about his early life. From
1469 to 1474 he was the master of St Willi-
brord's school at Wesel. In 1474 he moved to St
Martin's school at Emmerich, and in the same
year he was studying Greek with his friend
Rodolphus *Agricola (Ep 23; Allen I 55, 57;
Adagia I iv 39).

It can be assumed that he became headmaster
of St Lebuin's school at Deventer by 1483. In
an undated letter to him, Agricola refers to the
plague of that year and to Hegius' auspicious
beginnings in that position (rejecting a different interpretation by Kohls). In another letter
of 7 April 1487 to Antonius Liber, Agricola still
mentioned Hegius' headmastership at Deventer in terms which suggest that it had not as yet
become common knowledge. If Hegius did not
move to Deventer until 1483, Erasmus cannot
have benefitted a great deal from his instruction, since he himself appears to have left
Deventer when the plague struck again in
1484. Moreover, by that time Erasmus had not
reached the senior level at which Hegius was
teaching regularly and thus would have heard
him only on special occasions when the
headmaster was addressing the entire school
(Allen I 48; CWE 4 405). In the *Spongia* (ASD IX-1
196) Erasmus remarked in fact that he owed
little to Hegius, although he rarely mentioned
him without praise (see especially *Adagia* I iv
39). Clearly he had a high opinion of the man
under whose influence Deventer developed
into a centre of humanistic education (Allen I
48; CWE 4 404–5) and even did him the honour
of quoting from his poems (*Adagia* II ii 81; LB V
1253B). Hegius probably knew Erasmus' *Carmen bucolicum* (Reedijk poem 1), which dates
from the Deventer years; subsequently he
received other samples of Erasmus' literary
production (Ep 28).

Hegius spent the rest of his life at St
Lebuin's, where he was buried. He was a
regular visitor to Wessel *Gansfort's 'Academy' at Aduard, and at an advanced age he took
holy orders. He held fame in low regard and
this may be why he did not achieve real
greatness, as one of the speakers in Erasmus'
Ciceronianus points out (ASD I-2 683). As a
teacher, however, he was eminently success-

ful. At the time of his death St Lebuin's school
was attended by more than two thousand
pupils. Among the many prominent humanists
Hegius taught were Johannes *Murmellius,
Gerard *Geldenhouwer, Ortwinus *Gratius,
Tilmann Kemner, Jacobus Montanus, *Gozewijn of Halen (who heard him announce the
news of Agricola's death), Johann Butzbach,
and Hermannus *Buschius (who dedicated to
him his *Carmina*). After Hegius' death another
pupil, Jacobus *Faber, edited his literary
works, mostly from manuscript: *Carmina* (Deventer: R. Pafraet 1503; see Ep 174), and a
volume containing the *Dialogi*, the *Invectiva in
modos significandi*, and the *Farrago* (Deventer:
R. Pafraet 31 December 1503; NK 1041). The
Farrago had been printed earlier (Deventer: J.
de Breda c 1486; NK 1042). Hegius also
contributed to Jan *Synthen's commentary on
the *Doctrinale puerorum* by Alexander de Villa
Dei (Deventer: R. Pafraet 1488).

BIBLIOGRAPHY: Allen Ep 23 and I 580–1 / CWE
Ep 23 / ADB XI 283–5 / A.J. van der Aa et al
Biographisch woordenboek der Nederlanden (Haar-
lem 1852–78) VIII-1 388–9 / J. Wiese *Der
Pädagoge Alexander Hegius und seine Schüler*
(Berlin 1892) / A. Bömer 'Alexander Hegius'
Westfälische Lebensbilder 3 (1934) 345–62 / H.
Kronenberg 'Wanneer is Alexander Hegius te
Deventer gekomen?' *Verslagen en mededeeling-
en Vereeniging tot beoefening van Overijsselsch
regt en geschiedenis* 29 (1913) 1–7 / E.-W. Kohls
'Zur Frage der Schulträgerschaft der Brüder
vom gemeinsamen Leben und zum Rektorats-
beginn des Alexander Hegius in Deventer'
*Jahrbuch des Vereins für Westfälische Kirchenge-
schichte* 61 (1968) 33–43 / A.C.F. Koch *The Year
of Erasmus' Birth* (Utrecht 1969) 37 / J. IJsewijn
'Alexander Hegius († 1498), *Invectiva in modos
significandi*' *Forum for Modern Language Studies* 7
(1971) 229–318   C.G. VAN LEIJENHORST

Vincenz HEIDECKER or HEIDNECKER *See
Vincentius* OPSOPOEUS

Marx HEIDELIN *See Balthasar* HILTBRAND

Johann HEINZMANN of Basel, d before 1533
Johann Heinzmann (Heitzmann) was one of
the notaries employed by the bishop of Basel.
His name is frequently found at the end of
documents which he had drawn up or certified. In 1527 he assisted Erasmus in drawing up

his first will and certified the correctness of a copy to which he added a postscript (Allen VI 506). With the victory of the reform party he moved with the episcopal court of law to Altkirch, Upper Alsace, the traditional seat of one of the bishop's officials. On 7 June 1529 he officially renounced his Basel citizenship. He was survived by his wife, Küngolt Hess.

BIBLIOGRAPHY: *Aktensammlung zur Geschichte der Basler Reformation* ed E. Dürr et al (Basel 1921–50) III 109, 295, 543, IV 199, 272 / *Wappenbuch der Stadt Basel* ed W.R. Staehelin (Basel [1917–30]) s v Heitzmann   PGB

Matthias HELD of Arlon, d 1563

Matthias Held (Helt) was born at Arlon, in Belgian Luxembourg; other than that nothing is known about his early life until August 1527, when the Elector Joachim of Brandenburg nominated him for the post of an assessor at the imperial law court (*Reichskammergericht*). In 1530 he was persuaded to join the court of *Charles V, and henceforward his considerable ability and energy remained fully committed to the emperor. In 1531 Held was promoted to the position of imperial vice-chancellor, and in this office he soon commanded a considerable measure of influence within Hapsburg government circles. A faithful adherent of the traditional church, Held consistently advocated a policy of firm opposition to the Protestants throughout his years in office and was even prepared to resort, if necessary, to military coercion. He never approved of the policy of reconciliation which the imperial court initiated in 1531 and endeavoured at all times to place a restrictive interpretation on the concessions made to the Protestant estates at Nürnberg in 1532. In particular, he never failed to support the *Reichskammergericht*, whose administration of justice was frequently biased in favour of Catholic interests.

In November 1536 Held was sent to Germany and charged with a difficult mission, recently the subject of much controversy among historians. When negotiating with the members of the Schmalkaldic League in February 1537, he took advantage of an ambiguity created by two consecutive sets of instructions, preferring the deceptive stance recommended by the first set (in German) to the real concessions towards the Protestants advocated by the second (in

French). His blunt rejection of their requests prompted the Protestant estates to turn down in a similarly uncompromising manner the demands made by the emperor such as his call for their participation in a future council of the church. Held in turn found that the attitude of the Protestants fully confirmed his earlier suspicions that they were preparing for overt aggression. He now lent all his energies to the creation of a defensive alliance of Catholic estates; however, the Catholic League founded at Nürnberg on 10 June 1538 was joined by so few estates that Held had trouble persuading the emperor's government in Spain to ratify the alliance.

From this point on Held's influence waned as his personal enemies and political opponents such as Nicolas *Perrenot de Granvelle and Johann von Weeze, archbishop of Lund, kept strengthening their position at court. Fighting increasingly from a position of isolation, Held failed in the spring of 1540 in his last attempt to have the policy of reconciliation with the Protestants reversed. In June 1541 the office of imperial vice-chancellor was handed over to a protégé of Granvelle, Jean de Naves. Held, who had been knighted by the emperor in 1536, now retired to live at Cologne with his five children and their mother, his housekeeper, Magdalena Brandis, whom he married a year before his death. By the time of his dismissal he had gathered a fortune of two hundred thousand ducats, part of which he used to acquire the lordship of Zähringen.

There is no evidence of personal relations between Erasmus and Held, who was, however, a good friend of *Viglius Zuichemus (Epp 2767, 2854).

BIBLIOGRAPHY: Allen Ep 2767 / NDB VIII 465–6 / ADB XI 682–4 / de Vocht *Dantiscus* 330–1 / Karl Brandi *Kaiser Karl V.* new ed (Darmstadt 1959–67) I 335–40 and passim / L. Ennen 'Der Reichsvizekanzler Dr. Mathias Held' *Annalen des historischen Vereins für den Niederrhein* 25 (1873) 131–72 / Gustav Heide 'Die Verhandlungen des kaiserlichen Vizekanzlers Held mit den deutschen Ständen (1537–1538)' *Historisch-politische Blätter* 102 (1888) 713–38 / Gustav Heide 'Nürnberg und die Mission des Vizekanzlers Held' *Mitteilungen des Vereins für die Geschichte der Stadt Nürnberg* 8 (1889) 161–200 / W. Kampschulte 'Das Adelsdiplom des kaiserlichen Vicekanzlers Mathias Held vom Jahre 1536' *Forschungen zur deutschen Geschichte* 4 (1864) 604–8 / Peter Rassow *Die Kaiser-Idee Karls v.* (Berlin 1932) 299–316, 393–8 and passim   ALBRECHT LUTTENBERGER

Peter HELDUNG of Obernai, d 1561
Peter Heldung (Heldungus), born in Obernai, in Lower Alsace, was a layman who became steward (*canonicarius*) and treasurer of the cathedral chapter of Strasbourg. He is mentioned in the correspondence between Erasmus and *Wimpfeling as a member of the literary society of Strasbourg (Epp 302, 305). In 1536 Johann *Huttich criticized him for managing the chapter archives with an excess of protectiveness (BRE Ep 305). His epitaph in the church at Obernai provides scant biographical information.
    BIBLIOGRAPHY: Allen and CWE Ep 302 / Schmidt *Histoire littéraire* I xvii
                              MIRIAM U. CHRISMAN

HELIAS Marcaeus *See Helias MARCAEUS*

Robert HELLIN documented at Bruges from c 1519–d 15 January 1527
Robert Hellin (Hellyn) came from a family, perhaps of French origin, that had settled at Bruges, where one of his brothers was a canon of St Donatian's while another was secretary to the city council. Robert himself was a MA and pensionary, or legal consultant, to the city, an office previously held by Frans van *Cranevelt, a good friend of both Erasmus and Hellin. When *Christian II of Denmark and his wife *Isabella, the sister of *Charles v, arrived in Bruges in 1523, Hellin welcomed them with two Latin speeches, on 7 or 8 July.
    By the time Erasmus stayed at the Prinsenhof as the guest of Karel van *Hedenbault in the summer of 1519 (or 1520), Hellin had already joined Hedenbault's household as the husband of his young cousin, Eleanor van Fevijn. A son, Robert, was born to them in the spring of 1523, but another child died, together with the mother at the time of its birth on 12/13 October 1526. Robert, whose health was already failing, followed them soon after (Ep 2278).
    BIBLIOGRAPHY: Allen and CWE Ep 1012 / de

Vocht *Literae ad Craneveldium* Epp 51, 67, and passim   PGB

Matthias HELT *See Matthias HELD*

Paul HEMMERLIN of Andlau, documented 1486–1504
Paul Hemmerlin (Hämmerli, Paulus Malleiolus Andelocensis), of Andlau, in Lower Alsace, received a BA at Paris in 1486–7 and a year later a MA; he stayed on as a teacher in the Collège de Bourgogne. In 1488–9 he was also procurator and in 1497–8 receiver of the German nation at the University of Paris. He is known chiefly from his editions of Virgil (Paris: U. Gering 1489), Cicero's *De officiis* (Paris: G. Wolff and T. Kerver 1498), and Terence (Paris: J. Philippi 1499), all of which were reprinted several times. He also wrote a dedicatory epistle, addressed to Gillis van *Delft, for an edition of Niccolò *Perotti's *Rudimenta grammaticae* (Paris: J. Bade 1504). Erasmus made fun of him in an epigram about the rival editions of Virgil edited by Hemmerlin and Augustinus Vincentius *Caminadus (Reedijk poem 44).
    BIBLIOGRAPHY: Philippe Renouard *Imprimeurs et libraires parisiens du XVIe siècle* (Paris 1964–   ) I 174, 323, II 32, 37 / *Auctarium chartularii Universitatis Parisiensis* ed Charles Samaran et al (Paris 1894–1964) VI 639 and passim   PGB

Johann HENCKEL of Levoča, d 5 November 1539
Johann (János) Henckel (Henkel) was born at Levoča (Leutschau, Löcse, today in Czechoslovakia) of German-speaking parents. From the spring of 1496 he was able to attend the University of Vienna owing to the generosity of his uncle, who had bequeathed him his books and a yearly stipend for education. Henckel, who may also have studied in Cracow, received his BA in 1499 and MA in 1503 and eventually proceeded to Italy, where he studied at Padua (1508) and Bologna (1509). Although he was subsequently referred to as a doctor of laws, it is impossible to ascertain where he received his degree. In the meantime he acquired ecclesiastical preferment and was named archdeacon of Békes and canon of Oradea (Várad) and of the Spiš (Szepes). In 1513 he was back in Hungary and was

appointed parish priest in his native city of
Levoča. It was probably through his influence
that Leonard *Cox accepted a position as
headmaster of the municipal school in that city
(1520). Two years later both men were at Košice
(Kassa), where Henckel was the new parish
priest and Cox the headmaster.

Henckel's career took a major turn around
1524, when he was invited to become court
chaplain of Queen *Mary, the wife of *Louis II
of Hungary. At Buda he became a member of
the Erasmian circle which had developed
around Jacobus *Piso. One of his friends, Jan
*Antonin, praised him to Erasmus as an avid
collector of the works of the Dutch humanist
and indicated that Henckel's sermons were
always filled with the Erasmian spirit. Antonin
also forwarded a first letter and a gift spoon
from Henckel (Epp 1660, 1672, 1698). When the
news of the disaster of Mohács (29 August
1526) reached Buda, Henckel accompanied the
queen to Bratislava but soon left her entourage
and went back to his former parish at Kosiče.
Caught in the political divisions of Hungary
(Ep 1916), he resigned his commendatory
benefices and prepared for a visit to Erasmus in
the company of Antonin, his close friend (Epp
1803, 1810, 1824). However, the new king,
*John Zápolyai, would not let him go and
offered him a bishopric, which he declined (Ep
1810).

In 1528 Henckel rejoined the service of the
queen and became her confessor. Moved by
Mary's sorrow at the loss of her husband,
Henckel requested Erasmus to write a work of
consolation for her (Ep 2011). Erasmus responded by dedicating his *Vidua christiana* to
her in 1529 (Epp 2100, 2107). Henckel reacted
with a further gift of his own, a gilt-laminated
cup, and also intended to translate Erasmus'
work into German (Ep 2309). The queen was
temporarily residing at Znojmo (Znaim), in
Moravia, when Henckel rejoined her, but they
soon set out on a long journey which took them
to Linz, where Henckel met *Ursinus Velius
(Epp 2309, 2313), Passau, Innsbruck, and
finally to the diet held at Augsburg (1530).
Nicolaus *Olahus, another important admirer
of Erasmus from Hungary, was also in the
queen's retinue during these journeys. He and
Henckel both urged Erasmus to attend the diet

and help to heal the sectarian conflict by his
presence (Ep 2309, 2339), but, claiming ill
health, Erasmus did not go. At Augsburg
Henckel met the theologian Johann *Eck, who
accused him of being on friendly terms with the
'arch-heretic' *Melanchthon. Henckel, whose
religious views were deeply influenced by the
spirit of toleration preached by Erasmus, was
appalled by Eck's outburst and indicated that
he much preferred the gentle Melanchthon to
the crude and boorish Eck; he also had a brief
meeting with the Strasbourg reformers *Capito
and *Bucer (Ep 2392). The following year, 1531,
when Mary was appointed regent of the
Netherlands, Henckel was forced to leave her
service on the orders of *Charles v. His
orthodoxy was questioned and he was accused
of harbouring Lutheran sympathies. He settled
in Silesia, where Mary had secured for him a
canonry of the cathedral of Wrocław (Breslau)
and where he continued to reside until his
death. He also kept up his correspondence
with Erasmus. The last known letter dates from
1532 (Ep 2783), but many others are clearly
missing.

Henckel was an appealing, kind, tolerant,
and scholarly man. His library, which contained both scholastic and humanistic works,
has been scattered, but a number of his
volumes are preserved at the library of
Alba Iulia (Gyulafehérvár) in Transylvania.

BIBLIOGRAPHY: Allen Ep 1672 / *Matrikel Wien*
II-1 250 / Vilmos Fraknói *Henckel János, Mária
királyné, udvari papja* (Pest 1872) / Gusztáv
Bauch 'Dr. Johann Henckel, der Hofprediger
der Königin Maria von Ungarn' *Ungarische
Revue* (1884) 559–627 / Imre Trencsényi-
Waldapfel *Erasmus magyar barátai* (Budapest
1941) / A. Hudak 'Der Hofprediger Johannes
Henckel und seine Beziehungen zu Erasmus
von Rotterdam' *Kirche im Osten* 2 (1959) 106–
13 / Some of Henckel's letters are published by
Gusztáv Bauch 'Adalékok a reformácio és a
tudományok történetéhez Magyarországon a
XVI. században' *Történelmi Tár* (1885) 353–4,
521–3 / Concerning his library: Elemér Varju 'A
gyulafehérvári Batthány-könyvtár' *Magyar
könyvszemle* (1899) 217–345   L. DOMONKOS

HENLIN, HENNER *See Eucharius and Johannes
GALLINARIUS*

Jakob HENRICHMANN of Sindelfingen,
d 28 June 1561

Jakob Henrichmann (Hainrichman), born in
Sindelfingen, in Swabia, around 1482, was
encouraged to study by Heinrich *Bebel,
from whom he received his first instruction.
Henrichmann matriculated in Tübingen on 4
November 1497; he obtained his MA on 24 June
1502 and stayed on to teach until 1506, also
studying philosophy and law. In 1514 he became councillor to Heinrich von Lichtenau,
bishop of Augsburg, and canon at the cathedral in Augsburg (until 1521); from 1514 until
his death in 1561 he was parish priest in
Zusmarshausen, west of Augsburg, and vicar-
general of the bishopric under bishops Christoph von *Stadion and Otto von Truchsess.

In his first work, a Latin grammar, *Grammaticae institutiones* (Pforzheim: T. Anshelm
1506) Henrichmann referred to the encouragement he received from his friend Heinrich
Bebel. He also wrote a satire on clumsy
expressions which was published in a Latin
version, *Prognostica alioqui barbare practica
nuncupata latinitate donata* (Strasbourg: J. Grüninger 1504). A few Latin proverbs by him were
included in Bebel's *Opuscula* of 1508 (Strasbourg: J. Grüninger). He was a friend of
Ottmar *Nachtgall, who dedicated to him his
Ioci ac sales (Augsburg: S. Grimm 1524), and
was acquainted with Matthias *Kretz, who
wrote to Erasmus about Henrichmann's admiration for his writings (Ep 2402).

BIBLIOGRAPHY: Allen Ep 2402 / ADB XI 782-3 /
Matrikel Tübingen I 118   IG

HENRICUS (Epp 1689, 1690, etc) *See Heinrich
SCHÜRER*

HENRICUS (Ep 2240) *See Claudius
CANTIUNCULA*

Gerardus HENRICUS of Amsterdam,
documented 1532

In May 1532 Erasmus received at Freiburg a
visit from one Gerardus Henricus of Amsterdam, who was on his way home from Italy,
where he had obtained a medical degree.
Erasmus gave him letters for Joost *Sasbout and
Nicolaus *Olahus (Epp 2645, 2646). He also
recommended him to Olahus, who confirmed

Henry VII, by Michel Sittow

in July that the physician had called on him in
Ghent, giving him Erasmus' letters (Ep 2693).
Gerardus Henricus has not been identified.

Dom HENRIQUE *See* HENRY, *cardinal-king of
Portugal*

Alphonsus HENRIQUEZ *See Alonso
ENRÍQUEZ*

HENRY VII king of England, 1457–
21 April 1509

The son of Edmund Tudor, earl of Richmond,
and Margaret *Beaufort, the heiress of John of
Gaunt, Henry became king after defeating
Richard III at Bosworth in 1485. A Lancastrian,
Henry consolidated his dynasty by his marriage to *Elizabeth of York on 18 January 1486.
Henry was a gifted administrator, hard-
working himself and capable of choosing
capable administrators like John *Morton and
Richard *Foxe to work with him. Universally
thought a wise king, he was also a great
promoter of learning and a patron of the arts
(Ep 2435). He patronized humanists like Petrus

Henry VIII

year (Ep 657; *Panegyricus* ASD IV-1 56). In the *Adagia* (II v 18) and the *Lingua* (ASD IV-1 285) he reported anecdotes to illustrate the king's enlightened attitudes and quick wit, while Germain de *Brie, in his controversy with Thomas More, accused More of attacking Henry VII's memory in praising his son (Epp 1087, 1093).

BIBLIOGRAPHY: J. Gairdner in DNB IX 520–7 / *Memorials of King Henry VII* ed J. Gairdner (London 1858) / J. Gairdner *Henry the Seventh* (London 1889) / Polidoro Virgilo The '*Anglica Historia*' ed and trans Denys Hay (London 1950) / J.D. Mackie *The Earlier Tudors 1485–1558* (Oxford 1952) / Roberto Weiss *Humanism in England during the Fifteenth Century* 3rd ed (Oxford 1967) / S. Anglo *Spectacle, Pageantry, and Early Tudor Policy* (Oxford 1969)

R.J. SCHOECK

*Carmelianus and Andrea *Ammonio, poets like Bernard *André (Ep 2422), and playwrights like William Cornish. He had John *Colet appointed dean of St Paul's (Ep 1211). He completed St George's Chapel at Windsor and built the chapel in Westminster Abbey which bears his name. There is a portrait by Michel Sittow (see CWE 4 312) and another by an unknown Flemish artist, both dated 1505 and both in the National Portrait Gallery, London.

Even before going to England, Erasmus spoke of Henry in connection with an embassy to England undertaken by his bishop, Hendrik van *Bergen (Ep 77). During Erasmus' first trip to England in 1499 Thomas *More took him to meet the royal children at Eltham Palace (Ep 104). Shortly thereafter he wrote his *Prosopopeia Britanniae* in praise of Henry and his children (Reedijk poem 45; CWE 4 408). Subsequently he must have had personal contacts with the king, who by 1506 appears to have promised him an elusive benefice (Ep 189). Erasmus showed particular interest in Henry VII's meeting with Philip the Handsome of *Burgundy, which had occurred in the same

HENRY VIII king of England, 28 June 1491– 28 January 1547

Henry, the second son of *Henry VII, the first Tudor monarch, and his wife, *Elizabeth of York, the daughter of Edward IV, was born at Greenwich.

Erasmus first met Prince Henry in 1499. In his famous account (Allen I 6) Erasmus related how he was taken by Thomas *More from the country house of William *Blount, Lord Mountjoy, to Eltham Palace, where all of Henry VII's children except his eldest son, *Arthur, were assembled in the hall. More presented the nine-year-old prince with some writing; Erasmus, already struck by the boy's demeanor and dignity, was embarrassed that he had nothing to offer. Within three days he completed a laudatory poem, *Prosopopoeia Britanniae*. This was printed, together with a dedicatory epistle to Henry (Ep 104), at the end of the first edition of the *Adagia* (Paris 1500; see Reedijk poem 45).

Erasmus and Henry exchanged letters in 1506 and 1507 (Epp 204, 206). Erasmus later cited the fine style of Henry's Latin epistle as proof that Henry himself was capable of writing the *Assertio septem sacramentorum*. In fact the boy's letter was probably an exercise written under the eye of a tutor, possibly Mountjoy; another letter (Ep 1313) refers to Mountjoy's encouraging Henry to read Erasmus' works.

After the death of Prince Arthur in 1502 Henry became heir apparent to the English throne. His accession (22 April 1509) called forth Mountjoy's well-known panegyric 'Heaven smiles, earth rejoices; all is milk and honey and nectar' (Ep 215). Within a few months Erasmus returned to England, hoping for the patronage which Mountjoy promised. Throughout Erasmus' long sojourn (1509–14) Henry treated him with great respect, and Queen *Catherine of Aragon supposedly asked him to be her tutor. But the promised largesse failed to materialize, and Erasmus had to content himself with commenting on free time and royal favour (Ep 296).

In 1511 Henry joined Pope *Julius II and King *Ferdinand II of Aragon in the Holy League, promising war on France (Epp 236, 239). After Henry's victory at the battle of the Spurs (1513) Erasmus scoffed, in a jocular letter to Andrea *Ammonio, 'We are shut in by the plague and beset by highway robberies; instead of wine we drink vinegar and worse than vinegar, and our coffers are emptying; but "hurrah for victory!" – that is what we sing, being the world-conquerors we are' (Ep 283). A note in Erasmus' edition of Jerome adds the comment that another Thérouanne could be built for less than it had cost Henry to besiege it (Hieronymi opera, 1516, I 40 verso). Henry's involvement in the war is also discussed in Julius exclusus (Opuscula 111–14).

At about this time Erasmus translated Plutarch's De discrimine adulatoris et amici and sent a manuscript to Henry, together with a dedicatory preface expressing the hope that the treatise would be useful to the king (Ep 272). This should probably be read as revealing Erasmus' belief that Henry was being misled by flattering councillors who favoured bellicose policies. In 1517 Erasmus sent Henry a copy of the third published edition, with the comment that the king had originally been too busy with war to give attention to literature (Ep 657).

Shortly before leaving England in 1514 Erasmus attempted to call on Henry at Richmond but found him ill, although his physician said that the king was out of danger (Ep 287). Erasmus continued to oppose war, which he feared might break out again in 1514 (Ep 288), but he believed that Henry was not opposed to peace (Querela pacis LB IV 642C) and had been

persuaded to fight by the incautious remarks of the papal legate (Lingua ASD IV-1 277).

In 1516 More reported that Henry would soon give Erasmus some extraordinary preferment (Ep 388). Erasmus himself mentioned being asked to enter Henry's service upon generous terms (Ep 657), perhaps the handsome house and pension of six hundred florins referred to in a letter to *Pirckheimer (Ep 694). In 1518 Henry sent Erasmus a gift of sixty angels and offered him a living worth one hundred marks, on condition that Erasmus return to England (Ep 816). Erasmus thanked the king, praising his court and character, and said that he would not decline the offer but would shortly be able to devote himself wholly to Henry's service (Ep 834). He wrote Richard *Pace that he would like to go to England again (Ep 887) but told Cuthbert *Tunstall that he would need a higher offer from the king (Ep 886). In the end he did not return, although he continued to praise Henry's love for literature and his patronage of the universities and scholars (Epp 964–6, 968–70).

In 1520 Erasmus went to Calais as a result of invitations from More (Epp 1087, 1096, 1106) and Archbishop *Warham (Epp 1101, 1102). They evidently hoped that he would take part in the famous conference at the Field of Cloth of Gold, and that it might include *Charles V as well as *Francis I. But Charles did not attend – he met privately with Henry in and near Calais – and Erasmus played no major role in the parley. This has been interpreted as a sign that he had abandoned hope for a reconciliation of the European powers. He did greet More and *Wolsey and had a public interview with Henry (Epp 1118, 1132, 1184, 1342); this was the last time Erasmus saw his English friends.

During the same summer Erasmus' ire was aroused by Dr Henry *Standish, the conservative bishop of St Asaph, who had denounced Erasmus and his translation of the New Testament publicly at Paul's Cross in London and privately at court in the presence of Henry and Catherine. There is no evidence that Henry argued Erasmus' cause with Standish, but two friends of Erasmus, very likely More and perhaps Pace, took him to task, and he finally confessed that his zeal had outrun his learning (Epp 1126, 1162, 1196).

In 1520 Erasmus suggested that Henry VIII

nominate some of the arbiters in a panel to settle the dispute between Martin *Luther and the papacy (*Consilium, Opuscula* 359). Henry's *Assertio septem sacramentorum*, a long treatise attacking *Luther, was published in 1521 (London: R. Pynson; STC 13078). Wolsey held up a copy – presumably a manuscript – when some of Luther's books were burned at Paul's Cross on 12 May (LP III-1 1273–4; *Calendar of State Papers, Venetian* III 210). Such correspondents as George, duke of *Saxony, were convinced that Erasmus was the true author of the work (Ep 1298), a charge which Erasmus denied repeatedly (Epp 1275, 1313, 1342). But the king doubtless did have some scholarly help. According to William Roper, More admitted being a 'sorter out and placer of the principall matters therein contayned'; see *Lyfe of Sir Thomas More* (London 1935) 67. Several of Erasmus' letters show his resentment of Luther's attacks on the English king (Epp 1348, 1352), and his friendship was further demonstrated in 1523 by his dedication of the paraphrase on St Luke to Henry VIII (Epp 1381, 1385). This volume appeared, however, in an unimposing form, and there seems to have been some delay in its delivery (Allen Ep 1381 introduction).

By January 1524 Henry was pressing Erasmus to write against Luther (Epp 1408, 1415, 1495). Although Erasmus had wished to remain a spectator of the religious tragedy engulfing Europe, he finally yielded to such calls: *De libero arbitrio diatribe* appeared in September of the same year. Erasmus told Henry of its composition in a letter probably dispatched in March (Ep 1430). On 13 November Juan Luis *Vives reported the enthusiasm of the king and queen upon reading the treatise itself (Ep 1513). Erasmus was glad to hear of Henry's compliments but told Vives he would have preferred money (Ep 1531). Thomas *Lupset later sent him two gold rings which had been blessed by the king; these were probably of little value but were believed to be useful against convulsions (Allen Ep 1595:113n).

In 1527 Henry again invited Erasmus to return to England (Ep 1878). Erasmus was reluctant to leave the protection of the emperor, but he did send over his servant, Quirinus *Talesius, to ascertain the conditions of the

offer. On 1 June 1528 he wrote the king explaining why he felt unable to accept the invitation (Ep 1998).

The 'great matter' of Henry's divorce from Catherine of Aragon was of concern to Erasmus, perhaps as early as 1526, when at Catherine's request he wrote his elaborate *Christiani matrimonii institutio* (Basel: J. Froben, August 1526; see Epp 1727, 1754). As Allen comments (Ep 2846 introduction), the second half of this work, which deals with ethical considerations, contains some of Erasmus' best writing. In the first portion Erasmus trod cautiously in discussing the legal and theoretical aspects of divorce, but within a year he wrote More of his regret that he had allowed his pen to run away with him (Ep 1804). Since Catherine at first took no notice of the book, Erasmus supposed that she was displeased. In 1528 Erasmus, like Luther, suggested that bigamy might be preferable to divorce (Ep 2040). At one time he may have hoped that Henry would find an heir by marrying his daughter *Mary to an English nobleman (Ep 1727). By January 1530 he was looking at the issue more from Henry's point of view, perhaps as a result of an invitation to dedicate his commentary on Psalm 22 to *Anne Boleyn's father, Thomas *Boleyn (Epp 2232, 2266), and he asked Bonifacius *Amerbach whether a dispensation could be justified on grounds of public tranquillity (Ep 2256). Late in 1533 Erasmus reported a rumour of Henry's reconciliation with Catherine (Epp 2877, 2882), but this proved to be false. In the end he could do little but wring his hands and grieve that the king was trapped in such a labyrinth (Ep 2271).

In 1529 Henry had dismissed his chief minister, Thomas Wolsey, for failure to secure the divorce and had appointed Thomas More to the post of chancellor. On 28 October More wrote Erasmus with news of the king's immense favour and grace (Ep 2228). Erasmus mentioned his friend's preferment in a number of letters, commenting that learning, and More himself, stood to lose, although Henry and England would gain from his services (Epp 2263, 2287, 2295). More resigned the office in 1532, actually as a protest against the Submission of the Clergy, although he told Erasmus that his retirement was due to ill health and that Henry had accepted it unwillingly (Ep

2659). Erasmus commented on the resignation in letters to Johannes *Fabri and Jan *Łaski (Epp 2750, 2780). By February 1535 Erasmus had learnt that Henry had sent More and John *Fisher to the Tower, but he believed that the king was treating More gently (Ep 2996). In June he expressed fear for More's life (Ep 3025), and by the end of August he knew that More and Fisher had been executed (Epp 3037, 3041, 3042). While he decried the loss of his friends and held that England never had holier or better men (Ep 3049), and while he wrote a Latin lament for More (*Carmen heroicum*), his letters do not express indignation directed against the king. As late as September 1535 Erasmus received gifts from Henry's new minister, Thomas *Cromwell, and from Archbishop *Cranmer (Ep 3058), but after the fulsome praise of More and Fisher in Erasmus' preface to the *Ecclesiastes* (Ep 3036) reached England Erasmus realized that he could no longer expect support from the government there (Ep 3104).

Henry outlived Erasmus by a decade. His later years were marred by a revival of warfare, by religious unrest and factional dissension, and by the execution of two of Henry's wives and the tragic death of another following childbirth. Erasmian ideas remained influential at his court, however. As J.K. McConica has demonstrated in his *English Humanists and Reformation Politics* (Oxford 1965), the circles associated with Cromwell and with Henry's last queen, Catherine Parr, were permeated with Erasmianism. The king himself may have been following Erasmus, both in thought and in phraseology, when he argued for charity and moderation in religion rather than bitter division between the supporters of 'old mumpsimus and new sumpsimus,' as he put it in his last address to Parliament; see Allen Epp 456:72–82 and 619:83; S.E. Lehmberg *The Later Parliaments of Henry VIII 1536–1547* (Cambridge 1977) 229–31.

An early portrait of Henry, attributed to Joos van Cleve, is in the collection of Her Majesty the Queen. The most important likenesses were painted by Hans *Holbein the Younger between 1536 and 1543. See Paul Ganz *The Paintings of Hans Holbein* (London 1956); Roy Strong *Holbein and Henry VIII* (London 1967).

BIBLIOGRAPHY: James Gairdner in DNB IX

Henry II, king of France, by Primaticcio

527–45 / LP passim / A.F. Pollard *Henry VIII* (London 1902) / J.J. Scarisbrick *Henry VIII* (London 1968) / On Erasmus and the divorce see Hans Thieme 'Die Ehescheidung Heinrichs VIII. als europäischer Rechtsfall' in *Syntagma Friburgense ... Hermann Auben dargebracht* (Lindau-Constance 1956) 257–78

STANFORD E. LEHMBERG

HENRY II king of France, 31 March 1519– 10 July 1559
Henry was the second son of King *Francis I and *Claude of France. On 17 March 1526 Henry and his elder brother *Francis, were handed over to the Spaniards as hostages to secure the freedom of their father. They were allowed to return after the 'Ladies' Peace' of 3 August 1529. In 1533 Henry married *Catherine de' Medici, the niece of Pope *Clement VII and the daughter of Lorenzo de' *Medici, duke of Urbino (Ep 2917), but her dowry was never paid in full; he despised his wife and remained attached to his mistress, Diane de Poitiers. Since Henry's elder brother had died in 1536, Henry was proclaimed king on the death of his father on 31 March 1547.

In 1556 he sent an army to Italy to secure Naples for the French crown. Meanwhile the Spaniards advanced from the Netherlands and threatened to attack Paris but had to withdraw without deriving much benefit from their victory at Saint-Quentin. In January 1558 Calais, a stronghold of the English for two hundred years, fell to King Henry. His eldest son, the dauphin, Francis, married Mary, queen of Scotland. Hostilities between France and Spain were ended by the treaty of Cateau-Cambrésis signed on 3 April 1559. During the festivities that followed, celebrating the peace and the marriage of Henry's daughter Elizabeth to Philip II, Henry was wounded in a tournament and died on 10 July 1559.

BIBLIOGRAPHY: Allen Ep 2917 / L. Romier *Les Origines politiques des guerres de religion* (Paris 1913–14) passim   IG

HENRY cardinal-king of Portugal, 1512–31 January 1580
Henry (Henrique) was the son of King *Manuel I and his second wife, Maria, the sister of Isabella, his first wife; he was a younger brother of King *John III. In a letter to Erasmus, *Schets wrote of the king's brother who was very generous and learned and fond of Damião de *Gois (Ep 3042). The reference may be to Henry or, less likely, his brother Dom *Afonso.

Henry gathered around him noted scholars such as Pedro Nunes, the mathematician, and Jorge *Coelho, the poet, and engaged as teacher of ancient languages Nicolaus *Clenardus, the Flemish humanist. When the latter joined him in 1533 Henry was already archbishop of Braga. He founded a school there and made Clenardus its principal, greatly facilitating his studies of the Arabic language by granting him a stipend which enabled him to learn more Arabic and to read the Koran with Moslems in Africa. But as grand inquisitor Henry found it impossible to tolerate Clenardus' fraternization with Jews in Fez and consequently withdrew his support from him. When Gois published his *Fides, religio moresque Aethiopum* in 1540 (Louvain: R. Rescius) Henry, who had become a cardinal after the death of Dom Afonso, prohibited the book's circulation

in Portugal. On the other hand he put Gois in charge of writing the history of King Manuel's reign after his return to his home-country in 1545, despite the fact that he had already been denounced before the Inquisition.

Henry had great sympathy for the Jesuits. After John III's death he appointed a Jesuit as tutor to Dom Sebastian, the future king. In 1558 he asked the pope's permission to establish a Jesuit university in Evora. After Sebastian's death on the battlefield in North Africa in 1578, Henry became king, but he died two years later, the last of the house of Aviz. His personality, like that of King John III, reflected the intellectual conditions of an unsettled period which lasted until the final session of the council of Trent.

BIBLIOGRAPHY: Allen Ep 3042 / Fortunato de Almeida *História de Portugal* (Coimbra 1922–5) II and III passim / H.V. Livermore *A New History of Portugal* (Cambridge 1966) 158–62 and passim / B.W. Diffie and G.D. Winius *Foundations of the Portuguese Empire, 1415–1580* (Minneapolis 1977) 422–3 and passim / Elisabeth Feist Hirsch *Damião de Gois* (The Hague 1967) 153–4 and passim

ELISABETH FEIST HIRSCH

Nicolaus HERBORN *See Nikolaus* FERBER

Gerard van HEREMA documented 1515–30
Gerard von Herema, the father-in-law of Hector van *Hoxwier, was a member of the Friesland council. No doubt he is identical with Gerold van Herama (one of the wealthiest and foremost lords of Friesland) who was appointed councillor in 1515 and who remained in office after the reorganization of 29 July 1527. On 31 January 1530 Erasmus wrote a polite letter to Herema (Ep 2262), who was very grateful, despite the long delay before he received it (cf Ep 2624). Herema was married to Lucia Ziaerda; Allen suggests that the papal chamberlain Theophilus ab Herema, to whom *Viglius Zuichemus wrote a letter on 24 April 1558, was his son.

BIBLIOGRAPHY: Allen Ep 2262 / de Vocht CTL II 164 / *Naamrol der Edele Mogende Heeren Raden 's Hoffs van Friesland* (Leeuwarden 1742) 6, 9–10 / J.S. Theissen *Centraal gezag en Friesche vrijheid* (Groningen 1907) 148, 151 / S.A.

Gabbema *Illustrium et clarorum virorum epistolae selectiores* (Harlingen 1669) I Ep 76
                                      C.G. VAN LEIJENHORST

Konrad HERESBACH 2 August 1496–
14 October 1576
Heresbach (Hertzbach) was born on the
Heresbach estate near Düsseldorf, into a family
that was wealthy but did not belong to the
nobility. Through the marriages of his brothers
and sisters Heresbach was related to some
noble families of the duchy of Cleves as well as
to the Cologne chronicler Hermann Weins-
berg, who mentioned Heresbach in complimentary terms in his work.

The chronology of Heresbach's life can be
established from his diary, the documents in
the Stadtarchiv of Wesel, the matriculation
records of the University of Cologne, and his
voluminous correspondence. He received a
good education in the Latin schools of Wer-
den, on the Ruhr, and Hamm and Münster, in
Westphalia. In Münster he was taught by
Johannes *Murmellius. In October 1512 he was
accepted into the Bursa Montis at Cologne and
matriculated at the university as an arts
student. In Cologne he met *Glareanus and
*Haio Herman. Having graduated MA in 1515,
he proceeded to study law in France. In Paris
he met Thomas *Lupset and together with him
read Plato. In the summer of 1519 he returned
to Cologne.

Following Erasmus' visit to Cologne in
November 1520, and conceivably as a result of
it, Heresbach was working as a corrector for
Johann *Froben in Basel by December of that
year. Perhaps again on Erasmus' recommendation he was appointed lecturer in Greek at the
University of Freiburg in June 1521 (AK II 790).
His inaugural address, *De laudibus graecarum
literarum*, was later published together with
Johann Sturm's *De educatione principum* (Strasbourg: W. Rihel 1551). In the spring of 1522 he
became Erasmius *Froben's tutor for a while
(Ep 1316) and made the acquaintance of
Udalricus *Zasius. In the autumn of 1522
Heresbach left Freiburg for Italy, where he
obtained a doctorate of laws from the University of Ferrara on 22 October. Thereafter he
visited Padua and Venice and returned to
Freiburg, where he continued to teach Greek

until May 1523, when the university's refusal
to raise his salary induced him to resign. In this
period he revised Strabo and translated the
fourth book of the Greek grammar of Theodorus *Gaza (published in Basel by Valentinus
*Curio in March and August 1523
respectively).

Heresbach no doubt discussed his future
with Erasmus when the latter visited Freiburg
in March 1523. In June Erasmus sent him to the
papal nuncio Ennio *Filonardi at Constance
with an impressive recommendation (Ep 1364),
but apparently without success. Another
approach, however, proved more promising.
Heresbach had dedicated the Strabo to Johann
von *Vlatten, who was also in Freiburg during
Erasmus' visit in the same month; Vlatten and
Erasmus seem to have combined efforts in
finding appropriate employment for Heresbach (Ep 1390), and on 1 September 1523 he
was installed as tutor to the future William v
duke of *Cleves. To Erasmus' great satisfaction
(Ep 2189, 2431) Heresbach continued in this
position until 1534; he also remained in close
contact with Vlatten until 1536.

Heresbach's services were rewarded with
ecclesiastical preferment, including a canonry
at St Victor's, Xanten (1529), and a promise of
the provostship of Rees (Ep 2146). Although in
1535 and 1536 he resigned his benefices and
took a wife, he never wavered in his commitment to an irenic church policy and the
avoidance of a complete break with Rome.
Meanwhile in the autumn of 1532 he paid
another visit to Italy (Epp 2736, 2753). On 25
June 1535 he was named ducal councillor and
subsequently was engaged in important diplomatic missions on the eve of Duke William's
unsuccessful war to retain Gelderland (at
Hampton Court and Worms in 1540 and at
Regensburg in 1541) and defended Vlatten's
policy of peace in a pamphlet, *Defensio iuris ...
principis Wilhelmi* (14 February 1542). He also
participated in negotiations with Archbishop
Hermann von *Wied (at the castle of Hambach,
19 July 1543) and in the duke's retinue went to
Brussels to welcome the future Philip II (30
April 1549). When the duke was in financial
difficulties after losing the war and Gelderland, Heresbach was in a position to lend his
master eleven hundred gold florins, an indica-

tion of his wealth, which increased further with his second marriage in 1562.

At about this time Heresbach retired to his estate of Lorward on an island in the Rhine, near Wesel, and resumed his personal studies, although on occasion he continued to serve as a councillor. In 1562 he negotiated with Georgius Cassander, Georg *Witzel, and Julius *Pflug about a rapprochement between the Catholic and Protestant positions. Together with Vlatten and Heinrich Olisleger he pursued the project of a university at Duisburg which was to consolidate the Erasmian church reform in the United Duchies, and in January 1567 he participated in deliberations on the revised church ordinance. He died at Lorward and was buried in St Willibrod's, Wesel.

In his will of 13 January 1568 (preserved in the Stadtarchiv of Wesel), Heresbach added to an earlier educational endowment and made dispositions concerning his valuable library and his literary estate. All this is lost, however, except for a few of his books, which went to the Gymnasium of Wesel, and his diary, 1537–44, which is in the collection of the Bergischer Geschichtsverein at Wuppertal and is published in *Zeitschrift des Bergischen Geschichtsvereins* 23 (1887) 57–83.

Heresbach continued to correspond with Erasmus until the latter's death; apart from three extant letters (Epp 1316, 3031, 3031A), there are many references to missing ones (Epp 1549, 1775, 1934, 2234, 3041, 3071). Heresbach visited Erasmus at Freiburg in September 1532 to consult him about the new church ordinance for Cleves (Ep 2728). Heresbach's two reports (Epp 3031, 3031A) about the end of the Anabaptist kingdom of Münster have the value of an independent source. Among his other correspondents were *Melanchthon, *Bucer, and *Camerarius.

In addition to the Strabo and Gaza volumes mentioned above, Heresbach edited Herodotus and Thucydides in Latin (Cologne 1526, 1527). Among his own numerous writings may be noted: *Rei rusticae libri quatuor* (Cologne: J. Birckmann 1570), a delightful manual on farming (English trans London, R. Watkins 1577, STC 13196); *De educandis erudiendisque principum liberis* (Frankfurt: J. Feyerabend 1570); *Diarium seu quotidianae preces* (Basel

1574); and *Psalmorum Davidicorum simplex et dilucida explanatio* (Basel: P. Perna 1578).

BIBLIOGRAPHY: Allen Ep 1316 / NDB VIII 606–7 / ADB XII 103–5 / Albrecht Wolters *Konrad von Heresbach und der Clevische Hof* (Elberfeld 1867) / Anton Gail 'Johann von Vlatten und der Einfluss des Erasmus ... ' *Düsseldorfer Jahrbuch* 45 (1951) 1–109 passim / Jean-Claude Margolin in his introduction to Erasmus *Declamatio de pueris statim ac liberaliter instituendis* (Geneva 1966) 29–40 / J.A.R. von Stintzing *Geschichte der deutschen Rechtswissenschaft* 3rd ed (Munich 1880–1910) I 228ff, 543 / 'Freundesbriefe Conrads von Heresbach an Johann von Vlatten ... ' ed O.R. Redlich *Zeitschrift des Bergischen Geschichtsvereins* 41 (1905) 160–203 / O.R. Redlich *Staat und Kirche am Niederrhein zur Reformationszeit* (Leipzig 1938) 16–17 and passim / AK II Ep 825 and passim

ANTON J. GAIL

Jean d'HÉRINNES *See Johannes* AMMONIUS

Haio HERMAN *See* HAIO HERMAN

HERMANN *See Georg and Johann Georg* HÖRMANN

HERMANNUS Goudanus *See Herman* LETHMAET

HERMANNUS Phrysius *See* HAIO HERMAN

Willem HERMANS of Gouda, c 1469– 18 July 1510

Willem Hermans (Guilielmus Goudanus), a cousin of Cornelis *Gerard, was a native of Gouda. According to the superscription of the *Certamen Erasmi atque Guielmi* (Reedijk poem 9) he and Erasmus were of the same age, so he may have been born in 1469. He no doubt received his first schooling at Gouda, perhaps from Pieter *Winckel; he then became a pupil of St Lebuin's school at Deventer, where Alexander *Hegius was his teacher. It is likely that he first met Erasmus there, or even earlier (Erasmus held that they knew each other '"from tender nails" as the Greeks say,' Ep 49), but their friendship cannot be traced before they were both in the monastery of the Augustinian canons at Steyn (Allen I 57). They were separated when Hermans was sent to a cell at Haarlem (1489–90?; hence his praise of Haarlem's St Bavo, cf Ep 28). From this period, however, nothing of their correspondence remains; the first extant letter, Ep 33, seems to have been written just after Erasmus had joined Bishop Hendrik van *Bergen, and by that time Hermans had returned to Steyn. While Erasmus' horizons constantly widened, Hermans was virtually confined to his familiar circle (Gerard, Servatius *Rogerus, Claes *Warnerszoon, and others), although he found some compensation in several new acquaintances made through Erasmus, such as Fausto *Andrelini (Ep 84), Jacob *Batt (Ep 35), and, indirectly, *Johannes, the tutor of Philip the Handsome of *Burgundy (Ep 38). Presumably in the spring of 1495 Hermans, Batt, and Erasmus met at Halsteren, near Bergen op Zoom, thus creating the scene of the *Antibarbari* in its revised version (ASD I-1 38–9; CWE 23 19–21). There were moments when Erasmus feared he would be supplanted by Hermans in the favour of Batt and Batt's employer, Anna van *Borssele, who allowed Hermans to stay at Tournehem castle in the summer of 1500 (Epp 129, 130); Hermans' opinion of Batt was not altogether positive (Ep 92).

Around the end of 1493 Hermans had already sent some of his poems to Erasmus (Ep 34), and he gave him more of these when Erasmus visited him in 1496 (Allen I 50; CWE 4 408 and Ep 49); Erasmus paid other visits to him in 1498 (Ep 83) and 1499 (Ep 92). Probably without Hermans' knowledge, Erasmus edited his *Sylva odarum* (Paris: G. Marchand 20 January 1497); he added a dedicatory letter to Hendrik van Bergen (Ep 49) and two poems of his own (Reedijk poems 40, 43). The volume seems to have enjoyed considerable success in Paris (Epp 50, 51). Around 1500 Hermans was again living at Haarlem, where he tried to sell copies of Erasmus' *Adagia* (Epp 138, 139, 142). In 1501 Erasmus visited him there; he had taken books with him to initiate Willem in the mysteries of Greek, but his friend was anything but co-operative (Ep 157). Erasmus' friendships were seldom cloudless, and indeed the two regularly reproached one another, Hermans criticizing Erasmus for his way of life and Erasmus reproving Hermans for wasting

his talents (especially Ep 83; *Ciceronianus* ASD I-2 681). Nevertheless they maintained relations at least until 1506, when Erasmus referred in Ep 190 to a letter he had written to him; apparently Hermans was then at Steyn. According to the *necrologium* of Steyn, Hermans died 18 July 1510. A certain *Sasboudus informed Erasmus of his death (Ep 296).

Hermans' accomplishments were not only in the field of poetry. He also prepared a prose version of the fables of Avianus (the '*Apologi*'), probably printed in 1502 or 1503 (Epp 172, 178; cf Reedijk poem 76) but of which no copies survive; an enlarged edition was published ten years later under the supervision of Pieter *Gillis (Antwerp: D. Martens, 21 September 1513; NK 2243; cf Allen Ep 184n). More important, however, are his historical works: he wrote a history of Holland, now lost, which was a major source for Jan van Naaldwijk, Reyner *Snoy (*De rebus Batavicis*), and Cornelis Gerard (*Divisiekroniek*), and which was highly praised by Erasmus in his *Panegyricus* (ASD IV-1 34). His *Bellum Olandie Gelrieque*, dealing with contemporary history, was published posthumously around 1517 (Amsterdam: [P.J. Tyebaut?]; NK 1037) and reprinted in A. Matthaeus' *Analecta* I (The Hague 1738).

BIBLIOGRAPHY: Allen Ep 33 / A. Hulshof in NNBW III 480–1 and J. Romein in NNBW IX 358 / I. W[alvis] *Beschryving der stad Gouda* (Gouda-Leiden [1713]) I 239–44 / J. Romein *Geschiedenis van de Noord-Nederlandsche geschiedschrijving* (Haarlem 1932) 206–8 / Reedijk 54–7 / A. Baudet et al 'Lijst van werken van Nord-Nederlandse humanisten, gebooren voor … 1500' *Folium* 4 (1954) 3–28, esp 17

C.G. VAN LEIJENHORST

HERMICO, HERMINCUS *See Henrique CAIADO*

Georgius HERMONYMUS of Sparta, documented 1475–1508
Nothing is known of Georgius Hermonymus' life until he arrived in Rome in 1475 or 1476 at the court of *Sixtus IV, who sent him on a diplomatic mission to England. He reached Paris in 1476 and was still there in 1508. He taught Greek to Johann *Reuchlin (1478), Erasmus (1501), *Beatus Rhenanus, and Guil-

laume *Budé (c 1494, Ep 583), among others. Much of his life seems to have been devoted to copying Greek manuscripts (Ep 583), but he also translated pseudo-Aristotle's *De virtutibus et vitiis*, the *Dicta septem sapientium*, and Gennadius' *Via salutis*, besides writing a *Vita Machometi*. Erasmus had a rather low opinion of Hermonymus' mastery of Greek (Allen I 7; ASD I-4 48). Several other disparaging comments by Erasmus about a 'graecus' (Epp 149, 194) are generally thought to refer to him.

BIBLIOGRAPHY: Allen I 7 / H. Omont 'Georges Hermonyme de Sparte, maître de grec à Paris et copiste de manuscrits' *Mémoires de la societé de Paris et de l'Ile-de-France* 12 (1885) 65–98 / Ludwig Geiger 'Studien zur Geschichte des französischen Humanismus' *Vierteljahrsschrift für Kultur und Literatur der Renaissance* 2 (1887) 194–7 / L. Delaruelle *Guillaume Budé: Les origines, les débuts, les idées maîtresses* (Paris 1907) 69–73 and passim / R. Weiss *Humanism in England during the Fifteenth Century* 3rd ed (Oxford 1967) 145–7, 151–2, 198 / J. Irigoin 'Georges Hermonyme de Sparte: ses manuscrits et son enseignement à Paris' *Bulletin de l'Association Guillaume Budé* (1977) 22–7
CHARLES B. SCHMITT

HERVÉ de Portzmoguer *See Hervé de* PORTZMOGUER

Johann HERWAGEN of Waderdingen, 1497–c 1558
Johann Herwagen was born in Waderdingen, Hegau, north-west of Lake Constance. He was well educated, but it is not known where he acquired his learning. On 11 November 1522 he obtained the citizenship of Strasbourg, where he set up a successful press in the Elisabethenstrasse and between then and 1528 published more than a hundred books, many of them by *Luther and other reformers. In 1526 he asked Martin *Bucer to provide him with a Latin translation of Luther's German commentaries on New Testament readings in the mass. The translator took the liberty of inserting into the text that Herwagen printed direct attacks upon Luther's doctrine of the Eucharist, which the Wittenberg reformer countered by publishing a sharp letter addressed to Herwagen (Luther w XIX 462–73; z VIII Ep 554).

In 1528 Herwagen moved to Basel, where he was received as a citizen on 28 July and joined the 'Schlüssel' guild on 2 August. No doubt he was attracted to Basel by Gertrud *Lachner, the recent widow of Johann *Froben, who married Herwagen soon after his arrival (Ep 1962). At first he was a partner in the Froben publishing house (Ep 2033), but in 1531 he set up his own press at the Nadelberg, where he occupied Froben's house 'zur alten Treu,' until 1529 the residence of Erasmus (Epp 1316, 2945). He can hardly have been poor at the time of his marriage and by 1538 he was clearly well-to-do (AK v Ep 2266). Although the former partners confronted one another with conflicting claims (Ep 2945; AK v Epp 2264, 2287, 2290, 2300), they did on occasion renew their co-operation, as in the case of Sigismundus *Gelenius' editions of Pliny (1535) and Livy (1534, 1539, 1543), and again in 1546 (AK VI Epp 2681, 2823, 2840). In 1538 Herwagen published some books in partnership with his stepson, Erasmius *Froben, but this connection took an unfortunate turn in October 1541 when he was accused of adultery with Erasmius' wife. The trial ended on 19 January 1542 in his banishment after his friend and loyal supporter Bonifacius *Amerbach had assured the city council that Mosaic and civil laws offered no basis for treating the case as incest (AK v 485–8). Three years later the pleas of the university, Philip of *Hesse, and Ulrich of *Württemberg opened the way for his return from Strasbourg to Basel, although humiliating restrictions remained imposed upon him until 1547. After they had been lifted he obtained a coat of arms from *Charles v on 1 December. At the end of his career he was printing in partnership with his son-in-law, Bernhard Brand. He died before 31 January 1559.

At Basel Herwagen's book production shifted in emphasis to ancient and medieval history as well as other works by classical and patristic authors. In 1535 and 1541 he published editions of Homer in Greek, and with his Cicero edition of 1534 he endeavoured to rival the Augustine of the Froben firm (AK IV Ep 1602). To his friendship with Amerbach he owed his opportunity to publish Andrea *Alciati's *Parerga iuris* (1538); also among his legal output are editions of the *Corpus iuris* and Jakob *Spiegel's *Lexicon iuris civilis* (1549,

1554). In 1532 and 1537 he produced Simon *Grynaeus' *Orbis novus*.

From the time of his arrival in Basel Herwagen's contacts with Erasmus were inevitably frequent. In 1530, when he went to Venice in search of manuscripts, Erasmus recommended him to his friends there (Epp 2249, 2288, 2302). A year later Erasmus' *Epistolae floridae* (Ep 2518) were among the very first products of his independent press. However, insufficient discretion was used in editing these letters (Ep 2615), and henceforward Herwagen failed for the most part to obtain other texts by Erasmus (Ep 2945), although with great difficulty he succeeded enlisting his help with the Demosthenes of 1532 (Epp 2686, 2695) and the great Cicero edition (Epp 2764, 2765, 2775, 2788), and more easily perhaps with two other projects (Epp 3030, 3135).

BIBLIOGRAPHY: Allen Ep 2033 / Grimm *Buchführer* 1396–7 / Benzing *Buchdrucker* 34, 414 / Josef Benzing in NDB VIII 719–20 / R. Wackernagel *Geschichte der Stadt Basel* (Basel 1907–54) III 440 and passim / P. Heitz and C.C. Bernoulli *Basler Büchermarken bis zum Anfang des 17. Jahrhunderts* (Strasbourg 1895) xxix–xxx, 76–9
PGB

Johann HESS of Nürnberg, 23 September 1490–5 January 1547
Johann Hess (Hessus), the son of a Nürnberg merchant, studied from 1506 to 1510 at Leipzig and then moved to the University of Wittenberg, where he graduated MA in 1511. He stayed to teach there for a year, making the acquaintance of *Spalatinus and *Luther. In 1513 he became the secretary of Johannes (II) *Thurzo, bishop of Wrocław (Breslau), but returned to his studies in 1517 when he attended the University of Erfurt and established contacts with *Eobanus Hessus and his circle. In 1518 he matriculated at the University of Bologna, where he met Johannes *Crotus Rubianus. After receiving a theological doctorate from Ferrara, he again spent several weeks in Wittenberg late in 1519 and formed a close friendship with *Melanchthon. Subsequently he returned to the service of Thurzo, who provided him with a canonry of Wrocław. Thurzo died the following year, and his successor, Jakob von *Salza, proved unsympa-

thetic to Hess' pro-Lutheran views. Hess was forced to retire to Nürnberg, but on 20 May 1523 the city council of Wrocław appointed him parish priest of St Mary Magdalen in defiance of the bishop. In close co-operation with the council he led the Reformation to victory and won wide recognition as the leading representative of Lutheranism in Silesia (Ep 2601). On 8 September 1525 he married Anna Jopner of Wrocław. Firmly grounded in Lutheran doctrine, he also showed the caution and tolerance required by the ecclesio-political situation in Silesia.

There is no record of personal relations between Hess and Erasmus.

BIBLIOGRAPHY: Allen Ep 2601 / Schottenloher I 342, VII 95 / ADB XII 283–4 / NDB IX 7–8 / Knod 198 / *Melanchthons Briefwechsel* I Ep 75 and passim / *Christoph Scheurl's Briefbuch* ed F. von Soden and J.K.F. Knaake (Potsdam 1867–72, repr 1962) Epp 74, 80
MICHAEL ERBE & PGB

Philip, landgrave of HESSE 13 November 1504–31 March 1567
Philip's nominal rule of Hesse began when he was five years old after the death of his father, Landgrave William II (11 July 1509). He was brought up by his mother, Anna von Mecklenburg, who from 1514 also exercised the functions of regent until Philip was declared of age on 16 March 1518. By the time he attended the diet of Worms in 1521 he had established full control of his state and was showing a firm grasp of German problems in general. While making apt use of capable advisers such as his chancellor, Johann *Feige, he would throughout his life reach his decisions independently after thorough examination of the matter in question. At Worms he formed a rapport with Richard von *Greiffenklau, archbishop of Trier, which two years later led to Philip's decisive intervention in the war between Trier and Franz von *Sickingen, who had earlier threatened the integrity of Hesse as well, and to Sickingen's downfall. Also in 1523 Philip married Christina, a daughter of Duke George of *Saxony, as a token of close collaboration with the Saxon dynasty. Although his relations with George were soon troubled by the latter's firm commitment to Catholicism, and despite a number of differences later on, the

Philip, landgrave of Hesse, by Hans Brosamer

alliance between Hesse and Saxony proved decisive to the survival of the German Reformation.

Philip's commitment to the evangelical faith was personal and sincere. At Worms the sixteen-year-old landgrave had gone to see Luther at his inn, and he became an avid reader of Scripture. After the troubles of the peasant rebellion (1525), Philip proceeded with an orderly and complete reform of the church in Hesse, but he was careful to involve the estates, who heard François *Lambert argue the evangelical case at the synod of Homburg in 1526. While the monasteries were dissolved, four large civic hospitals were created and a university was founded in Marburg (1527). In 1528 the machinations of Otto von *Pack induced the landgrave to prepare for a military confrontation with the neighbouring ecclesiastical princes. While war was barely averted on this occasion, Philip had reason to conclude that his militancy had served him well. He again showed great firmness in his preparations before attending the diet of Augsburg in 1530 (Epp 2310, 2333), and he left secretly when he recognized that *Charles v was not

going to make concessions to the Protestants (Ep 2367). Even before the diet Philip had worked for a rapprochement between Luther and *Zwingli, and in the autumn of 1529 the two reformers met at his invitation in his castle at Marburg but failed to reach an agreement on the crucial question of the Eucharist and on political co-operation. Not troubled by theological minutiae, Philip was impressed by Zwingli's political militancy and, after the disappointing outcome of the diet of Augsburg, pressed harder than ever for a firm alliance with the evangelical cities of Switzerland and Southern Germany. Only Zwingli's death on the battlefield in 1531 persuaded him to devote his energies fully to the strengthening of the Lutheran Schmalkaldic League.

Of particular importance to the consolidation of Protestantism in Southern Germany and at the same time a political triumph for Philip was the restoration of duke Ulrich of *Württemberg. The landgrave was instrumental in achieving a common front among Württemberg's neighbours against the continued administration of the duchy on behalf of the Hapsburgs. Early in 1534 he secured the support of King *Francis I of France in a personal meeting at Bar-le-Duc and in April and May he led his army to victory on Ulrich's behalf over the Hapsburg governor of Württemberg, Philip count *Palatine. After the peace of Kadan (25 June 1534, Ep 2947) Philip visited King *Ferdinand at Vienna and offered his support in the war against the Turks. He was received with great honour (Ep 3049). Nearly a decade of friendly relations with the Hapsburg court followed. Charles v's sympathetic inaction proved beneficial to Philip in the troubles following his 'collateral' second marriage to his mistress, Margarethe von der Saal (4 March 1540), a step bound to aggravate the growing difficulties he was experiencing with the Saxon relatives of his principal wife, Christina.

At the same time as Philip intervened in Württemberg the troubles of Münster seemed to present him with an opportunity for strengthening the Protestant presence in Northern Germany. But his mediation failed to prevent the victory of Anabaptist radicals in that city (Epp 2957, 3031A), and subsequently his support of the Catholic bishop, Franz von

*Waldeck, did not, as he had hoped, induce the latter to join the reform camp. At the diet of Regensburg (1541) Philip loyally supported the Hapsburg efforts to promote reconciliation between Catholics and Protestants, but after the peace of Crépy (1546) he was obliged to alter his assessment of Charles v's intentions and urged his allies in the Schmalkaldic League to prepare for war. In the summer of 1546 he took the field together with the Elector John Frederick of *Saxony, but when the opportunity for decisive action was allowed to pass the disappointed landgrave withdrew by the end of the year to Hesse. After the emperor's victory at Mühlberg (24 April 1547), Philip's son-in-law, Maurice of Saxony, persuaded him to surrender to Charles v. Contrary to his expectation, he was arrested and remained imprisoned in the Netherlands until 1552, when Maurice's successful counter-attack led to his release.

Although Erasmus kept informed of Philip's political moves, he had no direct connections with the landgrave and his court.

BIBLIOGRAPHY: Allen Ep 2141 / W. Friedensburg in ADB XXV 765–83 / Schottenloher III 188–98, VII 340–1 / René Hauswirth *Landgraf Philipp von Hessen und Zwingli* (Tübingen-Basel 1968) / Hans J. Hillerbrand *Landgrave Philip of Hesse, 1504–1567* (St Louis 1967)   PGB

Christina, landgravine of Hesse, by Hans Brosamer

Jacob HESSELE of Nieuwkerke-les-Bailleul, 1506–4 October 1578
Jacob Hessele (Hesselus; Hessels is inappropriate) was born in Nieuwkerke-les-Bailleul, Flanders (now Département du Nord), the son of Nicolaas and Jacqueline Wicx. With his first wife, Elisabeth Monicx, he had eight children, all of whom died before reaching adulthood. After Elisabeth's death (12 September 1558), Jets van Hoytema, a niece of *Viglius Zuichemus, became his second wife; of her four children two survived infancy, Folcard and Maria. Hessele was lord of Ter Caemere, near Menin in West Flanders, and a knight of the Golden Fleece. He matriculated at the University of Louvain on 21 February 1527. In 1546 he became deputy councillor (*conseiller-commissaire*) of the council of Flanders in Ghent; in 1550 he was councillor-in-ordinary, and in 1554 proctor-general. In the course of

the religious riots he was hanged by the Ghent Calvinists on 4 October 1578.

On 12 July 1533 Hessele introduced himself to Erasmus with a letter (Ep 2843) mentioning his friendship with Karel *Uutenhove and Omaar van *Edingen and the death of Daniël *Tayspil.

BIBLIOGRAPHY: Allen Ep 2843 / BNB IX 322–7 / de Vocht CTL II 471–2 / *Matricule de Louvain* III-1 774 / P. van Peteghem 'Centralisatie in Vlaanderen onder keizer Karel (1515–1555)' (thesis, Rijksuniversiteit Ghent 1980)

                          MARCEL A. NAUWELAERTS

HESSELS *See* GHISBERT *and* Jacob HESSELE

Christiaan HEUSDEN *See* CHRISTIANUS *Hieronymita*

Simon HEXAPOLITANUS *See* Simon SCHAIDENREISSER

Berta HEYEN documented at Gouda, 1473–87
The name of Heyen (Heye, etc) is found frequently in the lists of Gouda magistrates in the fifteenth and sixteenth centuries, but

information on Berta is scant. Her maiden name is not known; she was married to Baert Jan Heyenzoon, who died before 1474. After the death of her husband Berta remained active; she is often recorded buying and selling houses between 1473 and 1487, and she used her wealth for charity. As *moeder* she supervised the hospital of St Elisabeth (18 February 1484; LB VIII 556B), but it was not only the hospital that profited from her munificence; so did Erasmus and his fellow monks, who regularly sat at her table. It seems that she had been particularly fond of Erasmus from his childhood and after the death of his parents accorded him her motherly affection. Erasmus praised her courage when one of her daughters, Margareta Honora *Heyen, died (LB VIII 557–8). Her own death may have occurred by 1489; Erasmus composed the *Oratio funebris in funere Bertae de Heyen* (LB VIII 551–60), which is probably the funeral speech mentioned in Ep 28. He also wrote two epitaphs for her (Reedijk poems 12, 13). As these documents are rather formal it is difficult to say how much Erasmus owed to Berta; however the writing in itself appears to have been an act of piety and probably did not bring him any benefits. Berta was survived by two or more daughters who were nuns in an Augustinian convent at Gouda; it is to them that Erasmus addressed the *Oratio funebris*. One may have been *Elisabeth, addressed in Ep 2.

BIBLIOGRAPHY: Allen Ep 28 / Reedijk poems 12, 13, with an introduction making use of the Gouda archives   C.G. VAN LEIJENHORST

Margareta HEYEN of Gouda, d c 1487–9
According to the *Oratio funebris in funere Bertae de Heyen* (LB VIII 557–8), Berta *Heyen lost one of her daughters, named Margareta, only six weeks after the girl's wedding. Margareta Heyen may well be identical with Margareta Honora, the wife of Guihelmus *Fiscinius, for whom Erasmus wrote an epitaph (Reedijk poem 10) after her premature death.

BIBLIOGRAPHY: Reedijk poem 10
          C.G. VAN LEIJENHORST

Theodoricus HEZIUS of Heeze, d 10 May 1555
Dirk Adriaans (Adriani) was called Hezius because he was born in Heeze, near Eindho-

ven (in the province of North Brabant, Netherlands). The date of his birth is unknown but must be assigned to the last quarter of the fifteenth century because he matriculated at the University of Louvain on 28 February 1504. Having become a MA in 1509, he taught philosophy at the College of the Falcon, where he was admitted as a paying student. He did not go beyond his baccalaureate in theology, but this did not seem to affect his career adversely. His career began in the shadow of his master and fellow-countryman, Adrian of Utrecht, whom he followed to Spain and later to Rome when he became Pope *Adrian VI in 1522. As secretary to the new pope Hezius in fact became his right hand. He was named apostolic protonotary and would have received the cardinal's hat had his master not died prematurely in 1523. A few months later Hezius left Rome and took up residence in Liège, the capital of the diocese in which he was born. He obtained a canonry at St Lambert's in Liège on 7 January 1524 and became vice-dean of that chapter in 1543, a position he held until his death. In Liège he carried out the functions of inquisitor at least from 1529 on. In this capacity he actively supported the prince-bishops Erard de la *Marck, Cornelis van Bergen, and *George of Austria. He also maintained friendly relations with Girolamo *Aleandro, Gian Matteo *Giberti, Johannes *Fabri, Gerard *Morinck, *Arnold of Tongeren, Frans van *Cranevelt, Ignatius of Loyola, and other well-known contemporaries. In the end he increasingly took on the role of the unconditional defender of the University of Louvain.

Hezius' relationship with Erasmus is marked by contrasts. The mutual admiration shown in the first years subsequently changed to reserve, mistrust, and finally hostility. Only one of Hezius' letters to Erasmus is extant, and two letters from Erasmus to Hezius (one of them only tentatively assigned): Epp 1339, 1386, 1483. In December 1522 Erasmus no doubt referred to Hezius when he informed his friend Johann von *Botzheim that he was grateful for the intercession of a theologian not known to him personally who advised Adrian VI against supporting Erasmus' enemies (Ep 1331). One month later, on 25 January 1523, Hezius himself wrote a very flattering letter to Erasmus in which he showed his familiarity with Erasmus' works and gave his advance approval to any future actions against *Luther (Ep 1339). No doubt Erasmus replied to Hezius, whom he called a most candid theologian (Ep 1353), but the letter is now lost and there is no further evidence of contacts between them until September 1523, when Erasmus wrote a letter (Ep 1386) to a friend who may be identified as Hezius. Finally, on 2 September 1524, Erasmus sent Hezius a copy of his *De libero arbitrio* together with Ep 1483.

A change in their relationship came about in 1525 when Giberti, the datary of *Clement VII, sent Hezius to Louvain with orders to take action against Erasmus' enemies *Baechem and *Theodorici (Ep 1589A). Hezius obeyed, but the letters which he sent to Rome show clearly that he sided with the theologians of Louvain and found fault with Erasmus. He feared Erasmus' pen, however, and bound his correspondents to secrecy. Nevertheless, from the middle of the following year Erasmus realized what was going on (Ep 1717). He called the former papal secretary a viper (Ep 1875). From there on Hezius declared himself openly an enemy of Erasmus, opposing his ideas and his writings. In August 1530 he effected the confiscation of Erasmus' books found in the school of the Brethren of the Common Life in Liège (Epp 2369, 2566). Erasmus seems to have written to him on this subject (cf Ep 2587) and was still complaining about Hezius in 1533 (Ep 2842). *Paul III's favourable attitude towards Erasmus did not deter Hezius. On the contrary, he wrote to Aleandro, whom he knew to be an opponent of Erasmus, saying that his books led to heresy. He even went so far as to suggest that the papal brief (Epp 3021, 3033, 3034) was Erasmus' own fabrication or that of his supporters. Finally, in 1545, he contrived to have several of Erasmus' works put on the Index drawn up by the public authorities of the principality of Liège.

Despite this, Hezius was not an uncultured person, nor did he close his mind to learning and progress. Johann *Eck dedicated to him his *De purgatorio* (Rome: M. Franck 1523), Bruno Loher his edition of the *Enarrationes* of Johann Justus Landsberg (Cologne 1541), and Nicolas van *Winghe his Flemish translation of *De imitatione Christi* (Antwerp: H. Peetersen 1548).

Towards the end of his life he asked to be admitted to the Jesuit order, but his age proved an obstacle. Hezius' friends described him as gentle, prudent, reserved, modest, and disinterested. Today he is recognized as an efficient and knowledgeable collaborator with his various superiors in Louvain, Rome, and Liège. He died in Liège.

BIBLIOGRAPHY: Allen Ep 1339 / de Vocht *Literae ad Craneveldium* Ep 228 / de Vocht MHL 509–31 / E. Fairon 'Un dossier de l'inquisiteur liégeois Thierry Hezius' *Bulletin de la Commission royale d'histoire* 88 (Brussels 1924) 99–160 / J. Paquier *Jérôme Aléandre et la principauté de Liège* (Paris 1896) 297–307 / P. Balan *Monumenta Reformationis Lutheranae* (Regensburg 1884) 552, 561 / L.-E. Halkin *Le Cardinal de la Marck, prince-évêque de Liège* (Liège-Paris 1930) 151, 283 / L.-E. Halkin *Histoire religieuse des règnes de Corneille de Berghes et de Georges d'Autriche, princes-évêques de Liège* (Liège-Paris 1936) 116–128, 345–361, 401   LÉON-E. HALKIN

Michaël HILLEN of Hoogstraten, d 22 July 1558

Michaël Hillen (Hillenius Hoochstratanus) was born around 1476 in Hoogstraten, between Antwerp and Breda. From 1506 he worked in Antwerp as a printer, publisher, bookseller, and bookbinder. In 1546 he handed the business over to his son-in-law, Jan Steels, but continued to live in Antwerp to his death. A man of great energy, Hillen published in excess of five hundred works, including edicts of *Charles V, almanachs, works by humanistic authors such as Erasmus, Adrianus Cornelii *Barlandus, Georgius Macropedius, and Cornelius *Grapheus, and also material both for and against the ideas of *Luther. From the time of Erasmus' residence in Louvain, 1517–21, Hillen began to publish various of his works and continued to do so even after Erasmus' death.

Hillen is often mentioned in the correspondence of Erasmus and in some of his works. In early 1519 he published Jacobus *Latomus' dialogues *De trium linguarum et studii theologici ratione*, which prompted Erasmus to reply with an *Apologia* (*Opuscula* 286; Ep 934). Later that year he eventually declined to print Edward *Lee's critique of Erasmus' New Testament at the same time that he produced an edition of

Erasmus' paraphrases to some of the Pauline Epistles, a coincidence eagerly debated in the quarrel between Lee and Erasmus (*Apologia invectivis Lei* in *Opuscula* 252–5, 286; Epp 1053, 1061). In 1534 Hillen angered Erasmus by publishing a book of sermons by the Franciscan Nikolaus *Ferber which contained vigorous attacks on Erasmus' orthodoxy (Ep 2896). To Erasmus' disappointment his complaints to the court of Brussels did not result in Hillen's being punished, although the court apparently succeeded in scaring him (Epp 2899, 2922, 2948, 2981, 3053).

BIBLIOGRAPHY: Allen Ep 1053 / A.G. Demanet in BNB IX 377–80 / A. Rouzet *Dictionnaire des imprimeurs, libraires et éditeurs des XVe et XVIe siècles dans les limites géographiques de la Belgique actuelle* (Nieuwkoop 1975) 94–6
MARCEL A. NAUWELAERTS & PGB

Theobald HILLWEG of Thann, c 1450–20 April 1535
In May 1524 Erasmus agreed to support Ambrosius *Kettenacker in his conflict with the Cistercian abbot of Wettingen, Andreas *Wengi; to do so he wrote Ep 1447, to another unnamed abbot expected to have some influence with Wengi. He was very probably the abbot of Lucelle (Lützel), in the Jura between Delémont and Porrentruy. Lucelle was the principal Cistercian house of that region and the mother house from which Wettingen had been founded; the abbots of the two houses visited one another frequently (Chèvre 45, 97, 118).

Theobald Hillweg (Hyllweg) of Thann, in Upper Alsace, had been cellarer of Lucelle when he was elected abbot on 14 or 15 October 1495. Faced with enormous problems, Hillweg showed exceptional ability. Twice he rebuilt his monastery after it had been destroyed, by Swiss troops in 1499 and again by rebelling peasants in 1525. By purchasing land he doubled the extent of Lucelle and brought two additional priories under the sway of its abbots. When iconoclasm swept through the streets of Basel at the height of the Reformation crisis, Hillweg personally carried a statue of the Virgin away to safety from the Lützelhof, the abbey's house at Basel. He resigned his abbacy on 20 May 1532 at the age of eighty-two.

BIBLIOGRAPHY: Allen Ep 1447 / André Chèvre *Lucelle* ([Delémont] 1973) 119–29 and passim
PGB

Balthasar HILTBRAND of Basel (Ep 2372 of 31 August 1530)
In this letter Bonifacius *Amerbach informed Erasmus of an expedition to Liestal, south-east of Basel, in which the *Oberzunftmeister* ('tribunus') took part. This office was held for the year beginning in June 1530 by Balthasar Hiltbrand. The passage is not clear, however, and it has also been suggested that Amerbach might be referring to Marx Heidelin or to Jakob *Meyer zum Hirzen, both of whom held the position in other years.

BIBLIOGRAPHY: Allen Ep 2372 / AK III Ep 1462 / BA *Oekolampads* II 466, 476–7
PGB

Hieronymus HIRSCHKOREN documented at Strasbourg, 1533
Hieronymus Hirschkoren has not been identified. In 1533 Johann *Löble stated (Ep 2808) that Hirschkoren and Johann *Ebel were holding money for Erasmus in Strasbourg; the two men were business associates of Friedrich *Prechter.
MIRIAM U. CHRISMAN

Toussaint d'HOCÉDY, Panagius HOCEDIUS
See Toussaint HOSSEY

HOCHSTRATUS, HOECHSTRATENSIS
See HOOGSTRATEN and Antoine de LALAING

Cornelis Henricxzoon HOEN d 1524
Cornelis Hoen (Hoon, Honius, Honnius), once a fellow-pupil of Maarten van *Dorp at St Jerome's school, Utrecht, was a lawyer attached to the council of Holland at The Hague. He may have been the man Dorp mentioned as a supporter of Martin *Luther in 1519 (Ep 1044). Among the books left by Dorp's uncle, Jacob Hoeck (Angularius, d 1509), Hoen had found Wessel *Gansfort's *De sacramento eucharistiae*, which incited him to reject transubstantiation and to interpret Christ's words 'This is my body' symbolically. By 1521 he included that view in his famous letter on the Eucharist which was carried by Hinne Rode to Germany and Switzerland. Luther disapproved of it, but it influenced Huldrych *Zwingli, who edited it in 1525 (Ep 1621): *Epistola christiana admodum* (n

p; modern facsimile edition by Eekhof). It was soon translated into German. In February 1523 Hoen was arrested on a charge of heresy and prosecuted by the Inquisitor Frans van der *Hulst; with a short intermission (Ep 1358) he was held in custody until October (Ep 1394). While he was in prison, Cornelis *Gerard sent him a consolatory letter, 'De patientia'. He also addressed his *Apocalypsis* to him. Erasmus followed these developments with interest – he seems to have been an old friend of Hoen – and still remembered him in 1533 (Ep 2800).

BIBLIOGRAPHY: Allen Ep 1358 / A. Eekhof in NNBW VI 787–8 / J.N. Bakhuizen van den Brink in RGG III 441 / O. Clemen in *Realencyklopädie für protestantische Theologie und Kirche* ed A. Hauck VIII (Leipzig 1900) 312–13 / *Biographisch woordenboek van protestantsche godgeleerden in Nederland* ed J.P. de Bie and J. Loosjes IV (The Hague 1931) 90–2 / N. van der Zijpp in *The Mennonite Encyclopedia* (Scottdale 1955–7) II 776 / A. Eekhof *De Avondmaalsbrief van Cornelis Hoen* (The Hague 1917) / M. van Rhijn *Studiën over Wessel Gansfort en zijn tijd* (Utrecht 1933) 38ff   C.G. VAN LEIJENHORST

Hendrik HOEVELMANS of Westerhoven, documented 1505–after 1521

Hendrik Hoevelmans (Hovelmans) of Westerhoven, in North Brabant, matriculated at Louvain in February 1505 as a student of the College of the Falcon. He was promoted licentiate in theology on 26 January 1518. In 1520 he was curate of the collegiate church of Notre Dame in Antwerp and, apparently on instructions received from the Louvain theologians, began to attack Erasmus from his pulpit (Ep 1165). Probably in July 1521 Hoevelmans wrote to the papal nuncio Girolamo *Aleandro, whose reply from Ghent is extant. An undated but apparently later record of Hoevelmans is in Molanus.

BIBLIOGRAPHY: Allen Ep 1165 / E. Reusens *Documents relatifs à l'histoire de l'Université de Louvain (1425–1797)* (Louvain 1881–1903) III 39 / H. de Jongh *L'Ancienne Faculté de théologie de Louvain* (Louvain 1911) 43* / *Matricule de Louvain* III-1 288 / *Lettres familières de Jérôme Aléandre* ed J. Paquier (Paris 1909) Ep 45 / Johannes Molanus *Historiae Lovaniensium libri XIV* ed P.F.X. de Ram (Brussels 1861) I 648   MARCEL A. NAUWELAERTS

Joost van der HOEVEN d 11/12 July 1536

Joost van der Hoeven, probably of Louvain, had obtained a MA by the time when he was appointed notary and beadle at the faculty of divinity at Louvain. He had married Katrien Maes before 14 August 1511, when they made a joint will. After his wife's death he became depressed and this seems to have caused him to neglect his duties. His performance was criticized by the faculty on 30 September 1515 and 30 September 1517. In 1520 he was given an assistant, who later succeeded him as beadle (30 September 1532). By 1520 Joost van der Hoeven had taken a second wife, Anna Loens, who became the mother of his son, Antoon. As counsel to St Martin's priory, on 29 February 1524 he requested the incorporation of that institute into the university, which was granted in 1525.

After being widowed for the second time, van der Hoeven was appointed president of the Collegium Trilingue on 1 December 1529, in succession to Nicolas *Wary. His experience in academic life and administration and his acquaintance with the members of the faculty and the trustees of Jérôme de *Busleyden's will, especially with Bartholomeus van *Vessem, enabled him to carry on successfully the management of the prosperous, well-regulated college Wary had left behind. He kept careful accounts which have survived and provide valuable insight into the history of the college at that time. In general, he was well liked, although in the case of Jan van *Campen, who left the Trilingue in 1531, he seems to have shown little patience. In his will he founded scholarships in the Trilingue and in the College of the Holy Ghost.

Joost van der Hoeven was well acquainted with Erasmus, who referred to him in Ep 2876.

BIBLIOGRAPHY: Allen Ep 2876 / de Vocht CTL II 103–4, 636, III 9–11 and passim / de Vocht *Busleyden* 460 / H. de Jongh *L'Ancienne Faculté de théologie de Louvain* (Louvain 1911) 39*, 60*–1*   IG

Hugo von HOHENLANDENBERG d 7 January 1532

Hugo von Hohenlandenberg (Landenberg), born in 1457 or 1460 in Oberwinterthur, came from an old family with estates in the territory

Hans Holbein the Younger, self-portrait

of Zürich. He was provost of St Mary's in Erfurt in 1484 and matriculated at Erfurt in 1487, being then a canon of Constance, Basel, and Chur. On 7 May 1496 he was elected bishop of Constance and was soon involved in difficult negotiations with the city, which was attempting to strengthen its authority amid interference both by the Swiss cantons and by the Emperor *Maximilian I. At first he took a stand against indulgences and sided with Huldrych *Zwingli; he introduced reforms in his diocese (Ep 1342), appointed Johannes *Fabri as his vicar-general, and did not obstruct the spread of *Luther's and Zwingli's ideas. But after Zwingli's publication of the *Apologeticus Archeteles adpellatus* [Zurich: C. Froschauer] in August 1522 (Epp 1315, 1331), he began to oppose the reformers. His efforts to dismiss Johann *Wanner, a Lutheran preacher at Constance, were thwarted by the citizens and the council (Epp 1382, 1401). He also seems to have been responsible for the investigation for heresy against Johann von *Botzheim on account of his sympathy with the reformers (Epp 1519, 1555; AK II Ep 989). If Botzheim is to be believed, Hugo's motives for doing so were

discreditable, since the action was designed to cover up the bishop's liaison with a burgher's wife (Ep 1555; AK II Ep 991).

All had been well when Erasmus visited Constance in September 1522; the bishop honoured him as best he could and in turn was praised by Erasmus as kind and noble, sincere and free from pride (Epp 1316, 1342). But between 1523 and 1527 Botzheim commented on the bishop's actions against him (Epp 1519, 1540) and against the Lutherans (Epp 1401, 1454, 1540). Antagonized by the growing reform movement in Constance, the bishop and the chapter withdrew from the city towards the end of 1526, and Hugo lived henceforward in his castle at Meersburg. Efforts at reconciliation between the bishop and the city in 1528 were unsuccessful, and Hugo von Hohenlandenberg resigned his see in 1529; however, the sudden death of his successor, Balthasar *Merklin, forced him to resume episcopal duties for the last months of his life.

BIBLIOGRAPHY: Allen 1316 / Rublack *Reformation in Konstanz* 2–10, 16–19, 45–6, and passim / Bernd Moeller *Johannes Zwick und die Reformation in Konstanz* (Gütersloh 1961) 52, 85–91 / E. Egli 'Hugo von Landenberg, Bischof von Konstanz' *Zwingliana* 1 (1897–1904) 185–91 / Jörg Vögeli *Schriften zur Reformation in Konstanz* ed A. Vögeli (Tübingen 1973) passim / *Matrikel Basel* I 89 / *Matrikel Erfurt* I 418   IG

Wilhelm von HOHENSTEIN *See Wilhelm von* HONSTEIN

Hans HOLBEIN the Younger of Augsburg, 1497/8–1543
Painter, miniaturist, designer of woodcuts and painted glass, jewellery, metalwork, etc, Hans Holbein the Younger was a son of the Augsburg painter Hans Holbein the Elder (c 1465–1524) and the younger brother of the painter Ambrosius (c 1494–1519?).

Holbein arrived in Basel from Augsburg by the end of 1515 and executed his first portraits there in 1516. In 1517 he worked on his first wall decoration on the façade of the Hertenstein-Haus, Lucerne, from where it has been assumed, on the slenderest of evidence, he made a brief visit to northern Italy. Returning to Basel he joined the painters' guild on 25 September 1519, and in addition to painting portraits he worked for the book printers. His principal commission in Basel was the decoration of the council chamber in the Rathaus in 1521 and 1522 and again in 1530. He visited France briefly in 1524 and by the autumn of 1526 was in England, where his chief patrons were Sir Thomas *More and Sir Henry *Guildford. He was back in Basel by 19 August 1528, when he bought a house. There he painted his renowned *Portrait of his Wife and Children* (Ganz *Paintings* no 52). He returned to England in 1532 and had certainly arrived by 2 September. There he remained until his death, except for a continental tour from March 1538 to January 1539, visiting mainly France and staying briefly in Basel from 10 September to 16 October, and a second continental trip in the summer of 1539. In London he worked chiefly for the Hanseatic Merchants until, possibly by 1535, certainly by 1536, he was appointed a court painter to *Henry VIII. His chief royal commission was the wall-painting of the Tudor dynasty that was formerly in the Whitehall Palace but was destroyed by fire in 1698. Its appearance is known from copies and from the survival of part of the original cartoon for the fresco. Holbein's will was dated 7 October 1543; he was buried on 29 November of that year.

Erasmus first encountered Holbein when the artist arrived in Basel from his native Augsburg as a young journeyman, most probably at the latest by the end of autumn 1515. An earlier date seems unlikely, since the attribution to him of the so-called 'Holbein' painted table-top, now in Zürich (Ganz *Paintings* no 152), is no longer tenable. Holbein's earliest surviving work appears to be drawings in the margins of a copy of the second edition of Erasmus' *Moria* (Basel: J. Froben spring 1515) that belonged to the humanist and schoolmaster Osvaldus *Myconius, originally Geisshüsler (1488–1552). The majority of these can be confidently attributed to Holbein, and only a few are by his brother, Ambrosius. According to Myconius' inscription on the first page, all the drawings were done in ten days at the end of 1515 and the beginning of 1516. By one of these, that of *Erasmus at work writing the Adages*, Myconius has noted that when Erasmus saw this drawing (Ganz *Handzeichnungen* L no 64) he said, 'Aha,

Elizabeth Binzenstock, wife of Hans Holbein, by Hans Holbein the Younger

aha, if Erasmus now looked like that he would immediately take a wife.' It may be that this prompted in reply the marginal drawing, *The Man* [perhaps Erasmus] *distracted by the Pretty Woman steps on the Egg-seller's Basket* (Ganz *Handzeichnungen* L no 3), which seems plausible in that this drawing is unrelated to the text. At this time Holbein evidently must have met Erasmus' Basel printer, Johann *Froben, for whom by October 1516 the artist was designing title-pages.

We have grounds for asserting that Ambrosius Holbein was then in Basel with his brother because they each painted a side of the Schoolmaster's Sign (Ganz *Paintings* nos 153, 154) dated 1516, evidently for Myconius, before the latter departed in the same year to teach in the Stiftsschule in Zürich.

In 1523 Holbein painted two portraits of Erasmus which were sent to England (Ep 1452), one of them destined for William *Warham, archbishop of Canterbury (Ep 1488). The archbishop's portrait could be that which depicts Erasmus resting his hands on a book bearing the inscription 'The Labours of Hercules' in Greek and is now in the collection of the earl of Radnor (Ganz *Paintings* no 34; Allen v 534). The second portrait may be that of Erasmus writing, now in the Louvre (Ganz *Paintings* no 36; Allen v 470). A third portrait of 1523, at Basel, shows even more clearly that Erasmus is writing his Paraphrase on Mark, published by Froben in 1523 (Ganz *Paintings* no 35). In the Louvre (Ganz *Handzeichnungen* 7) there is a sheet of silverpoint and black chalk studies of Erasmus's hands used in these portraits of 1523.

When Holbein, prompted by the rising tide of social and religious unrest in Basel, sought patronage in England for the first time, Erasmus played a key role. Holbein left for England bearing a letter dated 29 August 1526 to Pieter *Gillis at Antwerp (Ep 1740). In it, Erasmus recommended Holbein as 'insignis artifex' and asked that he might be introduced to Quinten *Metsys. Holbein cannot have been long in Antwerp because More wrote to Erasmus on 18 December 1526 (Ep 1770) singing the artist's praises and indicating that he already had proof of his genius. He warned Erasmus against having too high hopes of Holbein's advancement in England but undertook to do all he could to help him. More kept his word, introducing him into court circles and commissioning him to produce a group portrait of himself and his family, now lost. Its composition is most accurately recorded in a drawing by Holbein (Ganz *Handzeichnungen* no 24), which was sent to Erasmus, almost certainly borne by the artist himself on his return to Basel in 1528, with annotations by Nikolaus *Kratzer giving the identities of the sitters and their ages. Erasmus had certainly received it by 5 September 1529, when he mentioned it in a letter to More (Ep 2211). On 6 September he wrote a charming letter to Margaret *More (Ep 2212), sending greetings to the family and saying how vividly they were all brought into mind through Holbein.

Erasmus also turned to Holbein to produce various versions of his device, Terminus. In 1525 he gave to Basel University a glass painting of the Terminus, preserved now only in Holbein's preparatory design (Ganz *Handzeichnungen* 201; Allen VII 430), based on the reverse of Quinten Metsys' medal of 1519. Probably after 1532 Holbein executed a related painted version, now in Cleveland, Ohio (J.

Rowlands in *The Bulletin of the Cleveland Museum of Art*, February 1980, 50–4). The device makes a final appearance in Holbein's elaborate woodcut portrait, *Erasmus 'im Gehäus'* (Woltmann II 184, no 206; Allen XI 142). It can be dated approximately from the inscription on the first state of the print, consisting of the first two lines of a poem by Gilbert *Cousin which was published in Hieronymus *Froben's edition of the *Adagia* of 1535. The features, like those in the rounded woodcut portrait of 1533 (Woltmann II 185, no 207) are based on those of Holbein's image of the aged scholar, the roundel portrait, now in Basel (Ganz *Paintings* no 60; Allen IX 226), which must have been executed just before Holbein left for his second stay in England. To this time also belongs the series of portraits of Erasmus derived in their pose from his portrait of 1523 in the Radnor Collection and in their features from the roundel portrait. The best version is that now in the Lehmann Collection, the Metropolitan Museum, New York (Ganz *Paintings* no 57). Unfortunately, from the postscript, dated 10 April, to a letter of 22 March 1533 to Bonifacius *Amerbach (Ep 2788) we learn that Erasmus became disappointed in Holbein's behaviour. He complained about his delaying over a month in Antwerp en route to England in the previous year. Apparently Erasmus had only heard of the delay the following spring, after receiving letters of complaint from one or two English correspondents about the artist. There is no indication in the letter as to the way in which the unnamed friends of Erasmus were deceived by Holbein.

BIBLIOGRAPHY: Allen Ep 1397 / H. Reinhardt in NDB IX 515–20 / Alfred Woltmann *Holbein und seine Zeit* 2nd ed (Leipzig 1874–6) / Paul Ganz *Die Handzeichnungen Hans Holbein d.J.: Kritischer Katalog* (Berlin 1937) / Edgar Wind 'Aenigma Termini' *Journal of the Warburg Institute* 1 (1937–8) 68–9 / Paul Ganz *The Paintings of Hans Holbein* (London 1950) / Erwin Panofsky 'Erasmus and the Visual Arts' *Journal of the Warburg and Courtauld Institutes* 32 (1969) 200–7 / A. Gerlo *Erasme et ses portraitistes, Metsijs, Dürer, Holbein* 2nd ed (Nieuwkoop 1969) 45–67 / James McConica 'The Riddle of the Terminus' *Erasmus in English* 2 (1971) 2–7 / John Rowlands 'The Device of Erasmus of Rotterdam: a Painting by Holbein' *The Bulletin of the Cleve-*

land Museum of Art (February 1980) 50–4 / Hans Reinhardt 'Erasmus und Holbein' *Basler Zeitschrift für Geschichte und Altertumskunde* 81 (1981) 41–70   JOHN ROWLANDS

Lambertus HOLLONIUS of Liège, documented 1518, d before 25 May 1522
The earliest, and scanty, reference to Hollonius (Lambert de Hollogne, Hologne), 'personnage sans relief,' as he is called by Lucien Febvre, is found in *Beatus Rhenanus' preface (dated 22 November 1518; BRE Ep 80) to the first, unauthorized edition of *Familiarium colloquiorum formulae* (Basel: J. Froben, November 1518). This small book, which Erasmus thought permanently lost, was published 'thanks to a young and learned man from Liège, Lambertus Hollonius.' On 1 January 1519 Erasmus disowned the Basel edition in his preface (Ep 909) to the first authorized and expanded edition of the work (Louvain: D. Martens 1 March 1519), but this letter is hardly more informative about Hollonius. Erasmus declared his willingness to forgive Hollonius for having released the manuscript into Beatus' hands, if he in turn would render him a more valuable service. What Erasmus expected of Hollonius was efficient collaboration in the correction of the proofs for the New Testament, a task for which he had been sent to Basel together with *Menard of Hoorn at the end of October 1518 (AK II Ep 642). On 5 December 1518 Hollonius had written to Erasmus, 'his most beloved teacher,' to give an account of his mission: he made no mention of the publication of the *Formulae* but heaped compliment upon compliment, as if he wanted to appease Erasmus in advance. He also announced that he had entered the service of the printer Johann *Froben, at the request of Beatus Rhenanus, perhaps in exchange for Erasmus' unpublished manuscript (Ep 904). Erasmus later accused Hollonius of having threatened Froben with selling the manuscript to one of his competitors for a higher price (Ep 3100), but there is no evidence to corroborate this statement. Froben, who seems to have had a high opinion of his new proof-reader, does not provide us with any information on the manner in which the young man from Liège obtained possession of the *Formulae*. Hollonius may have purchased one of the copies circu-

lated by Augustinus Vincentius *Caminadus, or he may simply have taken the manuscript from Erasmus' rooms, where he lived in Louvain. In fact, Erasmus had recently recovered from Roger *Wentford what appears to be another manuscript of the work. The unpublished manuscript presented an unexpected opportunity to a young man who sought employment in a printing house. Hollonius may thus have been unable to resist the temptation to borrow the manuscript and submit it to Beatus Rhenanus, furnishing him with the information which he was able to gather about the history of the book. His unscrupulous action set a precedent and example for all who were in possession of an unpublished work by Erasmus. It was perhaps for this reason that the humanist, who had previously abused Vincentius Caminadius, now directed the full force of his anger against Hollonius, especially after the young man's death (Ep 1284).

In the preface to one of his three tragedies, Gregorius Hollonius, the neo-Latin poet, informs us that his uncle on his father's side was a 'perfect Latinist, but also versed in Greek and Hebrew,' who had studied theology and travelled to Italy to visit the holy places of Rome, where he had died. But he gives no precise date for his death. Nor does he provide information about his uncle's studies, although we know that the young Lambert was acquainted with Adrianus Cornelii *Barlandus and Rutgerus *Rescius and may well have been their student, as was his colleague Menard van Hoorn (Ep 904). His nephew hints that he left some writings of which he himself had seen only a few fragments. The only extant text by Lambertus Hollonius is Ep 904, in which he links Erasmus and *Luther in praise.

For a long time Lambertus Hollonius was considered the first printer of Liège. This error has its origin in a marginal note found in the preface (Ep 1284) of an edition of *De conscribendis epistolis* (n p 1534) which is kept in the library of the University of Liège. The note says: 'Hollonius of Liège, printer, the first to publish the *Colloquia*.' Hollonius was certainly from Liège, since his name derives from Hollogne, near Liège, but his involvement in printing is documented only for Basel. If Hollonius was not the first to print the

Formulae, one may at any rate consider, as did his contemporaries, that he was responsible for publishing the text that eventually became the *Colloquia*. This is his only claim to glory, and not a small one at that.

BIBLIOGRAPHY: Allen and CWE Ep 904 / BNB IX 436 / H. Helbig 'Les Holonius ou de Hologne' *Messager des sciences historiques* (1877) 201–4 / J. Brassinne 'L'imprimerie à Liège jusqu'à la fin de l'ancien régime' in *Histoire du livre et de l'imprimerie en Belgique des origines à nos jours* V (Brussels 1929) 13 / Xavier de Theux de Montjardin *Bibliographie liégeoise* (Bruges 1885) ii / Anne Rouzet *Dictionnaire des imprimeurs, libraires et éditeurs des XVe et XVIe siècles dans les limites géographiques de la Belgique actuelle* (Nieuwkoop 1975) 97 / Gregorius Holonius *Laurentias* (Antwerp: J. Bellerus 1556) ff A^ii verso-A^iii recto / Lucien Febvre *Un destin: Martin Luther* (Paris 1968) 81–2 / Franz Bierlaire *Erasme et ses Colloques: le livre d'une vie* (Geneva 1977) 13–20 / Franz Bierlaire 'Erasme, les imprimeurs et les *Colloques*' *Gutenberg-Jahrbuch* (1978) 106   FRANZ BIERLAIRE

John HOLT of Chichester,
d before 14 June 1504
There is strong reason to identify 'our friend Holt' spoken of by Erasmus in his letter to Andrea *Ammonio of December 1513 (Ep 283) with the John Holt (Holte, Holtigena, Holtt) of Chichester, Sussex, who was at Magdalen College, Oxford, from 1490 to 1496. Holt received his MA in 1494, was ordained priest in 1495, and around 1496 was schoolmaster in the archbishop's school at Lambeth Palace, London. This distinguished schoolmaster was a friend of Thomas *More and taught in Lambeth school immediately after More had been a student there. There is concrete evidence of friendship between More and this John Holt in More's letter to him of 1501 (Rogers Ep 2), which has much to say about William *Grocyn and his lectures on the *Hierarchia ecclesiastica* of Dionysius. That the relationship continued is manifest by the publication in 1510 of Holt's Latin grammar in English, the *Lac puerorum* (STC 13604), which is introduced and concluded by two verses composed by the young Thomas More. Meanwhile, in 1502 Holt had been appointed tutor to the future *Henry VIII

in succession to John *Skelton. From 1501 to his death he was also schoolmaster and prebendary at Chichester. His will was proved on 14 June 1504. The incident referred to in Erasmus' letter to Ammonio – of Holt showing him some pages on trivial subjects – must have occurred in 1499 during Erasmus' first visit to England, when it would surely have been More who introduced Erasmus and Holt.

However, the Holt mentioned in Ep 283 could also be one Nicholas Holt, master of the grammar school of St Anthony's Hospital, London (documented c 1491–5), who taught Thomas More and probably also John *Colet.

BIBLIOGRAPHY: Allen and CWE Ep 283 / Emden BRUO II 953–4 / Rogers Ep 2 / A.W. Reed 'Young More' in *Under God and the Law* ed R. O'Sullivan (London 1949) 1–8 / R.S. Stanier *Magdalen School* (Oxford 1940) 36   R.J. SCHOECK

Eucharius HOLZACH of Basel, 1486–13 November 1558
Eucharius Holzach was the son of another Eucharius (d 1521), who was mayor (*Schultheiss*) of Kleinbasel. After attending the school at Sélestat, the younger Eucharius was admitted to the University of Basel in 1500. From 1501 to 1506 he studied at Paris in the company of the *Amerbach sons, as he had done previously at Sélestat. On 1 September 1506 he matriculated at the University of Montpellier, where he received a medical doctorate in 1511. After his permanent return to Basel he practised medicine privately but was also appointed town physician, and was a member of the medical faculty from 1524. He was married first to Veronica Rispach and after her death to Lucia Gerolt, and had eight children. In 1535 he visited his sons, who were then studying at Paris, and revived memories from his own student days.

Holzach grew up and lived in the Rheingasse, not far from the home of Johann *Amerbach. Bonifacius *Amerbach's wife was related to him, and Bonifacius later took a friendly interest in Holzach's sons. In Ep 2323 Bonifacius reminded Erasmus that in his years in Basel he had entrusted himself to Holzach's medical care.

BIBLIOGRAPHY: Allen Ep 2323 / *Matrikel Basel* I 260 / *Matricule de Montpellier* 9 / *Wappenbuch der*

Stadt Basel ed W.R. Staehelin (Basel [1917–30]) / AK I Ep 65, III Ep 1183, IV Ep 1951, and passim / Albrecht Burckhardt *Geschichte der medizinischen Fakultät zu Basel* (Basel 1917) 21, 45

PGB

Jan de HONDT d 24 November 1571

Jan de Hondt (Hont, Canis, Canius) was said to be eighty-five at the time of his death and thus may have been born in 1486; most likely he was a native of Sint-Pauwels-Waas, in East Flanders. He matriculated as an arts student at the University of Louvain on 8 October 1503. In 1506 he described himself in a book he owned as a licentiate in arts and a cleric of the diocese of Tournai. In 1514 he was a chaplain of St Willebrord, Hulst (Zeeland, adjacent to the Waas district), and also a chaplain of Courtrai. In the same year he contributed a poem to Eligius Hockaert's *Tractatus de penitentia* (1514). Probably from 1 January 1517, he was a canon of Our Lady's, Courtrai, since Pierre *Barbier resigned to him a prebend against an annuity payable to Erasmus. On 20 October 1519 he was curate of St Martin's, Courtrai, and dean of the rural parishes of Courtrai (Ep 1094), functions which he resigned on 30 April 1520 to Jacob van *Thielt but held again later on. In 1534 he was secretary of his chapter and on 10 March 1541 he was elected precentor in succession to Jacob van Thielt. Musical talent evidently ran in his family, which also produced Cornelius Canis and other musicians. From 1545 to 1550 de Hondt also held the benefice of the parish of St Brice at Marche, in Belgian Luxembourg, and in 1551 he received a prebend of St Saviour's, Bruges, and the chaplaincy of the hospital of Hulst. He undertook various missions for the Courtrai chapter and liberally supported pious foundations both in his lifetime and by his will, dated 28 August 1571, which is extant. The inventory of his remarkable library has also survived. He owned many patristic volumes as well as works by Jan *Driedo, Frans *Titelmans, Stanislaus *Hosius, and others. His colleague and friend Frans Heeme (Haemus) celebrated his memory in his *Poemata* (Antwerp: C. Plantinus 1578).

Erasmus' contacts with de Hondt concerned for the most part the annuity in Erasmus' favour which was settled upon de Hondt's prebend (Epp 436, 751, 1094, 1458, 1621, 1862,

2404), and their correspondence dealing with the complicated transactions resulting from this arrangement awaits investigation by an expert in the field. Erasmus always found de Hondt reliable and prompt in his payments, even beyond the call of duty (Epp 794, 913, 1235, 1848, 1849, 1993, 2024, 2364, 2403, 2404, 2413, 2558), and responded with feelings of genuine friendship (Epp 1695, 1769, 2961). When delays occurred in the payments he was inclined to blame Barbier, through whose hands the money had to pass at least nominally (Epp 2243, 2356). After 1530 the correspondence offers no evidence of further payments by de Hondt. As Barbier, who was heavily in debt, owed him money, the Courtrai canon no longer felt obliged to make him payments for the benefit of Erasmus and evidently believed that it was now up to Barbier to settle Erasmus' annuity directly (Epp 2527, 2704).

The contacts between de Hondt and Erasmus were not entirely confined to financial matters. In 1520 de Hondt recommended to Erasmus a student by the name of *Soti who was setting out for Louvain (Ep 1094). Another common acquaintance was Michael *Bentinus, who often worked for the Basel printers between 1520 and 1527 and in 1524 persuaded Erasmus, needlessly perhaps, that he ought to reassure de Hondt about his attitude towards the reformers (Epp 1433, 1471).

BIBLIOGRAPHY: Allen Ep 751 / *Matricule de Louvain* III-1 266; cf 226, 453, 506 / de Vocht CTL III 513–14 and passim / de Vocht *Literae ad Craneveldium* Ep 134 and passim / P. Gorissen 'Het Kortrijkse pensioen van Erasmus' *De Leiegouw* 13 (1971) 107–51 / Cornelis van Auwater *Epistolae et carmina* ed H. de Vocht (Louvain 1957) 101–3 / C. Caullet *Musiciens de la Collégiale Notre-Dame à Courtrai* (Courtrai-Bruges 1911) 92–103 and passim / *Testaments d'une centaine de membres du Chapitre de Notre-Dame à Courtrai, 1328–1650* ed Cercle historique et archéologique de Courtrai (Bruges-Courtrai [1922]) 37, 49, 51, 74, and passim

PGB

Margareta HONORA *See Margareta* HEYEN

Antoine HONORAT *See Antoine Honorat, sieur d'*ORAISON

Wilhelm von HONSTEIN c 1470–
29 June 1541
Wilhelm von Honstein was the son of an
important noble family of Thuringia. Brought
up by his great-uncle, Berthold von Henne-
berg, archbishop of Mainz, Wilhelm was
trained both as a diplomat and as an ecclesiastical administrator. He attended the universities
of Erfurt (1486–8), Padua (1492), and Freiburg
(1494–5), following the law curriculum. By
1494 he already held benefices in the cathedral
chapters of Mainz, Cologne, and Strasbourg
and served as rector of the University of
Freiburg, as he had formerly done at Erfurt.
After being appointed vicar-general of Mainz
in 1505, he was elected bishop of Strasbourg in
1506 and held his solemn entry in October
1507.
    Honstein was pious and well educated. He
made a serious attempt to reform the diocese
through the renewal of monastic and clerical
discipline, but he lacked incisive leadership.
He took a firm position against the Reformation
and struggled to maintain the Roman Catholic
cause, especially in the territories under
episcopal sovereignty. In 1524 *Botzheim reported his presence at a gathering of princes in
Heidelberg (Ep 1454). In 1540 he presided at
the religious colloquy in Haguenau. He died at
the episcopal palace in Saverne. Wilhelm was a
patron of music and art rather than of letters.
He built St Martin's chapel in Strasbourg
cathedral.

BIBLIOGRAPHY: Allen Ep 1454 / ADB XLIII
205–7 / Johann Ficker and Otto Winckelmann
Handschriftenproben des sechzehnten Jahrhunderts
(Strasbourg 1902) I 37 / François Rapp *Réformes
et Réformation à Strasbourg, 1450–1525* (Paris
1974) 371–98 / *Matrikel Erfurt* I 411, 421 /
Matrikel Freiburg I 113

MIRIAM U. CHRISMAN

Jan HONT *See Jan de* HONDT

Andreas of HOOGSTRATEN
d 29 February 1528
Andreas of Hoogstraten (Hoochstratus,
Hoechstratensis) was named after his native
town of Hoogstraten, some thirty kilometres
northeast of Antwerp, where his family resided
and possessed property. The family name
apparently was Meeus or Meeussen. Andreas

himself went to live at Liège, where he was
appointed canon and subsequently dean of the
chapter of Saint-Denis. From Liège he may
have visited Orléans in 1504 for study. No
information has come to light about the
beginnings of his friendship with Erasmus. In
August 1514, when Erasmus went to Liège
and hoped to see him, he happened to be away
– perhaps he had gone to visit his family – so
Erasmus left a short note for him at his house
(Ep 299). Hoogstraten did not answer until
January 1516, when he had received a fresh
letter and a gift from Erasmus. As Erasmus had
missed him on his journey to Basel, Hoogstraten urged him to be his guest on his return,
especially since he would also find in Liège his
old friend Girolamo *Aleandro (Ep 381).
Whether he actually visited Liège is not
known. In December 1517 he had not heard
from Hoogstraten for some time (Ep 725); after
that Hoogstraten is not mentioned in Erasmus'
correspondence. His will, however, is preserved in manuscript. Dated 27 February 1528
it leaves to one of his nephews, Jan, the son of
his sister Antonia, a number of theological
works including Erasmus' paraphrases. Hoogstraten died two days later.

BIBLIOGRAPHY: E. Schoolmeesters 'Les
doyens de la collégiale de Saint-Denis' *Leodium*
9 (1910) 97, 128 / J. Deckers 'Le chapitre de la
collégiale Saint-Denis de Liège' *Bulletin de
l'Institut archéologique liégeois* 84 (1972) 178 / L.
Naveau and A. Poullet *Recueil d'épitaphes de
Henri van den Berch* (Liège 1925) I 128 /
Matricule d'Orléans II-1 248–9

LÉON-E. HALKIN

Jacob of HOOGSTRATEN d 21 January 1527
Jacob of Hoogstraten (Hoogstraeten, Hog-
stratus, Hoecstratus) was generally known by
the name of his native town, north-east of
Antwerp. Erasmus claimed to be older than he
was (Ep 1006), but that hardly seems possible
since Hoogstraten matriculated at the University of Louvain on 31 August 1479. In 1485 he
was promoted MA, with the highest standing at
that graduation. He taught for a while in the
College of the Falcon, where he had been a
student. He entered the Dominican order and
was ordained priest before moving on to
Cologne, where he enrolled on 10 September
1496, became a licentiate in theology on 5

March 1503 and took his doctor's degree on 10 February 1504. In 1500, 1505, and 1508 he was prior of the convent of Antwerp and in 1510 of that of Cologne. From 1505 to 1507 he was regent of the Dominican studium at Cologne, and he also taught theology at the university.

The first of several controversies in which he took an active part involved Petrus Ravennas (Pietro Tomasi of Ravenna) and broadened into a quarrel between humanists and conservative theologians. Following the publication of Hoogstraten's defensive tracts *Justificatio ... dissolvens rationes ... Petri Ravennatis* (Cologne: H. Bungart c 1507) and *Defensio scolastica* (Cologne: J. Landen 1508) and before his *Purgatorium detractorum* was published in October 1509, Ravennas had to leave Cologne. In the same year a new issue arose between Johann *Pfefferkorn, who wanted the destruction of all Hebrew books, and *Reuchlin, who defended the value of the study of the ancient languages. Hoogstraten, who in 1510 was appointed inquisitor of the archdioceses of Cologne, Mainz, and Trier, supported Pfefferkorn and his backers (Ep 615); he even went to Rome to plead their cause (1514–17). Although Erasmus was on excellent terms with Reuchlin (Epp 290, 300), he did not become involved in this quarrel and did not approve of the acrimonious language used by both sides (Ep 636). He had earlier had agreeable contacts with Hoogstraten, it seems (Epp 856, 1342).

After his return from Rome to Cologne, Hoogstraten went to Antwerp in June 1518 (Ep 849), and in September he was at Louvain while Erasmus was in Basel (Ep 884). Erasmus was informed of Hoogstraten's writings and read his *Apologia* (Cologne: H. Quentel February 1518). He regretted Hoogstraten's involvement in the Reuchlin controversy, which lowered his esteem of the Dominican (Epp 747, 856, 1006). For many years he repeated with evident delight a malicious anecdote about Hoogstraten's expulsion from Cologne by the relatives of Hermann von *Neuenahr (CWE Ep 877). In public, however, he kept silent until his own views on divorce were attacked in Hoogstraten's *Destructio cabalae seu cabalisticae perfidiae ab Ioanne Reuchlin Capnione iam pridem in lucem editae* (Cologne: H. Quentel April 1519). Erasmus then answered Hoogstraten with a mild letter (11 August 1519), which

he published without delay. He asked the Dominican to be more lenient in his attacks on Reuchlin and defended his opinion on marriage and divorce as redefined in the second edition of his New Testament (Ep 1006). As he received no answer, he tried in the autumn to ascertain Hoogstraten's reaction from Ortwinus *Gratius, a common friend (Ep 1022).

Meanwhile, Hoogstraten had arrived in Louvain on a confidential mission, carrying a sealed copy of *Luther's Latin writings (Basel 1518) and a condemnation thereof by the Cologne faculty of theology. On 12 October 1519 he appeared before the Louvain theologians and requested them to draw up a similar condemnation (CWE Ep 1030). He had also brought with him Erasmus' friendly letter to Luther (Ep 980) and showed it around in Louvain as well as at the court of Brussels to prove Erasmus' complicity with the German friar. As a result the Louvain theologians broke the peace they had recently concluded with Erasmus (Epp 1033, 1040; CWE Epp 1022, 1038 introductions). Early in 1520, Erasmus and Hoogstraten met and settled their differences (Ep 1064). At the same time Erasmus helped Hoogstraten to secure a truce with the bellicose count von Neuenahr (CWE Ep 1078 introduction). This reconciliation did not, however, prevent the publication of the anonymous lampoon *Hochstratus ovans*, intended as a vindication of Erasmus, who asked Wolfgang *Capito to suppress it (Ep 1165; ASD IX-1 142).

Erasmus remained suspicious of Hoogstraten (Epp 1141, 1166). Both before and after the death of the Dominican he indicted him together with Nicolaas *Baechem Egmondanus as a principal enemy of the *bonae literae* and deplored his unthinking zeal against Luther (Epp 1299, 1330, 2315, 2445). On the whole the statements he published in Hoogstraten's lifetime remained guarded, however, and in February 1523 he publicly protested against rumourmongers who were trying to stir up trouble between him and his 'old friend' Hoogstraten (Ep 1342). This statement did not escape the attention of Ulrich von *Hutten. In his *Spongia* against Hutten, published a few months later, Erasmus felt compelled to offer a lengthy analysis of his relations with the Dominican. In view of Hutten's charge that he had favoured Hoogstraten over Reuchlin, he was eventually prepared to call Hoogstraten a self-seeking trouble-maker, indifferent to *bonae literae* (ASD IX-1 134–42). Three years later, however, in a letter to Guillaume *Budé he noted that even old enemies of the *bonae literae*, such as Hoogstraten, had begun to polish their language (Ep 1794), and when relaying to a friend the news of Hoogstraten's death, he mentioned that the Dominican had apparently suffered pangs of conscience on his deathbed (Ep 1821).

Apart from a *Margarita moralis philosophiae* (Cologne: P. Quentel 1521), Hoogstraten's literary activity was largely devoted to the fanatical defence of orthodoxy against Luther. However, on account of his two dialogues *Cum divo Augustino colloquia* (Cologne 1521–2), he has been credited with a valuable effort to go beyond superficial polemic and trace the theological problem of original sin to its roots in St Augustine. Subsequent attacks on the Lutheran position included *De veneratione et invocatione sanctorum contra perfidiam Lutheranam* (n p 1524), *De fide et operibus adversus Martini Lutheri libertatem* (Cologne: P. Quentel 1526), and *Disputationes contra Lutheranos* (n p 1526). *Cum divo Augustino colloquia* and some other texts have been edited by Frederik Pijper in *Bibliotheca reformatoria Neerlandica* (The Hague 1903–14) III.

BIBLIOGRAPHY: Allen and CWE Epp 290, 849, 1006 / Hubert Jedin in NDB IX 605–6 / R. Coulon in DTC VII-1 11–17 / *Matricule de Louvain* II-1 403–4 / *Matrikel Köln* II 407 / de Vocht CTL I 418–41 and passim / K. Blockx *De veroordeling van Maarten Luther door de theologische faculteit te Leuven in 1519* (Brussels 1958) / Ludwig Geiger *Johann Reuchlin* (Leipzig 1871, repr 1964) 290–6 and passim   GILBERT TOURNOY & PGB

HOOGSTRATEN *See also Antoine de* LALAING

Jan HORÁK of Milešovka, d 1551
Jan Horák (Johannes Horatius, Hasenberg, Hasenbergius, Hoselburgianus) was born at Siřejovice, near Hasenburk in the district of Litoměřice (west of Prague), a son of Jakub Horák Horský. After preparatory training under the influence of the provost of Litoměřice, Jan Žák, a devout Catholic, Jan matriculated at Leipzig in the winter semester

of 1518 and received his BA on 6 March 1522 and his MA on 28 December 1523.

In 1534 Horák returned to Litoměřice as dean of the chapter, becoming provost in 1537. At his private school founded in Litoměřice for the children of the nobility, he combined humanistic methods of education with indoctrination in the Catholic faith. Among his students were Johann Jakob and Raimund Fugger. In April 1539 he assumed responsibility for the education of King *Ferdinand's children and from then on pursued a successful career at Ferdinand's court.

In 1541 Horák failed to be appointed bishop of Olomouc (Olmütz) in Moravia but was knighted with the title 'Milešovka' by the Emperor *Charles V. He accompanied Ferdinand's children on an extended visit to the Netherlands. On his return, the Bohemian diet on two occasions (in 1545 and again in 1549), nominated him as candidate for the archiepiscopal see in Prague, which had been vacant since the outbreak of the Hussite revolution in 1421. However, negotiations with the papal court were difficult, and the see was filled only in 1561, ten years after Horák's death. Horák was sent by King Ferdinand to the council of Trent in 1545 and later accompanied the king on the military expedition against Saxony during the war against the Schmalkaldic League (1546–7). In 1550 he attended the imperial diet in Augsburg and died there early in 1551, before 4 March.

Throughout his life, Horák maintained wide literary contacts with humanists in his homeland and in other countries, including Jan *Šlechta, Sigismundus *Gelenius, Julius *Pflug, Fridericus *Nausea, and Georg *Witzel. In his Leipzig years he co-operated especially with Johannes *Cochlaeus in the literary polemic against the Lutherans, using an approach that was particularly repulsive. His *Epistola Martino Ludero et suae parum legitimae uxori Catharinae a Bhor ... scripta* (Leipzig: V. Schumann 1528, also published in a German version), drew an equally unsparing reply, to which he responded with *Ad Luderanorum famosum libellum recens Wittenbergae editum responsio* (Leipzig: M. Blum 1528, with a dedicatory preface to Jan Žák). He followed up with a satirical play on *Luther's marital life, dedicated to Cochlaeus: *Ludus ludentem Luderum ludens* (Leipzig 1530). One of the two earlier tracts was sent to Erasmus by Cochlaeus; in his reply of April 1529 Erasmus politely regretted the violent tone of the piece without divulging its author (Ep 2143). Following the publication of this letter, Horák wrote on January 1530 to Erasmus, accepting the criticism. His letter, an admiring first approach, also referred to his connections with Hieronymus *Walther, whom he called his patron, and Conradus *Wimpina (Ep 2247).

BIBLIOGRAPHY: Allen Ep 2247 / *Matrikel Leipzig* I 565, III 346, and passim / Pflug *Correspondance* II Ep 308 and passim / *Epistolae ad Nauseam* 447, 453, and passim / Martin Spahn *Johannes Cochlaeus* (Berlin 1898, repr 1964) 139, 199, 202 / Götz von Pölnitz *Anton Fugger* (Tübingen 1958–   ) II 318, III 618, 757 / For a bibliography of MSS and published works, see Antonín Truhlář, Karel Hrdina, Josef Hejnic, and Jan Martínek *Rukovět' humanistického básnictví v Čechách a na Moravě – Enchiridion renatae poesis Latinae in Bohemia et Moravia cultae* II (Prague 1966) 332–6   J.K. ZEMAN

Guillaume de HORION documented 1530–40
A descendant of an old aristocratic family of Limburg, Guillaume de Horion (Horrion), lord of Ordingen, near St Truiden, was the father of Michel de Horion, who became a student of the Collegium Trilingue on 3 August 1530. Another 'dominus Wilhelmus de Horion' of St Truiden, presumably a relative, matriculated at the University of Louvain on 6 June 1522.

Michel de Horion was a student of Conradus *Goclenius, and it must have been in consultation with Goclenius that his father wrote to Erasmus in 1533. Only after a reminder from Goclenius did Erasmus send Horion an answer (Ep 2795) as well as a copy of his *Explanatio symboli* (Basel: H. Froben March 1533), which is now in Trinity College, Cambridge. Horion must have been a patron of scholars. On 13 March 1539 Gerard *Morinck dedicated to him his edition of Rudolf von *Langen's *Historia Hierosolymae* (Louvain: R. Rescius) and the following year a memoir that survives in manuscript.

BIBLIOGRAPHY: Allen Ep 2795 / de Vocht CTL

Georg Hörmann, by Christoph Amberger

III 232–4 / de Vocht MHL 487–9 / *Matricule de Louvain* III-1 674, III-2 258
                                        FRANZ BIERLAIRE

Georg HÖRMANN of Kaufbeuren,
26 February 1491–11 December 1552
Georg Hörmann (Hermannus) of Kaufbeuren, in Swabia, was descended from a highly respected family of wine merchants; he was a son of the patrician Hans Hörmann, a friend of Anton *Fugger. Georg matriculated on 31 August 1505 at the University of Tübingen and in 1512 married Barbara, a daughter of Ludwig Reihing and Veronika Imhof, who was a sister of Anton Fugger's mother. Hörmann was in the service of the Fuggers from 25 April 1520, at first in Antwerp, then in Schwaz in the Tirol, where he managed the mining and smelting enterprise owned by the Fuggers and their partner, Hans Stöckl. When this partnership was terminated on 31 December 1524 Hörmann worked out an equitable division of all assets. He stayed with the Fuggers and, as one of their most trusted factors, was eventually in charge of the mining operations in the whole region of

the Alps. He continued to reside in Schwaz, earning a substantial salary of fourteen hundred florins annually as well as the interest on capital invested in the Fugger firm in his own name and that of his wife. Although he had favoured the Protestant faith since approximately 1527, he enjoyed the full confidence of Anton Fugger and the respect of both the Emperor *Charles V, who issued a privilege for him in June 1520, and King *Ferdinand I. In 1545 he received valuable fiefs such as the castle of Waldegg on the Iller, near Memmingen.

During the Schmalkaldic war Hörmann followed the fate of the Protestant League with concern but remained loyal to the Fugger firm and thus the Hapsburgs. When Kaufbeuren accepted the harsh conditions of the Augsburg Interim in 1550, Hörmann was asked to use his and his employer's connection with the Hapsburg courts on behalf of the city. He did so, but was criticized by many of his fellow-citizens. Unable to cope with his heavy work-load on top of his personal problems, he retired from the Fugger firm on 8 June 1550 and returned to his native city; he died two years later on his estate, Gutenberg, near Kaufbeuren.

Hörmann, who considered a good Latin style a status symbol (Ep 3088), strove to provide the very best education for his sons. His eldest son, Johann Georg *Hörmann, studied under *Viglius Zuichemus, while Ludovicus *Carinus was the tutor of another son, Matthäus, who attended the University of Louvain. None of his sons, however, lived up fully to his expectations. Hörmann must have written to Erasmus at least once before he took up his pen again in January 1536 amid the worries caused by Johann Georg's mediocre academic performance. Hörmann's life is well summed up by the emblem he had chosen: a burning candle accompanied by the words 'Dienend verzer ich mich,' for which he desired an appropriate Latin translation (Ep 3088).

BIBLIOGRAPHY: Allen Ep 2716 / Götz von Pölnitz Anton Fugger (Tübingen 1958–) I 385–6, 479–80, III-1 111–13 and passim / Matrikel Tübingen I 149 / NDB VII 524 (s v Philipp Hainhofer) / de Vocht CTL III 461–5
IG & PGB

Johann Georg HÖRMANN of Augsburg, 6 June 1513–5 April 1562

Johann Georg, the eldest son of Georg *Hörmann, received his early schooling at Innsbruck, close to Schwaz, where his father managed the Fugger mines. In 1528 he was sent to France with two other youths who were distantly related to the Fugger family, Heinrich and Quirinus Rehlinger, the grandsons of Johann *Rehlinger. Returning from Bourges with their tutor, *Viglius Zuichemus, who was five years older than Johann Georg, they passed through Basel and Freiburg, where Viglius and Johann Georg visited Erasmus in the autumn of 1531 (Ep 2716). They continued their journey to Italy by way of Augsburg and Schwaz. Johann Georg did not show much promise in his studies, and his taste for wine and women caused great concern to his father. He remained at Padua in Viglius' care until 1533, and in 1535 Viglius took him to Speyer, where Johann Georg's father had secured him a position at the imperial law court. In November 1536 Johann Georg went back to Siena in the company of Ulrich Fugger. After his return from Italy he married Radegunde Hörwart (Herwart, d 20 August 1559) in 1539 and settled in Augsburg as an employee of the Fugger headquarters, although his position in the firm would never match the importance of that held by his father. As a loyal follower of Anton *Fugger, he supported the Hapsburgs during the Schmalkaldic war and was obliged to leave Augsburg temporarily. He was buried in St Anne's, Augsburg.

When Viglius noticed Johann Georg's flagging interest in studies, he coaxed him to write to Erasmus and asked the latter to send an encouraging letter to the young man (Ep 2716). The fact that Erasmus complied with this wish was much appreciated by Johann Georg's father, who urged his son to reply. After some delay he did so (Epp 3074, 3117), expressing great respect for the famous scholar and an awareness of his own mediocrity in the literary field.

BIBLIOGRAPHY: Allen Ep 2716 / Götz von Pölnitz Anton Fugger (Tübingen 1958–) I 480 and passim / de Vocht CTL III 462–3 / NDB VII 524 (s v Philipp Hainhofer)
IG & PGB

Maximiliaan van HORN d 3 February 1543
A descendant of the lords and counts of Horn
(Hornes, near Roermond) and Houtkerke
(near Ieper), Maximiliaan was the eldest son
of Arnoud van Horn and Marguerite, the
daughter of Jean de Montmorency, lord of
Nevele in Flanders. Born around 1475, Maximiliaan followed Philip the Handsome, duke of
*Burgundy, to Spain in 1501. On 15 May 1504
he married Barbara, the daughter of Jan van
Montfoort, and after the death of his father
succeeded on 1 March 1505 to the lordship of
Gaasbeek, near Brussels. He also obtained
Houtkerke and Horn, to which he added the
lordships of Hees, Hondschoote, and other
estates. He was also burgrave of Bergues
(today Département du Nord). On 12 November 1516 he was sworn in as lieutenant of the
court of Brabant and in the same year he was
made a knight of the Golden Fleece by the
future *Charles v during the eighteenth chapter of the order at Brussels.
   Maximiliaan had attended court and been
sent on diplomatic missions since before the
death of Philip the Handsome in 1506. In
general he preferred the court of Brussels to his
estates and family affairs in Flanders. Although he was the third member of a commission which supervised the appointment of
burgomasters and aldermen in Flanders, he
was rarely present at the commission's meetings between 1520 and 1541. The rise of
Hondschoote as an industrial town occurred
without much encouragement on his part, nor
did he derive any benefits from it. Maximiliaan
was laid to rest in a beautiful tomb at
Braine-le-Château. His wife, who died in 1528,
had borne him four children, among them
Hendrik, who in 1536 succeeded his father as
lieutenant of Brabant.
   Erasmus wrote Maximiliaan a short letter
from Anderlecht in May 1521, which shows
that he was personally acquainted with the
lord of Gaasbeek and his wife (Ep 1208).
   BIBLIOGRAPHY: Allen Ep 1208 / F. Vennekens
La Seigneurie de Gaesbeek, 1236–1795 (Affligem–
Hekelgem 1935) 63–5 / F. Goethals *Histoire
généalogique de la Maison de Hornes* (Brussels
1848) 241–6 / D. Schwennicke *Europäische
Stammtafeln* (Marburg 1936–) VI table 64 / E.
Coornaert *Un Centre industriel d'autrefois: La*

*draperie-sayetterie d'Hondschoote (XIVe–XVIIIe
siècles)* (Rennes 1930) 83–6 / Louis Galesloot
Inventaire des archives de la cour féodale de Brabant
(Brussels 1870) I 1x, 210, 270 / J. de Borchgrave
d'Altena 'Le gisant de Maximilien de Hornes à
Braine-le-Château' *Annales du Cercle historique
et folklorique de Braine-le-Château* 1 (1972–3) 1–8,
with an appendix by J.C. Ghislain, 8–13 / H.
Kervyn de Lettenhove *La Toison d'Or* (Brussels
1907) 95 and passim / W. van Hille in
Hornejaarboek (1977) 180–92
                                       PAUL VAN PETEGHEM

Johann HORNBURG of Brunswick,
d 16 June 1555
The identification of Johannes Hornburgius,
author of Epp 1779, 1935, with Johann Hornburg of Brunswick is based on the assumption
that Hornburgius' reference to 'Francia Orientalis' as his homeland (Ep 1935) was probably a
learned reference to the region south and west
of Saxony proper; see Charles du Fresne du
Cange et al *Glossarium mediae et infimae
Latinitatis* new ed (Niort-London 1885–7) IV s v
Francia Orientalis.
   Johann Hornburg (Horneborch), the second
son of Ludeke, burgomaster of Brunswick,
matriculated in Wittenberg in the summer of
1504, in Leipzig in 1507 (receiving a BA in the
following spring), and in 1515 in Bologna. By
1520 he laid claim to the rank of doctor of both
laws. He was secretary to Bernhard von *Cles
in 1527 and 1528 (Epp 1779, 1935). By 1530 he
was canon of Hildesheim and undertook an
embassy to dukes Ernest and Francis of
*Brunswick-Lüneburg on behalf of the imperial
vice-chancellor, Balthasar *Merklin. In 1535
Hornburg was councillor to Cardinal Albert
von *Brandenburg, who in 1538 leased to him
the copper-mine near Könnern, north of Halle,
for exploitation. He held numerous benefices
and was a canon of Halberstadt (after 1538),
Minden (from 1550), Merseburg, and Naumburg, and also non-resident provost of St
Peter's in Nörten, near Göttingen (1538–47).
On 29 December 1551 he became bishop of
Lebus (on the Oder below Frankfurt); he died
in his castle of Storkow.
   Hornburg was a convinced Catholic but was
tolerant and a patron of learning, as is evident
from *Melanchthon's letter to him dated 6

Stanislaus Hosius

December 1554 (*Corpus Reformatorum*, Halle 1834– , VIII Ep 5696). Writing from Vienna in 1527 (Ep 1778), Hornburg expressed his admiration for Erasmus, who replied in a letter now missing. In a second letter written from Buda the following year (Ep 1935), Hornburg apologized for the delay in answering Erasmus' letter, which had been caused by a long trip to his homeland and the lack of a messenger.

BIBLIOGRAPHY: Allen Ep 1779 / Knod 215 / *Matrikel Wittenberg* I 13 / *Matrikel Leipzig* I 477, II 436 / Pflug *Correspondance* I Ep 111 and passim / *Deutsche Reichstagsakten* Jüngere Reihe (Gotha-Göttingen 1893–) VII-1 378   IG

Stanislaus HOSIUS of Cracow, 5 May 1505–5 August 1579

Stanislaus Hosius (Stanisław Hozjusz) was the son of Ulryk, a Cracow burgher who was director of the Vilno mint, and his second wife, Anna. Hosius began his studies at the University of Cracow in 1519 and in 1520 received a BA. He remained in Cracow as a teacher first at the court of bishop Jan Konarski and then at

that of Piotr *Tomicki, who took a particular interest in him and sent him to Italy for further study. Hosius left Cracow in 1530 in the company of Anianus *Burgonius. They studied at Bologna and Padua, and in June 1534 Hosius received his doctorate of civil and canon law from Bologna. In September he returned to Poland and was appointed secretary to Tomicki. After Tomicki's death Hosius began to work in the royal chancery under the bishop of Płock and chancellor of the realm, Jan Chojenski. In 1534 Hosius was named chief secretary by *Sigismund I, and in the same year he took holy orders, already being in possession of numerous benefices including canonries of Warmia (Ermland), Cracow, and Sandomierz. On 3 February 1549 he was appointed bishop of Chełmno (Kulm) by *Sigismund Augustus and began to exercise a greater role in the political life of the kingdom. Above all, Hosius became the principal defender of papal authority and the chief organizer of the Counter-Reformation in Poland.

In January 1551 Hosius became bishop of Warmia. At the synod of Piotrkow (8–16 June 1551) he persuaded the Polish bishops to swear to a confession of faith he himself had drawn up, the *Confessio fidei catholicae christiana*, first published in 1553 and printed in numerous editions afterwards. In May 1558 Hosius left Poland for Rome at the request of Pope *Paul IV, to become an adviser to the curia in the matter of renewing the activities of the council of Trent. In March 1560 Pope Pius IV sent him to Vienna in connection with this matter, and on 26 February 1561 he was appointed cardinal. From 20 August 1561 he was at Trent as one of the papal legates to the council, and in 1563 he was chairman of proceedings. In 1564 Hosius returned to Warmia and undertook an energetic attack upon the Reformation. In Brunsberg, in the vicinity of Elbląg (Elbing), he founded the first Jesuit college in Poland. On 20 August 1569 he left for Rome once again, this time as the representative of the Polish king; there he became a member of several curial congregations. In 1573 he received the title of grand penitentiary from Pope Gregory XIII. By means of his copious correspondence he directed the Counter-Reformation in Poland and supported Catholicism in Germany and

Sweden. Hosius died in Capranica, near Rome, and was buried at the basilica of Santa Maria Trastevere.

During his years as a student and teacher at Cracow, Hosius was above all a humanist. He had close contacts with the group of Erasmus' admirers in Poland and was a friend of Andrzej *Krzycki, Leonard *Cox, and Jan (II) *Łaski, who recommended him to Erasmus in 1527 (Epp 1915, 1916). Hosius praised Erasmus in Latin poems which were published with reprints of Erasmus' De copia (Cracow: H. Wietor 1523) and Hyperaspistes (Cracow: H. Wietor 1526). In Cox's edition of Statius' Sylvae (Cracow: M. Scharffenberg 1527) Hosius published a long poem describing the journey of Jan (II) Łaski and his association with Erasmus. In 1527 Hosius published Erasmus' Ep 1819 to King Sigismund I (Cracow: M. Scharffenberg) with a long preface addressed to Piotr Tomicki. Two of Hosius' publications are particularly revealing of his debt to Erasmus: In Psalmum quinquagesimum paraphrasis (Cracow: H. Wietor 1528), dedicated to Piotr Tomicki, and his translation of John Chrysostom's Comparatio monachi cum rege (Cracow: M. Scharffenberg 1528). In his preface to the latter Hosius expressed his great respect for Erasmus. He had actually wanted to meet Erasmus personally and intended to visit him on his return journey from Bologna in 1534, but he was robbed on the way and prevented from travelling via Freiburg by lack of funds.

The bulk of Hosius' correspondence and works may be found in Opera omnia (Cologne: M. Cholinus 1584); Stanislai Hosii ... epistolae tum etiam orationes, legationes ... ed F. Hipler and T. Zakrzewski in Acta historica res gestas Poloniae illustrantia IV and IX (Cracow 1879–88); S. Hosii ... epistolae ab eo conscriptae et ad eum datae (1564) ed A. Szorc (Olsztyn 1976). Hosius' poems in Latin and in Polish translation are published as S. Hozjusz Poezje (Olsztyn 1980). Hosius' portrait by an unknown painter is in the Polish hospice in Rome.

BIBLIOGRAPHY: Allen Ep 1915 / PSB X 42–6 / LThK V 490 / A. Eichhorn Stanislaus Hosius (Mainz 1854–5) / K. Miaskowski 'Studienjahre des ermländischen Bischofs und Kardinals Stanislaus Hosius' Zeitschrift für die Geschichte und Altertumskunde Ermlands 19 (1916) 329–93 / J. Fijałek 'Przekłady pism św. Grzegorza z Nazyanzu w Polsce' Polonia Sacra I (Cracow 1918) 86–130 / L. Hajdukiewicz 'Im Bücherkreis des Erasmus von Rotterdam' Vierteljahresschrift für Geschichte der Wissenschaft und Technik (Warsaw) 5 (1960) Sonderheft 2, 73 / Erasmiana Cracoviensia in diem natalem Erasmi Roterodamensis quingentesimum edita Zeszyty Naukowe Uniwersytetu Jagiellońskiego CCL (Cracow 1971) 27, 60–1 / M. Borzyszkowski Materiały do twórczości poetyckiej i działalności wydawniczej Stanisława Hozjusza (Olsztyn 1970)

HALINA KOWALSKA

Toussaint HOSSEY of Valenciennes, d 30 July 1565

Toussaint Hossey (Hosey, d'Hocédy, Toussanus or Panagius Hoscedius or Hocedius) matriculated on 2 April 1511 at the University of Louvain and ranked first among those promoted to MA in 1514. He stayed on and taught arts courses at the College of the Falcon. Later, when he became abbot of Gorze, one of his monks claimed that for a while Hossey had shared accomodation and meals with Erasmus in Louvain (BRE Ep 328). Hossey also made the acquaintance of Juan Luis *Vives, who mentioned him as a common friend at the end of his Adversus pseudodialecticos (Louvain: D. Martens c 1519) addressed to Johannes *Fortis. By 1528 (Ep 2027) he had become a secretary to cardinal Jean de *Lorraine, a position which he retained until 1543. In 1539 his master resigned to him the abbey of Gorze, south-west of Metz, which he held in commendam until 1542 or 1543. In 1543 the Cardinal resigned to him the bishopric of Toul, in Lorraine, and in 1546 he received the abbey of Honnecourt, near Cambrai.

François *Dubois dedicated to Hossey an edition of Cicero's Pro Cn. Plancio (Paris: J. Bade 1531) and Louis des Masures, who was his nephew, dedicated to him some of his poems. In 1528 Hossey sent greetings to Erasmus through Gervasius *Wain (Ep 2027).

BIBLIOGRAPHY: Allen Ep 2027 / Matricule de Louvain III-1 411 / Eubel III 321 / Gallia christiana III 114, XIII 891, 1047–8 / de Vocht CTL II 210

PGB

Thomas Howard, by Hans Holbein the Younger

Johannes HOVIUS documented 1518–27
Johannes Hovius (Hovicus, Hovus) of unknown descent, was probably a MA when he
joined Erasmus in 1518 at Basel and in
September returned with him to Louvain (Epp
867, 902). He lived with his master in the
College of the Lily and was employed primarily, it seems, as a copyist (Epp 857, 897
introductions; Allen Epp 879, 883 introductions, Allen I 605–6). Although he remained in
Erasmus' service for several years he is rarely
mentioned in the correspondence (Epp 1109,
1222, 1256), since the more conspicuous role of
letter carrier and messenger was normally
reserved for his colleague, Lieven *Algoet.
Hovius left Erasmus' service, probably in 1523,
and went to Italy in hope of better things (Epp
1349, 1386, 1387, 1424). By early 1524 he was
living in Rome, where he apparently found
that Erasmus' introductions opened many
doors to him (Epp 1424, 1437). Although
Erasmus was then critical of the way Hovius
had served him (Ep 1437), their relations
remained quite friendly. Erasmus exchanged a
number of letters, none of which are extant,
with his former secretary and asked him to

hand other letters to their recipients in Rome
(Epp 1424, 1519, 1605, 1621, 1762, 1806A); he
also continued to recommend Hovius to
influential patrons (Ep 1509). In May 1525
Hovius belonged to the entourage of Felix
*Trophinus, bishop of Chieti (Ep 1575), but
nothing is known about the remainder of his
life.

BIBLIOGRAPHY: Allen Ep 867 / Bierlaire
Familia 54–5 / *Opuscula* 245 / BRE Ep 416

FRANZ BIERLAIRE

Thomas HOWARD duke of Norfolk, 1473–
25 August 1554
Howard was the eldest son of Thomas Howard
and Elizabeth Tylney. Because of the close
alliance between the Howards and Richard III,
he was betrothed in 1484 to Lady Anne, the
daughter of Edward IV. The marriage was
permitted by *Henry VII in 1495. Howard
served in Scotland under his father and was
knighted by him in 1497. In May 1512 he was
second in command of the army sent to Spain
and was created lord admiral for the invasion
of France in the following year. However, he
did not serve at sea but fought again under his
father, at Flodden. In 1514 he accompanied
*Mary Tudor to France and was created earl of
Surrey. In the following years he dared to
oppose Thomas *Wolsey in foreign policy and
other matters in council.

On the death of his first wife in 1513 he
married Elizabeth, the eldest daughter of
Edward *Stafford, duke of Buckingham. In
1520 he was sent to maintain order in Ireland
but was recalled to command the English fleet
against France the following year. In 1522 he
succeeded his father as high treasurer and, on
his father's death in 1524, became duke of
Norfolk.

Howard sided with the king on the divorce
issue and together with Charles *Brandon,
duke of Suffolk, gathered the evidence which
led to Wolsey's condemnation. For his part in
the dissolution of the monasteries he received
confiscated lands and other proceeds. In 1533
Thomas *More reported to Erasmus that *Henry
VIII had ordered Howard to state publicly that
the king had been reluctant to accept More's
resignation (Ep 2831). Although Howard was
the chief adviser to his niece *Anne Boleyn, he
was later to preside at her trial and execution.

Created earl marshal in 1533, he headed the opposition to Thomas *Cromwell and secured his arrest in 1540. In that year he arranged the marriage of his niece Catherine Howard to the king.

In 1546 Howard and his son were charged with treason by the new royal favourite, Edward Seymour, earl of Hertford. Howard's execution was prevented by the timely death of the king and the accession of Edward VI in 1547. He spent Edward's reign imprisoned in the Tower but was released when *Mary came to the throne. He was restored as duke of Norfolk in 1553. His portrait by *Holbein is in the royal collection.

BIBLIOGRAPHY: DNB X 64–7 / G.E. C[ockayne] *The Complete Peerage of England* ed V. Gibbs et al (London 1910–59) IX 615–20   CFG

Ausonius van HOXWIER documented 1528–42

Ausonius (Latin for Aesge) van Hoxwier was a younger brother of Hector van *Hoxwier. Hector recommended him to his former professor, Conradus *Goclenius (cf Gabbema III Ep 4), who directed Ausonius' studies from at least the spring of 1528. After some years Ausonius left Louvain for Bourges, where he met *Viglius Zuichemus, who was quite willing to extend his friendly feelings for Hector to his brother (cf Ep 2624). He travelled to Italy and, on hearing Andrea *Alciati lecture, encouraged Hector to attend his lectures too. Ausonius returned to Friesland and settled at Mantgum, near Leeuwarden, where he married not long before 1 March 1535 (Gabbema III Ep 10). There are some traces of his involvement in Frisian politics, but he seems not to be documented after 4 January 1542, when Viglius addressed a letter to him.

BIBLIOGRAPHY: de Vocht CTL II 453–5 / S.A. Gabbema *Illustrium et clarorum virorum epistolae selectiores* 2nd ed (Harlingen 1669) I Epp 73–5, III Epp 10, 11, 13   C.G. VAN LEIJENHORST

Hector van HOXWIER 1502–47

Hector (or Hette in the vernacular) van Hoxwier (Hoxvirius), a native of Mantgum, near Leeuwarden, was the eldest son of the noble Aesga van Hoxwier and Wick van Dekama, and a brother of Ausonius van *Hoxwier. He studied at Louvain under

Conradus *Goclenius (Ep 2586); his friendship with *Viglius Zuichemus presumably dates from this period. After his return he became a councillor of Friesland; in that capacity he delivered a speech to congratulate *Charles V in 1531 on his recent coronation. Surprisingly he resigned his office in 1534 in order to study law at Padua and Pavia under Andrea *Alciati, to whom Erasmus had recommended him (Epp 2972, 3022). Having taken his degree in civil and canon law in 1536, he continued his career in Friesland. He was sent on several embassies to Charles V, who afterwards employed him for similar missions. From 15 May 1538 he was again a member of the council of Friesland, and in 1541 he accepted the presidency of the council of Utrecht, in succession to Maerten van *Naerden. However, he did not lose the confidence of the Frisian people. In the year before his death he was created a knight of the Golden Fleece as a reward for his services. He was married twice: to Ath, the daughter of Gerard van *Herema, and to Doedt van Holdingen. He had several children.

In 1531, no doubt encouraged by Goclenius, Hoxwier wrote to Erasmus. This led to the exchange of a number of friendly letters, in which the two discussed, among other things, their common friends. Three of these letters have survived (Epp 2586, 2624, 3022), while at least three others have not (cf Epp 2586, 2851, 2972).

BIBLIOGRAPHY: Allen Ep 2586 / J. van Kuyk in NNBW II 612 / de Vocht CTL II 163–5 / S.A. Gabbema *Illustrium et clarorum virorum epistolae selectiores* 2nd ed (Harlingen 1669) I Epp 73–5, III Epp 4–6, 14–17 / J.S. Theissen *Centraal gezag en Friesche vrijheid* (Groningen 1907) 388–9 / J.J. Woltjer *Friesland in hervormingstijd* (Leiden 1962) 55 / *Naamrol der Edele Mogende Heeren Raden 's Hoffs van Friesland* (Leeuwarden 1742) 10   C.G. VAN LEIJENHORST

Johann von HOYA d 11 June 1535

Johann von Hoya's family owned sovereign territories in the region of the city of Hoya, on the Weser in Lower Saxony. When it died out in 1582 the county was added to Brunswick-Lüneburg. Johann was at first in the service of King *Christian II of Denmark, but he joined Gustavus Vasa when the latter established himself as the independent ruler of Sweden.

He married a sister of Gustavus Vasa and was made lord of the city of Wyborg, near modern Leningrad, as well as receiving estates in Finland. In 1529 he concluded a treaty with the city of Lübeck which aroused the suspicion of Gustavus Vasa and in 1534, ignoring a counter offer from the Swedish king, he agreed to join Lübeck in the so-called Count's war against *Christian III of Denmark. With the support of democratic forces in the Hanse towns and Denmark herself, Lübeck hoped to re-establish its former position of pre-eminence in the region. After an unsuccessful campaign in Skane (Schonen, today in southern Sweden), Johann von Hoya's army was decisively defeated and he was killed near Assens, on the Danish island of Fyn (Fünen); cf Ep 3041.

BIBLIOGRAPHY: Allen Ep 3041 / *Hanserezesse* (Leipzig etc 1870–   ) IV-1 ed Gottfried Wentz 411 / *Inventare Hansischer Archive des sechzehnten Jahrhunderts* III: *Danziger Inventar 1531–1591* ed Paul Simson (Munich and Leipzig 1913) nos 551, 570 / F.C. Dahlmann and D. Schäfer *Geschichte von Dänemark* (Gotha 1840–1902) IV 287 and passim / Georg Waitz *Lübeck unter Jürgen Wullenwever und die europäische Politik* (Berlin 1855–6) II 23 and passim / Bruno Gebhardt *Handbuch der deutschen Geschichte* 8th ed (Stuttgart 1954–9) II 90, 367, 461, 465   PGB

Antonio HOYOS de Salamanca d 1551
Antonio was the son of Juan de Hoyos, a Castilian nobleman who had travelled to Germany in 1526 in the retinue of *Charles V; he was also the nephew of Gabriel de *Salamanca, count of Ortenburg. According to Eubel, Antonio was at first coadjutor to Girolamo *Balbi, bishop of Gurk, who resigned the bishopric to him in 1526, when he attained the age of eighteen. Apparently, however, he did not occupy his see until 1533. Antonio went to Freiburg to study law, matriculating in April 1529. He wrote to Erasmus before 6 February 1529 asking him to recommend a tutor, and Erasmus suggested Peter *Bitterlin (Epp 2096, 2098). In March 1529 Antonio was also in contact with Bonifacius *Amerbach, whom he invited to dinner and asked to buy three textbooks on logic for him. After a further exchange of letters between Antonio and Erasmus in the following weeks (Epp 2104,

2118) there seems to have been no further contact. Antonio was still in Freiburg on 10 July 1529 (AK III Ep 1367). He is said to have died by violence in 1551.

BIBLIOGRAPHY: Allen Ep 2098 / NDB IX 673 / AK III Epp 1338–40, 1367 / *Matrikel Freiburg* I 274 / Eubel III 207   IG

Stanisław HOZJUSZ *See Stanislaus* HOSIUS

Balthasar HUBMAIER of Friedberg, d 10 March 1528
Balthasar Hubmaier (Pacimontanus), born in Friedberg, near Augsburg, attended the University of Freiburg from 1 May 1503 as a student of Johann *Eck in liberal arts and theology. After teaching briefly in Schaffhausen he returned to Freiburg and was ordained priest. When Eck accepted a call to the University of Ingolstadt, Hubmaier followed him, obtained a doctorate of theology, and in 1516 was appointed chaplain at the cathedral in Regensburg. After his involvement in the explosive new cult of the Virgin Mary at Regensburg, which was accompanied by Jewish pogroms, he became a parish priest in Waldshut, in the Breisgau, which was at that time under Austrian administration. At first Hubmaier was influenced by humanist scholars, in particular by Erasmus, whom he visited in Basel in 1522 (Allen Ep 1292 introduction), but he also began to study *Luther's writings.

In Waldshut Hubmaier's interest in *Zwingli's reforming ideas grew stronger; he introduced the German language in his services, helped to establish an evangelical congregation, and married Elisabeth Hügelin, the daughter of a citizen in Reichenau. He was in contact with *Oecolampadius, *Vadianus, and Zwingli, but soon disagreed with them on the question of the baptism of children. During the peasants' revolt of 1524–5 Hubmaier worked to connect the political and religious aspirations of Waldshut with the actions of the peasants and to win the support of Zürich for both. When the Anabaptist movement in Waldshut grew stronger he showed open sympathy and as a result had to flee, at first in the fall of 1524 temporarily to Schaffhausen, and finally to Zürich in December 1525, when Austrian troops occupied Waldshut. At Zürich he was arrested and had to recant his Anabaptist

convictions. Having regained his liberty in
1526, he passed through Augsburg, where he
met Hans *Denck; from there he proceeded to
Mikulov (Nikolsburg) in Moravia, where he
became the leader of a large Anabaptist
community and maintained, in opposition to
Hans Hut, that in view of the Turkish danger
and other factors limited co-operation with the
state was justified. The Austrian government
successfully demanded his extradition because
of his political involvement in Waldshut.
Hubmaier was imprisoned in Kreuzenstein
(Lower Austria) and burnt at the stake in
Vienna on 10 March 1528.

Hubmaier wrote a number of pamphlets,
among them *Achtzehn Schlussreden so betreffende
eyn ganz christlich Leben* (Waldshut 1524), *Von
Ketzern und ihren Verbrennern* (1524), *Vom
christlichen Tauf der Gläubigen* (1525), *Eine
christliche Lehrtafel* (1526/7, for the Mikulov
congregation), *Von der Freiheit des Willens*, and,
of particular importance, *Von dem Schwert* (both
Mikulov c 1527). All his preserved treatises
have been gathered in *Schriften,* ed G. Westlin
and T. Bergsten (Gütersloh 1962).

Hubmaier is mentioned by Erasmus in
passing. In his *Declarationes ad censuras Lutetiae
vulgatas* he pointed out that Hubmaier, like
other troublemakers, had been trained in
scholastic theology (LB IX 871, 919F), while
other remarks concern the disagreement between various reformers (Ep 1644; LB X 1263D,
1268F).

BIBLIOGRAPHY: Allen Ep 1540 / NDB IX 703 /
ADB XIII 264–7, XLV 463 / RGG III 463 / *Matrikel
Freiburg* I 150 / J. Loserth in *The Mennonite
Encyclopedia* (Scottdale 1955–9) II 826–34 / G.H.
Williams *The Radical Reformation* (Philadelphia
1962) 64–8 and passim / Ugo Gastaldi *Storia
dell'anabattismo dalle origini a Münster* (Turin
1972) 190–202 and passim / J.K. Zeman *The
Anabaptists and the Czech Brethren in Moravia
1526–1628* (The Hague-Paris 1969) 122–76
                                                              IG

Guillaume HUÉ d 31 July 1522
Guillaume Hué was perhaps originally from
Etampes, since an uncle, Cantien Hué, an
alumnus of the Collège de Navarre and a
doctor of theology of Paris in 1478, was from
there, but Guillaume Hué was later said to be
from Orléans. He probably studied arts at

Balthasar Hubmaier

Navarre and perhaps taught arts at the
Collège de Beauvais. He then studied in the
faculty of theology but did not advance beyond
the rank of bachelor. He became a canon of
Paris, and on 15 February 1518 was made dean
of the cathedral chapter. He was interested in
literature and was a friend of Nicolas *Bérault,
who tried to promote a friendship between
Hué and Erasmus (Ep 989). Erasmus wrote to
Hué in 1519 but apparently failed to receive a
reply (Epp 1003, 1185). Robert Fortuné, who
said Hué was from Orléans, praised his
learning in a letter to Louis *Ruzé in 1512.

Allen, following Renouard, has confused
Hué with the Franciscan doctor of theology
Guillaume Huet, and modern authors have
adopted this mistake. The two men died within
one week of each other, Guillaume Hué on 31
July and Guillaume Huet on 6 August 1522.
Oronce Finé's laudatory verse in *In quarto
sententiarum Joannis Bassolii* (Paris 1517) was
probably addressed to the secular Hué and not
to the Franciscan.

BIBLIOGRAPHY: Allen and CWE Ep 989 / Farge
no 246 / *Gallia christiana* VII 216 / Jean de Launoy
Regii Navarrae gymnasii Parisiensis historia (Paris

1677) II 979–80 / Rice *Prefatory Epistles* 294–5
JAMES K. FARGE

Lieven HUGENOYS of Ghent, 17 September
1457–1537
A Benedictine at the abbey of St Bavo, Ghent,
Hugenoys was elected abbot on 14 April 1517.
He was a patron of artists and scholars.
Probably in 1517, he showed Erasmus a
manuscript of the Gospels that was in his
abbey; at the time Erasmus was preparing the
second edition of the New Testament (Allen
Epp 373 introduction, 597:16n; LB IX 766F).
Erasmus travelled in his company from Ghent
to Dendermonde, perhaps in 1520, as he
recalled when writing to the abbot in June 1521
(Ep 1214). He wrote to thank Hugenoys for a
gift and to obtain access to an ancient
manuscript of St Jerome preserved in the
library of St Bavo. The following year the abbot
sent him greetings amid hints of further
generosity (Ep 1271). In the light of these
connections we do not know why Hugenoys
merited a passage in the colloquy *Synodus
grammaticorum* (published in 1529, ASD I-3
586–7) in which the splendour of the abbot's
personal books is described in stark contrast to
their useless content. As recently as 22 January
1527 Erasmus had set down in his first will that
the abbot was to receive a gift copy when his
collected works were printed (Allen VI 505).

BIBLIOGRAPHY: Allen Ep 1214 / E. Varenbergh
in BNB IX 651–2 / M.A. Nauwelaerts 'Erasme et
Gand' *Commémoration nationale d'Erasme, Actes*
(Brussels 1970) 171–2
MARCEL A. NAUWELAERTS

Ulrich HUGWALD of Wilen, 1496–
24 January 1571
It can be assumed that an unauthorized first
edition of Erasmus' *Formula* (CWE 25) was
accompanied by a letter from Hugwald to an
unidentified Petrus *Fabricius that also appears in a reprint (Basel: A. Petri September
1521). Erasmus mentioned the letter in Ep 3099,
where he appeared to blame Hugwald for the
unauthorized edition but refused to do him the
honour of revealing his name.

Ulrich Hugwald (also called Mutz, Mutius)
was born in Wilen, near Bischofszell in the
Thurgau, and matriculated in the University of
Basel for the spring term of 1519. He earned his

living as a private tutor and corrector in the
press of Adam Petri, and between 1520 and
1522 he published several works by *Luther
and, in co-operation with the printer Johannes
*Petri, several pamphlets of his own attacking
the church of Rome, which were noted by
*Lefèvre d'Etaples. Shortly thereafter he
adopted some Anabaptist views, but after two
brief spells of incarceration in May 1524 and
August 1525 he seems to have satisfied
*Oecolampadius and the Basel authorities of
his return to orthodoxy. During his Anabaptist
phase he had close contacts with Thomas
Müntzer, who had gone to Basel in the autumn
of 1524.

Hugwald owned and worked some agricul-
tural land near the city gates and as a member
of the 'Spinnwettern' guild he did military
service in October 1531. However, at the same
time he must have held a minor appointment in
the university which was cancelled on 15
December 1531 as an economy measure when
the university was reorganized after a prolonged crisis caused by the reformation of
Basel. In 1535 Hugwald taught at Basel's Latin
school and in 1540 he was the headmaster.
Meanwhile in 1538 he was awarded a scholarship from the Erasmus bequest and expected to
study theology; he received payments until
1546 but never obtained a theological degree.
He graduated MA, however, on 1 January 1541
and four months later joined the faculty of arts,
where he taught grammar and Aristotelian
ethics. He also was warden of a student
residence. He was dean of arts for a term each
in 1543, in 1563–4, and again in 1570, when he
died during his term in office. In his letters to
Bonifacius *Amerbach he showed some knowledge of medicine. His wife, Rosina Miles of St
Gallen, bitterly complained in a letter of 1549 of
his physical and mental cruelty and of his
failure to provide for her needs.

In 1539 Hugwald published a chronicle in
thirty-nine books, *De Germanorum prima origine*
(Basel: H. Petri), which he dedicated to the
physician Eustache du Quesnoy (Querce-
tanus), whom he identified as the source of his
medical and botanical knowledge.

BIBLIOGRAPHY: *Matrikel Basel* I 340, II 514–15 /
AK V Ep 2275, VII Ep 3196, and passim / BA
Oekolampads I 290–2, 330, 381–2, 387–90, and
passim / O. Clemen *Beiträge zur Reformations-*

geschichte aus Büchern und Handschriften der
Zwickauer Ratsschulbibliothek (Berlin 1900–3) II
45–85 / *Aktensammlung zur Geschichte der Basler*
Reformation ed E. Dürr et al (Basel 1921–50) I
126, II 33, and passim / Ugo Gastaldi *Storia*
dell'anabattismo dalle origini a Münster (Turin
1972) 62, 172–3 / Petrus Ramus *Basilea* ed H.
Fleig (Basel 1944) 43, 68   PGB

Frans van der HULST d 6 December 1530
Frans van der Hulst (Hulstus) studied in
Louvain and was promoted licentiate in law.
He was appointed to the council of Brabant in
Brussels, becoming an extraordinary member
on 5 December 1505 and an ordinary member
on 1 May 1508. Although a layman, he took a
special interest in matters of heresy. As early as
8 November 1511 he appeared – in the
company of the future Pope *Adrian VI – before
the University of Louvain in a matter related to
the Inquisition; in April 1522 he was appointed
inquisitor by *Charles V and confirmed in this
position by his old friend, who was now pope,
on 1 June 1523.

University matters also seem to have belonged to his field of special competence. In
January 1520 he was one of two members
delegated by the council of Brabant to settle
Wilhelm *Nesen's appeal against the university, which had refused his application to give
lectures (Ep 1057). The council's failure to
support Nesen may have confirmed Erasmus in
his opinion that Hulst was a sworn enemy of
the new learning, prepared to resist it more
fiercely even than he opposed the Lutherans
(Ep 1345). In December 1521 Hulst took an
active part in preparing the inquisitorial
proceedings against Erasmus' friends Cornelius *Grapheus and Jacob *Proost. In 1523 he
showed excessive zeal when preparing a
similar case against Cornelis *Hoen, another
friend of Erasmus (Ep 1358). Hulst was
prepared to disregard Hoen's privileged position as a member of the council of Holland and
even to forge documents. As a result, *Margaret of Austria asked him to resign, and on 17
June 1524 Pope *Clement VII confirmed Nicolas
*Coppin as his successor. He still had powerful
friends, but although Erasmus thought in
August 1525 that his period of disgrace might
have ended (Ep 1603), he was never restored to
a position of authority. Erasmus treated him as

an inseparable ally of his arch-opponent
*Baechem (Ep 1434) and could not conceal his
satisfaction at the commotions in Holland
which led to Hulst's demotion (Epp 1466, 1467,
1469).

BIBLIOGRAPHY: Allen Ep 1345 / de Vocht CTL I
463, III 377, and passim / de Vocht *Literae ad*
Craneveldium 556 / H. de Jongh *L'Ancienne*
Faculté de théologie de Louvain (Louvain 1911)
250, 17*–18* / J.G. de Hoop Scheffer *Geschie-*
denis der kerkhervorming in Nederland van haar
ontstaan tot 1531 (Amsterdam 1873) passim /
Recueil des Ordonnances des Pays-Bas II-2
(Brussels 1898) 189–91   PGB

Michael HUMMELBERG of Ravensburg,
1487–19 May 1527
Michael Hummelberg (Hummelberger, Hum-
melburg), the son of a tailor and guild master,
was born in Ravensburg, north-east of Lake
Constance. He attended the local Latin school,
matriculated in Heidelberg on 7 September
1501, and received his BA on 9 January 1503.
From 1503 to 1511 he studied in Paris under
*Lefèvre d'Etaples, learnt Greek from *Her-
monymus and *Aleandro, and helped Josse
*Bade with several editions (Ep 263). He
became a close friend of *Beatus Rhenanus,
obtained his MA in 1505, and presided over the
German nation in 1506 and 1511; he subsequently returned to Ravensburg. From 1514 to
1517 he studied and practised canon law in
Rome, where he also had the opportunity of
supporting the cause of *Reuchlin. After his
return from Rome he took holy orders and
received the chaplaincy of St Michael's, Ravensburg, which enabled him to continue his
humanist studies while working as a teacher.
Between 1517 and 1523 he was repeatedly in
Constance in the house of a kinsman, the
physician Johann *Menlishofer, introducing
Johann von *Botzheim and his friends to the
Greek language with the help of a summary of
the Greek grammar he had written, later to be
published as *Epitome grammaticae graecae*
(Basel: J. Herwagen 1532). During one of these
visits, in September 1522, he was introduced to
Erasmus (Epp 1316, 1342), who was impressed
by Hummelberg's knowledge and manners. He
kept in touch with Hummelberg through
Botzheim, who conveyed greetings from one to
the other (Epp 1454, 1782; Allen I 46), while a

letter from *Melanchthon to Hummelberg, which the latter had sent to Erasmus, played an unfortunate role in the quarrel with *Eppendorf (Epp 1496, 1934). Although he did not join the Reformation, Hummelberg kept up a friendly correspondence with Melanchthon as well as with *Peutinger and many other humanists. His religious ideals clearly resembled those of Erasmus and Botzheim. Very appropriately Beatus Rhenanus addressed to Hummelberg the dedicatory preface of the *Auctarium* of Erasmus' letters (1518; Allen II 602–3; CWE 2 352–3). Josse Bade dedicated to him his collection of *Annotationes doctorum virorum* (Paris 1511), while Beatus Rhenanus recalled his friend's life and work in the preface of Hummelberg's *Epitome grammaticae graecae* (BRE Ep 283).

BIBLIOGRAPHY: Allen and CWE Ep 263 / NDB X 56–8 / A. Horawitz *Michael Hummelberger* (Berlin 1875) / A. Horawitz in ADB XIII 388–9 / BRE Ep 3 and passim / AK I Ep 407 and passim / *Melanchthons Briefwechsel* I Ep 108 and passim / RE Ep 262 and passim / *Matrikel Heidelberg* I 442 / Rice *Prefatory Epistles* 120, 202–4, and passim / Helmut Binder 'Die Brüder Hummelberg' in *Lebensbilder aus Schwaben und Franken* ed R. Uhland et al (Stuttgart 1948–) XII 1–24

IG

HUMPIUS Phrysius *See* HAIO HERMAN

Martin HUNE of Gittelde,
documented 1508–33
Hune (Hunus) was born in Gittelde, fifteen kilometres to the north-east of Northeim, in the region of Brunswick, and matriculated at the University of Erfurt in the summer semester of 1508. He could not afford the entire matriculation fee and paid the remainder at the time of his examination for the baccalaureate, which he passed in the fall of 1509. Thereafter he seems to have left Erfurt, not to return until about 1517. He obtained his MA in 1518, placing first among the candidates; and around this time formed a close friendship with *Eobanus Hessus. At the end of the winter semester of 1519–20 the city of Erfurt proposed him as a member of the Collegium Maius, but the faculty council hesitated to accept him because he did not fully satisfy their requirements. The matter was relegated to the plenary

session of the university, which gave a favourable decision. In the summer semester of 1520 Hune was co-opted into the faculty council. In the summer semester of 1523 he was one of the councillors delegated to choose the new rector and voted for Georg Sturtz. In the winter of 1523–4 he was treasurer (*collector*) of the faculty of arts. At the end of the semester – the examinations for the baccalaureate took place at the beginning of March – he journeyed to Basel to see Erasmus, carrying a letter of recommendation from *Mutianus (Ep 1425) describing him as a humanist of impeccable character and critical of *Luther. He was probably accompanied by Johann *Moldenfeld and also took with him letters from Eobanus dated 1 March 1524 and addressed to *Pirckheimer and *Zasius.

The visit to Erasmus earned Hune a high reputation among Erfurt scholars, and on 18 April the faculty council elected him dean of arts. Erasmus had entrusted him with a letter to Duke George of *Saxony, but his new office detained him in Erfurt until the official inauguration in the church of the Austin Friars. It was only after this ceremony that he was able to take the letter to Duke George, who received it on 20 May (Ep 1448). The delay worried Erasmus, who wrote to Hune on 3 July (Ep 1462) inquiring about the letter since he had not received any answer.

Friendly letters continued to be exchanged between Erasmus and the two friends Hune and Eobanus until the summer of 1526 (Epp 1498, 1567, 1718). In the meantime Hune had completed his term as dean. On 30 September 1524 he presided over the BA examinations for four candidates and in the middle of October a new dean was elected. Hune does not appear to have served the faculty in any other function. In the fall of 1525 he left Erfurt, spent the summer of 1526 in Annaberg and Vienna, and travelled to Italy, where he obtained his doctorate of medicine in Padua in 1531. Thereafter he visited Ferrara (cf Giovanni *Manardo *Epistolae medicinales* book XIV Ep 1) and finally settled down as a physician in Graz. The last letters addressed to him by Eobanus are dated 1532 and 1533. From then on nothing further is known of him.

Eobanus introduced Hune as a speaker in his dialogue *Melaenus* (von Hase no 533), defending medicine. Joachim *Camerarius mentioned him as a close friend of Eobanus: 'But his closest friend was Martin Hune, to whom he dedicated the *Praise of Medicine*, a versification of Erasmus' oration.'

BIBLIOGRAPHY: Allen Ep 1462 / *Matrikel Erfurt* II 257 / F.W. Kampschulte *Die Universität Erfurt in ihrem Verhältnis zum Humanismus und zur Reformation* (Trier 1855–60) II 194ff / Carl Krause *Helius Eobanus Hessus* (Gotha 1879) I 241–2 / H.R. Abe 'Die Erfurter medizinische Fakultät in den Jahren 1392–1524' *Beiträge zur Geschichte der Universität Erfurt* 17 (1973–4) 124, 127–8, 191, 239 / J. Camerarius *Narratio de Helio Eobano Hesso* ed J.T. Kreyssig (Meissen 1843) 23 / E. Kleineidam *Universitas studii Erffordensis* (Leipzig 1964–   ) I 222 and passim / Martin von Hase 'Bibliographie der Erfurter Drucke von 1501–1550' *Archiv für Geschichte des Buchwesens* 8 (1967) 655–1096   ERICH KLEINEIDAM

Louis de HUSSON d 1537
A member of the important family of the counts of Tonnerre, east of Auxerre, Louis de Husson (Ludovicus de Tenodoro) was a son of another Louis and of Françoise de Rohan. He was barely eighteen years of age when he succeeded in 1521 to the see of Poitiers, which was vacated by the death of his uncle, Bishop Claude de Husson. During the years 1530–2, when Pierre *Du Chastel was in his service, the bishop-designate seems for the most part to have attended the royal court at Blois and Paris (Epp 2388, 2425), while the administration of Poitiers lay in the hands of a suffragan. Louis was licentiate in canon law but was never ordained priest; after the death of his elder brother, Claude, in the battle of Pavia (1525), he wished to marry and in 1532 was supported by *Francis I in his efforts to receive a papal dispensation. It seems that he succeeded, for shortly thereafter he resigned his see to Cardinal Gabriel de *Gramont. He died in Avignon.

BIBLIOGRAPHY: *Gallia christiana* II 1203, 1271 / Eubel III 273 / *Catalogue des actes de François I* (Paris 1887–1908) III 312 and passim
                                      MICHEL REULOS & PGB

Frowin von HUTTEN 1472–1529
Frowin, the son of Hans von Hutten and Margarete von Forstmeister, was an uncle of Ulrich von *Hutten. By 1510 he was appointed marshal and later *Hofmeister* at the archiepiscopal court of Mainz, and in 1516 he was named councillor to *Maximilian I. In the spring of 1517 he and Ludwig von *Hutten joined a troop of pilgrims going to Rome and Jerusalem under the leadership of Bernhard von Hirschfeld. In June, before setting sail, they arranged to meet Ulrich von Hutten in Venice (Ep 611). In July they were on their way back from Jerusalem to Jaffa when Frowin fell ill. He recovered, however, and subsequently joined Franz von *Sickingen in his feud against the archbishopric of Trier and as a result was deprived of all his estates in 1522. He was reinstated, however, in 1526 after having helped to quell the peasant rebellion. As he had no sons he sold his estates in 1528 to his cousins. He died the following year at Steinau, on the Main, where his tomb may be seen in the local church.

BIBLIOGRAPHY: Allen and CWE Ep 611 / NDB X 98 (genealogy) / Georg Landau *Die hessischen Ritterburgen und ihre Besitzer* (Kassel 1836, repr 1976) III / Damasus Fuchs *Beiträge zur Geschichte der Stadt, der Pfarrei und des Klosters Salmünster* (Frankfurt am Main 1946) 71ff, 84ff / Reinhold Röhricht *Deutsche Pilgerreisen nach dem Heiligen Lande* 2nd ed (Innsbruck 1900, repr 1967) 208–11   BARBARA KÖNNEKER

Ludwig von HUTTEN (Ep 611, 20 July 1517)
Frowin von *Hutten was in the company of one Ludwig von Hutten, said to be the son of another Ludwig, when he joined the pilgrimage to Jerusalem led by Bernhard von Hirschfeld in 1517 (Ep 611). The name of Ludwig was popular in several branches of the Hutten family, but the pilgrim may well have been Ludwig, a son of the Ludwig (d 1517) who had founded the Frankenberg branch. The younger Ludwig was a brother of Hans von Hutten, who was slain by Ulrich of *Württemberg in 1515. Ludwig was subsequently the official at Kitzingen, near Würzberg, then belonging to the margraves of Brandenburg-Ansbach, and died without offspring in 1547. The father of that Ludwig was among the patrons of Ulrich von *Hutten and had himself performed the pilgrimage to the Holy Land in 1482. Two other Ludwigs, father and son, belonged to the Stolzenberg branch; the latter died in 1571. At

Moritz von Hutten

the time of the imperial election of 1519 a
Ludwig von Hutten was in the service of
Albert von *Brandenburg, archbishop of
Mainz, and the name is also found in connec-
tion with subsequent diets.

BIBLIOGRAPHY: Georg Landau *Die hessischen
Ritterburgen und ihre Besitzer* (Kassel 1836, repr
1976) III 292 / Reinhold Röhricht *Deutsche
Pilgerreisen nach dem Heiligen Lande* 2nd ed
(Innsbruck 1900, repr 1967) 159, 209 / *Deutsche
Reichstagsakten* Jüngere Reihe (Gotha-
Göttingen 1893–) I 763–4 and passim
                                          BARBARA KÖNNEKER

Moritz von HUTTEN 26 November 1503–
6 December 1552
Moritz von Hutten was born in Arnstein, north
of Würzburg. His father was Bernhard von
Hutten, a magistrate of Würzburg and a cousin
of Ulrich von *Hutten. Assured in advance of a
canonry at Würzburg, Moritz studied from
1518 to 1530 in Leipzig, Wittenberg, Ingolstadt, Padua, Basel, and Freiburg. Having
been made canon of Würzburg and Augsburg
in 1530, he was received into the chapter of
Eichstätt in 1532. On 1 September 1536 he

became provost of Würzburg, an appointment
which caused a lengthy controversy with the
curia because of accumulation of benefices and
obliged him to reside in Rome for some time in
1537 while the problem was being settled. On
25 June 1539 he was elected prince-bishop of
Eichstätt. As a bishop he strove to restore
ecclesiastical discipline and at the same time to
restore Christian unity. In 1543 he was one of
the handful of bishops who responded to the
first, unsuccessful, convocation of the council
of Trent, and in 1546 he presided over the
religious colloquy held at Regensburg. He died
in Eichstätt and is commemorated by a monument with an inscription in the cathedral of
Würzburg.

Erasmus evidently met Moritz when he was
studying at Basel with a fellow canon from
Würzburg, Daniel *Stiebar (Ep 2322). Moritz
von Hutten deserves credit for collecting the
writings of his relative Ulrich. According to
*Eobanus many might have been lost to
posterity without the intercession of Moritz
(Hutten *Opera* II 440), who also had Ulrich's
dialogue *Arminius* posthumously published in
Haguenau by Johann Setzer in 1529.

BIBLIOGRAPHY: Allen Epp 2116, 2322 / Hein-
rich Grimm in NDB X 98 / Karl Ried *Moritz von
Hutten und die Glaubensspaltung* (Münster 1925)
/ Ludwig Weiss in *Würzburger Diözesange-
schichtsblätter* 16–17 (1954–5) 252–3 / *Matrikel
Freiburg* I 277 / *Matrikel Basel* I 362 / AK III Ep
1228 / A.J. Schmidlin *Geschichte der deutschen
Nationalkirche in Rom, S. Maria dell'Anima*
(Freiburg-Vienna 1906)
                                          BARBARA KÖNNEKER

Ulrich von HUTTEN 21 April 1488–end of
August 1523
Ulrich von Hutten, born at the castle of
Steckelberg, near Fulda, was the descendant of
a large clan of Franconian knights. His parents,
Ulrich von Hutten and Ottilie von Eberstein,
had destined him for the priesthood. In 1499 he
entered the monastery of Fulda, but left in 1505
(*Opera* II 145). Almost destitute, he spent the
next few years studying at the universities of
Cologne, Erfurt, Frankfurt an der Oder –
where he obtained a BA in 1507 (*Opera* I 5) –
Leipzig, and Greifswald. He also came into
contact with *Crotus Rubeanus and the circle
of humanists in Erfurt. A quarrel with Lötze,

his host in Greifswald, prompted him to publish the *Querelae* (Frankfurt an der Oder 1510), demonstrating for the first time his talents as a writer of satire and polemics. During a visit to Vienna in the summer of 1511 he was introduced to the patriotic and historico-political aims of the humanist circle founded by Conrad Celtis. In the same year he published his *Ars versificatoria* in Leipzig. In 1512 Hutten went to Italy to study Roman law, but returned to Germany one year later and presented a collection of epigrams to the Emperor *Maximilian, who crowned him poet laureate in 1517 (Ep 611).

From 1515 on Hutten was engaged in a controversy over the murder of a relative by Duke Ulrich of *Württemberg, and after the publication of five tracts against the duke (Mainz 1519) he emerged as the political champion of the free imperial knights. At about the same time he became involved in the controversy surrounding *Reuchlin. When George, count *Palatine, bishop of Speyer passed judgment in favour of Reuchlin, Hutten was inspired to compose the *Triumphus Capnionis* (published under a pseudonym, Haguenau 1518) on which he asked Erasmus' opinion at their first meeting (*Spongia* ASD IX-1 202–3). This took place in August 1514 in Mainz, where Erasmus stopped over on his journey to Basel and met Reuchlin, Hermannus *Buschius, and Hutten (Ep 300). A second meeting took place in Frankfurt am Main in April 1515 (*Opera* I 43–4). These two meetings marked the beginning of an alliance 'against the enemies of the languages and good literature' (ASD IX-1 202), a relationship that was all the more flattering for Hutten because Erasmus had already reached the zenith of his career.

In October 1515, when he was on his way back to Italy, Hutten wrote his first letter to Erasmus (Ep 365). He praised Erasmus as a 'German Socrates' at whose feet he would gladly sit to obtain knowledge, like 'Alcibiades.' In Ep 611 he told of the friendly reception he had been given in Italy by Erasmus' friends (cf Ep 588). Erasmus, for his part, mentioned Hutten in his annotations to the New Testament of 1516 (1 Thessalonians 1:2; Hutten *Opera* I 103 – in later editions Erasmus deleted this passage) and spoke of

Ulrich von Hutten, by Hans Weiditz

him in complimentary terms in letters to *Budé and *Eobanus Hessus (Epp 778, 874). Erasmus' earliest extant letter to Hutten (Ep 951) dates from April 1519 (for the lost correspondence of this time cf Kaegi 234–9 and CWE Ep 986 introduction).

In the summer of 1517 Hutten finally returned from Italy and entered the service of Archbishop Albert of *Brandenburg, to whom he had dedicated a *Panegyricus* on the occasion of his accession to the see of Mainz in 1514 (Tübingen 1515). Hutten's second trip to Italy had had a profound impact on his life: in the course of this journey he wrote a large part of his anonymous contributions to the *Epistolae obscurorum virorum* (Haguenau 1515; Cologne 1517) as well as *Phalarismus* (Mainz 1517), his first satirical dialogue aimed at Ulrich of Württemberg. Also during this time he made up his mind to direct his future literary production against the Roman church. His experiences with the papal curia had convinced him that this battle had to be fought in the name of liberty for the 'German nation.' In Mainz he devoted much time and energy to his writings, publishing *Valla's treatise *De falso* *credita et ementita Constantini donatione* in 1517 and in 1518 an address to the diet of Augsburg rejecting the taxation demanded by Rome to finance a crusade against the Turks (Augsburg 1518). In the fall of the same year he wrote his dialogue *Aula* (Augsburg 1518), a treatise *De guaiaci medicina et morbo gallico* (Mainz 1519), and *Febris prima* (Mainz 1519), the first of his dialogues attacking Rome. Within a year he followed it up with *Febris secunda, Vadiscus sive trias Romana*, and the dialogues *Inspicientes* (Mainz 1520; German translation *Gespräch-büchlin*, Strasbourg 1521). In the spring of 1519 he joined the army of the Swabian League for its war against Ulrich of Württemberg. This campaign led to a friendship with Franz von *Sickingen, whom he induced to protect Reuchlin (Ep 986).

The political orientation of Hutten's publications did not at first affect his friendship with Erasmus, although the latter expressed some reservations (Ep 967) and counselled moderation (Ep 951). In fact Erasmus valued Hutten more than ever because of his position in Mainz, even though Albert's efforts to attract Erasmus to his court remained unsuccessful (Epp 614, 661). Erasmus praised Hutten's talents repeatedly in letters to the archbishop (Epp 745, 968, and, with some qualifications, Ep 1009). Hutten sent Erasmus a valuable gift from the archbishop (Ep 986), and both men contributed prefatory letters to an edition of Livy dedicated to the archbishop in 1518 (Ep 919; Hutten *Opera* I 249). Erasmus continued to approve of Hutten's works (Ep 951; cf Ep 967) as they reached him: *Nemo* (Erfurt 1510, 2nd ed Augsburg 1518; Epp 961 and 967) and the dialogues *Phalarismus* and *Febris prima*, which Hutten sent him in 1519 (Ep 923). In July of the same year Erasmus addressed to him as a token of appreciation his famous letter about Thomas *More (Ep 999; cf Erasmus' later statements on this subject, Allen I 27). Their relationship was affected for the first time when Hutten published a letter addressed to Albert of Brandenburg (Ep 1033, of October 1519), in which Erasmus defended *Luther. Hutten had acted without Erasmus' authorization and even before the archbishop had seen the letter (*Spongia* ASD IX-1 192–3). Erasmus considered this a serious breach of trust (Epp 1152, 1153,

1167, 1217) because it forced him to take a stand, a situation which he had tried to avoid out of concern for the fate of humanistic studies. Hutten, however, had always considered Erasmus the founder and leader of the opposition to the church. He had admired him in this role (*Expostulatio, Opera* II 208–9; cf I 198) and evidently believed he was acting in accord with the unspoken wishes of Erasmus. He expected Erasmus to come out openly in favour of Luther, especially in view of the massive support he and other German admirers had given Erasmus in his quarrel with Edward *Lee (*Opera* I 346–8; cf Ep 1083 and *Spongia* ASD IX-1 160).

The third and last meeting between Erasmus and Hutten showed clear signs of the impending break-up. The meeting took place in Louvain in June 1520 (Ep 1113–15) during Hutten's journey to Brussels, where he hoped to win Archduke *Ferdinand's approval for his and Sickingen's plan for an armed attack against the church. Hutten had left the service of the archbishop of Mainz in the summer of 1519 but still received a pension from him. In the meantime he had formed a close alliance with Sickingen and during his visit discussed their common plans with Erasmus. Erasmus provided him with two letters of recommendation for the court in Brussels (Epp 1114, 1115) but adamantly refused to support his cause (*Spongia* ASD IX-1 202). When his mission to Brussels proved unsuccessful, Hutten had to flee from Mainz, his printer was arrested, and the pope demanded from Albert a full investigation into Hutten's conduct (*Opera* I 362–5). In August 1520 Hutten wrote to Erasmus from Steckelberg, for the first time attacking his cautious attitude and his manoeuvring between the two fronts (Ep 1135). Three months later, now a refugee in Sickingen's castle, the Ebernburg, he wrote his last extant letter to Erasmus (Ep 1161), this time warning him of the impending fight and begging him to flee to Basel, where he would be safe and free to serve the cause of humanistic studies. No further direct communication took place between Hutten and Erasmus until the winter of 1522. Erasmus' reaction may be gleaned from remarks he made in letters to other friends. He emphasized his impartiality (Epp 1166, 1195)

and regretted that 'this whirlwind of Luther'
had taken in Hutten, who was 'torn from us by
these tumults' (Epp 1184, 1202).

Meanwhile Hutten continued to pour out
numerous polemical pamphlets, among them
*Clag und Vormanung gegen dem übermässigen
unchristlichen Gewalt des Bapsts zu Rom* (1520),
Conquestiones (1520), *In incendium Lutherianum
exclamatio* (1521); *Anzoig, wie allwegen sich die
römischen Bischöff oder Bäpst gegen den teutschen
Kaisseren gehalten haben* (1521), *Dialogi novi*
(1521), and *Entschüldigung Ulrichs von Hutten
wyder etlicher unwarhafftiges Aussgeben von ym*
(1521). In Ep 1244 of November 1521 Erasmus
was clearly taking aim at this incessant
production when he commented 'Men who
write like this and utter those threats should
have had troops at their disposal, had they
wished to remain unharmed.'

To gather 'troops' for the impending battle
with the church had indeed been Hutten's
purpose since the autumn of 1520. After he
had appealed to the emperor, to Frederick,
elector of *Saxony, and to the 'common German
nation' both in Latin and German (*Conquestiones* and translation), he finally decided to
begin the battle with the help of none but
Sickingen. In preparation he fired off his
Dialogi novi, but the realization of his plans had
to be delayed time and again because of
Sickingen's hesitation and the restraining
tactics of the imperial government. Finally, in
the late summer of 1521, Hutten composed his
famous song 'Ich habs gewagt mit Sinnen'
announcing that he was going to begin on his
own the battle against the clergy. He accomplished no more than ambushes in the fashion
of the old *Raubritter* and extortion against the
Strasbourg Dominicans (cf *Spongia* ASD IX-1
176, 200–1). Hutten did not participate in the
more general revolt of the imperial knights and
Sickingen's expedition against the archbishopric of Trier in 1522. Even before the princes
gathered their troops to punish Sickingen,
Hutten fled to Switzerland. Sick and destitute,
he arrived in Basel in November 1522 and for
the time being was granted asylum by the city
council.

After Hutten's arrival in Basel Erasmus
refused to see him (Ep 1331), and thus their
conflict became evident to all. The reasons for

Erasmus' refusal (Epp 1342, 1356, 1496; *Spongia*
ASD IX-1 123–4), *Eppendorf's dubious role as a
go-between (Epp 1383, 1437, 1934), and the
validity of mutual accusations made in the
written polemic have been thoroughly analys-
ed by Werner Kaegi (461–83), who also
examined the aftermath of the quarrel and the
reaction of Erasmus' friends and opponents
(Ep 1443; Hutten *Opera* II 254, 258–9, 325–51,
373–8, 401). Of the correspondence between
Erasmus and Hutten during these months only
one of Erasmus' letters is extant (Ep 1356); in it
he tried to prevent Hutten from publishing his
Expostulatio (1523), the work which presents
his final reckoning with Erasmus. Hutten
wrote the work in Mulhouse, where he had
withdrawn after his expulsion from Basel in
January 1523. It was first circulated in manuscript (Ep 1384; Hutten *Opera* II 327) and
shortly afterwards printed in Strasbourg (Ep
1429). Erasmus reacted sharply in a letter to the
city council of Zürich, whose protection
Hutten had sought, demanding that the city
refuse Hutten asylum (Ep 1379). He wrote to
*Zwingli in a similar vein (Epp 1378, 1384) and
finally published his reply, the *Spongia* (ASD
IX-1 93–210; Epp 1388, 1389), in Basel a few
days after Hutten's death. Hutten died of
syphilis at the end of August 1523 on the island
of Ufenau in Lake Zürich (the date of 29
August given by Erasmus in Ep 1388 may not
be correct).

Unlike the controversy with Luther which
unfolded soon afterwards, the quarrel between Erasmus and Hutten as evidenced in
their writings consisted largely of personal
accusations, suspicions, and justifications.
Erasmus never overcame his bitter disappointment at the change in their relationship, which
had been based on common goals and causes
but had turned into bitter hatred and
suspicion; it determines and colours all his later
remarks about Hutten (Allen I 27, 31; Ep 1347,
1376, 1379, 1384, 1389, 1437, 1445, 1614). Their
mutual accusations document the breakdown
of their friendship as well as the fundamental
misunderstanding that governed their relationship from the beginning. They had never
assessed correctly one another's personalities,
aims, and motives. Hutten saw only cowardice
and hypocrisy in Erasmus' efforts to remain

Johann Huttich, by Friedrich Hagenauer

---

neutral for the sake of reason and peace, while Erasmus considered Hutten's determination and ensuing actions as a betrayal of the ideals of humanism. This misunderstanding is not only based on a clash of personalities, however; the *Expostulatio* and the *Spongia* are valuable documents of intellectual history. With the question of right or wrong no longer of importance, they are significant as expressions of opposing points of view, of two different directions in the development of humanism that were bound to clash at a certain point in history – the onset of the Reformation.

BIBLIOGRAPHY: Allen and CWE Ep 365 / Heinrich Grimm in NDB X 99–102 / Ulrich von Hutten *Opera omnia* ed E. Böcking (Leipzig 1859–70, repr 1963) / David Friedrich Strauss *Ulrich von Hutten* (Leipzig 1858–60, partial repr 1930) / Paul Kalkoff *Ulrich von Hutten und die Reformation* (Leipzig 1920, repr 1971) / Werner Kaegi 'Hutten und Erasmus: Ihre Freundschaft und ihr Streit' *Historische Vierteljahrsschrift* 22 (1924–5) 200–78, 461–514 / Hajo Holborn *Ulrich von Hutten* (Leipzig 1929; English trans R.H. Bainton 1937) / L.W. Spitz *The Religious Renaissance of the German Humanists* (Cam-

bridge, Mass, 1963) 110–29 and passim / Hutten's *Expostulatio* and Erasmus' *Spongia* are translated and annotated in R.J. Klawitter *The Polemics of Erasmus of Rotterdam and Ulrich von Hutten* (London-Notre Dame, Ind 1977) / For a detailed bibliography of Hutten's publications see Josef Benzing *Ulrich von Hutten und seine Drucker* (Wiesbaden 1956)

BARBARA KÖNNEKER

Johann HUTTICH of Strinz, d 4 March 1544
Allen's tentative identification of Johannes Eutychius with Johann Huttich (Huttichius) should be accepted in view of Eutychius' residence in Mainz (Ep 614) and the documented contacts of Huttich and many of his friends with Erasmus. It is true that the name form 'Eutychius' was not, it seems, otherwise used for Huttich, but neither can it be connected with any known contemporary of his.

Johann Huttich was born about 1490 in Strinz, in the Taunus. In Mainz he studied with Johannes Rhagius Aesticampianus, who took Huttich with him when called to the University of Frankfurt an der Oder in 1506. There Huttich joined *Hutten's circle and obtained a BA in February 1507 together with Wolfgang *Angst. In 1508 he followed Aesticampianus to Leipzig and taught there until 1511, arousing controversy by his advocacy of the *bonae literae*. In 1511 he returned to Mainz, was appointed vicar at the cathedral, and collaborated as corrector and editor with Johann *Schöffer. He supported *Reuchlin (RE Ep 276) and with Sebastian von *Rothenhan prepared the first edition of the chronicler Regino of Prüm (Mainz: J. Schöffer 1521). In 1519 he accompanied Frederick II, count *Palatine, to Spain to inform *Charles V officially of his election. After his return he became a citizen of Strasbourg in February 1521. From 1527 he was a canon of St Thomas' and from 1533 also held the position of choirmaster at the cathedral. His income enabled him to collect books and manuscripts. He became a good friend of *Beatus Rhenanus and gave much scholarly assistance to the printer Johann *Grüninger in Strasbourg.

Erasmus dedicated to Huttich his translation of Lucian's *Convivium* (1517, Ep 550). There is evidence of some correspondence between them, but no other letters have survived. Ep 614 mentions a letter from Erasmus to Huttich that reached Mainz in Huttich's absence and was read by Archbishop Albert of *Brandenburg. Huttich's edition of Dietrich Gresemund's *Collectanea antiquitatum in urbe atque agro Moguntino* (Mainz: J. Schöffer 1520) is dedicated to Albert's vicar-general, Theoderich *Zobel (Epp 919, 1054). His most important work, the well-illustrated *Imperatorum Romanorum libellus* (Strasbourg: W. Köpfel 1525), was often reprinted. While in Spain, Huttich had collected booklets dealing with the discovery of America; these were reprinted in Simon *Grynaeus' collection *Novus orbis regionum ac insularum* (Basel: J. Herwagen 1532).

BIBLIOGRAPHY: Allen and CWE Ep 550 / Heinrich Grimm in NDB X 105–6 / Heinrich Grimm 'Die Matrikel der Universität Frankfurt/ Oder ... als urkundliche Quelle für die Geschichte des Buchwesens' *Archiv für Geschichte des Buchwesens* 3 (1960) 398–512, esp 404–5 / BRE Ep 264 and passim / *Matrikel Frankfurt* I 490   IG

Werner HUYN van Amstenrade d before 23 April 1534

Werner Huyn van Amstenrade (Amstenrath, Anstenroed, Anstenroid) was descended from a noble family originating from Luxembourg and owning estates in Dutch Limburg. He was the nephew of Nicolaas Huyn van Amstenrade, canon of St Mary's in Aachen from 1472 to 1500. On 14 February 1500, apparently at a relatively young age (Ep 1170), Werner succeeded to his uncle's prebend. He matriculated in the faculty of arts of the University of Cologne on 21 April 1506 and was studying there in 1507. On 25 January 1517 he was appointed vice-provost of St Mary's. In this function he was also in charge of the provost's *Lehnkammer* (or *Mannkammer*). Extant evidence illustrates his management for the period 1521–33. In 1525 Huyn and his fellow-canon Leonardus *Priccardus went to the court of John III, duke of *Cleves, to seek his intervention on behalf of St Mary's in a litigation with the city council of Aachen. Werner Huyn died early in 1534 and was succeeded in his canonry by Werner von Vlatten on 23 April.

A friend of the noted Rhenish Erasmians Konrad von *Heresbach and Johann von *Vlatten, Huyn was a member of the circle of Erasmians in Aachen gathered around Priccardus. He met Erasmus, probably for the first time, during the latter's brief visit to Aachen in September 1518. Erasmus attended a meal at his house and afterwards made ambiguous remarks about the hospitality of the Aachen canons in a letter that soon attained wide circulation (Ep 867). Later he praised the civility of the youthful vice-provost (Ep 1170).

BIBLIOGRAPHY: Allen Ep 867 / *Matrikel Köln* II 591 / Luise Coels von der Brügghen *Die Lehensregister der probsteilichen Mannkammer des Aachener Marienstifts 1394–1794* (Bonn 1952) 49, 221, 315–16, 425, 749 / Anton Fahne *Geschichte der Kölnischen, Jülichschen und Bergischen Geschlechter in Stammtafeln, Wappen, Siegeln und Urkunden* (Cologne-Bonn 1848–53, repr 1965) I 184 / Hermann Ariovist von Fürth *Beiträge und Material zur Geschichte der Aachener Patrizier-Familien* (Aachen 1890) I 54–5 / Anton Gail 'Johann von Vlatten und der Einfluss des Erasmus auf die Kirchenpolitik der Vereinigten Herzogtümer' *Düsseldorfer Jahrbuch* 45 (1951) 1–109, esp 30 / *Nomina admodum reverendorum perillustrium atque generosorum dominorum canonicorum regalis ecclesiae B.M.V. Aquisgranensis* ed Antonius Heusch (Berlin 1892) 11–12 / 'Freundesbriefe Conrads von Heresbach an Johann von Vlatten (1524–36)' ed Otto R. Redlich *Zeitschrift des Bergischen Geschichtsvereins* 41 (1905) 170, 177

KASPAR VON GREYERZ

Jan HUYSMAN
(Ep 3053, of 2 September 1535)

According to Cornelius *Grapheus, Jan Huysman, a former curate of the collegiate church of Notre Dame at Antwerp, was in 1535 the principal priest of Edingen. Huysman recommended Erasmus' famulus Johannes *Clauthus to Grapheus in a letter, now lost, which Grapheus forwarded to Erasmus with Ep 3053. No more is known about Huysman.

BIBLIOGRAPHY: Allen Ep 3053 / de Vocht CTL III 394   MARCEL A. NAUWELAERTS

Rochus HYEMS documented at Louvain 1513–d 1531

Rochus Hyems (Hyeme) was a canon regular of St Augustine and is documented from 1513 in the monastery of St Maartensdal, Louvain, where he died; by 1527 he was sub-prior. Erasmus' good friend Maarten *Lips, who also lived at St Maartensdal, reported in 1527 that Hyems had not changed his opinion that Erasmus' writings were pernicious and heretical (Ep 1837).

BIBLIOGRAPHY: W. Lourdaux *Moderne devotie en christelijk humanisme: De geschiedenis van Sint Maarten te Leuven van 1433 tot het einde der xvie eeuw* (Louvain 1967) 155, 158, 191, 205, 208

E.J.M. VAN EIJL

Theobald HYLLWEG *See Theobald* HILLWEG

IACOBUS, IACOBI *See* JACOB, JACOBSZOON, *JACOBUS*

IASPARUS (Ep 83, to be dated 14 December 1497)
Iasparus (Jasper), a friend of Willem *Hermans, who had placed Erasmus 'deeply in his debt,' has not been identified.

Henricus IESKYN
(Ep 465 of 16 September [1516])
Ieskyn (Henry Jeskin), a servant of William *Warham, was sent to Thomas *More with Ep 465. He has not been identified.

IESUS *See Johann* BURCHARD

René d'ILLIERS d 8 April 1507
René, a son of Florent d'Illiers and Jeanne de Contes, belonged to a powerful family which dominated ecclesiastical appointments in the diocese of Chartres for a considerable time. While his brothers became dean and archdeacon, respectively, of the cathedral chapter, René obtained a licence in both laws and on 18 March 1486 succeeded an insane uncle as abbot of Bonneval and on 3 December 1492 another uncle as bishop. In 1498 he assisted in the annulment of the marriage of *Louis XII. In the summer of 1506, barefooted, he led a procession of thanksgiving to God for sparing the cathedral from the lightning and fire that had damaged the north tower. It was just at this time that Erasmus dedicated to him from Paris his translation of Lucian's *Alexander seu Pseudomantis* (Ep 199). An illustrated copy of Hartmann Schedel's *Liber chronicorum* (Nürn-

berg 1493) bearing René's coat of arms is in Besançon.

BIBLIOGRAPHY: Allen Ep 199 / *Gallia christiana* VIII 1186-7, 1244-5 / A. Castan *Catalogue des incunables de la Bibliothèque publique de Besançon* (Besançon 1893) 629   MICHEL REULOS & PGB

Hans IMHOF of Nürnberg, d 1526
Hans Imhof, the husband of Willibald *Pirckheimer's daughter Felicitas, may be referred to in Epp 1085, 1095; see CWE Ep 1085.

Johann INGENWINKEL 1469–23 July 1535
Johann Ingenwinkel (Vinchel, Ingen Winkel, etc), a native of the Lower Rhine region, is documented as a member of the Roman curia from 1496 and was at that time a MA and canon of Xanten. From then on he spent his entire life in the service of consecutive popes. He was a papal protonotary in 1505 and an apostolic scriptor in 1511 and eventually became the datary. As an able administrator he exercised considerable influence and reaped rich rewards from all sides. He secured benefices for some of his relatives and favours for the many ecclesiastical corporations with which he was associated. He was also a benefactor of the German institution of Rome, Santa Maria dell'Anima.

Among his contemporaries Ingenwinkel enjoyed a dubious reputation in view of the incredible number of benefices he held at one time or another, trading them rather like a portfolio of stocks. For the years up to 1521 a wealth of data for these transactions has been gathered by Schulte, who lists benefices in the dioceses of Utrecht, Cambrai, Tournai, Arras, Thérouanne, Liège, Trier, Cologne, Mainz, Constance, Münster, Lübeck, Verden, Paderborn, Spoleto, Veroli, Anagni, and Todi and in Rome. Among his Roman friends were Willem van *Enckenvoirt, Theodoricus *Hezius, and Albert *Pigghe.

In 1525 Ingenwinkel drew up Ep 1588, a papal brief enabling Erasmus to make a will; his signature appears beneath the draft. On 1 April 1519 *Leo x had granted Ingenwinkel the right of succession to the provostship of St Lebuin's at Deventer, where he held a canonry. After his death *Paul III nominated Erasmus to the provostship at Deventer (Epp 3033, 3034, 3047, 3061). Writing to Johannes

*Danticus on 6 December 1535, Cornelis de
*Schepper even spoke of three bishoprics
reserved for Erasmus, together with most of
Ingenwinkel's benefices.

BIBLIOGRAPHY: Allen Ep 1588 / Aloys Schulte
Die Fugger in Rom, 1495–1521 (Leipzig 1904) I
289–306 and passim / de Vocht *Dantiscus* 154,
254, 276 / de Vocht CTL III 208 and passim / de
Vocht *Literae ad Craneveldium* 257 and passim /
Pastor IX 49, 80–1 / Ludwig Geiger *Johann
Reuchlin* (Leipzig 1871; repr 1964) 421 / A.J.
Schmidlin *Geschichte der deutschen Nationalkirche
in Rom, S. Maria dell'Anima* (Freiburg-Vienna
1906) 360–1 and passim   PGB

Tommaso INGHIRAMI of Volterra, 1470–
6 September 1516
Tommaso Inghirami (Phaedra, Phaedrus,
Fedra), the son of Paolo and Lucrezia Barlet-
tani, was born in Volterra, in Tuscany. In 1472
his father, a prominent political figure in his
native town and a friend of the Medici, was
killed during a political uprising (cf Niccolò
Machiavelli *Istorie fiorentine* VII xxix). After
the murder, Paolo's children were taken to
Florence. While he was still very young
Tommaso was sent to Rome, where he was
under the protection of Bishop Jacopo
Gherardi and of his uncle, Antonio Inghirami,
a secretary to Pope *Sixtus IV. Early fame came
to Tommaso from his participation in the
memorable presentation of Seneca's *Hippolytus*, staged by Giovanni *Sulpizio under the
auspices of Cardinal Raffaele *Riario and with
the support of the members of the Roman
Academy of *Pomponius Laetus. The Senecan
tragedy was performed several times in 1486 (in
front of the cardinal's palace and presumably
in Campo de' Fiori); Inghirami, a pupil of
Pomponius Laetus, played the role of Phaedra
(Ep 1347), and his success was such that
thereafter he became known by the name of the
Greek tragic heroine. *Ariosto remembers
Inghirami (*Orlando Furioso* 46.13) as a member
of the Roman intellectual élite, and as such he
is praised by *Bembo, *Castiglione, Paolo
Giovio, Machiavelli, and *Colocci. In 1495
Inghirami was sent by *Alexander VI to be
orator to the Emperor *Maximilian I, who
created him count palatine and poet laureate.
In 1510 he became librarian of the Vatican
library; in 1513 he served as secretary to the

Tommaso Inghirami, by Raphael

college of cardinals in the conclave that elected
*Leo X and as secretary in the Lateran council.
    Inghirami's interest in the theatre continued
till the end of his life. He directed the
presentation of Plautus's *Poenulus*, staged
during the festivities organized to celebrate the
conferment of Roman citizenship on Giuliano
and Lorenzo de' *Medici in the new Teatro del
Campidoglio; he contributed to the stage
decoration and probably to the design of the
stage itself, and he supervised the design of
the costumes and the rehearsals. In 1514 he
devised the eighteen allegorical floats paraded
during the 'festa di Agone,' and we learn from
Paolo Giovio that his interests extended to
dramatic productions in Italian.
    Erasmus met Inghirami during his visit to
Rome in 1509; the two established a warm and
cordial relationship, which Erasmus vividly
remembered for a long time (Epp 1347, 3032;
Allen I 67, perhaps also Ep 216). In 1523 he
noted accurately that Inghirami's reputation
was based more on his prestige as an orator
than on his production as a writer (Ep 1347),
praising him for being a 'wonderfully copious
and effective speaker.' In Ep 3032 he again

emphasized Inghirami's rhetorical talent, saying that the Romans took him for a second Cicero. However, in both these letters he failed to remember Inghirami's Christian name correctly.

In the *Ciceronianus* of 1528 Erasmus noted in passing Inghirami's outstanding reputation as an orator, stating, however, that the force of Giulio *Camillo's eloquence was greater. This circumstantial statement is made in the context of his famous account of a Ciceronian lenten sermon he had heard at Rome (ASD I-2 637-9). The preacher is bitterly criticized, but his name is withheld. Suggestions that he was Inghirami (ASD I-2 639:17n) are unsubstantiated and fail to take into account the high praise given to Inghirami in Ep 1347. However, Erasmus' attitude towards a friend who had been dead for a number of years by the time he composed the *Ciceronianus* could have been influenced by factors which materialized after the date of Ep 1347. Among these elements particular consideration might be given to the possible influence of Jacopo *Sadoleto. In 1523 this friend of Erasmus completed the dialogue *Phaedrus*, the first section of his *De laudibus philosophiae*, where he assigned to Inghirami the role of his antagonist and, in the words of Richard M. Douglas, described him as a 'cynical mocker of speculative thought and a champion of the *vita negotiosa*, a straw philistine, whom Sadoleto intended to destroy in the *Hortensius*'; see Richard M. Douglas *Jacopo Sadoleto* (Cambridge, Mass., 1959) 78.

The number of works published by Inghirami during his lifetime is small: extant are an *Oratio de obitu Iohannis Hispaniae principis* (Rome: E. Silber 1498) and a *Panegyricus in memoriam Thomae Aquinatis* (Rome: E. Silber 1500). Girolamo Tiraboschi, in his *Storia della letteratura italiana* (Florence 1812) 1351, quotes Aulus Janus Parrhasius, who in his *Liber de rebus per epistulam quaesitis* maintains that he saw the following works written by Inghirami: *Luculentissimae scilicet orationes, In Horatii poetica vigilantissima commentaria, Annalium breviarium quo res omnes a Paulo Romano gestas complexus est, Apologia in Ciceronis obtrectatores*, and *In Plauti comoedias scrupulosissimae quaestiones*. Gaetano Feroci who compiled Inghirami's biography also accepts Parrhasius' list in the *Elogi degli uomini illustri toscani* (Lucca 1771)

237. The correctness of this account may be tested with the help of the most authoritative results of contemporary archival research. For this purpose the most relevant study is Isabella Inghirami 'Notizia dei codici, degli autografi e delle stampe riguardanti le opere dell'umanista volterrano Tommaso Inghirami, detto Fedro' *Rassegna volterrana*, 21-3 (1955) 33-41, supplemented by Roberto Weiss 'Un'orazione dimenticata di Tommaso Fedra Inghirami' *Rassegna volterrana* 21-3 (1955) 46-52 and by the indications on the manuscript material of Inghirami in Paul O. Kristeller's *Iter italicum* (London-Leiden 1965-).

Raphael painted the most famous portrait of Tommaso Inghirami, which is now in the Galleria Pitti (Florence), while another copy is in Boston.

BIBLIOGRAPHY: Allen Ep 1347 / The political events leading to the murder of Paolo Inghirami are described in Antonio Ivani of Sarzana *Historia de Volaterrana calamitate* ed F.L. Mannucci, XIII-iv of L.A. Muratori *Rerum Italicarum Scriptores* (Città di Castello 1913) 3-26 / Besides the already quoted eighteenth-century profile of G. Feroci and the biographical notations of Tiraboschi, a modern monograph on Inghirami is provided by Anna Maria Rugiadi *Tommaso Fedra Inghirami umanista volterrano* (Amatrice 1916) / For Inghirami's contributions to the development of the theatre in Rome during the second half of the fifteenth century and the early years of the pontificate of Leo X see F. Pintor *Rappresentazioni romane di Seneca e Plauto nel Rinascimento* (Perugia 1906), W. Creizenach *Geschichte des neueren Dramas* (Halle 1911-18) II 19-20, and M. Pastore Stocchi *Les Tragédies de Sénèque et le théâtre de la Renaissance* (Paris 1964) / For the theatrical activity of Pomponius Laetus and his pupils see Margret Dietrich 'Pomponius Laetus' Wiedererweckung des antiken Theaters' *Maske und Kothurn* 3 (1957) 3 / For the 1513 performance of Plautus' *Poenulus* see G. Palliolo *Le feste pel conferimento del patriziato romano a Giuliano e Lorenzo de' Medici* (Bologna 1885) and Fabrizio Cruciani *Le feste romane del 1513 in onore di Giuliano e Lorenzo de' Medici* (Milan 1968) / For the Florence and Boston copies of Raphael's portrait of Inghirami see P. Künzle 'Raffaels Denkmal für Fedro Inghirami auf dem letzten Arazzo' in *Mélanges Eugène Tisserant* (Vatican City 1964) / For the question of the lenten sermon see Silvana Seidel Menchi 'Alcuni atteggiamenti della cultura italiana di fronte ad Erasmo' in *Eresia e riforma nell'Italia del Cinquecento* (Florence-Chicago 1974) 69–133, esp 106–7   DANILO AGUZZI-BARBAGLI

Heinrich INGOLD of Strasbourg, documented 1484–1521(?)

Heinrich Ingold (Ingolt) came from a patrician Strasbourg family whose members served as senators, diplomats, and *Ammeisters*, or chief representatives of the guilds and chief administrators of the city. Heinrich was probably the son of Hans Ingold of Haguenau, who had bought the citizenship of Strasbourg on 27 March 1470. He married Klara Gerbott and, like other members of his family, was involved in Europe-wide trade. His interests in the manufacture and sale of paper led to a close business connection with the international publisher Anton Koberger of Nürnberg. On occasion he accepted books in return for his shipments of paper and thus he had some involvement in the book trade. In the years following his death the Ingold family formed a properly constituted trading company and dealt primarily in spices and precious metals.

From 1491 Heinrich served regularly on the Strasbourg city council, and in 1508 and 1514 he was elected *Ammeister*. In 1514 Erasmus was honoured by the *Ammeister* during his visit to Strasbourg and expressed his appreciation in a letter to *Wimpfeling (Ep 305). In 1515 Ingold was book censor. He died either in 1520 or in 1523; a document recording an anniversary gift in 1521 could mean that he was still alive at that time. A spurious letter from Erasmus to a Heinrich Ingold of Strasbourg, dated Basel, 1 March 1524, is printed in Allen v 618–21.

BIBLIOGRAPHY: Allen and CWE Ep 305 / François-Joseph Fuchs 'Richesse et faillite des Ingold, négociants et financiers strasbourgeois du XVI siècle' in *La Bourgeoisie alsacienne* (Strasbourg-Paris 1954) 203–23 / Grimm *Buchführer* 1434–5 / AK I Ep 126 / Oscar Hase *Die Koberger* 3rd ed (Amsterdam-Wiesbaden 1967) 69–70, 308–9   MIRIAM U. CHRISMAN & PGB

Doctor IOACINUS (Ep 256, [end of February] 1512)

Writing from Paris to Erasmus, who was then in London, Girolamo *Aleandro warmly recommended to him one 'doctor Joachim,' whose upright character and literary attainments had impressed Aleandro. Assuming that Aleandro had met Joachim recently in Paris, Allen proposed to identify the latter with Joachim Egellius of Ravensburg, who is documented in Paris in 1508 and 1510, studying with his cousin Michael *Hummelberg. Hummelberg, who had left Paris in 1511, had been a student of Aleandro's. Very little is known about Egellius (Egelensis, Eckel), who had also left Paris to matriculate at Montpellier on 20 May 1511, the same day as his countryman Johann *Menlishofer. The two went on to the University of Vienna, where they matriculated together in the autumn of 1511, perhaps attracted by the presence of Joachim *Vadianus. It was probably in Vienna that Egellius earned a medical doctorate, whereas in Paris he had only earned a MA. He practised medicine in his home town and remained in touch with Vadianus. Thus Allen's identification appears to be tenuous.

BIBLIOGRAPHY: Allen Ep 256 / BRE Ep 3 / AK I Ep 441 / *Matrikel Wien* II-1 392 / *Vadianische Briefsammlung* III Ep 116, IV Appendix Ep 10 / Bernhard Milt *Vadian als Arzt* (St Gallen 1959) 105, 124–6 / *Matricule de Montpellier* 20 ('Johannes Egelensis')   PGB

IOANNES, IOHANNES See JOHANNES

Franciscus IRENICUS of Ettlingen, 1495–1559/1564

Irenicus (Fritz, Friedlieb), of Ettlingen, near Karlsruhe, was a fellow student of *Melanchthon both at the Pforzheim Latin school under Georg *Simler and at the University of Heidelberg, where he registered in 1510. At Tübingen he matriculated on 16 May 1516 and was taught by Melanchthon. He returned to Heidelberg, graduated MA on 23 February 1517, and became a member of the university council in 1519. He was present when Martin *Luther debated at Heidelberg on 26 April 1518 and thereafter was sympathetic to the views of Luther. In 1522 at Baden-Baden he entered the service of Margrave Philip of Baden and was appointed canon and court preacher. In 1526 he accompanied the margrave to the diet of Speyer. In 1530 he became a minister in

Gemmingen, near Heidelberg, where he founded a Latin school and eventually died.

In 1517 Irenicus composed an *Exegesis Germaniae* (Haguenau: T. Anshelm 1518). Parts of it he may have shown to Erasmus in 1518 at Speyer, but it failed to impress him (Ep 877). The work, a historical and topographical compilation, was well received as a fervent expression of national sentiment. It was reprinted three times and praised by Willibald *Pirckheimer.

BIBLIOGRAPHY: Allen and CWE Ep 877 / NDB X 178–9 / ADB XIV 582–3 / *Matrikel Heidelberg* I 477, II 437 / *Matrikel Tübingen* I 211 / BA *Oekolampads* I 405, II 487–8, and passim / Hans Rupprich in *Geschichte der Deutschen Literatur von den Anfängen bis zur Gegenwart* ed H. de Boor and R. Newald (Munich 1960–1) IV-1 673   IG

IRENICUS Phrysius *See Rienck van* BURMANIA

Damian IRMI of Basel, d 24 October 1531
Damian Irmi (Irmy) entered the University of Basel in the autumn of 1502, graduated BA in 1506, and, after further studies in Freiburg in 1507 and Bologna in 1510, received his MA, again at Basel, in 1512. His intermittent studies notwithstanding, he was a man of action. A well-to-do merchant trading with Italy, he at one time owned the castle of Binningen, near Basel. In 1515 he was named interpreter to the Basel troops sent to Italy and fought in the battle of Marignano. Subsequently he was killed by the Swiss Catholics in the battle of Gubel during the second Kappel war. His support for *Oecolampadius and the reform party at Basel had often been forceful. In 1524 he caused a brawl when he confronted a monk who had just finished his sermon on St John's day. Three years later, at the height of the Reformation crisis, he was involved in another fight – perhaps the event alluded to by Erasmus in Ep 1780 – and afterwards seems to have visited the belligerent Guillaume *Farel in Aigle. Militancy did not, however, vanquish his respect for learning and at one time he endeavoured to secure Hebrew Bibles for his theologian friends. About 1518 he married a widow, Maria Rul, and they had two daughters.

BIBLIOGRAPHY: Allen Ep 1780 / BA *Oekolampads* I 603 and passim / *Matrikel Basel* I 268 /

Matrikel Freiburg I 179 / *Wappenbuch der Stadt Basel* ed W.R. Staehelin (Basel 1917–30) / R. Wackernagel *Geschichte der Stadt Basel* (Basel 1907–54) III 360, 450 / AK II Ep 914 / Herminjard I 468, II 13   PGB

ISABELLA of Austria queen of Denmark, 15 August 1501–18 January 1526
Isabella was born at Brussels, the daughter of Philip the Handsome, duke of *Burgundy, and of *Joanna of Castile, and a sister of the Emperor *Charles V. She was educated in Flanders. On 12 August 1515 she married *Christian II, king of Denmark, Norway, and Sweden. In 1523 Christian lost his dominions and fled with his wife to Flanders. In 1524 Isabella attended the diet of Nürnberg to seek assistance in regaining Denmark. After establishing residence at Lier, she died at Swynaerde, near Ghent. Her children were John, Dorothea, who married Frederick II elector *Palatine, and Christina, who married Francesco Maria *Sforza of Milan, then François I de Lorraine.

In the *Vidua christiana*, addressed to *Mary of Austria, queen of Hungary and Bohemia, Erasmus mentioned the sadness created by the exile and death of her sister Isabella (LB V 725F).

BIBLIOGRAPHY: Karl Brandi *Kaiser Karl V.* new ed (Darmstadt 1959–67) I 35 and passim / Julia M. Ady *Christina of Denmark, Duchess of Milan and Lorraine, 1522–1590* (New York 1913) 4–48 and passim   MILAGROS RIVERA

ISABELLA queen of Castile, 22 April 1451–26 November 1504
Isabella was born at Madrigal de las Altas Torres to John II of Castile and his second wife, Isabella of Portugal. She had a brother, Alfonso, who in the 1460s was the centre of a rebellion against their half-brother, Henry IV, king of Castile. When Alfonso died in 1468, Castile was divided between the partisans of Isabella and those of Joanna of Castile, Henry IV's daughter, called 'la Beltraneja' because the nobleman Beltran de la Cueva was thought to be her true father. Henry tried to have Isabella married to Pedro Girón, master of Calatrava, and later to Alfonso V of Portugal, but in 1469, without his consent, she married *Ferdinand II, subsequently king of Aragon. This marriage led to the union of the crowns of Castile and

Aragon. On the death of Henry in December 1474 civil war again flared in Castile, with Alfonso v of Portugal and *Louis xi of France allied with Joanna. The situation was further complicated by the position of Ferdinand, who had a claim to the Castilian throne on the grounds that he was the closest male relative of the deceased king. At Segovia, however, Ferdinand and Isabella agreed to govern Castile jointly. Their war with Joanna ended successfully in 1479, when Alfonso v and Joanna renounced their claims at Alcáçovas. Ferdinand and Isabella then turned to the pacification of the kingdom, using the Santa Hermandad to suppress rebellious nobles and bandits. From 1482 they also launched a series of campaigns for the kingdom of Granada, culminating in their triumphal entry into the city of Granada on 6 January 1492.

While Ferdinand directed a vigorous foreign policy, Isabella concentrated on the domestic affairs of Castile. With the collaboration of the Holy See, the crown received the mastership of the wealthy military orders. In 1478 *Sixtus iv authorized the establishment of the Inquisition in Castile, giving the monarchs power to appoint inquisitors. While the Inquisition prosecuted Jews who had converted to Christianity but then returned to the Jewish faith, in 1492 Ferdinand and Isabella took the further step of expelling all unconverted Jews from their kingdoms. During the final years of her life, Isabella dedicated herself to the conversion of the Moslems of her kingdom, relying on the advice of Francisco *Jiménez de Cisneros, since 1495 archbishop of Toledo, whose excessive zeal provoked a sanguinary rebellion in the Alpujarras. It was also Isabella who, in 1492, supported the venture of Christopher Columbus, whose discoveries gave new scope to the conquering energies of Castile. Finally she helped make the court of the Catholic monarchs a centre for humanistic studies and actively encouraged learning by studying Latin herself.

The children of Ferdinand and Isabella were Juan who died in 1497, Isabella, who married King *Manuel i of Portugal and died in 1498, *Joanna 'the Mad,' who married Philip the Handsome of *Burgundy and inherited the crowns of Castile and Aragon, Maria, who married Manuel of Portugal after the death of

Isabella, queen of Castile

Isabella, and *Catherine of Aragon, the wife of *Henry viii of England.

Erasmus frequently praised Isabella's piety and love of learning in *De pueris instituendis* (ASD I-2 52), in the *Vidua christiana*, addressed to her granddaughter *Mary, queen of Hungary and Bohemia (LB V 730D), and in letters to Catherine of Aragon (Ep 1727) and Francisco de *Vergara (Ep 1885). In the *Panegyricus ad Philippum* he mentioned the joyful welcome she gave her son-in-law Philip the Handsome when he first visited Spain in 1502 (ASD IV-1 42).

BIBLIOGRAPHY: Allen Ep 1727 / *Diccionario de historia de España* 2nd ed (Madrid 1968–9) ii / J.N. Hillgarth *The Spanish Kingdoms, 1250–1516* (Oxford 1976–8) ii

MILAGROS RIVERA & TBD

Empress ISABELLA of Portugal 4 October 1503–1 May 1539
Isabella was the daughter of King *Manuel i and his second wife, Maria, and thus the sister of *John iii of Portugal. She was married to her cousin *Charles v in Seville on 10 March 1526 (Ep 1647). Isabella, who identified herself

completely with the interests of Spain, governed the country during her husband's many absences (Epp 2208, 2523, 2757). A portrait of her is in the Prado.

BIBLIOGRAPHY: Allen Ep 1647 / Anselmo Braancamp Freire *Ida da Imperatriz D. Isabel para Castela* (Coimbra 1920) / F. Walser and R. Wohlfeil *Die spanischen Zentralbehörden und der Staatsrat Karls v.* (Göttingen 1959) 114–15 and passim / Karl Brandi *Kaiser Karl v.* new ed (Darmstadt 1959–67) I 164 and passim / Manuel Fernández Álvarez in *Historia de España* ed Ramón Menéndez Pidal XVIII (Madrid 1966) passim   ELISABETH FEIST HIRSCH

Anton and Salentin von ISENBURG
documented 1520–31

Anton and Salentin von Isenburg (Ysenburg, Isenborch) were the sons of Salentin VI von Isenburg-Grenzau and Elisabeth von Hunoldstein. From April 1525 their father was the judge of the nobility (*Ritterrichter*) in the county of Luxembourg and lived on his estate of Neumagen; he also had title to the estates of St Johannesberg, Broich, and Sechtendorf. Anton and Salentin matriculated at Cologne on 24 March 1520. In 1523 their tutor, Johannes *Caesarius, dedicated to them an edition of Horace's *Epistles* (Cologne: J. Soter); subsequently they were entrusted to Simon *Riquinus (Ep 2298). Anton received the estate of St Johannesberg in the duchy of Luxembourg, while Salentin received Neumagen in the archbishopric of Trier (Simon II 96). Anton von Isenburg attended the diet of Speyer in 1529 in the retinue of Richard von *Greiffenklau, archbishop of Trier. Anton died in 1531 as governor of Luxembourg, and Salentin may have been alive in May 1542; neither had any offspring.

BIBLIOGRAPHY: Allen Ep 2298 / de Vocht CTL II 387–8 / *Matrikel Köln* II-2 821 / *Deutsche Reichstagsakten* Jüngere Reihe (Gotha-Göttingen 1893–) VII-2 1384 / Gustav Simon *Die Geschichte des reichsständischen Hauses Ysenburg und Bündingen* (Frankfurt am Main 1865) II 95–6 / J.H. Zedler *Grosses vollständiges Universal-Lexikon aller Wissenschaften und Künste* (Halle-Leipzig 1732–50) XIV 1347   KONRAD WIEDEMANN

Wilhelm von ISENBURG documented
c 1470–1532

Wilhelm, count of Isenburg (Ysenburg, Eisenberg) and Grenzau, was born before 1470 and by 1491 had joined the order of Teutonic Knights in Prussia. He repeatedly held high office between 1495 and 1514, and tried to reorganize the order. In 1503 he returned to Cologne for reasons of health but was soon recalled to Prussia. As *Obermarschall* of the order in 1510, he was deeply involved in the election of Margrave Albert of *Brandenburg-Ansbach as high master and undertook diplomatic missions on behalf of the order until 1523. After several years spent in the Rhineland, Isenburg joined Albert in November 1517 at Berlin for negotiations that led Brandenburg to support the knights in their war against Poland. Subsequently Isenburg was dispatched to Duke George of *Saxony. In 1518 he was ordered to attend the diet of Augsburg. In 1519 he participated in the negotiations leading to the election of the Emperor *Charles V and then went to the Lower Rhine to enrol mercenaries for the war against Poland, although he was not given sufficient funds to pay them adequately. They reached Prussia after a long delay and besieged Gdansk. Isenburg was blamed when they failed to take the city.

On his way to Prussia in November 1519 he had visited *Luther in Wittenberg, and over the next decade, while in charge of the order's commandery of Koblenz and residing in Cologne, he published a series of German pamphlets and books on justification and related issues, among them *Hauptartikel aus göttlicher Geschrifft* (1526). He held that justification was by faith alone, and consequently he was attacked by Johannes *Cochlaeus and other Catholic controversialists; he never abandoned the traditional church and was treated with respect even by his opponents and by the city council of Cologne, which in 1529 begged him to desist from further pronouncements on religious matters.

His evangelism was evidently close to the views held by Erasmus. His name last appears in Ep 2663 (22 June 1532), in which Erasmus thanked him for the gift of an elegant dagger which may well have expressed his apprecia-

tion of Erasmus' *Enchiridion*. Caspar *Hedio
dedicated to Isenburg some translations from
St Augustine (Strasbourg 1532).

BIBLIOGRAPHY: Allen Ep 2663 / ADB XIV
622–5 / Luther w *Briefwechsel* I Ep 223 / Erich
Joachim *Die Politik des letzten Hochmeisters in
Preussen: Albrecht von Brandenburg* (Leipzig
1892–5; repr 1965) I 8–11, 147–57, II 25, 43,
70–2, 147–8, III 52–3, and passim   IG & PGB

Isidorus de ISOLANIS of Milan, c 1480–1528
Isidorus de Isolanis (Isolani) was born at Milan
and entered the Dominican convent of Santa
Maria delle Grazie in that city; he taught
theology in the houses of his order at Pavia,
Verona, Milan, and Cremona. In 1521 or 1522
he received the degree of bachelor of theology
from the University of Bologna, and for a time
was director of the *studium generale* of his order
at that university. He served as prior of Santa
Maria delle Grazie as late as 22 April 1528 but
died before 9 July 1528.

Isolanis was the anonymous Dominican who
wrote the book against *Luther mentioned by
Erasmus on 18 October 1520 (Ep 1153). The
*Revocatio Martini Lutherii Augustiniani ad sanc-
tam sedem* was completed by 22 November
1519 and published at Cremona by Franciscus
Richardus Luere with a dedication to its
bishop. Martin Luther mentioned the *Revocatio*
twice in his *Babylonian Captivity* in August
1520, identifying its author as 'a certain friar of
Cremona.' Isolanis later acknowledged his
authorship in the dedication to his second
work against Luther, the *Disputata catholica*
(Pavia: J. de Burgofranco 1522; Lyon 1528).
Although Erasmus listed the author of the
Revocatio with other rabid opponents of
Luther, Luther himself noted that the author
did not write with malice; nevertheless in
Luther's view he was an idiot and a simpleton,
not to be taken seriously.

Isolanis published a number of other works
on philosophical and theological topics, including two attacks on Averroist positions, *De
immortalitate animi humani* (Milan 1505) and *In
Averroistas de aeternitate mundi libri quattuor*
(Pavia 1513). His other works included *Libellus
contra magos, divinatores et maleficos* (Milan:
G.A. Scinzenzeler 1506), *Opus de veritate
conceptionis Immac. Virg. Mariae* (Milan 1510),

De imperio militantis ecclesiae libri IV (Milan: G.
da Ponte 1517), and *Summa de donis S. Joseph*
(Pavia: J. de Burgofranco 1522). His complete
works were published at Lyon in 1528 and
1580.

BIBLIOGRAPHY: Allen and CWE Ep 1153 / DTC
VIII 112–15 / LThK V 802–3 / Friedrich Lauchert
Die italienischen literarischen Gegner Luthers
(Freiburg 1912, repr 1972) 200–15   TBD

Pietro ISVAGLIES of Messina,
d 22 September 1511
Nothing is known of the early life of Pietro
Isvaglies (Isvales) except that he came from
Messina. Already an apostolic protonotary, he
was made governor of the city of Rome on 11
August 1496 and bishop of Reggio Calabria on
18 February 1497. After his appointment as
cardinal on 28 September 1500, he was known
as 'Reginus (Rheginus)' or the cardinal of
Reggio; his promotion may have been due to
the recommendation of King *Ferdinand II of
Aragon. In 1510 he may also have obtained the
bishopric of Messina. Pietro left Rome in
November 1500 as legate to Hungary, where he
met the aristocratic mining entrepreneur
Johannes (I) *Thurzo; Jacobus *Piso recalled
in 1526 that when Thurzo's death was announced in Rome, Isvaglies had praised him
very highly (Ep 1662). On 8 October 1503 Pietro
was received in Venice on his return journey;
he tried to obtain a grant from the Signoria for
his nephew, who was reading law at Padua.
He arrived back in Rome on 24 October.

Pietro continued in favour under *Julius II,
whom he accompanied to Perugia (having first
gone with Cardinal *Riario to Orvieto) and
Bologna in 1506; he took part in the pope's
triumphal entry into Bologna on 11 November.
His house in Rome was near the Campo dei
Fiori and is described by Albertini as adorned
with statues and paintings; he was a neighbour
and friend of Cardinal Riario, who may have
introduced him to Erasmus in 1509. In May
1510 he was appointed legate to Perugia and
had to raise infantry there; he joined the pope
at Bologna later the same year and was one of
the three cardinals who accompanied him in
the attack on Mirandola in January 1511. He
succeeded Cardinal *Alidosi as legate to
Romagna from May to September 1511. Pietro

had many contacts with secular rulers, including *Henry VIII, but after his death from intestinal disease at Urbino, Cardinal Bainbridge refused to perform the requiem mass for him in Rome. Paris de Grassis praised him as a friend of the oppressed, a promoter of literature, and a beloved (spiritual) father; Andrea *Ammonio notified Erasmus of his death in a letter of 27 October 1511 (Ep 236).

BIBLIOGRAPHY: Allen and CWE Ep 236 / Eubel II 24 and passim / Pastor VI 92 and passim / Sanudo *Diarii* III 857 and passim / D.S. Chambers *Cardinal Bainbridge in the Court of Rome* (Oxford 1965) passim / F. Albertini *Opusculum de mirabilibus novae et veteris urbis Romae* (1510) ed A. Schmarsow (Heilbronn 1866) / J. Burchardus *Liber notarum* ed E. Celani (Città di Castello 1906–59) passim / L. Frati *Le due spedizioni militari di Giulio II* (Bologna 1866) passim   D.S. CHAMBERS

IUSSELLUS (Epp 1354, 1760 of 1523?–1526) Iussellus, an acquaintance of Claude *Le Marlet and Thiébaut *Biétry, had visited Erasmus, probably at Basel. Iussellus is not identified; for a suggestion see Allen Ep 1354:4n.

JACOB of Aalst documented 1530–1 One Jacob, called Jacob of Aalst by Jakob *Jespersen (Ep 2570), had by 1530 been in the service of the printer Dirk *Martens for approximately ten years; Martens was also a native of Aalst, between Brussels and Ghent. In July 1530 Conradus *Goclenius sent Jacob from Louvain to Freiburg, where Erasmus was looking for a famulus. Jacob, who had taken with him Epp 2352, 2353, had not returned to Louvain by the end of August (Ep 2369). Writing from Brussels in November 1531, Jespersen reminded Erasmus of Jacob's visit the previous year and stated that Jacob had replaced him as a Greek teacher to Jacopo *Canta and that he had been sent to Italy, where he was in charge of a press (Ep 2570). No more is known about Jacob of Aalst.
                            MARCEL A. NAUWELAERTS

Jan JACOBSZOON (Ep 2571 of 19 November 1531) Jan Jacobszoon ('Magister Io. Iacobi') cannot safely be identified, since there must have been

many bearers of this name. Writing from Brussels, Maarten *Davidts assured Erasmus that this one was in good health; evidently he was a common acquaintance. A Jan Jacobj was said to be canon of Mechelen at precisely this time, late in 1531, and to be the host of Johannes Secundus (Everaerts) when the latter received a letter from Johannes *Dantiscus, which was delivered by Hilarius *Bertholf, Erasmus' former amanuensis.

BIBLIOGRAPHY: de Vocht *Dantiscus* 123
                                                        PGB

JACOBUS documented at Freiburg, 1532–3 Jacobus, who has not been identified, was a servant of Erasmus who eventually obtained a bursary for study at Freiburg. Erasmus accused him of theft and suggested (Ep 2868) that he was a native of Freiburg and had many disreputable relatives. See Epp 2652, 2653, 2694, 2696, 2735, 2788, 2868.

BIBLIOGRAPHY: Allen Ep 2652 / Bierlaire *Familia* 92–3

JAMES IV king of Scotland, 17 March 1473– 9 September 1513 James, the eldest son of James III and Margaret, the daughter of Christian I of Denmark, was crowned in 1488. Although only fifteen at the time, he took an active part in the affairs of the realm. Recognizing the importance of the navy, he encouraged its expansion, but at the same time he fostered literature and education and refused to execute heretics. His reign was marked by the frequent necessity to suppress rebellions in unsettled areas of the kingdom. James attempted to create a fixed court at Edinburgh. He concluded a truce with *Henry VII in 1491, and, although he supported the claim of Perkin Warbeck to the English throne, the resulting military actions were insignificant. In August 1503 he married *Margaret Tudor, the daughter of the English king. After the death of Henry VII, English-Scottish relations deteriorated; James concluded an alliance with *Louis XII of France in 1512, prepared to invade England, and was finally killed in the battle of Flodden (Ep 325).

Killed with him was Alexander *Stewart, his natural son (Epp 1992, 2018) by his mistress, Marion Boyd. Erasmus tutored Alexander in Italy in 1508 and 1509, together with James

*Stewart, earl of Moray, James IV's natural son by Janet Kennedy. The king also had a daughter, Lady Margaret, by Margaret Drummond.

Erasmus wrote of the failure of the English-Scottish alliance and lamented the invasion of England in 1513 in his *Institutio principis christiani* (ASD IV-1 208). In the *Adagia* and his letters he praised the policy of peace and cultural endowment that James had pursued through most of his reign and mourned his death at Flodden (*Adagia* II v 1; Epp 2283, 2886). Petrus *Carmelianus wrote an epitaph for James which Erasmus and Andrea *Ammonio criticized (Epp 280, 282).

James was succeeded by his son, *James V; a posthumous son, Alexander, duke of Ross, was born to Margaret Tudor in 1514.

BIBLIOGRAPHY: DNB X 582–90   CFG

JAMES V king of Scotland, 10 August 1512–14 December 1542
James, the son of *James IV by *Margaret Tudor, was only a year old when his father was killed in the battle of Flodden. Upon his coronation on 21 September 1513, the alliance with France was renewed. From 1513 until 1528 the queen mother, her second husband, Archibald Douglas, earl of Angus, and John Stewart, duke of Albany, fought over the regency. In 1528 James, then sixteen, managed to assert personal control; Gavin Dunbar, archbishop of Glasgow and James' former tutor, was named chancellor and exercised strong influence over the king throughout his reign.

The English did not follow up their victory at Flodden, and a peace treaty signed in 1534 ensured stability in the border region. At first James recognized the validity of *Henry VIII's divorce and received the order of the Garter as a reward. His foreign policy changed, however, in January 1537, when he married Madeleine, the eldest daughter of *Francis I of France. After her premature death in the same year, he married Mary, the daughter of Claude, duke of *Guise, in 1538. The old hostility towards England resumed, and, as a mark of newly gained papal favour, James was presented with a cap and sword on behalf of *Paul III. When Henry VIII declared war on Scotland in 1542, the king was

James IV, king of Scotland

abandoned by the Scottish nobles, part of whose lands he had confiscated two years before. James completed this alienation when, after falling ill, he assigned the command of the Scottish forces to a commoner; the result was a resounding English victory. In December 1542 Mary Stuart, his only legitimate child, was born, shortly before the death of her father.

Erasmus expressed the hope that James would follow his father's example and favour the cause of humanistic studies (Epp 964, 2283). In 1533, at the request of Johannes *Cochlaeus, he wrote a short letter of recommendation to James V (Ep 2886), who replied the following year (Ep 2950).

BIBLIOGRAPHY: DNB X 590–8   CFG

JAN of Brussels (Epp 60, 155)
Two of Erasmus' early letters, of 1497 and 1501 respectively, are addressed to one Jan of Brussels (Johannes Bruxellensis or Bruxellanus), apparently an old friend from the entourage of Hendrik van *Bergen, bishop of Cambrai. It seems that by the summer of 1497 Jan was familiar with Erasmus' domestic arrangements in Paris and that Erasmus ex-

pected to see him again before long. Jan of Brussels has not been identified. A 'Johannes Nepotis de Bruxellis' matriculated at the University of Louvain on 11 June 1496 (*Matricule de Louvain* III-1 139), within days of the matriculation of Bernhard *Schinkel and Heinrich *Northoff. Both Northoff and Schinkel were soon thereafter in Paris, where Northoff maintained close contacts with both Erasmus and Augustinus Vincentius *Caminadus. In Ep 155 Erasmus asked Jan for news of Caminadus and Nikolaus *Bensrott, another north-German student of the latter.   PGB

JAN of Brussels *See also Jan* MOMBAER

JAN of Delft d 25 May 1530
Jan (Johannes Petri) of Delft may have studied in Cologne in 1463 before joining the Carthusian order at the monastery near his native town. On 23 November 1495 he arrived in Louvain to supervise the establishment of a new convent of his order. Undismayed by a shortage of funds he moved ahead, and on 18 June 1501 the church was consecrated. Jan himself was elected first prior in 1504. During these difficult years he received help and advice from the future Pope *Adrian VI and from Willem *Bibaut. On 28 February 1521 he had the satisfaction of seeing his monastery incorporated in the university. In 1525 he resigned the priorate because of his advanced years but continued to live in the Louvain charterhouse until his death. When one of his monks, Jan of *Heemstede, corresponded with Erasmus in the fall of 1525, Jan sent greetings. Erasmus' warm response shows affection and respect which were evidently based on personal acquaintance (Ep 1646).
BIBLIOGRAPHY: Allen Ep 1646 / NNBW V 496–7 / de Vocht MHL 347–8 and passim / *Monasticon Belge* ed U. Berlière et al (Maredsous-Liège 1890–) IV-6 1468–73
PGB

JAN of Dokkum d 1541
Jan (Bogerman) of Dokkum (Ioannes Doccumensis Frisius) matriculated at Cologne, in the faculty of arts, in 1500 and afterwards studied at Bologna, where he seems to have taken his degree in civil and canon law on 22 March 1509. On 5 September 1511, after having taught

at Cologne for some time, he became an advocate and on 5 March 1516 assessor to the Reichskammergericht of Worms. In 1518 he returned to Cologne. This was to remain his home until his death, although at various times he was employed by John III, duke of *Cleves, and by Franz von *Waldeck, bishop of Münster (Ep 2957). He was a good friend of Bernard Bucho van *Aytta, and also of *Viglius Zuichemus, who adopted his eldest son, Hieronymus (d 1535), and dedicated his *Candela evangelica* to Jan.
BIBLIOGRAPHY: Allen Ep 2957 / A.J. van der Aa et al *Biographisch woordenboek der Nederlanden* (Haarlem 1852–78, repr 1965) V 202 / *Matrikel Köln* II 505 / Knod 94
C.G. VAN LEIJENHORST

JAN of Friesland documented 1516–17
Jan of Friesland (Johannes Phrysius) is known only during the year he was in Erasmus' service. It appears that he was with Erasmus when the latter visited Antwerp in September and October 1516 and accompanied him from there on (Epp 532, 534). He was used both as a messenger (Epp 616, 637, 638) and as a secretary and copyist (CWE Ep 480A and Allen Ep 771 introductions, Ep 683). In September 1517 he copied his last letters into the Deventer Letter-book (hand A, CWE Ep 665 introduction) and took them with him to England. Erasmus recommended the versatile man to his English friends (Epp 667, 668), since his many talents apparently could not secure him a living in the Low Countries (Ep 717). Soon thereafter Erasmus lost touch with him (Ep 740).
BIBLIOGRAPHY: Allen Ep 637 / Bierlaire *Familia* 51–2 / W.K. Ferguson in *Opuscula* 238
FRANZ BIERLAIRE

JAN of Głogów c 1445–11 February 1507
Jan (Johannes Glogoviensis) was born in Głogów (Glogau), Silesia. From 1468 he was a professor at the University of Cracow. He left many commentaries on works by Aristotle and also on John of Sacrobosco, in addition to works of his own in the fields of grammar, logic, philosophy, and geography. He also concerned himself with astrology and was the author of numerous prognostications. His scholarship is recalled with praise by Jan Benedykt *Solfa in Ep 2601.

BIBLIOGRAPHY: Allen Ep 2601 / PSB X 450–2 /
NDB X 552   HALINA KOWALSKA

JAN of Leiden 1509–22 January 1536

Jan of Leiden (Bockelson, Beuckelszoon, Beu-
kels, Bocaldus), the son of Beukel Gerijtszoon
of Leiden, learnt to read and write and became
a tailor. He tried his hand in commerce and
travelled as far as Lübeck and Lisbon, but with
little financial success. After his return he
married Maritge Ysbrantsdochter, a sailor's
widow, and kept an inn at Leiden. He soon
came under the influence of the radical
Anabaptist leader Jan *Mathijszoon, who
appointed him one of his 'apostles' and sent
him to visit Münster in 1533. Being well-read in
Scripture and a dynamic speaker, he had
considerable success in preaching his faith. In
January 1534 Jan returned to Münster for good.
The rule of the Anabaptists was established in
February, when Mathijszoon himself arrived
and Bernhard *Knipperdolling, in whose
house Jan of Leiden was living, was elected
burgomaster. After Mathijszoon's death in a
sortie on 5 April 1534 Jan became 'king of the
New Jerusalem.' These events and further
developments of the tragic fate of the Anabaptists in Münster aroused considerable interest
among the correspondents of Erasmus. Epp
2956, 2957, 3031, 3031A, and 3041 give detailed
accounts, while Epp 3060, 3071, 3111, and 3116
report the storming of the city, the capture of
Jan of Leiden on 24 or 25 June 1535, and finally
his execution in Münster on 22 January 1536.

Jan of Leiden, by Heinrich Aldegrever

BIBLIOGRAPHY: Allen Ep 2957 / NDB II 344–5 /
NNBW IX 62–3 / G.H. Williams *The Radical
Reformation* (Philadelphia 1962) 358–9, 368–75,
and passim / Ugo Gastaldi *Storia dell'anabattismo dalle origini a Münster* (Turin 1972) 222–3,
242–56, 556–7, and passim   IG

JAN of Louvain *See Jan* BIJL

JAN *See also* JOHANNES

Claudius JANANDUS documented 1529–52

Claudius Janandus (Iannandus, Janand) is first
documented when he came to Basel for a few
months in the winter of 1528/9, and studied
under Bonifacius *Amerbach (AK III Ep 1328).
He also met Christoph von *Carlowitz and
Erasmus, who wrote to him very warmly on 1
April 1529, shortly after his departure, on
which he carried a letter for Karel *Sucket in
Dole (Ep 2141). That same day Janandus wrote
to Amerbach from the house of his patron,
Charles Ludin, at Besançon (AK III Ep 1346). In
March 1531 Amerbach recommended him
warmly to Andrea *Alciati, who was then
teaching at Bourges. Perhaps in order to obtain
another recommendation Janandus had also
written to Erasmus, and he could conceivably
have carried Ep 2468 to Alciati (AK IV Epp 1504,
1506). No more is heard of Janandus except
that Gilbert *Cousin mentioned him in his
Burgundiae descriptio (1552) as a respected
lawyer at Lons-le-Saunier; earlier he had
praised him as a good friend.

BIBLIOGRAPHY: Allen Ep 2141 / Gilbert
Cousin *Opera* (Basel 1562) I 349, III 72 / Gilbert
Cousin *La Franche-Comté au milieu du XVIe siècle*
ed E. Monot (Lons-le-Saunier 1907) 173
                                                                        PGB

JANUS Pannonius 29 August 1434–
27 March 1472

Janus Pannonius (Janus of Czezmicze or Ivan
Česmički) was born near the river Drave. He

received his early education at the court of his uncle, Bishop János Vitéz of Oradea (Várad), who is considered the father of Hungarian humanism. Encouraged by Vitéz, Janus went to Italy in 1447 and remained there for the next eleven years. In Ferrara he attended the school of Guarino *Guarini of Verona and became one of his most famous students, praised by the master for the excellence of his Latin and Greek. Under the classical name of Janus Pannonius he became a poet of considerable renown, writing a number of epigrams, elegies, and panegyrics during this period. In the fall of 1454 he entered the University of Padua and studied canon law for four years, but it is uncertain whether he ever received a doctorate.

Upon the accession of *Matthias Corvinus to the Hungarian throne in 1458, Janus returned to Hungary and became a member of the humanistic circle around the young king. He was made canon of the cathedral chapter of Oradea and provost of Titel (1459) and in 1460 was elevated to the bishopric of Pécs (Fünfkirchen, Quinqueecclesiae). He was a member of the royal council and chancellor of the queen, and, together with János Vitéz, had considerable influence on the intellectual and artistic development of King Matthias. As royal ambassador he visited his beloved Italy for the last time in 1465. During this trip he presented Matthias' request for major financial aid against the Turks to Pope Paul II, who responded favourably. He also received the foundation bull for the University of Bratislava (Pozsony, Pressburg). An avid bibliophile, Janus returned to Hungary loaded down with precious Latin and Greek volumes. Although his health was failing, he accompanied the king on several military campaigns. In 1469 and 1470 Janus was *ban* (governor) of Slavonia. Because of disagreements with the foreign policy of King Matthias, who ignored the Turkish danger, Janus became involved in a plot against the king. It was soon discovered, and, fearing Matthias' wrath, he set out towards Italy but died near Zagreb. Janus was buried at the cathedral of Pécs. His tomb was destroyed during the course of the Turkish wars in the sixteenth century.

In 1483 Matthias ordered that the poems of Janus should be collected and entrusted the task to Péter Váradi, archbishop of Kalocsa. A veritable Janus cult developed in the sixteenth century. In 1505 an unsuccessful attempt was made by István *Brodarics to have the works of Janus printed by Aldo *Manuzio. In 1512 the first edition of his panegyric on Guarino was published in Vienna. Between 1512 and 1523 no fewer than eight editions of his poems were published, among them one prepared by *Beatus Rhenanus and printed by Johann *Froben at Basel in 1518. Janus' fame spread throughout Europe, and he was praised by Erasmus (Ep 943), Carducci, and others. The most complete Latin edition of his works is by Samuel Teleki, *Iani Pannonii poemata* (Utrecht 1784). The most recent edition is by Sandor V. Kovács, *Jani Pannonii opera latine et hungarice* (Budapest 1972).

BIBLIOGRAPHY: Allen Ep 943 / *Magyar irodalmi lexikon* (Budapest 1963–5) I 521–4 / *Magyar életrajzi lexicon* (Budapest 1967–9) I 802 / Jozsef Huszti *Janus Pannonius* (Pécs 1931) / Rabán Gerézdi 'Janus Pannonius, egy költöi hirnév története' *Irodalomtörténeti közlemények* (1962) 720–31 / Csaba Csapodi 'Die Bibliothek des Janus Pannonius' *Acta litteraria* (1972) 389–400 / Ivan Česmički *Piesme i epigrami* ed M. Komboi (Zagreb 1951) / Veljko Gortan 'Ivan Česmički. Pjesme i epigrama' *Ziva antika* (1953) 281–90

L. DOMONKOS

JASPER See IASPARUS

Henry JESKYN See Henricus IESKYN

Jakob JESPERSEN of Aarhus, documented 1526–49
Nothing is known of the early life of Jakob Jespersen (Iasperus, Jasperi, Jacobus Danus) of Aarhus, in Denmark. In 1526 he was in Cologne, and on 18 May 1529 he matriculated at the University of Louvain for study in the Collegium Trilingue, where Rutgerus *Rescius was among his teachers. In some later references he is addressed as MA (*Oláh Levelezése* 565). He began to teach Greek privately in Louvain and was engaged for this purpose by Jacopo *Canta, a member of Cardinal *Campeggi's entourage. He did not wish, however, to follow Canta to Italy, and by November 1531 he had entered the service of Nicolaus *Olahus, whom he followed in 1539 to Austria

and Hungary. By 1540 he seems to have lost his sight, although by 1543 he had recovered it at least partially. He left Hungary and from 1541 seems to have lived continually in Antwerp, where he published a series of complimentary poems addressed to famous men and women (see Allen Ep 2570 introduction). In the spring of 1531 he attempted to initiate a correspondence with Erasmus, sending him an assortment of his poems. When no reply came he wrote again in November from Brussels (Ep 2570), assembling a bulletin of news which he thought might interest Erasmus. Again no answer is known; instead Erasmus accused him in letters of May 1532 addressed to *Goclenius and Olahus of divulging to *Aleandro one of his letters to Johannes *Dantiscus (Epp 2644, 2646, 2849). Olahus apologized for him (Ep 2693), but Erasmus continued to distrust him (Epp 2762, 2785), and in his next letter to Olahus (Ep 2792) he wrote scornfully of Jespersen's verse, especially an attack upon Erasmus' detractor Julius Caesar *Scaliger. While the poem in question is not known to exist, Erasmus repeated elsewhere that Jespersen's support was not welcome (Ep 2736). In July 1533 Jespersen wrote again to reaffirm his innocence (Ep 2849) and may have succeeded in mollifying Erasmus, who sent him greetings in subsequent letters to Olahus (Epp 2877, 2898, 2922). Jespersen finally wrote an epitaph for Erasmus, which was published in 1537 together with a letter he addressed to Rescius (LB I preliminary pieces; de Vocht CTL III 412–14).

Before the end of 1536, Jespersen probably married (Oláh Levelezése 565). He appears to have been self-seeking, indiscreet, and sometimes slightly pathetic (Oláh Levelezése 224). His Latin verses show no outstanding talent, but among Danish humanists he is remarkable for his knowledge of Greek and oriental languages.

BIBLIOGRAPHY: Allen Ep 2570 / C.F. Bricka in *Historisk Tidskrift* 5th ser 4 (1883–4) 302–15 / de Vocht CTL III 244–7 and passim / de Vocht *Literae ad Craneveldium* Ep 281 and passim / de Vocht *Dantiscus* 111 and passim / See also Olahus' correspondence: *Oláh Levelezése* ed I. Arnold (Budapest 1875) passim / *Matricule de Louvain* IV-1 21

MARTIN SCHWARZ LAUSTEN & PGB

Francisco Jiménez de Cisneros, by Juan de Borgoña

Francisco JIMÉNEZ DE CISNEROS
of Torrelaguna, 1436–8 November 1517
Francisco Jiménez de Cisneros was born in Torrelaguna, in New Castile, and baptized Gonzalo by his noble but impecunious parents, Alonso Jiménez de Cisneros and Marina de Astudillo de la Torre. He began his education privately with his uncle, Alvaro, a cleric, before continuing at Alcalá and the University of Salamanca, where he graduated bachelor of laws. After his ordination he travelled to Rome, where he obtained title to the next benefice to fall vacant in the diocese of Toledo. On 22 January 1471, after a bitter legal struggle with the archbishop of Toledo – during which he was for a time imprisoned – Cisneros became the archpriest of Uceda. By January 1477 he had moved to Sigüenza as *capellán mayor* to the more congenial archbishop of Seville, Gonzalo de Mendoza, who befriended him and made him a vicar-general. Within the last four months of 1484 he left to enter the Franciscan order, taking the name Francisco. He resided at San Juan de los Reyes in Toledo, Castañar, and La Salceda, where he became guardian in 1492. In the same year, on

Mendoza's recommendation, he replaced Hernando de Talavera as confessor to Queen *Isabella of Castile. Enjoying the confidence of the queen and of her husband, *Ferdinand II of Aragon, he became provincial of the Franciscan order in Castile in 1494, archbishop of Toledo and primate of Spain in 1495, and cardinal and inquisitor-general in 1507. On the death of Ferdinand in January 1516 he served as regent of Castile. Among his more notable accomplishments were the reform of the Franciscans in Spain, the conquest of Oran from the Moslems in 1509, and the forcible conversion of the Granadine Moors. He died at Roa, near Burgos.

Although direct contacts between Cisneros and Erasmus were few, Cisneros' patronage and policies had a profound effect on the diffusion of humanism and more specifically of Erasmianism in Spain. He founded the University of Alcalá de Henares, which opened in 1508 after more than a decade of construction and became a seed-bed for religious studies and especially biblical scholarship. Cisneros' great project at Alcalá was the production of the Complutensian Polyglot Bible (named after the Latin name of Alcalá), with parallel passages in Latin, Greek, and Hebrew (Alcalá: A. Guillén de Brocar 1514–17). Among the scholars called upon to complete this work were Elio Antonio de *Nebrija, Diego *López, Zúñiga, Hernán Núñez, and Juan de *Vergara, the last a personal secretary and protégé of the cardinal. On two occasions Cisneros invited Erasmus himself to Spain to help place the final touches on the Polyglot Bible, but Erasmus declined (Epp 541, 597, 628, 809). Erasmus saw his biblical scholarship as similar in aim and effect to that sponsored by Cisneros (Epp 1789, 1858; LB VI [24]) and credited the cardinal with shielding him from the violent attacks of López Zúñiga (Ep 1128, 1216; ASD IX-2 60–2). There were, however, radical differences between the goals of the two men. While Cisneros wanted only to purify the Latin, Greek, and Hebrew texts of the Bible without using the Greek or Hebrew to correct the Vulgate, Erasmus in his *Novum instrumentum* (Basel 1516) produced a new Latin translation of the Greek New Testament. The Complutensian Polyglot Bible was a work of outstanding quality, but its sales did not rival those of

Erasmus' editions of the New Testament. Its printing, which began in 1514, was not completed until after the death of Cisneros in 1517. Only six hundred copies were produced, and these were not offered for sale until 1522, in part because of a delay in securing authorization from Rome. By then Erasmus' New Testament had undergone three editions. A second, revised, edition of the Complutensian Polyglot was printed only during the reign of Philip II (Antwerp: C. Plantinus 1569–73).

Cisneros was also an enthusiast for medieval works of mysticism and personal devotion. He sponsored translations and editions of the works of Catherine of Siena, Angela of Fulgino, Vincent Ferrer, Ludolph of Saxony, and Thomas à Kempis. He also extended friendship and protection to Spanish mystics. Although Cisneros left few original writings of his own, several volumes of official correspondence have been published: *Cartas del Cardenal ... Cisneros dirigidas a D. Diego López de Ayala* ed P. Gayangos and V. de la Fuente (Madrid 1867–75), *Cartas de los secretarios del Cardenal ... Cisneros durante su regencia* ed V. de la Fuente (Madrid 1875), and *Cartas inéditas del Cardenal Cisneros al cabildo de la catedral primada* ed J. Meseguer Fernández (Toledo 1973). Other letters are scattered in various works. Also printed are Cisneros' *Constituciones* for the archdiocese of Toledo (Salamanca 1498; Madrid 1905). His will survives in manuscript in the Archivo Histórico Nacional, Madrid, and his 'Instrucción según la qual el emperador Carlos V se habrá de haver en su llegada a España,' with its title added after Cisneros' death, in the Biblioteca Nacional, Madrid. Other principal collections of unpublished material relating to Cisneros are in the Archivo de la Universidad and Real Academia de la Historia, Madrid. He is portrayed in the fresco in the chapter house of Toledo cathedral by Juan de Borgoña and on a number of medallions.

BIBLIOGRAPHY: Allen Ep 541 / K.J. von Hefele *Der Cardinal Ximenes und die kirchlichen Zustände Spaniens ...* (Tübingen 1851), French trans 1856, Spanish trans 1869 / J.P.R. Lyell *Cardinal Ximenez, Statesman, Ecclesiastic, Soldier and Man of Letters, with an account of the Complutensian Polyglot Bible* (London 1914) / L. Fernández de Retana *Cisneros y su siglo* (Madrid 1929–30) /

Bataillon *Erasmo y España* 1–43 and passim / J. Babelón 'Medallones españolas del siglo XVI' *Numisma* 4 no 11 (1954) 57–67 / J. López de Toro *Perfiles humanos de Cisneros* (Madrid 1958) / J. García Oro *Cisneros y la reforma del clero español en tiempo de los Reyes Católicos* (Madrid 1971) / P. Sainz Rodríguez *La siembra mística del Cardenal Cisneros y las reformas en la iglesia* (Madrid 1979) / In addition, the Spencer Library, University of Kansas (MS C 238) has an early biography of Cisneros composed at Torrelaguna between 1517 and 1524

FELIPE FERNÁNDEZ-ARMESTO

JOANNA queen of Castile, 6 November 1479–12 April 1555
Joanna, the daughter of *Ferdinand II of Aragon and *Isabella of Castile, was born at Toledo. On 21 October 1496 she married Philip the Handsome of *Burgundy, the son of the Emperor *Maximilian I. After the deaths of her brother, Juan (1497), sister Isabella (1498), and nephew Miguel (1500), she became heiress of Castile and Aragon. Joanna was solemnly acclaimed as such by the Cortes of Toledo in May 1502 and by that of Saragossa in October of the same year. In 1503 she began to show signs of mental derangement. On the death of her mother in 1504, Philip and Ferdinand struggled for the regency, and Ferdinand was forced to retire to Aragon. Philip's death at Burgos on 25 September 1506 destroyed Joanna's sanity completely. From 1509 until her death the queen lived at Tordesillas. In August 1520 the town was occupied by the army of the *comuneros* who had rebelled against her son *Charles V. The queen received their representatives but refused to sign any legal document. She was attended on her deathbed by St Francisco de Borja. In addition to Charles, her children were *Eleanor of Austria, *Isabella, queen of Denmark, *Ferdinand the future emperor, *Mary of Austria, and *Catherine.
Erasmus mentioned Joanna in the *Panegyricus* (ASD IV-1 29, 35).
BIBLIOGRAPHY: Karl Brandi *Kaiser Karl V.* new ed (Darmstadt 1959–67)) I 32–7 / J.H. Elliott *Imperial Spain 1469–1716* (London 1963) 125–35 / Antonio Rodriguez Villa *La reina doña Juana la Loca: Estudio histórico* (Madrid 1892) / Luis Suarez in *Diccionario de historia de España* 3rd ed (Madrid 1968) II   MILAGROS RIVERA

Joanna, queen of Castile

Honoratus JOANNIUS of Valencia, 14 January 1507–30 July 1566
Honoratus Joannius (Joan) was the son of Caspar, a prominent citizen of Valencia. By 1523 he was a student of Juan Luis *Vives at Louvain with Diego *Gracián de Alderete. He stayed at Louvain for some time after Vives left for England in 1523, corresponding regularly with his master (Vives *Opera omnia* ed Gregorio Mayans y Siscar, Valencia 1782–90, repr 1964, VII, 137–41). He was in Paris in 1529 and by 1531 had returned to Valencia. Years later he became a tutor to Philip II's son Don Carlos and to Don Juan of Austria, both born in 1545. On 1 March 1564 he became bishop of Osma.
In 1526 Conradus *Goclenius sent Erasmus a packet of letters, including several translated from Spanish into Latin by Joannius, an admirer of Erasmus (Ep 1768). Juan Luis Vives praised Joannius in the introduction to his *De officio mariti* (Bruges: H. de Crook 1529) and referred to him in the *Varius dialogus de urbe Valencia* (Vives *Opera omnia* I 389). After his return to Spain Joannius helped the professor of Latin at Valencia, Laurentius Palmyrenus, replace manuals of Erasmus and of Lorenzo

*Valla with works more Ciceronian in style.

BIBLIOGRAPHY: Allen Ep 1768 / Eubel III 283 / de Vocht CTL II 404–8 / de Vocht *Literae ad Craneveldium* Ep 32   TBD

JODOCUS *See JOOST of Schoonhoven, Joyce PELGRIM, and THEODORICUS of Haarlem*

Konrad JOHAM of Strasbourg, d 1551
Konrad Joham (Joham von Mundolsheim, Conradus Johannes) was a member of a wealthy merchant family from Saverne, who resided in Strasbourg after 1486. A relative of his, Anshelm Joham, was knighted by *Maximilian I in 1506, and Konrad was granted hereditary nobility by *Charles V in 1536. He was a merchant-banker, involved in commerce in silk and metal, and played an active role in the government of Strasbourg, serving on the city council, or senate, and on the important and prestigious councils of Fifteen and Thirteen. He was a well-known host, receiving important guests in his mansion in the Judengasse.

Joham was acquainted with Erasmus, perhaps through Erasmus *Schets, and from July 1534 to February 1535 there were three occasions on which he received or forwarded mail for Erasmus. Thus the business network of one of the wealthiest families in Strasbourg was put at the disposal of the humanist (Ep 2955, 2972, 2992). When a crisis arose after Strasbourg's defeat in the Schmalkaldic war and the city was torn over the acceptance of the Augsburg Interim of 1548, Joham emigrated rather than jeopardize his wealth and his holdings by incurring the wrath of the emperor.

BIBLIOGRAPHY: Thomas Brady *Ruling Class, Regime and Reformation at Strasbourg, 1520–1555* (Leiden 1978) 106–7, 281–9, 323–4

MIRIAM U. CHRISMAN

JOHANNES (Epp 20, 21, 23) *See Jan Dirksz van der HAER*

JOHANNES (Ep 38 of [1494])
'Magister Johannes,' the tutor of Philip the Handsome, duke of *Burgundy, and the addressee of a letter from Willem *Hermans, has not been identified. The letter contained a recommendation of Erasmus.

JOHANNES (Ep 123 of [March 1500])
Among the household of Anthony of *Burgundy in the castle of Tournehem there was a valet (*cubicularius*) named Johannes. Erasmus sent greetings to him in Ep 123, but he has not been identified.   ANDRÉ GODIN

JOHANNES (LB X 1681D)
In his *Responsio adversus febricitantis libellum* of 1529, directed against Luis de *Carvajal, Erasmus recalled a scandalous story told to him about twenty-six years before at Antwerp in the house of *Nicolaas of Middelburg, an unidentified physician. His informant was a one-eyed Dominican, a teacher of theology, whose name may have been Johannes. Erasmus thought that he might still be alive. The Antwerp Dominican has not been identified.

MARCEL A. NAUWELAERTS

JOHANNES Andernacus (Ep 1303) *See Johannes GUINTERIUS*

JOHANNES Athenaeus (Ep 2570 of 19 November 1531)
'Ioannes Athenaeus seu Romanus' was probably a nickname given to this Austin canon in the priory of Bethlehem, near Herent in the district of Louvain. He sat up at night to study Greek authors. He has not been identified.

JOHANNES Confluentinus or JOHANN von Koblenz *See Jean de COBLENCZ*

JOHANNES a Greek (Ep 1096 of [May] 1520)
Johannes, a Greek, was held in high esteem by Thomas *More, who talked to him, probably in London. It may be assumed that Johannes normally resided at Paris since he gave More information about Germain de *Brie. Johannes is not identified.

JOHANNES of Lorraine documented in England, 1512–13
A Johannes of Lorraine, MA ('M. Ioannes Lothoringus'), is mentioned in Ep 281 as the carrier of letters between Erasmus in Cambridge and Andrea *Ammonio. References in Epp 273 and 282 seem to concern the same person and suggest that Johannes was closely associated with Ammonio, perhaps his famulus. Very similar references in Epp 255 and 262 would likewise appear to concern Johannes of

Lorraine, who has not otherwise been identified (but cf also John (II) *More).   PGB

JOHANNES a Mera *See Johannes a* MERA

JOHANNES the Pole (Ep 254 of
8 February [1512])
In a letter to the papal penitentiary Thomas
*Halsey, who was in Rome, Erasmus sent
greetings to Halsey's colleague 'D. Ioannes
Polonus' ('Master John, the Pole'). Johannes
has not been identified.

JOHANNES of Westphalia (Ep 867 of
[October] 1518)
Johannes, a canon of St Victor's, near Mainz,
was with Erasmus in September 1518 on a boat
journey from Mainz to Bonn and was evidently
splendid company (Epp 867 and probably 880).
For several canons of St Victor's whose first
name was Johannes, see CWE Ep 867.

JOHANNES *See also* JAN, JOHN

JOHANNES MARIA Armoricus (Ep 1845)
Very little is known about Johannes Maria
Armoricus, who composed three poems in
praise of Erasmus which he sent to him with an
undated letter. He seems to have been a native
of Ciriè, north of Turin, and must have
entered the service of *Margaret of Austria
prior to the death of her second husband,
Philibert II, duke of *Savoy. In a letter written
from Antwerp on 13 October 1529 Henricus
Cornelius *Agrippa refers to him as Margaret's
physician and mentions his use of a specific
medical treatment. In 1535 he was vicar of the
Benedictine monastery of Brou near Bourg-
en-Bresse, Margaret's cherished foundation,
where both Philibert and she herself lie buried.
   BIBLIOGRAPHY: Allen Ep 1845 / Max Bruchet
Marguerite d'Autriche (Lille 1927) 241 / Henricus
Cornelius Agrippa *Opera* (Lyons c 1600, repr
1970) II 936–7 (Correspondence book 5, Ep 85)
                                              PGB

JOHANNES Petrus *See Jean-Pierre* VARADE

Conradus JOHANNES *See Konrad* JOHAM

Georgius JOHANNIS of Rotterdam,
documented 1504–23
Very little is known about Georgius Johannis

John, prince of Denmark, by Claus Berg

of Rotterdam, who matriculated at the University of Cologne on 9 June 1504 and in 1512 was
a member of the Bursa Corneliana. In the
following year he entered the council of the
faculty of arts, and in 1514 he was an examiner.
He was still teaching at the University of
Cologne in 1523.
   In the summer of 1517 Erasmus sent him
greetings in a letter to Johannes *Caesarius (Ep
610); shortly thereafter he seems to have visited
his native region and, on his way back to
Cologne, called on Erasmus at Louvain,
handing him Epp 610, 611 (Ep 615).
   BIBLIOGRAPHY: Allen and CWE Ep 610 /
Matrikel Köln II 562   HANSGEORG MOLITOR

JOHN prince of Denmark, 21 February 1518–
11 August 1532
John (Hans), the only son of *Christian II of
Denmark and *Isabella, the sister of *Charles V,
was born in Copenhagen. In 1523 he accompanied his parents and two sisters to their
exile in the Netherlands, where the regent,
*Margaret of Austria, saw to it that he was
brought up in the Catholic faith. It is possible
that in 1526 Conradus *Goclenius was invited
to take an interest in the education of John and

John III, king of Portugal, by Hans Weigel the Elder

his sisters (Ep 1765); towards the end of his short life the prince was tutored by Gotskalk *Eriksen, who took him through Erasmus' *Apophthegmata* (Ep 2570). In the spring of 1524 he accompanied his mother to the court of Charles v at Nürnberg, and, like the regent, Margaret, the emperor took to his nephew. On 5 January 1532 John was recognized as heir to the throne of Norway by the council of the realm, but six months later he died after a short illness at the emperor's court in Regensburg; he was deeply mourned by Charles v. There is a portrait of John by Claus Berg on an altar piece at St Knud's church, Odense.

BIBLIOGRAPHY: Allen Ep 2570 / *Dansk Biografisk Leksikon* (Copenhagen 1933–44) IX 77 / C.F. Allen *Breve og Aktstykker til Christian II's og Frederik I's Historie* (Copenhagen 1872) v 296–301 / Karl Brandi *Kaiser Karl v.* new ed (Darmstadt 1959–67) I 156–7, 269, II 223

MARTIN SCHWARZ LAUSTEN

JOHN III king of Portugal, 1502–11 June 1557
Erasmus *Schets, the Antwerp banker, suggested to Erasmus in several letters that he dedicate a work to John III in the hope of being

rewarded with a generous stipend (Epp 1681, 1682, 1750). Schets, who had known King *Manuel I in Portugal, had been favourably impressed with the king's interest in the sciences and religion, and the same was true, he wrote to Erasmus, of his son and successor (in 1521), King John III. Schets assured Erasmus that John spent a great deal of money on the sciences and especially theology (Ep 1681). Erasmus finally dedicated his edition of St John Chrysostom to John, mixing praise with criticism of his spice monopoly (Ep 1800).

The great overseas event during John III's reign was the colonization of Brazil. In keeping with the tendency of the age, the king held the reins of government firmly. His personality is not easy to define. Contemporaries called him the 'pious' king because of his commitment to the Christian religion, and later scholars have criticized him for his religious fanaticism. This judgment is based on the fact that, after years of negotiation with Pope *Paul III, who was reluctant to give his permission, the Inquisition was introduced in Portugal in 1536. It was directed against 'new Christians' (superficially converted Muslims and Jews), whose possessions were confiscated if they were convicted. Since the king's treasury was always empty, it is possible that his motives in establishing the Inquisition were, in part at least, financial. Nevertheless, the king's actions in the academic domain were liberal. For example, he supported a group of Erasmian humanists that included Damião de *Gois and André de *Resende.

The king instituted academic reform on humanistic lines. In 1527 he had endowed fifty fellowships for Portuguese students to study at the Collège de Sainte-Barbe in Paris. At the same time he improved the teaching at the colleges and universities in Portugal. His most ambitious project was the foundation of the College of the Arts in Coimbra which was fashioned after Jérôme de *Busleyden's Collegium Trilingue in Louvain. John's most surprising act was his appointment to positions at the new college of a group of professors from the Collège de Guyenne at Bordeaux, led by André de Gouveia, who were known for their liberal religious views. He made these appointments in 1546 despite having been warned by Diogo de Gouveia, a strict conservative and an enemy of Erasmus. André was his nephew and had taught under him at Sainte-Barbe. But subsequently he and his colleagues were decried as 'Lutherans' by Diogo. Moreover, John III was interested in Erasmus and tried to get him to Coimbra at a time when some of his writings had already been condemned in Spain.

Nevertheless, this did not mean that the king neglected conservative scholars. They too played a role at court and at the colleges and universities, and it was he who established the Jesuits in the country. It was thus not long before the professors from Guyenne were denounced before the high tribunal of the Inquisition. André de Gouveia had already died in 1548. The others were found guilty and imprisoned for some time (1551). However, after their release the king appointed one of them, Diogo de Teive, principal of the College of the Arts, and so the strife among the various groups continued until eventually John turned the college over to the Jesuits (1555). His toleration of scholars adhering to various persuasions may be a sign of the king's openmindedness, but it also indicates a lack of clear vision as to the direction his academic reform was to take. During John III's reign many liberals were protected from prosecution, but after his death Portugal followed Spain in closing itself to 'modern' influences in the religious and intellectual spheres.

Schets saw to it that a presentation copy of Chrysostom was suitably bound and sent to Portugal for John (Ep 1850), but to his embarrassment there was no response (Ep 2243). Not until the summer of 1530 did Erasmus learn that the book had never been presented to the king for fear that he might take offence at Erasmus' criticism of the spice monopoly (Ep 2370). Besides Erasmus' Chrysostom, the following books were dedicated to John III: Jean Fernel *Cosmotheoria* (Paris: S. de Colines 1527), Jan *Driedo of Turnhout *De ecclesiasticis scripturis et dogmatibus* (Louvain: R. Rescius and B. Gravius 1533), and Juan Luis *Vives *De disciplinis* (Antwerp: M. Hillen 1531).

BIBLIOGRAPHY: Marcel Bataillon 'Érasme et la cour de Portugal' in *Etudes sur le Portugal au temps de l'Humanisme* (Coimbra 1952) 49–99 / Mário Brandão *A Inquisicão e as professores do*

Colégio das Artes (Coimbra 1948) I passim / José Sebastião da Silva Dias *A politica cultural da época de João III* (Coimbra 1969) / Ernest Gaullieur *Histoire du Collège de Guyenne* (Paris 1874) 145 and passim / Elisabeth Feist Hirsch *Damião de Gois* (The Hague 1967) 160–90 and passim / Alfredo Pimenta *Dom João III* (Porto 1936) / J.E.J. Quicherat *Histoire de Sainte-Barbe* (Paris 1860–4) / António José Saraiva *Historía da cultura em Portugal* (Lisbon 1955) II 555–6 and passim   ELISABETH FEIST HIRSCH

JOHN d'Albret king of Navarre, d 17 June 1516

John was the son of Alain d'Albret, called 'Le Grand,' count of Dreux, Gaure, and Castres, viscount of Tartas, and of Françoise de Bretagne. On 14 June 1484 he married the queen of Navarre, Catherine, the daughter of Gaston de Foix, prince of Viane, and of Madeleine de France. The royal couple did not in the long run succeed in maintaining the independence of their kingdom; in 1504 Béarn was occupied by the French and all of Navarre south of the Pyrenees was lost to *Ferdinand II of Aragon in 1512.

In his *Panegyricus* Erasmus praised both John and his father for the warm reception they accorded to Philip the Handsome, duke of *Burgundy, when he passed through Navarre in January 1502 (ASD IV-1 42–3). In March 1518 Erasmus mistakenly believed that John's daughter had married Lorenzo (II) de' *Medici, the future duke of Urbino (Epp 781, 786).

BIBLIOGRAPHY: ASD IV-1 43 / Allen and CWE Ep 781 / DBF VII 1416 (Catherine de Foix) / *Bulletin des amis du château de Pau* 57 (1973) 19–20
MICHEL REULOS & PGB

JOHN Zápolyai king of Hungary, 1487– 22 July 1540

János Zápolyai (Zapolya, Szapolyai), born at Szepesvár, near Spišske Podhradie, was the son of István Zápolyai, count palatine (*nádor*) of Hungary. The Zápolyai family was among the richest and most influential in the kingdom. John's first major role was at the diet of Rákos in September 1505, when he emerged as the leader of the 'national' party of the lesser nobility, opposed to foreign rule. The diet decreed that if King *Vladislav II died childless, the nobility would elect only a Hungarian-born

John Zápolyai, by Erhard Schoen

monarch to succeed him. As Zápolyai was the prime candidate of the national party to be the next king, the birth of the future *Louis II in 1506 was a major setback for his ambitions. To further his rise, Zápolyai made several attempts (1505, 1510, 1513) to marry Vladislav's daughter Anne, but without success. His appointment as *voivode* of Transylvania in 1511 might have been motivated by a desire to remove him from the court of Buda. His popularity among the nobility was greatly enhanced in 1514, when he was instrumental in putting down the greatest peasant revolt in Hungarian history. He was personally responsible for the execution, in a particularly horrible fashion, of the leader of the revolt, György Székely Dozsa, and his associates. In the following years the growing conflict between the national party and the great barons left the country paralysed. Even the fall of Belgrade on 29 August 1521 did not end the wrangling and alert the nobility to the danger of Turkish expansion.

In August 1526, when *Suleiman the Magnificent was advancing on Hungary, Zápolyai amassed a large army in Transylvania. Because

of contradictory orders from Louis II he did not advance to meet with the troops of the king and thus was not present at the battle of Mohács on 29 August 1526. As a result he was accused of being a traitor and was blamed for the débâcle in which Louis II and much of the Hungarian army perished (Ep 1917). There is no evidence that he stayed away from the battle on purpose, secretly hoping that Louis II would be killed and he could thus become king, but he did nothing to prevent the capture of Buda by Suleiman on 11 September. After the Turks withdrew from the capital on 30 September, a diet was called at Székesfehérvár where Zápolyai was elected king by the majority of the nobility and crowned on 10 November 1526. Archduke *Ferdinand of Hapsburg did not recognize Zápolyai's election, claiming that the dynastic agreements between the late Vladislav II and his family made him the legitimate heir to the Hungarian throne. To enhance his claim, Ferdinand had himself elected king at Bratislava (Pozsony, Pressburg) on 16 December 1526 by a small group of pro-Hapsburg nobles. Zápolyai began to seek diplomatic support for his claim as the legitimate king of Hungary among the anti-Hapsburg powers of western Europe and to counter the accusation that he was a usurper.

Ferdinand invaded Hungary in the summer of 1527, defeated the armies of Zápolyai, and forced him to flee to Poland in March 1528. In desperation Zápolyai allied himself with the Turks, did homage to Suleiman (18 August 1529), and was restored to his throne in Buda by the sultan (Ep 2211). Intermittent fighting continued until the peace of Várad (24 February 1538), which recognized the division of Hungary into two parts and accepted Ferdinand as king of the whole country if Zápolyai were to die childless. The following year, however, Zápolyai repudiated the treaty, married Isabella of Poland, and planned to establish a dynasty. A son, John Sigismund, was born on 7 July 1540, but Zápolyai died later in the month at Sebeş (Szászsebes). His body was carried to Székesfehérvár for burial on 27 September 1540. His tomb was desecrated by the Turks five years later. Although not a very intellectually oriented man, Zápolyai attracted a number of Hungarian humanists to his court, among them the historian István *Brodarics. He also owned a copy of the 1516 edition of Erasmus' *Institutio principis christiani.*

Erasmus' steady correspondence with friends in Poland caused him to see the quarrel between John Zápolyai and Ferdinand, in part at least, from their perspective, which was sympathetic to Zápolyai; in particular he was well informed on the involvement of Hieronim *Łaski and his brothers with the Hungarian national party (Epp 1810, 2862, 3014). In a letter of May 1527 addressed to *Sigismund I of Poland, he quite properly referred to Zápolyai as king of Hungary (Ep 1819). The letter was published right away and caused Erasmus trouble with the court of Vienna (Epp 2030, 2032), despite his efforts to remain impartial (Epp 1874, 2177).

BIBLIOGRAPHY: Allen Ep 1810 / *Magyar életrajzi lexikon* (Budapest 1967–9) II 707–8 / The most important contemporary sources for Zápolyai's reign are: Georgius Sirimiensis *Epistola de perditione regni Hungarorum* (Pest 1858) and Gábor Mindszenti *Diarium öreg János kiraly haláláról* (Kolozsvár 1837) / Ignac Acsády *Magyarország három részre szakadássának története* (Budapest 1897) / János Horváth *A reformacio jegyében* (Budapest 1957) / Gábor Barta and Antal Fekete-Nagy *Parasztháború 1514-ben* (Budapest 1973) / *Acta Tomiciana* (Poznań-Wrocław 1852–) VI–XVII passim
L. DOMONKOS

JOHN ALBERT king of Poland, 27 December 1459–7 January 1501
John Albert (Jan Olbracht, Johannes Albertus) was the third son of Casimir IV Jagiełło, king of Poland and grand prince of Lithuania, and Elisabeth of Hapsburg; one of his younger brothers became King *Sigismund I. John Albert was born in the royal castle of Cracow. He received a good education, and among his teachers was Filippo Buonaccorsi called Callimachus. From 1484 he was the favourite of his royal father, who prepared him to rule over Poland and Hungary. The following year he was given responsibility for the defence of the south-west frontier. After the death of *Matthias Corvinus in 1490 he received the votes of part of the Hungarian nobility, but he was obliged to step down in favour of his eldest brother, *Vladislav Jagiełło, king of Bohemia.

John Albert, king of Poland

On 27 August 1492 John Albert was elected king of Poland by an assembly of 40 voters and crowned on 30 September in Cracow. In 1493 and 1494 his personal political program began to take shape. He strove to increase the king's power and prerogative in the field of foreign policy, where his attention was directed towards relations with Turkey and the Hapsburgs. His ultimate aim was to unite Silesia with Poland (one of the titles he used was 'Supremus dux Silesiae') and to ensure that the Poles had access to the Black Sea by conquering Moldavia. The possibility that John Albert was planning a great expedition against the Turks cannot be ruled out, and he definitely wished to take over Matthias Corvinus' role as Turkey's main enemy in Europe. However, an expedition into Moldavia in 1497 ended in political and military defeat for the king.

John Albert never married. He died in Cracow and was buried in the cathedral; the likeness of him carved on his tomb in Hungarian marble, still visible today, is attributed to either Stanisław Stwosz or Hans Huber of Passau. Erasmus reported in his *Lingua* a dictum of John Albert (ASD IV-7 358).

*Justus Jonas, detail from group portrait
by Lucas Cranach*

BIBLIOGRAPHY: PSB X 405–10 / F. Papée *Jan
Olbracht* (Cracow 1936)

HALINA KOWALSKA

Justus JONAS of Nordhausen, 5 June 1493–
9 October 1555
Born in the free imperial city of Nordhausen,
eighty kilometres north of Erfurt, Jonas was the
son of a patrician and city councillor. His
original name was Jodocus Koch, but by 1515
Conradus *Mutianus was calling him 'Justus.'
He himself retained the name Jodocus until
1521; his adopted second name, Jonas, was his
father's first name. His mother died when he
was young, and his father married a widow
from Mühlhausen in Saxony by the name of
Wolfhagen. She had two sons by her previous
marriage: Mathes and Berthold. Mathes, who
was mayor of Mühlhausen, died in 1524 and
left a legacy of six hundred florins to the
University of Erfurt; Berthold, who was a
canon of St Mary's in Erfurt, appealed his
brother's will and became embroiled in a bitter
fight with the university in which Justus Jonas
tried to mediate.

In the summer semester of 1506 Jonas

matriculated at the university of Erfurt; he
obtained a BA in the fall of 1507 and a MA at the
beginning of 1510 at the age of sixteen. In 1509
he added laudatory verses to the *Bucolicon* of
*Eobanus Hessus (M. von Hase 251), and in
1510 he wrote some verses of his own: *Jocus
tumultuarius in defensionem Cupidinis adversus
Mistotheum*, ie, Ludwig Londergut of Rain (M.
von Hase 327). In the summer semester of 1511
he matriculated at the University of Wittenberg, where he studied law with Henning
Göde and obtained a legal baccalaureate. In the
spring of 1515 he returned to Erfurt. It was
probably at that time that he became closely
acquainted with Mutianus. At a time of plague
in Erfurt, in the fall of 1517, he was in
Nordhausen, enjoying the company of his
good friend Melchior of Aachen, who was a
canon and secretary to the city of Nordhausen.
On 16 August 1518 Jonas was made a licentiate
of civil and canon law in Erfurt, but he never
obtained a legal doctorate. At the end of 1518
he received a canonry at St Severin's which
served as the endowment of a university chair.

As a professor in the faculty of arts, Jonas
belonged to the intellectual society of Mutianus and Eobanus, but he also maintained
contacts with the influential circle around the
suffragan bishops Huthenne and Trutfetter, as
Christoph Scheurl's correspondence shows. In
the spring of 1519 he visited Erasmus in
Louvain in the company of Kaspar *Schalbe
(Ep 963). He carried with him a letter from
Frederick the Wise, elector of *Saxony, and
also one from Martin *Luther – the first one
he ever addressed to Erasmus (Ep 933). Jonas
and Schalbe proceeded to Antwerp, Brussels,
and other cities, so Erasmus did not get his
replies ready until 30 May. Erasmus wrote a
letter to Jonas (Allen Ep 985; CWE Ep 967A) in
which he advised him to study theology; he
had clearly formed a high opinion of his visitor
which was in keeping with Jonas' rich talents.
On his way back Jonas travelled first to Frankfurt
am Main, where Frederick the Wise was staying because of the imperial election, and did
not return to Erfurt until the middle of June.

In his absence Jonas had been elected (on
2 May) to serve as rector of the university for
the summer semester; moreover the university
had chosen a committee of eight men to reform
the philosophical faculty. The committee was

dominated by three theologians, Bartholomäus of *Usingen, Johann *Lang, and Maternus Pistoris; its reforms were not revolutionary, but they nevertheless meant a significant change in the teaching schedule, which now emphasized humanistic and language studies, as favoured by Erasmus. Jonas was surprised by this development, and on 24 June 1519 he wrote to his friend Melchior of Aachen that the University of Erfurt had not experienced such change in more than a hundred years (Jonas Ep 25). The Leipzig disputation between Luther and *Eck took place while he was rector of the university. Jonas did not fully grasp the theological significance of the disputation; what aroused his indignation most was Eck's attack on Erasmus (Ep 769), who in his opinion had revived the church and the whole world in only three years (Jonas Ep 27). On this basis Jonas at first viewed Luther's struggle within the framework of humanism. He followed Erasmus' advice to study theology, and also began to preach. His *Praefatio* to a course of lectures on Corinthians was published in Erfurt by Mathes Maler in 1520 (M. von Hase 407; Jonas Ep 35). A congratulatory letter from Petrus *Mosellanus (Jonas Ep 39) was published with the volume, but that same honour was not extended to Luther, who had also congratulated Jonas on his theological studies (w *Briefwechsel* II Ep 302). In April 1520 Erasmus wrote to Jonas asking his aid in the dispute with Edward *Lee (Ep 1088). Erasmus' circle of friends in Erfurt assumed the task with great zeal, but Jonas apparently did not participate in their efforts (CWE Ep 1083 introduction; M. von Hase 307).

Humanistic ideals had triumphed at the University of Erfurt; all the rectors succeeding Jonas were humanists. The first was Jacobus *Ceratinus, who had attended the school at Deventer; he was followed in the summer semester of 1520 by Ludwig *Platz of Melsungen, to whom Erasmus conveyed his satisfaction at the developments at the university (Ep 1127); and Platz was succeeded by *Crotus Rubianus, under whose leadership the tempestuous humanistic agitation reached a peak. Jonas was sent to Hildesheim by the faculty of arts to negotiate about the institution of the Saxon college at Erfurt; he also showed great dedication in mediating an unpleasant dispute within the medical faculty. When Henning Göde died on 21 January 1521, the Elector Frederick the Wise tried to persuade Mutianus to become his successor as provost of the chapter and professor of law in Wittenberg, but Mutianus demurred, preferring his 'blessed peace' in Gotha. Consequently Mutianus and *Spalatinus suggested Justus Jonas for the position at Wittenberg. Mutianus recommended him in a highly complimentary letter of 1 March 1521, and he was appointed.

In the meantime the intellectual and religious climate in Germany had changed considerably: the nationalistic-religious opposition to Rome and the papacy had won the upper hand, and Martin Luther was generally accepted as its leader. When he arrived in Erfurt on 6 April 1521 on his way to appear before the diet of Worms, Luther was officially welcomed by the rector, Crotus Rubianus, who met him with forty horsemen and led him into the city. Jonas had ridden as far as Weimar to meet Luther and subsequently accompanied him to Worms. There he met Johannes *Cochlaeus, to whom we owe this description of Jonas' person: 'an excellent young man, of tall stature and very cultured.' Jonas also accompanied Luther on his return journey and arrived back in Erfurt on 1 May 1521. Ten days later Erasmus, who had correctly assessed Jonas' qualities, wrote to him, admonishing him to keep the peace and avoid tumult (Ep 1202). Soon afterwards he wrote again; Jonas had asked for an account of John *Colet's life, since Erasmus had been greatly influenced by him. Erasmus complied with this request in a long letter (Ep 1211) in which he gave Jonas an account of the lives of Jean *Vitrier and John Colet. But Luther too vied for Jonas' attention at that time; on 8 June 1521 while at the Wartburg he dedicated to Jonas his treatise *Rationis Latomianae pro incendiariis Lovaniensis scholae sophistis redditae Lutheriana confutatio* (Wittenberg: [M. Lotter 1521]).

On 6 June 1521 Jonas was appointed provost of the Wittenberg chapter. His duties included lecturing on canon law at the university. However, he refused this task; in fact he returned to Erfurt to await clarification of the matter. On 26 June 1521 the elector requested that he move to Wittenberg; someone else would lecture on canon law, but Jonas would have to compensate this substitute. In July 1521 Jonas moved to Wittenberg but without officially resigning his canonry in Erfurt. On 21 September Andreas *Karlstadt promoted him licentiate in theology, and on 14 October 1521 he was made a doctor of divinity. This occurred during a period of stormy and polemical developments in Wittenberg in which Karlstadt played an important role, leading an intensive campaign for revolutionary changes in the liturgy. On 9 February 1522 Jonas married Katharina Falk (Ep 1258). From 1523 to 1525 he was dean of the theological faculty, and in the summer semester of 1526 and winter semesters of 1531 and 1536 he was rector of the university of Wittenberg.

Jonas was devoted to public life rather than to quiet scholarship. As late as 1544 the Saxon chancellor, Gregor Brück, criticized his lack of interest in teaching and university affairs in general (Jonas Ep 715). In 1529 he joined Luther at the religious debate in Marburg and in 1530 was present at the diet of Augsburg, but he did not attend the Schmalkalden meeting in 1537. Despite objections from the bishop he preached in the cathedral of Naumburg from April until September 1536. In 1538 he visited Zerbst, where he was instrumental in introducing a new church ordinance. On 23 May 1539 he gave the first Protestant sermon at St Thomas' in Leipzig. From 1541 to 1547 he was superintendent of Halle and carried through the reform of the city. He was present at Luther's death and gave the funeral oration in Eisleben. In 1547 he was forced by imperial troops to flee Halle; he moved to Nordhausen and later to Hildesheim, although he would have preferred to return to Erfurt, which he considered his second home. He went back to Halle for two years but was unable to regain his old position. In 1550 he left Halle, moved to Regensburg in 1552, and finally took over the parish of Eisfeld in Thuringia, where he gave his first sermon on 25 August 1553. He died in Eisfeld two years later.

Justus Jonas was not a leading theological light, but he defended Luther's position loyally and with skill. Cochlaeus regarded him as one of the 'four apostles of the new teachings' (Luther, *Melanchthon, Jonas, and *Bugenhagen). His main contributions to theology are his excellent translations of Luther's most important writings such as the Ninety-five Theses, De servo arbitrio (a very free and independent translation, Das der freye Wille nichts sey, Wittenberg: H. Lufft 1526). He also translated Melanchthon's Apologia for the Augsburg Confession (Wittenberg: G. Rhau 1531), and Loci communes (Wittenberg: G. Rhau 1536). His main opponents, with whom he carried on a continuous battle, were Johannes *Fabri, Johannes Cochlaeus, and especially Georg *Witzel (Ep 2768).

It was only very reluctantly and gradually that Jonas came to detach himself from the ideals of Erasmus. As late as 1527 Luther reported in his treatise Auf des Konigs zu Engelland Lesterschrift Titel Martin Luthers Antwort (Wittenberg: [M. Lotter]): 'My dear Dr Justus Jonas would not leave me in peace and kept urging me to deal sincerely with Erasmus and to write against him with due reverence. "Doctor, sir," he said to me, "you have no idea what a noble and reverend old man he is"' (w XXIII 30). But in the same year Luther wrote to Jonas on 19 October 1527: 'I congratulate you on your recantation. Finally you depict Erasmus in his proper colours, as a deadly viper full of stings. Before that, you honoured him with many complimentary epithets but now you recognize his true nature. I am glad that you have gained so much insight reading his Hyperaspistes, and that you have changed your opinion of him' (w Briefwechsel IV Ep 1160).

BIBLIOGRAPHY: Allen and CWE Ep 876 / Walter Delius Justus Jonas (Berlin 1952), with a complete bibliography of Jonas' writings / Der Briefwechsel des Justus Jonas ed Gustav Kawerau (Halle 1884–5, repr 1964) / For additional letters see Walter Delius in ARG 31 (1934) 133–6 and 42 (1951) 136–45 / NDB X 593–4 / LThK 1116 / Walter Delius 'Justus Jonas und Erasmus' Theologia viatorum 1 (1948–9) 71–9 / Matrikel Erfurt II 244 / Matrikel Wittenberg I 35 / Christoph Scheurl's Briefbuch ed F. von Soden and J.K.F. Knaake (Potsdam 1867–72, repr 1962) Ep 116 and passim / Martin von Hase 'Bibliographie der Erfurter Drucke, 1501–1550' Archiv für Geschichte des Buchwesens 8 (1967) 655–1096

ERICH KLEINEIDAM

JOOST of Schoonhoven documented in Bergen op Zoom from 1493, d 1502

It is safe to assume that 'Jodocus medicus,' a speaker in Erasmus' dialogue *Antibarbari* (ASD I-1 34–138), is Joost of Schoonhoven, between Rotterdam and Utrecht. Joost is documented in the Bergen archives as a local physician from September 1493. He was married to Kerstine Henric Clausdochter and died in 1502. As Erasmus had little contact with Bergen in his later years it is not impossible that he may have been unaware of Joost's death and that he was referring to his old friend in Bergen when inquiring after a Jodocus in 1525 (Ep 1562).

In Allen I 588 Joost is erroneously called 'John' and tentatively identified with Johannes a *Mera (also in ASD I-1 41). This mistake was corrected in Allen Ep 1562:15n.

BIBLIOGRAPHY: C. Slootmans 'Erasmus en zijn vrienden uit Bergen op Zoom' *Taxandria* 35 (1928) 113–23   C.G. VAN LEIJENHORST

Guy JOUENNEAUX d 1505 or 1507

Guy Jouenneaux (Jouennaux, Jouvenceaux, Guido Juvenalis) arrived in Paris from the region of Maine before 1490 and began to teach both publicly and privately. Among his students was Symphorien *Champier. He joined the circle of Robert *Gaguin and the brothers Charles and Jean *Fernand, which was devoted to humanistic studies as well as monastic reform. In 1492 he left his teaching position to become a monk at the Benedictine abbey of Chezal-Benoît in Berry, which had recently returned to the austere rules of the earliest Benedictine observance. He was soon joined there by the Fernand brothers, and as the reform movement of Chezal-Benoît began to spread, the abbey of St Sulpice outside the walls of Bourges was joined to the congregation of Chezal-Benoît. Abbots of St Sulpice were henceforward to be appointed for a term of three years, and upon the resignation of the titular abbot, Guillaume de Cambrai, archbishop of Bourges, Jouenneaux took over as abbot from 29 May 1497.

Among his publications one may note *Grammatica* (Lyon n d); *In latinae linguae elegantias tam a Laurentio Valla quam a Gelio memoriae proditas interpretatio* (Paris 1492 and repeatedly thereafter); a Latin translation of Terence's comedies (Rouen n d, etc); a French translation of the rule of St Benedict (Paris 1500); and his *Reformationis monasticae vindiciae*

seu defensio (Paris 1503), written in support of the efforts undertaken by his friends to reform the abbey of St-Germain-des-Prés.

When he lived at Paris Erasmus undoubtedly became aware of Jouenneaux's efforts and thirty years later recalled him in the *Ciceronianus* (ASD I-2 672).

BIBLIOGRAPHY: *Gallia christiana* II 129–30 / Renaudet *Préréforme* 125, 131–3, 354–5, 454–5, 563–4, and passim / *French Monasticism in 1503: An Abstract of the Plea for Reform ... by Guy Jouenneaux* ed and trans G.G. Coulton in his *Medieval Studies* XI (London 1915) / *Catalogue général des livres imprimés de la Bibliothèque Nationale, Auteurs* (Paris 1897–   ) LXXIX 180–2 / For a MS poem Jouenneaux addressed to Charles Fernand see the biography of the latter   PGB

Benedictus JOVIUS *See Benedetto* GIOVIO

JUAN MANUEL d 26 July 1543

Don Juan Manuel (Johannes Emmanuel), lord of Belmonte, a hundred kilometres west of Cuenca, and later marquis of Elche, was an illegitimate kinsman of the royal family of Castile. When Philip the Handsome, duke of *Burgundy, first visited Spain with his wife, *Joanna, Juan Manuel became his favourite. After the death of Queen *Isabella (1504) he supported Philip's claim to the regency of Castile and in return was named knight of the Golden Fleece (1505) and governor of Burgos. Philip's sudden death (25 September 1506) occurred in the wake of festivities at which he had been Juan Manuel's guest.

Fearing the wrath of *Ferdinand II of Aragon, Juan Manuel retired in 1507 to the Netherlands, where with a group of other Castilian émigrés he continued his opposition to the king of Aragon and approached the Francophile party at the Hapsburg-Burgundian court. Though small and inconspicuous in appearance, he was independent-minded and highly intelligent, and was apt to be viewed with some suspicion by his Netherlandish acquaintances. On 17 January 1514 the regent *Margaret had him arrested despite the protest of his fellow-knights of the Golden Fleece, including the future *Charles V. The move was designed to please King Ferdinand, and it seems that Juan Manuel did not regain his freedom until after the king's death (23 January 1516). After Charles had been elected emperor Juan Manuel was sent to Rome as his new ambassador, either because the critical situation called for his ability and experience or perhaps because Guillaume (I) de *Croy, lord of Chièvres, Charles' principal adviser, wished to be rid of him. He arrived in Rome on 11 April 1520 and served his master with great distinction in bringing about a convergence of papal and imperial policies with regard to both France and *Luther. His good rapport with *Leo x did not, however, extend to the next pope, *Adrian VI, whose election he had initially opposed and whose spiritual concerns he may have failed to understand. On 13 October 1522 he left Rome to continue his agitation against the pope from the kingdom of Naples, and by the end of the year Adrian VI had him excommunicated.

In 1523 Juan Manuel returned to Spain, joined the emperor's court, and was appointed to the council of state and the council of finance. Being advanced in years, he reserved to himself the right to retire to his estates whenever he felt that his advice was not welcome. Although he knew how to use that right, he became the weightiest opponent of Chancellor *Gattinara in Charles' council, challenging first his plans for Milan and subsequently his policy towards France. On Charles v's return from his disastrous expedition against Algiers in 1540, Juan Manuel received his monarch with rather dry commiseration.

Diego *Gracián de Alderete, who was Manuel's secretary from 1527 to 1529, assured Erasmus of his master's admiration and support at court (Epp 1970, 2297, 2300). Assisted by Gracián, the Spanish grandee spent his recreational hours reading Latin works of edification, including Erasmus' version of the New Testament. Juan Manuel's son, Diego, who was one of Charles' chamberlains, died in May 1521 of the plague, together with Chièvres and Luigi *Marliano.

BIBLIOGRAPHY: Allen Ep 1970 / Bataillon *Erasmo y España* 267–9 and passim / Karl Brandi *Kaiser Karl v.* new ed (Darmstadt 1959–67) I 43, 123–4, II 126 and passim / F. Walser and R. Wohlfeil *Die spanischen Zentralbehörden und der Staatsrat Karls v.* (Göttingen 1959) 249–50 and

passim / Pastor VIII 8–9, IX 4–5, and passim / de Vocht *Busleyden* 334, 405 / *Deutsche Reichstagsakten* Jüngere Reihe (Gotha-Göttingen 1893–) II passim / Herbert Kreitner in *Archiv für österreichische Geschichte* 96 (1907–8) 279

PGB

Hieronymus JUD of Pforzheim, d before 23 May 1530

Hieronymus Jud (Jod) registered at the University of Freiburg on 14 November 1515. He studied with Udalricus *Zasius, as did his friend Bonifacius *Amerbach, whom he visited at Basel in early May 1521. He was already a doctor of laws when on 1 October 1527 he wrote from Pforzheim to apply for the vacant chair of Institutions at Freiburg. He obtained the position and on 1 November 1528 became rector for a term. Twice thereafter he was dean of law. In May 1528 a payment to his wife at childbirth is recorded in the acts of the faculty of law. In July 1529, when the University of Basel had ceased to function in the Reformation crisis, Jud offered to go there with other Freiburg doctors so that a graduation might be held with proper decorum. On 23 May 1530 Erasmus reported Jud's death to Daniel *Stiebar (Ep 2322), and on 11 June the faculty of law recorded a payment for his funeral.

BIBLIOGRAPHY: Allen Ep 2322 / *Matrikel Freiburg* I 224, 272 / AK II Epp 542, 790, 793, III Epp 1298, 1362 / Schreiber *Universität Freiburg* II 324–5 / Winterberg 47–8 and passim

PGB

Leo JUD of Guémar, c 1482–19 June 1542

Leo Jud (Judae) was the son of the priest of Guémar, between Colmar and Sélestat; he went to the Latin school of Sélestat with *Bucer. When he matriculated at the University of Basel in the autumn of 1499 he called himself Leo Keller and indicated Basel as his home town, conceivably to conceal the position and the Jewish descent of his father. In 1507 he walked to Rome as a pilgrim and obtained his admission to the priesthood despite his illegitimate birth. From late 1507 until 1512 he was deacon at St Theodore's in Basel while continuing his studies. On leaving Basel in 1512 he obtained his MA and then returned to his native region to become the parish priest of Saint-Hippolyte. During his Basel years he had

formed a close friendship with *Zwingli, who
recommended him as his successor when he
left Einsiedeln in 1519. As a parish priest at
Einsiedeln Jud worked closely with the administrator of the abbey, Diebold von Geroldseck
(Ep 1120), who was also a follower of Zwingli.
Again on Zwingli's recommendation, Jud was
appointed to the parish of St Peter's, Zürich,
on 2 February 1523. He remained in this
position until his death, quickly establishing
himself as one of Zürich's leading churchmen.
While Zwingli was alive, Jud was his closest
associate, and after the reformer's death he
faithfully upheld his theological doctrine,
although in 1532 and 1533 he temporarily
adopted the radical views of Kaspar
Schwenckfeld.

It is possible that Jud caused the first edition
of the *Defensor pacis* of Marsilius of Padua to be
printed (Basel: V. Curio 1521), but above all his
scholarly work consisted of posthumous editions of Zwingli's Bible commentaries. He also
produced a revised German Bible (Zürich: C.
Froschauer 1540) and a new Latin translation
of the Old Testament which was completed by
his friends after his death and published
together with the New Testament (Zürich: C.
Froschauer 1543). In addition to his scholarly
work, Jud paid much attention to the practical
needs of the reformed church and its flock,
writing catechisms and hymns as well as translating into German works by St Augustine,
*Luther, Calvin, and Erasmus. At Einsiedeln
he translated the *Enchiridion*, the *Querela pacis*,
the *Institutio principis christiani*, the *Expostulatio
Iesu* (Reedijk poem 85), and the early paraphrases (all published in Zürich by C. Froschauer or in Basel by V. Curio, 1521–3);
probably in 1535 Froschauer published his
translation of the complete paraphrase of the
New Testament (n p, n d). As a translator, Jud
strove to retain the special merits of Erasmus'
style but contended that literal rendering could
not achieve this. Therefore he translated with
great freedom, always bearing in mind what he
perceived to be the needs of a reader lacking
higher education.

Towards the end of 1525 Jud reaffirmed his
concern for religious lay education by juxta-
posing the eucharistic views of Erasmus and
Luther in a German pamphlet published
anonymously with the date of 18 April 1526.

Leo Jud

This incensed Luther no less than Erasmus,
who replied first with Ep 1708 and a month
later with his *Detectio praestigiarum* (ASD IX-1
211–62), which was also published in a
German translation. Jud ignored Luther's
protests but wrote a rejoinder to those of
Erasmus: *Uf Entdeckung Doctor Erasmi ...
Antwurt und Entschuldigung* ([Zürich: C.
Froschauer] 1526). Jud's bluntest criticism of
Erasmus' position, however, was expressed in
a private letter in Latin, which is now lost (Epp
1737, 1741, 1744, 1804). Erasmus later referred
to Jud's attacks when he wished to present
evidence for his Catholic orthodoxy (Epp 1902,
2443, 2445). However, Jud's opposition to
Erasmus was far from total. At the end of his
life he showed his appreciation of Erasmus'
scriptural scholarship in his own Bible translations. In a preface to Froschauer's Latin Bible of
1543 Heinrich Bullinger expressed his admiration for Jud, who had recently died, and also
for Erasmus, whose work on the New Testament he too valued highly.

BIBLIOGRAPHY: Allen Ep 1737 / ADB XIV
651–4 / NDB X 636 / DHBS IV 295 / Leo Weisz *Leo
Jud* (Zürich 1942) / E. Egli 'Leo Jud und seine

Pope Julius II, by Raphael

Propagandaschriften' *Zwingliana* 2 (1905–12), 161–6, 198–208 / Karl-Heinz Wyss *Leo Jud: seine Entwicklung zum Reformator, 1519–23* (Bern 1976) / Irmgard Bezzel 'Leo Jud (1482–1542) als Erasmusübersetzer' *Deutsche Vierteljahrsschrift für Literaturwissenschaft und Geistesgeschichte* 49 (1975) 628–44 / z VII Ep 51 and passim / H. Bullinger *Werke* ed H. Büsser (Zürich 1974–) *Briefwechsel* I Ep 4 and passim / AK I Epp 108, 423, II Ep 658 / *Matrikel Basel* I 258 / *Ein Klag des Frydens: Leo Juds Übersetzung der Querela Pacis von 1521 zusammen mit dem lateinischen Original* ed A.M. Haas and U. Herzog (Zürich 1969) / Otto Herding in ASD IV-2 15 and passim

PGB

JÜLICH, JULIERS *See* CLEVES

Pope JULIUS II 5 December 1443–
21 February 1513
Giuliano, the son of Rafaello della Rovere, was a nephew of Pope *Sixtus IV. Details about his youth are uncertain. The story repeated by Erasmus that he spent it rowing the fishing boat of his humble father cannot be confirmed (*Adagia* III iv 86; *Julius exclusus, Opuscula*

71–2). Nor is there evidence that his mother was Greek (Brosch 3), or that he studied at Perugia under the supervision of his uncle, the future pope (Pastor IV 237). Jacopo of Volterra (1434–1516) described him in his diary in about 1480 as acute in intelligence but mediocre in literary learning.

On 15 December 1471 Giuliano was created cardinal priest of San Pietro in Vincoli (with which church he was to be continuously associated), also receiving the title of Santi Apostoli. He was raised to the cardinal bishoprics of Sabina (19 April 1479) and Ostia (31 January 1483). Episodes of violence characterized his career as cardinal and as pope, the feature that particularly fascinated Erasmus. As papal legate in Umbria in 1474 he authorized the sacking of Todi and Spoleto. Appointed bishop of Avignon on 23 May 1474, he began a long association with France and was sent on missions to *Louis XI in 1476 and 1480; in 1481 he confronted a hostile army which had invaded the Comtat Venaissin. But he also founded a college in Avignon, revised the university statutes, and improved the church of Notre Dame des Doms, providing a choir school. He added the bishopric of Bologna to his growing number of benefices on 3 November 1483, and the following year he returned to Rome and engineered the election of Cardinal Gianbattista Cibo, who became Pope Innocent VIII. Giuliano was a dominating figure during Innocent's pontificate; among his many services was the military defence of Rome from December 1486 to January 1487 against the attack of *Alfonso II of Naples and Virginio Orsini.

Giuliano's failure to be elected pope in 1492 and his bad relations with his rival, Cardinal Ascanio Sforza, and Pope *Alexander VI led him to depart secretly from his rebuilt fortress at Ostia in April 1494, whence he returned to France and joined his voice to those urging *Charles VIII to invade Italy. He accompanied Charles to Rome and Naples but in October 1495 returned to Avignon. Between December 1496 and March 1497 he was again in Italy and reconciled with the pope; in November 1498 he presented Cesare Borgia, the pope's son, to *Louis XII. Giuliano presided over the marriage of Louis XII and Anne of Brittany in January 1499 and in September joined the king at Turin and Milan; subsequently he stayed at Savona until the death of Alexander VI.

Giuliano was elected pope on 1 November 1503. The aggressive temporal policy for which Pope Julius became famous was first dictated by the need to redeem papal territory alienated to Cesare Borgia or annexed by Venice, and then by wider objectives, which he certainly intended should culminate in a crusade against the Turks. Accompanied by an army in September and October 1506 he regained Perugia and Bologna more by intimidation than by force. Erasmus, who had just arrived in Bologna, was driven by this display of papal militarism to take refuge at Florence and wrote to Servatius *Rogerus about it on 4 November (Ep 200); in 1526 he claimed he could still recall the sound of papal gunfire (Ep 1756). Julius' triumphal entry into Bologna first suggested to Erasmus the comparison with Julius Caesar (Epp 203, 205; cf Opuscula 85). No personal contact with Julius is recorded then, nor when Erasmus was in Rome in 1509, but he recalled having been present at a bullfight in Julius' palace, presumably the Vatican (Ep 3032).

In April 1509 Julius declared his support of the League of Cambrai, the alliance directed against Venice. The league defeated the Venetians at Agnadello in May; as a result Venice temporarily lost most of her mainland dominion. By February 1510, however, Julius had made peace with Venice and decided to reverse his longstanding pro-French policy, being enraged against Louis XII and in particular against his ally, Alfonso I d'*Este, duke of Ferrara, who was technically a papal vassal. On his second military expedition as pope, Julius reached Bologna on 22 September; the French advance on the city and his own severe illness in October were overcome by a determination to conquer that was visually expressed by his growing a beard, probably with ancient military commanders in mind. In January 1511 Julius was present at the siege of Mirandola; his headquarters were in a convent, the kitchen of which was struck by a cannon ball. In spite of such dangers and heavy snowfalls he entered Mirandola through a breach in its walls.

Bologna was lost by Julius in May 1511, and a schismatic council, sponsored by Louis XII and a number of rebel cardinals – not all of them

French – opened at Pisa in November. Although the council denounced Julius as a simoniac, the pope's fortunes were by then improving. Spain, Venice, and England had joined his Holy League against France, and his own plans were going forward to call a general· council, scheduled to open in Rome in April 1512. In spite of the French victory at Ravenna in April 1512, Louis XII's army suffered severe losses and withdrew under pressure. Julius was seen as Italy's liberator from the foreigner and was portrayed as Mars in a victory parade in Rome; he also shaved his beard. Fascinated by Julius' energy and belligerence, Erasmus had continued to ask for news of 'the most invincible Julius' (Ep 233) and whether he was really playing the part of Julius (Caesar) (Ep 262; cf ASD IX-1 172). Having at last obtained the Emperor *Maximilian's adherence in November 1512, as a counterweight to the threat of Spanish designs in northern Italy, Julius directed the fifth Lateran council to condemn French ecclesiastical policies and impose an interdict. His health was failing, however; after his severe illness of October–December 1510, he was again seriously ill in August 1511. Erasmus had then heard a rumour that 'Julius Maximus' was dead (Ep 228). The pope died at Rome eighteen months later.

Erasmus' characterization of Julius as a 'terrestrial Jupiter' remained fairly constant (Ep 1756). Writing to *Budé in June 1527 he recalled his anti-French policy (Ep 1840) and to *Krzycki in August 1528 his warlike character (Ep 2030). He also stooped to repeating stories of Julius' drunkenness (Lingua ASD IV-1 276). Whether or not there was any truth in such allegations, there is no doubt that Julius possessed an uncontrollably coarse tongue and manic bad temper. Erasmus vehemently denied writing the Julius exclusus (for example, Ep 622). On the other hand, he acknowledged to *Leo X in May 1515 that Julius had been 'a very great man' even though his wars had brought misery to others (Allen Ep 335:93–129). Conradus *Pellicanus reminded Erasmus in 1525 that Julius had also wished to reassert the universal spiritual authority of the papacy by means of the fifth Lateran council (Ep 1639).

Erasmus did not mention Julius' celebrated role as a patron of the arts – which included commissions to Michelangelo for the Sistine

chapel and Raphael for the Vatican 'Stanze' –
but he was certainly aware of the most famous
item in Julius' patronage of architecture, the
foundation in 1506 of a new St Peter's. Though
Erasmus recalled the pope's attendance at a
Ciceronian Latin sermon (ASD I-2 637–9), he
does not appear to have known that Julius had
an extensive private library, the display of
which is now widely believed to have been the
original function of the so-called Stanza della
Segnatura decorated by Raphael. Nor did he
know that Julius took pleasure in having
Bramante read Dante aloud to him. Among the
most celebrated of portraits of Julius are those
by Melozzo da Forlì (showing him as a young
cardinal with Sixtus IV) in the Pinacoteca
Vaticana and by Raphael in the National
Gallery, London, and in the 'Stanza' of
Heliodorus in the Vatican. His head appears
on many medals.

BIBLIOGRAPHY: The most useful biographical
article available is by G.B. Picotti in *Enciclopedia
Cattolica* (Vatican City 1949–54) VI 749–58 /
There is no comprehensive monograph; the
nearest attempt remains J. Brosch *Papst Julius
II. und die Gründung des Kirchenstaats* (Gotha
1878), and the relevant chapters in Pastor IV–VI
are indispensable / E. Rodocanachi *Le Pontificat
de Jules II* (Paris 1912) is lavish but unreliable /
Essential primary material is in F. Albertini
*Opusculum de mirabilibus novae et veteris urbis
Romae* ed A. Schmarsow (Heilbronn 1866); J.
Burchardus *Liber notarum* ed E. Celani (Città di
Castello 1906–59); *Le due spedizioni militari di
Giulio II* ed L. Frati (Bologna 1886) (extracts
from the diary of Paris de Grassis); Jacopo of
Volterra *Dispacci e lettere ...* ed E. Carusi (Rome
1909) 19; Sigismondo dei Conti *Le storie de' suoi
tempi dal 1471 al 1510* (Rome 1883): but much
remains unpublished.

The following secondary works include
some new material or interpretations: L. Dorez
'La bibliothèque privée de Jules II' *Revue des
bibliothèques* 6 (1896) 97–121 / Felix Gilbert *The
Pope, His Banker and Venice* (Cambridge, Mass-
London 1980) / L.H. Labande *Avignon au xve
siècle* (Paris 1920) / A. Luzio 'Federico Gonzaga
ostaggio alla corte di Giulio II' *Archivio della
R. Società Romana di Storia Patria* 9 (1886) 510–
82 / A. Luzio 'La reggenza d'Isabella d'Este
durante la prigonia del marito' *Archivio storico
lombardo* 37 (1910) 5–104 / A. Luzio 'Isabella

d'Este di fronte a Giulio II negli ultimi tre anni
del suo pontificato' *Archivio storico lombardo* 39
(1912) 55–144, 245–334 / F. Seneca *Venezia e
Giulio II* (Padua 1962) / J. Shearman 'The
Vatican Stanze: functions and decorations'
Proceedings of the British Academy 57 (1971) 3–
58 / R. Weiss 'The medals of Pope Julius II
1503–1513' *Journal of the Warburg and Courtauld
Institutes* 28 (1965) 163–82 / M.J. Zucker
'Raphael and the beard of Pope Julius II' *Art
Bulletin* 59 (1977) 524–33   D.S. CHAMBERS

JUSTINIANUS *See* GIUSTINIANI

Jakob of KALKAR *See Jakob* RIDDER

Adriaan van der KAMMEN of Mechelen,
d 20 September 1540
Adriaan van der Kammen (Kamen, Cammen,
Cammius) was a son of Bartholomaeus and
Maria Caluwaerts. He matriculated at the
University of Louvain on 23 November 1507
and he graduated in due course as a licentiate
in civil and canon law. He became legal
consultant ('pensionary') to the town of
Mechelen and was succeeded in this office by
his brother Jan.

Adriaan introduced himself to Erasmus with
Ep 2244 (26 December 1529), after having met
Erasmus' servant, Quirinus *Talesius, at Mechelen. The purpose of his letter was to
receive one from Erasmus in return.

BIBLIOGRAPHY: *Matricule de Louvain* III-1 344 /
de Vocht CTL II 494
MARCEL A. NAUWELAERTS

Nicolaas KAN of Amsterdam, d 1555
Nicolaas Kan (Cannius, Caninus, Caem), the
son of Jan, was a native of Amsterdam who
matriculated at the University of Louvain on 14
May 1524 and attended the lectures of Conradus *Goclenius and Rutgerus *Rescius at the
Collegium Trilingue. He is first mentioned in
the correspondence of Erasmus in the spring of
1527 but may have joined his household at
Basel somewhat earlier. He was particularly
useful to his master as a copyist of Greek
manuscripts (Ep 1832). In the first half of 1527
Kan was sent to England on two consecutive
missions and also visited Brabant on his return
from the second trip to England (Epp 1816,

1831, 1832, 1849, 1857, 1861, 1890, 2040). Ep
1832, sent after the departed famulus, clearly
shows Erasmus' loving concern for the young
man who had proved so useful to his master. In
June 1528 he again went to the Low Countries
(Epp 1999, 2014, 2015, 2025, 2026) and had not
returned by the beginning of September, not
wholly to Erasmus' surprise (Ep 2039). After
his return he persuaded Erasmus to introduce
him as a character in his colloquy *Cyclops sive
evangeliophorus* (ASD I-3 603–9; Epp 2147, 2196).
Kan assisted Erasmus on his move to Freiburg
in April 1529 (Ep 2202, 2229), and on occasion
received his share of his master's suspicion and
annoyance (Ep 2236; but cf Ep 2239). In January
1530 Kan left Erasmus to return home for good
and receive holy orders (Epp 2261, 2343, 2348,
2349); by July he had settled in Amsterdam (Ep
2352). On his return to the Netherlands
sickness had prevented him from carrying out
Erasmus' orders at once (Ep 2352), and when
the latter heard that Kan had visited the hated
*Geldenhower in Strasbourg he exploded (Ep
2356). Kan wrote a letter of apology, which
Erasmus accepted none too graciously; Kan
also asked *Viglius Zuichemus and Goclenius
to put in a word for him (Epp 2484, 3037, 3061),
but it seems that Erasmus was not persuaded;
he even associated Kan with the detested
*Quirinus Hagius (Ep 3052).

In Amsterdam Kan renewed his connections
with *Alaard, the *Occo family, and Cornelis
*Croock. He was a parish priest and adminis-
trator of the Ursuline convent, but also
devoted much of his time to teaching. By the
end of his life he was apparently priest of
Spaarnwoude, near Haarlem, and planned to
join the Society of Jesus. Croock dedicated to
Kan his *Colloquiorum puerilium formulae* (1534).
The dedicatory preface contained a statement
that has led to the erroneous claim that Kan
edited an expurgated edition of Erasmus'
Colloquia.

BIBLIOGRAPHY: Allen Ep 1832 / NNBW X 170 /
Matricule de Louvain III-1 725 / AK III Ep 1378 / de
Vocht *Literae ad Craneveldium* Ep 242 and
passim / de Vocht CTL II 139–42 and passim /
A.J. Kolker 'Biografische gegevens omtrent
Nicolaas Cannius' *Archief voor de Geschiedenis
van de katholieke kerk in Nederland* 7 (1965)
129–61 / Bierlaire *Familia* 72–6

FRANZ BIERLAIRE

Andreas Karlstadt

Andreas KARLSTADT of Karlstadt, c 1480–
24 December 1541
Andreas Rudolf Bodenstein called himself
Karlstadt (Carlstadt, Carolostadius) after his
native city, Karlstadt, on the Main near
Würzburg. He matriculated at Erfurt in 1499
and obtained a BA in 1502. On 17 June 1503 he
matriculated in Cologne, where he received a
thorough training in disputations and discussions. He moved to Wittenberg in 1505 and
obtained his MA on 15 August 1505; subsequently he began to teach, lecturing on St
Thomas Aquinas and Duns Scotus. He advanced rapidly, held a doctorate in theology in
1510, and was elected archdeacon of the All
Saints chapter. As he was dean of the faculty of
divinity in 1512, it was he who conferred a
doctorate in theology upon Martin *Luther.
Hoping to become provost of All Saints, a
position for which a doctorate in law was
needed, Karlstadt went to Italy in 1515 and,
after a pilgrimage to Rome, obtained a doctorate in law in Siena in March 1516. After his
return to Wittenberg Luther drew his attention
to the teachings of St Augustine; intensive
study of his writings and those of Johann von

*Staupitz inspired Karlstadt to post a list of 151 theses on 26 April 1517; they were primarily on grace and were highly praised by Luther. Around this time Karlstadt also began to be interested in medieval mystics, especially Johann Tauler.

Two further sets of theses, some of them questioning the pope's powers, led to the clash with Johann *Eck, who confronted Karlstadt and Luther at the Leipzig disputation of 1519 (Ep 911). The debate was continued in polemical pamphlets exchanged with Eck; among these, in October 1519, was Karlstadt's *Epistola adversus ineptam et ridiculam inventionem Joannis Eckii* (Leipzig: V. Schumann), dedicated to *Spalatinus. Karlstadt's *Confutatio* (Wittenberg: M. Lotter 28 February 1520) expressed his violent resentment to an extent that he himself soon regretted. Meanwhile student enrolment increased in Wittenberg in 1520 and, like those of Luther and *Melanchthon, Karlstadt's lectures proved highly popular. His scholarly book *De canonicis scripturis libellus* (Wittenberg: J. Rhau-Grunenberg August 1520) offered a moderate refutation of the infallibility of the pope; however, Karlstadt also rejected in it some views of St Augustine, preferring those of St Jerome, and he attacked Luther's disparagement of the Epistle of James, thus causing a minor rift between them. The two men were, however, on common ground in their opposition to the sale of indulgences and the emphasis on ceremonies which Karlstadt attacked in a number of pamphlets such as *Von geweihtem Wasser und Salz* (Leipzig: V. Schumann August 1520). When threatened with excommunication, he wrote the polemical pamphlet *Von päpstlicher Heiligkeit* (Wittenberg: M. Lotter) dated 17 October 1520. In January 1521 the rift deepened when Luther failed to support Karlstadt's candidacy for the vacant position of provost of All Saints, which subsequently went to Justus *Jonas. In May 1521 Karlstadt accepted an invitation from King *Christian II of Denmark to help with the reformation of Denmark and the reorganization of the University of Copenhagen. After the promulgation of the edict of Worms (26 May 1521) political considerations forced Christian to suspend his reforms (cf Ep 1241), and Karlstadt had to return to Wittenberg six weeks after he had left.

Karlstadt's regard for biblical literalism made him receptive to the more radical trends in the Reformation. He produced pamphlets and in June and July 1521 new sets of theses against celibacy, the Roman understanding of the Eucharist, and aural confession. On 15 December he introduced a shortened mass, partly in German, and the lay chalice; on 19 January 1522 he married Anna von Mochau, the daughter of a poor nobleman (Ep 1258). In the absence of Luther, who was detained in the Wartburg, Karlstadt took a leading part in formulating Wittenberg's precedent-setting church ordinance of January 1522, but he also preached iconoclasm. The publication of his *Von der Abthuung der Bilder*, on 27 January 1522 (Wittenberg: N. Schirlentz), aroused the ire of Hieronymus *Emser; in Wittenberg it coincided with radical agitation by Gabriel Zwilling and the 'Zwickau prophets' led by Nikolaus *Storch. Luther returned from the Wartburg in March 1522, reintroduced the Latin mass, and spoke against Karlstadt in several sermons. Karlstadt began to feel isolated in Wittenberg; he bought a farm in Wörlitz and in the summer of 1523 took personal charge of his parish of Orlamünde, south of Jena, which had hitherto been administered by a vicar. There he wrote a new series of pamphlets and treatises which were printed by Michael Buchführer in Jena. Although he was appalled by the fanaticism of Thomas Müntzer and rejected his approaches, Karlstadt did refuse to baptize children in Orlamünde. This and incidents of iconoclasm moved Luther to have Karlstadt expelled from Saxony in September 1524 after a memorable last encounter at Jena.

Leaving his pregnant wife behind, Karlstadt first went to Rothenburg ob der Tauber, then to Strasbourg, where, although he stayed there for only four days, he caused a violent commotion (Luther w *Briefwechsel* III Ep 796). He travelled on to Zürich for an indecisive meeting with the Anabaptist Swiss Brethren and on his return passed through Basel, where several pamphlets of his on the Eucharist, presenting a view to some extent similar to that of *Zwingli and *Oecolampadius, were printed by Thomas *Wolff and Johann *Bebel (Epp 1522, 1523, 1620, 1621). On the advice of Oecolampadius, however, they refused to print a further pamphlet on the subject of infant baptism. At the beginning of November Karlstadt visited Simon *Grynaeus, his son's godfather, in Heidelberg. When his application to Duke John of *Saxony for permission to return home was rejected, Karlstadt returned to Rothenburg. Meanwhile Luther had summed up his reasons for opposing Karlstadt in *Wider die himmlischen Propheten* (Wittenberg: L. Cranach and C. Döring, 2 parts, December 1524–January 1525), to which Karlstadt replied in three pamphlets especially *Anzeig etlicher Hauptartikel christlicher Lehre* (Augsburg: P. Ulhart 1525). Karlstadt's second child, Andreas, was born in January 1525, and when his wife refused to have the infant baptized, she also had to leave Saxony and joined her husband in Rothenburg.

During the peasant revolt (March–April 1525) Karlstadt tried without success to prevent the excesses of the peasants, but he continued to sanction iconoclasm. When the revolt broke down, he appealed to Luther for asylum in Saxony and was permitted to return after a formal recantation (Epp 1616, 1624). From 1526 to 1529 he tried to live as a farmer, first in Segrehna, then in the village of Bergwitz, near Kemberg, but he could not make ends meet. In 1528 he refused to write against Oecolampadius and Zwingli; new bitterness arose between him and Luther, and in February 1529 Karlstadt fled from Saxony and went first to Holstein and then to East Friesland, where he lived as a preacher until a new edict of Count Enno II *Cirksena of Friesland, a militant Lutheran, drove him to Strasbourg in February 1530. He was offered hospitality in *Bucer's house. Hoping for permission to stay, he sent for his wife and three children, but on 9 May 1530 he was ordered to leave Strasbourg. In Basel Oecolampadius received him warmly but was unable to find him a position. Karlstadt went to Zürich, where Zwingli secured him the position of deacon at the hospital. Also working as a corrector for the Froschauer press, Karlstadt settled down in Zürich with his family. Through Zwingli's influence he received a call as pastor to the parish of Altstätten in the Upper Rhine valley in September 1531, but although he was not present at the battle of Kappel – the false rumour that he had died there with Zwingli persisted for a while (Ep

2559) – in January 1532 the effects of the war drove him back to Zürich, where he assisted Heinrich Bullinger and Leo *Jud in the continuation of Zwingli's work and was again employed at the hospital. Highly recommended by Bullinger and *Myconius, Karlstadt was finally appointed as preacher of St Peter's in Basel and, on 1 July 1534, professor of Old Testament at the University of Basel. From 1536 to 1541 he was dean of the faculty of theology and for 1537–8 he was rector. He sided with Bonifacius *Amerbach and the Basel council when they insisted that the professors of theology should obtain a doctorate, offending Myconius and Grynaeus by taking this stand (AK V Ep 2436). In spite of this quarrel Karlstadt was highly respected and remained at Basel until the end of his life.

At the time of the Leipzig disputation of 1519 Karlstadt was an ardent admirer of Erasmus, praising him highly in his *Epistola adversus ... inventionem Joannis Eckii* (Barge I 168, 175). Erasmus sent polite greetings to Karlstadt when he wrote to Luther in 1520 (Ep 1127A). By this time Karlstadt's interests had changed, and he did not seek further contact. Erasmus was well aware of Karlstadt's conflict with Luther (LB X 1257B) and of his stand in the eucharistic debate. In his *Hyperaspistes* he frequently discussed the differences between Luther's and Karlstadt's views on grace and free will (LB X 1277B and passim). In many statements he took exception to Karlstadt's views, especially as they were echoed, he believed, by Leo Jud, Oecolampadius, and Conradus *Pellicanus. At one point he considered writing a pamphlet against Karlstadt lest his own stand on free will and the Eucharist might be confused with Karlstadt's (Epp 1616, 1640, 1708). Erasmus' many references to Karlstadt, and likewise Karlstadt's views on Erasmus, need to be investigated by theologians.

BIBLIOGRAPHY: Allen and CWE Ep 911 / NDB II 356–7 / ADB III 8–15 / RGG III 1154–5 / Hermann Barge *Andreas Bodenstein von Karlstadt* (Leipzig 1905, repr 1968) / Calvin A. Pater *Karlstadt as the Father of the Baptist Movement* (Toronto 1983) / *Matrikel Erfurt* II 212 / *Matrikel Wittenberg* I 16 / *Matrikel Basel* II 7 and passim / G.H. Williams *The Radical Reformation* (Philadelphia 1962) 38–44, 101–6, and passim / J.S. Oyer *Lutheran*

Georg Keck

Georg **KECK** of Hechingen, d 1547
The curate at the cathedral of Freiburg ('paro-chus Friburgensis,' Ep 2207) was Georg Keck of Hechingen, south of Tübingen, who held this position from 1519 to 1532. In 1533 he was a doctor of theology and by 1536 a member of the theological faculty. In 1537 Keck competed against Fridericus *Nausea for the provostship of the chapter of Waldkirch, north of Walds-hut. He was elected, but in 1539 the University of Freiburg was still pleading with Nausea to stand aside. The benefice was considered as a kind of retirement benefit for the old professor, and he rarely resided at Waldkirch. When he died in 1547 he was succeeded by Nausea. He left his house at Freiburg to the university.

BIBLIOGRAPHY: Allen Ep 2207 / AK III Ep 1377, VIII Ep 3494 / [August] Münzer in *Schau-ins-Land* 33 (1906) 61–2 (with a reproduction of a portrait at Waldkirch) / J.J. Bauer *Zur Frühgeschichte der theologischen Fakultät der Universität Freiburg i. Br.* (Freiburg 1957) 183
                                                        PGB

Reformers against Anabaptists (The Hague 1964) 21–8 and passim / David C. Steinmetz *Reformers in the Wings* (Philadelphia 1971) 175–85 / BA *Oekolampads* I 134 and passim / *Karlstadt's Battle with Luther* ed Ronald J. Sider (Philadelphia 1978)   IG

Alice KEBEL d 8 June 1521
Alice Kebel was the third wife of Erasmus' patron, William *Blount, fourth Baron Mount-joy, and the mother of his son and heir, Charles *Blount, the fifth baron. She was the daughter of Henry Kebel, lord mayor of London from 1510 to 1511, and had previously been married to William Browne, lord mayor from 1507 to 1508. She was buried in the church of the Grey Friars, London. Erasmus sent greetings to her in two epistles (Epp 783, 888) and mentioned her in a letter to Thomas *More (Ep 829).

BIBLIOGRAPHY: Allen and CWE Ep 783 / G.E. C[ockayne] *The Complete Peerage of England* ed. V. Gibbs et al (London 1910–59) IX 340–1
                                        STANFORD E. LEHMBERG

Cornelius KEISEPREISTER documented at Münster, 1532–5
The name 'Keespaep,' cited in Allen Ep 2957:86 as if it were a nickname, no doubt refers to Cornelius Keisepreister, who in 1532 was still listed among the Lutherans of Münster. In the so-called *Bichtbook*, however, he is called a *ketzer*, which is to say an Anabaptist. As such he came to be part of the court of 'king' *Jan of Leiden; in the *Hofordnung* his position is given as *Holzsetzer* or supervisor of supplies (no 22).

There is no basis for the identification of Keespaep with Johann Glandorp, as proposed in Allen Ep 2957:85–7n.

BIBLIOGRAPHY: K.H. Kirchoff *Die Täufer in Münster 1534/35* (Münster 1973) 18 / The *Bichtbook* is edited as 'Ein schoin gedicht off historie van den Mönsterschen wederdoepers' in *Die Schriften der Münsterschen Täufer und ihrer Gegner* II ed R. Stupperich (Münster 1980) 135 / 'Des Münsterischen Königs Johann von Leiden Hofordnung' (broadsheet 1534–5), repr in *Die Wiedertäufer zu Münster* ed K. Löffler (Jena 1923) 130–4   ROBERT STUPPERICH

Michael KELLER *See Michael* CELLARIUS

KEMPO of Texel, documented 1505–22
Kempo (Kempo Thessaliensis) was born on the
island of Texel and studied at Zwolle. He took
his degree in arts at Paris before 1 July 1505,
the publication date of the earliest known
edition of his commentary on the second part of
the *Doctrinale puerorum* of Alexander de Villa
Dei (Cologne: H. Quentel). This work, which
complemented the commentary on the first part
of the *Doctrinale* by Hermannus *Torrentinus,
earned Kempo a derogatory remark from Juan
Luis *Vives in Ep 1362 to Erasmus in 1523. On
10 December 1517, after teaching for some time
at Zwolle, Kempo was appointed rector of
the Alkmaar municipal school, succeeding
Johannes *Murmellius. In 1522 he succeeded
Gerardus *Listrius as rector at Zwolle. He was
probably still alive in 1530.

Kempo wrote many poems and published
Carmina et epigrammata ([Zwolle: P. Os c 1500];
NK 1278), *Carmen scholare* ([Alkmaar: J. Daventriensis c 1515]; NK 1277), and *De gloriosa virgine
Maria* (Alkmaar: J. Daventriensis c 1515; NK
1276). In addition he wrote an explanation of
the *Horae divae crucis* of Jean *Fernand, his
teacher at Paris (Zwolle: L. Rensinck c 1516;
NK 4152).

BIBLIOGRAPHY: Allen Ep 1362 / C.W. Bruinvis
in NNBW II 1421 / de Vocht CTL I 199 / H.E. van
Gelder *Geschiedenis der Latijnsche School te
Alkmaar* (Alkmaar 1905) I 109–13, 133–8
                                    C.G. VAN LEIJENHORST

Johann von KERSSENBROCK documented
1486–1540
A younger son of a noble Westphalian family,
Johann (Jürgen) von Kerssenbrock (Carsen-
brock) was intended for an ecclesiastical career
from an early age. In the winter term of 1486 he
matriculated at the University of Erfurt, being
listed in the register as canon of Osnabrück. He
is documented as a canon in 1491, after having
studied for a time in Greifswald. It seems that
by 1532 he was the scholaster of the cathedral
chapter and sympathetic to humanistic studies
(Ep 2687). Perhaps in that year he also became
vicar of the cathedral and at one time he held
the office of obedientiary. In 1540 he is
documented as canon of Osnabrück and
Minden.

BIBLIOGRAPHY: Anton Fahne *Geschichte der

Westfälischen Geschlechter (Cologne 1858) 2427 /
Matrikel Erfurt I 414; cf I 434 (1490) for a
Johannes Kersenbrock de Bilveldia, probably
another man   ROBERT STUPPERICH

Ambrosius KETTENACKER of Winterthur,
d 5 November 1541
Kettenacker (Suagrius, Syragrius, Swagrius,
Sauracker) registered at the University of Basel
for the winter term 1508–9 and soon became
friends with the *Amerbach brothers and Jakob
Salzmann, an older fellow student who acted
as his tutor, and also Johann *Zwick, *Beatus
Rhenanus, and Michael *Bentinus. By the end
of 1518 he was evidently a priest and had been
nominated to the parish of Riehen, just north
of Basel. From the beginning of his ministry he
was in touch with *Oecolampadius and
*Zwingli and was clearly committed to promot-
ing the Reformation. In 1522 he preached an
uncompromising sermon on Matthew 1 to
which Erasmus referred in Ep 1447.

The parish of Riehen was under the patronage of the abbot of Wettingen (Aargau), but the
village was acquired by the city of Basel in
1522. From August 1523 litigation developed
between Kettenacker and Andreas *Wengi,
the conservative abbot of Wettingen, which
continued for two years and led to Erasmus'
intervention in support of Kettenacker (Ep
1447). Erasmus, however, does not mention
the priest's support of the reformers or his
notorious disregard of celibacy. The abbot was
supported by the Swiss diet and Kettenacker
by the Basel council, which was eager to assert
its own jurisdiction but nonetheless requested
him to send his mistress away. He enjoyed the
support of a majority of his parishioners, albeit
against strong opposition from a conservative
minority led by Heinrich *Meltinger, and in
1528 he defeated Meltinger's efforts to reintro-
duce the mass at Riehen. In the same year he
accompanied Oecolampadius to the disputation at Bern. In 1530 he married Agathe
Niesslin of Zürich, formerly a nun at the
Gnadental convent near Mellingen (Aargau),
and in his will he left two hundred florins to
found a scholarship at Basel for poor students
of divinity from Riehen.

BIBLIOGRAPHY: Allen Ep 1447 / DHBS IV 347 /
A. Bruckner et al *Riehen: Geschichte eines Dorfes*

(Riehen 1972) 166–74 / R. Wackernagel *Geschichte der Stadt Basel* (Basel 1907–54) III 326 and passim / AK II Epp 568, 636, and passim / BRE Ep 58 / z VII Ep 131 and passim / *Matrikel Basel* I 294 / *Aktensammlung zur Geschichte der Basler Reformation* ed E. Dürr et al (Basel 1921–50) I 81–93 and passim / BA *Oekolampads* II 468–9 and passim   PGB

Robert de KEYSERE of Ghent, d 1532
Born before 1480 into a prosperous artisan environment, Robert de Keysere (Caesar, Caesaris, L'Empreur) was the son of Jan, a cooper, and of Kathelyne de Cleercq. Robert's sister Clara was widely known as an illustrator. Robert studied at Paris and may have received a MA there; the title of *magister* is given to him as early as 1496. On 29 October 1500 he bought a house named the 'Lintworm' on the Koornlei in Ghent and there opened a Latin school. His pupils included the historian Jacob de Meyere and the humanist Eligius Hockaert. He enjoyed an excellent reputation as a teacher (Ep 175) and may have been given a part in the education of the future *Charles v. For some years up to 1517, and possibly longer, he was the tutor of *Leopold, the natural son of *Maximilian I.

On 3 October 1508 de Keysere sold the 'Lintworm' and apparently returned to Paris. In 1510 he was head of the Collège de Tournai at Paris and in November of that year he dated from the college the introductory letter for his edition of Apuleius' *De asino aureo* (Paris: Collegium Italorum 1510). Some time after the appearance of this book, at least in the years 1511 and 1513, de Keysere became directly involved in printing. Although he did not operate a press himself, as was claimed by several of his biographers, he set one up and supplied it with capital and typographical material (Epp 175, 263). The actual printer of the 'praelum Caesareum' was probably Joris Biermans of Bruges, and the press may have been located either in de Keysere's college or perhaps in the premises formerly occupied by Petrus Caesarius, a native of Silesia. De Keysere's printing activities are explicitly mentioned by Josse *Bade (Ep 263) and also by Gervasius *Amoenus in a prefatory epistle addressed to de Keysere and published with Valerius Flaccus' *Argonauticon* (Paris: praelum

Caesareum for J. Bade and J. Petit 1512). The first edition of Erasmus' *Concio de puero Jesu* is commonly attributed to this press on the basis of type and printer's mark; more recently Machiels suggested that in view of the typographical material and the title woodcut *De ratione studii* (Paris: J. Biermans 1511; Ep 66; CWE 24 661–91) came from the same press.

In 1513 de Keysere was again in Ghent, where on 23 July he bought back the 'Lintworm' and at the same time rented another house, the 'Posteerne,' using both for a new 'praelum Caesareum.' Four books have been identified as products of this press, printed for different booksellers of Ghent. During this period Erasmus met Robert at Ghent in the summer of 1514 (Ep 301). In 1516 the press was taken over by Robert's nephew, Pieter de Keysere, who had formerly been in business as a bookseller. In the following years, living alone in the 'Lintworm' (Ep 525), de Keysere applied himself to the study of Roman law (Epp 524, 525, 530) and subsequently of Greek, the latter perhaps in the hope of an appointment to the newly founded Collegium Trilingue at Louvain (Ep 743). Afterwards he was associated with Pierre *Cotrel in efforts to found a humanistic college at Tournai. After a successful, if modest, start in 1521 these efforts were ultimately frustrated in 1530 through the intervention of the University of Louvain.

In 1526 de Keysere married Margriet Stoop, from a bourgeois family; by the time he died in 1532 they had three sons. For a scholar he did not write a great deal. We know of a work enigmatically entitled 'De nuptiis Leopoldi,' which he had composed as the tutor of Leopold of Austria and which treated, in Robert's own words, 'of the new learning and the French-Greek-Latin university to be founded in Tournai.' De Keysere apparently presented it to Maximilian I, but it is not known to exist today. When Charles v visited Ghent in June 1520, de Keysere offered him an equally curious 'Salomonis tria officia ex sacris desumpta,' which netted him a renumeration and is preserved as a manuscript in the Escorial. It presents the text of an office to be used by the emperor at sea with lessons taken from the Book of Wisdom.

Erasmus and de Keysere kept in touch for some years, mostly through Erasmus' correspondence with Antonius *Clava (Epp 585, 650, 665, 719, 743), and met again when Erasmus visited Ghent in the spring of 1518 (Ep 841). While always willing to encourage de Keysere's studies, Erasmus nevertheless expressed the wish that his various efforts might finally lead to more substantial achievements (Ep 530). After 1518 no more is heard of contacts between them.

BIBLIOGRAPHY: Allen Ep 175 / de Vocht CTL I 279–81 and passim / Reedijk 291–2 / A. Hocquet *Tournai et le Tournaisis au XVIe siècle* (Brussels 1906) 283–6 / V. van der Haeghen 'L'humaniste-imprimeur Robert de Keysere et sa soeur Clara la miniaturiste ... ' *Annales de la Société d'histoire et d'archéologie de Gand* 8 (1908) 325–81 / J. van den Gheyn 'Un manuscrit de l'imprimeur gantois Robert de Keyser à la bibliothèque de l'Escurial' *Annales de la Société d'histoire et d'archéologie de Gand* 8 (1908) 91–108 / Renouard *Répertoire* 63–4 / Philippe Renouard *Imprimeurs et libraires parisiens au XVIe siècle* (Paris 1964–) II 100 / F. van Ortroy 'Contribution à l'histoire des imprimeurs et des libraires belges établis à l'étranger' *Revue des bibliothèques* 35 (1925) 111–26, 282–97, 369–418, esp 370–80 / M.E. Kronenberg 'Robert de Keysere als drukker in Gent en in Parijs (1511–1514)' *Het Boek* 21 (1933) 1–22 / M.E. Kronenberg 'Nog iets over Robert de Keysere' *Het Boek* 24 (1936–7) 41–55 / M.A. Nauwelaerts 'Erasme et Gand' *De Gulden Passer* 47 (1969) 152–77, esp 160–3 / J. Tracy 'On the composition date of seven of Erasmus' writings' BHR 31 (1969) 355–64, esp 361–2 / J. Machiels 'Robert en Pieter de Keysere als drukker' *Archives et bibliothèques de Belgique* 46 (1975) 1–32

                          HILDE DE RIDDER-SYMOENS

KHAIR AD-DIN Pasha of Mytilene, d 4 July 1546
Khair ad-Din Pasha, called Barbarossa, the famous Turkish corsair and grand admiral of the Ottoman fleet, was born around 1466 at Mytilene, on the island of Lesbos, where his father, Yakub, a knight of Vardar Yeniçesi, had settled after the Ottoman conquest of 1462. His mother was Greek, and his real name was Khizir. He began his career by transporting goods between various points on the Aegean. Later he joined his brother Oruç at Djerba and engaged in pirate activities. Subsequently the

Khair ad-Din Pasha, called Barbarossa

two brothers made La Goulette their headquarters, and in 1516 they established themselves at Algiers, where Oruç proclaimed himself ruler. When Oruç died in 1518, Khizir succeeded to his position and immediately faced and repulsed the expedition of Ugo de Moncada, the Spanish viceroy of Sicily. Khizir then put to flight the sultan of Tlemcen, who had allied himself with the Spanish. In 1520 he retook the coastal city of Ténès. Henceforward the Christians gave him the name of Barbarossa – an allusion to the colour of his hair. He himself adopted the name of Khair ad-Din.

Although he assumed the title of sultan, Khair ad-Din's position was insecure, and he appealed to the Ottomans for aid. *Selim I accepted the proffered suzerainty, sending Khair ad-Din a decree of investiture, two thousand janissaries, and some artillery.

In 1520 Khair ad-Din was expelled from Algiers by a rebellion of the people supported by Muhammad, sultan of Tunis, and his local allies. In 1521 Khair ad-Din seized Collo, and in 1522 Annaba (Bone) and Constantine. Operating from his base at Djerba, he and his corsairs ravaged the coasts of the western

Mediterranean, seizing large quantities of booty and gaining a formidable reputation. In 1525 he recovered control of Algiers, establishing Ottoman domination on a permanent basis.

Khair ad-Din eliminated the Spanish threat to Algiers when in May 1529 he captured and dismantled the fortress on the island of Peñon, in the immediate vicinity of Algiers. He then sent assistance to the Moriscoes in Spain. In 1533 *Suleiman summoned him to Istanbul and in February 1534 appointed him Kapudan Pasha with the title of *Cezayir Beylerbeyi* (the beylerbey of the Islands). He was then dispatched with eighty-four ships to capture Tunis. He first seized La Goulette and on 18 August 1534 entered Tunis, which had been abandoned by Mawlay al-*Hasan. When he defeated the latter at al-Kayrawan, he seized control over all parts of Tunisia. But his triumph was short-lived, for in 1535 *Charles v launched an attack on Tunis with three hundred ships and about thirty thousand troops (Epp 3000, 3007), taking La Goulette on 14 June (Ep 3037) and on 20 June attacking Tunis with the support of the Arabs and some four thousand Christian captives who had broken their fetters (Ep 3047). Khair ad-Din was forced to fall back on Annaba, whence he made surprise attacks on Port Mahon and Palma on the Balearic Islands, taking thousands of captives and enormous quantities of booty.

In 1538 Khair ad-Din occupied a number of Venetian islands in the Aegean and also plundered Crete, taking over fifteen thousand captives. On 27 September his fleet of 120 ships defeated a combined Christian fleet of over 300 ships under the command of Andrea *Doria off Prevesa, assuring Ottoman domination of the Mediterranean until 1571.

As a result of the alliance between Suleiman and *Francis I, the Ottoman fleet under Khair ad-Din joined the French at Marseille in the summer of 1543 and proceeded to sack Villafranca, whereas Nice eluded them. Khair ad-Din spent the winter at Toulon, returning to Istanbul in 1544. Two years later he died and was buried at Beshiktas, near Istanbul.

Khair ad-Din gave the Ottomans a well-organized province in North Africa and made their fleet a formidable power in the Mediterranean. He was not only a remarkable seaman but a statesman whose prudence and other qualities were extolled even by his enemies. The collected letters of Pietro Aretino include a flattering exchange between the Italian humanist and the corsair.

BIBLIOGRAPHY: E.Z. Karal in *Islam Ansiklopedisi* (Istanbul 1940–   ) II 311–15 / A. Galotta in *Encyclopaedia of Islam* new ed (Leiden-London 1960–   ) IV 1155–8 (with full bibliography) / There is no good modern biography; E. Bradford *The Sultan's Admiral, the Life of Barbarossa* (London-New York 1968) is not recommended / The most important contemporary source, Sayyid Murad's *Ghazawat-i Khair al-Din Pasha*, is now available in a popular edition in Turkish, published by Tercüman; there is also an inadequate French translation / Albert P. Prieur *Les Barberousse, corsaires et rois d'Alger* (Paris 1943)   FEHMI ISMAIL

Richard KIDDERMINSTER c 1462–d after 3 November 1531

Kidderminster (Kedremyster) was probably a native of Worcestershire. At the age of fifteen he entered the Benedictine abbey of Winchcombe, in Gloucestershire, and at the age of twenty-two was sent to study at Gloucester College, Oxford. Shortly after his return to Winchcombe, he was elected abbot in 1488; the monastery flourished under his direction. Continuing to study theology on his own, he restored a discipline of study among the growing number of his monks. In 1525 he resigned his abbacy and continued to live as a monk in Winchcombe.

In 1497 Kidderminster received a doctorate of theology from Oxford. In 1511 he was court preacher at Greenwich and was appointed together with Silvestro *Gigli and John *Fisher to attend the Lateran council in 1512. It is not quite certain that he went to Rome, but according to one source he did so and preached repeatedly before the pope.

Kidderminster wrote Thomas *Wolsey in 1514, congratulating him on his preferment to York. In 1515 he opposed Henry *Standish with a much-noted defence of clerical privilege in the legal sphere. In 1530 he signed a petition to *Clement VII, asking the pope to expedite the king's divorce. A year later *Henry VIII had his representatives in Rome propose that Kidderminster and *Warham should be appointed judges to hear the divorce case in England. On 3 November 1531 Kidderminster wrote Thomas *Cromwell describing his advanced age and illness; he probably died not long thereafter. He wrote a history of Winchcombe and a work on the Benedictine rule which John *Longland hoped to see in all the Benedictine houses of his diocese, but both works appear to have perished in 1666. Longland dedicated to Kidderminster some sermons (London: R. Pynson? n d; STC 16797) that he had delivered before Henry VIII in 1517.

Respected by conservative churchmen and Christian humanists alike, Kidderminster was apparently a patron of Edward *Lee during his years as a student at Louvain. It seems that in his bitter controversy with Lee, Erasmus had attacked the abbot on this count, for in Ep 1061 Lee insisted that Kidderminster was no one's enemy. Although Erasmus did not mention his name, some of his subsequent statements imply that he had not changed his mind with regard to Kidderminster (Epp 1074, 1097, 1113, 1126, 1139).

BIBLIOGRAPHY: Allen and CWE Ep 1061 / DNB X 1185 / Emden BRUO II 1047 / David Knowles *The Religious Orders in England* (Cambridge 1948–59) III 91–5   CFG & PGB

Ludwig KIEL *See Ludovicus* CARINUS

Balthasar von KIENRING *See Balthasar von* KÜNRING

Johann KIERHER of Sélestat, d 19 July 1519
Johann Kierher (Kirher, Kyrherus) was born in Sélestat (Alsace). As a young man he lived in the house of the canon Thomas *Truchsess in Speyer. Having found a copy of Francesco *Filelfo's *Convivia* in Truchsess' library, he published it in 1508 (Speyer: K. Hist). In 1509 *Beatus Rhenanus dedicated to him his edition of George of *Trebizond's *Dialectica* (Strasbourg: M. Schürer 1509). In September of that year Kierher left for Paris to pursue an advanced degree. He earned his MA in 1510 and then remained in Paris until July 1512. About 1514 he was a fellow student of Bonifacius *Amerbach at Freiburg. By 1515 he had returned to Speyer, taken orders, and received a post as vicar in the cathedral. He was a good friend of Canon Maternus *Hatten,

in whose company he probably met Erasmus when he was passing through Speyer in 1514 or 1515. In March 1519 he bought a house from Hatten. At about this time Erasmus made a respectful mention of Kierher in his *Encomium Selestadii* (Reedijk poem 98). In September of 1515 he wrote to Erasmus asking his help in interpreting a passage in Jerome which assigned numerical values to the different states of matrimony, widowhood, and virginity. Kierher notes that he had sought out the theologians with his inquiry but 'you cannot think how tedious and barren were their replies' (Ep 355). Erasmus answered that the matter would be covered in the edition of Jerome he was then completing (Ep 361).

BIBLIOGRAPHY: Allen and CWE Ep 355 / Rice *Prefatory Epistles* Ep 67 / BRE Ep 8 and passim / AK I Ep 441, II Epp 536, 548 / Manfred Krebs *Die Protokolle des Speyerer Domkapitels* (Stuttgart 1968–) I 479, II 25   MIRIAM U. CHRISMAN

Hans KLARER *See Konrad* SCHMID

Mikuláš KLAUDYÁN documented 1504–22
Born in the region of Žatec (Saaz), west of Prague, Klaudyán must have suffered from a physical infirmity. His original Czech nickname, 'Kulha' or 'Belha' ('the limping one'), was translated as 'Claudianus' and then adapted into Czech as 'Klaudyán.' Nothing is known about his formal education except that he is described as 'magister' in his last will. His career reflects interests typical of a person with humanistic training.

Some time prior to 1504, Klaudyán settled as a self-taught physician in Mladá Boleslav (Jungbunzlau), east of Prague, and acquired extensive properties. The small city was the foremost centre of the radical religious group known as Unity of Bohemian or Czech Brethren (also fratres Waldenses, Picarti, Unitas fratrum) who had separated from the national Hussite (Utraquist) church in 1467 and formed an independent network of congregations throughout Bohemia and Moravia. Klaudyán was a member of the Unity and rendered important services to his church as a printer and envoy experienced in international contacts.

From 1507 or earlier Klaudyán collaborated with the printing shop of Hieronymus Höltzel in Nürnberg and was responsible for the publication of several Czech and Latin writings on the religious beliefs of the Brethren, including an *Apologia sacrae scripturae* (completed 16 December 1511). As a man of substantial means, he established his own printing shop in Boleslav but continued to use Höltzel's for more difficult projects. Beside publishing several humanistic, medical, liturgical, and theological books, including a Czech translation of the New Testament, he drew and produced the first printed map of Bohemia in 1518.

As a humanist with international contacts, Klaudyán might have been aware of the correspondence between Jan *Šlechta and Erasmus in 1518 and 1519, in the course of which Erasmus expressed a favourable opinion of the Brethren (Ep 1039). Probably through his own initiative, the leaders of the Unity sent him and Laurentius *Voticius to visit Erasmus in the summer of 1520. They found him in Antwerp, presented him with a copy of the *Apologia sacrae scripturae*, and requested his evaluation. Erasmus asked for time to study the book, and when the envoys returned a few days later he apparently expressed approval but declined to do so publicly for fear of jeopardizing his own cause (CWE Ep 1039 introduction). The accounts of this meeting by Jan Blahoslav and Joachim *Camerarius are confirmed in some measure by Erasmus' letter to Arkleb of *Boskovice of 28 January 1521, which mentions the visit and suggests a way in which the Brethren might be reconciled to the church of Rome (Ep 1183).

While on a business visit to Leipzig in 1521 Klaudyán fell ill and made his will. It was not entered in the Books of Inheritance at Mladá Boleslav until 24 November 1522. Neither the date nor the place of his death was recorded. His press appears to have been acquired, in part, by Oldřich Velenský and moved to nearby Bělá pod Bezdězem (Weisswasser). Part of the typographical equipment may have been used by the press 'Na Karmeli' ('In monte Carmeli') in Mladá Boleslav, operated since 1521 by Jiři Štyrsa under the auspices of the Brethren. Klaudyán's widow, Marketa, later married a physician, Jan, who was also a member of the Brethren and died in 1565.

BIBLIOGRAPHY: Allen Ep 1117 introduction /
CWE Ep 1039 introduction / *Ottův slovník naučný (Prague 1888–1909)* XIV 320 / On Klaudyán as a physician: G. Gellner 'Jan Černý a jiní lékaři čeští do konce doby Jagellovské' *Věstnik kral. české spolecnosti nauk* 3 (1934) 134–7 / On Klaudyán as a printer and cartographer Mirjam Bohatcová 'Počátky publikační činnosti Jednoty bratrské' *Acta Comeniana* 1 (1962) 44–60; Mirjam Bohatcová 'Vydavatel a tiskař Mikuláš Klaudyán' *Časopis Národního Muzea* 148 (1979) 33–67; František Horák *Pět století českého knihtisku – Five Hundred Years of Czech Printing* (Prague 1968) 130 (in English); *Early Maps of Bohemia, Moravia and Silesia* ed Karel Kuchař and Jindřich Svoboda (Prague 1961) (with a reproduction of Klaudyán's map of 1518); A.J. Lamping *Ulrichus Velenus and his Treatise against the Papacy* (Leiden 1976) 47–50 and passim; F. Spina 'Tschechischer Buchdruck in Nürnberg am Anfang des 16. Jahrhunderts' *Prager Deutsche Studien* 9 (1908); *Knihtisk a Universita Karlova* ed Lubomír Vebr (Prague 1972) 99–100.

The details of the visit with Erasmus in 1520 and the names of the two envoys were recorded by Jan Blahoslav (1523–71) in his 'Summa quaedam brevissima collecta ex variis scriptis Fratrum, qui falso Waldenses vel Piccardi vocantur, de eorundem Fratrum origine et actis' (1556) and published by Jaroslav Goll in his *Quellen und Untersuchungen zur Geschichte der Böhmischen Brüder* (Prague 1878–82) I 124–5 / With Blahoslav as his source Joachim Camerarius described the visit in his *Historica narratio de Fratrum orthodoxorum ecclesiis in Bohemia, Moravia et Polonia* (published posthumously by his grandson Ludwig, Heidelberg 1605) 124–6, reprinted by Allen with Ep 1117 and by Konrad Bittner 'Erasmus, Luther und die Böhmischen Brüder' in *Rastloses Schaffen: Festschrift für Friedrich Lammert* (Stuttgart 1954) 109–29, esp 115–16 / See also Josef Susta in *Český časopis historický* (Prague 1916) 188–92 / The *Apologia sacrae scripturae* (Nürnberg 1511) is reprinted in *Bekenntnisse der Böhmischen Brüder* ed Erich Beureuther and Alfred Eckert (Hildesheim-New York 1979) in Series I, vol III of *Nikolaus Ludwig von Zinzendorf: Materialien und Dokumente.*

P.S. Allen *The Age of Erasmus* (Oxford 1914) 276–98 / F.M. Bartoš 'Erasmus und die böhmische Reformation' *Communio Viatorum* 1

(1958) 116–23 and 246–57 / Amedeo Molnár
Boleslavští Bratří (Prague 1952) 85–92 / Joseph
T. Müller *Geschichte der Böhmischen Brüder* I
(Herrnhut 1922) 392–6 / Rudolf Říčan 'Die
tschechische Reformation und Erasmus' *Communio Viatorum* 16 (1973) 185–206 / Paul de
Vooght 'Un épisode peu connu de la vie
d'Erasme: sa rencontre avec les hussites
bohèmes en 1519–1521' *Irénikon* 47 (1974)
27–47 / Jarold Knox Zeman *The Anabaptists and
the Czech Brethren in Moravia* (The Hague-Paris
1969) 137–41   J.K. ZEMAN

Johann KLEBERGER of Nürnberg,
d 6 September 1546
Born in Nürnberg in 1485 or 1486 into a family
of middling affluence, Johann Kleberger
(Kléberg, Clebergius, Clebergerus) was the
son of Johann Kleberger and Agathe Zeidler.
He began his business career as an agent for
the Nürnberg house of Imhof, his commercial
activity taking him to the fairs of Lyon and to
Bern, where he acquired the status of burgher
in 1526. Soon afterwards he went into business
on his own, began to lend money to King
*Francis I, and built up an enormous fortune
through banking and other investments. In
October 1528 he finally persuaded the reluctant Nürnberg patrician Willibald *Pirckheimer
to consent to his marriage to his widowed
daughter, Felicitas. Although he had agreed to
live permanently in Nürnberg, Kleberger departed two years later for Lyon, creating great
bitterness between him and his father-in-law.
Felicitas refused to follow him and died shortly
afterwards. Kleberger visited Erasmus in Basel
in early 1528 during his period of courtship (Ep
1977). Erasmus did not sever his ties with
Kleberger after his departure from Nürnberg
and wrote him a courteous letter in October
1532, recalling their earlier visits and commenting on the state of the church (Ep 2731).
    Settling in Lyon as a royal banker, Kleberger
bought landed property, became a naturalized
French citizen, and was named *valet du roi*. In
1536 he married Pelonne Bouzin, the widow of
a Picard merchant burnt for Lutheran heresy in
Paris not long before; Pelonne herself was
saved only by abjuration. This marriage,
together with Kleberger's growing connections with Geneva, suggests an inner movement towards Protestantism, though the

Johann Kleberger, by Albrecht Dürer

banker made no formal break with the Catholic
church. In addition to Erasmus, Kleberger had
connections with other figures of cultural
importance: his portrait was painted by Albrecht *Dürer in 1526 (Kunsthistorisches Museum, Vienna), he patronized artists in Lyon,
and he was mentioned in *Le Cinquième Livre* of
*Rabelais (ch 30). When he died in 1546, his
enormous contributions to the new municipal
welfare organization in Lyon had won him
the title of 'le bon allemand.'
    BIBLIOGRAPHY: Allen Ep 1977 / NDB XI 718–
19 / ADB XVI 72–3 / R. Ehrenberg *Capital and
Finance in the Age of the Renaissance* (London
1928) / Eugène Vial *L'histoire et la légende de Jean
Cleberger dit 'le bon allemand' (1485?–1546)*
(Lyon 1914) / N.Z. Davis *Society and Culture in
Early Modern France* (Stanford, Ca, 1975) ch 2 /
Götz von Pölnitz *Anton Fugger* (Tübingen
1958–   ) I 46 and passim
                          NATALIE ZEMON DAVIS

Lukas KLETT of Rouffach, d after 1538
Lukas Klett (Paliurus, Philantropos) was the
son of Michael Klett, a schoolmaster at
Rouffach, Upper Alsace. In 1502 he and his

brother Gallus studied at Paris together with the *Amerbach sons, and in 1509 the Klett brothers matriculated at the University of Basel. In 1512 Lukas was a MA and in 1513 a member of the faculty of arts and regent of a residence; a year later he opened his own private school. He met Erasmus on his first visit to Basel and in November 1514 asked him for an introduction to Udalricus *Zasius (Ep 316). By that time he was probably well advanced in his legal studies, and in 1515 he graduated at Basel as a doctor of both laws. In this period Erasmus honoured him with an epigram (Reedijk poem 101). Perhaps in search of employment, in about 1516 he visited Ensisheim, the centre of the Hapsburg administration in Alsace (Ep 400), but his opportunity came in 1517 with his appointment as chancellor to the bishop of Basel (Epp 599, 626) in succession to Johannes *Fabri, a position which he held into old age. He also taught at the university and served as dean of law in 1520, 1523, and 1527. In the spring of 1526 Klett met with Fabri and King *Ferdinand at Tübingen (Epp 1690, 1709); no doubt they discussed the planned resignations of his master, Christoph von *Utenheim, and his coadjutor, Nikolaus von *Diesbach. After the Basel reformation Klett moved to the new episcopal residence of Porrentruy in the Jura. From there he corresponded with Bonifacius Amerbach, who in 1538 made a recommendation about a potential successor. A reply by Klett concerning this matter, dated 22 December 1538, is the last we hear of him.

BIBLIOGRAPHY: Allen and CWE Ep 316 / *Matrikel Basel* I 295, 372 / R. Wackernagel *Geschichte der Stadt Basel* (Basel 1907–54) III 162–3 and passim / Winterberg 48 and passim / BRE Ep 38 / AK I Ep 179, II Epp 492, 493, III Ep 1445, V Ep 2260 and passim / Öffentliche Bibliothek of the University of Basel, MS C VI^a 35 f 249: letter to U. Zasius, 22 August 1517
PGB

Johann KLOPREIS of Bottrop, d 1 February 1535
Johann Klopreis, born in Bottrop, near Essen in the Ruhr, studied at the University of Cologne between 1518 and 1521 and became a parish priest in Wesel and later in nearby Büderich. He preached the gospel, and he gave shelter to a fugitive lay preacher, Adolf

Clarenbach. When he was summoned to Cologne, Clarenbach went with him and was executed on 28 September 1529. Klopreis was imprisoned but escaped on 31 December and fled to Wassenberg in the duchy Jülich, where the tolerance of the local bailiff permitted the formation of the group of so-called Wassenberg preachers which included Hendrik *Rol. They began to advocate Anabaptism, and in January 1534, when the government of Jülich started to take measures against them, most of them fled to Münster, including Klopreis with his wife and children. He stayed for a few months, but then he was sent out to spread the Anabaptist message in an effort to reinforce the besieged community of Münster. Klopreis was arrested in Warendorf (Westphalia) on 14 October 1534 and burnt at the stake on 1 February 1535 in Cologne (Ep 2990).

BIBLIOGRAPHY: Allen Ep 2990 / *The Mennonite Encyclopedia* (Scottdale 1955–9) III 206–7 / Ugo Gastaldi *Storia dell'anabattismo dalle origini a Münster* (Turin 1972) 482, 569, and passim / G.H. Williams *The Radical Reformation* (Philadelphia 1962) 361, 365, 375   IG

Gerard van KLOSTER See GERARD of Kloster

Katharina van der KLUSEN d 16 January 1559
Katharina van der Klusen (Clusen) married Karl *Harst on 8 January 1527 in Louvain. According to Conradus *Goclenius, who was a good friend of both, she had earlier been his sweetheart for some time and was anxiously awaiting his return from Basel (Epp 1768, 1778, 1788). Harst was no less anxious to be reunited with her, and Erasmus let him go with a sympathetic smile (Ep 1724). Later he had high praise for Katharina's handling of Harst's pupils (Ep 2231). She bore Harst two sons and a daughter.

BIBLIOGRAPHY: Allen Ep 1215 / de Vocht CTL II 143–5 / NDB VII 705–6   PGB

Piotr KMITA 1477–31 October 1553
Kmita (Kmitha) came from a powerful family from Little Poland with the coat of arms of 'Szreniawa', and was the son of Stanisław, a Russian *voivode*, and Katarzyna Tarnowska, the stepsister of the grand hetman of the realm, Jan Tarnowski. His youth was spent at the court of the Emperor *Maximilian; after his

return to Poland he joined the court of King
*Sigismund I and was appointed marshal on 28
March 1518. Thanks to his military and
diplomatic skills he reached a position of
considerable political authority. His advancement was steady: in 1527 he was castellan of
Wojnicz and in 1532 of Sandomierz, and in
1535 he was *voivode* of Sandomierz. On 21 May
1529 he was appointed grand marshal of the
realm, in 1533 general prefect of Cracow, and
finally *voivode* of Cracow on 15 March 1535. In
1523 he was created count of Wiśnicz by the
Emperor *Charles v.

Kmita worked closely with Queen *Bona to
promote good relations with France in opposition to the Hapsburgs. In an attempt to prevent
a Hapsburg take-over of Hungary he supported *John Zápolyai and opposed war with
Turkey. Although critical of the policies of the
Roman curia he remained a Catholic to the end
of his life and founded churches on his estates.
As the last surviving member of the Kmita
family he accumulated in his hands the family's
vast estates in Little Poland. At his main
residence, the castle of Wiśnicz near Cracow,
he held a magnificient court where humanists,
lawyers, writers, and poets found patronage.
He collected a rich library in which some of
Erasmus' works were to be found. At the
suggestion of his Polish friends, Erasmus
dedicated to him in 1535 *De puritate tabernaculi*
(Ep 3046). Whether he received an answer is
not known.

Kmita was twice married but had no children. He was buried in Cracow cathedral,
where today a statue of red marble perpetuates
his memory. Among other homages from
humanists and poets, Simon Maricius from
Pilsno dedicated to him two of his editions of
Demosthenes' works: *De pace oratio* (Cracow:
Unglerowa 1546) and *Pro libertate Rhodiorum
oratio* (Cracow: M. Scharffenberg 1547),
Stanisław *Aichler inscribed to him his edition
of *Pomponius Laetus' *De Romanorum magis-
tratibus* (Cracow: F. Ungler 1544), and Josephus
*Tectander addressed to Kmita his *Elegiae tres
de peregrinationibus suis* (Cracow: F. Ungler
1542). Thirteen books from Kmita's library have
been identified; ten are today in the Biblioteka
Ossolineum in Wrocław, among them a volume
in which several works by Erasmus are bound
together (XVI Qu 1190–1). Two others are in the

Piotr Kmita

Muzeum Narodowe of Cracow, and one is in
the Bibliotece Czartoryskich in Cracow.

BIBLIOGRAPHY: Allen Ep 3046 / *Korespondencja
Erazma z Rotterdamu z Polakami* ed M. Cytowska
(Warsaw 1965) / PSB XIII 97–100 / H. Barycz
Kulturalna działalność Piotra Kmity (Przemyśl
1924) / W. Pociecha *Królowa Bona: Czasy i ludzie
Odrodzenia* (Poznań 1949–58) I–IV / J.A. Kosiń-
ski 'Fragment księgozbioru Piotra Kmity w
Bibliotece Ossolineum' *Ze skarbca kultury* 16
(1964) 114–31 / *Andreae Cricii Carmina* ed
K. Morawski (Cracow 1888) / Klemens Janicki
Carmina ed G. Krókowski (Cracow 1966)
                              HALINA KOWALSKA

William KNIGHT of London, 1476–
29 September 1547
Knight was born in London in 1476. Having
studied at Winchester School from 1487 and
New College, Oxford, from 1491, he went to
court in 1495 and was appointed secretary to
*Henry VII. He studied law at Ferrara in 1501
and by 1507 had received a doctorate in canon
law from an Italian university. In 1515 he was
chaplain to *Henry VIII and became protonotary apostolic the following year. Gradually he

Bernhard Knipperdolling, by Heinrich Aldegrever

assembled innumerable benefices, but he resigned many of them in 1541 when he was created bishop of Bath and Wells.

During Henry VIII's reign Knight was frequently employed on foreign embassies; he was in Spain in 1512 and 1513 and was ambassador to *Margaret of Austria in the Low Countries in 1514 and in 1518 and 1519. In 1514 he also went to Switzerland. He was appointed to succeed Cuthbert *Tunstall at the court of the future *Charles v (Ep 534), with whom he conferred in January 1517. He did not sail to Spain with Charles, but in 1520 he was present at the Field of Cloth of Gold. He knew Thomas *More well, having served with him at Bruges in 1515 and 1520 and at Calais in 1517. In 1522 he was ambassador to Switzerland and to the imperial court. He was appointed the king's secretary in 1526, and the following year he was sent by Henry personally on a confidential mission to Rome to promote the king's 'great matter,' although owing to the Sack he was unable to meet *Clement VII until 1 January 1528. While in Italy he was created canon of Westminster, but when he returned to London in 1528, his embassy was deemed a failure. He

went to Paris in 1529 in the embassy of Charles *Brandon, duke of Suffolk, but they were unable to prevent their French allies from settling their differences with Charles v in the treaty of Cambrai. In his will dated 12 April 1547, Knight left bequests to New College and to Winchester School.

Erasmus had evidently met Knight, whom he mentioned in Epp 534 and 2810.

BIBLIOGRAPHY: Allen and CWE Ep 534 / DNB XI 264–6 / Emden BRUO II 1063–4 / J.J. Scarisbrick *Henry VIII* (London 1968) 159–61 and passim / Rogers Epp 13–14, 51, 98, and passim   CFG

Bernhard KNIPPERDOLLING of Münster, d 22 January 1536

Bernhard (Bernt) Knipperdolling (Knipperdollink) was born in Münster of a good family around 1490. He was a merchant and guildmaster in 1527 when he took part in a riot to free a protester who had been imprisoned by Bishop Franz von *Waldeck. He paid a fine as requested, but was nonetheless imprisoned for a year and had to pay a heavy ransom to be released. His unsuccessful efforts to obtain justice before the Reichskammergericht increased his resentment. Knipperdolling joined the movement for civic autonomy and church reform, supported *Rothmann in 1532 against the town council, and subsequently supported *Jan of Leiden against Rothmann. After the Anabaptist take-over of Münster he was elected burgomaster on 24 February 1534. Hendrik *Rol lived in his house, and later so did Jan of Leiden and Jan *Mathijszoon. Knipperdolling organized the military defence of the city; he was captured during the final assault on 25 June 1535 and, together with Jan of Leiden and Bernhard *Krechting, he was displayed in a cage at fairs throughout Westphalia until all of them were executed in Münster on 22 January 1536.

Erasmus was informed about events in Münster by Konrad *Heresbach (Epp 3031, 3031A) and Tielmannus *Gravius (Ep 3041).

BIBLIOGRAPHY: Allen Ep 3041 / R. Stupperich in NDB XII 187 / ADB XVI 293–5 / *The Mennonite Encyclopedia* (Scottdale 1955–9) III 208 / Ugo Gastaldi *Storia dell'anabattismo dalle origini a Münster* (Turin 1972) 514–57 / G.H. Williams *The Radical Reformation* (Philadelphia 1962) 363–4 and passim   IG

Andreas KNOPKEN of Słońsk,
d 18 February 1539
Andreas Knopken (Knöpken, Knopius,
Cnopha) was born around 1468 in Słońsk
(Sonnenberg), east of Kostrzyn (Küstrin in
Brandenburg). Little is known about his life
until he made contact with Johann *Bugenhagen, who from 1504 directed the Latin school
of Trzebiatów (Treptow an der Rega, in
Pomerania). Bugenhagen may have sent him to
the University of Ingolstadt prior to the spring
term of 1512, when he matriculated at the
University of Frankfurt an der Oder. It is not
known when Knopken had been ordained, but
by 1492 he had been in charge of two parishes
consecutively in the neighbourhood of Kostrzyn, while between 1514 and 1517 he is
repeatedly mentioned as clerk of the Premonstratensian abbey of Belbuk, near Trzebiatów.
His brother Jakob was a canon of Riga in
Latvia, and in 1517 he secured a chaplaincy for
Andreas, which involved preaching in the
church of St Peter's. During his first sojourn at
Riga, 1517–19, he began to write to Erasmus
(Ep 1177), while a subsequent stay in Trzebiatów, 1519–21, led him to take an interest in
the writings of *Luther. From 1519 he taught
again at Trzebiatów, succeeding Bugenhagen
as rector of the Latin school in 1521. In the
summer of 1521 he settled permanently in Riga,
resuming his preaching at St Peter's. It was at
Bugenhagen's suggestion that *Melanchthon
recommended Knopken to the city council of
Riga (*Melanchthons Briefwechsel* I Ep 149). He
became the leader of the Lutheran party in
Riga, and on 12 June 1522 a disputation was
held at St Peter's, which served to strengthen
his position and the confidence of his followers. Riga took the lead among the Baltic cities in
adopting the Reformation, with Knopken
himself retaining a moderate stance and opposing iconoclastic excesses. In 1524 he published
at Wittenberg a commentary on Romans, to
which Bugenhagen contributed a preface. This
work contains several references to Erasmus'
writings and shows that Knopken had used
Erasmus to modify Luther's doctrine of justification. After he had written three letters to
Erasmus, all of them now missing, Erasmus
replied on 31 December 1520 with a message of
encouragement (Ep 1177).
BIBLIOGRAPHY: Allen Ep 1177 / NDB XII 215–

16 / ADB XVI 324–5 / RGG III 1684 / *Matrikel
Frankfurt* I 33 / F. Hörschelmann *Andreas
Knopken, der Reformator Rigas* (Leipzig 1896) /
Leonid Arbusow *Die Einführung der Reformation in Liv-, Est-und Kurland* (Leipzig 1921,
repr 1964) 171–85, 244–8, and passim / Schottenloher I 411, II 653, VII 107–8
                                    MICHAEL ERBE

Christian KNYVET d 1523
Dame Christian, the mother of Erasmus' friend
John *Colet, was a daughter of Sir John Knyvet
or Knevet of Norfolk and Alice Lynne. She was
probably born by 1445–50 and married Henry
*Colet by 1465. John was their eldest child and
the only one to survive past 1503 (Epp 1211,
2684). On 14 March 1493 Dame Christian was
in Rome with her husband and sons John and
Richard. After her husband died in 1505 she
continued to live in his house at Stepney, east
of London, until her own death. In 1510 she
received there, as her son's guest, the young
Henricus Cornelius *Agrippa of Nettesheim.
On 1 December 1510 she was granted letters of
fraternity by Christ Church, Canterbury. Her
will is dated 13 January 1523 and was proved
on 22 November 1523.
    Lady Colet survived both her husband and
her son. Erasmus spoke admiringly of her (Ep
1211) and in 1532 invoked her memory to
recommend her stoical example to Bonifacius
*Amerbach, whose infant daughter had just
died (Ep 2684). He may not have met her until
about 1504, when Colet moved to London. In
March 1512 Colet told Erasmus that he had
been staying with his mother 'in the country,'
no doubt at Stepney (Ep 258); and on 20 June
1516, from his mother's house at Stepney, he
assured his friend that Dame Christian, now
'in a happy old age,' spoke often of him,
'cheerfully and with pleasure' (Ep 423).
    BIBLIOGRAPHY: Allen 1211 / J.H. Lupton *Life
of Dean Colet* 2nd ed (London 1909) 13–14, 153,
199–200 / Mary L. Mackenzie *Dame Christian
Colet* (London 1923) / J.B. Trapp 'Dame
Christian Colet and Thomas More' *Moreana*
15–16 (1967) 103–114 / *Acts of Court of the
Mercers' Company, 1453–1527* ed L. Lyell and
F.D. Watney (Cambridge 1936) 672–3 / George
B. Parks *The English Traveler to Italy* (Rome
1954–) I 375   J.B. TRAPP

Johann **KOBERGER** of Nürnberg,
d 1 March 1543
Johann Koberger (Koburger, Copergus, Con-
bergus, Conpergius, etc) was born about 1454
in Nürnberg, a son of Sebald Koberger, a
baker, and a cousin to Anton Koberger (d
1513), the founder and head of Germany's
first-ranking publishing house. Johann probably learnt the goldsmith's trade, but before
the turn of the century most of his remarkable
energies and stamina were devoted to Anton's
firm. His great contribution was the systematic
expansion of the firm's trade with Italy and
France, and even with Spain. In the first
decade of the sixteenth century he travelled
incessantly between Nürnberg, Venice, Lyon
(where he regularly attended the fair), and
Paris. On the way south he often visited
Strasbourg and Basel, and of course he also
attended the Frankfurt fairs, thus establishing
personal contacts with many of the firm's major
suppliers of paper and printed books. On
Anton's death in 1513, Johann became largely
responsible for the firm's direction although
the working capital belonged primarily to
Anton's sons and heirs. Anton had already
phased out the printing operation at Nürnberg, and Johann continued to commission
whole editions or effected large bulk pur-
chases, dealing with such printers as Johann
*Froben and Adam Petri at Basel, and Thomas
*Anshelm in Haguenau, among many others.
    From 1507 Koberger was a member of the
town council of Nürnberg; he married Anna
Voit in 1492 and, after her death, Margarethe
Mäurl, the daughter of a town councillor.
Koberger, who was well educated and broad-
minded, was a friend of Christoph Scheurl,
Johannes *Cochlaeus, Willibald *Pirckheimer,
and Heinrich *Stromer, and had good connections with several bishops. He died in Nürnberg.
    Several references in the correspondence of
Erasmus may be taken to refer to the Koberger
firm rather than to Johann individually as its
head; these illustrate the important services the
Kobergers rendered Erasmus in forwarding
letters and gifts (Epp 1398, 1603, 1728, 1729). In
1517 Erasmus and *Beatus Rhenanus eagerly
followed Johann's negotiations – which were
eventually abortive – with Wolfgang *Lachner
about a reprint of Johann *Amerbach's great

edition of St Augustine (Ep 581). In 1525
Erasmus wrote to Pirckheimer expressing his
gratitude to and indeed friendship for Johann
Koberger, but at the same time complaining
forcefully how badly the guileless Froben was
treated by his business partners. Koberger's
main fault at that moment seemed to Erasmus to
be his business liaison with Franz *Birckmann.
    BIBLIOGRAPHY: Allen and CWE Ep 581 / Oscar
von Hase *Die Koberger* 3rd ed (Amsterdam-
Wiesbaden 1967) 32–5 and passim / Grimm
Buchführer 1213–17 and passim / AK I Ep 139
and passim   IG & PGB

Konrad KOCH *See Conradus* WIMPINA

Jan KOECHMAN documented at Zwolle,
1481–1520
Jan Koechman (Cocmannus), a member of the
Brethren of the Common Life, is documented in
1481 as a member of the Brethren's community
at Zwolle, in Overijssel. By November 1490 he
became the sixth rector of the Zwolle house.
When Gerardus *Listrius was appointed master of the Brethren's school in 1516 he lived
with Koechman. He sent Erasmus greetings
from Koechman who, he said, was praising
Erasmus to all the world (Ep 504). Koechman
continued to show kindness to Listrius during
his difficulties at Zwolle. His successor was in
office in March 1521.
    BIBLIOGRAPHY: Allen Ep 504 / H.C. Rogge in
Nederlands Archief voor Kerkgeschiedenis 7 (1899)
217   PGB

Ludwig KÖL documented at Constance
1491–1529
'Ludovicus, procurator consistorii nostri,' who
brought *Botzheim a letter from Erasmus in
about November 1524 (Ep 1519), was probably
Ludwig Köl, who around this time appeared
repeatedly as an attorney before the episcopal
court. He is documented at Constance from
1491, and from 1522 as a canon and the
bishop's fiscal. He was conceivably a relative of
Johannes Alexander *Brassicanus (Köl).
    BIBLIOGRAPHY: Manfred Krebs *Die Protokolle
des Konstanzer Domkapitels* (Karlsruhe 1952–9)
VI 253, 346, 353, 396 / Jörg Vögeli *Schriften zur
Reformation in Konstanz* ed A. Vögeli
(Tübingen-Basel 1972–3) II-2 964–5 / Rublack

Reformation in Konstanz 290 / *Vadianische Brief-sammlung* II Ep 234   PGB

Dietrich KOLDE of Münster, c 1435–
11 December 1515
Dietrich Kolde (Coelde, Theodoricus Monas-teriensis, Dietrich von Münster), the son of Hermann, belonged to an influential family in Münster (Westphalia). In 1453 he joined the Austin friars in Osnabrück and studied in Cologne. By 1479 he had entered the order of the Franciscan Observants and lived for several years in the convent of Bodendaal, near Brussels. During a violent outbreak of the plague in the area of Brussels in 1488 and 1489 he selflessly tended the sick and comforted the survivors. Kolde was named *praedicator gene-ralis* for the Rhineland and Westphalia in 1491 by the archbishop of Cologne, Hermann of Hesse. In 1497 he was warden of the Francis-can monastery of Brühl near Cologne; subse-quently he was transferred to the wardenship of Bodendaal in 1502, of Antwerp in 1508, and of Louvain in 1510. He died in Louvain.

Kolde – or Dietrich von Münster, as he called himself in his books – was acquainted with Bishop David of *Burgundy and had many contacts with leading humanist scholars; Rudolf von *Langen mentions in the preface to his *Rosarium* (1493) that the book was written at Kolde's suggestion. Johannes *Trithemius met him in 1494 at Cologne and mentioned some of his writings, especially his *Der Kerstenen Spegel* (*Cristenspiegel*), written and published before 1477, the first catechism written in Low German, and the Latin version of it, the *Manuale simplicium* (printed in Cologne, perhaps before 1477 and often reprinted).

Erasmus met Kolde at Bergen around 1493–4 and was impressed by his saintly life and preaching and his consideration for others, even at the time of his death (Epp 1347, 2700).

BIBLIOGRAPHY: Allen I 589, Ep 1347 / NDB III 307 / ADB IV 386–8 / *Der Christenspiegel des Dietrich Kolde von Münster* ed Clemens Drees (Werl 1954), a critical edition with a biographi-cal introduction   IG

Johann KOLER of Augsburg, d before
21 March 1538
From 1503 to 1533 Johann Koler (Choler, Coler) held the benefice of a parish priest of Lands-

berg, in Bavaria, which may have been his native city. He was also provost of Passau from 1508 to 1517 and canon of St Moritz in Augsburg from 1504, and had obtained a doctorate of canon law by 1512, when he became provost of Chur, in the Grisons. Although it is not certain that his contacts with Chur went beyond the occasional visit, he was appointed vicar-general of the troubled bishopric in 1529 and the following winter he accompanied its administrator, Paul *Ziegler, to Rome (Ep 2269). From at least 1524 he continued to reside in Augsburg. When the chapter of St Moritz left Augsburg in January 1536 because of the Reformation, Koler and some other canons stayed behind. In 1537 he married, and on 5 July 1537 Pope *Paul III conferred the vacant provostship of Chur on someone else. On 21 March 1538 Sixt *Birk reported that Koler had died a few days before (AK V Ep 2190).

Koler was a friend of Anton *Fugger, Konrad *Peutinger, Ottmar *Nachtgall, and Johann (II) *Paumgartner and corresponded with Fride-ricus *Nausea (1527–35) and *Viglius Zuiche-mus (1533–6). He contributed information to Bartholomaeus Amantius' and Petrus *Api-anus' *Inscriptiones sacrosanctae vetustatis* (In-golstadt: P. Apianus 1534). Aegidius *Rem dedicated to him an edition of Agathius' *De bello Gothorum* (Augsburg: S. Grimm and M. Wirsung 1519).

In the summer of 1529 Koler wrote to Erasmus urging him to accept Anton Fugger's invitation to take up residence in Augsburg. Erasmus' answer (Ep 2195) reflects the elo-quence of Koler's letter, which is lost, and shows that Erasmus was impressed, even though he declined to go. In Fugger's name Koler repeated this invitation periodically in years to come (Epp 2384, 2437, 2438, 2505), but like Fugger he respected Erasmus' reasons for declining and continued to offer warm friend-ship; this Erasmus accepted all the more readily because it facilitated his valued contacts with Bishop Christoph von *Stadion (Epp 2384, 2505, 2592), the *Rem family (Epp 2269, 2565, 2627, 2993, 3050), and the *Paumgartner family (Epp 2728, 2814, 2868, 2953, 2983, 2993, 3050). This latter connection, which Koler had helped to bring about (Ep 2438), also extended to Franciscus *Rupilius (Epp 2867, 2947, 2983,

3050). When Koler returned from Rome, where he had met – and liked – Diego *López Zúñiga and Johannes *Dantiscus he cordially replied to a letter of Erasmus that had arrived in his absence (Ep 2269). From this point on their lively and frequent correspondence continued without interruption until Erasmus' death (Ep 3095). Both discussed a variety of topics freely. When Erasmus faced difficulties with the lease of his house in Freiburg, Stadion instructed Koler to help by contacting Johann *Löble, treasurer to King *Ferdinand I (Epp 2470, 2505). All of Koler's preserved letters reflect a prevailing interest in politics, which at that time meant predominantly religious politics, whether locally in Augsburg or on the wider scene of Germany and beyond. Koler's report of the diet of Augsburg (1530), for instance, affords an interesting insight into his mentality, which perhaps seems more Machiavellian than Erasmian (Ep 2384). When *Luther attacked Erasmus in a letter to *Amsdorf, Koler expressed his indignation and urged Erasmus to reply; he was relieved to receive Erasmus' reply to Luther, although he found it almost too mild (Epp 2936, 2937, 2947).

In addition to his frequent letters, Erasmus rewarded Koler's friendship by dedicating to him his new translation of St Basil's two homilies De laudibus ieiunii (Freiburg: J. Faber Emmeus 1532; Ep 2617; LB VIII 535–46). It is doubtful that Erasmus and Koler ever met, although on one occasion the provost of Chur regretted that, contrary to his intention, he had been unable to travel by way of Freiburg (Ep 2505).

A Johann Koler of Landsberg – conceivably a relative of the provost – matriculated at Freiburg in 1514 and Vienna in 1515 (Matrikel Freiburg I-1 217, Matrikel Wien II-1 424).

BIBLIOGRAPHY: Allen Ep 2195 / AK IV Ep 2020, V Ep 2190 / Götz von Pölnitz Anton Fugger (Tübingen 1958–) I 502, 552, 683 / Friedrich Zoepfl Geschichte des Bistums Augsburg und seiner Bischöfe (Munich-Augsburg 1955–) II 93, 95 / de Vocht Dantiscus 52   IG & PGB

Georg von KOMERSTADT of Meissen, 28 March 1498–26 December 1559
A descendant of a patrician family of Meissen, in Saxony, Georg von Komerstadt (Comerstedt, Commerstadius) matriculated at the University of Leipzig in the spring term of 1515 and was promoted licentiate (5 April 1525) and doctor (10 July 1526) of civil and canon law there. From 1525 he was syndic and town councillor of Zwickau. He also served Duke George of *Saxony and his successors, Dukes Henry and Maurice, as a councillor. Especially under Maurice he was a member of the Hofrat and, although according to *Melanchthon he did not approve of the duke's religious policy, assumed a considerable measure of responsibility for ecclesiastical and educational matters, in particular for the administration of secularized religious institutions. He was a friend and patron of Georgius *Agricola, who dedicated to him De mensuris et ponderibus (Basel: H. Froben 1533), in the publication of which Erasmus had taken a hand, and De veteribus et novis metallis (Basel: H. Froben and N. Episcopius 1546). Komerstadt was raised to the nobility in 1538 and died on his estate of Kalckreuth, near Grossenhain.

Erasmus wrote to him in June 1531 at the suggestion of Christoph von *Carlowitz. Although he had never met Komerstadt, he was aware of his influence with Duke George and knew him to be friendly. Since Komerstadt had also had contacts with Heinrich *Eppendorf, his friendship was especially worth cultivating (Ep 2498).

BIBLIOGRAPHY: Allen Ep 2498 / NDB XII 479–80 / ADB XVI 498 / Matrikel Leipzig I 543, II 38, 49–50 / Pflug Correspondance I Epp 55–6 and passim / Georgius Agricola Ausgewählte Werke ed H. Prescher et al II (Berlin 1955) 294–5 / J. Reimers 'Aus dem Leben des Dr. Georg von Kommerstädt' Zeitschrift für Kirchengeschichte 54 (1935) 87–101   MICHAEL ERBE

Andreas von KÖNNERITZ
d after 21 May 1552
Andreas was a son of Heinrich von Könneritz (Conritz, Kienritz), Berghauptmann or superintendent of mines of Jáchymov (Joachimsthal), in the Bohemian Erz mountains, and the elder brother of Christoph and Erasmus von *Könneritz. The knights von Könneritz zu Zossen und Lobschütz were an old noble family from the region of Meissen. Andreas matriculated at the University of Leipzig in the spring term of 1517 together with his brother Johann. On 15 May 1520 both brothers matriculated at

Wittenberg and subsequently were among the students of *Melanchthon. From 1523 they studied at Bologna, where Andreas was procurator of the German nation in 1527, while Johann seems to have died in the course of his studies abroad. In Italy Andreas met Georgius *Agricola and thus was probably in touch with the circle of northern students at Padua who corresponded with Erasmus. After his return from Italy Andreas first went to Leipzig, where in early October 1528, in the company of Julius *Pflug, he met his old teacher, Melanchthon, who was visiting Leipzig; they talked about Erasmus and his *Ciceronianus*. On 2 December 1528 Andreas matriculated with his brother Christoph at Freiburg and became a student of Udalricus *Zasius. After Erasmus' arrival at Freiburg in April 1529 they lived for some time in his house, apparently before the arrival of a third brother, Erasmus (Ep 2450). Andreas' friendship with Georgius Agricola helped to bring about friendly contacts between the latter and Erasmus (Ep 2529), who addressed the Könneritz brothers in a commendatory letter written for Agricola's *Bermannus* (Ep 2274).

In March 1531 Andreas and Erasmus von Könneritz returned home, carrying letters from Erasmus that contained recommendations of Andreas to both Pflug and Duke George of *Saxony (Epp 2450–2). Pflug, an old friend of the Könneritz family, received Andreas kindly (Epp 2492, 2522), and the duke took him into his service. As soon as he had obtained a doctorate in both laws from the University of Leipzig (8 August 1531), Andreas was sent to the imperial law court (Reichskammergericht) of Speyer, where on 23 October he took his oath of office as a representative of ducal Saxony. From Speyer Andreas continued to exchange greetings with Erasmus (Epp 3060, 3071, 3117). After a decade with the Reichskammergericht, Könneritz resigned on 2 November 1541 to enter the service of King *Ferdinand. Before long he moved to Freiburg, where he seems to have purchased a house as early as 1544. The following year he bought a property near Freiburg and entered into negotiations for other estates situated in the prince-bishopric of Basel. While these ultimately failed, his property transactions and resulting litigations brought fresh contacts

with the Basel lawyer Bonifacius *Amerbach, whom he had already met between 1528 and 1531. In 1551 he was appointed Ferdinand's governor (*Landvogt*) of the region of Ortenau between the Rhine and the Black Forest. On his death he left his wife, Katharina Stör, and children to cope with very considerable debts.

BIBLIOGRAPHY: Allen Ep 2274 / NDB XII 363 (family) / *Matrikel Wittenberg* I 93 / *Matrikel Leipzig* I 557, II 38, 52–3 / Knod 266–7 / *Matrikel Freiburg* I-1 272 / AK V Ep 2156, VI Epp 2635, 2759, VII Ep 3023, VIII xxvi and passim / *Melanchthons Briefwechsel* I Ep 714 / Pflug *Correspondance* I 62–3, 326 and Ep 98, and passim / Georgius Agricola *Ausgewählte Werke* ed H. Prescher et al II (Berlin 1955) 59–60, 295 / Winterberg 48–50   PGB

Christoph von KÖNNERITZ d 14 August 1557

Christoph was a younger brother of Andreas von *Könneritz, with whom he matriculated on 2 December 1528 at the University of Freiburg to study law. Both brothers lived for a while in Erasmus' house and were honoured by their host, who in February 1530 addressed to them a commendatory letter published with Georgius *Agricola's *Bermannus* (Ep 2274). When Andreas returned to Saxony in March 1531 Christoph at first continued his studies at Freiburg (Epp 2450–2), but in 1532 he moved to the University of Ingolstadt and in 1534 to Bologna, where he was procurator of the German nation the following year. In 1539 he attended a diet at Worms on behalf of the bishop of Meissen, substituting for the ambassador, Christoph von der Strassen, who was unable to go. His mission led to energetic protests on the part of the electoral Saxony and to an ugly confrontation with the electoral representative. In 1542, like his brother Andreas, he joined the service of King *Ferdinand. He at first became a councillor attached to the government of Lower Austria, and later he rose to the position of *Oberst-Kammergraf*, or superintendent of the mines in Hungary and Bohemia. He was a Lutheran, was married to Agnes von Harrach, and acquired the estates of Haggenberg and Entzersdorf.

BIBLIOGRAPHY: Allen Ep 2274 / Knod 267 / Pflug *Correspondance* I Ep 49, II Ep 139, and p 69 / Georgius Agricola *Ausgewählte Werke* ed

Jan Koolman, by Maarten van Heemskerk

H. Prescher et al II (Berlin 1955) 59–60, 295 /
Winterberg 48–50   PGB

Erasmus von KÖNNERITZ d 1563
Erasmus (Erasmius, Asmus), a younger brother
of Andreas and Christoph von *Könneritz,
came to Freiburg while his brothers were
studying there and returned home with Andreas in March 1531 (Epp 2450, 2452). Erasmus
recommended him to Bernhard von *Cles, but
the latter replied in June from Prague that
Erasmus had not as yet appeared (Ep 2504).
Könneritz had not matriculated at Freiburg,
and it is not known where he studied
jurisprudence. In 1538 he participated in the
war against the Turks and was taken prisoner;
having regained his freedom he was knighted
by *Charles v. He became *Oberhauptmann* of the
district of Leipzig and a judge at the *Oberhofge-
richt* of electoral Saxony; in 1547 during the
Schmalkaldic war he conducted negotiations
between the government of the Elector John
Frederick of *Saxony, the estates of Bohemia,
and the mining town of Jáchymov (Joachimsthal). In 1550 he was a councillor to Duke
Maurice of Saxony and one of his ambassadors

to the diet of Augsburg. He also attended some
of the preceding and subsequent diets.
   BIBLIOGRAPHY: NDB XII 363 (family) / Georgius
Agricola *Ausgewählte Werke* ed H. Prescher et al
II (Berlin 1955) 295 / Pflug *Correspondance*
III 242, 732, 742 / Winterberg 48–50
                                MICHAEL ERBE & PGB

Jan KOOLMAN of Delft, d 1538
Jan Koolman (Colmannus, Coelmanus) was
promoted MA at Louvain on 17 March 1510 and
also obtained a doctorate of canon law. He was
the first secular priest to become confessor of
the convent of St Agatha at Delft, a post he
held from 1516 or earlier. He died early in 1538
and was succeeded on 12 March by the
well-known Cornelis Muys (Musius), whom
he had recommended. A fine portrait of
Koolman by Maarten van Heemskerk is now in
the Rijksmuseum, Amsterdam.
   Koolman had met Erasmus at Dorp's table in
Louvain and was said to be one of his admirers
(Ep 1044).
   BIBLIOGRAPHY: CWE Ep 1044 / *La Correspondance d'Erasme* ed A. Gerlo et al (Brussels
1967–) IV Ep 1044 / B.W.F. van Riemsdijk *Het
klooster van Sinte Agatha* (The Hague 1889)
10–12 / S.W.A. Drossaers *De archieven van de
Delftsche Statenkloosters* (The Hague 1917); see
index / de Vocht MHL 375
                                C.G. VAN LEIJENHORST

Gregor KOPP of Kalbe, documented 1500–20
Gregor Kopp (Copp, Coppus, Copus, Köppe),
born in Kalbe, in the Altmark north of
Magdeburg, matriculated in Leipzig in 1500,
obtained a BA in 1501, and studied in Wittenberg in 1502. In 1506 he matriculated in
Frankfurt an der Oder, where he is documented in the winter semester of 1509–10 as a
bachelor of medicine. In 1518 and 1519 he and
Heinrich *Stromer were physicians to Albert
von *Brandenburg, archbishop of Mainz. Here
he helped Ulrich von *Hutten in writing his
book *De guaiaci medicina et morbo gallico* (1519).
Kopp went to Magdeburg in August 1519 to
study Hebrew, a fact that he mentioned in a
letter in defense of Erasmus and humanistic
studies addressed to his friend Stromer (Magdeburg, 31 August 1520). It was printed in
*Duae epistolae Henrici Stromeri Auerbachii et
Gregorii Coppi Calvi medicorum* (Leipzig: M.

Lotter 1520). On 6 February 1520 he wrote to the chancellor, *Spalatinus, recommending his own Hebrew teacher, Werner of Bacharach, as a suitable candidate for a position at the University of Wittenberg.

Kopp wrote *Problema Aristotelis unum omnium iucundissimum causam huiusce ambiguitatis, cur omnes melancholici ingenio fuere singulari, graphice exponens* (Frankfurt an der Oder: J. Hanau 1509). His respected position at the court of Mainz and his admiration for Erasmus are mentioned in Epp 986 and 999.

BIBLIOGRAPHY: Allen and CWE Ep 986 / Hutten *Opera* I Ep 98 / Luther w *Briefwechsel* II Ep 257, III Ep 816 / *Matrikel Leipzig* I 436, II 385 / *Matrikel Wittenberg* I 5 / *Matrikel Frankfurt* I 8 / Gustav Wustmann *Der Wirt von Auerbachs Keller* (Leipzig 1902) 26, 37–9 / J.K. Seidemann 'Gregorius und Johannes Coppus' *Theologische Studien und Kritiken* 49 (1876) 728–34   IG

Wilhelm KOPP *See Guillaume* COP

Dirk KORTENHOEF *See Theodoricus* CORTEHOEVIUS

Katharina KRAPP *See Philippus* MELANCHTHON

Paweł Sebastian KRASSOWSKI d 2 October 1545
Krassowski (Krasowski, Crescentius, Decentius) came from a noble family with the coat of arms of 'Rogala' which lived at Krassow, in Little Poland; his father's name was Mikołaj. In 1507 Paweł was created apostolic notary. From 1516 he was a canon of the chapter of All Saints in Cracow and in 1538 he became its provost. From 1527 he was also a canon of the Cracow cathedral chapter, and from 1540 he was vicar *in spiritualibus* and general official of the bishop of Cracow. In addition he was canon of Lvov, provost of the Warsaw chapter, and precentor of that of Wiślica and held many less important benefices. In 1526 he was appointed secretary to King *Sigismund I.

Krassowski belonged to the Cracow circle of Erasmus' admirers (Ep 1916) and published two of Erasmus' translations of Chrysostom with a dedication to Chancellor Krzysztof *Szydłowiecki (Cracow: H. Wietor 1528).

BIBLIOGRAPHY: Allen Ep 1916 / J. Fijałek

Nikolaus Kratzer, by Hans Holbein the Younger

'Przeklady pism św. Grzegorza z Nazyanzu w Polsce' *Polonia Sacra* I (Cracow 1918) 78 / Zród ła do dziejów Wawelu IV: *Wypisy źródłowe do dziejów Wawelu z archiwaliów kapitulnych i kurialnych krakowskich, 1501–1515* ed B. Przybyszewski (Cracow 1965) 178 / *Acta Tomiciana* XII (Poznań 1906) Ep 57 / *Bibliografia polska* ed K. Estreicher et al (Cracow 1870–1951) XVIII 403   HALINA KOWALSKA

Nikolaus KRATZER of Munich, c 1487–after 3 August 1550
Nikolaus Kratzer studied at Cologne from 18 November 1506, obtaining a BA on 14 June 1509. Despite many speculations (cf Allen and CWE Ep 515), very little is known of his whereabouts over the next decade. In January 1517 he set out from Antwerp to Brussels, carrying a letter from Pieter *Gillis to Erasmus (Ep 515). In 1519 he is recorded in the employ of King *Henry VIII as astronomer and 'deviser of the King's horologes,' a position which he still held in 1545. In October 1520 he obtained leave to visit Antwerp, where Albrecht *Dürer drew his portrait, now lost, and where he was present when Erasmus sat for Dürer (Ep 1132

introduction). He also met there Cuthbert *Tunstall, who suggested that he be sent to Germany as an English agent (LP III 1018, 1019). In March 1521 he is documented as a tutor in the household of Thomas *More (Rogers Ep 101). On 9 March 1523 he was incorporated as a teacher at the University of Oxford and lectured thereafter on astronomy, the astrolabe, and Ptolemy's *Geographia*. He received houses in London from the king in 1544 and erected two sundials in Oxford, both of which have disappeared. Kratzer was acquainted with Hans *Holbein, who painted his portrait in 1528.

BIBLIOGRAPHY: Allen and CWE Ep 515 / Emden BRUO (1501–1540) 333 / Rogers Ep 101 / DNB XI 344–5 / NDB XII 678–9 / ADB LI 364–6 / *Matrikel Köln* II 603   IG

Bernhard KRECHTING of Schöppingen, d 22 January 1536

Bernhard (Bernd) Krechting, born at Schöppingen, north-west of Münster, was a priest and educator at the court of the count of Bentheim in Westphalia; later he was a priest at Gildehaus, between Osnabrück and Enschede, where he began to take an interest in the Anabaptist movement and therefore had to leave. He arrived in Münster before 15 February 1534 and took an active part in the establishment of the Münsterite Kingdom as one of the ministers of *Jan of Leiden. During the final assault on the city in June 1535 Krechting commanded the last cohesive force of defenders. He was caught, tortured, and finally executed with Jan of Leiden and Bernhard *Knipperdolling on 22 January 1536.

In Allen Ep 3031A:661–6 Konrad *Heresbach reports Krechting's capture and execution. Since he called Krechting one of the three principal leaders, he may have confused him with his brother Heinrich (Hinrich) Krechting, born at Schöppingen in 1501, who was also a priest at Gildehaus and in 1533 was appointed administrator of the territory of Sandwelle, near Ahaus, by the bishop of Münster, Franz von *Waldeck. After refusing to arrest one of the supporters of Bernhard *Rothmann and to have a Lutheran preacher executed, Heinrich Krechting fled to Münster on 15 February 1534. Here the brothers were joined by a large group of friends and relatives from Schöppingen, and

Heinrich became the chancellor in Jan of Leiden's kingdom. In the storming of the city he was probably the only leader of the Münster Anabaptists who managed to escape. He was in Oldenburg until 1538, then lived in Friesland, where he abandoned Anabaptism under the influence of Jan *Łaski. In 1545 he became the leader of a reformed church and died on 28 June 1580.

BIBLIOGRAPHY: *The Mennonite Encyclopedia* (Scottdale 1955–9) III 234–5 / Ugo Gastaldi *Storia dell'anabattismo dalle origini a Münster* (Turin 1972) 536, 556–7 / G.H. Williams *The Radical Reformation* (Philadelphia 1962) 381
                                                                        IG

Wolfgang KRESS (Ep 2475, of 3 April 1531)

No more appears to be known about Wolfgang Kress (Cressus) than is reported by Christoph *Freisleben, who associated with him at Augsburg. According to Freisleben, Kress, a doctor and the preacher of St Dominic's, Augsburg, was a rabble-rouser. By 1532 the Dominican monastery of Augsburg was in a state of decay and inhabited by no more than four monks; in 1534 it was closed down by the city council.

BIBLIOGRAPHY: Friedrich Roth *Augsburgs Reformationsgeschichte* (Munich 1901–11) II 187–8
                                                                        PGB

Matthias KRETZ of Haunstetten, d 1543

Matthias Kretz (Gretz, Kretzius) was born around 1480 in Haunstetten, near Augsburg. In the spring of 1502 he matriculated at Vienna and from 6 October 1504 he studied at Tübingen, graduating MA in 1506 and bachelor of theology on 30 March 1512. He knew Hebrew and Greek and taught at the monastery of Austin canons in Polling, Upper Bavaria, between 1513 and 1516. In 1516 he matriculated at the University of Ingolstadt, where Johann *Eck promoted him doctor of theology in 1519. In the same year he was appointed preacher at the cathedral of Eichstätt, and in 1521 he obtained the same position at Augsburg, succeeding Urbanus *Rhegius, whose sympathy for the reformers he did not at all share (Ep 2430). The citizens of Augsburg were shifting their loyalties in growing numbers, and in 1524 Kretz was repeatedly prevented from preaching. One of his main opponents was Michael *Cellarius. In

1526 he attended the disputation of Baden. At the diet of Augsburg in 1530 Kretz was one of the theologians who had to examine the Lutheran confession, and *Charles v requested him to recite the daily gospel readings without expounding them in a sermon.

Kretz first wrote to Erasmus in October 1530, assuring him of his admiration and also that of his bishop, Christoph von *Stadion. He hoped Erasmus would not mind that Eck had been among the many Catholic theologians who stayed in his house during the recent diet (Ep 2402). Erasmus replied with Ep 2414; at the same time, however, in Ep 2415, Erasmus wrote to Johann *Koler, asking him for further information about Kretz. Koler's answer (Ep 2437) was reassuring. Meanwhile Kretz wrote again in February 1531 (Ep 2430) to report his forthcoming move to Munich, where Duke William iv of *Bavaria had offered him an appointment. No evidence of further correspondence is available, but Erasmus sent greetings to Kretz in 1533 (Ep 2803) through Johannes *Agricola. Meanwhile Kretz had moved to Munich, where he became dean of the cathedral chapter in 1533. He attended the colloquy of Worms in 1540 and died in Munich.

BIBLIOGRAPHY: Allen Ep 2402 (with a list of Kretz's publications) / NDB XIII 16–17 / ADB IX 645 / Matrikel Tübingen I 144 / Matrikel Wien II-1 301 / Luther w Briefwechsel v Ep 1591 / F. Roth Augsburgs Reformationsgeschichte (Munich 1901–11) 100ff, 247 / BA Oekolampads I 324–5 and passim / Nikolaus Paulus 'Dr. Matthias Kretz' Historisch-politische Blätter 114 (1894) 1–19

IG

Hartmut von KRONBERG See *Hartmuth von* CRONBERG

Georg KRUSS See CRUSIUS

Andrzej KRZYCKI 1482–10 May 1537
Krzycki (Andreas Critius) came from a noble family with the coat of arms of 'Kotwicz,' whose family estates were in Greater Poland. He was the son of Mikołaj, the heir of Mały Krzyck, and Anna, the sister of the future vice-chancellor Piotr *Tomicki. Of his studies little is known, except that he attended the lectures of Codro *Urceo and Filippo (I)

*Beroaldo at Bologna, probably between 1498 and 1503. After his return to Poland he was retained at the humanist court of Bishop Jan Lubrański in Poznań. In 1504 he took holy orders and was elected canon of Poznań; in 1507 he was chancellor of the cathedral chapter of Poznań. Further preferment was secured for him by the efforts of his uncle, Piotr Tomicki. On 23 July 1512 he became a canon of Cracow, and subsequently he was appointed to be secretary to the first wife of King *Sigismund I, Queen Barbara Zápolyai. After her death in 1515 Krzycki took over the position of secretary to the king himself and soon found favour with his second wife, Queen *Bona Sforza. Thanks to her intervention he was appointed provost of the chapter of St Florian in Cracow on 30 November 1518.

Krzycki soon found that he had to divide his loyalties between Queen Bona, who favoured co-operation with France, and her political opponent, Piotr Tomicki. In this delicate situation he was often forced to compromise. In 1522 he received the bishopric of Przemyśl, an appointment that was confirmed by the pope on 4 June 1523. However, Krzycki, who lived mostly in Cracow, was rarely present in his diocese and called only one diocesan synod. He took part in the negotiations leading to the secularization of the state of the Teutonic Knights in Prussia and prepared an apology for the resulting treaty of Cracow (1525) in the form of a letter to the papal nuncio Giovanni Antonio *Buglio, *Ad Joannem Antonium Pulleonem ... de negotio Prutenico epistola* (Cracow: H. Wietor 1525). In it Krzycki defended his king against charges of supporting Lutheranism, underlining the distinctly political motives which had led to the secularization. Personally he was a strong opponent of the Reformation, but in political life he put the interests of his state and the king's will above the considerations that were due to Rome. Following the defeat and death of *Louis II of Hungary at Mohács in 1526, Krzycki advocated the assertion of Sigismund's claims to the Hungarian throne. Later he supported Queen Bona's policy of backing the rule of *John Zápolyai in Hungary. During the years 1531–3 he was the principal advocate of lasting peace with the Turks.

In April 1527 Krzycki was appointed bishop

of Płock and on 24 September held his solemn entry into the city. On 10 May 1528 he called a diocesan synod; yet, preoccupied with political affairs, he was not able to reside permanently in Płock and Pułtusk until 1531. He administered his diocese in an energetic manner, making personal visitations of his parishes, supporting the construction of new churches, taking care to preserve a uniform liturgy, and sharply countering the Reformation currents.

In mid-1535, owing to the intervention of Queen Bona, Krzycki was raised to the archbishopric of Gniezno. He was duly elected by the cathedral chapter on 29 October 1535, and his inauguration took place on 21 April 1536. He stayed at Gniezno for a short time only, returning to Cracow on 5 May. The death of his uncle, Piotr Tomicki, allowed him greater freedom of action. However, by then it was too late in Krzycki's career for him to play a political role commensurate with his talents and ambitions.

Krzycki was noted much more for his cultural interests and his literary production than as a statesman. His devotion to humanism is illustrated by his friendships with Leonard *Cox and Stanisław Biel, vice-chancellor of the University of Cracow, and by his close contacts with the young humanists gathered around Cox and Jan *Łaski the younger. Stanislaus *Hosius was one of his protégés. His residence in Cracow near St Florian's, known as 'Tusculum,' offered a meeting-place for men of letters. After his elevation to the see of Płock, Krzycki strove to follow Tomicki's example as a patron of art and culture. Between 1530 and 1535 he tried to convince *Melanchthon to settle in Poland. Appreciating his scholarly talents to the full, he wanted to draw Melanchthon away from Martin *Luther and made overtures to him with the approval of popes *Clement VII and *Paul III. Krzycki kept a magnificent court and had somewhat extravagant tastes. This caused him financial difficulties, despite the fact that the bishopric of Płock was very wealthy. In 1532 he commissioned the building of a new cathedral in Płock according to plans made by the Italian architect Bernardinus de Gianotis. He also enlarged the castle of Pułtusk, eagerly collected books and manuscripts, and was a patron of many poets. One of his clients was

Clemens Janicius, who in 1537 became his librarian.

Krzycki's own poetic career began in 1512 when he published an epithalamium in honour of the marriage of Sigismund I with Barbara Zápolyai, *In augustissimum Sigismundi regis Poloniae et reginae Barbarae connubium ... carmen* (Cracow: J. Haller 1512) and an excellent poem in praise of the king's victory over the Tartars, *Encomium divi Sigismundi regis Poloniae, post victoriam de Tartaris partam* (Cracow: J. Haller 1512). His reputation as a poet grew steadily as he published new works: a heroic poem glorifying the victory of Orsza, *Ad divum Sigismundum Poloniae regem ... post partam de Moscis victoriam carmen* (Cracow: J. Haller 1515); an epicedium for Barbara Zápolyai, *Deploratio immaturae mortis Barbarae, uxoris Sigismundi primi, regis Poloniae* (Cracow: J. Haller 1515), and, above all, his poem in honour of the marriage between Sigismund I and Bona Sforza, *Epithalamium divi Sigismundi primi regis et inclytae Bonae, reginae Poloniae* (Cracow: J. Haller 1518). This work has been acclaimed as one of the best neo-Latin poems written in Poland.

Another aspect of Krzycki's creative talent is shown by his epigrams and satiric verses, characterized by sharp wit and biting criticism. These were directed against his political and personal opponents and made fun of many highly placed dignitaries, including the pope. He wrote them in his youth but he did not publish them – as he also did not publish his earliest works, which include erotic verses, drinking songs in rhyme, and parodies of church hymns. Krzycki's early works also employ political satire and express his concern with the state of the church and the kingdom. Soon he joined the controversy against the reformers with his ironic *Encomia Lutheri* (Cracow: H. Wietor 1524, also Rome 1524), which contained epigrams by other authors as well. In *De afflictione ecclesiae, commentarius in Psalmum XXI* (Cracow: H. Wietor, January 1527, also Rome 1527) he took issue with Luther's *Cperatio in Psalmum XXI* (1523). This commentary signals a new period in Krzycki's literary career, characterized by a deep concern about the future of Christianity and a desire to improve his own reputation, which had been tarnished by his anticlerical satires and his apology for the secularization of the Teutonic state. In the same vein he composed a kind of pastoral letter to his diocesan clergy of Płock, *De ratione et sacrificio missae* (Cracow: M. Scharffenberg 1528), and many hymns, particularly Christmas carols.

Krzycki's unconventional Latin style is reminiscent of ancient Roman comedies. He also used prosodies, rhymes, and linguistic structures common to the Middle Ages. In his political verse he is indebted to the influence of Codro Urceo and Angelo *Poliziano. However, Krzycki did not follow classical literary forms; and classical topics, neo-Platonic mythology and Polish themes are blended in his works, giving them an individual touch. He was also famous amongst his contemporaries as an orator. Krzycki died in Cracow and was buried in the cathedral of Gniezno. His tomb is covered by a Renaissance slab presenting a portrait fashioned after his death mask.

Krzycki held Erasmus and his works in great respect. The title of his anti-Lutheran satire *Encomia Lutheri* may be a tribute to Erasmus' *Moriae encomium*, and Erasmus' opposition to Luther is noted in that work. It may be assumed that Krzycki took the initiative in sending it to Erasmus, and likewise *De negotio Prutenico*. The two books reached Erasmus with Hieronim and Jan *Łaski, who no doubt encouraged him to write to Krzycki. He did so in October 1525 (Ep 1629), sending the Polish bishop and diplomat as a gift a recent book by an English bishop and diplomat, Cuthbert *Tunstall. That Krzycki was eagerly expecting this kind of response from Erasmus is clear from his reaction. He at once sent Stanislaus Hosius a copy of Erasmus' letter and suggested that he be invited to settle in Poland (*Hosii epistolae* Ep 1). Such an invitation was in fact conveyed to Erasmus in Krzycki's long reply of December 1525 (Ep 1652). A month later Jan *Antonin sent Erasmus a book by Krzycki, perhaps *Religionis et reipublicae querimonia* (Cracow: H. Wietor 1522), and urged him to accept the invitation (Ep 1660). Erasmus was gratified (Ep 1697) but declined it (Ep 1753). Krzycki's answer is lost, as are his remaining letters to Erasmus. Not all of Erasmus' letters have been preserved either, and traces of their missing correspondence can be found in Epp 1810, 1825, 2030, 2174 and *Acta Tomiciana* x Ep 445. In

view of these missing letters a full evaluation of their relations is difficult. Krzycki certainly desired Erasmus' friendship and endeavoured to present himself in the best possible light. He sent Erasmus copies of some of his books, and also a poem, presumably in manuscript (Ep 1683). According to Jan (II) Łaski, Krzycki was a leading promoter of King Sigismund's generosity to Erasmus (Ep 1954). With the aim of establishing stronger ties with Erasmus Krzycki finally sent his nephew Andrzej *Zebrzydowski to Basel in the spring of 1528.

Erasmus, for his part, praised Krzycki highly in the *Ciceronianus* (ASD I-2 689–90), but his letters to him are written with a certain distance and seem to lack deeper feeling. Despite the similarity of their problems – both were being attacked by certain Catholic circles – a close understanding never developed, and Erasmus' polite letters to Krzycki may be due largely to his friendship with Tomicki, Krzycki's uncle. Zebrzydowski's visit was not a success, and although Erasmus tried not to show his discontent (Ep 2201) it did not improve his relations with Krzycki. They continued to exchange publications and Krzycki sent Erasmus a ring (Epp 2201, 2351, 2375). He also informed Erasmus of his invitation to Melanchthon (cf *Acta Tomiciana* xv Ep 269); the news intrigued Erasmus (Ep 2876) and may have caused him to write to Jan Łaski in curiously slighting terms about Krzycki (Ep 2911). Finally Erasmus congratulated Krzycki on his appointment to the archbishopric of Gniezno; however, most of this letter was a tribute to the deeply regretted Piotr Tomicki (Ep 3089).

Many of Krzycki's poems remained unpublished, and of these all but few appear to be lost. In the absence of a modern critical edition one may consult *Andreae Cricii carmina* ed Kazimierz Morawski (Cracow 1888).

BIBLIOGRAPHY: Allen Ep 1629 / *Korespondencja Erazma z Rotterdamu z Polakami* ed M. Cytowska (Warsaw 1965) / PSB xv 544–9 / *Bibliografia literatury polskiej Nowy Korbut* (Warsaw 1964–) II / H. Barycz *W blaskach epoki Odrodzenia* (Warsaw 1968) / Andrzej Krzycki *Poezje* (Warsaw 1962) / J. Fijałek 'Z dziejów humanizmu w Polsce' *Pamiętnik Literacki* 1 (1902) 421–32, 615–22 / L. Hajdukiewicz 'Im Bücherkreis des Erasmus von Rotterdam' *Vier-*

teljahresschrift für Geschichte der Wissenschaft und Technik (Warsaw) 5 (1960) Sonderheft 2 92–4 / L. Hajdukiewicz *Księgozbiór i zaintere-sowania bibliofilskie Piotra Tomickiego na tle jego działalności kulturalnej* (Wrocław 1961) / K. Morawski *Czasy Zygmuntowskie na tle prądów Odrodzenia* (Warsaw 1965) / J. Nowak-Dłużew-ski *Okolicznościowa poezja polityczna w Polsce: Czasy Zygmuntowskie* (Warsaw 1966) / W. Pociecha *Królowa Bona. Czasy i ludzie Odrodzenia* (Poznań 1949–58) I–IV / W. Pociecha 'Rzym wobec starań o sprowadzenie Melanchtona do Polski' *Reformacja w Polsce* (Warsaw) 9–10 (1937–8) 418–22 / *Stanislai Hosii Epistolae* ed F. Hipler et al in *Acta historica res gestas Poloniae illustrantia* (Cracow 1879–88) IV Ep 1 / *Acta Tomiciana* (Poznań-Wrocław 1852–) VII Ep 103, 104, IX Ep 158, X Ep 144, 445, XI Ep 123, XV Ep 269   HALINA KOWALSKA

Martin KÜGELIN of Birkenfeld,
d 1 September 1559
The 'Doctor Martin' mentioned in Ep 3045 with his colleagues Georgius *Amelius and Sebastian *Derrer for having offered help to Margarete *Büsslin is most likely Martin Kügelin (Kigelin, Orbilius) of Büchenbronn, near Birkenfeld, east of Pforzheim. He matriculated in 1520 at the University of Tübingen, where he became a MA in 1523 and rector in the spring of 1529. On 3 April 1528 and on 4 July 1531 he received preliminary theological degrees, while teaching in the faculty of arts, whose dean he was in the winter of 1529–30. After difficult negotiations about his salary, he was appointed professor of theology at Freiburg and matriculated on 15 April 1532. After taking holy orders he was promoted doctor of theology on 28 January 1533. He was many times dean and rector; there is, however, no known record of direct relations between him and Erasmus.

BIBLIOGRAPHY: *Matrikel Tübingen* I 228, 263 / *Matrikel Freiburg* I 281 and passim / H. Schreiber *Universität Freiburg* II 279–82 / J.J. Bauer *Zur Frühgeschichte der theologischen Fakultät der Universität Freiburg i. Br.* (Freiburg 1957) 47–8, 80, and passim   PGB

Balthasar von KÜNRING d 1547
The house of Künring (Kienring, Kieveringen, Khuenring, Chünring, Conrick) was a noble

family originally from Upper Austria which had spread into other regions as well (cf *Matrikel Wien* II-2 186 and passim). Balthasar's father, Johann v von Künring, lived in Vienna. Balthasar entered the Collegium Trilingue at Louvain on 11 May 1529 and was entrusted to the care of Conradus *Goclenius, who supervised his studies. On 7 February 1530 he matriculated at the University of Louvain. He left Louvain on 4 March 1531 and first went to Paris, where he stayed until 1532 or later and met former fellow-students of his from the Collegium Trilingue, among them Bartholomaeus *Latomus and Johannes Secundus (Everaerts). In 1535 he was registered in the University of Bologna and may have gone to Rome. On his return from Italy he arrived in Basel by the end of August 1535. He visited Erasmus, who appreciated his Latin conversation. Künring sent his servant to Louvain with Ep 3052 for Goclenius and with some books, including a copy of Erasmus' *Precationes aliquot novae* (1535) for his friend Johann (III) *Paumgartner (Epp 3061, 3111). He also visited *Capito in Strasbourg and *Zasius in Freiburg and intended to go to Frankfurt. In Italy he had married Anastasia de Zelking of the diocese of Padua after obtaining a papal dispensation dated 13 July 1535 removing the obstacle of a prohibited degree of kinship. In addition he evidently wished to consult lawyers and theologians both Protestant and Catholic, and obtained from the legal faculty of Freiburg an opinion on the validity of papal dispensations. That same summer, as he passed through Constance he was looking for a Protestant preacher to join his household, but apparently he did not find one until 1537.

BIBLIOGRAPHY Allen Ep 3052 / AK IV Epp 1974, 1978, 1981, 1988 / de Vocht CTL II 383–5 / Knod 283 / Bernd Möller *Johannes Zwick und die Reformation in Konstanz* (Gütersloh 1961) 167

IG

Antoine de LA BARRE d 12 January 1547
Antoine, a son of Jean de La Barre, seigneur d'Etampes, and Marie de La Primaudaye, was born at the family estate of Véretz, near Tours. He was an apostolic protonotary, was dean of St Martin's, Tours, from 1 August 1518, and in the same year was appointed commendatory abbot of St Catherine's (or Holy Trinity), near

Rouen. On 28 January 1524 he resigned his deanery to become bishop of Angoulême, a see which he held until his appointment to the archbishopric of Tours four years later. On 5 July 1528 he took possession of the see of Tours by procuration. Under his auspices the diocesan statutes were collected and published in 1537.

In February 1536 Pierre *Vitré informed Erasmus that he had been absent from Paris for three years in the service of the archbishop of Tours (Ep 3101).

BIBLIOGRAPHY: Allen Ep 3101 / *Gallia christiana* II 1020, XI 130, XIV 133, 183 / Eubel III 192–3, 321   PGB

Gertrud LACHNER of Basel, d 1560
In November 1510, Gertrud, the daughter of Wolfgang *Lachner, was married to the widowed Johann *Froben in a match that was intended to seal the close business association between her father and her husband. She was clearly conscious of her independent resources, economic and otherwise, as is indicated by the imprint of Henricus *Glareanus' *Duo elegiarum libri* (1516), which stated that the book was printed by Johann Froben at the expense of his wife, Gertrud Lachner. After her father's death she was well aware of the crucial role her money played in the destiny of the Froben firm. Again the independence of Gertrud and her family is reflected by the imprint of *Zasius' *Lucubrationes aliquot*, printed by Froben at the expense of Lachner's heirs in 1518. With frank misgivings Erasmus noted the 'petticoat government' in Froben's house (Ep 885), presumably referring to Gertrud, her mother, Ursula, and several unmarried sisters, who were all living together (Ep 2033). A quip attributed to Guillaume *Farel stated that Gertrud knew more theology than Erasmus (Ep 1510). In a moment of anger Erasmus accused Gertrud of having conspired with Hieronymus *Froben, her stepson, against her husband and of precipitate remarriage after her husband's death, although he also blamed Hieronymus for Gertrud's new marriage to Johann *Herwagen (Epp 1962, 2033, 2231). Normally, however, their relations appear to have been courteous; they exchanged greetings (Epp 330, 419, 635, 904; ASD I-3 129), and Gertrud even wrote Erasmus some polite lines (Ep 634). Ep

1209 mentions an 'unfinished shirt' she sent to Erasmus, no doubt as a gift. In her marriage to Froben Gertrud had three children, Erasmius *Froben, Justina *Froben, and Ursula (AK II Ep 916). Three more children were born in the first three years of her marriage to Herwagen, and another two thereafter.

BIBLIOGRAPHY: Allen Ep 419 / AK III Ep 1484, v Ep 2456, VI Ep 2219a / R. Wackernagel *Geschichte der Stadt Basel* (Basel 1907–54) III 168   PGB

Wolfgang LACHNER of Neuburg,
d 27 January 1518
Wolfgang Lachner, of Neuburg on the Danube, near Ingolstadt, probably took his first steps in the book business under the guidance of another bookseller from Neuburg, Wolfgang Krüss, who had business connections with Basel. It was there that Lachner, who had probably trained at Augsburg and Venice, established himself as an independent bookseller, acquiring citizenship on 22 April 1488 and three months later membership of the 'Safran' guild. Three years later he moved up to the distinguished 'Schlüssel' guild, and in 1515 he was among the Basel troops in the battle of Marignano. He was married to Ursula of Thus, also called Gasser (Ep 419) and had a number of children, predominantly daughters. His eldest daughter, Gertrud *Lachner, married Johann *Froben in November 1510, while another, Anna, became the wife of Hieronymus *Froben on 7 January 1524. Three more daughters died in September 1519 of the plague, which had already taken the life of their father (Ep 781).

In 1495 Lachner acquired the house 'zum roten Ring' on the Fischmarkt and from this basis developed an important book trade, attracting to Basel commercial buyers from many regions. He also travelled to, or was represented at, the fairs of Frankfurt, Strasbourg, and Lyon (Epp 575, 594; AK I Epp 348, 353). He specialized in the importation of books from Italy, above all the products of the Aldine press, and he maintained close links with the book-distributing network of Johann *Schabler and his associates in France and with that of the *Birckmann family in the Netherlands and in England. From 1508 there is growing evidence of his association with the presses of Johann Froben and his partners (AK I

Epp 394, 421), an association soon to be reinforced by the marriage of his daughter Gertrud. Although the arrangements between the partners are not known in detail, it seems clear that Lachner, in association with Schabler (AK I Epp 234, 323), accounted for a great many of Froben's sales, so much so that he came to exercise a decisive influence on Froben's publishing policy. In 1517 *Beatus Rhenanus complained about Lachner's preference for voluminous scholastic compilations (Ep 575; cf AK I Epp 268, 394), and large folio sizes retained a prominent place in the production of the Froben firm throughout its existence. At the same time it is evident that Lachner invested heavily in Froben's business, especially after the death in 1513 of Froben's partner, Johann *Amerbach. Many details in the correspondence of Erasmus point to his authoritative role in the press (Epp 352, 469, 575, 581, 594, 628, 732). The difficulties faced by Froben after Lachner's death were caused primarily by a lack of working capital, as some of Lachner's funds were apparently withdrawn while the rest were now controlled by Gertrud Lachner, her mother, Ursula, and other family members (Epp 795, 885).

Lachner's tough and decisive personality is reflected in his relations with Erasmus. When the scholar first appeared in Basel, Lachner took charge of him at once and looked after all his needs (Ep 305). Thereafter he repeatedly expressed his desire to publish anything Erasmus could produce (Epp 469, 581). He also determined Erasmus' remuneration, avoiding paying him cash whenever he could (Epp 469, 629, 732, 733, 795). Although not satisfied with these arrangements, Erasmus knew what he owed to the 'head' (Epp 781, 794) of the Froben press and often did not hesitate to deal with him in preference to Froben (Epp 629, 687, 733, 786). Others though, including Beatus Rhenanus and Jakob *Wimpfeling, did not like Lachner's way of doing business (Ep 575; AK I Ep 268). Lachner's attentions to Erasmus are perhaps reflected in a curious rumour of 1524 which reported Erasmus' death and had him buried in the bookseller's tomb (Ep 1518).

BIBLIOGRAPHY: Allen Ep 419 / F. Hieronymus in NDB XIII 377–8 / AK I Ep 234 and passim / Grimm Buchführer 1366–72 / R. Wackernagel Geschichte der Stadt Basel (Basel 1907–54) III

167–8 and passim / W.R. Staehelin Wappenbuch der Stadt Basel (Basel [1917–30]) PGB

LADISLAS II See VLADISLAV II, king of Bohemia and Hungary

Simon LAGNIER documented at Besançon 1531–6
Simon Lagnier (Laynier, Leignier, Lenius) is documented as a notary and citizen of Besançon in 1531. Erasmus wrote to him in November 1533 after he had received an unexpected gift of wine, and promised his assistance to Lagnier's sons Hugues and Ferry, young clerics who were soon to matriculate at Freiburg (Ep 2881). In March 1536 he expressed sympathy with Lagnier in view of his troubles (Ep 3104). A month later we learn that he and his wife were seriously ill (Ep 3115).

BIBLIOGRAPHY: Allen Ep 2881 / L. Febvre 'Un secrétaire d'Erasme: Gilbert Cousin et la réforme en Franche-Comté' Bulletin de la Société de l'histoire du Protestantisme français 56 (1907) 97–158, esp 109 / Matrikel Freiburg I 287 / Besançon Archives du Doubs MS G 191 ff 210 verso, 215 PGB

Jean-Baptiste de LAIGUE documented 1509–46
Jean-Baptiste was a younger brother of Antoine Honorat, sieur d'*Oraison. His father, Philibert de Laigue of Bourges, had been chamberlain to René d'Anjou, count of Provence, and his mother was Louise d'Oraison. Jean-Baptiste was bishop of Senez (Département des Alpes de Haute-Provence) from 1509 to 1546 and abbot of St Eusèbe at Apt (Département de Vaucluse) from 1517 to 1536. Two natural sons of Laigue were legitimated in 1539. In 1530 and 1531 Erasmus sent him greetings through the unidentified Franciscus *Cassander, who may have been in his service (Epp 2296, 2442).

BIBLIOGRAPHY: Allen Ep 2296 / Gallia christiana I 381, III 1261 / Eubel III 297 / Catalogue des actes de François I (Paris 1887–1908) VI 552 and passim MICHEL REULOS

Johann LAIR See John SIBERCH

Antoine de LALAING count of Hoogstraten, 1480–2 April 1540

Originally from Lallaing (Département du Nord, arrondissement de Douai). Antoine's family belonged to the higher Burgundian nobility and from the time of Philip the Good, duke of *Burgundy, included a number of occupants of high office and knights of the Golden Fleece. Antoine was the second son of Josse de Lalaing, lord of Montigny, and Barbe (Bonne) de Viefville. The lordship of Montigny was transferred to him in 1498 by his elder brother, Charles, who had acquired the lordship of Lalaing from an older branch of the family. Antoine was a member of the household of Philip the Handsome, duke of *Burgundy, by the age of sixteen, and he remained throughout his life in the service of Philip, of his son, the future *Charles v, and above all of *Margaret of Austria, regent of the Low Countries. As chamberlain he accompanied Philip on his two journeys to Spain (1501, 1506). After Philip's death he returned in 1507 to the Netherlands and joined the household of Prince Charles. In 1513 he was appointed second chamberlain and thus deputy of the grand chamberlain, who was the manager of the ducal household and the administrator of its finances. He was also appointed to the privy council and in 1515 became head of the council of finance, while in 1516 he received the order of the Golden Fleece.

During Charles v's second absence from the Netherlands, from 1522 to 1531, Lalaing reached the pinnacle of his career. With the title of *chevalier d'honneur* (from 1523), he managed Margaret's household, but his financial authority, as was mentioned above, went far beyond the spheres of court and household. Moreover, his functions permitted him to play a leading part in political decision-making. This is confirmed by a comparison with Henry iii of *Nassau, who as grand chamberlain held an analogous position at the court of Charles v. In short, Lalaing was the most influential member of Margaret's court and her personal confidant. He was also rumoured to be her lover, which may account for his unpopularity, as did the fact that he was responsible for mobilizing the Low Countries' resources in support of the emperor's costly wars. In the wake of the peace with France (Cambrai 1529) he also played a leading part in the acquisition of the temporalities of the bishopric of Utrecht and the temporary submission of Karel van *Egmond, duke of Gelderland.

The death of Margaret (1 December 1530) was followed by a reorganization of the central government of the Low Countries and the appointment of *Mary of Hungary as the new regent. As a result Lalaing lost much of his political influence and part of his revenues, although he retained his position as a member of the council of state and head of finances. On the other hand, his role in regional affairs was enlarged. From 1518 he had commanded one of the companies of *gens d'armes* and from 1522 he had been governor of Holland and Zeeland; now in 1530 he was also appointed governor of the new province of Utrecht. In this sphere of his activities he was confronted by such problems as the rise of Anabaptism and the economic consequences of the Hapsburg support for *Christian ii of Denmark. As far as the 'Danish troubles' were concerned, he deserves much credit for their eventual resolution.

Lalaing had three illegitimate children when he married Elisabeth van *Culemborg, the heiress of the lordship of Hoogstraten, in 1509. In 1518 he was created count of Hoogstraten after his wife had transferred that lordship to him. His wife's dowry and the income derived from his offices and generous rewards for his services to Margaret of Austria formed the basis of Lalaing's considerable wealth, which stood in sharp contrast to his beginnings as a younger son without claim to an inheritance. By prudent management of his wife's estates and his own, he was able to increase his properties steadily. As he had no legitimate children, he left the county of Hoogstraten to his nephew, Philippe de Lalaing.

Lalaing was clearly well educated, but it is not known where he had acquired his learning. As a young man he wrote an account in French of his first journey to Spain in the retinue of Philip the Handsome, which has been edited by Gachard. He also took a genuine interest in art and architecture, and the results of his building activity can still be admired in castles, town houses, and churches at Culemborg, Hoogstraten, Brussels, and Mechelen. After the death in 1524 of Philip (i) of *Burgundy, bishop of Utrecht, Lalaing bought his entire library.

Erasmus was personally acquainted with the powerful courtier, but the acquaintance was slight (Epp 1553, 1585), and from the time of a visit to Brussels by the inquisitor Jacob of *Hoogstraten (in October 1519), he remained uneasy about his personal standing with the count of Hoogstraten (Epp 1038, 1040, 1585). Fully aware of Lalaing's influence, he nonetheless hesitated to approach him direct in the matter of his unpaid pension (Epp 1545, 1585). In 1534, at a time when Erasmus was being attacked in the Netherlands by the Franciscan Nikolaus *Ferber, he emphasized that Lalaing was a special patron of the Franciscans (Epp 2906, 2961).

BIBLIOGRAPHY: Allen Ep 1038 / J. Lauwerys in NBW I 653–60 / BNB XI 80–5 / NNBW VIII 993–5 / de Vocht CTL I 430 and passim / de Vocht *Literae ad Craneveldium* Ep 126 and passim / M.L.J.C. Noordam-Croes 'Anton van Lalaing ... ' *Jaarboek van Koninklijke Hoogstratens Oudheidkundige Kring* 36 (1968) v–xix, 1–175 / J. Lauwerys in *Jaarboek van Koninklijke Hoogstratens Oudheidkundige Kring* 24 (1956) 24–61 / Michel Baelde *De collaterale raden onder Karel v en Filips II* (Brussels 1965) 272–3 and passim / *Collection des voyages des souverains des Pays-Bas* ed L.P. Gachard and C. Piot (Brussels 1874–82) I 121–340 (Lalaing's account of the journey to Spain) / Many letters addressed to him as *stadhouder* of Holland and Zeeland are in Brussels, Archives générales du Royaume, MSS Papiers d'état et de l'audience, and in The Hague, Algemeen Rijksarchief, MSS Hof van Holland   HEIDE STRATENWERTH

Sidrach de LALAING d 28 June 1533
Sidrach de Lalaing graduated as a licentiate in canon law, no doubt from the University of Paris, and became a canon of the chapter of Saint-Omer. On 14 March 1512 his fellow-canons elected him dean of the chapter despite the emperor's request that they should choose Jean de Renty. Apart from the imperial letter and the proxies tendered by some of the canons for this election, the chapter archives do not offer any documents that cast light on the reasons for this confrontation, which evidently went beyond the personal ambitions of the two candidates. Renty's stubborn refusal to yield and the general stir caused by the conflict made it necessary for Lalaing to

wait a full year before he could take possession of his office (30 March 1513). His duties as dean and his forceful personality caused him to play a significant part in the religious life of Saint-Omer. In 1529 the city council entrusted to him two sensitive missions to the convent of the nuns of St Margaret. The purpose of these visitations was to investigate and eventually to reform the lax discipline of this convent, which also figured frequently among the concerns of Jean *Vitrier. At the request of the emperor, Lalaing was also summoned to testify during the interminable proceedings against the head of that convent, Marie de Sempy. His own statements and some others which he entered into the record show that he was critical of the mother superior and shared the concern of Vitrier and Erasmus for religious reform. In turn Erasmus considered him 'a man of exemplary character and a great lover of literature' (Ep 273).

In his will, dated 1532 and written in French, Lalaing gave the most detailed instructions for his funeral. In compliance with these he was buried in the chapter church in front of the chapel of St John the Evangelist. A contract has been preserved in which his executors commissioned a 'tailleur d'ymaiges' to create a funeral monument representing the story of Shadrach ('Sidrac'), Meshach, and Abednego (Daniel 3) together with a praying man dressed as a canon. Although this monument no longer exists, its conception pays tribute both to his strong religious conviction that was firmly rooted in the Bible and to his determination to leave his mark even after his death, in the city where he had exerted such influence.

BIBLIOGRAPHY: Allen and CWE Ep 273 / *Gallia christiana* III 482 / Saint-Omer, Bibliothèque municipale, MS 932 'Catalogue des archives capitulaires' II G 407, 482; 'Archives de Saint-Omer' procès 64; 'Comptes du Magistrat 1529/30–1531' f 95   ANDRÉ GODIN

Jean LALEMAND d 18 September 1560
A native of the Franche-Comté, Jean Lalemand (L'Allemand, Alemannus) served in the Parlement of Dole in 1507. He began his career as clerk to Louis Barangier, secretary of *Margaret of Austria, and was himself appointed a secretary to Margaret on 21 June 1517. That same year, Lalemand went to Spain in the train

of the future *Charles v; specifically he was attached to Laurent de *Gorrevod. By 1520 he had become a secretary in the service of Charles himself; he also served as comptroller of Aragon. In 1522 Lalemand became the successor to Jean Hannart as secretary 'signant en finances,' a prominent position, to which was added that of secretary of the newly formed council of state. Until 1528 he was the emperor's first secretary. In 1524 Lalemand married Anne, the daughter of Philippe *Haneton. By that time he had also acquired the seigneurie of Bouclans, north-east of Besançon.

In 1526 Lalemand was an active participant in the negotiations leading to the peace of Madrid with *Francis I. Subsequently he fell out with Alfonso de *Valdés and, if the latter is to be believed (Ep 2163), took the lead in attacking Valdés' dialogue *Lactancio*. But soon he himself fell victim to court intrigues. In 1528 he was accused of treason and influence-peddling; his former protectors Gorrevod and Chancellor *Gattinara had by then turned against him. In December 1528 he lost his office and, after a short imprisonment (Ep 2083), was banished from court. Although an investigation cleared him of the charge of treason, he never regained the emperor's favour. He retired to the Franche-Comté, where he was appointed canon of Besançon on 21 January 1540 and died twenty years later.

Erasmus clearly thought that Lalemand was well disposed towards him; in 1524 and 1525 he addressed letters to Lalemand about his court pension and a plan for his return to the Netherlands (Epp 1431, 1554). He also appealed for his help against the theologians of Louvain (Epp 1554, 1747).

BIBLIOGRAPHY: Allen Ep 1554 / *Correspondance politique administrative de Laurent de Gorrevod* ed André Chagny (Mâcon 1913) / José Antonio Escudero *Los secretarios del estado y del despacho (1474–1724)* (Madrid 1969) 62–5, 70–7, 787–91 / Augustin Redondo *Antonio de Guevara (1480?– 1545) et l'Espagne de son temps: de la carrière officielle aux oeuvres politico-morales* (Geneva 1976) 377 / Fritz Walser *Die spanischen Zentralbehörden und der Staatsrat Karls v.* (Göttingen 1959) 245, 255–61 / Andreas Walther *Die burgundischen Zentralbehörden unter Maximilian I. und Karl v.* (Leipzig 1909) 155–61 /

Bataillon *Erasmo y España* 385–6 and passim / de Vocht *Dantiscus* 39–40 / de Vocht CTL II 247–8 and passim / Gauthier 131–3 and passim / Karl Brandi *Kaiser Karl v.* new ed (Darmstadt 1959–67) II 208 and passim / Vienna, Haus-, Hof- und Staatsarchiv, MS Belgien PA 24a

PETER MARZAHL & PGB

LA MARCK *See de la* MARCK

Jean LAMBELIN of Jussey, d 12 June 1538
Jean Lambelin, of Jussey in the Franche-Comté, was assistant secretary to the town council of Besançon from 1520 and shortly thereafter secretary and thus head of the chancery. In the course of his duties he was sent to the diet of Worms in 1521 to present the town's complaints against the archbishop, Antoine de *Vergy, as he did again in a submission of 1527. After his return from Worms he began to propagate the Lutheran reforms amid continued antagonism between the town on one side and the chapter and archbishop on the other. In 1525 he investigated a popular outburst against the canons' concubines. From 1527 he joined the political party of Simon Gauthiot d'Ancier and after Gauthiot's defeat at the polls in 1537 Lambelin was made the scapegoat. After he had signed an ambiguous council edict against the Lutheran sect, dated 3 February 1537, he was himself charged with heresy, embezzlement, and abuse of his political powers. He was tortured with a new instrument of his own invention and beheaded on the market square, giving witness to his Protestant faith. Four days earlier his books and other possessions were sold in public, including a Horace edited by Jakob *Locher (Strasbourg: J. Grüninger 1498).

In October 1532 Erasmus replied to a letter written by Lambelin on behalf of the council to encourage his move to Besançon (Ep 2733). Thereafter they kept in touch, partly through Lambelin's relative Etienne *Desprez (Epp 3104, 3115).

BIBLIOGRAPHY: Allen Ep 2733 / Claude Fohlen et al *Histoire de Besançon* (Paris 1965) I 615–22 and passim / A. Castan 'Granvelle et le petit empereur de Besançon 1518–1538' *Revue historique* 1 (1876) 85–139 passim / Auguste Castan *Catalogue des incunables de la Bibliothèque*

publique de Besançon (Besançon 1893) 440 /
Herminjard v Ep 725   PGB

LAMBERT of Torn d 1528 (?)
Little is known of the Franciscan Lambert of
Torn (Thoren), in Limburg, who was convicted
of Lutheran heresy in 1523 with two other
Franciscans, Hendrik *Vos and Jan van den
*Esschen. While these were executed on 1 July,
Lambert was apparently granted time for
reflection and remained in jail. It seems that he
remained there for five years, in very harsh
conditions, and died around 15 September
1528, without ever having recanted. Erasmus
had been told that Lambert was not executed
with his two fellow-sufferers but had been
killed secretly in prison a few days later (Epp
1382, 1384, 2188). Martin *Luther had at first
received the same information, but subsequently he learnt that Lambert was still alive
and wrote him a comforting letter on 19 January
1524 (Luther w *Briefwechsel* III Epp 635, 707).

    BIBLIOGRAPHY: de Vocht *Literae ad Cranevel-
dium* Epp 66, 213 / de Vocht MHL 238   PGB

François LAMBERT of Avignon,
d 18 April 1530
François Lambert was born at Avignon, probably in 1487; his family originated in the
Franche-Comté. At Avignon his father was
secretary of the legation and of the apostolic
palace. Shortly after his father's death, he
entered the Franciscan order (1501). Sixteen
years later he was named an apostolic preacher
and travelled extensively to preach a revival
based on the Gospel. In the next few years he
came under *Luther's influence. In 1522 he was
sent on a mission to the vicar-general of the
Franciscans in Germany. He proceeded
through Switzerland, met *Zwingli in Zürich,
and stayed for a while in Basel, where Erasmus
perhaps refused to see him. He went on to
Wittenberg, where he arrived in January 1523.
Having abandoned his cowl, he took a wife,
gave a course of lectures, and translated the
works of the German reformers into French
and Italian. Unable to find permanent employment in Saxony he moved first to Metz and
then to Strasbourg, where he was given
citizenship (1 November 1524). Here he lectured on the Scriptures, preached to French
residents of the town, and wrote books

designed to convert King *Francis I and the
French kingdom. In 1526 Phillip of *Hesse
entrusted him with introducing the Reformation in his territories. His theses or *Paradoxa*
(Erfurt 1527), which were drawn up on
Lutheran lines, were acclaimed by the estates
of Hesse. The same year Lambert was named to
a chair of theology in the newly created
University of Marburg. In the controversy over
the real presence Lambert sided with the
Zwinglian party (1529).
    Lambert's *In ... Oseam ... commentarii* (Stras-
bourg: J. Herwagen 1525) were written in
rebuttal to Erasmus' *De libero arbitrio*. In his
Hyperaspistes Erasmus claimed that Lambert
had misrepresented his thinking (LB X 1277D).
Notable among Lambert's other writings were
*Rationes propter quas minoritarum conversationem
habitumque rejecit* (written in Wittenberg
1522–3, published in 1730); *Evangelici in
minoritarum regulam commentarii* (Strasbourg: J.
Knobloch 1523?), *In divi Lucae evangelium
commentarii* (Nürnberg: J. Petreius 1524), and
Commentarii de sacro conjugio ... (Nürnberg: J.
Petreius 1525).
    BIBLIOGRAPHY: G. Müller in NDB XIII 435–7 /
J.W. Baum *Franz Lambert von Avignon* (Stras-
bourg 1840) / R.L. Winters *Francis Lambert of
Avignon, 1487–1530* (Philadelphia 1938) / G.
Müller *Franz Lambert von Avignon und die
Reformation in Hessen* (Marburg 1958) / E.V.
Telle 'François Lambert d'Avignon et son
abbaye de Thélème' BHR 11 (1949) 43–55 / A.
Möser 'Franz Lamberts Reise durch die
Schweiz im Jahre 1522' *Zwingliana* (1957)
467–71 / Herminjard I Epp 52–3 and passim / z
VII Ep 222 and passim / AK II Epp 924, 962
                            HENRY HELLER

Guilelmus Johannis LAMBERTI *See Willem of*
VIANEN

LAMBERTUS (Ep 1778 of 13 January [1527])
Lambertus, an unidentified secretary of
Henry, count *Palatine, bishop of Utrecht,
mentioned in conversation with Conradus
*Goclenius that Gerard *Geldenhouwer had
got married.

LAMBERTUS Carthusianus *See Lambertus*
PASCUALIS

Marcellus de LA MORE documented 1513–30
Marcellus de La More is documented as a
surgeon to *Henry VIII in 1513 and attended
the king on his French campaign the same
year. On 18 July 1513 he was appointed
'serjeant' (or chief) of the royal surgeons. In
1515 and on 29 September 1520 he was granted
annuities. He probably died before 20 April
1530, when his office and annuity were
granted to another surgeon (LP IV 6363.29). His
son, who has not been identified, was appointed in 1515 to a canonry in the chapter of
Tournai by Thomas *Wolsey, who was the
administrator of Tournai. The same prebend,
which was contested by a papal nominee, had
earlier been offered to Erasmus, who now had
to be content with a promise of future
compensation (Ep 371; LP II 889–90). In 1516
Marcellus' son was in possession of the
prebend, but Richard *Sampson, Wolsey's
vicar-general, thought that he was 'not in heart
so good English' as was desirable (LP II 2066).
BIBLIOGRAPHY: Allen Ep 371 / LP I 2222 (5),
2404, 2480, 2964 (46), 4390, III 999 and passim
PGB

Pierre LAMY d c 1525
Intriguingly little is known about Pierre Lamy
(Amicus, L'Amy), who, like his friend François
*Rabelais, was a Franciscan Observant at
Fontenay-le-Comte. Having been forced to
enter the order, Lamy fled from his monastery
not later than 1522 to find shelter and some
freedom to study in the Benedictine abbey of
Saint-Mesmin at Micy, near Orléans. His flight
evidently set an example for Rabelais himself,
who recalled it in *Pantagruel* III 10.
Like Rabelais, Lamy corresponded with
Guillaume *Budé (1520–4) and was also acquainted with François *Deloynes. In 1524 he
knew both Guillaume *Farel and Jacques
*Lefèvre d'Etaples, the latter not very well, it
seems. At about this time he received a letter
from Conradus *Pellicanus, the warden of the
Franciscan house at Basel, whom he must have
met some time before he left the Franciscan
order. When Pellicanus wrote neither he nor
Farel seems to have been aware of Lamy's
defection. In the light of Erasmus' Ep 2449 it
appears probable that he too had met Lamy
when he was still a friar, so the latter may well
have been a guest of the Basel Franciscans at

some time when Erasmus was at Basel. It is not
known whether any Basel connections were
operative when Lamy apparently came under
the patronage of Jan (II) *Łaski, who in the
spring of 1525 brought the young Frenchman
with him to Basel, or so Erasmus recalled in
1531 (Ep 2449). He also stated there that Lamy
died after a few months and was buried in the
Franciscan churchyard, although without the
'seraphic' cowl. The modest and scholarly
Frenchman had clearly impressed him. The
only other documentation we have of Lamy's
presence in Basel, and the only autograph of
his, is a short note to Bonifacius *Amerbach,
begging to borrow a Demosthenes (AK V
Ep 1013a).
BIBLIOGRAPHY: Allen Ep 2449 / Henry Meylan
D'Erasme à Théodore de Bèze (Geneva 1976)
47–51 / Herminjard I Ep 103 / Louis Delaruelle
Répertoire de la correspondance de Guillaume Budé
(Toulouse-Paris 1907) Epp 53, 68, 111, 142
PGB

Hugo von LANDENBERG *See Hugo von
HOHENLANDENBERG*

Cristoforo LANDINO of Florence, 1424–
24 September 1498
Cristoforo Landino was born in Florence to a
noble family originating in the Casentino. At
Florence he dedicated himself to the study of
law and, under the guidance of George of
*Trebizond, of Greek. He married an Alberti.
In 1458 he succeeded Cristoforo Marsuppini in
the chair of rhetoric and poetry at the
Florentine Studio. The students, who would
have preferred a more prestigious teacher,
opposed his appointment. Despite his limitations Landino was important in Florentine
cultural life as a disseminator of ideas. He belonged to Marsilio *Ficino's Platonic Academy
and was a teacher of Lorenzo (I) de' *Medici
and his brother Giuliano. He also held public
offices, in 1467 as chancellor of the Guelf party
and later as scriptor of public letters for the
Signoria. He enjoyed the protection of the
Medici, who gave him a number of gifts,
including the villa of Borgo Collina, where he
died.
Erasmus mentioned Landino in *Adagia* I i 9
and among Italian humanists in the *Ciceronianus* (ASD I-2 667).

Landino wrote three philosophical dialogues, *De anima* (1453), *De vera nobilitate* (1469), and the *Disputationes Camaldulenses* (c 1474). The latter was a discussion in the Camaldolese monastery between Landino, Giuliano de' Medici, Leon Battista Alberti, Ficino, and other humanists on the relative merits of the active and contemplative life. Landino also wrote three books of Latin poems under the name of the lady 'Xandra,' dedicated in 1458 to Piero de' Medici, and many letters and orations, including the *Elogium in funere Donati Acciaioli*, published in Italian in Venice in 1561. In addition he prepared commentaries on the *Aeneid* (1478) and the *Divine Comedy* (Florence: Niccolò di Lorenzo 1481). A proponent of the use of the vernacular, he commented on Petrarch in his lectures and published Italian translations of Pliny's *Historia naturalis* (Venice: N. Jenson 1476) and of Giovanni Simonetta's Latin life of Francesco Sforza (Milan: A. Zorotto 1490).

BIBLIOGRAPHY: The works of Cristoforo Landino are found in *Annali delle università toscane* 24–6 (1916–17), *Carmina omnia* ed A. Perosa (Florence 1939), and *Scritti critici e teorici* ed R. Cardini (Rome 1974) / For biographical information see R. Cardini *La critica di Landino* (Florence 1974) / Arthur Field 'A manuscript of Cristoforo Landino's first lectures on Virgil (1462–1463) ... ' *Renaissance Quarterly* 31 (1978) 17–20 / E. Garin 'Cristoforo Landino' in *Storia della letteratura italiana* (Milan 1965) IV 290–4 / P. Giannantonio *Cristoforo Landino e l'umanesimo volgare* (Naples 1971) / D. Lupi *Cristoforo Landino* (Naples 1924) / M. Santoro 'Cristoforo Landino e il volgare' *Giornale storico della letteratura italiana* 131 (1954) 501–47   MARCO BERNUZZI

Ortensio LANDO of Milan, c 1505–c 1555
The earliest documentary evidence concerning the Milanese writer Ortensio Lando (Hortensius Landus) is contained in the register of the Augustinian general Gabriele della Volta for the years 1525 to 1532. It records events in the academic and religious life of Fra Geremia da Milano, whose identification with Ortensio is established by the testimony of the German humanist Johann Albrecht *Widmanstetter. Fra Geremia studied at Padua in 1527, with a dispensation from morning service in order to follow Greek lectures, and at Bologna from 1531 to 1533, achieving the grade of *lector*; it is not clear whether he was ever ordained priest. Some time after May 1533, and probably before the end of 1535, he left the Augustinians, for unknown reasons, and thereafter assumed, or perhaps reverted to, the name Ortensio, often coupled with the ironic epithet Tranquillo. However, for such of his works as were not anonymous, he used in the main a different series of appellations, comprising the element 'Philalethes' and direct or indirect derivations from the name Utopia (for example, 'Philalethes Polytopiensis civis,' 'messer Anonimo d'Utopia').

Lando's first published work, *Cicero relegatus et Cicero revocatus* (Lyon: S. Gryphius 1534), a satirical comment on the debate provoked in Italy by Erasmus's *Ciceronianus*, aroused the great man's ire for its apparent attack on Cicero himself (Epp 3019, 3032; cf Ep 3005). His short dialogue *Desiderii Erasmi funus* (Basel: n pr 1540) is a lively fantasy, containing both strong criticism and extravagant praise of Erasmus; its correct interpretation is obscure, and currently in dispute. The several indications of Protestant affinities in these and other early Latin works – *Forcianae quaestiones* (Naples-Lyon 1535) and 'Disquisitiones in selectiora divinae scripturae loca' (Trent, Biblioteca Communale, MS 1002) – are confirmed by a letter of May 1543 to the Swiss reformer Joachim *Vadianus, in which he speaks of religious persecution and claims to have translated works of *Luther into Italian. Yet Lando, who from 1534 to 1545 seems to have lived a wandering life, as much outside as inside Italy, from 1545 settled on Venetian territory, establishing or renewing links with characteristic figures of the Venetian literary scene such as Pietro Aretino, Ludovico Domenichi, and Girolamo Muzio. He apparently remained unmolested for nearly a decade until he was again in trouble with religious authority, as testified by a letter to Cardinal Cristoforo Madruzzo, prince-bishop of Trent, dating from not before June 1553, which is also the last documentary evidence of his life.

The series of Lando's published Italian works begins with the *Paradossi* (Lyon: J. Pullon 1543), his best and most successful work; a partial French translation by Charles Estienne went through more editions that the Italian original. They continue with the first Italian translation of Thomas *More's *Utopia* (Venice: n pr 1548), with a travel work, *Commentario delle cose d'Italia* (n p, n pr 1548), a remote ancestor of Montesquieu's *Lettres persanes*, and with several works of compilation whose flexible structure allowed scope for his great erudition and paradoxical sense of humour. His Protestant affinities never weakened; indeed, according to one interpreter they became ever more markedly radical during the 1540s. They became explicit early in the 1550s in the *Vita del beato Ermodoro* (Venice: A. Arrivabene 1550) and the *Dialogo della Sacra Scrittura* (Venice: A. Arrivabene 1552). The name of 'Hortensius Tranquillus' appears in the Milanese and Venetian Indices of 1554, and the more accurate designation of 'Hortensius Tranquillus, alias Heremias, alias Landus' in the Roman Index of 1559.

BIBLIOGRAPHY: Ireneo Sanesi *Il cinquecentista Ortensio Lando* (Pistoia 1893) / Conor Fahy 'Per la vita di Ortensio Lando' *Giornale storico della letteratura italiana* 142 (1965) 243–58 / Paul F. Grendler *Critics of the Italian World 1530–1560: Anton Francesco Doni, Nicolò Franco, and Ortensio Lando* (Madison 1969) / Conor Fahy 'The two "Neapolitan" editions of Ortensio Lando's *Forcianae Quaestiones*' in *Collected Essays on Italian Language and Literature presented to Kathleen Speight* ed G. Aquilecchia, S.N. Cristes, and S. Ralphs (Manchester 1971) 124–42 / Silvana Seidel Menchi 'Sulla fortuna di Erasmo in Italia: Ortensio Lando e altri eterodossi della prima metà del Cinquecento' *Revue suisse d'histoire* 24 (1974) 537–634 / Silvana Seidel Menchi 'Spiritualismo radicale nelle opere di Ortensio Lando attorno al 1550' ARG 65 (1974) 210–76 / Myron P. Gilmore 'Anti-Erasmianism in Italy: the dialogue of Ortensio Lando on Erasmus' funeral' *The Journal of Medieval and Renaissance Studies* 4 (1974) 1–14 / Conor Fahy 'The composition of Ortensio Lando's dialogue *Cicero relegatus et Cicero revocatus*' *Italian Studies* 30 (1975) 30–41 / Conor Fahy 'Landiana: I. Ortensio Lando and the dialogue *Desiderii Erasmi funus* (1540)'; 'Landiana II. Lando's letter to Vadianus (1543)' *Italia medioevale e umanistica* 19 (1976) 325–87 / Ugo Rozzo 'Incontri di Giulio da Milano: Ortensio Lando' *Bollettino della società di studi valdesi* 140 (1976) 77–108 / Conor Fahy 'Il

dialogo *Desiderii Erasmi funus* di Ortensio Lando' *Studi e problemi di critica testuale* 14 (1977) 42–60 / Silvana Seidel Menchi 'Un inedito di Ortensio Lando: il *Dialogo contra gli huomini letterati*' *Revue suisse d'histoire* 27 (1977) 509–27 / Paolo Cherchi 'La fonte dei *Cathaloghi* di Ortensio Lando' *Studi e problemi di critica testuale* 18 (1979) 135–48   CONOR FAHY

Johann LANG of Erfurt, d 2 April 1548
Johann Lang (Lange, Langius), the son of a burgher family, was born in Erfurt around 1486. He matriculated at the university in the winter of 1500, paying only one half of his fees. In the spring of 1503 he graduated BA. During this time he may have come into contact with the circle of Nikolaus Marschalk, especially with the brothers Heinrich and Peter Eberbach, and he was already studying Greek. In 1505 or 1506, however, he entered the house of the Austin friars in Erfurt, probably shortly after *Luther, and in 1508 he was a priest. In a certificate of indulgence (18 April 1508) he is listed along with Luther, who was already a lecturer. At the end of August of 1511 he was transferred to Wittenberg, where he matriculated at the university and on 10 February 1512 graduated MA. He succeeded Luther as a lecturer on the *Nicomachean Ethics*, a course which he taught four times. At the same time he gave lectures in Greek and also became assistant regent of the study house of the Augustinians. *Eobanus Hessus wrote to him from Frankfurt an der Oder and visited him during his journey to Leipzig in 1513. In 1515 he went with Luther to the chapter of his order at Gotha, where Luther was preaching. On 20 November 1515 in Wittenberg he received his first theological degree of *baccalarius biblicus*. In this capacity he lectured on *Ecclesiastes* and *Titus*; perhaps he had previously begun his commentary on *Romans*. As early as 1514 he published in Wittenberg the *Enchiridion Sexti philosophi Pythagorici* and in 1515 two letters of St Jerome.

In February of 1516 his transfer to Erfurt was announced, but for the time being he continued his lectures on *Titus* in Wittenberg. At the end of May Luther installed him as prior of the Erfurt monastery. At that time he became *baccalarius sententiarius* at the University of Erfurt and began lecturing on the first book of

Peter Lombard's *Sentences*, progressing to the second book in the winter semester of 1516. He maintained close contact with the circle of *Mutianus and Eobanus, while Luther relied on him for advice and information. More than forty of Luther's letters to Lang are extant from the time between the end of May 1516 and September 1522. In August 1517 Lang was promoted licentiate of theology. In April of 1518 he participated in the debate at Heidelberg, and his order appointed him supervisor of a Saxon district in succession to Luther. In September 1518 he wrote to Erasmus, who did not save his letter but replied (Ep 872) with uncharacteristically bitter criticism of the papacy. Erasmus' letter was taken to Erfurt by Eobanus together with some others, but unlike most of the others it was not published in Eobanus' *Hodoeporicon*.

On 14 February 1519 Lang obtained his doctorate in theology. He encountered some opposition from the faculty but was accepted on the intercession of Bartholomaeus Arnoldi of *Usingen. Petrus *Mosellanus and his student Peter of Suaven came from Leipzig to attend Lang's graduation ceremony. Lang was appointed to an academic committee whose task it was to reform the university. He was present at the disputation between *Karlstadt, Luther, and *Eck that took place in Leipzig from 24 June to 15 July 1519 and immediately published the record of proceedings (Erfurt 1519, M. von Hase 388–90a). In the winter semester of 1519 he was requested by the philosophical faculty to take charge of the newly introduced course in Greek.

On 28 August 1520 *Staupitz resigned his office as vicar-general of the Augustinians, and Lang followed his example, resigning as vicar of his district. In 1521 he published in Erfurt his German version of the gospel of St Matthew, which he had translated from the Greek (M. von Hase 102–3). In a letter to the rector, Martin von der Marthen, published by Eobanus (M. von Hase 428) he defended himself against accusations that as an advocate of religious reform he had shown himself hostile to academic learning. He did not actively participate in the 'Pfaffensturm' riots of 1521. At the beginning of 1522 he left his order and in the summer of 1524 married a mature widow.

Thomas Müntzer opposed him, and his relationship with Eobanus Hessus also became strained as a result of his criticism that Eobanus encouraged the university to favour humanistic studies at the expense of all other subjects. During the peasant revolt of 1525, when all Erfurt's churches were taken over by the Lutherans, Lang became the minister and preacher at St Mary's, after Johann Eberlin of Günsburg had rejected the position. After the death of his first wife in 1524, Lang remarried in 1528 (Luther w *Briefwechsel* III Ep 1257). When St Mary's was returned to the Catholics, he became a preacher at the former Dominican church. If anyone can claim to be the reformer of Erfurt, it is Lang, and he was recognized as such by Luther and his friends at Wittenberg. In 1533 he carried out the visitation in the county of Schwarzburg; in 1537 he signed the articles of Schmalkalden. He died in Erfurt and was buried at St Michael's.

BIBLIOGRAPHY: For a list of Lang's works see E. Kleineidam *Universitas Studii Erffordensis* (Leipzig 1964–80) II 307–8 / Lang's commentary on Titus was published by R. Weijenborg in *Scientia Augustiniana: Festschrift für Adolar Zumkeller* (Würzburg 1975) 433–68 / Weijenborg also published his lectures on Romans: *Antonianum* 52 (1976) 394–494 / Allen and CWE Ep 872 / ADB XVII 635–6 / RGG IV 225 / M. Burgdorf *Johann Lange, der Reformator Erfurts* (Rostock 1911) / NDB XIII 540–1 / M.P. Bertram 'Doktor Johann Lang, Erfurts Kirchenreformator' *Erfurter Lutherbuch* (1917) 125–76 / L.F. Brossmann 'Die Matthäusübersetzung des Johann Lang im Jahre 1521' (unpublished thesis, Heidelberg 1955) / O. Clemen 'Aus dem Lebenskreis des Erfurter Reformators Johannes Lang: Die Gothaer Briefsammlung A 399' ARG 38 (1941) 34–54, 39 (1942) 151–69 / R.W. Scribner 'The Erasmians and the beginning of the Reformation in Erfurt' *Journal of Religious History* 9 (1976–7) 3–31 / J. Beumer 'Der Briefwechsel zwischen Erasmus und Johann Lang' in *Scrinium Erasmianum* II 315–23 / P.G. Bietenholz 'Erasmus and the German public, 1518–1520: the authorized and unauthorized circulation of his correspondence' *The Sixteenth Century Journal* 8 Supplement (1977) 61–78 / *Matrikel Erfurt* II 218 / *Matrikel Wittenberg* I 38 / Martin von Hase 'Bibliographie der Erfurter

Drucke von 1501–1550' *Archiv für Geschichte des Buchwesens* 8 (1967) 655–1096

ERICH KLEINEIDAM

Matthäus LANG of Augsburg, 1468–30 March 1540
Lang, the son of a burgher of Augsburg, studied in Ingolstadt, Vienna, and Tübingen. After receiving his MA at Tübingen in 1490, he entered the chancery of the Emperor *Frederick III. He may have planned to teach at a university and secured from *Maximilian I an unusual grant of *licentia docendi* on 18 December 1494, but he continued his political career and soon became one of the closest advisers of Maximilian I. He began to receive benefices and distinctions; in 1500 he was provost of Augsburg and in 1505 bishop of Gurk; in 1508 he was raised to the nobility (von Wellenburg); in 1511 he was a cardinal (public announcement on 19 November 1512), in 1515 coadjutor to the archbishop of Salzburg, and in 1519 archbishop of Salzburg. He was tough, ambitious, often unpopular, and loved displays of power and pomp. He was accompanied by a great train of followers when he came to Aachen to attend the coronation of *Charles V in 1520. Although he had at first retained his central position in the government of the Austrian states, his influence upon Charles and *Ferdinand I soon began to decline, and from 1521 he was chiefly concerned with the administration of his ecclesiastical principality of Salzburg. He was a stern opponent of the Lutheran reform and adhered to the Regensburg convention of 1524– designed to stop the further spread of Lutheranism – to the point of causing him difficulties with the Bavarian and Austrian governments. Lang's strictness gave rise to dissatisfaction among his subjects, but he was able to suppress a revolt of the citizens of Salzburg in 1523 as well as the peasant rebellion of 1525–6. Lang was active in politics up to 1538, when illness forced him to retire; he died in Salzburg.

In 1517 Erasmus seized the opportunity of sending humble greetings to Lang, who was at that time considered a patron of scholars (Ep 549). He continued to keep an eye on the cardinal's moves (Epp 584, 1166), and after the coronation of Charles V he was introduced to

Matthäus Lang, by Albrecht Dürer

Lang at Cologne thanks to the efforts of Rudbert von *Mosham, who was then in Lang's service; however, the interview went so badly that he preferred to forget it (Epp 1450, 1512). In later years Erasmus and his friends briefly mentioned Lang's difficulties during the peasant revolt (Epp 1603, 1606) as well as his important role in the restoration of an independent state of Württemberg (Epp 2947, 2993).

BIBLIOGRAPHY: Allen and CWE Ep 549 / L.H. Ulmann in ADB XX 610–13 / LThK VI 783 / Pastor VI 344–7, 425–6, VII 668–71 and passim / Eubel III 13 and passim / *Matrikel Wien* II-2 229 / *Matrikel Tübingen* I 73 / Hermann Wiesflecker *Kaiser Maximilian I.* (Munich 1971–   ) I 377 and passim   IG

Jean LANGE documented in Paris and Meaux, 1522–4
Jean Lange (Johannes Angelus), a native of Argonne, studied under *Lefèvre d'Etaples at the Collège du Cardinal Lemoine at Paris, and in 1522 he was teaching Greek there. That year he published an edition of Horapollo's *Hiero-*

glyphica (Paris: P. Vidoue). The dedication was to Jean de Mauléon, bishop of Comminges, in Gascony, whose patronage he was anxious to secure. At the beginning of 1524 he joined the entourage of Guillaume *Briçonnet, bishop of Meaux. On 1 January 1524 he wrote two letters addressed to Basel, one to Guillaume *Farel, formerly a colleague at Cardinal Lemoine, and the other to Erasmus. In the first (Herminjard I Ep 83) he urged Farel to carry on the struggle for the Gospel; in the second (Ep 1407) he took note of the esteem felt for Erasmus by the humanists of France and regretted Erasmus' quarrel with Lefèvre d'Etaples. According to Lange this remarkable letter was written at the suggestion of a nephew of François *Du Moulin de Rochefort. Lange subsequently became principal of the college of Troyes.

BIBLIOGRAPHY: Allen Ep 1407 / Herminjard I Ep 83 / Rice *Prefatory Epistles* Ep 133

HENRY HELLER

Johann LANGE of Karvinà, 16 April 1503–25 September 1567
Johann Lange (Langus) of Karvinà in Czechoslovakia (formerly Freistadt in Silesia) was the son of a clothmaker. After attending school at Nysa (Neisse), he obtained a BA at the University of Cracow and subsequently matriculated at Vienna in the summer term of 1523, studying Greek and jurisprudence. For a short time he taught the boys of the royal chapel at the court of Buda, but after the death of King *Louis II at the battle of Mohács (29 August 1526) he returned to Silesia and directed schools at Złotoryja (Goldberg; 1527–8) and subsequently Nysa. In 1532 he was appointed clerk to the town of Świdnica (Schweidnitz) and in 1535 secretary to Jakob von *Salza, bishop of Wrocław. Salza's successor, Bishop Balthasar von Promnitz, chose Lange as his chancellor in 1539. In 1543 he was attached to the household of Queen Elizabeth, the wife of *Sigismund II Augustus of Poland and the daughter of King *Ferdinand. Subsequently he served frequently as Ferdinand's ambassador to the Polish court. He was named one of Ferdinand's councillors and received other rewards on account of his scholarly work. In 1557 he retired to Świdnica, where he resided to his death. There is an *Epicedion in funere Ioannis Langi* (Görlitz 1568) by Daniel Scepsius.

Lange left a collection of Latin poetry and, especially in collaboration with the Wrocław printer Andreas Winkler, edited and translated a variety of texts, among them Greek Fathers and Byzantine authors. Of particular importance was his translation of the fourteenth-century *Historia ecclesiastica* by Nicephorus Callistus (Basel: J. Oporinus and J. Herwagen 1555 with protective privileges by kings Ferdinand and *Henry II of France). A list of his publications is found in C.G. Jöcher *Allgemeines Gelehrtenlexicon* Fortsetzung and Ergänzungen III (Delmenhorst 1810, repr 1961) 1214–15.

In December 1527 Erasmus sent his regards to Lange in response to greetings forwarded by either Jan *Antonin or Jan (II) *Łaski (Ep 1916).

BIBLIOGRAPHY: Allen Ep 1916 / Henryk Barycz in PSB XVI 478–81 / ADB XVII 638–9 / *Matrikel Wien* III-1 34 / Schottenloher I 429, V 148

MICHAEL ERBE

Johann LANGE, LANGIUS *See also Johann* LANG, *Jan de* LANGHE

Rudolf von LANGEN of Everswinkel, c 1438–25 December 1519
Rudolf von Langen (Langius), born in Everswinkel, near Münster, received his first instruction from his uncle, Hermann von Langen, a canon in Münster. Between 1456 and 1460 he studied at Erfurt, obtaining a BA and a MA. After spending some time at the court of Duke John I of Cleves, in 1462 he was appointed provost of the Münster cathedral chapter, where he had held a canonry from an early age. In 1466 he was sent to Rome on a diplomatic mission. He stayed in Italy for four years, returning with an extensive personal library. Together with such friends as Wessel *Gansfort, Alexander *Hegius, and Rodolphus *Agricola, he helped establish a centre for the new humanistic studies in the abbey of Aduard, near Groningen. From there he exchanged letters with Antonius Liber in 1469. The remainder of his life was spent mostly at Münster. Reports of a second journey to Italy, in 1486, this time in the company of Hermannus *Buschius, should be dismissed, according to Klemens Löffler.

Like Hegius and Liber, Langen took great interest in the improvement of education. By

1500 he was able to introduce a curriculum of humanistic studies in the school of the Münster chapter. In the same year he secured the appointment of Johannes *Murmellius as a teacher, while Hegius declined to move to Münster. Langen's school was the first in Germany to introduce instruction in Greek (1512) and Hebrew (1517).

Erasmus praised Langen repeatedly as one of the leading scholars of his native region (Epp 1237, 2073) and may have referred to Langen in Ep 23; the text, which is known only from its first publication in 1607, appears to be garbled. In 1498 he wrote to Langen, hoping to initiate a correspondence through the good services of Christian *Northoff (Epp 70, 72), but no letters are known today and no more is heard about the matter.

BIBLIOGRAPHY: Allen Ep 70 / Otto Herding in NDB XIII 578–80 / ADB XVII 659–60 / *Epistolae Rodolphi Langii* ed H.W. Crecelius (Elberfeld 1876) / Hermann Hamelmann *Geschichtliche Werke* ed H. Detmer et al (Münster 1902–13) I-4: the *Oratio* on Langen, ed Klemens Löffler / Klemans Löffler 'Zur Biographie R. von Langens' *Westfälische Zeitschrift* 69 (1911) 1ff / Klemens Löffler in *Westfälische Lebensbilder* ed Alois Boemer et al (Münster 1930–) II 344–57 / Hermann Rothert *Westfälische Geschichte* (Gütersloh 1949) I 487 / A. Hartlieb von Wallthor 'Höhere Schulen in Westfalen vom Ende des 15. bis zur Mitte des 19. Jahrhunderts' *Westfälische Zeitschrift* 107 (1957) 1–106, esp 18–19 / Georg Ellinger *Geschichte der neulateinischen Literatur Deutschlands* (Berlin 1929–33) I 420 / Albert Hyma *The Christian Renaissance* 2nd ed (Hamden, Conn, 1965) 202–3 and passim

ROBERT STUPPERICH & IG

Johann LANGENFELD *See Johannes LONGICAMPIANUS*

Jan de LANGHE d late October 1571
Jan de Langhe (Lange, Langius) was a secretary to Archbishop Jean (II) de *Carondelet in 1524 when he rendered a service to the faculty of arts of Louvain. In the spring of 1533 he still held a position of special trust as Carondelet's secretary and in this capacity negotiated with Nicolaus *Olahus and Nicolaus *Grudius about Erasmus' return to the Netherlands (Ep

2784). In fulfilment of a pledge he had received on 19 November 1532, he was appointed one of the secretaries of the privy council at the court of Brussels on 14 September 1538. He was lord of Beaulieu and was married to Antoinette de la Sale (d 30 September 1536); their son, Carolus Langius, became a renowned classical scholar at Louvain.

Jan de Langhe was a good friend of *Viglius Zuichemus and of the scholar Andreas Masius; he was also acquainted with Cornelis de *Schepper.

BIBLIOGRAPHY: Allen Ep 2785 / de Vocht CTL I 15, IV 180 / de Vocht *Literae ad Craneveldium* 702 / de Vocht *Dantiscus* 175, 388, 402 / Michel Baelde *De collaterale raden onder Karel v en Filips II* (Brussels 1965) 274–5 and passim   IG

Thomas LARKE d July 1530
Larke (Lark, Laracus, Larchus) was perhaps the son of Peter Larke, a Thetford innkeeper. He was a doctor of civil law, probably of Cambridge, where he was at the King's Hall 1508–9 and master of Trinity Hall 1517–25. His career prospered when his sister became mistress to Thomas *Wolsey at about the time of the latter's rise to power. Larke himself was the cardinal's chaplain and (by 1527) confessor as well as (by 1511) chaplain to King *Henry VIII. He was dean of Bridgnorth 1508–15, canon of St Stephen's, Westminster, 1511–30, canon of Lincoln 1514–17, archdeacon of Sudbury 1517–22, canon of Salisbury 1517–18, dean of Chichester 1517–18, and archdeacon of Norwich 1522–8. Among various parishes which he held was Winwick, Lancashire; this he resigned to his nephew Thomas *Winter in 1525. He accompanied the cardinal north at his fall, and died at Southwell.

From 1517 to 1521 Larke had been an agent of the king in funding the construction of Bridewell Palace; but it is in Wolsey's household that there is most record of his activities. By 1516 he was said by Andrea *Ammonio (also a canon of St Stephen's, Westminster) to have more influence than anyone with his master (Ep 429). He was mentioned in, and the recipient of, diplomatic correspondence, and it was to him that Dr John London reported on the progress of Cardinal College in 1526. In 1527 he received a pension of one hundred crowns from the French king – he and perhaps his father were the only recipients of such pensions outside the royal household and the great officers of state (Thomas *More, then chancellor of the duchy of Lancaster, had only fifty crowns). He was also in the pay of Thomas, Lord Darcy. Among his correspondents and avowed friends were Ammonio, John Tayler, and Abbot Kyrtin of Peterborough. Silvestro *Gigli remarked in 1516 on the widespread respect for his modesty and virtue. In 1513 Erasmus described him as the most courteous and truest friend of his English acquaintance (Ep 283) and in 1516 he was going to write to him (Ep 455), but no such letter is extant. In his will dated 20 April 1529 and proved 15 January 1533 he requested burial in the church of the London Blackfriars and left the residue of his estate to his kinsman Peter.

BIBLIOGRAPHY: Allen and CWE Ep 283 / Emden BRUC 353 (where Larke is not identified as the *magister* who incepted in civil law in 1478: such identification would make Larke nearly eighty at his death, but cf John Venn *Alumni Cantabrigienses*, Cambridge 1922–54) / A.F. Pollard *Wolsey* (London 1929) 306–7 / J. Le Neve *Fasti Ecclesiae Anglicanae 1300–1541* ed H.P.F. King, B. Jones, and J.M. Horn (London 1962–7) I 128, III 66, IV 28, 32, VII 5, XII 43 / LP I 1977, II 397, 2637, 4068, pp 1468, 1471, 1474, 1475, Ap 30, III 955, 1030(?), 1083, 1916, 1283*, 2483, pp 1535, 1537, 1544, IV 1083 (p 475), 1233, 1265, 1938, 2001, 2527, 2734, 3619, 4056, 5970, 6524, Ap 61, V 15 / Larke's will is in London, Public Record Office, PROB 11/25, f 47 (PCC 9 Hogen)   C.S. KNIGHTON

Gérard de LA ROCHE *See Gérard de PLAINE*

Constantinus LASCARIS of Constantinople, 1434–1501
Constantinus Lascaris was born at Constantinople to a family of importance in the military and administrative affairs of the Byzantine empire. Between 1444 and 1453 he studied under Johannes *Argyropoulos, who had returned to Constantinople after his first sojourn in Italy. Taken prisoner on the fall of the city to the Turks, Lascaris managed to win his freedom, perhaps on payment of a ransom, and migrated to Italy via Rhodes, Pherae (Velestinon), and possibly Crete and Corfu. In 1460 he was in Milan, where he taught Greek

publicly and was private tutor to Ippolita, the daughter of Duke Francesco I Sforza. In 1465, when Ippolita married *Alfonso II of Aragon, duke of Calabria, Lascaris accompanied her to Naples and was appointed to teach rhetoric by King Ferdinand I. He left Naples in June 1466, probably stopping in Rome to enjoy the patronage of Cardinal *Bessarion. His stay at Rome could only have lasted several months, for by the end of 1466, after considering a return to Greece, he accepted an invitation to go to Messina.

In December 1467 Cardinal Bessarion nominated Lascaris to teach at the Greek school of the Basilian monastery of San Salvatore of Messina, and he began his official duties some time after 4 February 1468 with an annual salary of eighty ducats. He remained at Messina for the rest of his life, making only brief trips to Naples in 1477 and 1478 and in 1481 and refusing an invitation to teach at Milan in 1488. His teaching attracted scholars from all over Italy, including Pietro *Bembo, Angelo Gabrielli, Umberto Bolzano, Bernardo Ricco, and Matteo Caldo. His will was dated 15 August 1501, and he was buried in the Carmelite church of Messina.

In addition to copying numerous manuscripts Lascaris composed a popular Greek grammar, first published by Demetrius Damilas at Milan in 1476 and, according to Geanakoplos, the first dated book to be printed entirely in Greek in Europe. The grammar was reprinted frequently, with a Latin translation by Giovanni Crastoni added to the Venetian edition of Aldo *Manuzio of 1494. In 1501 Erasmus tried in vain to obtain a copy of the grammar for Jacob de *Voecht (Ep 159).

BIBLIOGRAPHY: Allen Ep 159 / A. de Rosalia 'La vita di Constantino Lascaris' *Archivio storico siciliano* ser 3-3 (1957–8) 21–70 / Deno John Geanakoplos *Greek Scholars in Venice* (Cambridge, Mass, 1962) 57 and passim   TBD

Janus LASCARIS of Constantinople, 1445–7 December 1534
Janus (Johannes) Lascaris ('Ιάνος Λάσκαρις) was born in Constantinople; his family, a branch of the imperial house, came from Rhyndacus, in Asia Minor. Lascaris came through Crete to Italy soon after the fall of Constantinople. He studied with Demet-

rius *Chalcondyles at Padua and eventually
joined the entourage of Lorenzo (I) de'
*Medici, on whose behalf he made two visits
to the former Byzantine Empire in search of
manuscripts. His travels took him through
North Italy, Corfu, and Thessalonica, and to
Mount Athos and Constantinople. He bought
or arranged to have copied a very large number
of codices for the Medici library. From 1492 to
1495 he served as professor of philosophy and
poetry in the Florentine Studio. At the same
time he published with the Florentine firm
of Alopa the first editions of the Greek
Anthology, the *Hymns* of Callimachus, and
four tragedies of Euripides. His activity as a
teacher and editor did a great deal for the
diffusion of Greek texts in the West – in
particular, he did much to create the immense
vogue for Latin translations and adaptations of
the epigrams from the Greek Anthology.

When the French invaded Italy in 1494,
Lascaris transferred his allegiance to *Charles
VIII, whom he probably saw as the potential
leader of a crusade to free Byzantium from
Turkish rule. He quietly removed the dedicatory letter to Piero de' Medici from most copies
of his edition of the Greek Anthology and
followed the French home. In France he won
the friendship of Charles' successor, *Louis
XII, and entered the royal service. In 1503
Lascaris returned to Italy, on a mission to
Venice; the next year he became the French
ambassador there. He retained that post until
1509, enjoying close relationships with Aldo
*Manuzio and the Greek and Italian scholars in
his circle. From 1513 he directed the Roman
college for Greek studies that was founded by
the Medici pope, *Leo X. He wrote the statutes
for the college and supervised its editions of
unpublished Greek texts, notably the old
scholia on Homer and Sophocles. In 1518 he
left the papal service to found a similar
institution under French auspices in Milan. He
recruited Greek students for this college in
Venice in 1520 and supported them with his
own resources until it became clear that
*Francis I would not honour his promises to
support the college himself. Back in Rome
again, he undertook a mission to *Charles V
after the battle of Pavia, urging him on behalf of
the pope to show clemency to Francis I and to
lead a crusade against the Turks. The mission

Janus Lascaris

failed, though the impressive speech that
Lascaris delivered won wide diffusion. He
went to Paris in 1526 (Ep 1733), but after an
unsuccessful attempt to persuade Francis I to
found royal lectureships in 1527, he returned
to Rome, where he died.

As a scholar, Lascaris was both gifted and
prolific. His most original piece of sustained
writing seems to have been the preface to his
edition of the Greek Anthology, in which he
sketched a brilliant outline history of the Greek
alphabet. But his main work was as a disseminator of the Greek language and literature. He
taught Greek to such men as Guillaume *Budé
and Germain de *Brie (Epp 569, 583, 2727). He
edited many texts and provided the Latin base
texts from which Claude Seyssel translated
Appian, Xenophon, and Diodorus Siculus into
French. At the same time, he freely lent the
many manuscripts that he imported from the
East to other scholars, and he tried to ease the
way of younger exiles from Byzantine lands
who wished to make careers as teachers of
Greek in the West.

Lascaris and Erasmus met in 1508, when
Erasmus was overseeing the famous Aldine

edition of the *Adagia*. Lascaris, along with others, lent Erasmus unpublished sources for the work (*Adagia* II i 1). Erasmus in turn developed great admiration for Lascaris as one of the few exiles with real skill in Latin (Ep 1347). Indeed, in his *Apologia adversus rhapsodias Alberti Pii* (1531), Erasmus recalled that Lascaris had invited him to his own house and table if he wished to leave the noise and activity of Aldus' shop for the rest of his stay in Venice (LB IX 1137C). After Erasmus returned north, the two men remained on terms of respect. On 26 April 1518 Erasmus wrote to Lascaris (Ep 836), asking him to recommend a native Greek for the chair of Greek at the Collegium Trilingue of Louvain, and describing the terms of the appointment with so much enthusiasm that it seems likely that he hoped to attract Lascaris himself. If so, he failed, but he nonetheless retained a consistent interest in Lascaris' doings, sending him greetings through Germain de Brie (Ep 1736) and Budé (Ep 1794). Thomas *More believed – how correctly it is hard to say – that Lascaris was one of those who tried to persuade Brie not to publish his *Antimorus* (Epp 1087, 1096).

An unfortunate incident made his relationship change for the worse during the two men's last years. In the *Ciceronianus* Erasmus compared Lascaris' great friend and pupil Budé with the printer Josse *Bade in a manner that upset Budé's friends (ASD I-2 672–3). Lascaris replied with a 'sharp epigram' against Erasmus, as Gervasius *Wain hastened to report (Ep 2027). Erasmus, who had referred admiringly to Lascaris himself in the *Ciceronianus* (ASD I-2 664–5), complained bitterly about Lascaris' criticism in several letters (Epp 2038, 2040, 2105, 2291).

It is hard to measure the contribution Lascaris made to Erasmus' work. He was fond of quoting proverbs, according to Germain de Brie (Ep 2727); it is possible, then, that he supplied Erasmus with Greek proverbial matter from Byzantine paroemiographi. A 'Ianus' is mentioned by Sir Thomas Smith as arguing that the modern pronunciation of Greek should be reformed (*De recta et emendata linguae graecae pronuntiatione*, Paris: R. Estienne 1568, f 6 verso). If this Janus could be identified with Lascaris, then one might argue that Erasmus had derived some of his own views on the pronunciation of Greek from Lascaris in Venice. But as Knös and others have shown, serious chronological difficulties make this interpretation implausible.

BIBLIOGRAPHY: Allen Ep 269 / Emile Legrand *Bibliographie hellénique des xve et xvie siècles* new ed (Paris 1962) I cxxxi–clxii / Silvio Mercati in EI xx 556–7 / Cosenza III 1935–40 / Börje Knös *Un ambassadeur de l'hellénisme – Janus Lascaris – et la tradition gréco-byzantine dans l'humanisme français* (Uppsala 1945) / K.K. Müller 'Neue Mittheilungen über Janus Laskaris und die Mediceische Bibliothek' *Centralblatt für Bibliothekswesen* 1 (1884) 333–412 / Pierre de Nolhac 'Inventaire des manuscrits grecs de Jean Lascaris' *Mélanges d'archéologie et d'histoire* 6 (1886) 251–74 / Pierre de Nolhac *La Bibliothèque de Fulvio Orsini* (Paris 1887) / Pierre de Nolhac *Les Correspondants d'Alde Manuce* (Rome 1888) / Léon Dorez 'Un document nouveau sur la bibliothèque de Jean Lascaris' *Revue des bibliothèques* 2 (1892) 280–1 / Léon Dorez '"Joannes" Lascaris frère de "Janus" Lascaris' *Revue des bibliothèques* 5 (1895) 325–9 / Abel Lefranc *Histoire du Collège de France* (Paris 1893) / Karl Müllner 'Eine Rede des Joannes Laskaris' *Wiener Studien* 21 (1899) 128–43 / G. Mercati 'Quando morì G. Lascaris?' *Rheinisches Museum für Philologie* n s 65 (1910) 318 / G. Mercati 'Cenni di A. del Monte e G. Lascaris sulle perdite della Biblioteca Vaticana nel sacco del 1527' in *Opere minori* (Vatican City 1937–41) III 130–53 / L. Delaruelle 'La carrière de Janus Lascaris depuis 1494' *Revue du seizième siècle* 13 (1926) 95–111 / L. Delaruelle 'Notes complémentaires sur deux humanistes' *Revue du seizième siècle* 15 (1928) 311–23 / James Hutton *The Greek Anthology in Italy to the Year 1800* (Ithaca 1935) / James Hutton *The Greek Anthology in France and in the Latin Writers of the Netherlands to the Year 1800* (Ithaca 1946) / Vittorio Fanelli 'Il ginnasio greco di Leone x a Roma' *Studi romani* 9 (1961) 379–93 / E. Casamassima 'Per una storia delle dottrine paleografiche dall'umanesimo a Jean Mabillon, I' *Studi medievali* 3rd series 5 (1964) 525–78 / Armando Verde *Lo Studio fiorentino, 1473–1503: Ricerche e documenti* (Florence 1973–)   ANTHONY GRAFTON

Hieronim ŁASKI 27 November 1496–22 December 1541
Hieronim Łaski (a Lasco, Lascanus) was the

son of Jarosław, *voivode* of Sieradz, and the
elder brother of Jan (II) and Stanisław *Łaski.
He was born at the family estate of Łask, near
the town of Sieradz in Greater Poland. He was
brought up at the court of his uncle Jan (I)
*Łaski, archbishop of Gniezno, and it was
thanks to the latter that he was educated
abroad. He attached himself to the retinue of
his uncle when the archbishop attended the
fifth Lateran council at Rome in 1513. From
1514 to 1516 he studied at Bologna and the
following year he began, in the traditional
fashion of chivalry combined with pilgrimage,
a grand tour of France, England, Portugal
(where he probably fought the Muslims while
serving in the Portuguese army), and finally
the Holy Land. In the spring of 1519 he
returned to Poland and the same year married
Anna Kurozwecka of Rytwiany, who brought
him a huge dowry. When added to his own
family estates this represented a considerable
fortune.

Hieronim now began his career at the court
of King *Sigismund I. In 1522 he became *voivode*
of Inowrocław and in 1523 of Sieradz. In 1520
he was sent on an embassy to *Francis I of
France and also attended the coronation of
*Charles V at Aachen. It was in Brussels that he
met Erasmus of Rotterdam for the first time (Ep
1242), and perhaps they met again at Cologne.
By the end of 1521 Hieronim was back in
Poland and in the spring of 1523 was sent as a
delegate to Rome. The 'splendid embassy' of
Hieronim in 1524 at the French court coincides
with the peak of his diplomatic career. On the
way he and his brothers, Jan and Stanisław,
visited Erasmus, reaching Basel by the beginning of May. By agreement with his uncle his
aim was to test Erasmus' attitude towards
*Luther. He gave him copies of an edict of King
Sigismund I against Luther as well as the
anti-Lutheran writings of Bishop Andrzej
*Krzycki. In the course of an amusing incident
Erasmus and his guest finally discovered that
they stood on common ground with regard to
Luther. Erasmus gave Łaski copies of several
statements by Luther which showed him to be
critical of Erasmus and were suitable for
showing around at the Polish court. When he
left, Hieronim offered Erasmus a silver cup
(Allen I 31–2, Epp 1452, 1482, 1496, 1501).

Six months later Erasmus dedicated to

Hieronim his *Modus orandi Deum* (Ep 1502; LB V
1099–132), and he still recalled his visit after
several years (Ep 1805). The good relations
with the Łaski family became even closer
thanks to a prolonged stay by Hieronim's
younger brother Jan with Erasmus at Basel in
1525. In a letter to Hieronim (Ep 1622) Erasmus
praised Jan and lamented his recall from Basel.
In 1527 Erasmus sent Hieronim a copy of his
latest work, the *Christiani matrimonii institutio*
(Ep 1751).

Erasmus recalled Hieronim Łaski frequently
in his letters to other Poles, especially, of
course, to Hieronim's brother Jan. Their
reports enabled Erasmus to keep track of
Hieronim's adventures in the Balkans (Epp
1954, 2606, 2746, 2862, 3014); in return he
expressed a well-founded concern for Łaski's
safety (Epp 1915, 1916, 2033, 3049). Poland
officially remained neutral in the Hungarian
civil war that erupted in 1526, but Hieronim
Łaski committed himself to *John Zápolyai
and, backed by letters from Zápolyai, func-
tioned as his chief envoy, leaving on 26
April 1527 on a mission to France, England,
and Denmark, seeking to obtain support
against the Hapsburgs. Having achieved
nothing, he decided to approach the Turks
and undertook the first of his seven missions to Constantinople and other areas under
the sultan's jurisdiction. The negotiations,
conducted by Hieronim with great personal
courage, led in February 1528 to the conclusion of a treaty whereby the sultan bound
himself to bring aid to Zápolyai.

In 1529 *Suleiman I occupied Hungary and
put it under the control of Zápolyai. As his
reward Łaski received from Zápolyai the title
of *voivode* of Transylvania and occupied
one of the highest positions in Hungary
(1530). He also received large estates in Slovakia with the castle of Kiezmark, in which
he established his headquarters, ruling his
territories as a kind of private principality.
In October 1530 he participated as a representative of Zápolyai in a congress at Poznań,
where an attempt was made to stabilize the
situation in Hungary. Thereafter Hieronim
became convinced that he had been inade-
quately rewarded by Zápolyai and from
1531 he plotted secretly with the Hapsburg
commander while still officially in Zápol-

yai's service and conducting negotiations on his behalf. In 1532 he visited France and tried to organize an alliance of German princes against the Hapsburgs. He also conspired at Zápolyai's expense with Alvise *Gritti. But their coup aborted, and Zápolyai imprisoned Hieronim in the fortress of Buda (31 August 1534). Owing his life and liberty to the intervention of Jan Tarnowski, he was released in January 1535.

After long and humiliating bargaining, Hieronim agreed to serve with King *Ferdinand, who in 1536 named him a member of the council of the Kingdom of Hungary, then about 1540 *ban* of Croatia and Slovenia. He fought against Zápolyai's forces at Spisz. On 31 October 1540 he started out on his last mission to Constantinople, this time on behalf of Ferdinand. On 8 November 1540 he was imprisoned by the Turks and only survived through the intervention of the French. He had to accompany Sultan Suleiman as a prisoner throughout his expedition in Hungary in 1541. He was released in September 1541 on condition that he sever his connection with the Hapsburgs. In October 1541 he was at Linz to give an account of his mission. Seriously ill, he spent November at Kiezmark, and then was conveyed to Cracow, where he died. He was buried in the cathedral in the chapel of his wife's family. Before his death he allegedly revealed secret plans for a large-scale Turkish invasion of central Europe. His contemporaries liked to compare his adventures to those of Ulysses and Catiline.

BIBLIOGRAPHY: Allen Ep 1242 / PSB XVIII 225–9 (with a list of unpublished sources) / *Bibliografia polska* ed K. Estreicher et al (Cracow 1870–1951) 3rd part XXI 79 / O. Bartel *Jan Łaski* (Warsaw 1955) / I.A. Fesler *Geschichte von Ungarn* (Leipzig 1874) III / S. Katona *Historia critica regum Hungariae* (Buda 1793) IV-1 / J. Pajewski *Węgierska Polityka Polski w połowie XVI wieku* (Cracow 1932) / W. Pociecha *Królowa Bona 1494–1557* (Poznań 1949–58) / *Fontes rerum Transylvanicarum* ed A. Veress (Budapest 1914) IV / *Korespondencja Erazma z Rotterdamu z Polakami* ed and trans Maria Cytowska (Warsaw 1965) MARIA CYTOWSKA

Jan (I) ŁASKI March 1455–19 May 1531

Jan (Johannes a Lasco) was the son of Andrzej Łaski and the uncle of Hieronim, Jan (II), and Stanisław *Łaski; his coat of arms showed an arch ('Korab'). Jan was born on the family estate of Łask, near the city of Sieradz on the river Warta in Greater Poland. Without completing his formal education, he was apprenticed to a private lawyer, master Andrzej Góra. From 1479 to 1483 he was a secretary to the royal chancellor, Krzesław of Kurozweki. In 1484 he received a canonry at Poznań and in 1487 another at Gniezno; and in 1502 he was appointed secretary to King Alexander I. While holding the office of royal grand chancellor from 1503 to 1510, he played a considerable role in formulating the policies of the Polish crown. In 1510 he was appointed archbishop of Gniezno and primate of Poland and resigned the chancellorship, without, however, giving up his political influence.

A leading Polish statesman of his time, Łaski advocated a progressive program of internal reforms and close co-operation between the crown and the nobility in their efforts to control the magnates who placed themselves above the law. He possessed an expert knowledge of the law and was the first to publish a collection of Polish statutes, the *Commune incliti Poloniae regni privilegium* (Cracow: J. Haller 1506). He undertook a large number of diplomatic missions, going to Vienna in 1490 and to Flanders from 1496 to 1497; from 1500 to 1501 he performed a pilgrimage to Rome and Jerusalem. He strove to unify Prussia under the direct suzerainty of the Polish crown and advocated before the diet the removal of the Teutonic order from Polish territory and the re-unification of Western Pomerania with Poland. As a recognized expert in the question of the Teutonic order he presided over the congress of Poznań and, in 1511, conducted the peace negotiations at Torun. During the years 1513-15 he resided at Rome with orders to prevent any decisions in the matter of the Teutonic order that might be detrimental to the interests of Poland. He failed, however, in his personal efforts to secure a cardinalate and had to settle for the title of *legatus natus*, or permanent papal legate, for himself and his successors as primate of Poland. When he had left Poland for Rome he was accompanied by his nephews, Hieronim, Jan, and Stanisław, who had been brought up in his court and now proceeded to study abroad. The archbishop supported them financially and in years to come he would do all he could to promote their careers.

After 1515 Łaski's political influence was declining although he remained actively engaged in government affairs until 1525. He was an avowed opponent of Piotr *Tomicki's policy of co-operation with the Hapsburgs and staunchly resisted its implementation. In the Senate he also spoke out against the secularization of the Teutonic order, which he considered set a dangerous precedent. By 1524 his major preoccupation was the struggle against the reformers.

It was no doubt on the instruction of his uncle that Hieronim, when visiting Erasmus at Basel in 1524, endeavoured to probe Erasmus' true feelings with regard to *Luther. The archbishop's attitude towards Erasmus was reserved, and neither the friendship between the Dutch scholar and his nephew nor the compliments Erasmus was paying him in his correspondence (Epp 1593, 1805), nor indeed the dedication of Erasmus' edition of St Ambrose (1527), made him change his mind. He failed to send Erasmus a gift in return for the fine letter of dedication (Ep 1855), and a discreet reminder sent to Jan, the nephew (Ep 1915), merely produced excuses to the effect that his uncle was constantly preoccupied with weighty affairs (Ep 1954). All things considered, it was above all Erasmus' loyalty to the house of Hapsburg which antagonized Łaski, who held that the Hapsburgs were, and would always be, the enemies of his country. His opposition to the Hapsburg party induced the archbishop to side with Hieronim, who supported the claims of *John Zápolyai in Hungary. At the request of the imperial chancellor, Mercurino *Gattinara, Pope *Clement VII summoned Łaski to Rome (9 January 1530), where he was to answer severe charges of complicity with the Turks. Although King *Sigismund I rejected the papal summons for his archbishop, who had for years been of poor health, these developments may well have precipitated Łaski's death, which occurred at Kalisz. Following

his death, his nephew Jan sent Erasmus a ring, stating that this was done in compliance with the archbishop's request (Epp 2862, 2911). Appropriate tribute was paid to Łaski's patriotism and clear-sighted statesmanship by Frycz Modrzewski in his *De republica emendanda* (Cracow 1551).

BIBLIOGRAPHY: Allen Ep 1855 / PSB XVIII 229–36 / *Bibliografia polska* ed K. Estreicher et al (Cracow 1870–1951) 3rd part XXI 79–83 / *Nowy Korbut Piśmiennictwo staropolskie* (Warsaw 1963–5) II 481–4 / H. Schumauch 'Die kirchenpolitischen Beziehungen des Fürstbistums Ermland zu Polen' *Zeitschrift für die Geschichte und Altertumskunde Ermlands* 26 (1938) 5 and passim / E. Zivier *Neuere Geschichte Polens* (Gotha 1915) I passim / *Korespondencja Erazma z Rotterdamu z Polakami* ed and trans Maria Cytowska (Warsaw 1965) passim / *Acta Tomiciana* (Poznań-Wrocław 1852–1960) I–XIII passim / *Matricularum regni Poloniae summaria* (Warsaw 1905–61) III–IV passim / Gniezno, Archivum Archidioecesanum, MSS Archivum Capitulare fasc I–II / Cracow, Biblioteka Czartoryskich, MSS 239 p 429, 1596 p 39

MARIA CYTOWSKA

Jan (II) ŁASKI 1499–8 January 1560
Jan Łaski (a Lasco, Lascius) was a son of Jarosław, *voivod* of Sieradz, and thus a brother of Hieronim and Stanisław *Łaski. Jan Łaski, the archbishop of Gniezno, was his uncle. Born on the family estate of Łask, near Sieradz, Jan was educated at the episcopal court of his uncle and thanks to him was able to study abroad. When the archbishop left for Rome to attend the fifth Lateran council he took with him his older nephews, Hieronim and Jan. Jan probably began his studies at Vienna in 1514 and moved after a few months to Bologna. After a stay of almost four years (1514–18) in that city, he moved on to Padua and then Rome. By mid-March 1519 he had returned to Poland. During his studies he increased his knowledge of the ancient languages, acquired a mastery of German and Italian, and absorbed canon law. His uncle, who financed his studies, intended him for an ecclesiastical career, hoping he would succeed him as archbishop of Gniezno and primate of Poland. Even while he was still studying, the archbishop obtained several benefices for him; on

Jan (II) Łaski

covered most of the expenditure for the humanist's household (Epp 1622, 1674). To help the scholar in a material fashion, he also made arrangements to buy his library, leaving Erasmus the use of it for life (the sales contract is dated 20 June 1526). Apparently he used to read aloud to Erasmus during meals (Ep 1616); above all, Erasmus aroused in him concern for ethical problems and won him for his irenic approach to the religious controversy then raging. He always wrote about Jan with great warmth and high regard for his mind and spirit (Epp 1622–4, 1626, 1629, 1805, 1820, 1821, 1824, 1855). Although he showed interest in the eucharistic views of Conradus *Pellicanus, his Hebrew teacher (Ep 1637), and Claudius *Cantiuncula (Ep 1616) and had contacts with *Zwingli, *Oecolampadius, and *Farel, Jan remained under the dominant influence of Erasmus, as is confirmed by his marginal notes in a copy of Erasmus' New Testament (1522) which is now in the library of King's College, Cambridge. He also formed ties with the professors Ludwig *Baer and Bonifacius *Amerbach and with the printer Johann *Froben. *Beatus Rhenanus dedicated to him his annotations to Pliny (Basel: J. Froben 1526; BRE Ep 252) and Henricus *Glareanus his *De geographia* (Basel: J. Faber Emmeus 1527); in turn Łaski persuaded Erasmus to dedicate his *Lingua* to Krzysztof *Szydłowiecki (Ep 1593).

On his uncle's orders Łaski left Basel for Italy on about 5 October 1525 (Epp 1622, 1629); he was accompanied by Erasmus' secretary, Karl *Harst, and equipped with letters of introduction to some of Erasmus' correspondents (Epp 1626, 1650, 1707). After a stay in Padua and Venice, from where he sent letters to his friends in Switzerland, he returned to Poland at the beginning of April 1526, taking Anianus Burgonius back with him. In his absence he had been appointed *custos* of the Płock chapter (nomination dated 26 April 1525) and provost of that of Leczyca; on 6 November 1526 he was nominated provost of Gniezno. While he took his place alongside his uncle, the primate, he continued to display his distaste for Lutheranism as well as for the monks and to express his longing for the rebirth of the church. His service to the primate and his own ecclesiastical duties did not prevent him from pursuing further theological studies, and at the same

30 November 1517 he was confirmed as canon and *custos* of Łęczyca, canon of Płock, and coadjutor of the dean of Gniezno, becoming dean on 30 December. On 7 May 1518 he was appointed canon of Cracow. In 1521 he was ordained priest and received a post as royal secretary. It is unlikely that he was abroad in 1520 and accompanied his brother Hieronim to the coronation of *Charles v. On the other hand, he and Stanisław accompanied Hieronim in 1524 on his embassy to France, stopping by early May in Basel for a visit with Erasmus. Before the end of May Jan was in France, and after a brief visit to the royal court then at Blois, he went to Paris and stayed there for almost a year, attending courses at the university. He formed links with the circle grouped around *Margaret of Angoulême, the sister of *Francis I, and later maintained a correspondence with her (Ep 1615). He also met *Briçonnet, *Lefèvre d'Etaples, and Antonio Rincon, a Spaniard in the service of Francis I. In the spring of 1525 he returned to Basel and with his French famulus, Anianus *Burgonius, was a guest in Erasmus' house for six months.

During his stay with Erasmus, Jan may have

time he emerged as a leading figure in the circles of Polish Erasmians. He corresponded with Erasmus, who at his instigation addressed a letter to King *Sigismund I in May 1527 (Epp 1819, 1820, 1916, 1918, 1954).

When civil war broke out in Hungary and Hieronim Łaski committed himself to the cause of *John Zápolyai, Jan went to Hungary in 1529 as an aide to his brother. He was named bishop of Veszprém – a purely titular office, since that see was in territory occupied by the Turks – and entered Zápolyai's diplomatic service. As 'ambassador of King John' he addressed the Polish diet at Cracow on 9 March 1530 and pleaded for Polish support for his new master; in October he was one of John's two envoys to the congress of Poznań. For the next two years he refrained from corresponding with Erasmus since he knew his friend was devoted to the house of Hapsburg and thought that an exchange of letters might cause trouble for them both (Epp 2279–81, 2746).

When his uncle, the archbishop, died on 19 May 1531, Jan made the arrangements for his funeral and settled the inheritance, renouncing the share his uncle had left to him in favour of his brothers. He now divided his time between his functions as a royal secretary in Cracow and the estates of his brother Hieronim. At about this time Andrzej Frycz Modrzewski entered the service of the Łaski brothers and on Jan's orders went on a secret mission to Germany, where he had contacts with *Luther and *Melanchthon. Burgonius too was provided by his master with a letter of introduction to Melanchthon (dated 7 March 1534) and went off to study in Germany under Modrzewski's supervision. These events, however, do not indicate a decisive change of direction in Jan's religious outlook. Indeed at this time (1533–4) even Piotr *Tomicki, an avowed enemy of the reform movement, planned to attract Melanchthon to the University of Cracow.

The Łaski family's involvement in Hungary contributed to their political ruin and loss of popularity in Poland; it also cast a cloud over their relations with Erasmus. Not until two years after the archbishop's death was Jan able to send Erasmus a reward for his dedication of the works of Ambrose to his uncle (Ep 2862), nor had Jan, who was beset by debts, trans-

ferred the balance owing from the purchase of Erasmus' library. Erasmus, who had another potential buyer on hand, finally offered to cancel the agreement for sale (Ep 2780). However, Jan would not give up the purchase and wrote Erasmus in reassuring terms (Epp 2862, 2911); Erasmus did not change his will in which he reserved the library for Łaski on condition that he paid the arrears (Ep 3134; Allen XI 364). After Erasmus' death Modrzewski arranged the transfer of the books to Poland and Łaski acknowledged their arrival on 5 April 1537 (AK V Ep 2130).

From September 1534 to the end of January 1535 Jan spent his time in negotiations for the release of his brother Hieronim who had been jailed by John Zápolyai at Buda. Once Hieronim had regained his freedom, Jan went to King *Ferdinand to beg for a post for him in the Hapsburg service, a step that compromised the Łaskis even further. The sudden death of Anianus Burgonius in January 1535, while on a mission to Wittenberg, created more problems for Jan, whose ecclesiastical career was now stalling. He failed to secure the archbishopric of Gniezno which had been promised to him in 1530; in fact the nomination to the archdeaconry of Poznań (18 March 1538) was his last promotion. Besides a short journey to Germany in April 1537, in the course of which he met Melanchthon, Jan now lived in isolation on Hieronim's estates. In the middle of 1539 he left Poland and stayed for some time at Frankfurt am Main, where he met the young theologian Albert Hardenberg. He accompanied Hardenberg back to Louvain, attracted not so much by the conservative university as by the circles of the Brethren and Sisters of the Common Life. It is probable that the cloth-merchant's daughter named Gudula, whom he married in 1540, came from these circles. His marriage stripped him of his ecclesiastical benefices in Poland while at Louvain he had reason to fear the Inquisition. He moved on to Friesland and settled down at Emden. Faced with financial problems, he tried to sell part of his library which Modrzewski had had sent to him from Poland in the summer of 1541.

Towards the end of September 1541 Jan left for Linz and Kieżmark for a last meeting with Hieronim, who had fallen seriously ill. After Hieronim's death in December and in compliance with his last wishes, Jan resumed negotiations, begun earlier by Hieronim, concerning his return to Catholic orthodoxy. On 6 February 1542 he swore a solemn oath before Archbishop Piotr Gamrat that he had not forsaken the Catholic church, and on 3 March he did likewise before the chapter of Cracow. Soon afterwards he returned to Germany under the pretext of fetching Hieronim's children and setting his own affairs in order. On 12 May he was back in Emden, and now he broke openly with the Catholic church. How this new turn relates to the oaths he had sworn in Poland remains to be investigated more fully.

At the beginning of 1543 the regent, Anne of Oldenburg, appointed Jan minister of Emden as well as superintendant of the church of East Friesland, and in 1544 he prepared a general summary of its doctrine: *Epitome doctrinae ecclesiarum Frisiae orientalis*. In the same year he attempted to reconcile opposing views of the Lord's Supper in his *Epistola ad amicum quendam de verbis caenae domini*. Accused of Zwinglianism by the Lutherans and unwilling to endorse the Augsburg Interim when the regent adopted it, Jan prepared to leave East Friesland. A new king, *Sigismund Augustus, began to rule Poland, and Łaski offered him his services, hoping he would reform the church. When this proved an illusion he went to England in September 1548, where he made contact with William Cecil and John Cheke, the tutor of Edward VI, and attempted to promote a Protestant coalition against *Charles V. By April 1549 he was in Kaliningrad (Königsberg), from where he sent Sigismund Augustus a letter he had obtained from Edward VI. In spite of this he was not granted permission to return to Poland, and when he returned to Emden he was relieved of his position (2 October 1549). After several months of wandering (Bremen, Hamburg) he took his whole family to England, where he arrived on 13 May 1550. Thanks to the support of Bishop John Hooper, Edward VI appointed Łaski superintendant of the church for foreigners on 24 July. In this capacity he watched over the morals of his congregation and, avoiding any emphasis on dogma and theology, demanded agreement only on the fundamental principles of the faith. Two of his writings served to determine the organization and the liturgy of his church: *Compendium*

doctrinae (1551) and *Forma ac ratio tota ecclesiastici ministerii in peregrinorum ecclesia* (after 1550); in addition he composed catechisms, again avoiding controversial issues of doctrine such as the Lord's Supper. On 6 October 1551 he was appointed to the commission for the revision of ecclesiastical law in England. During his stay in England his wife died of sweating sickness in 1552 and he remarried in 1553.

When *Mary ascended the throne of England and reestablished Catholicism Łaski had to leave by the middle of September 1553. A gale in the Channel probably cost him part of his library before he and his companions were finally carried to the shores of Denmark. Asylum in Denmark would have been contingent on his acceptance of Lutheranism; thus Łaski and his party moved on to Friesland. After a short time in his old refuge of Emden, Lutheran agitators again caused him to depart in April 1555. He took refuge in Frankfurt am Main, where in June 1556 the Dutch church was placed in his charge. But once again his views on the Eucharist aroused the opposition of the Lutherans, and a disputation held at Stuttgart further aggravated the situation and put his followers in danger. He spent his last month at Frankfurt composing a justification: *Purgatio ministrorum in ecclesiis peregrinorum Francofurti* (Basel 1556). Meanwhile Bullinger and Calvin had urged him to return to Poland, hoping that he might influence the course of the Polish reform. To prepare for his return, he sent to Poland his *Forma ac ratio* with a dedication to King Sigismund Augustus. Permission to enter Poland was finally granted on condition that he show in writing that his views did not militate against the Augsburg Confession and that he delay his arrival until after the termination of a diet summoned to Warsaw for August 1556. After a meeting with Melanchthon in Wittenberg, he reached Little Poland by mid-December and stopped at Rabsztyn with his kinsman by marriage Jan *Boner. In February 1557 he was at Cracow, where he met with the Italian reformers Francesco Lismanino and Pier Paolo *Vergerio. In a letter of 28 December 1556 he had asked the king to grant him an audience; Sigismund Augustus received him at Vilna on 19 and 24 March but did not grant him authority to promote his cause other than by preaching the

Gospel as a private person. Under pressure from the Catholic clergy, the king issued a mandate on 8 July 1557 banning Łaski from any activity in favour of reform. Although it was not enforced, the mandate weakened his position. Only in Little Poland, where he directed the Calvinist church from 1557, did he meet with relative success. He worked towards the adoption of a confession and a liturgy and urged the translation of the Bible into Polish and the establishment of funds for the endowment of ministers and schools. He planned to remodel the school of Pinczow at the level of an academy. Struggling against Lutherans and Catholics alike, he continued to work for the unification of all evangelical churches, an achievement not realized until the so-called concord of Sandomierz of 1570. Constantly on the move, he was to be found at one time or another in Balice, Osiek, and Pinczow, where he died on 8 January 1560 and was buried.

BIBLIOGRAPHY: PSB XVIII 237–44 / LThK VI 803–4 / DNB XI 599–601 / *Bibliografia polska* ed K. Estreicher et al (Cracow 1870–1951) 3rd part XXI 83–90 / O. Bartel *Jan Łaski* part I: 1499–1556 (Warsaw 1955) / O. Bartel 'Johannes a Lasco und Erasmus von Rotterdam' *Luther-Jahrbuch* 32 (1965) 48–66 / H. Dalton *Beiträge zur Geschichte der evangelischen Kirche in Russland: Lasciana* (Berlin 1898) / U. Falkenroth *Gestalt und Wesen der Kirche bei Johannes a Lasco* (Göttingen 1957) / F.W. Kantzenbach 'Der Beitrag des Johannes Brenz zur Toleranzidee' *Theologische Zeitschrift* 21 (1965) 38–64 / H. Kowalska *Działalność reformatorska Jana Łaskiego* (Wrocław-Warsaw-Cracow 1969) / F.A. Norwood 'The Strangers' "Model Churches" in sixteenth century England' in *Reformation Studies: Essays in Honor of Roland H. Bainton* (Richmond, Va., 1962) 181–96 / *Die evangelischen Kirchenordnungen des 16. Jahrhunderts* ed E. Sehling (Tübingen 1963) VII-2 / Jan Łaski *Opera tam edita quam inedita* ed A. Kuyper (Amsterdam 1866) / *Korespondencja Erazma z Rotterdamu z Polakami* ed and trans Maria Cytowska (Warsaw 1965) / *Melanchthons Briefwechsel* II Ep 1416 and passim / AK III Epp 1026–8 and passim
MARIA CYTOWSKA

Stanisław ŁASKI d 29 March 1550
Stanisław Łaski (Stanislaus a Lasco, also known by the pseudonym Walenty Poddany) was born around 1500 on the family estates near Sieradz. Like his elder brothers, Hieronim and Jan (II) *Łaski, Stanisław was brought up at the court of their uncle, Jan (I) *Łaski, archbishop of Gniezno. After studies in Bologna with Jan (II) (1514–18), Stanisław probably accompanied Hieronim, who was sent to represent Poland at the coronation of *Charles V in 1520; it is thus possible that he too met Erasmus at Brussels. Later that year he undertook a pilgrimage to the Holy Land, returning early in 1521 as a knight of the Holy Sepulchre. There is no doubt about his visit to Erasmus in Basel in the spring of 1524, when he accompanied his two brothers on a diplomatic mission to the French court (Allen I 33). Erasmus liked him and later recalled him repeatedly in his correspondence, especially with his brothers (Epp 1502, 1805, 1821, 2911). In France Stanisław attached himself to the court of *Francis I and joined the king for his Italian campaign. Like Francis he was taken prisoner in the battle of Pavia (24 February 1525) but was soon freed on payment of a ransom. Eventually he returned to Paris and later accompanied *Margaret of Angoulême to Madrid for negotiations about the release of her brother. At the turn of 1526–7 the French sent him back to Poland with instructions to engage his country in an international league against Charles V. In April he was in Hungary at Hieronim's side and subsequently accompanied the latter on his mission to France and England in the name of *John Zápolyai; before his return from England he was knighted by King *Henry VIII. In 1528 he joined a French expedition against Naples, but after the treaty of Cambrai (3 August 1529) he left the French service and returned to Poland.

In 1530 Stanisław was again in Hungary, commanding mercenary troops in support of John Zápolyai; he also accompanied Hieronim on a mission to Constantinople. He had just returned to Poland when his uncle, the archbishop, died (19 May 1531), and in 1534 he was appointed castellan of Przemęt. After Hieronim's death (22 December 1541) Stanisław succeeded him as *voivode* of Sieradz. Until close to his death he was active in the diplomatic service of King *Sigismund I and subsequently King *Sigismund II Augustus. In 1539 he was sent on a mission to the Elector Joachim of Brandenburg and in 1547 and 1548 on another to the diet of Augsburg and Charles

v. In reward for his services Sigismund Augustus appointed him in 1548 *starost* of Leczyca. His diplomatic activity was also praised by contemporaries in such works as Bernardus Holtorpius' *De peregrinatione Stanislai a Lasco* (Regensburg 1548) and Stanisław Warszewicki's *Oratio de Stanislao a Lascy* (Wittenberg 1551).

Diplomacy was not, however, Stanisław's only talent. He also had literary gifts, producing as his most interesting work a political pamphlet reminiscent in style of Erasmus' *Colloquia*. Circulating anonymous in manuscript under the title *Dialogus de asiana diaeta vel potius de Piotrcoviensibus comitiis 1535 in mense Decembri habitis*, it was finally published in Andrzej *Krzycki *Carmina* ed K. Morawski (Cracow 1888). He also composed a treatise on military matters inspired by Vegetius' *De re militaria*, and finally he translated Erasmus' *Querela pacis* into Polish, transforming it in the process into a tract of anti-Turkish propaganda. He published it under the pseudonym Walenty Poddany as *Napomnienie polskie ku zgodzie do wszech krześcianów wobec, a mianowicie ku Polakom uczynione* (Cracow 1545).

BIBLIOGRAPHY: Allen Ep 1502 / PSB XVIII 253–5 / *Korespondencja Erazma z Rotterdamu z Polakami* ed and trans Maria Cytowska (Warsaw 1965) / *Bibliografia polska* ed K. Estreicher et al (Cracow 1870–1951) 3rd part XXI 90–3 / *Nowy Korbut: Piśmiennictwo staropolskie* (Warsaw 1963–5) II 489–91 / W. Pociecha *Królowa Bona (1494–1557)* (Poznań 1949–58) / O. Bartel *Jan Łaski: Część I: 1499–1556* (Warsaw 1955) 44–8 / Maria Cytowska 'Stanisław Łaski jako tłumacz Erazma z Rotterdamu' *Meander* 14 (1959) 362–8   MARIA CYTOWSKA

William LATIMER d before 17 October 1545
William Latimer (Latamer, Latomerus, Lotomer, Lottermarus, etc) was a scholar and humanist who in his day was highly regarded for learning, of which little but the report survived his death. He was born about 1460, and nothing is known of his origins. His life was spent mostly in Oxford and in Italy until the later years, when he seems unaccountably to have withdrawn from scholarly pursuits to live simply as a churchman. In June 1538 he was made canon of Sarum and prebendary of Woodford and Wilsford in Salisbury Cathedral, a living he vacated by August 1543. He died two years later at Saintbury, Gloucestershire, where he had been made rector in 1504.

Latimer was elected a fellow of All Souls College, Oxford, in 1489, and vacated his fellowship by 1497. In 1502 he proceeded MA at Ferrara and seems to have been in Italy until December 1503, when he returned to England. He wrote to Aldo *Manuzio from Padua on 4 November 1498, and, in company with Cuthbert *Tunstall there, he encouraged the studies of Richard *Pace, who remembered him in his *De fructu*. He also formed a friendship with Niccolò *Leoniceno, to whom he later commended Reginald *Pole as well. On his return to England he was ordained acolyte for the diocese of London on 23 December 1503, and priest on 21 December 1504.

In 1510 and 1511 he was back at Rome, where he was registered at the English hospice as 'doctor of arts' (MA) of Ferrara. He also borrowed volumes of Plutarch and Aristotle from the Vatican library. By 1513, however, he was again in Oxford as tutor to Reginald Pole (cf Thomas *Lupset's tribute, Ep 1595). He was also charged rent for rooms at Canterbury College, Oxford, in 1516–17, 1521–2, and 1528–9. At the sale of William *Grocyn's books (1520) he was appointed arbiter for the price of those acquired by Corpus Christi College from Grocyn's executor, Thomas *Linacre. He was incorporated MA at Oxford on 18 November 1513 and had taken his bachelor's degree in theology by 1531. In that same year he was mentioned as an Oxford scholar who might be consulted about the royal divorce. Like Linacre, he kept in touch with Niccolò *Leonico Tomeo at Padua until the latter's death in 1531, thus forging a link with another generation of English students that began to arrive in Padua with Reginald Pole.

Latimer first appears in Erasmus' correspondence (Ep 207) as one of those – with Linacre, Grocyn, and Tunstall – to whom Erasmus showed his translations from Euripides (cf Ep 1479). In 1512 he was one of the 'fellow-scholars,' with Grocyn, Linacre, and *More, remembered to Erasmus by Girolamo *Aleandro (Ep 256). On 5 June 1516 Erasmus wrote to Latimer to ask him for help in preparing the second edition of his New Testament (Ep 417), and shortly afterwards he and More attempted to recruit Latimer to help John *Fisher learn Greek (Epp 468, 481). When Latimer received these requests he had already decided to return to Oxford and could not be persuaded to stop with Fisher. His letter of explanation, written to Erasmus from Oxford on 30 January 1517 (Ep 520), also politely declined the help requested in the correction of the New Testament, on the grounds that he had neglected Greek and Latin for many years and was not competent for the task. The letter itself contains two passages in Greek. He also pointed out, however, that the Greek of the Gospels was so far from the language of the ancients 'that there is little enough in them that I can understand and nothing I dare guarantee.' As for Fisher, Latimer pointed out reasonably enough that a stay of a month or so with the bishop could accomplish little, and he suggested that More and Erasmus look in Italy for a suitable teacher, prepared to stay in Rochester long enough to ensure some gains.

Latimer's refusals were received by Erasmus with equanimity (Ep 540) and with the gentle rebuke that he and Grocyn should not allow their excessive modesty to deter them from advancing the cause of scholarship. Latimer does seem to have sent Erasmus some annotations, at least on the text of Matthew, and the fact that Edward *Lee sent his own animadversions on Erasmus' edition to Latimer, as to More and Fisher among Erasmus' friends (Ep 1061), suggests that Latimer may have been known to be interested (cf Ep 1175). In the Ciceronianus (1528) Erasmus mentioned him as a man who preferred theology to Ciceronian eloquence (ASD I-2 678–9).

Latimer was a witness to the will of Thomas Linacre, who died in 1524. He may also have been involved with Linacre and Grocyn in a project to translate the works of Aristotle, but if so nothing is known of Latimer's part in this. He was remembered by John Leland in his Encomia, and by other contemporaries like George Lily, as a man among the most eminent for learning of his day in England; but of his writings, only his letters to Erasmus survive.

BIBLIOGRAPHY: Allen Ep 207 / DNB XI 622–3 / Emden BRUO II 1106–7 / Montagu Burrows Collectanea, second series (Oxford 1890) / P.S. Allen 'Linacre and Latimer in Italy' English Historical Review 18 (1903) 514–17 / G.P. Parks

The English Traveler to Italy (Rome 1954–) I 469, 475, and passim / Francis Maddison et al Linacre Studies (Oxford 1977)

JAMES K. MCCONICA

Bartholomaeus LATOMUS of Arlon, d 3 January 1570

Latomus (Bartholomaeus Henrici Arlunensis), the son of Henri Mason (Masson, Lapicida), was born in Arlon, on the border between Belgium and Luxembourg, in about 1498. From childhood he was a friend of Matthias *Held, to whom he later dedicated his edition of Cicero's Oratio pro Aulo Cecinna (Paris and Strasbourg 1539). He matriculated in Freiburg on 10 March 1516 and obtained a BA in September 1516 and a MA on 31 October 1517. He studied law under Udalricus *Zasius, whose friend he became, and probably at about this time first met Erasmus at nearby Basel (Ep 3029). From 1518 he was a lecturer in the Freiburg faculty of arts and at the same time supervisor of a students' residence (Ep 1342). He was a lively youth and was repeatedly subjected to disciplinary measures. In November 1521, returning to Freiburg after a visit to his native city, he met Erasmus in Strasbourg and accompanied him as far as Sélestat (Ep 1342). Having already published some verse with Philipp *Engelbrecht's Carmen paraeneticum (Basel: J. Froben 1517), he now composed some more in honour of Erasmus, who thanked him through Zasius (Ep 1252) and praised him in a letter written for immediate publication (Ep 1342).

In the summer of 1522 Latomus went to Trier, where he may have continued his studies while tutoring other students. He secured some patronage from the archbishop, Richard von *Greiffenklau, whom he later honoured with a Declamatio funebris (Cologne 1531). He also took part in the defence of Trier against Franz von *Sickingen and described the events in his epic poem Factio memorabilis (Soest: N. Schulting 1523), which he dedicated to the future archbishop, Johann von *Metzenhausen. Subsequently he matriculated in Cologne on 28 August 1526 with his students, and soon was lecturing on Livy and Cicero. On 1 August 1530 he matriculated in Louvain – perhaps some time after his arrival – and continued his study of Latin authors in the Collegium Trilingue as a disciple and friend of

*Goclenius. In May 1531 he dedicated his edition of Terence to Goclenius from Trier (Cologne: J. Gymnich 1531?), while his *Carmen gratulatorium* (n p, n d) on the occasion of *Ferdinand I's coronation as Roman king was dedicated to Gilles de *Busleyden.

In July 1531 Latomus was appointed lecturer in the Collège de Sainte-Barbe in Paris under André de Gouveia, to whom he dedicated an *Epitome* of Rodolphus *Agricola's rhetoric (Cologne: J. Gymnich 1532). When Gouveia invited Latomus to follow him to the Collège de Guyenne at Bordeaux in 1533, *Budé retained him in Paris by securing a royal professorship in Latin for him. His inaugural lecture of 1 November 1534, *Oratio de studiis humanitatis* (Paris: S. Gryphius 1534), is dedicated to Budé. In Paris Latomus retained connections with former fellow students at the Trilingue such as Johann Sturm and Balthasar von *Künring.

In the autumn of 1539 Latomus was granted leave to visit Italy at the king's expense. In Bologna, where he is documented on 11 February 1540, he appears to have received a legal doctorate. On his way back to Paris he passed through Basel, visiting Johannes Oporinus, one of his printers. In July 1540 he stopped in Strasbourg with his friend Johann Sturm. He accompanied the Strasbourg reformers to the Haguenau conference before returning to Paris in October 1540. In the summer of 1541 he went to the diet of Regensburg and there met his former student Johann Ludwig von Hagen, now archbishop of Trier, whose service he entered in 1542 after resigning his chair at Paris. At about this time he married Anna Zieglein of Andernach at Koblenz. From 1543 to 1546 the Trier councillor was involved in a controversy with *Bucer, who was then collaborating with Hermann von *Wied, archbishop of Cologne. In his replies to Bucer he showed both firmness and dignity. In 1548 he accepted an imperial appointment as assessor at the Reichskammergericht in Speyer, taking his oath of office on 1 October; he resigned on 11 May 1555 to return to Trier. He attended the diet of Speyer in 1556 and was also a speaker for the Catholic party at the colloquy of Worms in 1557.

Latomus deserves his reputation as one of the leading Latin scholars of his day, particu-

larly in view of his work on Cicero. His commentaries to many of Cicero's orations appeared in numerous individual editions and were gathered by Johannes Oporinus in *Lucubrationes in ... Ciceronis orationes aliquot* (Basel: T. Platter and B. Lasius 1536–7; second edition Basel: R. Winter 1539). Among his other works are *Ad christianissimum Galliarum regem Franciscum ... bombarda* (Paris: F. Gryphius 1536) and *De docta simplicitate primae ecclesiae ... adversus ... insultationem Iacobi Andreae* (Cologne: M. Cholinus 1559).

After his early meetings with Erasmus Latomus had lost contact with the Dutch scholar and was pleasantly surprised (Ep 3029) when Erasmus responded to the publication of his *Oratio de studiis humanitatis* with an encouraging letter. Clearly aware of Latomus' gifts and pleased with the warmth of his tribute, Erasmus wrote again (Ep 3048) and published both letters with his last selection of correspondence in February 1536.

BIBLIOGRAPHY: Allen Ep 1252 / BNB XI 425–35 / ADB XVIII 14 / M.A. Kugener 'Barthélemy Latomus' *Latomus* 1 (1937) 1–2 / de Vocht CTL II 591–602 and passim / AK VIII Ep 2395a / *Matrikel Freiburg* I-1 225 / *Matrikel Köln* II 884 / *Matricule de Louvain* IV-1 40 / B. Latomus *Deux Discours inauguraux* ed and trans L. Bakelants (Brussels 1951) / B. Latomus *Zwei Streitschriften gegen Martin Butzer, 1543–1545* ed L. Keil (Münster 1924) / *Melanchthons Briefwechsel* II Ep 1336
IG & PGB

Jacobus LATOMUS of Cambron, d 29 May 1544

Latomus (Jacques Masson, Saxicida, Hephestion) was born at Cambron, between Ath and Mons, about 1475. Erasmus' statement that Latomus was three years younger than himself (Ep 2275) is questionable. Latomus first studied in Paris under Jan *Standonck. He was a MA when on 17 November 1500 he enrolled at the University of Louvain, where he was a student of Adrian of Utrecht (the future Pope *Adrian VI). In August 1502 he became head of a residence for poor students at Louvain, which had been founded by Standonck in 1500. This appointment was for three years and ended by Pentecost 1505. He earned a licence in theology while teaching in the faculty of arts, and in the latter capacity he was admitted to the council of

the university (29 November 1510). On 16
August 1519 he received a doctorate in
theology. The expenses for his promotion were
paid by his pupils Robert and Charles (II) de
*Croy (Epp 1694, 1695). In the same year he
was authorized to lecture in divinity and
entered the Collegium strictum of the faculty of
theology, becoming dean in the following year
and again in 1526 and 1529. In 1526 Bishop
Robert de Croy had provided him with a
canonry of Cambrai. In the summer of 1529 he
moved to Cambrai, where he resided until his
appointment in 1535 as professor of theology
and canon of St Peter's, Louvain, in succession
to Jan *Driedo (Ep 3037). He was rector of the
university in 1537 and remained at Louvain
until his death.

When Erasmus moved to Louvain in 1517,
Latomus and other Louvain theologians gave
him a friendly welcome. When preparing the
second edition of his New Testament Erasmus
asked some of them, including Latomus, to let
him have their comments on the first (Epp 1225,
1571, 1581), but none offered any serious
criticism. In April 1519 Erasmus stated that
until recently Latomus had been 'not particularly against the humanities and my good
friend' (Ep 948; cf Epp 936, 1225). The issue
which abruptly changed their relationship was
Latomus' opposition to the teaching of Greek
and Hebrew, which he believed to be dangerous rather than useful. In November 1518 the
Louvain printer Dirk *Martens published a
separate edition of Erasmus' *Ratio verae theologiae* (Ep 745 introduction). At about the same
time Petrus *Mosellanus' *Oratio de variarum
linguarum cognitione paranda* (Leipzig: V.
Schumann 1518) became known in Louvain.
Latomus reacted to both with his dialogue *De
trium linguarum et studii theologici ratione*
(Antwerp: M. Hillen 1519; CWE Ep 934 introduction). The controversy caused a stir in
Louvain, and although Latomus had not mentioned Erasmus by name, the latter decided to
answer with a temperate *Apologia contra Latomi
dialogum* (Antwerp: J. Thibault [1519]; LB IX
79–106). Writing in April to Bishop John
*Fisher, he suggested that some of Latomus'
anonymous criticisms might be seen as meant
for him although they were actually intended
for *Luther (Ep 936). Erasmus thought for some
time that Latomus had served as a mouthpiece

Jacobus Latomus, by Philip Galle

for other theologians, in particular Jan *Briart
of Ath (Epp 934, 993, 998). Even though
Erasmus probably had no share in the publication of the *Dialogus bilinguium ac trilinguium*
(CWE 7 appendix), which contained mordant
attacks upon Latomus and other Louvain
theologians, some of the ideas expressed in
that satire were certainly his. Latomus wrote a
final refutation of Erasmus' *Apologia* in which
he denied that his colleagues had had a part in
his earlier work and that his own view of the
question differed from Erasmus'. This *Pro
dialogo de tribus linguis apologia* was published
posthumously in 1550 in his *Opera* (Louvain: B.
Gravius) edited by his nephew and namesake.

Despite some moments of respite (Epp 968,
1022), the friction between Erasmus and the
Louvain theologians grew worse and influenced his decision to remove to Basel (autumn
1521). From 1519 some Louvain theologians
believed that he and Luther supported each
other and even suspected him of secret
collaboration in the writing of Luther's works.
The faculty of theology officially condemned
Luther (7 November 1519) and began an
investigation of the writings of Erasmus. In

private letters dating from the spring and summer of 1520 Erasmus described Latomus as an unrelenting, indeed his principal, opponent in Louvain (Epp 1088, 1113). He repeated his charges in another letter, which he published a year later, thinly disguising Latomus' name (Ep 1123). To Luther he wrote that Latomus was apt to break into abuse when attacking Luther in his lectures (Ep 1127A). At the same time he protested to the Louvain theologians about Latomus' attacks upon the *Consilium* he had drawn up with the Dominican friar Johannes *Faber (Epp 1149, 1217). In January 1522 Juan Luis *Vives confirmed that Latomus continued to rave against Erasmus and added that his arrogance was alienating his colleagues (Ep 1256).

In 1525 Erasmus learnt of another attack by Latomus which renewed his alarm. Latomus had published a volume at Antwerp (M. Hillen) which opened with a treatise *De confessione secreta*. This was an attack upon Johannes *Oecolampadius, but implicitly it also took issue with Erasmus' *Exomologesis*, published the preceding year. Concealed thrusts against Erasmus also occurred in the other tracts published with *De confessione secreta*, which were directed against the Lutherans (Epp 1581, 1582, 1585). This attack greatly agitated Erasmus, and over the next two years he referred to it in many letters. He complained to the Louvain theologians that anything he wrote was interpreted by Latomus in the sense of Lutheran heresy (Ep 1582), and he made analogous charges when writing to Francesco *Chierigati at the papal court (Ep 1686), Cardinal Jacopo *Sadoleto (Ep 2443), Chancellor Mercurino *Gattinara (Ep 1700), Archbishop Jean (I) de *Carondelet (Ep 1703), and others.

Meanwhile Latomus continued his campaign against heresy with unrelenting vehemence. In *De primatu Romani Pontificis adversus Lutherum* (Antwerp: M. Hillen 1526) he defended the divine origin of the papal primacy. In 1530 he published his *Libellus de fide et operibus et de votis atque institutis monasticis* (Antwerp: M. Hillen) and in 1544 his *Duae epistolae, una in libellum de ecclesia Philippo Melanchtoni inscriptum, altera contra orationem factiosorum in comitiis Ratisbonensibus habitam* (Antwerp: A. Coppenius).

He also sustained his misgivings about Erasmus, and in the last year of his life he was working on a refutation of Erasmus' *De concordia* that was published posthumously in Latomus' *Opera* of 1550.

While modern authors do not suggest that Latomus' zeal and conservatism were matched by the originality of his theological thought, Luther seemed to consider him a foremost antagonist. In his Table Talk he repeatedly called him the most formidable of his opponents, unequalled by Erasmus and other 'frogs' (de Jongh 179–80).

BIBLIOGRAPHY: Allen and CWE Ep 934 / DTC VIII-2 2626–8 / LThK VI 822 / de Vocht CTL I 324–34, II 249–53 and passim / H. de Jongh *L'Ancienne Faculté de théologie de Louvain* (Louvain 1911) 173–80, 69*–80*, and passim / J.H. Bentley 'New Testament Scholarship in Louvain in the Early Sixteenth Century' *Studies in Medieval and Renaissance History* n s 2 (1979) 53–79, esp 60–3 / J. Etienne *Spiritualisme érasmien et théologiens louvanistes: Un changement de problématique au début du XVIe siècle* (Louvain-Gembloux 1956) 163–86 / Karel Blockx *De veroordeling van Maarten Luther door de theologische faculteit te Leuven in 1519* (Brussels 1958) / Karel Blockx 'Een conflict tussen Erasmus en de Leuvense theologen in 1519' in *Nationale Erasmus-Herdenking: Handelingen* (Brussels 1970) 7–30 / Charles Béné 'Saint Augustin dans la controverse sur les trois langues à Louvain en 1518 et 1519' in *Colloquium Erasmianum* (Mons 1968) 17–32 / Georges Chantraine 'L'Apologia ad Latomum: deux conceptions de la théologie' in *Scrinium Erasmianum* II 51–76 / Leopold Vinken 'Jacobus Latomus en Maarten Luther: de botsing van twee visies op theologie' in *Facultas S. Theologiae Lovaniensis 1432–1797: Bijdragen tot haar geschiedenis* ed E.J.M. van Eijl (Louvain 1977) 299–311 / *Correspondance de Nicolas Clénard* ed A. Roersch (Brussels 1940–1) Epp 23, 24 and passim / BA *Oekolampads* I 366–7 and passim

GILBERT TOURNOY

LAURENS See *LAURINUS*

Laurens LAURENSEN d 1533
Laurens Laurensen (Laurentius Laurentii Phrysius), a native of Friesland, joined the

Dominican order at the Groningen convent
and was lector there from 1516 to 1518.
Erasmus later said that he had studied in
Louvain (Ep 2205), but his name has not been
found in the surviving university records. At
all events, he was a bachelor of theology (Epp
1147, 1165) when he took to attacking Erasmus'
Moria in July 1520 (Epp 1164, 1166, 1173). He
continued to do so for some six weeks until
temporarily silenced by Godschalk *Rose-
mondt (Epp 1166, 1581) and by Girolamo
*Aleandro (Epp 1581, 1582; ASD IX-1 152–3).
But Erasmus soon found that he had reason for
new complaints about Laurensen's attacks,
which by the beginning of October were aimed
specifically against the *Antibarbari* (Epp 1164,
1166, 1172, 1173). In an attempt to justify
himself, Laurensen called on his adversary at
the end of 1520, but Erasmus felt little
sympathy for the troublesome young man,
whom he judged to be conceited and stupid
(Epp 1164, 1166). He thought again of Laurensen when told of a sermon linking him with
*Luther that was preached at Louvain on 28
October 1521, at the time when Erasmus
himself was about to leave the Netherlands (Ep
1342), but subsequently he stated that Laurensen had never attacked him outside the walls of
his monastery (Ep 2205).

Soon after Erasmus' departure Laurensen
must have gone to Paris in quest of a doctorate
in divinity. In February 1523 he was appointed
prior of the Dominican house at Groningen (Ep
2205). On 12 March of that year he presided
over a debate at Groningen between Dominicans and Lutherans and afterwards answered
an attack by Ulrich von Dornum with *Een
antwoort op de disputacie ghedruct in de naem
Juncker Ulricx van Doernum* (Kampen: J.
Evertsz, 9 August 1527; NK 1330). In 1523 and
1533 he was *definitor* at the provincial chapters
of his order and in 1530 he was inquisitor for
the dioceses of Utrecht and Münster. In 1525
he conducted unsuccessful peace negotiations
with Karel van *Egmond, duke of Gelderland,
on behalf of Groningen. He signed his name to
the title page of a copy of Johannes Buridanus'
*Questiones super decem libros Ethicorum Aris-
totelis* (Paris: P. le Preux 1513), now in the
library of Groningen University.
BIBLIOGRAPHY: Allen Ep 1166 / P.F. Wolfs *Das*

*Groninger 'Religionsgespräch' (1523) und seine
Hintergründe* (Nijmegen 1959) 46–53 and
passim / G.A. Meijer in NNBW II 789
C.G. VAN LEIJENHORST

Johannes Baptista LAURENTIA documented
1535–6
Laurentia has not been identified. He is known
from Erasmus' letter of 18 March 1535 (Ep
3005), addressed to him and Petrus *Merbelius,
which answered individual letters received
from each of them, neither now extant. In
subsequent letters from Milan, Merbelius
acknowledged receipt of Erasmus' letter and
stated that Laurentia was ailing and that he
had not seen him for some time (Epp 3070,
3091).

Laurentius LAURENTII *See Laurens
LAURENSEN*

LAURENTIUS (Epp 2065, 2068) *See Lorenz
SCHLEHENRIED*

Hieronymus LAURINUS of Bruges, d 1509
Hieronymus was the father of Marcus,
Matthias, and Petrus *Laurinus. He held
several estates, among them the lordship of
Watervliet, north of Ghent. He was chamber-
lain and treasurer of Flanders (Ep 201) under
Philip the Handsome, duke of *Burgundy, and
had earlier been treasurer of the free district
(Vrije or Franc) of Bruges (1487–98). His first
wife, Jacqueline Pedaert, died on 4 May 1502;
Hieronymus himself died seven years later at
Ghent, where both are buried in St Bavo's. His
house at Mechelen, which he sold in 1507,
became a residence of *Margaret of Austria.
BIBLIOGRAPHY: Allen Ep 201 / de Vocht CTL II
67–8   PGB

Marcus LAURINUS of Bruges, 17 May 1488–
c 4 November 1540
Marcus Laurinus (Lauwerijns, Laurijn,
Laurin), the second son of Hieronymus
*Laurinus, was born at Bruges. With his
brothers, Matthias and Petrus *Laurinus, he
matriculated at Louvain on 31 August 1502.
They were boarders in the College of the Lily
and Erasmus may have met them at that time. In
1524 he wrote that he had known Laurinus

since his childhood (Ep 1512). Unless this is an exaggeration, it can hardly refer to an encounter in Bologna, where the brothers went for study in 1507, since Marcus was then a young man of nineteen years. He returned to his native city as a doctor of civil and canon law and spent the rest of his life there as a leading member of the chapter of St Donatian. In 1512 he became canon of the twentieth prebend, and on 24 September 1519 he was appointed dean. One of his first measures was the printing of a *Breviarium ad usum insignis ecclesiae Sancti Donatiani Brugensis* (Paris: A. Bonnemere 14 August 1520). Other benefices bestowed upon Laurinus were the parishes of Hoorn (Holland) and Flines, near Douai, and also a benefice at St Michael's, Ghent. Laurinus died at Bruges in 1540 and was buried in his church on 4 November.

Laurinus always remained in close contact with the court of Brussels and the University of Louvain. Thus he was at Louvain in 1518 and was able to visit Erasmus during his severe illness at the home of Dirk *Martens (Ep 867). On 12 July 1530 he attended the doctoral promotion of Pieter de *Corte in Louvain (Epp 2352, 2353), and in March 1522 he went to Brussels (Ep 1271). More important than these short journeys is the fact that his house served as a meeting place, a guest-house, and a post office for numerous humanists, politicians, diplomats, and other dignitaries – such as Erasmus, *Vives, Pieter *Gillis, *Cranevelt, *Fevijn, Guy *Morillon, Cornelis de *Schepper, and Thomas *More. Erasmus was his guest in 1517 (Ep 651) and again in August 1521 (Ep 1227). Laurinus was also trusted to receive payments for Erasmus from his prebend at Courtrai, but since he appeared to be rather careless and neglectful in such matters, Erasmus suffered some losses and ordered the Courtrai canon, Jan de *Hondt, to remit the annuity direct to his banker, Erasmus *Schets in Antwerp (Epp 1458, 1470, 1548, 1695, 1769, 1783, 1848, 1849, 1862, 1866, 2286).

Erasmus sent Laurinus his publications such as the *Apologia ad Fabrum* (Ep 651) and the *Paraphrasis in Romanos* (Ep 740). He repeatedly wrote long and important letters to Laurinus about his work (Ep 763 on the New Testament), his travels (Ep 1342 on his journeys to Basel and Constance), and his manifold troubles

with hostile theologians (Epp 809, 1342, 1792), in which he relied on Laurinus for support (Ep 2045). In his scholarly work too Erasmus could count on Laurinus' help. In 1524 the dean let him know that a very old codex of St Jerome's *In Psalmos* was kept at St Bavo's abbey, Ghent (Ep 1214). Erasmus' amanuenses were always welcome in his house, and on occasion he himself recommended a suitable young man to Erasmus, as he did with *Algoet (Ep 1091). Foreign scholars such as the Basel professor Simon *Grynaeus were entertained at his house, and on such occasions 'convivia docta' or learned dinner parties were held to which local scholars and humanists were invited (see Ep 2499 written by Adrianus *Chilius, who shortly afterwards dedicated his Latin translation of Aristophanes' *Plutus* to Laurinus). No wonder then that Laurinus was mourned by a host of Flemish Latin poets at the time of his death.

Notwithstanding his close and sustained contacts with so many leading humanists Marcus Laurinus was never a scholar and writer himself. Even his personal library does not seem to have been large or valuable in any respect.

BIBLIOGRAPHY: Allen Ep 201 / CWE Ep 651 / A. Dewitte in NBW VII 499–503 / de Vocht *Literae ad Craneveldium* 13–14 and passim / de Vocht CTL I 516 and passim   J. IJSEWIJN

Matthias LAURINUS of Bruges,
d 9 November 1540
Matthias, the elder brother of Marcus *Laurinus, was probably born at Bruges by 1486 and inherited from his father the lordship of Watervliet, north of Ghent. He was several times treasurer and burgomaster (for example, in 1528, 1533, and 1538) of the free district of Bruges (Vrije or Franc). As an official of the Hapsburg court he often resided at Brussels and Mechelen. In 1517 he accompanied the future *Charles v to Spain (Ep 651). He was married to Françoise, the daughter of Jean *Ruffault, who bore him two sons, Marcus and Guido. He died at Watervliet and was buried there.

Erasmus and Matthias knew each other fairly well. In Ep 1870 Erasmus appealed directly to the influential dignitary, who supported him in his conflicts with hostile theologians and on occasion offered his good services at court (Ep 1848). Juan Luis *Vives was likewise acquainted with him (Ep 1889).

BIBLIOGRAPHY: BNB XI 459 / de Vocht CTL II 68, IV 185 and passim   J. IJSEWIJN

Petrus LAURINUS of Bruges, 7 December 1489–27 February 1522
Petrus, the youngest brother of Marcus *Laurinus, died young. He had been married to Anna Isabella Donche, who after his death became the wife of the diplomat Cornelis de *Schepper. Erasmus knew Petrus (Ep 201) and sent greetings to him through Marcus (Epp 651, 789); he was informed of Petrus' death by Juan Luis *Vives (Ep 1271).

BIBLIOGRAPHY: CWE Ep 651 / Allen Ep 1271 / de Vocht CTL II 68   J. IJSEWIJN

Joost LAUWEREYNS of Bruges, d 6 November 1527
Joost Lauwereyns (Laureys, Jodocus), the son of Nicolaas, was lord of Terdeghem, near Cassel in France from 1522. An able jurist, he entered the service of *Charles V as an imperial councillor on 16 December 1515, when he became a member of the grand council (*senatus*) of Mechelen. He undertook several diplomatic journeys for the emperor and may be the Jodocus who followed the court to Spain, as Erasmus reported to Pierre *Barbier in Epp 695, 764. By letters dated 17 April 1522 Lauwereyns became president of the grand council. He took his oath on 15 May and by about the same time was appointed superintendent of the Inquisition for the Netherlands and made responsible for repressing Lutheranism. When Nicolaas *Baechem Egmondanus preached at Mechelen, renewing his charge that Erasmus was a Lutheran, especially because of the new *Froben edition of the *Colloquia* (March 1522), Erasmus felt the need to defend himself in a letter addressed to Lauwereyns and asked for his understanding and protection (Ep 1299). Lauwereyns' reaction was probably rather cool, and he subsequently took the side of anti-Erasmian theologians such as Jacobus *Latomus (Epp 1717, 1747), counteracting in this way Jean de *Carondelet's support of the Dutch humanist. Erasmus was inclined to think that the learned jurist lacked common sense (Ep 2191) and fostered unconcealed

hatred of all humanists. This may be a slightly biased view, however; *Vives found him a very human and friendly person (de Vocht *Literae ad Craneveldium* Ep 157). In an interview with the town secretary of Amsterdam, Andries Jacobs-zoon (April 1527), he took the view that as long as the edicts against heresy were obeyed religious thought was a private matter. Lau-wereyns died unexpectedly at Mechelen (de Vocht *Literae ad Craneveldium* Ep 250), leaving a widow, Jehanne de Gros of Bruges, and two children, Margaret and Ferry. Nicolaas *Everaerts succeeded him as president of the council.

BIBLIOGRAPHY: de Vocht *Literae ad Cranevel-dium* Epp 74, 133, and passim / de Vocht CTL II 253–4, 285, 436 / F. Walser and R. Wohlfeil *Die spanischen Zentralbehörden und der Staatsrat Karls V.* (Göttingen 1959) 136 and passim / *Corpus documentorum Inquisitionis haereticae pravitatis Neerlandicae* ed Paul Fredericq (Ghent-The Hague 1889–1903) v
                                                    J. IJSEWIJN

LAUWERIJNS See LAURINUS

LAXIANGUS (LB X 1684B)
In his *Responsio adversus febricitantis libellum*, Erasmus mentioned that Luis de *Carvajal's *Apologia diluens nugas Erasmi* (Paris n pr 1529) contained an appendix of epigrams exchanged between Juan de *Zafra and one 'frater Laxiangus,' who has not been identified.

LAZARUS (Ep 271) *See John (II) MORE*

LEBNA DENGAL emperor of Ethiopia, c 1497–1540
Lebna Dengal, the son of the Emperor Na'od, ascended the throne of Christian Ethiopia at the time of his father's death in 1508. His reign was dominated by a series of confrontations with Ethiopia's eastern neighbour, the Islamic kingdom of Adal. Towards the end of the 1520s, when Adal came to have a strong ruler in the person of the Imam Ahmed, it posed a serious threat to Ethiopia. Although Lebna Dengal routed Adal's army in 1516, he himself suffered a crushing defeat in 1529 in the battle of Shimbra-Kobe. During the remaining decade of his rule the defence of Ethiopia degenerated into incoherent actions led by

provincial chiefs and even guerilla warfare.

The Portuguese, who identified the Ethiopian ruler with the legendary Prester John, had sought to establish contacts with the Christian state in Africa since 1487, hoping eventually for military co-operation against the Muslim world. In reaction to the Portuguese approaches the Empress Eleni, acting as regent for Lebna Dengal, who was still a child, sent envoys to King *Manuel I of Portugal in 1513. The Portuguese responded with an embassy of their own, which actually arrived at Lebna Dengal's court in 1520 but at first received a very cautious welcome from the young ruler. All but two of the Portuguese envoys returned home in 1526, carrying letters and presents from Lebna Dengal and also 'a declaration of obedience to the pope, the significance of which the Ethiopians certainly did not understand' (Huntingford, in Alvarez I 4–5). The Portuguese were accompanied by an Ethiopian envoy. A member of this party, Father Francisco Alvarez, the author of a report on Ethiopia (first published in 1540), was sent to Italy in 1532 with the ambassador, Dom *Martinho. In February 1533 a correspondent informed Erasmus that he was present at the public audience in Bologna when Lebna Dengal's declaration of obedience was presented to Pope *Clement VII (Ep 2767).

It was not until 1541, after another, more desperate message from Lebna Dengal and after his death, that a Portuguese expeditionary force was dispatched to Ethiopia. The Portuguese fought alongside the Ethiopians in the battle of Woina-Deng (22 February 1543), where the Imam Ahmed was killed.

BIBLIOGRAPHY: *The Cambridge History of Africa* (Cambridge 1975–) III 167, 170–81 / Francisco Alvarez *The Prester John of the Indies* ed C.F. Beckingham and G.W.B. Huntingford (Cambridge 1961) / C.F. Beckingham *The Achievements of Prester John* (London 1966)   PGB

Antonio de LEBRIJA *See Elio Antonio de* NEBRIJA

Nicolas LE CLERC of Paris, d 1558
Nicolas Le Clerc (Clericus) was born in the diocese of Paris, the son of Jean Le Clerc, sieur d'Authézat in Auvergne and *conseiller* in the Châtelet of Paris, and Catherine de Vaudétard

of Issy. Several nephews held positions in the Parlement of Paris or in the royal bureaucracy. Le Clerc took his MA at the Collège des Bons-Enfants in Paris under Florentin Le Gambier, after which he taught arts at the same college. He was received as a *socius* of the Collège de Sorbonne in 1500 (the same year as his illustrious colleague Josse *Clichtove). He was the prior of the Sorbonne in 1505. Doctor Guillaume *Duchesne presided over Le Clerc's doctoral disputations in the faculty of theology, where he received his licence on 9 May 1506 and his doctorate on 19 November 1506. Le Clerc was ranked fifth of fifteen graduates.

Le Clerc was, after Noël *Béda, the most active member of the faculty of theology of Paris. He was one of four delegates from the University of Paris to the anti-papal council of Pisa-Milan of 1511–12. From May 1525 until January 1527, Le Clerc was on a special inquisitorial commission constituted by the regent, Louise of *Savoy, the pope, and the Parlement of Paris. In November 1533 he defended the faculty's prerogatives in the censure of *Margaret of Angoulême's *Miroir de l'âme pécheresse*, and this was probably the cause of his imprisonment from 17 March until September 1534 (Ep 2961) and his house detention until late November 1534. On 15 November 1539 the faculty of theology designated Le Clerc as the official university orator for the arrival of the Emperor *Charles V in Paris. Le Clerc served as dean of the faculty from September 1541 until his death. He was also named by the Parlement of Paris in 1542 to a panel constituted to receive accusations of heresy.

Le Clerc was a canon of the diocese of Thérouanne from about 1511 to at least 1527. He was the curé of several parishes (sometimes concurrently) in the dioceses of Le Mans and Paris. He held the parish of St André-des-Arts in Paris from 1519 until at least 1549. From 1533 until at least 1541 he was the archdeacon of Joinville in the diocese of Châlons-sur-Marne. He also stated that he was in the service of Jean de Guise and his brothers during their youth (perhaps as a tutor). Le Clerc was heir to a considerable fortune, and he used both this and his influence to further the careers of his nephews. But family intrigues about his money were the source of bitter personal disillusionment and long court battles in the 1540s. Le Clerc died in 1558, before 3 October.

No contemporary source authorizes the name 'Le Clerc, *dit* de Juigné' which Allen adopted from Féret and La Croix du Maine. Féret mistakenly makes Le Clerc the author of a French book on the Gospels censured by the faculty of theology.

Erasmus wrote to Le Clerc in 1528 (Ep 2043) to protest against a sermon in which Le Clerc linked Erasmus' name to *Luther's and to dissuade Le Clerc from pursuing a condemnation of Erasmus' works in the faculty of theology. At the same time Ludwig *Baer wrote to Le Clerc and apparently received an answer (Ep 2065). As early as 1526, however, Le Clerc had spoken of the books of 'Luther, Erasmus, and others' that were found in Louis de *Berquin's possession as being reprehensible.

Le Clerc is probably the translator of the following version of St Hippolytus' *Tractatus de consummatione saeculi: Vray discours de l'antechrist, de la consommation du monde, des miseres et calamitez qui adviendront aux dernier temps* (Paris: Nicolas Chesneau 1566). Bishop Robert *Céneau dedicated his *Opus super compescenda haereticorum petulantia* (Paris: J. Kerver 1557) to Le Clerc.

BIBLIOGRAPHY: Allen Ep 2043 / E. Campardon and A. Tuétey *Inventaire des registres des insinuations* (Paris 1902) nos 2471, 2518, 3357, and passim / Clerval 20, 76, and passim / Delisle passim / Farge no 275 / P.-Y. Féret *La Faculté de théologie de Paris et ses docteurs les plus célèbres. Epoque moderne* (Paris 1900–10) II 21–2 / Herminjard I 391, II 38, III passim, VIII 60 / Paris, Archives de l'Université (Sorbonne) Registre 89 f clxi verso / Paris, Archives Nationales MS MM 248–9 passim
JAMES K. FARGE

Etienne LECOMTE of Bailleul, d c 1544
Etienne Lecomte (le Comte, de Grave, Stephanus Comes) was born in Bailleul, north-west of Lille (and is therefore also called Bellocassius). He taught at the school at nearby Cassel, and in 1513 his first poems, *Primitiae*, were printed by Pieter de Keysere in Ghent. At about this time he seems to have criticized the work of Jan de Spouter (Despauterius), who mentions Lecomte's attacks in later editions of his *Ars versificatoria* (Paris 1515) and his

Syntaxis (Paris 1516–17). In 1519 he composed an *Oratio congratulatoria*, to be delivered by Pieter van Onderbergh (Submontanus), abbot of Our Lady of the Dunes, near Bruges, which he published together with a *Carmen heroicum* on *Charles v's election as emperor and other poems (Ghent: Pieter de Keysere 23 February 1520). In the same year he moved to Bruges, where he remained for the rest of his life, having been appointed secretary to the chapter of St Donatian's. Following his death a further collection, *Sylvula carminum* (Bruges: R. Wouters and E. Verreecken 1544), was published by his friend Antoon, the son of Cornelis van *Schoonhove. He was a friend of Frans van *Cranevelt, and apparently also of Marcus *Laurinus, the dean of St Donatian's. In July 1521 Juan Luis *Vives gave him a letter for conveyance to Erasmus, who was then at Anderlecht, near Brussels (Ep 1222).

BIBLIOGRAPHY: Allen VI xxi / de Vocht CTL I 210, 516, II 180–1 / de Vocht *Literae ad Craneveldium* Ep 39   IG & PGB

Edward LEE d 13 September 1544
Edward Lee (Leeus, Leus) was born, perhaps in 1482, of a good Kentish family. He was the son of Richard Lee, esquire, of Lee Magna, and paternal grandson of Sir Richard Lee, knight, lord mayor of London in 1461 and 1470. He was elected fellow of Magdalen College, Oxford, in 1500, and after graduating BA in 1501 he incorporated at Cambridge early in 1503. There he proceeded MA in 1504 and in that same year was ordained deacon with title to the church of Wells, Norfolk. Lee was collated to a prebend at Lincoln in 1512 and had a grace for the bachelor's degree in theology at Cambridge, although he was not admitted until 1515, when he was also proctor in convocation. Long after his controversy with Erasmus had cooled, he was incorporated doctor of divinity at Oxford in 1531.

It was Lee's desire to learn Greek that drew him to Louvain, where he matriculated on 25 August 1516, and resulted in Erasmus' first notice of him, on 17 July 1517 to Cuthbert *Tunstall: 'Lee is working very hard at his Greek' (Ep 607). Six months later Erasmus wrote Lee that it was not possible to incorporate his notes in the second edition of the New Testament (Ep 765). Upon that polite rejection hung a controversy which was to tax Erasmus severely and expose Lee first to notoriety and then to the ridicule of the humanist community.

Although Erasmus later said that Lee had attacked him even before their meeting (Ep 1074), he reports their early relations as amicable, stating how he aided Lee's progress in Greek and how as familiarity increased he shared with Lee his pending revisions of the *Novum instrumentum* (1516) and invited suggestions (*Opuscula* 242; Epp 886, 1074). Ambitious to secure fame by having Erasmus adopt his scholarship, Lee sporadically communicated scraps of notes (*Opuscula* 242; Epp 886, 1074), while Erasmus obtained others through Maarten *Lips (Epp 750, 843, 900, 901). Although modern scholarship has not yet evaluated those which Lee eventually published, Erasmus judged those that he saw to be largely worthless (Ep 886) and declined to use them. Lee, having misinterpreted what had been a senior scholar's kind encouragement of a novice as an invitation to collaborate, nurtured an enmity for Erasmus. An incident he published to substantiate his slight discloses his small character in the ensuing dispute: entering a tavern in which Erasmus was among friends, Lee supposed that they were ridiculing his notes (*Opuscula* 261:17n).

Before departing for Basel (c 1 May 1518) to facilitate the printing of his second edition of the New Testament, Erasmus acquired a further set of Lee's notes through Lips (Ep 750), which he answered in detail on 7 May in Ep 843. During Erasmus' absence Lee combined his own industry with common criticisms of the *Novum instrumentum* to compile three hundred refutations of it. He also accused Erasmus of using his initial notes without acknowledgment. When Erasmus returned to Louvain a bitter exchange developed which preoccupied him in futile attempts to obtain Lee's manuscript 'by every method, even underhanded' (*Opuscula* 250) and to mollify Lee – by personal interview (Epp 1225, 1581) and letter (Ep 998); by pleas for the intervention of common English friends (Epp 1026, 1029, 1030) and Lee's patron, Richard *Foxe (Ep 973); by the intercession of professors at Louvain, especially Jan *Briart (*Opuscula* 247–50), and even of Wilfred *Lee, Edward's

brother (*Opuscula* 267–8). By Erasmus' account, Lee refused to share the manuscript (Ep 998); by Lee's he was both ever willing to share it and concerned about its abuse (Ep 1061). When Erasmus could not obtain a personal copy of it, he urged Lee to publish. That failing, he negotiated with Briart for arbitration of the dispute, despite misgivings (*Opuscula* 247:205n). Lee agreeably submitted his notes to Briart, but the latter failed to make a decision before Erasmus had to return his own corrected proofs to *Froben. Erasmus next implored his English friends to intervene. Lee proposed that John *Fisher judge the case (Ep 1061; *Opuscula* 267) and supposedly sent a copy of his notes to him in March 1519, although More later claimed that Fisher never received Lee's letter of request or the manuscript (Rogers Ep 75:400–2; cf CWE Ep 1026).

Meanwhile, the publication of Erasmus' *Apologia contra Latomi dialogum* dated 28 March 1519 (LB IX 79B–106E) inflamed Lee with a reference (106A) which he took personally (Ep 993, 1061; *Opuscula* 268). Determined to publish against Erasmus he took his notes to Jean *Thibault and then to Michaël *Hillen, but they refused him. Lee alleged they had been bribed and threatened by Erasmus (Ep 1061). His attempt thwarted, he yielded to pressure from Fisher, Thomas More, Richard *Pace, and John *Colet to desist (Epp 936, 1061, 1074; *Opuscula* 250:279n). But another publication, the satiric *Dialogus bilinguium ac trilinguium* (*Opuscula* 206–24), maddened him again in July as he recognized himself (Ep 1061) as Phthonides, the enemy of the Muses (*Opuscula* 218–9), although Erasmus denied any connection with the *Dialogus* (*Opuscula* 269). When a placard attacking him was posted on the doors of a Louvain church, he appealed again to Hillen in October, but in vain (Ep 1061). Erasmus, however, was not deterring but urging publication of Lee's manuscript (Epp 1019, 1026, 1029, 1030), as he openly announced in Ep 998, which appeared in the *Farrago* in the same month (Basel: J. Froben). Coinciding with the arrival in Louvain of that volume appeared Dirk *Martens' edition of the *Colloquia*, with reference to a certain N and his sophistical riddling, his trumpery talk, his innuendoes, his arrogance, his bitterness, his sardonic laugh, his Thrasonical bragging, and his self-satisfaction. Lee assumed this person to be himself (Ep 1061; *Opuscula* 289–90). In December Erasmus published a long apologia as Ep 1053 to Thomas *Lupset. But Lee had already sent his manuscript off again, except for Ep 1061, this time to Gilles de *Gourmont in Paris, who published it for Konrad *Resch of Basel about 15 February 1520. In addition to Lee's *Annotationum libri duo*, which were 243 notes concerning Erasmus' first edition of the New Testament and 25 concerning the second, the volume contained a prefatory *Apologia E. Leei contra quorundam calumnias* addressed to the students of Louvain; an *Index annotationum prioris libri*; an *Epistola nuncupatoria ad D. Erasmum* (Ep 1037); and an *Epistola apologetica E. Leei: qua respondet duabus D. Erasmi epistolis* (Ep 1061, answering Epp 998, 1053). The version of the controversy which Lee recounts in the last has been judged by Wallace K. Ferguson as 'full of contradictions' (*Opuscula* 230).

Lee had imagined Erasmus to be attacking him surreptitiously as N, but soon he had open contempt to deal with, when within three days of receiving Lee's publication Erasmus composed an *Apologia invectivis Lei* (*Opuscula* 236–303). He published it with Hillen early in March; it was reprinted by Eucharius Cervicornus in Cologne during the same month, and later under the cover of the fictitious Vulcan Islands at the House of Brontes and Steropes (n d). Two further refutations quickly followed in April and May, again from the presses of Hillen and Froben detailing Erasmus' philological and theological disagreements with Lee (*Responsio ad annotationes Lei* LB IX 123–284B).

Deploring the controversy as one between Christians, priests, and friends, Erasmus also noted the impropriety of a senior scholar contending with a youth: it was like wrangling with a woman (*Opuscula* 236). Although Lee was past thirty-five at the time of their conflict, Erasmus correctly assessed his stature: 'He is young, so far distinguished by no remarkable literary service; as for theological affairs he neither has, I think, a doctorate nor has achieved for himself a single degree beyond mediocrity; he discharges no public office' (*Opuscula* 299). Erasmus pointed out that Lee sniffed impudently at his editions, which even the pope approved (*Opuscula* 271, 277; Ep 899).

And yet Erasmus' correspondence, especially from 1518 to 1520, is choked with concern over Lee's attacks. More than seventy letters in that period alone ventilate his irritation, importune friends, and defend himself. That Lee, with but months of Greek under his tonsure, could unsettle the most excellent scholar of the Renaissance is a matter for more consideration than can be offered here. Briefly, however, there is Erasmus' characteristically exaggerated attention to criticism, which has been charged variously to flawed character or scholarly concern. There is a deference to Lee required by mutual friendships, such as More's. Erasmus seemed especially troubled by Lee's accusation that he manifested through him a hatred of all Englishmen (Ep 899; *Opuscula* 266–7), and he even wrote to *Henry VIII denying this (Ep 1098) and enclosed a copy of the first *Responsio*. He may also have worried that Lee would stir up trouble for him politically, as may be gathered from the appeal to the lord mayor of London which Lee's principal supporter in England, Henry *Standish, made concerning Erasmus' translation of *logos* as *sermo* (John 1:1) in the New Testament of 1518–19; an early version of Erasmus' *Apologia de 'In principio erat sermo'* was published in the same binding with the *Apologia invectivis Lei* (Cologne: E. Cervicornus, March 1520; cf Ep 1072). The same fear is reflected in Erasmus' seeking Thomas *Wolsey's protection, which also mentions Lee (Ep 1060), and in his defence to Henry VIII through Thomas More (Ep 1126). There is Erasmus' suspicion that enemies at Louvain were encouraging Lee (Epp 973, 993, 998, 1074, 1097, 1098); to refute Lee would be to quell them also. Finally, there is his expressed fear lest his work cease to bear fruit if he did not respond to the critic (Ep 1139). Allen and Ferguson also emphasize a personal animosity between Erasmus and Lee.

While Erasmus' attention to Lee at this time was inflated, it was not incommensurate with the ecclesiastical power and diplomatic influence Lee would later acquire: as an ambassador of Henry VIII to *Charles V in Spain (1525–30) and also to Pope *Clement VII when he met the emperor in Bologna (1530); as royal almoner from 1523; and as archbishop of York from 1531. Early discerning Lee's ambitions ('He has a burning desire for reputation,' Ep 973), Erasmus perhaps assessed also where they might take him. Five years after these mutual recriminations, when on embassy in Spain, Lee again circulated a polemic against him (Epp 1744, 1747, 1864, 2094, 2198). Therefore Erasmus could feel justified in the severity of his earlier treatment of Lee, even though he had finally decided that few of Lee's original notes had been his own work (Ep 1581).

When friendly persuasion had failed, Erasmus saw added to his own publications against Lee the *Epistolae aliquot virorum* (first published by Hillen in May 1520 with his knowledge; then enlarged by Froben in August, which version he may have tried to withdraw later, Ep 1157), in which among others More, Lupset, Wilhelm *Nesen, Richard Pace, *Beatus Rhenanus, Johannes *Sapidus, *Zasius, Ulrich von *Hutten, Paul *Volz, Gerardus *Listrius, Marquard von *Hattstein, and Eucharius *Gallinarius criticized and sometimes abused Lee. Erasmus' fair warning to Lee about the violence of his German friends (Ep 998; cf Ep 1061) was also realized when the humanists of Erfurt lampooned him with epigrams and a recriminating pamphlet appeared 'against the raving sycophant' (CWE Ep 1083 introduction). Erasmus soon relented, however, and had Froben publish late in May 1520 a milder version of the controversy, purged of his *Apologia invectivis Lei* and Lee's letter to Louvain (Ep 1061), and with a new preface (Ep 1100). After that, references to Lee in Erasmus' writings, although still numerous in the correspondence, are brief, and they mostly review the controversy or note the progress of Lee's career. Exceptions are the letters written between 1526 and 1529 concerning Lee's collaboration with the Spanish monks, especially the pamphlet Erasmus attributed to him.

Lee survived Erasmus by nine years. He was buried in his cathedral church, which he had guided through the transition from Roman to Anglican discipline. In contrast to the published invectives which Erasmus and other humanists heaped contemptuously on him were two verses in his honour placed in the window of the founder's chamber at Magdalen College, where he had begun his career.

In addition to his publications against Erasmus, Lee wrote: 'Commentarium in universum Pentateuchum,' unpublished (Roger Ascham *Letters* II Ep 17); *Exhibita quaedam, per Eduardum Leum, oratorem anglicum in consilio caesareo ante belli indictionem* (Antwerp: J. Grapheus 1528); translations of 'Lives of divers Saints,' British Library MS Harl. 423 ff 9–55; resolutions of questions on the sacraments, printed in Gilbert Burnet *History of the Reformation* (London: Richard Chiswell 1681–3) I Records: Bk 3, 201–41 passim; letters, Epp 1037, 1061 and in John Strype *Ecclesiastical Memorials* (Oxford 1822) I 290–4, 330–1 with an oration at 64–5, and in the Harleian and Cotton MSS of the British Library and in the Record Office; with others, 'Articles about Religion set out by the Convocation and published by the King's Authority' and 'A Declaration made of the Functions and Divine Institution of Bishops and Priests,' Burnet 314, 324. DNB attributes to him a treatise concerning the dispensing power, Harl. MS 417 f 11.

BIBLIOGRAPHY: Allen and CWE 765 / Emden BRUO II 1122–3 / DNB XI 788–90 / de Vocht CTL I 324 and passim / de Vocht *Literae ad Craneveldium* Ep 254:31n / Augustus Bludau *Die beiden ersten Erasmus-Ausgaben des Neuen Testaments und ihre Gegner* (Freiburg 1902) 86–125 / On the possibility that Lee composed Henry VIII's book against *Luther, as the latter thought, see J.J. Scarisbrick *Henry VIII* (London 1968) 112 / On Lee's role during the so-called 'Pilgrimage of Grace' see M.H. Dobbs and R. Dobbs *The Pilgrimage of Grace 1536–1537 and the Exeter Conspiracy 1538* (Cambridge 1915) I 377–87 and passim   MARJORIE O'ROURKE BOYLE

Wilfred LEE documented 1519–20
Wilfred Lee (Galfredus) is not documented apart from his role in the conflict between his brother, Edward *Lee, and Erasmus, in which he acted as an arbitrator. Wilfred met Erasmus several times at Louvain (Ep 1053) and, according to a letter from Thomas *Lupset to Thomas Paynell which appeared in the *Epistolae aliquot virorum* (Basel: J. Froben 1520; cf Ep 1083), had also tried to assuage his brother's feelings. Erasmus reports that Wilfred seemed to embrace Erasmus' explanation concerning the passage in the *Apologia contra Latomi dialogum* (LB IX 106A) at which Edward took umbrage (*Opuscula* 268). Nevertheless it was

Wilfred who delivered Edward's manuscript to Michaël *Hillen in Antwerp on his second attempt to get it published in October 1519 (Ep 1061), although he was unsuccessful. It was also Wilfred who delivered the manuscript to Gilles de *Gourmont in Paris (Ep 1074), finally succeeding in getting it published. In his *Responsio ad annotationes Lei* (LB IX 205B) Erasmus likened this brotherly collaboration to the adage *Frater viro adsit* (*Adagia* I vii 92). Several months later he noted, however, that even his brothers disagreed with Edward (Ep 1126). Long after this controversy, but during a second one which flared when Edward collaborated with the Spanish monks, Erasmus wrote Thomas *More that during Wilfred's mission to Paris he secured, with the counsel and consent of Jacobus *Latomus, the assistance of Noël *Béda in completing the manuscript, since at that time Edward could not write a page on a theological subject (Ep 1804). Erasmus' final notice of Wilfred occurs in 1533, when he incorrectly identified him as More's successor as chancellor and recalled him as a friend in time past whose only nobility derived from the fact that he was a lawyer, since he was born in a village (Ep 2780).

BIBLIOGRAPHY: Allen and CWE Ep 1053 / *Opuscula* 267–8

                                    MARJORIE O'ROURKE BOYLE

Gerard LEEU of Gouda, d 1493
Born in Gouda, Leeu (Leeuw, Leew, Leo, Leonis) was active as a printer and publisher there from 1477 to 1484 and from then to his death in Antwerp. In 1485 he was admitted as a master to the guild of St Luke. His wife, Cornelia, bore him two daughters, Maria and Gheertruyde, who later lived at Gouda as nuns. Leeu published in excess of two hundred volumes; while works in Dutch prevailed during his Gouda years, works in Latin came to dominate his production at Antwerp. As the first Dutch printer to produce works in English and French, Leeu may be counted among the leading printers of his generation in the Netherlands.

By 1489 Erasmus had personal contacts with Leeu, whom he judged to be 'a very clever fellow' (Ep 32).

BIBLIOGRAPHY: Allen and CWE Ep 32 / M.E. Kronenberg in NNBW VI 918–21 / P. Bergmann

in BNB IX 642–5 / A. Rouzet *Dictionnaire des imprimeurs, libraires et éditeurs des xve et xvie siècles dans les limites géographiques de la Belgique actuelle* (Nieuwkoop 1975) 121–3

                                    MARCEL A. NAUWELAERTS

Jacques LEFÈVRE d'Etaples c 1460–1536
Jacques Lefèvre d'Etaples (Faber Stapulensis) was born about 1460 in the small Channel port of Etaples in Picardy. Having matriculated at the Collège de Boncour in Paris in 1474 or 1475, he moved to the Collège du Cardinal Lemoine, where he received a BA in 1479 and his licence and MA the following year. He became a teacher in the faculty of arts of the university, probably at the Collège du Cardinal Lemoine, and began to study Greek under the guidance of Georgius *Hermonymus. In 1490 he wrote an introduction to the *Metaphysics* of Aristotle, a work distinguished from its scholastic rivals by the endeavour to return to and make clear the teachings of Aristotle himself. By 1491 he was briefly tempted to retire from the world and enter a monastery, having been deeply stirred by reading the *Liber contemplationis* of Ramón Lull. In the winter of 1491–2 Lefèvre took the first of three trips to Italy. In Rome he met the Venetian humanist Ermolao I *Barbaro, and in Florence he visited Marsilio *Ficino and Giovanni *Pico della Mirandola. It was Barbaro who inspired Lefèvre to try to purify the understanding of Aristotle in the Paris schools by making available the philosopher's original texts. Ficino introduced Lefèvre to the writing of Dionysius the Pseudo-Areopagite, to the Hermetic writings, and to the Platonists. Lefèvre soon distanced himself from the latter school but became profoundly attached to the Pseudo-Areopagite and the Hermetic writings. Pico encouraged Lefèvre to approach the understanding of the sources of ancient wisdom, including Scripture, by a syncretic and contemplative method.

On his return to Paris Lefèvre resumed his lectures at the Collège du Cardinal Lemoine. Before the end of 1492 he published his first work, paraphrases of Aristotle's writings on natural philosophy (Paris: J. Higman), and in the course of the next few years he published humanist translations and fresh commentaries on the entire corpus of Aristotle. In 1493 and

Jacques Lefèvre d'Etaples

1494 he brought out his introduction to Aristotle's *Metaphysics* (Paris: J. Higman) and a commentary on the *Nicomachean Ethics* (Paris: A. Caillaut); subsequent years witnessed the appearance of new editions of Aristotle's *Nicomachean Ethics* (Paris: J. Higman and W. Hopyl 1497), *Organon* (Paris: W. Hopyl and H. Estienne 1503), *Politics* (Paris: H. Estienne 1506), and *Metaphysics* (Paris: H. Estienne 1515). Throughout, Lefèvre sought to use his commentaries on the text not in the scholastic manner, as a point of departure for philosophical disputation, but to assist students to understand Aristotle's philosophy. His understanding of other ancient philosophers, allusions to classical poetry, and references to historical examples from antiquity threw a new light on Aristotelian philosophy. At the same time his Aristotelianism remained profoundly Christian: in his view Aristotle had been inspired by divine illumination, and Aristotle's conception of the essence of essences was, according to him, identical to the Christian concept of God the Father and Creator.

Important as the study of Aristotle was to Lefèvre, he considered it only the first stage in the development of understanding. In the aftermath of his first Italian journey he had interested himself in astrology and the mystical understanding of numbers. In 1499 he published the writings of the Pseudo-Areopagite (Paris: J. Higman and W. Hopyl) and in 1505 an edition of the *Hermetica* (Paris: H. Estienne). Lefèvre's educational program, as outlined in his introduction to Aristotle's *Politics* (1506), called in the first place for the cultivation of a humanist understanding of Aristotle based on a sound training in the liberal arts. But the second and higher stage of understanding lay in the comprehension of the Scriptures. Moreover, just as an understanding of Aristotle depended on the prior study of Virgil, Cicero, and Boethius, an understanding of the sacred texts depended on comprehending the works of the Fathers of the church like Cyprian, Hilary, and Jerome. Beyond these authorities it was possible, according to Lefèvre, to gain insight into Scripture through studying the writings of Dionysius the Pseudo-Areopagite and Nicolaus *Cusanus.

By the first decade of the new century a humanist circle had emerged around Lefèvre, attracted by his lectures on Aristotle and by his humanist scholarship. The most important member of this circle was Josse *Clichtove, who over the following two decades became Lefèvre's collaborator in editing and publishing Aristotle's works as well as patristic texts and works on logic, music, mathematics, and mystical religion. Next in importance to Clichtove was Charles de Bovelles, who rediscovered the work of Cusanus and attempted to build a fresh philosophical synthesis out of it. Other followers, teachers in the colleges of the university, were Robert Fortuné, Guillaume Castel, Johannes de *Molendino, and Gérard *Roussel.

Lefèvre made two more journeys into Italy, in 1500 and again in 1507. Following his return from his second Italian visit he retired from his teaching post at the Collège du Cardinal Lemoine. His new patron, Guillaume *Briçonnet, abbot of Saint-Germain-des-Prés, invited him to take up residence in the abbey, which was in the process of reform. Lefèvre, now freed from the day-to-day routine of teaching, devoted himself single-mindedly to scholarship. Moreover, he was for the first time brought face to face with the necessity of relating his scholarship to the problem of reform of the monasteries – a problem which had preoccupied a generation of French reformers. Erasmus' *Enchiridion* (1503) had already enunciated the ideal of a purified Christianity founded on a return to the Gospel, and his edition of Lorenzo *Valla's *Adnotationes* on the New Testament (1505) provided a model for the textual criticism which would make this truer understanding possible. It was in this context that Lefèvre turned to scriptural studies. In 1509, anticipating the great work of Erasmus on the New Testament, Lefèvre published his critical study of a biblical text, the *Quincuplex Psalterium* (Paris: H. Estienne). In the commentaries on the Pauline Epistles which appeared three years later (Paris: H. Estienne) Lefèvre attempted to apply the same historical and philological principles to the text of St Paul as he had to the works of Aristotle. At the same time his approach to St Paul was strongly coloured by mysticism and in particular the teachings of Dionysius the Pseudo-Areopagite and Nicolaus Cusanus. His hermeneutic was distinguished by its Christocentricity, its stress on the need for spiritual incorporation in God's grace, and its emphasis on grace rather than exteriorized observances.

Erasmus had lived in Paris between 1495 and 1499, and he revisited the city at least six more times in the next decade. It was on the occasion of his seventh and last visit in 1511 that we have evidence of a meeting between him and Lefèvre. At that time Erasmus had just published the *Moriae encomium* and had established himself as among the most celebrated of European humanists. Lefèvre, among other notables, received him warmly. According to Erasmus' account they had a number of intimate conversations, but one is entitled to wonder how frank they actually were with each other since, as Erasmus pointed out, Lefèvre told him nothing of the impending publication of his commentaries on Paul (Allen Ep 337:837–52). Lefèvre wrote to Erasmus in 1514 enthusiastically welcoming him back to the continent following his third sojourn in England (Ep 315).

The publication of Erasmus' New Testament undoubtedly greatly affected Lefèvre. It led in the first place to a quarrel provoked in part by

the fact that Lefèvre felt intimidated by the evident superiority of Erasmus' scholarship. There can be no question that the latter was the better humanist; his erudition was deeper, his sense of grammar more exact, and his sense of history more profound. The dispute was nominally over a quite trivial point. Erasmus criticized Lefèvre for his reading of *Hebrews* 2:7 as 'Thou madest him a little lower than God' instead of ' a little lower than the angels.' Their disagreement, insignificant though it appeared, nevertheless reflected profound differences in spiritual outlook and temperament. Lefèvre based his view, among other things, on an extraordinary awareness of the dignity of Christ or, to put it in another way, on a deep sense of the gap separating God and man. On the other hand, Erasmus stressed the historical and theological significance of Christ's suffering on the Cross. There seems little doubt that Erasmus was right on both counts. The dispute was fought out in Lefèvre's second edition of the Epistles of St Paul (1515), Erasmus' *Apologia ad Fabrum*, and many letters, mostly on the part of Erasmus and his friends (Epp 597, 659, 680A, 778, 814; LB IX 17–80; index to CWE 5). The quarrel opened up a breach between Lefèvre and his followers and Erasmus that was really never bridged. Lefèvre and those who followed him, such as *Margaret of Angoulême, believed that Erasmus had sacrificed piety to scholarship.

Despite this quarrel Erasmus' achievement clearly had an important effect on Lefèvre. Even in overshadowing Lefèvre's more modest efforts Erasmus' New Testament confirmed them as pioneering works in scriptural study. Erasmus certainly saw them in this light. Moreover, Erasmus' scholarly principles evidently began to influence Lefèvre's approach to Scripture. In the *De Maria Magdalena et triduo Christi disceptatio* (Paris: H. Estienne 1518) and two subsequent works, Lefèvre tried to dispel the confusion common in the Middle Ages between the three Marys who appear in the Gospel narrative (Epp 765, 766, 936, 1030). Erasmus' technique of historical and textual analysis evidently influenced Lefèvre to a remarkable degree. Increasingly Lefèvre was coming to see Scripture as the most important standard determining authentic belief.

Under attack from the Paris faculty of

theology, Lefèvre withdrew from Paris at the beginning of 1521. He was called to assist in the reform of the diocese of Meaux, where his patron, Briçonnet, had become bishop in 1516. He was first made head of the *leproserie* (1521) and then vicar-general *in spiritualibus* (1523). In 1522 he published at Meaux (S. de Colines) his *Commentarii initiatorii* on the four Gospels. By 1524 Lefèvre and others at Meaux were corresponding with Guillaume *Farel in Basel and enthusiastically reading the Latin works of the German reformers. By 1525 when he came to write his *Commentarii in Epistolas catholicas* (Basel: A. Cratander 1527) and to oversee the composition of the *Epistres et Evangiles pour les cinquante et deux sepmaines de l'an* (Paris: S. Du Bois 1525?), Lefèvre was prepared to question the intrinsic spiritual authority of the priesthood, the efficacy of the sacraments apart from faith, the sacrificial character of the Eucharist, and the doctrine of the real presence. He rejected the practice of invoking the saints and the veneration of images. The contemporary forms of confession and extreme unction he held to be suspect on the basis of the Gospel.

Growing radicalization of the Meaux reform led to a reaction which forced Lefèvre to flee to Strasbourg in October 1525. The persecution of Lefèvre in France may have caused Erasmus to intervene on his behalf at Rome (Ep 1650A). It is not impossible that this act prepared the way for a meeting of the two at Basel prior to Lefèvre's return to France in the spring of 1526 (Ep 1713). Lefèvre was recalled to France by *Francis I, who appointed him head of the royal library at Blois and tutor of the royal children. In the ensuing years he finished translating the Bible into French and had it printed by Maarten de Keyser at Antwerp in 1530. That year he moved to Nérac to the court of Margaret, now queen of Navarre, where he lived in retirement until his death in 1536. Erasmus remained well disposed towards Lefèvre. He felt drawn to him by the fact that both were under attack by the syndic of the Paris faculty of theology, Noël *Béda. He referred to Lefèvre in 1529 as a 'bonus vir' (Ep 1821) and made efforts to keep in touch with him (Ep 1795; cf Epp 2052, 2077). But whether through fear, illness, or animosity, Lefèvre apparently did not respond.

The best-known portrait of Lefèvre is in the *Icones* of Théodore de Bèze published in 1580. There is also a miniature (Paris, Bibliothèque de l'Arsenal, MS 4009) in which the royal almoner, François *Du Moulin de Rochefort, is depicted as presenting Lefèvre to Louise of *Savoy. Lefèvre also appears in a sculpture in the Belle-Chapelle in the abbey of Solesmes. There he is represented as St Jerome attired in the dress of a cardinal of the Roman church.

BIBLIOGRAPHY: Allen and CWE Ep 315 / Apart from sixteenth century editions, see for Lefèvre's own writings Rice *Prefatory Epistles*, and the *Epistres et Evangiles pour les cinquante et deux dimanches de l'an* ed Guy Bedouelle and Franco Giacone (Leiden 1976) / The fullest account of Lefèvre's life may be found in Guy Bedouelle *Lefèvre d'Etaples et l'intelligence des écritures* (Geneva 1976); it is a scholarly but tendentious interpretation and ought to be supplemented by Henry Heller 'The evangelicism of Lefèvre d'Etaples 1525' *Studies in the Renaissance* 16 (1969) 42–77 / Also important are Eugene F. Rice 'The humanist idea of Christian antiquity, Lefèvre d'Etaples and his circle' *Studies in the Renaissance* 9 (1962) 126–60 / Eugene F. Rice 'Humanist Aristotelianism in France: Jacques Lefèvre d'Etaples and his circle' *Humanism in France* ed A.H.T. Levi (Manchester 1970) 132–49 / Eugene F. Rice 'Jacques Lefèvre d'Etaples and the Medieval Christian Mystics' *Florilegium historiale: Essays presented to Wallace K. Ferguson* ed J.G. Rowe et W.H. Stockdale (Toronto 1971) 89–124 / The dispute between Erasmus and Lefèvre may be approached through Margaret Mann *Erasme et les débuts de la réforme française: 1517–1536* (Paris 1934) 23–46; Helmut Feld 'Der Humanisten-Streit um Hebräer 2, 7 (Psalm 8, 6)' ARG 61 (1970) 5–33; John B. Payne 'Erasmus and Lefèvre d'Etaples as Interpreters of Paul' ARG 65 (1974) 54–83 / Guy Bedouelle *Le Quincuplex Psalterium de Lefèvre d'Etaples: Un guide de lecture* (Geneva 1979)   HENRY HELLER

Jacques LEFÈVRE *See also Jacobus* FABER

Simon LEIGNERIUS *See Simon* LAGNIER

Roberte LE LIEUR c 1491–c 1559
Roberte Le Lieur (Le Lyeur), the daughter of a family of well-educated dignitaries, married Guillaume *Budé around 1505 (Ep 583). She presided over the household of her humanistic

husband in the tradition being established by the Renaissance women of northern Europe. Although constrained by the mores restricting women from open scholarly activity, she apparently assisted Budé in his research and publications over the years while providing him with the delights of an idealized family circle. Some years after the death of her husband, she and three sons took up residence in Geneva close to Calvin's quarters in order to escape the sharp rebukes of those who rejected the radical directions of the reformers (1549). Eventually adopting Calvinism, she may have extended her influence at least partially to two sons who continued to write in the reformist vein without, however, ever attaining their father's prominence.

BIBLIOGRAPHY: Allen and CWE Ep 583 / E. de Budé *Vie de Guillaume Budé* (Paris 1884) / L. Delaruelle *Guillaume Budé* (Paris 1907) / D. McNeil *Guillaume Budé and Humanism in the Reign of Francis I* (Geneva 1975) / F. Watson *Vives and the Renascence Education of Women* (London 1912) quoting Juan Luis *Vives *De institutione feminae christianae*

ALICE TOBRINER

Claude LE MARLET of Dijon, documented 1503–34
Not a great deal is known about Claude Le Marlet (Marletus). His family was highly respectable; a Jean Le Marlet was mayor of Dijon from 1540 to 1542 and from 1543 to 1545, and Jean's brother Hugues was *bailli* of Dijon in 1556, but subsequently the family died out. Claude was *avocat* at the Parlement of Dijon. In February 1503 he obtained a letter of nobility from *Louis XII in recognition of services rendered. He published *Orationes duae Valentiae habitae, una in laudem divi Sebastiani, altera in funere ... Antonii Palmerii* (Lyon: S. Gryphius 1528, copy in the British Library, London) and *De felicissimo reginae adventu Divione celebrato enchiridion* (Dijon: P. Grangier, n d, copy in the Bibliothèque Nationale, Paris), following the marriage of *Eleanor, the sister of *Charles v, to *Francis I of France (4 July 1530). A *consilium* by Le Marlet is found in Barthélemy de Chasseneux *Consilia* (Lyon: N. Vincent 1588), and P.S. Allen discovered in Besançon a manuscript letter by him, dated 3 June 1534.

Le Marlet introduced himself to Erasmus with a complimentary letter, probably written in 1523 (Ep 1354), referring to *Iussellus as a common acquaintance; no reply is known.

BIBLIOGRAPHY: Allen Ep 1354 / Philibert Papillon *Bibliothèque des auteurs de Bourgogne* (Dijon 1742) II 25 / Jules d'Arbaumont 'Les anoblis de Bourgogne' *Revue nobiliaire* (1866), in the offprint page 46 / Dijon, Bibliothèque publique, MS 820: P. Palliot 'Mémoires généalogiques.' Monsieur P. Gras, Conservateur-en-chef of this library, has informed me that, contrary to Allen's conjecture, there is no connection between the families Le Marlet and Morelet du Museau; he has kindly supplied most of the information used for this article

PGB

Guillaume LE MOYNE documented 1521–4
Guillaume Le Moyne served under Jean Hannart in the chancery of *Charles v. In March 1521 Cuthbert *Tunstall informed Cardinal *Wolsey of a conversation between Le Moyne and the English agent Thomas Spinelly, and in October 1521 Le Moyne countersigned a letter from Charles v to Wolsey. In March 1524 Erasmus sent him greetings in a letter addressed to Guy *Morillon.

BIBLIOGRAPHY: Allen Ep 1431 / LP III 1668 / *Deutsche Reichstagsakten* Jüngere Reihe (Gotha-Göttingen 1893–) II 813–14   PGB

Jean LENGHERANT *See* BINTIUS

Pope LEO x 11 December 1475–
1 December 1521
Giovanni was the second son of Lorenzo (I) de' *Medici ('il Magnifico') and Clarice Orsini, and a first cousin of Giulio de' Medici, who became Pope *Clement VII. His education from the age of three was entrusted to notable teachers (Erasmus congratulated him on this in Ep 335): *Poliziano, Martino della Commedia, and Bernardo Michelozzi. He learnt Greek from Urbano *Valeriani and Demetrius *Chalcondyles and music from the Netherlandish composer Isaac. He received the tonsure and first minor orders on 1 June 1483 and on 12 June was created an apostolic protonotary. Giovanni was appointed a cardinal in secret in March 1489. This was announced publicly three years later, and he arrived in Rome on 22 March 1492. In the mean time he had studied canon law at the University of Pisa under Filippo *Decio, Bartolomeo Sozzini, and

Pope Leo X, by Raphael

others. He was appointed legate in the Patrimony of St Peter on 15 April 1492 and on 11 May legate to Florence and its dominion. He was in Rome for the conclave which elected *Alexander VI, leaving again for Florence on 2 September. After the invasion by *Charles VIII of France and the fall of his brother Piero de' Medici in November 1494, Giovanni left Florence with his brothers and his cousin Giulio, going first to Bologna then returning to Rome; he was in Milan in 1496 and Bologna in 1497, closely in touch with Piero in his attempts to restore the family in Florence. In August 1499 he visited Venice, making an unfavourable impression as fat and ugly (Sanudo *Diarii* II 1036, 1060) and subsequently travelled to Germany and Flanders. According to Paolo Giovio he was arrested at Ulm and then was given an imperial safe conduct to proceed; at Saint-Omer he stayed with the abbot of St Bertin, Antoon van *Bergen, though the latter's reply to Giovanni's thanks for his hospitality was not written until 30 July 1501 and the real author is believed to have been Erasmus (Ep 162). In it Giovanni was described as 'another Ulysses,' and two songs together

with a musical setting accompanied the letter. Saint-Omer may have been the place of the early meeting of Erasmus and the future pope referred to by the latter in his letter of 10 July 1515 to *Henry VIII (Ep 339). He continued his travels through France, returning by ship from Marseille; because of bad weather he put in at Savona, meeting there the future *Julius II, and re-entered Rome on 18 May 1500. The favour he was to enjoy from Pope Julius enabled Giovanni to make his household in Rome the rallying point for the Medici after 1503. In September 1506 he accompanied Julius to Perugia (where he was named governor) and Bologna, taking part in the triumphal entry on 11 November which Erasmus witnessed.

During Erasmus' stay in Rome in 1509 Giovanni was particularly kind to him: he recalled this in letters to Servatius *Rogerus (Ep 296), and to Leo himself (Ep 335), and this is also mentioned by *Beatus Rhenanus writing in 1540 (Allen I 62). The cardinal's palace was near the church of Sant' Eustachio: Albertini mentions that it had a library in which were statues and paintings; in fact most of the Medici library, repurchased in 1508 and 1509 from the friars of San Marco in Florence, was there. Indeed Erasmus was so appreciative of Giovanni's geniality and encouragement of learning that he overlooked his close involvement in Julius II's wars. Giovanni not only accompanied Julius to Bologna and Ravenna in 1510 and 1511 but on 1 October 1511 was appointed legate to Bologna and Romagna and was actively raising infantry at Imola in January 1512. While he was with the papal army at the battle of Ravenna in April 1512, he was captured by Albanian *stradiotti* and taken to Milan as a prisoner with the retreating French army; his subsequent escape at Pieve del Cairo, near Mortara, earned fame as an almost miraculous delivery. He was present at Mantua for the discussions in July and August 1512 leading to the league's invasion of Tuscany, the sack of Prato, and the restoration of the Medici to Florence, during which expedition Giovanni again accompanied the army as legate.

Elected Pope Leo X on 11 March 1513 (after which he was ordained a priest and bishop), he was favourably characterized by Erasmus. Erasmus described him to Antoon van Bergen

as scholarly and devout (Ep 288) and to
Cardinal *Riario as the restorer of peace (Ep
333), thus emphasizing the contrast with Julius
II; when writing to Leo himself on 21 May 1515
Erasmus elaborately compared him to Solomon
and reviewed the first nine popes who bore the
names Leo (Ep 335). In fact war had continued
after Leo's accession, and not until the French
defeats in the summer of 1513 was the situation
effectively changed. However, Leo's magna-
nimity towards the recently schismatic cardinals and his reopening of the fifth Lateran
council demonstrated his pacific intentions,
and his diplomacy did express a reluctance to
renew war against France. The accession of
*Francis I and the invasion leading to victory at
Marignano in September 1515 forced Leo to
make his position clearer. Negotiations, culminating in his interview with Francis at Bologna
in December, preserved the papal state and
Medicean interests in Tuscany, also gaining
some ecclesiastical advantage in France with
the abolition of the Pragmatic Sanction; but
Lombardy was again under French control.
Erasmus did not comment on this episode, or
on Leo's various schemes to establish his
brother Giuliano in a principality, or his
confiscation of the duchy of Urbino in 1516 and
conferment of it upon his nephew Lorenzo (II)
de' *Medici, leading to a calamitously expensive war in 1517. In a letter to *Tunstall (Ep
607), however, Erasmus did mention hearing
of the conspiracy in Rome against Leo's life in
which the cardinals *Petrucci, *Sauli, and
Riario were involved. Leo's crusade projects of
1517–18 were attributed by Erasmus to ruthless
political ambitions (Epp 781, 785, 786, 796; cf Ep
2285), but his genuine concern at this time to
obtain peace and concord in Europe was
acknowledged in the *Querela pacis* (LB IV
636C–D, 642B). He attempted to impose a
five-year truce and hoped in vain to prevent
either Francis I or Charles of Hapsburg from
becoming emperor. However, growing tensions in relations with Francis I in 1520,
culminating in the French attack upon Reggio
in June 1521, finally brought Leo into decisive
alliance with *Charles V (Ep 1228); the ensuing
military campaign led to the expulsion of the
French from Lombardy. After victoriously
returning to Rome on 25 November, Leo fell ill
with bronchial pneumonia and died on 1

December. He had suffered poor health for
many years; as well as chronic obesity, he had
an anal fistula which had even required
surgery during the 1513 conclave. Erasmus
heard of the pope's death by 14 December (Ep
1249); later, in a letter to Clement VII (Ep 1414),
he described it as untimely.

The levity and ostentation of Leo X and his
overriding concern for Florence and his Florentine relatives and dependents did not arouse
Erasmus' criticism. While music and hunting
were probably Leo's main diversions, as
Giovio also recorded, his was a golden age for
writers and scholars; and Erasmus was well
aware of the opportunities. He frequently
boasted in letters that Leo had liked the *Moriae
encomium* (Ep 673, 739, 749; LB IX 1109E).
According to Andrea *Ammonio, by February
1516 Leo was praising Erasmus to other
scholars and hoped he would visit Rome (Ep
389). Erasmus' main endeavour was to obtain
Leo's patronage for his edition of the New
Testament. In December 1515 he announced
that he had decided to dedicate it to him (Ep
377; cf Ep 384); eventually on 10 September
1518 the pope sent his blessings for the second
edition (Ep 864), which Erasmus happily
acknowledged (Ep 905), hoping Leo would
express his approval of Erasmus' endeavours
in an even more general form (Epp 1007, 1060,
1062). But rather some strain appeared in their
relationship. The trouble was partly due to
Erasmus' conservative critics and partly to the
militancy of *Luther and his friends (cf Ep
1033). Erasmus insisted he had no sympathy
for Luther and refused to support *Hutten
despite his appeals (Epp 1135, 1161); he urged
Leo on 13 September 1520 not to believe the
calumnies against himself, and also mentioned
that he had hoped to come and work in the
Vatican library that winter (Ep 1143). The
pope's answer (Ep 1180) was friendly, but it
showed that Erasmus' fears had been well
founded. Subsequently he wrote that he had
suspected *Aleandro of trying to turn the pope
against him (Epp 1213, 1236, 1496). Erasmus
continued to describe Leo as mild and just,
uncharacteristically provoked to anger by
Luther when he permitted the condemnation
of *Reuchlin's work to pass (Ep 1059). While
Leo was alive, his personality held out a last
spark of hope for a peaceful and just resolution

of the Reformation controversy (Ep 1205), but after his death Erasmus declared that he was not the judge of Leo (Allen Ep 1342:908).

BIBLIOGRAPHY: Leo has been the subject of several biographical studies, beginning with the basic one by his contemporary Paolo Giovio, *Vita Leonis x*, written before 1534 and published in many editions; further material appeared in A. Fabroni *Leonis x, Pontificis Maximi vita* (Pisa 1797), followed by W. Roscoe *The Life and Pontificate of Leo the Tenth* (1st ed, 4 vols, Liverpool 1805, subsequently revised). F. Nitti *Leone x e la sua politica* (Florence 1892) is mainly concerned with Leo's diplomacy, and the excellent, fully documented study by G.B. Picotti, *La giovinezza di Giovanni de' Medici* (Milan 1928), only goes up to 1494; however see also Picotti's biographical article in *Enciclopedia Cattolica* (Rome 1948–54) VII 1150–5. There is extensive coverage in Pastor VII–VIII and M. Creighton *A History of the Papacy from the Great Schism to the Sack of Rome* (London 1887–1902) V–VI; basic information in Eubel and much material in Sanudo *Diarii*, contemporary Florentine historiography, and the Diary of Paris de Grassis: apart from the sections published by Creighton, further extracts are in P. Delicati and L. Armellini *Il Diario di Leone x di Paride di Grassi* (Rome 1884) and *Le due spedizioni militari di Giulio II* ed L. Frati (Bologna 1886).

Further publications of importance include: F. Albertini *Opusculum de mirabilibus novae et veteris urbis Romae* ed A. Schmarsow (Heilbronn 1866) / G. Pieraccini *La stirpe de' Medici di Cafaggiolo* (Florence 1924) I 191–212 / A. Ferrajoli *La congiura dei cardinali contro Leone x*, Miscellanea della R. Società Romana di Storia Patria (Rome 1919) / G.L. Moncallero *Epistolario di Bernardo Dovizi* (Florence 1955–65) (correspondence of Giovanni's secretary) / P. Ravasio 'Memorie e cimelii inediti di Pieve del Cairo Lomellina circa la liberazione del Cardinale de' Medici della prigionia dei francesi' *Archivio storico lombardo* 10 (1883) 381–95 / E. Piccolomini *Intorno alle condizioni ed alle vicende della libreria medicea privata* (Florence 1875) / A. Luzio 'Isabella d'Este ne' primordi del papato di Leone x e il suo viaggio a Roma nel 1514–1515' *Archivio storico lombardo* 4th ser 6 (1906) 99–180, 454–89 / V. Fanelli 'Il ginnasio greco di Leone x a Roma' *Studi Romani* 9 (1961) / K.M. Setton 'Pope Leo x and the Turkish Peril' *Proceedings of*

the American Philosophical Society 113 (1969) 367–424 / J. Shearman 'The Vatican Stanze: functions and decorations' *Proceedings of the British Academy* 57 (1971) 3–58 / J. Shearman *Raphael's Cartoons in the Collection of H.M. the Queen and the Tapestries for the Sistine Chapel* (London 1972)   D.S. CHAMBERS

Ambrosius LEO *See Ambrogio* LEONI

LEODEGARIUS documented 1524–7
Leodegarius (Leodigarius, Leodegerius), who has not been identified, was associated with Ludovicus *Carinus and Heinrich *Eppendorf (Epp 1761, 1799). On 15 June 1524 he departed from Frankfurt am Main for his native region. This journey apparently took him through Wittenberg, where he delivered a letter to *Melanchthon; cf *Melanchthons Briefwechsel* I Ep 328.   PGB

Ambrogio LEONI of Nola, c 1459–c 1524
Little is known of the early life of Leoni (Leone, Ambrosius Leo) other than that he was born at Nola, east of Naples, the son of Marchesella Balletta and Marino Leoni, a merchant. He studied philosophy and medicine at Padua with Nicoleto Vernia, among others. He taught philosophy and later medicine at the University of Naples before returning to Padua some time after 1504, when he studied Greek with Marcus *Musurus. In 1507 he went to Venice, where he joined the household of Aldo *Manuzio, serving him both as editor and as physician. Leoni remained in Venice for the rest of his life, publishing voluminously during his later years. He wrote a history of his native Nola and several medical and philosophical works, and he translated Actuarius' *De urinis* and Pseudo-Aristotle's *De virtutibus* into Latin.

Erasmus and Leoni first met in Aldo's house about 1507, as Leoni himself said (Ep 854). The tone of the letters they exchanged (Epp 854, 868) is warm, indicating a close friendship between the two while they were together in Venice. Erasmus considered Leoni to be one of the foremost physicians of the age, along with *Linacre, *Cop, *Du Ruel, and *Leoniceno (Epp 541, 542, 868; LB IX 85F). He gave Erasmus particular help in explicating one of the *Adagia*; this is gratefully acknowledged, with Leoni referred to as 'philosophus huius tempestatis eximius' (I ii 63). Elsewhere Leoni's acuteness was praised (*Adagia* II iii 50, III vii 66), and Erasmus mourned his death in a letter of 3 October 1525 (Ep 1623).

BIBLIOGRAPHY: Allen Ep 854 / *Catalogus translationum et commentariorum* (Washington 1960–) I 117–18 / M. Dazzi *Aldo Manuzio e il dialogo veneziano di Erasmo* (Vicenza 1969) passim / P. de Montera 'La Béatrice d'Ambroise Leone de Nola: ce qui reste d'un "Beatricium" consacré à sa gloire' in *Mélanges ... offerts à Henri Hauvette* (Paris 1934) 191–210 / V. Spampanato *Vita di Giordano Bruno* (Messina 1921) 5–18 and passim

CHARLES B. SCHMITT

Niccolò **LEONICENO** of Vicenza, 1428–1524
Niccolò Leoniceno was born near Vicenza and educated first at the school of the humanist Ognibene da Lonigo and thereafter at Padua, where he took his doctorate of medicine in 1453. Early biographies state that he spent some time in England before returning to lecture at Padua, but neither of these facts can be proved: all that is certain is that Leoniceno was established in Ferrara by 1464, since an inscription (now lost) erected after his death stated that he had lectured continuously in that university for sixty years. Although he taught mathematics and Greek philosophy as well, Leoniceno's interests seem quickly to have become concentrated on medical problems, partly as a result of his own epileptic condition. In 1492 he challenged Pliny's use of Greek sources in *De Plinii et aliorum erroribus in medicina* (Ferrara: L. de Rossi and A. de Grassis), provoking a sharp academic controversy and promoting his own fame by applying humanist techniques to a specialist subject (Ep 2172). Recent research has proved that Leoniceno played a vital part in assembling and editing Greek texts for the press of Aldo *Manuzio; cf M. Sicherl *Handschriftliche Vorlagen der Editio Princeps des Aristoteles* (Mainz 1976). He also sent two short works of his own, *De tiro seu vipera* and *De morbo gallico*, to Aldo for publication in 1497. It was probably as a result of this editorial connection that Erasmus met Leoniceno at Ferrara in 1508 (Epp 216A, 1576), and Venetian presses remained interested in Leoniceno's work long after Aldo's death. From 1514 Leoniceno published translations of most of the works of Galen and Hippocrates into Latin, besides a version of

Ptolemy's *Inerrantium stellarum significationes* (Venice: house of A. Manuzio and A. Torresani 1533). Italian translations of several dialogues of Lucian (Venice: N. Zoppino 1529) and of Dio Cassius' Roman history (Venice: N. Zoppino 1533) show that his interests extended beyond the classical languages.

Erasmus invariably mentioned Leoniceno with respect, usually setting him alongside *Cop and *Linacre as one whose humanist convictions helped revive medicine (Ep 862; LB IX 85F; cf Ep 1810). He enquired after him in 1525 (Ep 1576) and received the news of his death as a disaster equal to the loss of *Pico or *Barbaro (Ep 1587). In the *Ciceronianus*, Leoniceno received the compliment of being called 'a doctor, not an orator' (ASD I-2 667–8). From Leoniceno's immediate reaction to the mention of Erasmus' name by Ulrich von *Hutten, it appears that he reciprocated this respect (Ep 611), but the two men's interests hardly converged, and most mentions are strictly formal.

BIBLIOGRAPHY: CWE Ep 216A / Allen Ep 541 / D. Vitaliani *Della vita e delle opere di Niccolò Leoniceno Vicentino* (Verona 1892) / A. Castiglioni 'The School of Ferrara and the Controversy on Pliny' *Science, Medicine and History* ed E. Underwood (Oxford 1953) I 269–79

M.J.C. LOWRY

Niccolò **LEONICO TOMEO** 1 February 1456–28 March 1531
Niccolò Leonico Tomeo (Leonicus Thomaeus) was born in Venice of Epirote Greek parentage and studied Greek in Florence under Demetrius *Chalcondyles. He had apparently been teaching at the University of Padua for some time when he was appointed its first official lecturer on the Greek text of Aristotle in 1497, since the Venetian senate's decree called him 'very popular and acceptable to the students.' Though elected to succeed Giorgio *Valla in the chair of Greek in Venice itself during 1504, he does not appear to have taken the post up seriously and was superseded by *Musurus in 1512. He returned to Padua as soon as the university reopened after the wars of the League of Cambrai, teaching there continuously until his death.

Leonico's published works all appeared in the latter part of his career: they include a translation of Ptolemy's treatise on planets, which was appended to the third volume of the Aldine Ovid (1516); a translation of Aristotle's *Parva naturalia* (Venice: B. and M. dei Vitali 1523); a volume of his own *Dialogi* (Venice: G. de' Gregori 1524); further translations from Aristotle and Proclus (1525); an editorial contribution to an edition of Aristotle and Theophrastus (Florence: heirs of F. Giunta 1527); a miscellany of his own entitled *De varia historia* (Basel: H. Froben and N. Episcopius 1531); and a translation and commentary on Aristotle's *De partibus animalium*, published posthumously in 1540 (Venice: G. de Farri). In spite of the strong scientific and Aristotelian bent of his scholarship, he was regarded by both *Bembo in a memorial inscription and Erasmus in the *Ciceronianus* as a Platonist, a man of deep religious conviction, and, for a philosopher, an unusually gifted writer (ASD I-2 677; cf Ep 2443).

Leonico seems to have been particularly friendly towards his English pupils at Padua, who included *Linacre, *Latimer, *Pace, and later *Lupset and Reginald *Pole. This may well have been the basis of Erasmus' unbroken respect for him. He named Niccolò as one of the most learned men in Venice and Padua (Ep 1479), read his works and valued his judgments (Epp 1675, 2347, 2443), and approved *Zebrzydowski's and *Utenhove's move to Padua to hear him lecture (Ep 2201). Perhaps Lupset's assurance (Ep 1595) that Leonico had been among the teachers of Erasmus' patron Pole strengthened this loyalty. Yet, even in his regretful mention of Leonico's death (Ep 2526), Erasmus never claimed to have met him.

BIBLIOGRAPHY: Allen Ep 1479 / F. Foffano 'Marco Musuro professore di Greco a Padova e a Venezia' *Nuovo archivio veneto* 3 (1892) 453–70 / References in D. Fenlon *Heresy and Obedience in Tridentine Italy: Cardinal Pole and the Counter-Reformation* (Cambridge 1972)

M.J.C. LOWRY

LEONTIUS (Ep 1136 of 1520)
Erasmus addressed Ep 1136 to a certain Leontius, who seems to have been a schoolmaster. Allen has tentatively identified him with the Nicolaus Leontius of Leiden appearing in *Geldenhouwer's list of famous 'Batavian' writers (in P. Scriverius *Batavia illustrata*, Leiden 1609, 69) and among the learned

citizens of Leiden mentioned by Arend van Buchell in his *Diarium* (in the edition of G. Brom and L.A. van Langeraad, Amsterdam 1907, 86); Geldenhouwer calls him *grammaticus*, Buchell *rhetor*.

BIBLIOGRAPHY: Allen Ep 1136

C.G. VAN LEIJENHORST

LEOPOLD of Austria d 27 September 1557
Leopold was an illegitimate son of the Emperor *Maximilian I. His funeral inscription at Córdoba suggests that he was born in 1504, and while a statement made by Robert de *Keysere seems to point to 1509, it makes sense to assume that Leopold was begotten after Maximilian arrived in the Netherlands, early in 1505, to take personal charge of the war against Gelderland. Even though nothing appears to be known about Leopold's mother, the fact that Robert de Keysere at Ghent was appointed to tutor him suggests that he was born in that region. In May 1517 de Keysere took Leopold from Ghent to meet his father, who was then paying his last visit to the Low Countries (Ep 585), and later recalled details of an interview between father and son at Maastricht on 31 May. At that time de Keysere presented to Maximilian a work of his entitled 'De nuptiis Leopoldi,' which is not known to exist now. The wedding referred to could have been a symbolical one, since de Keysere suggests that the work treated of the new learning and his efforts to found a humanistic college at Tournai.

Nothing is yet known of the subsequent course of Leopold's life until he was named bishop of Córdoba on 29 April 1541. From 1545 to 1547 he attended the council of Trent, but otherwise he seems to have devoted much attention to his diocese. He began to revise the missal and prepared a new *Breviarium ecclesiae Cordubensis* (Córdoba 1557), for which he had sought the advice of Juan Ginés de *Sepúlveda. He also carried out renovations at the cathedral in which he was to be buried.

BIBLIOGRAPHY: Allen Ep 585 / J. Coignet in DHGE V 889–90 / J. Van den Gheyn 'Un manuscrit de l'imprimeur gantois Robert de Keyser à la bibliothèque de l'Escurial' *Annales de la Société d'histoire et d'archéologie de Gand* 8 (1907) 91–108 esp 97–8 / Hermann Wiesflecker *Kaiser Maximilian I.* (Munich 1971–) III 284

PGB

Johannes LEOPOLITANUS of Lvov, 1482–
16/20 February 1535
Johannes Leopolitanus (Jan Leopolita, Jan of
Lvov), the son of Michał, was known after the
Latin name of his native city of Lvov (Lemberg). He came from a burgher family and
studied at the University of Cracow from 1495,
receiving a MA in 1500, after which he began to
lecture in the faculty of arts. About the year
1520 he began to study theology; on 28 August
1526 he was promoted licentiate, and on 10
January 1527 doctor, of theology. As a member
of the theological faculty he lectured on the
Bible. In 1524 he was appointed preacher at the
cathedral of Cracow, and from 10 June 1527 he
was canon and preacher of the chapter of St
Florian in Cracow, where he died.

He belonged to the group of Erasmus' Polish
admirers and was a faithful reader of his
works, many of which were found in his
library. He was recommended to Erasmus by
Jan *Antonin and Jan (II) *Łaski (Epp 1916,
2746). His sermons were published posthumously: *Vivificae passionis Jesu Christi historica
explanatio* (Cracow: Ungler 1537). Individual
works from his library are to be found in the
Biblioteka Jagiellońska in Cracow.
BIBLIOGRAPHY: Allen Ep 1916 / PSB XVII 73–4 /
Korespondencja Erazma z Rotterdamu z Polakami
ed M. Cytowska (Warsaw 1965) / *Erasmiana
Cracoviensia in diem natalem Erasmi Roterodamensis quingentesimum edita* Zeszyty Naukowe
Uniwersytetu Jagiellońskiego 250 (Cracow
1971) 25, 44, 105, 113, 116
                                        HALINA KOWALSKA

Catherine LE PICART *See Jean* BUDÉ

Pedro de LERMA of Burgos, c 1461–
11 August 1541
Pedro de Lerma was born at Burgos, in
northern Spain. He studied at the University of
Paris and before 1500 taught arts at the
Collège de Navarre. In 1500 he switched to the
Sorbonne, where he was prior in 1502. On 12
November 1504 he received his doctorate in
theology, and in 1506 he was appointed a
canon at Burgos. He returned to Spain and on
11 August 1508 delivered the inaugural lecture
of the University of Alcalá, founded by
Cardinal *Jiménez de Cisneros. He became the
university's first chancellor, and therewith
abbot of Sts Justus and Pastor. In 1527 Alonso

*Manrique, the inquisitor-general of Spain,
asked Lerma to take part in a conference at
Valladolid called to investigate a list of
doctrinal questions raised against Erasmus by
the heads of the major religious orders in
Spain. During the conference, which lasted
from 27 June to 13 August, Lerma and other
scholars from Alcalá formed an Erasmian block.
The Spanish humanist Juan Luis *Vives informed Erasmus of Lerma's support (Epp 1836,
1847). In 1535 Lerma resigned as chancellor to
return to his prebend at Burgos. In 1537 he was
tried by the Inquisition for heresy, accused of
introducing teachings of Erasmus into his
preaching; he was forced to recant publicly
eleven propositions that were declared heretical and scandalous. Late in 1537 he decided it
would be better to leave Spain and teach
theology at Paris, where he had begun his
career many years earlier. He took up residence at the Sorbonne and was dean of the
faculty of theology when he died.

Some verses by Lerma appear in Pedro
Ciruelo's edition of the *Sphera mundi* by
Johannes de Sacro Bosco (John of Holywood or
Halifax) (Paris: G. Marchant 1498–9). He is
probably the same Pedro de Lerma who pro-
duced the *Imitación del Planto de Hieremias
nuevamente traduzido en metro castellano y latino*
(Salamanca 1534). Lorenzo Balbo de Lillo, one
of Lerma's students, dedicated to him an
edition of Valerius Flaccus' *Argonautica* (Alcalá:
Miguel de Eguía 1524).
BIBLIOGRAPHY: Allen Ep 1836 / Bataillon
Erasmo y España 12–13 and passim / Farge no
295   LUIS A. PÉREZ & TBD

Jean (I) LE SAUVAGE January/February
1455–7 June 1518
Born in Lille, Jean Le Sauvage (Sylvagius) took
a licence in law at Louvain (1478) and rose in
the Burgundian legist hierarchy to become
councillor (1490) and president (1497) of the
council of Flanders, president of the privy
council (1508), and chancellor of Brabant
(1509). *Margaret of Austria, regent for the
future *Charles V, objected to his accumulation
of offices, but Le Sauvage found support from
Guillaume de *Croy, lord of Chièvres,
Charles' guardian. Together they worked out
an arrangement with *Maximilian I whereby
the emperor emancipated his grandson (thus
removing Margaret as regent) in return for a

generous subsidy from the states of Brabant (for Erasmus' thinly veiled comment, see *Scarabaeus aquilam quaerit, Adagia* III vii 1). As a result Le Sauvage became the first native of the Low Countries to hold the office of grand chancellor of Burgundy (1515). English observers (see LP I-2, II-1, II-2) as well as some in the Low Countries characterized the policy of Charles' 'two guardians' as pro-French, but it may be argued that good relations with France were especially necessary to ensure Charles' peaceful succession to the thrones of Castile and Aragon following the death of *Ferdinand II, 'the Catholic,'in 1516. In the same year Le Sauvage was appointed chancellor of Castile. Soon after the treaty of Noyon (1517) with France, he preceded his sovereign on the voyage to Spain; although he died there before a year had passed, Le Sauvage was prominent among the 'Flemings' whose great influence at the court of Castile helped provoke the revolt of the Comuneros (1520). He was lord of Escobecque, near Lille, and a 'golden knight,' and was remembered in a funeral monument erected in St Gudula's, Brussels. The claim in his epitaph that he showed 'integritas erga omnes' remains unsubstantiated, as do certain allegations of bribery and corruption which followed him all his life.

In 1514 Erasmus met 'the president of Flanders, a very well-read man' at Ghent (Ep 301). Although the president of the council of Flanders by then was Richard Reyngheer, the reference is more likely to Le Sauvage, president of the privy council, for the following spring Le Sauvage entertained him for three days (Ep 332). Thereafter he was anxious to keep in touch with the influential courtier (Epp 410, 412). It was apparently Le Sauvage who in 1515 obtained Erasmus' appointment as councillor to Charles (*Compendium vitae*, Allen I 51, CWE 4 409); in any case, it was Le Sauvage who paid Erasmus' stipend for the first year out of his own pocket (Epp 597, 621) and later procured for him a canonry at Courtrai (Epp 421, 436, 2407). That the two men had much in common is suggested by *Molendino's comment that the chancellor enjoyed the dialogue *Julius exclusus* (Epp 532, 543). Moreover, Erasmus' interest in peace was consistent with (though hardly provoked by) the foreign policy which Le Sauvage and Chièvres pursued; pointed criticisms of those who sought

war with France are to be found in both the *Institutio principis christiani*, which Erasmus wrote for Prince Charles, and *Querela pacis*, written at the express request of Le Sauvage (Allen I 19). In connection with the treaty of Noyon, Le Sauvage was hailed as a peacemaker by Erasmus (Allen I 18; cf Epp 532, 533) and by his good friend the Antwerp town secretary, Pieter *Gillis (in the dedicatory preface to his edition of *Summa sive argumenta legum diversorum imperatorum*, Louvain 1517). During the same year, Le Sauvage repeatedly promised Erasmus he would find a bishopric for him, perhaps in Sicily, to be held *in absentia* (Epp 470, 475, 597, 886). Perhaps in consequence of this prospect, Erasmus moved to Brussels, where he lived for six months in proximity to the court; he later recalled the humiliation of paying suit to the chancellor (Ep 2613). Though the bishopric never materialized, Erasmus deeply regretted the death of his 'Maecenas' and loyal protector against monkish critics who had their own powerful friends at court (Epp 852, 853, 886, 887, 893).

BIBLIOGRAPHY: Allen Ep 410 / BNB XXI 441–5 / de Vocht *Busleyden* 93–4 / LP I-2, II-1, II-2, especially the correspondence from the Low Countries of Thomas Spinelly, Cuthbert *Tunstall, and Charles Somerset, earl of Worcester / J. Buntinx *Inventaris van het archief van de Raad van Vlaanderen (1386-1795)* (Brussels 1964–79) passim / James D. Tracy *The Politics of Erasmus: A Pacifist Intellectual and His Political Milieu* (Toronto 1979) / Andreas von Walther *Die Anfänge Karls v.* (Leipzig 1911)

JAMES D. TRACY

Jean (II) and Antoine LE SAUVAGE
Jean and Antoine were the sons of Jean (I) *Le Sauvage, chancellor of Burgundy and Castile. Although they did not rise to a level of prominence comparable with that of their father, the younger Jean's career was progressing well by the time of the chancellor's death. He had been appointed to the privy council of the future *Charles v at the time of its foundation in July 1517; he was also named master of requests and assigned a higher salary than most of his fellow councillors. At his father's death he inherited Schoubeke and other lordships. Despite her disagreements with his father, *Margaret of Austria still found in her album a place for one of the younger

Jean's French epigrams. His own sons, Jean and François, matriculated in 1533 and 1535 at the Collegium Trilingue in Louvain.

Antoine Le Sauvage inherited the lordship of Sterrebeek, which his father had acquired in 1516. In November 1531 Maarten *Davidts informed Erasmus that he was at Sterrebeek as chaplain to Antoine, who had great admiration for Erasmus, and that Jean had died earlier (Ep 2571). On 29 June 1556 Charles v accepted the hospitality of the lord of Sterrebeek while the plague was ravaging Brussels.

BIBLIOGRAPHY: Allen Ep 2571 / BNB XXI 444 / de Vocht CTL III 239–41 / de Vocht Busleyden 93 / Alphonse Henne Histoire du règne de Charles-Quint en Belgique (Brussels-Leipzig 1858–60) II 201, 323, X 291 / L.P. Gachard and C. Piot Collection des voyages des souverains des Pays-Bas (Brussels 1874–82) II 504   PGB

Rafał LESZCZYŃSKI d 23 March 1527
Leszczyński (Raphael Letscintius) came from a noble family with the coat of arms 'Wieniawa' in Greater Poland and was the son of Kasper and Zofia of Oporów. He was connected with the king's court from his youth. In 1507 he was appointed secretary to King *Sigismund I, in which position he carried out diplomatic missions; in 1514 he was appointed royal envoy to the Emperor *Maximilian I, and in 1515 he took part in the conference of monarchs in Vienna and was ambassador to Venice. In 1517 he was again sent to the emperor's court. He was appointed castellan of Lad on 10 May 1518 and was a member of the Polish embassy to the German princes prior to the election of *Charles v (Augsburg and Frankfurt am Main, 1518–19). Thereafter he entered the ranks of the church and on 15 July 1520 was appointed bishop of Przemyśl by the king; on 26 October 1522 he advanced to the bishopric of Płock. He was, however, more a politician than a pastor of his diocese. He died in Pułtusk and was buried in the town's collegiate church. Andrzej *Krzycki succeeded him as bishop of Płock (Ep 1803).

BIBLIOGRAPHY: Allen Ep 1803 / PSB XVII 130–2
                                    HALINA KOWALSKA

Herman LETHMAET of Gouda, c 1492–
6 December 1555
Herman Lethmaet (Lethmaat, Lethmanus, Hermannus Goudanus or Gaudanus) was born at Gouda, near Rotterdam, the son of Hugo, a substantial burgher. After the usual schooling he went to the University of Paris, where he received his MA in 1509 and subsequently studied theology, receiving his theological doctorate on 16 April 1520 as the top candidate in that promotion. In 1521 he met Erasmus in Anderlecht, near Brussels, and gained his friendship and admiration, as is shown by a notable letter of recommendation Erasmus wrote on his behalf to Nicolaas *Everaerts, the president of the council of Holland (Ep 1238). In Ep 1320 Lethmaet expressed his sincere gratitude for two letters of recommendation, including, presumably, this one. They assisted him in his approach to the court for a position with Jean de *Carondelet at Mechelen. Erasmus' second letter of recommendation is missing, but if the 'Hermannus' mentioned in Ep 1277 may be identified with Lethmaet, that letter would show how warmly he reciprocated Erasmus' friendship in his early days in court circles. In reply to Lethmaet's request (Ep 1320), Erasmus on two occasions (Epp 1345, 1359) sent the fledgling courtier a number of suggestions for his conduct, which included the recommendation to keep away from the Lutheran controversy (Ep 1345). This point was well taken, for in his next letter (Ep 1350) Lethmaet admitted that the Louvain theologians tended to count him among the Lutherans. Erasmus, for his part, had other reasons to regret that the frank Ep 1345 was apparently circulating in print (Ep 1383). Erasmus owed to Lethmaet's position the strengthening of his ties with Jean de Carondelet, to whom he dedicated his edition of Hilary in 1523 (Ep 1334).

In September 1522 Pope *Adrian VI conferred upon Lethmaet a canonry of St Mary's, Utrecht, after having received a letter of recommendation from the young man's uncle (cf Ep 1350); the formal date of transfer is presumed to be 20 February 1523. In 1525 he was sent to Amsterdam to assist with the suppression of heresy, and on 11/12 October 1530 he was appointed dean of St Mary's. In 1535 he became involved in a widely discussed scandal which concerned the disappearance of one of three unicorn horns belonging to St Mary's. Lethmaet was accused of having given it to Karel van *Egmond, duke of Gelderland, so as to pay off Utrecht's war-debts. Although he denied any wrongdoing, he was imprisoned, but was freed after the regent, *Mary of Austria, had intervened on his behalf. In the same year he was appointed vicar-general to the new bishop of Utrecht, Joris van *Egmond, who sent him to Cologne in 1538 to attend meetings in preparation for the council of Trent. From 9/10 April to 15 October 1554 he acted as an inquisitor in Friesland with Franciscus Sonnius. He died at Utrecht and was buried at St Mary's; his portrait is to be seen on a stained-glass window which he donated to the church of St John in Gouda.

Although there is no record of direct contacts after 1523, Erasmus' respect for Lethmaet was enduring. In letters to Noël *Béda (Allen Ep 1581:300) and Nicolas *Maillard (Ep 2466) he referred to Lethmaet's authority in the field of theology, and in his will of 1527 he set out a legacy for him (Allen VI 505). Lethmaet, for his part, was very attached to Erasmus' letters, which he carried around with him. His own works show the degree to which he was guided by Erasmus' program of reforms within the Catholic church: *De instauranda religione libri IX* (Basel: J. Oporinus 1544), dedicated to *Charles V, and 'Suspirium sive desiderium matris ecclesiae super redintegranda religione' in thirty-five books, a work that was never published and is lost today. Oporinus would have liked to print it, but Lethmaet was waiting for the approval of the council of Trent, which never came.

BIBLIOGRAPHY: Allen Ep 1320, also I 612–13 / ADB XVIII 458–9 / A.J. van der Aa et al *Biographisch woordenboek der Nederlanden* (Haarlem 1852–78, repr 1965) XI 363–4 / I.W[alvis] *Beschryving der stad Gouda* (Gouda-Leiden [1713]) 250–8 / C.P. Hoynck van Papendrecht *Analecta Belgica* (The Hague 1743) III-1 292–3 / T.J. van Almeloveen *Amoenitates theologico-philologicae* (Leiden 1694) 61–93: ten letters addressed to Lethmaet / A. Matthaeus *Sylloge epistolarum* (Leiden 1708) 331–5 / Farge no 307 / A.J. Kölker 'Herman Lethmatius "Over de vernieuwing van de godesdienst"' in *Postillen over kerk en maatschappij ... aangeboden aan ... R.R.Post* (Utrecht-Nijmegen 1964) 284–313 / J.J. Woltjer *Friesland in hervormingstyd* (Leiden 1962) 111–17 / D. van Heel OFM *Doctor Herman Lethmaet* (Gouda 1950)

C.G. VAN LEIJENHORST

LEUS *See Edward and Wilfred* LEE

Jean LE VASSEUR *See Jean* VASSEUR

Elias LEVITA of Ipsheim, 1469/70–5 January 1549

Elias Levita, properly Eliyahu ben Asher ha-Levi, was a German Jew born in the village of Ipsheim on the Aisch, in Middle Franconia. The names Baḥur and Tishbi, by which he was sometimes known, come from the titles of two of his better-known works. Levita's father, who seems to have been his principal teacher, moved the family to nearby Neustadt while Levita was still quite young. Between 1492 and 1494 Levita migrated to Venice. The unstable civil fortunes of the Jews occasioned a series of moves: Padua, Venice again, then in 1515 Rome, where he enjoyed twelve years of relative tranquillity in the household of the Augustinian general and cardinal Egidio *Antonini of Viterbo. Levita copied and translated Hebrew and Aramaic manuscripts for his patron and guided him in language and cabbalistic studies, while he himself profited from the relationship to learn Greek and broaden his acquaintance with Italian humanism. The Sack of Rome in 1527 brought this period to a close. Levita returned to Venice, this time to an association with the great printer of Hebrew, Daniel Bomberg. There he remained until his death, save for an interval back in his native Württemberg in the small city of Isny, as the guest and collaborator in the publication of Hebraica of Paulus Fagius, an evangelical pastor and a student of Levita. Although this period has been supposed to be of several years' duration, it now seems established that the elderly Levita was in Isny less than a year (winter 1540–41 to fall 1541).

Levita's breadth of scholarship and openness to sharing his knowledge with Christian students meant a wide circle of contacts among the leading Christian Hebraists of the day: apart from those already mentioned, these included Jan van *Campen, Girolamo *Aleandro, Guillaume Postel, Lazare de *Baïf, Johann Albrecht *Widmanstetter, Johann *Eck, and Sebastian Münster. Erasmus, on the other hand, apparently did not know him (Ep 2447).

Levita's contributions to Hebrew and Aramaic scholarship are numerous: particularly notable is his work on Hebrew grammar, proceeding from an edition of the standard work of Moshe Kimḥi (1504) to his own magistral *Massoret ha-Massoret* (Venice 1538). Editions of several of Levita's works, the Latin translation furnished by Münster, appeared in Basel, contributing to the wide reputation of Levita among Christian scholars: amongst them were the *Grammatica hebraica absolutissima* (1525) and the *Capitula Cantici, specierum, proprietatum et officiorum* (1527). Levita also made significant contributions to Yiddish literature.

BIBLIOGRAPHY: Allen Ep 2447 / *Encyclopedia Judaica* (Jerusalem 1971–2) XI 132–5 / Gérard Weil *Elie Lévita humaniste et massorète* (Leiden 1963, Studia Post-Biblica VII)

R. GERALD HOBBS

Antonius LIBER *See Antonius* GANG

William LILY of Odiham,
d c 10 December 1522
William Lily (Lilius, Lilly, Lylly, Lyly, Lylye) was born at Odiham, Hampshire, probably in 1468. He was the godson of William *Grocyn and was remembered as such in Grocyn's will, proved 20 July 1522. Lily was admitted demy of Magdalen College, Oxford, by November 1486 at the age of seventeen. No record exists of his taking a degree, and he may have left before he could do so. As a youth Lily went on a pilgrimage to Jerusalem, after which he studied at Rhodes for some time, getting a thorough grasp of the rudiments of Latin and Greek, before travelling to Rome. There he attended the lectures of Giovanni *Sulpizio of Veroli and Julius *Pomponius Laetus. G.B. Parks conjectures that he travelled with Grocyn to Italy in the early summer of 1488, took the pilgrim galley to Jerusalem, and spent the latter part of that year and the greater part of 1489 in Rhodes, before returning to Italy. He was in Rome in November 1489 and may have returned to England in 1492, in which year a William Lily was presented to the living of Holcot, Northamptonshire. Thomas Stapleton says that he had, like Thomas *More, contemplated going into the church, but the inference that he was More's fellow in the Charterhouse is unjustified.
Lily married at an unknown date. His wife,

Agnes, predeceased him, having borne him fifteen children in seventeen years of marriage. Lily's will was made on 2 September 1522 and proved on 9 March 1523; a second copy (with codicil) was proved on 21 May. On 10 December 1522 the Mercers' Company took cognizance of his death and appointed John Ritwise his successor as high master of St Paul's School. Lily died from an operation for a boil (*verrucula*) on his hip, undergone against Thomas *Linacre's advice, and was buried in Pardon Churchyard, St Paul's, London. His will mentions an unspecified number of children dead, besides four sons and two daughters living. The dramatist John Lily was his grandson.

Lily and Thomas More made rival versions in Latin elegiacs of eighteen Greek epigrams. At least sixteen were done from the text of the *Greek Anthology* then current; one seems not to have been accessible until after 1508 and may have been brought to More in 1509 by Erasmus. In a letter of 1504, More calls Lily 'the dearest partner of my endeavours' (Rogers Ep 3), and Erasmus says that More, who was born in 1477/8, wrote epigrams 'as a very young man, or even (for many of them) a boy' (Ep 635; cf Ep 999). The two sets of translations were first printed, with the title *Progymnasmata Thomae Mori et Guilielmi Lilii sodalium*, in March 1518 (Basel: J. Froben) with More's other epigrams and his *Utopia*, a prefatory letter to the whole by Erasmus (Ep 635), and another to the *Epigrammata* by *Beatus Rhenanus in which Lily is praised for his knowledge of Greek and Latin (BRE Ep 72).

Other Latin epigrams by Lily are preserved in manuscript in the British Library (printed STC 15606.5 and 7), including verses on the storm which brought Philip the Handsome, duke of *Burgundy, accidentally to England and blew the eagle weather-vane off St Paul's Cathedral on 15 January 1506, and on the entry of *Charles V into London on 6 June 1522.

Lily was Colet's first high master of St Paul's School. He is already mentioned as such in a document drawn up by the cathedral chapter on 27 July 1510, although building was not complete until 1512 and he seems not to have been formally appointed until then, at a salary of a mark (13s 4d) per week, a livery gown, housing, and resort. For the school he wrote

Rudimenta, an elementary Latin syntax in English, often printed with Colet's *Aeditio.* His *De constructione,* a more advanced syntax in Latin (ASD I-4 105–43; cf CWE 24 450), also written for the school, was revised by Erasmus at Colet's request, so that neither man felt he could own it and it was first published as an anonymous work in 1513. Erasmus tells the story in a preliminary letter (Ep 341) added to the revised edition (Basel 1515), praising Lily as a scholar and teacher (Ep 277). Richard Pace in *De fructu* also praised him for virtue and learning. His pupils included Thomas *Lupset, John *Clement, and John Leland. More credits Lily with good Italian (Ep 499), and George Lily says that his father translated Lorenzo Spirito's *Libro della sorte* from that language for Sir Thomas More. More made English verses on it.

In the 'grammarians' war' of the early 1520s Lily, as Colet and Erasmus would have done, took the part of William Horman in favour of imitation of good examples as the road to good Latin, against Robert Whittington and John *Skelton, who were for inculcation of grammatical rules. Horman's *Antibossicon* (London: R. Pynson 1521) is dedicated to Lily, while Bernard *André praised him in his *Hymni christiani* (Paris: J. Bade 1517). Lily may have travelled to Louvain in 1520 to bring back Greek books for gifts in memory of Grocyn.

His reputation was great. William Camden speaks in his *Britannia* (1610) of an inscription too difficult even for Lily to read. His portrait was placed with those of Donatus, Servius, and Priscian as representatives of Grammar in Sir Nicholas Bacon's banqueting house at Gorhambury (c 1570, destroyed). No authentic portrait survives. Lily's library included Pliny's *Historia naturalis* (Brescia: A. and J. Britannicus 1496).

BIBLIOGRAPHY: Allen and CWE Ep 341 / DNB XI 1143–5 / Emden BRUO II 1147 / STC 156013–33 and passim / George Lily [William's son] in Paolo Giovio *Descriptio Britanniae* (Venice 1548) 47–8 / Rogers Ep 3 / BRE Ep 72 / Thomas Stapleton *Tres Thomae* (Douai 1588) 18 / More Y III-2 12, 78–95, 321–6 / William Camden *Britannia* (London 1610) 254 / J.H. Lupton *A Life of Dean Colet* new ed (London 1909) 166, 171, 238, and passim / A. Feuillerat *John Lily* (Cambridge 1910) 505–6 (William's will) and passim / G.B. Parks *The English Traveler to Italy* (Rome 1954) I 463–6 and passim / M.F.J. McDonnell *History of St Paul's School* (London 1909) passim / M.F.J. McDonnell *Annals of St Paul's School* (London 1959) 64 and passim / S. Anglo *Spectacle, Pageantry, and Early Tudor Policy* (Oxford 1969) 187–9 and passim / A.F. Leach 'St Paul's school before Colet' *Archaeologia* 62–1 (1910) 191–238, esp 203, 223 / J.B. Trapp in *Classical Influences in European Culture, 1500–1700* ed R.R. Bolgar (Cambridge 1976) 211 / H. Schulte Herbrüggen in *Lebende Antike: Festschrift für R. Sühnel* (Berlin 1967) 155–72 / W. Nelson *John Skelton Laureate* (New York 1939) 148–57 / Franklin B. Williams Jr *Index of Dedications and Commendatory Verses in English Books before 1641* (London 1962) 118 / Oxford Historical Society *Collectanea* 2 (1890) 327, 370 / J.G. Nichols *Progresses of Queen Elizabeth* (London 1823) II 59 / London, British Library MS Harl 540 (Latin epigrams) / C.R. Baskervill in *Huntington Library Bulletin* 9 (1936) 1–14 / G. Tournoy 'Twee ongepubliceerde gedichten bij portretten van Erasmus en Thomas More' in *Liber amicorum Prof. Dr. G. Degroote* (Brussels 1980) 159–62   J.B. TRAPP

Tilmann LIMPERGER of Mainz, c 1455– c 1535

Tilmann Limperger (Limberger, Limpurger, Telamonius) joined the friars of St Augustine and graduated MA at Mainz. In 1477 he was sent to study in London and subsequently in Bologna, where he became a bachelor of theology. In 1482 he was appointed lector and preacher at the Strasbourg house of his order. When transferred to Freiburg he registered at the university on 5 August 1487, and in 1489 he was chosen to be prior of the Freiburg monastery. On 11 February 1491 he received his theological doctorate and a few days later was appointed to the second chair of theology at Freiburg; however, he had to resign in August 1492 when he was appointed provincial of the Upper Rhine province of his order. He nevertheless remained a member of the Freiburg faculty of theology and was actually its dean for three semesters in 1494, 1496–7, and 1498.

On 1 October 1498 Limperger was appointed suffragan bishop of Basel and was consecrated three months later in Rome with the title of bishop of Tripolis. His salary was fixed at 200 florins annually; his duties in the diocese were mostly of a practical and pastoral nature. In 1514 he became a citizen of Basel; later when the religious debates began he was soon found to be in sympathy with the reformers. During the Easter week of 1523 he attended a series of public lectures given by *Oecolampadius and consequently was forbidden to preach. By the end of 1525 he had been suspended in all his ecclesiastical functions, including that of preacher at the cathedral, but, until his death in 1527, Bishop Christoph von *Utenheim continued to pay Limperger his salary as a suffragan. In 1526 Limperger excused himself on the grounds of age when he was invited by the Basel council to attend the disputation of Baden. When the Reformation triumphed in 1529 he was reappointed preacher at the cathedral, a position soon to be known by the title of archdeacon (the principal minister at the cathedral, or *antistes*, being Oecolampadius himself). On 14 February 1529 Limperger preached at a victory service of the reform party in the cathedral. In 1533 he appears to have retired from his position.

The change in his religious convictions is reflected in his writings. As a prior at Freiburg he edited the *Canones Aurelii Augustini* (Strasbourg: M. Schott 1490). In his early years at Basel he preached sermons on purgatory and also wrote them down in book form (not known to exist today), whereas in 1527 he published anonymously a polemical attack in German upon the institution of suffragan bishops. Oecolampadius dedicated to him a translation of Nicephorus Chartophylax (Basel: J. Froben 1518), Johannes *Lonicerus his Latin version of *Luther's commentary on Habakkuk (Strasbourg: J. Knobloch 1526), and *Myconius a posthumous edition of Oecolampadius' commentary on the Gospel of John (Basel: A. Cratander and J. Bebel 1533). Clearly in a jocular mood, Erasmus commented in 1527 on the old man's plans to take a wife, which are not otherwise known; soon thereafter he conveyed Limperger's greetings to *Pirckheimer (Epp 1883, 1893).

BIBLIOGRAPHY: Allen Ep 1883 / J. Bücking 'Die Basler Weihbischöfe des 16. Jahrhunderts' *Zeitschrift für schweizerische Kirchengeschichte* 63 (1969) 67–91, esp 67–73 / J.J. Bauer *Zur Frühgeschichte der theologischen Fakultät Freiburg* *i.Br.* (Freiburg 1957) 70 and passim / *Helvetia Sacra* ed A. Bruckner (Basel 1972–) I-1 229 / *Matrikel Freiburg* I 87 / BA *Oekolampads* I 77, 219–20, and passim / AK I Epp 424, 426 / Luther w *Briefwechsel* III Ep 574 / Z VIII Ep 319 / R. Wackernagel *Geschichte der Stadt Basel* (Basel 1907–54) III 57*–8* and passim   PGB

Thomas LINACRE c 1460–20 October 1524

Thomas Linacre (Linacer) was probably born in the diocese of Canterbury; nothing is known of his early life. He was at Oxford by 1481 and was elected a fellow of All Souls College in 1484. In 1487 Linacre went to Italy, remaining there until 1499. From about 1488 to 1490 he studied Greek and Latin at Florence with Demetrius *Chalcondyles and Angelo *Poliziano; he was a fellow student of William *Grocyn, William *Latimer, and Giovanni de' Medici, the future *Leo x. He was in Rome by 4 November 1490, when he was admitted to the English hospice, being named warden on 3 May 1491. In 1492 or 1493 he left Rome for the Venetian republic and studied at the University of Padua, taking a degree in medicine on 30 August 1496. During the period 1497–9 Linacre was in close contact with Aldo *Manuzio, helping in the publication of the *editio princeps* of Aristotle's works in Greek and participating in the cultural activities of Aldo's household. By 27 August 1499 he had returned to London, and on 15 October of the same year his Latin translation of Pseudo-Proclus' *Sphaera* appeared at the Aldine press dedicated to Prince *Arthur. At about the same time Linacre was charged with the education of the young prince. In 1500 Thomas *More studied Greek with Linacre in London, and the two read Aristotle's *Meteorologica* together.

In 1509 Linacre was appointed physician to *Henry VIII. Between that date and the end of his life various ecclesiastical benefices were bestowed upon him. In 1514 he became physician to *Mary Tudor, queen of France, travelling with her to Paris, where he met Guillaume *Budé. With the support of Henry VIII and Cardinal *Wolsey, Linacre founded the College of Physicians – later the Royal College of Physicians – at London in 1518, though its charter was not ratified until 1523. Linacre was president from its inception, a position he held until his death. The first meetings of the college were held in Linacre's own home in Knight Rider Street, and after his death it served as the headquarters of the college for some years. In 1520 he was ordained deacon and about 1523 was appointed tutor to the future Queen *Mary I. Although Erasmus referred to Linacre's declining health in 1521 (Ep 1230), he lived until October 1524. He was survived by two sisters and a brother. His will provided for the establishment of medical lectureships at both Oxford and Cambridge.

Linacre first met Erasmus after his return to England in 1499 (Ep 118). From that date until his death the relations between the two were warm and cordial. Three letters from Erasmus to Linacre survive (Epp 194, 415, 1230), and there was a now lost epistolary exchange in verse (ASD I-2 218). While in London Erasmus visited Linacre in his home (ASD I-3 347). Erasmus spoke of him frequently as one of the outstanding physicians of the age (Epp 541, 542, 855, 862) and showed a continuing interest in the publication of Linacre's translations of Galen (Epp 502, 687, 690, 726, 755, 785, 971). Moreover, he consulted Linacre for medical advice while in London and later wrote requesting a copy of the prescription for the treatment of fever (Ep 415). Erasmus also intervened with *Colet to smooth over the situation subsequent to the rejection of Linacre's grammar (Epp 227, 230; see below).

Linacre and Erasmus held each other in mutual esteem. Linacre obviously considered his Dutch friend to be a man of outstanding ability and integrity (Ep 415, 513) and in 1516 warmly praised Erasmus' abilities before Henry VIII (Ep 388). Although he once reproached Linacre for not publishing more (Ep 1230), Erasmus had the highest opinion of the Englishman's abilities, praising him frequently in an unstinted fashion (Ep 118, 971, 1005, 1117, 1175, 1558; ASD I-2 676–7; ASD IX-1 196; Adagia IV vi 52), at one point saying that Linacre's abilities were comparable with the best available in Italy (Ep 540).

Linacre's extant writings consist of a very few letters, several grammatical works, and various translations. Besides letters of dedication we have only three of Linacre's letters and seven others addressed to him. His first grammar book seems to be the work (now lost) submitted to John Colet for use at St Paul's

School, which was rejected (Ep 227). His published grammatical works include *Progymnasmata grammatices vulgaria* (London: J. Rastell c 1515; STC 15635) which may be a reworking of the earlier grammar; *Rudimenta grammatices* (London: R. Pynson c 1523; STC 15636); and *De emendata structura Latini sermonis* (London: R. Pynson 1524; STC 15634). The latter two were reprinted frequently until the end of the sixteenth century. Besides the version of pseudo-Proclus, which remained standard until the early seventeenth century, Linacre also translated into Latin Paulus Aegineta's *De crisi et diebus decretoriis* (Paris 1528) and, most important, the following works of Galen: *De sanitate tuenda* (Paris: G. Le Rouge 1517), *Methodus medendi* (Paris: G. Hittorp 1519), *De temperamentis et de inaequali intemperie* (Cambridge: J. Siberch 1521; STC 11536), *De naturalibus facultatibus* (London: R. Pynson 1523; STC 11533), *De pulsuum usu* (London: R. Pynson 1522; STC 11534) and *De symptomatum differentiis* (London: R. Pynson 1524; STC 11535). These were all reprinted frequently. As a translator Linacre exhibited a high level of precision and style consonant with his great proficiency in both Greek and Latin.

The edition of Julius Pollux's *Onomasticon* edited by A. Francino (Florence: B. Giunta 1520) was dedicated to Linacre, and some twenty books from his library have been identified (list given in Maddison et al 331–6). No authentic portrait is known to exist.

BIBLIOGRAPHY: Allen and CWE Ep 118 / DNB XI 1145–50 / Emden BRUO II 1147–9 / All previous literature is now superseded or explicitly referred to in *Linacre Studies: Essays on the Life and Work of Thomas Linacre* ed F. Maddison, M. Pelling, and C. Webster (Oxford 1977) which also contains a detailed bibliography of Linacre's writings and the secondary literature referring to him.   CHARLES B. SCHMITT

Bartholomew LINSTED documented 1513–53

There is no evidence of the early life and education of Bartholomew Linsted (alias Fowle) before his appointment as prior of the Austin house of St Mary Overey, Southwark (London) in 1513. Thereafter occasional references in the state papers indicate various payments and augmentations to Linsted,

through whom sums were dispatched to
Edward *Lee when he served as ambassador to
Spain from 1527 to 1528 (LP IV 2682, 2830, 2865,
2987, 3263, 5104, 6438). In October 1539
Linsted surrendered the house to *Henry VIII
but thereafter was awarded a yearly stipend of
one hundred pounds which was paid out to
him as late as 1553. A few of Erasmus' letters of
1520 refer to Linsted in the context of Erasmus'
controversy with Lee, who in February 1520
assured Erasmus that Linsted meant him no
harm (Ep 1061). Erasmus refused to accept
Lee's assurances and thereafter he occasionally alluded to Linsted – without, however,
mentioning him by name – as an abbot
supporting Lee (Epp 1074, 1097, 1113, 1126,
1139).

BIBLIOGRAPHY: Allen Ep 1061 / W. Dugdale
Monasticon Anglicanum ed J. Caley, H. Ellis,
and B. Bandinel (London 1830) VI 169

MORDECHAI FEINGOLD

Joost LIPS *See Maarten* LIPS

Maarten LIPS of Brussels,
d 23 March 1555/1559
Maarten Lips (Lypsius) was born at Brussels
about 1492 of a distinguished Brabant family to
which the famous philologist Justus Lipsius
(1547–1606) also belonged. The precise degree
of kinship between Maarten and Justus is not
quite clear. In his autobiography Justus calls
Maarten his 'propatruus' and this agrees with
the description of Petrus Trudonensis, the
chronicler of St Maarten's convent at Louvain:
'Iusti Lipsii patruus maior.' Both terms in Latin
normally mean the brother of the great-
grandfather. Yet Justus speaks of Maarten in a
context which clearly suggests that he was a
brother of his grandfather, Nicolaas, not of his
great-grandfather, Joost or Justus. In fact, he
mentions Maarten between Nicolaas and his
wife, Margareta van den Eekhout, then goes
on to discuss Joost and his wife, Anna van
Linkebeek. If, therefore, Maarten was Lipsius'
great-uncle, Nicolaas may be the brother
mentioned in Epp 902 and 1837. If this is
correct, the elder Joost and Anna van Linkebeek must be Maarten's parents. This would
very well agree with the lapse of time normally
required between three generations. Maarten's father died before 9 May 1527 without

making a will (Ep 1837). If, however, the elder
Joost was Maarten's brother, he must have
been about twenty years older than Maarten to
permit the accomodation of two more generations between him and his famous namesake
born in 1547.

Maarten's father had a brother, Jan, who
was a monk in the abbey of Egmond (Northern
Holland). He tried to have Maarten educated
in Egmond, but the boy was not accepted
because of his tender age. So in 1507 he was
taken to the priory of St Maartensdal at
Louvain, which was much closer to his home.
Since the house no longer had its own school,
his education must have been taken in hand by
some brethren of the community. In 1510
Maarten made his profession and in 1518 he
was ordained priest. It is uncertain whether he
attended courses at the university. No mention
is ever made of an academic degree, and his
name does not appear in the students' register
and other records. However, university professors such as Nicolaas van *Broeckhoven
also did some teaching in St Maartensdal, and
Lips may have benefitted from this kind of
arrangement. On the whole he seems to be
more or less a self-taught man, like Erasmus,
who frequently encouraged him to persevere
in his studies (Ep 750). In his way and using the
considerable resources of his convent's library
Maarten acquired a sound knowledge of
classical and particularly patristic literature.
He did not, however, become a humanist in the
Italian sense and declined to write Latin verses
(cf a letter to G. Gheershoven of February 1526,
Horawitz 785–8).

Lips made the acquaintance of Erasmus by
about 1516. Their friendship knew some
difficult moments, but it lasted until Erasmus'
death (AK V Ep 2379). It caused Lips much
trouble in his convent, especially on the part of
the sub-prior, Rochus *Hyems, and Nicolaas
van *Winghe. On account of these conflicts
he left Louvain (perhaps in May 1525) for the
Augustinian nunnery of Croix-à-Lens at Lens-
Saint-Rémy, in the Belgian province of Liège.
This move may well have been designed to
relegate a potentially dangerous Erasmian from
Louvain to a remote village where the people
spoke a different language. Maarten's illness
in 1526 and 1527 (Ep 1837) may have been
emotional as much as physical. The change

must have been great indeed. At Louvain he had been in charge of the rich convent library (there is, however, no evidence for Horawitz's assertion that he was prior), and as the librarian of St Maartensdal he was in continual and congenial contact with scholars at Louvain and at many monasteries all over Brabant. At Lens, however, he was merely an assistant to the prior for ten years. After a time he adjusted to his new milieu and may have begun to teach some Latin to local youths. He produced a French adaptation of a Latin grammar by Johannes *Custos of Brecht. He may also have been parish priest of the nearby hamlet of Abolens. After the death of the prior on 14 February 1535, he succeeded to the office, exercising it with skill and energy until his own death. The evidence for the year of his death is conflicting. Petrus Trudonensis gave 1555 in his chronicle but 1559 in his *Catalogus* of Windesheim authors. The latter date was also given by Valerius Andreas, who may have depended on the *Catalogus*. No other independent source seems to exist, and no obituary is preserved.

From Lens, Lips maintained contacts with Erasmus and also other humanists, above all *Goclenius, who for many years forwarded letters and messages between Erasmus and Lips. Lips visited him several times at Louvain, for example, in June 1527 (Ep 1837) and in November 1531 (Ep 2566) when he attended a farewell dinner for *Clenardus. He also saw Goclenius shortly after Erasmus' death (AK v Ep 2303), when false rumours had it that his name was mentioned in Erasmus' will. Lips also made other short journeys; he went to Liège in the autumn of 1531 to meet Paschasius *Berselius (Ep 2566), and to Antwerp in September 1547. When in 1542 the army of Gelderland invaded Brabant he temporarily fled to the abbey of Neumoustier, near Huy in the prince-bishopric of Liège.

A fine Latin scholar, Lips devoted his whole life to the study and editing of ancient ecclesiastical authors, mainly Augustine, the patron of his order. From the beginning he was associated with Erasmus' edition of the collected works of St Augustine (Basel: H. Froben 1528–9). No one did more to persuade Erasmus that he should undertake the huge task (Ep

922), and he became his principal collaborator in the enterprise. On the basis of many manuscripts preserved at St Maartensdal, Groenendaal, Park, and other religious houses in Brabant, he prepared for the press a great number of works including *De doctrina christiana*, *Confessiones*, and *De agone christiano*. He discovered twenty-two unknown letters and some sermons and sent Erasmus the information or the actual manuscripts he needed (Epp 1174, 1189, 1473, 1547, 1768). After Erasmus' death Lips carried on the work for Hieronymus *Froben, who rightly bestowed lavish praise on him in a new edition of 1543. Other works to benefit from Lips' careful study included those by Ambrose, Hilary, and Chromatius (for whom he used a manuscript of St Laurent, Liège, and another from the abbey of St Truiden) and the letters of Symmachus.

Lips also rendered other services to Erasmus, for example, making indexes to the Gospels and the Acts of the Apostles (Ep 1837). In all this, however, he remained the modest collaborator known only to his fellow monks and close friends. When Erasmus gave orders to his Antwerp banker, Erasmus *Schets, early in 1536 to pay forty guilders to Lips as a token of his gratitude, the banker had to make inquiries and ask Goclenius who Lips was, for he did not even know his name (Epp 3119, 3130; AK v Ep 2303).

BIBLIOGRAPHY: Allen Ep 750 / de Vocht CTL III 71–5 / W. Lourdaux in NBW III 507–10 / W. Lourdaux *Moderne Devotie en christelijk humanisme: de geschiedenis van Sint-Maarten te Leuven van 1433 tot het einde der XVIe eeuw* (Louvain 1967): includes abstracts of Lips' correspondence and a discussion of his work / An important collection of letters by Erasmus and his friends was gathered by Lips into a copy book and edited by A. Horawitz in *Sitzungsberichte der kais. Akademie der Wissenschaften* phil.-hist. Klasse 100 (Wien 1882) / Petrus Trudonensis *Catalogus scriptorum Windeshemensium* ed W. Lourdaux and E. Persoons (Louvain 1968) 170–2 / The chronicle of the same author is unpublished. The manuscript is in Louvain, Stadsarchief MS 4239

J. IJSEWIJN

Nicolaas LIPS *See Maarten LIPS*

Gerardus LISTRIUS of Rhenen, documented 1506–22

Gerardus Listrius (Lystrius, Lyster) was born at Rhenen, near Utrecht. The year of his birth is unknown; conjectures vary from 1470 to 1490, but a relatively late date seems to be probable. At any rate, he attended St Lebuin's school in Deventer when Alexander *Hegius (d 1498) was still alive. On 27 February 1506 he matriculated at Louvain, where Jean *Desmarez was one of his professors. He later studied at Cologne under Johannes *Caesarius. On 8 April 1514 he became a licentiate and doctor of medicine at Pavia. By August 1514 (AK II Ep 500) he was studying medicine at Basel, where he soon made the acquaintance of Erasmus, who thought highly of him (Epp 305–7). Listrius contributed several Greek verses to the title page of Erasmus' translations from Plutarch (Basel: J. Froben August 1514) and later corrected the 1515 edition of the *Adagia* for the press of Johann *Froben (Ep 322; AK II Ep 512). In March 1515 Froben also published a new edition of the *Moria*, with a commentary under Listrius' name, dedicated by Listrius to Jean Desmarez (Ep 337). Although Erasmus normally attributed this important commentary entirely to Listrius (Allen I 19; Epp 337, 641), his letter to Martin *Bucer of March 1532 indicates that he actually began the commentary himself when Listrius was unable to proceed quickly with the work (Ep 2615). To Erasmus Listrius also owed a certain familiarity with Udalricus *Zasius (Epp 306, 307) and Thomas *More (Ep 388).

In 1516 Listrius was appointed rector of the school of Zwolle and left Basel. However, he was eager to maintain contact with Erasmus and wrote several letters to him (Epp 495, 500, 504). For some time at least he lived in the *Fraterhuis* of Jan *Koechman (Ep 504). Having inaugurated his lessons with an *Oratiuncula habita in coetu scholasticorum Svollensium* (Zwolle: L. Rensinck c 1516; NK 3411), he took on his new task with great enthusiasm and energy. Skilled in Latin, Greek, and Hebrew, he introduced Greek in his school (Ep 500) and, usually in conjunction with the printer Simon *Corver, published many school books, such as *De figuris et tropis* (1 December 1519; NK 3408), dedicated to *Gerard of Kloster, *De octo*

figuris constructionis (c 1519; NK 3407), and *Commentarioli in dialecticen Petri Hispani* (c 1520; NK 1375), dedicated to *Gozewijn of Halen. He also edited several works by Erasmus for Corver, including the adage *Sileni Alcibiadis* (c 1520; NK 869).

Around 1519 Listrius married a certain Justina (BRE Ep 193), on which Erasmus congratulated him cordially (Allen Ep 660, IV 67; now CWE Ep 1013A). In 1520 Erasmus heard a rumour that some misfortune had befallen Justina and that Listrius had given up teaching Greek. Although this proved to be false (Ep 1140), Listrius' life at Zwolle was not easy, for over the years he had become involved in two extremely unpleasant affairs. First, Listrius was alleged by some to have poisoned Johannes *Murmellius, who had been his assistant briefly in 1517 but who had subsequently attacked him in the *Epigrammata paraenetica*, published only weeks before his sudden death on 2 October 1517. Although Listrius appears to have been innocent, he lived in an atmosphere of suspicion for some time and badly needed the comfort given by Erasmus in Ep 697. However, Listrius rejected Erasmus' advice not to defend himself in public (Ep 838; cf also Ep 830) and wrote a *Carmen in malas et venenosas linguas* (Deventer: J. de Breda c 1517; NK 3404). Shortly after this, Listrius came into conflict with the Dominicans of Zwolle over the question of the Reformation. The correspondence which Listrius conducted with Martin *Luther and his connections with Corver, who published several writings of Luther and of Wessel *Gansfort, made him susceptible to accusations of heresy. No doubt his counterattack, the *Epistola theologica … adversus Dominicanos Svollenses* (ed J.E. Kapp in *Kleine Nachlese*, Leipzig 1727–33, IV 515–31) did not silence his adversaries; perhaps they pressed him so hard that this was the decisive factor in his departure from Zwolle. While Corver disappeared from the northern Netherlands altogether, Listrius accepted the rectorate of the Latin school of Amersfoort in September 1522. After this nothing was heard of him.

Listrius' disputed position and the short duration of his rectorate made it impossible for him to achieve for the school of Zwolle anything comparable to what Hegius had done for St Lebuin's of Deventer. Only two of his pupils are known: a certain *Gerard of Friesland (Ep 2232) and Johannes *Longicampianus, who after being recommended by Erasmus studied Greek and mathematics under him (Epp 500, 504).

BIBLIOGRAPHY: Allen Ep 495, IV xxv / Matricule de Louvain III-1 307 / J. Lindeboom in NNBW III 782–3 / F.A. Hoefer and H.C. Rogge in Archief voor Nederlandsche Kerkgeschiedenis 7 (1899) 203–20 / M. Schoengen in De Dominikanen te Zwolle (Zwolle 1926) 88–98 / M.E. Kronenberg in Bijdragen voor Vaderlandsche Geschiedenis en Oudheidkunde 6th ser 9 (1930) 177–214 / P.F. Wolfs OP Das Groninger 'Religionsgespräch' (Nijmegen 1959) 34–9 / On the commentary on the Moria see J.A. Gavin and Th.M. Walsh 'The Praise of Folly in context: the commentary of Girardus Listrius' Renaissance Quarterly 24 (1971) 193–209 and G. Hess in Der Kommentar in der Renaissance ed A. Buck and O. Herding (Boppard 1975) 141–5

C.G. VAN LEIJENHORST

Pierre LIZET of Salers, c 1482–7 June 1554
A native of Salers (Auvergne), Lizet (Lizetius, Lysetus) contracted a marriage with Jeanne Hénard, the daughter of the paymaster of the Parlement of Paris. In 1514 he became a councillor in the Parlement, and on 29 July 1517 was made royal advocate. As such he pleaded for the crown against Constable Charles de Bourbon (1522) and against Guillaume *Briçonnet, bishop of Meaux (1525). In 1529 he was named first president of the Parlement in succession to Jean de *Selve, and his tenure was notable for its severity towards the evangelical cause. Although he had earlier clashed with Noël *Béda over the latter's attacks upon Erasmus (Ep 1763) and upon the divorce of *Henry VIII, Erasmus had grounds to complain of Lizet's support of the Sorbonne's hostility to him (Ep 2587). Among the more celebrated victims of Lizet's harshness was Etienne *Dolet. In 1549 and 1550 Lizet ran afoul of Cardinal Jean de *Lorraine and was forced to resign. Although not in orders at the time, he was given the abbey of St Victor near Paris in compensation for the loss of his post. He was buried in the choir at the abbey. Among others Lizet published the following

works: Adversum pseudo-evangelicam haeresim libri seu commentarii novem (Lyon: P. LePreux 1551), De auriculari confessione; de monastico instituto; de huiusce saeculi caecitate ac circumventione, dialogus inter spiritualem et mundanum (Lyon: S. Gryphius 1552), Briève et succinte manière de procéder, tant à l'institution et décision des causes criminelles que civiles (Paris: V. Sertenas 1555).

BIBLIOGRAPHY: Allen Ep 1763 / Edouard Maugis Histoire du Parlement de Paris (Paris 1916, repr 1967) III 146, 149, 188 / André Lebey Le Connétable de Bourbon, 1490–1527 (Paris 1904) 121–44 / R.C. Christie Etienne Dolet, the Martyr of the Renaissance (London 1899) 422–37 / V.-L. Bourrilly Guillaume du Bellay (Paris 1905) 102–6 and passim   HENRY HELLER

García de LOAYSA of Talavera, 1479– 22 April 1546
García, a son of Pedro de Loaysa and Caterina de Mendoza, was born in Talavera de la Reina, west of Madrid. He joined the Dominican order, taking his vows at Peñafiel in Old Castile in 1494. He quickly came to occupy high offices in the order and in 1518 was elected general in succession to Cardinal *Cajetanus. Paying special attention to the reform of the Dominican houses of Spain, he became personally acquainted with *Charles V when a chapter of the order was held at Valladolid in May 1523. As a result he was named confessor to the emperor in succession to Jean *Glapion. His new duties soon made it impossible for him to continue as the Dominican general; on the other hand, the emperor secured for him the bishopric of Osma (8 June 1524–1532). On 4 August 1524 he was also appointed president of the new council of the Indies at the request of Chancellor *Gattinara. In 1526 he entered the council of state and thus reached the summit of his career. Although Charles V allowed him to express frank criticism of his moral conduct, Loaysa's political career was cut short because of his lack of diplomacy. In 1528 he was removed from the council of state and, from 1530, Charles used Juan de Quintana as his personal confessor, although Loaysa too retained that title.

Loaysa accompanied the monarch to Bologna for his coronation in February 1530 and on

9 March was named cardinal with two other Hapsburg diplomats, Bernhard von *Cles and Iñigo *López de Mendoza. Loaysa remained in Rome until 1533, and the letters he dispatched to Charles v in this period are a valuable source of diplomatic history. A man of moral principles but ambitious and tactless, Loaysa was soon locked in a bitter feud with Charles' ambassador in Rome, Miguel *Mai, which continued until both were removed from the Holy City in 1533. In Spain, Loaysa resumed his activity in the council of the Indies (until 1543), lending his support to the proposals of Bartolomé de Las Casas. In 1538 he became archbishop of Seville and shortly before his death also inquisitor-general.

Loaysa denounced what he perceived to be heretical passages in Erasmus' *Enchiridion* when it was first translated into Spanish but failed to prevent the publication of that Spanish version in 1526. By 1527 Erasmus had been warned to see in him his principal adversary at the Spanish court (Ep 1903). Constantino Ponce de la Fuente dedicated his *Suma de doctrina cristiana* (Seville: J. Cromberger) to Loaysa in 1543.

BIBLIOGRAPHY: Allen Ep 1903 / Eubel III 21, 211, 265 / Bataillon *Erasmo y España* lxxix, 191–2, and passim / Agustin Redondo 'Luther et l'Espagne de 1520 à 1536' *Mélanges de la Casa de Velázquez* 1 (1965) 109–65, esp 110, 131 / José Luis G. Novalín *El Inquisidor General Fernando de Valdés (1483–1568)* (Oviedo 1968) I 162–3 / Otto Lehnhoff *Die Beichtväter Karls v.* (Alfeld 1932) 34–59 / F. Walser and R. Wohlfeil *Die spanischen Zentralbehörden und der Staatsrat Karls v.* (Göttingen 1959) 251–3 and passim / Karl Brandi *Kaiser Karl v.* new ed (Darmstadt 1959–67) I 216–17, II 157–8 and passim / Pastor IX 450, X 206–10, 228, and passim PGB

Jean LOBEL of Boulogne, d 1544
Jean Lobel (Lobbel, Lobellius), a native of Boulogne-sur-Mer, was appointed secondary ('pomeridianus') professor of canon law at Louvain in 1532 and received a doctorate in canon and civil law on 10 February 1534. A conservative, he happened to be rector of the university when it was decided that Rutgerus *Rescius had no right to use legal source texts for his Greek course at the Collegium Trilingue

García de Loaysa

(Ep 3111). In 1538 he resigned and accepted a canonry at St John the Baptist's, Louvain, and subsequently another at St Bavo's, Ghent, where he was elected dean in 1539.

BIBLIOGRAPHY: Allen Ep 3111 / de Vocht CTL III 128 and passim / de Vocht MHL 594–5 and passim ANDRÉ GODIN

Johann LÖBLE d before 24 July 1536
Johann Löble (Löblin, Leblin) was evidently a Swabian and served in the treasury of Württemberg under Hapsburg occupation in 1520 and 1521. By 1524 he was a member of the Hapsburg Austrian treasury, and in 1525 he was sent to Augsburg for the purpose of selling silver. He is given the titles of councillor and *Pfennigmeister* and in 1532 that of *Burgvogt* of Enns. On 21 January 1526 he received his letters of nobility. After the death of his first wife, Anna von Kageneck, he remarried by January 1530; his second wife was Jakob *Villinger's recent widow, Ursula *Adler, and through his marriage he came to have considerable influence upon the house 'zum Walfisch' at Freiburg where Erasmus was living (Epp

2256, 2462, 2505, 2808). In 1530 the city of Augsburg made him a gift of five hundred florins on the occasion of the diet. In June 1531 he wrote a letter in German (Ep 2497) to Erasmus from Stuttgart. Between 1532 and 1534 he is documented again at Augsburg, trying to secure huge loans for King *Ferdinand from the *Fuggers and the *Paumgartners and, in a political capacity, to secure Ferdinand's admission to the league Augsburg had concluded with Ulm and Nürnberg. Löble was also heavily involved in business of his own and granted large loans to his master. Shortly before Löble died Ferdinand owed him thirty-one thousand florins, and in 1540-2 the Fuggers and Löble's widow were engaged in efforts to secure repayment of the amounts owed by the king.

Several bearers of the name of Johann Löblin matriculated in the universities of Tübingen (1499, 1512) and Heidelberg (1504).

BIBLIOGRAPHY: Allen Ep 2497 / K.O. Müller *Quellen zur Handelsgeschichte der Paumgartner von Augsburg* (Wiesbaden 1955) 29, 159, 164, 182 / G. von Pölnitz *Anton Fugger* (Tübingen 1958–) I 315–16, II 137, 211, 319, 330, 473, and passim / AK VII Ep 3025 / *Die Chroniken der deutschen Städte* (Leipzig-Stuttgart 1862–) XXV 406 / *Matrikel Tübingen* I 125, 188 / *Matrikel Heidelberg* I 452   PGB

Jakob LOCHER of Ehingen, 1471–
4 December 1528
Jakob Locher (Philomusus) was born in Ehingen, on the Danube near Ulm, into a respected but relatively poor family. He attended the Latin school in Ulm and began his university studies in 1487–8 in Basel, where he was a student of Sebastian *Brant, and Freiburg; he continued in Ingolstadt in 1489, studying philosophy, theology, and law. In 1492 and 1493 he travelled in Italy, accompanying Margrave Jakob II von Baden; the name Philomusus was given to him in Bologna. After his return to Ulm he published two of Cicero's orations (1494); in 1495 he was in Freiburg, where he lectured on poetry and tutored Karl and Christoph von Baden. He received the poet's laurel from the Emperor *Maximilian I in 1497. A year later he was called to Ingolstadt as a lecturer in poetry in succession to Conradus Celtis. However, a fierce attack upon a

respected older theologian forced him to leave Ingolstadt and led to new quarrels with Jakob *Wimpfeling (Ep 224) and Udalricus *Zasius. After three years at Freiburg (1503–6) he resumed his teaching at the University of Ingolstadt, where he remained. He married in 1515 and Leonhard von *Eck was godfather to his first child. After fleeing to Ulm in 1521 from an outbreak of the plague, he became the victim of a lingering illness which eventually proved fatal.

Locher edited Latin authors, for example, Horace (Strasbourg: J. Grüninger 1498), Fulgentius (Augsburg: S. Grimm and M. Wirsung 1521), Pliny's *Historia naturalis* (Ingolstadt: A. Lutz 1522), and Claudianus (Nürnberg: F. Peypus 1518). He translated Sebastian Brant's *Narrenschiff* into Latin as *Stultifera navis* (Basel: J. Bergmann 1497, many reprints), and had several volumes of his own poetry published, for example *Epigramma de diva Katherina* (Basel: J. Bergmann 1496). He also wrote plays in Latin, four of which were successfully performed at Freiburg and Ingolstadt (1495–1502), and *Theologica emphasis sive dialogus super eminentiam quatuor doctorum ecclesiae* (Basel: J. Bergmann 1496) in verse.

BIBLIOGRAPHY: Allen and CWE Ep 224 / ADB XIX 59–63 / *Matrikel Basel* I 197 / *Matrikel Freiburg* I 91 / G. Ellinger *Geschichte der neulateinischen Literatur Deutschlands im sechzehnten Jahrhundert* (Berlin and Leipzig 1929–33) I 24 / H. Rupprich in *Geschichte der deutschen Literatur* ed H. de Boor and R. Newald (Munich 1957–) IV-1 passim   IG

LODOVICUS See LOUIS, LUDOVICUS

Georg von LOGAU of Świdnica,
d 2/11 April 1553
Georg, Freiherr von Logau (Logus, a Logus, the latter form permitting the pun Ἄλογος), was a Silesian nobleman born in Świdnica (Schweidnitz). He matriculated in 1514 at the University of Cracow, where he became a pupil of the humanist and poet Valentin Eck. The support of Johannes (II) *Thurzo, bishop of Wrocław, enabled Logau to register in April 1516 at the University of Vienna, and for the rest of his life he was to remain a faithful client of the Thurzo family. In Vienna Logau was closely connected with Caspar *Ursinus

Velius, another native of Świdnica. Subsequently he received a scholarship from King *Louis II of Hungary and Bohemia to cover the expense of three years of study in Italy. He registered at the University of Bologna in 1519 and was again at Bologna in 1526. In 1527 he returned to Cracow with the Hapsburg ambassador Georgius *Loxanus and became a friend of Justus Ludovicus *Decius. Two years later he entered the service of *Ferdinand I, who had succeeded Louis II as king of Bohemia. In 1530 he attended the diet of Augsburg in Ferdinand's retinue and there met Johannes *Dantiscus, whose help he solicited in his efforts to secure a canonry of the Holy Cross, Wrocław. In fact, he was to spend the last two decades of his life at Wrocław as a canon and later provost of the Holy Cross and a canon of St John's.

From Augsburg he went again to Italy and in September 1530 was in Padua. This journey was financed by his patron, Stanislaus *Thurzo, but Logau also appears to have been tutoring a young nobleman (Epp 2657, 2753, 2810). In Padua he made the acquaintance of Pietro *Bembo (Ep 2708) and *Viglius Zuichemus and his circle of friends. He also associated with such Polish Erasmians as Stanisław *Aichler and Jan *Boner. Viglius' letters to Erasmus often refer to him, sometimes without giving his name, and suggest that their relationship was ambiguous, in part no doubt on account of Logau's participation in the controversy over Erasmus' Ciceronianus during a visit to Rome from 1533 to 1534 (Epp 2568, 2657, 2716, 2753, 2791). After a trip to Naples in the company of Anselmus *Ephorinus (1535–6), Logau left Italy with the reputation of being a Ciceronian that he had acquired in Rome.

Before the publication of the Ciceronianus and his visit to Rome, Logau had composed verses for publication in the Cracow editions of Erasmus' Precatio dominica (1525) and of Ep 1819 addressed to King *Sigismund I of Poland (1527). Erasmus, who never met Logau (Ep 3005), sent him greetings in September 1533 when writing to Franciscus *Rupilius (Ep 2867). Six months later, however, he had learnt about a tract attacking the Ciceronianus that was circulating in manuscript at Rome and subsequently also at Padua; he also knew Logau to be its author (Epp 2906, 2961). It was never published, but by May 1534 Ambrosius von *Gumppenberg had dispatched a manuscript copy to Erasmus from Rome; Erasmus mentioned a year later that he had never read anything more insipid (Epp 2936, 3005). In 1534 Logau left Italy, but he returned there once more, receiving a doctorate in canon and civil law in Ferrara on 1 February 1538.

In Italy Logau met Johann Albrecht *Widmannstetter, who provided manuscripts of the Cynegetica by Nemesianus and Gratius as well as Ovid's Halieutica, all of which Logau edited (Venice: heirs of A. Manuzio 1534), with a dedication to Anton *Fugger. Two years later Logau was corresponding with Fugger's agent, Georg *Hörmann, and receiving payments from the Fugger firm. He was also a friend of the Zanchi family of Bergamo, editing the poems of Basilio (Petreius) (n p, n d) and receiving through Viglius in 1532 Giovanni Crisostomo *Zanchi's elegy on the death of his father. Logau was also a friend of Georg *Sauermann, for whom he composed an epitaph that was displayed in Wrocław. Although ridiculed by fellow scholars on account of his pride in his birth – he traced his descent from Achilles – Logau was esteemed for his neo-Latin poetry. His Hendecasyllabi (Vienna: H. Wietor 1529) were eventually followed by a posthumous collection of Carmina (Vienna 1599).

BIBLIOGRAPHY: Allen Ep 2568 / Maria Cytowska in PSB XVII 525–6 / Matrikel Wien II-1 431 / Knod 311–12 / de Vocht Dantiscus 60–1, 70 / Götz von Pölnitz Anton Fugger (Tübingen 1958–) II 316 / Hans Striedl in Festgabe der Bayerischen Staatsbibliothek [for] Emil Gratzl (Wiesbaden 1953) 103, 112–13 / Georg Ellinger Geschichte der neulateinischen Literatur Deutschlands im sechzehnten Jahrhundert (Berlin-Leipzig 1929–33) II passim / Pflug Correspondance I 491 and passim / Schottenloher I 450

MICHAEL ERBE & PGB

Jakob LOMPART of Basel, documented 1512–32
Jakob Lompart (Lampart, Lombard, Lumparth) was descended from a notable family of Fribourg in Switzerland, his father, Hans, having obtained the citizenship of Basel in 1494. Jakob registered at the University of Basel in 1512; because he was the famulus of a

professor he paid no fees. Subsequently he opened a bank and engaged in international transport and commerce, in 1522 working jointly with Martin vom Busch, perhaps to be identified with Martin *Lompart, who was managing the firm's office at Antwerp. From 1528 Jakob sat on the great council; he was also a prominent member of the 'Gartneren' guild and in this capacity participated in the Kappel wars of 1531. He was master of his guild in 1532 and probably died soon thereafter.

He first married Christiane vom Busch and subsequently, about 1529, a daughter of Bernhard Meyer zum Pfeil, who in March 1530 was a godmother to Irene, the daughter of Johannes *Oecolampadius. Jakob's sister Katharina was the second wife of Simon *Grynaeus.

Jakob is mentioned in Erasmus' correspondence with Erasmus *Schets between 1526 and 1529. Lompart's firm transferred sums of money and other gifts to Erasmus' full satisfaction (Epp 1658, 1671, 1676, 2193).

BIBLIOGRAPHY: *Wappenbuch der Stadt Basel* ed W.R. Staehelin (Basel [1917–30]) / BA *Oekolampads* II 416 / *Matrikel Basel* I 312 / *Aktensammlung zur Geschichte der Basler Reformation* ed E. Dürr et al (Basel 1921–50) II 362 and passim / AK III Ep 1165 / Traugott Geering *Handel und Gewerbe der Stadt Basel* (Basel 1886) 351   PGB

Martin LOMPART of Basel, documented 1526–31
Martin Lompart has not been identified adequately from the Basel sources. In his letters to Erasmus the Antwerp banker Erasmus *Schets described him as Jakob *Lompart's brother and associate living in Antwerp (Epp 1651, 1658, 1671, 2511). Erasmus is perhaps wrong in calling him Jakob's son (Ep 1676). He may be identical with one Martin Lompart, called vom Busch, whose wife was probably from Antwerp and who died before 12 January 1534. His son Christian was apparently brought up under the guardianship of Martin's father-in-law. A Martin vom Busch and his sisters are documented in Basel on 28 April 1494 after the death of their father, also called Martin.

BIBLIOGRAPHY: Staatsarchiv Basel-Stadt, MSS Privat-Archive 355 C 305   PGB

Noël de LONGASTIS See NATALIS
(*Epp 95 and 101*)

Johannes LONGICAMPIANUS
d 10 March 1529
Johann Gusebel called himself Longicampianus after his native village of Langenfeld in Bavaria, perhaps Burglengenfeld near Regensburg. Born around 1495, he studied at Cracow in 1512–13, graduating BA on 18 May 1513. On 13 December 1514 he matriculated at the University of Rostock, where he apparently received his MA. On 16 October 1516 he registered at Louvain. A few weeks later he travelled to Brussels to meet Erasmus, carrying an introduction from Maarten van *Dorp (Ep 496). Erasmus, in turn, sent him on to his friend Gerardus *Listrius in Zwolle, where he studied Greek and mathematics (Epp 500, 504; the chronological order is uncertain). During his stay in the Netherlands he also met Cuthbert *Tunstall and did some private teaching (Ep 867) but was evidently not able to secure satisfactory employment. In September 1518 he was at Mainz and had another encounter with Erasmus, who happened to be passing through the city (Ep 867). In the wake of this meeting he wrote to Erasmus and Dorp, presumably in another fruitless quest for a position in Louvain. Erasmus' brief answer indicates that Longicampianus knew *Eobanus Hessus and had connections with a circle of scholars around the press of Johann *Schöffer (Ep 881). In 1519 he went to Ingolstadt, and probably in 1523 he arrived in Wittenberg, where he won the esteem of *Melanchthon and at first directed a private school (*Melanchthons Briefwechsel* I Epp 366, 476). He married Anna Blankenfeld, who was well-connected in Wittenberg, and from the summer term of 1525 taught a course of mathematics at the university, although without obtaining a full academic position. He remained in Wittenberg until his premature death in a state of poverty.

Longicampianus' only extant writing is an oration given at Ingolstadt on 5 March 1520 to mark the beginning of Johann *Reuchlin's teaching at the university: *Oratio ... coram universitate Ingolstatensi habita pro D. Io. Capnione Phorcensi cum in lingua hebraica et graeca ludum ... aperiret* (Augsburg: S. Otmar 1520).

BIBLIOGRAPHY: Allen and CWE Epp 496, 881 / *Matrikel Rostock* II 59 / *Matricule de Louvain* III-1 545 / Luther W *Briefwechsel* V Ep 1396 / *Melanchthons Briefwechsel* I Ep 765 and passim / Hans Volz 'Johann Gusebel Longicampianus

...' in *Festschrift für Josef Benzing* ed E. Geek and
G. Pressler (Wiesbaden 1964) 456–75 / de Vocht
MHL 174 and passim   MICHAEL ERBE & PGB

John LONGLAND of Henley-on-Thames, 1473–7 May 1547

John Longland was born at Henley-on-Thames
to Thomas Longland, a servant of William
Lovell, Lord Morley. Presumably educated at
the local grammar school, Longland entered
Magdalen College, Oxford, in Michaelmas
term 1491 and was elected a demy of the college
in 1493 and a fellow in 1496. On 18 April 1500
he was ordained priest, and on 29 January 1504
he was presented to the rectory of Woodham
Ferrers, Essex, by Thomas Grey, marquis of
Dorset. Longland continued to reside in
Oxford, however, serving as a bursar at
Magdalen College in 1504–5 and principal of
Magdalen Hall from 1505 to 1507. By this time
Longland had embarked on his theological
studies, taking his bachelor's degree on 27
June 1509 and supplicating doctor of divinity
on 15 February 1511/12. By 1513 Longland's
abilities as a preacher began to attract increas-
ing attention, and in March of that year he was
preaching at court. Thereafter in quick succession he was installed as rector of Lifton,
Devon, on 6 June 1513, prebendary of North
Kelsey, Lincoln Cathedral, in 1514, and dean
of Salisbury, also in 1514. During this period
Longland continued to preach at court, and in
1520 he was made chaplain and confessor to
*Henry VIII as well as a member of the king's
council. In 1519 he had been made canon of
Windsor, while on 5 May 1521 he was
consecrated bishop of Lincoln. Even after his
elevation to the see of Lincoln, Longland spent
much of his time at court, maintaining his
membership in the king's council throughout
his life and serving as a judge both at the Court
of Requests and at the Star Chamber. In 1532 he
was made chancellor of Oxford.

Longland played a very active role in the
early stages of Henry's quest for a divorce,
helping to obtain the favourable report of
Oxford to the king's case and acting as
*Cranmer's assistant during the divorce pro-
ceedings at Dunstable during May 1533. His
advocacy of Henry's case may help explain
why the rebels of 1536 singled him out for
hostility. Longland was, however, essentially
a conservative man, and although he played a

very active role in the early stages of the case,
after 1534, when the full consequences of the
divorce were becoming increasingly apparent,
his views changed somewhat; at most he only
half-heartedly subscribed to the new order.
Despite his involvement at court, Longland did
not neglect his diocese; reputed to be somewhat cruel in his treatment of heretics, he
sought to raise the quality of the local clergy.
His abilities as both a preacher and a scholar
were applauded by Thomas *More and among
his friends were numbered Richard *Kidderminster, Robert *Aldridge, Thomas Robertson,
and Juan Luis *Vives with whom he corresponded. A catalogue of his writings is to be
found in Wood.

The first meeting between Longland and
Erasmus probably occurred during either
Erasmus' third or fourth visit to England, in
1509 or 1515. In any case by the time they met in
Calais in 1520 they were already close friends.
From Erasmus' letter to *Fonseca of 2 September 1527 (Ep 1874) it appears that Longland
was in the habit of writing to Erasmus twice a
year, although only two of these letters have
survived (Epp 1570, 2227). Erasmus dedicated
to Longland two sequels to his paraphrases on
the Psalms (Epp 1535, 2017) as well as his
translation of Athanasius' *Lucubrationes* (Ep
1790). The friendship between the two was not
without differences of opinion, however, and
on a few occasions Erasmus sought to vindicate
his *Colloquia* and other writings before his
critics, one of whom was apparently Longland.
The conservative bishop seems to have remained somewhat sceptical of Erasmus' attitude towards the Reformation and attempted
to persuade him to revise certain of his writings
(Epp 1704, 2037). These disagreements, however, did not threaten their friendship, and
Longland continued to act as Erasmus' patron
until the latter's death in 1536, frequently
supplying him with funds (Epp 1758, 1769,
2072, 2159, 2227, 3104, 3108).

BIBLIOGRAPHY: Allen Ep 1535 / DNB XII 120–1 /
Emden BRUO II 1160–2 / J.W. Blench 'John
Longland and Roger Edgeworth, two forgot-
ten preachers of the early sixteenth century'
Review of English Studies n s 18 (1954) 123–43 /
J.W. Blench *Preaching in England in the Late
Fifteenth and Sixteenth Centuries* (Oxford 1964) /
A. Wood *Athenae Oxonienses* (Oxford 1813–20)
I 161–4 (Longland's writings) / G.E. Wharhirst

'The Reformation in the Diocese of Lincoln as illustrated by the life and work of Bishop Longland (1521–1547)' *Lincolnshire Architectural and Archaeological Society*, reports and papers n s 1–2 (1936–8) 137–76 / M. Bowker *The Secular Clergy in the Diocese of Lincoln 1495–1520* (Cambridge 1968) 3, 6, and passim

MORDECHAI FEINGOLD

Gisbertus LONGOLIUS of Utrecht, 1507–30 May 1543

Gisbertus Longolius (Langenraet, Langenrak), a native of Utrecht, matriculated at the University of Cologne on 23 June 1524. His first publication was an annotated edition of Erasmus' *De civilitate* (Cologne: J. Gymnich 1530; cf NK 4145); this was followed quickly by a second edition, revised and enlarged (Cologne: J. Gymnich, October 1531), which was enormously successful. Longolius subsequently left for Italy, where he studied medicine. On his return north from Ferrara, probably in the autumn of 1535, he apparently intended to visit Erasmus (Ep 3113), but the letters from Johannes *Sinapius and Antoine de *Pons which he was supposed to deliver to Erasmus are not preserved, and his visit is not otherwise mentioned. From his return until about 1537 he held appointments in Deventer as town physician and headmaster and subsequently became a professor at the University of Cologne and personal physician to Archbishop Hermann von *Wied. Towards the end of 1542 he went to Rostock to participate in the restructuring of university programs. His *Studii literarii publici in Academia Rostochiensi diligens et accurata restauratio; una cum constitutione ludi puerilis, a clarissimo viro D. Gisberto Longolio professore medico* (Rostock: L. Dietz August 1544) was published after his death.

Longolius prepared a number of editions and commentaries of classical authors, but today he is known mostly as the annotator of Erasmus' *De civilitate*. It is evident that among his contemporaries he enjoyed a solid pedagogical reputation. The archives of the chapter of St Thomas at Strasbourg preserve a manuscript copy of 'Leges scholasticae ludi literarii Daventriensis authore G. Longolio Utricensi' (c 1536), which seems to have provided some inspiration for the founders of the famous Strasbourg Gymnasium. At the end of these

regulations Longolius inserted two prayers selected from Erasmus' *Precationes aliquot novae* (Basel: H. Froben August 1535). If his visit to Erasmus actually took place, it may be that he received a copy of this work in return for the letters he brought Erasmus.

BIBLIOGRAPHY: ADB XIX 155–6 / J. Revius *Daventriae illustratae sive historiae urbis Daventriensis libri sex* (Leiden 1651) 233–7 / *Matrikel Köln* II 867 / *Matrikel Rostock* II 104–5 / O. Krabbe *Die Universität Rostock im fünfzehnten und sechzehnten Jahrhundert* (Rostock 1854) 443–4 / H. Schnell *Das Unterrichtswesen der Grossherzogtümer Mecklenburg-Schwerin und Strelitz* I (Berlin 1907) 149 ff, III (Berlin 1909) 213 / F. Bierlaire and R. Hoven 'L'école latine de Deventer vers 1536: un règlement oublié' *Archives et bibliothèques de Belgique* 45 (1974) 602–17

FRANZ BIERLAIRE

LONGOLIUS *See also Christophe and Pierre de LONGUEIL*

Christophe de LONGUEIL c 1488–11 September 1522

The family of Christophe de Longueil (Longolius) belonged to the oldest nobility of Normandy. His grandfather was a member of the Parlement of Paris, *lieutenant-civil* of the Châtelet, and master of requests of the royal palace. His father, Antoine de Longueil, was bishop of Saint-Pol-de-Léon in Brittany and served Queen Anne of Brittany as her chancellor and almoner-in-chief. King *Charles VIII sent him on an embassy to the Netherlands, in consequence of which Christophe was born at Mechelen, about 1488, the son of a local girl. By 1497, despite his very young age, he was sent to Paris to study at the Collège du Plessis. However, after the death of his father in 1500 he abandoned studies for a life among the military. In 1501 he accompanied *Louis XII on the Italian campaign, and in 1504 he was in the Netherlands and joined Philip the Handsome, duke of *Burgundy, for his journey to England and Spain. When Philip died in the autumn of 1506 Longueil resumed his studies, reading law at Bologna in 1507 and at Poitiers from 1508 to 1510. At the same time he was keenly interested in science; at Poitiers he distinguished himself sufficiently to be chosen to lecture on the elder Pliny, who was then considered an encyclopaedic repository of information on science, and also on the twenty-eighth book of the Pandects.

Probably in 1510, on the occasion of the feast of St Louis, 25 August, he delivered a solemn oration in which he celebrated the genius of the French nation and expressed a measure of anti-Italian feelings, thus reflecting the contemporary tensions between Rome and France. This *Oratio de laudibus divi Ludovici atque Francorum* was published in 1512 (Paris: H. Estienne; repr Paris: P. Gromors 1520, with the introductory lecture to the commentary on the Pandects); in later years it was to cause trouble for its author. At Amboise Longueil was received by the future King *Francis I, to whom he gave some lessons. Thereafter he was again on the move, perhaps following Louis XII to Italy at the time of the council of Pisa (1511). Having been absolved from the consequences of his irregular birth by brief of *Leo X, he received a protonotaryship and a pension. Driven by the desire to verify his book-learning in the field, especially in ichthyology, he wandered all over Switzerland and in doing so met with several misadventures. After his return he received a doctorate in law in 1514 from the University of Valence and on this occasion delivered an oration in praise of jurisprudence (published in Valence: L. Olivetti 25 August 1514). Thereafter he went to Paris, and on 9 June 1515 he was appointed to the Parlement of Paris. He mingled with the Paris scholars and assisted Nicolas *Bérault in his edition of Pliny; he also enjoyed the patronage of Louis *Ruzé, who may have financed his earlier studies and seems to have treated him like a son. When he wished to learn Greek he begged Guillaume *Budé to be his teacher. According to Budé's first biographer, Louis Le Roy, the famous humanist refused, whereupon Longueil started for Rome in the company of Lazare de *Baïf.

In Rome he was taught by Janus *Lascaris and Marcus *Musurus, having been recommended to the latter by Budé in a letter of 10 June 1516. His patrons at Rome were Giulio Tomarezzo or Tomarozzi, whose son Flaminio was one of Longueil's favourite pupils, and Mario Castellano. He met Pietro *Bembo, who introduced him to the Ciceronian circles of the Roman Academy. Such was his mastery of

Latin that even the Romans could not refuse this 'arrival from the North' their admiration, but at the same time he encountered patriotic resentment. The offended pride of the Romans was particularly evident in the case of Celso Mellini, a young patrician. In the hope of ruining Longueil, his enemies drew attention to his oration in praise of St Louis. In an effort to gain indulgence for that work of his youth, Longueil composed five speeches in honour of Rome in August 1518. With these he succeeded so well in turning public opinion in his favour that on 31 January 1519 the city council proposed to accord him the title of 'civis Romanus.' The matter was taken up in a trial which took place on 16 June 1519 in the presence of Pope Leo X and the cardinals and aroused extraordinary passions and tensions. Longueil thought it advisable not to attend the trial in person, but he composed in his own defence the *Orationes duae pro defensione sua*. They were published at Rome and distributed on 9 August, although a request to have them read at the trial had not been granted.

As early as May Longueil had withdrawn to the abbey of Lérins, where he was granted hospitality by the abbot, Gregorio Cortese, and by Agostino Grimaldi, bishop of Grasse. From there he returned to Paris, accompanied by Lorenzo *Bartolini, abbot of Entremont. At the end of August he paid a visit to Budé at Marly, asking him for letters of recommendation addressed to some English humanists and to Erasmus. After a journey in England Longueil and Bartolini arrived in Louvain for a visit with Erasmus from 13 to 15 October 1519 (Epp 1011, 1023, 1024, 1026, 1187, 1706). Subsequently Longueil returned to Paris and let it be known that he intended to set out for Italy without delay; he had won his trial in Rome, his friends were calling for his return, and the pope had created him count palatine and apostolic protonotary. Accordingly he appealed to Budé, who was to ask Louis Ruzé to grant him leave. By the end of 1519 he was in Venice, and on 18 April 1520 he reached Padua. Giulio de' Medici, the future *Clement VII, offered him a chair of Latin at Florence, but he declined so as to devote himself exclusively to scholarship. It seems that by now his only ambition was to become ever more accomplished in perfect Ciceronian Latinity. In Padua he was at first the guest of Pietro Bembo at the villa Noniana, and subsequently of the Sauli family, having among his pupils the young Stefano Sauli; he also got together again with his former student Marcantonio Flaminio. At the pope's request he took up his pen in the service of the faith and late in 1520 composed an *Oratio ad Lutheranos quosdam iam damnatos* (Ep 1597). The death of Leo x left him without means, but this did not prevent him from taking in his friend Simon *Villanovanus, whom he helped to find a patron. From the beginning of July 1521 Longueil himself was the protégé of Reginald *Pole (Ep 1675), in whose house he died, covered with a Franciscan cowl (Epp 1347, 1597; ASD I-3 689).

Longueil's death was commemorated in verse by Germain de *Brie, Clément Marot, Jean *Salmon Macrin, and Guillaume Scève. Pole wrote a biography of him and published it together with such of Longueil's works as he knew the author would have wished to see gathered: the two speeches occasioned by the Roman trial (which had formerly been published by Nicolas Bérault in Paris in 1520), the oration against the Lutherans, and the correspondence comprising some one hundred and fifty of Longueil's letters, divided into four books, to which had been added a fifth with letters from Bembo and *Sadoleto to Longueil. This volume was first printed in Florence by the Giunta press in 1524; it was reprinted at Paris by Josse *Bade in 1526, and many times thereafter, enabling future generations of scholars to make a proper study of Longueil.

Longueil's written oeuvre is disproportionately small compared with the impact his personality made upon his contemporaries, including Erasmus. Only one letter from Erasmus to Longueil is known today, Ep 935, dating from 1 April 1519, but this one letter reflects the beginnings of a potential conflict between the two humanists. Erasmus' letter was prompted by his desire to blunt the impact of another letter (Ep 914) which Longueil had written two months earlier to Jacques *Lucas, dean of Orléans, who was then in Rome. It was a kind of show-piece in which Longueil compared Erasmus and Budé without concealing his preference for the Frenchman. In writing it, Longueil identified himself with

those slightly chauvinistic tendencies of French humanism which encouraged their partisans to see in Budé a model and a symbol. On reading this letter, which Ruzé had shown him in March 1519, Erasmus can hardly have been pleased. This letter also set the stage for his personal encounter with Longueil in October 1519. Writing to *Lupset (Ep 1026), he commented afterwards that Longueil had impressed him favourably in all respects but one: for one born in Brabant he was too French (cf *Ciceronianus* ASD I-2 692; Ep 3043). In fact it was Longueil's misfortune that he could claim successively to be associated with several nations, each of which later saw itself disappointed in the hopes it had set on him. Thus he was bound to cause controversy and to be accused of contradicting himself. A Frenchman by paternal descent, a Fleming by birth, and a Roman by choice, he could at the same time seem too French, or at least too Budean, to Erasmus and disappoint the French (Ep 1812) when he preferred to swell the ranks of the Italian Ciceronians rather than make his contribution to the glory of French letters. His progress in this direction could not but add to the distance that separated him from Erasmus. The latter was acquainted with Longueil's collected works (Epp 1595, 1675, 2059, 2329), which contained several negative assessments of himself; cf *Opera* (1524) 121, 128, 138. It is difficult to deny that he may have recalled the tone of those passages when he composed his *Ciceronianus*.

From the continuing scholarly debate devoted to the interpretation of the *Ciceronianus* only one crucial point needs to be touched on here, namely whether or not Nosoponus, one of the speakers in Erasmus' dialogue, should be identified with Longueil. Etienne *Dolet was convinced that he should when setting out to defend Longueil, but the ambiguity of Erasmus' dialogue permits, and perhaps calls for, a very different interpretation. Thus for Giovanni Toffanin and Angelo Gambaro, the *Ciceronianus* represents an animated defence and even a vindication of Longueil. Erasmus could no doubt have nourished some grudge against a man who had brilliantly challenged his fame; but he might just as well have taken Longueil's censures as a mere reflection of the typical Italian hostility to his work. In view of Longueil's sad fate and the excessive price he was made to pay for his Ciceronian perfectionism, Erasmus might even have felt a mixture of admiration and genuine pity. This hypothesis is supported by the fact that in 1535 Erasmus paid tribute to Longueil's memory and presented him as a native Hollander who had reaped honour for his nation, although like Homer he was claimed by several towns (Ep 3043). It is, however, improbable that Longueil was born at Schoonhoven in Holland, as Erasmus had been told by Pierre de *Longueil, the uncle of Christophe. Nonetheless, the widespread desire to adopt Longueil for one's own country reveals something of the fascination he must have aroused. To Erasmus, Longueil was a Christian soldier misled by the cult of Cicero and lost to the cause of Nordic humanism and the *philosophia Christi*. To Longueil himself, however, Ciceronianism probably meant not merely an aesthetic ideal but a highly demanding code of ethics, a kind of asceticism related to the Franciscan poverty with which he had fortified himself at the hour of his premature death.

BIBLIOGRAPHY: Allen Ep 914 / CWE Ep 1011 / BNB XII 349–59 / T. Simar *Christophe de Longueil, humaniste (1488–1522)* (Louvain 1911) / P.A. Becker *Christophle de Longueil, sein Leben und sein Briefwechsel* (Bonn-Leipzig 1924) / G. Budé *Correspondance* French trans by G. Lavoie and R. Galibois (Sherbrooke 1977) 181–221 / G. Vallese 'L'Umanesimo al primo cinquecento, da Cristoforo Longolio al *Ciceronianus* di Erasmo' in *Le parole e le idee* (Naples 1959) I 107–23; repr in *Da Dante ad Erasmo* (Naples 1962) / G. Toffanin *Storia dell'umanesimo* 2nd ed (Bologna 1964) / A. Gambaro *Il Ciceronianus di Erasmo di Rotterdam* (Brescia 1965) / P. Mesnard 'Un brabançon qui n'a pas son égal en Europe' in *Actes de la commémoration nationale d'Erasme* (Antwerp 1969) / P. Mesnard *Erasme, ou le christianisme critique* (Paris 1969) / M.-M. de la Garanderie *Christianisme et lettres profanes* (Lille-Paris 1976) I 112 (Le Cicéronianisme en France) / R. Aulotte 'Une rivalité d'humanistes; Erasme et Longueil traducteurs de Plutarque' BHR 30 (1968) 549–73 / E.-V. Telle *L'Erasmianus sive Ciceronianus d'Etienne Dolet (1535)* (Geneva 1974)   M.-M. DE LA GARANDERIE

Pierre de LONGUEIL documented 1465– after 1484

Pierre, paternal uncle of Christophe de *Longueil, was the third son of Jean III, seigneur de Longueil, Varangeville, Offrainville, Maisons, and Rancher au Maine (d 1466), by his wife, Marie, the daughter of Philippe de Morvilliers, first president of the Parlement of Paris. Like many other younger sons of the aristocratic Longueil family, Pierre made his career in the church. His uncle, Pierre de Longueil, bishop of Auxerre (1449–73) and grand master of the chapel of the duke of Burgundy, created him second archdeacon of La Puisaye in 1465. Later he served as vicar-general to his elder brother Antoine, bishop of Saint-Pol-de-Léon in Brittany (1484–1500). In 1535 Erasmus cited Pierre de Longueil's authority for the claim that Christophe de Longueil was born at Schoonhoven in Holland (Ep 3043). However, Christophe's biographers agree that his birthplace was Mechelen. Erasmus' personal contacts with Pierre must have occurred several decades earlier; if the nephew was, in fact, mentioned, Christophe may have come to Erasmus' attention earlier than the record of their connections suggests.

BIBLIOGRAPHY: *Gallia christiana* XII 330 / F.A. Aubert de la Chesnaye des Bois *Dictionnaire de la noblesse* 2nd ed (Paris 1770–86) IX 96–7 / N.V. de Saint-Allais *Nobiliaire universel de France* (Paris 1876) XIII 252–3 / T. Simar *Christophe de Longueil, humaniste (1488–1522)* (Louvain 1911) 3–4 / P.A. Becker *Christophle de Longueil, sein Leben und sein Briefwechsel* (Bonn-Leipzig 1924) 2–3   JUDITH RICE HENDERSON

Johannes LONICERUS of Artern, d 20 June 1569

Johannes Lonicerus (Lonitzer), of Artern, south-west of Eisleben in Saxony, entered the monastery of Austin friars in Eisleben and was sent to Wittenberg, where he graduated BA on 12 April 1519 and MA on 24 January 1521. In May 1520, under the influence of Martin *Luther and Philippus *Melanchthon, he wrote a pamphlet, *Contra Romanistam fratrem*, against Augustin von *Alveldt (Wittenberg: J. Rhau-Grunenberg). In December 1521, with a recommendation from Thomas *Blarer to Philipp *Engelbrecht, Lonicerus went to Freiburg, where he taught Hebrew. After a public attack upon the Franciscans he had to leave Freiburg in 1522 and went for a while to Esslingen, near Stuttgart. In 1523 he moved to Strasbourg, where he received hospitality from Nikolaus *Gerbel, to whom he had been recommended by Melanchthon. In the same year Lonicerus published in Strasbourg (J. Schott) a *Catechesis bona voluntate Dei*. He worked for the publishing houses of Knobloch, Köpfel, and *Herwagen and married the daughter of a Strasbourg citizen on 6 January 1524. Lonicerus translated a number of Luther's works into Latin to facilitate their circulation in France, for example, *Super Magnificat commentarii* (Strasbourg: J. Herwagen 1525). On 30 May 1527, as the result of a recommendation by Helius *Eobanus Hessus, he received a call to the University of Marburg, where he taught Greek and, from 1536, also Hebrew. He later became professor of medicine and in 1554 of theology. He died in Marburg.

Apart from his contributions to the literature of the Reformation, Lonicerus published in Strasbourg editions of Homer (W. Köpfel 1525) and the Septuagint (W. Köpfel 1524–6) in Greek. He also published, chiefly in Basel, many Latin translations of Greek authors, among them Pindar (Basel: A. Cratander 1528) and Sophocles' *Ajax* (Basel: J. Herwagen 1533), and the commentaries of Theophylact to the minor prophets (Basel: J. Bebel 1534) and to the Pauline Epistles (Basel: A. Cratander 1540). He wrote a Greek grammar (Basel: B. Westheimer 1536, revised 1540, 1551) and *Erotemata in Galeni de usu partium in hominis corpore libri xvii* (Frankfurt: C. Egenolff 1550). In Ep 1934 Erasmus mentioned that one of Lonicerus' publications referred to Heinrich *Eppendorf.

BIBLIOGRAPHY: Allen Ep 1934 / ADB XIX 158–63 / Luther w *Briefwechsel* II Ep 284, III Ep 739 / AK VI Ep 2862, VII 3062 / BRE Ep 248   IG

Iñigo LÓPEZ de Mendoza y Zúñiga
d 9 June 1535

Iñigo López de Mendoza y Zúñiga was a son of Pedro de Zúñiga y Velasco, second count of Miranda, and a brother of Francisco de *Zúñiga, third count of Miranda, and of Juan de Zúñiga y Avellaneda, commander of Castile. Educated at Salamanca, he became bishop of Coria in Estremadura in the 1520s. In

September 1526 the Emperor *Charles v sent him to England to help negotiate for universal peace. While in England, on 2 March 1529, he was nominated bishop of Burgos. He returned to Spain in about May 1529, but soon he accompanied Charles v to Italy, and in March 1530 he was secretly named cardinal by Pope *Clement VII. He served Charles on missions to Naples and Rome (1531–2) and returned to his diocese in 1533. He founded the college of St Nicholas at Burgos.

In 1529 and 1530 the correspondence between Erasmus and Alfonso de *Valdés was forwarded through López de Mendoza (Epp 2163, 2252). In 1532 the cardinal had a hand in sending to Erasmus critical notes of Diego *López Zúñiga on Erasmus' editions of the New Testament and Jerome (Epp 2705, 2905, 2951). López de Mendoza was also a patron of Juan Gines de *Sepúlveda (Ep 2810). Juan *Maldonado wrote his *Pastor bonus*, published in the *Opuscula quaedam* (Burgos: J. de Junta 1549), in homage to the bishop late in 1529.

BIBLIOGRAPHY: Allen Ep 2163 / Eubel III 143, 160 / Bataillon *Erasmo y España* 328–9 and passim / José M. March *Niñez y juventud de Felipe II* (Madrid 1941–2) I 83, II 249 and passim   TBD

Diego LÓPEZ PACHECO marquis of Villena,
d 6 November 1529

Diego was the eldest son of Juan Fernández Pacheco (1419/21–74), first marquis of Villena, duke of Escalona, and grand master of the knights of Santiago from 1469, by his second marriage, to María Portocarrero. Diego first married María de Luna and then Juana Enríquez, the daughter of the admiral of Castile. His father had accumulated one of the largest territorial holdings of any nobleman of his time. However, after the death of Henry IV of Castile in 1474, Diego's support for the claims of Juana la Beltraneja to the crown and his resistance to her rival, *Isabella of Castile, led to his forfeiture in 1480, under the terms of the royal pardon granted him that year, of many of the lands he had inherited. He recovered his position at court, was made captain general of the Catholic monarchs' troops investing Granada in 1490, and in 1492 was present at the surrender of the city. He was at court during *Charles v's first stay in Spain (1517–20) and, during the *Comunidades*, sought to re-establish the authority of the absent emperor in Toledo. He was obliged to flee the city in 1521 and thereafter, being of advanced age, passed his remaining years quietly in his castle at Escalona. The date of his death, as given on his tombstone, was 6 November 1529. He was buried in the Hieronymite monastery of El Parral at Segovia, founded by his father.

The marquis is remembered for the way in which, in the early 1520s, he made his residence a centre of religious activity directed towards the development of the inner Christian life. As early as 1493 he had founded a monastery for the Franciscan Observants, for whom he had particular regard. In 1527 he built a house for the Franciscans at Escalona. Following the reform of the order by Cardinal *Jiménez de Cisneros, the Franciscans of New Castile, in which Escalona was situated, were particularly associated with the cultivation of an inner spiritual state – recogimiento – sought by turning away from the popular form of meditation on the suffering humanity of Christ and by a radical detaching of the self from the whole created order, and even from all discursive thought, in the pursuit of union with God. The finest expression of this movement was Fray Francisco de Osuna's Tercer abecedario espiritual, which the author dedicated to the marquis, remarking in his preface on the marquis' great attachment to what he had written in this work. Its first edition (Toledo: Ramón de Petras 1527) bore the marquis' arms. The Franciscan movement was not hostile to the experience of elevated spiritual states, and in the first decades of the century Franciscans came to be especially associated with more or less dramatic demonstrations of such experience. Not a few were moved to prophesyings; others were credited with miracles. Two Franciscans notable in this way were taken by the marquis into his household in 1522: Juan de Olmillos, who provided him with spiritual counsel, and Francisco de Ocaña, who preached the need for reform of the church in notably extravagant terms.

In 1523, the marquis appointed Pedro Ruiz de Alcaraz as a domestic lay preacher. Alcaraz was of humble converso origins and a disciple of the illuminist Isabel de la Cruz. While possess-

ing no formal learning, he had a remarkable knowledge of the Bible and preached regularly to the marquis' household and in the vicinity. He had been of interest to the Inquisition since 1519. In February 1524 he was arrested and was imprisoned at Toledo. The charges against him formed the basis of the edict against the alumbrados of the archbishopric of Toledo of September 1525. His teaching appears to have displayed marked similarities in a number of respects to that of *Luther, though the nature of the connection between them, if any, continues to be debated. Together with Isabel de la Cruz, Alcaraz was eventually sentenced, in 1529, after recantation, to life-imprisonment; he was also to be publicly whipped in the places where he had preached, Escalona among them. One of those who had listened to Alcaraz's preaching there was Juan de *Valdés, whose anonymously published Diálogo de doctrina cristiana (Alcalá: Miguel de Eguía 1529) was dedicated to the marquis in the year of the latter's death and of Alcaraz's disgrace. No action was taken against the marquis himself. Two years earlier he had written to Alfonso de *Valdés to ask how he might best make known his admiration for Erasmus and to express his sorrow that old age and ill health prevented him from defending Erasmus against the calumnies of the religious orders, representatives of which were then assembled at the Valladolid conference to examine the humanist's works (Ep 1839).

BIBLIOGRAPHY: Allen Ep 1839 / Hernando de Pulgar Claros varones de Castilla ed R.B. Tate (Oxford 1971) 87–8 / L. Suárez Fernández and J. de Mata Carriazo Arroquia La España de los Reyes Católicos vol 17 of Historia de España ed R. Menéndez Pidal (Madrid 1969) 173–5, 337–41, and passim / Bataillon Erasmo y España 182–4 and passim / M. Serrano y Sanz 'Pedro Ruiz de Alcaraz, iluminado alcarreño del siglo XVI' Revista de archivos, bibliotecas y museos 7 (1903) 1–16, 126–39 / V. Beltrán de Heredia, OP 'El edicto contra los alumbrados del reino de Toledo (23 de septiembre de 1525)' Revista española de teología 10 (1950) 105–30 / A. Selke de Sánchez 'Algunos datos nuevos sobre los primeros alumbrados: El edicto de 1525 y su relación con el proceso de Alcaraz' Bulletin hispanique 54 (1952) 125–52 / Juan de Valdés Diálogo de doctrina christiana repr in facsimile ed M. Bataillon (Coimbra 1925) / Augustin Redondo 'Luther et l'Espagne de 1520 à 1536' *Mélanges de la Casa de Velázquez* 1 (1965) 109–65 / Milagros Ortega Costa de Emmart 'Las proposiciones del Edicto de los alumbrados. Autores y calificadores' *Cuadernos de investigación histórica* 1 (1977) 23–36 / J.C. Nieto *Juán de Valdés and the Origins of the Spanish and Italian Reformation* (Geneva 1970, rev ed Madrid-Mexico 1979) passim / J.C. Nieto 'The Franciscan alumbrados and the prophetic-apocalyptic tradition' *Sixteenth Century Journal* 8 (1977) 3–16 / J.C. Nieto 'The heretical alumbrados dexados: Isabel de la Cruz and Pedro Ruiz de Alcaraz' *Revue de littérature comparée (Hommage à Marcel Bataillon)* nos 2–4 (April–December 1978) 293–313   R.W. TRUMAN

Diego LÓPEZ ZÚÑIGA d 1531

Little is known about the early life of Diego López Zúñiga (Stunica) except that he was a member of a distinguished Spanish family. Prior to 1502 he studied under Aires Barbosa, who held the chair of Greek at the University of Salamanca from 1490 to 1503. A competent scholar in Greek, Latin, and Hebrew, and with some Aramaic and Arabic, López Zúñiga was one of the experts gathered at the University of Alcalá by Cardinal *Jiménez de Cisneros to prepare the Complutensian Polyglot Bible. Although his exact role in the project is unknown, de Jonge has argued that he made part of the interlinear Latin version of the Septuagint and collated Greek manuscripts of the gospels with the Latin Vulgate. In the mid-1510s, out of a desire to defend the Latin Vulgate and Christian orthodoxy, he prepared a series of criticisms on the commentaries on St Paul of Jacques *Lefèvre d'Etaples (1512) and the first edition of Erasmus' New Testament (1516). Jiménez de Cisneros advised him not to rush into print, at least not until after he had written to Erasmus. After the cardinal's death in 1517, however, López Zúñiga proceeded, issuing his attack on Lefèvre in 1519 and his *Annotationes contra Erasmum Roterodamum in defensionem tralationis Novi Testamenti* in 1520, both through the Alcalá press of Arnao Guillén de Brocar, printer of the Complutensian Polyglot.

In 1520 López Zúñiga travelled to Rome, describing his trip in the *Itinerarium ab Hispania* (Rome: M. Silber 1521). He was teaching Greek at the Roman university in 1521, and in the next year published an *Epistola* to the recently elected *Adrian vi (Rome: n pr). Meanwhile Erasmus published his first *Apologia* against López Zúñiga (Louvain: D. Martens 1521; ASD IX-2 58–267). Despite the efforts of Juan de *Vergara to make peace (Allen IV 623–31), the Spaniard replied with the *Erasmi Roterodami blasphemiae et impietates* (Rome: A. Bladus 1522), an abridged version of a manuscript which he had submitted to Pope *Leo x in 1521. Until then the controversy between the two scholars, though bitter, had been conducted on the basis of scholarly attack and riposte. According to Bataillon, the *Blasphemiae et impietates* marked the first occasion on which anyone had publicly criticized the entire religious program of Erasmus to prove that he was a radical heretic. To it López Zúñiga added the *Libellus trium illorum voluminum praecursor* (Rome: A. Bladus 1522), intended to be a warning that he would soon be publishing in full the original three books of the *Blasphemiae et impietates*. Erasmus' reply to the *Blasphemiae et impietates* was at the press in June 1522 when the *Libellus* arrived. He quickly added an appendix entitled *Apologia ad prodromon Stunicae*, and both were printed by Johann *Froben with the *Epistola de esu carnium* at Basel in August 1522 (LB IX 355–81).

Although López Zúñiga found some support in his compatriot Sancho *Carranza de Miranda, who published an *Opusculum in quasdam Erasmi annotationes* in March 1522 (Rome: A. de Trino), the violence of his attack alienated people who might otherwise have been disposed to accept his criticisms of Erasmus (Allen IV 631; Ep 1582), and Adrian vi imposed silence on him. After the pope's death, however, López Zúñiga published the *Conclusiones principaliter suspectae et scandalosae quae reperiuntur in libris Erasmi* (Rome: [A. Bladus] 1523; LB IX 381B–382F), soon followed by the *Loca quae ex Stunicae annotationibus ... in tertia editione Novi Testamenti Erasmus emendavit* (Rome: n pr 1524) and the *Assertio ecclesiasticae translationis Novi Testamenti* (Rome: n pr 1524). The frequency of his publications is partially explained by the fact that all his works were short and were the outpourings of considerable emotional fervour. Once again silence was imposed on him, this time by *Clement VII.

Erasmus, meanwhile, replied to López Zúñiga's *Conclusiones* with another *Apologia*, printed with the *Exomologesis* by Froben at Basel in March 1524. His final rejoinder to the Spanish scholar was in the form of a letter to Hubertus *Barlandus of 8 June 1529 (Ep 2172, published with the *Opus epistolarum*, Basel: H. Froben 1529). This reply was occasioned by the discovery of a copy of the *Assertio ecclesiasticae translationis* among his papers when he moved to Freiburg. Erasmus often referred to López Zúñiga in his letters as an arch-enemy ranking with Edward *Lee and Noël *Béda (Ep 2111) and as a kind of pestilence of which he could not rid himself (Epp 1278, 1294, 1311, 1411).

After 1524 López Zúñiga continued working on Erasmus' editions of the New Testament and of St Jerome with the purpose of refuting his errors. However he did not publish his material, and in his last years the controversy between him and Erasmus moderated. In 1529 he was with Cardinal Francisco de *Quiñones in the welcoming party which met *Charles V at Genoa. Before his death, on a visit to Naples, he asked that his notes, which had been left to Quiñones, be sent to Erasmus (Epp 2637, 2701). This wish was fulfilled by Iñigo *López de Mendoza y Zúñiga, bishop of Burgos (Epp 2705, 2905, 2951).

BIBLIOGRAPHY: Allen Ep 1128, IV 621–2 / H.J. de Jonge in ASD IX-2 1–57 / Nicolás Antonio *Bibliotheca Hispana nova* (Madrid 1783–8) I 295–6 / Bataillon *Erasmo y España* lxxx, 22–3, 115–32, and passim

                              WILLIAM B. JONES & TBD

Etienne LORET *See Jean de* GAIGNY

LORITI *See Henricus* GLAREANUS

Nicaise de L'ORME *See Nicaise* DELORME

Antoine, duke of LORRAINE 4 June 1489–14 June 1544
Antoine, the eldest son of Duke René II, became duke of Lorraine and Bar at the death of his father in 1508. He had spent the seven preceding years at the court of *Louis XII of

Antoine, duke of Lorraine,
by Hans Holbein the Younger

France, and he remained a faithful ally of the French crown, to which he was tied further by his marriage and by the careers of his brothers, Claude, duke of Guise (1496–1550), and Jean, cardinal of *Lorraine. In 1538 he claimed the duchy of Gelderland by virtue of his maternal lineage but soon abandoned his claim in the train of a general political realignment that led him to friendship with the house of Hapsburg; however, he continued his policy of peace and mediation between France and the Hapsburgs, as was to be expected from the location of his territories. He endeavoured to consult the representatives of his subjects; only in his opposition to the Lutheran movement did he show no flexibility, even though he avoided excessive severity. He is mentioned casually in Epp 2177, 2217, 2299, 3032. In Ep 3032 Erasmus also seems to recall how in the peasant rebellion of May 1525 Antoine was joined by his younger brother, Claude, who commanded the French troops in Champagne and was prominently involved in the defeat of the peasants.

BIBLIOGRAPHY: Allen Ep 3032 / DBF III 7–12
                                                        PGB

Jean, cardinal of LORRAINE 9 April 1498–
10 May 1550
Jean was the second son of René II, duke of
Lorraine and Bar. Before he had reached the
age of three he was designated coadjutor to the
bishop of Metz, who was his great-uncle, and
in 1517 he received his first bishopric, the see of
Toul, which he possessed intermittently until
1543. In 1518 he was admitted to the see of
Metz and created cardinal with the title of
Sant'Onofrio. Subsequently he was archbishop
of Narbonne (1524–50), Reims (1532–8) and
Lyon (1537–9) and bishop of Die and Valence
(1521–4), Thérouanne (1522–35), Verdun
(1523–44), Albi (1535–50), Agen (1541–50),
and Nantes (1542–50); he also held a number of
abbeys, including Cluny (from 1529). This
extraordinary accumulation of ecclesiastical
preferment reflects his skill in rendering
himself indispensible at the court of *Francis I.
Together with his younger brother, Claude,
created duke of Guise, he enjoyed the king's
fullest confidence and was involved in many
diplomatic negotiations such as the peace with
the Hapsburgs, in 1538, after he had been
unable to prevent the outbreak of the war (Ep
3121). He was at his monarch's side on many
state occasions, including the Field of Cloth of
Gold (Ep 1006), and at a similar meeting in 1532
he duly lost to *Henry VIII both at dice and the
jeu de paumes. He also pursued the interests of
France during his visits to Rome, and after the
death of *Paul III in 1549 he was the
unsuccessful French candidate for the papacy,
although by that time he was already somewhat overshadowed by his brilliant nephew,
Charles, cardinal of Lorraine. Jean was noted
as a patron of scholars and poets such as
Lazare de *Baïf (Ep 1962), Symphorien *Champier, Etienne *Dolet, and Nicolas *Bourbon.
He corresponded with *Sadoleto, and Benvenuto Cellini created a portrait medal of him.
    When Erasmus considered moving to Paris
in 1522 the cardinal of Lorraine was among
those who helped arrange for a royal safe-
conduct (Epp 1319, 1342). By February 1524
they had begun corresponding (Ep 1424), and
a year later in the first preserved letter Erasmus
pleaded with the cardinal to help Pierre
*Toussain (Ep 1559). In June 1527 Erasmus
dedicated to him the Latin translation of John
Chrysostom's commentary on Galatians (Ep

1841), as he had been urged to do by
*Cantiuncula, who was in the cardinal's
service (Epp 2063, 2240). Thirteen months later
Erasmus reminded Jean of the gift he had
promised in return (Epp 1884, 2009), but soon
he had reason to praise his generosity since the
cardinal had sent two hundred crowns (Epp
2027, 2217, 2370, LB VIII 265–318). Erasmus also
appealed to the cardinal for protection against
Noël *Béda and his other critics at the Paris
faculty of theology (Epp 1911, 1914), and he
recommended to him Gervasius *Wain (Ep
1911), who was visiting Basel on the eve of his
activities as a French political agent, and Egli
*Offenburg (Ep 2217), who had fled Basel
because of his opposition to the reformers.
    BIBLIOGRAPHY: Allen Ep 997 / Eubel III 18 and
passim / Pastor VII 241 and passim / Albert
Collignon Le Mécénat du cardinal Jean de
Lorraine (Paris-Nancy 1910) 11–36 and passim /
Martin Meurisse Histoire des évesque de l'église
de Metz (Metz 1634) 600–8 / J.C. Russell The
Field of Cloth of Gold (London 1969) 76–7
                                                    PGB

Johann (I) LOTZER of Horb, documented
1508–32
Johann Lotzer (Locerus) was born in Horb, in
Württemberg; his elder brother, Sebastian,
was a tanner and the author of popular
Reformation pamphlets. Johann matriculated
in Tübingen on 25 October 1508; by 1519 he
had obtained a doctorate of medicine and was
physician to Wilhelm von *Honstein, bishop of
Strasbourg. His book Ein nützlich Regimen
(Haguenau 1519), containing suggestions as to
how one could avoid catching the plague, was
dedicated to his father. In 1529 he was
physician to Louis V, elector *Palatine. After
the death of Ulrich von *Hutten, Lotzer bought
his library. Erasmus did not know him when he
wrote to him in 1529 (Ep 2116) referring to a
previous acquaintance between Lotzer and
Johann *Froben and requesting the loan of a
manuscript of Quintilian, which Hutten had
discovered in Fulda. It is not known whether
the request was granted, but the continuation
of Lotzer's friendship with Erasmus is evident
from Ep 2306, an introductory letter for
Lotzer's son, Johann (II), and his son's friend
Johann *Fichard, who were going to study in
Freiburg, where they matriculated on 20 June

1530. In 1531 Erasmus sent greetings to Lotzer when writing to Johannes *Sinapius (Ep 2461), a common friend who had recently dedicated to Lotzer his *Declamatio contra ignaviam* (Haguenau: J. Setzer 1530). There is no information about the subsequent career of Johann (II) Lotzer.

BIBLIOGRAPHY: Allen Ep 2116 / ADB LII 97–8 / *Matrikel Tübingen* I 166 / *Matrikel Freiburg* I 278

IG

Johann (II) LOTZER *See Johann (I) LOTZER*

LOUIS XI king of France, 3 July 1423–30 August 1483

Louis, the son of King *Charles VII of France and Marie d'Anjou, received a good education under the guidance of Jean Majoris, a friend of Jean Gerson, the chancellor of the University of Paris. In 1436 Louis married Margaret of Scotland, who died in 1445. Soon after his marriage, Louis was sent on a successful mission against rebellious noblemen in Languedoc. From 1440 he was involved in plots against his father, who exiled him in 1447 to his apanage, the Dauphiné. The tensions between Louis and his father increased when, after the death of his first wife, Louis married Charlotte of Savoy. The Dauphiné was annexed by the king and Louis settled in Genappe, near Brussels, from 1451 to 1461, under the protection of Philip the Good, duke of *Burgundy. He was crowned king on 15 August 1461 and at once became involved in struggles against his chief vassals. His defeat of Charles the Rash, duke of *Burgundy, in 1477, leading to the annexation of Bourgogne, Picardie, and Boulogne, contributed greatly to the strengthening of the French monarchy. In 1479 he suffered a stroke and withdrew to his castle, Plessis-les-Tours, where he died. He was succeeded by *Charles VIII, his son by Charlotte of Savoy.

Anecdotes about King Louis are related in the colloquy *Convivium fabulosum* (ASD I-3 443–6). He is also mentioned in *De conscribendis epistolis* (ASD I-2 286).

BIBLIOGRAPHY: Thomas Basin *Histoire de Louis XI* ed C. Samaran (Paris 1963–6) / Pierre Champion *Louis XI* (Paris 1927) / Philippe de Commines *Mémoires* ed J. Calmette (Paris 1925, repr 1964)   IG

Louis XI, king of France

LOUIS XII king of France, 27 June 1462–1 January 1515

Louis, the son of Charles, duke of Orléans, and Mary of Cleves, was born at Blois and succeeded his father as duke in 1465. In 1476 he was constrained to marry Jeanne de France, the deformed daughter of his second cousin, *Louis XI. When the sickly *Charles VIII became king in 1483, Louis was next in line for the throne. However, during the minority of Charles he joined the rebellion of Brittany against the crown and was captured at Saint-Aubin-du-Cormier on 28 July 1488. After a period of imprisonment he was restored to royal favour in June 1491 and participated in Charles' invasion of Italy. Louis XII succeeded Charles on 8 April 1498 and in the same year divorced Jeanne of France to marry Charles' widow, Anne of Brittany, thus preserving the union of the duchy to France. In 1499 he asserted his claim to be heir to the Visconti by invading Italy and capturing Milan. Although Duke Ludovico *Sforza managed to recover the city in early 1500, he was taken prisoner at Novara after his Swiss mercenaries refused to fight their compatriots in the pay of the French.

Louis XII, king of France, by Jean Perréal

Louis also renewed the French claim to Naples, and in November 1500 he signed the secret treaty of Granada with *Ferdinand II of Aragon to partition the kingdom. Louis conquered Naples in the summer of 1501 but soon fell out with Ferdinand and by early 1504 had lost the kingdom completely. By the treaty of Blois of 12 October 1505 he resigned Naples to his niece *Germaine de Foix, who married Ferdinand. In December 1508 he joined the Emperor *Maximilian I, Ferdinand, and Pope *Julius II in the League of Cambrai against Venice, and on 14 May 1509 he participated in the decisive French victory at Agnadello. By 1510, however, Julius II had turned against Louis, organizing a Holy League with Spain, Venice, England, and later the emperor in order to drive the French from Italy. Louis replied not only by force of arms but also by promoting the council of Pisa and Milan. Although the French under Gaston de Foix were victorious at Ravenna, they were driven from Milan by the Swiss in the summer of 1512, and in 1513 they were defeated at Novara by the Swiss and in the battle of the Spurs by *Henry VIII. His Italian policy in a shambles and his country

invaded, Louis reconciled himself with the recently elected *Leo x in 1513 (Ep 355) and made peace with England in 1514, marrying the sister of Henry VIII, *Mary Tudor. By Anne of Brittany Louis had two daughters, *Claude, who married the future *Francis I in 1514, and Renée, who married Ercole II d'*Este, duke of Ferrara.

Erasmus mentioned Louis XII on numerous occasions in his letters and works, usually to denounce the futility of his wars with Venice and with Julius II (Epp 240, 355; *Adagia* II v 1; *Opuscula* 91, 98, 102; ASD IV-1 213, 276). In a letter to Bonifacius *Amerbach of 6 January 1530 Erasmus contrasted Henry VIII's grounds for divorce with those of Louis in 1498 (Ep 2256).

BIBLIOGRAPHY: John S.C. Bridge *A History of France from the Death of Louis XI* 5 vols (Oxford 1929–36; repr New York 1978) / R. Doucet in *New Cambridge Modern History* ed G.R. Potter (Cambridge 1957–70) I 292–315   TBD

LOUIS II king of Hungary and Bohemia, 1 July 1506–29 August 1526
Born at Buda, Louis was the son of King *Vladislav II and his queen, Anne de Candale, who died of complications following Louis' birth. He was a frail child and remained sickly throughout his brief life. During his father's lifetime he was crowned king of Hungary at Székesfehérvár on 4 July 1508 and king of Bohemia on 11 March 1509 at Prague. His education was entrusted to the humanist scholars Girolamo *Balbi, Jacobus *Piso (Ep 850), and Johannes Dubravius. Louis showed himself to be a capable student and learnt to speak Hungarian, Czech, German, and Latin. When Vladislav II died on 13 March 1516, a regency was established for the ten-year-old king, which ran the affairs of government amidst increasing financial and political difficulties. The kingdom was on the brink of bankruptcy and the conflict between the lesser nobility and the great barons was on the verge of erupting into open warfare. It was under these circumstances that Louis was declared of age on 11 December 1521 and prepared for his forthcoming marriage. As early as 1515 Vladislav II had taken the first steps designed to tie the family fortunes of the Jagiełło kings of Hungary and Bohemia to the House of Haps-

burg. On 22 July 1515 Louis was married to
Archduchess *Mary, the sister of the future
*Charles v and *Ferdinand i. According to the
agreement reached in 1515, if Louis died with-
out a male heir, as in fact he did, Hungary and
Bohemia were to pass into the hands of the
Hapsburgs. The marriage between Louis ii
and Mary was formally blessed in Buda on 13
January 1522.

Although a pleasant and well-meaning
young man, the king was incapable of dealing
with the pressing problems of the kingdom and
proved to be a passive monarch. Added to the
internal difficulties was the ever-increasing
threat of the Turks. With the accession of
*Suleiman the Magnificent in 1520 the Ottoman
expansion on Hungary's southern borders
became more serious. The strategic fortress of
Belgrade fell to the Turks in 29 August 1521.
Urgent appeals for help were made to western
European powers, but no aid was forthcoming.
In 1526 Suleiman advanced on southern
Hungary with an immense army; to meet this
threat Louis ii left Buda with a small, hastily
collected, and ill-equipped army and headed
south to meet the enemy. On 29 August 1526
the two armies met at Mohács, and the battle
was a complete disaster for the Hungarian
forces. Although Louis fought valiantly, his
army was overwhelmed and almost completely
annihilated. When all seemed hopeless, the
king attempted to flee but fell into a swollen
stream and drowned. His body was temporarily buried on the banks of the creek, but it
was later returned to Székesfehérvár, where it
was solemnly interred on 10 November 1526.
The most reliable eyewitness account of the
battle of Mohács and the death of King Louis ii
is István *Brodarics' De conflictu Hungarorum
cum Turcis. The events in Hungary and the
tragic fate of Louis ii had a profound effect
upon Erasmus, who remembered the king in
several of his writings (LB V 352D–E, 359A, 725B;
Epp 2211, 2285). Although the reign of Louis ii
is generally characterized as one of decadence,
the person of the king is viewed with
sympathy. The seeds of humanistic culture
sown in the period of *Matthias Corvinus bore
some fruit during the reign of Louis ii. The king
and queen were great admirers of Erasmus
(Epp 1154, 1297). The Erasmian influence is
also evident in the presence at Buda of men

Louis ii, king of Hungary

such as Piso, Nicolaus *Olahus, Brodarics,
Johann *Henckel, and Alexius *Thurzo (Epp
1572, 1660). The battle of Mohács greatly
weakened Buda's significance as a humanistic
centre.

Some of the letters of Louis ii were edited
by Elemer Mályusz in 'ii Lajos levelei a hg.
Batthyány család körmendi levéltáraban' *Leve-
tári közlemények* (1927) 80–93. The best surviving portrait of Louis is by an anonymous
Flemish master and is now in the museum of
fine arts in Budapest.

BIBLIOGRAPHY: Allen Ep 850 / *Magyar életrajzi
lexikon* (Budapest 1967–9) ii 15 / Jozsef Fógel *ii.
Lajos udvartartása* (Budapest 1917) / Vilmos
Fraknói *A Hunyadiak és Jagellok kora 1440–1526*
(Budapest 1896) / Jane de Iongh *Mary of
Hungary* (New York 1951) / Ferenc Szalkály *A
Mohácsi csata* (Budapest 1977) / *Acta Tomiciana*
(Poznań-Wrocław 1852–) i–vi passim
                                                                 L. DOMONKOS

LOUIS *See also* LUDOVICUS

LOUISE de Savoie *See Louise of* SAVOY

Thomas Lovell

Thomas LOVELL documented from 1501, d 1524

Thomas Lovell (Louellus), of the diocese of York, is first mentioned as a student in Cambridge, where he became a bachelor of civil law in 1502 and of canon law in 1506–7 and went on to receive a doctorate in canon law by 1513. On 23 December 1503 he was ordained priest after having been appointed rector of Belton, Lincolnshire, earlier in that year. In September he resigned as vicar of Cornwood, Devonshire, after he had been appointed canon of Wells on 31 July 1513. In 1516 he became subdean of the chapter of Wells, an office which he retained until his death. He was vicar-general of successive bishops of Bath and Wells (cardinals Adriano *Castellesi and Thomas *Wolsey, who both held that see *in commendam*, and John *Clerk) in 1513, 1517, and 1522 and from September 1523 to his death.

Erasmus was at Cambridge by the time Lovell received his doctorate there and his prebend at Wells. A sincere friendship must have formed (Ep 1138), although there are no traces of correspondence between them. In 1524 Lovell sent Erasmus a gift of money, while Erasmus had high praise for his love of learning at an age when others had their careers foremost in their minds (Ep 1491).

BIBLIOGRAPHY: Allen and CWE Ep 1138 / Emden BRUC 374–5 / LP II 2852 and passim

PGB

Georgius LOXANUS documented 1527–50

Georgius Loxanus (Georg von Logkschau, Loschau) was a Silesian nobleman in the service of *Ferdinand I. In 1527 he went to Cracow as an ambassador to the Polish court. During two years of residence in Cracow he was accompanied by Georg von *Logau. In 1534 he apparently took advantage of a visit to Freiburg made by Desiderius a *Simandris to introduce himself to Erasmus presumably with a letter accompanied by a portrait medal. Erasmus' brief acknowledgment is extant (Ep 2986). Loxanus was a friend of Johannes Ludovicus, the brother of Johannes Alexander *Brassicanus. When Johannes Ludovicus set out for Padua in 1536 Loxanus gave him a letter by which he introduced himself to Pietro *Bembo. Over the following year a correspondence between Bembo and Loxanus ensued in the course of which the latter sent Bembo too a silver coin with the likeness of himself and his wife of recent date. Johannes Ludovicus Brassicanus and Celio *Calcagnini had composed verses on the occasion of Loxanus' marriage. After Brassicanus' death in 1549 Johannes Pedioneus addressed to Loxanus an elegy on the loss of his friend (in Johannes Pedioneus *Hymnorum liber* ... , Ingolstadt: A. Weissenhorn 1550). Loxanus was also a friend of Joachim *Camerarius, who dedicated to him his *Hippocomicus* (Tübingen: U. Morhart 1539).

Although in his short letter Erasmus addressed Loxanus as vice-chancellor of Bohemia, his vice-chancellorship was actually of Silesia. In May 1540 he arrived in Augsburg with Anselmus *Ephorinus, who gave him a letter for Bonifacius *Amerbach (AK V Ep 2399), since Loxanus evidently intended to continue his journey in the direction of Basel.

The Georgius Silesius mentioned by Caspar *Ursinus Velius in his *Varia epigrammata* appended to his *Oratio dominica* (Vienna: J. Singren 1524) was probably Logau rather than Loxanus (as suggested in Allen).

BIBLIOGRAPHY: Allen Ep 2986 / Franz von

Bucholtz *Geschichte der Regierung Ferdinands des Ersten* (Vienna 1831–8) III 214–23 / *Die Korrespondenz Ferdinands I.* ed W. Bauer et al (Vienna 1912–) II-1 160 / Götz von Pölnitz *Anton Fugger* (Tübingen 1958–) I 674

MICHAEL ERBE

Jacques LUCAS documented 1510–19
Jacques Lucas was elected dean of the chapter of Ste Croix, Orléans, in 1510; it is not known when his successor was appointed. Between February and May 1519 he was in Rome as a member of a mission sent to promote the canonization of St Francis of Paola. Probably during his visit to Rome, Christophe de *Longueil addressed to him a famous letter comparing Erasmus and *Budé (Ep 914). Nicolas *Bérault dedicated to him his *Metaphrasis ... in Oeconomicon Aristotelis* (Paris: J. Barbier 1515?).

BIBLIOGRAPHY: Allen Ep 914 / *Gallia christiana* VIII 1509 MICHEL REULOS

Philibert de LUCINGE documented 1523–9
The Lucinges were a noble family of the Bugey region, east of Geneva. Philibert was a close relative, probably the son, of Bertrand de Lucinge, a councillor of the duke of Savoy who visited Geneva from 1518 to 1519 on business for his master. Bertrand was a friend of Aymon de *Gingins, in whose house at Geneva he met Henricus Cornelius *Agrippa of Nettesheim. In the autumn of 1522 Philibert was sent to study in Basel, and in October Agrippa was persuaded to address a letter to the young man, encouraging him to take his studies seriously, especially in Greek. Probably on 10 November 1523 Philibert de Lucinge was a guest at Erasmus' dinner-table together with *Cantiuncula (Agrippa *Opera* II 752). At the time of his stay at Basel he was already canon of Geneva and protonotary apostolic.

Subsequently Lucinge returned to Geneva and February 1526 was among the canons who sympathized with the duke of Savoy and were compelled by mob action to leave Geneva. In April the chapter sent him to Bern in efforts to oppose Swiss support for the Geneva council in its conflict with the church and Savoy. He never returned to live in Geneva but kept his capitular house. The last that is heard of him is that on 13 August 1529 he allegedly murdered a

Geneva craftsman near Lyon at the time of the Lyon fair.

Philibert wrote to Erasmus in January 1524 after Erasmus' servant Hilarius *Bertholf had called on him at Geneva, perhaps on his return from Paris. In his letter Philibert mentioned that *Luther had written to Duke Charles II of *Savoy (Ep 1413).

BIBLIOGRAPHY: Allen Ep 1413 / H. Cornelius Agrippa of Nettesheim *Opera* (Lyon n d, repr 1970) II 740–2, 752 / Henri Naef *Les Origines de la réforme à Genève* (Geneva 1968) I 317–18, II 12, 20, 208 / Henri Naef in *Bulletin de la Société d'histoire et archéologie de Genève* 7 (1938–42) 47, 65–6, 74, 78–9, 89 / Henri Jougla de Morenas *Grand Armorial de France* (Paris 1934–52) III 343
PGB

Antonio LÚCIO of Evora, documented 1525–36
Antonio Lúcio came from Evora in Portugal and studied medicine under the French doctor Pierre *Brissot. He edited and published Brissot's *Apologetica disceptatio qua docetur per quae loca sanguis mitti debeat in viscerum inflammationibus praesertim in pleuritide*, with his own preface (Paris: S. de Colines 1525). He later served as physician to Renée of France, duchess of Ferrara, probably from 1527 to 1528. On 1 July 1533 he was living in the household of Johannes *Sinapius, a German professor of medicine at Ferrara. On 3 April 1536 Sinapius (Ep 3113) sent greetings from Lúcio to Erasmus. Lúcio is probably the physician mentioned by Erasmus in Ep 2956 as sending him a letter. Lúcio's wife was named Parthenea.

BIBLIOGRAPHY: Allen Ep 3113 TBD

LUDOLPHUS (Ep 94) *See Adolf* GREVERADE

LUDOVICUS (Ep 167 of winter 1501)
The man addressed by Erasmus in this letter had been one of his earliest servants until he was let go in November 1500 when Erasmus was at Orléans (Epp 135, 138). For a year he was maintained by Erasmus' friend Jacob *Batt at the castle of Tournehem (Ep 166), during which time he continued to serve Erasmus as a messenger (Epp 138, 139, 146, 155, 157, 163). He was also asked to copy the letters from Erasmus that were in Batt's possession (Epp 151, 163). In the autumn of 1501 Erasmus sent

him to Saint-Omer with a recommendation to
*Adrianus (Ep 166), and he seems to have
remained there for a while, doing a great deal
of copying for Erasmus and also for others (Ep
167). No more is heard of him thereafter, unless
he is indeed identical with the *Ludovicus at
Bruges.

BIBLIOGRAPHY: Allen and CWE Ep 167 /
Bierlaire *Familia* 47–8   FRANZ BIERLAIRE

LUDOVICUS documented at Bruges 1517–18
Ludovicus, a friend of Marcus *Laurinus, has
not been identified. He lived in Bruges, was
married, and had played host to Erasmus (Epp
651, 666, 789, 790). There is no evidence to
suggest that he might have been identical with
the *Ludovicus of Ep 167.

LUDOVICUS Volterranus (Ep 1519 of
26 November 1524)
Ludovicus Volterranus was a physician who
was host to Johannes *Hovius, the former
servant of Erasmus, at Rome. In 1524 Johann
von *Botzheim used his name in relaying a
letter from Erasmus to Hovius. No more
appears to be known about him.

ANNA GIULIA CAVAGNA

LUDOVICUS *See also* LOUIS, Ludwig KÖL

Fileno LUNARDI of Bologna
Fileno Lunardi was a friend and companion of
Giovanni Angelo *Odoni, who described him
as being 'of Bologna.' He studied law for six
years at the University of Bologna, probably
between 1528 and 1534. He was a member of a
small evangelical circle, headed by a man –
possibly Battista *Fieschi – who used the
pseudonym Eusebio Renato, which professed
an admiration for Erasmus and espoused reforming ideals infiltrating Italy from Strasbourg. In 1534, armed with letters of introduction from Johannes *Sinapius to Simon
*Grynaeus and Erasmus, Lunardi and Odoni
went to Strasbourg to study theology under
Martin *Bucer and Wolfgang *Capito. In 1535
he helped Odoni compose a letter to Erasmus
which was also a manifesto of the Erasmian
reformers of Italy (Ep 3002). In company with
Odoni he visited Erasmus at Freiburg in 1535.
He travelled to Germany with Capito and

translated unspecified works of Erasmus into
Italian. He returned to Italy in 1537 to spread
the ideas of the Reformation, probably at
Ferrara.

According to Alberto Merola, whose study
has not yet been published, Fileno Lunardi
was the important reformer who wrote under
the pseudonyms Lisia Fileno and Camillo
Renato.

BIBLIOGRAPHY: Allen Ep 3002 / L. Perini 'Gli
eretici italiani del '500 e Machiavelli' *Studi
storici* 10 (1969) 883–901 / S. Seidel Menchi
'Sulla fortuna di Erasmo in Italia' *Revue suisse
d'histoire* 24 (1974) 537–634 / S. Seidel Menchi
'Passione civile e aneliti erasmiani di Riforma
nel patriziato genovese del primo Cinquecento'
Rinascimento 18 (1978) 119–21 / On the identi-
fication of Lunardi with Lisia Fileno see C.
Ginzburg *Il nicodemismo* (Turin 1970) 140 n 2 /
On Lisia Fileno, alias Camillo Renato, see
D. Cantimori *Eretici italiani del Cinquecento*
(Florence 1939 repr 1967) 71–87 and passim; C.
Renato *Opere* ed A. Rotondò in *Corpus
Reformatorum Italicorum* (Florence-Chicago
1968)   SILVANA SEIDEL MENCHI

Gerardus de LUPABUS of Saint-Dié, d before
22 February 1518
The doctor of laws named Gerardus who was
greeted by Erasmus in Ep 541 was probably
Gerardus de Lupabus (de Sancto-Thomaeo), of
Saint-Dié in the Vosges, who matriculated at
Basel in the winter of 1494–5, obtained his
doctorate in 1496, taught civil law, and was
elected dean of the legal faculty for 1508–9 and
1513–14. In the latter year, however, he was
absent and unable to carry out his functions.
Little else is known about him except that he
was the son-in-law of a legal professor at Basel,
better known than himself, Fridericus de
Guarletis, and that he acquired the castle of
Bottmingen, south of Basel. At the time of his
death he was negotiating the sale of Bottmingen to the city, which bought it from his seven
children on 22 February 1518.

BIBLIOGRAPHY: Allen Ep 541 / *Matrikel Basel* I
241, 371 / R. Wackernagel *Geschichte der Stadt
Basel* (Basel 1907–54) III 71, 130 / *Urkundenbuch
der Stadt Basel* ed R. Wackernagel et al (Basel
1890–1910) IX 410–12   PGB

Alice and William LUPSET *See Thomas* LUPSET

Thomas LUPSET of London, c 1498–
27 December 1530

Thomas Lupset (Lupsett) was born in St
Mildred's parish, Bread Street, London. His
father, William (d 1522), was a goldsmith and a
citizen of London, and his mother, who
survived her son by fifteen years, was named
Alice (Ep 1229).

Lupset attended the grammar school of St
Paul's Cathedral, and by 1508 had entered the
household of John *Colet. He was introduced
to Latin and Greek by William *Lily and
subsequently attended Cambridge as a member
of Pembroke Hall. It was there that Lupset met
Erasmus, who, referring to him as Colet's
protégé, told Colet in 1513 that Lupset helped
him daily with texts for his editions of the New
Testament and the letters of St Jerome (Ep 270;
cf Ep 279). Later, in 1517, Lupset referred to
Erasmus as his teacher to whom he was greatly
indebted (Ep 664). It is clear that the chief
formative influence was that of Colet, on
whose death Erasmus told Lupset that he
should seek to resemble Colet in learning and
piety (Ep 1053). In his will Colet left Lupset 'all
suche Bookes prynted as may be most necessary for his lernyng.'

Lupset's movements between 1513 and 1516
are obscure, although P.S. Allen, like Louis
Delaruelle, concluded that he accompanied
Richard *Pace 'to Italy' in 1515 (Allen Ep
270:60n). Pace returned to England from Rome
in March of that year and the following
October was dispatched again, not to Italy but
to deal with the Swiss. Wegg (p 65) thought
that Lupset accompanied Pace back from Italy
in early 1515 'at least part of the way,' but there
is no support for these conjectures in the
Calendars of State Papers.

What is clear is that in June 1516, Lupset
returned to Erasmus notebooks of his that he
had been keeping, and he admitted having
withheld them from the trusted scribe and
messenger Pieter *Meghen because he had
thought it safer to keep them until Erasmus
himself returned to England (Ep 431). In
December Thomas *More wrote Erasmus that
Lupset had returned 'some notebooks of
yours,' among them, 'the *Julii genius*' (Ep 502),

and on 1 March 1517 Erasmus asked More to
forward them (Ep 543). In September 1517
Lupset was still apprehensive about Erasmus'
anger over this episode (Ep 664), and it is
possible that these letters have to do with the
unexplained circumstances through which the
text of the *Julius exclusus* reached the printer.

In 1517, Lupset went to Paris to study. While
there he supervised the printing of two of
Thomas *Linacre's translations from Galen, *De
sanitate tuenda* and *Methodus medendi* (Epp 726,
764), as well as the second edition of More's
Utopia. He also made the acquaintance of
Guillaume *Budé, probably through the offices
of Linacre. In 1519 Lupset returned to England
by way of Louvain, at the height of the
controversy between Erasmus and the future
archbishop of York, Edward *Lee, who was
then a student at Louvain. Lupset perhaps
rather presumptuously attempted to dissuade
Lee, his senior, from publishing his notes on
Erasmus' New Testament, incurring Lee's
hostility; see Ep 1026 and Gee Ep 5 for Lupset's
later account of the matter to Wilhelm *Nesen.
It was to Lupset that Erasmus then addressed
his account of the controversy in December
1519 (Ep 1053). Three letters written by Lupset
are printed in the *Epistolae eruditorum virorum*
(Basel: J. Froben 1520; cf Ep 1083 introduction),
a collection of letters from various hands
directed against Lee and probably edited by
Wilhelm *Nesen, with substantial assistance
from Lupset.

By October 1519 Lupset was resident at
Oxford, where in 1520 he succeeded John
*Clement as *Wolsey's reader in humanity.
According to Thomas More, he commanded an
enthusiastic audience (Ep 1087). Lupset resided in Corpus Christi College, until at least
June 1522. On 2 June 1521 he supplicated for
the MA degree at Oxford on the strength of four
years' study at Paris and Oxford; it is presumed
that his BA was taken earlier in Paris.

On 6 February 1522, as royal nominee,
Lupset was granted a pension due to be
provided by the abbot-elect of St Mary's, York
(LP III–2 p 871). He had already (1508) been
appointed rector of the free chapel of St
Margaret, Hilborough, in Norfolk, a living
held earlier by Colet, and rector of Claypole,
Lincolnshire, a living he vacated by 1523,

probably on his departure for Italy. On 24 March 1523 he was made chaplain of St Nicholas' chapel in the parish of Stanford le Hope, Essex, and this living he held until his death.

Lupset left Oxford in the spring of 1523 in order to assist in the education of Wolsey's natural son, Thomas *Winter, who was conducted from Louvain to Padua that year. It is probable that in April, en route, he called on Erasmus in Basel (Ep 1360; cf Allen Ep 1595:114–16). At Constance, where the party arrived by 21 April, they met Johann von *Botzheim, canon of the cathedral. In a letter thanking Botzheim for his hospitality, written on 27 April from Innsbruck (Ep 1361), Lupset asked Botzheim to inform Erasmus as soon as possible that an unbound copy of the paraphrase on the Gospel of St John had been given to its dedicatee, Archduke *Ferdinand, by an unknown messenger. The paraphrase had been published by Froben the previous February; the informal presentation was apparently a mischance, and Erasmus subsequently sent a copy properly bound to the prince (Ep 1376).

Lupset and Winter reached Padua about 8 May and joined the household of Reginald *Pole not long after his arrival; it was from a letter of Lupset of 23 August 1525 that Erasmus received his introduction to the future cardinal (Ep 1595). The ensuing friendship with this royal scholar probably lies behind Lupset's further promotion while still abroad. On 21 April 1526 he was collated to the rectory of Great Mongeham in the diocese of Canterbury, a living, worth £20 a year, that he held until a few months before his death. On 3 July 1526 he was also appointed to the rectory of St Martin's, Ludgate, London, worth £140 per annum. This lucrative living Lupset held until his death.

Meanwhile, in the winter of 1524–5 Lupset had accompanied Winter back to Padua, where Pole visited them in early 1525. In April of that year he was present at Edward Wotton's examination for the degree of MA. Lupset also renewed his acquaintance with Pace at this time and evidently visited him in Venice shortly after his return to Italy. In 1525 he joined John Clement as one of four Englishmen who assisted with the Aldine edition of the works of Galen in Greek (*Galeni librorum pars v*,

Venice 1525). Late that year he was in Paris, according to a letter from Erasmus to Pole (Ep 1675), although the reason for this visit is not clear. He returned to Padua and accompanied Pole back to England from Italy in the autumn of 1526, visiting Botzheim at Constance on the way (Ep 1761). Pole arrived in England early in 1527; Lupset may have returned to Paris first. On 10 May 1527, Germain de *Brie wrote to Erasmus in a vein suggesting that at some recent time he and Lupset had become well acquainted in Paris (Ep 1817).

The final years of Lupset's brief life were spent chiefly as tutor to Thomas Winter, although according to a contemporary, George Lily, he had intended to devote all his time to study. Nevertheless he managed to complete several works and translations. During most of 1527 he seems to have been teaching in London; the Edmund Withypoll to whom he dedicated *An exhortacion to young men* (London: T. Berthelet 1535; STC 16936–8) may have been one of two pupils there. The other referred to in that work, Christopher Smith, was the son of Andrew *Smith, a prominent notary who was an acquaintance of Erasmus.

Lupset arrived in Paris before February 1528 to take up his duties towards Winter. He returned to England by 24 August 1529, having been with Winter still in March of that year. By December Winter himself was in England following the downfall of Wolsey the month before. Lupset's *A treatise of charitie* (London: T. Berthelet 1533; STC 16939–41) was perhaps written in the first half of 1529; he then joined the household at the More, Wolsey's seat in Hertfordshire, and the colophon of *An exhortacion* is signed there on 24 August 1529. It is likely that he then accompanied Pole, who left England in October of that year for Paris, and wrote there *A compendious … Treatyse teachinge the waye of dyenge welle* (London: T. Berthelet 1534; STC 16934–5), whose colophon reads, 'at Paris the .x. day of Januarye.' Although the topic was a commonplace of both humanist and medieval spirituality, it may reflect Lupset's own awareness of his approaching end. He had some part in the mission with which Pole was charged, to obtain from the theology faculty at Paris a decision favourable to Henry VIII in the matter of the royal divorce. On 1 August 1530 he was collated by Wolsey to the parish of Cheriton in the diocese of Worcester, and on 6 August he became a canon of Salisbury. On 27 December 1530, however, he died of consumption at his mother's house in London. He was buried in the church of St Alphege, London Wall, with the following inscription, 'Hic situs est Thomas Lupsetus, vir Grece et Latine, atque in sacris literis eruditissimus … ' Erasmus referred to his death in a letter to Reginald Pole the following August (Ep 2526; cf Ep 2496).

In addition to the works already mentioned, Thomas Lupset translated *The Sermon of Doctor Cole Made to the Convocation of Paulis* (London: T. Berthelet 1530; STC 5550), St John Chrysostom's *A Sermon that No Man is Hurted but of Hym Selfe* (London: T. Berthelet 1542; STC 14639), and *A Swete Sermon of St Cyprian of the Mortalitie of Man, The Rules of the Christian Life Made by John Picus the Elder Earle of Mirandula,* and *Gathered Counsayles oute of S Isidore,* all of which were printed in 1546, in *Th. Lupsets workes* (London: T. Berthelet; STC 16932–3).

The fictional *Dialogue between Pole and Lupset,* written by Thomas Starkey, may have been based on a visit by Lupset to Pole at Bisham in 1529; see *Starkey's Life and Letters* ed J.M. Cowper (Early English Text Society, Extra Series xxxii, 1878).

BIBLIOGRAPHY: Allen Ep 270 / Emden BRUO 1501–40 366–7 / J.A. Gee *Life and Works of Thomas Lupset* (New Haven 1928) which also prints the texts of his original treatises and letters / L. Delaruelle *Répertoire analytique et chronologique de la correspondance de Guillaume Budé* (Paris-Toulouse 1907) Ep 12 and passim / McConica passim / J.K. McConica 'Erasmus and the *Julius' The Pursuit of Holiness in Late Medieval and Renaissance Religion* ed Charles Trinkaus with Heiko A. Oberman (Leiden 1974) 444–71 / Jervis Wegg *Richard Pace, a Tudor Diplomatist* (London 1932) / LP II-1 273, 1067, 1094, 1105 II-2 4421, 4422, III-1 435, III-2 2029, IV-2 3955, 4015, 4022, 4064, 4216, 4848, IV-3 5382, 5563, 5642, 6505 / *Calendar of Patent Rolls Henry VII* (London 1914–16) II 607 / Nancy Lee Beaty *The Craft of Dying Well* (New Haven 1970) 54–107 / G.B. Parks *The English Traveler to Italy* (Rome 1954–) I passim

JAMES K. MCCONICA

Otmarus LUSCINIUS *See Ottmar* NACHTGALL

Johann LÜTHARD of Lucerne, d 8 July 1542 Lüthard (Lüthart, Sündli), the son of a prominent citizen of Lucerne, apparently joined the Franciscans in his native city. He first appears in 1520 as the preacher of the Franciscan monastery at Basel. His popular style proved highly offensive to the opponents of the reform party. In April 1523 the Basel chapter persuaded his superiors to transfer him and his close friend Conradus *Pellicanus to another monastery, but the civic authorities supported him, expelling the visiting Franciscan official and suspending the professorial salaries of his chief antagonist, Moritz *Fininger, and three others. After the reformation of 1529 he was confirmed as minister at the Franciscan church and to the hospital. He also served as chaplain with the Basel troops joining the expedition against Giangiacomo de' Medici, lord of Musso, in 1531.

On 1 October 1528 Erasmus noted that the Franciscan had married, following the example of *Oecolampadius (Ep 2054). In 1533 his wife, Elisabeth, formerly a Franciscan nun, resisted the schemes of a bath attendant who had been paid to seduce her. Lüthard's matriculation at the university in 1539 was probably a gesture to satisfy the civic authorities, who had fallen out with the ministers over their refusal to obtain academic degrees.

BIBLIOGRAPHY: Allen Ep 2054 / Willy Brändly 'Johannes Lüthard "der Mönch von Luzern"' *Zwingliana* 8 (1944–8) 305–41 / *Matrikel Basel* II 22–3 / *Aktensammlung zur Geschichte der Basler Reformation* ed E. Dürr et al (Basel 1921–50) II – VI passim / R. Wackernagel *Geschichte der Stadt Basel* (Basel 1907–54) III 326–33 passim / BA *Oekolampads* I 220 and passim   PGB

Hans LUTHER of Möhra, c 1459–29 May 1530 Hans Luder or Ludder, the father of Martin *Luther, was born about 1459 in Möhra, near Eisenach. He belonged to a peasant family, worked as a miner, and married Margarete Ziegler or Lindemann. The family moved to Eisleben before Martin was born, and in 1484 to Mansfeld, a centre of the mining industry. There Hans Luther was able to lease a little foundry in partnership with another man. Hard work and thrift helped him to succeed in his venture. In 1491 he was one of the town councillors, and in 1511 he was part-owner of

Hans Luther, by Lucas Cranach

Margarete Luther, by Lucas Cranach

two foundries and at least six shafts. He was able to send Martin, the eldest of his numerous children, to university. Hans Luther wanted his son to study law and strongly disapproved when Martin entered monastic life. Although he still had some reservations, he accepted Martin's invitation to attend his first mass on 2 May 1507. Luther's booklet *De votis monasticis* (Wittenberg, 21 November 1521) is dedicated to his father. Hans Luther approved of his son's marriage in 1525. He became ill in February 1530 and died on 29 May.

In Ep 1672 Erasmus suggests a fanciful connection between the form of the family name chosen by Martin and his father's smelting operation.

BIBLIOGRAPHY: Allen Ep 1672 / ADB XIX 660 / Hermann Grisar *Luther* trans E.M. Lamond (London 1914–17) I 5 and passim / Heinrich Boehmer *Martin Luther, Road to Reformation* (New York 1957) 5 and passim / E.H. Erikson *Young Man Luther* (New York 1962) passim / W. Möllenberg 'Hans Luther' *Zeitschrift des Harzvereins für Geschichte und Altertumskunde* 39 (1906) 191 ff   IG

Katharina LUTHER *See Katharina von* BORA

Martin LUTHER 10 November 1483–18 February 1546

Martin Luther (Lutherus, Eleutherus) was born in Eisleben, in Thuringian Saxony. He was the son of Hans *Luther, who saw that Martin had a good education and sent him to the University of Erfurt to study law. Without consulting his parents, Martin abandoned these studies to enter religion, in the order of Augustinian hermits. He was selected for further studies and succeeded his teacher, Johann von *Staupitz, in the chair of biblical studies in the new University of Wittenberg, and for the rest of his life served both town and gown in that place. As a young professor he became involved in a program of humanistic biblical reform, but in November 1517 his Ninety-five Theses questioning the value of indulgences led to public controversy which both widened and deepened in the next few years, leading him to ever sharper protest against abuses in the church – in both morals and doctrine. Condemned by the papal bull

Exsurge Domine in 1520 he replied with vehement manifestos which found a response in German people of all classes. In April 1521 he appeared before the imperial diet at Worms but refused to recant. He spent the next months in hiding at the Wartburg, where he began his version of the German Bible, a great achievement which had a deep and lasting influence on German language and faith. In the next few years he had to fight on two fronts, against the Roman church and against a radical ferment within the ranks of the reformers. The year 1525 was in some ways a watershed for him, with the peasant war, his marriage to Katharina von *Bora, the eucharistic controversy, and his debate with Erasmus (see below).

By this time the Reformation movement had become an international and many-sided schism in which Luther himself played a less and less dominant role. While continuing to pour out an immense flood of commentaries, sermons, and polemical and edifying writings, he left the ecclesiastical diplomacy and practical reform more and more to his colleagues, *Melanchthon and *Bugenhagen. While it is not right to contrast too sharply the young, the mature, and the ageing Luther, the effects of constant illness were evident in his later years, while the recovery of power by the papacy (initiated by the council of Trent) and the Hapsburg empire sharpened the apocalyptic tone in his last writings. When he died in February 1546 in Eisleben, the Reformation movement was little affected by his passing from the scene, despite his great and often critical importance in earlier years.

Assessing the relations between Erasmus and Luther is, as the military historians would say, a matter of balance. The years 1513 to 1518 when the young Luther was giving formidable lectures on the Psalms, Romans, Galatians, and Hebrews were years when Erasmus was swiftly gaining fame as the foremost humanist in Northern Europe, as an outspoken critic of contemporary religion, and as a bold exponent of new biblical studies. Like many others, Luther turned to him for the latest expository and exegetical tools of Erasmus' New Testament, his edition of Jerome, his *Adagia*, and the satire of his *Enchiridion* and *Moria*. And though

Martin Luther, by Lucas Cranach

not as close to Erasmus as his friends Staupitz, *Spalatinus, *Jonas, and Melanchthon, he too spoke of 'our Erasmus.' Yet he was early aware of a difference of approach. In October 1516 (w *Briefwechsel* I Ep 27) he said, 'in the exposition of the Scripture I put Jerome as far behind Augustine as Erasmus puts Augustine behind Jerome.' In a letter to Lang in March 1517 (w *Briefwechsel* I Ep 35) he put his finger on a deeper issue: 'I am at present reading our Erasmus, but my mind is moving more and more away from him ... I fear he does not spread Christ and God's grace sufficiently abroad ... the human is of more importance to him than the divine ... although unwilling to judge him I beg you not to read blindly what he writes ... those who ascribe something to man's freedom of will regard those things differently from those who know only God's grace.' In January 1518 he wrote to Spalatinus, 'I find much in Erasmus which sounds strange and unhelpful to the knowledge of Christ, if I speak as a theologian, rather than as a grammarian' (w *Briefwechsel* I Ep 57). But when Luther got into trouble in the following months, Erasmus

was among many humanists who showed
sympathy and even agreement with much of
his protest. In March 1518 Luther ventured to
approach Erasmus personally and with deference: 'Who is there in whose heart Erasmus
does not occupy a central place, to whom
Erasmus is not the teacher who holds him in
thrall? ... And so, dear Erasmus ... accept this
younger brother of yours in Christ' (Ep 933).
Erasmus sent a polite reply in May beginning:
'Dearest brother in Christ. Your letter gave me
great pleasure ... and breathed the spirit of a
Christian' (Ep 980).

The relationship between Luther and Erasmus was bedevilled not only by events that
drove Luther to ever-greater vehemence and
boldness, but by the gossip and tactlessness of
friends and enemies, who circulated and even
printed the private comments of one about the
other. Moreover, from the first Erasmus had
his own enemies in the Catholic fold – those
from Girolamo *Aleandro to Josef Lortz who
regarded him as worse than Luther and who
subscribed to the epigram, quoted by Erasmus
himself at the end of his life (Ep 2956), that
Erasmus laid the egg which Luther hatched.
With Luther's condemnation and impenitent
defiance (1520), Erasmus was under new
pressure from friends like Thomas *More to
declare himself against Luther, while others,
like *Hutten, tried to draw him openly to
Luther's support.

Yet with a firm consistency that belies
Luther's poor opinion of him, Erasmus held to
his own course, refusing to express outright
condemnation of all Luther had done and said
while deploring schism and Luther's violence.
The result was that in the fateful months of
1520 and 1521 he did Luther a real service. He
tried to arrange some kind of arbitration (cf Ep
1149 introduction) and wrote out some Axiomata pro causa Lutheri (Opuscula 329–37; cf
Ep 1155 introduction) which are surprisingly
sympathetic to Luther and his case. But the
papal condemnation, Luther's reply, and the
furore surrounding his appearance at the diet
of Worms brought a new alignment among the
humanists, and Erasmus expressed himself
with more and more reserve to Luther's friends
and with open condemnation to his Catholic
colleagues. In his own position, painfully and
precariously reached, as an independent

scholar, he would not get involved. As he
wrote to Richard *Pace in July 1521: 'Even had
all he [Luther] wrote been religious, mine was
never the spirit to risk my life for the truth.
Every one has not the strength needed for
martyrdom ... Popes and emperors when they
make the right decisions I follow, which is
godly; if they decide wrongly I tolerate them,
which is safe. I believe that even for men of
good will this is legitimate, if there is no hope of
better things' (Ep 1218). In 1523 Luther
criticized Erasmus in a letter to the Basel
reformer *Oecolampadius, which was unfortunately published: 'He [Erasmus] has accomplished what he was called to do: he has
introduced sacred letters among us and called
us from sacrilegious studies. Perhaps he will
die with Moses in the plains of Moab, for he
does not go on to better studies (which have to
do with piety)' (w Briefwechsel III Ep 626). In
1524 Erasmus let it be known that he would
respond to the pressure of friends and patrons
and write against Luther's doctrines. A very
alarmed Luther wrote a warning letter to
Erasmus in April (Ep 1443) to which Erasmus
wrote a non-committal reply (Ep 1445). In
August Erasmus published his diatribe De
libero arbitrio (LB IX 1215–48), and in his reply, in
November 1525 (w XVIII 600ff), Luther praised
his opponent for choosing a theme which went
to the root of the great argument between
them. Both tried to keep their argument within
a scriptural frame, with the result that both
treatises contain important hermeneutical discussions – Erasmus' on the 'mystery' of
Scripture and Luther's on the 'external and
internal certainty of the Word of God.'
Erasmus was sufficiently upset by Luther's
reply to write a further treatise, in two parts,
the Hyperaspistes (LB X 1249–536). Luther did
not retort, but many allusions by both scholars
in letters and in Luther's Tischreden ('Table
talk') show how the controversy had ended
any cordialities between them, although their
common friends Jonas and Melanchthon contrived to keep in contact with Erasmus. To the
end Erasmus affirmed that there were some
things which Luther stood for which he had all
along supported and that he had chiefly
deplored his violent tongue. Luther never
ceased to pay tribute to the learning and
eloquence of Erasmus and his contribution to

sacred letters, but he took Erasmus' caution for cowardice and his discretion for cunning artifice: 'Erasmus is an eel. Only Christ can grab him. Est vir duplex' (w *Tischreden* I no 131, cf 108, 446, 811). Like many others he believed that Erasmus' sacramental views were more negative than he would admit. His wit he took to be levity, if not downright profanity, and at the end he classed him in the ranks of those he contemptuously derided as 'Epicureans' and 'sophists.' Both henceforth listened to and passed on malicious gossip – Erasmus in nasty references to the pregnancy of Luther's wife in the autumn of 1525 (Ep 1633; but cf Ep 1677) and Luther about the tale that Erasmus had died unshriven and without the last sacraments. The suggestion made by some of their friends that the two men might meet was never taken up. It might have cleared up misunderstandings. But it would more likely have been disastrous.

BIBLIOGRAPHY: Allen Ep 933 / Martin Luther *Werke* (Weimar 1883–) / Martin Luther *Works* ed J. Pelikan (St Louis 1955–) / Josef Benzing *Lutherbibliographie* (Baden-Baden 1966) / Among many examinations of the relations between Erasmus and Luther, and of their theological differences may be mentioned: *Luther and Erasmus: Free Will and Salvation* ed and trans E.G. Rupp and P.S. Watson (Philadelphia 1969); M. Richter *Desiderius Erasmus und seine Stellung zu Luther* (Leipzig 1907); E.G. Rupp *The Righteousness of God* (London 1953); R.H. Murray *Erasmus and Luther* (London 1920); K.S. Meissinger *Erasmus* (Berlin 1948); E.W. Kohls *Luther oder Erasmus* (Basel 1973); D. Kerlen *Assertio* (Wiesbaden 1976); H. Bornkamm 'Erasmus und Luther' in *Das Jahrhundert der Reformation* (Göttingen 1961); R. Herrmann *Von der Klarheit der Heiligen Schrift* (Berlin 1958)   E. GORDON RUPP

Louis de LUXEMBOURG 1467– 31 December 1503

Louis de Luxembourg, count of Ligny, was born of the second marriage of the more famous Louis de Luxembourg, count of Saint-Paul and constable of France, who was executed in 1475. The younger Louis thus grew up under a cloud but regained royal favour when his cousin, *Charles VIII, ascended the French throne in 1483. In preparation for the king's expedition

to Naples he was sent to Rome for negotiations with Pope *Alexander VI and subsequently, when Charles was in Italy, Louis de Luxembourg was given important military commands. Under King *Louis XII he was made a knight of the order of St Michael and grand chamberlain; he served again with the army that conquered Milan in 1499 and 1500. As governor of Picardy he welcomed Philip the Handsome, duke of *Burgundy, on his arrival on French soil on 16 November 1501 and conducted him from Saint-Quentin to Lyon (ASD IV-1 39).

Louis de Luxembourg also took the title of prince of Altamura, having married Eleanor of Guevara and Beaux, princess of Altamura. His interests extended to cultural developments and he employed as his secretary the poet and chronicler Jean Lemaire de Belges.

BIBLIOGRAPHY: Nicolas Vignier *Histoire de la maison de Luxembourg* (Paris 1617) 294, 302–6, 448 / F.A. Aubert de la Chenaye-Desbois *Dictionnaire de la noblesse* 3rd ed (Paris 1863–76) XII 600–2   PGB

Philippe de LUXEMBOURG 1445– 2 June 1519

Philippe was a son of Thibaut de Luxembourg, lord of Fiennes and count of Brienne, and Philippa de Melun, the aunt of *Louis XI of France. He was canon and archdeacon of the cathedral chapter of Le Mans and on 13 May 1476 succeeded his father as bishop of Le Mans and abbot of St Vincent-du-Mans, but not apparently as abbot of Ourscamp and Igny (*Gallia christiana* IX 303, 1133; Canivez). On 12 September 1480 he was named commendatory prior of Saint-Georges-d'Oléron in the diocese of Saintes, again in succession to his father. On 18 March he received the abbey of San Martino Sacri Montis in the diocese of Genoa. At the request of the French crown, he was made a cardinal on 21 January 1495. His election to the see of Thérouanne by the cathedral chapter was, however, contested by Cardinal Federigo Sanseverino, who had been provided with the same bishopric by the pope. Not until after the resignation of Sanseverino was Philippe finally confirmed as bishop of Thérouanne on 12 November 1498. His solemn entry took place on 29 May 1502, and by this time the events came to pass which affected Jean *Vitrier and were reported by Erasmus in his life of Vitrier

(Ep 1211). For some years Philippe held the sees of Thérouanne and Le Mans concurrently, but on 27 January 1507 he resigned Le Mans in favour of his nephew, François de Luxembourg, bishop of Saint-Pons. With the death of François, he regained Le Mans and Saint-Pons on 9 September 1509, while three months earlier, on 3 June, he had received the bishopric of Albano, near Rome. The latter he resigned on 20 January 1511 in exchange for Frascati, and subsequently he also gave up Saint-Pons. In November 1516 he exchanged Thérouanne for Arras, a see which had been held by his uncle, François de Melun. On 10 March 1518 he exchanged Arras for Maillezais, and fourteen days later he resigned the latter to Geoffroy d'Estissac. From then on to his death he kept only the bishopric of Le Mans, where he carried out reforms that brought him the admiration of Josse *Clichtove (Paris, Bibliothèque Mazarine, MS 1068, f 289 recto). He had liturgical books, in particular missals and breviaries, printed in Le Mans (1503), Rouen, and Paris.

Philippe supported the Benedictine reform of Chezal-Benoît and introduced it in his abbeys, thereafter permitting reformed monks to take his place as abbot in return for financial compensation for himself. Such transfers occurred in 1502 at St Vincent-du-Mans; in 1517 at St Pierre, Jumièges, an abbey he had held from 1511; and especially in 1513 at St Martin, Séez, where he had held the abbacy from 1506 and where his efforts were supported by Charles *Fernand, who dedicated to him an *Epistola paraenetica observationis regulae Benedictinae ad Sagienses monachos* (Paris: J. Bade 1512). In this course of action he was also assisted by Marguerite de Lorraine, the friend of saints Jean de Valois and Francis of Paola.

From August to December 1498 he was a member of the commission which annulled the first marriage of King *Louis XII. In 1511 he participated, cautiously and only by procuration, in the schismatic council of Pisa. In 1516 he succeeded Georges (I) d'*Amboise as papal legate-extraordinary in charge of the reform of French monasteries, but the university and the Parlement of Paris, which were opposed to the concordat of Bologna, obtained a reduction of his powers to act in this capacity. His mission was also obstructed by the legate-in-ordinary,

Bernardo Dovizi, Cardinal Bibbiena. Philippe's career was a typical example of the exorbitant and selfish demands placed upon the church by the leading families of the French nobility at that time.

BIBLIOGRAPHY: Allen Ep 1211 / Eubel II 24, 59, 73, 139, 217, III 6, 122, 162, 234, 250, 277 / *Catholicisme: Hier, Aujourd'hui, Demain* (Paris 1976–7) VIII 5–6, 446 / *Gallia christiana* II 1375, III 346–7, VI 249, X 1569, XI 715, 973–4, XIV 411–13, 464 / P. Imbart de la Tour *Les Origines de la Réforme* 2nd ed (Paris 1946–8) I 113, II 149, and passim / A. Renaudet *Le Concile Gallican de Pise-Milan* (Paris 1922) passim / Renaudet *Préreforme* 189 and passim / Pastor V 460, VI 92, and passim / J. Lestocquoy *Les Evêques d'Arras: leurs portraits* ... (Fontenay-le-Comte 1942) 58–61 / A. Angot *Le Catéchisme au diocèse du Mans depuis 1508* (Laval 1914) 8–13 / G.M. Oury 'Les Bénédictins réformés de Chezal-Benoît' *Revue d'histoire de l'Eglise de France* 65 (1979) 89–106 / U. Berlière 'La congrégation bénédictine de Chezal-Benoît' in his *Mélanges d'histoire bénédictine* III (Maredsous 1901) 97–178 / *Statuta capitulorum generalium ordinis Cisterciensis* ed J.M. Canivez (Louvain 1933–41) V 105, 112, VI 512   JEAN-PIERRE MASSAUT

Arnold LUYD, LUYDIUS *See Arnold Luyd of* TONGEREN

LYPSIUS *See* LIPS

Petrus LYSETUS *See Pierre* LIZET

Gerard LYSTER, LYSTRIUS *See Gerardus* LISTRIUS

Niccolò MACHIAVELLI of Florence, 3 May 1469–22 June 1527
Niccolò, the son of Bernardo Machiavelli and Bartolomea Nelli, was born at Florence. In the spring of 1498, in a reshuffling of the Florentine government after the death of Girolamo *Savonarola, he became head of the second chancery. While serving in this capacity he undertook diplomatic missions to *Louis XII of France, Caesar Borgia, Pope *Julius II, and the Emperor *Maximilian I. He also promoted the formation of a Florentine militia. However, when the Medici returned to power in 1512 Machiavelli's career in the chancery came to an

abrupt end. In February 1513 he was implicated in a plot against the Medici and was
imprisoned, tortured, and finally pardoned.
Confined for most of his last fourteen years to
his villa near San Casciano, he benefitted from
his forced leisure to compose a series of works
which established his reputation as the foremost political thinker of the Renaissance. His
most famous works included *Il Principe*, written in 1513 and printed in 1532 (Rome: A.
Bladus), *Discorsi sopra la prima deca di Tito Livio*
(Rome: A. Bladus 1531), *Arte della guerra*,
printed soon after completion in 1521 (Florence: heirs of F. Giunta), and *Istorie Fiorentine*,
commissioned by Giulio de' Medici (*Clement
VII) and published at Rome (A. Bladus) and
Florence (B. Giunta) in 1532.

There is no clear reference to Machiavelli in
the works and correspondence of Erasmus
other than the words of praise expressed by
Giovanni Angelo *Odoni in his letter of March
1535 (Ep 3002).

BIBLIOGRAPHY: Federico Chabod *Machiavelli
and the Renaissance* trans D. Moore (London
1958) / Federico Chabod in EI XXI 778–90 / Felix
Gilbert *Machiavelli and Guicciardini* (Princeton
1965) / J.R. Hale *Machiavelli and Renaissance
Italy* (London 1961) / Niccolò Machiavelli *Opere*
ed S. Bertelli and F. Gaeta (Milan 1961–8) /
Roberto Ridolfi *The Life of Niccolò Machiavelli*
trans Cecil Grayson (Chicago 1963) / Roberto
Ridolfi in *Encyclopedia Britannica* (Chicago-
London 1973) XIV 518–21 / Leo Strauss *Thoughts
on Machiavelli* (Glencoe, Ill, 1958) / *Studies on
Machiavelli* ed Myron P. Gilmore (Florence
1972)   TBD

Johannes MACIOCHIUS *See Giovanni*
MAZZOCCHI

Salmon MACRIN *See Jean* SALMON

Jean de la MADELEINE documented at
Besançon 1505–38
Jean de la Madeleine was appointed canon of
Besançon and precentor of the chapter on 21
April 1505, following the resignation of his
uncle, of the same name, who had held the
same positions. In turn Jean resigned them on
12 June 1538 to François de la Palud, abbot of
Luxeuil. As the third-ranking dignitary of the
chapter he attained some notoriety when his

Niccolò Machiavelli

'maid' died in 1532, for he placed on her tomb a
funeral slab with her effigy, his own coat of
arms, and a Latin epitaph in humanistic style.
The chapter had the monument removed, but it
soon reappeared in a different location, with a
scriptural verse added that seemed to censure
the detractors of the good maid. It caused
considerable scandal before it disappeared
again, this time for good.

Erasmus met the precentor during his visit to
Besançon in the spring of 1524 (Ep 1610).

BIBLIOGRAPHY: Besançon Archives du
Doubs, MS G 250 / Gauthier 121, 126 / Claude
Fohlen et al *Histoire de Besançon* (Paris 1965) I
615 / A. Castan 'Granvelle et le petit empereur
de Besançon 1518–1538' *Revue historique* 1
(1876) 78–139, esp 106–7   PGB

Vincentius MADIUS *See Vincenzo* MAGGI

Mario MAFFEI of Volterra, 1459–24 June 1537
Mario Maffei (Maffeus Volaterranus), a son of
Gherardo and the brother of Antonio and
Raffaele *Maffei, came from an established
curial family. Mario entered curial service and
was sent on a legation to France from 1506 to

1507; he also held a canonry at St Peter's in Rome. He was well educated, a man of great humour and fine artistic discrimination. An important humanist in Rome, he belonged to the academy of Johannes *Corycius, was a poet, and maintained his own informal academy devoted to archaeological topics. Both Medici popes favoured him: *Leo x appointed him bishop of Aquino (1516) and *Clement VII translated him to the see of Cavaillon (1525). *Julius II made him supervisor of the building of the new St Peter's; he performed a similar function for the Medicean Villa Madama. His friends included cardinals Alessandro *Farnese and Jacopo *Sadoleto, and bishops Gian Matteo *Giberti and Paolo Giovio, as well as Tommaso (Fedra) *Inghirami, Baldesar *Castiglione, and *Ariosto. He accumulated enough wealth to own land and houses in Rome and Volterra. He died in Volterra and was buried in its cathedral, where a handsome monument commemorates him.

There is no indication that Mario and Erasmus ever met, even though they had common friends, especially Inghirami. Mario was one of the Roman humanists who urged Pietro *Corsi to write his Defensio pro Italia ad Erasmum Roterodamum (Rome: A. Bladus 1535). In his defence against Corsi, Erasmus credited Maffei with a moderating influence upon Corsi (Allen Ep 3032:175–6). The source of Mario's hostility towards Erasmus was probably Erasmus' critical remarks on his brother Raffaele's scholarship, especially the criticisms of Raffaele's translation of Basil the Great addressed to Mario's close friend Sadoleto (Allen Ep 2611:119ff).

BIBLIOGRAPHY: Allen Ep 3032 / The Fondo Maffei of the Biblioteca Guarraciana, Volterra, has much unexplored manuscript material on Maffei / Luigi Peschetti 'Mario Maffei' Rassegna volterrana (1932) 65–91 / Pio Paschini 'Una famiglia di curiali: I Maffei di Volterra' Rivista di storia della chiesa in Italia 7 (1953) 356–376 / Renato Lefevre 'Un prelato del '500, Mario Maffei e la costruzione di Villa Madama' L'Urbe 33, no 3 (1969) 1-11 / John F. D'Amico Renaissance Humanism in Papal Rome: Humanists and Churchmen on the Eve of the Reformation (Baltimore-London 1983) 78, 85–8, and passim / John F. D'Amico, 'Papal history and curial reform in the Renaissance: Raffaele Maffei's

Breuis historia of Julius II and Leo x' Archivum Historiae Pontificiae 18 (1980) 157–210

JOHN F. D'AMICO

Raffaele MAFFEI of Volterra, 17 February 1451–25 January 1522

Raffaele Maffei (Raphael Volaterranus), a son of Gherardo and the brother of Antonio and Mario *Maffei, was educated in Rome and Volterra. He entered the curia as apostolic scriptor and accompanied Cardinal John of Aragon to Hungary in the winter of 1479–80. He married before 1490 and had one surviving child, a daughter. He retired to Volterra in 1502 and seems not to have left that city after 1506. His home in Volterra was a centre for learned men. Lorenzo (I) de' *Medici, *Poliziano, Tommaso (Fedra) *Inghirami, Paolo *Cortesi, and Ermolao (I) *Barbaro were among his friends. He devoted his last years to monastic retreat and religious scholarship in Volterra where he died.

Maffei's Commentaria urbana (Rome: J. Besicken 1506) is an enormous encyclopedia which enjoyed great popularity among humanists. He translated works by Procopius, Xenophon, Basil the Great, Homer, and others into Latin. He composed a theological treatise De institutione christiana, dedicated to *Leo x and printed with a philosophical tract, De prima philosophia (Rome: J. Mazzocchi 1518). He also wrote the unfinished 'Stromata' (autograph in the Biblioteca Apostolica Vaticana, MS Barb. Lat. 753), and an attack on *Luther. His learning was generally admired.

Erasmus and Maffei probably never met. Maffei does not mention Erasmus in his writings. Erasmus was familiar with Maffei's publications, especially the Commentaria urbana, and mentioned him occasionally (Epp 1479, 2446; Adagia I i 2, mistranslated in CWE 31:35; cf LB II 16E). Maffei's life of Jerome from the Commentaria urbana is criticized in the Vita Hieronymi (Opuscula 138). Erasmus gave extensive critical consideration to Maffei's translation of Basil the Great (Rome: J. Mazzocchi 1515), faulting him for his mistranslations from the Greek (Epp 2611, 2617). This criticism might account for the hostility shown by Maffei's brother, Mario towards Erasmus.

Allen confuses Raffaele Maffei with Raffaele *Regio.

BIBLIOGRAPHY: E. Garin 'Alessandro d'Alessandro e Raffaele da Volterra' *Rinascimento* 1
(1950) 102–103 / Luigi Peschetti 'Raffaele
Maffei non Rhegius' *Rassegna volterrana* 20
(1952) 1–8 / Pio Paschini 'Una famiglia di
curiali: I Maffei di Volterra' *Rivista di storia della
chiesa in Italia* 7 (1953) 337–376 / Jose Ruys-
schaert 'Recherches des deux bibliothèques
romaines Maffei des xve et xvie siècles' *La
Bibliofilia* 60 (1958) 306–55 / Carlo Dionisotti *Gli
umanisti e il volgare fra quattro e cinquecento*
(Florence 1968) ch 4 / John F. D'Amico 'A
humanist response to Martin Luther: Raffaele
Maffei's *Apologeticus' Sixteenth Century Journal*
6 no 2 (1975) 37–56 / John F. D'Amico
*Renaissance Humanism in Papal Rome: Humanists
and Churchmen on the Eve of the Reformation*
(Baltimore-London 1983) 10–11, 82–5, and
passim / John F. D'Amico 'Papal history and
curial reform: Raffaele Maffei's *Breuis historia* of
Julius II and Leo x' *Archivum Historiae
Pontificiae* 18 (1980) 157–210
                                                JOHN F. D'AMICO

Vincenzo MAGGI of Brescia, documented
1520–63

After the studies of Tiraboschi, reconfirmed by
Guerrini, the subject of this article should not
be confused with another Vincenzo Maggi
(Madius), also a native of Brescia, who went to
Constantinople as a French agent, visited Basel
in 1556 (*Matrikel Basel* II 97), and inclined
towards heterodoxy.

Vincenzo Maggi (Madius, Magius) was born
in Brescia, or in Pompiano near Brescia, about
1498. The availability of data on his life is
limited. In 1520 Maggi was studying philosophy at the University of Padua. After a journey
in northern Europe (Epp 2154, 2166) he
returned to Padua and taught philosophy at
the university, where by 1540 he met Benedetto Varchi, who read, or heard, some of his
lectures on Aristotle's *Poetics*. In 1542 Ercole II
d'*Este invited Maggi to Ferrara, where he
became the tutor of Ercole's son Alfonso and
professor of philosophy at the Studio. One of
his new pupils was Giambattista Giraldi
Cintio, who praised highly the range and
excellence of his philosophical teaching. Another student of Maggi at the Studio of Ferrara,
Giulio Castellani, remembered the philosopher
warmly in his *De humano intellectu* (Venice: D.

Nicolini 1567). The opinion of previous biographers (including Paolo Guerrini) that Maggi
remained in Ferrara after the closing of the
Studio in 1557 is contradicted by evidence
provided by Bernardino Telesio; this also
illustrates the prominence of Maggi's position
in the cultural world of sixteenth-century Italy.
In the preface to the 1565 edition of his *De
rerum natura juxta propria principia* (Rome: A.
Bladus), Telesio states that in 1563 he 'left for
Brescia to meet' Maggi and discuss in detail the
content of his masterpiece. Tiraboschi and
Guerrini maintain that Maggi died about 1564,
but in the light of Telesio's declaration their
conjecture that he died in Ferrara is
questionable.

In May 1529 Maggi visited Erasmus, carrying
a letter from Emilio de' *Migli (Ep 2154).
Evidently impressed, the Dutch scholar described the young Italian philosopher as a
pious and sincere man (Ep 2166). There is
reason to believe that subsequently they
corresponded directly – if at no other time,
at least during the period when *Viglius
Zuichemus was in Padua and witnessed the
success of Maggi's courses at the university
(Ep 2854). He mentioned a lost letter from
Erasmus to Maggi written about 1533. Although at the present stage of research there is
no evidence to sustain the hypothesis that
Maggi answered Erasmus' letter, it is only
logical to think that he did. Unfortunately no
light is shed on this problem by the extant
works of the Italian philosopher, which contain no reference to the Dutch humanist. Given
this lack of basic information it becomes
difficult to evaluate the merits of the statement
in Allen Ep 3002:644, where Giovanni Angelo
*Odoni includes Maggi among the Italian
admirers of Erasmus.

Maggi's main contribution is a commentary
to the *Poetics* of Aristotle, written in collaboration with Bartolomeo Lombardi until the
latter's death (1542): *In Aristotelis librum de arte
poetica communes explicationes* (Venice: V. Val-
grisi 1550). The cultural significance of this
work – after Robortello's the most important of
the great sixteenth-century Italian commentaries in Latin on Aristotle's *Poetics* – has been
established in contemporary scholarship after
the pioneering investigations of J.E. Spingarn,
Ciro Trabalza, Baxter Hathaway, and Bernard

Weinberg. The edition of the commentary includes Maggi's short treatise *De ridiculis*. Other known works by Maggi are an introduction to his courses at the University of Ferrara entitled *De cognitionis praestantia oratio* (Ferrara 1557) and the now very rare *Trattato dell'eccellentia delle donne ... di lingua latina in italiana tradotto* (Brescia: D. de Turlini 1545), which seems to have been originally read in the presence of Calvin's protector, the Duchess Renée of France. Allen's statement that in this work Maggi 'translated from Latin into Italian Plutarch's *De praestantia mulierum*' appears to be in need of verification. MS A Q 6 14 of the Biblioteca Estense (Modena) contains notes taken by Alessandro Sardi on the lectures delivered by Maggi at the University of Ferrara on Aristotle's *Poetics*. Maggi's notes on the *Physics* of Aristotle are also located in the Biblioteca Estense.

BIBLIOGRAPHY: Allen Ep 2154 / References to biographical data on Vincenzo Maggi in older collections may be found in F. Niccolini 'Tre lettere inedite di Iacopo Bonafadio' *Giornale storico della letteratura italiana* 74 (1919) 92–3 n 3 and Paolo Guerrini 'Due amici bresciani di Erasmo' *Archivio storico lombardo* 50 (1923) 176 n 2 / The identity of the two Vincenzo Maggis is discussed in G. Tiraboschi *Storia della letteratura italiana* VII (Florence 1812) 1464 and confused by Giovanni Busino 'Italiani all' Università di Basilea' BHR 20 (1958) 497–526, esp 517 / For the relations between Maggi and Telesio see Eugenio Garin *La cultura filosofica del Rinascimento italiano* (Florence 1961) 444 and *Storia della filosofia italiana* II (Turin 1972) 645–6 / For Maggi's contributions to the literary criticism of the age of the Counter-Reformation see J.E. Spingarn *History of Literary Criticism in the Renaissance* (New York 1899); Ciro Trabalza *La critica letteraria* (Milan 1915); Baxter Hathaway *The Age of Criticism* (Ithaca 1962); and Bernard Weinberg *A History of Literary Criticism in the Italian Renaissance* (Chicago 1961) / For the relations between Maggi and Benedetto Varchi see Umberto Pirotti 'Benedetto Varchi e l'aristotelismo del Rinascimento' *Convivium* n s 3 (1963) 280–311, repr in English translation in *The Late Italian Renaissance* ed Eric Cochrane (New York 1970) 168–208

DANILO AGUZZI-BARBAGLI

Johannes MAGNUS of Linköping, 19 March 1488–22 March 1544

Johannes Magnus (or Store, which is the Swedish translation of Magnus) was the son of Måns and Kristina Pedersson, citizens of Linköping, Sweden. A canon of Linköping and Skara, he studied at Louvain, where he gained the attention of the future Pope *Adrian VI, and from August 1519 in Cologne. In 1520 he received a doctorate in theology from the University of Perugia. In 1523 Adrian VI sent him as apostolic legate to the new king of Sweden, Gustavus Vasa. Magnus was appointed provost of the Strängnäs chapter and bishop of Västerås. To counter Rome's support for the pro-Danish archbishop of Uppsala, Gustaf Trolle, who had fled Sweden, Gustavus Vasa nominated Magnus himself to the archdiocese. He was elected on 15 August, but papal confirmation was refused, although *Clement VII recognized him as administrator in 1524. From 1527 king and country gradually adopted the Reformation and in 1531 a Protestant archbishop was in office. Meanwhile Magnus had left Sweden in 1526. He settled in Gdansk and in 1527 he met there Damião de *Gois, whom he encouraged to write on the subject of the Ethiopians and the Lapps. Gois' *Legatio ... Presbyteri Ioannis* (Antwerp: J. Grapheus 1532) is dedicated to Magnus, and when approached by Gois, Erasmus too took a warm interest in this work and did his best to draw additional attention to the Lapps (Epp 2826, 2914; LB V 813–15). Apart from that, there is no indication of contact between him and Magnus, who later visited Venice and lived in Rome from 1541 to his death. On 27 August 1533 Clement VII confirmed him as archbishop of Uppsala. He worked untiringly to save Sweden for the Catholic church and wrote a history of the metropolitan see of Uppsala, which his brother and successor Olahus Magnus, published at Rome in 1557, and *Historia ... de omnibus Gothorum Sueonumque regibus* (Rome: G.M. de Viottis 1554), also edited by Olahus.

BIBLIOGRAPHY: Allen Ep 2826 / *Svenskt Biografiskt Lexicon* (Stockholm 1918–) XX 220–6 / *New Catholic Encyclopedia* (New York 1967–79) IX 74–5 / de Vocht CTL II 22, III 56–62, and passim / de Vocht *Dantiscus* 264–6 and

passim / *Briefe von Johann und Olahus Magnus* ed
Gottfried Buschbell (Stockholm 1932)
MARTIN SCHWARZ LAUSTEN & PGB

MAGNUS (Ep 1454 of 6 June 1524)
Johann von *Botzheim could remember only
the surname of the young man who had been in
Constance for three days and was expected to
take Ep 1454 to Basel for Erasmus. Magnus has
not been identified; his name in German was
presumably Gross.

Miguel MAI *See Fernando de* SILVA

Nicolas MAILLARD documented c 1508–
18 January 1565
Nicolas Jérôme Maillard (Mallarius) was born
in the diocese of Rouen. He took his MA under
Nicolas Ansoult at the Collège d'Harcourt in
Paris about 1508, and then taught first at
Harcourt and later at the Collège de Justice.
He began to study canon law but abandoned
this for theology, receiving his licence on 24
March 1522 (he ranked seventh of thirty-six)
and his doctorate on 10 July 1522. Maillard was
a *boursier* of Harcourt, but his theological
studies were directed by Nicolas *Le Clerc of
the Collège de Sorbonne. In 1512 he attended
the lectures at the Collège de Navarre of
Jacques Almain on Gabriel *Biel, which he later
edited. He was rector of the university in 1521
and was frequently called on by the university
for diplomatic functions, approaching the king
on at least three occasions in his career.
Maillard delivered public orations on several
important occasions.

As a doctor of theology, Maillard was very
active in 1523 and 1524. He was delegated to
examine an unnamed work of Erasmus and
spoke in favour of a limited use of translations
of the Bible. He also publicly advocated the
necessity of Greek and Latin for all theologians. Maillard had obviously embraced at
least part of the Erasmian program. After a
challenge and rebuke by Noël *Béda, syndic of
the theological faculty, Maillard disappeared
from faculty proceedings until 1533. During
that time, he explained to Erasmus (Ep 2424),
he studied Greek and passed at least part of the
time at the château of Saint-Bel near Lyon, the
home of his patron, Antoine d'*Albon, abbot *in*

commendam of Savigny and l'Isle-Barbe. He
also visited Erasmus at Freiburg early in 1530
(Ep 2410), and in the following years they
exchanged two long letters of great interest
(Epp 2424, 2466; cf Ep 2472).

It was probably Nicolas Maillard – and not
the Franciscan Olivier Maillard, as Pierre
Mesnard conjectures; cf *Studies in the Renaissance* 13 (1966) 203 – who approached Johann
Sturm in 1533 about collaborating on a paraphrase of St Paul's Epistle to the Romans. In
that same year, however, Maillard resumed an
active role on the faculty of theology of Paris
and was from that time on involved in many
issues of importance. He performed a censor's
function many times, notably in Nantes in
1544, and an inquisitor's role in Meaux in 1546.
He became the dean of the faculty of theology
in 1558 and attended the colloquy of Poissy in
1561, where he defended traditional forms of
piety in debates with Théodore de Bèze. In
October 1562 he led the first and only
delegation of Paris theologians to the council of
Trent, where his first intervention shocked
Gallican theorists as conceding too much
authority to the pope. In a second speech
Maillard denied that the sacrament of matrimony was founded in the Bible.

Throughout his career Maillard held several
offices in the Collège d'Harcourt and the
Collège de Justice. In 1530 he styled himself
'comes Lugdunensis, theologus.' In 1531 he
was commendatory abbot of the Benedictine
priory of Saint-Lambert in the diocese of
Rouen, a position which led Allen to conclude
wrongly that he became a Benedictine. By 1545
Maillard was a canon and official theologian of
the diocese of Paris and was also a canon of
Evreux by 1549. He was a close confidant of
Pierre *Lizet, *premier président* of the Parlement
of Paris.

Maillard wrote verse which appeared in
several books other than his own. Charles de
Bouelles and Joachim Périon each dedicated a
book to him. His works include the following
editions: Pliny the Elder *Naturalis Hystoriae libri
xxxvii*, comment Ermolao (1) *Barbaro (Paris:
Nicolas Des Prez et al 1511, 1514); St Jerome
Epistolarum codicilli tres (Paris: Poncet Le Preux
1512). He edited, alone or with others,
Eutropius and Paul the Deacon *De inclytis*

totius Italiae provinciae gestis libri xviii (Paris: Geoffroy de Marnef, Gilles de Gourmont, and Galliot Du Pré 1512); Jacques Almain *Acutissimi divinorum archanorum scrutatoris ... in tertium Sententiarum utilis editio* (Paris: Jean Granjon 1516; Lyon: Jacques Myt 1527); Jacques Almain *Moralia* [*Et Questio in vesperiis habita*] (Paris: Claude Chevallon et al 1516); Martin Le Maistre *Contemplatio super Salve Regina* (Paris: Josse Bade 1519); *Mallarii epistola musarum graecarum apologetica ad Erasmum. Erasmi ad Mallarium epistola* (n p 1531); 'De morte Lutheri' *Le Catalogue des livres censurez par la Faculté de Théologie de Paris, 1544. Avec accession et addition ... 1547* (Paris: Jean André 1547).

BIBLIOGRAPHY: Allen Ep 2424 / H.-L. Bouquet *L'Ancien Collège d'Harcourt* (Paris 1891) / Farge no 323 / B. Moreau *Inventaire chronologique des éditions parisiennes du xvie siècle* (Paris 1972–)
JAMES K. FARGE

Guilhelmus MAINUS *See Guillaume*
DU MAINE

Johannes MAIUS of Sélestat, 31 March 1502–16 July 1536
Maius (Maier, Meier), the son of Hans Meier, a baker, and of Magdalena, the sister of Jakob *Wimpfeling, was a half-brother of Jakob *Spiegel, who directed his education with Wimpfeling's help (Ep 2088). He studied in Heidelberg (1516) and Freiburg (1518). Like his half-brother, he belonged to the literary society of Sélestat (BRE Ep 163). Maius entered the imperial chancery in 1520 and succeeded Spiegel as secretary to King *Ferdinand in 1526. Later he became provost at the Cistercian abbey of Zwettl in Lower Austria; he was buried at Hall, in the Inn valley.

There is no record of personal contact between Maius and Erasmus but in 1531 he and Spiegel expedited an exchange of letters between Erasmus and Cardinal Bernhard von *Cles (Epp 2572, 2590). Like Spiegel he was a friend of Girolamo *Aleandro, and in a letter to Fridericus *Nausea of 15 August 1535 he wrote of Erasmus with enthusiasm (*Epistolae ad Nauseam* 155).

BIBLIOGRAPHY: Allen Ep 2088 / ADB XXXV 157 / Schmidt *Histoire littéraire* I 88 / Joseph Knepper *Jakob Wimpfeling* (Freiburg 1902, repr 1965) 219 and passim / *Matrikel Heidelberg* I 506 / *Matrikel*

Freiburg I 239 / BRE Ep 140 and passim / AK V Ep 2107 / Winterberg 84 and passim   IG

Nicolas de MALAISE d 19 January 1538
Nicolas de Malaise (Malesius) is known only as abbot of the Benedictine house of Saint-Hubert in the Ardennes, near the Belgian frontier with Luxembourg, a dignity he held from 1503 to his death. He restored discipline among his monks, endeavoured to increase the temporalities of his abbey, and devoted his last years to the rebuilding of the church which had been partially destroyed by fire. It was no doubt Paschasius *Berselius who advised Erasmus to seek contact with 'this man of wonderful generosity' (Ep 884). To secure the abbot's patronage Erasmus dedicated to him the *Argumenta* for the apostolic epistles (Louvain 1518, Ep 894). Malaise is not actually known to have shown favours to Erasmus, or to other scholars, but Gillis van *Delft also dedicated a work to him, namely his *Conclusiones in Sententias* (Louvain: D. Martens June 1519).

BIBLIOGRAPHY: Allen Ep 894 / U. Berlière et al *Monasticon belge* (Maredsous-Liège 1890–) V 62–4   FRANZ BIERLAIRE

Juan MALDONADO of Bonilla, c 1485–c 1554
Juan Maldonado (Maldonatus), of Bonilla (Cuenca), studied at the University of Salamanca, where he was a pupil of Antonio de *Nebrija; afterwards he also studied with Christophe de *Longueil. Having received holy orders, he lived at Burgos from the age of twenty-five. He enjoyed the favour of Bishop Juan de Fonseca, who appointed him one of the *examinadores* in charge of diocesan visitation and also vicar-general (*administrador*). In Burgos Maldonado found a second patron in the person of Diego *Osorio, *corregidor* of Cordoba; during an outbreak of plague in the winter of 1519–20 Osorio invited him to his castle at Vallejera. While staying with Osorio he compiled a selection from Pliny, Livy, and other classical writers; he also dedicated to Osorio his Latin comedy *Hispaniola* (Valladolid 1525). Meanwhile he had also begun to apply the principles of humanistic historiography to current events. In a work completed in 1522 but not printed until much later, *De motu Hispaniae* (Rome 1572), he described the Comuneros rebellion. A manuscript of this work is

preserved in the Escorial and contains a dedication to Prince Philip dated 1 December 1545. Maldonado also composed a history of the reign of *Ferdinand II of Aragon and *Isabella of Castile, the manuscript of which was at Burgos in 1783 in the possession of Diego de Lerma.

Maldonado belonged to the circle of Erasmians at Burgos, where he taught from 1532 at the Latin school. In September 1527 he addressed a long letter to Erasmus, assessing in general terms his impact upon Spanish society (Ep 1742). Erasmus was impressed and shared the contents of Maldonado's letter with Thomas *More (Ep 1804); *Goclenius who had forwarded it to Erasmus, also retained a copy (Ep 1768). Erasmus' long answer (Ep 1805) was held back by Alfonso de *Valdés, who thought that it was too indiscreet to please Maldonado (Ep 1839). It continued to be mentioned in subsequent letters (Epp 1908, 1971, 2250) as Erasmus showed some reluctance to supply Maldonado with another copy. By 1534 Maldonado had ceased to admire Erasmus; in his *De felicitate christiana* and *Praxis sive de lectione Erasmi* (Burgos: Juan de Junta 1541) he rejected the *Colloquia* as dangerous to the faith and retained only the New Testament paraphrases as suitable reading matter. This change of mind is all the more significant because from 1532 Maldonado was publicly teaching the humanities at Burgos.

Maldonado's other works include *Paraenesis ad politiores literas adversus grammaticorum vulgum* ([Burgos] 1529) and *Opuscula quaedam* (Burgos: [Juan de Junta?] 1549), with a second, enlarged edition the same year containing his *Pastor bonus*, which offers an unsparing examination of the life of the clergy.

BIBLIOGRAPHY: Allen Ep 1742 / Bataillon *Erasmo y España* lxxxii, 215–18, and passim / Nicolas Antonio *Bibliotheca Hispana nova* (Madrid 1783–8) / Juan Maldonado *La revolución comunera* ed Valentina Fernández Vargas (Madrid 1975) / Juan Maldonado *Paraenesis* ed with a Spanish trans and a biographical intro by Eugenio Asensio and Juan Alcina Rovira (Madrid 1980)   MILAGROS RIVERA & PGB

Nicolas MALLARIUS *See Nicolas* MAILLARD

Paulus MALLEOLUS *See Paul* HEMMERLIN

François de MAMINES *See Frans van* MASSEMEN

Marcus MAMUCETUS (Ep 1842 of 29 June [1527])
Marcus Mamucetus (or Mamuretus) was a young man who associated in Paris with Jacques *Toussain. Toussain gave him a generous recommendation in a letter to Erasmus, which Mamucetus was expected to take to Basel. Manucetus has not been identified.

Meynard MAN of Wormer, d 4 December 1526
Meynard (Menardus) Man was born at Wormer, north of Amsterdam; both *Alaard of Amsterdam (Ep 676) and Erasmus' servant-pupil Quirinus *Talesius were relatives. He studied arts at Louvain, where he matriculated on 8 December 1485 but never, it seems, took a degree. Probably in 1492 he became vice-curate of Graft, near Alkmaar, and in 1501 he entered St Adalbert's, the famous Benedictine abbey of Egmond. On 10 November 1509 Man was elected its thirty-sixth abbot; he was consecrated at Antwerp on 17 March 1510 and installed on 24 March. As abbot he combined a great interest in spiritual reform with the promotion of arts and learning. On his death Alaard of Amsterdam wrote two epitaphs.

Man was a patron of Maarten van *Dorp, who in 1521 addressed to him a letter (de Vocht MHL 75–112) in defence of the publication of his introductory lecture on Paul (Antwerp: M. Hillen 27 September 1519; NK 739), which had drawn the ire of theologians and which Man himself had questioned. Man had earlier received dedications to Johannes *Murmellius' *Charoleia* (Louvain: D. Martens c 1515; NK 3556), to Dorp's *Oratio de laudibus disciplinarum* (Louvain: D. Martens for H. a Diegheem October 1513; NK 738), and to an edition, again by Dorp, of the *Quaestiones quodlibeticae* of the future *Adrian VI (Louvain: D. Martens March 1515). In addition Dorp asked Erasmus to dedicate one of his works to Man, but vague promises to that effect were never fulfilled (Epp 304, 337, 347). Still, Man and Erasmus held each other in high esteem (Epp 676, 1044), and, had his will of 1527 been his last, Erasmus would have bequeathed a set of his *Opera omnia* to the library of Egmond (Allen VI 505).
BIBLIOGRAPHY: Allen Ep 304 / A.J. van der Aa

et al *Biographisch woordenboek der Nederlanden* (Haarlem 1852–78, repr 1965) XII-2 816 / *Matricule de Louvain* III-1 5 / de Vocht MHL 64–120 and passim / V.J.G. Roefs *De Egmondsche abtenkroniek* (Sittard 1942) 253–4 / J. Hof *De abdij van Egmond van de aanvang tot 1573* (The Hague-Haarlem 1973) 136–49 / J. Bruyn in *Oud Holland* 81 (1966) 145–72, 197–227

C.G. VAN LEIJENHORST

Giovanni MANARDO of Ferrara, 24 July 1462–7 March 1536
Giovanni, the son of the notary Francesco Manardo (Manardi), was born at Ferrara. He studied at the University of Ferrara under Battista Guarino, Niccolò *Leoniceno, and Francesco Benzi, the son of the physician Ugo Benzi. On 17 October 1482 he received his doctorate in arts and medicine. He lectured in medicine at Ferrara until 1493, when he went to Mirandola to serve as physician and tutor to Gianfrancesco *Pico. He helped Gianfrancesco edit the works of his famous uncle, Giovanni *Pico, in particular the *Disputationes adversus astrologiam divinatricem* (Bologna: B. Hector 1495). When Gianfrancesco temporarily lost control of Mirandola in 1502, Manardo began a period of travel in Italy, possibly teaching at Perugia, Padua, and Pavia. In 1507, 1509, and 1512 he was again teaching at Ferrara. In 1513, through the influence of Celio *Calcagnini and Cardinal Ippolito d'*Este, he was named physician to *Vladislav II of Hungary and his son, the future *Louis II. In 1518 he returned to Ferrara, where he again taught at the university, succeeding to the chair of Leoniceno in 1524. He was also personal physician to Duke Alfonso I d'*Este. He was married first to Samaritana del Monte, by whom he had a son, Timoteo, and later, at the age of seventy-three to the widow Giulia di Sassoli of Bergamo, who survived him.

One of the most important physicians of the first half of the sixteenth century, Manardo collaborated in the restoration of ancient medical texts, publishing a popular edition of the *Ars medicinalis* of Galen (Rome: F.G. Calvo 1525; republished frequently thereafter). He also developed new methods for the analysis and classification of diseases, for example arguing that syphilis was strictly venereal in nature. His most important work was the *Epistolae medicinales*, a collection of medical discussions based on case histories and personal observations. First published in six books in 1521 (Ferrara: B. de Odonino), the *Epistolae* were expanded to eighteen books in 1535 (Basel: J. Bebel) and to twenty books in 1540 (Basel: M. Isengrin). The 1540 edition was reprinted for the seventh time in 1611. Manardo was also interested in botany and wrote a critical commentary on *In medicamina simplicia et composita*, attributed to Johannes Mesue the Younger, published with the *Epistolae* in 1535.

Manardo included among his correspondents Battista *Mantuanus, Pietro *Crinito, Girolamo*Fracastoro, and Symphorien*Champier. He was praised by many, including Ludovico *Ariosto, who mentioned him in the *Orlando furioso* (XLVI 14). Erasmus was also among his admirers. In July 1525 Celio Calcagnini praised the physician in a letter to Erasmus, offering to send a copy of the *Epistolae medicinales* should he not already possess one (Ep 1587). Erasmus in turn recommended the book to Hubertus *Barlandus, who in 1529 supervised a new edition at Strasbourg by Johann *Schott (Ep 2172). In the early 1530s Erasmus recommended Johannes *Sinapius as a student to Manardo (Ep 2956), whom he praised as one of the most knowledgeable physicians of the day (Ep 2968). Manardo sent greetings to Erasmus in December 1534 through Konrad *Nyder (Ep 2984). In April 1536 Sinapius informed Erasmus of the physician's death (Ep 3113).

BIBLIOGRAPHY: Allen Ep 1587 / J.H. Cotton in *Dictionary of Scientific Biography* ed C.C. Gillispie (New York 1970–80) IX 74–5 / A. Castiglioni *Storia della medicina* (Milan 1927) 443 / A. Pazzini *Storia della medicina* (Milan 1947) I 626 / C. Calcagnini *Opera* (Basel: H. Froben 1544) 51, 62, 89 / *Atti del Convegno internazionale per la celebrazione del V centenario della nascita di Giovanni Manardo* (Ferrara 1963); see in particular the contributions of L. Munster and A. Ostoja / P. Zambelli 'Giovanni Manardo e la polemica sull'astrologia' in *L'opera e il pensiero di Giovanni Pico della Mirandola nella storia dell'umanesimo* (Florence 1965) II 206–55

ANNA GIULIA CAVAGNA & TBD

Antonio MANCINELLI of Velletri, 1452–1505
Antonio Mancinelli was born in Velletri to Giovanni and Angela Mancinelli. He studied

at the universities of Perugia and Pisa, obtaining doctorates in law and medicine. He taught grammar and rhetoric in Venice, Rome, Orvieto, and other Italian cities. He wrote numerous popular grammatical and moral treatises, including *De oratore Brachylogia* (Rome: [B. Guldinbeck] c 1477), *De poetica virtute* (Rome c 1492), *Scribendi orandique modus* (Venice: S. Bevilacqua 1493), *De componendis versibus opusculum* (Venice 1496), and *De parentum cura in liberos* (Rome: E. Silber 1503). He also published commentaries on Virgil (Venice: B. Zanni 1493), Horace (Venice: P. Pincius 1492), Juvenal (Venice: J. Tacuinus 1494/5), and other classical authors and edited Strabo's *De situ orbis* (Venice: J. Rubeus 1494). Important biographical information is found in his poem *Vitae silva* (1492). Collections of his works were published frequently, the first perhaps at Paris (A. Denidel 1499).

Erasmus mentions Mancinelli as an Italian Ciceronian in the *Ciceronianus* (ASD I-2 667).

BIBLIOGRAPHY: Cosenza III 2099–106 / Marie-José Desmet-Goethals 'Die Verwendung der Kommentare von Badius-Mancinellus, Erasmus und Corderius in der "Disticha Catonis"-Ausgabe von Livinus Crucius' in *Der Kommentar in der Renaissance* ed August Buck and Otto Herding (Boppard 1975) 73–88 / Jacob Wimpfeling *Adolescentia* ed Otto Herding (Munich 1965) 43–7 and passim / Remigio Sabbadini 'Antonio Mancinelli: saggio storico-letterario' *Cronaca del R. Ginnasio di Velletri* (1878) 1–40
                                                        JOHN F. D'AMICO

Petrus MANIUS (Ep 1147 of 1 October 1520) Petrus Manius, a Dominican and perhaps a resident of Holland, has not been identified. Erasmus replied at length to a friendly letter from him, which is lost.

Alonso MANRIQUE de Lara c 1460– 28 September 1538
Alonso was a son of Rodrigo Manrique de Lara (1406–76), first count of Paredes de Navas and grand master of the knights of Santiago from 1474, and of his third wife, Elvira de Castañeda, the daughter of Pedro López de Ayala, count of Fuensalida. He was thus a half-brother of the poet Jorge Manrique. According to Allen, Alonso studied at Salamanca and, about 1488, expressed the wish, which was denied him, to join the Austin

friars. He subsequently became a canon of Toledo and master of the cathedral school at Salamanca. In 1499 he was appointed bishop of Badajoz.

After the death of Queen *Isabella of Castile in 1504, Manrique was prominent in public affairs, being associated with the nobles who opposed the rule of *Ferdinand II of Aragon in Castile, favouring instead the cause of his son-in-law, Philip the Handsome of *Burgundy, the husband of *Joanna of Castile and the father of the future *Charles V. Manrique appears among the witnesses of the document setting up a regency council under the presidency of the archbishop of Toledo, *Jiménez de Cisneros, on the death of Philip in September 1506. Manrique was one of those who now wished either Prince Charles or his grandfather, the Emperor *Maximilian, to come to Castile and claim the throne. When Ferdinand returned to Castile in 1507, Manrique decided to remove himself to the Burgundian court at Brussels. Early in 1508 he was taken prisoner on Ferdinand's orders in the vicinity of Santander and conveyed first to the castle of Atienza and then to Illescas. After being brought before the archbishop of Toledo, he returned to his diocese of Badajoz. From there he soon made his way to Portugal and thence to Brussels. Having been, as it appears, a member of Philip's council in Spain, he was well received at the Burgundian court. By 1511 he was both a member of the council of *Margaret of Austria and principal chaplain to Prince Charles. In March 1516 he wrote to Cisneros on the subject of the Spanish Inquisition: he feared that the complaints against it by recent arrivals from Spain and their pleas that it be abolished or at least deprived of royal support would have some effect at Brussels. Manrique's view was that the Inquisition should be not only preserved but strengthened. After being appointed bishop of Córdoba in August 1516 he returned to Spain with Charles in 1517. In 1523 he was nominated archbishop of Seville and in September of that year became inquisitor-general. He was created cardinal in February 1531.

As inquisitor-general Manrique was active in attempts to seize and destroy the substantial number of Lutheran works infiltrating Spain. In September 1525 he signed an edict against the *alumbrados*, or illuminists, of the archdiocese of Toledo. In the same year he was involved in the increasingly severe measures adopted to secure the effective christianization of the *moriscos* of the kingdom of Valencia. Whereas in April 1524 he had instructed local inquisitors not to proceed against these new Christians save in matters clearly indicative of heresy, he now issued a catalogue of points relating to *morisco* practice and belief that required delation to the Inquisition; the catalogue was of the kind that already existed for the Jews.

In contrast to his activity against Lutheran works, the *alumbrados*, and the *moriscos*, Manrique established himself as one of the chief protectors of Erasmus in Spain. In September 1526 the second edition of Alonso *Fernández de Madrid's translation of Erasmus' *Enchiridion* was published with a dedication to Manrique, whose coat of arms as inquisitor-general it bore on the reverse of its title page. The dedication explained that the work had been examined on Manrique's instructions and had been found 'very profitable and highly edifying.' Despite protests from the religious orders of Spain against Erasmus and the *Enchiridion*, the council of the Inquisition continued to favour the humanist's writings. Early in 1527 Manrique summoned the superiors of the religious orders to repeat to them the prohibitions already issued against public attacks on Erasmus: if the orders wished to bring charges of heresy against him, they must submit specific textual evidence to the Inquisition. When they complied Manrique convened an assembly of theologians at Valladolid to examine the evidence adduced. This conference of up to thirty divines met in twenty-one sessions from 27 June to 13 August under the presidency of Manrique (Ep 1814, 1846, 1847). Bataillon suggests that Manrique enlarged the gathering with a view to protracting its deliberations and obtaining an inconclusive outcome. When the conference was curtailed in August after an outbreak of plague, judgment was not passed for or against Erasmus; this was a moral victory for the Spanish Erasmians. At the end of the year Charles v sent Ep 1920, drafted by Alfonso de *Valdés, to Erasmus, in which he expressed his admiration for him and, referring to the Valladolid assembly, expressed his confidence in Erasmus' 'Christian disposition.'

Meanwhile Erasmus had appealed directly to Manrique in August 1527 (Ep 1864) and in the following autumn dedicated his *Apologia ad monachos quosdam hispanos* (Basel: H. Froben 1528) to the prelate (Epp 1877, 1879, 1888, 1967, 1980). In March 1529 he sent Manrique a copy of his edition of Augustine (Basel: H. Froben 1529; Ep 2126), and in March 1530 he wrote again to complain about the attacks of the Franciscan Luis de *Carvajal and to request action against the clandestine printer of his works (Ep 2301).

In 1528 Manrique defended Alfonso de Valdés' *Diálogo de las cosas ocurridas en Roma* (published c 1529) against the protests of the papal nuncio, Baldesar *Castiglione (Ep 2163). In the following year, Juan Luis *Vives dedicated his *De pacificatione* (Bruges) to Manrique, praising him for the favour he showed to men of learning, among them Luis Núñez *Coronel (Manrique's secretary) and Juan del Castillo. In 1531 the anonymous Spanish version of Erasmus' commentaries on Psalms 1 and 4 was dedicated to him. But from December 1529 until Charles v's return to Spain in 1533, Manrique had to withdraw from the court to Seville, having incurred the disfavour of the Empress *Isabella by using his position to secure, against her wishes, the marriage of his kinsman, the count of Treviño, to a young lady, Doña Luisa de Acuña, who had been left in her care. During this period he was no longer in effective personal control of the council of the Inquisition. He appears to have fallen into disfavour again in 1534 and to have withdrawn to Seville for his remaining years. In 1533 he made only a feeble effort to come to the aid of Juan de *Vergara, who had been imprisoned by the Inquisition. Later that year, Manrique's son, Rodrigo, moved by Vergara's troubles, wrote to Vives of his indignation at seeing 'silence imposed' on all men of learning in Spain. Again in 1533, Juan del Castillo, whom Manrique had brought from Seville to the court in 1525 and who had subsequently associated not only with Erasmus' followers there but also with leading illuminists, was brought back from Italy by the Inquisition. After making confessions of heresy before his former protector, he was burnt as a Lutheran heretic in 1535. The Blessed Juan de Avila enjoyed Manrique's support during the first years of his preaching 'apostolate of Andalusia,' but in the years 1531–3 he found himself under investigation on grounds of 'illuminism.' Manrique's failure in 1534 to obtain the vacant primatial see of Toledo may be seen as a sign that his time of influence and success was past and his role as protector of the Spanish Erasmian movement of the 1520s, so largely centred on the court, was at an end.

BIBLIOGRAPHY: Allen Ep 1846 / P. Rubio in *Diccionario de historia eclesiástica de España* (Madrid 1972–5) II 1408 / Eubel II 232, III 23, 194, 227 / J. Solano de Figueroa *Historia eclesiástica de la ciudad y obispado de Badajoz* (Badajoz 1933) V 37–145 / Erasmus *El Enquiridión o manual del caballero cristiano* ed Dámaso Alonso, with prologue by Marcel Bataillon (Madrid 1932, repr 1971) 100–3 / Bataillon *Erasmo y España* 165, 236–47, and passim / Jerónimo de Zurita *Historia del rey don Hernando el Cathólico* (Saragossa 1580) II 159 recto–verso / D. Ortiz y Zúñiga *Annales eclesiásticos y seculares de la ciudad de Sevilla* (Madrid 1677) 481 / K.J. von Hefele *Der Kardinal Ximenes und die kirchlichen Zustände Spaniens* ... (Tübingen 1851) 375 / A. Walther *Die Anfänge Karls v.* (Leipzig 1911) 81–2, 112 / A. Rodríguez Villa *La reina Juana la loca* (Madrid 1892) 189–91, 295–8 / L.-P. Gachard *Compte-rendu des séances de la Commission royale d'histoire* (Brussels 1844–50) X 5–35 / A. Redondo 'Luther et l'Espagne de 1520 à 1536' *Mélanges de la Casa de Velázquez* 1 (1965) 109–65 / V. Beltrán de Heredia OP 'El edicto contra los alumbrados del reino de Toledo (23 septiembre de 1525)' *Revista española de teología* 10 (1950) 105–30 (also given by A. Márquez *Los alumbrados: orígenes y filosofía, 1525–1559*, Madrid 1972) 273–83 / P. Boronat y Barranchina *Los moriscos españoles y su expulsión* (Valencia 1901) I 135–6 / R. García Cárcel *Orígenes de la inquisición española: el tribunal de Valencia, 1478–1530* (Barcelona 1976) 121–8 / L. Cardaillac *Morisques et chrétiens: un affrontement polémique (1492–1640)* (Paris 1977) 110–14 / J.E. Longhurst 'The Alumbrados of Toledo: Juan del Castillo and the Lucenas' ARG 45 (1954) 233–53 / J.C. Nieto 'Luther's ghost and Erasmus' masks in Spain' BHR 39 (1977) 33–49

R.W. TRUMAN

Baptista MANTUANUS of Mantua, 17 April 1447–20 March 1516
Baptista Mantuanus (Giovanni Battista Spa-

gnolo, Battista Mantovano) was born to Petrus Mantuanus and Constanza de' Maggi in Mantua. He studied in his home town with Gregorius *Tiphernas and Giorgio *Merula, and later at the universities of Padua and Bologna. At the age of sixteen he entered the Carmelite order. He was active in the affairs of the order and in 1513 was elected its prior-general. He died in 1516 and was beatified in 1885.

Mantuanus was a prolific poet and enjoyed enormous popularity both in Italy and in northern Europe. His poetry was especially prized for its combination of Christian material with classical form, as seen in his *De sacris diebus* and *Parthenicae*. His ten eclogues proved particularly influential. His reputation was high among Erasmus' friends. *Beatus Rhenanus edited some of his poems in 1510 (BRE Ep 17), Josse *Bade produced an edition of his *Opera* in 1513, and John *Colet required his students to study his religious poetry at St Paul's School.

Erasmus' attitude towards Mantuanus was a very positive one. He admired his style (Ep 47) and his treatment of Christian subjects (Ep 145; *Ciceronianus* ASD I-2 700). He referred to the Italian as a 'Christian Virgil' (Ep 49). He especially contrasted Mantuanus' Christian poetry with the 'pagan' poetry of Michael *Marullus (Epp 385, 1479).

BIBLIOGRAPHY: Allen Ep 47 / Cosenza III 2127–33 / EI XXXII 294 / Edmondo Coccia *Le edizioni delle opere del Mantovano* (Rome 1960) / William Ernest Painter 'Baptista Mantuanus, Carmelite Humanist' (doctoral thesis, University of Missouri 1961) / Hans Trümpy *Die Fasti des Baptista Mantuanus von 1516 als volkskundliche Quelle* (Nieuwkoop 1979)

JOHN F. D'AMICO

Petrus MANTUANUS *See Pietro* POMPONAZZI

MANUEL I king of Portugal, 3 May 1469–13 December 1521
Manuel was the son of the Infante Dom Fernando and Doña Beatriz. He was the brother of Leonor, the wife of King John II. At the time of John's death (25 October 1495) Manuel was duke of Beja and a contender for the throne, since the king left only a natural son, Jorge. It was due to the energy and determination of Leonor that, after many

intrigues Manuel was finally proclaimed king. Manuel reaped a rich harvest from the Portuguese discoveries overseas. Under him Francisco de Almeida was appointed the first viceroy of India, Pedro Alvares Cabral set foot on Brazilian soil for the first time, Portuguese navigators reached China and Japan, and the Negus of Ethiopia offered Manuel his assistance against the Moslems in Africa.

Lisbon had become a cosmopolitan city. Merchants from many European countries took up residence there and emissaries and visitors from overseas contributed colour and animation to the life of the metropolis. Among the many gifts which overseas rulers presented to the king none stirred the imagination of the people more than the rhinoceros and elephants. As a devout Catholic Manuel sent precious gifts from overseas to Rome and kept the pope informed about the progress of the explorations. He succeeded in consolidating the government against the nobles and centralizing his administration. The Portuguese economy prospered thanks to the overseas imports, so Manuel decided to open a 'factory' in Antwerp from which merchandise of all kinds was sold throughout Europe. Among the Portuguese merchants residing in Antwerp were many *marranos*.

Manuel was introduced to humanism by the Italian Catáldo Parísio Siculo, who had come to Portugal under John II; he developed a great liking for history and requested his courtiers to read the ancient chronicles. But the king's artistic inclinations exceeded by far his interest in learning, and he undertook an ambitious building program for which he engaged the best artists. Among his great monuments the tower of Belem, the church and cloisters of St Jerome in Lisbon, and the church of the convent of Tomar are vivid examples of the exuberant spirit that pervaded the period. The architecture has become known as the Manueline style; because of its sumptuous details it is often considered high Gothic or early Baroque.

King Manuel married three times. His first wife was Isabella, the daughter of *Ferdinand II of Aragon and *Isabella of Castile and the widow of Dom Afonso, the son of John II of Portugal. She made it a condition of the marriage contract that Jews who did not convert to Christianity were to be expelled from Portugal. In his chronicle of the king's reign Damião de *Gois reports that Manuel acceded to his future wife's wishes despite the opposition of his advisers, who pointed out that many European countries tolerated the Jews and that their expertise in arms-making was to Portugal's advantage. Gois describes the heartbreaking scenes that took place at the departure of the Jews when their children were taken from them to be brought up as Christians in Portugal.

Erasmus praised Manuel's achievements in Ep 1800; there are brief references to him in Epp 1108 and 1681 and in the *Julius exclusus* (*Opuscula* 112).

BIBLIOGRAPHY: Fortunato de Almeida *História de Portugal* II and III (Coimbra 1923–5) / H.V. Livermore *A History of Portugal* (Cambridge 1947) 222–39 / Charles Beazley 'The colonial empire of the Portuguese to the death of Albuquerque' *Transactions of the Royal Historical Society* 8 (1894) 109–27 / Damião de Gois *Chrónica do félicissimo rei D. Manuel* ed D. Lopez (Coimbra 1949–55) / J.A. Goris *Etude sur les colonies marchandes méridionales … à Anvers de 1488–1567* (Louvain 1925) 235–43 and passim / Manuel I king of Portugal *Cronicas e Cartas* (Lisbon 1977) / Américo da Costa Ramalho *Estudos sobre a época do Renascimento* (Coimbra 1969) passim / Elaine Sanceau *The Reign of the Fortunate King, 1495–1521* (Hamden, Conn. 1969–70) / Reynaldo dos Santos *L'Art portugais* (Lisbon-Porto 1949) 15–19 / Robert C. Smith *The Art of Portugal 1500–1800* (New York 1968) 22–56   ELISABETH FEIST HIRSCH

Don Juan MANUEL *See* JUAN MANUEL

Aldo MANUZIO of Bassiano,
d 6 February 1515
Aldo Manuzio (commonly called Aldus, also Aldus Pius Senior Manutius) was born in Bassiano, near Rome, probably in 1452. Although the details of his early life are lost, it seems that until about 1490 Aldus was a wandering scholar and teacher who was slowly building a respectable but second-class position. In the preface to his edition of Statius (1502) he mentioned a period of study with Domizio *Calderini in Rome, which must have fallen between 1473 and 1477; he then moved

to Ferrara, where he both worked under
Battista Guarino and taught on his own
account until the outbreak of war with Venice
in 1482. At this point he was drawn into the
orbit of the young Giovanni *Pico della
Mirandola and took the opportunity of improving his Greek, making contact with *Poliziano
and securing a post as tutor to Pico's nephews,
Alberto and Lionello *Pio of Carpi; see Angelo
Poliziano *Opera omnia* (Aldus 1498) Ep VII 7.
Aldus remained at the court of Carpi until
about 1490, and his earliest published work, an
open letter to the princes' mother setting out
his educational principles, was probably written at this time: it reflects a strong commitment
to Greek studies but makes no mention of
printing, and Aldus' reasons for abandoning a
successful career when approaching the age of
forty remain mysterious.

Arriving in Venice about 1490, Aldus seems
to have supported himself partly by teaching,
since his high connections with the Pio family
and his links with the Florentine humanists
gave him an easy introduction to Venetian
intellectuals such as Bernardo Bembo and
Girolamo *Donato. But he began preliminary
work on his program of publications immediately: letters of Codro *Urceo and Giorgio
*Valla show him assembling manuscripts as
early as 1491; see Domenico Vitaliani *Della vita e
delle opere di Niccolò Leoniceno* (Verona 1892)
276–7. In 1493 his future partner Andrea
*Torresani printed the first edition of Aldus'
Latin grammar. With its highly developed
printing industry, Venice offered a ready
source of technical expertise, but at this
moment it still lacked Greek presses which
could be found in both Florence and Milan.
Aldus' plans for a comprehensive series of
Greek editions quickly attracted interest, and
by 1495 he had formed a company with Pier-
francesco Barbarigo, the nephew of the doge
Agostino, and Torresani, one of the most
successful publishers in Venice at the time.
From a fragmentary account-book and from the
notarial acts which liquidated the company's
assets in the 1540s, it is apparent that Aldus
held only the smallest financial stake in the
enterprise, that his patron, Alberto Pio, was
not involved, and that the capital was almost
entirely controlled by Barbarigo and Torresani.
This bears out Erasmus' later statement that

Aldo Manuzio, by Antoine Lafrey

Aldus was in the power of his partners (LB IX
1137C), though it should be added that his
moral hold over them seems to have been
remarkable.

Between 1495 and 1515 Aldus produced one
hundred and twenty-six editions. They include a small number of ephemera and that
masterpiece of illustration, the *Hypneroto-
machia Polifili*, but the bulk comprises ninety-
four first issues of classical or post-classical
Greek authors dispersed through various
volumes, a large range of Latin authors in
octavo format, and a small selection of Italian
authors. Although the humanist emphasis is
obvious throughout, the program divides into
several phases. Until 1500 the Aldine press
was an important but not dominant feature of
the Venetian industry. Its activity was focused
on the five-volume edition of the Greek
Aristotle and a number of introductory Greek
texts, grammars, and dictionaries: four cursive
types were commissioned, and the techniques
were protected by copyright in 1496. Latin and
Italian played a subordinate role, the works
published being either small in scale or
financed by outside capital. But after 1500

Aldus' opportunities widened. The collapse of two merchant banks at the outset of the Turkish war left many of his competitors without funds, so Aldus was able to move into the wider market for Latin literature and make his press by far the most productive in Venice. The Latin cursive or italic types, designed by Francesco Griffo and first used in 1500, were turned in the following year to the production of octavo texts in editions which have usually been reckoned at one thousand copies but were in some cases as large as three thousand (Hieronymus Avantius' preface to Catullus, 1502). Although they were not uniformly cheaper than other editions, were quickly undercut by forgeries, and were probably aimed at the busy rather than the impecunious reader, these octavos played a great part in emancipating reading from the study. However, in seeking to combine them with his Greek texts and printing twenty-eight editions in 1502 and 1503, Aldus may have overreached himself. By 1505 his output had declined to seven editions, and the reports of Johannes *Cuno suggest that too much capital had been invested in Greek texts which did not sell easily (*Pirckheimer Briefwechsel* Ep 86).

Aldus reacted by attaching himself more closely to Andrea Torresani, whose daughter Maria he married in early 1505. By 27 March 1506, when he drew up his first will, Aldus had abandoned his house in Sant'Agostino and was living with his wife's family in San Paternian: the following day he and Andrea signed an agreement which amalgamated all their assets, assigning one fifth of the total to Aldus. The eighteen months of inactivity which followed these arrangements were a period of planned retrenchment which had no connection with the politics of the time. Aldus used them to gather new material and to settle a lawsuit, probably with Filippo Giunti (Junta) over the right to print in italic. By the time of Erasmus' first approach to Aldus on 28 October 1507 (Ep 207), work had clearly been resumed, and it was not until the following winter (Ep 213) that the threat of a European war became serious. Aldus continued work through the spring of 1509, but left Venice immediately after the disastrous Venetian defeat at Agnadello and seems to have planned a complete withdrawal from commerce, since he appoint-

ed agents in all the main centres of Italy and rescinded the union of his assets with Torresani's. Over the next three years his principal aim was to safeguard his own and Andrea's property on the mainland through his considerable influence at the French, papal, and imperial courts. Centring his efforts on Ferrara he travelled widely to canvass support and was able to summon a personal appeal from *Maximilian I to Francesco Gonzaga on his behalf. By the summer of 1512 these plans had come to nothing, and Aldus was persuaded by his Venetian friends to resume printing. Somewhat to his surprise, he found that an influx of refugees such as *Musurus, *Regio, and *Becichemo, had stimulated both the book market and the level of intellectual activity in Venice, and the last two years of his life saw the press almost as busy as it had been in the first years of the century. But towards the end of 1514 Aldus fell ill, and he died on 6 February of the following year. For a short time before being carried to his chosen, but now unknown, burial-place in Carpi, he was laid ceremonially in the Venetian parish church of San Paternian, surrounded by copies of his books. He left three sons and a daughter, whose arrival after his late marriage demanded modifications in 1511 and 1515 to the will he had drawn up in 1506. His liquid assets remained steady at around two thousand ducats, suggesting neither wealth, want, nor any obvious commercial success.

Long after his own death, Aldus' name was dropped into the quarrel between his old patron, Alberto Pio, and Erasmus: as a result the relationship between them has been somewhat distorted. In the *Moria* (ASD IV-3 140) Erasmus took a friendly dig at Aldus as an over-scrupulous grammarian who published his work five times, and this was taken by Alberto as a sign of ingratitude for the scholarly debts that Erasmus owed the printer and his circle. In 1531 Erasmus replied that he had learnt no Greek in Venice and owed nothing to Italy (LB IX 1136–7; see also Ep 3032). He also incorporated Aldus in his attack on Andrea Torresani under the name of 'Orthrogonus' (ASD I-3 676–85) and made a number of disparaging references to his editions (*Adagia* II iv 53, ix 76, IV viii 92; Ep 1437). But this assumed hostility is not borne out by earlier references. Erasmus' request to Aldus for an edition of his translations from Euripides is extremely deferential (Ep 207), and the Aldine text of the *Adagia* expanded the Parisian version of 1507 from 841 sections to 3260, transforming the work from a minor success into a best seller. The bulk of the new material was in Greek, and Erasmus declared that much of it had been made available to him by Aldus and his associates (*Adagia* II i 1). The quip in the *Moria* cannot be taken as evidence of a quarrel: Aldus did indeed re-issue his Latin grammar four times, in 1493, 1501, 1508, and 1514, while a Greek grammar was edited posthumously in 1515. In 1513 the printer admitted that he had never produced a book that satisfied him completely. Erasmus' joke was accurate as to the facts, and Aldus would probably have taken its implications as a compliment.

On the other hand no special relationship can be established between the two men on the grounds of Erasmus' assumed membership in Aldus' Academy. A statute forming an association of individuals determined to improve their Greek was printed by Aldus, probably in 1502, and mentioned in colophons over the next two years. But no rota of membership was drawn up, and after failing to secure imperial patronage for a humanist college, supported by a press, which he hoped to found in Germany, Aldus dropped the subject to the level of a domestic joke (Ep 868). At the time of Erasmus' visit the Aldine press was in fact working at reduced intensity, after a year's intermission. Erasmus was definitely active as an editor and received twenty crowns for his services, a fact which his opponents later seized upon as evidence that he had been an academic drudge (Epp 212, 1460, 2682, 3032). But such payments were usual, and the evidence only makes Erasmus one other member of a loosely defined editorial circle consisting of twenty or thirty scholars.

In his own time Aldus evidently enjoyed a respectable reputation as a scholar as well as a printer. A woodcut portrait attributed to Ugo da Carpi and now in the Kupferstichkabinet, Berlin, represents Aldus in his thirties, well before he gained fame as a publisher. A silver medallion and another woodcut, also in Berlin, belong to the early sixteenth century, and two portraits in oil, now lost, are mentioned in

contemporary correspondence. But Erasmus' character-sketch (*Adagia* II i 1) of an industrious, gentle, and self-effacing grammarian seems largely accurate. Aldus' first will directed his executors to burn his compositions as unfit for publication, and a three-page essay on the mispronunciation of diphthongs, which was printed with some of Erasmus' minor works at Basel in 1528, presumably appeared in spite of this request. An open letter to Alberto Pio's mother, Caterina, which Aldus seems to have published soon after his arrival in Venice in 1489 or 1490, and a number of short linguistic essays which he attached to his grammatical editions, all reflect the same profound interest in the variation of usage in speech or writing and in the selection of the correct form. Although Greek was his chief love, an introduction to Petrarch shows that Aldus was also intrigued by the potential of the Italian vernacular. His Latin grammar brought the fourth-century pattern laid down by Donatus up to date by adding material from contemporaries such as Guarino *Guarini or Niccolò *Perotti: it enjoyed a certain vogue during the first part of the sixteenth century but did not succeed, as Aldus had hoped, in replacing the twelfth-century *Doctrinale* of Alexander de Villa Dei. The Manuzio library was called a 'treasure house' by Erasmus (*Adagia* II i 1). Its contents during Aldus' own time cannot be reconstructed precisely, but the inventories drawn up at the end of the sixteenth century do not reveal any manuscripts of any obvious age or interest (Biblioteca Apostolica Vaticana, MS Latinus 7121). Aldus himself confessed to finding an uncial Latin script difficult to read (Orlandi I 94, introduction to Pliny's *Letters*), and it seems doubtful that his enthusiasm for antiquity was equalled by his understanding of it. The merit of his own classical texts, which Erasmus questioned later in his life, remains a matter for dispute. Some points of fact are ambiguous, and Aldus' responsibility for any one text is often blurred by the system of group editorship in which all his friends participated. Erasmus was not justified in criticizing the edition of Hesychius (*Adagia* II ix 76), which was based on the only complete manuscript. But it is now thought unlikely that Aldus had regular access to the vital source of early Greek manuscripts in the Biblioteca Marciana of

Venice, and his critical sense of the relationship between different manuscripts does not
seem to have been as sharp as that of Poliziano:
see E.J. Kenney *The Classical Text* (London
1976). Aldus' greatest quality was his gift for
friendship, and his influence was always very
personal.

BIBLIOGRAPHY: Allen and CWE Ep 207 / A.
Firmin-Didot *Alde Manuce et l'hellénisme à Venise*
(Paris 1875) / E. Pastorello *L'epistolario Manuziano* (Florence 1957) / E. Pastorello 'Di Aldo Pio
Manuzio: testimonianze e documenti' *La biblio-
filia* 67 (1965) 163–220 (comprehensive guide to
source material) / On Aldus' writings and
publications: A.-A. Renouard *Annales de l'im-
primerie des Alde* 3rd ed (Paris 1834, repr 1953);
Aldo Manuzio editore ed G. Orlandi (Milan
1976); P. de Nolhac 'Les correspondants d'
Alde Manuce' *Studi e documenti di storia e diritto*
8 (1887) 247–99, 9 (1888) 203–48 / On the
Aldine circle and Erasmus' place in it: D.
Geanakoplos *Byzantium and the Renaissance,
Greek Scholars in Venice* (Hamden, Conn, 1973),
first published as *Greek Scholars in Venice*
(Cambridge, Mass 1962); M.J.C. Lowry *The
World of Aldus Manutius* (Oxford 1979)

M.J.C. LOWRY

Antonio MANUZIO of Venice, 1511–59
Antonio, the second son of Aldo *Manuzio,
was expected when Aldus wrote his second
will of 25 August 1511 and born shortly
afterwards. He cannot have known Erasmus,
and the formal greeting conveyed by his
grandfather, Andrea *Torresani, in 1517 (Ep
589) must be regarded as a gesture only.
Educated in Asola with his brothers, Antonio
was unable to settle in Venice after Torresani's
death, since a misdemeanour had caused his
temporary banishment. During the 1530s he
followed a military career; thereafter he began
to take an active interest in publishing and by
the mid-1550s had settled in Bologna, where he
acted as agent for his younger brother, Paolo
*Manuzio. He was not, however, successful
in business and died in 1559, mentally un-
balanced and encumbered by debts.

BIBLIOGRAPHY: Allen and CWE Ep 589 / E.
Pastorello *L'epistolario Manuziano* (Florence
1957)   M.J.C. LOWRY

Manuzio MANUZIO of Venice, May 1506–
November 1568
Manuzio was the eldest son of Aldo *Manuzio
and Maria Torresani, expected when his father
wrote his will of March 1506 and born in May.
The only one of Aldus' children whom
Erasmus can have known personally, he sent a
formal greeting via his grandfather, Andrea
*Torresani, in 1517 (Ep 589) and was later
remembered by Erasmus in the colloquy
Opulentia sordida as the brat who got his
chicken liver (ASD I-3 683). After spending his
youth in Asola, he returned to Venice with his
brothers in 1529 in an attempt to revive the
family business after his grandfather's death.
But he soon gave way before the difficulties
encountered and drifted disconsolately from
Asola to Rome and so back to Venice,
attempting to secure a share of the property of
his brothers and *Torresani cousins; he was in
constant difficulty with his health, his wanted
or unwanted women, and his improperly held
ecclesiastical benefice. He died in November
1568, deeply in debt.

BIBLIOGRAPHY: Allen and CWE Ep 589 / E.
Pastorello *L'epistolario Manuziano* (Florence
1957)   M.J.C. LOWRY

Paolo MANUZIO of Venice, 12 June 1512–
6 April 1574
Paolo was the third and ablest son of Aldo
*Manuzio (Aldus) and his true successor as a
publisher. Born in 1512, he cannot have known
Erasmus personally, though he sent a formal
greeting to him, along with his brothers, in
1517 (Ep 589) and received one in return via
Ambrogio *Leoni the following year (Ep 868).
Although he spent much of his youth with his
brothers in Asola, Paolo must have been
educated partly in Venice, since he was
mentioned as an able pupil by the schoolmaster
Stefano Piazzone in 1526. From 1531 he was
deeply involved in litigation over the estates of
his father and maternal grandfather Andrea
*Torresani, and by 1533, though only twenty-
one, he had revived the Aldine press. Until
about 1540 he seems to have been supported by
his *Torresani cousins; afterwards he operated
independently, concentrating on Latin texts
and still able to call on a number of his father's
collaborators, including Giambattista *Egnazio. He became official printer to the Venetian

Academy in 1558 but moved to Rome three years later when the institution failed after serious financial irregularities. Paolo was able to use his contacts at the curia to gain a very lucrative monopoly of publication rights to the Tridentine catechism and reformed breviary, and he operated successfully at Rome until his death in 1574. As an editor he concentrated on the Latin prose authors, especially Cicero, never acquiring his father's expertise in Greek. But his own Latin and Italian letters were regarded as models of style and frequently reprinted during the sixteenth century, while his *Antiquitates Romanae* (first part published in 1557) remained popular for two centuries.

BIBLIOGRAPHY: Allen and CWE Ep 589 / A.-A. Renouard *Annales de l'imprimerie des Alde* 3rd ed (Paris 1834, repr 1953) 425–60, 520–43, and passim / Guide to sources in E. Pastorello *L'epistolario Manuziano* (Florence 1957) / References in P. Grendler *The Roman Inquisition and the Venetian Press 1540–1605* (Princeton 1977) 171–3 and passim / Francesco Barberi *Paolo Manuzio e la stamperia del Popolo Romano (1561–1570) con documenti inediti* (Rome 1942)
                                                                M.J.C. LOWRY

Jean MAQUET of Binche, d 1535
Jean Maquet (Macket, Maketus) of Binche, in Hainaut, studied at Louvain and subsequently was a member of the academic council from 31 August 1507, when he became promoter of discipline. He resigned on 23 December 1508 but was again appointed on 22 December 1512. From 1519 until his death he was syndic of the university, continuing also to carry out the duties of promoter after that office had been abolished. His name appears on numerous documents, and he introduced some useful changes: for instance, the rule that seats be provided for all students in all lecture halls (1532). From 1525 he also served as a notary to the Inquisition.

A reference to Maquet in Erasmus' Ep 1342 suggests friendly and familiar relations between them in 1521, and his jovial manner appears to be confirmed by Jan van *Campen, who in 1531 jokingly referred to his inquisitorial zeal, although on this occasion Maquet was not amused.

BIBLIOGRAPHY: Allen Ep 1342 / H. de Jongh *L'Ancienne Faculté de théologie de Louvain* (Lou-

vain 1911) 29*–30* and passim / de Vocht CTL I 450–2 and passim, III 164 / de Vocht *Dantiscus* (Louvain 1961) 74–5, 83 / de Vocht MHL 415 and passim / *Correspondance de Nicolas Clénard* ed A. Roersch (Brussels 1940–1) Ep 27   IG & PGB

Jean de MARAIS *See Jean* DESMAREZ

de MARCA *See de la* MARCK

Helias MARCAEUS of Mertz, d before 27 August 1527
Helias Marcaeus (Elias Mertz, Helias Faber de Juliaco, Helias de Luna) was born in Mertz, near Jülich, and matriculated at the University of Cologne on 18 May 1474 as an arts student. He graduated BA on 12 June 1476 and MA on 2 April 1479. He may have gone on to study theology, while also teaching arts courses. He became the rector and confessor of a convent of Benedictine nuns at Cologne which took its name from the possession of relics of the Maccabeans. He showed great zeal in promoting the cult of the seven Maccabean martyrs and their mother, himself composing a short account entitled *Sent Salome Martyr seben Kinder Macabeen* (n p, n d), which he dedicated to Sibyl of Brandenburg (d 1524), the widow of Duke William III of Jülich-Berg. It was subsequently translated into Latin by Johannes Cincinnius. He also arranged for the publication of his source, a text attributed to Josephus, and persuaded Erasmus to contribute a prefatory letter to this volume published at Cologne in 1517 or 1518 (Ep 842). Friendly contacts between Helias and Erasmus seem to have continued, and after the Benedictine nuns had sent him a gift of sweetmeats, Erasmus wrote for them in 1523 his *Virginis et martyris comparatio* (Epp 1346, 1475; LB V 589–600). Together with Ortwinus *Gratius, Helias also strove to win recognition for the Maccabean convent as the oldest and most prestigious shrine for the veneration of St Ursula and her eleven thousand virgins (Ep 842). Their claims rested on shaky foundations but should be seen in the light of a certain rivalry between the Maccabean convent, which accepted burghers' daughters, and the convent of the Holy Virgins, whose nuns were of noble descent.

From 1505 Helias was also in contact with Abbot Johannes *Trithemius. He contributed

generously to the rich apparel of the Maccabean convent, and his will, dated 1527, is
extant in the copy book of that convent preserved in the Staatsarchiv at Düsseldorf. On 27
August 1527, in a letter to Tielmannus *Gravius, Erasmus noted Helias' death and paid
tribute to his sincerity, also mentioning a last
exchange of letters between them, which must
have taken place during Helias' final illness
(Ep 1865). A funeral inscription for Helias,
composed by Ortwinus Gratius, is recorded in
Cologne, Historisches Archiv der Stadt Köln,
MS Chroniken und Darstellungen 181a.

BIBLIOGRAPHY: Allen Ep 842 / ADB XX 294 /
Matrikel Köln I 868 / Joseph Hartzheim *Biblio-
theca Coloniensis* (Cologne 1747) 111 / T. Ilgen
'Kritische Beiträge zur rheinisch-westfälischen
Quellenkunde des Mittelalters V' *Westdeutsche
Zeitschrift für Geschichte und Kunst* 30 (1911)
141–296 esp 232, 238

HANSGEORG MOLITOR

Antoine de la MARCK c 1495–August 1528
Antoine was the third or fourth son of Robert
(II) de la *Marck and thus a nephew of Erard de
la *Marck, prince-bishop of Liège (Ep 748). At
an early age he began to accumulate ecclesiastical preferment, being from 1506 prior of
Saint-Marcel near Chalon-sur-Saône, from
1507 abbot of Beaulieu-en-Argonne, south-
west of Verdun, from 1508 canon of St Lambert,
Liège, and subsequently archdeacon of Brabant (1515–21), archdeacon of Chartres from
1515, and prior of Saint-Séverin-en-Condroz
by 1520.

Antoine's life was adventurous. In the wake
of the political manoeuvres of his father, he
conspired with the French against his uncle in
1521 and lost the archdeaconry of Brabant. On
20 May 1525 he fought with the army of
Lorraine that defeated the Alsatian peasant
rebels in the battle of Scherwiller near Sélestat.
In 1525 he reverted from the French camp to the
Hapsburg alliance and in 1527 undertook a
campaign into Champagne in the name of
*Charles V. French revenge came when
Claude, duke of Guise, besieged and sacked
his abbey; Antoine himself was killed, it is said,
by a man whose wife he had abducted.

With the assistance of Paschasius *Berselius,
Antoine had made moves to offer patronage to
scholars. In the spring of 1519 when all the de

la Marck family was on the side of the
Hapsburgs and Antoine enjoyed the confidence of his uncle, Erasmus dedicated to him
his *Paraphrasis in Galatas* (Ep 956). A subsequent letter to Antoine (Ep 1065) suggested
that the dedication was the result of efforts
undertaken by the prelate to secure Erasmus
preferment and that Berselius had provided
the liaison. There had been no results,
however, and after Antoine's defection to
France in February 1521 Erasmus both published the very blunt Ep 1065 and withdrew the
dedication of his paraphrase. It is therefore
unlikely that a reference to 'Verdunius' in Ep
1257 concerns Antoine.

In addition to Erasmus' paraphrase, Antoine
received in 1520 the dedication of Adrien
*Amerot's *Compendium graecae grammatices*
(Louvain: D. Martens) and in 1527 of a *Syntaxis
graeca* (Paris: G. Gourmont) by Johannes
*Guinterius of Andernach. In each case Berse-
lius is mentioned again and may have provided
the contacts.

BIBLIOGRAPHY: Allen and CWE Epp 956, 1065 /
Paul Harsin *Recueil d'études* (Liège 1970)
163–7 / R. Hoven 'Antoine de la Marck,
dédicataire d'Erasme, d'Amerot et de Gonthier
d'Andernach' *Leodium* 57 (1970) 5–17 / de
Vocht CTL IV 256 and passim / J. de Chestret de
Haneffe *Histoire de la maison de la Marck* (Liège
1898) 167–9 / *Le Journal d'un bourgeois de Paris* ed
V.-L. Bourrilly (Paris 1910) 306–7 PGB

Erard de la MARCK 31 May 1472–
16 February 1538
Erard de la Marck (de Marca) was descended
from a noble family that owned many estates
in Lorraine and adjacent regions. Being a
younger son, he was directed towards an
ecclesiastical career from childhood and began
to accumulate benefices and dignities. As he
grew up, he moved from Sedan to Cologne,
Rome, Paris, and Liège. At Cologne he
matriculated in 1485 as a student in the faculty
of arts. In 1503 his correspondence shows that
he was in Rome and had been ordained
subdeacon. His presence in the holy city
enabled him to acquire useful connections at
the papal curia. Subsequently he moved to
Paris, where he gained the support of Cardinal
Georges (I) d'*Amboise and the patronage of
the Most Christian King, who named him royal

councillor. Finally he went to Liège and took up residence among the members of the cathedral chapter so as to be able to vote, and to stand for election himself, when the episcopal see fell vacant.

He did not have to wait for long; on 30 December 1505 he was elected prince-bishop of Liège. Following his ordination as a priest and his consecration as a bishop, he was ready to take over the spiritual as well as the temporal reigns of the ecclesiastical principality which was part of the Empire. French support, which had helped to bring about his election, continued to aid his advancement until 1517; in particular, a recommendation of *Louis XII prompted the chapter of Chartres to elect him to that see on 28 June 1507. On the other hand, the cardinal's hat eluded him for a long time, and his frustrated ambition to obtain it was one of the reasons for his spectacular political coup in 1518, when he abandoned his alliance with *Francis I and turned towards the future *Charles V. The first prince-bishop of Liège to apply the rules of modern statecraft, he accomplished a considerable degree of pacification and unification. A man of taste rather than scholarly interest, he dispensed his patronage freely and built the famous episcopal palace in Liège.

In 1520 Erard lost his French see of Chartres while Charles V secured for him the archbishopric of Valencia and the abbey of St Michael's at Antwerp. Finally, on 9 August 1521, he was appointed cardinal with the title of St Chrysogonus. While it seems that he took no more interest in his Spanish see than he had formerly taken in his French one, Liège reaped the benefits of his careful administration according to the principles of Catholic reform. At this time the diocese of Liège included the entire eastern region of present-day Belgium together with large parts of the adjacent provinces of Brabant and Limburg, Luxembourg, and the Prussian Rhineland of the future. Moreover, the bishop's ecclesiastical authority reached far beyond the frontiers of his principality and extended as far as 's Hertogenbosch, Roermond, Aachen, and Louvain.

From the very beginning of his rule Erard strove to suppress the immorality of the clergy and to reform the monasteries, but his efforts

Erard de la Marck, by Jan Cornelisz Vermeyen

were delayed and hampered by countless jurisdictional conflicts with various chapters and the University of Louvain. He had no choice but to attack the exemptions claimed by the secular chapters and the privileges of nomination claimed by the university. To strengthen his stand against these bodies he took into his service the famous Girolamo *Aleandro, past rector of the University of Paris. And towards the end of his rule he was still contriving to obtain the title and powers of a papal legate, largely in order to oppose the exemptions of his clergy with greater efficacy. However, he gained no advantages and had to be content with maintaining the status quo.

In 1520 Pope *Leo X appointed Aleandro papal nuncio to the imperial court. When he arrived in the Netherlands, carrying in his luggage the bull *Exsurge Domine*, his old friend Erard introduced him to the emperor. He also collaborated with Aleandro on a first edict ordering the seizure and burning of Lutheran books. This earliest version is lost today, but on 17 October 1520 Erard promulgated at Liège another edict to this effect, which is extant and as the earliest of its kind remains a document of great importance. In 1521 the prince-bishop participated actively in the sessions of the diet of Worms. In 1523 he tried unsuccessfully to have the famous imperial edict of Worms proclaimed in his diocese. Two years later the first heretic was imprisoned at Liège and apparently put to death. In 1526 Erard promulgated a new mandate concerning above all the causes of heresy and attempting to check the disastrous effects of clerical misconduct and non-residence, points on which he invoked the example of the Regensburg reform issued by the papal legate Lorenzo *Campeggi (7 July 1524). In 1527 the edict of Worms was finally proclaimed at Liège, and in the following year a priest was burnt at the stake. Other executions followed throughout the diocese; the total number for the reign of Erard is about fifty, many of them Anabaptists. The decisive battle for Catholic orthodoxy, however, was not to take place until the second half of the century and was to end with the progressive elimination of Protestantism in the territory of Liège.

Erard's efforts to check the reformers, though efficient and systematic to a point, were on occasion tainted by cruelty and, above all, they remained uneven. More impressive for their principles than for their results, they achieved as much success as could be expected in a diocese so beset by painful conflicts and of a prelate whose genuine zeal was counterbalanced by ambition and greed for honours.

Of the correspondence between Erard and Erasmus, only a few letters have been preserved: eight by Erasmus and a single one by Erard. All but the first were published by Erasmus. For all his travelling, Erasmus seems to have visited Liège only once. On his journey from Louvain to Basel in 1514 he went via Liège, intending to visit his friend Andreas of *Hoogstraten, canon of St Denis. Hoogstraten, who was away at the time, later implored him to come back, particularly since Erasmus' old friend Aleandro was in town as chancellor to the prince-bishop (Ep 381). But for unknown reasons Erasmus waited until 1517 before bringing himself to Erard's attention. By then Aleandro had left Liège, and we know nothing of Hoogstraten's having brought about a connection, as he might well have done. Rather it was the Benedictine

Paschasius *Berselius whom Erasmus asked to hand a letter and a book to the prince-bishop (Epp 738, 746). Erasmus' first preserved letter to Erard (Ep 738) dated from December 1517 and adroitly mentioned as common friends Aleandro and Etienne *Poncher, bishop of Paris. Erard's prompt reply (Ep 746), generous and carefully couched in rhetorical language, brought an invitation to Liège. Erasmus answered at once that he hoped to visit Erard before Lent, signing himself 'Your Highness' most devoted servant' (Ep 757). He mentioned the flattering invitation freely, but it does not seem that he went to Liège. The summer of 1518 was spent at Basel, and on his return a grave illness forced Erasmus to travel to Louvain by the most direct route (Epp 867, 893). While Erard showed disappointment, Erasmus was quick to sing his praises (Epp 884, 894), and before long they actually got together for a few days. Erasmus recalled this meeting in enthusiastic terms when dedicating to Erard his *Paraphrasis in Corinthios* (Ep 916, 5 February 1519) with a remarkable letter anticipating the style of *Epistola de esu carnium*. A copy of the printed paraphrases and an accompanying letter of 19 February were taken to Liège by Pieter *Gillis (Ep 918). Thereafter Erasmus met the prince-bishop again in March and May of 1519 (Epp 927, 952, 978, 1001).

The cordiality of their relations was suddenly threatened as a result of a line in Erasmus' letter to *Luther of 30 May 1519: 'There are some here too, the bishop of Liège among them, who favour your views' (Ep 980). In July this compromising letter was unfortunately published at Leipzig, provoking Erard's wrath. The trouble started early in October when Jacob of *Hoogstraten, the inquisitor of Cologne, was on a visit to Louvain and drew attention to Erasmus' statement. The faculty of theology, justifiably concerned, sent a delegation to Erard, who hastened to reassure the theologians of his orthodoxy. Erard happened to be in Louvain, and between 11 and 17 October Erasmus had an audience with him (Ep 1030). By the end of the month he wrote to Erard to apologize for his failure to bid him farewell, without even so much as hinting at the affair (Ep 1038). Either during the interview at Louvain or at some other time, perhaps by letter, Erasmus must have succeeded in appeasing the prince-bishop. In the same month he saw to it that Johann *Froben reprinted the embarrassing letter at Basel, suppressing Erard's name. The prince-bishop appears to have been satisfied with this subterfuge, or at least this is what Erasmus later wrote to Luther (Ep 1127A); at any rate their reconciliation was complete. In September Erasmus wrote to Pope *Leo x to exonerate the prince-bishop (Ep 1143), and the following month he addressed to Erard a letter recommending a friend (Ep 1151). The case was closed.

Erasmus' relations with Erard took a new turn for the worse from 1521, when the bishop had finally attained his cardinalate and Erasmus had left Louvain for Basel. Erasmus complained of Erard being influenced by Aleandro, now supposedly his enemy (Epp 1268, 1482, 1496). Despite the assurances of *Vives and *Morillon that Erard was always ready to defend Erasmus (Epp 1281, 1287), it is clear that they were growing suspicious of one another. This mistrust found striking expression in Erasmus' long letter to *Botzheim printed in April 1523. There Erard could have read that he had promised the world to Erasmus and given him nothing (Allen I 43–4); it is easy to imagine the extent of Erard's resentment. With the passing of years the mutual distrust became somewhat blunted as the two men came to realize that they shared their opposition to Luther as well as their concern for the Catholic reform. In 1527 Erasmus paid homage to Erard in the preface of the fourth edition of his New Testament, calling the prince-bishop perceptive in accordance with his prominence ('cordatissimus simulque oculatissimus'). In 1528 and 1530 he addressed two more letters to Erard, treating him as a patron rather than a friend (Epp 2054, 2382); no more is heard after that. In August 1530 when Theodoricus *Hezius ordered Erasmus' books confiscated from the Liège school of the Brethren of the Common Life, the prince-bishop was at Augsburg; more than likely he had nothing to do with the incident (Epp 2369, 2566). Erasmus had apparently said in a letter that he had no wish to live in Erard's neighbourhood (Ep 2360), but on 7 September he did write to him, soliciting his support for the Collegium Trilingue in Louvain and send-

ing him a copy of the *Epistola ad fratres Inferoris Germaniae* (Ep 2382). Perhaps it was the zeal of the Dominican Eustachius van der *Rivieren that finally brought Erasmus and Erard to the parting of the ways. He dedicated to Erard his sharp attack on Erasmus, *Apologia pro pietate* (Antwerp: W. Vorsterman 1531; Ep 2522), and despite the bishop's assurances that he had nothing to do with the book (Ep 2629), Erasmus remained severely critical of him (Epp 2590, 2906, 2961).

Among several portraits of Erard, the finest is the work of Jan Cornelisz. Vermeyen. He is also represented in one of the large stained-glass windows which he gave to the abbey of Herkenrode (Hasselt) and which are now in the cathedral of Lichfield, Staffordshire.

BIBLIOGRAPHY: Allen and CWE Ep 738 / L.-E. Halkin in DHGE XV 663–6 / L.-E. Halkin *Le Cardinal de la Marck, prince-évêque de Liège* (Paris 1930) / E. Buchin *Le Règne d'Erard de la Marck* (Paris 1931) / P. Harsin *Etudes critiques sur l'histoire de la principauté de Liège* (Liège 1955–7) II / J. Hoyoux 'Les relations entre Erasme et Erard de la Marck' in *Chronique archéologique du Pays de Liège* 36 (Liège 1945) 7–22 / A. Van Hove *Etude sur les conflits de juridiction dans le diocèse de Liège à l'époque d'Erard de la Marck* (Louvain 1900) / L.-E. Halkin *Les Conflits de juridiction entre Erard de la Marck et le chapitre cathédral de Chartres* (Paris 1933) / H. de Jongh *L'Ancienne Faculté de théologie de Louvain* (Louvain 1911) / de Vocht CTL II 276, 283, III 91–93 / K. Blockx *De veroordeling vam Maarten Luther te Leuven in 1519* (Brussels 1958) / J. Paquier *Jérôme Aléandre et la principauté de Liège* (Paris 1896) / J. Puraye *La Renaissance des études au pays de Liège au XVIe siècle* (Liège 1949) / S. Collon-Gevaert *Erard de la Marck et le palais des princes-évêques à Liège* (Liège 1975)   LÉON-E. HALKIN

Philippe de la MARCK d 1545
Philippe, a son of Robert II de la *Marck, was clearly present at a family gathering in the castle of Huy when his uncle, Erard de la *Marck, prince-bishop of Liège, was given a copy of Erasmus' *Paraphrasis in Romanos* (Ep 748) by Paschasius *Berselius. The following year Erard designated Philippe his eventual successor and subsequently named him archdeacon of Valence. On 16 February 1527 Philippe was installed as canon of St Lam-

Robert III de la Marck

bert's, Liège. In 1530 he became archdeacon of Hesbaye and prior of Saint-Séverin-en-Condroz. He was also canon of St Servasius', Maestricht, but failed to obtain the prince-bishopric. He died in the ancestral castle of Givonne, near Sedan, shortly after having made his will, which was dated 21 July 1545 and is conserved in Liège, Archives de l'Etat, MSS Cathédrale de Saint-Lambert, Secrétariat, Reg 268, f 113–14.

Philippe's elder brother, Robert III, sieur de Florange and from 1526 maréchal de France, was probably not present at the family gathering in Huy since he was educated at Blois and spent his entire life in the service of the French crown.

BIBLIOGRAPHY: Allen and CWE Ep 748 / U. Berlière et al *Monasticon belge* (Maredsous-Liège 1890–) II 128   FRANZ BIERLAIRE

Philippine de la MARCK *See Robert (II) de la MARCK*

Robert II de la MARCK d 1536
The elder brother of Cardinal Erard de la *Marck, Robert inherited the lordships of

Sedan, Florange, and Saulcy on the death of his father in 1487. As head of a powerful clan, he came to spearhead the opposition against the prince-bishop of Liège, Jean de Hornes, and on 2 November 1490 he was elected 'capitaine et mambour de la Cité' of Liège. As councillor and chamberlain of the king of France, he fought in the Italian wars on the side of *Louis XII, but in 1517 broke with Louis' successor, *Francis I. In the secret treaty of St Truiden (27 April 1518) he committed himself to supporting the future *Charles V, but in 1521 he reverted to the French alliance. In a dedicatory preface addressed to Robert's son, Antoine de la *Marck (Ep 956), Erasmus praised the martial skills of that unruly soldier, who continued to practise them right to his death.

Robert II was married to Catherine de *Croy. They had eight children, three of whom were present with their parents at a family gathering in the castle of Huy at the end of 1518 (Ep 748). These were Philippe and Antoine de la *Marck and a daughter, Phillippine (d 1537), described in 1518 as 'a maiden already of marriageable age, and in her looks the picture of Diana' (Ep 748). She became a lady-in-waiting to the regent *Margaret of Austria and married Reinout van Brederode.

BIBLIOGRAPHY: Allen and CWE Ep 748 / BNB XIII 542–7 / J. de Chestret de Haneffe *Histoire de la maison de la Marck* (Liège 1898) 152–62, 169 / Paul Harsin *Etudes critiques sur l'histoire de la principauté de Liège* (Liège 1955–7) I and II passim / P. Congar et al *Sedan et le pays sedanais* (Paris 1969) 129–47   FRANZ BIERLAIRE

Robert III de la MARCK *See Philippe de la MARCK*

MARCUS (Ep 2288 of 23 March 1530)
Marcus has not been identified. He had met Erasmus in Freiburg and was expected to meet Karel *Uutenhove in Padua, giving him Erasmus' letter as well as further information by word of mouth.

MARGARET of Angoulême queen of Navarre, 11 April 1492–21 December 1549
Margaret was the daughter of Louise of *Savoy and Charles, duke of Angoulême. Her childhood was overshadowed by the birth of her

brother, the future *Francis I (1494), and the
death of her father (1498). Louise of Savoy
based her hopes on the possibility that the
young duke of Angoulême might succeed
*Louis XII on the throne. For years the fate of
the family depended on whether or not Louis
XII produced a male heir. While Francis
received most of the attention, Margaret was
given an extraordinary education through the
efforts of her tutors, François *Du Moulin de
Rochefort and Robert Hurault. In 1509 she
married Charles, duke of Alençon. Margaret
apparently loved her husband dutifully but
remained childless until his death in 1525. Her
real concern lay with her brother, who on 1
January 1515 ascended the throne as Francis I.
Together with her brother and mother,
Margaret constituted a kind of royal trinity.
She extended the protection of the court to
writers, poets, and humanists. Already
strongly attracted to mysticism, she began in
1521 to patronize the Meaux reformers. The
bishop of Meaux, Guillaume (II) *Briçonnet,
opened her eyes to the evangelically based
mysticism of *Lefèvre d'Etaples. At the end of
1524, following the death of Queen *Claude
and her daughter Charlotte, she wrote the
Dialogue en forme de vision nocturne (Alençon: S.
Du Bois 1533). In 1525 she travelled to Madrid
to negotiate the release of her brother, who
had been captured at the battle of Pavia. In
1527 she married Henri d'Albret, king of
Navarre, a prince younger than herself whom
she loved passionately but who did not return
her affection. Only one of their children,
Jeanne d'Albret, survived infancy.

Following the death of Louise of Savoy in
1531, Margaret's influence at court gradually
declined. In 1533 Francis had to intervene to
protect her from persecution by the Paris
theologians (Ep 2961) following the publication of her Miroir de l'âme pecheresse (Alençon:
S. Du Bois 1531). After the placards affair
(1534) Margaret retired to her estates at Nérac,
in Béarn, surrounding herself with poets,
reformers, and men of letters. Her final break
with Francis I came over the marriage of her
daughter. Margaret and Henri were determined that Jeanne should marry Philip of
Spain, but Francis forced his niece to marry
William V, duke of *Cleves (1541).

Following this conflict Margaret rarely left

Margaret of Angoulême

her estates. It is in this final period that she
composed the Héptameron (Paris 1559) and the
Marguerites de la Marguerite (Lyon: J. de
Tournes 1547). Her religious opinions reflect
the evangelism of Meaux and later the influence of *Luther. She became the chief defender
at court of evangelicals like Marot, *Berquin,
and *Roussel and promoted a rapprochement
between France and the German Protestants.
However, her religious views, while heterodox, remained eclectic and individualistic.
Towards the close of her life she retired into a
quietistic evangelism that led to a break with
Calvin (1545). She died at Odos, near Tarbes in
Béarn.

As far as we know, Erasmus wrote two
letters to Margaret. The first, dated 28 September 1525 (Ep 1615; cf Ep 1599), relates to the
time when the trusted Hilarius *Bertholf had
left his household to enter Margaret's service.
It coincided with her journey to Madrid to the
side of her brother. While taking note of his
loyalty to the Emperor *Charles V, Erasmus
professed his love for the king of France. In
particular, having heard of Margaret's virtue
and piety, he asked for her friendship.

Margaret of Austria, by Berend van Orley

Margaret failed to respond to his overture. A second overture two years later (Ep 1854) likewise failed to produce a reaction other than a greeting (Ep 2213). Margaret did not feel the same admiration for Erasmus as he did for her. Already in the *Dialogue en forme de vision nocturne* she rejected Erasmus' conception of free will and in particular what she believed to be his intellectual religion: 'Laissez parler ceux qui se cuident sages.' Echoing the idea of Lefèvre d'Etaples she stressed the need to experience grace and the love of God. Margaret had little interest in humanistic learning for its own sake. Indeed, she was distrustful of the kind of critical humanistic learning practised by Erasmus, especially as it touched spiritual matters. Reflecting a viewpoint common to those associated with Lefèvre, she looked upon Erasmus as a proud and overly rational scholar whose teaching could undermine rather than illuminate religion.

For his part, Erasmus continued to receive news about Margaret (Epp 1884, 2168) and in 1528 sent her his compliments through Pierre *Toussain (Ep 2042).

BIBLIOGRAPHY: Allen Ep 1615 / Pierre Jourda *Marguerite d'Angoulême, duchesse d'Alençon, reine de Navarre (1492–1549)* (Paris 1930) / Lucien Febvre *Amour sacré, amour profane: autour de l'Heptaméron* (Paris 1944, repr 1971) / Abel LeFranc *Les Idées religieuses de Marguerite de Navarre* (Paris 1898) / Henry Heller 'Marguerite of Navarre and the reformers of Meaux' BHR 33 (1971) 271–310 / Jules Gelernt *World of Many Loves: The Héptameron of Marguerite of Navarre* (Chapel Hill 1966) / Guillaume Briçonnet and Margaret of Angoulême *Correspondance* ed C. Martineau, M. Veissière, and H. Heller (Geneva 1975–)   HENRY HELLER

MARGARET of Austria 10 January 1480–1 December 1530

Margaret, the daughter of the future Emperor *Maximilian and Mary of Burgundy, came to be recognized as one of the most astute sixteenth-century governors of Europe. Betrothed as a child to the Dauphin, the future *Charles VIII, she grew up in France amid the niceties of royal tradition. When repudiated by Charles, who moved to protect the vital interests of France by his marriage with Anne of Brittany, Margaret was again a pawn in political negotiations, first (1497) as wife to Juan, the son of *Isabella of Castile and *Ferdinand II of Aragon and heir to the Spanish thrones, and then after his death as wife to Philibert II, duke of *Savoy (1501). Three years later, in her second widowhood, she simply refused to re-enter the politics of marriage. Her talents as a bargainer were nevertheless utilized in her appointment as regent of the Netherlands by her father, and later (1517) by her nephew, the future *Charles V. Throughout her regency she exerted her efforts generally in favour of the English, at the same time taxing the Netherlands provinces heavily to support Charles and his continental campaigns. She drew the admiration of diplomats as a skilful mediator in disputation, as at Cambrai in 1508 when she represented Maximilian, or again at Cambrai in 1529 as Charles' delegate to the 'Ladies' Peace' negotiated with Louise of *Savoy, the mother of *Francis I (Ep 2167). In her singlemindedness she laboured incessantly for the aggrandizement of the house of Hapsburg. As godmother to four children of *Joanna of Spain and her brother, Philip the Handsome of *Burgundy, Archduchess Margaret reared the heirs of Europe effectively to the royal offices they were to fill in the future as emperor (Charles), queen of Portugal and of France (*Eleanor), queen of Hungary (*Mary), and queen of Denmark (*Isabella). She conducted all her affairs from her residence in Mechelen, which she offered as a centre for the new learning, with her collections of books and manuscripts and her patronage of literature and the arts. Her support of the northern humanists through stipends and pensions could stretch even to the point of a hardly subtle bribery, as in her efforts to persuade Erasmus to return to Brabant. Her political contemporaries acknowledged without reference to her sex her shrewdness as an administrator, her energy in the causes she favoured, and her fierceness in those she rejected, such as that of the Lutheran Reformation.

As early as 1504 Erasmus recognized Margaret as an important political figure whom he honoured by a reference to her first marriage in his poem in praise of Philip of Burgundy (Reedijk poem 78), as well as by two references to her as duchess of Savoy in his *Panegyricus ad Philippum* (ASD IV-1, 30, 46). Ten years later, in the preface to his first edition of the New Testament (Ep 373, 1515), he took the opportunity to thank her for permission to use, among other manuscripts, the 'Aureus Codex,' an eleventh-century Latin manuscript of the Gospels that had originally belonged to the library of *Matthias Corvinus and had been brought to the ducal library at Mechelen through Margaret's influence; the use of this valuable manuscript had obviously impressed him, as a much later reference in his *Apologia adversus Petrum Sutorem* shows (LB IX 766E). In 1514 he showed some interest in a rumour concerning plans for a possible third marriage for her (Ep 287), but the sentence in question was quickly removed from published versions of that letter. In later years he was careful not to mention her opposition to some of the dynastic plans for the future Charles V (CWE Ep 917 introduction) but noted that she conferred with Erard de la *Marck (Ep 1001) prior to his departure for the imperial election.

The bulk of Erasmus' correspondence with members of Margaret's court falls between 1522 and 1527 and concerns Erasmus' pension

which he no longer received after he had left Louvain. Referring to a letter from Charles V to his aunt (Ep 1380), Erasmus hoped that payments would continue in view of his merits as a scholar even if he did not return to the Low Countries. Meanwhile, however, Margaret had realized what an asset Erasmus' return would be for her in her endeavours to stop the spread of the Reformation. In addition to his former pension she offered considerably increased support (Epp 1408, 1416, 1431, 1553, 1585). Erasmus, however, had no intention of complying with her wishes, giving as a reason the hostility of some theologians in the Low Countries, especially Nicolaas *Baechem (Epp 1417, 1418, 1422). In 1524 he asked Archduke *Ferdinand to intervene with Margaret in order to put a stop to Baechem's hostility (Ep 1515). Although this was done (Epp 1553, 1581), he decided not to return, even if it meant losing all hope that the payments would be resumed (Ep 1871). Erasmus continued to refer to the pension in subsequent letters (Epp 2192, 2613, 2792).

BIBLIOGRAPHY: Allen Ep 287 / L.M.G. Kooperberg in NNBW VIII 1104–25 / ADB XX 323–4 / Léopold Godenne *Malines jadis et aujourd'hui* (Mechelen 1908) / K. Brandi *Kaiser Karl V.* new ed (Darmstadt 1959–67) I 37–44, 265–6, II 73–9, and passim / Jane de Iongh *Margaret of Austria* trans M.D. Herter Norton (London 1954) / Max Bruchet *Marguerite d'Autriche* (Lille 1927)

ALICE TOBRINER & IG

Lady MARGARET Beaufort *See Margaret BEAUFORT*

MARGARET of Parma June/July 1522– 18 January 1586
Margaret, *Charles V's natural daughter, received the same affection from her imperial father as his other children. Her mother, Johanna van der Gheynst, had attracted the conqueror of Tournai and Milan after his return to Brussels in 1522. When the child was born *Margaret of Austria, then regent of the Netherlands, brought her namesake under the influence of the household at Mechelen. Like the girls of all royal families of the period, the child became a pawn in negotiations for imperial political power. Betrothed to Alessan-

Margaret of Parma, by Alonso Sanchéz Coello

dro de' *Medici as a child in 1529 (Ep 2753), she was married in June 1536. When Alessandro died six months later, the emperor ignored the suit of Cosimo de' Medici, the new duke of Florence, and gave her in 1538 to Ottavio Farnese, the grandson of *Paul III, whom she did not love and in whose household she apparently played the spy for her father. In time, she was appointed by her half-brother, Philip II of Spain, to the regency of the Netherlands (1559–67) assuming the same role of governance as her dynamic godmother, Margaret of Austria, but under circumstances so difficult that, notwithstanding her courage, devotion, and independence of mind, all her efforts were doomed to end in frustration. She was the mother of Alessandro Farnese (1545–92), duke of Parma and regent of the Netherlands from 1578 until his death.

BIBLIOGRAPHY: Allen Ep 2753 / J.R. Romein in NNBW X 545–51 / ADB XX 324–8 / K. Brandi *Kaiser Karl v.* new ed (Darmstadt 1959–67) I 136, II 335, and passim / F. Rachfahl *Margaretha von Parma, Statthalterin der Niederlande* (Munich 1898)   ALICE TOBRINER

MARGARET Tudor queen of Scotland, 29 November 1489–18 October 1541
Margaret was the second child and elder daughter of *Henry VII and *Elizabeth of York, daughter of Edward IV, and the favourite grandchild of Lady Margaret *Beaufort. Her marital potential was of great political importance, and as early as 1495 negotiations were begun for her marriage to *James IV of Scotland in order to deter him from supporting the pretender Perkin Warbeck. This plan failed, but the scheme was revived two years later. Protracted dealings, involving a papal dispensation, were finally successful in January 1502, when a peace treaty was signed and the couple were married by proxy. In July 1503 (by which time she had become second in line to the English throne by the death of her elder brother, *Arthur) Margaret left for Scotland, where she was received with great ceremony and married in Edinburgh on 8 August. Her coronation took place in the following March. Two sons died in infancy, but in 1512 the future *James v was born. Margaret's relations with her husband were at first cordial but became progressively soured by the king's unfaithfulness and the worsening of Anglo-Scottish relations, exacerbated by the English refusal to transmit the queen's legacy from Prince Arthur. War broke out in September 1513 and James IV was killed in the battle of Flodden. Margaret became regent for her infant son and in August 1514 married Archibald Douglas, earl of Angus – a union which alienated a large section of the Scots nobility and strengthened the pro-French party. During the remaining twenty-seven years of her life Margaret was deeply involved in constant political tussles, leaning on the support of her brother, *Henry VIII, whose robust but fickle character she in many ways shared. Her marriage with Angus produced a daughter (to become the mother of Henry Stewart, Lord Darnley, the second husband of James v's daughter, Mary Queen of Scots) but was dissolved in 1527; the queen then married Henry Stewart, created Lord Methven, who survived her.

Margaret's education was interrupted by her early marriage, but it is said that she could write an 'evil hand' and play the clavichord and the lute. The court of James IV was notable for its cultural tone, and the queen was a patron of the poet William Dunbar. Erasmus, who had been introduced to the children of Henry VII in 1499 (Allen I 6; Reedijk poem 45) helped in the education of her illegitimate stepson, Alexander *Stewart, archbishop of St Andrews, and in *Adagia* II v 1 praised the queen's beauty, prudence, and devotion to her husband.

There is a portrait of the queen at Hampton Court Palace.

BIBLIOGRAPHY: Allen I 6 / DNB XII 1035–42 / J.J. Scarisbrick *Henry VIII* (London 1968) 57 and passim / I.A. Taylor *The Life of James IV* (London 1913) 122 and passim / H.W. Chapman *The Sisters of Henry VIII* (London 1969) / N.L. Harvey *The Rose and the Thorn* (New York 1975)
C.S. KNIGHTON

MARGARETA, mother of Erasmus *See* ERASMUS' *family*

MARGARETA (ASD V-1 78–9) *See* THEODORICUS *of Haarlem*

MARGARETA, Erasmus' housekeeper *See Margarete* BÜSSLIN

MARGARETA Honora *See Margareta* HEYEN

MARGUERITE de Navarre *See* MARGARET *of Angoulême, queen of Navarre*

MARIA *See* MARY

Johannes MARIA *See* JOHANNES MARIA *Armoricus*

MARIANUS Siculus *See Mariano* ACCARDO

Augustinus MARIUS of Ulm, 1485– 25 November 1543
Marius was born at Lehr, near Ulm, the son of a farmer, Johann Mayer (or Mair), and his wife, Margarethe Haiferlin. In 1502 he entered the Wengen house of the canons regular of St Augustine at Ulm. In the fall of 1513 he registered at the University of Vienna, studying there until the summer of 1519, when he went to Padua. A year later he had returned,

Margaret Tudor, queen of Scotland

having obtained a theological doctorate, and became a member of the Vienna faculty of theology. In the fall of 1521 he moved to Regensburg as preacher at the cathedral and on 25 February 1522 he was appointed suffragan to the bishop of Freising, Philip, count *Palatine, moving to Freising only in 1523. In the fall of 1525 the Basel chapter was looking for a cathedral preacher to replace Tilmann *Limperger, who had cast in his lot with the reformers. Johannes *Fabri, who was a non-resident canon and followed the events at Basel very closely, suggested Marius. In December 1525 the latter was in Basel to discuss the position. Returning to Freising he accepted, and the appointment was confirmed on 3 April 1526 at an annual salary of two hundred and fifty florins. With the accession of a new bishop he was also nominated suffragan bishop of Basel in March 1527.

Marius' activities at Basel were dominated by the religious conflict. *Oecolampadius received him with friendly overtures, but Marius left no doubt about his opposition to the innovators and soon emerged as a theologically competent and highly polemical spokesman for the Roman party. In 1527, when the city council requested opinions for and against the mass, Marius and Oecolampadius exchanged a series of polemical tracts in German. Another pamphlet, directed against the Anabaptist Karl Brennwald in 1527, was published in 1530; finally his Latin sermons of December 1528 on the first Epistle of John remain unpublished (Ep 2615). When the reformers triumphed Marius left Basel (Ep 2722) for Freiburg and on 3 March 1529 conveyed to Bonifacius *Amerbach a proposal by Udalricus *Zasius that Amerbach might replace the latter at the University of Freiburg. On 8 May the Würzburg chapter confirmed Marius' appointment as cathedral preacher at a salary of three hundred florins, to be paid in part by the bishop, and on 17 July he took an oath of office. When he left Freiburg for Würzburg, he obtained from Erasmus a letter to Bishop Konrad von *Thüngen and another to Daniel *Stiebar (Epp 2161, 2164). There is repeated praise for Marius in subsequent letters exchanged between Erasmus and Thüngen (Epp 2303, 2314, 2361). With Ep 2321 (cf Ep 2615) Erasmus sent Marius some copies of his public letter against some Franciscans (Ep 2275). Passages in Epp 2029, 2722, and the *Epistola ad fratres Inferioris Germaniae* (ASD IX-1 383–4) suggest that relations between Marius and Erasmus were close at times. In a letter to Thomas *More, however, Erasmus charged that two monks, one the cathedral preacher and the other a Dominican, had been largely responsible for stirring up the people of Basel and thus preventing a return to moderation (Ep 2211). This was challenged by the Dominican Ambrosius *Pelargus, for good reason convinced that the two monks were Marius and himself (Epp 2721–3).

In 1530 Marius attended the diet of Augsburg with Bishop von Thüngen, Stiebar, and Bartholomaeus of *Usingen. In 1535 he was briefly considered for a joint appointment as suffragan in the dioceses of Strasbourg and Basel. In 1536 he was made suffragan bishop of Würzburg, mostly, it seems, to put an end to his preaching in the cathedral, which had become an embarrassment. He died at Würzburg. In addition to Stiebar, Christoph von *Stadion (Epp 2029, 2064), Henricus *Gla-

reanus, *Beatus Rhenanus, and Bonifacius *Amerbach were common friends of Marius and Erasmus.

BIBLIOGRAPHY: J. Birkner *Augustinus Marius* (Münster i.w. 1930) / J. Bücking 'Die Basler Weihbischöfe des 16. Jahrhunderts' *Zeitschrift für schweizerische Kirchengeschichte* 63 (1969) 67–91 esp 73–8 / *Helvetia sacra* ed A. Bruckner (Bern 1972–) I-1 230 / *Matrikel Wien* II-1 404 / *Matrikel Basel* I 359 / BA *Oekolampads* II 134–9, 297–301 and passim / *Aktensammlung zur Geschichte der Basler Reformation* ed E. Dürr et al (Basel 1921–50) II 290–3, 579–611, 639–78, and passim / AK III Epp 1102, 1173, 1337, 1345, IV Epp 1727, 1746, and passim / BRE Ep 270 / Z VIII Ep 542 and passim   PGB

Claudius MARLETUS See Claude LE MARLET

Luigi MARLIANO of Milan, d 10/11 May 1521
Luigi (Aloysius) Marliano sprang from a well-known Milanese family whose members had been notable as scholars, diplomats, and ecclesiastics. In 1484 he was a member of the college of physicians of his native town; he was also appointed court physician to Duke Ludovico *Sforza and his family. After the expulsion of the Sforzas from Milan (1499–1500), if not by the time of the wedding between Bianca Maria Sforza and *Maximilian I (1494), Marliano moved north. In 1506 he was physician to Philip the Handsome, duke of *Burgundy, accompanying Philip and his wife, Queen *Joanna, on their journey to Spain. He won great respect for his treatment of Philip during his fatal illness (d 25 September 1506) and produced a medical report on his treatment and the autopsy. Although with Philip's help Marliano had recovered his property in Milan, he could not consider returning to the French-occupied city since he was well known for his opposition to France. He thus went back to the Netherlands, where he became councillor and physician to the future *Charles V. He is said to have invented Charles' device, 'plus oultre.' As the young prince was of frail health, Marliano's influence was naturally great, and when in 1511 Maximilian I wished to send him on an embassy to Italy with Matthäus *Lang, *Margaret of Austria and Charles intervened and persuaded the emperor to let Marliano return to Mechelen (Innsbruck MS).

Nothing is known of Marliano's wife, but two sons, Daniel and Jean-Antoine de Marlian, are recorded as members of the Netherlands court in 1517 and 1521. After the death of his wife, Marliano took orders around 1513. In the same year he seems to have received the provostship of Our Lady's at Bruges, while in 1514 he withdrew his application for the provostship of St Vincent's in Soignies. A close confidant of *Gattinara, according to Pietro Martire d'Anghiera, he was also on good terms with Jacopo *Bannisio, Jakob *Spiegel, and other leading advisers of Maximilian I and corresponded with Jérôme de *Busleyden and Pietro Martire d'Anghiera, who was his relative by marriage.

With Charles' coming of age (1515) and his succession to the Spanish kingdoms (1516), Marliano's influence entered its zenith. He was appointed to Charles' privy council and received the episcopal see of Tuy in Galicia (Ep 506; confirmed by *Leo x on 7 February 1517). A skilled Latinist, he gave an oration during the chapter of the Golden Fleece in 1516 and was largely in charge of Charles' diplomatic correspondence with foreign, especially the Italian, governments. In 1517 Marliano accompanied Charles to Spain; with his support he laid claim to La Magione, a rich commandery of the Teutonic Knights in Sicily. His claim was contested, and the ensuing legal proceedings may have strengthened his resolve to show himself as a firm opponent of the reformers. After Charles' return to the Netherlands in 1520 he was among those responsible for the publication of the bull Exsurge Domine. His hard line gained him the friendship of *Aleandro and the gratitude of Pope Leo x. He went with the emperor to the diet of Worms, where he supplied Aleandro with information about the proceedings. In Worms he contracted the plague and died.

From 1516 Marliano's personal acquaintance with Erasmus and the progress of their relations are reflected by Erasmus' correspondence (Ep 411). When Marliano was in Spain Erasmus repeatedly sent him greetings in his letters to Pierre *Barbier (Epp 695, 794, 803), while Marliano used that same common friend to warn Erasmus against engaging in controversies (Ep 1198). On Marliano's return Erasmus expected him to be his warm sup-

porter at court; he recommended *Hutten to the bishop and sent him the Apologia de 'In principio erat sermo' (Ep 1114). When they met at Brussels in the autumn of 1520, Erasmus was made aware of Marliano's overriding concern with the Lutheran danger (Ep 1198). During the diet of Worms, when criticism of Erasmus' religious position hardened, he endeavoured to justify himself in letters to Marliano (Ep 1195) and other members of the court. In his reply Marliano referred to his own two orations against *Luther, of which only the first and more moderate one is known today, and encouraged his friend to follow his example (Ep 1198).

Marliano's writings (see also de Vocht) include a Silva de fortuna (Bressanone: A. Britannicus May 1503); an account of Philip the Handsome's journey to Spain, addressed to Bannisio and published in Spiegel's edition of Isocrates' Ad Nicoclem (Vienna: H. Wietor and J. Singriener 1514); Oratio in comitiis Aurei Velleris ... aedita (n p, n d); and In Martinum Lutherum oratio (Rome [ie Strasbourg 1519–20?]).

BIBLIOGRAPHY: Allen Ep 411 / de Vocht Busleyden 358–61 and passim / Paul Kalkoff Der Wormser Reichstag von 1521 (Munich-Berlin 1922) 152–66 / A.J.G. Le Glay Négociations diplomatiques entre la France et l'Autriche durant les trente premières années du XVIe siècle (Paris 1845) passim / Deutsche Reichstagsakten Jüngere Reihe (Gotha-Göttingen 1893–   ) I and II passim / Pietro Martire d'Anghiera Opera (Graz 1966) 467–8, 640, and passim / Luis Fernandez de Retana Cisneros y su siglo (Madrid 1929) I 377 / Karl Brandi Kaiser Karl v. new ed (Darmstadt 1959–67) 46 and passim / Innsbruck, Tiroler Landesarchiv MSS Maximiliana Akten 17/3 f 91 verso   PETER KRENDL

Johannes MARQUARDUS (Allen Ep 2513: 728; 25 July 1531)
Johannes Marquardus is mentioned by Agostino *Steuco among other German intellectuals whose acquaintance he had made, presumably in Italy. Marquardus has not been identified. The name is frequent among both noble and burgher families in many regions of Germany (cf P.S. Allen's note), and bearers of the name Johann Margward, or similar, matriculated in 1510 at Heidelberg and in 1512 at Tübingen

(*Matrikel Heidelberg* I 487, *Matrikel Tübingen* I 193). PGB

Antonius MARQUES *See Antoine de* METTENEYE

Pietro MARSO of Cese, 1442–1512

The Italian humanist Pietro Marso was born at Cese, near Avezzano. Early in life he took holy orders and then went to Rome, where he became one of the students of Johannes *Argyropoulos and of Julius *Pomponius Laetus. His association with the Roman Academy brought him a brief imprisonment in 1468, but it also involved friendships of long standing with Pomponius, as well as with Bartolomeo *Platina and Argyropoulos. On Pomponius' recommendation, Marso became tutor to Cristoforo Piccolomini, the nephew of Cardinal Iacopo Ammanati, in 1472. Some time between 1472 and 1481 he was also appointed a teacher of rhetoric at the University of Rome. His most famous student was Paolo *Cortese. Marso died in Rome.

During his long tenure at the Studio of Rome Marso produced numerous textual commentaries, notably on Cicero's *De officiis* (Venice: Baptista de Tortis 1481) and *De senectute* (Venice: O. Scoto 1494), and on Silius Italicus (Venice: Baptista de Tortis 1483). In addition, Marso took responsibility for posthumously editing Argyropoulos' translation of Aristotle's *Nicomachean Ethics* (Rome: E. Silber 1492) and delivered several orations, including one at the funeral of Pomponius Laetus.

Erasmus met Marso in Rome when the latter was already near seventy, although he thought he was almost eighty. He admired Marso's industriousness, but did not have a high opinion of his work, wishing that Marso had been more selective (Epp 152, 1347; ASD I-2 667).

BIBLIOGRAPHY: Allen Ep 152 / J.H. Fabricius *Bibliotheca latina mediae et infimae aetatis* ed J.D. Mansi (Florence 1858–9) V 252 / Arnaldo della Torre *Paolo Marsi da Pescina* (Rocca S. Casciano 1903) / G. Lumbroso 'Gli accademici nelle catacombe' *Archivio della R. Società Romana di storia patria* 12 (1889) 215–40 / Egmont Lee *Sixtus IV and Men of Letters* (Rome 1978) 173, 189–90, and passim EGMONT LEE

Dirk MARTENS of Aalst, d 28 May 1534

Dirk Martens (Martinus, Theodoricus Alustensis; old Dutch forms vary: Dieric, Dieryck, Martins, Mertins, etc) was the only son of Joos Martens and Johanna (?) de Proost, who also had two daughters, Johanna and Margareta. Dirk was born, perhaps in the ancestral home on Lange Zoutstraat, at Aalst, a Flemish country town between Brussels and Ghent. The family had been established in the town for several generations: the great-grandfather, Heinricke Martens, is mentioned in 1394 and 1395 in the municipal accounts. Martens was also a relative of the Coeckes of Aalst, a family of artists.

Dirk was probably born about 1446–7; the date is not recorded. Nothing is known about his youth either, but it is generally assumed that he received his first education in the local convent of the Williamite Brethren, where he was also to spend his last years and to which he bequeathed his library. The books perished in a fire on 22–3 April 1582, when the Beggars (*Geuzen*) occupied the town. There is no information as to when, how, and why Martens went to Italy and came into contact with his compatriote Girardus de Lisa (Verleyen?) of Ghent, who had settled as a teacher and occasional printer in the region of Venice, mainly at Treviso. A close scrutiny of the books printed by Girardus at Treviso in 1471 and by Martens at Aalst in 1473 led Karel Heireman to the conclusion that either Martens had learnt his craft from Girardus or both had been trained in the shop of the same Venetian printer.

By 1473 Martens had returned to Aalst and established a press, printing works by *Denis the Carthusian, Pseudo-Augustine, and Aeneas Sylvius (Pope *Pius II). From late in 1473 to May 1474 Martens worked in partnership with John of Westphalia, a recent arrival from Cologne, whom he may have met in Venice. In the second half of 1474 Martens was again the sole printer at Aalst. Then all trace of him vanishes until 1486. There are indications that he went to Spain, and some scholars are inclined to identify him with a Teodorico Aleman who obtained a royal privilege for the selling of books (Seville, 25 December 1477) and seems to have been at Murcia in 1478.

In 1486, or 1487 at the very latest, Martens was again established as a printer at Aalst, producing mainly devotional and scholastic books until 1492. In 1491 his edition of Alexander de Villa Dei's *Doctrinale* (Heireman 18) is the first book printed in the Netherlands which includes Greek characters. During this period Martens may already have had some relations with the court at Brussels. In 1493 he moved to Antwerp and settled in the Steenhouwersvest, taking over the premises and part of the equipment of Gerard *Leeu. His publications of this period (which lasted until 22 May 1497) clearly show connections with the court in Brussels, but we have no evidence to prove that he came into contact with Erasmus at or through the court.

On 15 June 1497 Martens registered at the University of Louvain (*Matricule de Louvain* III-1 156) and opened a press in Proefstraat (now Naamsestraat) in front of University Hall. There he worked for four years, but he retained his connections with Antwerp and in 1502 returned to the commercial metropolis for another decade. During these years the young Pieter *Gillis was working for him as a corrector and through his work became acquainted with Erasmus in 1504, for in Antwerp Martens printed his earliest editions of books by Erasmus: the *Lucubratiunculae* (Heireman 54) on 15 February 1503 (which may be 1504, new style) and again on 6 November 1509 (Heireman 69), the *Panegyricus* in 1504 (Heireman 57), and an edition of the *Moria* in January 1512 (Heireman 77). Generally speaking, the proportion of humanistic books among Martens' publications increased notably in this period.

In the summer of 1512 Martens transferred his business definitively to Louvain, where he published Erasmus' translations from Lucian on 14 August (Heireman 81) and *De ratione studii* on 24 September (Heireman 82). In the course of the following years Erasmus and Martens became very close friends, as may be seen not only from the over fifty books by Erasmus which Martens printed but also by the friendly services they rendered each other (Ep 637, 638). The strongest proof of Martens' friendship for Erasmus was given in September 1518, when Erasmus arrived from Basel in very bad health and, unable to stay in his college room, lay sick for several weeks in Martens'

house. The friendly printer took care of him even though two doctors had diagnosed his illness as the plague (Ep 867; Allen Ep 1061:773–9). On other occasions when Erasmus was absent from Louvain Martens' shop served as a holding address for the humanist and his friends. In Ep 852 (14 July 1518) *Dorp reported that he had lunch with Martens and Erasmus' messenger, Jacobus *Nepos, in order to hear the latest news about Erasmus.

Martens' books were vital to the diffusion of humanist studies at the time of the foundation of Louvain's Collegium Trilingue. Apart from the work of scores of Latin authors, classical as well as humanist – such as Dorp, *Vives and *More (*Utopia* 1516) – he produced the badly needed Greek and Hebrew grammars and also dictionaries (Ep 795). Sometimes, however, Erasmus did not agree with Martens' decisions, and in November 1520 he expressed disappointment at the printer's refusal to publish a work of the theologian Jan *Driedo (Ep 1163). Finally, Erasmus studiously tried to avoid commercial conflicts between his publishers at Louvain and Basel. Ep 732 is a perfect illustration of his attitude towards both Martens and *Froben.

By June 1524 Martens left his business to his son, Pieter *Martens. When the latter died in October or November of the same year, the old printer resumed his activity for another five years. Probably in 1529 he published his last book, *Clenardus' *Tabula in grammaticen hebraeam*, then returned to his native town. He retired to the Williamite convent, where he died and was buried in the church. In 1527 Erasmus had composed an epitaph for him (Ep 1899; Reedijk poem 115). This was engraved in copper and placed above the tomb. In 1784, when the convent was suppressed, Martens' tombstone was removed to St Martin's, the principal church of Aalst, where it can still be seen as renovated in 1877. No original portrait of Martens is preserved, but a fine statue was erected in 1856 in the market square of Aalst. Martens' printer's emblem was an anchor.

BIBLIOGRAPHY: Allen and CWE Ep 263 / K. Heireman in NBW VI 633–7 / Biographical information including details from manuscript sources, a carefully revised chronological list of the books printed by Martens, and a bibliography of modern studies is given in the exhibition catalogue *Dirk Martens 1473–1973* (Aalst 1973). It is based on information gathered by K. Heireman, who also compiled the list of Martens' publications

J. IJSEWIJN

Joachim MARTENS of Ghent, documented 1527–c 1540
The correspondence of Erasmus apart, very little is known about Joachim Martens (Martinius, Martianus, Joachimus Gandavus). On 15 September 1527 he matriculated at Montpellier. In the summer or early autumn of 1528 he was with Jacopo *Sadoleto at Carpentras and from there wrote to Erasmus. His letter, which is missing, is mentioned by Bonifacius *Amerbach (AK III Ep 1300) and was answered by Erasmus with Ep 2049. Perhaps as early as the autumn of 1528 Martens moved to Paris; he may well be the 'Gandavus' of whom Simon *Riquinus reported that he battled valiantly against Noël *Béda and his friends (Ep 2077). Evidently impressed by the young man, Erasmus praised him and Riquinus as medical scholars of great promise in a dedicatory preface he contributed to Georgius *Agricola's *Bermannus* (Ep 2274 of 18 February 1530). In that same year Martens maintained contacts at Paris with a fellow-countryman, the printer Gerard *Morrhy, and with the circle of Erasmians around Philippus *Montius (Ep 2311). He also published his Latin translation of Galen's *De alimentorum facultatibus* (Paris: S. de Colines 1530), dedicating it to Sadoleto. In August 1532 he visited Erasmus in Freiburg and Amerbach in Basel, expecting to be on his way to Italy (Epp 2703, 2706, 2709). But then he changed his mind and returned to his ailing mother in Ghent (Epp 2728, 2799). Some time after his return he visited Levinus *Ammonius (Ep 2817). He seems to have died around 1540.

BIBLIOGRAPHY: Allen Ep 2049 / V. Jacques in BNB XIII 908–9 / *Matricule de Montpellier* 52

MARCEL A. NAUWELAERTS & PGB

Pieter MARTENS documented 1517–24
Very little is known about Pieter, the son of Dirk *Martens, the printer. He is perhaps identical with a Pieter Martens of Antwerp who matriculated at the University of Louvain on 23 April 1517, since Antwerp was where

Dirk had lived from 1493 to 1512, although not without interruption. On 15 June 1522 Pieter set out from Louvain for Basel with a letter from Conradus *Goclenius to Erasmus (Ep 1296), and in the course of 1524 his name is found in the colophon of some books published by the Martens press in Louvain (NK 223, 229, 2168, 3426). It may be assumed that he died in October or November of that year; at any rate in his epitaph for Dirk Martens (1527), Erasmus mentioned that the printer had survived his own offspring (Reedijk poem 115).

BIBLIOGRAPHY: Allen Ep 1296 / Reedijk poem 115 / *Matricule de Louvain* III-1 557   PGB

MARTINHO of Portugal, 1490– 15 November 1547
Dom Martinho was a natural son of Dom *Afonso, then bishop of Evora, a brother of King *John III. He studied in Paris in 1520 at the same time that *Vives was there. According to a letter Vives wrote to Erasmus, Dom Martinho showed a strong dislike of the 'sophists,' with whose manner of argumentation he was familiar (Ep 1108). Indeed, Dom Martinho belongs to the group of Erasmian devotees in Portugal who were active under John III. In 1525 the king sent him as his ambassador to Rome. After the Sack of Rome in 1527 *Clement VII appointed him his legate for Portugal, but he returned to Rome in 1532 and remained there until 1535. During this period he had to negotiate with the pope about the introduction of the Inquisition in Portugal. However, Dom Martinho sided with the pope, who hesitated to grant permission for an inquisitional tribunal because of the bad impression the institution had made in Spain. Since John III was in a desperate financial situation, he may have wanted to establish the Inquisition in part because he hoped to fill his empty treasury with the money and goods confiscated from the new Christians. Dom Martinho had strong feelings against such a policy, which he considered unjust. In 1536 Dom Martinho was called back to Portugal in disgrace, and John III reproached him for having looked after his own interests rather than the king's. Despite this, Dom Martinho's ecclesiastical career continued. He was a canon of Evora and in April 1538 received the see of Funchal on

Madeira, which was raised for him to an archbishopric.

During his residence in Italy Dom Martinho had had close relations with a number of cardinals, among them such friends of Erasmus as *Sadoleto and *Bembo. Perhaps under their influence, he wanted very much to meet the great humanist and asked Rui *Fernandes, the Portuguese factor in Antwerp, about his whereabouts (Ep 1681). If it is true, as John III alleged, that he was eager to have Pope *Paul III make him a cardinal, Dom Martinho tried as hard for the same honour to be bestowed on Erasmus (Epp 3047, 3052). A letter Erasmus sent him is lost (Ep 3050).

Dom Martinho showed his liberal religious views in two remarkable instances. One was in connection with the Ethiopian question. In 1520 an embassy led by Rodrigo de Lima had reached Ethiopia. A member of the group was Father Francisco Alvares, who had brought home with him a manuscript describing his experiences in that country. We know from Damião de *Gois' dedicatory letter of his Fides ... Aethiopum (Antwerp: R. Rescius 1540) addressed to Pope Paul III that Dom Martinho assigned to Paolo Giovio the task of publishing Alvares' report in a Latin translation. Although the project did not materialize, it is noteworthy that Dom Martinho should have been interested in it because eagerness to spread knowledge about Ethiopia had considerably lessened once the country had been discovered. Before the discovery Europeans had been very excited about the prospect of finding a Christian ruler in Africa, but when contact was established great disappointment was felt because the religion of the Ethiopians was considered heretical, especially in Rome, but also in Portugal. The second incident was in connection with Nicolaus *Clenardus, whom Dom Martinho knew in Portugal. The Flemish humanist had one goal, which he pursued passionately: he wanted to learn Arabic and read the Koran in order to promote a discussion between Moslems and Christians. He was against the forced conversion practised on the Iberian Peninsula. Clenardus received support in this matter from Dom Martinho, but he mentioned in a letter to Jean *Petit that this antagonized the monks.

BIBLIOGRAPHY: CWE Ep 1108 / Allen Ep 1681 /

Jose Sebastiao da Silva Dias *A politica cultural de epoca de Joao III* 1-2 (Coimbra 1969) 106–26 / Marcel Bataillon 'Erasme et la cour de Portugal' in *Etudes sur le Portugal au temps de l'humanisme* (Coimbra 1952) 60–70, 95–7 / Elisabeth Feist Hirsch *Damião de Gois* (The Hague 1967) 156, 178–9 / *Correspondance de Nicolas Clénard* ed Alphonse Roersch (Brussels 1940–1) Epp 34, 43, 53, and passim

ELISABETH FEIST HIRSCH

MARTINIUS, MARTINUS See MARTENS

MARTINUS (Epp 19–21 of c 1489)
Martin, who is called a lay brother ('conversus') in Allen Epp 20:77, 21:42, roused Cornelis *Gerard's desire to make friends with Erasmus and for some time acted as a messenger between the two Austin canons in their monasteries of Steyn and Lopsen, near Leiden, respectively. Afterwards he cunningly played them off against each other and by creating suspicion and envy almost undid what he had brought about. He is probably identical with a Martinus mentioned in a letter from Willem *Hermans to Cornelis Gerard (Gouda MS 1323 f 18 verso), who showed himself as unreliable in his handling of manuscripts that were entrusted to him as did the lay brother, according to Ep 20.

BIBLIOGRAPHY: Allen Ep 19 / P.C. Molhuysen in *Nederlands Archief voor Kerkgeschiedenis* n s 4 (1907) 65   C.G. VAN LEIJENHORST

MARTINUS (addressed in Ep 76 of [July? 1498])
Erasmus addressed this letter to Master Martin, a physician. Since it was included in a collection made by Erasmus' friend Franciscus *Theodoricus, a monk at Steyn, near Gouda, Martinus may have been a resident of Gouda. Walvis and Bik mention three physicians who were active in Gouda about 1520–5, among them one Joachimus Martinus Gregorius. As the Latin names of Gouda and Ghent are easily confused, this may, however, be a misleading reference to the Ghent physician Joachim *Martens (Martinius). At any rate, the physician Martin addressed by Erasmus in 1498 remains to be identified.

BIBLIOGRAPHY: Allen Ep 76 / I.W[alvis] *Beschryving der stad Gouda* (Gouda-Leiden) [1713]) I

226, 249–50 / J.G.W.F. Bik *Vijf eeuwen medisch leven in een Hollandse stad* (Assen 1955) 24

C.G. VAN LEIJENHORST

MARTINUS Sydonius Transsylvanus
documented 1522–7
Martinus Sydonius Transsylvanus is documented as a colleague of Alfonso de *Valdés in the imperial chancery in 1522. He was probably still attached to the chancery in 1527 when Alonso *Fernandez used him to forward a letter to Erasmus (Ep 1904). He is not otherwise known but could conceivably be connected with Maximilianus *Transsilvanus.

    BIBLIOGRAPHY: Allen Ep 1904   PGB

Raffaele MARUFFO of Genoa, documented 1497–1535
Raffaele Maruffo, who was Genoese by birth, arrived in England in 1497, having been granted leave to act as a merchant. On 21 August 1503 Maruffo was issued a three-year grant allowing him to keep the 'change, exchange & rechange' in Calais and in England in so far as they were directed at 'foreign parts,' and in 1506 the grant was extended for an additional three years. By 1509 he was involved in the financial transactions arising from the marriage of *Henry VIII to *Catherine of Aragon, and on 24 May 1513 he was granted denization for life. Thereafter he gained increasing prominence as a banker. In 1516 Thomas *More informed Erasmus that Archbishop *Warham always availed himself of Maruffo's services for his transfers of money and occasionally employed him as his personal banker (Ep 388). A considerable number of references to Maruffo in Erasmus' correspondence during the years 1516–18 relate to the remittance of Erasmus' Aldington annuity. Having developed a banker's sense of prudence, Maruffo on one occasion provoked some blunt talk on the part of More (Ep 424), while business rivals were repeatedly prepared to undercut his rate of exchange (Epp 424, 474, 491, 499).

    Maruffo also transferred the proceeds of indulgences to the papal curia; as early as 1509 Warham used him to remit to Rome 1309 ducats towards the building of St Peter's while in 1522 he remitted the sum of £1144, the result of five years' collections towards the same purpose. A

letter of John *Allen to Cardinal *Wolsey the following year indicates that Maruffo had raised funds in Ireland. Subsequent mention of Maruffo was made in 1527, when Sir Henry Wyatt settled with him the debts of Alberto da Prato. In 1532 Sir Robert Batty secured Maruffo's services, at the cost of £32, to obtain from the pope a dispensation allowing him to hold more than one living retroactive from the previous year. In a letter of 1533 to Sir Andrew Baynton, Hugh Latimer remarked upon the zealousness with which Maruffo advocated the supremacy of the pope, predicting that such a stance would lead the banker to martyrdom. Maruffo, however, appears to have preferred to leave England, and on his return journey to Genoa he visited Erasmus in Freiburg in the spring of 1535. He brought sad news about More and John *Fisher, and apparently took with him the original of Giovanni Angelo *Odoni's Ep 3002 (Epp 3025, 3042). No more is known of Maruffo after that date.

    BIBLIOGRAPHY: Allen Ep 387 / *Calendar of the Patent Rolls ... Henry VII* (London 1916) II 112, 318, 479 / A. Schulte *Die Fugger in Rom, 1495–1523* (Leipzig 1904) I 59 / LP I 1948 (83), II 689 p 1484, III 923, 2163, IV 3121, and passim to V 1784 / *The Acts and Monuments of John Foxe* ed G. Townsend VII (London 1847) 498

MORDECHAI FEINGOLD

Michael MARULLUS Tarcaniota
of Constantinople, c 1453–10 April 1500
Michael Marullus was born in Ancona to Manilius Marullus and Eufrosina Tarcaniota, who had fled from Constantinople when it fell to the Turks in 1453. In his writings he referred to himself as being of Byzantium or Constantinople. He combined the wandering life of a soldier of fortune with the writing of Latin poetry and was one of the few Greek exiles to master the Latin idiom. Around 1470 he served against the Turks in Bessarabia and other regions near the Black Sea. He returned to Italy around 1480 and probably fought in the war of Ferrara of 1482–4. He spent a good part of the 1480s in Naples, where he befriended Giovanni *Pontano, Jacopo *Sannazaro, and other important literary figures. He found patrons among the feudal barons of the kingdom of Naples, among them Antonello Sanseverino,

and probably left Naples around 1486–7, when King Ferdinand I suppressed a conspiracy in which Sanseverino was involved. He was briefly in Rome in 1488 and 1489 but by August 1489 was in Florence, where he found a patron in Lorenzo di Pier Francesco de' Medici, a relative of Lorenzo (I) de' *Medici. At Florence he enjoyed the leisure necessary to compose the first two books of his *Epigrammata*, published without place or date at Florence between 1490 and 1493. He also engaged in a bitter controversy with Angelo *Poliziano.

In May 1494, as *Charles VIII of France prepared his expedition against the kingdom of Naples, Marullus went to Lyon to join Antonello Sanseverino and other Neapolitan exiles in Charles' entourage. Marullus did not travel south with the French army but joined it later in southern Italy after a hazardous sea voyage. He served with Sanseverino's men in the campaign for Naples but was later disillusioned by the sudden retreat of Charles VIII from Italy. He returned to Florence, where around 1497 he married Alessandra, the learned daughter of Bartolomeo *Scala. In 1497 he collected his *Epigrammata* and *Hymni naturales*, addressed to the gods of Greece and Rome, and published them in a single volume at Florence (Societas Colubris). In January 1500 he was again in arms, unsuccessfully trying to defend Forlì in the Romagna from Caesar Borgia and the French troops provided him by *Louis XII. In April he visited Raffaele *Maffei at Volterra, but shortly after his departure he was drowned while trying to ford the river Cecina.

Erasmus did not have a high opinion of Marullus' poems finding them too pagan (Ep 1479; ASD I-2 700). He much preferred Baptista *Mantuanus as a poet (Ep 385). *Beatus Rhenanus held a similar view, preferring the epigrams of Thomas *More to those of Marullus (Ep 1087).

Marullus' *Epigrammata et hymni* were printed several times in the sixteenth century. A number of other epigrams were published by Marcantonio Flaminio at Fano (G. Soncino) in 1515. His 'De principum institutione' was first edited by Belisario Aquaviva di Aragona for the *Aliquot aureoli vere libelli* (Basel: P. Perna 1578). A modern edition of his *Carmina* was prepared by Alessandro Perosa (Verona 1951).

BIBLIOGRAPHY: Allen Ep 385 / Michael Marullus Tarcaniota *Le elegie per la patria perduta ed altri suoi carmi* ed Benedetto Croce (Bari 1938) / Deno John Geanakoplos *Interaction of the 'Sibling' Byzantine and Western Cultures in the Middle Ages and Italian Renaissance (330–1600)* (New York-London 1976) 112 and passim / Francesco Tateo *L'umanesimo meridionale* (Bari 1972) 62–72, 76   TBD

Nicolaus MARVILLANUS *See Nicolas* WARY

MARY of Austria queen of Hungary and Bohemia, 17 September 1505–18 October 1558
Mary, a sister of *Charles V, was born in Brussels and spent her early childhood mostly in Mechelen, where she and her sisters, *Eleanor and *Isabella, were brought up in the care of her aunt, Archduchess *Margaret. In 1514 her grandfather, *Maximilian I, summoned her to Austria to play her part in dynastic politics. The wedding between Mary and the future *Louis II of Hungary took place on 22 July 1515 during the gathering of monarchs in Vienna, but because of the youth of both spouses the consummation was deferred. At the same time Maximilian acted as proxy for one of his grandsons in a wedding ceremony with Louis' sister Anna; eventually she would be given to *Ferdinand. This double wedding was to give weight to the Hapsburg dynasty's claims to the crowns of Bohemia and Hungary.

Mary and Anna were educated in Vienna until 1516 and in Innsbruck until 1521. It appears that her grandfather encouraged Mary's passion for hunting, while early lessons prompted her love of music, which she was later to demonstrate impressively as regent of the Netherlands.

In June 1521 Mary went to Hungary, and on 11 December she was crowned queen. Because of her youth the queen at first had little political influence, but her court, which was replete with Germans and Netherlanders, formed a power-base for the Hapsburg interests represented by the ambassador Andrea da *Borgo, who was actually accredited to her. At the beginning of 1524 the queen's position strengthened when her servants took charge of the most valuable part of her rich Hungarian endowments: the seven mining towns in

Mary of Austria

central Slovakia with the royal mining authorities in Kremnica (Körmöchbánya, Kremnitz) and in Banská Štianvnica (Selmecbánya, Schemnitz), and the country of Zvolén (Zólyom, Altsohl). These possessions gave the queen a stronger voice in the struggle of the Hungarian factions. Moreover, Andrea da Borgo was replaced by Dr Johann Schneidpöck, who saw in the queen a potential spearhead of the pro-Hapsburg forces and supported her accordingly. In a spectacular coup (1525) the queen and her helpers had the Fugger-Thurzo mining and trading interests expropriated. It is with some justification that contemporary observers rated the queen's political abilities higher than those of her ineffectual husband. Her policies, however, failed to unify the country in the face of the Turkish threat. On the eve of the battle of Mohács Hungary was weak and divided. Thus the defeat was a foregone conclusion. Mary's husband, the young king, lost his life in the battle, on 29 August 1526.

In the ensuing struggle between Ferdinand and *John Zápolyai, Mary, with her large following and rich estates, was of crucial

importance to her brother. He named her regent, and in the summer of 1527 she assisted him in securing a significant portion of the country, including Buda. Her regency ended in June 1527 and she declined to resume it the following year. Although she had left Hungary, never to return, she retained her important possessions there until 1548 and on occasion even played a political role by mediating between Ferdinand and the Hungarian nobles.

Mary rejected all plans for a new marriage – her brothers eyed such candidates as *James v of Scotland and Count Frederick, subsequently elector *Palatine – and remained childless. But in 1531, after the death of her aunt Margaret, she agreed to take the regency of the Netherlands. Two factors dominated her rule, which was to last twenty-five years: her determination to centralize the government of the provinces and her struggle with the military threats and financial burdens laid on the Netherlands by the European politics of Charles v. Under her regency the country did, in fact, move towards greater internal unity as well as towards fuller independence from the Empire and France. But there were also external problems which demanded her attention. Her brother-in-law, *Christian ii, the exiled king of Denmark, dragged her into a confrontation with Denmark and Lübeck, which, if it had not been swiftly ended, might have had disastrous economic consequences. In August 1535 she met her sister Queen Eleanor of France in Cambrai, but they found no formula to end the Franco-Spanish war, and Mary's efforts to negotiate the neutrality of the Netherlands failed as well (Epp 3037, 3049). As the wars continued Mary herself took a hand in organizing the country's defence in 1537, 1543, and 1553. But her main task was to collect huge funds to support her brother's armies. The resulting economic crisis did not, however, come to a head until the reign of Philip ii.

When the question of Charles' succession led to sharp disagreement between the emperor and his brother, Ferdinand, Mary played an important role as mediator. Charles went before the estates general and resigned the government of the Netherlands in favour of Philip (25 October 1555), and Mary also stepped down as the regent. Departing from

Flushing on 14 September 1556, she accompanied Charles and Eleanor to Spain, where she died two years later. Shortly before her death Philip wanted to appoint her co-regent of Spain in his absence and had even persuaded her to resume the regency of the Netherlands. In 1574 he had her remains transferred to the Escorial.

Even while she was in Hungary questions were raised about Mary's religious leanings. Some of her courtiers and some princes with whom she took counsel were, in fact, Lutherans. She read some of *Luther's writing, and after Mohács he dedicated to her *Vier tröstliche Psalmen an die Königin von Ungarn* (Wittenberg, 1 November 1526, Luther w xix 542–615). Moreover, two evangelical hymns are attributed to her. On several occasions her religious views caused her brothers alarm. In 1530 she requested Johann *Henckel to contact Luther through *Melanchthon and consult him on five questions, which were indicative of her religious concerns. Concerning communion, she asked if it was sufficient for a believer, if circumstances so demanded it, to partake publicly of the host alone, and if that same believer could, without public confession, take communion in both forms in the privacy of his chamber. In other words, Mary was prepared to adopt the new doctrine in her private life, but not in public. Luther answered in the negative: he did not accept the dichotomy of private religiosity and public appearance. Mary, for her part, was unwilling to sacrifice her political duty – that is her service to the cause of Hapsburg imperialism – to her religious inclinations. As regent of the Netherlands she did not oppose the measures ordered by Charles to suppress the new doctrine, but in several instances she reduced their impact.

From an early time Mary was an admirer of Erasmus. It may be that Jacobus *Piso, the tutor of Louis ii, first introduced her to Erasmus' ideas (Ep 1297 of summer 1522). Another link was Johann Henckel, Mary's court preacher from 1525 to 1531. In 1528 he told Erasmus of Mary's bent for serious study and her great interest in his paraphrases of the New Testament (Ep 2011). He prompted Erasmus to write the *Vidua christiana* (lb v 723–66) and to dedicate it to Mary (Epp 2011, 2086, 2100, 2110). Felix *Rex took copies of the work to

Ferdinand and Mary (Ep 2211), but Erasmus had to make do without a return present. The queen, who was in financial difficulties, expressed her thanks in a message written in her own hand, while Henckel sent a cup (Epp 2309, 2345, 2350). From July 1530 (Ep 2339) Mary's secretary, Nicolaus *Olahus, maintained a lively correspondence with Erasmus. When Mary became regent of the Netherlands she directed Olahus and Jean de *Carondelet to effect Erasmus' return to his native country. Erasmus himself had for some time wanted to return, but he feared new attacks by friars and theologians and worried about his income – payments of his court pension were evidently not forthcoming. Olahus tried to eliminate all obstacles (Ep 2785) and Mary issued a personal invitation in June 1533 (Ep 2820). It was taken to Freiburg by Levinus *Ammonius together with travel funds, but Erasmus' health had deteriorated so much that the journey had to be delayed. In the end he only reached Basel (Ep 3141).

BIBLIOGRAPHY: L.M.G. Kooperberg in NNBW x 551–81 / W. Maurenbrecher in ADB xx 374–8 / E. de Borchgreve in BNB xiii 673–85 / Christiaan Sepp 'De bibliotheek eener koningin' in his *Bibliographische Mededeelingen* (Leiden 1883) 110–82 / Tivadar Ortvay *Maria ii. Lajos magyar kiraly neje (1505–1558)* (Budapest 1914) / Wilhelm Stracke *Die Anfänge der Königin Maria von Ungarn* (Göttingen 1940) / Ghislaine de Boom *Marie de Hongrie* (Brussels 1956) / Jane de Iongh *Mary of Hungary* (London 1959) / Ramón Carande 'Maria de Hungaria en el mercado de Amberes' in *Karl v. Der Kaiser und seine Zeit* ed Peter Rassow and Fritz Schalk (Cologne-Graz 1960) 38–50 / Gernot Heiss 'Politik und Ratgeber der Königin Maria von Ungarn in den Jahren 1521–1531' *Mitteilungen des Instituts für Österreichische Geschichtsforschung* 82 (1974) 119–80 / Gernot Heiss 'Die ungarischen, böhmischen und österreichischen Besitzungen der Königin Maria (1505–1558) und ihre Verwaltung' *Mitteilungen des Österreichischen Staatsarchivs* 27 (1974) 61–100 and 29 (1976) 52–121 GERNOT HEISS

MARY I queen of England, 18 February 1516–17 November 1558
Mary, the only surviving child of *Henry viii's marriage with *Catherine of Aragon, was born

Mary I, queen of England, by Anthonis Mor

on 18 February 1516, as Erasmus at once learnt from Andrea *Ammonio (Ep 389). The girl was thus heiress presumptive to the throne, but it was confidently expected that she would eventually be superseded in the succession by the birth of a male heir. Her first importance was therefore as the potential bride for some European prince, and the successive spouses proposed for her reflect the shifts in English foreign policy. In 1518 she was destined to marry the dauphin as part of *Wolsey's design for European peace; subsequently *James v of Scotland and the Emperor *Charles v, to whom she was actually betrothed in 1522, were considered, as well as many lesser figures. Charles repudiated the marriage treaty in 1525, as Erasmus discovered from Erasmus *Schets in November (Ep 1647). In the following year, when a French marriage was again in prospect, Erasmus wrote to Queen Catherine holding out great expectations of her daughter's erudition (Ep 1727). In 1528 he advised the young Charles *Blount to model himself on the learned princess (Ep 2023), and the next year he praised her skill in Latin (Ep 2133). In fact Mary was probably the least intellectually

gifted of Henry viii's children. Her first tutor had been Thomas *Linacre, and Juan Luis *Vives had written *De institutione feminae christianae* (Antwerp: M. Hillen 1524) for Queen Catherine as a syllabus for her daughter's training. Mary learnt French and Latin but no Greek or Spanish. She excelled in music but otherwise, in childhood and later life, showed little enthusiasm for or patronage of humanist culture, her interests and amusements remaining those of the old aristocracy. From 1525 she had exercised nominal responsibility as princess of Wales, holding her own court at Ludlow with a household supervised by Margaret Pole, the countess of Salisbury. Her education continued there in the charge of John Fetherstone.

Meanwhile none of the proposed marriages came about; nor did the hoped-for prince. Mary's fate was inevitably involved with that of her mother, to whom she was devoted. Erasmus wrote to Bonifacius *Amerbach in January 1530 of the king's impending divorce (Ep 2256), and when this became a reality in 1533 Mary was stripped of her titles and household and declared illegitimate. In December she suffered the humiliation of being sent to attend on her three-month-old stepsister, Elizabeth, the daughter of the new queen, *Anne Boleyn. Forbidden access to her mother, Mary found consolation in her fervent Catholicism and the support of the imperial ambassador, Eustache *Chapuys. Even her marital potential was now lost, and we may probably discount a rumour passed to Erasmus in November 1533 that a French marriage was again being considered for her (Ep 2882). At first Mary followed her mother in refusing to repudiate papal jurisdiction and accept the succession of Elizabeth as enacted by Parliament in 1534. During 1535 her position was extremely dangerous, and schemes were entertained by her friends to spirit her out of the country. The deaths of both Catherine and Anne in 1536 opened the way for a sort of reconciliation between the king and his elder daughter. By the summer Mary's resistance was broken, probably in part by the ill health to which she was always subject: she submitted to the king's demands and was received at court. With the birth of Prince Edward in 1537 Mary ceased to be a focal point for conservative opposition, and for the remaining years of her father's reign she was accepted into the royal family, though secretly disapproving of the progress of the Reformation, in particular of Henry's last wife, Catherine Parr, with whom she corresponded in Latin and at whose suggestion she began a translation of Erasmus' paraphrase of St John's Gospel. In 1544 she was reinstated in the order of succession (though not legitimated). With the accession of her brother as Edward VI in 1547 she again became heir to the throne. In 1549 and 1551 she resisted attempts to stop the Catholic services in her household. The ill-devised scheme of the king and the duke of Northumberland to prevent her succession had the effect of uniting the country behind her, and she ascended the throne in 1553 as England's first queen regnant. However, her early popularity was soon lost because of her determination to restore Catholicism and her unpopular marriage to Philip II of Spain. The Spanish alliance brought England into an unwelcome war with France, which led to the loss of Calais. The savagery of her persecution of Protestants – some three hundred were executed, including *Cranmer and other bishops as well as many humbler folk – was more than anything else responsible for the anti-Catholic prejudices which remained so strong in the English consciousness for many generations.

The classic portrait of the queen is that by Anthonis Mor (1554) in the Prado, Madrid.

BIBLIOGRAPHY: Allen Ep 389 / DNB XII 1218–39 / D.M. Loades *The Reign of Mary Tudor* (London 1979) is the most recent work on Mary's life and reign / C. Erikson *Bloody Mary* (London 1978) is the latest popular biography
C.S. KNIGHTON

MARY Tudor queen of France,
c March 1496–24 June 1533
Mary, the third child and second daughter of *Henry VII and *Elizabeth of York, daughter of Edward IV, was probably born in March 1496, though she was described as four years old by Erasmus when he visited the royal nursery in 1499 (Allen I 6; Reedijk poem 45). Her education encompassed French, Latin, music, and dancing as well as the more womanly accomplishment of embroidery; her tutors were William Hone and John *Skelton, probably

chosen by Lady Margaret *Beaufort on the advice of Bishop John *Fisher. In 1507 she was proposed as a bride for the future emperor, *Charles V and was indeed married to him by proxy in December of that year. The match was still in prospect in 1512 when Erasmus wrote of her imminent departure from England (Epp 252, 287). But two years later a shift in English foreign policy produced a treaty with France, as part of which Mary was married to the elderly *Louis XII. In September 1514 she left for Paris in the company of John *Palsgrave as tutor (Ep 499) and in October was crowned at St Denis. The king died on 1 January 1515, and despite favours from his successor, *Francis I, Mary secretly married Charles *Brandon, duke of Suffolk, *Henry VIII's close friend, who was at that time on an embassy to congratulate Francis on his accession. Henry's anger at this clandestine and somewhat improper union was assuaged by *Wolsey's intervention and the promise of a large sum of money. Mary returned to England in April and the following month she and Suffolk celebrated a second and public wedding. Her only son, Henry, was born in London on 11 March 1516. Thereafter she generally avoided court save on great occasions (she was, for example, present at the meeting of Henry and Francis at the Field of Cloth of Gold in 1520). She showed some favour to men of learning, and in 1532 Thomas Paynell dedicated to her his version of Erasmus' *De contemptu mundi* (STC 10471). Mary's daughter Frances Brandon (who became the mother of Lady Jane Grey) was also a patron of humanists. Mary was sympathetic to the cause of her sister-in-law, *Catherine of Aragon, whom she and Suffolk joined in a pilgrimage to Walsingham in 1517, but her husband's closeness to the king placed her in an unenviable position. She died shortly after the divorce of Henry and Catherine.

Several portraits of Queen Mary are extant, including one at Woburn Abbey and one by Anthonis Mor in the Prado, Madrid. Her book of hours is preserved in the library of The Queen's College, Oxford.

BIBLIOGRAPHY: DNB XII 1282–5 / J.J. Scarisbrick *Henry VIII* (London 1968) 20–1, 81, 84, 86 / McConica 55, 115, 120, 138 / H.W. Chapman *The Sisters of Henry VIII* (London 1969) / W.C. Richardson *Mary Tudor, the White Queen*

Galeotto Marzio

(Seattle 1970) / R. Ormond *The Face of Monarchy* (Oxford 1977) 185 / N.L. Harvey *The Rose and the Thorn* (New York 1975)   C.S. KNIGHTON

Galeotto MARZIO of Narni, c 1427–c 1494
Galeotto Marzio (Martius) was born at Narni, in Umbria, about 1427. After studying elsewhere for several years, he resided from 1447 to 1449 in Ferrara, where he became a pupil of Guarino *Guarini and a close friend of *Janus Pannonius. While in Ferrara he began his literary career by writing a Latin poem, 'De origine dominae Stellae domus et de ipsa domina Stella' (Ferrara, MS Estense lat 66.2) in honour of the mother of Leonello d'Este. In 1449 Galeotto travelled to Padua to teach humanities and study medicine. He was resident there until at least 1460, at which time he became a friend and protégé of John Tiptoft, earl of Worcester. From Padua he moved to Bologna, where he was professor of rhetoric and poetry from 1463 to 1465. In that year, Galeotto, having been recommended to King *Matthias Corvinus, accompanied his friend Janus Pannonius to Buda, where the Italian

took up the positions of secretary to King Matthias, tutor to his illegitimate son, Johannes, and first royal librarian. About 1470, Galeotto produced his fist major work, *De homine et eius partibus* (Venice: N. Jenson 1471?), dedicated to a Hungarian friend, János Vitéz (d 1471), archbishop of Gran (Strigonia). It was reprinted by Johann *Froben in 1517 (Ep 581). Like so much of Galeotto's work, this text is heavily influenced by astrology.

By 1473 Galeotto had returned to Italy and to his professorship at Bologna, which he was to hold until 1477. In 1474 Giorgio *Merula, one of his students, published an elaborate critique of *De homine* under the title *In librum 'De homine' Galeotti* (Venice: J. de Colonia and J. Manthen), to which Galeotto replied in 1476 with his *Refutatio objectorum in librum De homine* (Venice: J. Rubeus 1476). Nor was this the last of his literary debates. Some time later Galeotto produced 'Invectivae in apologiam Francisi Philelphi' (Biblioteca Apostolica Vaticana MS Lat. 3411) in response to criticism from the celebrated humanist Francesco *Filelfo.

In 1477 Galeotto completed 'De incognitis vulgo' (Paris, Bibliothèque Nationale MS 6563) addressed to his former patron, King Matthias. The intent of the work was to illustrate where philosophers and theologians differ. It was this dangerous subject and his alleged dealing with the Hussites when in Bohemia which led to his arrest and imprisonment by the Venetian Inquisition for heresy in late 1477. On 17 May 1478 Galeotto wrote 'ex carcere' to Lorenzo (I) de' *Medici imploring him to intervene with the doge or the pope on his behalf. *Sixtus IV, who was perhaps once his pupil, examined the book and pronounced Galeotto innocent. It was at this time that he appears to have returned to Hungary; and while in Buda he probably began (c 1485) his *De dictis et factis Matthiae regis* (Vienna 1563) in honour of his patron.

Galeotto returned to Italy by 1488 at the latest. Between 1488 and 1490 he wrote *De doctrina promiscua* (Florence: L. Torrentinus 1548), which he dedicated to Lorenzo the Magnificent. Like 'De incognitis vulgo,' this is a curious, rambling work of rough style and wide but scattered erudition, both Latin and Greek. The date and circumstances of Galeotto's death are uncertain. Near the end of his life he appears to have entered the service of *Charles VIII in France, where he may have died from a fall. However, Paolo Giovio in his *Elogia virorum literis illustrium* (Basel 1544) said that Galeotto's death occurred in Italy, near Este, precipitated by his great bulk. It is most unlikely, though, that his death, in about 1494, occurred in Bohemia, as suggested by Allen.

Besides the works discussed above, Galeotto wrote a treatise 'De chiromantia' (Padua, MS Antoniana XXII 560) and the relatively unknown *De excellentibus* of about 1490. Together with Girolamo Manfredi and others, he corrected Johannes Angelius' translation of Ptolemy's *Geography* (Bologna: G. de Lupis 1462). Also, there are extant his *Carmina* (ed L. Juhász, 1932) and *Epistolae* (ed L. Juhász, 1930).

A portrait of Galeotto by the Florentine Berto Linaiuolo survives in the dome of Matthias Corvinus' library at Buda.

BIBLIOGRAPHY: Allen Ep 581 / Cosenza III 2213–16 / Girolamo Tiraboschi *Storia della letteratura italiana* (Florence 1807) VI-1 380–9 / Lynn Thorndike *A History of Magic and Experimental Science* (New York 1923–58) IV 399–405 / Mario Frezza 'Introduzione al Pomponazzi: Galeotto Marzio da Narni' *Italica* 26 (1949) 136–40 / G. Saitta 'A proposito di Galeotto Marzio e di un suo storico e traduttore' *Giornale critico della filosofia italiana* 29 (1950) 249–51 / E. Garin 'Il Trattato di chiromanzia [di Galeotto Marzio da Narni]' *Giornale critico della filosofia italiana* 30 (1951) 156 / Carlo Malagola *Della vita e delle opere di Antonio Urceo detto Codro, studi e ricerche* (Bologna 1878) 63–5 / G. Bertoni *Guarino da Verona fra letterati e cortigiani a Ferrara (1429–1460)* (Geneva 1921) 54–5

KENNETH R. BARTLETT

Bartolomeo MASCARA of Brescia, documented 1532–5
Bartolomeo Mascara (Maschera) taught grammar at the cathedral school of Brescia. In 1532 he published an Italian translation of Aesop's fables (Brescia: Ludovico Britannico) and an edition of the *Epigrammaton libri quatuor* of Michael *Marullus Tarcaniota (Brescia: Damiano and Giacomo Filippo Turlini). His son

Florentino (d 1580 or 1584) was a pupil of the composer Claudio Merulo and became a noted violinist and organist at the cathedral of Brescia.

Given Bartolomeo's literary interests and the fact that an Italian translation of the *Enchiridion* of Erasmus had been published at Brescia in 1531 by Emilio de' *Migli, it is not surprising that Vincenzo *Mitelli described Bartolomeo as an admirer of Erasmus in his letter of 13 September 1535 (Ep 3057).

BIBLIOGRAPHY: EI XXII 490 / *Storia di Brescia* III (Brescia 1963) 912   ANNA GIULIA CAVAGNA

Pedro de MASCARENHAS 1484(?)–1555
Pedro was the son of Fernão Martins Mascarenhas, who served the crown of Portugal in Africa, where Pedro spent his youth. In 1531, Pedro Mascarenhas, then ambassador in Brussels, gave shelter to André de *Resende, who had left Louvain in protest against the growing intellectual repression (Ep 2570). In December the ambassador celebrated in his residence the birth of Manuel, the son of *John III of Portugal. The festivities at which Damião de *Gois and Resende were present lasted for three days and were attended by *Charles V and his court. The highlight was the presentation of the *Jubileu de amores* by Gil Vicente. Although the play is lost we know Girolamo *Aleandro's reaction to it; the cardinal, who participated in the celebration, complained about its attack on Rome and the pope, and the play was put on the Index in Portugal in 1551. Resende described the events in a poem dedicated to Mascarenhas, the *Genethliacon principis Lusitani* (Bologna: G.B. Phaelli 1533), which Erasmus mentioned (Ep 2914). Perhaps it was Resende who persuaded Mascarenhas to send Erasmus a gift of sugar (Ep 2704) before he left Brussels, taking Resende with him. Apparently they accompanied Charles V to Germany and Vienna (September 1532), where a round of warfare against the Turks was nearing its end. In 1539 Mascarenhas became ambassador in Rome. In 1554 he was appointed viceroy of India, where he died the following year. He had the reputation of being an honest and just man.

BIBLIOGRAPHY: Allen Ep 2500 introduction / I.S. Révah 'Recherches sur les oeuvres de Gil

Vicente' in *Bibliothèque du Centre d'Histoire du Théâtre Portugais* (Lisbon 1951), introduction 4ff / *Dicctionário de História de Portugal* ed Joel Sarrão (Lisbon 1975–8) IV 219

ELISABETH FEIST HIRSCH

Christiaan MASSEEUW of Warneton, 13 May 1469–25 September 1546
Christiaan Masseeuw (Christianus Massaeus Cameracenas), a native of Warneton, joined the Brethren of the Common Life at Ghent, where he taught for some time. In 1509 Bishop Jacques de *Croy called him to Cambrai. He spent the rest of his life there (hence 'Cameracenas') as a teacher in the Collège des Bons Enfants. Masseeuw was the author of a Latin grammar, *Grammatistice*, in three parts (Paris: R. Chaudière 1534–5) – which also contained an 'Ars versificatoria' heavily censured by Jan de Spouter (Despauterius) for plagiarism – and of twenty books of *Chronica*, begun in 1502 but not printed until 1540 (Antwerp: J. Crinitus; NK 1500). The dialogues Noël *Béda referred to in Ep 1609 were never published.

BIBLIOGRAPHY: Allen Ep 1609 / A. Roersch in BNB XIII 933–5 / de Vocht CTL I 210 n 2

C.G. VAN LEIJENHORST

Frans van MASSEMEN d 22 August 1529
Very little is known about Frans van Massemen (Massemius, de Mamines), who was grand bailiff of Ghent; he may have been related to Bartholomeus van Massemen, a member of the council of Flanders (d 30 March 1502 or 1503). In 1513 Frans was sent to greet *Henry VIII on his arrival at Calais. He was a faithful patron of the Carthusian Levinus *Ammonius, who mentioned him frequently in his letters and left a detailed description of Massemen's death from heart failure on returning from his estate of Herseghem, where he had gone to attend the dedication of a church (letter of 24 August 1529 printed by Pil 175–6). Ammonius also preserved the copy of a letter by Massemen, who took care to put him in touch with Jacobus *Ceratinus and Johannes de *Molendino. In Ep 2197 Ammonius assured Erasmus that he would be a welcome visitor to the country houses of Omaar van *Edingen, Jérôme *Ruffault, and Massemen, which were all situated in the same neighbourhood.

BIBLIOGRAPHY: Allen Ep 2197 / Albert Pil 'Vijf brieven van Levinus Ammonius ... ' *Horae Tornacenses* (Tournai 1971) 157–76

MARCEL A. NAUWELAERTS & PGB

Jacques MASSON *See Jacobus* LATOMUS

Richard MASTER of Maidstone, 1484–1552/8
Richard Master (Masters) was born at Maidstone, Kent, and was educated at Eton, where he was a king's scholar from about 1484 to 1502, and at King's College, Cambridge, to which he was admitted as a scholar in 1502, and where he was a fellow from 1505 to 1515. He took his BA in 1507, his MA in 1510, and his bachelor of divinity in 1515, having meanwhile incorporated at Oxford as MA in 1513. He served as junior proctor of Cambridge University for the year 1513–14, whereupon he concluded his university career. On 18 November 1514 he was collated to the rectory of Aldington, Kent, in succession to Bishop John *Thornton, and became responsible for the annuity of £20 assigned to Erasmus on his resignation of the living in 1512. Erasmus made favourable reference to the new rector's learning and respectability (LB V 811F), and his incumbency would have been noted only for the erection of the church tower had not one of his parishioners begun, in 1525, to see visions.

This was Elizabeth Barton, the celebrated 'nun of Kent' whose pronouncements aroused much popular interest. She was soon removed to a convent, but Master was briefly her confessor, and this all but caused his downfall. In 1533 the nun attacked the king's remarriage, and all her former associates were rounded up and charged with treason. On 29 September Master was arrested by Christopher Hales and brought to the Tower for interrogation. But Hales was impressed by the rector's good reputation, and nothing incriminating was found at his house. His failing health caused him to be moved to *Cranmer's custody at Forde Manor. Perhaps the archbishop's influence saved him, for although the nun and several of her supporters were executed in April 1534, Master was pardoned in July and returned to his parish. He subsequently sent a gift to *Cromwell, thanking him for his clemency but pleading that his troubles had caused his financial ruin.

Master's troubles had repercussions for Erasmus, who had already complained in 1530 that he did not receive the full extent of his (two) English pensions (Ep 2332). During 1535 he told correspondents that one of his creditors refused payment entirely and that the other had sent only half in the previous year because his goods had been seized by the crown (Epp 2996, 2997, 3028). Although Master was restored to his goods and living in July 1534, his difficulties continued. In September 1535 Thomas *Bedyll (who had assisted in Master's arrest two years before) wrote to Erasmus that the pensioner (presumably Master rather than the incumbent of Erasmus' other and unknown former benefice) denied the obligation of payment, but that Cranmer and Cromwell had promised their aid (Ep 3058). In the following March Erasmus wrote directly to Cromwell pointing out that Master had paid only half the money in the previous year and nothing at all in the current one, pleading distress. Probably aware of Master's fortunate escape from the scaffold, Erasmus suggested that a few words from Cromwell would open the rector's purse (Ep 3107). Nothing further is known of these negotiations. Master survived a further crisis in 1542 or 1543, when he was reported to the archbishop for failing to preach in favour of the royal supremacy and for continuing with various proscribed ceremonies. He remained at Aldington until at least 1552, and probably until 1558, when the next rector was appointed.

BIBLIOGRAPHY: Emden BRUO 1501–40 390 / DNB I 1263–6 / A.D. Cheney 'Richard Masters, parson of Aldyngton, 1514 to 1558' *The Journal of the British Archaeological Association* n s 10 (1904) 15–28 (which corrects previous accounts, including that of the DNB, which had claimed that Master was executed along with Barton and the others) / LP VI 1149, 1169, 1468, 1512, 1531, 1666, VII 71, 1026(10) / Some references in the correspondence do not make it clear which defaulting rector of the two English benefices is intended

C.S.KNIGHTON

Jean MATAL of Poligny, d 1597
Jean Matal was a close friend of Gilbert *Cousin and is perhaps one of the youths whose visit to Freiburg he mentioned in Ep 3123. But is there

Jan Mathijszoon

any evidence for Matal's presence at Freiburg? See Allen Epp 2381 introduction, 3123; Gilbert Cousin *La Franche-Comté au milieu du XVIe siècle* ed E. Monot (Lons-le-Saunier 1907) 158; Gilbert Cousin *Opera* (Basel 1562) I 217–18, 295, 302–4, 315–19, 412, 419; AK V Epp 2194, 2208, and passim, VII Ep 3035; Auguste Castan *Catalogue des incunables de la Bibliothèque publique de Besançon* (Besançon 1893) 322; Winterberg 53.   PGB

Jan MATHIJSZOON of Haarlem,
d 5 April 1534
Jan Mathijszoon (Matthys, etc), a baker in Haarlem, was a disciple of the Anabaptist Melchior Hofmann, but in 1532 refused to follow Hofmann's instruction that rebaptism should be temporarily suspended. Claiming exceptional spiritual powers, he left his unbelieving wife in 1533, married a young girl of Haarlem, and fled with her to Amsterdam. He gathered a considerable following in Holland, Overijssel, and Friesland. He claimed to be the prophet Enoch (Ep 2956) and ordained twelve apostles, among them *Jan of Leiden, whom he sent out to baptize the believers in the

Matthias Corvinus

neighbouring communities. The success of his disciples in Münster induced them to urge him to come to that city. Jan Mathijszoon arrived in Münster on 24 February 1534 and helped establish the rule of radical Anabaptism, assuming the leadership of the movement. A few weeks later, on Easter Sunday, he was killed in a sortie against the besieging army of Bishop Franz von *Waldeck.

BIBLIOGRAPHY: Allen Ep 2956 / NNBW IX 654–6 / ADB XX 600–2 / George H. Williams *The Radical Reformation* (Philadelphia 1962) 357–9, 368–71, and passim / Ugo Gastaldi *Storia dell'anabattismo dalle origini a Münster, 1525– 1535* (Turin 1972) 504–10, 531–42, and passim / A.F. Mellink *De wederdopers in de Noordelijke Nederlanden 1531–1544* (Groningen 1953) passim   IG

MATTHAEUS (Ep 2963, 25 August [1534])
Matthaeus, who is not identified, was one of two famuli who accompanied Damião de *Gois on his visit to Freiburg in 1534. When Gois was on his way to Italy Matthaeus fell sick and Gois sent him back to Freiburg (Epp 2963, 2970). But he was worried about the boy, as Erasmus

reported to *Melanchthon, and therefore returned to Freiburg. We do not know whether Matthaeus was the famulus Gois sent in 1535 from Italy to Portugal, where he delivered letters from Erasmus (Epp 3019, 3043).

BIBLIOGRAPHY: Allen Ep 2963 / Elisabeth Feist Hirsch *Damião de Gois: The Life and Thought of a Portuguese Humanist 1502–74* (The Hague 1967) 75   ELISABETH FEIST HIRSCH

MATTHIAS Corvinus king of Hungary and Bohemia, 23 February 1443–6 April 1490
Matthias Corvinus was born at Cluj (Kolozsvár, Klausenburg), the second son of János Hunyadi, the governor of Hungary. His election as king on 24 January 1458 signaled the triumph of the lesser nobility over baronial oligarchy. Matthias ruled for thirty-two years with great skill and energy. His internal policies were motivated by the desire to break the power of the great nobles and to create a centralized monarchy. His efforts met with massive opposition and although he was able to crush visible resistance, the power of the barons was not broken and reemerged after his death. To carry out his ambitious foreign policy, he levied heavy taxes on the land and relied increasingly on foreign mercenaries. Although the burdens he placed on the kingdom were heavy, he was able to retain much of his popularity because of his evenhanded administration of justice to rich and poor alike.

Matthias' foreign policy involved Hungary in major conflicts with the Turks, with Bohemia, and with the Emperor *Frederick III. In the early years of his reign he undertook a series of offensive campaigns against the Ottoman empire and met with considerable success. He was supported in these efforts by Pope *Pius II, who was preparing a full-scale Christian crusade in order to force the Turks out of Europe. When Pius II died (1464) and the crusade did not materialize, Matthias felt betrayed and abandoned his aggressive policy against the Ottomans, although later he inflicted a number of defeats upon Turkish armies and garrisons in the border regions.

Encouraged by Rome's efforts to break the power of the moderate Hussites, Matthias became involved in the political-religious controversies in Bohemia and was elected Bohemian king by a group of Catholic nobles and towns in 1469. He conquered and occupied much of Moravia and Silesia in a series of campaigns, but was outmanoeuvered diplomatically when the Jagiellonian Prince *Vladislav II was elected king by the majority of the Czech estates in 1471. Matthias' aggressive policies in Bohemia aroused the fears of Frederick III, who tried to isolate Hungary by the creation of a Hapsburg-Jagiellonian alliance. In the subsequent hostilities Matthias inflicted a series of defeats on Frederick and captured Vienna in 1485, but was unsuccessful in breaking the power of the Hapsburgs. His premature death left Hungary open to domination by the Jagiellonian-Hapsburg coalition.

Matthias was married twice. His first wife was Catherine Podebrady, whom he wed on 1 May 1463 and who died in childbirth the following year. His second marriage, with Beatrix of Aragon, took place on 22 December 1476. She survived him and died at Naples in 1508. Neither of his wives was able to provide Matthias with an heir. He did have an illegitimate son, Johannes Corvinus, and the last great effort of his reign was to have this young man recognized as his heir. He was prevented from consolidating his dynasty by his sudden death in Vienna. His body was returned to Hungary for burial at Székesfehérvár. His tomb was destroyed during the course of the Turkish wars.

Matthias is remembered as Hungary's greatest Renaissance ruler. An avid book collector, the king had one of the finest manuscript libraries north of the Alps. His court was sought out by numerous scholars and artists from all parts of Europe. He employed many foreigners in diplomatic and administrative positions; among his councillors was Johann (I) *Paumgartner (Epp 2602, 2879). He was a liberal patron of the arts and letters and made his court at Buda a centre of humanism.

BIBLIOGRAPHY: Mátyás király levelei ed Vilmos Fraknói (Budapest 1893–5) / Mathiae Corvini Hungariae regis epistolae ad Romanos Pontifices datae et ab eis acceptae, 1458–1490 ed Vilmos Fraknói (Budapest 1851) / Magyar életrajzi lexikon (Budapest 1967–9) II 169–71 / Magyar irodalmi lexikon (Budapest 1963–5) II 203–14 / Jolán Balogh A múvészet Mátyás király udvarában (Budapest 1966) / Karl Nehring Matthias

Corvinus, Kaiser Friedrich III. und das Reich (Munich 1975) / Vilmos Fraknói Hunyadi Mátyás király (Budapest 1890) / Mátyás király emlékkönyv ed Imre Lukinich (Budapest 1940) / Lajos Elekes Mátyás és kora (Budapest 1956) / Eva H. Balázs Mátyás a kortársak között (Budapest 1957) / Tibor Kardos A magyarorszagi humanizmus kora (Budapest 1955) / Csaba Csapodi The Corvinian Library, History and Stock (Budapest 1973)

L. DOMONKOS

Jan MATTHYS See Jan MATHIJSZOON

Johannes MAUBURNUS See Jan MOMBAER

Daniel MAUCH of Ulm, 27 June 1504– 19 May 1567
Daniel Mauch (Mach) was the son of another Daniel Mauch, a well-known sculptor and engraver. He studied at the universities of Heidelberg (from 1520) and Tübingen (1522–3), where he took his BA, as well as Cologne and Vienna (1521). He entered the service of Cardinal Lorenzo *Campeggi when that prelate came to Germany on his way to Hungary (1524). Mauch accompanied Campeggi's secretary, Floriano *Montini, on the papal embassy to Muscovy from 1525 to 1527. In 1529 he continued his studies at Erfurt till 1530, when he re-entered Campeggi's service, accompanying him to the diet of Augsburg. In 1531 he passed to the service of *George of Austria, bishop of Bressanone. While in George's service he took a doctoral degree in law at Pavia (1536), and with the same prelate visited France and Spain (1540). When George went to Denmark in 1534, Mauch for some time frequented the University of Louvain, associating with *Goclenius, *Viglius Zuichemus, and *Dantiscus. He also kept in touch with Sigismund von Herberstein, whom he met at the time of the Russian embassy, and in 1560 expressed high regard for Herberstein's Rerum Muscovitorum commentarii. In 1542 he was made an advocate of the imperial court (Reichskammergericht) at Speyer, and upon entering orders he became a canon of Worms and from 1545 to his death at Worms he was the scholaster of his chapter.

In October 1525 Erasmus sent a brief but friendly reply to a missing letter with which Mauch had approached him (Ep 1633).

BIBLIOGRAPHY: Allen Ep 1633 / Anton Naegele 'Aus dem Leben eines schwäbischen
fahrenden Scholaren im Zeitalter des Humanismus und der Reformation: Briefe und Akten
zur Biographie des Dr Daniel Mauch aus Ulm,
Domscholasticus in Worms' *Römische Quartals-
schrift* 25 (1911) 3*–26*, 38*–109*, 139*–161*,
203*–226* / Anton Naegele 'Daniel Mauch von
Ulm, Reisebegleiter des Russlandentdeckers
Sigismund von Herberstein 1526–27' *Mitteilungen des Vereins für Kunst und Altertum in Ulm
und Oberschwaben* 31 (1941) 158–70 / *Matrikel
Wien* III-1 23 / *Matrikel Erfurt* II 335 / de Vocht
CTL III 364–5 and passim / de Vocht *Dantiscus*
209–10 / S. von Herberstein *Description of
Moscow and Muscovy, 1557* ed B. Picard, trans
J.B.C. Grundy (London 1969) 2 / Pflug *Corres-
pondance* II Ep 238 and passim / *Epistolae ad
Nauseam* 95 and passim   JOHN F. D'AMICO

MAURICIUS (Epp 263, 273 of 1512–13)
Mauricius, who is not identified, was Erasmus'
famulus in the spring of 1512 when he was sent
from Cambridge to Paris with printer's copy for
Josse *Bade (Ep 263). He was probably French
and may have returned to his native region
after this errand, for in September 1513
Erasmus assumed that his friends at Saint-
Omer might have some news about his former
famulus (Ep 273).

BIBLIOGRAPHY: Allen Ep 263 / Bierlaire
Familia 48–9 / J.-C. Margolin in ASD I-2 425
                                                         PGB

Jacobus MAURICIUS *See Jacob* MAURITSZOON

MAURITIUS (Epp 1256, 1303) *See Maurice*
BIRCHINSHAW

Jacob MAURITSZOON of Gouda,
d 30 January 1522
Jacob Mauritszoon (Mauritius) of Gouda matriculated at Louvain on 12 October 1493 and
Orléans on 17 January 1500; at Orléans he
became procurator of the German nation on 7
January 1501. In the same year he received his
licence in canon and civil law and returned to
Gouda, where he was appointed town pensionary (Ep 1044). From 9 January 1514 to 29
October 1515 and from 23 July 1516 until his
death he was an ordinary councillor of the
council of Holland at The Hague. Mauritszoon

died at The Hague; his wife survived him and
married Heyman Claeszoon some time before
14 January 1529.

Erasmus was probably acquainted with
Mauritszoon during his years at Steyn, and
they remained in contact thereafter. Ep 176 of
28 September 1503 even shows Erasmus
prepared to undertake a 'tiresome' and 'useless' task Mauritszoon had set him – the nature
of the task is not quite clear. Erasmus wrote
two other letters to him in 1506 (Epp 190, 202).
Maarten van *Dorp sent Mauritszoon's greetings to Erasmus in 1519 (Ep 1044), and Erasmus
remembered him twice in letters to Nicolaas
*Everaerts in 1520 and 1521 (Epp 1092, 1188).
There appears to be little basis for identifying
Mauritszoon with the Jacobus mentioned by
Erasmus in Ep 83 without reference to past
acquaintance; also Mauritszoon was not the
Mauritius of Ep 1256. Franciscus *Theodoricus
of Gouda dedicated his *Precatiuncule* (Gouda:
Collaciebroeders [1512]; NK 1756) to
Mauritszoon.

BIBLIOGRAPHY: Allen Ep 176 / *Matricule de
Louvain* III-1 102 / *Matricule d'Orléans* I-2
199–200 / I.W[alvis] *Beschryving der stad Gouda*
(Gouda-Leiden [1713]) I 231–2 / J. Taal *De
archieven van de Goudse kloosters* (The Hague
1957) no 818   C.G. VAN LEIJENHORST

MAURUS *See Hartmann* MOER, *Friedrich*
MORMANN, *Antoine* MORELET *de Museau*

Emperor MAXIMILIAN I
22 March 1459–12 January 1519
Maximilian of Hapsburg, the son of the
Emperor *Frederick III and Eleanor of Portugal,
was born in Wienerneustadt and educated at
the court of his father. While thus acquiring
some Latin and an elementary knowledge of
several modern languages, he was not significantly reached by the new learning of humanism. On the other hand, the training deemed
useful for the future ruler included diplomacy,
some manual skills, and above all the handling
of weapons. Throughout his life Maximilian
was to be a passionate hunter and an eager
participant in chivalric tournaments. More
significantly, he developed into a talented
commander, highly imaginative in his use of
artillery and *Landsknecht* mercenaries. On 19
August 1477 in Ghent he married Mary,

daughter and heiress of Charles the Rash, duke of *Burgundy, who had lost his life in battle six months earlier. This match was the single most important step in the rise of the house of Hapsburg to great power status. At the same time, entering the world of the Burgundian court proved to be a decisive experience for Maximilian. As a result of it the rich culture of Burgundy and the Netherlands, its literature, music, art, and elaborate court ceremonial, came to have a lasting influence upon the older Hapsburg states, as did Burgundian techniques in administration, diplomacy, and warfare. After the untimely death of his wife in 1482 Maximilian continued for more than a decade to defend the unity of the states she had inherited. In this he had considerable success, although the French held on to the duchy of Burgundy proper as well as the region of Boulogne, and in the end Gelderland eluded him too. His task was rendered more difficult by the hostility of large segments of the people and the nobility, who after Mary's death tended to see him as a foreigner. In 1488 he was even captured by the rebels and imprisoned in Bruges until his father managed to free him.

Emperor Maximilian I, by Albrecht Dürer

In 1490 Maximilian pursued a policy of encircling France by offering his hand to Anne of Brittany, thus causing the French to occupy the duchy so as to oblige Anne to marry *Charles VIII of France. In that same year Maximilian left the Netherlands and began to devote his attention to the Hapsburg territories in Austria. Well aware of the significance of its Alpine passes and silver mines, he acquired the Tirol from a relative and chose Innsbruck for his capital. Following the death of King *Matthias Corvinus, he also reconquered Vienna, with Lower Austria, Styria, and Carinthia, from the Hungarians. He even advanced towards Budapest and put in his bid for the crown of Hungary. Although the Hungarians elected *Vladislav II of Bohemia, he succeeded in the peace of Bratislava (Pressburg, 1491) in laying the groundwork for the subsequent Hapsburg succession in Hungary. From then on he styled himself king of Hungary.

Meanwhile, Maximilian had been elected and crowned king of the Romans in 1486 and, when Frederick III died in 1493, succeeded him

as emperor and sole ruler of all Hapsburg states. In 1494 he married Bianca Maria, the niece of Ludovico *Sforza, thus establishing closer ties with the duchy of Milan, which was a singularly important fief of the empire. Maximilian's ambition was to re-establish the imperial power in Italy. Faced with Charles VIII's expedition to Naples (1494), he entered into a Holy League with Pope *Alexander VI, Venice, Milan, and Aragon, and although his Italian campaign of the following year was a fiasco, he never abandoned his hopes of gaining an Italian base for his emperorship. For this and other reasons he endeavoured to strengthen his political ties with the Spanish kingdoms and in 1496 and 1497 succeeded in negotiating matches for his two children: *Margaret with Juan, the presumptive heir of Castile and Aragon, and Philip the Handsome of *Burgundy with Juan's sister, *Joanna, thus laying another cornerstone for the universal empire of his grandson, *Charles V.

In the pursuit of his policies for Germany, however, Maximilian encountered great difficulties. In 1495 a diet at Worms largely failed to achieve the badly needed reforms. It is true that it came up with agreements on continuous territorial peace and the imperial law court, which, despite many flaws, were of enduring value, but powerful opposition on the part of the princes prevented any strengthening of either the emperor's central authority in Germany or his international role beyond Germany. As the member states of the empire usually refused him any subsidies, Maximilian had to burden the Hapsburg territories with the cost of his policies and very nearly succeeded in reducing them to financial ruin. Even at this price, however, lack of funds often prevented the success of his plans and earned him a reputation for wishful thinking and ineffectual plotting. The Swiss defeated him in 1499 and for all practical purposes ceased to be part of the empire. The Aragonese occupied Naples and King *Louis XII of France took Milan. Maximilian was unable to help Ludovico il Moro, who was to end his life in a French prison. The emperor's loss of face abroad had repercussions in Germany. In 1500 the diet of Augsburg subjected him to the authority of a supervisory body, the *Reichsregiment*, which in turn, however, ceased to function after two years, owing as much to lack of support from the princes as to Maximilian's opposition. In 1504 and 1505 he reached an understanding with France in the treaties of Blois and Haguenau, and in the following year intervened decisively in the Bavaro-Palatine war of succession. Both successes went some way towards restoring his prestige, and the following diets of Cologne (1505) and Constance (1507) permitted him to negotiate with the estates from a position of relative strength. He at once renewed earlier attempts to go to Rome for his coronation as emperor, but unfortunately the sudden death of his son, Philip the Handsome, delayed his departure, and Pope *Julius II offered opposition. As the German states failed to pay the subsidies they had granted him for the Roman expedition, Maximilian found the progress of his weak force blocked by superior Venetian and French armies. To make up losses the Venetians had caused him in Istria and Friuli and to reconquer territory traditionally subject to the empire, he entered into the League of Cambrai (December 1508) with France, Spain, and the

papacy, all committed to effect the dismemberment of the Venetian republic. Between 1508 and 1516 he conducted a series of campaigns against Venice, at first in alliance with the French, but later in the face of their opposition (*Julius exclusus, Opuscula* 109). Once again his lack of funds prevented him from honouring the commitments he had undertaken towards his allies, and Venice weathered the threat with relative ease. Verona, which Maximilian had taken, was returned to Venice in 1516, and the emperor had to settle for a small territorial gain in southern Tirol.

When Julius II's death seemed imminent in August 1511 (Ep 240), Maximilian toyed with the idea of becoming pope (cf ASD IX-1 172), but Julius recovered. In fact the schismatic council of Pisa offered to elect Maximilian in opposition to Julius. Personally devout, although at times strongly influenced by national and anticurial currents, Maximilian speculated that as an anti-pope he might be able to secure the backing and desperately needed financial support of the German clergy. But *Ferdinand II of Aragon persuaded him to desist from seeking the papal office and instead recognize the fifth Lateran council, which Julius II convened in 1512 (*Julius exclusus, Opuscula* 90–1, 95). After the collapse of his alliance with France, Maximilian concluded another Holy League with *Leo X, Spain, England, and the Swiss cantons. The Swiss drove the French from Milan and effected a short-lived restoration of the Sforza dynasty, while Maximilian joined *Henry VIII of England for the Thérouanne campaign of August 1513, which ended in the battle of the Spurs.

After King *Francis I had reconquered Milan in 1515 and Maximilian had failed to retake it the following year, a truce of Brussels (4 December 1516), negotiated by Prince Charles, left the French in possession of Milan. But this was no more than a truce; the goals Maximilian had defined and pursued unsuccessfully in his Italian policy would eventually be accomplished by Charles V, with his superior resources.

In the east Maximilian repeatedly dispatched ambassadors to Muscovy. He hoped that a co-ordinated policy against Poland would force King *Sigismund I to ease his pressure on the state of the Teutonic knights in Prussia. But when his support of the knights proved ineffectual, he came to terms with the Jagiełło rulers with a treaty at Vienna in July 1515. The negotiations at Vienna also led to the marriages of his grandchildren *Mary and *Ferdinand with the future *Louis II of Hungary and his sister Anne, as well as to an inheritance pact which was in effect the charter of the future Hapsburg monarchy in central Europe.

In his own hereditary domains the emperor reformed the administration after the model of Burgundy. He grouped single territories into larger units and in the face of opposition from the princes created a central council (*Hofrat*) and treasury for both the Hapsburg states and the Empire at large (1498). This was followed by a grouping of the German states into six *Reichskreise* (1500). He repeatedly summoned joint estates of the Austrian provinces and at the last of these to be held in his reign (Innsbruck 1518) had to face bitter criticsm of his financial mismanagement. Maximilian offered remedies, but it remained for his successors to reduce the enormous debt he had accumulated in his Venetian wars. The same wars prompted the convening of several imperial diets as Maximilian attempted again and again to secure subsidies. No cash was forthcoming, nor was any progress made in bringing constitutional reform to the empire beyond the creation of *Reichskreise*.

Maximilian's last diet at Augsburg in 1518 was in part devoted to appeals for a crusade against the Turks, a project always dear to his heart and recently promoted by Leo x (Epp 863, 891). But the estates procrastinated, and his move to have Charles elected king of the Romans also got nowhere. Even so, Maximilian's intensive negotiations about his succession may have benefited the Hapsburg strategy after his death. Martin *Luther, who was present at Augsburg, did not meet the emperor, who had shown some interest in him. After the conclusion of the diet, Maximilian travelled by way of Innsbruck to Wels, in Upper Austria, where he died on 12 January 1519. His will was limited to pious dispositions, without otherwise tying the hand of his heirs. It had been Maximilian's dream to restore to the imperial office the universal respect it had commanded in past centuries; instead he laid the concrete foundations for the great power of the Spanish and Austrian Hapsburgs in early modern Europe.

Maximilian was a generous patron of artists and scholars. Although a child of the waning Middle Ages, he was open to new ideas and even came to support the new learning. He sponsored a number of works on the history of his dynasty and expected them to perpetuate the fame of his own deeds. He himself was responsible for a number of works, either dictating the text or causing trusted collaborators to write it under his close supervision. His literary creations, many of which were never completed, sometimes served as a record of his personal experiences, as was the case with a secret book on hunting and a book on fishing in the Tirol (both ed M. Mayr, Innsbruck 1901). More typically, however, they were intended to acquaint posterity with his various actions and designs. In Latin he dictated points to serve as the basis for an autobiography (edited by Alwin Schultz in *Jahrbuch der Sammlungen des Allerhöchsten Kaiserhauses* 6, 1888). Autobiographical features are also found in the *Theuerdank* (published in 1517, re-edited by Sigmund Laschitzer in *Jahrbuch der Sammlungen* 8, 1890) and the more famous *Weisskunig* (latest edition by H.T. Musper et al, 1956).

The same features of self-glorification and personal direction characterize some works of art commissioned by Maximilian, such as the *Triumph* (published in 1526, re-edited by S. Appelbaum, New York 1964), the *Ehrenpforte* (*Triumphal Arch*, published in 1517), and his monumental tomb at Innsbruck watched by dozens of free-standing statues of his ancestors, cast in bronze. Numerous portraits of Maximilian by Hans Striegel and other contemporary artists are preserved, above all the famous painting by *Dürer (Vienna, Kunsthistorisches Museum) which was executed from a sketch taken at the time of the diet of Augsburg in 1518.

Erasmus never met Maximilian personally, but his works and letters contain many references to political and cultural developments involving the emperor, and also to the connections between Maximilian and the men who surrounded him, among them a number of correspondents and friends of Erasmus, such as cardinals Matthäus *Lang and Matthäus *Schiner, Jakob *Spiegel, Konrad *Peutinger, Willibald *Pirckheimer, Gregor *Reisch, and Jacopo *Bannisio. He was also aware of Maximilian's interest in *Hutten and *Reuchlin. His judgments of the emperor and his policies tended to be critical. The *Julius exclusus* gives several examples of Maximilian's shift in alliances (*Opuscula* 90–1, 95, 109). In a eulogy of the city of Strasbourg Erasmus' praise of Maximilian may sound more ironical now than was intended at the time: Strasbourg 'is blest with the mildest of princes, whose power it never feels except when it receives some benefit from his wisdom and generosity' (Ep 305). The same is true of Erasmus' assessment, following the peace of Cambrai (Epp 505, 532), of 'Emperor Maximilian who in his old age, wearied by so many wars, has decided to relax in the arts of peace' (Ep 541). Erasmus was bound to disapprove of Maximilian's wars and some critical statements in the *Querela pacis* (ASD IV-2 78) and the adages *Scarabeus aquilam quaerit* and *Dulce bellum inexpertis* (*Adagia* III vii 1, IV i 1) may be recognized as veiled references to Maximilian. There can be no doubt that Erasmus took exception to the events accompanying Maximilian's last visit to the Low Countries (Ep 543). The same visit, incidentally, led to a reunion between Maximilian and his illegitimate son, *Leopold, who was tutored by Erasmus' friend Robert de *Keysere. The colloquy *Convivium fabulosum* (1524, ASD I-3 446–7) offers an anecdote to illustrate how officials and courtiers were apt to take advantage of Maximilian's carelessness in financial matters. In September 1517 Erasmus was approached on behalf of Maximilian about some business 'which the man who committed it to me thought was of the greatest importance' (Ep 670; cf Ep 669). The nature of that business and the identity of the emperor's emissary – conceivably Bannisio – are a matter of speculation (CWE Ep 670 introduction) since the records of the imperial chancery and Erasmus' further correspondence offer no clues whatsoever.

BIBLIOGRAPHY: Heinrich Ulmann in ADB XX 725–36 / Hermann Wiesflecker *Maximilian I. Das Reich, Österreich und Europa an der Wende der Neuzeit* (Vienna-Munich 1971–) /

Heinrich Ulmann *Kaiser Maximilian I.* (Stuttgart 1884–91) / J.D. Tracy *The Politics of Erasmus* (Toronto 1978) 37–8, 92–4, 152–3, and passim / Louise Cuyler *The Emperor Maximilian and Music* (London 1973) / Otto Herding in ASD IV-2 14–15 and passim / *Katalog der Ausstellung: Maximilian I.* (Innsbruck 1969)

INGE FRIEDHUBER

Claudius MAY of Bern, d between 11 October 1527 and 3 April 1528
Claudius (Glado) May (Mey, Meyer), the son of Bartholomäus, belonged to a notable family. He was a member of Bern's great council and in 1502 he was bailiff (*Landvogt*) of Lenzburg. He owned Strättlingen and several other estates and with Niklaus von *Wattenwyl, his son-in-law, was one of the leading promoters of the Reformation in Bern. His death and, presumably, his daughter Clara, a former nun who had married Wattenwyl, are mentioned in Ep 1988.

BIBLIOGRAPHY: Allen Ep 1988 / DHBS IV 695 / Z VIII Ep 424 and passim / *Schweizerisches Geschlechterbuch* 2 (Basel 1907) 328–31   PGB

Giovanni MAZZOCCHI of Bondeno, documented 1509–22
Giovanni Mazzocchi (Maciochius) of Bondeno, in the territory of Ferrara, was active as a printer in Ferrara from 1509 to 1517 and in Mirandola from 1519 to 1522. His production was for the most part scholarly; it included an edition of Erasmus' *Adagia* (1514) and a Greek *Thesaurus* (1510) by Giovanni Maria Tricaglio, which Erasmus appreciated and of which he later tried to acquire a copy (Ep 885). Mazzocchi also published *Savonarola's *Prediche* and the first edition of Ariosto's *Orlando furioso*, both in 1516.

Giovanni may have been related to the Roman printer Jacopo Mazzocchi. In 1521 and 1522 Ariotto da Trino printed in Rome a Latin Xenophon and Sancho *Carranza's *Opusculum* against Erasmus for the publisher Giovanni Mazzocchi of Bergamo.

BIBLIOGRAPHY: Allen Ep 885 / Fernanda Ascarelli *Annali tipografici di Giacomo Mazzocchi* (Florence 1961) 14–15 and passim / *Short-Title Catalogue of Books Printed in Italy ... now in the British Museum* (London 1958) 888–9 and passim   PGB

Silvestro **MAZZOLINI** *See Silvester* PRIERIAS

MEDARDUS documented 1530–2
In 1530 the imperial secretary Adriaan *Wiele
was attending the diet of Augsburg, and on 16
November, during the last phase of the diet
with only the Catholic estates in attendance,
he wrote to Erasmus about Medardus (Metar-
dus), a Franciscan friar, who was attacking
Erasmus in his sermons (Ep 2408). According to
Wiele, Medardus was a court preacher to King
*Ferdinand; according to Preserved Smith and
the Allen edition, his name was Medardus von
(der) Kirchen. Erasmus seems to have pursued
the matter seriously. In June 1531 Johannes
*Fabri, bishop of Vienna, assured Erasmus that
he had rebuked Medardus, while Cardinal
Bernhard von *Cles declared that during the
entire diet he had not been aware of any
attacks by Medardus (Epp 2503, 2504). In a
new edition of his *Colloquia* (September 1531)
Erasmus published an insolent dialogue with
the title *Concio sive Merdardus* (ASD I-3 653–66;
Ep 2566). Medardus continued his attacks,
perhaps from Bavaria (Ep 2640), and in August
1532 Erasmus reported that in reply to his
colloquy Medardus had addressed a letter of
complaint to the court of Ferdinand, expressing a desire to continue the controversy (Ep
2700). No more is known about Medardus.
BIBLIOGRAPHY: Allen Ep 2408 / Preserved
Smith *A Key to the Colloquies of Erasmus*
(Cambridge, Mass, 1927) 51   PGB

Alessandro de' MEDICI d 6/7 January 1537
Alessandro de' Medici, first duke of Florence,
was born in Florence, probably in 1512. He was
reported to be the natural son of Lorenzo (II)
de' *Medici, duke of Urbino; however, Alessandro's contemporaries and many later historians attributed his paternity to Giulio de'
Medici, later Pope *Clement VII. This relationship may have been the reason why the pope
passed over Ippolito de' *Medici, Alessandro's
cousin and lifelong rival, and in 1531 conferred
on Alessandro, already duke of Penne, control
of recently conquered Florence. In addition
Clement arranged for Alessandro to marry
*Margaret of Parma, a daughter of the Emperor
*Charles V (Epp 2753, 2767).

Alessandro's ambiguous position in Florence was clarified on 4 April 1531 when the

Alessandro de' Medici, by Bronzino

government was restructured and the ancient
office of *gonfaloniere* was abolished and Alessandro became duke of Florence. The new
government excluded the leading Florentine
families, who formed an active opposition to
the duke, particularly in Rome. The dissidents
found their champion in Ippolito, who refused
to be content with a cardinal's hat and
regarded his cousin as a usurper.

Although advised by capable men such as
Francesco Guicciardini, Alessandro soon abandoned moderation, engaging in the persecution of his enemies and, accompanied by his
erratic cousin Lorenzino, giving himself over to
sexual excesses. More Florentines defected to
Ippolito. The dissidents, citing violations of
the terms of Florence's surrender, appealed
to the emperor, who agreed to consider their
complaints upon his return from an expedition
to Tunis. In June 1535 Alessandro survived an
assassination attempt which was quickly
traced back to Ippolito. Fearing attack from the
dissidents, Alessandro increased Florence's
fortifications, erecting the formidable Fortezza
da Basso. Ippolito, on his way to the imperial
court, sickened suddenly and died on 10

Ippolito de' Medici, by Titian

August 1535. Alessandro was widely condemned for poisoning him (Ep 3039), but modern authorities attribute Ippolito's sudden death to natural causes.

Ippolito's death failed to quell the Florentine dissidents, who in Naples in January 1536 presented their case to the emperor. Alessandro was summoned to answer the allegations. Guicciardini, Alessandro's eloquent spokesman, dismissed the charges as malicious. Determining that Florence's stability and dependability could best be assured under his future son-in-law, Charles v decided in Alessandro's favour. Vindicated, Alessandro returned in triumph to Florence, and in June 1536 he married the emperor's daughter, Margaret. Alessandro's victory was short-lived. On the night of 6 or 7 January 1537 he was assassinated by Lorenzino, who in an impassioned *Apologia* defended the murder as an act to liberate Florence from its tyrant. His actual motive may have been ambition. However, Alessandro's successor was not Lorenzino, but another cousin, eighteen-year-old Cosimo. Alessandro's illegitimate children died obscurely. In Alessandro's portrait in the Uffizi he is swarthy, petulant, and wary.

BIBLIOGRAPHY: Allen Ep 3039 / Eric Cochrane *Florence in the Forgotten Centuries 1527–1800* (Chicago 1973) 14–16 and passim / Cecil Roth *The Last Florentine Republic* (London 1925) 12, 32, and passim / Pastor IX 426, X 56 and passim, XI 312 and passim / J.R. Hale 'The end of Florentine liberty: the Fortezza da Basso' *Florentine Studies: Politics and Society in Renaissance Florence* ed N. Rubenstein (London 1968) 501–32   DE ETTA V. THOMSEN

Ippolito de' MEDICI 23 March 1511–
10 August 1535
Ippolito de' Medici was born in Urbino, the illegitimate son of Giuliano de' Medici, duke of Nemours. His mother is alleged to have been Pacifica Brandano of Urbino. He was educated in Rome under the direction of his uncle, Pope *Leo x. In 1524, under orders from another Medici pope, *Clement VII, also his uncle, Ippolito went to Florence as nominal head of the city, although control stayed in the hands of Cardinal Silvio *Passerini and, ultimately the pope. On 10 January 1529, at the age of eighteen, Ippolito became a cardinal and a few months later legate of Perugia. Endowed with numerous benefices, he maintained a sumptuous palace and led the life of a secular prince.

The treaty of Barcelona signed on behalf of *Charles v and Pope Clement on 29 June 1529 restored the Medici to power in Florence. Ippolito's dreams of returning to Florence as its ruler were, however, thwarted. After early proofs of favour, Pope Clement switched his preference to Alessandro de' *Medici, Ippolito's cousin, arranged for Alessandro to marry the emperor's daughter, and gave him pre-eminence in Florence. Ippolito was relegated to an ecclesiastical career.

Clement's reasons for passing over the older and more gifted Ippolito in favour of Alessandro have been variously interpreted. Some claim that Alessandro was the natural son, not of Lorenzo (II) de' *Medici, but of the pope himself. Others cite Ippolito's extravagance, which kept him indebted to and out of favour with the pope. Another theory is that Clement, realizing his death was imminent, wanted to secure his family's future in the church by nominating the urbane Ippolito to the college of cardinals. Whatever the pope's motivation, Ippolito's lifelong antagonism towards his cousin is evidence of his sense of being deprived of his 'birthright.' The remainder of Ippolito's life was spent trying to regain what he regarded as his rightful place as head of Florence.

In 1531 Ippolito sought to resign his cardinalate. Clement placated him with added honours and an increased allowance. On 3 July 1532 Ippolito was named vice-chancellor of the church. A few days later, as legate to the emperor's court, Ippolito went to Germany to enlist troops for the Hapsburg war against the Turks (Ep 2713). After several inconclusive skirmishes, thousands of troops, whose pay was months in arrears, rebelled. The emperor, fearing, perhaps with justification, that the affluent Ippolito meant to commandeer the rebels for his own political purposes, arrested the Cardinal and after a day released him.

Ippolito persisted in attempts to renounce the ecclesiastical life (Ep 2967) and continued to seek support for the ouster of Alessandro. Clement spent the last months of his life opposing his nephew's resolution by alternating threats and rewards. On 5 September 1534 Ippolito was nominated legate of the Marches. On 25 September 1534 Pope Clement VII died. Freed from the pope's restraint, Ippolito gathered about him the Florentine dissidents and appealed directly to the emperor for Alessandro's removal. Some of these dissidents proclaimed Ippolito to be the guardian of Florentine freedom, while others supported any means to end Alessandro's tyranny. Ippolito's intent was to substitute himself for Alessandro, and his plans for restoring Florence's freedom were undefined. The new pope, *Paul III, encouraged the strife between the cousins for his own purposes. Alessandro prepared to defend himself. The emperor, readying an expedition to Tunis, agreed to consider the question of Florentine rule upon his return.

In June 1535 Ippolito was implicated in, but not accused of, an assassination attempt against Alessandro. Determined to plead his case personally to the emperor, Ippolito left Rome on 11 July 1535 and proceeded towards Naples to embark for his meeting. At Itri he stopped to visit Giulia Gonzaga. He suddenly became ill and died. Rumours of poisoning by order of Alessandro were rampant in Europe, as seen in Ep 3039 and 3059, the latter speculating on the involvement of Antonio

*Pucci, bishop of Pistoia. However, most historians hold Ippolito's death to have been natural – from malaria, his own excesses, or the ignorance of an attending doctor.

The portrait by Titian in the Palazzo Pitti, Florence, captures the essence of the young cardinal, portraying him in the jaunty uniform of a Hungarian soldier. Handsome, robust (Ep 2713), cultivated, a writer of verses and translator of classics, and a generous patron of artists and musicians, Ippolito embodied the magnificence of his ancestors. His political ambitions and personal pride, also characteristic of the Medici, clashed with the will of his elders and made his brief life a futile quest.

BIBLIOGRAPHY: Allen Ep 2713 / EI XXII 699 / Pastor x 200–3 and passim / Giuseppe Moretti 'Il Cardinale Ippolito dei Medici dal trattato di Barcellona alla morte (1529–1535)' *Archivio storico italiano* 1 (1940) 137–78

DE ETTA V. THOMSEN

Lorenzo (I) de' MEDICI ('il Magnifico')
1 January 1449–8/9 April 1492
Lorenzo, the elder son of Piero de' Medici and Lucrezia Tornabuoni, was twenty when his father died. In a smooth transition he assumed the dominance of Florence and exercised it in the same unobtrusive fashion as had his father and grandfather, respecting the democratic intitutions as long as he controlled them. Sorely tried in the days of the Pazzi conspiracy (1478), this system essentially survived until after Lorenzo's death, although the European states, if not the Florentines themselves, increasingly accorded him the status of a ranking sovereign. At the same time, the Medici banking empire, the indispensable source of the wealth required to fulfil the family's political ambitions, was permitted to decline. As a result Lorenzo had to modify the traditional Medici munificence in sponsoring public projects of social relief and especially of cultural patronage; however, such modifications were compensated for by his personal knowledge and profound understanding of culture. Among those who came to enjoy his patronage were the philosophers *Ficino and *Pico, the poet and humanist scholar *Poliziano, and the painters Botticelli, Verrocchio, Leonardo da Vinci, and perhaps the young Michelangelo. Lorenzo himself wrote vernacular poetry which is among the best of his age.

Lorenzo (1) de' Medici

However, several aspects of his achievement as an intellectual and an Italian statesman are subject to differing interpretations.

In 1469 Lorenzo married Clarice Orsini; their middle son was Giovanni, the future Pope *Leo x. There is a passing reference to Lorenzo in Ep 145.

BIBLIOGRAPHY: EI XXII 699–702 / Lorenzo de' Medici *Opere* ed A. Simoni (Bari 1913–14) / Lorenzo de' Medici *Lettere* ed R. Rubinstein and R. Fubini (Florence 1977–   )   PGB

Lorenzo (II) de' MEDICI duke of Urbino, 12 September 1492–4 May 1519

Lorenzo (II) de' Medici was born in Florence to Piero, the eldest son of Lorenzo (I) de' *Medici, and Alfonsina Orsini. After the expulsion of the Medici from Florence in 1494 and the death of his father in 1503, he was raised in Rome by his mother. He studied classical letters under Favorino Camerte but preferred the princely pursuits of hunting and feasting. In 1512 the Medici returned to Florence, and on 11 March 1513 Lorenzo's uncle Giovanni was elected Pope *Leo x. Lorenzo, then twenty-one, was given control of the Florentine government.

Lorenzo's role in subsequent Medici politics is debatable. Some see him as a reluctant pawn manipulated by Leo x, while others argue that the pope considered his nephew incompetent and agreed to give him power only out of necessity and under pressure from Alfonsina. Leo, hoping to revive the informal system of government practised by Cosimo, Piero, and Lorenzo (I) de' Medici in the fifteenth century, sent Lorenzo back to Florence without a formal title. Not content with this role, Lorenzo turned his aspirations elsewhere. Denied Piombino by the pope, he was elected captain-general of the republic of Florence on 6 June 1515. In the summer of 1515, owing to the illness of his uncle Giuliano, he assumed command of a papal-Florentine army sent to engage *Francis I of France, who had invaded Lombardy. Lorenzo's sensibility to the pro-French sympathies of the Florentines hampered his freedom of action and contributed to the French victory at Marignano in September, where the pope's Swiss allies were decisively defeated. Meanwhile, contention had arisen in the Medici family over the duchy of Urbino. Lorenzo's uncle Giuliano, recently made lord of Parma, Piacenza, and Modena, resisted Leo x's plans to conquer Urbino, citing the hospitality that Urbino had given the exiled Medici and the popularity of its present duke, Francesco Maria *della Rovere. Peace with France in the autumn of 1515 and the death of Giuliano on 17 March 1517 cleared all obstacles to an attack on Urbino, and by 30 May 1517 a papal army, under the command of Lorenzo, had taken the state. The conquest was costly, for Lorenzo sustained a serious wound and continued control of Urbino was uncertain and expensive. Florence, which had little affection for its absent leader, chafed at supporting this dubious and disruptive enterprise. When Lorenzo returned as duke of Urbino, he was judged too arrogant for his origins.

On 28 April 1518 Lorenzo married Madeleine de la Tour d'Auvergne, a wealthy relative of the king of France, in a spectacular ceremony at Amboise (Epp 781, 786). On 29 April 1519 Madeleine died after giving birth to *Catherine, later queen of France. Lorenzo's death followed within the week and was variously attributed to the effects of his wound, a disorder of the spleen, syphilis, and the plague.

Handsome (a sixteenth-century Tuscan portrait exists, and he was also reported to have been painted by Raphael), an able horseman though an inept military commander, alternatively praised for moderation and reproached for excess, Lorenzo remains an elusive figure. Like his uncle Giuliano, he was buried in the new sacristy of San Lorenzo. Michelangelo's magnificent monument, commissioned by Leo x, bears no resemblance to the man it commemorates. Perhaps best remembered for being the recipient of the dedication of *Machiavelli's *The Prince*, Lorenzo did little to fulfil the author's hopes.

BIBLIOGRAPHY: Allen and CWE Ep 781 / EI XXI 501–2 / A. Giorgetti 'Lorenzo de' Medici, Duca d'Urbino e Iacopo v d'Appiano' *Archivio storico italiano* 4th series, 8 (1881) 222–38, 305–25 / A. Giorgetti 'Lorenzo de' Medici capitano generale della Repubblica Fiorentina' *Archivio storico italiano* 4th ser, 11 (1883) 194–215, 310–20 / R. Devonshire Jones 'Lorenzo de' Medici, Duca d'Urbino, Signore of Florence?' *Studies on Machiavelli* ed Myron P. Gilmore (Florence 1972) 297–315 / Pastor VII 36 and passim / 'Sommario della storia d'Italia dal 1511 al 1527 composto da Francesco Vettori' *Archivio storico italiano* 1st ser, 6 (1848) 309–29

DE ETTA V. THOMSEN

Lorenzo (II) de' Medici, duke of Urbino

MEDICI *See also* CATHERINE de' *Medici, queen of France, Pope* CLEMENT VII, *Pope* LEO X

Peter MEDMANN of Cologne, 11 November 1507–28 September 1584
Peter Medmann (Mettmann), the descendant of a respected Cologne family, attended the Latin school of Emmerich and from 1522 the University of Cologne, where he graduated MA. In 1526 he matriculated at the University of Wittenberg. By the spring of 1528 he had returned to Cologne, as is shown by an autograph marginal note in a copy of Erasmus' Cyprian (Basel 1540) which belongs to the library of the Grosse Kirche, Emden. In this note Medmann records that he was a witness to some of the proceedings for heresy against Adolf Clarenbach and also provides clear evidence of his own Protestant convictions.

Medmann began his career as a tutor in the families of Anton von *Isenburg and subsequently Johann von Wied, a brother of Hermann and Friedrich von *Wied. In 1536 he was appointed priest of Puderbach in Wester-

wald, a living within the gift of the dowager Countess Elisabeth von Wied. Not until 1550 did he give up a rent settled on this living. His duties as a family tutor were quickly outweighed by his political and diplomatic services to Archbishop Hermann. From 1539 he was in contact with *Melanchthon and *Bucer and by means of frequent correspondence ensured their involvement in Hermann's plans for the secularization of his ecclesiastical principality. During the Haguenau conference of 1540 he arranged the personal meetings between the archbishop and Bucer and in January 1543 he travelled to Wittenberg. Apart from their letters, proof of his enduring friendship with Melanchthon is found in the latter's dedication of *De coniugio* on the occasion of Medmann's wedding in 1550. Bucer too dedicated several writings to him. Diplomatic missions to diets and princely courts continued until 1547, when Archbishop Hermann was forced to resign and Medmann followed him to his family estates.

From the autumn of 1548 Medmann was at the court of the regent, Countess Anna of Oldenburg, in Emden; again he was engaged in a series of diplomatic missions but also tutored the sons of Enno II *Cirksena, count of Eastern Friesland. As early as 1545 he had been in touch with Jan (II) *Łaski: however, the common stand which had initially united them was to give way to disagreement and polemic. After Łaski's removal from Emden in 1554, Medmann eventually secured the appointment of his old friend Albert Hardenberg, who became preacher at Emden in 1567. In 1550 Medmann married Anna, the daughter of the Emden burgomaster, Heinrich Buttel, and from 1553 to his death he was himself burgomaster, fortifying the city against the military threat of Fernando, duke of Alva, but also opposing in his old age the rigour of Calvinist preachers.

Medmann's sympathy for Erasmus is reflected in a short letter of 1530, written from Strasbourg (Ep 2304). He had hoped to visit Erasmus in Basel but was unable to continue his journey and forwarded letters by Johannes *Caesarius and Simon *Riquinus (Ep 2298) that he had taken with him from Cologne. Medmann bequeathed his library to the city of Emden and persuaded his friend Hardenberg to do likewise. Seventy-eight volumes once in Medmann's possession are now in the library of the Grosse Kirche, Emden; the majority cover theological subjects and many bear marginal notes in his hand.

BIBLIOGRAPHY: Allen Ep 2304 / H.K. Hesse 'Leben und Wirken des Petrus Medmann' *Monatshefte für rheinische Kirchengeschichte* 26 (1932) 321–41 / E. Koch 'Die Bibliothek der Grossen Kirche in Emden' *Jahrbuch der Gesellschaft für bildende Kunst und vaterländische Altertümer in Emden* 24 (1936) 42–54 / P. Bartels 'Zur Erinnerung an den Emdener Rathausbau 1574' *Jahrbuch der Gesellschaft für bildende Kunst und vaterländische Altertümer in Emden* 1 (1874) 70–106 / H. Schilling 'Reformation und Bürgerfreiheit. Emdens Weg zur calvinistischen Stadtrepublik' in *Stadt und Kirche im 16. Jahrhundert* ed B. Moeller (Gütersloh 1978) 128–61
                              DIETER RIESENBERGER

Jan MEERHOUT d 10 October 1550
Jan Meerhout was probably born in Meerhout, a village in the Kempen, in about 1480–5. He taught for a short time at the school of the Brethren of the Common Life at Brussels and afterwards entered the Carthusian order. He took his vows at Scheut on 4 February 1508 and

was successively sacrist (1509–16) and procurator (16 November 1516–18 April 1517). In 1517 he became prior of the Brussels monastery, in 1532 *convisitator* of the province, and in 1539 *visitator*.

In a letter to the Carthusian Gabriël *Ofhuys dated 14 October 1521, Erasmus sent his greetings to the Brussels prior (Ep 1239).

Jan Meerhout is not to be confused with his more famous namesake, a canon regular of St Augustine at Korsendonk and the author of several grammatical and historical works.

BIBLIOGRAPHY: Allen Ep 1239 / Jan de Grauwe *Prosopographia Cartusiana Belgica (1314–1796)* (Ghent-Salzburg 1976) 202 (with further bibliography)   GILBERT TOURNOY

Pieter MEGHEN of 's Hertogenbosch, 1466–1540
Pieter Meghen (Mighen, Petrus Monoculus, Petrus Magius) was born in Brabant. A 'Petrus de Meghem Leod[iensis dioecesis]' matriculated at the University of Louvain on 15 June 1497. Almost everything that is known of this one-eyed scribe and courier, however, comes from the colophons of his manuscripts, the letters of Erasmus, and – for the last ten years of his life – the household accounts of *Henry VIII. In the colophons he styles himself 'Monoculus theuto brabantinus oppidi Buschiducensis dioecesis Leodiensis' or a variant such as (Petrus) Monoculus, Petrus Magius (Unoculus), or Petrus (de) Meghen; he sometimes signs himself P.M. Erasmus calls him Petrus, Petrus Cocles, Petrus Unoculus, Unoculus, Luscus, Cocles, and Cyclops; Johannes *Sixtinus styles him Monoculus (Epp 430, 438); and Richard *Pace also calls him 'luscus' (Ep 937).

Meghen's date of birth is established by the colophon of Oxford, Bodleian Library, MS Lat. misc. f 51 (Nikolaus *Kratzer 'Canones horoptri baculi' and 'Epitoma specierum arithmetice'), written in 1537, when he was seventy. By that time he had already been seven years in the service of Henry VIII, having been appointed Writer of the King's Books as from 25 March 1530. He held this post until his death between 29 September and 25 December 1540.

Twenty-nine manuscripts have been claimed for Meghen, including the part of the Deventer Letter-Book written by Hand B, which Bierlaire tentatively identifies as his. All are in Latin. All but two use an upright humanist script, the pen-strokes being thinner in some of the earlier and smaller codices than in the larger and later productions, where the letters are bold and bulky. Meghen also wrote at least three forms of humanist cursive. His vernacular hand can be identified in occasional scribbled marginal notes.

Meghen's first recorded patrons are Englishmen: Christoper *Urswick, for whom he wrote in 1503 a manuscript of Cicero's *De officiis*, as well as eight others later, including codices for Hayles Abbey in memory of Sir John Huddleston, and John *Colet, for whom he transcribed both stately Vulgate Bible manuscripts as well as the plain 'collected edition' of Colet's own works. In the 1520s, before entering Henry VIII's service, he was taken up by Thomas *Wolsey and Kratzer. Many of his codices were handsomely decorated by Flemish artists. The most imposing of these are the New Testament manuscripts in which the Vulgate text is written parallel with Erasmus' translation (Vulgate Epistles and Gospels for Colet, 1506–9, Erasmus' translation being added, by Meghen, at a later date, probably in the 1520s; Acts and Apocalypse for Henry VIII and *Catherine of Aragon, 1530?; complete Testament for an unknown patron, 1520s); the twin lectionary and epistolary for Wolsey (illuminated 1528–9); and the Huddleston manuscripts (a Psalter, 1514 and a Chrysostom, 1517). His transcript of Kratzer's 'Canones horoptri' was decorated by Hans *Holbein the Younger (1528) and his manuscript of two others of Kratzer's works by an accomplished but less eminent hand (1537).

The first mention of Meghen in Erasmus' correspondence is in a letter to Colet of 5 October 1511, when Meghen was in London (Ep 231; cf Ep 245 to Andrea *Ammonio) and the last in 1519 (see below). He was a frequent courier between Erasmus and his friends and patrons. His recorded journeys are all between the Low Countries and England, but it has been thought that he may have taken the *Novum instrumentum* to *Leo x in Rome (Ep 701). In early June 1516 he certainly carried letters for Erasmus to Wolsey (Ep 424:75), William *Warham (with four volumes of his St Jerome: Epp 416, 424, 425), Thomas *Ruthall

(Ep 437), Colet (Ep 423), Sixtinus (Ep 430), John *Watson (Ep 450), and Thomas *Lupset (Ep 431). Meghen also carried Erasmus' letters of 1 June 1516 to More (Ep 412) and of 5 June to John *Fisher (Ep 413), Ammonio (Ep 414), Thomas *Linacre (Ep 415), Urswick (Ep 416), and William *Latimer (Ep 417). In the letter to Urswick Erasmus spoke of finding Meghen, Urswick's protégé ('tuus alumnus'), pale and almost dead from overwork in copying, unwontedly abstemious and almost disliking wine. By 9 July (Ep 437) Meghen was back in the Netherlands with letters to Erasmus from Colet (Ep 423, 20 June), More (Ep 424, 21 June), Warham (Ep 425, 22 June), Thomas *Bedyll (Ep 426, 22 June), Ammonio (Ep 429, 26 June), Sixtinus (Ep 430, 26 June; cf Ep 448), Lupset (Ep 431, 28 June), and Fisher (Ep 432, c 30 June). Erasmus asked Pieter *Gillis in Antwerp to consult Meghen about the binding of his Jerome (Ep 477, 17 October 1516), complained about a length of cloth received from him, and later reported to Gillis that Meghen had been robbed and beaten (Ep 491, 18 November 1516). About the middle of September 1517 Erasmus sent books and letters by Meghen to Fisher and other friends (Epp 667, 668). He also entrusted Meghen with Quinten *Metsys' diptych, containing his own portrait and Gillis', and a letter, to be taken to More (CWE Ep 653 introduction). Gillis mentioned the mission in a letter to Erasmus (Ep 681), and More thanked both his friends for their gift from Calais (Epp 683, 684, 7 October), remarking later that he had had no news of Pieter since his departure for England (Ep 688). About 5 March 1518 Erasmus mentioned Pieter in letters from Louvain to Fisher, More, and *Pace (Epp 784, 785, 787; cf Ep 772 introduction), at the same time resolving to Bedyll never again to conduct business through 'natives of Gelderland or thirsty men with one eye' (Ep 782) and wondering whether Meghen had brought back no letter from Colet because he could not spare the time from drinking (Ep 786). Meghen was perhaps back in England by 5 April 1519 when Pace told Erasmus he could secure no commission for the scribe from the king (Ep 937). Probably on 6 June 1519 but perhaps on 2 May (Allen Ep 1061:599–600; *Opuscula* 255) Edward *Lee saw Meghen with Erasmus at Mechelen or Louvain, and it may have been Meghen who

Mehmed II

---

carried books in that year from Erasmus to Lorenzo *Campeggi in London (Epp 995, 996, 4–14 July).

BIBLIOGRAPHY: Allen Ep 230 / *Matricule de Louvain* III-1 156 / G. Dogaer in NBW I 707–8 / Bierlaire *Familia* 29 / McConica 69–71 / J.B. Trapp 'John Colet, his manuscripts and the ps.-Dionysius' in *Classical Influences in Western Culture 1500–1700* ed R.R. Bolgar (Cambridge 1976) 205–21 / J.B. Trapp 'Notes on manuscripts written by Pieter Meghen' *The Book Collector* 24 (1975) 80–96 / J.B. Trapp 'Pieter Meghen 1466/7–1540 scribe and courier' *Erasmus in English* 11 (1981) 28–35 / L. Campbell et al 'Quentin Metsys, Erasmus, Pieter Gillis, and Thomas More' *Burlington Magazine* 120 (1978) 716–24 / J.B. Trapp 'A postscript to Matsys' *Burlington Magazine* 121 (1979) 435–7, esp 434–5 / A.J. Brown 'The date of Erasmus' Latin translation of the New Testament' *Transactions of the Cambridge Bibliographical Society* 8, 4 (1984) 351–80   J.B. TRAPP

MEHMED II Ottoman sultan, 30 March 1432– 3 May 1481

Mehmed II (Machometes), known as *Fatih*, the Conqueror, was the son of *Murad II and Hüma Khatun and was born at Edirne. He was appointed governor of Manisa in 1443 and became sultan in August 1444, when Murad renounced the throne in his favour. The Christian states considered his accession a good opportunity for driving the Ottomans out of Europe and invaded Bulgaria, penetrating as far as Varna. Murad was recalled from retirement and given command of the Ottoman forces. He won a resounding victory at Varna on 10 November 1444. After this Murad retired to Manisa, but the state of crisis continued, so that in August 1446 Mehmed was deposed and Murad resumed the throne.

Mehmed's second and substantive period of rule began in February 1451. Under the influence of advisers who advocated expansion, Mehmed made the conquest of Constantinople his first objective, accomplishing this aim on 29 May 1453. Thereafter Mehmed regarded himself as the sole heir of the imperial tradition of Rome, claimed absolute power, and pursued a relentless policy of centralization, greatly extending the *kul* (slave) system. His great aim was the creation of a universal empire with Istanbul, the renamed imperial city, which he repopulated, expanded, and enriched, as its capital. Whereas Murad II had been content to exact tribute and exercise a loose control over newly conquered territories, Mehmed sought to annex and bring under his immediate control central Anatolia and all the areas to the south of the Danube. This policy brought him into conflict with Hungary and Venice in the Balkans and with Uzun Hasan, the powerful Ak-Koyunlu ruler, in Anatolia. Between 1454 and 1459 he brought Serbia under his direct control, in 1460 the Peloponnese (Morea), and in 1463 Bosnia, in the process fighting many indecisive engagements. Despite a long siege in 1456 he failed to capture Belgrade. The Venetian war lasted intermittently from 1463 to 1479, with the Ottomans raiding deep into Venetian territory, ejecting the Venetians from Albania, the Peloponnese and the northern Aegean, except for certain strongholds.

The greatest emergency of Mehmed's reign occurred in the early 1470s, when an alliance between Uzun Hasan and Venice confronted him with the prospect of fighting on two fronts simultaneously. After enormous exertions, Mehmed emerged victorious, decisively defeating Uzun Hasan at the battle of Otluk-Beli in Anatolia in August 1473. He further consolidated his position with the conquest of Karaman in 1474.

The possession of the Bosphorus and the Dardanelles gave Mehmed command of the Black Sea, and he sought to subjugate all the territories on its shores. In 1459 he annexed Amastra, in 1461 Sinope and Trebizond; in 1475 he occupied Feodosiya (Kaffa) and all other Genoese colonies in the Crimea, followed by Azov; in 1479 he occupied Anapa, Cofa, and Matrida. The khans of the Crimea submitted to Ottoman suzerainty. Moldavia agreed to pay Mehmed tribute in 1454 but then defaulted, obliging Mehmed to launch a campaign into Moldavia in 1476.

An Ottoman fleet under Gedik Ahmed Pasha conquered the Ionian Islands in 1479 and also took Otranto in southern Italy. When surveying recent Turkish history in *De bello turcico*, Erasmus emphasized this success to the point of claiming that Pope *Sixtus IV had been driven to flee to France (LB V 351E–F). A Turkish attempt against Rhodes was unsuccessful. In 1481 Mehmed had already set out on a campaign, the aim of which was yet unknown, when he died suddenly at Hünkâr Çayiri on 3 May.

Mehmed was warlike by nature and considered the waging of *ghazwa* (war against the infidels) as the most sacred duty of a Muslim ruler. From 1466 he claimed primacy in the Muslim world. He had an alert mind and was a patron of literature and the scientific studies of his day. He was interested in western culture and summoned Gentile Bellini to Istanbul to do his portrait. His name is associated with the first Ottoman *Kanunname* or collection of laws. He built many edifices, including the Rumeli Hisari and the castles of the Dardanelles. The finest architectural achievement of the reign was the Fatih mosque in Istanbul.

BIBLIOGRAPHY: M. Süreyya *Sicill-i Osmânî* (Istanbul 1890–7) / J.H. Kramers in *Encyclopaedia of Islam* (Leiden-London 1913–38) III 658–60 / The best accounts are H. Inalcik in *Islam Ansiklopedisi* (Istanbul 1940–   ) VII 506–35, and H. Inalcik *Fatih Devri Üzerinde Tetkikler ve Vesikalar* (Ankara 1954) / Franz Babinger *Mehmed the Conqueror and His Time* trans R. Manheim (Princeton 1978) / S. Tansel *Osmanli kaynaklarina göre Fatih Sultan Mehmed'in siyasî ve askerî faaliyeti* (Ankara 1953)   FEHMI ISMAIL

Yahya-Pasha-zade MEHMED Bey d 1548
Yahya-Pasha-zade Mehmed Bey or Pasha (Mechmethbecus) was the second son of Yahya Pasha who had served as Beylerbey of Anatolia and Rumelia and attained the rank of *vezir*, marrying a daughter of *Bayezid II. His elder brother, Bali Bey, attained great fame for the important part he played at the battle of Mohács in 1526, later serving as Beylerbey of Buda. Information on Mehmed Bey's early years is scanty. Later, in 1529, when *Suleiman I launched his campaign which took him to the gates of Vienna, Mehmed Bey was the governor of Smederevo (Semendria) and served in the vanguard of the Ottoman forces – a position he also held during Suleiman's Hungarian campaign of 1532. In 1530, when an Austrian force sent by King *Ferdinand besieged Buda, Mehmed Bey marched into Hungary, forcing the enemy to withdraw. Mehmed Bey then made raids into Hungarian territory held by Ferdinand and into Austria, taking some fifteen thousand captives. A record of the cruelties attributed to him is in Ep 2396, where his rank is given as governor of Belgrade.

In 1532 Andrea *Doria had seized Koroni (Coron). Mehmed Bey, who was appointed governor of the Peloponnese (Morea) for the occasion, was given the task of recovering Koroni and achieved his aim in April 1534. When Ottoman-Hapsburg hostilities were resumed in Hungary in 1535, Mehmed Bey occupied the fortress of Požega in Slavonia and made raids into Austrian territory. Ferdinand reacted by sending a force, said to have been forty-five thousand strong, into Hungary. Mehmed Bey defeated this force at Vertizo on 1 December 1537, attaining great fame. In August 1543 Mehmed succeeded his brother Bali as Beylerbey of Buda. He followed up Suleiman I's Hungarian campaign of 1543 by taking a number of strongholds in the region of Nógrád and also Hatvan.

BIBLIOGRAPHY: Some scattered information may be found in I.H. Danismend *Izahli Osmanli Tarihi Kronolojisi* (Istanbul 1971) II and Joseph von Hammer-Purgstall *Geschichte des Osmanischen Reiches* (Pest 1827–35) passim
                                                        FEHMI ISMAIL

MEIER *See Johannes* MAIUS, *Adalberg and Jakob* MEYER

Philippus Melanchthon, by Lucas Cranach

Konrad MEIT of Worms, d 1551
Konrad Meit (Meijt) must be the talented
sculptor employed by *Margaret of Austria in
the construction of the church of Brou, who
was showing around a portrait medal of
Erasmus (Epp 1963, 1985). He was not a
Hollander though, as stated in Ep 1963, but a
native of Worms. After working at Wittenberg
in the atelier of Lukas Cranach, he became
sculptor at Margaret's court in Mechelen by
1512, working in the Netherlands approximately from 1510 to 1526. In 1514 he married
Berthelmina La Paige at Mechelen.

Meit's sculpture includes portraits of Margaret and *Charles v. Between 1526 and 1531
he was working in Brou in the Franche-
Comté and subsequently at Lons-le-Saunier
before returning to the Netherlands, where
he worked and died at Antwerp.

BIBLIOGRAPHY: Allen Ep 1963 / J. Duverger
Conrad Meijt (Brussels 1934) / de Vocht *Literae
ad Craneveldium* Ep 54 / Ulrich Thieme and Felix
Becker *Allgemeines Lexikon der Bildenden Künste*
(Leipzig 1907–50) XXIV 349–51 / Schottenloher
II 18, VII 164   MARCEL A. NAUWELAERTS

MEJÍA *See Cristóbal and Pero* MEXÍA

Philippus MELANCHTHON of Bretten,
16 February 1497–19 April 1560
Melanchthon was born in Bretten (Palatinate),
the son of the armourer Georg Schwarzerd
(Schwartzerdt) and Barbara Reuter, the niece
of Johann *Reuchlin. He was taught privately
by Johann Unger and acquired a thorough
knowledge of Latin. For a year after the death
of his father in 1508 he attended the Latin
school in Pforzheim whose director, Georg
*Simler, encouraged his studies in Greek.
Reuchlin rewarded him for his achievements
and on 15 March 1509 bestowed on him the
Greek name of Melanchthon, an elaborate
rendering of Schwarzerd. The boy honoured
his great-uncle by arranging a production of
one of Reuchlin's Latin comedies. On 14
October 1509 he matriculated at the University
of Heidelberg and soon was in contact with
*Wimpfeling, who in 1510 included two poems
by the thirteen-year-old among his own publications (*Supplementa Melanchthoniana* VI-1 1–3).
On 10 June 1511 Melanchthon obtained his BA
in the *via antiqua*. On 17 September 1512 he
matriculated at the University of Tübingen,
where he obtained his MA on 25 January 1514,
this time in the *via moderna*. His comprehensive studies also included scholastic theology.
Beyond taking the statutory courses he read
classical and neo-Latin poets, especially Angelo
*Poliziano. Among his academic teachers,
Franciscus Stadianus and Johann *Stöffler
awakened his enduring interest in Aristotelian
dialectic and astronomy respectively. He was
also indebted to Rodolphus *Agricola's *Dialectica*, a copy of which was given to him by an
older friend, Johannes *Oecolampadius (*Briefwechsel* III Ep 2780). From 1514 to 1516 he
divided his time between the university, where
he taught some courses, and the press of
Thomas *Anshelm, who employed him as a
corrector and printed his first publications,
among them his editions of the *Clarorum
virorum epistolae ... ad Joannem Reuchlin* (March
1514) and of Terence (March 1516). Moreover,
his academic teaching led him to compose
textbooks on Greek grammar (May 1518),
rhetoric (1519), and dialectic (1520).

In 1518 Melanchthon was appointed to the
new chair of Greek at the University of
Wittenberg. His inaugural lecture, *De corrigen-
dis adulescentiae studiis*, given on 28 August,
aligned him with the proponents of a curricu-

lum reform recently set in motion. In addition to his own humanistic program, he soon was to support *Luther's call for the reform of theology. In his Greek lectures he treated the New Testament and, substituting for the Hebrew teacher, he also lectured on the Psalms. In his disputation for the degree of *baccalaureus biblicus* (9 September 1519) he defended theses based on the reform program. Earlier on he had begun to defend Luther in his publications, and during Luther's stay at the Wartburg castle (1521–2) Melanchthon was his *alter ego* in Wittenberg. At this time Melanchthon's main theological work, the *Loci communes rerum theologicarum*, was being published in sections. He also continued to work for curriculum reform along humanistic lines. On 26 November 1520 he married (Ep 1168) Katharina Krapp (1497–1557), the daughter of a late cloth merchant and burgomaster of Wittenberg. In defiance of the statute which required the rector to be celibate he was elected to that office for the winter term of 1523–4. With the support of Frederick the Wise, elector of *Saxony (represented by Georgius *Spalatinus), he introduced student declamations as a regular practice, thus creating a solid base for rhetoric in the Wittenberg curriculum. These humanistic declamations at first replaced, but later came to co-exist with, disputations in the scholastic fashion. Melanchthon lectured on the New Testament to capacity audiences, while also reading difficult Greek authors with some talented students. Despite Luther's urgings he persistently refused to teach exclusively in the theological faculty and never accepted the supplemental pay offered by the elector for the theology courses he taught additionally. Under the university's new constitution of 1536 he, like Luther, received the special privilege of setting his own course independent of faculty regulations. In addition to a generous annual salary of two hundred florins, the elector had a spacious house built for him. His activities as a consultant to several princes netted additional income.

For a time Melanchthon's preoccupation with theology caused him to neglect Aristotle, but soon the latter's moral and political writings regained an important place in his studies, which also came to include anthropology and physics. His lectures formed the basis for commentaries and systematic textbooks. Most of these were rewritten and revised several times during his lifetime and continued to be reprinted afterwards.

The scholarly work of the *praeceptor Germaniae* was frequently interrupted by his involvement in ecclesiastical politics. For the benefit of his own sovereign as well as other princes and cities, he prepared memoranda and undertook journeys of varying duration, not to mention his frequent visits to locations in the vicinity of Wittenberg such as Torgau, Leipzig, Dessau, and Berlin. In the spring of 1524 he went to Bretten for a vacation, accompanied by Joachim *Camerarius, Franz Burchard, and Johann Silberborner, and let his friends ride on to Basel for a visit with Erasmus (see below). In October and November 1525 and May and June 1526 he was in Nürnberg to found a new school. In the summer of 1527 and the winter of 1528–9 he participated in church and school visitations in Thuringia; from August 1527 to March 1528 and again from July 1535 to February 1536 he was mostly in Jena, since epidemics in Wittenberg had forced a temporary relocation of the university. From February to May 1529 he accompanied the Elector John of *Saxony to the diet of Speyer, and in September and October 1529 he took part in the Marburg colloquy. From March to October 1530 Melanchthon devoted his time to preparing for and attending the diet of Augsburg. He composed the *Confessio Augustana*, conferred with other theologians, and afterwards wrote an *Apologia* for the *Confessio*. In late December 1534 he met with Martin *Bucer at Kassel to prepare a mutually acceptable definition of the Eucharist. In September and October 1536 he again visited Bretten en route for Tübingen, where he helped reorganize the university. In December 1535 and February and March 1537 he attended political meetings in Schmalkalden. He was also invited to visit France and England, but after lengthy consultations he declined. In 1539 he accompanied the elector to Frankfurt for a conference of princes. On the way back they visited ducal Saxony, which had recently joined the reformed camp following the death of Duke George of *Saxony. In particular, Melanchthon's advice was sought about the reorganization of the University of Leipzig. Early in 1540 he went again to Schmalkalden and on his way there had to attend the bigamous wedding of Philip of *Hesse. In June he was to attend the religious colloquy in Haguenau but suffered a nervous breakdown in Weimar when he learnt that, against the advice of the Wittenberg reformers, Landgrave Philip had failed to keep his bigamy secret. Melanchthon regained his strength in time to pull his weight at the colloquy of Worms (October 1540 to January 1541), where he faced the opposition of Johann *Eck. Subsequently in Regensburg (March to July 1541) a compromise on the question of justification was worked out with Johann Eck, Johann *Gropper, and Julius *Pflug, but final agreement eluded the parties, who could not resolve their differences concerning the mass and ecclesiology. From April to August 1543 Melanchthon and Bucer were at Bonn to advise Archbishop Hermann von *Wied on his plans for the reformation of the state of Cologne.

The war of Schmalkalden (1546–7) led to the siege and occupation of Wittenberg. The university had to be closed, and Melanchthon moved his family at first to Zerbst and finally to Nordhausen. There they were taken in by Michael Meienburg, who later on combined on his epitaph the portraits of Erasmus and the Wittenberg reformers. Melanchthon himself was constantly travelling, attending manifold negotiations. After the war he was asked to help found a university at Jena but declined and thus succeeded in persuading his new sovereign, Maurice of Saxony, to reopen the University of Wittenberg and rehire the former professors. Melanchthon's advice also induced Maurice to reject the emperor's Augsburg Interim in favour of the so-called Leipzig Interim which permitted Saxony to retain Protestant doctrines under the cover of conservative rites. On this count as on others Melanchthon came under sharp criticism from such intransigent Lutherans as his former pupil Matthias Flacius Illyricus, who took exception to the humanist component of his theology. Nevertheless, his authority remained great. He composed the Confessio saxonica for presentation to the council of Trent, but his journey to Trent (January to March 1552) was interrupted in Nürnberg because of the new round of warfare. From August to December 1557 he attended at Worms his last religious

colloquy, which, like the preceding ones, ended in failure.

If consensus with the Catholics proved elusive, Melanchthon rendered great services to his fellow evangelicals. In October 1557 he helped reorganize the University of Heidelberg. His textbook Examen ordinandorum, composed in 1552 for Mecklenburg, became a part of many other church ordinances. For electoral Saxony he gathered his most important theological writings into a Corpus doctrinae. He also translated his Loci communes into German (1555), dedicating the work to Anna Camerarius. The last years of his scholarly activity were mainly devoted to historical work such as a revision of the chronicle of Johannes Carion.

Melanchthon's relations with Erasmus were at all times characterized by deep mutual respect even though the initial enthusiasm was bound to wear off after Melanchthon had joined Luther. When Melanchthon was a lecturer in Tübingen at the age of nineteen he acknowledged the authority of Erasmus in his edition of Terence (Corpus Reformatorum I 12). Erasmus, for his part, gave extravagant praise to the young scholar in his Annotationes to the New Testament of 1516 (page 555, later removed). It would seem that this praise was occasioned by Melanchthon's Terence, which Erasmus must already have seen although both works were published in March 1516. On 27 August he advised Reuchlin to send the young Melanchthon to John *Fisher in England rather than to Italy (Ep 457). Melanchthon remained, however, in Tübingen. In the same month he composed an elaborate Greek poem in honour of Erasmus (Ep 454) which was forwarded to the latter by *Beatus Rhenanus (Ep 556) and given a prominent place in the Basel edition of Erasmus' and *More's Epigrammata (March 1518). Melanchthon also asked Oecolampadius to recommend him to Erasmus. Oecolampadius was glad to do so and Erasmus fully concurred with his high opinion of the young man (Epp 563, 605).

Under the influence of Luther, Melanchthon began to loosen his dependence on Erasmus. He made some critical remarks, apparently about the Paraphrasis in Romanos, which were at once transmitted to Louvain (Ep 877), but Melanchthon apologized in January 1519 (Ep 910) and Erasmus' benevolent reply showed that he was not offended (Ep 947). In his publications and letters of 1519 Melanchthon took the view that Luther and his followers agreed with Erasmus and were in fact his disciples (*Briefwechsel* I Epp 40, 46, 47, 57, 58, 65). At the time Erasmus' statements on Luther were not unfriendly; as for Melanchthon, Erasmus merely warned him against overworking (Epp 933, 947, 1113). As late as December 1521 Melanchthon was pleased to relay a report from *Pellicanus at Basel, who believed that Erasmus was still sympathetic to Luther (*Briefwechsel* I Epp 182, 191). However, he now made a firm distinction between Luther and Erasmus: whereas Luther had shown that the biblical message of salvation surpassed all rational thinking, Erasmus remained a teacher of civic virtues, much like the ancient philosophers, although preferable to them on account of his Christian faith (*Corpus Reformatorum* xx 700). Melanchthon presented this distinction in a short piece appeasingly entitled *De Erasmo et Luthero elogion*. It was published with his *Ratio discendi*, most likely in the first half of 1523, and was at once translated into German. The same publication also contained a piece by Luther, however, and when Erasmus saw the book, he judged it to be hostile (Ep 1348). Meanwhile the earliest version of Melanchthon's theological *magnum opus*, the *Loci communes*, had been published in 1521. It presented an approach to scriptural studies which Erasmus himself had encouraged in the *Ratio verae theologiae* (LB V 130F–131B), yet as an exercise in systematic theology it differed greatly from the priorities Erasmus had set for himself.

Despite this parting of the ways Erasmus and Melanchthon continued to treat each other with consideration, although they did not correspond for four years. Erasmus was kept informed by third parties of Melanchthon's personal affairs and publications (Epp 1128, 1168, 1199), though not always correctly (Ep 1258). An important letter defining Erasmus' position with regard to Luther (Ep 1202) was addressed to Justus *Jonas but intended for Melanchthon as well. In his numerous critical remarks about the Lutherans he did not mention Melanchthon by name; on the other hand, he was glad to inform his correspondents of Melanchthon's rejection of

Ulrich von *Hutten's *Expostulatio* (Epp 1429, 1437, 1477; Allen I 29; cf *Briefwechsel* I Epp 279, 282, 287–9, 292, 297, 319). In his opinion it was Melanchthon who, next to Luther, drew the line against the radicals (Ep 1432).

Nevertheless, the public controversy between Erasmus and Luther drew irrevocably closer. When Luther asked Erasmus in April 1524 to refrain from public criticism (Ep 1443), Melanchthon remained in Bretten rather than accompany Camerarius, who took Luther's letter to Erasmus at Basel. He did not write to Erasmus direct but expressed his continued admiration for him in a letter to Pellicanus (Ep 1496). While sending Luther a rather harsh reply (Ep 1445), Erasmus expressed his regrets at not having been able to meet Melanchthon (Epp 1445, 1452, 1466). When *De libero arbitrio* was published in September, Erasmus sent it to Melanchthon rather than Luther, with a long and reassuring letter (Ep 1496). Melanchthon replied at once that Erasmus' book was received with equanimity in Wittenberg and that Luther would be quick and moderate in his reply (Ep 1500). Erasmus replied on 10 December 1524 with another long letter (Ep 1523), in which Melanchthon discovered renewed bitterness (*Briefwechsel* I Ep 371). If there was indignation, it was not directed against Melanchthon personally, whose earlier report about the reception of *De libero arbitrio* Erasmus eagerly communicated to his friends (Epp 1519, 1528, 1529, 1531). Melanchthon apparently did not reply, and no more letters were exchanged for a period of more than three years, while references to Melanchthon were rare in Erasmus' letters to others (Epp 1624, 1729, 1806, 1934).

By this time Melanchthon had attained his own philosophico-theological position, taking an intermediary stance between Luther and Erasmus. He adopted Luther's view of Scripture and his distinction between law and evangel (*Briefwechsel* II Ep 2302), pointing out that Erasmus had not made a clear pronouncement on the doctrine of justification (*Briefwechsel* I Ep 332). He continued, however, to oppose attacks on Erasmus (*Briefwechsel* I Ep 339) and, despite occasional criticism (*Briefwechsel* I Ep 473), valued his writings (*Briefwechsel* I Epp 411, 436). It is significant that after the publication of *De libero arbitrio* Melanchthon moderated the emphasis on predestination maintained in his earlier writings. When Erasmus continued the controversy with Luther in publishing the *Hyperaspistes* (1526–7), Melanchthon was saddened by this intensification of the quarrel (*Briefwechsel* I Epp 457–60, 492, 540). In response to some complex references to himself in the first part of the *Hyperaspistes*, he asked Sigismundus *Gelenius to assure Erasmus that he had had no hand in the writing of Luther's *De servo arbitrio* (*Briefwechsel* I Ep 474; but cf Ep 475). By the time the second part of the *Hyperaspistes* was published, Melanchthon had spelt out his own position on free will in his commentary on Colossians (*Werke in Auswahl* IV 222–5) and in his *Articuli ... per visitatores* (*Corpus Reformatorum* XXVI 26–8; cf *Briefwechsel* I Epp 597–9, 603, 606, 616). His experience in visiting parishes led him to emphasize man's ability and duty to act morally, relegating to second place the insufficiency of all human action before God. Luther's preface to the German version of the *Articuli* (1528) gave these teachings an official stamp of approval; they were also incorporated in the *Confessio Augustana*. In this manner Melanchthon safeguarded against any excessive reliance on freedom derived from the gospel, realizing that his own former emphasis on predestination might have encouraged some radicals. Erasmus could accept this position. A journey to Saxony by Frans van der *Dilft gave him an opportunity to write to Melanchthon in February 1528 after three years of silence (Ep 1944). In so doing, he praised Melanchthon's *Articuli* by contrasting them with Luther's views. Melanchthon thanked him warmly, and, even though he defended Luther and the late Wilhelm *Nesen, professed his support for Erasmus' humanistic goals (Epp 1981, 1982). At the same time he continued to view Erasmus' theology with frank disapproval (*Briefwechsel* I Epp 807, 830).

Melanchthon did not share the indignation displayed by Camerarius and Julius Pflug over Erasmus' *Ciceronianus* (1528; *Briefwechsel* I Epp 693, 696, 714, II Epp 2018, 2051). In fact the *Ciceronianus* was correct in pointing out that Melanchthon's splendid literary gifts were never fully developed because of his preoccupation with other matters (ASD I-2 686).

Melanchthon continued to take an interest in Erasmus' writings (*Briefwechsel* I Epp 669, 678, 762, 816) and in October 1528 received a further letter from Erasmus, which is not extant (*Briefwechsel* I Epp 712, 714). Although in July 1529 he had promised Camerarius to terminate his correspondence with Erasmus (*Briefwechsel* I Ep 807), the diet of Augsburg occasioned a new exchange of letters, apparently initiated by Melanchthon (Epp 2343, 2355, 2357, 2358, 2363, 2365). Erasmus, however, was unable to come to Augsburg or otherwise fulfil the high hopes in him (*Briefwechsel* I Epp 948, 985, 991, 1064). In any case, Melanchthon's theological reserve towards Erasmus remained unchanged (*Briefwechsel* I Ep 1002).

Erasmus' judgment resembled Melanchthon's: in the *Epistola ad fratres Inferioris Germaniae* (published in August 1530; ASD IX-1 412), he stood by his praise for Melanchthon's character and promotion of *bonae literae* but rejected his faith. At the same time he emphasized that despite his repeated attacks on Luther, Melanchthon was still his friend and had never published a bitter word about him. The only true humanist at Wittenberg (ASD IX-1 396), Melanchthon is nevertheless criticized for his hesitant support of public schools and his silence about the expropriation of church property (ASD IX-1 392). In his *Epistola contra pseudevangelicos* of November 1529 (ASD IX-1 298; cf 400) Erasmus had even praised Melanchthon for his zeal in mending the damage caused by Luther.

In the following years the correspondence was carried on casually with letters of recommendation and polite answers, some of them missing (Epp 2732, 2970, 3120, 3127). The two friends shared their feelings about the direction of the humanistic and reformatory movements. Erasmus noted Melanchthon's invitation to Poland by Bishop Andrzej *Krzycki but realized that he would never separate himself from Luther (Epp 2876, 2911). Although he once called him more Lutheran than Luther himself (Ep 2911), he continued to credit Melanchthon with a moderating influence on Luther (Epp 2937, 2947). In fact Melanchthon voiced disapproval (*Briefwechsel* II Epp 1420, 1421; Luther w *Tischreden* IV 573) of the virulent *Epistolae ... Amsdorfii et ... Lutheri de Erasmo Roterodamo* (Wittenberg 1534), while Erasmus sent gift copies of Melanchthon's *Commentarii* *in epistolam Pauli ad Romanos* (1532) to bishops Christoph von *Stadion and Jacopo *Sadoleto, although he could not fully approve of the work (Epp 2818, 2970, 2971, 3043). Finally Melanchthon's new edition of the *Loci communes* (1535) seems to have offended the sensitive Erasmus, but he was soon appeased by Melanchthon's moderate stance and words of heartfelt admiration (Epp 3120, 3127), and thus their correspondence ended with Erasmus' death.

In Melanchthon's biographical preface to the second volume of Luther's Latin works (1 June 1546) Erasmus is presented as a humanist forerunner of the Reformation, sharing Luther's concerns but opposed to his vehemence (*Corpus Reformatorum* VI 161, 163). On 5 August 1557 Melanchthon honoured Erasmus with a formal address given at an academic function in Wittenberg, presenting him again as a supporter of the Reformation (*Declamatio de Erasmo, Corpus Reformatorum* XII 264–71). Even on his deathbed, Melanchthon was moved to repeat Erasmus' last prayer (*Corpus Reformatorum* X 233, 278; Flitner 17).

BIBLIOGRAPHY: Allen Ep 454 / ADB XXI 268–79 / DTC X-1 502–13 / RGG IV 834–41 / *Philippi Melanthonis opera quae supersunt omnia* ed C.G. Bretschneider and H.E. Bindseil (Halle and Brunswick 1834–60, repr 1963) *Corpus Reformatorum* vols 1–28 / *Supplementa Melanchthoniana* (Leipzig 1910–29, repr 1968) / *Melanchthons Werke in Auswahl* ed R. Stupperich (Gütersloh 1951–   ) / *Melanchthons Briefwechsel* ed H. Scheible (Stuttgart-Bad Cannstatt 1977–   ) / Werner Zimmerman 'Melanchthon im Bildnis' in *Philipp Melanchthon 1497–1560* ed Georg Urban (Bretten 1960) 127–158 / Oskar Thulin 'Melanchthons Bildnis und Werk in zeitgenössischer Kunst' in *Philipp Melanchthon, Forschungsbeiträge* ed Walter Elliger (Göttingen 1961) 180–193 (with 33 illustrations) / Sibylle Harksen 'Bildnisse Philipp Melanchthons' in Leo Stern et al *Philipp Melanchthon, Humanist, Reformator, Praeceptor Germaniae* (Berlin 1960) 270–287 with plates I–XII / Wilhelm Hammer *Die Melanchthonforschung im Wandel der Jahrhunderte. Ein beschreibendes Verzeichnis* (Gütersloh 1967–   ) / Peter Fraenkel and Martin Greschat *Zwanzig Jahre Melanchthonstudium. Sechs Literaturberichte (1945–1965)* (Geneva 1967) / Karl Hartfelder *Philipp Melanchthon als Praeceptor Germaniae* (Berlin 1889, repr 1964) /

Clyde L. Manschreck *Melanchthon The Quiet Reformer* (New York–Nashville 1958) / Peter Meinhold *Philipp Melanchthon. Der Lehrer der Kirche* (Berlin 1960) / Robert Stupperich *Melanchthon* (Berlin 1960, English trans 1966) / Wilhelm Maurer *Der junge Melanchthon zwischen Humanismus und Reformation* (Göttingen 1967–9) / Heinz Scheible 'Philip Melanchthon, der bedeutendste Sohn der Stadt Bretten' in *Geschichte der Stadt Bretten von den Anfängen bis zur Zerstörung 1689* ed Alfons Schäfer (Bretten 1977) 257–82 / Andreas Flitner *Erasmus im Urteil seiner Nachwelt* (Tübingen 1952) 14–17 / Wilhelm Maurer 'Melanchthons Anteil am Streit zwischen Luther und Erasmus' ARG 49 (1959) 89–114, repr in Wilhelm Maurer *Melanchthon-Studien* (Gütersloh 1964) 137–62
HEINZ SCHEIBLE

Dionysius MELANDER of Ulm, 1486– 10 July 1561
In Allen Ep 2806:111n an unnamed advocate of heretical teachings on the Eucharist is tentatively identified with Dionysius Melander, an evangelical minister at Frankfurt. However, the tenets professed by the heretic cannot be attributed to Melander, who enjoyed the confidence of the Frankfurt council and was never jailed. Two years before the composition of Ep 2806 (5 May 1533) Melander had endorsed the moderate eucharistic position of *Bucer; see G.E. Steitz 'Luthers Warnungsschrift an Rath und Gemeinde zu Frankfurt (1533) und Dionysius Melanders Abschied von seinem Amt (1535) ... ' *Archiv für Frankfurts Geschichte und Kunst* n s 5 (1872) 257–81.
KONRAD WIEDEMANN

Bernardus MELIN (Ep 2652 of 31 May [1532])
Bernardus Melin, who was supposed to transmit a letter to Andrea *Alciati, has not been identified. Alfred Hartmann (AK IV Epp 1651, 1915) suggested Johann Bernhard Rumelin (Rymili) of Rheinfelden.

Petrus MELLIS of Antwerp, documented 1507–28
Petrus Mellis (Melis) joined the Dominican order at his native city of Antwerp. In 1507 the chapter general of his order meeting at Pavia instructed him to go to Cologne for study and, presumably following a period of study at the Dominican monastery, on 11 September 1511

he matriculated at the University of Cologne. In 1515 he was as *magister studentium* in charge of the Dominicans studying in Cologne and on 26 May 1517 he received his doctorate in theology, with Jacob of *Hoogstraten acting as promoter. He taught divinity at Cologne until 1520, when he returned to Antwerp. He was no doubt identical with a Dominican who criticized Erasmus' work at a dinner party. Erasmus was quite forthright in stating: 'He gets his name from honey [*mel* in Latin] though his remarks are nothing but bitter aloes' (Allen Ep 1196:510–15; c March 1521). In 1528 the provincial chapter meeting at Antwerp condemned him as an apostate and fugitive from the order.

BIBLIOGRAPHY: *Acta capitulorum provinciae Germaniae Inferioris ordinis Fratrum Praedicatorum ab anno* MDXV *usque ad annum* MDLIX ed S.P. Wolfs (The Hague 1964) 25–6, 29, 94 / *Matrikel Köln* I 68*, II 682   PGB

Francisco de MELO 1490–27 April 1536
Melo's father, Dom Manuel, was at some time Portuguese governor of Tangier; his mother was Beatriz da Silva. Francisco studied first at the University of Lisbon and then went to Paris, where *Vives knew him in 1520. In a letter to Erasmus Vives counted him among those whose example was 'a great stimulus to better things' (Ep 1108). Melo had a wide range of interests, including theology, mathematics, and poetry. During his stay in France he annotated and published (Lyon: S. Gryphius) some verses of Ausonius Decimus Magnus of Bordeaux (310?–95?), who was celebrated as a Christian poet although his poetry was often inspired by pagan divinities. Melo explained the reason for this work in a letter to Joanna Vaz, to whom he sent a copy: Ausonius was mainly known for his love poems, but Melo wanted to show another side of him which had mathematical implications. This letter is a learned letter directed to a learned woman. Joanna belonged to the circle of ladies around the court of Princess Maria, the sister of King *John III of Portugal, and was famous for her proficiency in five languages, among them Arabic. She also was an admirer of Erasmus and composed a poem on his death. After his return to his homeland in 1524, Melo played an important role as counsellor to John III. In 1534

he was appointed the first bishop of Tangier, but whether he went there is not established.

Melo's speeches before the assembled estates of Portugal are interesting documents. Firmly against tyranny, he believed aristocracy to be the best form of government. The king's actions, Melo held, should be guided by reason and motivated by the virtues of justice, prudence, constancy, and determination. Melo further stated that the king must always be ready to accept advice since, according to Socrates, no other person was in greater need of truthful information than a ruler. He strongly recommended that assemblies be summoned at regular intervals, citing the example of the Jewish kings. He favoured the decisions of the council of Basel to convene general councils of the church every tenth year. Melo proposed ecclesiastical reform on humanist lines: better knowledge of the ancients and emphasis on eloquence.

BIBLIOGRAPHY: Allen and CWE Ep 1108 / Marcel Bataillon 'Erasme et la cour de Portugal' in *Etudes sur le Portugal au temps de l'humanisme* (Coimbra 1952) 97–99 / André de Resende *Oração de Sapiência* (Lisbon 1956), notes by A. Moreira de Sá 106–21 where some of Melo's speeches are also printed / Carolina Michaelis de Vasconcellos *A Infanta D. Maria de Portugal (1521–77) e as suas damas* (Porto 1903) 37–38 (on Joanna)   ELISABETH FEIST HIRSCH

Heinrich MELTINGER of Basel, d 1529
Meltinger matriculated in the University of Basel in the autumn of 1485. As the son of a leading merchant and city councillor whose career had ended in a sentence for embezzlement, Heinrich was not encouraged to continue the family business. He therefore left Basel and joined the Swiss mercenaries in the pay of France. When he returned home after the turn of the century he joined the city aristocrats organized in the 'Hohen Stube,' married the daughter of one of them, Martha Meyer von Baldersdorf, and entered the service of the bishop of Basel, becoming his official in the Birs valley in 1504. In 1509 he took service with the city and administrated the district of Waldenburg in Basel's territory until 1512. When Riehen was subsequently acquired by the city he was appointed bailiff of that village. In 1512 he was elected to the city

council, becoming *Oberzunftmeister* in 1516 and burgomaster in 1523. His military skills too were now employed for the benefit of Basel. In the battles of Novara (1513) and Marignano (1515) he was one of Basel's captains and fought in the frontline of the Swiss armies. At Marignano he was seriously wounded.

Meltinger's reputation as the city's outstanding statesman was severely put to the test by the religious conflicts of the 1520s. He soon emerged as the political leader of the papal party and in the city council he strongly opposed the toleration advocated by a majority of his colleagues. In 1528 he made a fruitless attempt to re-establish the mass at Riehen, which was under his jurisdiction. When his life appeared threatened at the height of the popular agitation (Epp 2158, 2162, 2201) he left Basel quietly in the night of 8/9 February 1529, hours before the council voted to deprive him and his allies of their membership and to accede to the other demands of the Protestant party. Broken-hearted, he died at Colmar shortly thereafter. After the death of his first wife he had married Margarete Gottschalk and after her death, about 1508, Magdalena Hüssy. He had a son and three daughters.

Meltinger lived at the Nadelberg just opposite Erasmus and was evidently in familiar contact with him. When Erasmus commended the prudent handling of the peasant rebellion by the Basel government it was clearly Meltinger he singled out for special praise (Ep 1585). He also noted his eloquence and diplomatic skill on other occasions (ASD IX-1 386, Ep 2158) and expressed pity for him at his downfall.

In the *Epistola ad fratres Inferioris Germaniae* Meltinger's name was given as 'Melchior,' but Erasmus himself corrected the mistake of his secretary Quirinus *Talesius, who had copied the text for printing (ASD IX-1 386–7, LB X 1614, Ep 2378). As a result of incomplete information supplied by the editors, 'Melchior' was wrongly identified as Melchior *Ergesheimer in *Contemporaries of Erasmus* I.

BIBLIOGRAPHY: Allen Epp 1585, 2112 / *Wappenbuch der Stadt Basel* ed W.R. Staehelin (Basel [1917–30]) / DHBS IV 713 / R. Wackernagel *Geschichte der Stadt Basel* (Basel 1907–54) III 121, 419, 513, and passim / *Matrikel Basel* I 189 / AK III Ep 1025 and passim   PGB

Gregor MELTZER *See Gregorius* HALOANDER

MENARD of Hoorn d before 5 December 1518
Menard (Menardus Hoernensis) is documented only for the last few months of his short life. A native of Hoorn in North Holland, he seems to have received a MA from the University of Louvain (AK II Ep 642), no doubt as a student of Rutgerus *Rescius (Ep 904). Towards the end of October 1518 Erasmus sent him to Basel, perhaps together with Lambertus *Hollonius. He carried several letters and, above all, the final sections of the text of Erasmus' New Testament, which was then being reprinted by Johann *Froben, who was expected to employ Menard (Epp 882, 885). Highly recommended by Erasmus for his character and knowledge of Greek and Latin, Menard was in fact employed by Froben but died of the plague about a month after his arrival in Basel (Ep 904).

BIBLIOGRAPHY: Allen and CWE Ep 885 / de Vocht CTL II 24 / Bierlaire *Familia* 54 / Franz Bierlaire *Erasme et ses Colloques: le livre d'une vie* (Geneva 1977) 17–18   FRANZ BIERLAIRE

Genesius MENDESIUS (Ep 2951 of 3 July 1534)
Mendesius, an unidentified scholar, sent Erasmus a letter in Greek from Rome.

Francisco de MENDOZA y Bobadilla
25 September 1508–26 November 1566
Born in Cuenca, Francisco de Mendoza y Bobadilla (Bobadilla y Mendoza) was the uncle of Mencia de *Mendoza. He studied arts at Alcalá and law at Salamanca, where he was a favourite student of Hernán Núñez, known as 'el Comendador griego' or 'el Pinciano'. Mendoza was archdeacon of Toledo and from 1533 bishop of Coria. On 19 December 1544 he was created cardinal, and on 27 June 1550 was elected bishop of Burgos, on each occasion at the request of *Charles V. He represented Spanish interests in Rome from the time of his admission to the college of cardinals and in Siena from the time of the collapse of the Republic in 1555. In Italy he had the reputation of being a shrewd and tough diplomat. At Rome he lived in state in a palace on the Campo di Fiore (Palazzo Pio), built on the ruins of Pompey's theatre, and was known as a patron of the Jesuit order. In 1557 he returned to

Spain, reformed his diocese according to the decrees of the council of Trent, founding the first seminary, and devoted himself to theology.

In March 1527, when Mendoza was eighteen and archdeacon of Toledo, Erasmus considered him as one of his loyal supporters in Spain (Ep 1805). In 1531 he was with the imperial court in the Netherlands. Henry de Vocht identified him with the brilliant young archdeacon of Toledo who had come to Regensburg to attend the diet and was described to Erasmus in August 1531 as his admirer (draft of an undated letter, attributed to Johannes *Dantiscus). Bataillon found proof of Mendoza's Erasmianism in his *Constituciones y actos* for the diocese of Coria, which he introduced in 1537. He considered Mendoza as one of the leading representatives of aristocratic humanism in Spain. El Pinciano dedicated his *Observationes* on Pliny's *Historia naturalis* (Salamanca 1544) to Mendoza. Juan Luis *Vives dedicated his *De ratione dicendi* (Louvain: B. Gravius 1533) to him, addressing him as rector of the University of Salamanca. Bonaventure, the son of Petrus *Vulcanius of Bruges, was his secretary in 1558. Mendoza wrote *De naturali cum Christo unitate*, ed A. Piolanti (Rome 1947).

BIBLIOGRAPHY: Allen Ep 1805 / *Enciclopedia Cattolica* (Vatican City 1949–54) VIII 678–80 / de Vocht CTL III 23–8 / de Vocht *Dantiscus* 104–6 / Bataillon *Erasmo y España* 338–9 and passim / N. López Martínez 'El cardenal Mendoza y la reforma tridentina en Burgos' *Hispania sacra* 16 (1963) 61–137 / Pastor XII 93–5, XIII 383, and passim / Eubel III 28, 143, 160

MILAGROS RIVERA & PGB

Francisco de MENDOZA y Córdoba
d 29 March 1536

Francisco de Mendoza y Córdoba was successively bishop of Oviedo (6 November 1525–1527), Zamora (3 April 1527–1534), and Palencia (18 January 1534 to his death); he was also count of Pernia. From 1525 he presided over *Charles v's treasury council (*Consejo de hacienda*), which under his direction was well organized and efficient. As inspector-general of the 'Cruzada' (until his death) he also supervised the ecclesiastical revenue of the court. His secretary, Diego *Gracián de Alde-rete, described him as chief counsellor to the Empress *Isabella in the absence of the emperor and as a fervent supporter of Erasmus (Ep 2297, 28 March 1530). However, no direct relations between Mendoza and Erasmus have come to light. Under Mendoza's patronage Alonso *Fernández published the service book of the church of Palencia in 1536.

BIBLIOGRAPHY: Allen Ep 2297 / Eubel III 265, 267, 339 / Antonio Paz y Mélia 'Otro erasmista español, Diego Gracián de Alderete' *Revista de archivos, bibliotecas y museos* 3rd ser, 5 (1901) 27–36, 125–39, 608–25 / Milagros Ezquerro *Diego Gracián de Alderete* (Toulouse 1968) / F. Walser and R. Wohlfeil *Die spanischen Zentralbehörden und der Staatsrat Karls v.* (Göttingen 1959) 191, 218–19   MILAGROS RIVERA & PGB

Mencia de MENDOZA marchioness of Zenete, documented 1525–41

Mencia (Menzia) de Mendoza was the granddaughter of Pedro González de Mendoza, the powerful cardinal-archbishop of Seville and Toledo, and a niece of Francisco de *Mendoza y Bobadilla. The only daughter of Rodrigo, marquis of Zenete (Cagnete, Canete, Cenete), she received an excellent education and was considered a girl of great promise by Juan Luis *Vives, who had met her in Valencia; see his *De institutione feminae christianae libri tres* (Antwerp: M. Hillen 1524) I chapter 4. She inherited her father's rich estates in Spain and married Henry III, count of *Nassau-Dillenburg, on 30 June 1524. Her interest in humanist studies did not stop with her marriage. In 1529 she left Spain with her husband, often residing thereafter in the Low Countries, especially at Breda, where she studied with the renowned Spanish humanist scholar Hernán Ruiz de Villegas (probably a student of Vives), who dedicated to her an eclogue on the death of Vives (in *Ferdinandi Ruizii Villegatis Burgensis quae extant opera*, Venice 1743). She was also an able administrator of her estates, and, since her marriage was childless, these were not joined to the Nassau territories. After Henry III's death in 1538 she married Ferdinand of Aragon, duke of Calabria (1488–1550). On this occasion the Belgian poet Petrus Nannius, impressed by her knowledge of Greek, dedicated to her his *Dialogismi heroinarum* (Paris: C. Wechel 1541).

Mencia de Mendoza, an ardent admirer of Erasmus, happened to be present in Louvain in 1536 when *Goclenius had to resort to litigation over a prebend at Antwerp. Taking a personal interest in the matter, she brought it to a satisfactory conclusion (Ep 3111). Consequently Goclenius urged Erasmus to write to her; although willing to do so, Erasmus was unable to comply with his wish since he did not know where she resided (Ep 3130).

BIBLIOGRAPHY: Allen Ep 3111 / ADB XI 552 / DBI III 693 / de Vocht CTL III 101–2, 461 / de Vocht *Busleyden* 21 / Amédé Polet *Une Gloire de l'humanisme belge, Petrus Nannius* (Louvain 1936) 268–9 / F. Walser and R. Wohlfeil *Die spanischen Zentralbehörden und der Staatsrat Karls v.* (Göttingen 1959) 48–9   IG

Francisco de MENESES of Salamanca
Francisco de Meneses was a Franciscan of Salamanca who in the mid-1520s collaborated with Francisco *Castillo in preparing a collection of errors found in the works of Erasmus (Ep 2094). He was praised by Luis de *Carvajal in his *Apologia monasticae religionis diluens nugas Erasmi* (Salamanca: n pr 1528) as an eminent Scotist but at the same time a humanist so learned that Elio Antonio de *Nebrija would publish nothing without consulting him. His only other known work was a manual entitled *Difficilium accentuum compendium* (Paris: R. Estienne 1527), later republished as the *Brevis ac dilucida accentuum collectio* (Salamanca: J. de Junta 1546).

BIBLIOGRAPHY: Allen Ep 2094 / Bataillon *Erasmo y España* 219, 319, 723   TBD

Johann MENLISHOFER of Überlingen, d 5 August 1548
Johann Menlishofer (Mänishofer, Menlishoverus) of Überlingen, on Lake Constance, matriculated at Freiburg on 26 February 1506, graduating BA in 1507 and MA in 1508–9. On 20 May 1511 he matriculated at the University of Montpellier, the same day as his countryman Joachim Egellius (see Doctor *Ioacinus) of Ravensburg. In the autumn of 1512 they matriculated together at the University of Vienna, attracted no doubt by the presence of Joachim *Vadianus. In Vienna both may have completed their medical studies. Menlishofer was sworn in as town physician of Constance

on 16 May 1516. He was a kinsman of Michael *Hummelberg and belonged to the humanist circle of Johann von *Botzheim. In April 1518 he married the daughter of the burgomaster, Jakob Gaisberg. By 1523 he was favouring the reform movement of Constance and soon became one of its leaders. In 1542 he gave advice to Johann *Zwick as to how to avoid the plague. He was killed when Spanish troops stormed Constance after *Charles v's victory at Schmalkalden.

When Erasmus visited Constance in 1522 he met Menlishofer in Botzheim's house and was impressed by his knowledge and modesty (Allen Ep 1342:418–20). He sent greetings to Menlishofer in Ep 1331 and Ep I (Allen I 46).

BIBLIOGRAPHY: Allen Ep 1335 / *Matrikel Freiburg* I 168 / *Matricule de Montpellier* 20 / *Matrikel Wien* II-1 392 / Rublack *Reformation in Konstanz* 211–13 and passim / Bernd Moeller *Johannes Zwick und die Reformation in Konstanz* (Gütersloh 1961) 102, 240 / Bernhard Milt *Vadian als Arzt* (St Gallen 1959)   IG & PGB

Johannes a MERA (Ep 2700 of 9 August 1532)
Erasmus recalled having met the friar Dietrich *Kolde, probably around 1493–4 at Bergen op Zoom in the house of a highly respected citizen by the name of Johannes a Mera. This man has not been identified; Jan van der Meer, Meeren, etc is a common name.

Petrus MERBELIUS documented 1509–48
Petrus Merbelius (Merbel, Marbel, Merbeglio) matriculated at Erfurt in 1509 with his brother Johannes and later spent twenty years in the service of Francesco II *Sforza of Milan (Ep 3070). On Sforza's death in 1535 his appointment as secretary was continued by the government of *Charles v at Milan. In 1541 he was arrested on suspicion of heresy but was freed and soon reinstated.

On 18 March 1535 Erasmus wrote to Merbelius and Johannes Baptista *Laurentia discussing the recent attacks on him by Etienne *Dolet, Georg von *Logau, and Julius Caesar *Scaliger (Ep 3005). Merbelius later sent Erasmus at least three letters, informing him of the deaths of Cardinal Ippolito de' *Medici (Ep 3039) and Sforza (Ep 3070) and of his good fortune in being employed by the imperial government at Milan (Ep 3091). He also acted

Balthasar Merklin

---

as a contact between Erasmus and Ambrosius von *Gumppenberg at Rome (Ep 3047).

Merbelius was also a friend of Francesco Giulio *Calvo, *Beatus Rhenanus, and Conradus *Pellicanus. Between 1543 and 1546 he sent thirteen letters to Beatus Rhenanus, discussing political and religious events in Italy and the Empire, in one of them stating that a number of Erasmus' works were burnt as heretical at Milan on 29 January 1543 (BRE Ep 362). Fourteen letters to Pellicanus dated 1540–8 are found at Zürich.

BIBLIOGRAPHY: Allen Ep 3005 / *Matrikel Erfurt* II 262 / BRE Ep 362 and passim / AK V Ep 2539 / Federico Chabod *Per la storia religiosa dello stato di Milano durante il dominio di Carlo v* 2nd ed by Ernesto Sestan (Rome 1962) 144–5 and passim / *Christoph Scheurl's Briefbuch* ed F. von Soden and J.K.F. Knaake (Potsdam 1867–72, repr 1962) I Ep 280   TBD

Estéban Gabriel MERINO d July 1535
Merino was appointed archbishop of Bari on 9 May 1513 and resigned this see in 1530; he was also bishop of León (17 December 1516–1523) and of Jaén (12 June 1523 until his death), and

Patriarch of the Indies in 1530. Even before leaving Spain for Rome, the newly elected Pope *Adrian VI appointed him to go to Paris as his nuncio, and by the autumn of 1522 he was in France. This appointment is mentioned in a dedicatory letter by Juan de Celaya, who ascribed to him in 1523 his commentary on Aristotle's *Ethics*. In 1526 he became an adviser to Fadrique *Alvarez de Toledo, duke of Alba, and in 1529 *Charles v's envoy to Pope *Clement VII. At the emperor's request he was named to the college of cardinals on 21 February 1533 and was known thereafter as the cardinal of Bari.

Although no direct exchange of letters between Erasmus and Merino is on record, the Spanish prelate had shown an interest in Erasmus' writings even before the conference of Valladolid (1527), as is shown by two letters he addressed to Alfonso de *Valdés in which he requested information about the steps undertaken in Erasmus' favour and pledged his support, especially for the edition of St Augustine. Allen suggested that he might be the author of the anonymous letter in support of Erasmus mentioned by Valdés in Ep 2198, but this hypothesis is not accepted by either Fermín Caballero or Bataillon. Merino spent his last years in Rome, where he died. In April 1535 *Gumppenberg suggested that Erasmus should write to Merino and some other cardinals (Ep 3011), but four months later he informed Erasmus of Merino's death (Ep 3047).

BIBLIOGRAPHY: Allen Ep 2198 / Bataillon *Erasmo y España* 229, 273, 323, 431, and passim / Pastor IX 56, 93–4, and passim / Fermín Caballero *Alonso y Juan de Valdés* (Madrid 1875) documents 20 and 23 / Eubel III 21, 129, 203, 221 / Emile Legrand 'Bibliographie hispano-grecque' I no 47 in *Bibliographie hispanique 1915* (New York 1915)   MILAGROS RIVERA

Balthasar MERKLIN of Waldkirch, c 1479–28 May 1531
Balthasar Merklin (Mercklin), born in Waldkirch, near Freiburg, received his education in Sélestat. In 1495 he was a canon of St Simeon's in Trier, and later he was dean. He matriculated in Bologna in 1498 and obtained a doctorate in canon law on 14 August 1500. After his return to Germany he was a canon in

Constance, one of *Maximilian I's councillors in 1507, and provost in Waldkirch in 1508. Most of his life was spent in the diplomatic service of the Hapsburgs. In September 1521 he went to Constance as an imperial envoy; he was to press for the execution of the edict of Worms but had to leave the city in the face of popular agitation. From 1522 to 1527 he was in Spain with the Emperor *Charles v. In 1527 he was vice-chancellor of the Empire and bishop of Malta as well as administrator of Hildesheim. In the summer of 1528 the emperor sent him to Nürnberg in an effort to restrain the reformers; in 1529 and 1530 he attended the diets of Speyer and Augsburg. He also used his diplomatic skill in efforts to reconcile the city of Constance with Bishop Hugo von *Hohenlandenberg and was elected coadjutor to the bishop in 1527. When Hohenlandenberg retired, Merklin succeeded him as bishop of Constance on 9 March 1529 (Epp 2310, 2316). In 1531, travelling to the Low Countries, he died suddenly in Trier.

Merklin was a friend of *Zasius, *Pirckheimer, and *Vadianus. In 1523 Johann von *Botzheim, accused him of hostility towards Erasmus (Ep 1382), but in 1529 Erasmus knew him to be sympathetic and corresponded with him (Epp 2123, 2166). With Ep 2284 he dedicated to Merklin his edition of a treatise on the Eucharist by Alger of Liège (d c 1131). Merklin had advised Erasmus not to attend the diet of Augsburg (Epp 2371, 2375), and Erasmus praised him in his colloquy *Concio* (ASD I-3 666) for supporting him during the diet against the attacks of the Franciscan *Medardus.

BIBLIOGRAPHY: Allen Ep 1382 / ADB XXI 445–6 / Knod 344 / Rublack *Reformation in Konstanz* 209–10 and passim / Bernd Moeller *Johannes Zwick und die Reformation in Konstanz* (Gütersloh 1961) 106–7 / H. Buck and E. Fabian *Konstanzer Reformationsgeschichte in ihren Grundzügen I: 1519–1531* (Tübingen 1965) 29 and passim / Adolf Engelhardt *Die Reformation in Nürnberg* (Nürnberg 1936–7) II 65–8 / Karl Brandi *Kaiser Karl v*. new ed (Darmstadt 1959–67) I 154 and passim / Valentin von Tetleben *Protokoll des Augsburger Reichstages 1530* ed H. Grundmann (Göttingen 1958) 30 and passim   IG

Jan van MERLEBERGE of Diest,
d December 1533
Jan van Merleberge (Merleberghe, Merliberch) of Diest, in Brabant, was already in orders when he matriculated at the University of Louvain on 27 January 1491. In 1497 he entered the monastery of St Maartensdal at Louvain, which belonged to the Windesheim congregation of the canons regular of St Augustine. At some date between about 1518 and 1520 Erasmus gratified the ageing monk by composing at his request an inscription in verse for a painting of Saints Mary Magdalen and John (Ep 1130, Reedijk poem 111).

BIBLIOGRAPHY: Allen and CWE Ep 1130 / *Matricule de Louvain* III-1 67 / W. Lourdaux *Moderne Devotie en christelijk humanisme: de geschiedenis van Sint-Maarten te Leuven van 1433 tot het einde der XVIe eeuw* (Louvain 1967) 148, 299, 325   PGB

Jacques MERLIN of Saint-Victurnien,
documented 1490–1541
Jacques Merlin was probably the 'I.M.' who was a student of Girolamo *Balbi about 1490–1 in Paris and who published a defence of Balbi against Fausto *Andrelini's charges which had forced Balbi to leave Paris. If so, Merlin returned to his native Limousin but came back again in about 1497 to Paris, where he studied Scotist philosophy at the Collège de Reims under Pierre *Tartaret. In 1502 he became a *bursarius theologus* of the Collège de Navarre and received his licence in theology on 5 February 1510, ranking fourteenth of twenty-nine, and his doctorate on 17 October 1510. He became the principal of the Collège de Saint-Michel (Collège de Chenac) in Paris and was the curé of Montmartre by 1514, at which time he was involved in an attempted reformation of discipline at the abbey of Saint-Victor. Merlin was fairly active in affairs of the faculty of theology, the university, and the diocese of Paris.

From 1522 to 1528 Merlin was engaged in a bitter dispute with Noël *Béda, syndic of the faculty of theology, over Merlin's *Apologia* for Origen which appeared in his edition of Origen's works. This dispute was debated in over fifty meetings of the faculty and was intensified when Merlin publicly ridiculed Béda for attempting to stifle the works of

Erasmus (Ep 1763). The case was allowed to drop when Merlin was sentenced to prison for opposing a heavy tax on Parisians to ransom *Francis I's sons from Madrid and for criticizing Louise of *Savoy's inadequate military defence of Paris. After two years in prison and before a subsequent exile of one year in Nantes, Merlin exercised his office as canon and penitentiary of Paris by assisting Louis de *Berquin at his execution at the stake. Merlin also served as a *proviseur* of the Hôtel-Dieu of Paris from 1522 until his death. In 1530 he was named vicar-general of the bishop of Paris, a position of importance since Bishop François *Poncher was in prison. But Merlin lost this appointment in 1532, when Jean *Du Bellay became bishop. Merlin probably died on 26 September 1541, although one source (perhaps misreading the manuscript) indicates he was still alive in 1544. There is no evidence to suggest that Merlin was the Merlinus who was in Bologna in 1508 and intended to visit Erasmus and Aldo *Manuzio in Venice (Ep 210).

Merlin's works include *Invectiva in Faustum Balbi calumniatorem* (n p [1495]); his editions of Pierre d'Ailly *Questiones super primum, tertium, et quartum Sententiarum* (Paris: Jean Barbier for Jean Petit c 1508, c 1515); Durandus de Saint-Pourçain *In quattuor Sententiarum libros questionum ... decisiones* (Paris: Josse Bade for self and Jean Petit 1508, c 1515); Origen *Opera* (Paris: Josse Bade for self and Jean Petit 1512, c 1515, 1519, 1522, 1530; Lyon: Jacques Giunta, Nicolas Parvi, and Hector Penet 1536); Richard of Saint-Victor *Omnia opera* (Paris: André Bocard for Jean Petit and Josse Bade 1518); Pierre de Blois *Insignia opera* (Paris: André Bocard for Jean Petit 1519); and *Tomus primus quatuor conciliorum generalium. Secundus tomus quadraginta septem conciliorum provincialium* (Paris: Jean Cornillau for Galliot Du Pré 1524; Cologne: Peter Quentel 1530; Paris: François Regnault 1535; Paris 1675; Lyon 1701, 1723). He also wrote *L'Exposition de l'évangile 'Missus est Gabriel,' contenant le mystère de la réparation de nature humaine* (Paris: Yolande Bonhomme for self and Jean Petit 1539).

BIBLIOGRAPHY: Allen Ep 1763 / Clerval passim / Farge no 343 / Renaudet *Préréforme* 123–4 and passim / D.P. Walker 'Origène en France au début du xviᵉ siècle' in *Courants religieux et humanisme à la fin du xve et au début du xvie siècle*

(Paris 1959) 107–10 / Max Schär *Das Nachleben des Origenes im Zeitalter des Humanismus* (Basel and Stuttgart 1979) 191–208

JAMES K. FARGE

Elias MERTZ *See Helias* MARCAEUS

Gaudenzio MERULA of Borgolavezzaro, 1500–22 March 1555
Merula was born of a humble family in Borgolavezzaro, near Novara. By 1524 he had moved to Milan, from where he dated dedicatory epistles in 1534, 1537, and 1538, and where he also lived as a teacher at the beginning of 1543. In that same year he returned to his native town and subsequently began to teach in the Academy of Novara, as mentioned in the dedicatory preface of his *Terentianus dialogus*. The Franco-Spanish war seems to have interferred, however, with the success of his school. There followed two appointments as a master in municipal schools, the first in Vigevano, between Novara and Piacenza, where in 1545 he succeeded a schoolmaster dismissed for Lutheran heresy. In March 1550 he was suspended, apparently for lack of funds, and moved to a similar position in Turin, which was occupied by the French.

In between his teaching appointments, or alongside them, Merula must have sold books. A letter to the Basel printer Johannes Oporinus (Milan, 11 July 1544, edited by Steinmann) shows him engaged in the distribution of Oporinus' products. In 1554 Merula was charged with Protestant heresy, first before the bishop of Novara and subsequently in Milan. His *Memorabilium liber* was prohibited until purged of anticlerical passages, but other than that he was cleared by his judges, only to fall ill and die shortly after the termination of his second trial.

An admirer of Andrea *Alciati, Merula was a good friend of Ortensio *Lando, who introduced him, together with Etienne *Dolet and others, as a character in the second book of his *Quaestiones Forcianae* (Naples: M. de Ragusia 1536). Benedetto *Giovio was among his patrons and received him in his house at Como. Marcantonio Majoragio accused him of plagiarism, and in later editions of his *De Gallorum cisalpinorum antiquitate* he had to add an *Apologia* against such charges. In June 1536 Erasmus mentioned casually that Merula had attacked him without daring to sign his name to the tract (Ep 3127) and, mistakenly no doubt, suspected *Aleandro of having caused the attack (Ep 3130). Merula's work is probably the 'Bellum civile inter Ciceronianos et Erasmicos' mentioned in the preceding year (Ep 3019). It was probably never printed and is not known to exist now, but its title is reminiscent of the positions taken by Lando and Dolet.

Among Merula's works the encyclopaedic *Memorabilium liber* (Venice: G. Giolito 1550) and *De Gallorum cisalpinorum antiquitate* (Lyon: S. Gryphius 1538) met with considerable success and were reprinted a number of times. The former also appeared in an Italian translation: *Nova selva di varia lezione* (Venice 1559). Merula also composed *Terentianus dialogus* (Forlì 1543); a comedy 'Gelastinus,' and a 'Cronica de claris familiis' were never published, while his *Cronica suae aetatis rerum gestarum*, composed in 1540, was eventually printed (Milan 1876).

BIBLIOGRAPHY: Allen Ep 3127 / Attilio Butti 'Vita e scritti di Gaudenzio Merula' *Archivio storico lombardo* 3rd ser 12 (1899) 125–67, 333–92 / Cosenza III 2296 / Martin Steinmann 'Aus dem Briefwechsel des Basler Druckers Johannes Oporinus' *Basler Zeitschrift für Geschichte und Altertumskunde* 69 (1969) 103–203, esp 117–19   PGB

Giorgio MERULA of Alessandria, 1430/1–19 March 1494

The Italian humanist Giorgio Merula was known to Erasmus as a skilled translator of Greek into elegant Latin. Born in Alessandria (Piedmont) – not Alexandria in Egypt, as Erasmus (ASD I-2 665–6) seems to have believed – Merula received his early education in Milan and later studied in Rome, Padua, and Mantua. His teachers included Francesco *Filelfo and Gregorius *Tiphernas; in Padua he also seems to have attended the lectures of Galeotto *Marzio.

Merula taught at the school of San Marco in Venice (1465–82) and then was invited by Lodovico *Sforza to take up a teaching position in Milan. Intermittently he also lectured at Pavia but remained at Milan for the rest of his life. His students at various times included

Alessandro Minuziano, Eusebio Scutario, Tristano Calchi, and Baldesar *Castiglione. In addition to securing his teaching assignment, Lodovico Sforza commissioned Merula to write a history of the Milanese dynasty, of which fourteen books were completed and published under the title *De antiquitate Vicecomitum* (Milan: Guillaume de Siguerre for A. Minuziano c 1500). Merula's authorship of the final four books has sometimes been questioned.

Apart from translating Xiphilinus' epitome of Dio Cassius' lives of Nerva, Trajan, and Hadrian (Venice: Bernardino dei Vitali 1500; Milan: de Legnano brothers 1503), Merula was responsible for several editions of Latin authors. These include a collection of *Scriptores rei rusticae*, including Cato, Varro, Columella, and Palladius (first printed in Venice by Nicolas Jenson, 1472), Martial (Venice: Vendelinus de Spira n d, but c 1469–73), and Cicero *De finibus* (Venice: Johannes de Colonia and Vendelinus de Spira 1471), as well as the *editio princeps* of Plautus (Venice: Johannes de Colonia and Vendelinus de Spira 1472).

His many textual commentaries on such authors as Cicero, Juvenal, Martial, Virgil, and Pliny, as well as a historical essay on the siege of Skutari (Scodra), frequently provoked controversy with other humanists and led to polemics which Merula pursued with much warmth, sometimes with bitterness. His most notable antagonists were Filelfo, Domizio *Calderini, Galeotto Marzio, and Angelo *Poliziano.

Merula died in Milan and was buried in the church of Sant'Eustorgio. Cristoforo *Landino composed an epitaph for his tomb.

BIBLIOGRAPHY: Allen Ep 1587 / Ferdinando Gabotto and Angelo Badini Confalonieri *Vita di Giorgio Merula* (Alessandria 1893) / Filippo Argelati *Bibliotheca scriptorum mediolanensium* (Milan 1745) II-2 2134–6 and passim / Frank-Rutger Hausmann 'Martial en italien' *Studi medievali* 3rd ser, 17 (1976) 173–218 / Alessandro Perosa 'Documenti di polemiche umanistiche' *Rinascimento* 1 (1950) 178–82
                                        EGMONT LEE

Laurentius MERUS of Feldkirch, documented 1521–46

Laurentius Merus (Mör, Mär, Fabula) of Feldkirch, in Vorarlberg, is sometimes given

Quinten Metsys, by Jan Wierix

the title of doctor of divinity. In 1518 he preached at Zürich, apparently as a candidate for the position *Zwingli was soon to occupy; hence Zwingli's uncharitable comments about him (z vII Epp 46, 47). In 1521 Merus was parish priest of St Martin's, Chur, and wrote to *Vadianus on 18 March, apologizing for mislaying a letter from *Luther to Vadianus which a common friend had given him to read (*Vadianische Briefsammlung* II Ep 249). When Zwingli vacated the position of Leutpriester at Zürich on 12 November 1522 Merus renewed his candidature against Zwingli's advice (z vII Ep 265), and this time he succeeded. But in the autumn of 1523 he moved, now with Zwingli's assistance, to the parish of Baden in Aargau. In the Baden disputation of 1526 he sided with the Catholics, but at the same time he quarrelled with Andreas *Wengi, the abbot of Wettingen, over the monastery's financial obligations towards him. The conflict was taken to the Swiss diet, which supported the abbot, and Merus resigned on 23 July 1527 to become a parish priest, first in Überlingen, on Lake Constance, and from 1533 to his death in his native Feldkirch. *Botzheim had apparently

praised him highly when giving his greetings to Erasmus, who returned them cordially (Ep 2516). His admiration for Erasmus and his friendship with Botzheim serve to reinforce other indications of antagonism between the parish priest of Überlingen and Melchior *Fattlin, who attacked Erasmus in his popular sermons.

BIBLIOGRAPHY: z vII Ep 46, vIII Ep 317, and passim / T. Schiess 'Jakob Salzmann, ein Freund Zwinglis aus älterer Zeit' *Zwingliana* 1 (1897–1904) 167–74, esp 169–70 / T. Schiess 'Zwei Zeitbestimmungen betreffend Comander' *Zwingliana* 1 (1897–1904) 227–8 / E. Egli 'Wer war Laurentius Fabula?' *Zwingliana* 2 (1905–12) 147–51 / A. Semler in *Freiburger Diözesan-Archiv* 74 (1954) 185   PGB

MESIA *See Cristóbal and Pero* MEXÍA

METELLUS *See Jean* MATAL, *Vincenzo* MITELLI

Quinten METSYS of Louvain, d before 6 September 1530

Quinten Metsys (Metsijs, Massys) was born in Louvain by 1466, the son of Joost, a blacksmith; he too is said to have started out in that trade. He moved to Antwerp, where he set up shop as a painter and metal engraver, becoming a master in the painters' guild of St Luke in 1491. In 1492 he married Adelaide van Thuylt (d 1507), and after her death Catherina Heyns in 1508; he had three children by his first marriage and two by his second and died in Antwerp. Conservative in his technique but gifted with subtle powers of expression, Metsys was probably the most talented painter of his generation in Flanders. His principal works are two multiple altar pieces (now in Brussels and Antwerp respectively) for St Peter's church in Louvain and for the chapel of the carpenters' guild in the cathedral of Antwerp; the former is signed and dated 1509, while the latter can be dated 1508–11 on the basis of documentary evidence.

A friend of Pieter *Gillis, Metsys was commissioned in 1517 to produce the famous twin portraits of Erasmus and Gillis (Allen and CWE Ep 584, with reproductions), which the two friends presented as a gift to Thomas *More (Epp 616, 654, 669). More's enthusiastic reaction (Ep 684) reflects the great importance the artistic taste of that time attached to accuracy of detail. In 1519 Metsys produced the famous medal of Erasmus with the god Terminus on the reverse, which is often mentioned in the correspondence over a number of years (Epp 1092, 1408, 1452, 1985). In 1526, when Hans *Holbein passed through Antwerp on his way to London, Erasmus gave him a letter for Gillis, suggesting that he might introduce Holbein to Metsys (Ep 1740).

BIBLIOGRAPHY: Allen and CWE Epp 584, 616 / E. van Even in BNB XIV 639–67 / M.J. Friedländer in *Allgemeines Lexikon der bildenden Künstler* ed U. Thieme, F. Becker, et al (Leipzig 1907–50) XXIV 227–8 / J.B. Trapp et al 'Quentin Metsys, Erasmus, Pieter Gillis, and Thomas More' *Burlington Magazine* 120 (1978) 716–25 / E. Treu *Die Bildnisse des Erasmus von Rotterdam* (Basel 1959) / A. Gerlo *Erasme et ses portraitistes, Metsijs, Dürer, Holbein* 2nd ed (Nieuwkoop 1969) / L. Smolderen 'Quentin Metsys, médailleur d'Erasme' in *Scrinium Erasmianum* II 513–25   MARCEL A. NAUWELAERTS & PGB

Antoine de METTENEYE of Bruges, d c December 1522

Antoine de Metteneye, sieur of Marques (or Marcke) and Marquillies, belonged to an old and influential family of Bruges. As the oldest son he inherited the titles of his father, Pierre (d 1494), who had been captain of Oudenaarde and a member of the Bruges council in 1474. His mother was Marguerite de Baenst. Antoine was a canon of St Donatian's, Bruges, and an apostolic protonotary. In 1517 he was named to *Charles V's privy council constituted to govern the Netherlands in his absence and in July he assisted in the transfer of a sum of money from Pierre *Barbier to Erasmus (Epp 613, 621, 652, 695). His youngest brother Jean, accompanied Charles V to Spain in 1522 and corresponded with Jan van *Fevijn.

BIBLIOGRAPHY: Allen Ep 613 / de Vocht *Literae ad Craneveldium* 107, 174, 349–50 / Henne II 201, 323, X 389 / *Deutsche Reichstagsakten Jüngere Reihe* (Gotha-Göttingen 1893–   ) I 320 and passim (on Jean)   PGB

Johann von METZENHAUSEN 1492–22 July 1540

Johann, the son of Heinrich von Metzenhausen and Margarete Boos von Waldeck,

received preferment from an early age in the cathedral chapter of Trier, being domciliar in 1505 and canon in 1511. In 1512 he was elected precentor, in 1517 dean, and in 1518 provost of the chapter. On 27 March 1531, his fellow canons chose him to be the next archbishop and elector of Trier in succession to Richard von *Greiffenklau. Although he was a strict adherent of the papal church, Metzenhausen advocated a religious policy of moderation and compromise. He worked to improve the training and conduct of his clergy and to reform the ailing University of Trier (Ep 2966). He also directed the preparations for joint military action against the Anabaptists of Münster. In 1540 he went to the religious colloquy of Haguenau and served as one of the presidents of the conference; he died suddenly in the course of a visit to the castle of Thanstein, near Haguenau.

In the summer of 1533 Erasmus saw no reason to write to Metzenhausen, whom he had never met (Epp 2834, 2835), but Ambrosius *Pelargus, who had by then moved to Trier, kept encouraging him (Ep 2966), and he finally did send a letter to the archbishop (Ep 2968) by means of the Koblenz physician Konrad *Nyder; the letter was apparently well received (Ep 2984).

BIBLIOGRAPHY: Allen Ep 2968 / ADB XIV 423 / Benedikt Caspar *Das Erzbistum Trier im Zeitalter der Glaubensspaltung bis zur Verkündigung des Tridentinums in Trier im Jahre 1569* (Münster 1966) / Sophie-Mathilde Gräfin zu Dohna *Die ständischen Verhältnisse am Domkapitel von Trier vom 16. bis zum 18. Jahrhundert* (Trier 1960) / *Nuntiaturberichte aus Deutschland* 1. Abteilung 1533–1559, 1. Ergänzungsband 1530–1531 ed Gerhard Müller (Tübingen 1963)
                                                             ROLF DECOT

Cristóbal MEXÍA of Seville, documented 1529–33

Cristóbal is known only as the brother of Pero *Mexía (Epp 2299, 2300, 2892).

BIBLIOGRAPHY: Allen Ep 2299 / Bataillon *Erasmo y España* 492–3 and passim   TBD

Pero MEXÍA of Seville, 1499–7 January 1551

Pero Mexía (Mejía, Mesia), of a noble family of Seville, studied Latin in his native city and law at Salamanca. He later held various positions in the administration of Seville, including that of *regidor*. Hernando Colón (Columbus) and Juan Luis *Vives were among his friends.

Pero was an admirer of Erasmus and with his brother, Cristóbal *Mexía, wrote a letter of encouragement to him in late 1529 or early 1530, sending a copy, probably in manuscript, of Luis de *Carvajal's *Dulcoratio amarulentiarum Erasmicae responsionis* (Paris: S. de Colines 1530). On 30 March 1530 Erasmus wrote letters to both brothers (Epp 2299, 2300), using the occasion to make an indirect reply to Carvajal and Frans *Titelmans. He soon published these letters in the *Epistolae floridae* (Basel: J. Herwagen 1531). He again replied to letters from the Mexía brothers on 24 December 1533, sending greetings to Christophorus *Fontanus and stating that he sought only peace after the many attacks of his enemies and accusations that he was the precursor of *Luther (Ep 2892).

Pero Mexía published a number of works in Spanish, beginning with the *Silva de varia lección* (Seville 1540), a widely read and much-translated miscellany drawn from ancient and contemporary sources including Erasmus, and dedicated to *Charles v. More ambitious were his *Coloquios o diálogos nuevamente compuestos* (Seville: D. de Robertis 1547), inspired by the *Colloquia* of Erasmus and republished in 1548 (Seville: D. de Robertis) with a translation of the *Ad Demonicum* of Isocrates. He also wrote the *Historia imperial y cesárea* (Seville: J. de León 1545), dealing with the lives of emperors from Julius Caesar to *Maximilian I. This last work especially attracted the attention of the imperial court, and on 8 July 1548 Mexía was named a chronicler of Charles v. His *Historia de Carlos Quinto* was published by J. Deloffre in *Revue hispanique* 44 (1918) 1–556 and more recently by Juan de Mata Carriazo (Madrid 1945).

BIBLIOGRAPHY: Allen Ep 2300 / Bataillon *Erasmo y España* 265, 327, and passim / *Enciclopedia universal ilustrada europeo-americana* (Barcelona, Madrid 1907?–) xxxiv 256–7 / A. Morel-Fatio *Historiographie de Charles-Quint ...* (Paris 1913) 16–17, 73–9   TBD

Adelberg MEYER zum Pfeil of Basel, 1474– 8 June 1548
Meyer was descended from an aristocratic and influential Basel family. Following in his father's footsteps, he entered the cloth trade and in 1514 became a member of the city council. From 1521 to his death he was burgomaster every second year, the first to hold this office without confirmation by the bishop. He lacked originality but was capable of decisive action and represented Basel frequently at the Swiss diet and on other foreign missions. Exercising personal restraint and urging moderation upon others, he was a leading influence behind Basel's step-by-step adoption of the Reformation, and Erasmus' only unquestionable reference to him (Ep 1744) expressed disappointment at his shrewd handling of one instance of the religious controversy that concerned Erasmus personally.

From his father and from an uncle who was a canon Meyer inherited a collector's taste for books and manuscripts. In particular he had some of the older Basel chronicles copied and himself began the composition of a family chronicle (*Basler Chroniken* vi 343–78).

BIBLIOGRAPHY: Allen Ep 1744; cf Epp 1934, 2372 / DHBS IV 738–9 / ADB XXI 555 / *Wappenbuch der Stadt Basel* ed W.R. Staehelin (Basel [1917–30]) II / R. Wackernagel *Geschichte der Stadt Basel* (Basel 1907–54) II-2 914, III 262–3, 418, 84* / *Basler Chroniken* vi 381–6 / AK VI Epp 2749, 2962, VII Ep 3194, VIII Ep 3533, and passim   PGB

Jakob MEYER zum Hirzen of Basel, 1473– 4 October 1541
A prosperous clothier, Jakob Meyer was master of the 'Schlüssel' guild in 1510. From 1517 he sat on the city council for the guild 'zu Hausgenossen.' In 1521 he was one of the small minority of Basel magistrates who showed moral fibre in refusing the individual subsidies offered them by the French government in its eagerness to recruit mercenaries. In his case the refusal may represent an early indication of his sympathy with the views of *Zwingli. From 1522 he was *Oberzunftmeister* and from 1530 to his death burgomaster in alternate years.

Meyer quickly emerged as the recognized political leader and spokesman of the reform party (Epp 2158, 2328). He was a close friend of *Oecolampadius, after whose death he brought about the appointment of *Myconius as the next antistes; subsequently he supported the latter's preference for an understanding

with the Lutherans. He helped to find the
consensus expressed in the first Helvetic
Confession of 1536 and was instrumental in
reorganizing the university after the Reformation crisis of 1529 and in attracting Simon
*Grynaeus to the chair of Greek. Grynaeus
later died of the same plague epidemic as
Meyer. There is a monument in the cathedral
cloister honouring the two men together with
Oecolampadius. Meyer was married to Anna
von Dachsfelden in 1492, and after her death in
1518 he married Verena Husmann (d 1543) in
1521. He had a son and four daughters.

When Erasmus was preparing to leave Basel
in 1529 Meyer joined Oecolampadius in
attempting to retain him for the sake of the
city's reputation; he also appealed to *Beatus
Rhenanus for help (Epp 2158, 2196, 2328).
After Erasmus' return in 1535, however,
following a denunciation by Myconius, he
took exception to a passage in the *Ecclesiastes*
but allowed himself to be reassured by *Capito,
an old friend (AK IV Epp 1958, 1960).

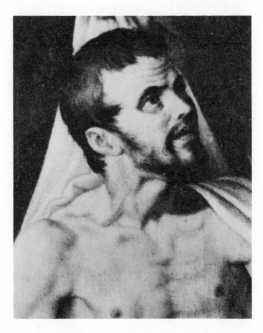

Jean Micault, by Jan Cornelisz. Vermeyen

BIBLIOGRAPHY: ADB XXI 582 / DHBS IV 738 /
Paul Meyer 'Bürgermeister Jakob Meyer zum
Hirzen, 1473–1541' in *Basler Zeitschrift für
Geschichte und Altertumskunde* 23 (1925) 97–142 /
AK IV Ep 2024, V Ep 2461, and passim / R.
Wackernagel *Geschichte der Stadt Basel* (Basel
1907–54) III 419 and passim / *Wappenbuch der
Stadt Basel* ed W.R. Staehelin (Basel [1917–30]) /
BA *Oekolampads* II 7–8 and passim / Petrus
Ramus *Basilea* ed H. Fleig (Basel 1944) 51
                                                               PGB

Matthias MEYNER of Karl-Marx-Stadt,
c 1475–c 1523
Matthias Meyner (Meiner) of Karl-Marx-Stadt
(Chemnitz), in Saxony, matriculated at the
University of Leipzig in the spring term of 1493;
he received a BA the following year and
subsequently also a MA, it seems. He entered
the service of Duke George of *Saxony and
married Anna, the daughter of Hans Arnold,
mayor of Chemnitz. In 1515 he was appointed
collector of mining revenue (*Zehntner, decimarius*) at Schneeberg, south-east of Zwickau,
and leased his house in Chemnitz. In 1522
Petrus *Mosellanus, professor of Greek at
Leipzig, dedicated to him an edition of
Prudentius' *Liber καϑημερινῶν* (Leipzig: N.
Schmidt n d). His connection with the circle of

Mosellanus is also demonstrated by the fact
that his widow later became the wife of
Georgius *Agricola. On 30 and 31 July 1520
Erasmus replied to letters received from Mosellanus and one Matthias, *decimarius* of Duke
George (Epp 1122, 1123). Matthias' letter was
accompanied by a gift of three lumps of silver,
taken to Louvain by Heinrich *Eppendorf.
Allen was clearly right in identifying Matthias
with Meyner.

BIBLIOGRAPHY: Allen and CWE Ep 1122 /
Matrikel Leipzig I 394, II 344 / Georgius Agricola
Ausgewählte Werke II ed Hans Prescher (Berlin
1955) 260, 301–2   MICHAEL ERBE & PGB

Jean MICAULT d 7 September 1539
Jean Micault (Michault) was born in Burgundy,
where his father, Philibert (d 1521), was castellan of Pommard (Côte-d'Or). Jean's mother
was Philibert's first wife, Jeanne de Conroy.
Jean is mentioned for the first time in 1506,
when he accompanied Philip the Handsome,
duke of *Burgundy, on his second journey to
Spain. As *argentier* Micault was in charge of the
chattels; he also kept the accounts of the
travelling party. On 14 July 1507 he succeeded

Simon Congin as receiver-general of the Burgundian states. He kept this office for close to three decades, having been confirmed in it at the time of the establishment of the Collateral Councils in 1531. On 1 August 1531 he resigned as receiver-general in favour of Hendrik Stercke, following his appointment to the Brussels audit office, where he was made a deputy auditor-general with special responsibility for the duchy of Luxembourg and the county of Chiny. In the following year he succeeded Maximilien Quarre as auditor--general.

Micault owned estates at Indevelde, Oister-steyn, and elsewhere in the regions of Brussels and Mechelen. On 3 December 1531 he was knighted, while from 1528 he was also treasurer of the order of the Golden Fleece. He was married to Livine van Welle, who bore him seven children, among them Nicolas (1518–89), who became a member of the privy council, and Marguerite, who married Lambert de *Briaerde. A touch of his character may be revealed by the fact that as late as 1545, during a chapter of the Golden Fleece at Utrecht, complaints were voiced about the former treasurer's mockery and swearing. Jean was buried in a chapel of St Gudula's, Brussels (now St Michael's cathedral). His children had Jan Cornelisz. Vermeyen paint a triptych for the altar of St Lazarus in this chapel, on which the entire family is portrayed. The piece is now in the Musée des Beaux-Arts, Brussels.

Briaerde and other friends of Erasmus attempted to win Micault's assistance in obtaining payments of Erasmus' annuity from the imperial court, on one occasion at least with some success (Epp 2571, 2767).

BIBLIOGRAPHY: Allen Ep 2571 / BNB XXXVII 585–7 / de Vocht Literae ad Craneveldium Ep 140 / J.T. de Raadt 'Le triptyque de la famille Micault: notes complimentaires' and 'Encore un mot sur le triptyque de Micault' Annales de la Société archéologique de Bruxelles 4 (1890) 455–466 and 9 (1895) 415–17 / J. Gaillard Bruges et le Franc ou leur magistrature et leur noblesse (Bruges 1857–64) I 243, 365, II 161, 467 / J. Verkooren Inventaire des chartes et cartulaires du Luxembourg: comté puis duché v (Brussels 1921) 301, 481 / C.P. Hoynck van Papendrecht Analecta Belgica: Vita Viglii ab Aytta Zuichemii

(The Hague 1743) I-2, 747, III-2 313 / J. Bartier Légistes et gens de finances au xve siècle: les conseillers des ducs de Bourgogne sous Philippe le Bon et Charles le Téméraire (Brussels 1955) 53 / J.P. Christyn Jurisprudentia heroica sive de jure Belgarum circa nobilitatem et insignia (Brussels 1668) I 502, II 164 / A. de Reiffenberg Histoire de l'Ordre de la Toison d'Or, depuis son institution jusqu'à la cessation des chapitres a généraux (Brussels 1830) 331–2, 372, 376 / A. von Wurzbach Niederländisches Künstler-Lexikon (Vienna-Leipzig 1910, repr 1974) II 778–80

HILDE DE RIDDER-SYMOENS

MICHAEL don Lope (Ep 2083 of 6 January 1529)

Although he is described by Guy *Morillon as a man of distinction and great influence among Spanish court circles, 'Michael don Lope, advocatus regius' has not yet been identified. Morillon cited him for his admiration of Erasmus. Allen mentioned in this connection one Don Lope de Urea, a gentleman of the household of *Charles v.

MICHAEL of Pavia See Michel PAVIE

Theoderich MICHWAEL of Caster, d before 3 March 1519

Theoderich Michwael (Wichwael, Wijggell, Theodericus de Castro, Pictorius) was born in Caster, in the region of Bedburg, west of Cologne and matriculated at the University of Cologne on 26 October 1478. He joined the Hermits of St Augustine and from 1495 was for many years prior of the Austin friar house at Cologne as well as professor of theology in the university. Under his direction the monastery became a centre for humanistic studies. A friend and correspondent of Cornelius *Agrippa, he reacted enthusiastically when the humanist Johannes Aesticampianus lectured in Cologne on St Augustine. He also supported Johann *Reuchlin in his conflict with the Dominicans. On 24 March 1500 a recently elected vicar-general of the order named Michwael his vicar for the region of Cologne, and on 4 June 1501 he was confirmed as magister regens. On 2 August 1504 Pope *Julius II created him suffragan to the archbishop of Cologne, Hermann of Hesse, with the titular see of Cyrene. Michwael was buried in the church of St Augustine at Bedburg, where another Austin friar, Adolf Michwael, was parish priest.

In June 1516 Erasmus mentioned the suffragan bishop of Cologne among other theologians he had found to be sympathetic to the study of Greek and Hebrew (Ep 413). In August 1519, apparently unaware of Michwael's recent death, he praised the suffragan of Cologne again in a manner that suggests personal contact at some point in the past and thus would seem to preclude the possibility that he was referring to Michwael's successor, Quirinus Op dem Velde, who was in office by 16 March 1519 (Ep 1006).

BIBLIOGRAPHY: Allen and CWE Ep 413 / *Matrikel Köln* II 49 / Adalbero Kunzelmann *Geschichte der deutschen Augustiner-Eremiten* IV: *Die kölnische Provinz bis zum Ende des Mittelalters* (Würzburg 1972) 47–8 and passim / Justus Hashagen 'Hauptrichtungen des rheinischen Humanismus' *Annalen des Historischen Vereins für den Niederrhein* 106 (1922) 1–56, esp 27 / Eubel III 184, 345 / Paola Zambelli 'Cornelio Agrippa, Erasmo e la teologia umanistica' *Rinascimento* 2nd ser 10 (1970) 29–88, esp 46–7 / Henricus Cornelius Agrippa *Opera* (Lyon c 1600, repr 1970) II 618–19, 664–9 (Epistolae I Ep 21, II Ep 19) / *Handbuch des Erzbistums Kölns* 26th ed (Cologne 1966) I 56
                                        HANSGEORG MOLITOR & PGB

MIDDELBURGENSIS, MIDDELBURGUS
See Jacob ANTHONISZOON, PAUL *of Middelburg*

Alice MIDDLETON documented 1509–34
Alice Middleton, the daughter of Dame Alice *More, was educated in the household of her stepfather, Sir Thomas *More. While very young she was married to Thomas *Elryngton, and after his death she married Giles (later Sir Giles) Alington, some time before 1524. Her correspondence with Margaret *More Roper in 1534 manifests her affection for Thomas More and her sharing in the family affections and tribulations (Rogers Epp 205, 206).

Erasmus seems to have confused Alice Middleton with More's second daughter, Elizabeth *More in both Epp 999 and 2432.
BIBLIOGRAPHY: Allen Ep 1233 / Rogers Ep 101

and passim / William Roper *Life of More* ed E.V. Hitchcock (London 1935) xli–ii / R.J. Schoeck in *New Catholic Encyclopedia* (New York 1967–78) IX 1142   R.J. SCHOECK

Emilio de' MIGLI of Brescia, c 1480–July 1531
Emilio de' Migli (Emilio Emigli, Aemilius de Aemiliis), the son of Girolamo, was born in Brescia. He married Chiara Soraga before 1517 and they had three children: Virginia, Caterina, and Luca. In 1526 Migli unsuccessfully sought election to the communal chancellorship of Brescia, which was assigned instead to Vincenzo Pedrocca. After Pedrocca's resignation in 1529 Migli was elected to the position, which he held until his death two years later.

Migli is best known for his translation into Italian of Erasmus' *Enchiridion*, which he had completed by May 1529. On 4 May 1529 he wrote to Erasmus, begging him to send a letter of approval for his work, adding that he had written four months earlier without receiving an answer (Ep 2154). This letter was carried to Erasmus by Vincenzo *Maggi. Erasmus replied with Ep 2165, expressing the hope that Migli's work would not stir up trouble similar to that caused by the translation of the *Enchiridion* in Spain, and encouraging the translation of the paraphrases and other works by him into Italian. Migli published both letters with his translation of the *Enchiridion* (Brescia: L. Britannico 1531). A second edition was issued by the same publisher in 1540. Migli dedicated his work to Altobello Averoldo, bishop of Pola, then legate to Venice, and at the end of his volume he added a poem (*Canzone di penitenza*) dealing with the themes presented in the Erasmian treatise.

Migli's other works were few. Some of his poems were included in Girolamo Ruscelli's anthology *Rime di diversi eccellenti autori bresciani* (Venice: P. Pietrasanta 1553).
BIBLIOGRAPHY: Allen Ep 2154 / Paolo Guerrini 'Due amici bresciani di Erasmo' *Archivio storico lombardo* 5th ser, 10 (1923) 172–80 / Silvana Seidel Menchi 'Alcuni atteggiamenti della cultura italiana di fronte ad Erasmo' *Eresia e riforma nell'Italia del cinquecento* (Florence-Chicago 1974) 74 / S. Caponetto 'Fisionomia del nicodemismo italiano' *Atti del convegno italo-*

Elisabeth de Mil, by Michael Coxie

---

polacco: Firenze 22–24 settembre 1971: Movimenti ereticali in Italia e in Polonia nei secoli XVI–XVII (Florence 1974) 208 / J.V. Pollet *Martin Bucer* (Paris 1958–62) II 478

DANILO AGUZZI-BARBAGLI

Elisabeth de MIL d 20 December 1552
Elisabeth was probably descended from a family of Bruges which counted among its members several civic officials and civil servants. Her name, however, does not appear in the known genealogy of that family, nor could it be traced elsewhere in the archives of Bruges. She was married to Guy *Morillon between 18 February and 5 June 1517 (Epp 532, 587) and seems to have been known to Erasmus at this time. She stayed behind when her husband went to Spain later that year (Ep 794) and was apparently likewise in the Netherlands in 1524 when her husband had returned to Spain (Ep 1507). Elisabeth, who survived her husband by four years, had six children.
BIBLIOGRAPHY: CWE 5 340–1 (plates) / de Vocht CTL III 46–50 / J. Gaillard *Bruges et le Franc ou leur magistrature et leur noblesse* (Bruges 1857–64) II 63–76 (genealogy of the family de

Mil) / Bruges, Stadsarchief MS P. le Doulx 'Levens der geleerde en vermaerde Mannen der Stad Brugge' I 142, II 153
HILDE DE RIDDER-SYMOENS

Johannes MILIO (documented 1524)
In Ep 1540 of January 1525 Johann von *Botzheim wrote that his unnamed adversary was greatly dependent on Jacopo *Sadoleto. In a letter to Sadoleto of September 1524 Bonifacius *Amerbach stated that Botzheim had been summoned to Rome by Mercurius de Vipera, a judge of the Rota, at the request of one Johannes Milio or de Miliis, a cleric of Cremona and 'litterarum apostolicarum sollicitator' (AK II Ep 970). Amerbach's letter was answered by Sadoleto's secretary, who stated that the bishop had spoken to Milio (AK II Ep 989). Allen suggested that Milio rather than Vipera could be the adversary mentioned in Ep 1540.

MILO (Ep 194 [c 12 June] 1506)
Milo, a Frenchman, had gone to England to join the household of William *Blount, Lord Mountjoy, and soon thereafter died of the plague. He is not identified.

Karl von MILTITZ c 1490–20 November 1529
Karl von Miltitz (a Milticis), the son of Sigismund, a district official in Meissen, matriculated in Cologne in 1508 to study law; in 1510 he studied in Bologna. He was a canon of Mainz, Trier, and Meissen. From 1514 he was in Rome as papal scriptor, chamberlain, and notary. In 1518 he was sent as papal nuncio to Frederick the Wise, elector of *Saxony, to bring him the Golden Rose, a rare distinction conferred by the popes. Miltitz attempted to influence Martin *Luther in a conciliatory way. During 1519 and 1520 he had three interviews with Luther, who was invited to submit his cause to the archbishop of Trier, Richard von *Greiffenklau (Luther w *Briefwechsel* I Ep 169). Miltitz returned to Rome in 1520, still hoping for a peaceful settlement. On another visit to Germany in 1529 Miltitz drowned in the Main near Steinau.
   In his brief references (Epp 1040, 1188; cf Ep 2445 and *Opuscula* 323) Erasmus showed little regard for Miltitz.
BIBLIOGRAPHY: Allen and CWE Ep 1188 / ADB XXI 759–60 / Luther w *Briefwechsel* I Epp 122,

152, II Ep 331 / *Matrikel Köln* II 628 / Knod 348 /
DTC x-2 1765–7 / Pastor VII 380 / H. Grisar
Martin Luther, His Life and Work adapted by F.J.
Eble (St Louis 1930, repr 1971) 103–4 / E.G.
Schwiebert *Luther and His Times* (St Louis, Mo,
1950) 361–4, 370–84 / R.H. Fife *The Revolt of
Martin Luther* (New York 1957) 307–26, 524–5
                                                              IG

MINDESIUS (Ep 1479 of 31 August 1524)
In a letter to *Haio Herman of Friesland, who
was then at Padua, Erasmus promised that he
was going to write to Mindesius. No such letter
is known to exist and Mindesius has not been
identified.

Simon MINERVIUS *See Simon
SCHAIDENREISSER*

Vincenzo MITELLI of Brescia, documented
1532–71
Called 'most erudite' by Quirini and 'friend of
the muses' by Peroni, Vincenzo Mitelli (Metellus) was a citizen of Brescia who wrote to
Erasmus in 1535, praising him and ranking him
among Origen, Augustine, and other great
Fathers of the church and ancient scholars (Ep
3057). An informal scholar rather than an
academic, Mitelli participated in the literary
circle of the 'Occulti' which arose in Brescia in
1542. Although his activity was restricted
almost entirely to his native city, he was among
those who praised the virtues of Donna Juana
of Aragon, a natural daughter of *Ferdinand II
of Aragon and the wife of the patrician Ascanio
Colonna, in the *Del tempio alla divina Signora
Donna Giovanna d'Aragona*, edited by Girolamo
Ruscelli (Venice: P. Pietrasanta 1555). He also
wrote an epic poem celebrating the Christian
victory at Lepanto in 1571: *Il Marte ... ove sotto
bellissime favole et inventioni si descrive la guerra di
Cipro con la rotta dell'armata de' Turchi* (Venice:
Venzoni 1582), dedicated to Bianca Capello,
the wife of Francesco I de' Medici, grand duke
of Tuscany. Ranked by Belloni among the tired
imitations of the poetry of Torquato Tasso,
Mitelli's epic was a mixture of history and
myth, inferior in scope and in religious
sentiment to other poems written in the wake
of Lepanto. Other works published by Mitelli
included an introduction to Bartolomeo *Mascara's edition of Aesop's fables (Brescia: L.

Britannico 1532), an *Oratio in funere Matthei
Advocati habita* (Brescia: L. Britannico 1547),
and seven sonnets included in Ruscelli's *Rime
di diversi eccellenti autori bresciani* (Venice: P.
Pietrasanta 1553).
  BIBLIOGRAPHY: Allen Ep 3057 / Antonio
Belloni *Il poema epico e mitologico* (Milan c
1908–11) 279 / A.M. Quirini *Specimen variae
literaturae quae in urbe Brixiae florebat* (Brescia
1739) II 249 / V. Peroni *Biblioteca Bresciana*
(Bologna 1818–23) II 276 / F.S. Quadrio *Della
storia e della ragione di ogni poesia* (Bologna-Milan
1739–52) II 360, IV 668 / E. Caccia in *Storia di
Brescia* II (Brescia 1961) 510, 522
                                                  PAOLO PISSAVINO

Jean de MIXON (Ep 73 of [April 1498?])
Allen proposed to identify Jean de Mixon,
archbishop of the nominal see of Tarsus, with
the 'reverend Father' whose arrival at Paris
was expected at this time; cf CWE Ep 73:14n.

Hartmann MOER of Linn,
d 23 August 1537
Hartmann Moer (Mor, Maurus), of Linn, near
Krefeld, matriculated at Cologne on 30 October
1506 and was a BA in 1512, a licentiate in 1514,
and a doctor of civil and canon law in 1521. In
his *Coronatio* (A 1 verso) he refers to himself
modestly as the most junior of legal professors.
In 1520 he was in the service of Archbishop
Hermann von *Wied when he attended the
coronation of *Charles V at Aachen as a member
of the Cologne delegation. His description of
the ceremonies, *Coronatio invictissimi Caroli*,
was published at Nürnberg (F. Peypus 1523). It
contains formulations (E 5 verso) that indicate
his adherence to the traditional church, at least
until the time of publication. In the course of
his subsequent activity at the imperial court
(*Reichskammergericht*) no criticisms of his religious attitudes can be found in the visitation
reports. He may actually have been in orders,
for on 27 December 1521 Charles V requested
unsuccessfully that the dean and chapter of
Cologne appoint Moer to a prebend.
  When the *Reichskammergericht* was reopened
in 1521 Moer was appointed assessor on behalf
of the ecclesiastical principality of Cologne, but
not until 1523 did he move away from Cologne
for good. He was at Nürnberg until 1524 and
afterwards followed the *Reichskammergericht* to

Esslingen (1524–7) and Speyer, where he eventually died and was buried in the cloister of St Guido's. On 15 January 1532 he signed a receipt for eighty-six Rheingulden and thirty-five Kreutzer, representing his salary for nine months. In June 1535 Udalricus *Zasius named him among those who had encouraged him to write his *Usus feudorum epitome* (Basel: J. Bebel). It seems quite possible that Moer met Erasmus at the time of the coronation at Aachen or immediately afterwards in Cologne, but the only known hint of personal relations dates from 1529, when Moer conveyed to Erasmus his disappointment at Erasmus' failure to dedicate to him a work he had recently published (Ep 2130; cf Ep 2103).

In addition to the *Coronatio* Moer published *De necessario bello adversus Turcos* (n p 1530). The chronicle of the lords of Zimmern mentioned a treatise by him on the customs of courtiers. On the last page of his books Moer had his coat of arms printed, which shows the head of a moor twice.

BIBLIOGRAPHY: Allen Ep 2130 / *Matrikel Köln* II-2 601 / Johann Heinrich Harpprecht *Staats-Archiv des Kayserl. und des H. Röm. Reichs Kammer-Gerichts* ... (Ulm 1760) V / *Die Reichsregisterbücher Karls V.* ed Lothar Gross (Vienna-Leipzig 1913–30) I no 1667 / Konrad Braun *Annotata de personis Iudicij Camerae Imperialis a primo illius exordio usque ad annum Domini 1556* (Ingolstadt 1757) / *Thesaurus practicantium omnibus in imperialis camerae judicio postulantibus, causasve agentibus* ... ed Simon Günther (Speyer 1608) / *Die deutschen Pfälzer Handschriften des 16. und 17. Jhd. der Universitätsbibliothek in Heidelberg* ed Jakob Wille (Heidelberg 1903) = *Katalog der Handschriften der Universitätsbibliothek in Heidelberg* II / Udalricus Zasius *Opera* (Frankfurt a. M. 1590) IV 76 / AK VII 197 / *Zimmerische Chronik* ed Karl Barack and Paul Hermann (Meersburg-Leipzig 1932) III 116 / *Deutsche Reichstagsakten* Jüngere Reihe (Gotha-Göttingen 1893–) II 79–97 passim / Heidelberg, Universitätsbibliothek MSS Germ. 493–4, 829 (*Katalog* II 69, 72, 129)   KONRAD WIEDEMANN

Johann MOLDENFELD of Marzhausen, documented 1520–4
Johann Moldenfeld (Moldefelt, Moldenvel-dius, Molthanveldius) of Marzhausen, near Witzenhausen in Hesse, matriculated at the University of Erfurt in the autumn of 1520. He may have been the son of another Johann Moldenfeld of Marzhausen who studied at Leipzig from 1484 to 1486. When the Erfurt professor Martin *Hune travelled to Basel in the spring of 1524 to visit Erasmus he took a companion with him who was probably Moldenfeld. At any rate the latter was at Basel in July (Ep 1462) and probably returned to Erfurt for the beginning of the winter term, taking with him letters from Erasmus to Duke George of *Saxony and *Melanchthon, as well as others which recommended the bearer to *Spalatinus and *Eobanus Hessus (Epp 1495–8). No more is known about Moldenfeld.

BIBLIOGRAPHY: Allen Ep 1462 / *Matrikel Erfurt* II 319 / *Matrikel Leipzig* I 345, II 293 / T.F. Freytag *Virorum doctorum epistolae selectae* (Leipzig 1831) 27 / *Udalrici Zasii epistolae* ed J.A. Riegger (Ulm 1774) II 503   PGB

Johannes de MOLENDINO documented 1501–29 May 1534
Johannes de Molendino (Jean Molinier, Molinaris, Molinus) was a Fleming from the diocese of Tournai. He was probably the person of this name from Tournai who took his MA at the Collège de Navarre in Paris about 1490 under Louis Le Coq (Galli) and then was regent in grammar and arts at the Collège de Bourgogne for about ten years. He was the rector of the University of Paris for a term in 1501. By this time he was in the circle of humanist scholars around *Lefèvre d'Etaples and wrote to Lefèvre from the Collège du Cardinal Lemoine on 25 January 1504. Josse *Clichtove praised him as 'bonarum literarum studiis deditissimus' in 1503. In 1508 he was still at Cardinal Lemoine when he dedicated to Jean de Ganay, chancellor of France, a Latin version of a description of Italy composed in French by the chancellor's nephew Germain, who was perhaps Molendino's pupil. He also composed two epitomes of Cicero's *De legibus*, which he dedicated to Germain de Ganay; both works remained in manuscript. Molendino became a canon of Tournai, where he was a familiar of William *Blount, Lord Mountjoy, and was involved with Pierre *Barbier in procuring an annuity for Erasmus at Courtrai. Jan de

Spouter dedicated his *De figuris liber* to
Molendino on 2 February 1519 (Paris: Josse
Bade 1519; Ghent: Pieter de Keyser 1520). He
was still living on 29 May 1534, when his
kinsman Levinus *Ammonius wrote to Nicolaus *Olahus to request relief from taxation for
Molendino in consideration for his studies and
the outstanding library he was assembling.

In 1515 it fell to Molendino to inform
Erasmus of *Wolsey's change of mind concerning the offer of a canonry at Tournai (Ep 371).
Thereafter they corresponded intermittently
until the time of Molendino's death (Epp 755,
2407, 2841). Many letters may be missing,
however, since they dealt primarily with
Erasmus' annuity. He evidently trusted Molendino and used him as an agent to receive
payments on his behalf (Epp 1470, 1471, and
many references in other letters). In the end,
however, Molendino's intimacy with Barbier
apparently caused Erasmus to suspect Molendino's friendship too when he concluded that
Barbier was playing him false (Epp 2793, 2961).
Molendino was united with his kinsman
Ammonius in their admiration for Erasmus'
writings (Epp 371, 486, 806, 2841) and their
opposition to Erasmus' critics among the Paris
theologians (Epp 1763, 2016), but he took
exception to Erasmus' *Apologia* against Lefèvre d'Etaples (Ep 755).

BIBLIOGRAPHY: Allen and CWE Ep 371 / NK II
2761–2, 2767 / Rice *Prefatory Epistles* Epp 34, 37 /
de Vocht CTL II 497 and passim / Paris, Archives
de l'Université (Sorbonne) MS Registre 89 f 1
[50] recto / See also bibliography for Levinus
Ammonius   JAMES K. FARGE & PGB

Jean MOLINIER *See Johannes de* MOLENDINO

Franciscus MOLINIUS *See François*
DU MOULIN

Ulricus MOLITORIS *See Ulrich* WIRTNER

Jan MOMBAER of Brussels,
d c 29 December 1501
Jan Mombaer (Mauburnus, or Jan of Brussels)
was probably born between 1460 and 1463. His
earliest schooling was in the cathedral school
of Utrecht, where he was exposed to classical
texts and studied chant under Jacob Obrecht.
Two relatives were already Augustinian

canons, and Mombaer took the habit about
1480 at St Agnietenberg (Mount St Agnes) near
Zwolle, an abbey of the reformed Windesheim
congregation in the *Devotio Moderna* tradition.
There he possibly came under the influence of
Wessel *Gansfort and composed devotional
works, the most important being the *Rosetum
exercitiorum spiritualium*, in which he outlined
an ideal of asceticism and contemplation, with
a method for the art of meditation dependent
on both the spirit and the senses which, some
have said, influenced the *Spiritual Exercises* of
Ignatius Loyola. Mombaer was one of the first
to insist that Thomas à Kempis, not Jean
Gerson, composed the *Imitatio Christi*. Mombaer was appointed confessor to the nuns of
Bronope and later was sub-prior of Gnaden-
thal (duchy of Jülich). The congregation
frequently appointed him to inspect libraries of
its member convents.

Upon invitation by the Paris reformist party
of Jan *Standonck, Mombaer led a group of six
canons from the Windesheim congregation to
Paris in September 1496. There they hoped to
be agents of strict monastic discipline in
Augustinian priories of the region. Initial
opposition and severe hardships at St Séverin
of Château-Landon, near Fontainebleau, almost forced Mombaer to abandon the effort,
but new reformist statutes were effected on 7
December 1497, and Mombaer became the
prior. A similar effort at St Victor in Paris
headed by Erasmus' friend Cornelis *Gerard
was not successful. The persistence of Standonck, Mombaer, and Nicolas de *Hacqueville, canon of Notre-Dame de Paris, claimed
the abbey of Livry on 10 February 1500.
Mombaer succeeded Hacqueville as abbot, and
after almost a year of illness he died in Paris.

Mombaer was only mildly attracted to
humanist authors and endeavours but preferred patristic texts and medieval spiritual
writers. He abhorred the critical spirit of
Lorenzo *Valla but was intensely concerned
about a corrected version of the Bible.
*Lefèvre d'Etaples claimed to have been
influenced by Mombaer (preface to *Contempla-
tiones* of Ramón Lull, Paris: J. Petit 1505).
Erasmus was impressed by Mombaer's joining
of culture with monastic ideals and expressed
sympathy for his reforming efforts at Livry
(Epp 52, 73). Renaudet suggests that Erasmus'

association with Mombaer in Paris was a last attempt to keep himself within the Augustinian obedience.

Mombaer composed the following works: *Exercitia utilissima pro horis solvendis et sacra communione cum considerationibus variis de vita et passione domini et sacramento eucharistiae* (Zwolle: Pieter de Os 1491); *Rosetum exercitiorum spiritualium et sacrarum meditationum. In quo etiam habetur materia predicabilis per totum anni circulum* (Zwolle [?] 1491; Basel: Jakob Wolff 1504; Paris: Josse Bade for Jean Petit and Johann Schabler 1510; Milan 1603; Douai 1620). Mombaer also left ten manuscripts, five of which are extant, on Augustinian spirituality and hagiography.

BIBLIOGRAPHY: Allen and CWE Ep 52 / ASD I-1 89 / BNB X 368–71 / P. Debongnie *Jean Mombaer de Bruxelles, abbé de Livry: ses écrits et ses réformes* (Louvain 1927) / J. Donndorf *Das Rosetum des Johannes Mauburnus* (Halle 1929) / Renaudet *Préréforme* 219–21 and passim / Rice *Prefatory Epistles* 141, 228–30   JAMES K. FARGE

Pierre MONDORÉ documented 1532–5
Pierre Mondoré (de Mondore, Montaureus, Monsaureus) was a French student who called on Erasmus at Freiburg in the winter of 1531–2. He made a good impression, and as he was on his way to Venice and Rome Erasmus gave him some letters to carry, none of which seem to have survived. In March 1532 *Viglius Zuichemus reported that Mondoré had changed his plans and was studying in Padua (Epp 2604, 2632). In September he was still in Padua and talked to Viglius about Giulio *Camillo's attack on Erasmus' *Ciceronianus* (Ep 2716). In April 1555 Mondoré was in charge of the library at the royal castle of Fontainebleau, where the 'Grec du Roi,' a famous set of Greek type, had been deposited.

Mondoré translated Euclid's *Elementorum liber decimus* (Paris: M. de Vascosan 1551) and composed Latin poems to be found in Ranutius Gherus' *Delitiae poetarum Gallorum* ([Frankfurt] 1609) II.

BIBLIOGRAPHY: Allen Ep 2604 / Philippe Renouard *Documents sur les imprimeurs, libraires ... à Paris de 1450 à 1600* (Paris 1901, repr 1969) 91 / *The British Library General Catalogue of Printed Books to 1975* (London 1979–) CCXXV 162   PGB

Petrus MONSAUREUS *See Pierre* MONDORÉ

Philippus MONTANUS of Armentières, d 22 May 1576
Philippus Montanus (de la Montagne, Montaigne) was born around 1498 (Ep 2890) at Armentières, in Flanders (now in the French Département du Nord). On 26 February 1518 he matriculated in the University of Louvain together with other students from Armentières and Douai. No more is known about him until the summer of 1528, when he visited Erasmus at Basel and was invited to stay for some time in his house. In the autumn he left for Paris in the company of Daniel *Stiebar, whom he had met at Erasmus' table. On arrival in Paris he delivered a number of letters Erasmus had given him and was hired by Jean de *Tartas, the principal of the Collège de Lisieux, to teach Greek in his college (Epp 2065, 2069, 2311). In April 1529 he witnessed the execution of Louis de *Berquin and reported the event in great detail to Erasmus, who in turn wrote to Karel *Uutenhove, another young scholar Montanus had met under Erasmus' roof (Ep 2188). In 1530 Montanus was, like Jacobus *Omphalius, his colleague at the Lisieux, in close contact with the printer Gerard *Morrhy, another Netherlander (Ep 2311), while Erasmus recommended him for patronage to the rich Guilhelmus *Quinonus (Ep 2380). Three years later Erasmus asked the influential abbot François *Bonvalot to find Montanus a benefice, declaring that he was ready to assume pastoral duties (Ep 2890).

Erasmus also commemorated Montanus' visit to Basel by giving his name, Philip, to one of the speakers in his colloquy *Impostura* (ASD I-3 601–2), first published in 1529. Montanus continued to correspond with Erasmus and his famulus, Gilbert *Cousin, but none of these letters seem to have survived (Epp 3101, 3104; AK IV Ep 2039). In 1534 he sent them both copies of *Alciati's *Emblemata*, informing them at the same time of Chrétien *Wechel's Paris reprint of Erasmus' *De praeparatione* and other matters of interest (AK IV Ep 1857). It is generally assumed that in 1535 Montanus collaborated with Erasmus and Cousin in producing the famous *Expositio fidelis* about the death of Thomas *More and his fellow martyrs, which was perhaps printed in Basel, although the extent of Montanus' collaboration is a matter of controversy (Allen XI 368–78). At the time of Erasmus' death Montanus was closely connected with Erasmus' old friend Pierre *Vitré, who taught at the Collège de Navarre (Ep 3101; AK IV Ep 2062), and both corresponded with Bonifacius *Amerbach (AK IV 2097, V Epp 2116, 2129) about the bequest of 150 gold crowns set out for each of them in Erasmus' will (Allen XI 364). Montanus' receipt, signed with the French form of his name, is preserved in Basel. As his subsequent correspondence with Amerbach shows, he continued to show his gratitude by assisting young people from Basel who went to Paris for their studies (AK VI Epp 2739, 2822, 2823, 2832, VII Ep 3082).

At some time before July 1536 (AK IV Ep 2039) Montanus had moved from the Collège de Lisieux to the Collège de Tournai, where he continued to combine his teaching with work on the Greek Fathers. In 1532 he had assisted Germain de *Brie in preparing a Latin edition of some homilies by St John Chrysostom (Ep 2727), and for a subsequent edition (Paris: C. Chevallon 1536) he revised the translation of other homilies. He undertook further revisions for a Chrysostom published by Chevallon's widow in 1543 and in 1556 edited the same author again for her, with a dedication to Odet de *Coligny. He also devoted great attention to Theophylact, who was often consulted by Erasmus. His Latin edition (Paris: J. Loys of Tielt 1546) contained a dedicatory letter to Claude Dodieu, bishop of Rennes, which combined a clear rejection of Protestantism with sharp attacks upon corruption within the church of Rome, as was perhaps fitting during the earliest phases of the council of Trent. The same letter was reprinted in a second edition (Basel: J. Herwagen 1554), which included a revised translation of Theophylact's commentaries on the Pauline Epistles. The revision was carried out with the help of a Greek manuscript sent from Basel, of which he had become aware when reading Erasmus' *Annotationes* to the New Testament (AK VII Ep 3082).

In 1562 Montanus returned to Flanders and became rector of Queen's College in the recently established University of Douai. He died at Douai and was buried in the church of St James, where his portrait was shown on a stained-glass window. He founded three scholarships in the university.

BIBLIOGRAPHY: Allen Ep 2065 / *Matricule de Louvain* III-1 578 / Bierlaire *Familia* 81–2 / AK III Ep 1397, IV Ep 2039, VII Ep 3082, and passim / P.G. Bietenholz *Basle and France in the Sixteenth Century* (Geneva-Toronto 1971) 178–9, 313, and passim / H. de Vocht *Acta Thomae Mori* (Louvain 1947) 61–71 and passim / *Correspondance de Nicolas Clénard* ed A. Roersch (Brussels 1940–1) Ep 10 and notes   PGB

Nicolaus MONTENSIS *See Nicolas* COPPIN

Baptista MONTEZA documented October 1535–39/44
Baptista Monteza (Monteso, Monteys) was a secretary and steward to the imperial ambassador in England, Eustache *Chapuys. In Allen's edition he is tentatively identified with an imperial secretary attached to Chapuys whom *Goclenius met at Louvain in early 1535 (Ep 2998).

BIBLIOGRAPHY: LP IX 595, 966, 1037, and passim to XIV-2 781; cf also XVII 596, XIX-2 353   PGB

Barbara van MONTFOORT *See Maximiliaan van* HORN

Jacob Gerritszoon van MONTFOORT
documented 1515–32
Jacob van Montfoort, the son of Gerrit, belonged to an influential Haarlem family. Pieter van *Montfoort, his son, mentioned him to Erasmus in Ep 2389 of 20 September 1530. At that time Jacob was one of the four mayors ('consuls') of Haarlem who were elected annually. He also held that office in the years 1515–23, 1526–7, and 1531–2.

BIBLIOGRAPHY: W.P.J. Overmeer in *Algemeen Nederlandsch Familieblad* n s 17 (1905) 206–7
                          C.G. VAN LEIJENHORST

Lodewijk van MONTFOORT
d 10 November 1505
Lodewijk was a son of Hendrik IV, viscount of Montfoort, south-west of Utrecht, and Marie (or Margaretha) de Croy, and a younger brother of Hendrik's heir, Jan III. He received the minor orders and from 1498 to 1500 often served as deputy for Friedrich von *Baden,

bishop of Utrecht. In fact he was so busy with these functions that he neglected his duties as a canon of Utrecht, as he admitted in a letter of July 1499 to his dean, Ludolf van den Veen. In 1502 he gave up his ecclesiastical career and resigned his benefices to marry the widowed Anna van *Borssele. His installation as lord of Veere took place at Flushing on 22 June 1502.

Erasmus was vehemently opposed to this marriage because he anticipated correctly that it would end Anna's patronage of himself (Epp 146, 172). Lodewijk van Montfoort died in 1505 and was buried with his ancestors at Montfoort. He had several natural children, among them Willem, who was to become bailiff of Domburg and Westkapelle on the island of Walcheren, and Hendrik (*Matricule d'Orléans* II-1 273–4), who pursued an ecclesiastical career.

BIBLIOGRAPHY: Allen Ep 80 / L.M.G. Kooperberg in *Archief* of the *Zeeuwsch Genootschap der Wetenschappen* (1938) 77–8 / C.A. van Kalveen *Het bestuur van bisschop en Staten* (Utrecht 1974) passim   C.G. VAN LEIJENHORST

Pieter van MONTFOORT of Haarlem, documented 1530–7
Pieter van Montfoort (Petrus Montfoert ab Hoeff) was the son of Jacob van *Montfoort, who often served as one of the four mayors of Haarlem. In the late 1520s and early 1530s he was in the service of Albert of *Brandenburg, the archbishop of Mainz, and of the Emperor *Charles v in Germany (Epp 2389, 2812). Pieter had once visited Erasmus at Basel (cf Ep 2818) and wrote to him on 20 September 1530 encouraging him to write a letter recommending Quirinius *Talesius, Erasmus' famulus, for the position of pensionary of Haarlem (Ep 2389). Three years later, in May 1533, Montfoort was sent to present Erasmus with a gift of money from the six states of Holland. He stayed with Erasmus at Freiburg for six days, using the opportunity to obtain letters recommending him to *Mary of Austria (Ep 2812) and Nicolaus *Olahus (Ep 2813) for the provostship of Haarlem. However, Montfoort's friendship with Erasmus was soon destroyed by confusion over the exact amount of the Dutch gift. On 16 August 1532 the states of Holland had set aside 240 florins for the gift; according to the minutes of 24–5 April 1533 Gerrit van

*Assendelft and Joost *Sasbout had ordered Aert van der *Goes to give Erasmus *Schets 200 florins to be taken to Erasmus by Montfoort. Erasmus, however, had heard that the amount of the gift was 300 florins, and he grew suspicious when Montfoort only offered him 200 (Epp 2818, 2819). Erasmus wrote on the matter to Vincent *Cornelissen (Ep 2819) and to Aert van der Goes (cf Ep 2896), but by April 1534 contented himself with 240 florins (Epp 2913, 2923). However, he remained convinced that someone had swindled him of 60 florins, and his prime suspect remained Montfoort, whom he now bitterly denounced in a letter to Olahus as a sycophant and a cheat (Ep 2922).

Meanwhile, in July 1533 Montfoort had returned from Germany via Louvain, where he visited Conradus *Goclenius (Ep 2851). When Anabaptists took control of Münster, the Burgundian court authorized Montfoort to open negotiations with them in order to win the town for Charles v. It is not clear whether he was a double agent or whether he was cunningly misled, but after the Anabaptist attempt of 10 May 1535 on Amsterdam he fell under suspicion and was imprisoned at The Hague on the charge of treason (Ep 3111). Sentenced to death by the council of Holland, he was pardoned by Charles v in March 1537. Montfoort was probably the author of the *Carmen gratulatorium in novum praesulem Leodiensem D. Cornelium a Bergen* (Leiden: P. Claeszoon van Balen March 1539; NK 3542); he is there called a licentiate in canon and civil law.

BIBLIOGRAPHY: Allen Ep 2389 / E.M. ten Cate in *Doopsgezinde Bijdragen* 39 (1899) 1–19 / A.F. Mellink *De wederdopers in de Noordelijke Nederlanden 1531–1544* (Groningen 1953) 94–8, 128–31, 178, 182 / N. van der Blom *Erasmus en Rotterdam* (Rotterdam-The Hague 1969) 15–18
                        C.G. VAN LEIJENHORST

Floriano MONTINI of Ferrara, d 13 May 1533
Little is known of the early life and education of Floriano Montini. By 1524 he was secretary to Cardinal Lorenzo *Campeggi, who used him on diplomatic and family errands. He accompanied his master on his missions to Germany, Eastern Europe, and England as an important adviser and was rewarded with a prebend in his diocese of Salisbury. Like his master he

opposed *Henry VIII's suit for a divorce from *Catherine of Aragon. While in the service of Campeggi he was deputed to accompany the papal mission of Franciscus de Potentia to Muscovy (1525–7). A man of some learning Montini was in contact with Italian humanists and apparently had a special interest in philosophy (Ep 1552). He died in Italy.

Erasmus knew Montini through Campeggi. Montini acted as an intermediary between Erasmus and some Italian humanists; he passed on Erasmus' *De libero arbitrio* to his Ferrarese friends, including Celio *Calcagnini, and in turn sent Erasmus a manuscript of Calcagnini's work on the same topic (Ep 1552). Erasmus had it published in Basel with a prefatory letter addressed to Montini (Ep 1578). Montini knew of Erasmus' desire to foster a moderate Catholic reaction towards the Lutherans, although he may not have agreed with it. He signed a dispensation from Campeggi for Erasmus (Ep 1542). Montini's name appears in Erasmus' correspondence with other members of Campeggi's *familia* (Epp 1577, 1587, 1633, 1673).

BIBLIOGRAPHY: Allen Ep 1552 / William E. Wilkie *The Cardinal Protectors of England* (Cambridge 1974) 119 and passim / Sanudo *Diarii* XLV 94–5   JOHN F. D'AMICO

Philippus MONTIUS (documented 1517–18) Montius is known only from the correspondence of Erasmus, who met him in 1517 and greatly liked him. Montius was then the court chamberlain (*procurator aulae*) of Philip (I) of *Burgundy, bishop of Utrecht, and he was married (Epp 727, 759, 811).

Antoine MONTRIVEL of Besançon, d 10 September 1534
Antoine, the second son of Guillaume Montrivel, received a canonry at Montbéliard, half-way between Besançon and Basel, in 1507 and was elected dean of that chapter in 1515. On 22 December 1508 he received a canonry at Besançon and on 24 July 1533 succeeded Désiré *Morel, who had died the day before, as archdeacon of Luxeuil; he thus took over one of the leading positions within the Besançon chapter at a time when it was embroiled in conflicts with the municipality. On 26 January 1534 a brief composed by Jean *Lambelin was

Lady Alice More, wife of Sir Thomas More, by Hans Holbein the Younger

presented to the imperial court on behalf of the town; one of the grievances was the allegation that Montrivel had embezzled four to five thousand francs in moneys collected for a crusade against the Turks. In February the chapter appointed Montrivel to present their own position to *Charles v, and he died at Valencia while carrying out this mission, leaving to the chapter his silver and his paintings.

Erasmus met Montrivel at Besançon during his visit in the spring of 1524 (Ep 1610).

BIBLIOGRAPHY: Allen Ep 1610 / A. Castan 'Granvelle et le petit empereur de Besançon 1518–1538' *Revue historique* 1 (1876) 78–139, esp 129–30 / J. Viénot *Histoire de la réforme dans le pays de Montbéliard* (Montbéliard 1900) I 34 / Gauthier 129–30   PGB

Anna MOONS *See Rutgerus* RESCIUS

Alice MORE 1471–after 1543
Dame Alice's maiden name is not known. She was the widow of John Middleton, a prosperous merchant of London and the Staple at Calais (d 1509), when she married Thomas

Elizabeth More, by Hans Holbein the Younger

Cecily More, by Hans Holbein the Younger

*More in August or September 1511 (Ep 232), a month after the death of his first wife, Jane *Colt. Alice had a daughter, Alice *Middleton, who came to live with her mother in More's household. More obviously cared for, though he continually teased, his second wife.

Erasmus' relations with Dame Alice for some years seem to have been clouded by some incident or incidents. In Ep 236 a friend of his refers rather sharply to her by the phrase 'the harpy's crooked beak.' More seems to have ignored (or been ignorant of) the strained relations between his wife and his best friend; in Ep 388 he sent Erasmus her respects. But in Ep 451 Erasmus writes Andrea *Ammonio that 'More's lady somewhat resents me as a guest of rather long standing.' After further exchanges of greetings and news (Epp 502, 584, 623) Erasmus refers in a humorous passage to Dame Alice's devotion to Christian continence (Ep 785); but in his famous description of More (Ep 999) he speaks of More's marrying more to care for his family than for pleasure and praises Dame Alice as a mother to the family, as he does in Ep 1233, speaking of her careful shepherding of More's 'school.' Thereafter Erasmus continued to commend Dame Alice and to

exchange greetings with her (Epp 2212, 2223, 2233, 2735). In his last known letter to Erasmus (Ep 2831) More sent his own epitaph, which also refers to Alice. After his death she was granted an annuity of twenty pounds in 1536 and retained her husband's property at Battersea, near London.

BIBLIOGRAPHY: Allen Ep 999 / Rogers Ep 174 and passim / DNB XIII 878 / R.W. Chambers *Thomas More* (London 1935) / E.E. Reynolds *Thomas More* (London 1953) / William Roper *Life of More* ed E.V. Hitchcock (London 1935) xli–xlii / Thomas Stapleton *The Life of Sir Thomas More* ed E.E. Reynolds (London 1966)

R.J. SCHOECK

Elizabeth and Cecily MORE of London
Sir Thomas *More's second and third daughters, Elizabeth and Cecily, were born in about 1506 and about 1507 respectively. They were educated at home as part of the 'school' of More and are, as Routh has written, 'known rather as members of a brilliant group than individuals.' On 29 September 1525 Elizabeth married William Daunce and Cecily married Giles Heron, who were both elected to represent Thetford in the Parliament of 1529.

Heron had been More's ward since May 1524; he was executed in 1540, a loyal defender of More's own cause. Both Elizabeth and Cecily had several children and continued to live with their families in More's home. Both were alive at the time of his death (Rogers Ep 218).

In Erasmus' correspondence Elizabeth and Cecily are regulary mentioned together (Epp 1233, 1402, 2233). They addressed letters to Erasmus (Ep 1404), but he did not preserve them, although some of his correspondence with their elder sister, Margaret *More, is extant. In Epp 999 and 2432 Erasmus calls Elizabeth Aloysia, perhaps confusing her with Alice *Middleton, More's stepdaughter. Erasmus also praised the sisters' learning in the colloquy *Abbatis et eruditae*, first published in March 1524 (ASD I-3 407). Juan Luis *Vives did likewise in his *Institutio feminae christianae*, I iv (Antwerp: M. Hillen 1524), also including in his commendation Margaret *More and Margaret *Giggs.

BIBLIOGRAPHY: Allen and CWE Ep 999 / R.W. Chambers *Thomas More* (London 1935) passim / E.E. Reynolds *St Thomas More* (London 1953) passim / E.M.G. Routh *Sir Thomas More and his Friends* (London 1934) 136 / Rogers Ep 43 and passim / R.J. Schoeck in *New Catholic Encyclopedia* (New York 1967–78) IX 1142

R.J. SCHOECK

John (I) MORE of London, c 1451–1530
The father of Sir Thomas *More, Sir John was still a lawyer when Erasmus first visited England in 1499; in 1503 he was made serjeant-at-law, and in 1518 was judge of Common Pleas and by 1523 judge of King's Bench. Erasmus mentioned Sir John in Ep 999, describing More and his family, and in Ep 1233 he referred (inaccurately) to Sir John's age. In Ep 2750 Erasmus spoke of More's family and his father's distinction as a lawyer. In Ep 2831 (the last letter which survives of the correspondence between Erasmus and More) More sent Erasmus a copy of his epitaph, which mentions his father.

On 24 April 1474 Sir John married Agnes Graunger, who became the mother of Sir Thomas and four other children, Jane, John (II), Edward, and Elizabeth More. After the death of his first wife Sir John married first Johanna Marshall (d 1498) and then Elizabeth Bowes (d 1505), who were both widows of

John (I) More, by Hans Holbein the Younger

wealthy mercers. His last wife, Alice Clerke, another widow, survived him (Ep 999).

Sir John appears in the *Holbein family portrait, and there is a drawing by Holbein (now in Windsor Castle). The painting itself, 'of cardinal importance in the development of portraiture,' is lost, but a pen and ink drawing of the More family is in the Kunstmuseum, Basel.

BIBLIOGRAPHY: Allen and CWE Ep 999 / DNB XIII 871–2 / Margaret Hastings 'The Ancestry of Sir Thomas More' in *The Guildhall Miscellany* 2 (1961) repr in *Essential Articles for the Study of Thomas More* ed R.S. Sylvester and G. Marc'hadour (Hamden, Conn, 1977) 92–103, 599–601 / R.W. Chambers *Thomas More* (London 1935) / E.M.G. Routh *Sir Thomas More and His Friends* (London 1934) / Nicholas Harpsfield *Life of Sir Thomas More* ed Elsie V. Hitchcock (London 1932) / K.T. Parker *The Drawings of Holbein at Windsor Castle* 2nd ed (Oxford 1945) 35 (1) / Stanley Morison *The Likeness of Thomas More* (New York 1963) 18–21

R.J. SCHOECK

John (II) MORE of London, 6 June 1480–c 1512
A son of Sir John (I) *More and brother of Sir

Anne Cresacre, wife of John (III) More,
by Hans Holbein the Younger

John (III) More, by Hans Holbein the Younger

Thomas *More, John More was apparently a skilled scribe – though nothing is known of his education – and probably his brother's secretary in early years. In Ep 243 Andrea *Ammonio wrote Erasmus about John's bringing Erasmus' letter, and in Ep 246 Erasmus wrote Ammonio to complain about the poor handwriting at Cambridge and to ask that More arrange to give a manuscript to his brother for copying. Little more is known of John More, but it is possible that the John of Ep 255 is John More in his last illness, to whom Erasmus sends his good wishes (but cf also *Johannes of Lorraine). It is also possible that John was mentioned in a letter of uncertain date addressed to Thomas More (Ep 271, of July 1513?). In it Erasmus sent greetings to 'Lazarus, a man plainly born for the muses and graces,' who was copying manuscripts for him. John might be either the poor, suffering Lazarus or Lazarus brought back to life after a severe illness.

BIBLIOGRAPHY: Allen Ep 243 / R.W. Chambers *Thomas More* (London 1935) 53 / E.M.G. Routh *Sir Thomas More and His Friends* (Oxford 1934) 42–3   R.J. SCHOECK & PGB

John (III) MORE of London, c December 1508–c November 1547
The only son and last child of Sir Thomas *More, John was educated at home, but he seems to have been outshone by his sister Margaret *More. He is mentioned in Ep 999, along with his sisters, and greeted in Ep 2211. Ep 1402 is a dedication to John More of Erasmus' commentary on the poem *Nux*, attributed to Ovid (ASD I-1 145–74; cf Allen I 12). In addition, both the second editions of Aristotle and Plato in the Greek were dedicated to young John – the former corrected by Simon *Grynaeus with a preface by Erasmus (Ep 2432), the latter with a preface by Grynaeus (Basel: J. Walder March 1534).

About 1529 John married Anne Cresacre (1511–77), a ward of Sir Thomas, and the biographer Cresacre More (1572–1649) was his grandson. In 1533 John translated from the Latin Damião de *Gois' *Legatio*, an account of the mission of Matthew, an Ethiopian envoy, to Portugal, and also a sermon by Fridericus *Nausea on the sacrament of the altar (both printed by William Rastell in 1533, STC 11966 and 18414). After the execution of his father two years later, John was temporarily imprisoned. In April 1544 John and his brother-in-law William Daunce were pardoned after an abortive attempt to have Thomas *Cranmer charged with heresy. John enjoyed a comfortable living on account of his wife's estate of Barnborough in Yorkshire. A fine portrait sketch by Hans *Holbein, 1526–7, is in Windsor Castle.

BIBLIOGRAPHY: Allen Ep 999 / DNB XIII 894 / Rogers Ep 107 and passim / E.E. Reynolds *St Thomas More* (London 1953) passim / Ro. Ba. *The Lyfe of Syr Thomas More ...* ed E.V. Hitchcock and P.E. Hallett (London 1950) 29, 50, and passim / A.W. Reed *Early Tudor Drama* (London 1926) 79–80 / R.W. Chambers *Thomas More* (London 1935) 181, 184, 189, 282 / R.J. Schoeck in *New Catholic Encyclopedia* (New York 1967–78) IX 1142   R.J. SCHOECK

Margaret MORE before October 1505–Christmas 1544
Margaret was the eldest child of Sir Thomas *More. The brightest star of the 'school' of More and doubtless her father's favourite child, she married William *Roper on 2 July 1521 (Ep 1233) and remained at her husband's side until her death. There were five Roper children, three daughters and two sons. Roger Ascham revealed in a letter of 15 January 1554 to one of the daughters, Mary Roper Clarke, that about twenty years earlier Margaret Roper had tried to persuade him to become a tutor in Greek and Latin to her children. After the execution of her father she was temporarily imprisoned.

Margaret corresponded with Erasmus, and several letters between them are extant. Erasmus praised her learning very highly, and along with her sisters she seems to have exercised great influence upon his ideas concerning the education of women. On Christmas day of 1523 Erasmus dedicated to her his commentary on Prudentius' hymns for Christmas and Epiphany (Ep 1404; Allen I 13), and in Ep 2212 he commented on her reading of his *Vidua christiana*. Margaret replied (Ep 2233, 4 November 1528), but curiously did not mention her father's promotion to the lord chancellorship, which had taken place two weeks earlier. In the *Colloquia* of March 1524, Margaret almost certainly figures as the Mag-

Margaret More, by Hans Holbein the Younger

dalia of *Abbatis et eruditae* (ASD I-3 403–8).

The same year Margaret translated Erasmus' *Precatio dominica* as *A Devout Treatise upon the Paternoster* (London: W. de Worde n d), and for it Richard Hyrde wrote an introduction dedicated to a Frances S. (probably Margaret's cousin, Frances Staverton) and described Margaret's virtue and learning. Margaret also translated the *Ecclesiastical History* of Eusebius (the first book into Latin, the first five books into English), and Thomas More's *Treatise on the Passion* into English for his 1557 *Works*. It appears that she further wrote a devotional treatise, 'De quattuor novissimis,' thus selecting a topic which her father had hoped to treat and which Erasmus treated in *De praeparatione ad mortem*.

Margaret's learning was widely praised: for example by John Coke (in *The Debate between the Heraldes of Englande and Fraunce*, London: R. Wyer 1550) and by Jan Coster of Louvain (in editing Vincent of Lérins, Louvain: A.M. Bergaigne 1552). Erasmus mentioned her in his famous accounts of More (Epp 999, 1233).

BIBLIOGRAPHY: Rogers Ep 43 and passim / William Roper *Life of More* ed E.V. Hitchcock

Thomas More, by Hans Holbein the Younger

(London 1935) / E.E. Reynolds *Margaret Roper*
(London 1960) / L.V. Ryan *Roger Ascham*
(Stanford 1963) 40   R.J. SCHOECK

Thomas MORE of London, 6/7 February
1477/8–6 July 1535
Thomas, the son of Sir John (I) *More, was
educated at St Anthony's School, London,
under Nicholas Holt, and next placed as a page
in the household of John *Morton, archbishop
of Canterbury. He attended Oxford University
for about two years, approximately 1492 to
1494, when he may have been a student of
*Grocyn and *Latimer, although he probably
did not begin to learn Greek until after he had
left Oxford.

Thomas More began his legal studies at one
of the lesser legal inns of chancery in London
about 1494, and in February 1496 he was
admitted to Lincoln's Inn, one of the four inns
of court for the study of English common law
(Ep 124). He advanced rapidly from student to
lawyer, residing for about four years in the
London Charterhouse (c 1500–4), and then
became a royal servant. During this period
More probably began his studies in Greek with

Grocyn and *Linacre; he also took up theology,
lecturing on Augustine's *De civitate Dei* at the
end of his Charterhouse years. Late in 1504 or
early 1505 he married Jane *Colt, and there
were four children – Margaret, Elizabeth,
Cecily, and John (III) *More – all known to
Erasmus. High points in the earlier phase of
More's distinguished legal and public career
are the following: member of Parliament in 1504
(and again in 1523, when he was elected
speaker of the house); under-sheriff of London
(1510–19); Reader and Bencher of Lincoln's
Inn; and member of an embassy to Flanders in
1515, on which mission he began to compose
his *Utopia*.

The first meeting of More and Erasmus took
place in 1499 during Erasmus' first visit
to England, and their friendship quickly
deepened and continued until death, although
they did not see each other in later life. Having
met Erasmus in London or Greenwich, More
took him to meet the future *Henry VIII (Ep
104). Erasmus' first surviving letter to More
dates from October 1499 (Ep 114) and shows
that it was preceded by other letters not known
to us. More's first preserved letter dates from
1516 (Ep 388), and throughout their correspondence a substantial number of exchanges are
missing. What struck Erasmus in these earliest
encounters was what he called More's 'sweet-
ness' (Epp 118, 120). From this date onwards,
the lives and intellectual development of the
two friends are closely intertwined. All More's
early humanistic works are the result of a close
collaboration with Erasmus – as in the case of
the translations from Lucian – or reflect
Erasmus' concepts of the classics and his
program of study – as do *Utopia* and *Richard III*
(although the latter is a work which Erasmus
never mentioned). Conversely, a number of
Erasmus' writings, among them the *Enchiridion*, bear marks of the influence of More.
More's translation of the life of Giovanni *Pico
(written c 1504 and published in 1509 or 1510,
London: J. Rastell) is another product of his
period of humanistic studies and achievements
from 1500 to 1516, and to these works must be
added the splendid letters in defence of
Erasmus and humanism which he wrote to
*Dorp, to Oxford University, and to the monk
John *Batmanson during the years 1515–19
(Rogers Epp 15, 60, 83).

Erasmus paid his second visit to England in 1505 and 1506, and by this time both he and More had been studying Greek for several years and had begun to translate Lucian; More was perhaps also translating the epigrams from the Greek Anthology. Several of Erasmus' letters (Epp 187, 191–3) dedicated individual translations which were published in their joint collection of *Luciani opuscula* (Paris: J. Bade 1506). Ep 192, like many other letters of these years, praised More for his learning. In 1509, upon his return from Italy, Erasmus lived with More – and his second wife, Alice *More – in their home at Bucklesbury in the city of London and at that time he revised his *Moria* (Paris: G. de Gourmont for J. Petit [1511]), with its pun upon More's name and its dedication to More (Epp 222, 337).

After a visit to Paris Erasmus again lived in England from June 1511 to 1514, when he was at Cambridge (Ep 211), and in August 1516 and April 1517. During this period More was working on *Richard III*, but neither his English nor his Latin version was published in his lifetime. Throughout these years More frequently advised or helped Erasmus on matters pertaining to his annuity from the benefices of Aldington and other moneys. In Erasmus' *De copia* (Paris 1512) More's name is added to many examples demonstrating the use of copious praise (CWE 24:355–64). The years 1515–17 are filled with correspondence between More and Erasmus, much of it concerned with the composition and publication of *Utopia*, from the composition and the sending of the manuscript to Erasmus (Ep 461) to arranging for the first edition (Louvain: D. Martens [December 1516]) and for the Basel edition by Johann *Froben in 1517 (Epp 550, 584, 634, 635). Erasmus was deeply involved in the initial conception of the work as well as the choice of publishers, but his role in the composition and publication of *Utopia* remains to be established definitively.

It is now clear that More entered the king's service before Erasmus was aware of the move; he thought that when More visited Calais in the autumn of 1517 (Ep 623) he was not yet in the council, but More had become a councillor not later than August of 1517. Towards the end of April 1518 Erasmus wrote More that he was lost to literature (Ep 829). He was appointed a judge in the Court of Requests and took up regular duties with the king's council in 1518. In 1521 he was knighted and named under-treasurer of the king's exchequer. Erasmus seems to have thought that he had not sought this office (Ep 1233) and to have confused this with the office of lord treasurer. In the same context he spoke of More's light duties and high salary and seems to have had an exaggerated notion of More's influence.

On 30 September 1525 More left the office of under-treasurer and became the chancellor of the Duchy of Lancaster, an important administrative and judicial office which he held until October 1529. During this period he was also high steward of Cambridge and Oxford. On 25 October 1529 More received the great seal from the king and was lord chancellor until his resignation was accepted on 16 May 1532 (Ep 2659), the day following the 'Submission of the Clergy,' which subjected the holding of synods to royal approval. In the next two years More was extraordinarily occupied writing massive works of polemic in defence of orthodoxy and the church – notably the *Apology* (London: W. Rastell 1533; STC 18078) and the *Debellation of Salem and Bizance* (London: W. Rastell 1533; STC 18081), both addressed to Christopher St German. They were written and published in English; Erasmus appears not to have read them, while in the *Debellation* More gives evidence of not being familiar with Erasmus' recent patristic scholarship.

After refusing to subscribe to the new oath required by the Act of Succession (1534), More was named in a bill of attainder and examined by the king's council. On 17 April 1534 More was committed to the Tower, where in perfect peace of mind he wrote a number of devotional and meditative works, of which the greatest is the *Dialogue of Comfort* (London: R. Tottel 1553; STC 18082). He was examined again in May 1535 by the king's council. On 1 July he was tried for treason and convicted on perjured testimony. On 6 July he was beheaded. After his head had been exhibited on London Bridge, it is believed that his body was transferred to the tomb in the Chelsea parish church for which More himself had composed an epitaph when he retired in 1532 (Epp 2831, 2865).

The news of More's execution shocked all Europe. Cardinal Reginald *Pole, in a forceful protest sent to the king and subsequently published as *Pro ecclesiasticae unitatis defensione*, asserted that strangers wept at hearing the news. Pope *Paul III praised More as excelling in sacred learning and courageous in the defence of truth. *Charles V is reported to have said that he would have preferred to lose his best city rather than such a councillor.

After Erasmus' visit to England in the spring of 1517 the nature of his contacts with More had changed. More's diplomatic mission to Calais later in that year allowed him to visit Erasmus' friends at Bruges (Ep 740–2) but surprisingly did not lead to a meeting with Erasmus, who was toiling at Louvain over the revision of his New Testament. Not until the summer of 1520 did they see each other again, at least in passing, when both attended the encounter of their monarchs at Calais and subsequent gatherings at Bruges (CWE Ep 1106). Apart from a similar meeting, again at Bruges, in August 1521 (Ep 1233), they never met thereafter but made sure they could behold each other to their hearts' content through the exchange of outstanding portraits: Quinten *Metsys' diptych of Erasmus and Pieter *Gillis (Epp 584, 654, 683, 684) and *Holbein's composite drawing of More in the middle of his family (Epp 2210, 2211). Erasmus, moreover, rivalled the painters in his masterly pen portraits of More and his household (Epp 999, 1233, 2750), which are indispensable for any historical assessment of More's character. More knew how to create for himself and those dear to him a domestic environment which was unique, in keeping with his personality – features that are well expressed in Erasmus' description of More's life in his home at Chelsea (Ep 2750), although Erasmus had never visited the latter.

The friends played similar roles when each tried to resolve, or at least defuse, a literary controversy that caused the other much excitement; More acted in this way during Erasmus' bitter quarrel with Edward *Lee (Epp 1026, 1083, 1090, 1097; Rogers Epp 75, 84, 85), while Erasmus endeavoured to reciprocate in More's quarrel with Germain de *Brie (Epp 1045, 1087, 1093; Rogers Ep 86). On the other hand,

Erasmus deplored in his *Spongia* (1523) the harshness of More's anonymous *Responsio ad Lutherum* (ASD IX-1 168–9), whereas More was instrumental in helping to persuade Erasmus to take up the pen against *Luther; in a letter of December 1526 (Ep 1770) he urged his friend in forthright language to proceed with the second part of *Hyperaspistes*, and preceding exchanges may have been similarly frank. This might partially explain the long gap of over five years in their preserved correspondence (Epp 1220, 1770). In his last extant letter to Erasmus (Ep 2659) More informed him of his resignation from the chancellorship, although he concealed the true reasons. Erasmus probably failed to understand at first that More's disgrace was caused by a matter of conscience (Ep 3048). More's discretion made it easy for Erasmus to persevere in his good opinion of Henry VIII as well as continue friendly relations with some of his chief advisers, while cautiously refraining from writing to More, who was jailed in the Tower (Ep 2997). From the summer of 1534, however, his attitude was slowly changing (Epp 2948, 2961, 2965, 3000, 3025), and after the news of More's execution (Ep 3037) he quickly published statements expressing his shock, grief, and indignation with the king (Epp 3036 [predated], 3049). Together with Philippus *Montanus and Gilbert *Cousin he seems to have been involved in the publication and circulation of the *Expositio fidelis de morte D. Thomae Mori et quorundam aliorum insignium virorum in Anglia* (Epp 3076, 3137; Allen XI 368–78).

BIBLIOGRAPHY: DNB XIII 876–96 / Emden BRUO II 305–8 / *The Yale Edition of the Complete Works of St Thomas More* (New Haven 1963–) / *The Correspondence of Sir Thomas More* ed E.F. Rogers (Princeton 1947) / William Roper *Life of More* ed E.V. Hitchcock (London 1935) / Nicholas Harpsfield *Life of More* ed E.V. Hitchcock (London 1932) / R.W. Chambers *Thomas More* (London 1935) / E.E. Reynolds *Thomas More and Erasmus* (London 1965) / Stanley Morison *The Likeness of Thomas More* ed and supplemented by Nicholas Barker (London 1963) / K.T. Parker *The Drawings of Hans Holbein … at Windsor Castle* (Oxford 1945) / *St Thomas More: Action and Contemplation* ed R.S. Sylvester (New Haven 1972) / J.H. Hexter

More's Utopia … The Biography of an Idea
(Princeton 1952) / *Thomas More's Prayer Book* ed
R.S. Sylvester and Louis L. Martz (New Haven
1969) / D.F.S. Thomson and H.C. Porter
Erasmus and Cambridge (Toronto 1963) / *Essen-
tial Articles for the Study of Thomas More* ed R.S.
Sylvester and G. Marc'hadour (Hamden,
Conn, 1977) / P.G. Bietenholz *History and
Biography in the Work of Erasmus of Rotterdam*
(Geneva 1966) / R.J. Schoeck 'Sir Thomas More
and Lincoln's Inn Revels' *Philological Quarterly*
29 (1950) repr in *Essential Articles for the Study of
Thomas More* / R.J. Schoeck *The Achievement of
Thomas More: Aspects of his Life and Works*
(Victoria, BC, 1976) / J.B. Trapp and H. Schulte
Herbrüggen *'The King's Good Servant' Sir
Thomas More* exhibition catalogue (London
1977) / G.P. Jones 'Recent Studies in More'
English Literary Renaissance, 9 (1979) 442–58
                              R.J. SCHOECK & PGB

Désiré MOREL at Besançon, d 23 July 1533
Désiré Morel (Morellus) was a canon of
Besançon from 20 December 1494 and succeeded Guillaume *Guérard, who died in January
1529, as official to the archdeacon. He also
became archdeacon of Luxeuil and thus a
ranking dignitary of the Besançon chapter. On
22 August 1509 he returned from Rome, having
obtained a judgment by the Rota in support of
his chapter against the citizens of Salins, and
on 10 May 1510 he was appointed priest of
Choisey. Erasmus met him during his visit to
Besançon in the spring of 1524 and recalled him
in polite terms (Epp 1534, 1610). He was a
great-uncle of Gilbert *Cousin (Ep 3123) and,
being unaware of his death, Erasmus wrote to
him in October 1533 when he sent Cousin to
Besançon to fetch wine (Epp 2870, 2895).
    BIBLIOGRAPHY: Allen Ep 1534 / L. Febvre in
*Bulletin de la Société de l'histoire du protestantisme
français* 56 (1907) 109 / Besançon, Archives du
Doubs MS G 250 / Gauthier 116, 122   PGB

Jean MOREL of Embrun, 1511–
18 November 1581
A native of Embrun, Hautes-Alpes, Jean Morel
(Morellus), sieur de Grigny, appeared in 1533
and 1534 at Basel, where he matriculated at the
university and presented himself to Bonifacius
*Amerbach, and at Freiburg, where he visited

Erasmus with an introduction from Jacopo
*Sadoleto, then at Carpentras. It is conceivable
that he was the trusted messenger who
brought Erasmus a manuscript of Sadoleto's
commentary on Romans in August 1533.
Subsequently he was living, and probably
working, with Hieronymus *Froben when
Amerbach recommended him as famulus to
Erasmus, who did not, however, think he
would do (Epp 2865, 2872; cf AK IV Epp 1783,
1785, 1791). He was also known to Amerbach's
friend Jean Montaigne at Avignon (AK V Ep
2128). His coming to Basel was probably
connected with the diplomatic efforts of
Guillaume Du Bellay, sieur de Langey, who
built up a network of agents with the purpose
of allying France to the Protestant princes and
cities and consequently of reconciling the old
faith and the new. Morel, who possessed the
agent's virtue of self-effacement, was still, or
again, at Basel in April 1537. In the summer he
paid a visit to Embrun and was promptly
investigated for heresy, so that Langey had to
come to his rescue, explaining the diplomatic
reason for his stay abroad and his 'professional' interest for the writings of the reformers.
Later that year he followed Langey to his new
post in Piedmont, where he had the opportunity of associating with *Rabelais. While at Basel
Morel had been in contact with the scholar and
printer Johannes Oporinus and contributed a
remarkable preface (addressed to Antoine
*Morelet de Museau) to a volume of commen-
taries on Cicero published by Oporinus and his
printing partners in 1537. The friendship
endured, and in 1541 Oporinus informed
Morel, then staying at Turin with Langey, of
the death of Simon *Grynaeus, their common
friend and adviser.
    When Erasmus returned to Basel in 1535
Morel probably maintained some contacts
with him. Conceivably he could thus be the
Grynaeus (Grigny) who, according to letters
by *Capito and *Bucer (20 and 22 July 1536),
claimed to have been present at Erasmus'
death. This claim, whoever made it, should be
viewed with scepticism, as should a similar one
made by Lambert *Coomans. The fact, presumably well known to contemporaries, that Morel
was, or had been, living at Froben's house,
where Erasmus died, would serve to enhance

an imaginary as well as a true claim. In two epigrams in honour of Erasmus, written after his death, Morel does not give any hint of special familiarity; these epigrams are reprinted among the preliminary pieces in LB I.

After Langey's death in 1543 Morel is documented at Paris, where he lived as a neighbour of Michel de L'Hospital in the rue Pavée and played congenial host to gatherings of the early Pléiade, being especially close to Joachim Du Bellay. Before 1547 he was *maréchal des logis* of *Catherine de' Medici, and he introduced L'Hospital at court; the latter became Catherine's chancellor when she was the regent. With his wife, Antoinette, the daughter of François *Deloynes, Morel had three daughters, to whom he gave a careful education, engaging Karel *Uutenhove as s their tutor in 1556. Morel himself took Greek lessons from Jean Dorat and supervised the education of a natural son of *Henry II. He died, according to Pierre de l'Estoile, discoursing in Latin of his faith in salvation.

BIBLIOGRAPHY: Allen Ep 2865 / E. Droz in BHR 21 (1959) 563–8 (cf 20, 1958, 132–4), reviewing C. Reedijk 'Das Lebensende des Erasmus' *Basler Zeitschrift für Geschichte und Altertumskunde* 57 (1958) 23–66, esp 62–4 / P.G. Bietenholz *Basle and France in the Sixteenth Century* (Geneva-Toronto 1971) 108–11, 206, and passim / V.-L. Bourrilly *Guillaume du Bellay* (Paris 1905) 224, 322–3, and passim   PGB

Thierry MOREL of Vitry-en-Perthois, documented 1520–6
Morel (Theodoricus Morellus) taught from 1520 to 1525, or possibly longer, at the Collège de la Marche in Paris, and was probably the principal of that college. He also seems to have been connected with the Collège de Saint-Michel, also called Collège de Chanac, from where he dated in 1523 a preface for a selection of Erasmus' letters, *Breves epistolae* (Paris: P. Gromors 1525), in which he praised the addressee, Pierre Pineau, canon of Reims, for his fervent admiration of Erasmus. In the winter of 1519–20 he went to Châlons-sur-Marne because the plague had infested Paris, and there he found an anonymous manuscript which he published after his return as *Oratio paraenetica in pressuras ecclesiae* (Paris: N. de la Barre 1520). Of his various school books the

most important is an *Enchiridion ad verborum copiam* (Paris 1523, reprinted several times). The title already acknowledges the work's debt to Erasmus' *De copia*, and in a final note to the reader Erasmus was praised along with Cicero and Quintilian as the authors most worthy of study. This book is dedicated to Robert de Lenoncourt, archbishop of Reims, and Morel's special patron. Morel also edited for use in schools the letters of *Poliziano and Francesco *Negro as well as other works, including the *Elegantiae* of Lorenzo *Valla, the *Bucolica* of Baptista *Mantuanus, and Pierre d'Ailly's *Tractatus de anima*.

In 1534 Jean *Lange included Morel in his list of Erasmus' friends and admirers in Paris (Ep 1407).

BIBLIOGRAPHY: Allen Ep 1407 / M.-M. de la Garanderie *Christianisme et lettres profanes (1515–1535)* (Lille-Paris 1976) I 103–8, 113, 167 / M.-M. de la Garanderie 'Recueils parisiens de lettres d'Erasme' BHR 31 (1969) 449–65
MICHEL REULOS

Antoine MORELET du Museau c 1500–17 October 1552
Antoine Morelet (Maurus Musaeus), sieur de la Marche-Ferrière, came from a distinguished Burgundian family and was the son of Jean(?) Morelet, *général des finances*, treasurer of the army, and from the beginning of 1522 frequently French ambassador to the Swiss (d c May 1529). Antoine's mother was Marie, the sister of Guillaume (II) *Briçonnet, and Nicolas *Bérault took a hand in his education. The name of Jean is also given to Antoine's uncle, who was a royal secretary and had met Janus *Lascaris in Paris (Delaruelle Ep 1). In 1526, when the Swiss tired of waiting for promised moneys, Antoine's father, the French ambassador, had to secure his own release from prison by offering Antoine as a hostage.

Meanwhile in 1523 Antoine became royal secretary, and Guillaume *Budé, a good friend of the Morelet family, thanked Erasmus for the warm reception accorded to Antoine at Basel (Ep 1370). In 1524 *Oecolampadius wrote to him at Paris. In 1533 or 1534 Antoine had to flee Paris because of his evangelical convictions and returned to Basel, where he lived for four years, apart from visits to Geneva, and met Jean Calvin. He was admitted to the citizenship of Basel on 16 June 1535. The Basel government was persuaded to intervene in his favour, and in the summer of 1537 *Francis I pardoned him. In 1541 and 1542 he undertook a mission to the German Protestants, visiting Worms and Speyer, and from 1543 he belonged to the team of French diplomats in Switzerland, sometimes as regular ambassador and sometimes as special envoy. In 1546 he bought a house on the Nadelberg at Basel, where he resided as often as circumstances permitted and where he died.

Antoine corresponded with Calvin and *Bucer. He was also a patron of scholars and had several books dedicated to him: a commentary to Cicero's orations with a preface by Jean *Morel (Basel: J. Oporinus 1537), Sebastianus Castellio's *Sibyllina oracula* (Basel: J. Oporinus 1546) and Guillaume Plancy's editions of Plutarch's *De superstitione* (Lyon: S. Gryphius 1552). He presented a gold-plated bowl to Katharina Klein, the widow of Konrad *Resch, who was his landlady, and Calvin's, during the early days at Basel.

BIBLIOGRAPHY: Allen Epp 1354, 1370 / Herminjard I 248–50, III 194–200, 204–8, IV 76–7, 268–9, VII 27, 113, and passim / AK VI Ep 2832, VII Epp 3157, 3336, VIII Ep 2395a, and passim / *Basler Chroniken* VIII 230–3 / E. Rott *Histoire de la représentation diplomatique de la France auprès des cantons suisses* (Bern 1900–35) I 274, 295, 308–15, 411–13, and passim / L. Delaruelle *Répertoire de la correspondance de Guillaume Budé* (Toulouse-Paris 1907) 2–3, 196 / V.-L. Bourrilly *Guillaume du Bellay* (Paris 1905) 314, 344, and passim / J.V. Pollet *Martin Bucer* (Paris 1958–62) II 9 and passim / P.G. Bietenholz *Basle and France in the Sixteenth Century* (Geneva-Toronto 1971) 58–9 and passim   PGB

Claude MORELET du Museau *See Claude* LE MARLET

MORELLUS *See* MOREL

Guy MORILLON d 2 October 1548
Guy Morillon, a Burgundian who was apparently of modest origins, is first documented in Paris in 1507 and 1508. Laying claims to a MA, he tutored young students and published, in part for their benefit, Horace's *Epistolae* (January 1507), Ovid's *Heroides* and *Ibis* (August

Guy Morillon, by Michael Coxie

1507), and, from a manuscript belonging to the abbey of St Victor, Suetonius (August 1508). Morillon knew Guillaume *Budé and, likewise in Paris, may have made the acquaintance of Erasmus. By June 1515 he had returned to the Netherlands and was living in Brussels, where he became secretary to the chancellor, Jean *Le Sauvage, and also a good friend to the chancellor's chaplain, Pierre *Barbier (Epp 532, 565). Like Barbier, Morillon did his best to sustain the chancellor's interest in Erasmus' person and work (Epp 532, 587). It can be assumed that Morillon accompanied his master to Spain in 1517, where he attended the court of the future *Charles V, kept in touch with Erasmus (Epp 695, 752, 794, 847), and, after Le Sauvage's death, was taken into the monarch's service as one of Charles' secretaries. He remained attached to Charles when the latter returned to the Netherlands and in the spring of 1522 was preparing to accompany him back to Spain by way of England, where he expected to meet Thomas *More (Ep 1287). Thereafter he seems to have remained in Spain until 1531 (Epp 2163, 2523), keeping in touch with Erasmus through a frequent exchange of letters, most of which are lost, however (Epp 1287, 1302, 1431, 1470, 1585, 1791, 2083, 2404, 2523). By the end of 1531 he returned to the Netherlands and lived in Louvain, but when Erasmus wrote his last known letter to him in August 1534, he was again in Spain and had been there, it seems, for a considerable time (Ep 2965). On 1 June 1538 he bought a house at Louvain in the Predikherenstraat, where he spent the last decade of his life surrounded by his family.

Like other executive members of the Hapsburg courts, Morillon did not visibly take sides in the political questions of the day, and his name is rarely found in works treating the general history of the Low Countries. In the spring of 1517 he married Elisabeth de *Mil, who bore him six children. Those who survived their parents erected a monument for them in the nave of St Peter's church, Louvain, which remained in place until 1807. It was adorned by a triptych by Michael Coxie which shows Guy and members of his family on the outer panels (now in the Stadsmuseum of Louvain).

Erasmus relied on Morillon repeatedly in financial transactions and problems related to his annuity from Courtrai (Epp 1254, 1287, 1470, 1507). A certain caution notwithstanding (Ep 1287), Morillon also seems to have supported Erasmus in the struggle against theological opponents (Ep 1814); especially in Spain he may have played a significant role in arranging contacts with other members of the imperial court such as Luis *Coronel (Ep 1274) and Alfonso de *Valdés (Ep 2163). Although his extant exchanges with Erasmus scarcely treat of scholarly and literary matters, Morillon had numerous contacts with the world of humanism. He knew Erasmus' friends Pieter *Gillis (Epp 532, 587) and Marcus *Laurinus (Ep 1287). In the years of his retirement at Louvain he associated with Damião de *Gois and Erasmus' admirers at the Collegium Trilingue such as Rutgerus *Rescius and Petrus Nannius. His sons, who matriculated at Louvain in 1532, studied at the Trilingue. At this time he also resumed his own studies, which after his departure from Paris he had sacrificed to the duties of his office. In particular he devoted himself to Livy, on whom he consulted Guillaume *Budé; Nannius acknowledged

Morillon's assistance when commenting on some passages by Livy in his *Miscellaneorum decas una* (Louvain: S. Zassenus 1548), published shortly before Morillon's death.

BIBLIOGRAPHY: Allen Ep 532 / NBW IX 563–4 / BNB XV 265–7 / de Vocht CTL III 44–50 and passim / de Vocht *Literae ad Craneveldium* Epp 86, 140, 142, 159 / Bataillon *Erasmo y España* 82–3 and passim / E. van Even 'Le Mausolée de la famille Morillon' *Messager des sciences historiques* (Ghent 1857) 269–84 / F. Neve *La Carrière de Guy Morillon* (Ghent 1858) / E. van Even 'Nouveaux renseignements sur le séjour à Louvain de Guy Morillon et sa famille' *Messager des sciences historiques* (Ghent 1877) 136–68 / A. Polet *Une Gloire de l'humanisme belge, Petrus Nannius, 1500–1557* (Louvain 1936) 50, 152, 158–9, 266, 275, 284 / P. Reckmans and F.A. Lefever 'De grafmonumenten en epitafen van de Leuvense Sint-Pieterskerke' *Medelingen van de Geschied- en Outheidkundige Kring voor Leuven en Omgeving* 14 (1974) 111–12

HILDE DE RIDDER-SYMOENS

Jean MORIN documented 1523–35
Apart from his official career little seems to be known about Jean Morin. He was an *avocat* in the Parlement of Paris when, at Easter 1523, he was appointed lieutenant to the royal bailiff of Paris, a newly created position given to Jean de La Barre. While retaining this office Morin is also referred to in 1525 as provost of the Paris merchants. In the following year he succeeded La Barre as bailiff, and on 28 December 1529 he was appointed royal *lieutenant criminel* for the city of Paris in succession to Guillaume Maillart; he still held the position in 1535. His functions apparently included issuing royal printing privileges, and Erasmus protested to him in 1531 because Julius Caesar *Scaliger's book against him had been licensed (Epp 2577, 2587). Erasmus seems to have learnt from Jacobus *Omphalius that the protest bore results, and in the spring of 1532 he addressed a letter of thanks to Morin (Ep 2635). In 1534 after the placards affair Morel personally conducted the hunt for the 'heretics,' pronounced death sentences, and inevitably attracted the hatred of the Protestant chroniclers. In October 1553 his heirs are mentioned in a legal document.

BIBLIOGRAPHY: Allen Ep 2577 / *Le Journal d'un bourgeois de Paris* ed V.-L. Bourrilly (Paris 1910) 12, 210, 226, 246, 332, and passim / *Inventaire des registres des insinuations du Châtelet de Paris: Règnes de François Ier et de Henri II* ed E. Campardon and A. Tuety (Paris 1906) 634 / Henry Meylan et al *Aspects de la propagande religieuse* (Geneva 1957) 85–6, 88, 100–1

PGB

Gerard MORINCK of Zaltbommel, d 9 October 1556

A native of Zaltbommel on the river Waal, Gerard Morinck (Moringus) matriculated at Louvain on 12 December 1510. He received his BA on 26 January 1510, his licence in arts on 27 January 1511, and his MA in 1513, standing first in a class of 155. Still at Louvain, he lectured in arts and studied theology under Jan *Briart, and became the amanuensis and intimate friend of Maarten van *Dorp, then president of the College of the Holy Spirit. He was living away from the college when Dorp died on 31 May 1525, but at the end of that year the faculty of theology appointed him a lecturer at Holy Spirit, although he would not acquire his licence in theology until 5 February 1527. In 1527 and 1529 he was procurator of the Holland nation. From 1529 to 1533 he seems to have been a tutor at the abbey of St Gertrude at Louvain. In 1533 Abbot George Sarens engaged his services for the Benedictine abbey of St Trudo at St Truiden, where he remained until his death.

In 1526 Morinck wrote a biography of the recently deceased Dorp and sent a manuscript copy to Erasmus, whom he greatly admired (Ep 1994A). According to letters written by Morinck in later years (de Vocht MHL 507, 508, 578–82), Erasmus scorned the work, perhaps because Morinck reduced his relations with Dorp to a few lines, saying nothing about their controversy over the new learning and their subsequent reconciliation of 1514–16. Morinck's life of Dorp remained unpublished until Henry de Vocht included it in MHL with notes (257–348). In 1528 Erasmus, having heard from Jan of *Heemstede that Morinck had begun a biography of St Augustine, suggested that the biography might be included in the coming Froben edition of the Father's works. Morinck replied with Ep 1994, stating that he had set aside his work on Augustine because he believed Erasmus was writing his own biography and wished to defer to the superior skills of the great humanist. However, when the works of Augustine appeared in 1529 without the anticipated biography, Morinck resumed his original project, completing it in 1532 and publishing it in August 1533 (Antwerp: J. Grapheus; NK 1543).

Morinck also wrote lives of Jan Briart (1522), Pope *Adrian VI (Louvain: R. Rescius November 1536; NK 1545, also in C. Burmannus' *Analecta*, Utrecht 1727), and saints Trudo, Eucherius of Orléans, and Libert of Mechelen (Louvain: S. Zassenus June 1540; NK 1546). His exegetical works included a commentary on Ecclesiastes dedicated to Joris van *Egmond (Antwerp: M. Hillen 1533; NK 1541). Five of his letters were published by de Vocht in MHL (499–584), and other works including a series of lectures on the New Testament, are found in a folio manuscript, autograph, formerly housed at Brussels but now in the Rijksarchief in Hasselt, Belgium. Although he was a conservative in theological matters, especially opposed to the Lutheran reformers, Morinck's lectures reveal that he was inclined towards humanism and shared Erasmus' faith in scriptural studies as a means to reform.

BIBLIOGRAPHY: Allen Ep 1994 / BNB XV 272–3 / J. Fruytier in NNBW VI 1036–7 / *Matricule de Louvain* III-1 404 / de Vocht *Literae ad Craneveldium* Ep 194 / de Vocht CTL II 504–5 and passim / de Vocht MHL 459–99 and passim / J.H. Bentley 'New Testament scholarship at Louvain in the early sixteenth century' *Studies in Medieval and Renaissance History* n s 2 (1979) 53–79, esp 63–9

C.G. VAN LEIJENHORST

Richard MORISON of Chardswell, d 17 March 1556

A political writer and diplomatist, Richard Morison (Morasyne, Morysin, Moryzinus) was born in Chardswell, Yorkshire, at a date unknown. His career began in *Wolsey's service. About 1526 he was admitted a canon of Wolsey's great Oxford foundation, Cardinal College; on 5 November 1528 he was admitted to the BA degree. Some three years later he removed to Cambridge, where he met William *Gonnell, the friend of Erasmus, and Thomas *Cranmer. Like many of his generation he then went to Italy to study Greek, and he wrote to Cranmer from Venice in December 1533, asking for a benefice. Three years later he joined the household of Reginald *Pole in the same city. By this time he was already in the service of Thomas *Cromwell and, on the latter's instruction, left Italy for England by May 1536. He became one of Cromwell's leading propagandists, and his *Apomaxis calumniarum* (London: T. Berthelet 1537; STC 18109) replied to Johannes *Cochlaeus' attack on the royal divorce of 1535. He figures in the correspondence of Erasmus only indirectly, since Cochlaeus cited two comments by Erasmus about the divorce in his *Scopa ... in Araneas Ricardi Morysini Angli* (Leipzig: N. Wolrab 1538); Ep 3001.

After Cromwell's fall he was a member of Parliament and gentleman of the king's privy chamber, ambassador to Denmark and the Hanseatic league, and from 1550 to 1553 ambassador to *Charles v. About 1550 he was knighted. He joined the English Protestant refugees under *Mary and was in Strasbourg by April 1555, where he died the following year. He married Bridget, the eldest daughter of John, Lord Hussey of Sleaford, by whom he had a son and three daughters.

BIBLIOGRAPHY: DNB XIII 957–8 / Emden BRUO 1501–40 405–6 / W.G. Zeeveld *Foundations of Tudor Policy* (Cambridge, Mass, 1948) / F. Le Van Baumer *The Early Tudor Theory of Kingship* (New Haven 1940) / G.B. Parks *The English Traveler to Italy* (Rome 1954–   ) I passim / G.R. Elton *Policy and Police* (Cambridge 1972)

JAMES K. MCCONICA

Friedrich MORMANN of Emden, d 1482
Friedrich Mormann (Fredericus Maurus) of Emden joined the Brethren of the Common Life and at one time was a teacher in the school of Münster. In 1479–80 Mormann addressed to Wessel *Gansfort a poem in praise of Rodolphus *Agricola's return from Italy (edited by M. van Rhijn). Subsequently he was one of the scholars who gathered around Gansfort at Aduard. A letter from Agricola to Alexander *Hegius shows that not long before 20 September 1480 Mormann was put in charge of a convent of nuns at Marburg. He died there two years later, and his death occasioned a poem by Rudolf von *Langen. Information about Mormann's life is scanty; even in Erasmus' youth

(Ep 23), he may have been a somewhat obscure representative of the group of early Westphalian and Frisian humanists.

BIBLIOGRAPHY: Allen Ep 23 / P.S. Allen 'The letters of Rudolf Agricola' *English Historical Review* 21 (1906) 302–17, esp 316–17 / P.S. Allen *The Age of Erasmus* (Oxford 1914) 25–6 / H.E.J.M. van der Velden *Rodolphus Agricola* (Leiden 1911) 124–8 / M. van Rhijn *Wessel Gansfort* (The Hague 1917) 138–40

C.G. VAN LEIJENHORST

Pierre de MORNIEU documented 1526–54
Little is known about Pierre de Mornieu (Mornyeus, Morniosus), abbot of the Cistercian house of Saint-Sulpice near Chambéry, Savoy. He was descended from a noble family with estates in the Bugey, and as abbot was still pursuing his studies when he visited Basel and Erasmus in 1526 (Ep 1777). His tutor was Hieronymus *Gemuseus, a protégé of the law professor Bonifacius *Amerbach, whom Mornieu also met at Basel. On leaving Basel Gemuseus and the young abbot went on to Avignon, where Amerbach's friend the famous jurist Andrea *Alciati was then teaching. From there they left by the beginning of 1527 either to go on to Turin or to return to Mornieu's home (AK III Epp 1178, 1192). Gemuseus was still with Mornieu in 1529 (Ep 2162) and, even in 1534, while living in Turin, was in touch with him, or indeed was staying with him (AK IV Ep 1875).

In January 1529 Erasmus wrote to Mornieu by way of Albanus *Torinus, who was, like Gemuseus, a medical humanist and was then travelling to meet the abbot, whom he probably knew from his visit to Basel (Ep 2084). Four months later Erasmus wrote again to thank Mornieu for the kindness he had shown Torinus and for having issued an invitation to Erasmus himself as he prepared to leave Basel in the wake of the Reformation (Ep 2162). In 1531 Mornieu again invited him to Savoy (Ep 2473). Both Gemuseus and Torinus dedicated works to him, and he was also acquainted with the *Alardet brothers.

BIBLIOGRAPHY: Allen Ep 1777 / *Gallia christiana* xv (i) 653 / Henri Jougla de Morenas *Grand Armorial de France* (Paris 1934–52) supplement 400

PGB

Gerard MORRHY of Kampen, documented
1525–56
A native of Kampen, in Overijssel, Morrhy
(Morrhe, Morrhius Campensis) is first documented as a student in Paris; he graduated BA
in 1525–6 and was procurator of the English
and German nation in 1527. At first he
remained in Paris and set up shop as a printer
near the Collège de Sorbonne; he published
more than fifty books from 1530 to 1532, mainly
Greek and Latin classics but also a few
contemporary authors such as Henricus Cornelius *Agrippa, Alessandro d'*Alessandro,
Oronce Finé, and Jean *Salmon Macrin. Subsequently Morrhy returned to Kampen, where
he was a town councillor from 1536 to 1548.

It seems that Morrhy was an old friend of
Erasmus; two letters which he wrote to him
have been preserved. The first one (Ep 2311),
written from Frankfurt, evidently while attending the spring fair of 1530, was accompanied by a gift copy of Morrhy's recent
publication of John Chrysostom's *Comparatio
regii potentatus et divitiarum* (Paris 1530), edited
by Polidoro *Virgilio, who had dedicated it to
Erasmus (Ep 2019). Two years later Morrhy
sent Erasmus Ep 2633.

BIBLIOGRAPHY: Allen Epp 2311, 2633 / Renouard *Répertoire* 318 / H. Omont 'Gérard
Morrhe' *Bulletin de la société de l'histoire de Paris
et de l'Ile-de-France* 18 (1891) 133–44, 22 (1895)
35–9 / Paris, Bibliothèque Nationale, Réserve
des livres imprimés, MS Philippe Renouard
'Bibliographie parisienne' 18
                                    GENEVIÈVE GUILLEMINOT

John MORTON c 1420–15 September 1500
Born in Dorset of an old Nottinghamshire
family and educated at a Benedictine house,
Cerne Abbey, in Dorset, Morton studied at
Balliol College, Oxford, where he proceeded
doctor of civil law. As an ecclesiastic he was a
pluralist; he was bishop of Ely from 1478 to
1479 and archbishop of Canterbury from
October 1486 until his death and was made a
cardinal in 1493. A staunch Lancastrian, he
was a royal councillor as early as 1464 and
master of the rolls from 1472, being reappointed in 1475. After two years of political exile in
Flanders he returned to England in 1485
following the victory of *Henry VII, who
appointed him archbishop of Canterbury and

on 6 March 1487 lord chancellor of England.
Morton's connections with the universities
were significant: he was chancellor of Oxford
from 1495 until his death and of Cambridge
from 1499 to 1500.

Erasmus must have known of Morton's
strong influence upon Thomas *More, who
was Morton's page from 1490 to 1492, and
upon More's *Richard III* and *Utopia*. In Ep 77
Erasmus mentions Morton as a benefactor of
his bishop, Hendrik van *Bergen.
BIBLIOGRAPHY: Allen Ep 77 / DNB XIII 1048–
50 / Emden BRUO II 1318–20 / *Calendar of State
Papers, Venetian* I 537, 743   R.J. SCHOECK

Richard MORYSIN *See Richard* MORISON

Guillaume de MOSCHERON of Bruges,
d 1527
Guillaume de Moscheron (Moscroen, Mouscron, Mouqueron, Moscronius), a relative of
Jean Louis de *Moscheron, was the son of Jean
de Moscheron (d 1498) and Heilwich de Mol (d
1493). His family had built up an important
trade with Italy, and Guillaume carried on in
this tradition. He married a young Italian
beauty whose name is given as Louisa Veneta.
She died on 17 June 1523, leaving nine
children. In September 1525 he was elected
treasurer of his native Bruges for a year. In the
same year he entrusted three of his sons to
Leonard *Casembroot, who was to be their
tutor at Padua. They arrived in Padua prior to
23 August 1525 (Ep 1594). In November,
however, Guillaume visited Padua and removed his sons from Casembroot's custody,
allegedly because of the financial burden (Ep
1650). On a later journey to Italy, in 1527, he
was killed during the Sack of Rome.
BIBLIOGRAPHY: de Vocht *Literae ad Craneveldium* Ep 243   IG

Jean Louis de MOSCHERON of Bruges,
d 1535
Jean Louis de Moscheron belonged to an
influential merchant family of Bruges. From
1502 he studied at Padua, where he obtained a
legal doctorate. On 8 February 1503 he was
present at the doctoral promotion of Jérôme de
*Busleyden, his fellow student and lifelong
friend; at that time he was already archdeacon
of Cambrai. In 1507 he also obtained a canonry

of St Donatian's at Bruges. Jean Louis remained in Rome until at least the summer of 1509 (Ep 216). After his return to the Netherlands he was an ecclesiastical member of the grand council of Mechelen from 16 October 1511 until early 1513. Thereafter he lived in Bruges, where in the spring of 1515 Erasmus visited him and perhaps was a guest in his house (*Busleyden* Ep 77).

BIBLIOGRAPHY: Allen Ep 216 / de Vocht *Busleyden* Epp 15, 59, 77 / de Vocht *Literae ad Craneveldium* Ep 243 introduction IG

Petrus MOSELLANUS of Bruttig, d 19 April 1524

Petrus Mosellanus (Peter Schade) was born in Bruttig, a village on the Mosel about thirty-five kilometres above Koblenz. After schooling in Beilstein, Luxembourg, Limburg, and Trier he matriculated at the University of Cologne on 2 January 1512. Among his teachers at Cologne were Johannes *Caesarius and Jacobus *Sobius, but it was mostly by private study that he learnt Greek. In 1514 he moved to Freiburg (Saxony) as a teacher of Greek at the grammar school of that town, directed by Johannes Aesticampianus. In the spring term of 1515 he matriculated at Leipzig, where he perfected his knowledge of Greek with the assistance of Richard *Croke. After Croke's departure in 1517 Mosellanus succeeded him as a lecturer in Greek; on 3 January 1520 he was formally admitted to the faculty of arts after completing his MA. In the same year he became a bachelor of theology and was admitted to teach in that faculty. In 1520 and 1523 he was rector of the University of Leipzig. He sympathized with *Luther and would have liked to move to the University of Wittenberg, but in preference to him *Melanchthon was appointed professor of Greek there in 1518. After years of weak health Mosellanus died prematurely at Leipzig in April 1524.

When Croke left Leipzig in the spring of 1517 he encouraged Mosellanus to write to Erasmus, whom he intended to visit on his way to England. This first approach (Ep 560) led to a correspondence (Epp 911, 948, 1123, 1305) that deals mainly with the advancement of Greek studies and its opponents in Leipzig and Louvain, who pursued both humanists with comparable animosity. On 6 January 1519

Mosellanus described the preparations for the Leipzig disputation to be held in June and July (Ep 911), which he was to open with a speech, *De ratione disputandi praesertim in re theologica* (Leipzig: M. Lotter 1519). Later he complained that Erasmus had published this lively and unguarded letter (Ep 1123). In a long answer to it (Ep 948), which was also printed without delay, Erasmus deplored the ignorance and hostility encountered by scholars and praised Mosellanus' recently published *Oratio de variarum linguarum cognitione paranda* (Leipzig: V. Schumann 1518), which argued that Hebrew and Greek as well as Latin studies were a necessary part of true theological learning. This speech aroused the theologians of Louvain, who were already suspicious of Erasmus and the newly founded Collegium Trilingue in their own university (CWE Ep 934 introduction). Jacobus *Latomus took it upon himself to voice their concerns in a dialogue, *De trium linguarum et studii theologici ratione* (Antwerp: M. Hillen 1519), which caused Erasmus to reply with his *Apologia contra Latomi dialogum* (Antwerp: J. Thibault 1519). In his letter of 31 July 1520 Erasmus was still bitterly resentful of Latomus and drew Mosellanus' attention to the neighbouring University of Erfurt, where Erasmus' admirers had rallied to his support against Edward *Lee (Ep 1123); in fact his friends in Leipzig did likewise (CWE Ep 1083 introduction). In his last known letter to Mosellanus (Ep 1305 of 8 August 1522) Erasmus dealt with the latter's projected trip to Italy. Erasmus was looking forward to seeing him at Basel on his way south (Ep 1326), but that trip, and their encounter, never came to pass. Erasmus greatly esteemed Mosellanus' learning (Ep 1125) and regretted his untimely death (Ep 1480; cf Epp 1448, 1452, 1462). In fact, Mosellanus had helped him in his conflicts with the Louvain theologians as well as with *Hutten and *Eppendorf (Ep 1437). Duke George of *Saxony consulted Erasmus about a suitable successor (Ep 1448), and after much correspondence (Epp 1520, 1526, 1550, 1717) Jacobus *Ceratinus was appointed upon Erasmus' recommendation (Epp 1561, 1564, 1565, 1567, 1568).

In addition to the two orations mentioned above, Mosellanus wrote *Tabulae de schematibus et tropis* (Frankfurt 1516), a textbook on rhetoric that proved very popular (CWE 24 488–9); *Paedagogia in puerorum usum conscripta* (c 1518); *Oratio de concordia praesertim in scholis publicis litterarum professoribus tuenda* (Leipzig 1520) on the occasion of his first rectorate; and *Praeceptiuncula de tempore studiis impartiendo* (Leipzig 1521), an introduction to chronology. He produced editions and commentaries of Aristophanes, Gregory of Nazianzus, Isocrates, Lucian, Theocritus, Aulus Gellius, Quintilian, and Lorenzo *Valla. Mosellanus maintained wide epistolary contacts, corresponding among others with Julius *Pflug, his former student, who later wrote a funeral oration for his teacher. Several unpublished letters to *Mutianus Rufus and Johann *Lang are extant in the Collectio Cameriana at Munich.

BIBLIOGRAPHY: Allen Ep 560 / ADB XXII 358–9 / *Matrikel Köln* II 689 / *Matrikel Leipzig* I 542, II 25–6, 543–4 / Pflug *Correspondance* I Ep 2 and passim / *Der Briefwechsel des Justus Jonas* ed G. Kawerau (Halle 1884–5, repr 1964) I Ep 28, 39, and passim / de Vocht CTL I 306–12 and passim / O.G. Schmidt *Petrus Mosellanus: Ein Beitrag zur Geschichte des Humanismus in Sachsen* (Leipzig 1867) / Reinhold Weier 'Die Rede des Petrus Mosellanus "Über die rechte Weise, theologisch zu disputieren"' *Trierer Theologische Zeitschrift* 83 (1974) 232–45 / Schottenloher II 67–8   MICHAEL ERBE

Rudbert von MOSHAM 24 September 1493–1543

Mosham (Moshan, Moshaim) was descended from a noble family of the region of Lungau, in Styria, but he also owned the castle of Viechtenstein, near Passau in Bavaria. On 21 August 1510 he matriculated in Vienna, and from 1514 to 1517 he studied in Bologna, where he met *Hutten and was elected procurator of the German nation. Later he laid claim to a doctorate in civil and canon law. On his return he entered the service of Matthäus *Lang, archbishop of Salzburg, and accompanied him to the coronation of *Charles V in Aachen (1520) and to the diet of Worms (1521). Soon afterwards he was attached to the court of Prince *Ferdinand, but court life did not satisfy him and by 1524 he had withdrawn to Passau, where he was dean of the chapter. Apparently ecclesiastical life did not satisfy him either, and in discussion with his friend Willibald *Pirck-

heimer he considered marriage and a move to Nürnberg. However, in 1529 he was provost of Głogów (Glogau) and in 1530 a councillor of King Ferdinand, but he failed to obtain the deanery of Wrocław. Meanwhile in Passau he caused a scandal by allowing his dogs to accompany him to church, and in 1536 he defended the lay chalice from the pulpit. In 1537 he presented his peculiar views on Christian unity to Ferdinand and Cardinal Giovanni Morone. The conflicts at Passau came to a head in 1539, when he was driven from his deanery by the chapter and Ernest of *Bavaria, administrator of the see of Passau. He then went to Nürnberg, where he quarrelled with the reformed minister, and thereafter he remained on the move, visiting Haguenau in 1540, Worms in 1541 at the time of the religious colloquies, and Speyer at the time of the diet (1542). He was also in Strasbourg (1541) and in Switzerland. In 1542 he was imprisoned by Cardinal Albert of *Brandenburg and died in jail the following year, it was rumoured by his own hand. Mosham's efforts to achieve reforms within the church and to reconcile Catholic and Protestants were ill received by both sides.

Mosham met Erasmus in Louvain and Cologne before and after the coronation of Charles V in 1520. In Cologne he arranged an audience for Erasmus with Cardinal Matthäus Lang (Epp 1450, 1512). He wrote to Erasmus from Passau in 1524, referring to their encounters and pleading for friendship and correspondence (Ep 1450). Erasmus replied (Ep 1512), but no subsequent letters exist although it seems that Erasmus wrote again in March 1525 (Ep 1560; cf Ep 1558).

Most of Mosham's publications in Latin and German were launched in 1539 and 1540 in an effort to promote his views on Christian unity; they include such titles as *Memoriale microsynodi Norimbergensis* and *Hierusalem nova*. In 1535 his brother Jakob published Rudbert's translation of a treatise on the breeding and keeping of dogs, *Kynosophion*, together with his *Encomium canis* (Vienna: J. Singriener).

BIBLIOGRAPHY: Allen Ep 1450 / Knod 359–60 / ADB XXII 393–4 / *Matrikel Wien* II-1 367 / BRE Ep 357 / *Epistolae ad Nauseam* 232 and passim / Pflug *Correspondance* I Ep 57 and passim   IG

Pedro Ruiz de la MOTA of Burgos,
d c 19 September 1522

Pedro Ruiz de la Mota was a native of Burgos
and a priest. Although he has been noted for
his erudition and is frequently referred to as
'Dr Mota' by modern historians, chroniclers
know him as 'maestro Mota.' After serving
Philip the Handsome, of *Burgundy between
1504 and 1506 he emigrated to Brussels prior to
the return to Castile of *Ferdinand II of Aragon
in 1507. He was in the service of the Emperor
*Maximilian and *Margaret of Austria and is
known to have taken part in embassies to
France (1510) and England (1512, 1514, 1521).
Around 1507 he headed the 'Felipista' party in
Brussels with *Juan Manuel and came to be
closely associated with Guillaume (I) de *Croy,
lord of Chièvres, who later relied exclusively
on Mota to determine his policies in Spain. In
1511 he became chaplain and almoner to the
future *Charles V; it is considered that from this
period onwards his influence on Charles
steadily increased. In about July 1516 he
became bishop of Badajoz, and in 1520 he was
transferred to the see of Palencia. In 1517 he
was a member of the council of Flanders and
remained on the royal council until his death.
He followed Charles to Spain in September
1517. In February 1518 he presided over the
cortes of Valladolid with Jean *Le Sauvage,
whom he defended against the criticisms of Dr
Juan Zumel of Burgos and the duke of Alba,
Fadrique *Alvarez de Toledo. At the cortes of
Santiago in April 1520 he presided with
Mercurino *Gattinara and read the speech from
the throne which is considered to be the
fundamental outline of Charles' imperial program. Whether this speech reflects the inspiration of Mota or Gattinara has been the subject
of extensive controversy. Mota took part in the
diet of Worms in April 1521. In September 1521
*Leo X had promised to make him a cardinal,
and it was rumoured that he might become the
chancellor of the Golden Fleece. After the
death of Guillaume (II) de *Croy he hoped to
become archbishop of Toledo; however, upon
arriving in Santander with the emperor on 28
July 1522, he fell ill and died at Reinosa two
months later.

When Erasmus wrote to Mota in April 1522
(Ep 1273), the latter was the most powerful man
at the imperial court after Gattinara. In spite of

Mota's encouragement of Erasmus (Epp 1269,
1299, 1300, 1331), Erasmus' suspicions about
Mota's attitude towards him (Epp 1268, 1302)
may have been well founded. Chroniclers
point out that Mota was 'more ambitious than
honest' (Sandoval I 122). His ability to maintain
an ambiguous position can be seen in his relations with Margaret of Austria and Chièvres,
and Chièvres and Cardinal *Jiménez de
Cisneros. As a candidate for the archbishopric
of Toledo, Mota may have tried to ingratiate
himself with Girolamo *Aleandro while still
encouraging Erasmus in order to maintain
favour with Gattinara and his circle.

Jakob *Wimpfeling's *Expurgatio* (Strasbourg:
J. Prüss 1514) contains a prefatory letter from
Jakob *Spiegel to Mota, while Georg *Sauermann dedicated his *Hispaniae consolatio* (n p
1520) to the Spanish prelate.

BIBLIOGRAPHY: Allen Ep 1273 / LP III 866 and
passim / K. Brandi *Kaiser Karl V.* new ed
(Darmstadt 1959–67) I 40, 70, 72 II 144, and
passim / P. Chaunu *L'Espagne de Charles Quint*
(Paris 1973) I / M. Fernández Álvarez in *His-
toria de España* ed R. Menéndez Pidal (Madrid
1966) XVIII / Pedro Girón *Crónica del emperador
Carlos V* ed J. Sánchez Montes (Madrid 1964) /
Francisco López de Gómara *Anales de Carlos
Quinto* ed R.B. Merriman (Oxford 1912) / J.A.
Maravall *Carlos V y el pensamiento político del
renacimiento* (Madrid 1960) / R. Menéndez-
Pidal *Idea imperial de Carlos V* (Madrid 1941) /
R. Merton *Cardinal Ximénes* (London 1934) /
Pedro Mexía *Historia del Emperador Carlos
V* ed J. de Mata Carriazo (Madrid 1945) /
Joseph Pérez *La Révolution des 'Comunidades'
de Castille (1520–1521)* (Bordeaux 1970) /
Prudencio de Sandoval *Historia de la vida
y hechos del emperador Carlos V* ed C. Seco
Serrano (Madrid 1955–8) / Alonso de Santa
Cruz *Crónica del emperador Carlos V* ed R.
Beltrán y Razpide and A. Blázqued y Delgado
(Madrid 1920–5) I   LOUIS P.A. MAINGON

François de MOULIN or MOULINS *See
François DU MOULIN de Rochefort*

MOUNTJOY *See Charles and William BLOUNT,
Barons Mountjoy*

MOUQUERON, MOUSCRON *See Guillaume
and Jean Louis de MOSCHERON*

MULEY HASSAN *See al-HASAN ben Muhammad*

Johann MÜLLER *See Johannes REGIOMONTANUS*

Leonhard MÜLLER abbot of St Georgenberg, d 10/14 April 1525
Leonhard Müller (Miller) was a monk in the Benedictine monastery in Scheyern, Upper Bavaria, in 1510 when he was sent to St Georgenberg in the Tirol at the request of the Emperor *Maximilian I; at St Georgenberg Müller became coadjutor to the abbot, Konrad Rues, and subsequently abbot after Rues had died on 18 March 1515. The manuscript chronicle of the abbots reports that he was a good administrator, well versed in all the necessary skills and especially knowledgeable in the art of building. This served him well, since in a fire in 1448 the monastery had suffered heavy damage that had not yet been repaired. Müller almost rebuilt the monastery, including the church, the cloister, and the library.
When a monk from St Georgenberg, Kilian *Praus, returned to Basel in the spring of 1522, Müller gave him a letter for Erasmus expressing his admiration (Ep 1279).
BIBLIOGRAPHY: Allen Ep 1279 / Maurus Kramer, OSB *Geschichte der Benediktinerabtei St. Georgenberg–Fiecht* (Fiecht 1954) 31, 63 / Fiecht, Archives of the Benedictine abbey (formerly of St Georgenberg) MS L 46: 'Catalogus Germanicus omnium abbatum monasterii Sancti Georgi per F. Bernhardum Empedium Priorem summa diligentia exaratus atque in unum collectus' (information kindly supplied by P. Maurus Kramer, Stiftsarchivar)   IG

Jan de MUNTER of Ghent, documented 1510–28(?)
Writing from Louvain, Conradus *Goclenius informed Erasmus of rumours concerning the disappearance, apostasy, and marriage of Nicolaas van *Broeckhoven, 'Johannes Munterus,' and other priests of Antwerp (Ep 2063, 7 October 1528). It appears that he expected Erasmus to be familiar with the name of Munterus. Munterus may therefore be identical with Jan de Munter (Muntere, Minter, Munterius). Like Broeckhoven, de Munter was

a good friend of Adrianus Cornelii *Barlandus, to whom he addressed a letter (from Louvain, 24 October 1513) which was published in a reprint of Barlandus' edition of the ancient *Fabule* (Louvain: D. Martens 22 October 1513). Jan de Munter matriculated at Louvain on 28 February 1510, and other university records show him to have been in orders by 1515. Otherwise he is known only for a number of Latin poems printed in works by other authors.
BIBLIOGRAPHY: Allen Ep 2063 / P. Bergmans in BNB XV 352–3 / de Vocht CTL I 227–8 / de Vocht *Literae ad Craneveldium* 153 / Etienne Daxhelet *Adrien Barlandus* (Louvain 1938, repr 1967) 246 / *Matricule de Louvain* III-1 389
MARCEL A. NAUWELAERTS

MURAD II Ottoman sultan, June 1404–3 February 1451
Murad II (Ammurates), a son of Mehmed I, was governor of the province of Rum from 1414 to 1421, residing at Amasya. He ascended the throne on 25 June 1421. In the first two years of his reign he eliminated rival claimants to the throne, including his younger brother Mustafa, and regained the allegiance of his rebellious vassals. In 1422 he besieged Constantinople, which had supported his opponents, but was unable to sustain the operation. Then he obliged the Palaeologi of the Peloponnese (Morea) to renew their allegiance. Faced with his relentless pressure, the Byzantines found it expedient to cede Salonika to Venice. This led to a war with Venice (1423–30) which culminated in Murad's capture of Salonika. His intense rivalry with the Hungarians over influence in Serbia and Wallachia also turned to Murad's advantage: the princes of Wallachia, Serbia, and Bosnia reaffirmed their allegiance to him in 1428, although the struggle was renewed in 1431.
In 1435 Murad turned his attention to eastern Anatolia, where complicated local feuds had provoked the intervention of his nominal overlord, Shah Rukh, the son of Timur. After Shah Rukh's departure from Anatolia, Murad invaded and annexed parts of Karaman.
In 1438 Murad led an expedition into Hungary, encountering no resistance. In 1439, owing to the recalcitrance of Djuradj Branković, he invaded and annexed the whole of

Serbia. In 1440 he unsuccessfully besieged Belgrade. In 1441 and 1442 János Hunyadi, the Hungarian commander, inflicted defeats on the Ottomans in Bosnia and Transylvania, and in 1443 he and Branković crossed the Danube and occupied Niš and Sofia. Murad repulsed the enemy at Izladi and in June 1444 made peace, restoring to Branković all the gains he had made since 1427. He also signed a new peace with Karaman restoring the gains he had made in 1438.

Confident that he had secured lasting peace, in August 1444 Murad voluntarily renounced the throne in favour of his son *Mehmed, partly because he wished to see his only remaining son firmly established as his successor. The step was ill conceived, however, since it encouraged Orkhan, a claimant to the throne, to rebel, while the Christian states perceived in it a good opportunity to drive the Ottomans out of Europe and renewed their attacks. A Hungarian-Wallachian army crossed the Danube and penetrated as far as Varna, while a Venetian fleet held the Dardanelles. Murad was recalled from retirement and given command of the Ottoman forces. He won a resounding victory at Varna on 10 November 1444. King Ladislas III of Hungary and Poland was amongst those killed (*De bello turcico* LB V 351D–E). After this victory, Murad retired to Manisa. However, the crisis was not over yet; a powerful faction at court led by the grand vizier, Çandarli Khalil Pasha, preferred to regard Murad as the real sultan and even instigated a Janissary rising in his favour, while hostilities with the Christian neighbours continued. Consequently Mehmed was deposed and Murad resumed the throne in August 1446.

In November 1446 Murad led an expedition to the Peloponnese (Morea) and forced the Palaeologi to renew their allegiance. In 1448 he invaded Albania but hastily returned to defeat the Hungarians under Hunyadi at Kosova in Albania in October. In 1450 he launched a second unsuccessful expedition against Iskender Bey of Albania.

Murad was basically peace-loving, industrious, and just, but also much given to pleasure. His reign was one of prosperity and saw the development of a specifically Turkish culture. The greatest architectural achievements of his reign were the magnificent Üç-Şerefeli Mosque at Edirne and the massive bridge at Ergene known as Uzun Köprü.

BIBLIOGRAPHY: There is no full-scale biography. The best accounts are H. Inalcik in *Islam Ansiklopedisi* (Istanbul 1940–   ) VIII 598–615 and H. Inalcik *Fatih Devri Üzerinde Tetkikler ve Vesikalar* (Ankara 1954) / J.H. Kramers in *Encyclopaedia of Islam* (Leiden-London 1913–38) III 728–30, contains some errors / N. Iorga *Geschichte des Osmanischen Reiches* (Gotha 1908–13) is useful   FEHMI ISMAIL

Johannes MURMELLIUS of Roermond, 1480–2 October 1517
Johannes, the only son of Theodoricus (Dirk) Murmellius, was born at Roermond, in Limburg. From about 1493 he was educated at Deventer in the school of Alexander *Hegius. On 14 April 1496 he matriculated at the University of Cologne, where he became a licentiate in arts on 14 March 1500. With the support of Rudolf von *Langen he was appointed assistant headmaster of the cathedral school of Münster but returned to Cologne to take a MA (26 March 1504). He resumed his duties at Münster and succeeded in replacing medieval schoolbooks with humanistic ones, many of which were his own work. They include *Opuscula duo ... ad puerorum usum* (Cologne: H. Quentel 1504), *Enchiridion scholasticorum*, and later the highly successful Latin primer *Pappa puerorum* (Deventer: T. de Borne 1513), which was reprinted many times. After a conflict with his headmaster he left the cathedral school for the rectorate of St Ludgerus' school, Münster, where he introduced the study of Greek. During his years at Münster he worked occasionally as an editor for the printer Eucharius *Cervicornus at Cologne. In 1513 he accepted an appointment to succeed Bartholomäus *Zehender as rector of the grammar school of Alkmaar, which was soon to gain an excellent reputation. Among his assistant teachers were Hermannus *Buschius, Rutgerus *Rescius, and *Alaard of Amsterdam. His fame spread widely; when Johann *Bugenhagen was rector of the school of Trzebiatow in Pomerania he was glad that two of his teachers had studied under Murmellius.

In June 1517 Alkmaar was sacked in the

course of the wars with Gelderland (Ep 628), and Murmellius lost all his possessions. With his wife and son, Johannes, he went to Zwolle, where he taught briefly under Gerardus *Listrius, and Deventer, where he was appointed to St Lebuin's school. His sudden death there gave rise to a persistent rumour that he had been poisoned by Listrius (Epp 697, 838). Although the two men had quarrelled at Zwolle the charge against Listrius seems unfounded. No personal relations between Erasmus and Murmellius are recorded, but in 1512 Murmellius stated in a letter to Bugenhagen that Erasmus was without equal in matters of Latin style and interpretation as well as a fairly good theologian.

Murmellius' writings are numerous; no fewer than fifty have been listed by Nauwelaerts. Working at great speed he produced, apart from his pedagogical works, many editions of classical and Renaissance authors, mostly intended for use in schools. His annotated edition of Boethius, however, is a creditable piece of philological scholarship. He also composed many poems, such as *Elegiarum moralium libri quattuor* (1507; only known in Quentell's reprint, Cologne 1508), dedicated to Langen, and the *Charoleia* (Louvain: D. Martens 1515), dedicated to Meynard *Man (dedicatory letter reprinted by Van Gelder 157); an ode to Münster is edited and discussed by H. Bücker in *Westfälische Zeitschrift* 111 (1961) 51–74.

BIBLIOGRAPHY: Allen and CWE Ep 838 / NNBW I 1348–51 / ADB XXIII 65–6 / D. Reichling *Johannes Murmellius* (Freiburg 1880) / A. Bömer 'Johannes Murmellius' in *Westfälische Lebensbilder* II (Münster 1931) 396–410 / H.E. van Gelder *Geschiedenis der Latijnsche School te Alkmaar* (Alkmaar 1905) I 90–106 / M.A. Nauwelaerts in *Historische opstellen over Roermond en omgeving* (Roermond 1951) 201–34 / Anthologies of Murmellius' poems were edited by D. Reichling (Freiburg 1881) and A. Bömer (Münster 1892–5, in five parts) / *Dr. Johannes Bugenhagens Briefwechsel* ed Otto Vogt et al, new ed (Hildesheim 1966) Ep 2

C.G. VAN LEIJENHORST & IG

Thomas MURNER of Obernai, 24 December 1475–1537
Thomas Murner was born in Obernai

(Oberehnheim), in Lower Alsace, where his family owned property. By 1481 his father and uncle had moved to Strasbourg and had purchased citizenship. Thomas was admitted as a novice to the Franciscan convent in Strasbourg in 1490 and attended the University of Freiburg from 1495 to 1497, receiving instruction in poetry from the humanist Jakob *Locher. He moved on to Paris, returning with a MA degree in 1499. For ten years he travelled from university to university – Cracow, Cologne, Rostock, and Prague. By 1502 he was already embroiled with *Wimpfeling on the issue of the latter's German nationalism. Murner criticized Wimpfeling for placing the geographic boundaries of ancient Gaul on the western side of the Vosges, excluding Alsace. In 1506 Murner received his doctorate of theology from Freiburg. He taught there but continued to move around from city to city; he was at Berne in time to comment on the affair of Johann Jetzer and the Dominicans, which was later recalled by Erasmus (Ep 1033). In 1509 or 1510 he was appointed warden of the Franciscan convent in Speyer. He preached a series of Advent sermons in Frankfurt (1511) and was tangentially involved with the Franciscan support for *Reuchlin. His life was itinerant. He was in Basel in 1518 studying for his doctorate in canon law, which was granted despite the active opposition of *Zasius. After a visit to Italy he returned to Strasbourg in 1520.

Murner's earliest writing was pedagogical or theological in nature. That he was an ingenious teacher is reflected in two card games he invented and published which covered the rules of logic and the fundamental principles of the *Corpus juris civilis*. In 1512 he began his literary career, publishing several long satirical poems in German. These were moral tracts, but Murner revealed himself as a bitter and unsympathetic critic of his fellow man. In 1520 he took up the gauntlet for the Catholic cause in the Reformation and emerged as one of the major Catholic polemicists. His poem *Vom grossen Lutherischen Narren* was so violent that the Strasbourg magistrates forbad the printer, Johann Grüninger, to release it. Murner visited England in 1523 and was instructed by *Henry VIII to chastise the magistrates for taking a Lutheran stand. It was after this visit that Erasmus reported that Murner had returned from England a rich man (Ep 1397).

In March 1524 Murner laid off his habit, assuming the dress of the secular clergy but remaining in the Franciscan monastery. Later he resumed the habit and went to Switzerland, receiving a pension from the Strasbourg magistrates when the monastery was formally disbanded. In 1530 he returned to his birthplace, Obernai, where he served as priest of St John's church until his death. In an age which delighted in controversy Murner was more controversial than most. His effectiveness as a social critic was dulled by his personal quarrels and his subjectivity but has recently become the subject of positive reappraisals.

BIBLIOGRAPHY: Allen Ep 1397 / E. Martin in ADB XXIII 67–76 / Hans Rupprich in *Geschichte der deutschen Literatur* ed H. de Boor and R. Newald (Munich 1957–   ) IV-1 585–90 and passim / Adalbert Erler *Thomas Murner als Jurist* (Frankfurt 1956) / Frauke Büchner *Thomas Murner: sein Kampf um die Kontinuität der kirchlichen Lehre und die Identität des Christenmenschen in den Jahren 1511–1522* (n p 1974) / Johann Ficker and Otto Winckelmann *Handschriftenproben des sechzehnten Jahrhunderts* (Strasbourg 1905) II 53 / Waldemar Kawerau *Thomas Murner und die Kirche des Mittelalters* (Halle 1891) / Schmidt *Histoire littéraire* II 209–315, full bibliography of Murner's works: II 419–31   MIRIAM U. CHRISMAN

Maurus MUSAEUS *See Antoine* MORELET *de Museau*

Domenico MUSSI documented c 1525–c 1533
Mussi (Domenicus de Musis) was private secretary to Girolamo *Aleandro from about 1525 until about 1533, but we have no information about his birth, education, or even the precise circumstances of his entering Aleandro's service. His temporary dismissal for gross incompetence over the accounts on 28 June 1527 and his attempt, when reinstated about a year later, to hack his employer's nephew Francesco to pieces in a quarrel over a plate of plums do not suggest that he was a man on whom much reliance could be placed. But he was described by *Jespersen in 1531 (Ep 2570) as a good scholar in both ancient

languages, who smiled rather pityingly at an effort to turn a conversation with his master in Erasmus' favour. Erasmus never met him, and he is most unlikely to be the 'Dominicus' who delivered a letter in December 1531 (Ep 2582). Firmly in Aleandro's favour after delivering useful dispatches to his master on the state of affairs in Rome during 1530, Mussi secured a benefice in Louvain through his good offices and dropped out of sight thereafter.

BIBLIOGRAPHY: Allen Ep 2570 / References in *Journal autobiographique du Cardinal Jérôme Aléandre* ed H. Omont (Paris 1895)
M.J.C. LOWRY

Marcus MUSURUS of Iraklion, c 1470–17 October 1517
Marcus Musurus was born at Iraklion (Candia) in Crete. He probably studied under Aristobulos Apostolides, with Johannes Gregoropoulos a fellow-student. At an early age he went to Italy, probably to Venice, which then controlled Crete. In 1486 he travelled to Florence, where he studied under Janus *Lascaris and possibly Demetrius *Chalcondyles. In 1493, after a visit to Crete, Musurus travelled to Venice, where he became a collaborator of the printer Aldo *Manuzio. For the next two decades, even when absent from Venice, he assisted Aldus in editing and translating numerous Greek works. In July 1499 he went to Ferrara to obtain manuscripts for Zacharias *Calliergis, who also managed a Greek press at Venice. In late 1499 or early 1500 he moved to Carpi, near Ferrara, to serve as teacher and companion to Alberto *Pio and curator of the Pio library. Musurus' residence at Carpi did not preclude visits to Venice, where he was a member of the circle of Aldus. In July 1503 Musurus became professor of Greek at the University of Padua, where he remained six years and established a reputation as the foremost Greek teacher of his day. His many students included Lazzaro *Bonamico, Bernardino Donati of Verona, Raffaele *Regio, Girolamo Negri, Girolamo Borgia of Naples, Girolamo *Aleandro, Andrea *Navagero, Gasparo *Contarini, and Germain de *Brie. Musurus left Padua for Venice in June 1509 because of the war of the League of Cambrai. In January 1512 he was appointed to the public lectureship in Greek at Venice,

where he taught Jean de *Pins, *Janus Pannonius, Matteo Grimani, and Pietro *Alcionio, among others. With Giambattista *Egnazio he also acted as librarian of Cardinal *Bessarion's collection of Greek manuscripts. In 1516 Musurus moved to Rome, where on 19 June 1516 *Leo x had appointed him archbishop of Monemvasia in Greece. He was also appointed bishop of Hierapetra and Herronesou in Crete but never visited his sees, remaining in Rome to teach Greek. Here his pupils included Lazare de *Baïf and Christophe de *Longueil. Musurus died at Rome after an illness of several months and was buried at Santa Maria della Pace.

Erasmus met Musurus on his trip to Italy of 1506–9 and according to *Beatus Rhenanus heard some of his lectures (Allen I 63). He dined at Musurus' house at Padua and met his father (Epp 1347, 2447), and later credited Musurus with assisting in the preparation of the 1508 Aldine edition of the *Adagia* (*Adagia* II i 1; Ep 269; LB IX 1137C). Although Paolo *Bombace once wrote that Musurus was Erasmus' enemy and spoke ill of the *Adagia* (Ep 223), Erasmus always spoke highly of the Greek scholar. He was informed of Musurus' appointment as archbishop (Epp 556, 574, 584) and after his death (Epp 729, 854) remembered him as a Greek friend at Venice whose place as a teacher would be difficult to fill (Epp 803, 855, 868).

Musurus' association with the Aldine press began with the publication of Musaeus' poem *Hero and Leander* in 1494, for which he provided a Latin translation and two introductory epigrams. He prepared or collaborated in numerous first editions for Aldus, including Aristophanes the poet (1498), Euripides (1504), Alexander of Aphrodisias' commentaries on the *Topics* of Aristotle (1514), Hesychius' *Lexicon* (1514), Athenaeus' *Deinosophistae* (1514), Gregory (1516), and Pausanias (1516). His most important philological work was, however, the complete works of Plato in Greek, prefaced by a long 'Hymn to Plato' addressed to *Leo x (Aldo Manuzio 1513). He also edited or collaborated in the *Epistolae diversorum philosophorum oratorum rhetorum sex et viginti* (A. Manuzio 1499), the *Etymologicum magnum* (Venice: Z. Calliergis 1499), Cicero's letters (A. Manuzio 1513), the Aldine grammar

Marcus Musurus, by Tobias Stimmer

(1515), and a treatise on gout, *De podagra* (Venice 1517).

BIBLIOGRAPHY: Allen Ep 223 / Deno John Geanakoplos *Greek Scholars in Venice* (Cambridge, Mass, 1962) 111–66 and passim / Deno John Geanakoplos *Interaction of the 'Sibling' Byzantine and Western Cultures in the Middle Ages and Italian Renaissance (330–1600)* (New Haven-London 1976) 225–30 and passim / M. Lowry *The World of Aldus Manutius* (Oxford 1979) 29, 62, and passim / M. Sicherl *Johannes Cuno* (Heidelberg 1978) 53, 87–106   TBD

Conradus MUTIANUS Rufus of Homberg, 15 October 1470–30 March 1526
Konrad Muth was born into a patrician family in Homberg, in Hesse. From about 1478 on he was a fellow pupil of Erasmus at the school in Deventer. In the spring term of 1486 he and his younger brother, Johann, matriculated at the University of Erfurt together with Count Wilhelm von *Honstein, who subsequently became bishop of Strasbourg. Mutianus obtained his BA in the spring of 1488 and his MA at the beginning of 1492, ranking twelfth out of thirteen candidates. He taught for the required

two years at the philosophical faculty of Erfurt, studying law concurrently.

In 1494 Mutianus went to Italy and studied first in Bologna, where he became a close friend of the younger Thomas Wolf of Strasbourg. He also made the acquaintance of Filippo (1) *Beroaldo and Baptista *Mantuanus. He continued his studies in Rome and subsequently in Ferrara, where he obtained a doctorate in canon law on 16 November 1501. On this occasion he already styled himself 'Mutianus Rufus,' and, despite the degree he had chosen to obtain, his true interests were directed primarily towards humanistic studies. On his return to Germany he met Johannes *Trithemius.

In 1502 Mutianus found employment in the chancellery of Landgrave William II of Hesse, where his brother, Dr Johann Muth, held the position of chancellor, but in 1503 he moved to Gotha, where he became canon of St Mary's. This prebend, combined with several other benefices, permitted him to live in ease, pursuing his studies in his house, which he had named 'beata tranquillitas.' Henceforward he declined all positions that were offered to him and would not move from Gotha, even when the Elector Frederick the Wise of *Saxony proposed to appoint him provost and professor at Wittenberg in succession to Henning Gödes. In the years before 1520 many regarded Mutianus as the third great German humanist after Erasmus and *Reuchlin. Although he did not publish any writings, he exercised great influence, for he had the ability to attract a circle of disciples in whom he instilled his own enthusiasm for the culture of classical antiquity. His correspondence, which remains an important source for the history of German humanism, has been edited by Karl Krause (Kassel 1885) and Karl Gillert (Halle 1890). Among his close friends were Henricus *Urbanus and Georgius *Spalatinus (Ep 501), for whom he obtained the schoolmaster's position at the abbey of Georgenthal. Others were Johannes *Crotus Rubianus, Ulrich von *Hutten, Heinrich and Peter Eberbach, Herbord von der Marthen, Euricius *Cordus, *Eobanus Hessus, and the Augustinian Johann *Lang.

Subtle and open-minded, Mutianus was a fine judge of literature and critical of traditional religious practice. Under the influence of Giovanni *Pico della Mirandola and Marsilio *Ficino, he recognized elements of revealed truth in every religion. His views captivated the most lively minds among a young generation at the University of Erfurt, and he led them to do battle whenever he saw intellectual freedom endangered, in support first of Jakob *Wimpfeling, then of Reuchlin, and finally of Erasmus. Initially he also took the side of *Luther but later came to share Erasmus' misgivings about Luther's aggressive stance and the tumultuous behaviour of some of his followers. After 1521 the last years of his life were over-shadowed by poverty and the depressing knowledge that he had been left behind by developments and by many of his friends (Ep 1425).

The contacts between Mutianus and Erasmus were mostly the result of the latter's connections with the humanist circle of Erfurt. Twice he sent short replies to letters Mutianus had sent him by a member of the Erfurt circle (Epp 870, 1438A); of Mutianus' letters only the second is preserved (Ep 1425).

BIBLIOGRAPHY: Allen Ep 501 / Matrikel Erfurt I 411 / ADB XXIII 108–9 / RGG IV 1226–7 / LThK VII 706–7 / Schottenloher II 82–3, VII 176 / Fritz Halbauer Mutianus Rufus und seine geistesgeschichtliche Stellung (Leipzig 1927, repr 1972) / L.W. Spitz The Religious Renaissance of the German Humanists (Cambridge, Mass, 1963) 130–54 / Erich Kleineidam Universitas Studii Erffordensis (Leipzig 1964–80) II 223–5 and passim / R.W. Scribner 'The Erasmians and the beginning of the Reformation in Erfurt' Journal of Religious History 9 (1976–7) 3–31 / There are also three doctoral dissertations, not printed: F.W. Krapp 'Der Erfurter Mutiankreis und seine Auswirkungen' (Cologne 1939); H.R. Abe 'Der Erfurter Humanismus und seine Zeit' (Jena 1953); R.W. Scribner 'Reformation, society, and humanism in Erfurt c 1450–1530' (London 1972) / Ferrara, Archivio di Stato, MS Notarile Tommaso Meleghini, Protocollo 1501, end ERICH KLEINEIDAM

Ulricus MUTIUS See Ulrich HUGWALD

Osvaldus MYCONIUS of Lucerne, 1488–
14 October 1552
Oswald Geisshüsler, better known as
Myconius, was descended from an old-
established family and registered at the University of Basel in 1510. Four years later he
graduated BA. His knowledge of theology was
the fruit of private studies and left him
painfully aware of some inadequacies. For this
reason and because of a natural disposition he
sometimes appeared insecure in his relations
with others.

From 1514 Myconius taught at the Basel
schools of St Theodor's and St Peter's; in 1516
he was called to the Grossmünster school at
Zürich and in 1519 to the chapter school of his
native Lucerne. At this time he was in touch
with *Zwingli, whose positions he adopted
faithfully, and as a result he was dismissed
from Lucerne in 1522. After an interlude at the
school of Einsiedeln abbey, he was called back
to Zürich and there directed the Fraumünster
school until his return to Basel in 1531 in the
wake of the city's reformation. There he
became minister of St Alban's and a year later,
with the political help of Jakob *Meyer zum
Hirzen, but still somewhat surprisingly, the
successor to *Oecolampadius (d 1532) as
antistes and professor of divinity. Tough and
practical-minded, he was at his best as the
architect of a new church structure in the city
and territory of Basel. Politically and theologically he advocated a compromise with the
Lutherans of Germany, much like his colleagues at Strasbourg. As a result he was
viewed with grave misgivings by Heinrich
Bullinger of Zürich, whose intellectual superiority he feared. The conflict was later played
down in view of the Catholic show of strength
after *Charles v's victory in the Schmalkaldic
war, but at its height Bullinger had ordered
some Zürich students who were living at
Myconius' house to leave.

In his youth Myconius had been friendly
with Henricus *Glareanus and had written a
commentary (published in Zürich in 1737) to
his *Descriptio Helvetiae*; he also published a
short biography of Zwingli and a commentary
on Mark (Basel: T. Platter 1538). After the
death of Oecolampadius he edited several of
his exegetical works and supported the publication of the Koran in Latin (Basel: J. Oporinus
1543). Initially Erasmus' friend Bonifacius
*Amerbach showed little regard for Myconius,
but later a modus vivendi was found between
the two fellow professors. Erasmus very likely
met Myconius at the time of his first visit to
Basel (1514–16). In spite of *Holbein's marginal
sketches in Myconius' copy of the *Moria*
(1515), there is no indication of intimacy
between the two scholars. In 1518 Erasmus
sent Myconius a short but friendly reply to a
letter now missing (Ep 861), treating him above
all as a friend of Glareanus (cf Epp 440, 463,
490). Much later he commented laconically and
contemptuously on his accession to the office
of antistes (Epp 2613, 2728). In 1535 Myconius
took exception to a passage in the *Ecclesiastes*,
but the matter was settled through the good
offices of Amerbach and *Capito (AK IV Epp
1958, 1960). On 12 July 1536, when Erasmus
was carried to his grave at Basel cathedral,
Myconius spoke briefly in his praise and may
be assumed to have spoken again a week later
at a more solemn commemoration (Ep 3135).

Myconius married at Basel in about 1514; his
wife, whose name is not known, was remembered with gratitude by former students (AK VI
576).

BIBLIOGRAPHY: Allen and CWE Ep 861 / ADB
XXIII 127–9 / RGG IV 1230 / R. Wackernagel
Geschichte der Stadt Basel (Basel 1907–54) III
161–2 and passim / Paul Burckhardt in *Basler
Chroniken* VIII 40–7 / *Matrikel Basel* I 300–1 / AK II
628, IV Ep 1728, v Ep 2557, and passim / E.
Bonjour *Die Universität Basel* 2nd ed (Basel
1971) 209–10 / J.V. Pollet *Martin Bucer* (Paris
1958–62) II 235–69 / Many unpublished letters
are in the Öffentliche Bibliothek of the University of Basel.   PGB

Bertinus MYRS or MYSS *See Nicolas* BOISSEL

WORKS FREQUENTLY CITED

SHORT TITLE FORMS OF ERASMUS' WORKS

CONTRIBUTORS

ILLUSTRATION CREDITS

Works Frequently Cited

This list provides bibliographical information for works referred to in short title form. The reader should notice, however, that the text of certain biographies contains additional short title references to works listed in the bibliography of the specific article in question. That bibliography should be consulted in the first place. For Erasmus' writings see the short title list, pages 484–6.

ADB	*Allgemeine Deutsche Biographie* (Leipzig 1875–1912)
AK	*Die Amerbachkorrespondenz* ed A. Hartmann and B.R. Jenny (Basel 1942–)
Allen	*Opus epistolarum Des. Erasmi Roterodami* ed P.S. Allen, H.M. Allen, and H.W. Garrod (Oxford 1906–58)
ARG	*Archiv für Reformationsgeschichte. Archive for Reformation History*
ASD	*Opera Omnia Desiderii Erasmi Roterodami* (Amsterdam 1969–)
BA Oekolampads	*Briefe und Akten zum Leben Oekolampads* ed E. Staehelin, Quellen und Forschungen zur Reformationsgeschichte vols 10 and 19 (Leipzig 1927–34; repr 1971)
Basler Chroniken	*Basler Chroniken* (Leipzig-Basel 1872–)
Bataillon *Erasmo y España*	Marcel Bataillon *Erasmo y España: Estudios sobre la historia espiritual del siglo xvi* tr A. Alatorre, 2nd ed (Mexico City-Buenos Aires 1966)
Benzing *Buchdrucker*	Josef Benzing *Die Buchdrucker des 16. und 17. Jahrhunderts im deutschen Sprachgebiet* (Wiesbaden 1963)
BHR	*Bibliothèque d'Humanisme et Renaissance*
Bierlaire *Familia*	Franz Bierlaire *La familia d'Erasme* (Paris 1968)
Blarer Briefwechsel	*Briefwechsel der Brüder Ambrosius und Thomas Blaurer* ed T. Schiess (Freiburg 1908–12)
BNB	*Biographie nationale* (Académie royale des sciences, des lettres et des beaux-arts de Belgique, Brussels 1866–)
BRE	*Briefwechsel des Beatus Rhenanus* ed A. Horawitz and K. Hartfelder (Leipzig 1886, repr 1966)
Calendar of State Papers, Milan	*Calendar of State Papers and Manuscripts existing in the Archives and Collections of Milan* ... ed A.B. Hinds (Hereford 1912)
Calendar of State Papers, Spanish	*Calendar of Letters, Despatches and State Papers relating to the Negotiations between England and Spain preserved in the Archives of Simancas and elsewhere*, with supplements, ed G.A. Bergenroth et al (London 1862–)
Calendar of State Papers, Venetian	*Calendar of State Papers and Manuscripts relating to English Affairs existing in the Archives and Collections of Venice and other Libraries of*

	Northern Italy, 1202–1672 ed R.L. Brown et al (London 1862–1940, repr 1970)
Clerval	*Registre des procès-verbaux de la faculté de théologie de Paris* ed J.-A. Clerval (Paris 1917)
Colloquia Erasmiana Turonensia	*Colloquia Erasmiana Turonensia* Douzième stage international d'études humanistes, Tours 1969, ed J.-C. Margolin (Paris-Toronto 1972)
Cosenza	Mario Emilio Cosenza *Biographical and Bibliographical Dictionary of the Italian Humanists and the World of Classical Scholarship in Italy, 1300–1800* (Boston, Mass 1962–7)
CWE	*Collected Works of Erasmus* (Toronto 1974–)
DBF	*Dictionnaire de biographie française* ed J. Balteau et al (Paris 1933–)
DBI	*Dizionario biografico degli Italiani* ed A.M. Ghisalberti et al (Rome 1960–)
Delisle	Léopold Delisle 'Notice sur un régistre des procès-verbaux de la faculté de théologie de Paris pendant les années 1505–1533' *Notices et extraits des manuscrits de la Bibliothèque Nationale et autres bibliothèques* 36 (1899) 317–407. Offprint ed (Paris 1899)
DHBS	*Dictionnaire historique et biographique de la Suisse* (Neuchâtel 1921–34), simultaneously published in a very similar but not identical German version: *Historisch-Biographisches Lexikon der Schweiz*
DHGE	*Dictionnaire d'histoire et de géographie ecclésiastiques* ed A. Baudrillart et al (Paris 1912–)
DNB	*Dictionary of National Biography* ed Sidney Lee et al (London 1885– , repr 1949–50)
DS	*Dictionnaire de spiritualité ascétique et mystique, doctrine et histoire* ed M. Viller et al (Paris 1932–)
DTC	*Dictionnaire de théologie catholique* ed A. Vacant et al (Paris 1899–1950)
EI	*Enciclopedia Italiana* ed D. Bartolini et al (Rome 1929– , repr 1949)
Emden BRUC	A.B. Emden *A Biographical Register of the University of Cambridge to AD 1500* (Cambridge 1963)
Emden BRUO	A.B. Emden *A Biographical Register of the University of Oxford to AD 1500* (Oxford 1957–9)
Emden BRUO 1501–40	A.B. Emden *A Biographical Register of the University of Oxford, AD 1501–1540* (Oxford 1974)
Epistolae ad Nauseam	*Epistolarum miscellanearum ad Fridericum Nauseam Blancicampianum ... libri x* (Basel 1550)
Eubel	*Hierarchia catholica medii aevi summorum pontificum, S.R.E. cardinalium, ecclesiarum antistitum series* ed C. Eubel et al (Münster 1901–)
Farge	James K. Farge *Biographical Register of Paris Doctors of Theology, 1500–1536* Subsidia Mediaevalia 10 (Toronto 1980)
Gallia christiana	*Gallia christiana in provincias ecclesiasticas distributa* ed D. Sammarthanus et al (Paris 1715–1865, repr 1970)
Gauthier	Jules Gauthier *Département du Doubs: Inventaire sommaire des archives départementales antérieures à 1790: Archives ecclésiastiques série G I* (Besançon 1900)
Grimm *Buchführer*	Heinrich Grimm 'Die Buchführer des deutschen Kulturbereichs und ihre Niederlassungsorte in der Zeitspanne 1490 bis um 1550' *Archiv für Geschichte des Buchwesens* 7 (1965–6) 1153–1772

Herminjard	*Correspondance des Réformateurs dans les pays de langue française* ed A.-L. Herminjard (Geneva-Paris 1866–97, repr 1965–6)
Hill	G.F. Hill *A Corpus of Italian Medals of the Renaissance before Cellini* (London 1930)
Hutten *Opera*	*Ulrichi Hutteni equitis Germani opera* ed E. Böcking (Leipzig 1859–61, repr 1963)
Hutten *Operum supplementum*	*Ulrichi Hutteni equitis Germani operum supplementum* ed E. Böcking (Leipzig 1869–71)
Knod	Gustav C. Knod *Deutsche Studenten in Bologna (1289-1562)* (Berlin 1899, repr 1970)
LB	*Desiderii Erasmi Roterodami opera omnia* ed J. Leclerc (Leiden 1703–6, repr 1961–2)
LP	*Letters and Papers, Foreign and Domestic, of the Reign of Henry VIII* ed J.S. Brewer et al (London 1862–1932)
LThK	*Lexikon für Theologie und Kirche* 2nd ed by J. Höfer and K. Rahner (Freiburg 1957–)
Luther w	*D. Martin Luthers Werke: Kritische Gesamtausgabe* (Weimar 1883–)
Matricule de Louvain	*Matricule de l'Université de Louvain* ed E. Reusens, A. Schillings, et al (Brussels 1903–)
Matricule de Montpellier	*Matricule de l'Université de Médecine de Montpellier (1503–1599)* ed M. Gouron (Geneva 1957)
Matricule d'Orléans	*Premier Livre des procurateurs de la nation germanique de l'ancienne Université d'Orléans, 1446–1546* ed C.M. Ridderikhoff, H. de Ridder-Symoens, et al (Leiden 1971–)
Matrikel Basel	*Die Matrikel der Universität Basel* ed H.G. Wackernagel et al (Basel 1951–)
Matrikel Erfurt	*Acten der Erfurter Universität* ed J.C.H. Weissenborn et al (Halle 1881–99, repr 1976)
Matrikel Frankfurt	*Ältere Universitäts-Matrikeln* I: *Universität Frankfurt a.O.* ed E. Friedländer et al (Leipzig 1887–91, repr 1965)
Matrikel Freiburg	*Die Matrikel der Universität Freiburg i. Br. von 1460–1656* ed H. Mayer (Freiburg 1907–10, repr 1976)
Matrikel Greifswald	*Ältere Universitäts-Matrikeln* II: *Universität Greifswald* ed E. Friedländer et al (Leipzig 1893–4, repr 1965)
Matrikel Heidelberg	*Die Matrikel der Universität Heidelberg von 1386 bis 1662* ed G. Toepke (Heidelberg 1884–93, repr 1976)
Matrikel Köln	*Matrikel der Universität Köln* ed H. Keussen (Bonn 1919–31, repr 1979)
Matrikel Leipzig	*Die Matrikel der Universität Leipzig* ed G. Erler (Leipzig 1895–1902, repr 1976)
Matrikel Rostock	*Die Matrikel der Universität Rostock* ed A. Hofmeister et al (Rostock-Schwerin 1889–1922, repr 1976)
Matrikel Tübingen	*Die Matrikeln der Universität Tübingen* ed H. Hermelink et al (Stuttgart-Tübingen 1906–)
Matrikel Wien	*Die Matrikel der Universität Wien* (Publikationen des Instituts für österreichische Geschichtsforschung VI. Reihe, 1. Abteilung, Vienna-Graz-Cologne 1954–)
Matrikel Wittenberg	*Album Academiae Vitebergensis: Ältere Reihe ... 1502–1602* ed K.E. Förstemann et al (Leipzig-Halle 1841-1905, repr 1976)
Melanchthons Briefwechsel	*Melanchthons Briefwechsel: Kritische und kommentierte Gesamtausgabe* ed Heinz Scheible (Stuttgart-Bad Cannstatt 1977–)

McConica   J.K. McConica *English Humanists and Reformation Politics under*
                        Henry VIII and Edward VI (Oxford 1965)

More Y   *The Yale Edition of the Complete Works of St Thomas More* (New
                        Haven-London 1961–   )

NBW   *Nationaal Biografisch Woordenboek* ed J. Duverger et al (Brussels
                        1964–   )

NDB   *Neue Deutsche Biographie* (Berlin 1953–   )

NK   Wouter Nijhoff and M.E. Kronenberg *Nederlandsche Bibliographie*
                        van 1500 tot 1540 (The Hague 1923–71)

NNBW   *Nieuw Nederlandsch Biografisch Woordenboek* ed P.C. Molhuysen,
                        P.J. Blok, et al (Leiden 1911–37, repr 1974)

Opuscula   *Erasmi opuscula: A Supplement to the Opera omnia* ed W.K. Ferguson
                        (The Hague 1933)

Pastor   Ludwig von Pastor *The History of the Popes from the Close of the*
                        Middle Ages ed and tr R.F. Kerr et al, 3rd ed (London 1938–53)

Pflug *Correspondance* Julius Pflug *Correspondance* ed J.V. Pollet (Leiden 1969–   )

Pirckheimer Briefwechsel *Willibald Pirckheimer Briefwechsel* ed Emil Reicke (Munich 1940–   )

PSB   *Polski Słownik Biograficzny* (Cracow, etc 1935–   )

RE   *Johann Reuchlins Briefwechsel* ed Ludwig Geiger (Stuttgart 1875,
                        repr 1962)

Reedijk   *The Poems of Desiderius Erasmus* ed C. Reedijk (Leiden 1956)

Renaudet *Préréforme*   Augustin Renaudet *Préréforme et Humanisme à Paris pendant les*
                        premières guerres d'Italie (1494-1517) 2nd ed (Paris 1953)

Renouard *Répertoire*   Philippe Renouard *Répertoire des imprimeurs parisiens, libraires,*
                        fondeurs de caractères et correcteurs d'imprimerie ... jusqu'à la fin du
                        seizième siècle ed J. Veyrin-Forrer and B. Moreau (Paris 1965)

RGG   *Die Religion in Geschichte und Gegenwart* 3rd ed (Tübingen 1956–62)

Rice *Prefatory Epistles* *The Prefatory Epistles of Jacques Lefèvre d'Etaples and Related Texts* ed
                        Eugene F. Rice, jr (New York–London 1972)

Rogers   *The Correspondence of Sir Thomas More* ed E.F. Rogers (Princeton
                        1947)

Rublack *Reformation*   Hans-Christoph Rublack *Die Einführung der Reformation in*
   in Konstanz   *Konstanz von den Anfängen bis zum Abschluss 1531* (Gütersloh-
                        Karlsruhe 1971)

Sanudo *Diarii*   *I Diarii di Marino Sanuto* ed N. Barozzi et al (Venice 1879–1903,
                        repr 1969–70)

Schmidt *Histoire*   Charles Schmidt *Histoire littéraire de l'Alsace à la fin du XVe et au*
   littéraire   *commencement du XVIe siècle* (Paris 1879, repr 1966)

Scrinium Erasmianum   *Scrinium Erasmianum: Mélanges historiques publiées sous le patronage*
                        de l'Université de Louvain à l'occasion du cinquième centenaire de la
                        naissance d'Erasme ed J. Coppens (Leiden 1969)

Schottenloher   Karl Schottenloher *Bibliographie zur deutschen Geschichte im Zeitalter*
                        der Glaubensspaltung 2nd ed (Stuttgart 1956–66)

Schreiber *Universität* Heinrich Schreiber *Geschichte der Albert-Ludwigs-Universität zu*
   Freiburg   *Freiburg i. Br.*: second part of his *Geschichte der Stadt und Univer-*
                        sität Freiburg im Breisgau (Freiburg 1857–60)

STC   *A Short-Title Catalogue of Books Printed in England, Scotland, and*
                        Ireland and of English Books Printed Abroad ed A.W. Pollard and
                        G.R. Redgrave (London 1926); 2nd ed revised by W.A. Jackson et
                        al (London 1976–   )

Vadianische Briefsammlung	*Vadianische Briefsammlung* ed E. Arbenz and H. Wartmann : Mitteilungen zur vaterländischen Geschichte, vols 24–5, 27–30, and supplements (St Gallen 1890–1908)
de Vocht *Busleyden*	Henry de Vocht *Jérôme de Busleyden, Founder of the Louvain Collegium Trilingue: His Life and Writings* (Turnhout 1950)
de Vocht *Dantiscus*	Henry de Vocht *John Dantiscus and his Netherlandish Friends as Revealed by their Correspondence, 1522–1546* (Louvain 1961)
de Vocht *Literae ad Craneveldium*	*Literae virorum eruditorum ad Franciscum Craneveldium, 1522–1528* ed Henry de Vocht (Louvain 1928)
de Vocht MHL	Henry de Vocht *Monumenta Humanistica Lovaniensia: Texts and Studies about Louvain Humanists in the First Half of the xvith Century* (Louvain 1934)
de Vocht CTL	Henry de Vocht *History of the Foundation and the Rise of the Collegium Trilingue Lovaniense, 1517-1550* (Louvain 1951–5)
Winterberg	Hans Winterberg *Die Schüler von Ulrich Zasius* (Stuttgart 1961)
z	*Huldreich Zwinglis Sämtliche Werke* ed E. Egli et al, Corpus Reformatorum vols 88–101 (Berlin-Leipzig-Zürich 1905–)

Short Title Forms for
Erasmus' Works

Titles following colons are longer versions of the same, or are alternative titles. Items entirely enclosed in square brackets are of doubtful authorship. For abbreviations, see Works Frequently Cited, pages 479–83.

Adagia: Adagiorum chiliades 1508 (Adagiorum collectanea for the primitive form, when required) LB II / ASD II-5, 6 / CWE 30-36
Admonitio adversus mendacium: Admonitio adversus mendacium et obtrectationem LB X
Annotationes in Novum Testamentum LB VI
Antibarbari LB X / ASD I-1 / CWE 23
Apologia ad Fabrum: Apologia ad Iacobum Fabrum Stapulensem LB IX
Apologia ad Caranzam: Apologia ad Sanctium Caranzam, or Apologia de tribus locis, or Responsio ad annotationem Stunicae ... a Sanctio Caranza defensam LB IX
Apologia ad viginti et quattuor libros A. Pii LB IX
Apologia adversus Petrum Sutorem: Apologia adversus debacchationes Petri Sutoris LB IX
Apologia adversus monachos: Apologia adversus monachos quosdam hispanos LB IX
Apologia adversus rhapsodias Alberti Pii LB IX
Apologia contra Latomi dialogum: Apologia contra Iacobi Latomi dialogum de tribus linguis LB IX
Apologiae contra Stunicam: Apologiae contra Lopidem Stunicam LB IX / ASD IX-2
Apologia de 'In principio erat sermo' LB IX
Apologia de laude matrimonii: Apologia pro declamatione de laude matrimonii LB IX
Apologia de loco 'Omnes quidem': Apologia de loco 'Omnes quidem resurgemus' LB IX
Apologia invectivis Lei: Apologia qua respondet duabus invectivis Eduardi Lei Opuscula
Apophthegmata LB IV
Appendix respondens ad Sutorem LB IX
Argumenta: Argumenta in omneis epistolas apostolicas nova (with Paraphrases)
Axiomata pro causa Lutheri: Axiomata pro causa Martini Lutheri Opuscula

Carmina varia LB VIII
Catalogus lucubrationum LB I
Christiani hominis institutum, carmen LB V
Ciceronianus: Dialogus Ciceronianus LB I / ASD I-2 / CWE 28
Colloquia (Familiarum colloquiorum formulae for the primitive form, when required) LB I / ASD I-3
Compendium vitae Allen I / CWE 4
[Consilium: Consilium cuiusdam ex animo cupientis esse consultum Opuscula]

De bello turcico: Consultatio de bello turcico LB V
De civitate: De civilitate morum puerilium LB I / CWE 25
De concordia: De sarcienda ecclesiae concordia LB V

De conscribendis epistolis LB I / ASD I-2 / CWE 25

De constructione: De constructione octo partium orationis, or Syntaxis LB I / ASD I-4

De contemptu mundi: Epistola de contemptu mundi LB V / ASD V-1

De copia: De duplici copia verborum ac rerum LB I / CWE 24

De immensa Dei misericordia: Concio de immensa Dei misericordia LB V

De libero arbitrio: De libero arbitrio diatribe LB IX

De praeparatione: De praeparatione ad mortem LB V / ASD V-1

De pueris instituendis: De pueris statim ac liberaliter instituendis LB I / ASD I-2 / CWE 26

De puero Iesu: Concio de puero Iesu LB V

De ratione studii LB I / ASD I-2 / CWE 24

De recta pronuntiatione: De recta latini graecique sermonis pronuntiatione LB I / ASD I-4 / CWE 26

De tedio Iesu: Disputatiuncula de tedio, pavore, tristicia Iesu LB V

De virtute amplectenda: Oratio de virtute amplectenda LB V

Declamatio de morte LB IV

Declamatiuncula LB IV

Declarationes ad censuras Lutetiae vulgatas: Declarationes ad censuras Lutetiae vulgatas sub nomine facultatis theologiae Parisiensis LB IX

Detectio praestigiarum: Detectio praestigiarum cuiusdam libelli germanice scripti LB X / ASD IX-1

[Dialogus bilinguium ac trilinguium: Chonradi Nastadiensis dialogus bilinguium ac trilinguium Opuscula] CWE 7

Dilutio: Dilutio eorum quae Iodocus Clithoveus scripsit adversus declamationem suasoriam matrimonii

Divinationes ad notata Bedae LB IX

Ecclesiastes: Ecclesiastes sive de ratione concionandi LB V

Elenchus in N. Bedae censuras LB IX

Enchiridion: Enchiridion militis christiani LB V

Encomium matrimonii (in De conscribendis epistolis)

Encomium medicinae: Declamatio in laudem artis medicae LB I / ASD I-4

Epigrammata LB I

Epistola ad Dorpium LB IX / CWE 3

Epistola ad fratres Inferioris Germaniae: Responsio ad fratres Germaniae Inferioris ad epistolam apologeticam incerto autore proditam LB X

Epistola ad graculos: Epistola ad quosdam imprudentissimos graculos LB X

Epistola apologetica de Termino LB X

Epistola consolatoria: Epistola consolatoria virginibus sacris LB V

Epistola contra pseudevangelicos: Epistola contra quosdam qui se falso iactant evangelicos LB X / ASD IX-1

Epistola de esu carnium: Epistola apologetica ad Christophorum episcopum Basiliensem de interdicto esu carnium LB IX / ASD IX-1

Exomologesis: Exomologesis sive modus confitendi LB V

Explanatio symboli: Explanatio symboli apostolorum sive catechismus LB V / ASD V-1

Expostulatio Iesu LB V

Familiarum colloquiorum formulae (see Colloquia)

Formula: Conficiendarum epistolarum formula (see De conscribendis epistolis)

Hymni varii LB V

Hyperaspistes LB X

Institutio christiani matrimonii LB V

Institutio principis christiani LB IV / ASD IV-1 / CWE 27

[Julius exclusus: Dialogus Julius exclusus e coelis *Opuscula*] CWE 27

Lingua LB IV / ASD IV-1
Liturgia Virginis Matris: Virginis Matris apud Lauretum cultae liturgia LB V / ASD V-1

Methodus: Ratio verae theologiae LB V
Modus orandi Deum LB V / ASD V-1
Moria: Moriae encomium LB IV / ASD IV-3 / CWE 27

Novum Testamentum: Novum Testamentum 1519 and later (Novum instrumentum for the first
   edition, 1516, when required) LB VI

Obsecratio ad Virginem Mariam: Obsecratio sive oratio ad Virginem Mariam in rebus adversis
   LB V
Oratio de pace: Oratio de pace et discordia LB VIII
Oratio funebris: Oratio funebris Berthae de Heyen LB VIII

Paean Virgini Matri: Paean Virgini Matri dicendus LB V
Panegyricus: Panegyricus ad Philippum Austriae ducem LB IV / ASD IV-1 / CWE 27
Parabolae: Parabolae sive similia LB I / ASD I-5 / CWE 23
Paraclesis LB V, VI
Paraphrasis in Elegantias Vallae: Paraphrasis in Elegantias Laurentii Vallae LB I / ASD I-4
Paraphrasis in Matthaeum, etc (in Paraphrasis in Novum Testamentum)
Paraphrasis in Novum Testamentum LB VII / CWE 42–50
Peregrinatio apostolorum: Peregrinatio apostolorum Petri et Pauli LB VI, VII
Precatio ad Virginis filium Iesum (in Precatio pro pace)
Precatio dominica LB V
Precationes LB V
Precatio pro pace ecclesiae: Precatio ad Iesum pro pace ecclesiae LB IV, V
Progymnasmata: Progymnasmata quaedam primae adolescentiae Erasmi LB VIII
Psalmi: Psalmi, or Enarrationes sive commentarii in psalmos LB V
Purgatio adversus epistolam Lutheri: Purgatio adversus epistolam non sobriam Lutheri LB IX

Querela pacis LB IV / ASD IV-2 / CWE 27

Ratio verae theologiae: Methodus LB V
Responsio ad annotationes Lei: Liber quo respondet annotationibus Lei LB IX
Responsio ad collationes: Responsio ad collationes cuiusdam iuvenis gerontodidascali LB IX
Responsio ad disputationem de divortio: Responsio ad disputationem cuiusdam Phimostomi de
   divortio LB IX
Responsio ad epistolam Pii: Responsio ad epistolam paraeneticam Alberti Pii, or Responsio ad
   exhortationem Pii LB IX
Responsio ad notulas Bedaicas LB X
Responsio ad Petri Cursii defensionem: Epistola de apologia Cursii LB X
Responsio adversus febricitantis libellum: Apologia monasticae religionis LB X

Spongia: Spongia adversus aspergines Hutteni LB X / ASD IX-1
Supputatio: Supputatio calumniarum Natalis Bedae LB IX

Vidua christiana LB V
Virginis et martyris comparatio LB V
Vita Hieronymi: Vita divi Hieronymi Stridonensis *Opuscula*

Contributors

Danilo Aguzzi-Barbagli
Rosemarie Aulinger
Kenneth R. Bartlett
Marco Bernuzzi
Franz Bierlaire
Marjorie O'Rourke Boyle
Virginia Brown
Fritz Büsser
Leo van Buyten
Virginia W. Callahan
Anna Giulia Cavagna
D.S. Chambers
Miriam U. Chrisman
Brian P. Copenhaver
Elizabeth Crittall
Maria Cytowska
John F. D'Amico
Natalie Zemon Davis
Rolf Decot
Jan De Grauwe
Rosemary Devonshire Jones
L. Domonkos
Paul J. Donnelly
Richard M. Douglas
K.-H. Ducke
E.J.M. van Eijl
Edward English
Michael Erbe
Conor Fahy
James K. Farge
Mordechai Feingold
Felipe Fernández-Armesto
R.M. Flores

Inge Friedhuber
Stephan Füssel
Anton J. Gail
Marie-Madeleine de la Garanderie
Veronika Gerz-von Büren
André Godin
Frank Golczewski
Anthony Grafton
Kaspar von Greyerz
Gordon Griffiths
Hans R. Guggisberg
Geneviève Guilleminot
Léon-E. Halkin
John M. Headley
Gernot Heiss
Henry Heller
Judith Rice Henderson
Elisabeth Feist Hirsch
R. Gerald Hobbs
Eugen Hoffmann
Irmgard Höss
J. Hoyoux
Jozef IJsewijn
Marie-Thérèse Isaac
Fehmi Ismail
Denis R. Janz
William B. Jones
James M. Kittelson
Erich Kleineidam
C.S. Knighton
Alfred Kohler
Barbara Könneker
Georges Kouskoff

Halina Kowalska
Peter Krendl
Egmont Lee
Valeria Sestieri Lee
Stanford E. Lehmberg
C.G. van Leijenhorst
M.J.C. Lowry
Albrecht Luttenberger
James K. McConica
Franz Machilek
David Mackenzie
Louis P.A. Maingon
Peter Marzahl
Jean-Pierre Massaut
C. Matheeussen
Hansgeorg Molitor
Gérard Moreau
Marcel A. Nauwelaerts
José C. Nieto
John C. Olin
Arsenio Pacheco
Luis A. Pérez
Paul van Peteghem
Paolo Pissavino
Michel Reulos
Hilde de Ridder-Symoens
Dieter Riesenberger
Milagros Rivera

Steven Rowan
John Rowlands
Hans-Christoph Rublack
Gordon Rupp
Beat von Scarpatetti
Hans Schadek
Heinz Scheible
Charles B. Schmitt
R.J. Schoeck
Martin Schwarz Lausten
Harry R. Secor
Silvana Seidel Menchi
Heide Stratenwerth
Robert Stupperich
Hans Thieme
De Etta V. Thomsen
Alice Tobriner
Gilbert Tournoy
Godelieve Tournoy-Thoen
James D. Tracy
J.B. Trapp
Charles Trinkaus
Ronald W. Truman
Rainer Vinke
Hartmut Voit
Manfred E. Welti
Konrad Wiedemann
J.K. Zeman

Illustration Credits

National Gallery, London 422
National Gallery of Art, Washington 133
Nationalmuseet, Copenhagen, St Knud's Church, Odense/Photo Lennart Larsen 239
National Portrait Gallery, London 178
Öffentliche Kunstsammlung Basel 59, 195, 289
Österreichische Nationalbibliothek, Vienna 360 (Photo Lichtbildwerkstätte 'Alpenland,'
   Vienna), 6, 90
Palazzo Riccardi, Florence 415 and 419 (Photo Fratelli Alinari/Art Resource, Inc)
Państwowe Zbiory Sztuki Na Wawelu, Cracow 243 (Photo L. Schuster), 265 (Photo Stanisław
   Michta)
Photo Más, Barcelona 227, 337
Rijksmuseum, Amsterdam 272, 305, 383, 400, 473
Società Colombaria, Florence/Photo Fratelli Alinari 365
Society of Antiquaries, London 177
Staatliche Kunsthalle Karlsruhe 170
Staatliche Lutherhalle Wittenberg/Photo Wilfried Kirsch, Wittenberg 206
Staatliche Museen Preussischer Kulturbesitz, Berlin/Photo Jörg P. Anders, Berlin 22, 217, 349
Staatliche Museen zu Berlin 220, 244
Stadsmuseum, Leuven/Photo P. Laes 444, 461
Stadtarchiv, Stadt Freiburg im Breisgau 256
Sterling and Francine Clark Art Institute, Williamstown, Massachusetts 203
Thomas Fisher Rare Book Library, University of Toronto 142, 188, 189, 240, 242, 266
Universitätsbibliothek, Basel 253
University of Michigan Library, Ann Arbor 293
University of Warsaw Library, Collection of King Stanisław August Poniatowski/Photo Maria
   Piwowarska 298
Verwaltung der Staatlichen Schlösser und Gärten, Berlin/Photo Jörg P. Anders, Berlin 96
Wartburg-Stiftung, Eisenach 360
Windsor Castle, Reproduced by gracious permission of Her Majesty the Queen 36 (Photo R.
   Todd-White Ltd, London), 208 (Photo A.C. Cooper Ltd, London), 97, 150, 352, 454, 452,
   453, 454
Zentralbibliothek, Zürich 249

Cover illustration: From *Commentarii linguae Graecae* (Paris 1529), by Guillaume Budé, courtesy
   Thomas Fisher Rare Book Library, University of Toronto